THE CLARETS CHRONICLES

THE DEFINITIVE HISTORY OF BURNLEY FOOTBALL CLUB

1882-2007

THE CLARETS CHRONICLES

THE DEFINITIVE HISTORY OF BURNLEY FOOTBALL CLUB 1882-2007

by

RAY SIMPSON

BURNLEY FOOTBALL CLUB HISTORIAN

with

DARREN BENTLEY, WALLACE CHADWICK,
EDWARD LEE AND PHIL SIMPSON

PUBLISHED BY BURNLEY FOOTBALL CLUB

First published in Great Britain by
Burnley Football Club
Turf Moor
Harry Potts Way
Burnley, Lancashire
BB10 4BX

2007

ISBN 978-0-9557468-0-2

Printed by Nayler Group Ltd, Church, Accrington, Lancashire
Jacket design by Adam Riding

Photographs supplied courtesy of Burnley FC, the Burnley Express Group, Lancashire Telegraph, PA Photos (formerly Empics) and various sources included within the acknowledgements.

This work is dedicated to a group of men who met in a pub all those years ago. The story continues........

Contents

Foreword by Barry Kilby

How time flies!
I have only held the privileged position of Chairman for eight of Burnley's illustrious years, but just like most supporters, this great football club has dominated much of my life.
My father Roy first introduced me to the club in 1962, when I watched us win 1-0 at Sheffield United in the FA Cup.
Ever since then I've been hooked. The gloriously rich claret and blue shirts, the line-up of household names and the fact that this was a club steeped in tradition, all made up my mind immediately that there could be no other
The great names to play for the club roll off the tongue: Halley, Boyle and Watson, McIlroy and Miller, Lochhead and Pointer, James and Fletcher, and more latterly, Payton, Wright, Gascoigne and Little.
As we celebrate 125 years it is right that we should reflect on a glorious history. Founder members of the inaugural Football League in 1888, crowned League Champions twice in 1921 and 1960, FA Cup winners in 1914 and finalists in 1947 and 1962.
The sixties were, of course, our halcyon days – and a quarter of a century later it was unthinkable that we could have lost our league status altogether on another momentous day in May 1987.
All these memories make up a rich tapestry that few other football clubs can rival. And as we move forward, I believe this great club is again on the verge of making history.
The Premiership has changed the English game beyond all recognition, but it remains the ultimate goal.
Hopefully in the not too distant future, we will achieve it and, along with the plans to re-develop Turf Moor, have a stadium, and a team, fit for another 125 great years.
Enjoy the story of Burnley Football Club so far. It makes for great reading.
Thanks for your support.
Barry Kilby
Chairman, Burnley FC

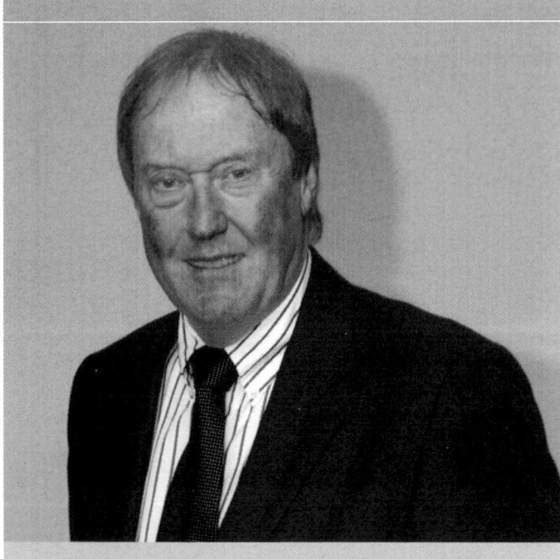
Barry Kilby, guiding the Clarets into the new millennium

Chairmen of Burnley Football Club, 1882 to 2007

1882	Albert Jobling
1883	John Rawcliffe
May 1885	John Bradley
Mar 1887	B Wyatt Granger
May 1896	Charles Sutcliffe
Jun 1899	Edwin Whitehead
Jun 1909	Harry Windle
Mar 1930	William E Bracewell
Jan 1932	Edward J Tate
Jul 1934	Tom Clegg
Jun 1948	Ernest D Kay
Oct 1952	Wilfred Hopkinson
Jun 1955	Robert W Lord
Oct 1981	John E Jackson
May 1985	Frank J Teasdale
Dec 1998	Barry C Kilby

Albert Jobling, Burnley FC's first Chairman

Bob Lord, in the chair for more than a quarter of a century

Foreword by Jimmy McIlroy

Here we go again with yet another book featuring Burnley Football Club, which must place the Clarets among the top Football League clubs immortalised in print.

I've joked for years that there are more books about this club than about the Second World War and, surprisingly, most of them have proved a hit with the fans.

Now comes "The Clarets Chronicles" which to some supporters may seem to be nothing more than a re-write of all the previous books, which of course, is far from the truth.

In fact, I predict that this book will turn out to be the "bible" of them all.

It stands out because it describes in minute detail, just about everything that is newsworthy about this famous old club since its formation 125 years ago.

Students of football history will be amazed that it records every senior match from 1888, including half-time scores, goalscorers, attendances, line-ups, league tables and much, much more, which isn't really surprising considering that it was produced by five lifelong Burnley supporters.

Editor and main contributor is the club's Historian, Ray Simpson, author of a number of Turf Moor books including the companion book "The Clarets Collection", and he is supported by local sports journalists Edward Lee, an author and co-author with Ray of past Clarets' books, Darren Bentley, the club's PR and Communications Manager and Phil Simpson, sports journalist from the Burnley Express (who just happens to be the son of aforementioned club Historian – chip off the old block, you might say!)

The quintet is made up by Ray's lifelong friend, chartered accountant Wallace Chadwick, who has been collecting information on the Clarets, alongside Ray, since his schooldays.

With talent and enthusiasm on this scale, it isn't surprising that by further delving into records, a mass of entirely new and exciting information has come to light, which makes this book a "must have" for every fan.

Personally, I would like to congratulate Burnley Football Club on maintaining Football League status since 1888 and for the recognition and glory it has brought to our town.

May I also thank the club for giving me the finest 13 years of my life.

To those people who voted me the best Burnley player they had seen, I have a little anecdote that keeps my feet firmly on the ground.

Some years ago, while walking in the park with my little grand daughter, I met an old chap I'd known for quite a while. His name, believe it or not, was Bob Lord (no, not THE Bob Lord).

Well into his nineties, Bob turned to me with a glint in his eye.

"McIlroy", he said, "you weren't a bad player".

Then, raising his hand, with a 3 inch space between index finger and thumb, he chuckled and said, "but Bob Kelly was that much better than you".

With that he walked on, having put a bemused Paddy firmly in his place.

Jimmy McIlroy

Penalty. McIlroy. Spot. Goal!

Introduction

There are obviously many thousands of facts, figures and statistics within the pages of this work. With five people contributing to the content, consistency was always going to be a major consideration, as there was invariably a danger that details of incidents, dates, scores, or any number of things referred to more than once, might vary.

Every effort has been made to try to ensure that everything that appears is accurate and consistent.

The majority of the book's historical content has been gleaned from the pages of the "Burnley Express", originally established in 1852. Much early detail has been cross-checked with the "Burnley Gazette" and "Burnley News", then separate news organs but both later absorbed into the Express.

In addition many regional and national newspapers have been scrutinised, in particular the Lancashire (Evening) Telegraph and the (Manchester) Guardian.

The club's own records have also been used.

Research into football statistics can be very frustrating, particularly before the turn of the nineteenth century. There are many inconsistencies in early match reporting, with often the most cursory of references to things that we consider crucial today, not least the identity of goalscorers.

Nevertheless every single match that Burnley has played since 1882 has been researched again for the purposes of this book. Detail that appeared in "Burnley, a Complete Record"(BACR), published in 1991, has been re-checked for accuracy and a number of interesting, in some cases significant, differences have emerged.

I would say immediately that most of the differences that are highlighted here are not because of poor initial research but because, originally, only a single newspaper was checked. When Wal Chadwick and I undertook the original research in the sixties and seventies (as young men), we thought, perhaps naively, that a team line-up was a team line-up, a goalscorer was a goalscorer, no matter which newspaper was researched. Wrong. It was only some time after the fruits of our early labours had appeared in BACR that we began to discover that there were certainly many variations in goalscorers, some variations in team line-ups and even one difference in a final score!

Research on the life and times of Burnley Football Club has been an ongoing process for many years but, as far as this publication is concerned, all previous information has been re-checked and now corrected where necessary.

In the course of my latest research two new players have emerged. A player called William McKay, who appeared in BACR with 14 games and 6 goals in 1888-89 is in fact two different players. Luckily their Turf Moor careers didn't overlap, the second one, Christian name unknown, appeared as the first one was injured, his Burnley career at an end. In some, but not all, newspaper reports (inconsistency again) their names are spelt differently and I have shown these players with different spellings to make it easier for the reader. Also Robert Henderson who, according to BACR, played three games in 1929 and 1930, is in fact two different players. William Henderson played the second and third of those games.

One of my objectives for this book was to try and identify the scorer of every single Burnley goal and particular effort has been made in respect of all previously unknown goalscorers in Football League and FA Cup matches, referred to in BACR as scrimmages. Regretfully this has simply not been possible. Many goals previously recorded as scrimmages have indeed been able to be applied to a specific player but alas, no matter how many different newspaper reports are scoured, it seems there are some goals that must remain forever untraced. Where a scorer is simply not mentioned, (Burnley scored again, the visitors' citadel later yielded to a vigorous assault, etc) the scorer is shown as "unknown". Goals "as a result of a hot/almighty/desperate scrimmage" continue as "scrimmages". Scrimmages and unknown goals are grouped as "untraced" goals in the various totals.

In addition some goals, just a few, have changed ownership from BACR. In the post-war period there are four such goals with Ray Harrison gaining a League goal in 1948 that appeared previously as an own goal. Unfortunately the other three changes are all goals previously credited to players that have now been identified as own goals. Bill Holden loses one in December 1954, John Connelly loses one in August 1960 and Ray Pointer loses an FA Cup goal in January 1961. The players involved can rest assured that much research and soul-searching has taken place before such a momentous decision. Sorry chaps!

There are also a number of earlier changes and a significant one occurs in a match played on 15 September 1888, a 4-3 win at Bolton, only Burnley's second-ever League fixture. Additional research, initially prompted by the Bolton Wanderers historian Simon Marland, reveals that Burnley's William Tait scored three goals in this match, not two (as in

BACR). This means that our friend Tait hit the first-ever hat-trick in a Football League game, a record previously credited to Aston Villa's Albert Allen in a match two weeks later.

Perhaps the most significant change however relates to the Burnley goal scored in a 1-5 defeat at Chesterfield on New Years Day 1932. The "Burnley News" credits Burnley's consolation to Billy Harker and this was the newspaper used for our original research. Harker therefore appears as the scorer in BACR. However the "Burnley Express", the "Guardian" and the "Derbyshire Times", researched via Chesterfield library, all confirm that the goalscorer in question was a certain George Beel!

Beel of course is Burnley's all-time leading scorer and his goalscoring record for Burnley is phenomenal. However in all the books I have read on him his League total has been set at 178 and this figure also appeared in BACR, supported by a total of 11 goals in the 1931-32 season.

This new evidence means that Beel actually scored 12 goals in 1931-32, so unless there is another goal somewhere between 1923 and 1932 that all previous researchers have also got wrong, George Beel's total of League goals for Burnley was actually 179.

As "the Clarets Chronicles" goes to print this new record figure is being publicised.

From the start, the objective of this work, commemorating as it does 125 years since the foundation of Burnley Football club, was for it to emerge as the most comprehensive study ever undertaken of a renowned sporting organisation.

I think it has achieved its objective.

Jimmy McIlroy has been kind enough to refer to it as the Burnley FC "Bible" and I would like to think that readers will agree.

Please enjoy THE CLARETS CHRONICLES.

Ray Simpson
September 2007

Notes

Not really guidance notes as such, but a few comments here regarding the seasonal stats pages might be useful.

The shading around the names of some of the players indicates a Burnley debut that season.

From the advent of a single substitute in 1965-66, the (used) sub is shown as S★, and the player replaced is shown as 7★.

Two substitutes were allowed from 1986-87 (FA Cup only at first) and the first (used) sub is shown as S★, the second (used) sub as S★★. The first player replaced appears as 8★ and the second as 9★★.

Three substitutes were allowed from 1993-94 (goalkeepers only at first) with symbols for the first two (used) subs as before. The third (used) sub appears as S^ with the third player to come off shown as 10^.

Shirt numbers didn't appear until 1939 but, from the very earliest matches, team line-ups were shown in traditional "W"(2-3-5) formation with (originally pseudo) shirt numbers 1 to 11. In most statistical records this continued until at least 1999, even though formations had long since changed.

With the emergence of the squad number concept in 1999, I felt it was time for a re-think on how team line-ups appeared statistically.

In "The Clarets Chronicles" from season 1999-2000 onwards, letters have replaced numbers, and all line-ups are shown in 4-4-2 formation, one goalkeeper (G), four defenders (D), four midfielders (M) and two forwards (F). Obviously not all formations these days are 4-4-2, and even the ones which start that way invariably change mid-match, but the system attempts to impose a degree of conformity.

On the few occasions where a substitute replaces a previous substitute, the names of both players appear alongside the team line up.

All information and statistics contained in this book are correct as of 30 June 2007.

Acknowledgements

This book is the product of a lot of hard work by a large number of people and this section attempts to acknowledge that hard work. Instead of a rider at the end that refers to people I might have forgotten to mention, I'll put it here, sorry if you have been overlooked or felt you deserved a personal mention.

If you're not here consider yourself here.

I must first of all thank the Chairman, Barry Kilby, and the Directors of Burnley Football Club, for inviting me to write "The Clarets Chronicles". I feel privileged to have been entrusted with the responsibility of capturing, in print, as much as possible of the first 125 years of history, the highs, and the lows, of this wonderful club of ours.

When I was first invited to a meeting to discuss the book, it was at the instigation of Darren Bentley, the club's PR and Communication manager. Even during that first meeting I probably realised that, to do the project justice in the time available, there would have to be more than one scribe.

The way I felt the book should be written, particularly the history of the club, detailed season by detailed season, meant that the end product was always going to be far more than just an update of previous books. I decided it needed a team of people who were passionate Burnley fans, knew a great deal about the club, were competent around a keyboard, and, obviously, who wanted to be involved.

Quite frankly the rest of our five-a-side team picked itself, and I want to place on record my thanks and appreciation to the skill, hard work and sheer dedication of my co-writers, Wallace Chadwick, Edward Lee, Darren Bentley and, my son, Phil Simpson.

Their original brief was to write, between them, the narratives on the post-war seasons, but they all ended up contributing to other aspects of the book as well. The reader might spot understandable differences in style here and there but that should not detract from his or her enjoyment of the content. I don't think it's necessary to ascribe any particular section of the book to one or other of the contributors although I'm sure the other three guys won't mind me mentioning that, as well as penning narratives on some of the more recent seasons, Phil undertook the meticulous checking (and re-checking) of all the seasonal statistics.

Suffice it to say that the finished product is a tribute to collaboration and teamwork by everyone involved.

That team of course includes the production team at Nayler's, Alastair Nayler, Debbie Gerrard, John Riding and Mohammed Ansar as well as the rest of the team, including Suzanne Geldard, who stepped in to provide valuable expertise on page design. Adam Riding at Burnley FC was always available on the graphics side and also designed the book's dust jacket and the original publicity leaflet. Many of the staff at Burnley FC have, perhaps unknowingly, done their bit towards the book, especially Sarah Meakin, but special mention must go to the staff in the club shop, manager Paul Stanworth, Lisa Merrifield and Tom Mackie, who have expertly handled all the incoming subscribers' forms and remittances.

As far as the research itself was concerned the dusty file rooms at the Burnley Express, Nelson Leader and Lancashire Telegraph have proved absolutely invaluable. It simply would not have been possible to write the book without putting the hours in poring over the newspapers mentioned and the staff involved have been kindness itself. The same is true of the staff of Burnley Reference Library, their patience has been remarkable and again, without the time spent in their company, the book would never have seen the light of day.

The Lancashire Football Association, the Football League and the Football Association have all been very helpful, with David Barber at the FA actually confirming as 3-3 the troublesome FA Cup score against Astley Bridge in October 1886.

I really appreciated Jimmy McIlroy agreeing to write the foreword and it was a joy for both Phil and I to spend time with the late Albert Maddox reliving his Turf Moor memories. Thanks to Muriel for making us both so welcome.

Veronica Simpson and the team at Ex-Clarets in Sport lent their assistance as did Mike Townend at Towneley Hall with rare photographs. Margaret Potts has always been very supportive of all my previous books, and she came up trumps again, this time with a number of unique photographs. I was also contacted from Sheffield by Julia Hatfield who provided lots of information and a family photograph of her grandfather, Albert Jobling, Burnley FC's first Chairman.

Other people who have provided help include Peter Mulligan, Jan Gedzielewski, Peter Bibby, Tony Scholes and the team at Clarets Mad, together with Kathryn Nelson who was kind enough to let me have her collection of scrapbooks and cuttings from the Seventies and Eighties.

I must also thank collectively the many football journalists, historians and statisticians whose works I have consulted to varying degrees and who are not individually mentioned here or in the Bibliography. Also the numerous librarians and staff at other newspaper offices who spent time trying to help Phil and I unravel as many of the "scrimmage" mysteries as possible.

Almost finally I am very grateful to all the subscribers who have parted with their hard-earned cash up front to see their names and messages in "The Clarets Chronicles".

Last, but most important of all, my grateful thanks go to my long-suffering wife Glenys who has lived and breathed this publication ever since it was first conceived in the spring of 2006. She has been extremely supportive all the way through and has had to live with my frustrations, which, particularly in the final few weeks before deadline, became ever-increasing, in inverse proportion to the amount of time left, which of course, was ever-reducing.

Not only that, she has been a tower of strength as she has coped with mountains of proof-reading and looked after the administration of the subscribers' copies. Even as I write this, she is now busy planning ahead to make sure that the official launch, the evening where subscribers will collect their numbered copies of "The Clarets Chronicles", will pass off smoothly.

A heartfelt thanks to one and all.

Ray Simpson
Burnley FC Historian
September 2007

Bibliography

There are some excellent reference works around these days on all aspects of football history, as well as on facts and figures relating to the beautiful game. The following is as comprehensive a list as possible of the sources used. There are other references included in the "acknowledgements" section.

Rothmans/Sky Sports Football Yearbooks 1970-2007.

PFA Footballers' Factfile/Who's Who 1995-2007. Football League Records by Gordon Smailes (Breedon). Football Managers by Dennis Turner and Alex White (Breedon).

Football League Players' Records (Post-war) by Barry Hugman (Tony Williams). The Official History of the Football Association by Bryon Butler (Queen Anne Press). The Official History of the Football League by Bryon Butler (Colour Library Books). The Football League Jubilee Book by Ivan Sharpe (Stanley Paul).

Various club histories in the Complete Record series (Breedon Books), also in the Official History series (Yore Publications). Book of Football (Marshall Cavendish). English Football Internationalists' Who's Who and Scottish Internationalists' Who's Who, by Doug Lamming (Hutton Press). England Football Factbook by Cris Freddi (Guinness). 100 Years of the FA Cup by Tony Pawson (Heinemann). The Football Grounds of Great Britain by Simon Inglis (Collins Willow). The Guinness Record of the FA Cup by Mike Collett (Guiness). Welsh International Soccer Players by Gareth Davies and Ian Garland (Bridge Books). Rejected FC by Dave Twydell (Yore Publications). The Daily Telegraph Chronicle of Football by Norman Barrett (Index). Soccer at War by Jack Rollin (Collins Willow). To the Palace for the Cup by Ian Bevan, Stuart Hibberd and Michael Gilbert (Replay). Football Firsts by Tony Matthews (Capella). He always Puts it to the Right by Clark Miller (Orion). The Football Fact Book by Jack Rollin (Guinness). The Port Vale Record by Jeff Kent (Witan). The History of Burnley by W.Bennett (Burnley BC). East Lancashire Derbies by Dean Hayes (Sigma). The Ultimate Drop by George Rowland (Tempus). The Soccer Companion by David Pickering (Cassell). Of Fossils and Foxes by Dave Smith and Paul Taylor (Polar). The United Alphabet by Garth Dykes (ACL & Polar). An Alphabet of the Celts by Eugene MacBride, Martin O'Connor and George Sheridan (ACL & Polar). Various publications in the Images of Sport series (Tempus). Up the Clarets by David Wiseman (Robert Hale). A case of vintage Claret by David Wiseman (Hudson & Pearson).

To all students of the history of football and of football clubs, who have penned major works, written articles or produced anything that might have been consulted -

Keep up the good work!

In the Beginning

The origins of Burnley Football Club, that is as a club playing association football, date back to 18 May 1882, the date generally accepted as the point that the club came into being. However the origins of that group of men, the members of Burnley Rovers who made the decision to change from rugby to association, date back a little further.

Rugby football was played by a number of clubs in the Burnley area in the 1870's before association football began to assume greater popularity. Two of the rugby clubs at that time were Burnley Rovers and Calder Vale who decided to amalgamate, the new club confusingly using the name Burnley Rovers but playing at Calder Vale. After a few years that club was disbanded but some of the members, who were also members of the Young Men's Christian Association, set up a new rugby club under the title Y.M.C.A., also playing at Calder Vale. That name was soon changed back to Burnley Rovers and it was the rugby-playing members of that club who eventually decided to switch to the round ball game.

Padiham are believed to have been the first rugby club in the area to change to the association code, in 1879, and they were followed by a number of other local clubs over the next few years, the last of which was Burnley Rovers.

In April 1882 the Lancashire Football Association, on the look out for new members, were shrewd enough to arrange the final of their main competition, the Lancashire Senior Cup, at Turf Moor. The protagonists were Accrington, who were the Lancashire Cup holders and Blackburn Rovers, who emerged as 3-1 winners, lifting the trophy for the first time.

Turf Moor diehards will have realised, but may not relish the fact, that Blackburn Rovers played at the famous old ground before Burnley did. The fact remains, however, that this was almost certainly the match, a Rovers victory, that finally convinced the watching members of the Burnley Rovers committee that association football was the coming thing.

On the evening of Thursday 18 May 1882, a special meeting of the members of Burnley Rovers was held at the Bull Hotel, Burnley.

The Bull Hotel, where it all began......

The secretary, George Waddington, read his report of the rugby season just ended, then the members discussed various matters of business relating to the report. The treasurer, Mr Baron, then submitted his balance sheet showing that income for the past season was £48-12-4, and expenditure £56-12-7, leaving a shortfall on the season of £8-0-3.

He thought the club had done very well considering the damage that had been sustained at the Calder Vale ground, - "in consequence of the unpropitious season". The tent (changing facilities) had been blown down as well as the bridge (access to the ground) washed away and this had incurred expenditure of £15-10-0. Had not the bridge been swept away the balance sheet would have presented a different aspect."

The members applauded and the report and balance sheet were adopted unanimously.

Then committee member Mr. Ernest Bradshaw moved that the recommendation of the club committee be adopted that – "the club, in future, play under association rules"

Mr. Barratt seconded the motion and, after a vote amongst the members, the motion was carried.

Rugby football was out, association football was in.

A few days after that historic decision was taken, a group of committee men were summoned to a meeting by the secretary, George Waddington. He was of the opinion that, now all the football clubs in the Burnley area were going to be playing association football, and there were quite a number, there would be a struggle to assume superiority.

He had a theory that eventually one club would have to emerge as the dominant force in Burnley and become, as he put it, the town's premier club.

He wanted that dominant force to be Burnley Rovers, as the new association football club was still called at that point, and he put forward a simple, but crucial suggestion. His proposal was to drop Rovers from the club's name so that the club would just be known as Burnley, thereby adopting the psychological high ground by carrying the name of the town.

The committee men all agreed, voted unanimously, and Burnley Football Club, born just days earlier, was now christened.

In July 1882, with the new season just around the corner, it was announced in the local press that -

"Burnley Football Club, which has now adopted association rules, has arranged a list of matches for the ensuing season, among which are engagements with Blackburn Rovers ('A' team), Haslingden and other local clubs".

All very well but what about the players? Originally it had been assumed that the players who had represented Burnley Rovers at Rugby would simply change codes, adapt smoothly to the round ball game and all would be well.

With the fixture list in place, loosely, the committee met to select possible teams and discuss tactics for the new challenge ahead. It soon dawned on these association pioneers that it was vital for new blood to be injected into the club or the infant Burnley FC may struggle to prosper or even to survive.

Another announcement in the local press –

"The Committee of Burnley Football Club have decided to play evening trial matches with several local clubs, to enable them to select the best possible elevens for the coming season. Any person desirous of participating in these practices will oblige by sending his name and address as early as possible to the Honorary Secretary of Burnley Football Club, George C. Waddington."

The new club, with new players, a new future and a new game to play, was just about ready to emerge into the association sunshine.

Burnley FC milestones

What constitutes a milestone is, of course, a matter of opinion. Within the pages of this book there are many milestones in the club's history which are highlighted in the coverage of each season. In compiling this list some of the more obvious highlights, which are well covered elsewhere, have been avoided, although no apologies are made for any duplication... some good things are best tasted more than once! Every Burnley fan will have his/her own personal milestones, and there are bound to be omissions, but hopefully this list will capture some of the flavour of the changing life and times of our great club.

1885 Oct 17 Best to get the bad news out of the way first! The 11-0 Cup defeat against Darwen Old Wanderers remains Burnley's record defeat in a major competition. The match remains somewhat shrouded in mystery, however, and probably for that reason is seldom given its place in infamy in football record books.

1887 Oct 15 Two years on, Burnley's first-ever victory in an F.A. Cup match, fittingly perhaps against those same Darwen Old Wanderers.

1888 Sep 8 The start of League football, with Burnley beaten 5-2 at Preston by the side destined to win the double in that inaugural season.

Sep 15 Only the second Saturday of League football and Burnley are making history. The Turfites come from 3 goals down to win 4-3 at Bolton with William Tait helping himself to the first-ever hat-trick in League football.

Oct 6 After four away games, Turf Moor staged its first League match. A 4-1 win against Bolton completed the club's first-ever double, following the earlier 4-3 win at Bolton.

Nov 3 Fred Poland, normally a centre-forward, appeared in goal. It was not an occasion to remember for Poland, who let in seven against Blackburn Rovers. He never played for the side again.

1889 Mar 2 Jack Yates became Burnley's first England international. He scored three times in a 6-1 win against Ireland, and was never capped for his country again!

1890 Mar 1 Claude Lambie scored the first League hat-trick seen at Turf Moor in a 7-0 win over Bolton, the club's first victory of the season at the eighteenth attempt.

Nov 15 The same Lambie became the first "Turfite" to score four in a game, in a 6-1 win against Derby.

1891 Mar 7 Preston were beaten 6-2, and Tom Nicol scored a hat-trick on his debut. He is still the only Burnley player to have achieved this in a League game.

1892 Jan 9 A 9-0 League win against Darwen, which still stands as Burnley's record victory in the League (it has been equalled three times in the F.A. Cup). Later that same season, Burnley beat Darwen 6-2 to complete the club's highest-scoring double.

Nov 26 Sandy Lang became the first player to reach 100 League appearances for Burnley. Up to this point, he had missed only six matches since the League's inauguration four years earlier.

1894 Mar 1 Burnley-born James Crabtree became the club's second England international. He won three caps while at Turf Moor before moving to Aston Villa in 1895 in what is often referred to as the first transfer between clubs involving a fee.

1897 Sep 4 Burnley's first match as a Second Division club, a 5-1 win at home to Blackpool.

Oct 2 Billy Bowes' goal against Newcastle was his 50th League goal for Burnley, making him the first to reach that milestone. He went on to score 79 in the League in total.

1898 Mar 28 Jimmy Ross scored five as Loughborough were hammered 9-3. He was the first nap-hander for the club, and this was (to date) the last time Burnley have scored nine in a League game. Ross's second goal was his twentieth of the season, another club landmark.

Apl 30 Promotion was secured in the famous "shotless" Test Match against Stoke, with both sides needing only a point and ensuring they both got just that. This led to the abolition of Test Matches, though they were revived in improved form (just!) 89 years later as play-offs.

Nov 26 Another milestone for Billy Bowes, as he became the first to reach 200 League appearances for the club. He failed to mark the occasion with a goal, but Blackburn were beaten 2-0.

1900 Apl 28 The infamous last-day defeat at Nottingham Forest when goalkeeper Jack Hillman attempted to buy safety for Burnley. With a final scoreline of 4-0 to Forest, it clearly didn't work... Burnley were relegated, and Hillman was banned for the whole of the following season.

1903 Nov 14 Defeat at Darwen (them again!) meant that Burnley failed to reach the first round proper of the F.A. Cup. This fate befell them only one other time, in the following season.

1904 Nov 26 Burnley fielded only ten men in a League game at Chesterfield, after defender Hugh Moffat missed his train connection. (The squad system was still several decades away).

1906 Jan 6 Defender Joe Taylor set a new club mark with his 300th League appearance.

1908 Apl 25 Dick Smith's goal in the final game of the season took his League tally to 24, beating Jimmy Ross's club record set a decade earlier.

1910 Sep 3 "The Clarets" were born as Burnley turned out in claret and blue for the first time. The story goes that they adopted the colours of then reigning champions Aston Villa in an attempt to improve the club's fortunes. Whatever the reason, the next few years certainly saw things change for the better.

1911 Apl 1 In his final game for the club, Fred Barron reached a new milestone of 400 League appearances.

1912 Mar 30 Bert Freeman scored his 30th League goal of the season. His final total of 32 smashed the previous club record. Within three years of his arrival from Everton in 1911, Freeman had set a new overall scoring record at Turf Moor, overtaking Billy Bowes.

1913 Jan 18 A 3-1 win at Lincoln completed a run of ten consecutive League victories, still the club record. Bert Freeman scored 14 of the 37 goals in that glorious sequence, the key factor in Burnley's return to the top flight at the end of the season.

Jan 25 A 3-5 defeat against Nottingham Forest was the first at Turf Moor since March 1911. The unbeaten run had stretched for 34 League games, another club record.

Mar 15 For the first time, Burnley's side included a half-back line of Halley, Boyle and Watson.

Mar 29 A first F.A. Cup semi-final appearance. A goalless draw against Sunderland at Bramall Lane was sadly followed by defeat in the replay at St. Andrew's.

1914 Apl 25 Too obvious, I hear you cry, but could we really ignore Burnley's first F.A. Cup final and only victory SO FAR in that famous competition, Bert Freeman's goal doing the necessary against Liverpool, with, yes, the reigning monarch in attendance for the first time and the medals mistakenly inscribed "English Cup".

1920 Feb 21 Bert Freeman became the first Burnley player to score a century of League goals, in only his 152nd appearance. No player since has reached the 100-goal mark so quickly. Only fourteen games and three goals later, his Turf Moor career was over.

Sep 4 Defeat at Bradford City meant that Burnley, with no points from three games, had equalled their worst start to a League season, BUT...

1921 Mar 25 Still only three defeats on the record as the unbeaten League run reached 30 matches. The following day saw the run end, but it remained the record within a single season for 83 years, until Arsenal's unbeaten Premiership campaign of 2003/04.

Apl 23 A 1-1 draw at Everton clinched Burnley's first Football League championship success.

1924 Feb 23 A third round F.A. Cup tie against Huddersfield attracted a crowd of 54,775, Turf Moor's biggest ever.

1925 Aug 29 The season began with a 10-0 defeat at Aston Villa, as Burnley failed to grasp the principles of the new offside law. It remains the club's biggest League reverse, equalled only once, against Sheffield United three seasons later.

Nov 7 Goalkeeper Jerry Dawson became the first (and still only) Burnley player to feature in 500 League games for the club.

1926 Apl 10 Louis Page, a winger played out of position at centre-forward, scored a double hat-trick in a 7-1 win at Birmingham. He remains the only Burnley player to have scored six in one game.

Apl 17 The first goal conceded against Bury was the 100th goal against of the season. The final figure in the "A" column for 1925-26 was 108, a club record. 1928-29 was the only other season when Burnley leaked a century.

1927 Nov 28 Turf Moor staged a full international for the first and so far only time. Burnley's Jack Hill and Louis Page were in the England side beaten 2-1 by Wales.

1928 Aug 29 The second of George Beel's three in a 7-2 win against Newcastle was his 104th League goal for Burnley, breaking Bert Freeman's record. Beel went on to score 179 before bowing out in 1932, and his record has never been remotely threatened since.

Dec 25 Jerry Dawson's 522nd and final League appearance. He remains the only 40-year-old to have played for Burnley at first-team level.

1930 Apl 26 Relegation with style... a 6-2 victory against Derby on the season's final day was insufficient to save the Clarets, as the bottom five sides all won.

1936 Mar 28 A debut for Tommy Lawton, aged 16 years and 163 days, Burnley's youngest-ever player. Nine months later, he moved to Everton, destined for greatness.

1947 Apl 26 Wembley! Burnley's first appearance underneath the Twin Towers, as a Second Division side, but First Division Charlton were the victors by 1-0 in the F.A. Cup final.

June 7 A curiosity... the only game Burnley have ever played in the month of June, a 1-1 draw against Millwall. The season had been extended after a notoriously harsh winter.

Oct 11 A crowd of 52,869 watched the First Division game against Blackpool, Turf Moor's highest-ever attendance for a League match.

1951 Mar 23 Goalkeeper Jimmy Strong's 203rd consecutive League appearance, a run dating back to the restart of League football after the war and a club record.

Sep 1 The debut of left-winger Billy Elliott, Burnley's new record signing at £25,000.

1952 Jan 19 Open to discussion, but possibly the best goal seen at Turf Moor? Many thought so... it was one of only three scored by Tommy Cummings in 434 League games for Burnley.

1955 Feb 15 The fourth round F.A. Cup tie against Chelsea was decided at the fifth attempt. In the course of 18 days, the two sides played 540 minutes of football before the London side progressed to the last sixteen. On only one other occasion (v Scunthorpe, 1989) have Burnley been taken past a first replay in the F.A. Cup.

1957 Jan 5 Ian Lawson, aged 17, scored four times on his debut in a third round F.A. Cup tie against Chesterfield. Lawson added another three in the next round against New Brighton, but then only another eight in his entire Clarets first-team career.

1960 May 2 Champions for the second time, as a 2-1 win at Maine Road clinched the First Division title. Burnley had not previously led the table prior to that final match.

Oct 24 Burnley's first-ever match in the League Cup, a low-key affair at Cardiff which the Clarets won 4-0. Despite two First Division clubs competing, the crowd was little over 8,000.

Nov 16 A much higher-key event as the Clarets made their European Cup debut with a 2-0 win at Turf Moor against French champions Reims.

Dec 3 Probably the greatest comeback in the club's history. Four goals down at Tottenham, Burnley came back to draw 4-4 against the side on its way to the League/Cup double.

1961 Mar 11 Another 4-4 draw, as a virtual Burnley reserve side held Chelsea. The club was fined £1,000 for fielding a weakened side in the build-up to a European quarter-final against Hamburg and an F.A. Cup semi-final against Tottenham.

Apl 27 Jimmy Adamson's goal at Birmingham was the Clarets' 100th League goal of the season. The final tally was 102, a club record. The only other time the century was reached was in the following season.

May 2 The League Cup semi-final replay against Aston Villa was Burnley's 62nd match of the club's busiest-ever season. Not only modern players are "overworked", and squads were much smaller in 1961!

Sep 30 A 5-3 win at Fulham made it seventeen goals scored from the last three away games.

1962 May 5 Wembley again, with Jimmy Robson scoring the 100th Cup final goal at the stadium as Burnley went down 1-3 to Tottenham.

1965 Aug 28 Ian Towers became the first Burnley player to appear as a substitute. In the 1965-66 season, subs were allowed only in cases of injury and were a comparative rarity.

1966 Sep 20 Burnley's debut in the Inter Cities Fairs Cup, the forerunner of the UEFA Cup. They would have qualified for the competition earlier but for the strict imposition of the "city clubs only" rule in its early years.

1967 May 13 16-year-old David Thomas made his League debut, becoming the youngest Claret first-teamer since Tommy Lawton, and still the youngest of the post-war era.

June Frank Casper was signed for £30,000, the first significant transfer fee paid by Burnley in over eight years. The fee broke the club record, which would fall again on several occasions over the next few years.

1968 May 10 Burnley beat Coventry 2-0 to win the F.A. Youth Cup. Nine of the eleven players in the starting line-up went on to play for the first team.

Aug A transfer milestone, as a six-figure fee was paid to Burnley for the first time, by Manchester United for Willie Morgan.

Nov 9 The eighth consecutive victory (League and League Cup) for a Clarets side largely consisting of youngsters, including Youth Cup winners David Thomas and Steve Kindon. The run included a memorable 5-1 win against that season's runaway League champions Leeds.

1971 May 1 The end of 24 seasons of top-flight membership after a season in which only 29 goals were scored in 42 League games and both cup "runs" ended at the first hurdle against lower division sides.

1972 Nov 4 The last game of a 22-match unbeaten League run, the best since the record-breaker of 1920-21. It included the first sixteen games of the 1972-73 season that would end in the Clarets' promotion back to the First Division.

1974 Aug 24 The sale of Martin Dobson to Everton for £300,000, a new club record which would be equalled the following year by Leighton James' move to Derby.

1975 Jan 4 Not Burnley's first defeat against a non-League side, but the one that hurt most, the Clarets then being high in the First Division and Wimbledon a mere Southern League outfit. It was the first home defeat suffered by a top-flight team against a non-League club since the 1920 League extension, and would prove a major stepping stone in Wimbledon's eventual rise to top-flight status themselves.

1976 Feb 7 The debut of Tony Morley, Burnley's first £100,000 signing.

Apl 24 A 1-3 home defeat against Coventry remains, at the time of writing, Burnley's last match in the top flight of English football.

1978 Sep 12 The worst crowd trouble ever seen at Turf Moor as many Celtic fans in a crowd estimated at 30,000 spilled over into the "Burnley section" of the Longside, forcing supporters on to the pitch and causing a 15-minute hold-up in play.

Nov 7 Having beaten Celtic both at Turf Moor and at Parkhead in the Anglo-Scottish Cup, the Clarets went on to a less glamorous semi-final tie against Mansfield. The second leg was decided by Turf Moor's first-ever penalty shoot-out, Burnley qualifying for a final against Oldham which they went on to win.

1979 Nov 24 A League win (5-3 v Cambridge) at the 25th attempt, following the longest sequence in the club's history without a victory.

1980 Aug 16 Burnley's first match as an associate member of the Football League, relegation to the Third Division having cost the club its full membership for the first time.

1983 Jan 19 Arguably the Clarets' greatest giant-killing act as, bottom of the Second Division, they travelled to Tottenham and won 4-1 to reach the semi-final of the League Cup.

June The appointment of John Bond brought to an end 29 years in which Burnley had always been managed by one of the club's former players.

July Following relegation to the Third Division, 19-year-old Trevor Steven was sold to Everton for a fee usually quoted at £300,000, equalling the Burnley record.

1984 Nov 17 Somewhat out of context with the depressing events of the period, Burnley's 9-0 F.A. Cup win at Penrith set a new club record away victory.

1985 Aug 17 The Clarets' first-ever match in the Fourth Division.

1986 Nov 4 Turf Moor's lowest confirmed attendance for a League game, just 1,696 turning out for a Tuesday night game against Colchester. They were rewarded with a 2-1 win.

1987 May 9 We all know this one! "The Orient Game", further comment unnecessary.

1988 May 29 A crowd of 80,841 at Wembley to see Wolves beat Burnley 2-0 in the final of the Sherpa Van Trophy. The gate was never subsequently equalled at the old stadium, and is likely to remain the biggest crowd ever to watch a match involving two sides from the League's bottom division.

1991 Nov 30 A 2-1 win at Northampton completed a run of nine successive League victories, the best of the post-war era. They were the first nine games after Jimmy Mullen took over as manager... has any manager, anywhere, had a better start?

1992 Apl 28 Goodbye to the basement as Burnley clinched the Fourth Division championship with a thrilling last-minute win at York.

1994 May 29 Promotion via the play-offs, with a 2-1 win at Wembley against Stockport (who had finished the season twelve points ahead of Burnley).

1995 Sep 16 Farewell to the Longside. A 2-1 win against Hull was the last match prior to the demolition of the famous old terrace, in preparation for the building of what is now the James Hargreaves Stand.

1996 Mar 30 Adrian Heath's appearance at Wycombe meant that he became Burnley's first player-manager. Only Chris Waddle has since repeated this.

1998 Dec 30 Steve Davis's return to the club made him Burnley's record incoming transfer at £850,000. He was already the club's record sale following his 1995 move to Luton for £750,000.

2000 Nov Ian Moore became the first player for whom Burnley paid a £1 million transfer fee.

2005 Jan Robbie Blake became the club's first £1 million sale. Within the same month, Richard Chaplow became the second.

Fourth Division Champions 1991-1992
Back: Chris Pearce, John Pender, Mark Yates, Andy Farrell, Paul McKenzie, Mark Monington, Ian Measham, John Deary,
Front: Robbie Painter, David Williams, Mike Conroy, John Francis, Joe Jakub, Steve Davis, Jimmy Mullen (manager)

1882-83

After a number of trial matches the Burnley committee were satisfied that the playing staff was in place for the new season, a combination of former Burnley Rovers rugby players and new arrivals from other clubs with association football experience.

The first recorded fixture of the infant Burnley Football Club was played at Calder Vale on the evening of Thursday 10 August 1882. Burnley Wanderers were the opponents and it was advertised and subsequently described as another trial match. Although it may have been the latest in a series of such matches it was certainly the one most vigorously contested by the players who had previously impressed the most.

The Burnley Committee were delighted with a 4-0 victory for their team on its first "serious" outing although sadly neither the actual line-up nor the goalscorers are recorded for posterity.

However, it seemed rather unsatisfactory not to at least speculate on the personnel involved on this historic occasion so the Simpson thought processes have been at work.

Assuming that the strongest available team was selected, the likely line-up was as follows : (2-3-5 formation)

R.B.Chase, Samuel Hargreaves, J.T.Marsland, Harry Walton, Tom French, George Waddington, Harry Culpan, Tom Midgley (capt), William Brown, Arthur Birley, Tom Bryce.

Burnley's fixtures for that inaugural historic season had been arranged mainly against a combination of local sides and relatively junior clubs within a reasonable travelling distance. All opponents were in Lancashire with the longest trip made to and by Kirkham FC. Three senior clubs were to be faced, Accrington, Blackburn Olympic and, the club who would go on to become public enemy number one for all supporters of Burnley FC, Blackburn Rovers. There was a twist however, it had been agreed that against the newcomers to the round ball game the senior clubs would not field their strongest line-ups. The opponents would be billed as an "A" team, perhaps not necessarily a reserve side but certainly with some key players missing.

Arthur Birley
scored the winner in the first Hospital Cup final

The first of these fixtures was at Calder Vale against Blackburn Rovers A, an out and out Rovers reserve team, but who were good enough to give Burnley a football lesson, cruising to a 10-0 win and showing the Burnley players, as well as the spectators just how much improvement was needed.

This was a week after Astley Bridge, a well established and, importantly, well trained team came to Calder Vale in Burnley's first-ever Lancashire FA Cup tie, and crushed the homesters 8-0.

It was by no means all doom and gloom however, there were some victories. Brierfield had been beaten 2-0 early on and Read were overcome 5-0 at Calder Vale at the end of October after Burnley introduced some new players into the team. This provoked an indignant reaction from the Read club which perhaps illustrates just how far football has come since those early days. The Secretary of Read FC wrote to the Burnley Express complaining that when the fixture had originally been arranged, it was against Burnley, not North East Lancashire, and in future would they play as agreed. Burnley's crime, as Read saw it, was to include "non Burnley" players in the team. The new players Burnley had imported from afar were Moorhouse and Bury from Darwen, Clegg from Enfield and Waddington from Accrington!

The club was beginning to find its feet and at the turn of the year discussions began with Burnley Cricket Club that the two clubs should join forces with the ultimate aim of sharing the facilities at the town's premier sporting venue, Turf Moor, Burnley CC's home for more than 50 years.

On 3 February 1883 Burnley FC played its final first team match at Calder Vale, beating Haslingden 1-0. The following week the club used Calder Vale for the last time when Burnley Seconds hosted Clitheroe Seconds, losing 2-4.

On Saturday 17 February 1883 Burnley Football Club played its first-ever match at Turf Moor against Rawtenstall. A large crowd gathered to enjoy the game and to witness the dawn of a new era with "the Turfites" as the team soon became known, getting off to a winning start against opponents they had already beaten. Alas it didn't happen. Not for the first time and certainly not the last, Burnley failed to perform on the big day, Rawtenstall raining on the Turf Moor parade with a 6-3 victory.

Padiham was undoubtedly the big club in local terms in the early 1880's and they were not about to make it easy for the newcomers, handing out 6-0 and 7-0 beatings, although Blackburn Olympic A and Accrington A were both overcome at Turf Moor.

As the first season of association football in Burnley drew to a close it was announced that a trophy was to be donated by Dr Dean, to be played for by local clubs, with proceeds to be donated to a fund for a proposed new hospital to be built in Burnley. It began by being known, logically enough, as Dr Dean's Cup but later became the Burnley Hospital Cup, believed to be the oldest charitable football tournament in the world.

It seems appropriate that Burnley FC were the inaugural winners of that competition, the first trophy "on the Turf Moor sideboard" at the end of a historic first season of association football.

1882-83

Managed by Club Committee

	Date			Opponents	Result		Goalscorers
	Aug	10	h	BURNLEY WANDERERS	W	4-0	unknown (4)
	Sep	23	h	BRIERFIELD	W	2-0	unknown (2)
		30	a	Read	L	3-7	unknown (3)
Burnley's first Lancs Cup tie	Oct	14	h	ASTLEY BRIDGE	L	0-8	
		21	h	BLACKBURN ROVERS A	L	0-10	
		28	h	READ	W	5-0	French (2), Lathom, Clegg, Bury
	Nov	4	a	Great Harwood	L	0-1	
		11	h	KIRKHAM	W	3-1	unknown (3)
		18	a	Rawtenstall	W	1-0	unknown
		25	h	BLACKBURN OLYMPIC A	L	1-4	unknown
	Dec	2	a	Accrington A	D	2-2	scrimmage, Clegg
		16	h	IRWELL SPRINGS	W	2-1	French, Duckworth
		23	h	BURNLEY WANDERERS	W	7-3	Birley, Sutcliffe, scrimmage, Brown (2), Culpan, Barlow
longest trip of the season		30	a	Kirkham	W	2-0	Bryce, unknown
	Jan	6	a	Haslingden	L	1-3	Sutcliffe
		13	a	Blackburn Rovers A	L	1-4	Birley
		20	h	CLITHEROE	W	2-0	Wilkinson, Cross
	Feb	3	h	HASLINGDEN	W	1-0	Newsome
		10	a	Clitheroe	L	1-3	unknown
first game at Turf Moor		17	h	RAWTENSTALL	L	3-6	unknown (3)
		24	a	Padiham	L	0-6	
	Mar	3	h	BLACKBURN OLYMPIC A	W	4-2	Wilkinson (2), scrimmage, Avery
		10	h	ACCRINGTON A	W	2-1	scrimmage, Wilkinson
		17	a	Irwell Springs	L	0-5	
		23	h	GREAT HARWOOD	W	4-2	unknown (4)
		24	h	PADIHAM	L	0-7	
	Apr	7	h	BRIERFIELD	L	0-3	
Dr Dean Cup		14	h	PENTRIDGE ROVERS	W	3-0	unknown (3)
Dr Dean Cup	May	12	a	Loveclough	W	2-0	unknown (2)
Dr Dean Cup		24	h	TRINITY	W	5-2	unknown (5)
Dr Dean Cup		31	h	BURNLEY UNION STAR	W	3-1	unknown (3)
Dr Dean Cup	Jun	7	h	FULLEDGE	W	8-0	unknown (8)
Dr Dean Cup final		11	h	BURNLEY RAMBLERS	W	2-1	Eastwood, Birley
		18	h	BLACKBURN ROVERS XI	L	0-3	

1883-84

As the players and officials of Burnley FC were preparing for the club's first full season at Turf Moor, Burnley Ramblers FC, one of Burnley's main rivals for the position of "the town's premier club", announced that they were to use Calder Vale, Burnley's former home, as their own home ground.

A number of new players appeared in Burnley's ranks as the new campaign got under way, including defender James Harper from Halliwell who was soon appointed as club captain, and Jack Gair, another defender, who had previously played for Hearts. Burnley also recruited goalkeeper James Wigglesworth, a native of the town who had developed a fine reputation with Burnley Ramblers and Burnley Olympic.

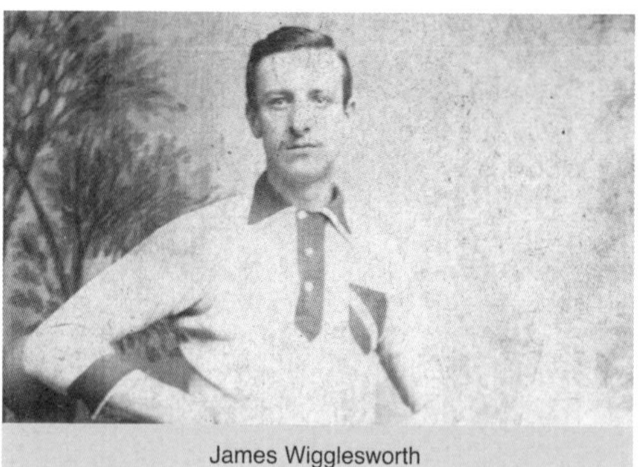

James Wigglesworth

After some encouraging early results, including an 11-0 victory against Kirkham, Burnley were crushed 1-9 by Padiham. That was followed by a 1-3 defeat by Blackpool, Burnley's first visit to the seaside, and a 1-4 home defeat by another Blackpool team, South Shore, in the Lancashire Cup. The Burnley committee decided it was time for further recruitment and the club's Scottish Agents again approached Hearts, signing two forwards, Ronaldson and William Gair the younger brother of recent arrival Jack Gair.

Then in October 1883 Burnley secured the services of a player who would emerge as the dominant personality at Turf Moor in the 1880's and whose Burnley career would continue into the days of league football. Dannie Friel had been recruited by Accrington from West of Scotland club Vale of Leven early in 1883 but was persuaded to switch his allegiance to Turf Moor. Friel was the most versatile of players, equally comfortable in defence or in attack and was to become almost a permanent fixture in Burnley's team for many years.

Dannie Friel's home debut proved to be the most controversial match so far played by Burnley in their short existence. Blackburn team, Witton, were the Turfites' opponents and the match kicked off in torrential rain with a gale blowing behind the visitors, who had been fortunate enough to win the toss. The weather made good football impossible and Witton spent the first half camped around the Burnley goal, scoring just once. During the half time interval the rain became even heavier and as the Burnley players prepared for their turn with the elements in their favour, all the Witton players suddenly emerged from the changing rooms, fully dressed. The Turf Moor fans were not impressed and proceeded to boo and hoot at the visitors as they left the ground. "Soft Blackburners", "Summer football players" and "Hothouse plants" were among the more polite cries aimed in their direction as the departure of the Witton players and officials effectively caused the match to be abandoned.

In December Burnley began their defence of the Hospital Cup but already such were the demands of an already hectic fixture list that the club fielded its second team when the cup ties clashed with "ordinary" matches.

On New Years Day 1884 there was a milestone in Burnley FC's history when the club entertained its first visitors from "cockneydom" as London was referred to in those days by the populace "up north". London Scottish were the club that had accepted the invitation of the Turf Moor committee and the 2-2 draw that the two teams fought out was said to be the best attended match so far played at Turf Moor as well as one of the most exciting.

Then on 2 February 1884 came the Turf Moor fixture that Burnley supporters had dreamed about since the club was formed. Preston North End were the visitors, "the Invincibles", by far the best team around in those far off days. The Turfites had been unbeaten in 15 matches since the fiasco with Witton in the previous November and there was genuine belief among the Burnley faithful that their team could give "the Preston cracks" a severe test. Alas it was not to be and a spirited display by the Burnley team was not enough as North End ended the unbeaten sequence with a 6-2 victory.

At the end of February Burnley paid a nostalgic visit to Calder Vale, the club's former home, to play Burnley Ramblers. It was a mid-week friendly, "well attended by shop assistants and others who enjoy the benefit of the Tuesday half-holiday". The Ramblers were no match for their visitors who cruised to a 10-1 victory.

In three previous encounters with fierce local rivals Padiham, Burnley had conceded 22 goals and scored just once. For the latest contest at Turf Moor, the Turfites felt they were ready to replace "the Pads" as the area's leading club. Twelve thousand spectators packed the ground with all other local football being called off to allow the players to attend and to perhaps witness a shift in the balance of football power. Almost, but not quite. Burnley led 1-0 and 2-1 but tired in the final quarter and Padiham scored three late goals to take the honours 4-2.

As the campaign drew to a close Burnley, fielding mainly their second team players, managed to retain their hold on the Hospital Cup, Trinity being defeated in the final at Turf Moor.

"The game was very pleasantly contested throughout, there being an utter absence of all rowdyism, both teams meeting together after the match in social harmony and good will."

1883-84

Managed by Club Committee

	Date			Opponents	Result		Goalscorers
	Jul	30	h	NELSON	W	7-1	unknown (7)
	Aug	2	a	Nelson	L	5-7	unknown (5)
		16	a	Accrington	W	3-2	Towler, Brown, Gallocher
	Sep	15	a	Blackburn Park Road	L	0-7	
		22	h	KIRKHAM	W	11-0	Birley, Cross, Bryce (5), unknown (4)
		29	a	Witton	L	2-4	Birley, Towler
	Oct	6	h	GREAT HARWOOD	W	4-2	unknown (4)
		13	a	Padiham	L	1-9	unknown
		20	a	Blackpool	L	1-3	unknown
Lancs Cup		27	h	BLACKPOOL SOUTH SHORE	L	1-4	unknown
	Nov	3	a	Clitheroe Low Moor	D	1-1	Swarbrick og
aban 45m, heavy rain		10	h	WITTON	aban	0-1	
		17	h	RISHTON	W	3-0	unknown (3)
		24	h	EAGLEY	W	5-0	opp og, Friel 2, Hartley, Bryce
	Dec	1	a	Clitheroe	W	3-0	Friel (2), Walton
		8	h	ENFIELD	W	7-0	Ronaldson (3), unknown (4)
		15	h	CLITHEROE LOW MOOR	D	1-1	scrimmage
Hospital Cup		15	a	Hapton Green	W	4-0	unknown (4)
		22	a	Church	D	1-1	unknown
		25	a	Lower Darwen	W	1-0	unknown
		29	a	Great Harwood	W	6-1	unknown (6)
first London opponents	Jan	1	h	LONDON SCOTTISH	D	2-2	unknown (2)
		2	h	BOLTON ASSOCIATION	W	2-0	unknown (2)
		5	h	BLACKBURN PARK ROAD	D	1-1	unknown
		12	h	RAWTENSTALL	W	6-0	Friel (2), Bryce (2), Marshall (2)
		19	h	CHURCH	W	3-1	Marshall, scrimmage, Ronaldson
		26	h	BLACKBURN OLYMPIC	W	3-0	Marshall, Friel (2)
	Feb	2	h	PRESTON N E	L	2-6	Marshall, Friel
		9	h	IRWELL SPRINGS	W	3-0	unknown (3)
		16	a	Eagley	W	1-0	unknown
		23	a	Irwell Springs	L	0-4	
		26	a	Burnley Ramblers	W	10-1	unknown (10)
aban 70m, disputed goal	Mar	1	h	CLITHEROE	aban	3-0	Culpan, Ronaldson (2)
		8	a	Rawtenstall	W	5-4	Bryce, Friel, Marshall, Ronaldson (2)
		15	h	BLACKPOOL	W	4-2	Bryce (2), Marshall, Whiteside
		22	a	Enfield	D	1-1	Marshall
Hospital Cup		22	h	NELSON	W	3-1	unknown (3)
		25	h	BURNLEY UNION STAR	W	4-2	unknown (3), Bryce
Attendance 12000		29	h	PADIHAM	L	2-4	Friel, Bryce
	Apr	5	a	Great Lever	L	2-3	unknown (2)
		11	h	GREAT LEVER	L	0-4	
		12	h	LOWER DARWEN	W	3-1	Dowds, opp og, Friel
		19	h	WITTON	W	6-1	Marshall (2), Dowds (3), Birtwistle
Hospital Cup		19	a	Hapton	W	2-1	Birley (2)
Hosp Cup semi, at Rake Head	May	12	n	Lowerhouse	W	4-0	opp og, Midgley, Walton, unknown
J Whiteside benefit		16	h	GREAT LEVER	W	4-2	Brown (2), unknown (2)
Hospital Cup final		26	h	TRINITY	W	3-1	unknown (3)

1884-85

Among the new players recruited for the new season by the Burnley Committee was rugged half-back Jack Keenan, signed from Clitheroe. Keenan had played against the Turfites during the previous campaign and had been earmarked as a player with some potential. He would go on to wear the Burnley colours with distinction for almost a decade.

Jack Keenan

Another new arrival was Alex McClintock, a defender from the Scottish club Vale of Leven, who had won three full caps for Scotland during the 1880's. Such was his versatility that most of his appearances for Burnley would be in goal !

Dannie Friel had been appointed as club captain following James Harper's departure for Rawtenstall.

This was perhaps the season that Burnley FC began to come of age and more and more fixtures were arranged with established senior clubs. In September 1884 Burnley travelled to play Bolton Wanderers for the first time and, although Bolton won 3-1, Burnley were by no means disgraced against a club who had been around since 1877 and were one of football's biggest names.

A few weeks later Burnley's visitors to Turf Moor for the first time were opponents who would become "the old enemy", FA Cup holders Blackburn Rovers. Once again Burnley had to admit defeat, Rovers coming out on top 4-2, but the Turfites' committee, and, especially the fans, were not despondent. They could all see that tremendous progress was being made.

Around this time matters were starting to come to a head in respect of the payment by football clubs to their players. Professionalism was still not accepted by the Football Association and, although most clubs provided expenses, many were much more generous with "additional remuneration".

Burnley FC were reasonably honest about their stance and decided against joining the FA. The club was soon in danger of being ostracised as FA members were instructed not to play against non-members and pre-arranged fixtures began to be cancelled.

Suddenly both Preston North End and Accrington were expelled from the FA for apparently making illegal payments to players. Other clubs were later suspended and, from being very much in the minority, Burnley FC were suddenly part of the Northern, mainly Lancashire, movement rebelling against the edict of the Football Association that players should not receive any payment.

A meeting of many Northern clubs was convened in Bolton to discuss the possible formation of a breakaway movement in competition with the FA, to be called the British Football Association.

The FA could see the writing starting to appear on its wall, and it read that professionalism was the way forward. There was a truce, uneasy at first, but the first blows for a major change in the structure of the game had been struck.

In December four new players arrived at Turf Moor, all Scots, defenders Jack Beattie and Hunter and forwards Arthurs and J McNee.

Over the New Year the Burnley Committe once again demonstrated that they were determined that more illustrious opponents should be invited to Turf Moor. Scottish clubs Cowlairs, Kilmarnock and Glasgow Northern all appeared in opposition to the Turfites with varying success for the locals. It was unfortunate that the matches co-incided with a spell of arctic weather in the Burnley area and it appeared that many people preferred the attractions of the numerous local ponds that were frozen solid, providing a haven for ice skating enthusiasts.

In late January 1885 the FA seemed at last to accept that professionalism in football was inevitable and a sub-committee recommended that it be legalised. A vote took place and although it was narrowly in favour of the recommendation the proposal was lost as, under FA rules, a two thirds majority was required.

In February another former international arrived at Turf Moor, Alf Jones had played for both Walsall Swifts and Great Lever and had won three England caps at left back in the early 1880's.

In the game against a Blackburn Select X1 Burnley fielded two internationals in their team for the first time, Jones making his Turfites' debut alongside Alex McClintock.

Then at the end of March 1885, came a significant milestone along the Burnley FC road to success. Blackburn Rovers sent a full strength team to Turf Moor - and were soundly beaten 5-1, the first success by the Turfites against one of the strongest teams around at the time. It was certainly a morale booster for the players, the Burnley Committee and the supporters as another season drew to a close and with the prospects of major changes ahead.

1884-85

Managed by Club Committee

	Date			Opponents	Result		Goalscorers	Att.
	Aug	1	a	Burnley Union Star	W	4-0	unknown (4)	
		12	h	BURNLEY UNION STAR	W	4-2	unknown (4)	
		16	a	Preston N E	L	0-1		10000
		19	h	BLACKBURN XI	W	2-1	Bryce, Ronaldson	
		23	a	Rawtenstall	W	7-2	unknown (7)	
		30	a	Accrington	W	3-0	Worthington, Dewhurst, Friel	
	Sep	6	a	Bolton W	L	1-3	Dewhurst	2500
		13	a	Blackpool	W	4-0	Friel, unknown, Crawford, Strachan	
		20	h	ASTLEY BRIDGE	W	4-0	scrimmage, Bryce (2), Strachan	
Lancs Cup		20	a	Bradshaw	L	1-2	unknown	
		27	h	BLACKBURN R	L	2-4	Gemmell (2)	
	Oct	4	h	WITTON	W	1-0	Keenan	
		6	h	PRESTON ZINGARI	W	2-0	Crawford, scrimmage	
		11	h	GREAT LEVER	W	4-0	Bryce (2), Strachan (2)	
		18	a	Clitheroe	W	4-2	unknown (4)	
		25	a	Halliwell	W	1-0	Logan	2000
		27	h	BOLTON W	L	0-2		
	Nov	1	h	RAWTENSTALL	W	5-0	Crawford, opp og, Aspden, Strachan, Bryce	
		3	a	Bolton W	L	1-3	Conway	4000
		8	a	Great Lever	L	0-3		2000
		10	h	PRESTON N E	W	2-1	Keenan, Strachan	
Hospital Cup		10	a	Robin Hood Swifts	W	11-0	unknown (11)	
		15	h	BLACKBURN PARK ROAD	W	2-1	Aspden (2)	
		17	a	Preston N E	L	1-3	Strachan	4000
		22	a	Astley Bridge	W	3-1	Thompson, scrimmage, Walmsley og	
		24	h	HALLIWELL	D	2-2	Gallocher, McFetridge	moderate
		29	h	DERBY MIDLAND	W	8-0	McNee (2), Friel (3), Bryce, Keenan, unknown	large
Hospital Cup		29	a	West End	L	1-2	unknown	
	Dec	2	a	Halliwell	L	1-4	Bryce	
		6	h	GREAT LEVER	D	1-1	Bryce	3000
		8	a	Blackburn Olympic	W	2-1	Strachan, unknown	
		13	a	Padiham	W	4-0	Hudson og, scrimmage (2), Bryce	9000
		15	h	BLACKBURN OLYMPIC	L	2-3	unknown, scrimmage	
		20	a	Accrington	W	1-0	unknown	3000
		25	h	BOLTON W	W	3-2	unknown (3)	
		27	a	Witton	L	0-1		800
first Scottish opponents	Jan	1	h	COWLAIRS	D	2-2	Arthurs, Strachan	1000
		2	h	KILMARNOCK	L	2-3	unknown (2)	
		3	h	GLASGOW NORTHERN	W	4-0	Balshaw (2), opp og, Aspin	
		10	h	NORTHWICH V	W	4-1	Bryce, Strachan, Mackereth (2)	2000
		17	h	ACCRINGTON	L	2-4	Arthurs (2)	4000
		24	a	Clitheroe	W	3-0	Bryce, Woods (2)	
		26	h	BLACKPOOL SOUTH SHORE	W	8-0	unknown (8)	
		31	h	HALLIWELL	W	3-2	Crawford, McCrae, Strachan	3000
	Feb	2	a	Bolton W	W	2-1	Arthurs, unknown	2000
		7	h	PADIHAM	L	0-1		7000
		14	h	BLACKPOOL	W	3-2	Arthurs, scrimmage, Bryce	
		16	h	BOLTON W	W	3-2	Keenan, McCrae, Strachan	4000
		21	a	Blackburn Park Road	D	1-1	unknown	
		23	h	BLACKBURN SELECT XI	W	4-0	Woods, Arthurs (2), Bryce	fair
		28	a	Preston N E	D	4-4	Arthurs, Strachan, Bryce (2)	8000
	Mar	7	a	Great Lever	L	0-3		4000
		9	h	GREAT LEVER	L	1-3	unknown	
		14	a	Accrington	L	1-4	Arthurs	4000
		21	h	PADIHAM	D	2-2	unknown, Beattie	5000
		23	h	BLACKBURN R	W	5-1	Friel, Strachan (2), Cowell og, Kennedy	2500
		28	h	BOLTON W	L	0-4		large
		30	h	MANCHESTER	W	10-1	Bryce (2), Arthurs (2), Kennedy (2), McCrae (2), Strachan (2)	
	Apr	4	a	Blackburn Olympic	D	2-2	Strachan, scrimmage	
		6	h	ACTON	W	7-0	Strachan (2), Woods, unknown, Beattie (2), Bryce	800
		11	h	BURSLEM P V	W	4-1	scrimmage, Arthurs, Bryce (2)	large
		16	h	BURNLEY RAMBLERS	W	7-1	unknown (7)	
		18	a	Padiham	D	3-3	Arthurs, Woods, Bryce	5000
		20	h	BURNLEY UNION STAR	W	4-0	Woods, Strachan (2), Kennedy	3000
		25	h	BLACKBURN OLYMPIC	D	1-1	Woods	5000
	Jun	5	h	BLACKBURN OLYMPIC	W	2-1	Bryce (2)	
		8	h	BURNLEY UNION STAR	D	1-1	Strachan	
		27	a	Irwell Springs	D	1-1	unknown	
		29	h	ACCRINGTON	D	1-1	Bryce	large

1885-86

The big football news of the summer of 1885 was the formal acceptance by the Football Association of professionalism in football. It had finally been ratified by the FA at a meeting in July, although there were certain conditions attached to the decision. Professionals could only play in the FA Cup and County FA competitions, if they had been born, or had resided for a minimum of two years, within six miles of their club's ground.

As the season got under way it was announced that the well known cricketer Frank Sugg had been engaged as Burnley FC secretary and as a player. Sugg had been playing County Cricket for Derbyshire and had been signed by Burnley Cricket Club for the 1885 campaign, joining his brother Walter Sugg who was the Burnley CC professional.

Sugg made his first appearance for the Turfites in a resounding 9-0 win against Derby St Lukes in which "the visitors met with a most crushing defeat, during the second half they were quite exhausted and over-matched"

A crowd of over 6,000 squeezed into Turf Moor for the season's first encounter with Padiham in late September. The match was originally intended to be a Lancashire Cup clash but was eventually played as a friendly fixture, Burnley winning 4-2, their first-ever success against "the Pads" at Turf Moor.

As mid-October came around it was time for the first round of the FA Cup, Burnley FC's first entry into the competition being away to Darwen Old Wanderers.

Because of the FA's ruling on professionals the lack of priority given to the tie is apparent as Burnley had already arranged a friendly fixture at Turf Moor for the same day when Wolves were to be opposed by the Turfites' strongest team. Partly as a gesture of protest Burnley fielded their entire reserve side at Darwen - and were crushed 0-11.

As the season progressed the Turfites were certainly winning many more games than they were losing but they could get nowhere near the best team around in that first season of open professionalism, Preston North End "the Invincibles". During that campaign the sides met four times with North End winning all four, scoring 23 goals against the Turfites and conceding just five.

The Turf Moor pitch got progressively worse as the weather during that particularly harsh winter deteriorated. There were letters to the local Press complaining about the state of it after heavy rain and asking the Burnley Committee to arrange for it to be drained in the summer. According to one scribe the pitch was "a veritable slough of despond that was not fit for a good team to play good football on". The pitches of many other clubs were no better, particularly in icy weather, when watching football as well as playing it could be an arduous task. On one especially raw winter's day in 1886 Burnley had a fixture against the 1883 FA Cup winners Blackburn Olympic at their Hole I' Th' Wall ground. The pitch was covered with snow and there was a biting wind cutting into every one of the 600 hardy souls who had braved the elements. One of those "enjoying" the game was the Burnley Express correspondent who reported thus "....a more comfortless day could not be imagined and the shivering spectators were only too glad when half time came so they could rush off to an adjacent hostelry to imbibe a hot scotch or buttered rum or two".

The Burnley Committee were determined to continue to strengthen their pool of players whenever possible. During the winter of 1885-86 an agent was instructed to visit Alexandria in the West of Scotland, home of Vale of Leven, a club that had proved to be fertile soil in the past for recruiting players. Now that professionalism was legal, the English clubs were more open about their approaches to Scottish talent. The trouble was the English view of professionalism was not yet shared by the Scots and there was a great deal of bitterness that their top players were going south in droves, lured by attractive offers of wages and jobs. On this occasion the Burnley representative was left in no doubt as to the views of the locals "as those in the town, on hearing what his mission was, followed him up the street and sent his hat into the gutter". The visitor was "conveyed" to the railway station and sent on his way with a message to Burnley FC that "if they sent any other person to try to take away their best players that person would be harshly treated."

On the whole the 1885-86 campaign was a successful one for the Turfites. Far more games were won than were lost and of the 107 goals conceded 34 came in just five matches from the players of Preston and Darwen Old Wanderers!

Announcements.

SPECIAL FOOTBALL MATCH
AT TURF MOOR
ON MONDAY EVENING NEXT, MAY 24TH,
in aid of the Hospital Funds.

PADIHAM V. BURNLEY DISTRICT.

Kick-off 6-15. Admission 3d.

District Team: —— (Wanderers), goal; Whitaker and Birnie (Wanderers), backs; Grimshaw, Robin (Stars), and Keenan (Burnley), half-backs; McNee, M'Crae, Friel (Burnley), McAulay and Trafford (Stars), forwards.

1885-86

Managed by Club Committee

	Date			Opponents	Result		Goalscorers	Att.
	Aug	15	a	Everton	W	4-2	unknown (4)	
		22	a	Clitheroe	W	4-2	unknown (4)	
	Sep	5	a	Rawtenstall	W	3-1	unknown (3)	
		12	a	Astley Bridge	L	0-3		
		19	a	Bolton W	L	1-2	Abrahams	
		21	h	DERBY ST LUKES	W	9-0	Friel (2), NcNee (2), McCrae, Sugg, Woods (2), Kennedy	
		26	h	PADIHAM	W	4-2	McNee, McConnell og, Kennedy, Woods	6000
		28	h	EVERTON	W	4-0	Beattie, Friel (3)	
	Oct	3	a	Blackburn R	D	2-2	Woods (2)	
		5	h	SHEFFIELD	W	8-1	unknown (8)	
		10	h	CHURCH	L	2-3	Friel (2)	4000
first game out of Lancashire		12	a	Burslem Port Vale	L	2-5	unknown (2)	2000
Burnley's first FA Cup tie		17	a	Darwen Old Wanderers	L	0-11		
note friendly on the same day!		17	h	WOLVERHAMPTON W	W	4-1	Friel, McNee, Woods, unknown	
		19	h	BLACKBURN R	D	1-1	scrimmage	
		24	h	BLACKBURN PARK RD	W	5-0	Friel (3), Beattie, Kennedy	1000
		31	h	PRESTON N E	L	3-8	Woods, Friel, Abrahams	6000
	Nov	7	h	ACCRINGTON	W	4-1	Friel (2), Kennedy, McCrae	3000
		14	h	PADIHAM	W	4-1	Friel, unknown (3)	3000
		16	a	Great Lever	L	1-2	Kennedy	
		21	h	BOLTON W	D	2-2	unknown (2)	great
		23	a	West Bromwich A	W	3-0	unknown (3)	
		28	a	Accrington	L	0-2		1000
	Dec	5	a	Aston Villa	D	1-1	Woods	3000
		7	a	Leek	L	2-4	unknown (2)	
		12	h	WALSALL TOWN	W	3-1	Friel (3)	
		14	a	Blackburn R	W	2-0	Howett, unknown	thousands
		19	a	Church	W	4-1	Howett, unknown (3)	
		22	h	CORINTHIANS	W	3-2	Friel (2), Kennedy	
		25	h	WELSH DRUIDS	W	5-0	unknown (5)	
		26	h	NOTTS RANGERS	W	5-0	McNee, unknown (4)	
		28	h	LONDON CASUALS	D	2-2	Kennedy, Friel	meagre
	Jan	2	h	HALLIWELL	W	8-2	Woods (2), Miller (3), McCrae, Beattie, Friel	
		4	h	BOOTLE	W	3-1	Woods, Kennedy, Friel	
		9	a	Wolverhampton W	D	0-0		
		11	h	GREAT LEVER	D	1-1	Friel	1000
		16	h	CLITHEROE LOW MOOR	W	3-0	Beattie, Friel, Parkinson	
		18	h	BLACKBURN OLYMPIC	W	2-0	Bryce, McNee	1000
		23	a	Darwen	L	1-3	unknown	1500
		25	h	STAVELEY	W	3-0	Woods, Lang, Friel	300
		30	a	Great Lever	W	2-1	Friel, McNee	meagre
	Feb	1	a	Blackburn Olympic	W	1-0	Friel	
		6	h	BLACKBURN R	W	1-0	unknown	4000
		8	a	Bolton W	L	0-3		
		13	h	RAWTENSTALL	W	3-0	Woods (2), Miller	
		20	a	Padiham	D	1-1	Miller	immense
		22	a	Preston N E	L	1-9	McNee	3000
		27	h	ASTON VILLA	W	2-1	Abrahams, Friel	
	Mar	6	a	Accrington	L	1-2	Keenan	
		13	h	GREAT LEVER	W	7-1	Keenan (2), Miller (2), McNee, McCrae, Woods	
		15	h	PRESTON N E	L	1-2	Woods	great
		20	a	Blackburn Olympic	W	3-2	Woods, McCrae, Friel	300
		27	h	WALSALL TOWN	W	3-1	Woods, Miller, McCrae	
		29	h	BOLTON W	W	3-2	McCrae (2), Keenan	2000
	Apr	3	h	BLACKBURN OLYMPIC	W	3-0	Friel (2), Woods	3500
		5	h	ACCRINGTON	W	3-1	McCrae, Woods, Friel	
		10	h	PADIHAM	W	5-0	Woods (2), Kennedy (3)	
		17	h	RAWTENSTALL	W	1-0	McCrae	
		19	a	Preston N E	L	0-4		
		24	h	DARWEN	W	3-2	Friel, Woods, scrimmage	
		26	h	LEEK	D	1-1	Kennedy	1000
Hospital Cup	May	3	a	Colne	D	1-1	Beattie	1000
		22	a	Padiham	L	3-4	McNee, McCrae, Waugh	
Hospital Cup		31	h	PADIHAM	W	2-0	Kennedy, Friel	2000

1886-87

The approach of the new season brought a number of new players, many coming from big local rivals Padiham, with goalkeeper James McConnell, the versatile William McFetridge and forwards Pat Gallocher and David Waugh all transferring their allegiance to Turf Moor from The Arbories.
The major event in the Autumn of 1886 was the arrival in Burnley of Prince Albert Victor, Queen Victoria's grandson who was invited to officially open the town's brand new hospital, to be named in Her Majesty's honour.
The Prince duly performed the opening ceremony and then, as part of the programme of events meticulously planned during the visit, the Royal party proceeded to Turf Moor to enjoy a match arranged especially for the occasion.
Bolton Wanderers provided the opposition for what was almost certainly the first-ever visit by a member of the Royal Family to a first-class association football match at a senior ground.
It had been arranged for the Royal party to watch the first twenty minutes of the match and then continue with their hectic schedule. The Prince was enjoying himself enormously however and insisted on staying until half-time. Perhaps he was a closet Bolton supporter as Wanderers had swept into a 3-goal lead and were 3-1 in front when the Royal visitors departed. The Turfites rallied somewhat in the second half but lost 3-4. For some considerable time afterwards Burnley FC enjoyed a certain level of celebrity status, being referred to as "the Royalites".
It was FA Cup time again and Burnley were drawn away to Astley Bridge, a team from Bolton, and the Turfites came away with a draw. The Burnley Committee had obviously anticipated a win and had arranged a match with Blackburn Olympic for the day of the replay. In the event both fixtures were fulfilled, a 4-0 win in Blackburn and a 2-2 draw with Astley Bridge in the FA Cup replay at Turf Moor.
Subsequently, for reasons still not fully explained, both Burnley and Astley Bridge decided to scratch from the FA Cup.
After Bolton came to Turf Moor again, this time in the Lancashire Cup, and won 5-1, 18 matches into what was becoming an excellent campaign, the Turfites had been beaten only three times, and on each occasion it had been by Bolton!
At the end of November Turf Moor hosted an inter-county match, Lancashire v Nottinghamshire. Four Burnley players were selected to represent the County Palatine, William McFetridge, Pat Gallocher and David Waugh together with Jack Keenan who was to captain the side. The game turned out to be somewhat one-sided with the Lancashire Lads overpowering their Nottinghamshire counterparts 7-1 with Pat Gallocher scoring one of the goals. The Burnley committee felt able to send a team out to fulfil a fixture at Church on the same day but, perhaps not surprisingly, the Turfites went down 1-3.
The Christmas period brought the usual hectic fixture programme with Redcar paying their first visit to Turf Moor during an East Lancashire tour, having already suffered a heavy defeat at Church. A combination of good goalkeeping and bad finishing kept the score down to 2-0 in the first half, at the end of which captain Jack Keenan, who had been limping from an early heavy challenge, went in goal with James McConnell slotting into the defence. Keenan was hardly troubled as the Turfites' forwards found their shooting boots with a vengeance, scoring an incredible 11 goals after the interval to record a 13-0 victory against a team clearly out of their depth.
Christmas Day brought a visit from Bolton side Halliwell and, incisive and clinical as the Turfites had been against Redcar, clueless and lethargic they were against Halliwell who won the encounter 1-0. Burnley were so poor that it was mooted by one observer that "perhaps this miserable exhibition was due to celebrating the advent of the festive season with more joviality than discretion". Whatever the reason the Turfites were in a far more purposeful mood two days later when London Hotspur paid their first visit to Turf Moor..... and were hit for 10!
As the new year unfolded letters began to appear in the local press about the lack of information coming from Turf Moor on the proceeds from "The Royal football match" and eventually a balance sheet was produced showing a profit to be given to the new Victoria Hospital of £62.3s.8d.
This in turn brought another flurry of correspondence accusing the club of being less than generous with their list of expenses. The final letter in the saga was written to the Burnley Express by the new Burnley FC Chairman B. Wyatt Granger, insisting that the club had acted fairly and had no intention of entering into a newspaper debate with complainants who did not have the courage to sign their names to letters.

Walter Place senior
On the mark with Burnley's first-ever FA Cup goal

A new arrival at Turf Moor in March was the much admired Padiham full-back William Bury, a player who was to go on and give some years of sterling service to the Turfites well into the coming days of League football.
The season officially ended with a match at Turf Moor in June against Accrington to mark the Golden Jubilee of the accession to the throne of Her Majesty Queen Victoria, in 1837.

1886-87

Managed by Club Committee

	Date			Opponents	Result		Goalscorers	Att.
	Aug	21	a	Bolton W	L	1-5	scrimmage	
	Sep	6	h	THE CLOWNS	W	9-1	McFetridge, Lang, Gallocher (2), Waugh (2), Miller, scrimmage (2)	
		11	a	Walsall	W	3-0	Gallocher (2), Howarth	
		13	h	RAWTENSTALL	W	4-0	Miller (2), McFetridge, unknown	
		18	a	Church	W	7-0	Miller (4), Waugh (2), Robinson og	
		25	a	Leek	W	3-0	Waugh, McCrae, unknown	
		27	h	COWLAIRS	D	0-0		
	Oct	2	h	BLACKBURN PARK ROAD	W	7-1	Friel (2), unknown (5)	2000
Lancs Cup, opps disqualified		9	a	Burnley Union Star	D	2-2	Norman og, unknown	3000
		13	h	BOLTON W	L	3-4	Waugh, Friel (2)	9000
		16	a	Grimsby T	W	2-1	unknown (2)	
FA Cup 1	Oct	23	a	Astley Bridge	D	3-3	Place sen (2), unknown	
		30	a	Blackburn Olympic	W	4-0	unknown (4)	
FA Cup 1 replay		30	h	ASTLEY BRIDGE	D	2-2	unknown, Keenan	
	Nov	1	h	BLACKBURN OLYMPIC	W	4-0	unknown (4)	
Lancs Cup		6	h	BOLTON W	L	1-5	Keenan	
		13	a	Accrington	W	3-1	unknown (2), scrimmage	
		15	h	BLACKBURN R	L	0-1		
		20	h	BLACKPOOL SOUTH SHORE	W	5-0	Friel, unknown (4)	2000
		27	a	Church	L	1-3	unknown	
	Dec	4	a	Blackpool South Shore	D	2-2	unknown (2)	
		6	a	Preston N E	L	3-6	Friel (2), Gallocher	
		11	h	ACCRINGTON	W	2-0	unknown (2)	
		13	h	PRESTON N E	L	0-2		
		18	a	Bolton W	D	2-2	Friel, Sugg	
		20	h	REDCAR	W	13-0	Gallocher (3), Miller (4), Sugg (4), Waugh (2)	
		25	h	HALLIWELL	L	0-1		
		27	h	LONDON HOTSPUR	W	10-0	Waugh (3), opp og, Friel (3), Sugg (2), McNee	
	Jan	1	h	KILMARNOCK	W	3-2	Friel (2), Waugh	
		3	h	ACCRINGTON	L	0-1		1500
		8	h	BURSLEM P V	W	5-1	Waugh (2), McCrae, Gallocher, Sugg	
		15	a	Accrington	D	0-0		large
		22	h	BLACKBURN R	W	4-0	Abrahams, Friel (2), Gallocher	thousands
		24	a	Blackburn R	L	0-1		
		29	h	EVERTON	W	5-0	McNee, Waugh, Sugg (2), Gallocher	
	Feb	5	h	CHURCH	W	6-2	Sugg (2), Friel (2), unknown (2)	
		7	a	Stoke	W	2-0	unknown (2)	
		12	a	Preston N E	D	1-1	Waugh	5000
		14	a	Bootle	W	3-1	unknown (3)	
		19	a	Burslem P V	L	1-3	unknown	
		22	a	Nottingham F	D	0-0		
		26	h	HALLIWELL	L	2-3	Gallocher, Waugh	large
		28	h	NOTTS JARDINES	L	2-4	Friel, Abrahams	
	Mar	5	h	BOLTON W	W	6-0	Gallocher, Friel (2), McFetridge, McCrae, unknown	
		12	h	LEEK	W	5-1	McFetridge (2), Gallocher (2), Friel	
		19	h	ACCRINGTON	W	3-2	Howarth, McFetridge, Stevenson og	3000
		26	h	WALSALL T	W	3-1	Gallocher, Friel, Howarth	6000
	Apr	2	a	Blackburn R	W	2-0	McFetridge (2)	2500
		8	h	NOTTINGHAM F	D	0-0		6000
		9	h	RENTON	D	2-2	Gallocher (2)	7000
		11	a	Everton	W	3-0	Keenan, McFetridge, Gallocher	enormous
		16	h	BLACKBURN OLYMPIC	L	2-3	Sugg, McFetridge	1000
		18	h	BLACKBURN R	W	2-1	Gallocher, Howarth	
		23	h	PRESTON N E	L	0-2		large
		25	h	BOLTON W	W	1-0	Gallocher	
		30	h	HALLIWELL	L	0-2		large
Hospital Cup	Jun	10	a	Colne	D	1-1	opp og	1000
		20	h	ACCRINGTON	D	1-1	Hay	3000

Both Burnley and Astley Bridge withdrew from the FA Cup.

1887-88

Burnley's team for the new season would be substantially the same as in 1886-87 although Frank Sugg had taken over the captaincy from Jack Keenan.

There were early season victories, home and away, against local rivals Padiham before a visit to Deepdale once again reminded the Burnley players and their supporters the considerable gulf that existed between them and "the Invincibles". Goals from David Waugh and Bob McCrae were mere consolation as Preston showed their vast superiority with a 7-2 victory. Burnley were also beaten 2-3 at Blackburn but there was a morale-boosting 4-1 victory at Pikes Lane against Bolton, with Dannie Friel scoring twice.

After a Turf Moor victory against Burslem Port Vale and a 7-0 demolition of Blackburn Olympic it was time for the FA Cup again with Burnley drawn against their old friends Darwen Old Wanderers. Following a 4-0 victory at Turf Moor it was revealed that the Football Association had ordered the tie to be replayed at Darwen as Frank Sugg was ineligible under the residential qualification. It later emerged that it was not the Darweners who had protested and ,to save any further ill-feeling, the Old Wanderers scratched from the competition leaving the way clear for Burnley to progress to the next round.

Stoke, Church, Bolton again, and Newton Heath were all negotiated unbeaten before the second round of the FA Cup. Accrington were Burnley's opponents, the first-ever competitive meeting between the clubs, with the match to take place at Thorneyholme Road, then shared with Accrington Cricket Club. A crowd of 7,000 packed the ground and saw the men from Turf Moor on top from the first whistle, goals from William McFetridge and David Waugh establishing a 2-0 lead by half time. Then it all went wrong, the "Owd Reds" turned it round completely and the Turfites had contrived to snatch defeat from the jaws of victory, with their interest in the FA Cup at an end for another season.

Around the turn of the year Burnley had a particularly successful run with ten victories in eleven games, the sequence beginning with wins at Turf Moor against a team from Cambridge University and the famous Corinthians. It also included an overwhelming 10-1 success at Turf Moor against Thornliebank, a Scottish team touring in England.

At the end of January 1888 the club President Charles Massey organised and funded a southern tour during which return matches were arranged against the Corinthians and Cambridge University. The game against the Corinthians was played at Kennington Oval and refereed by the famous Major Francis Marindin, then the President of the Football Association. A 2-2 draw was followed by a 2-1 victory at the Leys Ground against Cambridge University and the Burnley FC party returned to Lancashire well satisfied with their efforts.

Over the Easter holiday period of 1888 Burnley played host to Scottish visitors Dumbarton and Vale of Leven, both clubs touring Lancashire, to show the Sassenachs how the game should be played. Dumbarton arrived with just ten men but were still able to put one over on the Turfites, albeit relying heavily on an inspired display by their custodian. Vale of Leven, source of many of Burnley's stars in those early days, including current players McCrae, Friel and Abrahams, played like men possessed and well deserved their 3-2 victory. Maybe it was playing against the English that brought the best out of the Scots. More likely it was an opportunity to catch the eye of the English scouts in their own backyard and secure a professional contract with one of the wealthy English clubs.

It was in the early Spring of 1888 that English football began to realise that to prosper, perhaps even to survive, the game had to change. Although the game was now professional, the organisation was haphazard, friendly or "club" matches, the mainstay of a club's footballing year, were subject to last-minute cancellations on all sorts of pretexts. Fixtures were often called off at short notice if key players were injured or unavailable or because of bad weather. Communication was invariably poor and spectators frequently turned up at grounds only to be told that their game, for which they might have travelled some distance, had been cancelled.

The man who would come to be called the father of league football, William McGregor of Aston Villa, decided to act in the best interests of the game he loved. He wrote to a number of established professional clubs with the suggestion that they get together to arrange home and away fixtures each season. A meeting took place in London, as a result of which twelve clubs were formally invited to become members of the new "Football League or Union". A second meeting was held in Manchester on 17 April 1888, at which "the clubs selected as the most suitable 12 were all represented". Six clubs had been invited from Lancashire, Accrington, Blackburn Rovers, Bolton Wanderers, Burnley, Everton and Preston North End, and six from the Midlands, Aston Villa, Derby County, Notts County, Stoke, West Bromwich Albion and Wolverhampton Wanderers. No southern clubs had been invited as, at that time, there was no professional football south of Birmingham. From that date, the date accepted as the establishment of the Football League, the world of professional football was changed forever. Burnley Football Club, younger only than Derby County in that historic roll-call of "the Original Twelve", had played its part in a significant development in football history. It would certainly not be the last time.

William McFetridge

1887-88

Managed by Club Committee

	Date			Opponents	Result		Goalscorers	Att.
at Blackpool	Aug	1	n	Halliwell	W	2-0	scrimmage, Gallocher	
		13	a	Padiham	W	2-1	unknown (2)	
	Sep	3	a	Preston N E	L	2-7	Waugh, McCrae	
		5	h	PADIHAM	W	1-0	unknown	
		10	a	Blackburn R	L	2-3	Waugh, Elston	2000
		17	a	Bolton W	W	4-1	Friel (2), Unsworth og, Elston	
		24	a	Halliwell	L	0-4		
	Oct	1	h	BURSLEM P V	W	4-1	Rawson og, Gallocher, Friel, Lang	3000
		8	h	BLACKBURN OLYMPIC	W	7-0	Elston (2), Friel (2), Gallocher, scrimmage (2)	small
FA Cup 1		15	h	DARWEN OLD WANDERERS	W	4-0	Friel, McFetridge (2), unknown	2000
		17	a	Stoke	D	1-1	unknown	3000
		22	h	CHURCH	D	3-3	Pilkington, unknown (2)	
		24	h	BOLTON W	W	3-2	unknown (3)	
		29	a	Newton Heath	D	0-0		
FA Cup 2	Nov	5	a	Accrington	L	2-3	unknown, Waugh	7000
		12	h	ACCRINGTON	L	0-1		
Lancs Cup, at Turf Moor		19	a	Astley Bridge	L	1-3	unknown	
		21	a	Grimsby T	D	0-0		
		26	h	SHEFFIELD W	W	5-0	Waugh, Sugg, McCrae, McFetridge, Gallocher	moderate
	Dec	3	a	West Bromwich A	L	0-3		numerous
		5	h	PRESTON N E	L	0-2		
		10	a	Bootle	D	1-1	unknown	
		12	a	Bolton W	L	3-4	unknown (3)	
		17	h	CAMBRIDGE UNIVERSITY	W	2-0	Elston, McFetridge	
		20	h	CORINTHIANS	W	4-1	Gallocher, McFetridge, McCrae, Elston	
		24	a	Accrington	W	1-0	scrimmage	
		26	h	HALLIWELL	W	1-0	scrimmage	enormous
		27	h	WALSALL T	W	5-1	McCrae, Elston (2), Lacey og, Gallocher	2000
		31	a	Church	L	0-1		
	Jan	3	h	THORNLIEBANK	W	10-1	Gallocher (3), McFetridge, Waugh, McCrae (2), Friel, Keenan, Elston	
		7	h	BURNLEY UNION STAR	W	3-1	Waugh, Gallocher, scrimmage	
		14	h	DARWEN	W	5-1	Waugh, scrimmage, Elston (2), McFetridge	moderate
		16	h	ACCRINGTON	W	1-0	McCrae	
		21	h	LONG EATON RANGERS	W	5-0	Waugh (3), Elston, Hine	
		28	a	Corinthians	D	2-2	McFetridge, Gallocher	
		30	a	Cambridge University	W	2-1	Waugh, opp og	
		31	a	Long Eaton Rangers	D	1-1	Elston	
	Feb	4	h	ACCRINGTON	L	0-3		
		11	a	Darwen	D	2-2	Waugh, scrimmage	
		14	a	Nottingham F	W	2-1	Gallocher, unknown	
		18	h	STOKE	W	6-1	Waugh, McFetridge, Elston (2), Pilkington, Gallocher	
		20	h	NOTTS JARDINES	W	7-1	McFetridge (3), Pilkington, scrimmage, Gallocher, Elston	
		25	a	Burnley Union Star	W	3-0	Gallocher, Pilkington, Elston	numerous
	Mar	3	a	Everton	L	1-2	McFetridge	
		10	h	PRESTON N E	L	1-5	Waugh	very large
		12	h	HALLIWELL	L	0-1		
		17	h	BOOTLE	D	0-0		moderate
		19	h	ASTON VILLA	D	2-2	McFetridge, Gallocher	
		24	h	BOLTON W	W	3-1	Pilkington (2), Howarth	
		30	h	NOTTINGHAM F	W	3-1	Townley, Friel, Waugh	large
		31	h	DUMBARTON	L	1-2	McCrae	
	Apr	2	h	VALE OF LEVEN	L	2-3	Howarth, scrimmage	
		3	a	Derby C	L	0-1		
		7	h	NEWTON HEATH	W	7-1	Struthers, Gallocher, Poland (2), Howarth (2), Waugh	moderate
		9	h	NORTHWICH VICTORIA	W	2-1	Poland, opp og	
		14	h	HALLIWELL	W	2-1	Waugh, Poland	great
		16	h	WEST BROMWICH A	L	0-1		large
		21	a	Everton	L	0-2		
		23	h	BRIERFIELD	W	2-0	McFetridge, Poland	2500
		28	h	BLACKBURN R	W	3-1	Holden, Poland, Howarth	
		30	h	WITTON	L	1-3	scrimmage	
	May	5	a	Bolton W	L	1-4	unknown	
		7	a	Preston N E	L	1-5	Poland	
Hospital Cup	Jun	6	h	BURNLEY UNION STAR	W	6-0	Howarth, Friel, Gallocher, Crombie, Hibbert, scrimmage	
Hospital Cup final		8	h	BRIERFIELD	D	2-2	Crombie, Hibbert	

1888-89

Less than six months after an inaugural meeting to discuss "League" football, the world's first such organised competition kicked off on Saturday 8 September 1888 and Burnley made the comparatively short journey to play Preston North End at Deepdale.

Not for nothing were North End known as "the Invincibles" and they began their League campaign in style (and as they meant to go on) with a 5-2 victory against the men from Turf Moor. It was Scotsman Pat Gallocher who claimed the honour of scoring Burnley Football Club's first ever League goal after 21 minutes. By this time however his team were already two goals down and heading for something of a hiding and a football lesson against the side who would go on to win the first Football League Championship.

Within days of the advent of League football, the committee decided that it was time for the Burnley players to apply themselves a little more seriously and that a permanent trainer would be appointed for the first time. Joseph Law had spent five years as West Brom's trainer and had been a prominent athlete with Birchfield Harriers.

Burnley's next fixture was at Bolton and, perhaps lifted by the new training regime, the players gave a much improved display to win 4-3. They recovered magnificently from a 3-0 deficit at half time with inside right William Tait ensuring he was an early entry in the Burnley FC record books with the club's first League hat-trick and the first to be scored anywhere in League football.

Alec Brady

Following an erratic month of fixture scheduling, Turf Moor staged its first-ever Football League match on Saturday 6 October 1888, the return with Bolton ended 4-1. The distinction of scoring Turf Moor's first ever league goal fell to centre foward Fred Poland, on target after just 5 minutes and, after the match, the Burnley supporters made their way home in happy mood.

It didn't last however and the Turfites conceded 21 goals in their next four matches with Notts County winger Robert Jardine helping himself to five of them in a 6-1 win at Trent Bridge.

Perhaps the most bitter pill to swallow however was Blackburn Rovers' 7-1 victory at Turf Moor, one of rather too many heavy defeats by the old enemy over the years. Centre forward Fred Poland had been selected to play in goal for this game, the third different custodian of the season so far. Sadly the experiment was not a conspicuous success and Poland never played for the senior team again in any position.

After the first nine games of the campaign, Burnley had not yet managed to prevent any opponents scoring and had conceded 38 goals, more than any other club. Enter goalkeeper William Cox, signed from Hibernian, and the ship steadied, or at least, after a welcome clean sheet on Cox's debut against West Brom, the torrent of goals against slowed from a torrent to a steady flow.

After a draw and a defeat against Everton, Burnley made the season's shortest trip, down the road to play Accrington, only to suffer another heavy defeat, 1-5 against the "Owd Reds".

A welcome 2-1 win at home against Stoke was followed by the visit of Preston to Turf Moor. North End were still unbeaten, had only lost two points and had conceded just 10 goals, two of which Burnley had scored on the season's opening day. The Burnley supporters feared the worst but, not for the first time, or the last, the Turfites rose to the occasion, scoring another two goals against the Invincibles and taking another point from the Champions-elect in a 2-2 draw.

Another not unexpected defeat followed, 2-4 at second in the table Aston Villa, then a single goal victory at home against Notts County, before a visit to Turf Moor by Villa for the return fixture. "The Villans" were pushing Preston hard for supremacy in that historic first league season and had only been defeated twice thus far.

Once again the Turfites upset the odds and, playing their best football of the season in front of their own supporters, crushed the visitors 4-0. It has to be said that Villa were not helped by having to start the game with only eight men, three players having been mislaid in a thick Manchester fog as the party changed trains for East Lancashire. The scheduled kick off time of 2.30pm was delayed to give the wanderers time to arrive but at 3.05pm the referee insisted that the game must start. Two more Villa players did arrive just ten minutes into the match and after a quick change, were ushered on to the field of play. As it happens Jack Yates did not score Burnley's first goal until 20 minutes had elapsed so the visitors could obviously not have felt at too much of a disadvantage, particularly as we consider some dismal future performances by Burnley teams against 10 men (and even nine!). The final Villa absentee arrived, breathless from his travails, at four o'clock but the referee (a Mr Cooper from, whisper it, Blackburn) would not allow him to take part in the proceedings. Second half goals from Gallocher, Alec Brady and William McKay completed a marvellous afternoon for the Burnley team and their fans as they celebrated a famous victory.

A 2-2 draw at home against Accrington and a 1-0 win against Derby, also at home, completed the best sequence of League results of the season and the run continued with a 4-3 victory against Old Westminsters in the first round of the FA Cup.

The campaign went on to finish a little disappointingly with the Turfites ending their first League season in ninth place, Alec Brady top-scoring with seven goals. Winger Jack Yates became Burnley Football Club's first ever full international when he was selected for England against Ireland at Anfield, then the home of Everton, in March 1889. Although Yates

Jack Yates, Burnley's first international

showed his skill and pace to full effect, scoring three goals in a 6-1 win for England, he was never chosen to represent his country again.

After Burnley's first league season had come to an end early in March there was plenty of football still to be played. Over the Easter holiday the Turf Moor fans welcomed Scottish visitors, first of all from Vale of Leven who, over the years provided countless players to many English clubs, including Burnley. Vale were beaten 4-0 but the following day Burnley entertained for the first time a club who would go on to become one of the most famous in the world and who, nearly 80 years later would become the first British club to lift the European Cup. Glasgow Celtic were at the end of their first full season and had already flirted with success, reaching the Scottish Cup final where they had been beaten by Third Lanark. Celtic won that historic encounter 3-1 and inflicted on Burnley their first Turf Moor defeat in any match since the 1-7 debacle against Blackburn Rovers more than five months earlier.

In the summer of 1889 it was time for a number of players who had become stalwarts in those early days of Burnley FC to move on. Pat Gallocher who had first played as a guest for Burnley way back in 1882, left in March 1889 to join Accrington and in fact went on to appear against the Turfites on many occasions. Jack Abrahams and Bob McCrae had both played for Burnley for some years but neither were in the first flush of youth. Both men joined Burnley Union Star, one of the most prominent clubs in the town.

Burnley FC had completed that first historic campaign of League football in 9th position out of twelve. All the bottom four were required to apply for re-election and all four received the support of their fellow founder members to continue.

1888-89

		P	W	D	L	F	A	Pts
1	Preston NE	22	18	4	0	15	15	40
2	Aston Villa	22	12	5	5	43	43	29
3	Wolverhampton W	22	12	4	6	37	37	28
4	Blackburn R	22	10	6	6	45	45	26
5	Bolton W	22	10	2	10	59	59	22
6	West Bromwich A	22	10	2	10	46	46	22
7	Accrington	22	6	8	8	48	48	20
8	Everton	22	9	2	11	35	46	20
9	BURNLEY	22	7	3	12	42	62	17
10	Derby C	22	7	2	13	41	61	16
11	Notts C	22	5	2	15	40	73	12
12	Stoke	22	4	4	14	26	51	12

1888-89

Managed by Club Committee

Football League (9th)
Re-elected

	Date			Opponents	Result		h/t	Goalscorers/times	Opp. goal times
1	Sep	8	a	Preston N E	L	2-5	1-2	Gallocher 21, Poland 89	2, 3, 55, 65, 70
2		15	a	Bolton W	W	4-3	1-3	Tait (3) 44, 65, 75, Poland 54	5, 30, 33
3		22	a	Wolverhampton W	L	1-4	0-2	A.Brady 60	15, 20, 70, 80
4		29	a	West Bromwich A	L	3-4	3-2	Tait 10, Gallocher (2) 25, 44	38, 43, 65, 88
5	Oct	6	h	BOLTON W	W	4-1	3-0	Poland (2) 5, 33, A.Brady 25, Tait 60	80
6		13	h	WOLVERHAMPTON W	L	0-4	0-3		15, 30, 43, 85
7		20	a	Stoke	L	3-4	0-3	Poland 50, unknown 55, opp 87og	20, 30, 43, 89
8		27	a	Notts C	L	1-6	0-2	Yates 60	9, 11, 62, 70, 77, 85
9	Nov	3	h	BLACKBURN R	L	1-7	1-4	McKay 30	15,20,25,43,80,84,87
10		10	h	WEST BROMWICH A	W	2-0	1-0	McKay 20, scrimmage 65	
11		17	h	EVERTON	D	2-2	2-1	Gallocher 10, McKay 17	25, 50
12		24	a	Everton	L	2-3	0-3	McKay 65, A.Brady 72	38, 42, 45
13	Dec	1	a	Accrington	L	1-5	0-2	Horne 55og	3, 5, 65, 80, 85
14		8	h	STOKE	W	2-1	1-0	W.Brady 15, Yates 60	80
15		15	h	Preston N E	W	2-2	2-1	Mackay 30, W.Brady 45	43, 49
16		22	a	Aston Villa	L	2-4	1-2	A.Brady 25, unknown 80	35, 44, 47, 70
17		29	h	NOTTS C	W	1-0	0-0	Abrahams 75	
18	Jan	5	h	ASTON VILLA	W	4-0	1-0	Yates (2) 15, 85, Gallocher 55, A.Brady 70	
19		12	h	ACCRINGTON	D	2-2	1-1	Yates 25, A. Brady 53	43, 65
20		19	h	DERBY C	W	1-0	0-0	Mackay 85	
21	Feb	4	a	Blackburn R	L	2-4	2-3	Gallocher 34, A.Brady 36	30, 32, 44, 75
22	Mar	2	a	Derby C	L	0-1	0-0		75

FA Cup

1	Feb	2	h	OLD WESTMINSTERS	W	4-3	3-1	W.Brady 20, Gallocher (2) 23, 75, Lang 42	1, 55, 60
2		16	a	West Bromwich A	L	1-5	0-4	Gallocher 75	5, 25, 35, 42, 60

Final, Preston N E 3-1 Wolverhampton W, at Kennington Oval.

Other matches (friendlies and/or as detailed)

Hosp Cup final replay, 1887-88	Aug	27	a	Brierfield	W	3-1	scrimmages (2), McCrae
	Sep	1	a	Witton	W	7-2	Tait, Gallocher (3), Poland, Yates, opp og
		3	a	Bootle	L	0-3	
		10	a	Walsall T	L	0-1	
	Oct	1	a	Burslem P V	L	0-2	
		8	h	EVERTON	W	3-0	Gallocher (2), Lang
		15	h	NORTHWICH V	W	10-2	Tait, Yates (3), Brady (2), Friel, Poland (2), Gallocher
		22	h	DAVENHAM	W	8-2	opp og, Gallocher, Yates, scrimmage, Poland (2), McFetridge, Hibbert
		29	h	HALLIWELL	L	4-8	Keenan, Gallocher (2), Hibbert
Lancs Cup	Nov	10	a	Halliwell	L	4-9	unknown (4)
	Dec	24	h	NOTTS JARDINES	W	9-0	A.Brady (4), W.Brady, Yates (2), Gallocher, Mackay
friendly aban 10m, storm		25	h	HALLIWELL	aban	1-0	A.Brady
		31	h	WALSALL T	W	2-1	A.Brady (2)
	Jan	4	h	LONDON CASUALS	W	4-0	Gallocher, unknown, scrimmage, Mackay
		26	a	Darwen	L	1-2	Yates
	Feb	9	h	BOLTON W	W	2-1	Robinson og, Ashworth
		23	a	Bolton W	L	1-2	Yates
	Mar	9	h	WOLVERHAMPTON W	W	7-1	Mackay, Lang (2), McFetridge, Yates, W.Brady, Gallocher
		16	a	Nelson	W	6-0	W.Brady (3), Mackay, Ashworth, Yates
		18	h	HALLIWELL	D	3-3	unknown (3)
		23	h	DARWEN	W	2-1	Gallocher (2)
		30	a	Sheffield W	L	1-3	Lang
	Apr	6	h	CREWE A	W	3-1	W.Brady, Duckworth, Crossley
		8	h	WARWICKS COUNTY	W	8-0	Crossley (2), Yates, Binns (2), Lang (2), W. Brady
		13	h	WITTON	D	1-1	W.Brady
		19	h	VALE OF LEVEN	W	4-0	W.Brady (2), Keenan, Grant
		20	h	CELTIC	L	1-3	Duckworth
		22	h	HALLIWELL	W	1-0	Yates
		27	h	SHEFFIELD W	W	5-0	Duckworth, Friel, Campbell (2), Yates
		29	a	Everton	W	1-0	Duckworth
	May	29	h	NELSON	W	5-1	unknown, Heyes, Lang, Campbell, Haresnape

Att.	Pos	W Smith	Lang	Bury	Abrahams	Friel	Keenan	A Brady	Tait	Poland	Gallocher	Yates	McFetridge	Ridsdale	Duckworth	Kay	Midgley	Hibbert	W McKay	McCrae	Cox	McMahon	Kavanagh	Woods	W Brady	Mudie	Mackay	Hargreaves		
6,000		1	2	3	4	5	6	7	8	9	10	11																		1
		1		3	4	5	6	7	8	9	10	11	2																	2
4,000		1	2			5	6	7		9	10	11	3	4	8															3
2,100			2	3	6	5	4	10	11	9	8	7				1														4
6,000			2	3	6	5	4	10	11	9	8	7				1														5
4,000			2	3	4	5	6	7	8	9	10	11				1														6
			3	2	4	5	6	7		9	11	10				1	8													7
5,000			3	2		5	6	8		9	10	11	4			1		7												8
3,000			2	3	6	5	4			1	11	10	9						7	8										9
5,000			3	2	4	5	6	7			10	11							8		1	9								10
	8		3	2	4	5	6	7			10	11	9						8		1									11
			3	2	6	5	4	7			10	11	9						8		1									12
5,000	9		3		6	5		7				11	4						8		1	9	2	10						13
6,000	8		3	2		5	6	7				11	4								1				8	9	10			14
10,000			3	2		4	5	7			9	11	6								1				8		10			15
2,000	9		2	3		5	4	7			9	11	6								1				8		10			16
			2	3	4	5		7			9	10	6								1				8		11			17
6,000	8		2	3		4	5	7			9	10	6								1				8		11			18
6,000			3	2		5	6	7			9	11	4								1				8		10			19
3,000	8		2	3		5	4	7			9	10	6								1				8		11			20
2,000	9		2	3		5	4	8			9	11	6								1				7		10			21
3,000			3	2	5	11	6				10		4							8	1				7		9			22
Appearances		3	21	20	13	22	20	20	5	9	20	21	16	1	1	5	1	1	5	2	13	2	1	1	9	1	9			
Goals (42)					1			7	5	5	6	5							4						2		2		2	ogs

3 untraced

Att.	W Smith	Lang	Bury	Abrahams	Friel	Keenan	A Brady	Tait	Poland	Gallocher	Yates	McFetridge	Ridsdale	Duckworth	Kay	Midgley	Hibbert	W McKay	McCrae	Cox	McMahon	Kavanagh	Woods	W Brady	Mudie	Mackay	Hargreaves
		2		4	5	6				8	11	10								1	9			7			3
5,104		3	2		5	6				10	11	4							7	1	9			8			
Appearances		2	1	1	2	2				2	2	2							1	2	2			2			1
Goals (5)		1								3														1			

1889-90

One of Burnley's new signings during the summer of 1889 was inside forward Robert Haresnape who arrived from Blackburn Rovers after being unable to command a regular first team place at Leamington Road. Haresnape was one of five new arrivals to make their Burnley debuts at Villa Park on the opening day of the new season and he was on target in a 2-2 draw.

Aston Villa had finished the previous campaign as runners-up to Preston so there was initial optimism in the Burnley camp and after a defeat at Everton there was another 2-2 draw at Turf Moor, against Accrington. This was the match that launched the League career of one of the all-time greats of the English game, a man who would go on to play regularly for England and to become a key figure in Aston Villa's virtual domination of the game around the turn of the nineteenth century.

James Crabtree was born in Burnley in 1871 and was to play briefly for the first team as a teenage amateur before moving to Rossendale United to cut his teeth in the tough non-league arena.

Danny Spiers

Three more home defeats then followed including a 2-6 drubbing by Aston Villa, exacting sweet revenge for their own hammering at Burnley the previous season. A welcome draw at Accrington was followed by another crushing defeat, 1-7 at Blackburn, then a demoralising three match sequence saw the Turfites defence concede 21 goals with six at West Brom and another six at Preston. Early in December 1890 the Turfites hit rock bottom when they journeyed to Molineux to play the Wolves on an icy treacherous pitch. After an even first half it was 1-1 at the interval, then Burnley were hit by a real storm. In less than forty minutes Wolves found the Turfites' net eight times, running out 9-1 winners, even the Burnley goal in the first half had been scored by a Wolves player !

In November 1889 one of Burnley's all-time greats announced that it was time for him to leave Turf Moor. Dannie Friel had been a permanent fixture in the Burnley side since arriving from Accrington in 1883 when his experience had been hugely important as association football first began to take hold in the town. Friel was one of many talented Scots who had begun their football journey with Vale of Leven before taking the road South and in six years at Turf Moor he had played over three hundred games for Burnley, a large number as captain.

After the disaster at Wolves the time was right for a foray into the transfer market and the Burnley scouts in Scotland had being doing their homework, and were particularly vigilant on the banks of the Clyde. Three new players were signed from Greenock Morton and they all arrived in Burnley on the same day, ready to celebrate Christmas and Hogmanay south of the border, before the next League game at Derby on 4 January 1890. Centre half Danny Spiers and inside forwards William McColl and Alex Stewart all made their Burnley debuts in this match, but unfortunately it was more of the same with a 1-4 defeat.

For the game at home to Stoke there were two more newcomers in the side, another two Scots, goalkeeper James McConnell, signed from Padiham and left winger James Hill who arrived from St Mirren. Hill would go on to enjoy a distinguished career at Turf Moor but could make no significant impression on his debut, the Potters winning 3-1.

After a 1-2 defeat at non-league Sheffield United in the FA Cup there was a new Scottish centre forward for the next League match, with Claude Lambie arriving from Glasgow Thistle. "Lambie the Leap" was a former Scottish Junior International who came to East Lancashire as a 21-year-old with a reputation as a prolific goalscorer, and evidently he was, as his nickname suggested, exceptionally good in the air. Lambie appeared in the Burnley team for the first time against Everton at Turf Moor, but his goalscoring prowess was not immediately apparent, with his new team going down 0-1.

Another game, another new player, another Scot, another goalkeeper, as Archibald Kaye was signed from Glasgow Thistle ready for the home match against Blackburn. Alas, another defeat, Rovers winning 2-1, although after a controversial late winner for the Rovers, the Burnley crowd turned their venom on the referee, especially when a rumour spread around the ground that the man in the middle was the brother of a Blackburn player. Sure enough referee Richard Horne was the brother of John Horne, making his League debut in goal for Rovers. John Horne had actually played for Burnley occasionally, as a guest when he was with Accrington.

Needless to say the men from Turf Moor were bottom of the League with only four points from four draws, had lost their last nine games and had not won a League match for over a year. With only five League games still to play and with the bottom four clubs once again having to apply for re-election there was a very real danger that the second season of League football might be Burnley's last.

Suddenly there was a break in the clouds. Bolton were the next visitors to Turf Moor and the Turfites fielded the same side that had lost to Blackburn in their previous outing. Some players may have been warned by the Burnley committee that a number of heads were about to roll but no matter, something had brought about a dramatic improvement in performance. Bolton were no match for a rampant Burnley team and were swept away 7-0, Claude Lambie hitting a hat-trick, with his fellow Caledonian newcomers, McColl, Stewart and Hill all on target along with Robert Haresnape.

Derby were also beaten, 2-0 at Turf Moor, then another of the strugglers Stoke were overcome in an epic encounter at the Victoria Ground. Lambie and Haresnape both scored twice in a 4-3 victory, the Turfites first win away from home since September 1888. The League season ended with another victory, 3-0 at home against Notts County and a 2-2 draw at Bolton. After no League victories at all and only four draws in over a year, Burnley had now won four League fixtures in a row and were unbeaten in five. Even though Burnley finished in the last four again and had to apply for re-election to the League, the victory at Stoke ensured that the Potters and not the Turfites finished at the very bottom. Stoke failed to win re-election and Sunderland were admitted in their place.

Away from the League competition Burnley had certainly been enjoying some success in other matches, particularly in the Lancashire Cup. After three victories against perhaps modest opposition, including Haydock who were beaten 15-0, Blackburn Rovers were to be the opponents in the final at Accrington in April 1890. Both teams fielded full-strength line-ups and Rovers, having beaten Burnley twice in the league and finished third, were overwhelming favourites. It should be mentioned in passing that Rovers had also won the FA Cup just a few weeks earlier, beating The Wednesday 6-1 in the final at the Kennington Oval.

In Lancashire's own Cup Final a crowd of over 15,000 saw Burnley upset the odds with a 2-0 win, Alex Stewart scoring both goals. "A Glorious Victory" proclaimed the Burnley Express and the Turfites' faithful naturally concluded that, as Rovers had won the FA Cup and Burnley had beaten them, their favourites were obviously the best team in the land!

Alex Stewart
2 goals in the Lancashire Cup final

Over Easter 1890 a quirk of fate introduced to Burnley Football Club a player who was destined for fame and notoriety in just about equal measure. On Good Friday Burnley Reserves were due to meet Manchester Welsh at Turf Moor but this fixture had to be called off when the opposition missed their train and could not get to East Lancashire. An alternative game was quickly arranged for the Reserves against a scratch team of local league players who turned up at Turf Moor to play under the epithet of the Young Pilgrims. Their goalkeeper was 19-year-old John Hillman, who was outstanding as the youngsters beat Burnley Reserves 3-2 and he was asked to sign for Burnley on amateur forms there and then. He played his first game for Burnley Reserves just three days later and made his first senior appearance the following January. He went on to play for Burnley, on and off, for more than a dozen years, and was associated with the club until after the Great War. Jack Hillman's story was remarkable, for a man who first arrived at Turf Moor by accident!

1889-90

		P	W	D	L	F	A	Pts
1	Preston NE	22	15	3	4	71	30	33
2	Everton	22	14	3	5	65	40	31
3	Blackburn R	22	12	3	7	78	41	27
4	Wolverhampton W	22	10	5	7	51	38	25
5	West Bromwich A	22	11	3	8	47	50	25
6	Accrington	22	9	6	7	53	56	24
7	Derby C	22	9	3	10	43	55	21
8	Aston Villa	22	7	5	10	43	51	19
9	Bolton W	22	9	1	12	54	65	19
10	Notts C	22	6	5	11	43	51	17
11	BURNLEY	22	4	5	13	36	65	13
12	Stoke	22	3	4	15	27	69	10

1889-90

Managed by Club Committee

Football League (11th)
Re-elected

Note	No	Month	Day	Venue	Opponents	Result	Score	h/t	Goalscorers/times	Opp. goal times
	1	Sep	7	a	Aston Villa	D	2-2	1-2	Heyes 30, Haresnape 65	3, 33
	2		14	a	Everton	L	1-2	0-2	Ashworth 65	25, 28
	3		21	h	ACCRINGTON	D	2-2	2-2	Campbell 3, Duckworth 15	6, 20
	4		28	h	PRESTON N E	L	0-3	0-3		15, 20, 25
	5	Oct	5	h	ASTON VILLA	L	2-6	1-4	Friel 20, scrimmage 87	10, 12, 30, 35, 50, 75
	6		12	h	WEST BROMWICH A	L	1-2	1-1	Yates 35	44, 85
	7		19	a	Accrington	D	2-2	0-1	McFetridge 55, Haresnape 88	20, 60
	8		26	a	Blackburn R	L	1-7	0-6	Campbell 80	10,15,20,25,30,40,70
Friel's last game	9	Nov	2	a	Notts C	D	1-1	1-1	Heyes 34	37
	10		9	h	WOLVERHAMPTON W	L	1-2	0-2	Murray 84	5, 32
	11		23	a	West Bromwich A	L	1-6	1-2	Crabtree 15	40, 42, 55, 65, 70, 80
	12		30	a	Preston N E	L	0-6	0-2		25, 35, 50, 60, 70, 80
	13	Dec	7	a	Wolverhampton W	L	1-9	1-1	Fletcher 15og	5,46,50,55,65,70,75,80,85
	14	Jan	4	a	Derby C	L	1-4	0-1	Campbell 60	7, 50, 53, 75
	15		11	h	STOKE	L	1-3	1-1	Ashworth 20	44, 57, 76
	16	Feb	8	h	EVERTON	L	0-1	0-0		65
	17		22	h	BLACKBURN R	L	1-2	1-1	Stewart 6	30, 80
	18	Mar	1	h	BOLTON W	W	7-0	2-0	Lambie (3) 2, 22, 47, Haresnape (2) 50 ,85, Hill 65, McColl 75	
	19		8	h	DERBY C	W	2-0	0-0	Hill 75, McColl 85	
	20		10	a	Stoke	W	4-3	3-1	Haresnape (2) 6, 42, Lambie (2) 25, 60	15, 65, 75
	21		15	h	NOTTS C	W	3-0	1-0	Stewart (2) 44, 53, scrimmage 75	
	22		17	a	Bolton W	D	2-2	0-1	McFetridge 60, Hill 65	30, 55

FA Cup

Round	Month	Day	Venue	Opponents	Result	Score	h/t	Goalscorers/times	Opp. goal times
1	Jan	18	a	Sheffield U	L	1-2	1-2	Bury 25	10, 20

Final, Blackburn R 6-1 Sheffield W, at Kennington Oval.

Other matches (friendlies and/or as detailed)

Note	Month	Day	Venue	Opponents	Result	Score	h/t	Goalscorers
	Sep	2	h	DERBY C	D	2-2		Crabtree, Haresnape
		3	a	Brierfield	W	3-0		unknown (3)
		16	h	HALLIWELL	W	4-3		Caldow, Heyes, Crabtree, scrimmage
	Oct	14	h	NEWTON HEATH	D	0-0		
		21	h	BOOTLE	W	2-0		Murray, Haresnape
Lancs Cup		28	h	ROSSENDALE U	W	4-3		Heyes (2), scrimmage, Crabtree
	Nov	4	h	EVERTON	L	2-3		Murray, Campbell
		16	h	BOOTLE	L	0-3		
	Dec	21	a	Stoke	L	1-2		Glancey
		25	h	BRIERFIELD	L	2-4		scrimmage, Murray
		28	a	Bolton W	L	3-6		Coyle, unknown (2)
		31	a	Middlesbrough	W	4-1		unknown (4)
	Jan	1	a	Newcastle West End	W	3-2		McColl, Stewart, unknown
		2	a	Darlington	W	2-0		unknown (2)
Lancs Cup		20	h	HAYDOCK	W	15-0	7-0	Haresnape(2),Murray(5),McColl(2),Campbell(2),Lang(2),Heyes(2)
		25	h	PRESTON N E	W	2-1		Hill, Haresnape
		27	a	Blackburn Park Road	W	5-2		Stewart, White, Campbell (3)
	Feb	1	a	Halliwell	W	4-2		scrimmage, Hill, unknown (2)
		15	h	HALLIWELL	W	6-4		Keenan, Lambie (3), Haresnape, Stewart
	Mar	22	a	Accrington	W	4-2		Hill, McColl, Haresnape, McLardie
		29	h	BOLTON W	L	1-3		Lambie
	Apr	4	h	VALE OF LEVEN	W	4-3		McLardie, scrimmage, Stewart, Lambie
		5	h	ACCRINGTON	W	3-2		Haresnape, Stewart, Lambie
Lancs Cup semi, at Bury		12	n	Higher Walton	W	7-0		Hill (2), unknown, McLardie (2), Lambie, Spiers
		14	a	Blackpool S Shore	W	2-1		Lambie, Hill
		19	h	NOTTINGHAM F	W	4-1		Haresnape, Lambie (2), Hill
Lancs Cup final, at Accrington		26	n	Blackburn R	W	2-0	1-0	Stewart (2) 29, 74
		28	h	DARWEN	W	5-1		Bryce (2), Lambie (2), McFetridge
	May	3	a	Bury	W	2-1		Lambie, Stewart
		5	a	Ardwick	W	2-0		Lambie, scrimmage
		10	a	Darwen	L	3-4		Lambie (2), unknown
		12	a	Everton	D	0-0		
East Lancs Charity Cup semi	Jun	3	a	Darwen	L	0-2		

Att.	Pos	Cox	Bury	White	McFetridge	Lang	Keenan	Campbell	Haresnape	Caldow	Heyes	Yates	Friel	Ashworth	Duckworth	Crabtree	Murray	W Smith	Coyle	Spiers	McColl	Stewart	McConnell	Hill	C Lambie	A Kaye	McLardie		
4,000		1	2	3	4	5	6	7	8	9	10	11																	1
12,000	8	1	2	3		5	6	8	7	9	10		4	11															2
3,000	7	1	3	2	6	5	4	9	8		10				7	11													3
7,000	10	1	2	3	4	5	6	8	7	9	10	11																	4
8,000	11	1	2	3	4		6	9	7		10	11	5		8														5
6,000	11	1	3	2	6	5	4	9	7		10	11			8														6
2,000	11	1	3	2	6	5		7	8	11		10	4				9												7
4,000	11	1	2	3	4	5	6	8	7			11	10				9												8
1,000	11	1	2	6	4	3		8	7	10	11		5				9												9
4,000	12	1	2	5	6	3	4	8	7	10	11						9												10
7,100	12	1	3	4	6	2	5	8	7		11					10	9												11
	12		2	5	4	3	6		7		10				8	11	9	1											12
2,000	12	1	2	5	4	3	6	11	7		10						9		8										13
3,000	12	1	2		4	3	6	9	7										11	5	8	10							14
			2	5	4	3	6	9						7							8	10	1	11					15
6,500	12		3	5	6	2	4		7									1			8	10		11	9				16
7,000	12		2	5	4	3	6		7												8	11		10	9	1			17
	12		2	5	6	3	4		7												8	10		11	9	1			18
2,000			2	5	6	3			7											4	8	10		11	9	1			19
	11		2	5	4	3			7											6	8	10		11	9	1			20
	11		3	5	6	2	4														7	10		11	9	1	8		21
			2	5	4	3	6														7	10		11	9	1	8		22
Appearances		13	22	21	21	21	18	14	19	6	11	6	5	2	4	3	7	2	2	3	9	9	1	8	7	6	2		
Goals (36)					2			3	6		2	1	1	2	1	1	1				2	3		3	5			1	og

2 untraced

Att.		Cox	Bury	White	McFetridge	Lang	Keenan	Campbell	Haresnape	Caldow	Heyes	Yates	Friel	Ashworth	Duckworth	Crabtree	Murray	W Smith	Coyle	Spiers	McColl	Stewart	McConnell	Hill	C Lambie	A Kaye	McLardie	
2,000			2	5	4	3	6	11	7		10					9					8		1					1
Appearances			1	1	1	1	1	1	1		1					1					1		1					
Goals (1)			1																									

1890-91

The new League season started with a 1-1 draw at Accrington, with summer signings John Walker, a right back, and right winger John Oswald both making Burnley debuts. A week later Burnley journeyed to the North East for a historic meeting with Sunderland, the Football League's newest club, at their Newcastle Road ground. The Wearsiders had not played on the opening Saturday, so Burnley were the first club to oppose them in a league fixture and Alex Stewart became the first player to score a league goal in Sunderland, giving the Turfites the lead after just five minutes. After Sunderland then went 2-1 ahead, more history was made when goals from Claude Lambie and Alex McLardie gave Burnley a 3-2 victory.

After a 2-1 win against Aston Villa and a 3-3 draw in the return against Sunderland, Burnley were still unbeaten and Claude Lambie had scored in each of the season's opening four games and had bagged nine goals in his first eleven outings. It didn't last however and the next four games were all lost, the run including the usual hammering in the league by Blackburn, this time 1-6 at Turf Moor.

Lambie the Leap was soon back amongst the goals, a hat trick in a 4-4 draw at Aston Villa and four more in a 6-2 victory against Derby at Turf Moor. Lambie had now scored twelve goals in just ten games and he was by this time developing an understanding with another new Scottish signing Alex McLardie, who had arrived at Turf Moor from St Mirren at the end of the previous season. McLardie enjoyed a purple patch alongside Lambie, scoring thirteen goals in thirteen games as the Turfites strived to improve upon two decidedly uninspiring campaigns.

Although Burnley went 2-0 in front against Blackburn at Ewood, the Rovers still managed to inflict yet another heavy defeat on the Turfites, coming back strongly to win 5-2. Accrington were then beaten 2-0 at Turf Moor and the Burnley fans looked forward to the visit of West Brom on the first Saturday of December 1890. That game has gone down in Burnley FC history as one of the most exciting matches ever seen at Turf Moor and arguably the greatest ever recovery by any Burnley team. Albion scored early on and although the Turfites equalised through Robert Marr, the visitors hit three more before half time and the Burnley players trooped off at the interval 1-4 down and facing a huge task to get anything at all out of the game. As can be imagined the Turf Moor fans were less than complimentary about what they had seen from their team thus far and there was a chorus of boos as the players disappeared into the dressing rooms. What followed would live for a long time in the memory of all the fans who were at Turf Moor that day.

James Hill pulled one back after just three minutes of the second period but, despite laying siege to the West Brom goal, Burnley struggled to break through again and with 15 minutes to go they still trailed 2-4. Then, it all happened, John Oswald crashed a shot home to make it 3-4 and three minutes later Alex McLardie equalised. The Turf Moor crowd roared on their favourites and, with eight minutes to go, McLardie delivered the perfect response with his second goal, ultimately the winner, to make it 5-4 to the Turfites. McLardie and his team mates were cheered to the echo as the last few minutes were safely negotiated, the final whistle blew and Burnley had secured a quite astonishing victory that at half time, and even fifteen minutes earlier, had seemed impossible.

After four wins and just one defeat in seven games the Turfites were now fifth and the supporters were confident, as Burnley fans invariably are, that a successful season was on the cards. Two weeks later and very much after the Lord Mayor's Show, Notts County visited Turf Moor and won 1-0. Spirits were somewhat dampened especially after twenty goals were shipped in the following four League games, including seven at both Everton and Preston.

Tom Nicol
The only Burnley player ever to score a hat-trick on his league debut

Claude Lambie
top scorer in 1890-91

Two more defeats by Notts County, one of which ended Burnley's FA Cup hopes for another season, were followed by a visit to Turf Moor by Preston in early March 1891. North End of course had been champions for the past two years and were now vying with Everton for the title to make it three in a row. Centre forward and Turf Moor crowd favourite Claude Lambie had suddenly decided to return to Scotland but the Burnley Committee were once again able to call on their Scottish connections for a replacement. Tom Nicol was signed from Mossend Swifts, a prominent junior club in Glasgow and he arrived in East Lancashire with a reputation as a prolific goalscorer. The Burnley scouts north of the border had by no means finished searching for talent however and Nicol was immediately joined at Turf Moor by Billy Bowes, another young goalscorer, then playing his football with Edinburgh club Broxburn.

Both Nicol and Bowes made their first appearances in English league football against Preston and, once again, the form book was turned upside down as North End were crushed 6-2, with both new signings playing their part to the full in a superb team performance. Tom Nicol was unstoppable and scored a hat-trick with Robert Marr adding two goals and James Hill also on target. Preston only conceded 23 league goals altogether during the entire season but the six with which Burnley hit them at Turf Moor ultimately cost them the chance to clinch their third successive league championship and they finished second, a crucial two points behind Everton. Everton themselves were the next visitors to Turf Moor and were now well on course for their first league crown with Burnley having demolished Preston so convincingly. In a match played in almost continuous sleet and snow the Burnley players once again demonstrated their durability as they came from 2-1 down to score twice in the last five minutes, Haresnape, Bowes and Stewart on target in a 3-2 victory. After heavy defeats at both Goodison and Deepdale, the Burnley players had shown real character in bouncing back to overcome the best teams in the land in 1890-91. Perhaps good times were ahead after all for the long suffering Turf Moor faithful.

The season ended with a single goal defeat at Bolton but for the first time the Turfites finished outside the Football League's bottom four and did not have to apply for re-election.

At the League's annual meeting it was decided to increase the number of clubs from twelve to fourteen. All the bottom four were re-elected, Stoke were re-admitted after a year's absence and Darwen were elected, to increase the Lancashire contingent to seven.

THE WORLD OF FOOTBALL

Following Sunderland's admission to the League for the 1890-91 campaign, their first two home games in September 1890 were both lost, including their very first, at home to Burnley. From that point the Wearsiders, nicknamed "the Team of all the Talents," were defeated in only one other League game at home in the next six years, claiming three League Championships in that period.

1890-91

		P	W	D	L	F	A	Pts
1	Everton	22	14	1	7	63	29	29
2	Preston NE	22	12	3	7	44	23	27
3	Notts C	22	11	4	7	52	35	26
4	Wolverhampton W	22	12	2	8	39	50	26
5	Bolton W	22	12	1	9	47	34	25
6	Blackburn R	22	11	2	9	52	43	24
6	Sunderland	22	10	5	7	51	31	23
7	BURNLEY	22	9	3	10	52	63	21
8	Aston Villa	22	7	4	11	45	58	18
10	Accrington	22	6	4	12	28	50	16
11	Derby C	22	7	1	14	47	81	15
12	West Bromwich A	22	5	2	15	34	57	12

1890-91

Managed by Club Committee

Football League (8th)

Note	No	Month	Day	Venue	Opponents		Result	h/t	Goalscorers/times	Opp. goal times
	1	Sep	6	a	Accrington	D	1-1	1-1	Lambie 22	2
	2		13	a	Sunderland	W	3-2	3-2	Stewart 5, Lambie 38, McLardie 42	15, 30
	3		20	h	ASTON VILLA	W	2-1	1-0	Lambie 30, McLardie 75	55
	4		27	h	SUNDERLAND	D	3-3	2-3	Lambie 1, Spiers 35, McLardie 60	22, 30, 36
	5	Oct	4	a	West Bromwich A	L	1-3	1-1	Yates 38	3, 65, 80
	6		11	h	BOLTON W	L	1-2	1-0	Hill 40	55, 70
	7		18	h	BLACKBURN R	L	1-6	1-2	McLardie 20	5,15,50,55,70,80
	8		25	a	Wolverhampton W	L	1-3	1-3	Mason 20og	25, 37, 42
	9	Nov	1	h	WOLVERHAMPTON W	W	4-2	3-1	McLardie (2) 3, 80, Lambie 12, Place sen 30	5, 65
	10		8	a	Aston Villa	D	4-4	3-2	Lambie (3) 15, 42, 87, McLardie 8	20, 35, 50, 89
	11		15	h	DERBY C	W	6-1	3-0	Lambie (4) 25, 35, 44, 80, McLardie 52, Marr 85	68
	12		22	a	Blackburn R	L	2-5	2-0	Place sen 9, McLardie 20	55, 65, 67, 75, 81
	13		29	h	ACCRINGTON	W	2-0	2-0	McLardie 23, Lambie 30	
	14	Dec	6	h	WEST BROMWICH A	W	5-4	1-4	Marr 25, Hill 48, Oswald 75, McLardie (2) 78, 82	12, 35, 39, 43
	15		20	h	NOTTS C	L	0-1	0-0		55
	16		27	a	Everton	L	3-7	2-3	Hill 25, McLardie (2) 28, 70	10,35,43,55,65,86,87
	17	Jan	25	a	Derby C	W	4-2	2-1	Lambie (3) 11, 65, 70, scrimmage 40	5, 75
	18	Feb	2	a	Preston N E	L	0-7	0-3		14,30,35,55,58,70,80
	19		10	a	Notts C	L	0-4	0-3		22, 24, 40, 80
	20	Mar	7	h	PRESTON N E	W	6-2	4-0	Nicol (3) 7, 40, 80, Marr (2) 20, 24, Hill 60	50, 65
	21		14	h	EVERTON	W	3-2	0-0	Haresnape 51, Bowes 85, Stewart 87	55, 60
Kaye's last game	22		21	a	Bolton W	L	0-1	0-1		20

FA Cup

Note	Round	Month	Day	Venue	Opponents		Result	h/t	Goalscorers/times	Opp. goal times
after extra time, 2-2 at 90m	1	Jan	17	h	CREWE A	W	4-2	1-0	Lambie 23, Oswald 90, Hill 110, McLardie 115	55, 70
Bury's last game	2		31	a	Notts C	L	1-2	1-1	McLardie 10	38, 50

Final, Blackburn R 3-1 Notts C, at Kennington Oval.

Other matches (friendlies and/or as detailed)

Note	Month	Day	Venue	Opponents		Result	h/t	Goalscorers
	Sep	1	h	DARWEN	W	3-2		Oswald, Lambie (2)
		8	h	SHEFFIELD W	W	8-1		Lambie, Stewart (2), McLardie, Hill (3), Oswald
		9	a	Darwen	D	2-2		Oswald, unknown
		15	a	Stockton	L	2-6		unknown (2)
		22	h	NEWTON HEATH	L	3-4		Stewart, Walker, scrimmage
		29	a	Wolverhampton W	L	1-2		unknown
	Oct	6	h	WOLVERHAMPTON W	L	1-2		Stewart
		13	a	Sheffield W	L	1-4		Oswald
Hospital Cup final, 1889-90		20	h	NELSON	W	9-2		Haresnape (2), Lambie (3), McFetridge, Keenan, Stewart, McLardie
	Nov	3	h	STOKE	W	4-2		Haresnape, Lambie, McLardie, Stewart
		17	h	PRESTON N E	L	1-3		McLardie
	Dec	1	a	Stoke	L	1-4		Spiers
		13	a	Preston N E	L	0-3		
		18	a	Nottingham F	W	4-3		Lambie (2), Marr (2)
		25	h	WREXHAM	W	12-1	7-1	Lambie (5), Hill (2), McLardie (2), Keenan, Oswald (2)
		31	a	Newcastle East End	L	1-4		unknown
	Jan	1	a	Middlesbrough Ironopolis	L	1-5		scrimmage
		3	a	Bolton W	D	1-1		Hill
		10	h	LINFIELD ATHLETIC	W	6-2		McLardie (3), Oswald, opp og, Lambie
Lancs Cup	Feb	7	h	DARWEN	L	2-3		Hill, Place jun
		14	h	PRESTON N E	L	0-2		
		21	a	Bury	W	1-0		Yates
		28	a	Derby C	L	1-3		Nicol
	Mar	9	h	BLACKPOOL	L	2-4		Bowes, Hill
		16	h	NELSON	W	4-2		unknown (3), Yates
at Burslem Port Vale		23	n	Stoke	D	3-3		Nicol, Haresnape, McFetridge
		27	h	GLASGOW LINTHOUSE	W	7-2		Nicol (4), Hill, McFetridge, Bowes
		28	h	ACCRINGTON	W	4-1		Nicol, Haresnape (2), Marr
		30	a	Newcastle West End	L	1-3		Nicol
		31	a	Sunderland	L	0-5		
	Apr	4	h	GAINSBOROUGH T	W	5-1		Lambie (4), Hill
		6	h	BOLTON W	W	2-1		Hill, Lambie
		8	a	Blackpool South Shore	D	3-3		unknown (3)
		11	h	BIRMINGHAM ST GEO.	W	3-1		scrimmage, Haresnape, Lambie
		13	a	Newton Heath	W	2-1		Nicol, Yates
		15	a	Bootle	D	0-0		
		18	a	Rotherham Town	L	0-1		
		20	h	BLACKPOOL S SHORE	W	3-1		Marr, Nicol (2)
		25	h	DERBY C	D	2-2		Marr, Haresnape
		27	h	NOTTINGHAM F	W	3-0		Nicol, Haresnape, Bowes
		29	a	Blackpool	L	1-2		Hill
		30	h	ACCRINGTON	W	4-1		unknown (4)
Burnley Hospital Benefit	May	11	h	BLACKBURN R	W	4-1		Hill, Nicol (2), scrimmage
E L C Cup semi, at Blackburn		16	n	Darwen	W	2-0		McFetridge, Nicol
E Lancs Charity Cup final		30	a	Blackburn R	L	2-3		Marr, Bowes

Att.	Pos	A Kaye	Walker	Lang	McFetridge	Spiers	Keenan	Oswald	McLardie	C Lambie	Stewart	Hill	Yates	Carr	Haresnape	Duerden	W Place senior	Nash	Patterson	Marr	Bury	Brodie	Crossley	Bowes	Nicol	
8,000		1	2	3	4	5	6	7	8	9	10	11														1
5,000	4	1	2	3	4	5	6	7	8	9	11	10														2
10,000	2	1	2	3	4	5	6	7	8	9	10	11														3
8,000	4	1	2	3	4	5	6	7	8	9	11	10														4
6,000	5	1	2	3	4	5	6	7	8	9	11		10													5
7,500	6	1	2		6	5	4	7	8	9	10	11		3												6
10,000		1	2	3	4	5	6	8	9		10	11			7											7
3,000	8	1	3		4	5	6		8	9	10				7	2	11									8
3,500	7	1	2		4	5	6	7	8	9	10					3	11									9
5,000	7	1	3			5	6	7	8	9	10					2	11	4								10
6,000	7	1	2	3	4		6	7	8	9							11		5	10						11
4,000	8	1	2	3	4	5	6	7	8	9							11			10						12
6,000	6	1	2	3	4	5	6	7	8	9		11								10						13
5,500	5	1	2	3	4	5	6	7	8	9		11								10						14
4,500	6	1	2	3	4	5	6	7	8	9		11								10						15
12,000	7	1	3	2	4		6	7	8	9	10	11							5							16
2,500	7	1		2	6		4		10	9	8	7			11			5			3					17
3,000		1	2	3	4		6			9	10	11			7			5				8				18
4,000	8	1	2	3	6	5				9		11						4		10		8	7			19
7,000	8	1	2	3	4	5					6	11			7					10				8	9	20
10,000		1	2	3	4	5					6	11			7					10				8	9	21
4,500	8	1	2	3	4	5					6	11			7					10				8	9	22
Appearances		22	21	18	21	18	18	15	17	18	16	16	1	1	7	3	5	4	2	9	1	2	1	3	3	
Goals (52)						1		1	14	16	2	4	1		1		2			4				1	3	1 og
																										1 untraced

Att.		A Kaye	Walker	Lang	McFetridge	Spiers	Keenan	Oswald	McLardie	C Lambie	Stewart	Hill	Yates	Carr	Haresnape	Duerden	W Place senior	Nash	Patterson	Marr	Bury	Brodie	Crossley	Bowes	Nicol	
		1		3	4		6	7	8	9	10	11						5			2					1
9,500		1		3	4		6		8	9	10	11			7			5			2					2
Appearances		2		2	2		2	1	2	2	2	2			1			2			2					
Goals (5)								1	2	1		1														

1891-92

For the new campaign there were significant changes introduced by the football authorities. It seems inconceivable that it was only now that the decision was taken that goal nets might be a good idea to prevent disputes as to whether the ball had entered the goal or not and the League instructed all the clubs to provide nets "before 1 November 1891".

Previously each club had provided an umpire to try to uphold the laws and to ensure fair play but now referees were to be in sole charge of the games, assisted by linesmen.

Also the law regarding the penalty kick was substantially re-framed to make it more or less as we know it today.

Burnley's major signing during the summer of 1891 was a goalkeeper who would become one of the club's most famous, as well as most notorious players and who would go on to play for England. Even at 20 years old, Jack Hillman was a huge man and had been signed as a professional after a year playing as an amateur in Burnley's reserve team. Hillman was born near Tavistock in Devon in 1870 and had moved to Burnley with his parents as a young child. He had already played for the senior team in a friendly against Linfield in January 1891 and was now seen as the Turfites' first choice custodian for the new campaign. Jack Hillman replaced Archie Kaye, an ever-present between the sticks since February 1890, and who had now returned to Scotland.

The season began with a defeat at Accrington but home wins against Preston and Stoke boosted confidence before the return at Preston, another Deepdale demolition, this time 1-5, brought the first controversy of the campaign. North End captain Billy Stewart was sent off for violent conduct to become the first player ever to be dismissed in a League match involving Burnley. Played throughout in a strong blustery wind, the game very quickly deteriorated into a war of attrition as both sets of players were guilty of "rough play and unnecessarily hard tackling". Early in the second half, with North End leading 2-0, the referee called all the players together and warned them that he would not tolerate any more violent play. His words of authority seemed to do the trick and certainly benefited Preston who quickly scored three more goals to establish an unassailable 5-0 lead after 70 minutes. With 15 minutes to go Burnley's Tom Nicol pulled a goal back, little more than a consolation, but Nicol was then hacked down by Stewart who was immediately ordered off.

A welcome 3-3 draw at Blackburn, the first League point Burnley had taken from Rovers in seven matches, was soon followed by a fine 4-1 victory against Aston Villa at Turf Moor with two goals from Tom Nicol and one each from Billy Bowes and James Matthew. Centre half Matthew was making his Burnley debut and was yet another Scot in the Burnley squad, signed from non-League Lincoln City. This was the match in which goal nets were used at Turf Moor for the first time and, with just five minutes of the game gone, Billy Bowes was the first Burnley player who had the pleasure of seeing his shot "hit the net".

More Burnley FC history was made on the last day of October 1891 when a representative team from Canada visited Turf Moor on their tour of the UK. The Canadians were rather better footballers than expected and scored twice in the first twenty minutes. Tom Nicol was twice on target for the Turfites but it was only late in the game that his second goal ensured a draw for the hosts.

The new penalty law affected Burnley for the first time at Sunderland in November 1891. Tom Nicol had given the visitors an early lead, but five minutes before half time James Matthew was adjudged to have fouled Sunderland's centre forward Campbell in the Burnley penalty area. Up stepped Hugh Wilson and crashed the spot kick past Jack Hillman. Later in the game, with Burnley trailing 1-2, a second penalty was awarded to Sunderland but this time Hillman was equal to Wilson's effort, the first-ever penalty save by a Burnley FC custodian.

The following week, against West Brom at Turf Moor, our favourites were at last able to benefit themselves from the new penalty law. After 77 minutes, with the score at 1-1, it was Burnley captain Sandy Lang who stepped up to smash the first spot kick seen at Turf Moor past Albion's future England keeper Joe Reader. Tom Nicol scored Burnley's other two goals in a well-deserved 3-2 victory.

Sandy Lang
on target with Burnley's first ever penalty

There have been some exciting, eventful and notorious clashes between Burnley and Blackburn Rovers over the years but surely none more controversial than Rovers' visit to Turf Moor on 12 December 1891. It was a bitterly cold day with a biting wind and snow had been falling since early morning. In the first half, after losing the toss, the Blackburn team played in the face of a terrific snowstorm and were powerless to prevent goals from Tom Nicol, Hugh Galbraith and Billy Bowes establishing a healthy 3-0 lead for Burnley by half time. The Rovers players were slow in returning for the second half and four minutes after the scheduled start time, there were only seven members of the team on the pitch. Undeterred, the referee blew his whistle for the restart but within minutes the mood turned ugly when Rovers' Joe Lofthouse scythed down Sandy Lang. After a number of violent clashes between various players Lofthouse was again at the centre of the controversy when he brought down Alex Stewart then kicked the Burnley wing half as he tried to get to his feet. Stewart retaliated by flooring Lofthouse but by this time the referee had had enough and promptly sent off both protagonists. They were followed to the dressing rooms by all Rovers' remaining outfield players, only goalkeeper Herby Arthur remaining on the field. Amazingly, after waiting a few moments, the referee re-started proceedings and the Burnley players bore down on the Rovers goal with Arthur appealing loudly for offside. The whistle blew and, farcically, Arthur kept placing and replacing the ball for a free kick but never actually got around to kicking it. The referee eventually blew his whistle as a sign that he had abandoned the match. Both Alex Stewart, the first-ever Burnley player to be dismissed in a competitive match, and Lofthouse were later suspended by the Football Association. The Football League decided that the 3-0 scoreline in Burnley's favour should stand as a result and Blackburn were instructed to play a "penalty match" at Turf Moor.

In January 1892 Burnley established what is still the club's record victory in a senior competitive peacetime fixture when Darwen were beaten 9-0 at Turf Moor, with Tom Nicol and Alex McLardie both hitting hat-tricks.

The Turfites began their FA Cup campaign with a magnificent 4-2 victory at Everton in the first round, only for the tie to be subsequently downgraded to a friendly fixture because of the hard, bumpy pitch. A week later, in the re-match, there was no escape for the Merseysiders when Burnley again turned in an exceptional performance to go through 3-1.

Just two weeks later Everton were beaten for the third time in a month when a James Hill goal was enough give the Turfites the points. By this time however Burnley were out of the FA Cup, beaten 1-3 at Turf Moor by Stoke, who took advantage of some complacency by the Turfites and scored three times in the last twelve minutes.

Burnley's final away match of the season was at Darwen and the Turfites inflicted yet another heavy defeat on their near neighbours. This time they cruised home 6-2 making it fifteen in total against the men from Barley Bank, the highest aggregate score against any League opponents in Burnley FC history.

It had been the Turfites' best campaign of League football so far, seventh position, the first time the club had finished in the top half and also the first time more goals had been scored than had been conceded.

Jack Hillman
ever present in goal in his first season at Turf Moor

1891-92

		P	W	D	L	F	A	Pts
1	Sunderland	26	21	0	5	93	36	42
2	Preston NE	26	18	1	7	61	31	37
3	Bolton W	26	17	2	7	51	37	36
4	Aston Villa	26	15	0	11	89	56	30
5	Everton	26	12	4	10	49	49	28
6	Wolverhampton W	26	11	4	11	59	46	26
6	BURNLEY	26	11	4	11	49	45	26
7	Notts C	26	11	4	11	55	51	26
8	Blackburn R	26	10	6	10	58	65	26
10	Derby C	26	10	4	12	46	52	24
11	Accrington	26	8	4	14	40	78	20
12	West Bromwich A	26	6	6	14	51	58	18
13	Stoke	26	5	4	17	38	61	14
14	Darwen	26	4	3	19	38	112	11

1891-92

Managed by Club Committee

Football League (7th)

Note	No	Date		h/a	Opponents	Result		h/t	Goalscorers/times	Opp. goal times
	1	Sep	5	a	Accrington	L	0-1	0-1		32
	2		7	h	PRESTON N E	W	2-0	2-0	Bowes 20, Haresnape 25	
	3		19	h	STOKE	W	4-1	3-0	Bowes (2) 8, 30, Nicol 40, Place sen 88	90
	4		21	a	Preston N E	L	1-5	0-2	Nicol 75	35, 45, 60, 65, 70
	5		26	a	Blackburn R	D	3-3	1-2	Lang 35, Nicol 65, McLardie 78	2, 9, 87
	6	Oct	10	a	Stoke	L	0-3	0-2		10, 40, 85
1st Turf Moor match with nets	7		17	h	ASTON VILLA	W	4-1	2-1	Bowes 5, Matthew 35, Nicol (2) 65, 70	40
	8		24	a	Bolton W	L	0-2	0-1		35, 83
	9	Nov	7	a	Wolverhampton W	D	0-0	0-0		
	10		14	h	ACCRINGTON	W	2-1	1-0	Graham 8, McLardie 65	80
1st penalty conceded	11		21	a	Sunderland	L	1-2	1-1	Nicol 10	40p, 70
1st penalty scored	12		28	h	WEST BROMWICH A	W	3-2	1-1	Nicol (2) 32, 80, Lang 77p	35, 88
	13	Dec	5	a	Aston Villa	L	1-6	0-3	Hill 75	30,35,40,55,58,85
	14		12	h	BLACKBURN R	W	3-0	3-0	Nicol 7, Galbraith 22, Bowes 35	
	15		19	a	Derby C	W	1-0	0-0	Galbraith 60	
	16		26	a	West Bromwich A	L	0-1	0-1		30
	17	Jan	2	a	Everton	D	1-1	0-0	McLardie 89	65
	18		9	h	DARWEN	W	9-0	2-0	Nicol (3) 12, 50, 85, McLardie (3) 43, 65, 80, Hill (2) 48, 55, Espie 78	
	19	Feb	13	h	EVERTON	W	1-0	1-0	Hill 21	
	20	Mar	1	a	Notts C	L	1-5	0-2	Espie 89	5, 20, 51, 52, 70
	21		5	h	BOLTON W	L	1-2	1-1	Nicol 35	2, 70
	22		26	h	WOLVERHAMPTON W	D	1-1	1-1	Nicol 12	30
	23	Apr	2	a	Darwen	W	6-2	4-2	Nicol (2) 8, 10, Bowes 25, McLardie (2) 42, 85, Hill 70	2, 33
	24		15	h	NOTTS C	W	1-0	1-0	Nicol 17	
	25		16	h	DERBY C	L	2-4	0-2	McLardie 63, Graham 65	3, 27, 49, 60p
	26		30	h	SUNDERLAND	L	1-2	1-2	McLardie 30	22, 32

FA Cup

No	Date		h/a	Opponents	Result		h/t	Goalscorers/times	Opp. goal times
1	Jan	23	a	Everton	W	3-1	2-0	Hill (2) 25, 30, Nicol 70	60
2		30	h	STOKE	L	1-3	1-0	Hill 30	78, 82, 86

Final, West Bromwich A 3-0 Aston Villa, at Kennington Oval.

Other Matches (friendlies or as detailed)

Note	Date		h/a	Opponents	Result		Goalscorers
	Sep	1	h	ACCRINGTON	L	1-2	Nicol
		11	a	Stockton	W	2-0	McLardie, Spiers
		12	a	Middlesbrough Ironopolis	L	0-3	
	Oct	3	h	SUNDERLAND ALBION	W	6-1	Hill (2), McLardie, Place sen, Colyer, opp og
		31	h	CANADIAN XI	D	2-2	Nicol (2)
	Dec	17	h	BRIERFIELD	W	6-2	Matthew, McLardie, Bowes (2), Nicol, Lang
		25	h	BELFAST DISTILLERY	W	8-3	unknown (4), McLardie, Espie (2), Bowes
	Jan	1	a	Accrington	L	1-3	Hill
		16	a	Everton	W	4-2	McLardie (2), Nicol, Hill
Lancs Cup	Feb	6	h	BLACKPOOL	W	6-2	Hill (2), Nicol, Graham (2), McLardie
Lancs Cup		20	a	Darwen	L	0-1	
		22	h	SHEFFIELD U	L	0-1	
		27	h	PRESTON N E	L	2-7	McLardie, Hill
	Mar	12	a	Darwen	L	1-2	scrimmage
penalty match		14	h	BLACKBURN R	D	1-1	McLardie
		19	a	Sunderland Albion	L	0-4	
		28	a	Sheffield U	L	1-8	Bowes
	Apr	9	a	Newcastle East End	W	2-1	McLardie, Graham
		18	a	Linfield Athletic	L	0-2	
		19	a	Ulsterville Rangers	L	0-2	
		23	h	EVERTON	L	0-3	
		25	a	Nelson	D	2-2	unknown, Espie

Att.	Pos	Hillman	Jeffrey	Lang	McFetridge	Spiers	Stewart	Bowes	McLardie	Nicol	Graham	Hill	Haresnape	W Place senior	Walker	Matthew	Galbraith	Keenan	Espie	No.
7,000		1	2	3	4	5	6	7	8	9	10	11								1
8,500	8	1	2	3	4	5	6	9	8			11	7	10						2
5,500		1	2	3	4	5	6	9	8	7		11		10						3
	7	1	2	3	4	5	6	9	8	7		11		10						4
4,000	5	1		3	4	5	6	9	8	7		11		10	2					5
3,000	11	1		3	4	5	6	9	8	7		11		10	2					6
5,000	6	1		3	4		6	9	8	7		11		10	2	5				7
8,500	10	1		3	4		6	9	8	7		11		10	2	5				8
1,200	9	1	2	3	4		6		8	9	7	11		10		5				9
7,000	8	1		3	4		6	8	10	7	9	11			2	5				10
5,000		1		3	4		6	8	10	7	9	11			2	5				11
8,000		1		3	4		6	8	10	7	9	11			2	5				12
5,000	10	1		3	4		6	8	10	7	9	11			2	5				13
5,000	7	1		3	4		6	8	10	7	11				2	5	9			14
4,000	5	1		3	4		6	8	10	7	11				2	5	9			15
5,000	8	1		3	4			8	10	7	11				2	5		6	9	16
8,000	9	1		3	4			8	10	7	11	9			2	5		6		17
5,000	6	1		3	4			8	10	7		11			2	5		6	9	18
8,000	5	1	2	3	4		6		10	7	11	8				5			9	19
2,000	6	1		3	4			8		7	11	10			2	5		6	9	20
5,000	7	1	2	3	4			8		7	11	10				5		6	9	21
4,000		1		3	4			8	10	9		11			2		7	6	5	22
3,000	8	1		3	4		6	8	10	7	11	9			2				5	23
8,500		1		3	4			8	10	9	11				2		7	6	5	24
6,000		1		3	4			8	10	9	11				2		7	6	5	25
8,000		1		3			4	8	10	7	11	9			2			6	5	26
Appearances		26	7	26	25	6	18	24	24	25	17	21	1	8	19	15	5	9	10	
Goals (49)				2				6	10	17	2	5	1	1		1	2		2	

Att.	Pos	Hillman	Jeffrey	Lang	McFetridge	Spiers	Stewart	Bowes	McLardie	Nicol	Graham	Hill	Haresnape	W Place senior	Walker	Matthew	Galbraith	Keenan	Espie	No.
10,000		1		3	4			8	10	7	11	9			2	5		6		1
6,000		1		3	4			8	10	7	11	9			2	5		6		2
Appearances		2		2	2			2	2	2	2	2			2	2		2		
Goals (4)										1		3								

1892-93

The major departure from Turf Moor in the summer of 1892 was Alex McLardie who returned to Scotland to play for Paisley Abercorn. In two years at Burnley McLardie had been among the goals and his partnership with Claude Lambie had been very successful. Also leaving office was secretary Tom White who hoped to continue as a player but that did not turn out to be the case, at least not at senior level.

Burnley's new secretary was to be Arthur Sutcliffe, a local solicitor.

Among the new arrivals were defender George King and inside forward Robert Buchanan, both Scotsmen and both signed from Sunderland Albion. Another relatively fresh face at Turf Moor, although he had been around in the past, was Burnley-born James Crabtree. Crabtree had played briefly as an amateur with Burnley in 1889 but, whilst still a teenager, had left to hone his skills in the Lancashire Combination. Now he was back at Turf Moor and a wonderfully successful career lay in front of him.

After the first two league matches of the season both ended in defeat at the hands of Wolves and Aston Villa, Burnley journeyed to Manchester to take part in the very first Division One match to take place in the city. The Turfites' opponents were to be Newton Heath, newly elected to the Football League, at their North Road, Monsall ground. When they arrived the men from Turf Moor were somewhat disconcerted to discover that changing facilities for both teams were in a pub, some 800 yards from the ground! Hugh Boyd's goal for Burnley in a 1-1 draw was the first League goal at the ground as well as the first top flight goal to be scored in the city of Manchester. Boyd was another of the Turfites' new signings but his historic goal against Newton Heath was his only claim to fame, at least in his brief spell as a Burnley player, before he was transferred to West Brom.

There was controversy in Burnley's match at Preston when the Turfites, 0-2 down thanks to two own goals, were applying pressure on the North End goal. The Burnley Express reported that "during a melee in the Preston goalmouth, an ungloved hand was seen to fist out the ball, the custodian wore gloves, further comment is unnecessary".

After a home defeat by Accrington, Burnley travelled to Wearside to play Sunderland, reigning Champions and on their way to another league title. As if the task in hand was not difficult enough, full back Tom Nicol and inside forward William Chambers contrived to miss the train, not arriving at the ground until early in the second half. Playing with nine men the Turfites had perhaps done rather well to be only 0-2 down and the full complement at least managed to prevent Sunderland scoring again. The day, indeed the weekend, was complete when, on the return journey to Lancashire, the railway carriage containing the Burnley players somehow became detached from the rest of the train at Durham. It was late on the Sunday before the party arrived back at Turf Moor.

On the weekend before Christmas 1892, the Burnley players and supporters travelled to Ewood Park for their regular joust with the old enemy. With Rovers on top and deservedly 2-0 ahead, the game seemed destined to end without the controversy and ill-feeling that invariably surrounded the East Lancashire derby fixtures. Then with barely five minutes to play, Sandy Lang was hit with a ferocious tackle by Rovers' centre forward Jack Southworth. Lang slowly got to his feet but was then kicked again, at which point he was heard to "remonstrate with Southworth in language more forcible than polite". Lang then head-butted Southworth and the two players began to trade blows before both were sent off by the referee. A few minutes later the final whistle blew and as the Burnley players left the field they were jostled by the home supporters who then proceeded to hurl bricks, stones and mud. Both Lang and Southworth were later suspended for their actions.

After a fine 5-0 win against West Brom at Turf Moor on New Years Eve, there was more controversy the following week when the Turfites travelled to the Midlands for the return. In a season of mishaps on railway journeys, goalkeeper Jack Hillman decided to leave the train carriage after a brief stop at Stockport. After the window in the carriage door "somehow" got broken, Hillman was detained by the railway authorities and the train, containing the rest of the Burnley party, steamed off without him. He eventually arrived at Stoney Lane, then West Brom's home, at half time to find his team 1-4 behind with Billy Bowes having played in goal. The game was effectively already over but West Brom rubbed it in by adding three more goals against a dispirited Burnley team.

Billy Bowes
emergency goalkeeper at West Brom

In the interests of the team the Burnley Committee decided not to suspend Hillman but he was severely censured and warned as to his future conduct.

It was not the first time that Jack Hillman had crossed swords with authority and it would certainly not be the last.

After the West Brom debacle there was an upturn in level of performance by the Burnley team with a run of seven victories in eight league games. The team had been strengthened by the arrival of a new centre forward, Peter Turnbull from Third Lanark and his team mate, wing half Archie Livingstone. Livingstone in particular would provide sterling service to the Turf Moor cause over the coming years. Both FA Cup finalists, Wolves and Everton, were beaten at Turf Moor and Preston, destined to finish as runners-up, were overcome 4-2, also at Turf Moor, in one of the season's most exciting and entertaining matches. There was also a groundbreaking 3-1 win at Aston Villa, three goals in nine pulsating second half minutes, Burnley's first-ever competitive victory at Villa Park against the team who, over the next few years, would emerge as very much the dominant force in English football.

On the final day of the season Burnley again entertained Sunderland who had once more, as in 1891-92, already clinched the League Championship. The Wearsiders arrived at Turf Moor declaring that their intention was at least three goals to become the first side to score 100 goals in a League season. They had achieved their aim before half time but a spirited second half revival from the Turfites, goals from James Crabtree and James Hill, almost pegged it back, but not quite. Sunderland "the team of all the talents" were now the team setting the standard but it was to be some time before the team from Turf Moor would be mounting a challenge at the very top.

In the weeks following the end of the League season Burnley again took part in the East Lancashire Charity Cup Competition. After defeating Blackburn 2-0 at Ewood Park in the semi final, Accrington were overcome 4-1 in the final at Turf Moor in front of a crowd of 4,000.

After perhaps exceeding expectations with a sixth place finish in the First Division, the Turfites had ended the campaign by collecting some silverware and the fans were already looking forward to the new season with some confidence.

Winger James Hill

1892-93 - First Division

		P	W	D	L	F	A	Pts
1	Sunderland	30	22	4	4	100	36	48
2	Preston NE	30	17	3	10	57	39	37
3	Everton	30	16	4	10	74	51	36
4	Aston Villa	30	16	3	11	73	62	35
5	Bolton W	30	13	6	11	56	55	32
6	BURNLEY	30	13	4	13	51	44	30
7	Stoke	30	12	5	13	58	48	29
8	West Bromwich A	30	12	5	13	58	69	29
9	Blackburn R	30	8	13	9	47	56	29
10	Nottingham F	30	10	8	12	48	52	28
11	Wolverhampton W	30	12	4	14	47	68	28
12	Sheffield W	30	12	3	15	55	65	27
13	Derby C	30	9	9	12	52	64	27
14	Notts C	30	10	4	16	53	61	24
15	Accrington	30	6	11	13	57	81	23
16	Newton Heath	30	6	6	18	50	85	18

1892-93

Managed by Club Committee

Note	No.	Date		Venue	Opponents	Result		h/t	Goalscorers/times	Opp. goal times
	1	Sep	3	a	Wolverhampton W	L	0-1	0-0		85
	2		5	h	ASTON VILLA	L	0-2	0-0		60, 77
	3		10	a	Newton Heath	D	1-1	0-0	Boyd 60	85
	4		17	h	NEWTON HEATH	W	4-1	3-1	Crabtree 25, Hill (2) 35, 42, Bowes 60	15
	5		24	h	STOKE	W	3-2	2-1	Espie 10, Buchanan 30, Stewart 85	45, 60
	6	Oct	1	a	Sheffield W	L	0-2	0-1		11, 49
	7		3	h	DERBY C	W	2-1	1-1	Crabtree 43, McNab 70	23
	8		15	a	Preston N E	L	0-2	0-2		35, 38
	9		22	h	NOTTS C	W	3-0	1-0	Hill 40, Bowes 61, McNab 88	
McFetridge's last game	10		29	h	ACCRINGTON	L	1-3	0-0	Buchanan 50	60, 80, 87
	11	Nov	5	a	Sunderland	L	0-2	0-2		5, 25
	12		12	a	Derby C	L	0-1	0-1		44
Keenan's last game	13		19	a	Stoke	L	1-4	1-3	Chambers 44	1, 38, 41, 65
	14		26	h	NOTTINGHAM F	D	1-1	1-1	Crabtree 33	20
	15	Dec	3	h	BLACKBURN R	D	0-0	0-0		
	16		8	a	Notts C	L	1-3	1-2	Crabtree 40	10, 30, 70og
	17		10	a	Nottingham F	D	2-2	1-1	Graham 38, Crabtree 80	11, 48
Lambie's last game	18		17	a	Blackburn R	L	0-2	0-2		30, 39
	19		24	a	Everton	W	1-0	0-0	McNab 85	
	20		31	h	WEST BROMWICH A	W	5-0	2-0	Nicol 30, Chambers 40, Hill 50, McNab 65, Buchanan 85	
	21	Jan	7	a	West Bromwich A	L	1-7	1-4	Chambers 1	15,18,35,38,60,65,85
	22		14	a	Accrington	W	4-0	2-0	Bowes 30, Buchanan (2) 40, 71, Chambers 61	
	23	Feb	11	h	BOLTON W	W	3-0	2-0	Bowes 4, King 35, Hill 80	
	24		25	a	Bolton W	L	0-1	0-0		85
	25	Mar	18	h	PRESTON N E	W	4-2	3-2	McNab 11, Brady 25, Bowes 30, Turnbull 60	16, 20
	26		31	h	SHEFFIELD W	W	4-0	3-0	Buchanan 15, Bowes 25, Turnbull 35, Livingstone 75	
	27	Apr	1	h	WOLVERHAMPTON W	W	2-0	0-0	Turnbull 75, scrimmage 85	
	28		4	a	Aston Villa	W	3-1	0-1	Bowes 60, Buchanan 64, Turnbull 69	44
	29		8	h	EVERTON	W	3-0	3-0	Buchanan 3, Brady 15, Bowes 44	
	30		15	h	SUNDERLAND	L	2-3	0-3	Crabtree 60, Hill 76	32, 35, 40

FA Cup

No.	Date		Venue	Opponents	Result		h/t	Goalscorers/times	Opp. goal times
1	Jan	21	h	SMALL HEATH	W	2-0	2-0	McNab 33, Hill 45	
2	Feb	4	a	Sheffield W	L	0-1	0-0		60

Final, Wolverhampton W 1-0 Everton, at Fallowfield, Manchester.

Other matches (friendlies and/or as detailed)

Note	Date		Venue	Opponents	Result		Goalscorers
	Sep	1	h	BOOTLE	W	4-1	Buchanan (3), Graham
		19	h	SHEFFIELD U	L	1-3	Boyd
		29	h	WHITTLEFIELD TEMP.	W	7-1	Galbraith (2), Chambers (3), Crabtree (2)
	Oct	3	a	Bootle	W	4-2	McNab, Galbraith, Hill, Espie
	Dec	26	h	DARWEN	W	3-0	Hill, Bowes, scrimmage
	Jan	2	a	Darwen	L	1-3	unknown
Lancs Cup		28	a	Preston N E	L	3-7	McNab (2), Buchanan
	Feb	18	a	Newton Heath	L	1-2	Place sen
		20	a	Sheffield U	W	1-0	Hargreaves
	Mar	3	h	ROYAL SCOTS	W	4-0	Turnbull, Buchanan, Brady, scrimmage
		11	h	NEWTON HEATH	W	3-0	Turnbull, Bowes, scrimmage
cotton trade distress fund		14	h	BLACKBURN R	W	2-1	Turnbull, Connolly
		25	h	ROYAL SCOTS	W	7-1	Turnbull (2), Bowes (3), opp og, scrimmage
East Lancs Charity Cup semi	Apr	20	a	Blackburn R	W	2-0	Turnbull, Hill
		22	h	STOKE	W	3-2	Brady, McNab, Buchanan
		24	a	Bootle	D	3-3	Bowes (2), Espie
East Lancs Charity Cup final		28	h	ACCRINGTON	W	4-1	Hill, Brady (2), Bowes
		29	a	Macclesfield	W	3-0	Lang, unknown (2)

Att.	Pos	Hillman	Nicol	Lang	King	Matthew	Stewart	Crabtree	Bowes	Boyd	Hill	Graham	Mullineux	Buchanan	Espie	Keenan	W Smith	Ryan	Chambers	McNab	McFetridge	C Lambie	Nash	W Place Senior	Sawers	A Brady	Turnbull	Livingstone	
10,000		1	2	3	4	5	6	7	8	9	10	11																	1
8,000		1	2	3		5	6	7	8	9	10	11	4																2
10,000	14	1	2	3	4	5	6	7	8	9	10	11																	3
6,500	8	1	2	3	4	5	6	7	10	9	11			8															4
5,500	8	1	2	3		4	10	7	9		11			8	5	6													5
12,000	9		2	3		4	10	7	9		11			8	6	5	1												6
7,000	9		2	3		4	6	7			11			8	5			1	9	10									7
4,000	9	1	2	3		4	6		10		11			7	5				8	9									8
7,000	7	1	2	3			6		10		11			7	5				8	9	4								9
7,000	7	1	2	3			6		10		11			7	5				8	9	4								10
6,000	11	1	2	3	4		6	10	11					7	5				8	9									11
5,000	11	1	2	2	6		4	10	11					8	5				7	9									12
2,000	12	1	2	3	4		10	7				11		8	5	6			9										13
4,000	12	1	2	3	4		10	7	6		11			8	5				9										14
10,000	12	1	2	3	4	5		7	6		10	11							8			9							15
4,000		1	2	3	4	5		7	6		10	11							8			9							16
8,000	13	1	2	3	4			7	6		10	11							8			9	5						17
7,500	14	1	2	3	4	5		7	6		10								8			9		11					18
10,000	14	1	2	3	4			7	10		11		6	8	5					9									19
4,500	14	1	2	3	4			5	10		11		6	8					7	9									20
1,000	15	1	2		4			5	10		11		6	8					7	9					3				21
6,000	15	1	2	3	4			5	10		11		6	8					7	9									22
5,000	13	1	2		4			5	10		11		6	8					7	9					3				23
5,000	14	1	2	3	4			5	10		11			8	6					9				7					24
8,000	12	1	2	3	4			5	10		11				6					9						7	8		25
9,500		1	2	3	4				10		11			8	5											7	9	6	26
8,000		1	2	3					10		11		4	8	5											7	9	6	27
8,000	8	1	2	3					10		11		4	8	5											7	9	6	28
7,000	6	1	2	3					10		11		4	8	5											7	9	6	29
10,000		1	2	3				7	10		11		4	8	5												9	6	30
Appearances		28	30	28	19	11	14	23	28	4	27	7	10	22	18	3	1	1	16	13	2	4	1	2	2	5	6	5	
Goals (51)			1		1		1	6	8	1	6	1		8	1				4	5						2	4	1	

1 untraced

Att.	Pos	Hillman	Nicol	Lang	King	Matthew	Stewart	Crabtree	Bowes	Boyd	Hill	Graham	Mullineux	Buchanan	Espie	Keenan	W Smith	Ryan	Chambers	McNab	McFetridge	C Lambie	Nash	W Place Senior	Sawers	A Brady	Turnbull	Livingstone	
7,500		1	2	3	4			5	10		11		6	8					7	9									1
9,500		1	2		4			5	10		11		6	8					7	9					3				2
Appearances		2	2	1	2			2	2		2		2	2					2	2					1				
Goals (2)											1									1									

1893-94

There were no significant departures from Turf Moor in the summer of 1892 and just one major new arrival, full back Tom McLintock from Kilmarnock. McLintock was seen as the long term replacement at left back for Sandy Lang and he would emerge as one of Burnley FC's true legends over the coming seasons.

Tom McLintock
new arrival from Kilmarnock

In the first game of the new campaign Burnley travelled to Manchester to play Newton Heath who had finished bottom of the First Division at the end of the previous season but had not been relegated due to their success in the iniquitous Test Matches. They would again end the season at the very bottom but, on that opening day when all teams start equal and with sky high aspirations, they gave Burnley a two-goal start and came back to beat them 3-2.

There were impressive Turf Moor victories against both Darwen and Preston before a crushing 0-5 defeat at the Town Ground by Nottingham Forest. A 1-1 draw at West Brom was followed by an impressive 4-0 win against Stoke at Turf Moor and a 2-1 victory against an Everton side containing nine full internationals. They included inside forward Edgar Chadwick, one of football's biggest names in the 1890's, who would go on to play for Burnley later in his career. Billy Bowes and James Hill then got the goals in an historic 2-1 win against Preston, Burnley's first-ever league victory at Deepdale, a result against the inaugural Football League Champions that would not be equalled for a quarter of a century. Unusually a Lancashire local derby passed off without any unpleasant incidents, although there was a lighter moment when, as he scored Burnley's winner, James Hill collided with an upright which promptly collapsed. The game was held up for a time until a joiner could be found to effect temporary repairs to the frame of the goal.

Early in November 1893, Burnley came from a goal behind to beat Nottingham Forest 3-1 at Turf Moor, avenging a crushing defeat at Nottingham earlier in the season. In fine form in the Turfites' half back line was James Crabtree, now in his second season as a first team regular and destined for international honours later in the campaign. However, later on that Saturday evening, as he celebrated with his friends, Crabtree was involved in a violent argument with a drunken weaver that ended with the young footballing star being stabbed in the chest. Crabtree was not seriously hurt but the wound was sufficient to make him miss Burnley's next two games. Also "in the wars" was goalkeeper Jack Hillman, injured during Burnley's 2-4 defeat at Stoke, although, tough as he was, he insisted on finishing the game between the posts. For the following fixtures, including the local derby at Ewood Park, Walter Place senior was chosen in goal as Hillman's replacement. Place had not yet established himself as a regular first teamer, but demonstrated his versatility with a competent performance in a 2-3 defeat for the Turfites. He also appeared between the sticks at Everton but outfield defensive lapses rather than goalkeeping errors were responsible for a 4-3 victory for the Merseysiders.

The Burnley supporters were glad to see big Jack back in goal against Sunderland at Turf Moor and he was determined to show how much he had been missed. He was unbeatable in a 1-0 win, as he was in the following match, a 3-0 victory against West Brom. He followed that with an inspired display at Sunderland as the Turfites came back from 0-2 down to draw 2-2 thanks to two goals from Peter Turnbull.

The Christmas fixtures, so often over the years a disappointment to Burnley and their supporters, provided an excellent return, with December 1893 being as successful a month as the club had ever experienced. A crowd of over 13,000 turned up at Turf Moor on the Saturday before Christmas to see the homesters collect both points thanks to a goal from James Hill. Two days later, on Christmas Day, four second half goals found the Sheffield United net, with the only disappointment being the size of the crowd, just 8,000 hardy souls braving the most wretched Christmas weather imaginable. On Boxing Day Burnley ended their 1893 League programme with another success, a 1-0 victory at Olive Grove, then the home of Sheffield Wednesday. Billy Bowes was on target and the two points were enough to lift the Turfites into second place in Division One. The players were soon brought back down to earth however after a Turf Moor visit by the famous Corinthians, inspired by the peerless C.B.Fry, then only 21. The visitors, all amateurs of course, were rather too good for their professional hosts who went down 0-2 after being given something of a football lesson.

In January 1894 it was time for the FA Cup again and, in the first round at Trent Bridge, Burnley were expected to dispose of Second Division Notts County with some comfort. County had other ideas and scored an early winner in a match that deteriorated into a war of attrition with Burnley's John Espie and County's David Calderhead being sent off for fighting. County went on to win the FA Cup that season.

In February 1894 James Crabtree's excellent performances for Burnley at last brought him to the attention of the international selectors and he won his first representative

James Crabtree
England's first Burnley-born international

honour playing for the Football League in Belfast. It was the League's first-ever meeting with the Irish League and Crabtree was accompanied on his journey by Burnley Manager Harry Bradshaw. Ostensibly Bradshaw was looking after Crabtree but he was also intent on seeking out Irish talent, in particular a young Glentoran player who had been referred to him called Tom Morrison. It was a successful trip across the water for both men, Crabtree was impressive in a 4-2 win for the Football League, and within days, Tom Morrison was on his way to Turf Moor.

Just three weeks later James Crabtree travelled back to Belfast, having been selected for the full England team to play against the Irish. Once again he was in superb form, helping his side to a 2-2 draw and ensuring he would be an integral part of his country's plans in the coming years. Crabtree was only the second Burnley player to be chosen for his country, after the great Jack Yates five years earlier, and he was also the very first Burnley-born England international. Jack Yates himself appeared for Burnley's senior team for the final time in March 1894 against Derby at Turf Moor.

After a run of poor results Wolves were beaten 4-2 at Turf Moor on the last day of the season, two of Burnley's goals coming from top scorer Peter Turnbull. It was only the second victory by the Turfites since early February and it meant a fifth place finish, the club's highest ever. However just a modest points return in the final weeks of the season would have seen the men from Turf Moor end the campaign as runners-up to Aston Villa, themselves embarking on a sequence of five League Championships in seven years. Villa clinched their first League title with a 6-3 victory at Turf Moor on the penultimate Saturday of the season, a disappointing performance from the Turfites but a ruthless display of finishing power from Villa, showing how it should be done.

1893-94 - First Division

		P	W	D	L	F	A	Pts
1	Aston Villa	30	19	6	5	84	42	44
2	Sunderland	30	17	4	9	72	44	38
3	Derby C	30	16	4	10	73	62	36
4	Blackburn R	30	16	2	12	69	53	34
5	BURNLEY	30	15	4	11	61	51	34
6	Everton	30	15	3	12	90	57	33
7	Nottingham F	30	14	4	12	57	48	32
8	West Bromwich A	30	14	4	12	66	59	32
9	Wolverhampton W	30	14	3	13	52	63	31
10	Sheffield U	30	13	5	12	47	61	31
11	Stoke	30	13	3	14	65	79	29
12	Sheffield W	30	9	8	13	48	57	26
13	Bolton W	30	10	4	16	38	52	24
14	Preston NE	30	10	3	17	44	56	23
15	Darwen	30	7	5	18	37	83	19
16	Newton Heath	30	6	2	22	36	72	14

1893-94

Managed by Club Committee

Division One (5th)

	No	Date			Opponents	Result		h/t	Goalscorers/times	Opp. goal times
	1	Sep	2	a	Newton Heath	L	2-3	2-2	Brady 25, Hill 35	38, 45, 75p
Darwen goal 46m	2		4	h	DARWEN	W	5-1	2-0	Bowes 38, scrimmage (2) 44, 67 Turnbull 72, King 78	
	3		9	h	PRESTON N E	W	4-1	1-0	Brady (2) 5, 50, Buchanan 58, Turnbull 87	65p
	4		16	a	Nottingham F	L	0-5	0-2		5,15,60,70,75
	5		23	a	West Bromwich A	D	1-1	1-1	Brady 25	42
	6		30	h	STOKE	W	4-0	1-0	Espie 4, scrimmage 55, Turnbull (2) 75, 87	
	7	Oct	7	h	EVERTON	W	2-1	1-1	Brady 35, Hill 77	5
	8		14	a	Preston N E	W	2-1	1-1	Bowes 40, Hill 70	2
	9		21	h	NEWTON HEATH	W	4-1	1-0	Turnbull (2) 8, 75, Espie 60, Hill 65	87
	10		28	a	Aston Villa	L	0-4	0-2		20, 35, 65, 87
	11	Nov	4	h	NOTTINGHAM F	W	3-1	1-1	Nicol 35, Bowes 51, Brady 70	6
	12		11	a	Stoke	L	2-4	2-3	Bowes 25, Hill 40	20, 30, 35, 65
	13		18	a	Blackburn R	L	2-3	1-2	Hill 40, scrimmage 65	3, 20, 60
	14		25	a	Everton	L	3-4	1-1	Brady 30, Turnbull 47, Hill 64p	15, 55, 60, 87
	15	Dec	2	h	SUNDERLAND	W	1-0	0-0	Hill 80p	
	16		9	h	WEST BROMWICH A	W	3-0	2-0	Hill 20, Turnbull 23, Espie 75	
	17		16	a	Sunderland	D	2-2	1-2	Turnbull (2) 43, 59	7, 25
	18		23	h	BLACKBURN R	W	1-0	0-0	Hill 60	
	19		25	h	SHEFFIELD U	W	4-1	0-0	Bowes 60, Buchanan (2) 65, 86, Espie 80	83
	20		26	a	Sheffield W	W	1-0	1-0	Bowes 35	
	21	Jan	6	a	Bolton W	L	0-2	0-1		10, 80p
	22	Feb	3	h	BOLTON W	W	2-1	1-0	Place jun 30, Turnbull 50	65
	23		6	a	Darwen	D	0-0	0-0		
	24	Mar	3	a	Wolverhampton W	L	0-1	0-1		23
	25		10	h	DERBY C	W	3-1	2-0	Egan 30, Hill 43, Morrison 51	60
Yates' last game	26		23	h	SHEFFIELD W	L	0-1	0-1		20
	27		26	a	Sheffield U	L	0-1	0-1		15
	28	Apr	2	a	Derby C	D	3-3	1-2	Turnbull 30, unknown (2) 60, 85	5, 25, 50
	29		7	h	ASTON VILLA	L	3-6	1-1	Turnbull 45, Buchanan 51, Place jun 75	20,47,55,65,80,85
Buchanan's last game	30		14	h	WOLVERHAMPTON W	W	4-2	3-0	Place jun 17, Espie 20, Turnbull (2) 44, 46	65, 89

FA Cup

Rd	Date			Opponents	Result		h/t	Goalscorers/times	Opp. goal times
1	Jan	27	a	Notts C	L	0-1	0-1		7

Final, Notts C 4-1 Bolton W, at Goodison Park.

Other matches (friendlies and/or as detailed)

	Date			Opponents	Result		Goalscorers
benefit for Keenan and Hill	Sep	11	h	BLACKBURN R	L	0-3	
	Nov	15	a	Blackpool	W	2-0	Bowes, Wright og
		21	h	BLACKPOOL	W	7-3	Espie (2), Place jun (3), unknown, Turnbull
	Dec	30	h	CORINTHIANS	L	0-2	
	Jan	1	a	Accrington	L	2-3	Place jun (2)
		8	a	Liverpool	L	0-2	
County Palatine League		13	h	DARWEN	W	1-0	Turnbull
Lancs Cup		20	a	West Manchester	W	2-0	Espie, Turnbull
County Palatine League	Feb	10	a	Darwen	W	4-0	Turnbull (2), Bowes, Place jun
		17	a	Everton	W	2-1	King, Espie
County Palatine League		24	h	PRESTON N E	D	1-1	Espie
Lancs Cup		26	a	Everton	L	0-5	
County Palatine League	Mar	12	h	LIVERPOOL	W	4-2	Turnbull, Espie (2), scrimmage
County Palatine League		17	a	Preston N E	L	0-4	
		24	h	ACCRINGTON	W	3-1	Buchanan (2), Turnbull
		31	a	Heart of Midlothian	L	0-2	
County Palatine League	Apr	11	a	Liverpool	W	2-0	Turnbull, scrimmage
East Lancs Charity Cup semi		17	h	DARWEN	W	1-0	Turnbull
		18	a	Lincoln C	W	2-1	Turnbull (2)
		19	a	Grimsby T	W	4-1	unknown (4)
		21	a	Woolwich A	L	0-2	
		23	a	Millwall Athletic	W	3-1	Turnbull, Egan, Morrison
		24	a	Uxbridge	W	6-2	Egan, Crabtree, Morrison, Buchanan, Turnbull, Place jun
County Palatine League final		28	h	BURY	L	1-2	Place jun

Att.	Pos	Hillman	Nicol	McLintock	Mullineux	Espie	Livingstone	A Brady	Buchanan	Turnbull	Bowes	Hill	King	Crabtree	Lang	McNab	W Place senior	Watson	W Place junior	Morrison	Egan	Johnson	Yates	
10,000		1	2	3	4	5	6	7	8	9	10	11												1
6,500	6	1	2	3		5	6	7	8	9	10	11	4											2
9,000	3	1	2	3		5	6	7	8	9	10	11	4											3
7,000	11	1	2	3		5	6	7	8	9	10	11	4											4
3,000	9	1	2	3	4	5	6	7	8	9	10	11												5
6,000	4	1		2	4	5	6	7	8	9	10	11		3										6
10,000	4	1		3	4	5	6	7	8	9	10	11		2										7
6,000	3	1		2	6	5	4	7	8	9	10	11		3										8
7,000	3	1		3	4	5	6	7	8	9	10	11		2										9
10,000	3	1		3	4	5	6	7	8	9	10	11		2										10
6,000	3	1	2	3		5	6	7	8	9	10	11		4										11
5,000	5	1		2		5	6	7	8		10	11	4		3	9								12
5,000	5			2		5	6	7	8	10	9	11	4		3		1							13
10,000	5		2	3		9	6	7		8	10	11	4	5			1							14
9,500	5	1	2	3	4	9	6			8	10	11		5				7						15
4,500	4	1	2	3	4	9	6			8	10	11		5				7						16
7,000	4	1	2	3	4	9		7		8	10	11	6	5										17
13,000		1	2	3	4	9	6	7		8	10	11		5										18
8,000		1	2	3	4	9	6	7	8		10	11		5										19
10,000	2	1	2	3	4	9	6	7		8	10	11		5										20
	3	1	2		4	9	6	7		8		11		5	3				10					21
6,000	3	1	2	3	4	9	6			8	10	11		5					7					22
3,000	3	1	2	3		9	6			8	10	11	4	5					7					23
4,000	5	1	2	3		9	6					11	4		5				8	7	10			24
4,500	3	1	2	3		9	6			8		11	4		5					7	10			25
8,000			2	3		5	6			8			4						11	7	9	1	10	26
10,000	4	1		3		5	6		8	9			4	2					10	7	11			27
3,000	4	1	2	3		9	6		7	8					5		4		10		11			28
6,000	6	1	2	3		9	6		7	8			4		5				10		11			29
5,000		1	2	3		9			7	8			4	6	5				10		11			30
Appearances		27	22	29	15	30	28	19	18	27	22	25	14	18	8	1	3	2	9	4	7	1	1	
Goals (61)			1			5		7	4	15	6	11	1						3	1	1			

6 untraced

Att.	Hillman	Nicol	McLintock	Mullineux	Espie	Livingstone	A Brady	Buchanan	Turnbull	Bowes	Hill	King	Crabtree	Lang	McNab	W Place senior	Watson	W Place junior	Morrison	Egan	Johnson	Yates	
8,000	1	7	3	4	9	6			8	10	11		2	5									1
Appearances	1	1	1	1	1	1			1	1	1		1	1									
Goals (0)																							

1894-95

WANTED, by the BURNLEY FOOTBALL CLUB, a Gentleman to act as TEAM MANAGER. A statement of his duties can be seen at the office (as under) on Wednesday, Thursday, and Friday, Aug. 1st, 2nd, and 3rd, from 6-30 to 7-30 p.m.—Applications, in writing, stating age, present occupation, and salary required, to be sent to the undersigned, endorsed "Team Manager," by Monday, Aug. 6th. —Arthur F. Sutcliffe, 88, St. James's-street, Burnley, July 27th, 1894.

The big news in the summer of 1894 was that Burnley FC was to have a team manager for the first time, with club secretary Harry Bradshaw eventually appointed to the position.

One of the real Burnley FC stalwarts Sandy Lang decided not to re-sign for the new campaign and to seek re-instatement as an amateur. He would still be available for selection for the Turfites but in fact, would make his farewell appearance late in the season.

Three games into the new campaign came the first real crisis of Harry Bradshaw's managership when he had to recommend to the Burnley committee that Tom Morrison be discharged for misconduct. Morrison had only been at Turf Moor since the previous March and, although a brilliant player, had let himself down once too often with his volatile temperament. Morrison returned to Ireland but his path and that of Burnley FC would cross again in the future with unfortunate consequences.

After two draws and two defeats in the League, Burnley came from behind to win their first league game, 2-1 against Wolves at Turf Moor. They followed that with a 2-0 win against Derby but, once again, discipline was a problem when Walter Place junior was sent off for fighting with Derby defender Jack Cox, who was also dismissed. Little Walter was subsequently suspended for three matches.

In September 1984 the Turfites again won the East Lancashire Charity Cup when Blackburn were beaten 3-0 at Ewood Park in the final, held over from the previous season. Tom Nicol, John McKnight and Walter Place junior got the goals but the victory celebrations were overshadowed by an early injury to William Egan who was carried off after just ten minutes. It later emerged that Egan had broken his leg and in fact he never appeared again in Burnley's senior team.

By Christmas, after five wins in six league matches Burnley were fourth in the table and the fans began thinking seriously of the First Division title. It was a home defeat by Sheffield United that began the slide down the league, a game played in a gale force wind which damaged the hoardings surrounding the ground and caused play to be held up after blowing over one set of goalposts! The supporters could tell it was destined not to be their day when the Blades scored three goals in four minutes before half time including a sliced clearance from their hero James Crabtree that curled high into the air and dropped into his own net behind Jack Hillman.

After a Turf Moor friendly on Christmas Day with Paisley St Mirren, James Hill's previous club, Burnley played two League games in the Black Country before journeying north for an encounter with Celtic on New Year's Eve. The match was won thanks to two goals from Peter Turnbull and the Burnley party stayed in Glasgow to enjoy the Hogmanay festivities but this trip began a chain of events that led to one of Burnley's star players leaving Turf Moor.

While the main party returned to Burnley on New Year's Day Scotsman Jock Espie was given special permission by the Burnley committee to stay behind in Scotland for another day. In their wisdom the committee allowed Jack Hillman to stay with him, a strange decision considering the somewhat chequered career of "the Burly One" in terms of his relationship with authority in general. Predictably the pair were late returning to Burnley and both were fined by the committee as a result. Although both players were selected for the next few matches, there were reports of altercations between Hillman and members of the committee which apparently came to a head during and after a Lancashire Cup game at Turf Moor against Liverpool. Jock Espie's mind may also have been elsewhere during this game, he put through his own goal in a 0-4 defeat! Jack Hillman was not selected for Burnley's next game and although he was reported to be injured, within a few days it was reported that he had been "suspended indefinitely for insubordination". He was soon expressing his dissatisfaction and desire to leave Burnley to anyone who would listen, with apparently a preference for "a Lancashire club near the sea "

Within three weeks Hillman had been signed by Everton for an undisclosed transfer fee and a share of the proceeds of a match between the two clubs. His first appearance for his new club was against Burnley at Goodison Park in that transfer match, Everton winning 4-1. Oddly enough his first two League games for Everton were both against Burnley as well, the Merseysiders winning both matches although the Turfites let slip a two goal lead in the 2-3 defeat at Goodison. Immediately afterwards Hillman began to stir up the rivalry between the clubs, expressing his contempt for some of the Burnley players, obviously not considering that he may well return to Turf Moor in the future !

One of Burnley's most promising young reserves, locally born half back Joe Taylor made his league debut in the heavy defeat at Preston in January 1895. The Turfites lost every one of the games that Taylor played towards the end of that season but his potential was plain to see and he went on to enjoy a long and distinguished Turf Moor career well into the next century.

As one new Burnley FC talent was just getting into his stride, another, rather more mature one was reaching the end of the road. Sandy Lang made his final league appearance for Burnley in the defeat at Small Heath and then played in front of his beloved Burnley fans for the last time on the first day of April, in the benefit match for John Espie. Lang had been with Burnley since 1885, signing from Padiham as a 21 year old and had played over 300 games for the club, many as a well-respected captain.

It was a very disappointing end to the season with just one point gained from the last nine matches - the final seven were all lost - to finish in ninth position, only four points off the very bottom. As the end of the season approached, the Turfites' captain James Crabtree was again selected for England for the Home International series of 1895. He won his second cap in a 9-0 demolition of Ireland at Derby and his third in a 3-0 victory against Scotland at Goodison Park, playing at right back on both occasions. He also appeared for the Football League in a 4-1 win against the Scottish League in Glasgow. These representative appearances meant Crabtree missed Burnley matches of course which led to opportunities for others to try to make their mark. It was a chance for local youngster William "Titch" Tattersall to step into the right back role, at least temporarily, and John Espie, a natural leader, was given the captaincy during the skipper's absence on international duty.

When James Crabtree returned for Burnley's final match of the season, at home to Stoke, most of the Turf Moor crowd had heard the rumours that a number of big clubs had him in their sights and it was probably only a matter of time before he left his home town club. When he led the team on to the field he was cheered to the echo, the supporters appreciating the huge natural talent of one of their own. When they saw that he was wearing his international cap, which he kept on for the duration of the game, they knew the writing was on the wall and it read "Farewell and thanks for the memory".

Joe Taylor
a stalwart in the Burnley defence for a dozen years

1894-95 - First Division

		P	W	D	L	F	A	Pts
1	Sunderland	30	21	5	4	80	37	47
2	Everton	30	18	6	6	82	50	42
3	Aston Villa	30	17	5	8	82	43	39
4	Preston NE	30	15	5	10	62	46	35
5	Blackburn R	30	11	10	9	59	49	32
6	Sheffield U	30	14	4	12	57	55	32
7	Nottingham F	30	13	5	12	50	56	31
8	Sheffield W	30	12	4	14	50	55	28
9	BURNLEY	30	11	4	15	44	56	26
10	Bolton W	30	9	7	14	61	62	25
11	Wolverhampton W	30	9	7	14	43	63	25
12	Small Heath	30	9	7	14	50	74	25
13	West Bromwich A	30	10	4	16	51	66	24
14	Stoke	30	9	6	15	50	67	24
15	Derby C	30	7	9	14	45	68	23
16	Liverpool	30	7	8	15	51	70	22

1894-95

Manager : Harry Bradshaw

Division One (9th)

Note	No.	Date			Opponents	Result		h/t	Goalscorers/times	Opp. goal times
	1	Sep	1	a	Nottingham F	L	1-2	1-2	McKnight 10	12, 14
	2		3	h	LIVERPOOL	D	3-3	1-1	Crabtree 40, Hill 47, Egan 51	10, 48, 75
	3		8	a	Sunderland	L	0-3	0-1		20, 50, 55
	4		15	a	Sheffield U	D	2-2	1-0	Nicol (2) 25, 72	70, 88
	5		22	h	WOLVERHAMPTON W	W	2-1	1-1	Nicol (2) 40, 73	18
	6		29	h	DERBY C	W	2-0	2-0	Espie 38, Nicol 40	
	7	Oct	6	a	Sheffield W	L	3-4	3-3	Hill 10, Nicol 25, Place jun 39	17, 20, 43, 80
	8		13	h	SMALL HEATH	W	3-1	2-1	Nicol 22, Place jun 35, Bowes 70	25
	9		20	a	Bolton W	D	1-1	1-0	Paton 15og	85
	10		27	h	NOTTINGHAM F	L	0-1	0-0		65
	11	Nov	3	a	Liverpool	W	3-0	1-0	Nicol 20, Turnbull 55, Livinstone 75	
	12		10	h	SHEFFIELD W	W	3-0	3-0	Bowes 20, McKnight (2) 32, 40	
	13		17	a	Blackburn R	L	0-1	0-0		70
	14		24	h	WEST BROMWICH A	W	2-0	1-0	Bowes 25, McKnight 70	
	15	Dec	8	h	PRESTON N E	W	2-1	1-0	Crabtree 30, Bowes 60	52
	16		12	a	Derby C	W	2-0	1-0	Turnbull 5, McKnight 65	
	17		22	h	SHEFFIELD U	L	2-4	0-3	Nicol 50, scrimmage 65	41, 43og, 45, 84
	18		26	a	Wolverhampton W	L	0-1	0-0		55
	19		29	a	West Bromwich A	W	1-0	0-0	Nicol 70	
	20	Jan	5	h	BOLTON W	W	1-0	1-0	Bowes 20	
	21		12	h	BLACKBURN R	W	2-1	2-0	Bowes 24, McLintock 30	72
	22		26	a	Preston N E	L	0-4	0-1		5, 55, 70, 90
	23	Feb	23	h	ASTON VILLA	D	3-3	2-0	scrimmage 25, Nicol 30, Place jun 50	75, 80og, 87
	24	Mar	16	h	EVERTON	L	2-4	0-1	Place jun 81, Bowes 86	45, 53, 65, 70
	25		21	a	Everton	L	2-3	2-0	Bowes 25, McKnight 35	60, 70, 89
	26		23	a	Small Heath	L	0-1	0-0		65
	27		30	a	Stoke	L	1-5	0-2	Place jun 60	2, 35, 55, 65, 85
	28	Apr	6	a	Aston Villa	L	0-5	0-1		35, 50, 80, 85, 90
	29		13	h	SUNDERLAND	L	0-3	0-1		40, 68, 78
Crabtree's last game	30		20	h	STOKE	L	1-2	1-2	Hill 30	15, 44

FA Cup

No.	Date			Opponents	Result		h/t	Goalscorers/times	Opp. goal times
1	Feb	2	a	Newcastle U	L	1-2	1-1	Bowes 10	20, 80

Final, Aston Villa 1-0 West Bromwich A, at Crystal Palace.

Other first team matches (friendlies and/or as detailed)

Note	Date			Opponents	Result		Goalscorers
Millward (Everton) benefit	Sep	10	a	Everton	L	1-4	Turnbull
		12	a	Manchester C	W	1-0	unknown
		17	h	CLYDE	D	2-2	Turnbull, unknown
E L Charity Cup final, 1893-94		24	a	Blackburn R	W	3-0	Nicol, McKnight, Place jun
	Oct	9	a	Darwen	W	3-1	Hill, unknown, Place jun
	Dec	15	a	Nelson	W	4-1	Crabtree, Bowes (2), Place jun
		25	h	PAISLEY ST MIRREN	W	5-1	unknown (5)
		31	a	Celtic	W	2-0	Turnbull (2)
Lancs Cup	Jan	19	h	LIVERPOOL	L	0-4	
County Palatine League	Feb	9	h	DARWEN	W	4-0	Parker, Place jun, Turnbull (2)
County Palatine League		26	a	Darwen	D	1-1	scrimmage
County Palatine League	Mar	2	h	PRESTON N E	D	2-2	Turnbull, Bowes
Jack Hillman transfer match		4	a	Everton	L	1-4	Adams og
County Palatine League		9	h	BLACKBURN R	L	0-1	
County Palatine League		11	a	Preston N E	L	0-2	
poor children charity match		26	a	Bury	L	0-1	
John Espie benefit	Apr	1	h	BURY	W	4-2	Bowes (2), McKnight, Brimblecombe
County Palatine League		8	a	Blackburn R	L	3-4	unknown (3)
		12	h	DARWEN	W	5-0	Bowes, Lindsay, Crabtree, unknown, Hargreaves
		27	a	Bacup	W	4-1	Stirling, Knowles og, unknown (2)

Att.	Pos	Hillman	Nicol	McLintock	Munn	Crabtree	Livingstone	Morrison	Egan	McKnight	Bowes	Sutherland	W Place junior	Hill	Mullineux	Espie	Turnbull	Johnson	W Place senior	Parker	Taylor	Lang	Hargreaves	W Smith	Tattersall	Porterfield	Lindsay		
9,000		1	2	3	4	5	6	7	8	9	10	11																	1
10,000		1	2	3	4	5	6	7	9		10		8	11															2
7,000	15	1		3		2	6	7	8		10			11	4	5	9												3
5,000	12		7	3		2	6			8	10		11			5	9	1	4										4
6,000	9	1	7	3		2	6			8	10		11			5	9		4										5
6,000	8	1	7	3		2	6			9	10		11	8		5			4										6
	9	1	7	3		2	6			9	10		11	8		5			4										7
5,000	8	1	7	3		2	6			9	10		11			5			4	8									8
	7	1	7	3		2	6			9	10		11			5			4	8									9
4,000	8	1	7	3		2	6			9	10		11			5			4	8									10
8,000	7	1	7	3		2	6				10		11	8		5	9		4										11
4,500	7		7	3		2	6			8	10			11		5	9	1	4										12
7,000	9	1	7	3		2	6			8	10			11		5	9		4										13
6,000	7	1	7	3		2	6			9	10		11	8		5			4										14
6,000	5	1	7	3		2	6			9	10		11			5	8		4										15
1,750	4	1		3		2	6			9	10		11			5	8		4	7									16
2,000	4	1	7	3		2	6			9	10		11			5	8		4										17
5,000	8	1	7	3		2	6			9	10		11	8		5			4										18
2,535	7	1	7	3		2	6				8		10	11		5	9		4										19
4,500	7	1	7	3		2	6				8		11	10		5	9		4										20
10,000	5	1	7	3		2	6				8		11	10		5	9		4										21
5,000	8			3		2	6				8		11	10		5	9	1		7	4								22
7,000	8		7	3		2	6			9	10		11	8		5		1	4										23
9,000	8			3		2	6			9	10		11	7		5		1	4		8								24
8,000	8			3		2	6			9	10		11	8		5		1	7		4								25
5,500	8			3		2	6			9	10		11					1	7		4	5	8						26
2,000	9			3		2	6			9	10		11	8		5		1	7		4								27
4,000	9			3			5			9	10		11	8					4		6		7	1	2				28
8,000	9		7	3			6			8	10			11		5			4						2	1	9		29
			7	3		2	6				10		11	8		5			4							1	9		30
Appearances		19	22	30	2	28	30	3	3	22	30	1	25	20	1	26	13	8	26	5	6	1	2	1	2	2	2		
Goals (44)			11	1		2	1		1	6	8		5	3		1	2											1	og

2 untraced

Att.	Hillman	Nicol	McLintock	Munn	Crabtree	Livingstone	Morrison	Egan	McKnight	Bowes	Sutherland	W Place junior	Hill	Mullineux	Espie	Turnbull	Johnson	W Place senior	Parker	Taylor	Lang	Hargreaves	W Smith	Tattersall	Porterfield	Lindsay	
8,000		7	3		2	6				10		11	8		5	9	1	4									1
Appearances		1	1		1	1				1		1	1		1	1	1	1									
Goals (1)										1																	

1895-96

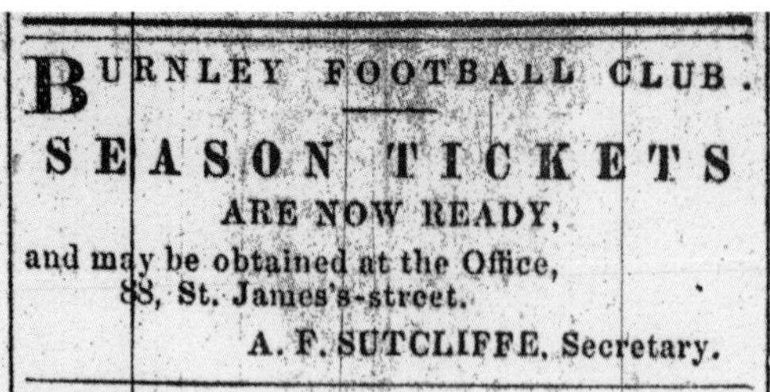
BURNLEY FOOTBALL CLUB.
SEASON TICKETS
ARE NOW READY,
and may be obtained at the Office,
88, St. James's-street.
A. F. SUTCLIFFE, Secretary.

After weeks of speculation it was finally confirmed that Burnley's very first home grown International, James Crabtree, had signed for Aston Villa for a fee of £250, a huge sum at the end of the Victorian era. Crabtree was the most versatile of defenders but had settled into the right back position at Turf Moor, winning three England caps. It was as a wing half however that he went on to achieve greatness with Villa and England and many critics regard this product of Burnley's cobbled streets as one of the best players these islands have ever produced.

Crabtree's replacement at right back was to be Jerry Reynolds, a Celtic stalwart since 1889, who won Scottish Championship medals in 1893 and 1894. Another local youngster, custodian Willie Tatham, would also make his mark in Burnley's First Division campaign, although for the Turfites' opening match at Wolves it was another young goalkeeper, Walter Napier, signed from Scottish junior football, who would don the gloves. The season got off to the worst possible start when left half Archie Livingstone missed the train connection at Manchester and did not arrive at Molineux until 20 minutes into the game. The Turfites were 0-2 down by then and never recovered, losing 1-5 with only a late consolation goal from James Hill. The misery was compounded when Napier received a kick on his knee late in the game and ended the day with it badly swollen. He was roundly congratulated on a fine debut performance by the senior players who all agreed he was not to blame for any of the goals. Such is the fickle nature of football however, that Walter Napier, apparently on the threshold of a promising career, was laid up for weeks – and never played for Burnley's senior team again.

Enter 18 year old Willie Tatham, a product of the Burnley Sunday School League, who certainly never let the Turfites down, only conceding two goals in his first six League outings, and he was Burnley's first choice, when available, for the rest of the season.

After a promising start to the campaign, matters deteriorated and from October until the turn of the year Burnley did not win a single league match, picked up only three points and dropped into the bottom three. Captain James Hill was injured in the early stages of the home defeat by Bolton and was out for a month. Such was his influence on the rest of the team however that he insisted on attending training and matches when instructed by his doctor to stay at home and rest. The Burnley committee became exasperated at Hill's keen but cavalier attitude to his own well-being and formally suspended him until he was fit again for selection.

As results continued to be poor, various committee members were reported to be "fishing in strictly preserved waters" and, sure enough, another Scottish import arrived at Turf Moor. Half back Charles McEleny had been a team mate of Jerry Reynolds at Celtic and was currently a fringe member of the Parkhead squad on its way to another Scottish title. He was described as a powerhouse with an unquenchable thirst for work and there is no doubt his mate Reynolds played no small part in persuading McEleny to follow him south where there was undoubtedly a place in the Burnley side for his talents. When word of his departure got out, the Celtic fans were astonished that a player of his calibre had been allowed to leave Parkhead.

Following the turn of the year, Burnley's fortunes suddenly changed with Bury beaten 4-3 at Gigg Lane on New Year's Day, James Hill hitting a hat trick, his first goals since September. Sheffield Wednesday and West Brom were both beaten with fine team performances, good preparation for the FA Cup first round tie with Second Division Woolwich Arsenal. The Gunners had made the Burnley committee a handsome offer to stage the match at Plumstead but the offer, a perfectly acceptable practice and very common in those days, was declined. It was a good decision, Woolwich were beaten 6-1 and completely outplayed, with Tom Nicol and Hugh Robertson each scoring twice.

The Turfites were also making progress in the Lancashire Cup, with wins at Bolton and Everton before the FA Cup second round tie with Stoke came around. The Turfites had warmed up for this clash with a league encounter with the Potters, cruising at 4-0 ahead when it was abandoned because of fog just 16 minutes from time. The Burnley Committee put in a request to the Football League that the match had almost been won and the points should be awarded to them. As an alternative, the committee proposed that the last 16 minutes of the abandoned match be played on the day of the forthcoming FA Cup tie between the clubs, but before the tie kicked off. In those far-off days this method was occasionally used in the case of abandoned matches, with the two sections of the fixture concerned sometimes months apart with a number of different players. A statistician's worst nightmare!

As it happened the League ordered this particular match to be replayed from scratch the following month, justice prevailing with Burnley winning it 2-0.

It was a different story in the FA Cup match however, with the Turfites labouring to a 1-1 draw, then being hit for seven in the replay at the Victoria Ground. The conditions for the match were as bad as they could be, pouring with rain, a mudheap of a pitch, and the ground enveloped in a damp smoky mist. The Burnley Express correspondent described his whole day as "a horrible experience. Is this what I have travelled from Lancashire to see, crushed 18 to a railway carriage?"

The season was petering out and Burnley's last hope of silverware disappeared when they lost in the semi final of the Lancashire Cup to Blackburn who went on to lift the trophy. There had been a number of consistent performers during the season and Tom McLintock was certainly one of them.

Not before time he was chosen to play for the Anglo Scots in a trial match against a Home based Scots X1 in Glasgow. The Scottish selectors very rarely picked England based players for their international team and although McLintock was selected as reserve for the Home International against England in Glasgow, he was never awarded the full cap his endeavours undoubtedly deserved.

The League campaign ended with a home match against Blackburn Rovers and the Burnley players signed off with something special in front of their own supporters, a 6-0 demolition of the "old enemy". Walter Place senior started the scoring after just ten minutes with only his second league goal of the season. Tom Nicol got two more before half time, both from good approach work by Charlie McEleny, bidding farewell to the Burnley supporters before his return to Celtic. Five minutes after the break Hugh Robertson was in on the act, following up when the Rovers' custodian spilled his shot. Just minutes later it was five when a cross from young Walter Place was met on the volley by Tom Nicol, completing his hat trick with the best goal of the match. In the last five minutes Nicol turned provider for Hugh Robertson to head home his second and Burnley's sixth to complete the rout. After a difficult campaign, especially early on, the players had reserved their finest performance for the very end and most of the 5,000 crowd went home feeling all was right with the world.

An end of season Scottish tour was arranged and three defeats in four matches demonstrated that there were still good players around north of the border, most of whom would be only too ready to listen to offers to ply their trade in the south. Needless to say Turfites' manager Harry Bradshaw was once again indulging in some "fishing in Scottish waters".

During the summer a rumour began to circulate around the town that Burnley FC were to leave Turf Moor and re-locate to the new Athletic Company's grounds in Towneley Park! The very idea!

Willie Tatham
locally born goalkeeper, a regular in his first season

1895-96 - First Division

		P	W	D	L	F	A	Pts
1	Aston Villa	30	20	5	5	78	45	45
2	Derby C	30	17	7	6	68	35	41
3	Everton	30	16	7	7	66	43	39
4	Bolton W	30	16	5	9	49	37	37
5	Sunderland	30	15	7	8	52	41	37
6	Stoke	30	15	0	15	56	47	30
7	Sheffield W	30	12	5	13	44	53	29
8	Blackburn R	30	12	5	13	40	50	29
9	Preston NE	30	11	6	13	44	48	28
10	BURNLEY	30	10	7	13	48	44	27
11	Bury	30	12	3	15	50	54	27
12	Sheffield U	30	10	6	14	40	50	26
13	Nottingham F	30	11	3	16	42	57	25
14	Wolverhampton W	30	10	1	19	61	65	21
15	Small Heath	30	8	4	18	39	79	20
16	West Bromwich A	30	6	7	17	30	59	19

1895-96

Manager : Harry Bradshaw

Division One (10th)

No	Date			Opponents	Result		h/t	Goalscorers/times	Opp. goal times
1	Sep	2	a	Wolverhampton W	L	1-5	0-4	Hill 75	6, 11, 30, 38, 80
2		7	a	West Bromwich A	W	2-0	1-0	Bowes 15, Place jun 65	
3		9	h	SUNDERLAND	D	0-0	0-0		
4		14	h	BURY	W	3-0	2-0	Nicol 2, Bowes 43, Place jun 89	
5		21	a	Bolton W	L	0-1	0-1		25
6		28	h	PRESTON N E	W	1-0	1-0	Bowes 33	
7	Oct	5	a	Blackburn R	L	0-1	0-1		30
8		12	h	BOLTON W	L	1-2	0-2	Place jun 49	2, 42
9		19	a	Preston N E	D	1-1	1-0	Place jun 15	85
10		26	h	EVERTON	D	1-1	0-0	H.Robertson 90	50
11	Nov	2	a	Aston Villa	L	1-5	0-1	H.Robertson 80	35, 50, 60, 70, 89
12		9	a	Derby C	L	1-5	0-2	H.Robertson 50	26p,44p,60,75,90
13		23	h	ASTON VILLA	L	3-4	3-3	Nicol 5, Bowes 10, Patterson 25	3, 20, 30p, 87
14		30	a	Everton	L	1-2	0-0	McEleny 70	82, 90
15	Dec	7	a	Stoke	L	1-2	0-1	Patterson 85	25, 50
16		14	a	Sheffield W	L	0-1	0-1		15
17		21	h	NOTTINGHAM F	D	0-0	0-0		
18		26	a	Small Heath	L	0-1	0-1		40
19	Jan	1	a	Bury	W	4-3	1-3	Hill (3) 42, 50, 64, Bowes 75	2, 22, 30
20		4	h	SHEFFIELD W	W	2-0	0-0	H.Robertson (2) 65, 80	
21		11	h	WEST BROMWICH A	W	3-0	1-0	Nicol 25, unknown 55, Davidson 75	
22	Feb	3	h	SHEFFIELD U	W	5-0	1-0	Place jun 26, Place sen 60, Davidson 62, Patterson 85, Bowes 88	
23		18	a	Sunderland	L	1-3	1-1	Johnson 15og	42, 70, 80
24		22	h	WOLVERHAMPTON W	W	3-1	0-1	McLintock 53p, H.Robertson 59, Taylor 80	30
25	Mar	7	a	Nottingham F	L	1-2	0-1	Nicol 50	15, 70
26		16	h	STOKE	W	2-0	2-0	Clawley 20og, H.Robertson 30	
27		30	a	Sheffield U	D	1-1	0-0	Place jun 86	62
28	Apr	3	h	SMALL HEATH	D	1-1	0-1	H.Robertson 58	5
29		4	h	DERBY C	D	2-2	1-0	Nicol 40, Place jun 55	65, 75
30		13	h	BLACKBURN R	W	6-0	3-0	Place sen 10, Nicol (3) 25, 37, 54, H.Robertson (2) 50, 85	

FA Cup

Note	Rd	Date			Opponents	Result		h/t	Goalscorers/times	Opp. goal times
Woolwich goal 80m	1	Feb	1	h	WOOLWICH A	W	6-1	4-0	Nicol 3, Place sen 25, Place jun (2) 27, 57, H.Robertson (2) 35, 47	
	2		15	h	STOKE	D	1-1	0-0	scrimmage 78	20
	rep		20	a	Stoke	L	1-7	0-5	Bowes 65	3,5,30,38,45,75,87

Final, Sheffield W 2-1 Wolverhampton W, at Crystal Palace.

Other matches (friendlies and/or as detailed)

Note	Date			Opponents	Result		Goalscorers
James Crabtree transfer match	Sep	16	a	Aston Villa	L	1-2	Hill
	Dec	25	h	DUNDEE	L	1-2	Paterson
Div 1 fixture aban 65m, storm		28	h	SHEFFIELD U	aban	1-0	Davidson
Lancs Cup	Jan	18	a	Bolton W	W	2-1	Hill, Bowes
Div 1 fixture aban 74m, fog		25	h	STOKE	aban	4-0	opp og, unknown (3)
Lancs Cup	Feb	8	a	Everton	W	2-1	Hill, Nicol
		29	a	Liverpool South End	W	4-3	unknown (4)
Lancs Cup semi, at Preston	Mar	14	n	Blackburn R	D	1-1	scrimmage
L Cup semi replay, at Man City		19	n	Blackburn R	L	1-2	H.Robertson
McQue (Liverpool) benefit	Apr	6	a	Liverpool	L	3-4	scrimmage, McLintock p, Nicol
		11	h	LIVERPOOL	D	3-3	H.Robertson, Nicol, unknown
		25	a	Dundee	L	1-2	unknown
		27	a	Motherwell	W	2-0	Nicol, Landless
		28	a	Celtic	L	1-2	Hill
		29	a	Paisley St Mirren	L	0-3	

Att.	Pos	Napier	Reynolds	McLintock	W Place senior	Espie	Livingstone	J Davidson	Stirling	Provan	W Place junior	Hill	Tatham	Nicol	Bowes	H Robertson	Taylor	P Robertson	McEleny	Paterson	Tattersall	Haddow		
6,000		1	2	3	4	5	6	7	8	9	10	11												1
5,000			2	3	4	5	6				10	11	1	7	8	9								2
10,000	6		2	3	4	5	6				10	11	1	7	8	9								3
5,500	4		2	3	4	5	6				10	11	1	7	8	9								4
7,000	7		2	3	5		6		8		10	11	1	7		9	4							5
6,000	6		2	3	5		6	9			10		1	7	8	11	4							6
3,500	9		2	3	5		6	9			10		1	7	8	11	4							7
5,000	11		2	3	5		6	8			11	9	1	7	10		4							8
7,000	10		2	3	4		6	8			11		1	7	10	9	5							9
8,000	11		2	3	4		6	8			11		1	7	10	9	5							10
6,500	11		2	3	4		6			8	11		1	7	10	9	5							11
6,000	12		2	3			6	7		9	11		1		10	8	5	4						12
7,000	13		2	3			6				10	11	1	9	8		5		4	7				13
14,000	14		2	3		5		8			10	11	1		9		6		4	7				14
2,500	14		2	3		5					10	11	1	9	8		6		4	7				15
5,000	14		2	3		5					10	11	1	9	8		6		4	7				16
4,500	13		2	3		5	6				10	11	1	9	8				4	7				17
5,000				3			6	8				11	1	9	10		5		4	7	2			18
				3			6				11	8	1	7	10	9	5		4		2			19
6,000	12		2	3	4		6				11	8	1	7	10	9	5							20
6,000	12		2	3	4			8			11		1	7	10	9	6		5					21
3,000			2	3	4			8			11		1		10	9	6		5	7				22
3,000	12		2	3	4	5	6	8			11			7	10	9						1		23
4,000	10		2	3			6	10		9		11	1	7		8	5		4					24
5,000	13			3	4		6				11	8	1	7	10	9	5				2			25
1,500	11		2	3	4		6	8			11		1	7	10	9			5					26
2,000			2	3	4		6	8			10	11		7		9			5			1		27
5,000			2	3	4		6	10			11	8		7		9			5			1		28
6,000	12		2	3	4			10			11	8		7		9	6		5			1		29
5,000			2	3	4			10			11	8	1	7		9	6		5					30
Appearances		1	27	30	21	9	23	18	2	4	28	20	25	26	23	22	21	1	15	7	3	4		
Goals (48)				1	2			2			7	4		8	6	10	1		1	3			2	ogs

1 untraced

Att.	Napier	Reynolds	McLintock	W Place senior	Espie	Livingstone	J Davidson	Stirling	Provan	W Place junior	Hill	Tatham	Nicol	Bowes	H Robertson	Taylor	P Robertson	McEleny	Paterson	Tattersall	Haddow	
6,000		2	3	4						11	8	1	7	10	9	6		5				1
13,000		2	3	4						11	8		7	10	9	6		5			1	2
10,915		2	3	4						11	8		7	10	9	6		5			1	rep
Appearances		3	3	3						3	3	1	3	3	3	3		3			2	
Goals (8)				1						2			1	1	2							

1 untraced

1896-97

FOOTBALL PRACTICE MATCHES at TURF MOOR DURING AUGUST.

LOCAL FOOTBALL PLAYERS desirous of taking part are requested to give in their names and particulars on MONDAY EVENING between 7 and 9 o'clock.

H. BRADSHAW.

23, St. James's Row.

The Burnley committee, fans and players went into the new season with confidence, determined to make it the best campaign so far, with genuine hopes of winning at least one of the major trophies. They came out of it having endured the worst season in the club's history, bottom of the league by some distance and facing the prospect of football in the Second Division for the first time ever.

There were some highlights of that depressing season, not many, but the astonishing and unexpected 3-0 win at Aston Villa just two days into the New Year was undoubtedly the high spot. Two goals from David Black, a new signing from Wolves, in only his third league outing, and a late strike from Billy Bowes saw the Turfites cruise to a thoroughly deserved victory against a Villa side who were the reigning League Champions and who were on their way to a League and FA Cup double. Not only that, Villa had lost only one league match at home since September 1894 and incredibly, had not failed to score at home in a league game in almost six years! There was deep disappointment among Midlands supporters and understandable speculation that one or two of the Villa players had enjoyed their New Year festivities a little too much!

During the summer one of Burnley's key defenders, left half Archie Livingstone, had been told by his specialist that his knee injury was serious and he must take anything up to a year out of the game, or his career may be in jeopardy. It was depressing news for Livingstone and for the Turfites, but not such bad news for young Joe Taylor who would step in to the breach as his own career began to flourish.

As the season began to unfold it was apparent that some of the players at the club's disposal, indeed one or two of the regular first team, were simply not good enough and a difficult winter lay ahead. After a scrambled 1-0 win at home to Bury early on, Everton were beaten 2-1 at Turf Moor in October and these were the only league victories that the Turfites managed before Christmas. Everton had their revenge at the end of October with a crushing 6-0 win that sent the Turfites to the foot of the league, a position from which they never really recovered. Burnley did not win a single point away from home before the turn of the year but the 1-1 draw at Bury on New Year's Day followed by the extraordinary success at Villa Park must have raised the supporters' hopes as the Turfites climbed out of the bottom two up to the giddy heights of 14th place. It was a false dawn however and Burnley had hit rock bottom again by the middle of February – and there they stayed.

Two of the club's longest serving players bade farewell to Turf Moor during that difficult season. After almost six years Tom Nicol appeared in the last of his 149 League and FA Cup games at Wolves in November 1896 before moving to Blackburn Rovers. Nicol had scored 44 goals in his Burnley career, very impressive for a player who had played many of his games at full back. Tom Nicol had recently married and become a publican in Blackburn and his relationship with the Burnley committee had, it was said, become "somewhat strained" as a result. Nicol was soon followed out of Turf Moor by James Hill, a Burnley player for more than seven years and a virtual ever-present since his arrival from Paisley St Mirren in 1889. Hill had played in 162 league and cup games, scoring 41 goals as a left winger or an inside forward and had captained the side on many occasions, he was transferred to Stoke in exchange for a fee of £60. As some of the old guard moved on, new players were arriving. Centre forward Wilf Toman made his debut on Boxing Day 1896, scoring in a 4-1 win against Liverpool, another of that campaign's few highlights. Toman would find the net for the Turfites on a regular basis over the next two seasons. Irishman Tom Morrison returned to Turf Moor after spells with Glentoran and Celtic, with his previous misdemeanours having apparently been forgiven by the Burnley committee. Morrison too would give sterling service to the Burnley cause, although not without his share of controversy.

With just four League matches to play Burnley were at the foot of the table with participation in the end of season Test Matches looking inevitable. To qualify for this series of games, first introduced to decide promotion and relegation when the Second Division was formed in 1892, players had to have appeared in at least four League matches. With this in mind, Burnley signed three more new players to bolster their squad including Robert Brown, a central defender loaned by Bolton, and Malcolm McVean, a short term acquisition from Liverpool.

The third member of the trio was Jimmy Ross, also signed from Liverpool and one of the most famous players of his day. Ross had been a member of the Preston "Invincibles" and had played and scored against Burnley many times and would emerge as a significant asset in the Turf Moor ranks. All three made their debuts, ironically in the case of Ross and McVean, at Liverpool and it proved to be another of the season's few highlights, a 2-1 win at Anfield. It was a glimmer of hope, but it was soon extinguished and the Turfites' place in the end of season Test Match drama was confirmed after the penultimate match, a 2-3 home defeat by Derby. With typical irony Burnley reserved their best Turf Moor display of a forgettable league campaign for their curtain call, a 5-0 thrashing of West Brom. Jimmy Ross scored his first Burnley goal, orchestrating an excellent display that at least sent the Turfites into the Test Matches with some optimism.

For the 1896-97 season the Test Match format had been changed with the bottom two in the First Division, Burnley and Sunderland, playing the top two in the Second Division, Notts County and Newton Heath on a home and away basis. Burnley's first opponents were Newton Heath, who had finished as runners-up in Division Two, with the first encounter at Turf Moor. The Turfites rose to the occasion with early goals from Billy Bowes and William Ferguson earning a 2-0 victory, an encouraging start. Two days later Newton Heath turned the tables with a 2-0 win on a gluepot of a pitch at Clayton. All now rested on two matches against Second Division Champions Notts County with the first match at the Town Ground, then the home of Nottingham Forest. A crowd of 15,000 saw a fighting performance from the Turfites who came back from a goal down to equalise thanks to a dramatic goal from Robert Brown just three minutes from time. The stage was set for a last day drama, with Burnley at home to Notts County and Newton Heath at Sunderland with none of the protagonists yet sure of their destiny. A Burnley win would give the Turfites a real chance of survival and a draw might also be enough, depending on the result at Sunderland. County, who didn't seem to have read the script properly, scored after just 10 minutes but after that Burnley roared back and piled on the pressure with attack after attack. County were penned back in their own half for long periods with the goalkeeper on top form making brilliant save after brilliant save. At last Jimmy Ross wriggled free of the Notts defence and crashed in a shot that looked certain to find the net. Agonisingly for Burnley it hit the inside of the post and bounced away to safety. In the second half the pattern was the same with Burnley relentless in their search for an equaliser that the efforts of the players undoubtedly deserved. With ten minutes to go there was an almighty scrimmage in the County goalmouth and, as reported in the Burnley Express "the ball was fisted out by a player other than the goalkeeper, who wore gloves, whereas the hand that did the trick was naked". The Burnley players and the fans beseeched the referee for a penalty but he remained unmoved and the last chance had gone.

The players had given their all but in vain. In the event Sunderland had beaten Newton Heath 2-0 so if any of the Burnley chances had counted and the match had been drawn they would have survived. As it happened Notts County were promoted and Sunderland stayed up, Newton Heath stayed down and Burnley were relegated. Turf Moor would stage Second Division football for the first time.

At the Football League's annual meeting in Manchester in May 1897, in a desperate attempt to stave off the inevitable, Burnley submitted a proposal to extend the League, to increase the number of clubs in each Division from sixteen to eighteen.

The proposal received a majority of votes in favour, but not the required 75%, and the motion was lost. At the end of the most traumatic season in the club's history, Burnley Football Club had dropped out of the Football League's top flight for the first time.

Time would tell whether or not the club could bounce back to join the elite.

An interesting season lay ahead.

Walter Place junior
a hard act to follow after his senior cousin

1896-97 - First Division

		P	W	D	L	F	A	Pts
1	Aston Villa	30	21	5	4	73	38	47
2	Sheffield U	30	13	10	7	42	29	36
3	Derby C	30	16	4	10	70	50	36
4	Preston NE	30	11	12	7	55	40	34
5	Liverpool	30	12	9	9	46	38	33
6	Sheffield W	30	10	11	9	42	37	31
7	Everton	30	14	3	13	62	57	31
8	Bolton W	30	12	6	12	40	43	30
9	Bury	30	10	10	10	39	44	30
10	Wolverhampton W	30	11	6	13	45	41	28
11	Nottingham F	30	9	8	13	44	49	26
12	West Bromwich A	30	10	6	14	33	56	26
13	Stoke	30	11	3	16	48	59	25
14	Blackburn R	30	11	3	16	35	62	25
15	Sunderland	30	7	9	14	34	47	23
16	BURNLEY	30	6	7	17	43	61	19

1896-97

Manager : Harry Bradshaw

Division One (16th)

Relegated via Test matches

Note	No.	Date		Venue	Opponents	Result		h/t	Goalscorers/times	Opp. goal times
	1	Sep	5	a	Sheffield U	L	0-1	0-1		40
	2		7	h	SUNDERLAND	D	1-1	1-1	Bowes 20	30
	3		12	h	BURY	W	1-0	1-0	Chambers 35	
	4		19	h	NOTTINGHAM F	D	2-2	1-1	Nicol 45, Bowes 62	1, 60
	5		26	a	Preston N E	L	3-5	1-2	Hill 10, Robertson 65, Chambers 80	5, 42, 55, 58, 70
	6	Oct	3	a	Blackburn R	L	2-3	2-0	Bowes 1, McLintock 20p	60, 65p, 75
	7		10	h	EVERTON	W	2-1	2-0	Chambers 10, Bowes 32	78
	8		17	h	PRESTON N E	D	2-2	2-1	Bowes 18, Chambers 40	32, 85
	9		24	a	Nottingham F	L	1-4	1-3	scrimmage 20	2, 15, 20, 87
	10	Nov	7	h	BLACKBURN R	L	0-1	0-1		45
	11		14	a	Derby C	L	2-3	1-2	Robertson 35, Place jun 75	12, 22, 48
Nicol's last game	12		21	a	Wolverhampton W	L	0-2	0-2		20, 30
	13		28	a	Everton	L	0-6	0-3		5,20,30,55,70,80
Hill's last game	14	Dec	19	h	SHEFFIELD W	D	1-1	1-1	Brady 23og	20
	15		26	h	LIVERPOOL	W	4-1	3-1	Toman 1, Bowes (2) 35, 45, Chambers 72	5
	16	Jan	1	a	Bury	D	1-1	1-0	Black 25	86
	17		2	a	Aston Villa	W	3-0	1-0	Black (2) 10, 58, Bowes 80	
	18		9	h	STOKE	L	1-3	1-1	Toman 25	30, 67, 87
	19		16	h	SHEFFIELD U	D	1-1	1-0	Taylor 23	72
	20	Feb	6	h	BOLTON W	L	0-2	0-0		57, 65
	21		8	h	ASTON VILLA	L	3-4	2-3	Robertson 32, Toman 33, Black 77	4, 9, 15, 60
	22		27	a	Stoke	L	2-3	0-3	Black 59, scrimmage 88	10, 20, 42
	23	Mar	2	a	Sunderland	D	1-1	1-0	Bowes 25	70
	24		6	a	Sheffield W	L	0-1	0-1		41
	25		13	a	Bolton W	L	1-2	0-0	Place jun 68	46, 65
	26		20	h	WOLVERHAMPTON W	L	0-3	0-1		37, 50, 60
	27		27	a	Liverpool	W	2-1	2-1	Toman 27, Brown 30	35
	28	Apr	3	a	West Bromwich A	L	0-3	0-2		30, 43, 51
	29		5	h	DERBY C	L	2-3	1-1	Bowes 40, Morrison 50	22, 55, 85
	30		10	h	WEST BROMWICH A	W	5-0	3-0	Robertson (2) 35, 50, Ross 38, Ferguson 40, Bowes 67	

FA Cup

No.	Date		Venue	Opponents	Result		h/t	Goalscorers/times	Opp. goal times
1	Jan	30	h	SUNDERLAND	L	0-1	0-1		3

Final, Aston Villa 3-2 Everton, at Crystal Palace.

Other matches (friendlies and/or as detailed)

Note	Date		Venue	Opponents	Result		h/t	Goalscorers	Opp. goal times
	Sep	1	h	BLACKPOOL	W	2-0		Place jun, Brae	
Walter Place junior benefit	Oct	19	h	BLACKBURN R	L	3-4		Robertson, Bowes, Ellis	
		31	a	Newcastle U	L	1-4		Chambers	
Lancs Cup	Dec	5	h	BLACKPOOL	W	3-0		Beveridge (2), Robertson	
Div 1 fixture aban 30m, flood		12	h	ASTON VILLA	aban	1-2		Hartley	
		25	h	EDINBURGH HIBS	W	2-1		Beveridge, Bowes	
Lancs Cup	Jan	23	h	NEWTON HEATH	W	2-1		Barrett og, McLintock p	
	Feb	13	a	Millwall	L	0-4			
Lancs Cup semi		20	a	Everton	L	1-5		Robertson	
in aid of Indian famine fund	Mar	8	h	NELSON	W	3-1		scrimmage, Place jun, Ferguson	
		24	a	Blackpool	W	1-0		Ferguson	
McVean transfer match	Apr	12	a	Liverpool	D	1-1		Ross	
		16	h	DUNDEE	W	2-1		Beveridge, Warburton	
Test match	Apr	19	h	NEWTON HEATH	W	2-0	2-0	Bowes 5, Ferguson 20	
Test match		21	a	Newton Heath	L	0-2	0-2		18, 28
Test match		24	a	Notts C	D	1-1	0-0	Brown 87	50p
Test match		26	h	NOTTS C	L	0-1	0-1		10
		27	a	Oldham County	L	0-1			

Att.	Pos	Tatham	Nicol	McLintock	W Place senior	Brae	Taylor	Hill	Chambers	D Brown	Bowes	W Place junior	Reynolds	H Robertson	Haddow	Warburton	Davidson	Longair	Black	Hartley	Dunn	Beveridge	Toman	Hargreaves	Almond	Morrison	Ferguson	J Ross	McVean	R Brown		
5,000		1	2	3	4	5	6	7	8	9	10	11																				1
9,000	14	1	2	3	4	5	6	7	8	9	10	11																				2
4,000	8	1	2	3	4	5	6	7	8	9	10	11																				3
4,000	10	1	7	3	4	5	6	8			10	11	2	9																		4
7,000	11	1	2	3	4	5	6	8	7		10	11		9																		5
9,000	13		2	3	4	5	6	8			10	11		9	1	7																6
9,000	9	1	5	3	4		6	8	7		10	11	2	9																		7
8,000	10	1	5	3	4		6	8	7		10	11	2	9																		8
4,000	11	1	5	3	4		6	8	7		10	11	2	9																		9
5,000	13	1	5	3	4		6	8			10	11	2	9			7															10
6,000	14	1	7	3	4		6	5	8		10	11	2	9																		11
4,000	15	1	7	3	4		6	5	8		10	11	2	9																		12
	16	1		3	4		6	5		8	10	11	2	9			7															13
5,000	16			3	4		6	8			10	11	2		1			5	7	9												14
9,000	16	1		3	4		6		8		10	11						5			2	7	9									15
8,700	16	1		3	4		6				10	11	2					5	8			7	9									16
14,000	14	1		3	4		6				10	11						5	8		2	7	9									17
3,000	16	1		3	4		6				10	11						5	8		2		9	7								18
6,000	13	1		3	4		5				10	11	2	7					8				9		6							19
5,500		1			4		6				10	11	2					5	8		3	7	9									20
4,000	15	1		3	4		6				10	11	2	9				5	8				7									21
10,000	16	1		3	4		6				8	10	2	9				5	11							7						22
4,000				3	4		6				8	10	2	9	1			5	11							7						23
5,000	16			3	4		6				10	11	2	9	1			5	8							7						24
4,000	16			3	4		6				10	11	2	9	1			5	8							7						25
3,000				3	4		6					10	2	9	1			5	8							7	11					26
12,000	16			3	4		6					10	2		1								9				11	8	7	5		27
3,100				3	4		6				9	10	2		1												11	8	7	5		28
3,000	16				4		6				10	11	2		1						3					7		9	8	5		29
4,900					4		6				10		2	9	1						3						11	8	7	5		30
Appearances		20	12	27	30	6	30	14	10	4	28	29	22	18	10	1	2	12	12	1	6	4	8	1	1	6	4	4	4	4		
Goals (43)			1	1			1	1	5	1	11	2		5					5				4			1	1	1			1	og

2 untraced

Att.	Pos	Tatham	Nicol	McLintock	W Place senior	Brae	Taylor	Hill	Chambers	D Brown	Bowes	W Place junior	Reynolds	H Robertson	Haddow	Warburton	Davidson	Longair	Black	Hartley	Dunn	Beveridge	Toman	Hargreaves	Almond	Morrison	Ferguson	J Ross	McVean	R Brown		
8,000		1		3	4		6				10	11	2					5	8			7	9									1
Appearances		1		1	1		1				1	1	1					1	1			1	1									
Goals (0)																																

1897-98

The Turfites approached the new season with supreme confidence, determined to show the football world that their demotion to the Second Division was merely temporary. The committee, players and especially the supporters, felt that the club's rightful place was among the football elite and that at the end of the campaign First Division football would return to Turf Moor.

In the event the optimism was justified, Burnley were top of the table from November onwards, suffered just two League defeats all season, dropped only one point at home, and the Second Division Championship was duly clinched in the very last match. That was by no means the end of the story however, even Championship status did not guarantee promotion, it simply gained entry into the dreaded series of Test Matches with one other candidate hoping to go up and two others dreading they might go down.

Burnley's participation in the Test Matches of 1897-98 would indeed end in promotion back to the big time, but it would also prove to be one of the most controversial episodes in the history of Burnley Football Club and lead to a radical change in the ground rules regarding promotion and relegation.

One change of rule for the season ahead was a little more protection for goalkeepers, custodians could no longer be charged unless the ball was in their hands. Strangely a proposal that goalkeepers should wear different coloured shirts from their team-mates was rejected!

The most high profile arrival at Turf Moor in the summer of 1897 was half back Peter O'Rourke from Celtic, essentially a reserve in his time at Parkhead but a Scottish Junior International and a man with a prominent future in English football. O'Rourke slotted into the Burnley half back line alongside Joe Taylor and Archie Livingstone in a defence that was to remain virtually unchanged until the New Year.

New captain Jimmy Ross led the Turfites into the new campaign with two goals in a comfortable win against Blackpool at Turf Moor. The first league fixture being at home was an event in itself, under an arrangement with Burnley Cricket Club the Turfites' match on the first Saturday in September had traditionally been away from home. Five goals against Blackpool began the promotion push and they were followed by another five against Woolwich, in Burnley's first ever league encounter with a London club, four against Walsall and three against Newcastle who would emerge as Burnley's main competition at the top of Division Two. After their defeat at Turf Moor the Magpies reported Burnley to the Football League for allowing a local theatrical celebrity, who rejoiced in the name of Witty Watty Walton, to perform the kick off. Mr Walton set the ball rolling, kicked it straight to a Burnley player and within 40 seconds it was nestling in the Newcastle net. As a result the League advised the clubs that celebrity kick-offs were illegal and should be discouraged.

The Turfites continued to perform impressively although there was a slight setback when they suffered their first defeat, 1-2 at Grimsby in October 1897. The early season pace-setters Manchester City were then beaten 3-1 at Turf Moor, Burnley's performance being described as one of the best-ever from a Turf Moor team. The match itself was, according to the Burnley Express, "an event long to be remembered". Darwen were then beaten 1-0 at Barley Bank and the Turfites hit the top of the league. They would not be overtaken again. The goals were going in on a regular basis, especially at Turf Moor and Burnley managed 16 in the next three home matches and were six points clear of Manchester City as Christmas approached. In January 1898 it was time for the FA Cup and the success kept coming with wins against Woolwich and Burslem Port Vale carrying the Turfites into the quarter finals for the first time ever and a clash with First Division Everton. The record crowd of 20,500 who squeezed into Turf Moor witnessed a bruising encounter that was won by the Merseysiders who scored three goals in a devastating five minute spell midway through the first half.

As well as a disappointing exit from the FA Cup Burnley suffered with injuries, losing both Walter Place junior and Archie Livingstone, who broke a collarbone and didn't play again until the Test Matches.

The League was very much the priority however and there were victories against Burton Swifts and Newton Heath before a dip in home form led to a 1-1 draw against Gainsborough, the first and only point dropped at Turf Moor all season. That was followed by what was becoming almost unthinkable, a defeat, 0-2 at Luton. It looked as though the pressure might be beginning to tell, even though the Turfites had brought back Jack Hillman from Dundee to provide extra confidence and stability at the back.

There was an emphatic response, to what was becoming a minor crisis, in the next match at Turf Moor. The visitors were Loughborough, struggling and destined to finish at the very bottom of the League. Burnley were at their scintillating best from the first minute and Jimmy Ross had completed a hat trick before a quarter of an hour had been played. By half time it was 7-1 and after a little more than an hour it was 9-1 with Jimmy Ross having scored five. Whether the Turfites ran out of steam or felt sorry for the visitors wasn't clear but the players made it very plain afterwards that from early on their target had been at least double figures. It just didn't happen however and Loughborough scored two late goals themselves. The nine goals Burnley scored in that match are still a league record for the club and the twelve goals scored

Archie Livingstone
sorely missed after a broken collar bone

altogether are also a record for a league match in which Burnley has taken part.

The Turfites had now clinched a place in the Test Matches, along with Newcastle, but it was not until their very last league game, at Gainsborough, that the Second Division Championship was finally secured, a drab 0-0 draw being in stark contrast to the exhilarating football that Burnley had played throughout the season.

The two First Division clubs who would contest the Test Matches were not decided until a week after Burnley had clinched the Second Division title. All the bottom five clubs ended the season on the same number of points but Stoke, one of the Turfites' bogey teams, finished at the very bottom on goal average, with the second bottom club, who Burnley would meet first, home and away, emerging as none other than the old enemy, Blackburn Rovers.

The first Test Match was at Ewood Park and after Rovers had gone ahead on the half hour, a second half hat-trick from Wilf Toman, all the goals coming from right wing crosses from Tom Morrison, saw the Turfites cruise home 3-1. Rovers had to win the return at Turf Moor to have a realistic chance of staying up but, after a featureless and goalless first half, Jimmy Ross set Burnley on their way after the break, with Toman putting the issue beyond doubt ten minutes from time. Perhaps unexpectedly, Burnley then lost at home to Stoke with the Potters scoring in the first five minutes and again five minutes from time. Two days later Newcastle lost at Blackburn and this meant that all four Test Match combatants had just one game to play, with Burnley and Stoke both on four points and Newcastle and Blackburn each on two points. In the final series of fixtures Burnley would visit Stoke and Newcastle would entertain Blackburn. The Newcastle and Blackburn fans didn't need to be trained mathematicians to realise that if the Stoke v Burnley game ended in a draw, the result of the Newcastle v Blackburn clash was irrelevant, Stoke would avoid relegation and Burnley would be promoted.

In the lead up to the final crucial matches, the local press speculated that Newcastle would probably beat Blackburn so that "Burnley's aim must be one point – the men must make up their minds to come away with at least one point". They studiously avoided mentioning that Stoke's aim must also be one point!

Wretched weather greeted the Burnley players and supporters as they arrived at the Victoria Ground, Stoke on the day of destiny. Rain fell incessantly throughout the match and the pitch very soon became a quagmire. Even if the 22 players had intended to provide a feast of entertainment on such an important occasion, it would have been almost impossible. The spectators played their part to the full, holding on to the ball whenever it went into the crowd or kicking it on to the roof of the stand. The players soon cottoned on to this new game and when replacement balls were produced, into the crowd they went. One ball even found its way into the nearby River Trent. Goalmouth incident was in short supply, in fact the match, some scribes called it a farce, would come to be known as the game without a shot at goal.

After 90 minutes of meaningless inaction the final whistle blew to mark the end of the match and of the season. Burnley and Stoke had both collected the point they needed and the Turfites were back in the First Division.

Jimmy Ross
captain and top scorer

In the weeks following the farcical end to the campaign there was much comment that the system had been abused and that Burnley and Stoke had manipulated the rules for their own ends. The clubs themselves were never actually accused of any kind of "gentlemen's agreement" but everybody knew that a tacit understanding between the players had been in place between the players from the first whistle.

At the Football League's annual meeting in May 1898, Burnley, no doubt feeling duty bound, once again proposed that the Football League be extended from 16 to 18 clubs in each Division. They also proposed that the Test Match system be abolished and that, in future, the bottom two clubs in the First Division be automatically replaced by the top two in the Second Division. Both proposals were voted upon and carried with a substantial majority with Blackburn and Newcastle being elected back into Division One and four new clubs coming in to Division Two.

At the end of this rather unfortunate episode, Burnley were back amongst the elite and it seemed that no real harm had been done. It was very much a case of "All's well that ends well!"

1897-98 - Second Division

		P	W	D	L	F	A	Pts
1	BURNLEY	30	20	8	2	80	24	48
2	Newcastle U	30	21	3	6	64	32	45
3	Manchester C	30	15	9	6	66	36	39
4	Newton Heath	30	16	6	8	64	35	38
5	Woolwich A	30	16	5	9	69	49	37
6	Small Heath	30	16	4	10	58	50	36
7	Leicester F	30	13	7	10	46	35	33
8	Luton T	30	13	4	13	68	50	30
9	Gainsborough T	30	12	6	12	50	54	30
10	Walsall	30	12	5	13	58	58	29
11	Blackpool	30	10	5	15	49	61	25
12	Grimsby T	30	10	4	16	52	62	24
13	Burton S	30	8	5	17	38	69	21
14	Lincoln C	30	6	5	19	43	82	17
15	Darwen	30	6	2	22	31	76	14
16	Loughborough T	30	6	2	22	24	87	14

1897-98

Manager : Harry Bradshaw

Division Two (1st)
Champions
Promoted via Test matches

Note	No	Month	Day	Venue	Opponents	Result	Score	h/t	Goalscorers/times	Opp. goal times
	1	Sep	4	h	BLACKPOOL	W	5-1	3-0	Ross (2) 15, 48, Taylor 25, Bowes (2) 35, 80	70og
	2		6	h	WOOLWICH A	W	5-0	4-0	Livingstone 15, McEvey 31og,Toman 35, Place jun 40, Taylor 55	
	3		11	a	Blackpool	D	1-1	1-1	Ross 11	5
	4		18	h	WALSALL	W	4-1	1-1	Toman 3, Morrison 55, Ross 75, Taylor 90	6
	5		25	a	Walsall	W	2-1	1-1	Bowes 35, Place jun 84	5
	6	Oct	2	h	NEWCASTLE U	W	3-0	3-0	Place jun 1, Ross 32, Bowes 38	
	7		9	a	Leicester F	W	1-0	1-0	Bowes 35	
	8		16	h	BURTON S	W	2-0	0-0	McLintock 82, scrimmage 86	
	9		23	a	Grimsby T	L	1-2	0-0	Bowes 68	55, 65
	10		30	h	MANCHESTER C	W	3-1	0-1	Ross 68, Toman (2) 73, 90	24
	11	Nov	6	a	Darwen	W	1-0	1-0	Ross 3	
	12		13	h	LUTON T	W	4-0	2-0	Bowes 16, Place jun 22, McCartney 70og, Toman 80	
	13		20	a	Manchester C	D	1-1	0-1	Williams 50og	17
Darwen goal 3m	14		27	h	DARWEN	W	6-1	4-1	Ross 18, O'Rourke 27, Toman 40, Place jun 43, McLintock 57p, Morrison 80	
	15	Dec	11	h	GRIMSBY T	W	6-0	2-0	Toman (2) 20, 50, Morrison 26, Ross (2) 48, 57, Place jun 68	
	16		27	a	Newcastle U	W	1-0	0-0	Toman 85	
	17	Jan	1	h	LINCOLN C	W	2-1	1-1	Bowes 43, Toman 51	15
	18		8	a	Small Heath	D	2-2	1-1	Place jun 31, Morrison 55	21, 46
	19		12	a	Newton Heath	D	0-0	0-0		
	20		15	h	LEICESTER F	W	4-0	2-0	Ross (3) 19, 35, 89p, Walker 55og	
	21		22	a	Loughborough	W	2-0	1-0	Morrison 38, Toman 50	
	22	Feb	5	h	SMALL HEATH	W	4-1	3-0	Ferguson 16, Taylor 23, McLintock 30, Ross 65	76
	23	Mar	5	a	Burton S	W	2-0	2-0	Toman 29, Ross 42	
Newton H goals 46, 50, 72	24		7	h	NEWTON HEATH	W	6-3	3-0	Toman (2) 6, 22, Ross (2) 21, 60, unknown 70, Ferguson 85	
Haddow's last game	25		12	h	GAINSBOROUGH T	D	1-1	0-1	Ross 52	30
	26		19	a	Luton T	L	0-2	0-1		20, 65
L'boro' goals 30m, 75m, 80m	27		28	h	LOUGHBOROUGH	W	9-3	7-1	Ross (5) 5, 6, 14, 35, 62, Morrison 15, Toman 40, Taylor 42, Ferguson 57	
-	28	Apr	2	a	Woolwich A	D	1-1	1-0	McInnes 25	65
	29		8	a	Lincoln C	D	1-1	1-1	Taylor 20	40
	30		9	a	Gainsborough T	D	0-0	0-0		

FA Cup

No	Month	Day	Venue	Opponents	Result	Score	h/t	Goalscorers/times	Opp. goal times
1	Jan	29	h	WOOLWICH A	W	3-1	1-1	Place jun 25, Ferguson 55, Taylor 80	24
2	Feb	12	h	BURSLEM P V	W	3-0	2-0	Bowes 7, Beveridge 24, Ross 67	
3		26	h	EVERTON	L	1-3	0-3	Place jun 86	16, 17, 21

Final, Nottingham F 3-1 Derby C, at Crystal Palace.

Other matches (friendlies and/or as detailed)

Note	Month	Day	Venue	Opponents	Result	Score	h/t	Goalscorers/times	Opp. goal times
	Sep	1	h	BLACKBURN R	W	3-1		Toman, Morrison, Ross	
Lancs Cup	Dec	4	a	Bury	L	2-4		unknown (2)	
		25	h	KILMARNOCK	W	6-0		unknown (6)	
	Feb	16	h	NELSON	W	7-3		Ross (3), Toman, Place jun (3)	
Benefit for McLintock & Livingstone	Mar	21	h	MANCHESTER C	D	2-2		scrimmage, McInnes	
		26	a	Derby C	D	3-3		scrimmage (2), McInnes	
	Apr	11	a	Reading	W	2-1		McLintock p, Bowes	
Test Match	Apr	21	a	Blackburn R	W	3-1	0-1	Toman (3) 50, 61, 66	33
Test Match		23	h	BLACKBURN R	W	2-0	0-0	Ross 53, Toman 80	
Test Match		26	h	STOKE	L	0-2	0-1		3, 85
Test Match		30	a	Stoke	D	0-0	0-0		

Att.	Pos	Haddow	Reynolds	McLintock	O'Rourke	Taylor	Livingstone	Morrison	J Ross	Toman	Bowes	W Place junior	Dunn	W Place senior	Beveridge	Ferguson	Arnott	Hillman	McInnes	
2,000		1	2	3	4	5	6	7	8	9	10	11								1
3,000	top	1	2	3	4	5	6	7	8	9	10	11								2
4,000	2	1	2	3	4	5	6	7	8	9	10	11								3
3,000	2	1	2	3	4	5	6	7	8	9	10	11								4
3,500	2	1	2	3	4	5	6	7	8	9	10	11								5
8,000	2	1	2	3	4	5	6	7	8	9	10	11								6
9,000	2	1	2	3	4	5	6	7	8	9	10	11								7
3,000	top	1	2	3	4	5		7	8	9	10	11	6							8
4,000	2	1	2	3	4	5	6	7	8	9	10	11								9
12,000	2	1	2	3	4	5	6	7	8	9	10	11								10
4,500	top	1	2	3	4	5	6	7	8	9	10	11								11
		1	2	3	4	5	6	7	8	9	10	11								12
20,000	top	1	2	3	4	5	6	7	8	9	10	11								13
3,000	top	1	2	3	4	5	6	7	8	9	10	11								14
4,000	top	1	2	3	4	5	6	7	8	9	10	11								15
24,959		1	2	3		5	6	7	8	9	10	11		4						16
4,000	top	1	2	3		5	6	7	8	9	10	11		4						17
12,000	top	1	2	3		5	6	7	8	9	10	11			4					18
7,000	top	1	2	3		5	6	7	8	9	10	11			4					19
4,000	top	1	2	3		5	6	7	8	9	10	11			4					20
2,000	top	1	2	3		5	6	7	8	9		11			4	10				21
4,000	top	1	2	3		5	6	7	8	9		10			4	11				22
		1	2	3		5		7	8	9	10			6	4	11				23
3,000	top		2	3		5		7	8	9	10			6	4	11	1			24
4,000	top	1	2	3	6	5			8	9	10	7			4	11				25
3,000	top		2	3		5		7	9		10	11		6	4	8		1		26
	top			3		5		7	8	9	10	6		2	4	11		1		27
12,000	top		2			5		7		9	10	6		3	4	11		1	8	28
			2	3		5		7		9	10	6		4		11		1	8	29
			2	3		5		7		9	10	6		4		11		1	8	30
Appearances		24	29	29	16	30	21	29	27	29	28	28	1	9	11	10	1	5	3	
Goals (80)				3	1	6	1	6	23	15	8	7				3			1	4 ogs

2 untraced

Att.	Pos	Haddow	Reynolds	McLintock	O'Rourke	Taylor	Livingstone	Morrison	J Ross	Toman	Bowes	W Place junior	Dunn	W Place senior	Beveridge	Ferguson	Arnott	Hillman	McInnes	
6,000		1	2	3		5	6	7	8	9		10			4	11				1
11,000		1	2	3		5	6	7	8	9	10	11			4					2
20,500		1	2	3		5	6	7	8	9	10	11			4					3
Appearances		3	3	3		3	3	3	3	3	2	3			3	1				
Goals (7)						1			1		1	2			1	1				

1898-99

In the summer of 1898, with First Division football in prospect once again, it was decided that the old 'Stars' Stand had had its day and it was duly demolished. It was replaced by a new Grandstand 'to increase comfort and accommodation' which was ready for use, although not complete, in time for 'The First' the term used at the time by all football fans for the opening match of the season. In the years before the Great War, the football season always officially started on the first day of September and ended on the last day of April.

After a win and a draw in the first two home games put the Turfites at the top of the League, the Burnley fans were looking forward to a successful campaign, which indeed they got. It could have been so much more successful however but for an unnecessary chain of events which rocked Turf Moor and led to the Club's star player and driving force being transferred.

Fred Barron
in the Burnley team to stay

As the season began to take shape, three of Burnley's younger players experienced very different emotions with 19-year-old Fred Barron making his debut at right half at Sheffield United. Barron had been signed in the summer from Stockton St Mary's and had been described as 'the best back in the Northern League'. From then on Fred Barron was one of the very first names on the Burnley team sheet for a dozen years and can rightly be described as one of the finest players in the club's history. Another of Burnley's young defenders with a big future was Joe Taylor but Taylor had an aggressive streak about him that one or two of the Burnley Directors found unacceptable. After the opening match of the season in which some of his tackling was apparently seen to be a little over-exhuberant, he was suspended. The Board then issued a somewhat mysterious official statement that 'they were taking a stand against blackguardly conduct on the field and ruffianism off it'. Joe Taylor was soon back in favour but later in the season was again on the sidelines after being hit in the face by flying glass when a dressing room window was smashed by a stray football. Taylor spent over a week in hospital and for a time, permanent damage to his sight was a grim possibility. Thankfully he made a complete recovery and was a regular in the Burnley team well into the next century.

Young goalkeeper Willie Tatham came into the side for Burnley's game at Stoke, conceding four goals but he kept his place for the next match at home to Aston Villa. His afternoon proved to be the proverbial nightmare as he again had to pick the ball out of his net four times. For Villa's opener he let a hopeful punt slip through his hands and the ball rolled over the line and for the second goal he dropped a cross at the feet of a Villa forward who just had to tap the ball into Burnley's net. His misery was complete in less than an hour when a bread and butter shot just hit him and bounced into the net for Villa's fourth. Tatham was pilloried by the Turf Moor fans who made their feelings very clear. The Burnley Directors agreed enough was enough and it was two years before the young custodian again appeared in a League match.

After eight games Burnley, were ninth in the League and playing well. With three different goalkeepers used already however it was felt that, to mount a real challenge for the title, more experience was needed between the sticks. A familiar figure soon turned up at his spiritual home to see what he could do, 'the Burly One', Jack Hillman, returning for his third spell at Turf Moor after his relationship with Dundee had deteriorated rapidly. Following his successful loan spell at Turf Moor at the end of the previous season Hillman had been obliged to return to Scotland after the euphoria of Burnley's Test Match series. He had continued to endure a difficult relationship with the Dundee Committee who eventually suspended him and made him available for transfer.

The ship was well and truly steadied and the Turfites suffered just one defeat in the next nine matches, climbing to second position in the table after a 4-2 victory against Wolves at Turf Moor in December. Centre forward Wilf Toman had continued his fine form in front of goal with eleven up to Christmas but the previous season's goal machine, captain Jimmy Ross, did not find the net at all in the league until December. His early season form, orchestrating Burnley's play, was brilliant but he was simply unable to find the net until he hit four goals in just half an hour in the 5-0 hammering of Sheffield Wednesday.

January was a disastrous month however with just a 4-1 win

in a friendly at Newcastle. Then, after the drawn FA Cup tie against Sheffield United, there began to be rumours of discontent in the dressing room, with certain players reported to be 'at loggerheads' with each other. During the match against the Blades it had been noticed by various observers that Jimmy Ross had rarely fed the ball to his right wing partner Tom Morrison and it transpired that apparently a rift had been developing between the two players. After a successful partnership on Burnley's right flank that had included the Second Division Championship campaign in which they both played in virtually every match, they would appear together just once more in a Burnley team. Tom Morrison himself became Burnley's first-ever Irish International when he helped his country to 1-0 victory against Wales in Belfast in March 1899. The 'Belfast Flier' had already had one spell at Burnley but had left the Club under something of a cloud in 1894, returning to Glentoran where he earned his first three caps for his country in 1895. Two weeks before Morrison's fourth game for Ireland, there had been more international recognition for Turf Moor when Jack Hillman was selected for the first time by England against the Irish at Sunderland. It was the first senior international match played at Roker Park and England won it 13-2, equalling their highest-ever score in a full international. Tom Morrison must have been pleased his recall hadn't been two weeks earlier but 'the Burly One' probably felt he had done enough to further his international aspirations when he saved a penalty, although he was unlucky that the ball broke back to an Irish forward who found the net. In April 1899, along with Wilf Toman, Hillman played for the Football League in a 4-1 win against the Scottish League in Glasgow. He also appeared once more for the Football League but never won another England cap.

Jeremy Reynolds
a stalwart at right back

In February 1899 the Burnley directors solved the problem of the dressing room upheaval by reluctantly transferring captain Jimmy Ross to Second Division Manchester City for a reported fee of £160. Ross promptly demonstrated what the Turfites had sacrificed by scoring twice on his debut for the Blues, playing alongside one of the all-time greats, Billy Meredith. Ross hit seven goals altogether as City remained unbeaten for the rest of the season and cantered to the Second Division Championship.

Back in East Lancashire, Derby and Sheffield United were defeated at Turf Moor and a William Ferguson goal was enough to bring back the points from West Brom. At that stage the Turfites still had realistic hopes of the Championship, just a point behind Aston Villa, although Villa had two extra games still to play.

In the event Burnley scored only two goals in the final five league matches of the season, with just one victory in that sequence, eventually finishing in third place. Although it had been comfortably the club's best-ever campaign in the top flight, the drive for a possible first-ever league title had run out of steam at the vital stage in the season and the team had ultimately been badly affected by the loss of Jimmy Ross, followed by the sudden departure of Wilf Toman, transferred to Everton.

Burnley had briefly flirted with real success in the First Division, it was to be almost a generation before Turf Moor would experience a similar challenge at the very top of the English game.

1898-99 - First Division

		P	W	D	L	F	A	Pts
1	Aston Villa	34	19	7	8	76	40	45
2	Liverpool	34	19	5	10	49	33	43
3	BURNLEY	34	15	9	10	45	47	39
4	Everton	34	15	8	11	48	41	38
5	Notts C	34	12	13	9	47	51	37
6	Blackburn R	34	14	8	12	60	52	36
7	Sunderland	34	15	6	13	41	41	36
8	Wolverhampton W	34	14	7	13	54	48	35
9	Derby C	34	12	11	11	62	57	35
10	Bury	34	14	7	13	48	49	35
11	Nottingham F	34	11	11	12	42	42	33
12	Stoke	34	13	7	14	47	52	33
13	Newcastle U	34	11	8	15	49	48	30
14	West Bromwich A	34	12	6	16	42	57	30
15	Preston NE	34	10	9	15	44	47	29
16	Sheffield U	34	9	11	14	45	51	29
17	Bolton W	34	9	7	18	37	51	25
18	Sheffield W	34	8	8	18	32	61	24

1898-99

Manager : Harry Bradshaw

Division One (3rd)

		Date			Opponents	Result		h/t	Goalscorers/times	Opp. goal times
	1	Sep	3	h	NOTTS C	D	1-1	1-1	Toman 42	15
	2		5	h	PRESTON N E	W	3-1	2-0	Morrison (2) 22, 25, Place jun 86	89
O'Rourke's last game	3		10	a	Stoke	L	1-4	1-2	Morrison 10	17, 30, 68, 71
	4		17	h	ASTON VILLA	L	2-4	2-3	Bowes 8, Toman 28	15, 17, 30, 55
	5		24	a	Bury	D	1-1	1-0	Place jun 43	80
	6	Oct	1	a	Sheffield U	D	1-1	0-1	Bowes 77	32
	7		8	h	NEWCASTLE U	W	2-1	1-0	Toman (2) 43, 88	60
	8		15	a	Preston N E	D	1-1	1-1	Toman 40	15p
	9		22	h	LIVERPOOL	W	2-1	1-1	Toman 30, Place jun 52og	7
	10		29	a	Nottingham F	W	1-0	1-0	Place jun 16	
	11	Nov	5	h	BOLTON W	W	2-0	2-0	Ross 30, Lee 43og	
	12		12	a	Derby C	L	1-2	1-0	Toman 12	46, 48
	13		19	h	WEST BROMWICH A	D	1-1	1-0	Toman 35	60p
	14		26	h	BLACKBURN R	W	2-0	1-0	McLintock 5p, Toman 82	
	15	Dec	3	h	SHEFFIELD W	W	5-0	5-0	Ross (4) 12, 15, 35, 44, Toman 28	
	16		10	a	Sunderland	W	1-0	1-0	Bowes 5	
	17		17	h	WOLVERHAMPTON W	W	4-2	1-0	McInnes 25, Bowes (2) 55, 70, Place jun 57	65, 89
	18		24	a	Everton	L	0-4	0-4		20, 30, 38, 41
	19		26	a	Blackburn R	W	2-0	1-0	Toman 15, Ross 80	
	20		31	a	Notts C	D	2-2	1-0	Place sen 30, Bowes 52	46, 67
	21	Jan	3	a	Bolton W	L	0-2	0-2		20, 30
	22		14	a	Aston Villa	L	0-4	0-3		15, 25, 38og, 70
	23		21	h	BURY	W	2-1	1-0	Bowes (2) 10, 89	73
Jimmy Ross' last game	24	Feb	4	a	Newcastle U	L	1-4	1-2	Bowes 25	15, 35, 60, 70
	25		18	a	Liverpool	L	0-2	0-1		10, 70
	26	Mar	6	h	NOTTINGHAM F	D	1-1	1-1	Place jun 15	30
	27		11	h	DERBY C	W	2-1	1-1	Place jun 8, Bowes 56	43
	28		18	a	West Bromwich A	W	1-0	1-0	Ferguson 30	
	29		31	h	SHEFFIELD U	W	1-0	1-0	McLintock 34p	
	30	Apr	1	a	Sheffield W	L	0-1	0-0		48p
Toman's last game	31		8	h	SUNDERLAND	W	1-0	0-0	Ferguson 60	
	32		15	a	Wolverhampton W	L	0-4	0-0		55, 65, 75, 80
	33		17	h	STOKE	D	1-1	0-1	Ferguson 75	14
	34		22	h	EVERTON	D	0-0	0-0		

FA Cup

				Opponents	Result		h/t	Goalscorers/times	Opp. goal times
1	Jan	28	h	SHEFFIELD U	D	2-2	1-2	Toman 23, Bowes 51	4, 36
rep	Feb	2	a	Sheffield U	L	1-2	1-2	Ross 22p	6, 28

Final, Sheffield U 4-1 Derby C, at Crystal Palace.

Other matches (friendlies and/or as detailed)

				Opponents	Result		Goalscorers
Lancs Cup	Dec	14	a	Chorley	W	1-0	unknown
	Jan	2	a	Newcastle U	W	4-1	Ross (2), Toman, Barron p
Div 1 fixture aban 69m, bad light		7	h	STOKE	aban	1-2	Bowes
Lancs Cup	Feb	11	a	Bolton W	L	2-3	Ferguson, Ross p
		25	a	Bristol C	L	1-2	Morrison
	Mar	25	a	Wrexham	W	5-0	Place jun, Toman, Bowes, unknown (2)
Walter Place senior benefit	Apr	4	h	ASTON VILLA	W	8-0	Toman, Place jun (2), McMillan, Ferguson, McLintock (2), Taylor
East Lancs Charity Cup final		24	a	Blackburn R	W	3-2	Beveridge, Jenkinson, Crompton og
Jimmy Ross transfer match		29	a	Manchester C	D	2-2	unknown (2)

Att.	Pos	Pinnell	Reynolds	McLintock	Beveridge	Taylor	Livingstone	Morrison	J Ross	Toman	Bowes	W Place junior	O'Rourke	McInnes	Tatham	W Place senior	McMillan	Ferguson	Arnott	Barron	Hillman	Nunnick	Jenkinson	Watkins	Nicol	Lester	Brearley		
6,500		1	2	3	4	5	6	7	8	9	10	11																	1
	top	1	2	3	4		6	7		9	10	11	5	8															2
	8			3	4		6	7		9	10	11	5	8	1	2													3
8,000			2	3		5	6	7	8	9	10				1		4	11											4
8,000	12	1	2	3	4	5	6	7	8	9	10	11																	5
10,000	14		2	3		5	6	7	8	9	10	11							1	4									6
6,000	10		2	3		5	6	7	8	9	10	11							1	4									7
8,000	9	1	2	3		5	6	7	8	9	10	11								4									8
10,000	7		2	3		5	6	7	8	9	10	11								4	1								9
5,000	6		2	3		5	6	7	8	9	10	11								4	1								10
6,000	4		2	3		5	6	7	8	9	10	11								4	1								11
8,000	7		2	3		5	6	7	8	9	10	11								4	1								12
7,500	5		2	3		5		7	8	9	10	11								4	1	6							13
12,000	3			3		5	6	7	8	9	10	11				2				4	1								14
6,000	3			3			6	7	8	9	10	11				2	5			4	1								15
8,500	3		2	3			6	7	8	9	10	11				5				4	1								16
4,000	2		2	3			6	7			9	10		8		5		11		4	1								17
20,000				3		5	6	7	8	9	10	11				2				4	1								18
20,000	2		2	3			6	7	8	9	10	11				5				4	1								19
12,000			2	3			6	7	8	9	10	11				5				4	1								20
8,000	3		2	3			6	7		8	9	11				5		10		4	1								21
22,000	5			3		2	6	7	8	9	10	11				5				4	1								22
2,000	4			2		5	6	7	8		9	10						11		4	1		3						23
20,000	4	1	2	3		5	6	7	8	9	10	11								4									24
12,000	4			3		5	6	7		9	10	8				2		11	1	4									25
2,000	4		2	3		5	6	7		9	10	8						11		4	1								26
7,000	4		2	3		5	6	7			9	10						11		4	1			8					27
2,330	4		2	3		6		7		9	8	10				5		11		4	1								28
7,000			2	3		5	6				9	10						11	1	4				8	7				29
6,000			2	3		5	6					10						11	1	4				8	7	9			30
6,000			2	3	7	5	6			9	8	10						11	1	4									31
5,000			2	3		5	6	7				10						11	1	4			9	8					32
4,000	3		2	3		5	6				10							11	1	4			9	8			7		33
	3		2	3		5	6				9	10						11		4	1			8			7		34
Appearances		5	27	34	5	26	32	29	20	26	32	32	2	3	2	12	2	14	8	29	19	1	3	6	2	1	2		
Goals (45)				2				3	6	11	10	7		1		1		3										1	og

Att.	Pos	Pinnell	Reynolds	McLintock	Beveridge	Taylor	Livingstone	Morrison	J Ross	Toman	Bowes	W Place junior	O'Rourke	McInnes	Tatham	W Place senior	McMillan	Ferguson	Arnott	Barron	Hillman	Nunnick	Jenkinson	Watkins	Nicol	Lester	Brearley		
11,500			2	3		5	6	7	8	9	10	11								4	1								1
11,000		1	2	3			6		8	9	10			7		5		11		4									rep
Appearances		1	2	2		1	2	1	2	2	2	1		1		1		1		2	1								
Goals (3)									1	1	1																		

1899-1900

Jack Hillman
failed attempt at bribery, banned for a full season

After an excellent campaign despite the strife within the camp, Burnley had finish third in Division One, the club's highest placing in eleven years of league football. Hopes were high at Turf Moor that the progress could be built upon with more success as the century turned.

However before the new season had even begun the Turfites were stunned by the resignation of their team manager, Harry Bradshaw, a blow from which the team never really recovered and the campaign ended with the dreadful disappointment of another relegation.

At the end of the season however, before the supporters had even fully taken in the implications of football out of the top flight once again, Burnley Football Club was enveloped in more controversy with accusations of attempted bribery against one of their star players, arguably the biggest scandal ever to hit the club.

It had all started so well with Harry Bradshaw securing the transfer of Edgar Chadwick, one of football's very top names of the 1890's. Inside forward Chadwick had been a regular at Everton for over ten years, playing more than 300 games for the Blues, scoring well over a hundred goals, and had been an ever present in Everton's League Championship success of 1891. He had also won seven England caps.

Within days of Chadwick arriving at Turf Moor however, Harry Bradshaw tendered his resignation after five years as Team Manager, during the last two of which he had also acted as Club Secretary. He was to take up a similar position at Woolwich Arsenal, a Second Division club with lofty ambitions after six years in the Football League with no real success. Bradshaw had been offered a generous salary which would be supplemented by a hefty bonus if Woolwich won promotion.

The Burnley first team squad had a number of new players including right back Tom Woolfall from Darwen, who would step in to replace the aging Jerry Reynolds. Waiting in the wings was defender Billy Bannister, a strapping local youngster who would go on to play for England.

Edgar Chadwick was an instant success with three goals in the first four matches and the quality of his all round play was excellent. He quickly became a crowd favourite and, as the campaign unfolded, was consistently the team's best performer, along with captain Jack Hillman, also on top form between the sticks. In the main however, the season developed into a struggle with only occasional encouraging performances. It had been decided not to appoint a team manager to replace Harry Bradshaw, with selection duties, for the time being, to be undertaken by the Directors.

At the end of October a South African touring team "the Kaffirs" turned up at Turf Moor and, as far as the Burnley Express was concerned the proceedings were very much a 'burlesque show'. The Burnley players soon realised that there was some fun to be had and 'toyed with their opponents', deliberately giving penalties away and scoring own goals. The match ended 7-6 in favour of the Turfites and the Express was outspoken in its criticism of the fixture -

"The prime object of the match was an educational one, the intention of the promoters being to educate Kaffirs in the winter pastime in order to popularise the game in Africa. Education, like charity should begin at home however, when people pay to see a football match they expect to see one, not a farce!"

Burnley hovered in the lower reaches of the First Division for almost all of the season but there were high spots. Edgar Chadwick continued his superb form with a hat-trick in a 3-1 win against Glossop in December 1899. It was the only hat-trick of the season and was a fitting finale to football at Turf Moor in the nineteenth century. In January 1900 Burnley's FA Cup was over almost before it began with a 0-1 defeat by eventual winners Bury at Turf Moor. That match was the last senior appearance of almost certainly the most versatile sportsman ever to play for Burnley Football Club. Walter Place senior (Big Walter) had played in just about every position during his Burnley career that had begun in the days before league football and he was also proficient in a number of other sports. He had announced his retirement in April 1899 but had kept himself fit, in case the call came in an emergency, and had continued to play frequently for the reserves.

In March 1900 the appointment of a new team manager was announced. Bolton-born Ernest Mangnall had been an amateur goalkeeper in his younger days and came to Burnley having been a director at Bolton Wanderers. He was a keen athlete and cyclist and among his accomplishments were cycle rides from John O'Groats to Lands End.

Ernest Mangnall could not claim much credit for it but soon after his arrival Burnley were playing in the Lancashire Cup final for the first time since they had won the trophy in 1890. After wins against Everton and Darwen, the Turfites met Southport Central in the semi final at Bolton, winning 2-0. The final against Preston had also been arranged originally for a neutral ground, Manchester City's Hyde Road, but, unfortunately City had arranged a friendly fixture on the date chosen. The clubs tossed a coin for choice of venue, Burnley lost, and the final was played at Deepdale, Preston collecting the trophy after a 1-0 win.

Into April 1900 and Burnley had not won for six matches. They had dropped into the bottom three, just one point above Preston who had struggled all season and seemed destined to accompany Glossop into Division Two. A fine performance at Liverpool, another struggling side, ended in a 1-0 win for the Turfites, thanks to an early goal from Abe Hartley and an inspired performance from Jack Hillman who saved two penalties.

On the penultimate Saturday of the season, Burnley's visitors were none other than Preston themselves. Roared on by a sizeable Turf Moor crowd the Burnley players battled from first whistle to last and deserved at least a draw. Alas it was not to be and a single goal late on was enough to take the points back to Deepdale.

Even at this late stage the Turfites were still not in the bottom

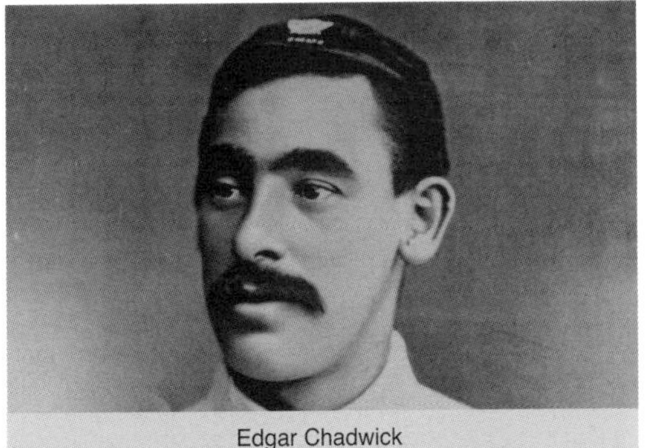

Edgar Chadwick
England international signed from Everton

two and if they won their last two games, they would stay up, no matter how Preston performed in their last three matches. The final game at Turf Moor was a rearranged fixture against Sheffield United who could still finish as League Champions – provided they beat Burnley by eight goals! On the day it was Burnley who looked like potential champions, playing some of their best football of the season. The Blades never really looked like scoring even one goal, let alone the eight they needed for the title. The Burnley front men just could not make the breakthrough however and the game looked like finishing goalless, a result that would be of no real benefit to either side. Then, in the very last minute, with the Turfites attacking yet again, the ball broke to James Davidson on the edge of the penalty area. Davidson let fly with a ferocious shot that flew past the legendary United keeper Billy Foulke into the net. The Burnley crowd went wild and the cheering had not even begun to subside when the referee blew for full-time. The Burnley supporters felt that the hard work had been done and relegation was sure to be avoided. The Turfites were three points ahead of Preston with their final fixture to come, at Nottingham Forest. A win at Forest would guarantee safety but even if Burnley lost, surely Preston would not win both their last two matches, both at home, against Wolves, who were fourth – and Blackburn Rovers. In the event it all went horribly wrong, Forest completely outclassed the men from Turf Moor, cruising home 4-0, while Preston beat Wolves 2-0. North End still needed at least a point from their last game with Blackburn but the Burnley fans just knew how it would end. Sure enough it finished Preston 2-0 Blackburn, North End were safe and Burnley were down, for the second time in two years.

Then, as if relegation were not bad enough, the Burnley Express reproduced a statement that had appeared in the Nottingham Evening Post to the effect that a Burnley player had attempted to bribe the Forest players to lose the match. Allegedly the, thus far un-named, Burnley player had, via the Forest captain, offered to guarantee the Forest players £2 per man if they would let Burnley win the match. The offer was said to have been 'indignantly declined' but when half time arrived with Burnley losing 0-2, the offer was raised to £5 per man, with the same response. At the end of the match, with Burnley having lost 0-4, and with relegation now confirmed, the facts were reported by their captain to the Forest committee.

The Forest officials, in turn, advised the Football League who because of the seriousness of the accusations deferred judgement to the Football Association.

The Burnley player at the centre of the controversy turned out to be the captain and goalkeeper Jack Hillman and he and the Forest captain, John MacPherson, together with senior representatives of both Burnley FC and Nottingham Forest FC, were summoned to an FA Commission hearing in Manchester. In his defence Jack Hillman admitted that he had indeed used the words of which he had been accused, but it had been a joke and he had not meant his offer to be taken seriously. Unfortunately MacPherson had not seen the funny side, and neither did the FA Commission. They decided that Burnley Football Club had no knowledge of, nor were they responsible for, Jack Hillman's actions. The verdict on Hillman himself was that "he had offered a bribe to affect the result of the match" and he would be suspended from football until the end of the 1900-01 season. The Commission added that, but for his previous good conduct, they would have considered banning him from all involvement in football for life!

Just to heap even more misery on the deflated Burnley FC camp, once more contemplating life in Division Two, and without one of their star players, the former Burnley manager Harry Bradshaw, now at Woolwich Arsenal, came calling and signed another of the Turfites' stars, Walter Place junior.

1899-1900 - First Division

		P	W	D	L	F	A	Pts
1	Aston Villa	34	22	6	6	77	35	50
2	Sheffield U	34	18	12	4	63	33	48
3	Sunderland	34	19	3	12	50	35	41
4	Wolverhampton W	34	15	9	10	48	37	39
5	Newcastle U	34	13	10	11	53	53	36
6	Derby C	34	14	8	12	45	43	36
7	Manchester C	34	13	8	13	50	44	34
8	Nottingham F	34	13	8	13	56	55	34
9	Stoke	34	13	8	13	47	45	34
10	Liverpool	34	14	5	15	49	45	33
11	Everton	34	13	7	14	47	49	33
12	Bury	34	13	6	15	40	44	32
13	West Bromwich A	34	11	8	15	43	51	30
14	Blackburn R	34	13	4	17	49	61	30
15	Notts C	34	9	11	14	46	60	29
16	Preston NE	34	12	4	18	38	48	28
17	BURNLEY	34	11	5	18	34	54	27
18	Glossop	34	4	10	20	31	74	18

1899-1900

Managed by Club Directors June 1899 to March 1900, then J Ernest Mangnall

Division One (17th)
Relegated

		No.	Date			Opponents	Result		h/t	Goalscorers/times	Opp. goal times
	1	Sep	2	a	Glossop	L	0-2	0-1		25, 60
	2		9	h	STOKE	D	2-2	2-1	Chadwick 20, Bowes 44	30, 75
	3		16	a	Sunderland	L	1-2	0-0	Chadwick 70	46, 80
	4		23	h	WEST BROMWICH A	W	2-0	2-0	Chadwick 31, Morrison 40	
	5		30	a	Everton	L	0-2	0-1		28, 60
	6	Oct	7	h	BLACKBURN R	W	1-0	0-0	Bowes 60	
	7		14	a	Derby C	L	1-4	0-2	Chadwick 87	25, 44, 65, 70
	8		21	h	BURY	W	1-0	1-0	Bowes 22	
	9		28	a	Notts C	L	1-6	0-2	Chadwick 65	5,29,48,55,69,73
	10	Nov	4	h	MANCHESTER C	W	2-0	2-0	Jenkinson 2, Taylor 30	
	11		11	a	Sheffield U	D	0-0	0-0		
	12		18	h	NEWCASTLE U	L	1-3	0-1	Jenkinson 83	40, 60, 75
	13		25	a	Aston Villa	L	0-2	0-1		41, 75
	14	Dec	2	h	LIVERPOOL	W	2-1	0-0	Bowes 49, Miller 70	72
	15		9	h	WOLVERHAMPTON W	L	0-1	0-0		60
Reynolds' last game	16		16	a	Preston N E	D	1-1	1-0	Bowes 25	65
	17		23	h	NOTTINGHAM F	D	2-2	1-2	Hartley 40, Miller 55	3, 13og
	18		26	a	Stoke	L	0-3	0-1		35, 65, 80
	19		29	h	GLOSSOP	W	3-1	2-0	Chadwick (3) 12, 14, 70	50
	20	Jan	1	a	Blackburn R	L	0-2	0-1		25, 50
	21		13	h	SUNDERLAND	W	3-1	2-1	Hannigan 18, Chadwick 33, Hartley 50	20
	22		20	a	West Bromwich A	L	0-2	0-0		50, 75
	23	Feb	3	h	EVERTON	W	3-1	1-0	Morrison 40, Hartley 55, Chadwick 75	89
	24		17	h	DERBY C	L	1-2	0-1	Hartley 84	40, 65
	25	Mar	3	h	NOTTS C	W	3-0	0-0	Hannigan (2) 49, 80, Morrison 50	
	26		10	a	Manchester C	L	0-1	0-0		85
	27		14	a	Bury	D	1-1	0-1	Place jun 65	30
	28		24	a	Newcastle U	L	0-2	0-2		14, 30
	29		31	h	ASTON VILLA	L	1-2	1-1	Bowes 10	13og, 75
	30	Apr	7	a	Liverpool	W	1-0	1-0	Hartley 20	
	31		14	a	Wolverhampton W	L	0-3	0-1		25, 57, 62
	32		21	h	PRESTON N E	L	0-1	0-0		83
	33		23	h	SHEFFIELD U	W	1-0	0-0	Davidson 90	
last games for Livingstone & Place junior	34		28	a	Nottingham F	L	0-4	0-2		30, 43, 65, 69

FA Cup

	No.	Date			Opponents	Result		h/t	Goalscorers/times	Opp. goal times
Place senior's last game	1	Jan	27	h	BURY	L	0-1	0-0		72

Final, Bury 4-0 Southampton, at Crystal Palace.

Other matches (friendlies and/or as detailed)

	Date			Opponents	Result		h/t	Goalscorers
	Sep	4	h	BOLTON W	D	0-0		
		26	a	Grimsby T	W	1-0		Chadwick
	Oct	30	h	KAFFIRS	W	7-6		Savage, Taylor, Chadwick, Barron, unknown (2), Jenkinson
Lancs Cup	Dec	18	h	EVERTON	W	2-1		Chadwick, Watkins
		25	a	Bolton W	L	0-2		
	Jan	6	a	Southport Central	W	1-0		Hartley
Lancs Cup		16	a	Darwen	W	5-0		Hartley (2), Bowes, Place jun, Morrison
Lancs Cup, tie replayed	Feb	20	a	Darwen	W	2-0		Place jun (2)
		24	a	Blackburn R	L	0-2		
Lancs Cup semi, at Bolton	Mar	5	n	Southport Central	W	2-0		Bowes, Sutherland
Lancs Cup final		17	a	Preston N E	L	0-1	0-0	
	Apr	13	a	Woolwich A	L	0-2		
		16	a	Reading	W	1-0		Bowes

Att.	Pos	Hillman	Reynolds	McLintock	Barron	Taylor	Livingstone	Morrison	Chadwick	Bowes	Fairburn	Ferguson	Woolfall	W Place junior	Greenwood	Bannister	Arnott	Swainston	Jenkinson	McMillan	H Ross	Watkins	Miller	Hartley	Hannigan	Sutherland	J Davidson	W Place senior	
6,000		1	2	3	4	5	6	7	8	9	10	11																	1
6,500	14	1		3	4	5	6	7	8	9		11	2	10															2
12,500	15	1		3	4	5	6	7	9	8		11	2	10															3
10,027	12	1		3	4	5	6	7	9	8		11	2	10															4
15,000	15	1		3	4	5	6		9	8		11	2	10	7														5
12,855	12	1		3	4	9	6	7	10	8			2	11		5													6
10,000	15			3	4	5	6	7	10	8			2	11			1	9											7
6,500	13	1		3	4	9	6	7	10	8			2	11		5													8
10,000	14			3	4	5	6	7	10	8			2				1		9	11									9
5,000	12	1		3	4	5	6	7	10	8			2	11					9										10
6,000	12			3	4	5	6	7	10	8			2	11			1		9										11
5,000	12	1		3	4	5	6		10	8			2	11					9		7								12
10,000	12	1		3	4	5	6	7		10			2	11				9				8							13
5,000	12	1		3	4	5	6	7	8	9			2	10									11						14
5,000	12	1		3		5	6	7	8	9			2	10					4				11						15
7,000	11	1	2	3		5	6	7	9	10			4									8	11						16
5,000		1		3	4	5	6	7	8	10			2										11	9					17
10,000	13	1		3	4	5	6	7	8	10			2										11	9					18
		1		3	4	5	6	8	9	10			2										11		7				19
14,000	13	1		3	4	5	6	8	9				2	10									11		7				20
5,000	12	1		3	4	5	6	8	10				2										11	9	7				21
3,427	14	1		3	4	5		8	10	6			2										11	9	7				22
4,000	12	1		3	4	6		8	10				2			5							11	9	7				23
5,000	12	1		3	4	6		8	10				2			5							11	9	7				24
4,000	11	1		3	4	5	6	7	10				2											9	8	11			25
13,000	12	1		3	4	5	6	7	10	8			2	11										9					26
2,000		1		3	4	5	6	7	10	8			2	11										9					27
12,000	15	1		3	4	5	6		10	8			2	11										9	7				28
6,000	16	1		3	4	6		7	9	8			2	10		5							11						29
10,000	16	1		3	4	5	6	7		8			2	10									11	9					30
5,000	16	1		3	4	5	6	7		8			2	10									11	9					31
8,000		1		3	4	5	6	7	10	8			2										11	9					32
6,000	16	1		3		5	6	7	10	9			2						4				11				8		33
3,000	17	1		3		5	6	7	10	9			2	11					4								8		34
Appearances		31	2	34	30	34	30	31	31	29	1	5	33	21	1	5	3	2	7	1	1	2	16	13	8	1	2		
Goals (34)						1		3	10	6				1					2				2	5	3		1		

Att.	Pos	Hillman	Reynolds	McLintock	Barron	Taylor	Livingstone	Morrison	Chadwick	Bowes	Fairburn	Ferguson	Woolfall	W Place junior	Greenwood	Bannister	Arnott	Swainston	Jenkinson	McMillan	H Ross	Watkins	Miller	Hartley	Hannigan	Sutherland	J Davidson	W Place senior	
6,000		1		3	4	5	6	8	10	9			2										11					7	1
Appearances		1		1	1	1	1	1	1	1			1										1					1	
Goals (0)																													

1900-01

Even with Jack Hillman unavailable for the entire season and Edgar Chadwick deciding not to re-sign for the Turfites, everyone at Turf Moor was confident that Second Division football at Turf Moor would once again be a short term affair, promotion simply had to be achieved under new club captain Joe Taylor.

The new season started with two new full backs in place. Following just one season at Turf Moor Tom Woolfall had been transferred to Bolton with George Lockhart getting his chance after himself coming from Bolton in March 1900. After seven years as a fixture at left back Tom McLintock stepped aside for Jimmy Lindsay, signed from Newcastle, although McLintock would certainly make his presence felt in the season ahead.

After two years in the Turf Moor shadows, Willie Tatham started the season between the sticks but he was not seen even as the short term replacement for the suspended Jack Hillman. With just four matches gone he was replaced by another newcomer, 24 year old Harry Collins, signed in June 1900 from Hebburn Argyle. Collins would go on to make the position his own until "the Burly One" returned from the wilderness.

Burnley started the campaign well enough and indeed on the opening day they overpowered Grimsby who went on to lift the Second Division Championship. The Turfites were always up with the leaders, top for a spell, second for a time, but there was a distinct lack of consistency which would ultimately prove to be their downfall. A match in which the players did perform was away at Barnsley but on that occasion the fates, and it has to be said, the referee, conspired against them.

It was Burnley's first visit to Oakwell and, on a dark November afternoon, their train was five minutes late arriving. When the players got to the ground, the referee, in his wisdom, had not yet started to get changed and all the players were ready to kick off a good five minutes before the referee appeared. The ball was finally set in motion ten minutes after the allotted time and those ten lost minutes were to prove crucial. An early own goal put the Turfites ahead and when William Watkins doubled the lead just past the hour there was only going to be one winner. However as the match moved towards its conclusion the light, which had never been very good, deteriorated to the point where none of the spectators could see anything and the players could barely make out team mates from opponents. With 82 minutes played the whistle wielder decided enough was enough, and abandoned the match just eight minutes short of two points in the Burnley bag. The game was eventually replayed in full at a time when the Turfites were not in good form – and Barnsley won 2-1!

There was another successful campaign in the Lancashire Cup but, once again the Turfites were beaten at the final hurdle, Blackburn Rovers cruising home 4-0 in the final at Hyde Road, home of Manchester City. At that point in the season Burnley were finding some form in the league with successive five-goal victories against Glossop and Chesterfield at Turf Moor. After a spell out of the team Billy Bowes scored his only Burnley hat-trick against Glossop, following that with another goal against Chesterfield to send the Turfites back to the top of the league.

James Savage
another promising youngster

On 22 January 1901 came the sad news that all the country had been anticipating for some time, the death of Her Majesty Queen Victoria at Osborne House on the Isle of Wight. As a mark of respect the Football Association postponed for two weeks all the FA Cup first round ties due to be played on the following Saturday, including Burnley's clash with Newton Heath. To avoid fixture congestion, all the league matches due to be played on that second Saturday in February were brought forward by two weeks, which seemed to defeat the object somewhat. The Queen's funeral on Saturday 2 February 1901 brought most of the country to a standstill and there was no organised football played anywhere, all football fixtures being postponed until later in the season.

The Turfites and Newton Heath played out a goalless draw in their delayed FA Cup tie at Clayton and Burnley produced their best performance of the season in the replay, demolishing the Mancunians 7-1. It was Burnley's biggest-ever win in the FA Cup and it meant the Turfites had scored 17 goals in three home games, with local youngster William Jenkinson helping himself to five of them in his first full season. Burslem Port Vale were then beaten 1-0, with a goal from James Savage, yet another promising local youngster making the most of his opportunities in the senior team. Burnley were now top of the league again and looking favourites for promotion.

It was as good as it got however and with only one win in the next eight matches, the Turfites were out of the FA Cup and struggling to keep up with the Second Division front runners, Grimsby and Small Heath. With just three matches to play Burnley were four points behind second-placed Small Heath and needing a lift for the home match with Blackpool.

It had seemed a measure of desperation when left winger Jimmy Savage was rested for the match with Barnsley and veteran full back Tom McLintock brought in in his place. McLintock had been solid however, had tucked away a penalty in a 4-0 win and had kept his place in the team on merit. McLintock proceeded to play Blackpool on his own and by half time had scored twice as Burnley led 2-0. After the break the Seasiders goalkeeper Dorrington decided to lend a hand in Burnley's quest for promotion. After launching himself feet first at Tom McLintock in a goal mouth skirmish, a penalty was awarded against Dorrington and McLintock duly obliged to make the score 3-0. Dorrington then delivered a stream of invective in the direction of the referee who promptly sent him off. Incredibly, just five minutes later there was a careless handball in the Blackpool penalty area, another whistle, another spot kick, another goal for Tom McLintock. 4-0 to Burnley, the gods had smiled but would they continue to do so?

After the Tom McLintock show, Burnley were still third with just two matches left and, mathematically at least, could still be promoted. It was not to be. The players sensed the task was hopeless and, with the impetus gone, were very much second best in their penultimate match at Stockport, going down 2-3. The two most consistent teams of the campaign, Grimsby and Small Heath, would be going up to Division One but, with only one match to play, the championship was still undecided. Burnley, at home to Small Heath on the last Saturday of the season, would have a part to play in that decision.

Small Heath's only home defeat of the season had been 0-1 against Burnley and the Turfites were determined to make it a double. For their part the Heathens needed a better result than Grimsby to clinch the Second Division title. In the event Small Heath were outplayed and the Burnley players, with no other incentive than to finish the campaign in style, were worthy winners thanks to yet another goal from Tom McLintock.

Third position then, but it could, and should, have been so much better. Excellent performances, in general, against the leading lights had been nullified by poor results against all the bottom four. In addition, the unfortunate loss of two points in the abandoned game at Barnsley had been costly.

Confidence was still high in the Turf Moor camp however, surely the eagerly awaited promotion back to the top flight had only been delayed by a year.

Alas it would be more than a decade before even the modest heights of 1900-01 would be reached again.

Billy Bannister
another local find to go on to play for his country

1900-01 - Second Division

		P	W	D	L	F	A	Pts
1	Grimsby T	34	20	9	5	60	33	49
2	Small Heath	34	19	10	5	57	24	48
3	BURNLEY	34	20	4	10	53	29	44
4	New Brighton T	34	17	8	9	57	38	42
5	Glossop	34	15	8	11	51	33	38
6	Middlesbrough	34	15	7	12	50	40	37
7	Woolwich A	34	15	6	13	39	35	36
8	Lincoln C	34	13	7	14	43	39	33
9	Burslem PV	34	11	11	12	45	47	33
10	Newton Heath	34	14	4	16	42	38	32
11	Leicester F	34	11	10	13	39	37	32
12	Blackpool	34	12	7	15	33	58	31
13	Gainsborough T	34	10	10	14	45	60	30
14	Chesterfield	34	9	10	15	46	58	28
15	Barnsley	34	11	5	18	47	60	27
16	Walsall	34	7	13	14	40	56	27
17	Stockport C	34	11	3	20	38	68	25
18	Burton S	34	8	4	22	34	66	20

1900-01

Manager : J Ernest Mangnall

Division Two (3rd)

Note	No	Date		Venue	Opponents	Result		h/t	Goalscorers/times	Opp. goal times
	1	Sep	1	h	GRIMSBY T	W	3-0	1-0	Davidson 25, Bowes 55, Morrison 86	
	2		3	h	BURTON S	W	2-1	2-1	Morrison 2p, unknown 5	30
	3		8	a	Lincoln C	L	0-2	0-1		22, 65
Tatham's last game	4		15	h	NEWTON HEATH	W	1-0	0-0	Bowes 70	
	5		22	a	Glossop	W	1-0	0-0	Sutherland 55	
	6		29	h	MIDDLESBROUGH	W	2-0	1-0	Morrison 40, Bannister 60	
	7	Oct	6	a	Chesterfield	W	3-1	0-1	scrimmage 65, Hancock 67og, Bowes 89	25
	8		13	a	Burslem P V	L	0-1	0-0		65
	9		20	h	LEICESTER F	D	0-0	0-0		
	10		27	a	New Brighton T	L	1-2	0-1	Savage 86	25, 65
	11	Nov	3	h	NEW BRIGHTON T	W	2-1	1-0	Watkins 16, Mole 90	65
	12		10	a	Walsall	L	0-2	0-2		20, 22
	13		17	a	Leicester F	D	1-1	0-0	Davidson 60	63
	14	Dec	1	h	WOOLWICH A	W	3-0	1-0	Watkins 12, Jenkinson 60, Morrison 65	
	15		8	a	Blackpool	W	1-0	0-0	Watkins 60	
	16		15	h	STOCKPORT C	W	3-1	1-0	Jenkinson 44, Watkins (2) 52, 70	60
	17		22	a	Small Heath	W	1-0	1-0	Savage 30	
	18		25	h	GAINSBOROUGH T	W	2-1	1-1	Jenkinson 22, Savage 71	17
	19		29	a	Grimsby T	L	1-2	0-2	Savage 65	5, 44og
	20	Jan	5	h	LINCOLN C	W	1-0	1-0	Bannister 2	
	21		12	a	Newton Heath	W	1-0	1-0	Jenkinson 27	
	22		19	h	GLOSSOP	W	5-1	4-0	Bowes (3) 23, 40, 62, Jenkinson 35, Mole 43	89
	23		26	h	CHESTERFIELD	W	5-1	3-0	Barron 15, Jenkinson (2) 25, 35, Bowes 52, Savage 85	50
	24	Feb	16	h	BURSLEM P V	W	1-0	1-0	Savage 40	
	25	Mar	9	a	Gainsborough T	L	0-3	0-2		10, 35, 75
	26		16	h	WALSALL	D	0-0	0-0		
	27		23	a	Burton S	L	0-1	0-0		80
	28		30	h	BARNSLEY	W	4-0	1-0	Jenkinson 25, Bowes 50, McLintock 80p, Watkins 90	
	29	Apr	5	a	Barnsley	L	1-2	0-1	Barron 75	15, 65
	30		6	a	Woolwich A	L	1-3	0-1	Bowes 86	44, 60, 70
	31		9	a	Middlesbrough	D	0-0	0-0		
	32		13	h	BLACKPOOL	W	4-0	2-0	McLintock (4) 31, 38, 68p, 73p	
	33		20	a	Stockport C	L	2-3	1-1	Bannister 30, Jenkinson 80	40, 65, 75
Bowes' last game	34		27	h	SMALL HEATH	W	1-0	1-0	McLintock 42	

FA Cup

Note	Rd	Date		Venue	Opponents	Result		h/t	Goalscorers/times	Opp. goal times
	1	Feb	9	a	Newton Heath	D	0-0	0-0		
Newton Heath goal 21m	rep		13	h	NEWTON HEATH	W	7-1	4-1	Mole 4, Bannister 24, Taylor 35, Morrison (2) 40, 82, Jenkinson (2) 70, 85	
	2		23	a	Small Heath	L	0-1	0-1		16

Final, Tottenham H 3-1 Sheffield U, at Bolton, after a 2-2 draw, at Crystal Palace.

Other matches (friendlies and/or as detailed)

Note	Date		Venue	Opponents	Result		h/t	Goalscorers
	Sep	17	h	BOLTON W	W	3-1		McLintock, Astin, Miller
Lancs Cup	Oct	1	a	Liverpool	W	2-0		Davidson, Morrison
		15	a	Bolton W	D	2-2		Sutherland, Bannister
Lancs Cup		22	h	BOLTON W	W	5-0		Bowes (3), Savage (2)
Lancs Cup semi final	Nov	12	a	Manchester C	D	2-2		Davidson, Bannister p
Div 2 fixture aban 82m, bad light		24	a	Barnsley	aban	2-0		Stephenson og, Watkins
Lancs Cup semi replay at Bury		26	n	Manchester C	W	2-1		Savage, Davidson
Lancs Cup final at Man City	Jan	14	n	Blackburn R	L	0-4	0-3	

Att.	Pos	Tatham	Lindsay	Lockhart	Barron	Bannister	Taylor	Morrison	J Davidson	Mole	Bowes	Sutherland	Jenkinson	Miller	Watkins	McLintock	Collins	Howarth	Savage	H Ross	Parkinson	Driver	Sawley		
4,000		1	2	3	4	5	6	7	8	9	10	11													1
3,500	top	1	2	3	4	5	6	7	8	9	10	11													2
	2	1	2	3	4	5	6	7	8		10		9	11											3
4,000	top	1	2	3	4	5	6	7			10			11	8	9									4
2,000	top		2	3	4	5	6	7			9	11			8		1	10							5
4,500	top		2	3	4	5	6	7			9	11			8		1	10							6
3,000	top		2	3	4	5	6	7	8		9	11					1	10							7
1,000	top		2	3	4	5	6	7	8		9	11					1	10							8
4,000	top		2	3	4	5	6	7			9	11			8		1	10							9
3,000	3		2	3	4	5	6	7			9	10			8		1		11						10
4,000	top		2	3	4	5	6	9		7		10			8		1		11						11
5,000	3		2	3	4	5	6	7	10				9		8		1		11						12
10,000	2		2	3	4	5	6	7	10				9		8		1		11						13
4,000	3		2		4	5	6	7	10				9		8		1		11	3					14
4,500	3		2	3	4	5	6	7	10				9		8		1		11						15
3,000	3		2	3	4	5	6		10	7			9		8		1		11						16
10,000	2		2	3	4	5	6	7	10				9		8		1		11						17
7,000			2	3	4	5	6	7	10				9		8		1		11						18
7,000	3		2	3	4	5	6	7				10	9		8		1		11						19
4,000	3		2	3	4	5	6	7			10		9		8		1		11						20
10,000	3		2	3	4	5	6	7			10		9		8		1		11						21
2,000	2			3	4	5	6	8		7	10		9				1		11	2					22
1,000	top			3	4	5	6	8		7	10		9				1		11	2					23
4,000	top		2	3	4	5	6	8		7	10		9				1		11						24
3,000	3		2	3	4	5	6	8	10	7			9				1		11						25
3,000	3		2	6	4		5		10	7			9		8		1		11	3					26
	3		2	3	4	5	6						9		8		1		11		7	10			27
400	3		2	3	4	5	6	7			10		9		8	11	1								28
			2	3	4	5	6	7			10		9		8	11	1								29
7,000			2	3	4	5	6	7			10		9		8	11	1								30
6,000	3		2	3	4	5	6	7			10		9		8	11	1								31
2,000	3		2	3	4	5	6				10		9		8	11	1				7				32
1,000	3			3	4	5	6	7			10		9		8	11	1			2					33
5,000				3	4	5	6	7			10				8	11	1			2			9		34
Appearances		4	30	33	34	33	34	30	14	9	22	10	23	2	25	8	30	5	18	6	2	1	1		
Goals (53)					2	3		4	1	2	9	1	9		6	6			7					1	og

2 untraced

Att.	Pos	Tatham	Lindsay	Lockhart	Barron	Bannister	Taylor	Morrison	J Davidson	Mole	Bowes	Sutherland	Jenkinson	Miller	Watkins	McLintock	Collins	Howarth	Savage	H Ross	Parkinson	Driver	Sawley		
8,000			2	3	4	5	6	8		7	10		9				1		11						1
4,000			2	3	4	5	6	8		7	10		9				1		11						rep
11,000			2	3	6	5	4	10		11	8		9				1		7						2
Appearances			3	3	3	3	3	3		3	3		3				3		3						
Goals (7)						1	1	2		1			2												

1901-02

For the first time in a decade there was no Billy Bowes in the Burnley squad for the new season. After almost 300 league and FA Cup games and over 80 goals Bowes, now in his thirties, had decided to step down from league football.

Matt Brunton
new arrival from Accrington

The only newcomer to the Turfites' ranks in the summer of 1901 was Burnley-born Matt Brunton, who arrived at Turf Moor after a season with Accrington in the Lancashire Combination. He went straight into the senior team for his first taste of league action, oddly enough replacing another Burnley native, William Jenkinson, who had decided to move to the capital to join West Ham, then in the Southern League.
There was also a familiar face back on the Turf Moor scene with Alex Stewart returning to the fold after nine years with a brief to coach the reserve team, although he also went on to provide valuable cover for the senior team.
After just one season goalkeeper Henry Collins had been transferred to Queens Park Rangers, as Jack Hillman was now available again after his year on the sidelines. "the Burly One" immediately re-assumed the team captaincy.
At the end of August 1901 the issue of the club's balance sheet sent a bleak message out to supporters. After Burnley FC's worst ever season of league football in 1900-01, the club was in financial difficulties and poor gates had led to a loss of over £800.
The Burnley Express did not mince its words –
"First class football in Burnley is not a paying proposition and cannot be continued for much longer"
There was a definite suggestion that, not for the first time, and by no means the last, one or more of the club's best players would have to be sold.
The season started off reasonably well, especially at home, where the Turfites were defeated only once in the league until March 1902. That defeat came in October 1901 and it was Burnley's old friends Preston North End, newly relegated themselves, who demonstrated just how difficult the campaign was going to be, cruising home 3-0. Amazingly that was Burnley's first ever home defeat in Second Division football after more than two full seasons at that level.
The Turfites had been hoping to field a new Scottish signing in the Preston match. A native of Hamilton, 23-year-old William Lambie came well recommended, a junior international, with experience at both Clyde and Queens Park. In the event it was reported that Lambie had twisted his knee and was unable to leave Scotland for the time being. He eventually arrived in Burnley and was immediately selected at outside right for the match against Burton United at Turf Moor. The game ended goalless, "a wretched display" according to the Burnley Express, "possibly the worst ever performance by a Burnley team". As for William Lambie "his knee gave way after a few minutes and he left the field, later returned briefly, then retired at half time". In the days following the match it was revealed that William Lambie had been released as he was "clearly not fit". However it was subsequently admitted by Burnley FC Directors that the club had been duped and "William Lambie" or whoever he was, had been in fact, an imposter! He had been able to convince Burnley's Scottish representative that he was the Queens Park international winger with a fierce shot and an eye for goal. The Burnley Express was scathing -"Lambie's exhibition was such as to suggest that he had never before donned a jersey on a football field!"

OBITUARY
ALEXANDER (SANDY) LANG
DIED 8 NOVEMBER 1901, AGED 38.

Former Burnley FC fullback and captain, Sandy Lang sustained fatal injuries after a fall whilst working at the Dog and Duck public house in the centre of Burnley where he was the landlord.
Born at Bridge of Weir, near Paisley in 1863, Sandy Lang first came to Lancashire in 1884, joining Padiham FC, then one of the leading clubs in the county. He was transferred to Burnley in 1885 and first appeared at Turf Moor in a 9-0 win against Derby St Lukes in September 1885, a game which was also the Burnley debut of the famous cricketer Frank Sugg.
Sandy Lang was a regular in the Burnley team in the late 1880's and formed a formidable full back partnership with his close friend William Bury well into the days of league football. He was the Turfites' first captain in the Football League, was the first Burnley player to appear in 100 League matches and scored the club's first ever goal from a penalty kick in November 1891. After over 300 games for Burnley, including 123 League games, Sandy Lang left Turf Moor in 1895 and went on to contribute to Nelson's Lancashire League Championship success of 1896 before becoming a publican.
'Sportsman' of the Burnley Express was moved to write thus "If Burnley had had a team of players of the calibre of Sandy Lang, there would have been no descent to the Second Division. Alas poor Sandy, we will not look upon his like again"

RIP

Once again Burnley reached the Lancashire Cup final and once again they were to meet up with the old enemy, Blackburn Rovers. The final was again staged at Manchester City's ground and the Turfites were hoping for revenge after their walloping by the Rovers in the 1900-01 final at the same venue. It was the third time that the clubs had met in the County showpiece and it was almost twelve years since Burnley's one and only triumph in the competition, the famous 2-0 victory over Rovers, then the FA Cup holders, in the final of 1890, at Accrington. Alex Stewart had scored both goals on that memorable day and, following his return to Turf Moor, was the only member of either team who had played in the 1890 final. He was hoping that history would repeat itself but it was not to be, Burnley were second best on the day to their First Division opponents and a single goal, mid way through the second period, was enough to take the trophy back from whence it came, to Ewood Park.

Blackburn's ground was also the scene of Burnley's first defeat in the East Lancashire Charity Cup since 1891 when, ironically they had been beaten by Rovers in the final. Burnley had won it on every occasion that the Cup had been competed for since that season and had held it since beating Blackburn themselves in the 1899 final. On this occasion it was Darwen who triumphed 2-1 after an arduous three-game saga in which the stars had been the ex-Burnley goalkeeper James Arnott and the Darwen centre forward Duckworth who was born in Burnley.

In November 1901 came the inevitable sale of Burnley's star player, centre half Billy Bannister, transferred to Bolton for a fee of £300. Another Burnley-born Turfite, Bannister had enjoyed a rapid rise to stardom since making his First Division debut in October 1899 and going on to play for both the Football League and for the full England side during his first full season of league football in 1900-01. He would undoubtedly be missed but as one door closed another opened with the promotion to the senior team of another local youngster, Arthur Dixon from Barrowford. Dixon, along with Joe Taylor and Fred Barron would be a part of the Turfites' defence for many years to come.

After the season's solitary away win in the League at Stockport, Burnley managed to negotiate a tricky FA Cup qualifying round tie at Bishop Auckland. It was the first time ever that Burnley had had to enter the FA Cup at that stage and the Northern League Champions of 1901 and FA Amateur Cup winners of 1900 made it very difficult for the Turfites. The first two goals of his Burnley career from new signing Cornelius Hogan, however, helped the league side squeeze through to the first round proper, and a trip to Midland League Walsall. This time there was no happy ending and the chance of a lucrative FA Cup run disappeared after a 0-1 defeat.

With Burnley still losing money, out of the FA Cup and becalmed in mid-table with no realistic prospects of promotion, the directors decided to cash in on another of the club's assets. After more than ten years at Turf Moor, in three separate spells, the colourful and controversial Jack Hillman was on his way again, transferred to Manchester City for a much needed fee of £350.

The season was petering out and attendances were still very

Arthur Dixon
more local talent continuing to emerge

poor, only 400 hardy souls bothering to turn up at Turf Moor to witness the 6-0 victory against Gainsborough in March 1902. At Easter, traditionally a popular time for football, there was an attendance of just 500 for the visit of Scottish side St Bernards.

As a difficult campaign drew to close, it was announced from Turf Moor that, amongst other cost-saving measures, including stopping summer pay for the players, Burnley would be withdrawing their Reserve team from the Lancashire Combination for season 1902-03. Negotiations had taken place with Burnley Belvedere FC and Belvedere would play their home matches in the Lancashire Amateur League at Turf Moor, with a number of the Belvedere players signing league forms to be able to turn out for Burnley, if required, as amateurs.

After Burnley FC's worst-ever season, drastic measures had had to be taken to ensure the club's survival.

Surely things could not get any worse.....or could they?

1901-02 - Second Division

		P	W	D	L	F	A	Pts
1	West Bromwich A	34	25	5	4	82	29	55
2	Middlesbrough	34	23	5	6	90	24	51
3	Preston NE	34	18	6	10	71	32	42
4	Woolwich A	34	18	6	10	50	26	42
5	Lincoln C	34	14	13	7	45	35	41
6	Bristol C	34	17	6	11	52	35	40
7	Doncaster R	34	13	8	13	49	58	34
8	Glossop	34	10	12	12	36	40	32
9	BURNLEY	34	10	10	14	41	45	30
10	Burton U	34	11	8	15	46	54	30
11	Barnsley	34	12	6	16	51	63	30
12	Burslem PV	34	10	9	15	43	59	29
13	Blackpool	34	11	7	16	40	56	29
14	Leicester F	34	12	5	17	38	56	29
15	Newton Heath	34	11	6	17	38	53	28
16	Chesterfield	34	11	6	17	47	68	28
17	Stockport C	34	8	7	19	36	72	23
18	Gainsborough T	34	4	11	19	30	80	19

1901-02

Manager : J Ernest Mangnall

Division Two (9th)

	No	Date			Opponents	Result		h/t	Goalscorers/times	Opp. goal times
	1	Sep	7	a	Lincoln C	L	0-1	0-1		17
	2		9	h	STOCKPORT C	W	3-0	2-0	Morrison 14, Brunton (2) 35, 63	
	3		14	h	WEST BROMWICH A	D	0-0	0-0		
	4		21	a	Woolwich A	L	0-4	0-2		10, 18, 55, 60
	5		28	h	BARNSLEY	W	2-0	1-0	Watkins 31, Brunton 60	
	6	Oct	5	a	Leicester F	L	1-2	0-2	Stewart 82	25, 43
	7		12	h	PRESTON N E	L	0-3	0-3		3, 15p, 35
	8		19	h	BURTON U	D	0-0	0-0		
	9		26	a	Burslem P V	D	1-1	0-1	Davidson 52	35
	10	Nov	2	h	CHESTERFIELD	D	0-0	0-0		
	11		9	a	Gainsborough T	D	1-1	1-0	Sawley 20	70
	12		16	h	MIDDLESBROUGH	D	2-2	0-1	Davidson 55, Brunton 67	7, 65
	13		30	h	BLACKPOOL	W	2-0	2-0	Savage 5, Brunton 29	
	14	Dec	7	a	Stockport C	W	2-1	0-1	Morrison 52, McLintock 60p	7
McLintock's last game	15		21	a	Glossop	D	0-0	0-0		
	16		28	h	DONCASTER R	W	7-0	4-0	Brunton (3) 15, 42, 80, Savage (2) 18, 47, Hogan (2) 40, 66	
	17	Jan	1	a	Barnsley	D	2-2	2-1	Morrison 30, Hogan 43	2p, 89p
	18		4	h	LINCOLN C	W	1-0	0-0	Morrison 76p	
	19		11	a	West Bromwich A	L	0-3	0-1		25, 60, 75
	20		18	h	WOOLWICH A	D	0-0	0-0		
	21	Feb	1	h	LEICESTER F	W	1-0	1-0	Taylor 30	
	22		11	a	Newton Heath	L	0-2	0-1		18, 70
	23		15	a	Burton U	L	2-5	1-2	Hogan 32, Savage 60	10,30,65,70,75
	24		22	h	BURSLEM P V	W	4-1	2-1	Morrison (2) 10, 20, Hogan (2) 65, 85	32
	25	Mar	1	a	Chesterfield	L	0-3	0-1		42, 50, 87
last goal Taylor 87m	26		8	h	GAINSBOROUGH T	W	6-0	2-0	Morrison 23, Davidson 35, Barron 66, Hogan 71, Birchall 75	
	27		15	a	Middlesbrough	L	0-3	0-3		15, 30, 45
	28		22	h	BRISTOL C	L	0-1	0-1		25
	29		28	h	NEWTON HEATH	W	1-0	1-0	Barron 35p	
	30		29	a	Blackpool	L	1-2	0-2	Hogan 70	7, 35
	31	Apr	7	a	Preston N E	L	1-3	0-2	Hogan 75	35, 38, 60
	32		12	a	Bristol C	L	0-1	0-0		65
	33		29	h	GLOSSOP	D	1-1	1-0	Hogan 35	75
James Davidson's last game	34		26	a	Doncaster R	L	0-3	0-1		10, 65, 75

FA Cup

	Rd	Date			Opponents	Result		h/t	Goalscorers/times	Opp. goal times
	Q	Dec	14	a	Bishop Auckland	W	3-2	1-1	Hogan (2) 5, 58, Barron 49	20, 65p
Hillman's last game	1	Jan	25	a	Walsall	L	0-1	0-0		68

Final, Sheffield U 2-1 Southampton, at Crystal Palace, after a 1-1 draw, also at Crystal Palace.

Other matches (friendlies and/or as detailed)

	Date			Opponents	Result		Goalscorers
East Lancs Charity Cup semi	Sep	16	h	ACCRINGTON	W	3-0	Savage, Watkins, Barron
Lancs Cup	Oct	1	a	Stalybridge C	W	2-0	Sawley (2)
East Lancs Charity Cup final		8	h	DARWEN	D	3-3	Savage, Taylor, Sawley
EL Charity Cup final replay		15	a	Darwen	D	1-1	Bannister p
Lancs Cup		21	a	Bolton W	D	1-1	Sawley
ELCC final 2nd rep at B'burn		29	n	Darwen	L	1-2	Watkins
Lancs Cup replay	Nov	4	h	BOLTON W	W	3-2	Brunton, Savage, Bannister
Lancs Cup semi final		18	h	SOUTHPORT C	W	1-0	Brunton
Lancs Cup final at Man City	Dec	2	n	Blackburn R	L	0-1	
	Mar	31	h	ST BERNARDS	W	3-0	Hogan (2), Brunton
Ibrox Disaster Match	May	2	a	Accrington	L	1-4	unknown

Att.	Pos	Hillman	H Ross	Lockhart	Barron	Bannister	Taylor	Morrison	Watkins	Brunton	J Davidson	McLintock	Stewart	Savage	Sawley	Dickinson	W Lambie	C Hogan	Dixon	Howarth	Sugden	Ridsdale	Birchall	H Brown	
		1	2	3	4	5	6	7	8	9	10	11													1
3,500		1	2	3	4	5	6	7	8	9	10	11													2
4,992		1	2	3	4	5	6	7	8	9	10	11													3
10,000	12	1	2	3	4	5	6	7	8	9			10	11											4
3,000	10	1	2	3	4	5	6	7	8	9			10	11											5
3,000	11	1	2	3	4	5	6	7		9			10	11	8										6
5,500	13	1	2	3	4	9	5	7		8		6	10			11									7
2,000	13	1	2		4	5	6	8		10		3			9	11	7								8
4,000	13	1	2		4	5		7	8		10	3	6	11	9										9
1,000	13	1	2		4	5		7	8		10	3	6	11	9										10
	11	1	2		4	5	6	7		8	10	3		11	9										11
2,000	9	1	2		4	5	6	7		8	10	3		11				9							12
600	9	1	2		4		5	7		8	10	3	6	11				9							13
	6	1	2		4		5	7		8	10	3	6	11				9							14
	8	1	2		4		5	7		8	10	3	6	11				9							15
800	7	1	2	3	4		5	7		8	10			11				9	6						16
3,000		1	2	3	4		5	7		8	10			11				9	6						17
	6	1	2	3	4		5	7		8	10			11				9	6						18
9,149	7	1	2	3	4		5	7		8	10			11				9	6						19
4,000	7	1		3	4		5	7		8	10			11				9	6	2					20
700	7		2	3			5	7	8		10							9	6		1	4	11		21
1,000			2	3	4		5	7	8		10			11				9	6		1				22
3,000	7		2	3	4		5	7		8	10			11				9		6	1				23
2,500	7		2	3	4		5	7		8	10							9	6		1		11		24
4,000	7		2	3	4		5		8	7	10							9	6		1		11		25
400	7		2	3	4		5	7		8	10							9	6		1		11		26
10,000	7		2	3			5	7		8	10							9	6		1	4	11		27
1,000	7		2	3	4		5		7	8	10							9	6				11	1	28
3,000			2	3	4		5	7		8	10			11				9	6					1	29
3,000	7		2	3	4		5	7		8	10							9	6				11	1	30
600	7		2	3	4		5	7		8	10							9	6				11	1	31
4,000	8		2	3	4		5	7		8	10							9				6	11	1	32
1,000	9		2	3	4		5	7		8	10							9	6				11	1	33
			2	3	4		5	7		8	10							9	6				11	1	34
Appearances		20	33	26	32	12	32	32	11	30	29	12	9	18	5	2	1	23	17	2	7	3	11	7	
Goals (41)					2		2	7	1	8	3	1	1	4	1			10					1		

Att.	Pos	Hillman	H Ross	Lockhart	Barron	Bannister	Taylor	Morrison	Watkins	Brunton	J Davidson	McLintock	Stewart	Savage	Sawley	Dickinson	W Lambie	C Hogan	Dixon	Howarth	Sugden	Ridsdale	Birchall	H Brown	
4,000		1	2		4		5	7		8	10	3	6	11				9							Q
9,000		1	2	3	4		5	7		8	10			11				9	6						1
Appearances		2	2	1	2		2	2		2	2	1	1	2				2	1						
Goals (3)					1													2							

1902-03

As Burnley Football Club embarked upon the new campaign, little did anyone connected with the club realise that it was very near to being their last season as a member of the Football League. Season 1901-02 had been a poor one but new depths were about to be plumbed and only four years after ending the campaign third in Division One, Burnley would finish the season at the very bottom of Division Two with their future as a league club very much in the hands of others.

OBITUARY
JAMES DANIEL (JIMMY) ROSS
DIED 12 JUNE 1902, AGED 36.

One of the great talents of the early days of professional football, Jimmy Ross, passed away suddenly after contracting an acute skin disease.

Born in Edinburgh in 1866, Jimmy Ross came south to join Preston in 1884 and in his 10 years at Deepdale, helped establish North End, 'The Invincibles,' as the first great power in English professional football. Ross was a key member of the Preston team that won the League and FA Cup double in 1888-89 and the Football League Championship again in 1889-90. After a spell at Liverpool, it was a great coup for Burnley when Jimmy Ross came to Turf Moor in 1897. He was the Turfites' leading scorer and undoubtedly the team's inspiration when the Second Division Championship was secured in 1898. He joined Manchester City in 1899 and immediately helped the Blues to the Second Division title. Ross was playing league football as recently as January 1902 and in fact played for City's reserves at Turf Moor in March 1902. The final word on Jimmy Ross must come from all-time great Billy Meredith who played alongside him at Manchester City –

'King James will always be my all-time hero...what he didn't know about football just wasn't worth knowing!'

RIP

After just one season at Turf Moor the talented Matt Brunton had decided not to re-sign for the Turfites and returned to Accrington in the Lancashire Combination. Winger Jimmy Savage had also moved on, signing for Trawden Forest also in the Combination. Former Turf Moor stalwarts Billy Bowes and Tom McLintock also turned up at Trawden along with Walter Place junior, returning north after two years at Woolwich. Meanwhile Walter Place senior had been appointed club captain at Burnley Belvedere.

Burnley's season began with yet another new pair of hands between the sticks, Fred Wynne stepping up from the previous season's Reserve team. Three draws to start the season seemed promising and then a Turf Moor win against Small Heath, one of the promotion favourites, saw Burnley in fifth place. Although the Turfites suffered some heavy defeats away from home, including a 0-5 drubbing at Preston, the home form was holding up quite well. Following the second win of the season, 3-2 at home to Gainsborough early in November, Burnley were in ninth position and still unbeaten at home.

It could not, and did not last. As the old year turned Burnley hadn't won another match and had been dumped out of the FA Cup, again at the qualifying stage, and again by a non-league club. This time it was Reading, going well in the Southern League, but still almost two decades away from becoming members of the Football League.

Another series of poor Turf Moor gates, only 600 against Blackpool, meant that Burnley simply had to cash in on the value of their star players and this time it was Irish international Tom Morrison who joined Manchester United. Burnley's problem was starkly illustrated by the comparison between Morrison's last league games for Burnley, against the Reds with a reasonably healthy attendance, for Burnley, of 4,000 and his first game for United in front of 40,000, ten times as many, against Manchester City.

Early in the New Year there was huge controversy when a friendly match was arranged at Turf Moor between Burnley and their new bedfellows Burnley Belvedere. From the first whistle there appeared to be bad feeling developing between the two sets of players and also among the rival supporters. Belvedere scored early on and when a second goal from the amateurs' pacy winger Cuthbert Storey was disallowed, the Belvedere section of the crowd began to barrack the referee. In the second half, after more violent confrontations between rival players, Storey was heard to address remarks to the referee best described as 'uncomplementary'. He was immediately ordered off the field but insisted his tirade had been directed at a team mate and refused to go. The referee would not allow the game to continue until Storey departed

Henry Ross
ever present at right back in 1902-03

which he eventually did, slowly and reluctantly. Before the referee had time to blow his whistle however, Belvedere captain Walter Place senior, a prominent ex Turfite of course, followed Storey to the touchline and beckoned his players to do the same. After a few moments the referee decided he had no choice but to abandon the game. The Burnley players left the field and one unnamed Turfite was seen to confront a group of Belvedere supporters, one of whom was seen to fall to the ground.

There were bridges to build between the two clubs and a start was made when Cuthbert Storey immediately offered his services to Burnley for the following Saturday's Second Division match. Storey's offer was accepted, he made his debut at Turf Moor against Lincoln City and an amazing sequence of events was completed when last week's villain became this week's hero when, astonishingly, he scored the only goal of the match!

Although Cuthbert Storey's goal earned two priceless points, it was another Belvedere debutant, inside forward Arthur Bell who had not played in the 'friendly' match, who would go on to make much more of an impact at Turf Moor, at football as indeed he had already done at cricket.

Following another home defeat, by Leicester, Burnley dropped into the Second Division's bottom three for the first time ever. With only three victories all season they already looked like having to apply for re-election with a dozen matches still to play. A 0-6 thrashing at Champions-elect Manchester City was followed by defeats at Blackpool and at home to Barnsley and the Turfites slumped to second bottom with only Stockport below them.

When Burton United visited Turf Moor in mid-March 1903, Burnley had won only one game in more than five months and a 4-1 victory was a tonic for the 600 or so spectators who bothered to turn up. Into April and a 0-4 defeat at Manchester United guaranteed, if it wasn't a certainty already, that Burnley would finish in the bottom three and be obliged to apply for re-election.

Oddly enough, Burnley's last three fixtures were all to be against the other two clubs destined to finish in the last three and Doncaster made sure they would at least be on top of that mini-league with a 2-1 win against Burnley on Good Friday.

When the Turfites came from behind to deny fellow-strugglers Stockport a deserved draw in their penultimate fixture, amazingly it was Burnley's third successive home win. Although a place in the bottom two was a certainty, a win in their final match, at Stockport, would guarantee the wooden spoonists would be County, not Burnley. It was not to be, the Turfites were completely outplayed, losing 0-3, and when Stockport drew their own final match with Preston, Burnley slipped to the very bottom of Division Two, rock bottom of the Football League.

Alas league tables never lie. It was official, Burnley were the worst team in the Football League. Only six games had been won out of 34, all at home. Only a single point had been picked up away from home, a 0-0 draw at Burton on the opening day of the season, how long ago that now seemed, and in fact the Turfites had only won one league match on an opponents' ground since January 1901! Just 30 goals had been scored during this miserable campaign, only five of which were away from home, and one of those was an own goal!

The annual meeting of the Football League was held on 25 May 1903 at the Tavistock Hotel, Covent Garden. The Burnley FC delegation felt sure that, as founder-members of the Football League back in 1888, their Club had the pedigree to be successful in the voting for re-election.

There were eight applications for just three places and when the votes were counted brand new club Bradford City received most votes with Stockport County in second place....... and Burnley third! It had been so close but the club who were to lose their league status, somewhat unfairly, would be Doncaster Rovers, who had ended the campaign third from bottom, five points ahead of both Burnley and Stockport County. It had been a close call but Burnley Football Club's league status was secure, at least for the time being, and the club could move forward with cautious optimism.

Arthur Bell
an impact for Burnley FC on and off the field

Despite the traumas of the campaign that ended with 'the Orient Game' 84 years in the future, the 1902-03 season arguably has the edge as Burnley FC's worst ever and, interestingly, the club has never since finished bottom of any Division.

1902-03 - Second Division

		P	W	D	L	F	A	Pts
1	Manchester C	34	25	4	5	95	29	54
2	Small Heath	34	24	3	7	74	36	51
3	Woolwich A	34	20	8	6	66	30	48
4	Bristol C	34	17	8	9	59	38	42
5	Manchester U	34	15	8	11	53	38	38
6	Chesterfield	34	14	9	11	67	40	37
7	Preston NE	34	13	10	11	56	40	36
8	Barnsley	34	13	8	13	55	51	34
9	Burslem PV	34	13	8	13	57	62	34
10	Lincoln C	34	12	6	16	46	53	30
11	Glossop	34	11	7	16	43	58	29
12	Gainsborough T	34	11	7	16	41	59	29
13	Burton U	34	11	7	16	39	59	29
14	Blackpool	34	9	10	15	44	59	28
15	Leicester F	34	10	8	16	41	65	28
16	Doncaster R	34	9	7	18	35	72	25
17	Stockport C	34	7	6	21	39	74	20
18	BURNLEY	34	6	8	20	30	77	20

1902-03

Manager : J Ernest Mangnall

Division Two (18th)
Re-elected

		Date			Opponents	Result		h/t	Goalscorers/times	Opp. goal times
	1	Sep	1	a	Burton U	D	0-0	0-0		
	2		6	h	DONCASTER R	D	1-1	1-1	McInnes 30	40
	3		8	h	CHESTERFIELD	D	1-1	1-0	Hogan 30	57
	4		13	a	Lincoln C	L	1-4	0-1	unknown 88	30, 82, 84, 86
	5		20	h	SMALL HEATH	W	2-1	1-0	Barron 15p, Lee 76	88
	6		27	a	Leicester F	L	1-2	1-0	Hogan 43	55, 75
	7	Oct	4	h	MANCHESTER C	D	1-1	0-1	McInnes 80	35
	8		11	a	Chesterfield	L	0-2	0-1		25, 60
	9		18	a	Preston N E	L	0-5	0-2		30p, 35, 55, 65, 80
	10		25	h	BURSLEM P V	D	3-3	1-2	Lee 5, Barron 60p, Duckworth 65	3, 42, 55
	11	Nov	8	h	GAINSBOROUGH T	W	3-2	2-1	Morrison 27, Baron 36p, Crawford 53	16, 80
	12		15	h	WOOLWICH A	L	0-3	0-1		10, 65, 78
	13		22	h	BRISTOL C	D	0-0	0-0		
	14	Dec	2	a	Glossop	L	0-2	0-0		50, 65
	15		6	h	MANCHESTER U	L	0-2	0-2		5, 43
	16		20	h	BLACKPOOL	D	1-1	0-0	Hogan 65	55
	17		27	a	Woolwich A	L	1-5	0-2	Ashcroft 60og	10, 15, 50p, 70, 75
	18	Jan	1	a	Barnsley	L	0-3	0-0		60, 80, 85
	19		10	h	LINCOLN C	W	1-0	1-0	Storey 38	
	20		17	a	Small Heath	L	0-3	0-1		43, 55, 75
	21		24	h	LEICESTER F	L	1-3	1-2	Dixon 29	16, 42, 49
	22		31	a	Manchester C	L	0-6	0-2		25,44,50,56,70,89
	23	Feb	7	a	Blackpool	L	0-2	0-2		25p, 43
	24		14	h	PRESTON N E	D	1-1	0-0	Ross 76p	70
	25		28	h	BARNSLEY	L	1-2	1-1	Duckworth 35	37, 65
	26	Mar	7	a	Gainsborough T	L	0-3	0-3		5, 30, 44
	27		14	h	BURTON U	W	4-1	2-1	Crawford (2) 40, 74, Hogan 44, Driver 80	25
	28		21	a	Bristol C	L	0-3	0-1		3, 60, 70
	29		28	h	GLOSSOP	W	2-1	2-1	Hogan 30, Driver 37	8
	30		30	a	Burslem P V	L	1-3	1-0	Lee 42	47, 61, 77
	31	Apr	4	a	Manchester U	L	0-4	0-2		18, 32, 60, 74
	32		10	a	Doncaster R	L	1-2	0-1	Duckworth 75	3, 65
	33		11	h	STOCKPORT C	W	3-2	1-2	Hogan (2) 5, 75, Arridge 69og	12, 30
last games for Lockhart and Cornelius Hogan	34		18	a	Stockport C	L	0-3	0-3		15, 25, 35

FA Cup

	Date			Opponents	Result		h/t	Goalscorers/times	Opp. goal times
1	Dec	13	a	Reading	L	0-1	0-1		20

Final, Bury 6-0 Derby C, at Crystal Palace.

Other matches (friendlies and/or as detailed)

				Opponents	Result		Goalscorers
Lancs Cup	Oct	6	h	STALYBRIDGE R	W	5-0	Crawford, Hogan (3), Morrison
Lancs Cup		20	h	BLACKBURN R	L	1-2	scrimmage
East Lancs Charity Cup semi	Nov	5	a	Accrington	D	2-2	Driver, Dixon
E Lancs Charity Cup semi rep		10	h	ACCRINGTON	L	1-3	Driver
	Dec	25	a	Darwen	L	2-5	unknown (2)
		26	a	Brentford	D	1-1	Barron
Fdly aban 70m, 'disagreement'	Jan	3	h	BURNLEY BELVEDERE	aban	0-1	
Div 2 fixture aban 13m, storm	Feb	21	a	Burslem P V	aban	0-0	
	Mar	23	a	Aberdare	W	1-0	unknown

Att.	Pos	Wynne	H Ross	Lockhart	Barron	Taylor	Dixon	Morrison	Sawley	Crawford	McInnes	Birchall	Lee	C Hogan	Duckworth	Welsh	Whittaker	Howarth	Driver	Towler	Storey	Bell	Edmondson		
		1	2	3	4	5	6	7	8	9	10	11													1
2,000		1	2	3	4	5	6	7	10	9	8		11												2
2,000		1	2	3	4	5	6	7		9	8		11	10											3
	10	1	2	3	4	5	6			10	8		11	9	7										4
3,000	5	1	2	3	4	5	6	7		10	8		11	9											5
3,000	9	1	2	3	4	5	6	7		10	8		11	9											6
4,000	9	1	2	3	4	5	6	7		10	8		11	9											7
3,000	10	1	2	3	4	5	6	7		10	8		11	9											8
3,000	12	1	2	3	4	5	6	7		10	8		11	9											9
1,200	11		2	3	4	5	6	7	8	10			11		9	1									10
600	9		2	3	4		6	7		9	8		11				1	5	10						11
2,500	9	1	2	3	4	5	6	7		9	8		11						10						12
1,000	10		2	3	4	5	6	7		9	8		11						10	1					13
	10		2	3	4	5	6	7		9	8		11						10	1					14
4,000	11		2	3	4	5	6	7		10	8			9					11	1					15
600	13		2	3	4	5	6			10	8		11	7				9		1					16
13,000	15		2	3	7	5	6			10	8		11		9			4		1					17
4,000	15		2	3	7	5	6		9	10	8		11					4		1					18
1,500	14		2	3	7	5	6			9			11					4		1	8	10			19
6,000	15		2	3	4	5	6			9	7		11						10	1	8				20
1,200	16		2	3	4	5	6		7	9	8									1		10	11		21
16,000			2	3	4	5	6			9	7								10	1	8		11		22
600	16		2	3	4	5	6			7	11		10	9					8	1					23
1,200	16		2	3	4	5	6			7	11			9					10	1	8				24
1,000	17		2	3	4	5	6		8	7	11				9				10	1					25
			2	3	4	5	6			7	11			9	8				10	1					26
600	17		2	3	4	5	6			7	11		8	9					10	1					27
5,000	17		2	3	4	5	6			7	11		8	9					10	1					28
500			2	3	4	5	6			7	11		8	9					10	1					29
	17		2	3	4	5	6			7	11		8	9					10	1					30
5,000	17		2	3	4	5	6			8	11		7	9	10					1					31
			2	3	4	5	6			8	11		7	9	10					1					32
	17		2	3	4	5				8	11		7	9	10			6		1					33
2,000			2	3	4	5			7	8	11			9	10			6		1					34
Appearances		10	34	34	34	33	32	14	7	34	32	1	26	20	9	1	1	7	15	22	4	2	2		
Goals (30)			1		3		1	1		3	2		3	7	3				2		1			2	ogs

1 untraced

Att.	Pos	Wynne	H Ross	Lockhart	Barron	Taylor	Dixon	Morrison	Sawley	Crawford	McInnes	Birchall	Lee	C Hogan	Duckworth	Welsh	Whittaker	Howarth	Driver	Towler	Storey	Bell	Edmondson		
5,000			2	3	4	5	6	7		10	8		11	9						1					1
Appearances			1	1	1	1	1	1		1	1		1	1						1					
Goals (0)																									

1903-04

With the trauma of the re-election application out of the way and thankfully with a successful outcome, the Turfites' secretary and team manager Ernest Mangnall turned his attention to the forthcoming campaign. Hopefully it would be one to bring some much-needed and overdue success to Turf Moor after a period in the doldrums since relegation from the top flight in 1900.

Following the disastrous 1902-03 season a number of first team regulars had left Turf Moor including centre forward Cornelius Hogan who had been the club's top scorer in both his seasons at Burnley. Other forwards Edward Lee and Harry Duckworth, both regulars, had also been released and George Lockhart, a virtual ever present at left back in his three years at Turf Moor, had obviously had enough of struggling in the English Second Division, and never returned from spending the summer in his native Scotland.

Dugald McFarlane
new centre forward from Barrow

A new centre forward Dugald McFarlane was signed from Barrow, along with his colleague inside forward William Jackson. Wingers Tom Aspden from Kettering and Henry Williams from Bolton also arrived. Goalscoring had indeed been a problem but keeping them out at the other end had also been difficult so Ernest Mangnall reckoned a goalkeeper and a centre half were very much a priority. William Green, Brentford's 21 year old custodian, was soon Turf Moor bound and Green would go on to give years of excellent service to Burnley FC, his career continuing until the arrival of a certain Jeremiah Dawson. The picture was completed with the signature of yet another Barrow player, rugged centre half David Walders.

Turf Moor finances were still stretched and as the new campaign got under way there, Burnley still did not have a reserve team. The groundshare with Burnley Belvedere was to continue for another season with a number of Belvedere players once again registering to play for Burnley, as amateurs. The arrangement had obviously suited the Belvedere camp in 1902-03, they had finished as runners-up in the Lancashire Amateur League and had won the North East Lancashire Combination Shield.

After a promising first month of the new season, rumours began to circulate that another of the Burnley players was about to be sold to balance the Turf Moor books. Speculation was rife about the stars who would be obvious targets, new captain Fred Barron, popular local hero Arthur Dixon and full back Henry Ross, all of whom were predicted to have big futures in the game, possibly away from Turf Moor.

The news finally broke that a familiar face was indeed to leave, but it wasn't a player, it was secretary/manager Ernest Mangnall who had resigned to take up a similar position with Manchester United! Given that Burnley and United had already met twice, once in a friendly at the Reds' Clayton ground and also in the opening Turf Moor League fixture of the season, there were disgruntled mutterings among the Burnley faithful that Mangnall had been "tapped up". The natives were particularly restless because Ernest Mangnall's immediate predecessor, Harry Bradshaw, had left Turf Moor in similar circumstances four years earlier to join Woolwich Arsenal.

The Burnley directors wasted no time in appointing a successor to Ernest Mangnall. Within days the chairman/secretary of Oswaldtwistle Rovers, Spencer Whittaker was in the Turf Moor hot seat. Whittaker, forever known as Spen, would be responsible purely for first team matters with director W.R.Thornton taking over the club's secretarial duties. Spen Whittaker certainly came from a footballing family, his brother Nat Whittaker had been the secretary of the Southern League since 1894 and a member of the FA Council since 1897.

Whittaker inherited a team that had lost only once in seven games, were still unbeaten at home and lay in fourth position. It was still very early in the season but, after the first half hour or so of his first game in charge, against Blackpool at Turf Moor, he must have thought the job was going to be easy. His side was a goal up, completely in charge and looking as though they might end the day in second place in Division Two. Alas, the fat lady then started to sing, Blackpool turned the game on its head with four goals, and David Walders crashed a late penalty high over the crossbar.

Welcome to professional football team management!

During the early days of Spen Whittaker's tenure, there were plenty of goals in Burnley's matches but unfortunately too many of them went in at the wrong end. The FA Cup started promisingly with a qualifying round tie against non-league Keswick eventually being switched to Turf Moor and the Turfites cruising home 8-0, although it took until the second half to open up the Cumbrians' defence. In the following three matches, all away, the Burnley defences were breached fifteen times, with three of the goals scored by Lancashire Combination side Darwen, to end Turf Moor interest in the FA Cup for another season.

A new player was added to the squad when Rochdale inside forward Jimmy Hogan was signed in November 1903. Hogan was a native of Nelson and had already played for his home town club and as a teenage amateur for Burnley Belvedere. Although he would blossom into an accomplished player for a number of clubs, Jimmy Hogan would go on to become famous as an innovative and influential coach, particularly on the continent where he was idolised as something of a football genius.

After the turn of the year, the apparently ubiquitous Burnley scouting system unearthed another gem when 19-year-old defender Hugh Moffat arrived at Turf Moor from his home town club, Congleton. Moffat was an extremely skilful left back but was equally comfortable at left half back and would go on to feature prominently in the Burnley defence for many years and would also play for his country.

Hugh Moffat
signed from Congleton, would go on to play for England

In February, after a 2-1 win at Burton United and following an unbeaten League run stretching back to mid-December, Burnley were in second place their best position of the season, and just about in touch with runaway leaders Preston. It was as good as it got however and a crushing 0-4 defeat at Woolwich was the beginning of something of a slump as the campaign approached its climax. Five defeats and just two victories in the final ten matches put paid to any hopes of a promotion that would have been remarkable after the bitter disappointment of 1902-03.

The campaign concluded, for the second season in succession, with a visit to Edgeley Park. Perhaps summing up Burnley's progress under Spen Whittaker the result was a 2-2 draw, an improvement on April 1903 when the Turfites had been thrashed 3-0 by Stockport to just about confirm that the wooden spoon was destined for Turf Moor. It was not enough for County however who subsequently lost their league status.

The final Second Division table demonstrated just how tight the competition at the top had been. Ironically Burnley, frustratingly inconsistent, had beaten all the top three at Turf Moor, and had dropped points against all the bottom four!

The Turfites had been up in the top six for almost the whole season and a fifth place finish undoubtedly represented a significant improvement on the catastrophic 1902-03 campaign. In truth however Burnley were almost always just off the pace and although it had been an encouraging start for the new man in charge, Spen Whittaker, things had to get worse before they got better.

More difficult times lay ahead.

1903-04 - Second Division

		P	W	D	L	F	A	Pts
1	Preston NE	34	20	10	4	62	24	50
2	Woolwich A	34	21	7	6	91	22	49
3	Manchester U	34	20	8	6	65	33	48
4	Bristol C	34	18	6	10	73	41	42
5	BURNLEY	34	15	9	10	50	55	39
6	Grimsby T	34	14	8	12	50	49	36
7	Bolton W	34	12	10	12	59	41	34
8	Barnsley	34	11	10	13	38	57	32
9	Gainsborough T	34	14	3	17	53	60	31
10	Bradford C	34	12	7	15	45	59	31
11	Chesterfield	34	11	8	15	37	45	30
12	Lincoln C	34	11	8	15	41	58	30
13	Burslem PV	34	10	9	15	54	52	29
14	Burton U	34	11	7	16	45	61	29
15	Blackpool	34	11	5	18	40	67	27
16	Stockport C	34	8	11	15	40	72	27
17	Glossop	34	10	6	18	57	64	26
18	Leicester F	34	6	10	18	42	82	22

1903-04

Manager : J Ernest Mangnall until October 1903, then Spencer (Spen) Whittaker

Division Two (5th)

	No	Date			Opponents	Result		h/t	Goalscorers/times	Opp. goal times
	1	Sep	5	a	Chesterfield	D	0-0	0-0		
	2		7	h	MANCHESTER U	W	2-0	2-0	McFarlane 20, Dixon 40	
	3		12	h	BOLTON W	D	0-0	0-0		
	4		19	h	BURSLEM P V	W	1-0	1-0	Crawford 33	
	5		26	a	Preston N E	L	0-2	0-2		13p, 43
	6	Oct	3	h	GRIMSBY T	W	2-0	2-0	Jackson 26, Aspden 35	
	7		10	a	Leicester F	D	0-0	0-0		
	8		17	h	BLACKPOOL	L	1-4	1-2	Jackson 15	35, 38, 50, 70
	9		24	a	Gainsborough T	W	2-1	1-1	Jackson 5, Jenkinson 70	43
	10	Nov	7	a	Bristol C	L	0-6	0-4		10p,13,24,35,60,75
	11		21	a	Glossop	L	2-6	2-1	Walders 12, Williams 26	10,51,62,73,79,84
	12		28	h	BRADFORD C	W	3-2	2-1	Jackson 10, Whittam 35, Walders 87	25, 60
	13	Dec	19	a	Lincoln C	L	1-3	0-2	Williams 84	30, 43, 49
	14		25	h	BURTON U	W	2-1	1-0	McFarlane 22, Dixon 70	55p
	15		26	h	STOCKPORT C	W	2-0	2-0	Jackson 1, McFarlane 42	
	16	Jan	2	h	CHESTERFIELD	W	2-1	1-0	Dixon 25, Aspden 58	48
	17		9	a	Bolton W	D	1-1	1-1	Williams 32	37
	18		16	a	Burslem P V	D	2-2	0-0	Hogan 83, Williams 85	47, 51
	19		23	h	PRESTON N E	W	2-1	0-1	Aspden (2) 75, 81	21
	20		30	a	Grimsby T	D	0-0	0-0		
	21	Feb	6	h	LEICESTER F	W	2-1	0-1	Williams 52, Dixon 74p	30
	22		13	a	Blackpool	W	5-0	2-0	Dixon (2) 17, 82p, McFarlane (2) 35, 72, Hogan 63	
	23		20	h	GAINSBOROUGH T	W	2-0	1-0	Williams 25, Bell 50	
	24		27	a	Burton U	W	2-1	1-1	Hogan 44, McFarlane 63	30
	25		29	a	Woolwich A	L	0-4	0-3		6, 28, 37, 68
	26	Mar	5	h	BRISTOL C	L	2-3	1-1	Hogan 7, Williams 48	15, 70, 76
	27		12	a	Manchester U	L	1-3	0-3	Bell 85	10, 22, 43
	28		19	h	GLOSSOP	L	2-4	1-1	Hogan 41, Williams 70	29, 60, 64, 80
	29		26	a	Bradford C	L	0-3	0-2		20, 35, 85
	30	Apr	1	h	BARNSLEY	D	2-2	0-1	Barron 58, Jackson 63	35, 61
	31		2	h	WOOLWICH A	W	1-0	0-0	Ross 56p	
Jenkinson's last game	32		9	a	Barnsley	D	1-1	1-0	McFarlane 43	80
	33		16	h	LINCOLN C	W	3-1	1-0	McFarlane 23, Moffat 55, Bell 57	70
Henry Ross' last game	34		23	a	Stockport C	D	2-2	0-1	McFarlane 62, Hall 82og	21, 86

FA Cup

	Rd	Date			Opponents	Result		h/t	Goalscorers/times	Opp. goal times
At Turf Moor	Q3	Oct	31	a	Keswick	W	8-0	0-0	Walders (3) 50, 70, 78, Jackson (4) 52, 55, 86, 89, Crawford 72	
	Q4	Nov	14	a	Darwen	L	0-3	0-1		30, 60, 68p

Final, Manchester C 1-0 Bolton W, at Crystal Palace.

Other matches (friendlies and/or as detailed)

	Date			Opponents	Result		Goalscorers
	Sep	1	a	Manchester U	L	0-1	
East Lancs Charity Cup semi	Oct	19	h	ACCRINGTON	L	0-2	
Div 2 fixture aban 63m-fog	Dec	5	a	Woolwich A	aban	0-1	
		7	a	Tottenham H	L	0-4	
		12	h	ROYAL ARTILLERY	W	4-0	Hogan (2), McFarlane, Wilkinson
Lancs Cup	Jan	18	h	MANCHESTER C	W	2-1	McFarlane, Jackson
Lancs Cup		25	a	Preston N E	L	1-5	McFarlane
	Apr	25	a	Barrow	W	1-0	J.Walders og

Att.	Pos	W Green	H Ross	Jenkinson	Barron	D Walders	Dixon	Aspden	Crawford	McFarlane	Jackson	Williams	Taylor	Booth	Towler	J Hogan	Whittam	Bell	Swain	Moffat	Lowe		
3,000		1	2	3	4	5	6	7	8	9	10	11											1
5,000		1	2	3	4	5	6	7	8	9	10	11											2
7,000	3	1	2	3	4	5	6	7	8	9	10	11											3
6,000	3	1	2	3	4		6	7	8	9	10	11	5										4
10,000	5	1	2	3	4	5	6	7	8	9	10	11											5
5,000	4	1	2	3	4	5	6	7	8	9	10	11											6
5,000	4	1	2	3	4	5	6	7	8	9	10	11											7
4,500	6	1		3	4	5	6	7	8	9	10	11		2									8
	6	1	2	8	4	5	3		7	9	10	11	6										9
6,000	8		2	9	4	5	3		7		10	11	6		1	8							10
	8	1	2		4	5	3		10	9	7	11	6			8							11
1,000	6	1	2		4	5	3			9	7	11	6			8	10						12
2,000	8	1		3	4	5	2	7		10		11	6			8	9						13
4,000		1	2		4	5	3	7		10		11	6			8	9						14
3,000	6	1	2		4	5	3	7		9	10	11	6			8							15
3,000		1	2		4	5	3	7		9	10	11	6			8							16
6,000	4	1	2		4	5	3	7		9	10	11	6			8							17
	5	1	2		4	5	3	7		9	10	11	6			8							18
10,000	4	1	2		4	5	3	7		9	10	11	6			8							19
4,000	4	1	2	9	4	5	3	7				11	6			8		10					20
4,000	4	1	2		4	5	3	7		9		11	6			8		10					21
2,000	4	1	2		4	5	3	7		9		11	6			8		10					22
4,000	2	1	2		4	5	3	7		9		11	6			8		10					23
	2	1	2		4	5	3	7		9		11	6			8		10					24
4,000	3	1	2		4	5	3	7		9		11	6			8		10					25
4,000	3	1	2	6	4	5	3	7				11				8	9	10					26
14,000	4	1	2	6	4	5	3	7		9	11					8		10					27
3,000	4	1	2		4	5	3	7		9		11				8		10	6				28
10,000	5	1	2		4	5	3	7		9		11	6			8		10					29
3,000	5	1	2	10	4	5	7			9	6	11				8				3			30
5,000	5	1	2	10	4	5		7		9	6	11				8				3			31
	5	1	2	10	4	5	3	7		9	6	11				8							32
3,500	5	1	2		4	5	3	7		9						8		11		6	10		33
2,000		1	2		4	5	3	7		9		11				8				6	10		34
Appearances		33	32	17	34	33	33	29	11	31	21	32	19	1	1	25	4	11	1	4	2		
Goals (50)			1	1	1	2	6	4	1	8	6	8				5	1	4		1		1	og

Att.	W Green	H Ross	Jenkinson	Barron	D Walders	Dixon	Aspden	Crawford	McFarlane	Jackson	Williams	Taylor	
	1	2	9	4	5	3	7	8		10	11	6	Q3
3,000	1	2		4	5	3	7	8	9	10	11	6	Q4
Appearances	2	2	1	2	2	2	2	2	1	2	2	2	
Goals (8)					3			1		4			

1904-05

THE WORLD OF FOOTBALL

On 21 May 1904 was held the inaugural meeting of Federation Internationale de Football Association (FIFA) in Paris. Nations represented at that historic gathering were Belgium, Denmark, The Netherlands, Sweden, Switzerland and the hosts France. Conspicuous by their absence were the English FA who had treated their letter of invitation with some disdain. With that peculiar short-sightedness that has occasionally characterised British, in particular English, thinking, the FA Council decided they could see no need for such a body. The following year attitudes softened, an FA representative attended a meeting in Berne, in Switzerland and England's football rulers were convinced. Within another year the FIFA Presidency was in the hands of FA Treasurer D.B. Woolfall, evidence of England's accepted standing and importance in the world game.

Preparations for Burnley's new season were somewhat disrupted with the departure, in the summer of 1904, of one of Turf Moor's bright young stars. Henry Ross had been firmly established in the right back position and a virtual ever present for the past three difficult seasons following his arrival from Brechin Harps in 1899. Ross had been lured to Fulham, then in the Southern League, but ambitious enough to have appointed former Burnley Manager Harry Bradshaw to lead them in their quest for membership of the Football League. Bradshaw felt ready for a new challenge after leading Woolwich Arsenal to promotion from the Second Division to become the first London Club to compete in the Football League's top flight. Following Ross out of Turf Moor, after just a single season, were Tom Aspden, William Jackson and Henry Williams, all forwards, and William Jenkinson who had returned to Burnley in 1903 after a year at West Ham. There were rumours that Arthur Dixon had also been attracted to the bright lights of London but Dixon eventually decided his future lay at Turf Moor, for the time being at least. One other departure was long serving trainer Jack Stuttard who had also moved to Fulham.

Team-building began with the arrival of left back Jack Walders from Barrow, brother of David Walders who had himself moved from Barrow a year earlier and had created such a favourable impression in making the Turfites' centre half position very much his own. Ironically Jack's last game for Barrow had been in a friendly match against Burnley in April 1904, part of the transfer arrangement that had taken brother David to Turf Moor, and he had signed off by scoring a goal.....unfortunately it was in his own net and it gave the Turfites a 1-0 win! Jack Walders was followed to Turf Moor by two more players with Cumbrian connections, Joe Smith from Keswick and his namesake Richard Smith from Workington, who would go on to score plenty of goals for Burnley as the club slowly but surely began to build the most successful side in Turf Moor history.

After two years Burnley's Reserve team was resurrected and entered in the North East Lancashire Combination and Turf Moor bade farewell to Burnley Belvedere who continued life in the Lancashire Amateur League at a new ground at Heasandford.

The first match of the season was against West Brom at Turf Moor. It was a disappointing opening to the campaign, with the Baggies coming from behind to win 4-1 with four second half goals. Jack Walders made his Burnley debut at left back in that game and with David Walders at centre half they became the first brothers to play alongside each other for Burnley in a league fixture. Brothers had actually appeared together for Burnley before, when Jack and William Gair lined up alongside each other during 1883, but it was not to happen again until Vince and Richard Overson appeared in the same Burnley side in 1979, more than 75 years later.

After ten defeats in eleven matches Burnley had slumped to second bottom, above only Doncaster, who had been the Turfites' only victims in that dismal run. A welcome win at home to Glossop, themselves in the re-election zone, set Burnley up for a crucial visit to Chesterfield on the last Saturday of November 1904, a day that was to prove unique in Burnley Football Club history.

David Walders
joined at Turf Moor by his brother Jack

On a foggy morning the main Burnley party set off by train and would change at Manchester for Chesterfield. Left back Hugh Moffat was to join up with the group on the station platform but missed the connection and found he could not catch another suitable train for more than two hours. Moffat eventually arrived in Chesterfield just after the final whistle, to discover that his ten team mates had managed reasonably well without him and had secured a point in a 1-1 draw The Spireites had even decided to try to balance things out a little by missing an early penalty. It was more than sixty years before substitutes would be introduced, no twelfth man had accompanied the team and the new trainer, J H Barker, had not been registered as a player. It was a fiasco but at least the players had shown their battling qualities on a day of adversity.

Richard Smith
early goalscoring hero

Although there have been cases of Burnley playing with a man or men short for part of matches, the game at Chesterfield is the only occasion in the Club's history when the team competed in the whole of a senior match with only ten players. There was a rap over the knuckles to come from the Football League, who fined Burnley one guinea for not travelling to Saltergate with a twelfth man.

Ironically that day seemed to be the turning point in the season for the Turfites. Although after the Chesterfield match they were still in 17th place, four successive victories in December improved the situation somewhat and ensured a climb into mid table. One of those wins was a hard earned 2-1 victory at Barnsley on Christmas Eve, Burnley's first ever success at Oakwell. It was the Turfites' only victory on the road that season other than at Doncaster who finished some way adrift at the bottom and failed to win re-election.

Another rare highspot of a mediocre season came at Turf Moor in February 1905 when Burnley's visitors were Burslem Port Vale who were struggling and were destined to finish in the bottom three. The Turfites hit top form that day and were 4-0 up by half time thanks to a purple patch of four goals in just seventeen minutes, including two from Dick Smith. Smith completed his hat-trick near the end, the first of his Burnley career and he went on to become one of Turf Moor's early goalscoring heroes.

During the final week of the League season Burnley enjoyed a morale boosting 3-0 win against old adversaries Blackburn Rovers in the final of the East Lancashire Charity Cup, the first time that the Turfites had won the trophy, any trophy, since 1899.

Burnley's final League fixture was at Anfield against Liverpool, already Second Division Champions and on their way back to the top flight. The Reds' impressive performance as they cruised to a 3-0 victory demonstrated how far the Turfites had yet to go in their crusade to climb back into the top flight. It was still to be seven long years before the men from Turf Moor would take their place among football's elite.

1904-05 - Second Division

		P	W	D	L	F	A	Pts
1	Liverpool	34	27	4	3	93	25	58
2	Bolton W	34	27	2	5	87	32	56
3	Manchester U	34	24	5	5	81	30	53
4	Bristol C	34	19	4	11	66	45	42
5	Chesterfield	34	14	11	9	44	35	39
6	Gainsborough T	34	14	8	12	61	58	36
7	Barnsley	34	14	5	15	38	56	33
8	Bradford C	34	12	8	14	45	49	32
9	Lincoln C	34	12	7	15	42	40	31
10	West Bromwich A	34	13	4	17	56	48	30
11	BURNLEY	34	12	6	16	43	52	30
12	Glossop	34	10	10	14	37	46	30
13	Grimsby T	34	11	8	15	33	46	30
14	Leicester F	34	11	7	16	40	55	29
15	Blackpool	34	9	10	15	36	48	28
16	Burslem PV	34	10	7	17	47	72	27
17	Burton U	34	8	4	22	30	84	20
18	Doncaster R	34	3	2	29	23	81	8

1904-05

Manager : Spen Whittaker

Division Two (11th)

Note		Date			Opponents	Result		h/t	Goalscorers/times	Opp. goal times
	1	Sep	3	h	WEST BROMWICH A	L	1-4	1-0	Moffat 28	48, 65, 75, 84
	2		5	h	CHESTERFIELD	W	2-0	1-0	Hogan 38, J.Smith 80	
	3		10	a	Bolton W	L	0-4	0-3		20, 28, 37, 85
	4		17	a	Grimsby T	L	0-1	0-0		87
	5		24	h	BLACKPOOL	L	0-1	0-1		31
	6	Oct	1	a	Doncaster R	W	2-0	0-0	R.Smith 50, McFarlane 75	
	7		8	h	GAINSBOROUGH T	L	1-3	1-0	Ross 8	60, 85, 87
	8		15	a	Burton U	L	1-3	1-2	J.Smith 19	5, 37, 60
	9		22	h	LIVERPOOL	L	0-2	0-0		49, 84
	10		26	a	Gainsborough T	L	1-3	0-1	Barron 63p	2, 52, 77
	11		29	a	Burslem P V	L	1-3	1-0	McFarlane 15	58p, 68, 77
	12	Nov	5	h	BRISTOL C	L	2-3	1-1	McFarlane 42, Barron 55p	4, 65p, 85
	13		12	a	Manchester U	L	0-1	0-0		50
	14		19	h	GLOSSOP	W	3-1	3-0	Hogan 4, McFarlane (2) 7, 25	84
10 players only	15		26	a	Chesterfield	D	1-1	0-0	Hogan 86	57
	16	Dec	3	h	BRADFORD C	W	2-1	2-0	Ross 12p, Marshall 23	79
	17		17	h	LEICESTER F	W	2-0	0-0	Marshall 52, McFarlane 78	
	18		24	a	Barnsley	W	2-1	1-0	R.Smith 22, McFarlane 75	87
	19		26	h	GRIMSBY T	W	1-0	0-0	Dixon 48p	
	20		31	a	West Bromwich A	D	1-1	0-1	McFarlane 70	30
	21	Jan	7	h	BOLTON W	L	0-1	0-0		58
	22		21	a	Blackpool	L	0-2	0-1		29, 60
	23		28	h	DONCASTER R	W	4-3	1-2	Hogan (2) 35, 53, D.Walders 77, McFarlane 78	1, 20, 83
Burnley's 500th League game	24	Feb	11	h	BURTON U	D	1-1	0-1	Marshall 89	15
	25		25	h	BURSLEM P V	W	5-0	4-0	R.Smith (3) 23, 40, 87, McFarlane 27, Marshall 29	
	26	Mar	4	a	Bristol C	D	0-0	0-0		
	27		11	h	MANCHESTER U	W	2-0	0-0	J.Walders 59, Hogan 87	
	28		18	a	Glossop	D	0-0	0-0		
	29	Apr	1	a	Bradford C	L	1-4	0-2	McFarlane 50	10, 23, 65, 70
	30		8	h	LINCOLN C	W	2-1	1-0	R.Smith 2, McFarlane 80	75
	31		15	a	Leicester F	D	2-2	1-2	Hogan 20, R.Smith 70	42, 44
	32		21	a	Lincoln C	L	0-2	0-1		15, 84
	33		22	h	BARNSLEY	W	3-0	2-0	McFarlane 29, Barron 39, R.Smith 80	
Jimmy Hogan's last game	34		29	a	Liverpool	L	0-3	0-1		40, 65, 75

FA Cup

	Date			Opponents	Result		h/t	Goalscorers/times	Opp. goal times
Q	Jan	14	h	LINCOLN C	D	1-1	1-1	Marshall 30	22
rep		18	a	Lincoln C	L	2-3	1-1	Marshall 43, J.Smith 60	44, 63, 80

Final, Aston Villa 2-0 Newcastle U, at Crystal Palace.

Other matches (friendlies and/or as detailed)

Note	Date			Opponents	Result		Goalscorers
Lancs Cup	Oct	7	a	Liverpool	L	1-7	McFarlane
	Dec	10	a	Southport C	W	2-1	Thornley, Hogan
East Lancs Charity Cup semi	Jan	2	a	Accrington	W	3-2	Marshall (2), Hogan
	Mar	25	a	Woolwich A	L	0-3	
East Lancs Charity Cup final	Apr	24	h	BLACKBURN R	W	3-0	Hogan (2), Taylor
		25	a	Congleton	L	0-1	

Att.	Pos	W Green	Dixon	J Walders	Barron	D Walders	Moffat	Atkinson	J Hogan	McFarlane	Bell	Lowe	J Taylor	J Smith	Beard	Hutchinson	Henderson	A Ross	Driver	R Smith	Jackson	Marshall		
5,389		1	2	3	4	5	6	7	8	9	10	11												1
4,000		1	3		4	5	2	7	8	9	10		6	11										2
13,000	15	1	2		4	5	3	8		9			6	11	7	10								3
5,000	17	1	2	8	4	5		7		9			6	11			3	10						4
4,000	17	1	2		4	5		7		9			6	11			3	10	8					5
2,000	15	1	2		4	5		7		9			6	11			3	10		8				6
3,000	16	1	2	3	4	5		7		10			6	11				9		8				7
	15	1	2		4	5		7		10			6	11			3	9		8				8
9,000	16	1	3		4	5	6	7			10			11			2	9		8				9
4,000		1	3	8	4	5	6	7						11			2	10		9				10
1,500	17	1	3		4	5	6	7	8	10			2	11						9				11
3,000	17	1	2		4	5	3	7	8	10			6	11						9				12
15,000	17	1			4	5	3	7	8	10			6				2			9	11			13
2,200	17	1	2		4	5	3	7	8	10			6	11						9				14
	17	1	2		4	5			8	10			6					3		9		7	10 players only	15
3,000	14	1	2		4	5	3		8	10			6					11		9		7		16
3,000	13	1	2	6	4		3		8	10			5					11		9		7		17
2,000		1	2		4	5	3		8	10			6					11		9		7		18
		1	2		4	5	3		8	10			6					11		9		7		19
7,374	10	1	2	6	4		3		8	10			5					11		9		7		20
9,000	11	1	2		4	5	3		8	10	11		6							9		7		21
3,000	14	1	2	6		4	3			9	10		5	11						8		7		22
2,000	11	1	2		4	5	3		8	10			6	11						9		7		23
2,000	12	1	2	6	4	5	3		8	10								11		9		7		24
1,000	11	1	2		4	5	3		8	10			6					11		9		7		25
4,000	10	1	2	11	4	5	3		8	9			6					10				7		26
7,000	10	1	2	7	4	5			8	10			6				3	11		9				27
2,000	9	1	2	7	4	5			8	10			6				3	11		9				28
8,000	10	1	2	7	4	5			8	9			6	11			3	10						29
5,000	9	1	2	7	4	5	3		8	10			6					11		9				30
5,000	10	1	2	7	4	5	3		8	10			6					11		9				31
	11	1	2	7	4	5	3		8	10			6					11		9				32
3,000	10	1	2	7	4	5	3		8	10			6					11		9				33
10,000		1	2	7	4	5	3		8	10			6					11		9				34
Appearances		34	33	17	33	32	25	14	25	32	5	1	30	15	1	1	10	24	1	27	1	12		
Goals (43)			1	1	3	1	1		7	13				2				2		8		4		

Att.	Pos	W Green	Dixon	J Walders	Barron	D Walders	Moffat	Atkinson	J Hogan	McFarlane	Bell	Lowe	J Taylor	J Smith	Beard	Hutchinson	Henderson	A Ross	Driver	R Smith	Jackson	Marshall	
4,000		1	2		4	5	3		8	10			6					11		9		7	Q
		1	2		4	5	3		8	9			6	11				10				7	rep
Appearances		2	2		2	2	2		2	2			2	1				2		1		2	
Goals (3)														1								2	

1905-06

The main arrival in the summer of 1905 was defender Jack Cretney from Newcastle. Cretney was a fierce competitor who would go on to provide many years of sterling service to the Burnley cause as the club slowly began to build foundations for a solid future. Other new signings included two Scots, Andrew Davidson from Clyde and Bernard Murphy from Duntocher Hibernians. It was Murphy who scored Burnley's first goal of the season on his league debut, a 2-1 win at West Brom, Burnley's first ever victory at The Hawthorns since Albion had moved there in 1900.

Jack Cretney
new signing from Newcastle U

As the season got into its stride one of Burnley's star players of 1904-05, Jimmy Hogan, left Turf Moor after a dispute over wages. He went to play for Nelson but was subsequently lured south to join the growing ex-Burnley contingent at Fulham led by former Turfites' manager Harry Bradshaw. Bradshaw had already attracted Henry Ross and trainer Jack Stuttard to Craven Cottage and he saw Hogan as a key player in Fulham's quest for Football League membership which was indeed gained in 1907.

At the end of November 1905, after a single goal victory against Gainsborough at Turf Moor, the Turfites were up to fifth position and still very much in the hunt for the promotion craved by all at Turf Moor. It was as good as it got however and Burnley won just one of the next twelve matches in League and FA Cup and the season was destined to be another campaign of anti climax.

On Christmas Day 1905 Burnley's present to their long suffering fans was their best performance and biggest win of the season, 4-1 against Blackpool at Turf Moor. Centre forward Alf Wood, signed from Blackpool's reserves in the summer, scored on his debut either side of two goals from Dugald McFarlane, with the Seasiders making it 3-1 to the Turfites at half time. It was a second half goal from winger Jack Walders however that got the crowd talking and comparing it to other memorable goals in the past. Walders had been signed as a defender but was extremely quick and quite often played on the right wing. After an hour's play Walders broke up a Blackpool attack on the edge of his own penalty area and sprinted down the middle evading tackle after tackle. When he reached the visitor's penalty area he let fly with a ferocious ground shot which crashed into the net just inside the post giving the keeper absolutely no chance. The Turf Moor crowd cheered Jack Walders to the echo with even the Blackpool contingent applauding a very special goal. It was speculated in the Burnley Express that the goal, Jack Walders' first of the season and only the second of his Burnley career, was possibly the finest ever seen at Turf Moor.

In January 1906 Burnley paid their first ever visit to London for an FA Cup tie when they travelled to White Hart Lane for the first of many epic confrontations with Tottenham Hotspur. Spurs were then playing in the Southern League but were too good for the Turfites on the day and eased into the next round with a 2-0 win. A crowd of 20,000, the largest attendance at any Burnley match that season, saw a polished performance from the celebrated England international Vivian Woodward, an amateur all his football career, who scored one of Tottenham's goals.

It was a disappointing FA Cup exit but perhaps not unexpected with the Turfites in the middle of a poor run of form, the win against Blackpool had been their only success since November. Two more defeats followed including a 0-5 hammering at Lincoln before the losing run was halted with draws at Leeds and Burslem. Burnley were now twelfth and, after a promising start to the season, the dream of promotion had, once again, almost certainly faded away. A 2-1 win against Barnsley, only the second victory since November, was a tonic but then the Turfites travelled to Clapton Orient, the League's bottom club, and were ignominiously thrashed 3-0. It was only Orient's second victory since September and their biggest win of the season in their first campaign as a league club.

Perhaps the season's most exciting game was a seven goal thriller against Leeds at Turf Moor. Burnley were irresistible early on and soon established a 3-0 lead with two goals from Andrew Davidson and one from Arthur Bell. City pulled one back before Albert Smith made the score 4-1 and, with almost half an hour still to play, the points seemed to be Burnley's for sure. The Turfites relaxed a little too much however and Leeds scored what seemed little more than a consolation to make it 4-2. When they pulled another goal back, 4-3, the Burnley crowd began hooting at the referee to blow the final whistle, which he eventually did to the relief of the fans and the players. Two of the Leeds goals that day were scored by a young centre forward called David Wilson. Less than six months later he and his team would come up against the men from Turf Moor again, this time with tragic consequences.

The victory against Leeds was the start of a decent run-in to the end of the season although all realistic hopes of promotion had gone. Dugald McFarlane scored his first Burnley hat-trick in a 3-1 win at Burton United and League newcomers Chelsea were beaten 2-0 at Turf Moor with goals from Arthur Bell and Dick Smith. A 1-0 win at Gainsborough was followed by a visit to Turf Moor by the League leaders Bristol City who were unbeaten away from home since the first day of the season. In front of a crowd of 10,000, Turf Moor's biggest of the season, Burnley came back from a goal down with goals from Dick Smith and Andrew Davidson to be within five minutes of a memorable victory before City equalised to earn a deserved 2-2 draw.

In the last week of the season Burnley and Blackburn Rovers met in the final of the East Lancashire Charity Cup competition, drawing 2-2 at Turf Moor. Burnley were quite willing to play a period of extra time and a replay if necessary. For some reason Rovers refused so Burnley were able to hold on to the trophy they had won in 1905. At least the campaign had produced a trophy but the real triumph, promotion back to the top flight, had eluded the Turfites yet again.

OBITUARY

JACK KEENAN

DIED 16 MARCH 1906, AGED 42.

Jack Keenan was born in Clitheroe, of Irish extraction, in 1864 and played for his home town club before his transfer to Burnley in 1884. He very quickly established himself in the half back line of Burnley's senior team and was quite often the sole Englishman in a side that otherwise consisted entirely of Scots. His consistent play brought him to the notice of the international selectors and he was called up to join the England party for the match against Scotland in Glasgow in March 1888. He was not chosen to play however and never got another chance to represent his country. Jack Keenan was a hard man and regularly appeared alongside the equally formidable Dannie Friel well into the days of league football and was a key member of the side that won the Lancashire Cup in 1890 when Blackburn Rovers were defeated in the final. After around 300 senior games Keenan made his final league appearance for Burnley in November 1892 and continued to assist the Turfites' reserves before retiring from the game in 1893. He had worked in a local brewery for a number of years but had been ill for some time before his death.

RIP

Jimmy Hogan
a short career at Burnley, a huge influence in Europe

1905-06 - Second Division

		P	W	D	L	F	A	Pts
1	Bristol C	38	30	6	2	83	28	66
2	Manchester U	38	28	6	4	90	28	62
3	Chelsea	38	22	9	7	90	37	53
4	West Bromwich A	38	22	8	8	79	36	52
5	Hull C	38	19	6	13	67	54	44
6	Leeds C	38	17	9	12	59	47	43
7	Leicester F	38	15	12	11	53	48	42
8	Grimsby T	38	15	10	13	46	46	40
9	BURNLEY	38	15	8	15	42	53	38
10	Stockport C	38	13	9	16	44	56	35
11	Bradford C	38	13	8	17	46	60	34
12	Barnsley	38	12	9	17	60	62	33
13	Lincoln C	38	12	6	20	69	72	30
14	Blackpool	38	10	9	19	37	62	29
15	Gainsborough T	38	12	4	22	44	57	28
16	Glossop	38	10	8	20	49	71	28
17	Burslem PV	38	12	4	22	49	82	28
18	Chesterfield	38	10	8	20	40	72	28
19	Burton U	38	10	6	22	34	67	26
20	Clapton O	38	7	7	24	35	78	21

1905-06

Manager : Spen Whittaker

Division Two (9th)

Note	No	Date		h/a	Opponents	Result		h/t	Goalscorers/times	Opp. goal times
	1	Sep	2	a	West Bromwich A	W	2-1	0-1	Murphy 70, McFarlane 72	30
	2		4	h	BRADFORD C	D	0-0	0-0		
	3		11	h	CHESTERFIELD	D	1-1	0-0	A.Smith 71	62
	4		16	a	Hull C	D	1-1	1-0	Cretney 15	65
	5		23	h	LINCOLN C	W	2-1	2-0	Barron 34, Murphy 37	78
	6		30	a	Chesterfield	L	0-3	0-2		10, 40, 51
	7	Oct	2	h	LEICESTER F	L	0-2	0-1		25, 53
	8		7	h	BURSLEM P V	L	1-3	1-1	R.Smith 30	42, 64, 70p
	9		14	a	Barnsley	W	2-1	0-1	Davidson 75, R.Smith 83	22
	10		21	h	CLAPTON O	W	3-0	1-0	Cretney (2) 5, 62, R.Smith 66	
	11		28	h	GRIMSBY T	D	0-0	0-0		
	12	Nov	11	h	BURTON U	W	1-0	1-0	A.Smith 10	
	13		18	a	Chelsea	L	0-1	0-0		85
	14		25	h	GAINSBOROUGH T	W	1-0	1-0	McFarlane 29	
	15	Dec	2	a	Bristol C	L	0-2	0-1		25, 70
	16		9	h	MANCHESTER U	L	1-3	1-1	Cretney 41	3, 60, 75
	17		16	a	Glossop	D	1-1	1-0	R.Smith 4	73
	18		23	h	STOCKPORT C	L	0-1	0-1		24
	19		25	h	BLACKPOOL	W	4-1	3-1	McFarlane (2) 6, 29, Wood 23, J.Walders 63	38
	20		30	h	WEST BROMWICH A	L	0-2	0-1		43, 89
	21	Jan	6	a	Leicester F	L	0-2	0-0		75, 88
	22		20	h	HULL C	L	1-3	0-2	McFarlane 75	15, 30, 78
	23		27	a	Lincoln C	L	0-5	0-3		8,14,20p,60,80
	24	Feb	3	a	Leeds C	D	1-1	1-0	McFarlane 42	46
	25		10	a	Burslem P V	D	2-2	1-2	Bell 23, McFarlane 82	25, 35
	26		17	h	BARNSLEY	W	2-1	2-1	Davidson (2) 29, 44	5
	27		24	a	Clapton O	L	0-3	0-2		30, 43, 46
	28		27	a	Bradford C	W	1-0	0-0	Moffat 65	
	29	Mar	3	a	Grimsby T	L	0-2	0-1		18, 75p
	30		10	h	LEEDS C	W	4-3	3-1	Davidson (2) 9, 12, Bell 17, A.Smith 65	35, 84, 89
	31		17	a	Burton U	W	3-1	2-0	McFarlane (3) 33, 43, 70	86p
	32		24	h	CHELSEA	W	2-0	2-0	Bell 11, R.Smith 21	
	33		31	a	Gainsborough T	W	1-0	0-0	R.Smith 85	
	34	Apr	7	h	BRISTOL C	D	2-2	0-0	R.Smith 70, Davidson 80	56, 85
	35		13	a	Blackpool	W	1-0	1-0	Davidson 41	
	36		14	a	Manchester U	L	0-1	0-0		88
Jack Walders' last game	37		21	h	GLOSSOP	W	1-0	0-0	A.Smith 75	
David Walders' last game	38		28	a	Stockport C	L	1-3	0-2	Moffat 55p	20, 30, 75

FA Cup

No	Date		h/a	Opponents	Result		h/t	Goalscorers/times	Opp. goal times
1	Jan	13	a	Tottenham H	L	0-2	0-0		70, 80

Final, Everton 1-0 Newcastle U, at Crystal Palace.

Other matches (friendlies and/or as detailed)

Note	Date		h/a	Opponents	Result		Goalscorers	
Div 2 fixture aban 75m, flood	Sep	9	h	LEICESTER F	aban	1-0	Wood	
Lancs Cup		18	a	Bolton W	L	0-4		
Div 2 fixture aban 53m, fog	Nov	4	a	Leeds C	aban	1-1	Marshall	
East Lancs Charity Cup semi	Apr	23	h	ACCRINGTON	W	2-0	Davidson, Taylor	
East Lancs Charity Cup final		26	h	BLACKBURN R	D	2-2	R.Smith, J.Walders	Burnley hold Cup

Att.	Pos	W Green	Dixon	Moffat	Barron	D Walders	Cretney	J Walders	A Davidson	R Smith	McFarlane	Murphy	Marshall	A Smith	J Taylor	Parker	Greenwood	Campbell	Bell	Wood	Lovett	Riley	McNab	Whiteley	Mooney	Hargreaves	Whittaker	
7,223		1	2	3	4	5	6	7	8	9	10	11																1
8,000		1	2	3	4	5	6	7	8	9	10	11																2
1,500	4	1	2	3	4	5	6	11	8	9			7	10														3
6,000	4	1	2	3	4	5	10	7	8	9		11			6													4
6,000	5	1	2	3	4		10	7	11	9		8			6	5												5
4,000		1	2	3	4		10	7	11	9		8			6	5												6
1,500		1	2	3	4		10	7	11	9		8			6	5												7
3,000	10	1	2	3	4	5	6		8	9	10		7	11														8
4,000	7	1	3	6	4	5			8	9	10		7	11			2											9
3,500	5	1	3	6	4	5	10		8	9			7	11			2											10
4,000	5	1		6	4	5	10		8	9	11		7				2	3										11
3,000	5	1	3	6	4	5		7	8	9	10			11				2										12
8,000	5	1	3	6	4	5		7	8	9	10							2	11									13
4,000	5	1	3	6	4	5		7	8	9	10							2	11									14
8,000	5	1	3	6	4	5	10	7	8	9								2	11									15
8,000	8	1	3	6	4	5	10	7	8	9								2	11									16
2,000	7	1	3	6	4	5	9		8	10			7				2		11									17
2,000		1	3	6	4	5	9	7		10	8						2		11									18
6,000		1	3	6	4	5		7	10		8						2		11	9								19
6,500		1	3	6	4	5		7	10		8						2		11	9								20
		1	3	6	4		10	7		11	8				5		2			9								21
3,000	11		3	6	4		8	7		9	10				5			2	11		1							22
2,000	13	1	3	6			4		8		9		7	11		5		2	10									23
7,129	11	1	3	6	4		5	11	8		9		7					2	10									24
	12	1	3	6	4		5	11	8		9		7						10			2						25
4,000	10	1	3	6	4		5	11	8		9		7				2		10									26
		1		3	4		5	11	8	10			7		6		2			9								27
4,000	11	1		3	4	5		11	8	9				10	6		2						7					28
4,000	10	1	2	3	4	5		11	8	9				10	6									7				29
5,000	10	1		3	2	5	4	7	8	9				11	6				10									30
3,000	10	1		3	2	5	4	7	8	9	10			11	6													31
8,000	9	1		3	2	5	4	7	8	9				11	6				10									32
	8	1		3	2	5	4	7	8	9				11	6				10									33
10,000	9	1		3	2	5	4	7	8	9				11	6				10									34
5,000	9	1	3	6	2	5		7	8	9				11	4				10									35
12000	9	1	3	6	2	5		7	8	9				11	4				10									36
2,000	9	1	3	6		5		7	8	9	10			11	4							2						37
		1	3	6	4	5			10					11						9					2	7	8	38
Appearances		37	30	38	36	28	26	31	35	31	19	6	11	17	17	4	11	9	19	5	1	2	1	1	1	1	1	
Goals (42)				2	1		4	1	7	7	10	2		4					3	1								

Att.	Pos	W Green	Dixon	Moffat	Barron	D Walders	Cretney	J Walders	A Davidson	R Smith	McFarlane	Murphy	Marshall	A Smith	J Taylor	Parker	Greenwood	Campbell	Bell	Wood	Lovett	Riley	McNab	Whiteley	Mooney	Hargreaves	Whittaker	
20,000		1	3	6	4		10	7			8				6			2	11	9								1
Appearances		1	1	1	1		1	1			1				1			1	1	1								
Goals (0)																												

1906-07

The main departures from Turf Moor in the summer of 1906 had been the Walders brothers, both of whom had been prominent members of the Burnley first team squad, Jack for two seasons, David for three, since arriving from Barrow. They both moved to Oldham Athletic, then in the Lancashire Combination, but ambitious for Football League membership. David and Jack both played their part in fulfilling the Latics' dreams with the Lancashire Combination Championship in 1907 and with it election to Football League Division Two.

Rupert Cawthorne, signed from Clitheroe, was David Walders' initial replacement at centre half, with winger Joe Kenyon being transfered from Failsworth. Another 'new signing', ostensibly making his Turfites' debut on the opening day of the season, was outside right Stephen Trainer, a young Scot signed from Coatbridge. It later emerged however that he had already appeared in a league match for Burnley against Bradford City in February 1906, using the name 'McNab'!

With the departure of Mr Barker to pastures new, there was also a new first team trainer who was reserve team trainer T.H.Holden who was to be assisted by a Turfite of old, Tom 'Ching' Morrison who had been signed on a free transfer from Manchester United, primarily as a coach but available, if necessary, as a player.

Rupert Cawthorne
new signing from Clitheroe

After the first three games of the new season ended in defeat and with no goals scored, Burnley were bottom of the league but the Turfites had not played that badly and soon pulled it round with three successive wins. Then came a real tonic for the long suffering Turf Moor fans, the best display and biggest win for some time when Burslem Port Vale were hit for six. Centre forward Richard Smith was unstoppable and scored the second league hat trick of his Burnley career. The Vale defenders must have been sick of the sight of him, his first Burnley hat trick had been against them in February 2005! A special cheer was reserved for the Turfites' fifth goal, a piledriver from the very popular local hero, now veteran, Joe Taylor. Joe no longer scored many goals but when he hit a ball, it stayed hit!

In October 1906 a late goal from Arthur Bell clinched the points at Leeds and at the final whistle the Burnley players trooped into the dressing room, justifiably satisfied with their efforts. The shocking news that greeted them however made them forget all about football and put everything into stark perspective. One of the Leeds players was lying dead in the adjacent dressing room.

OBITUARY
DAVID 'SOLDIER' WILSON
DIED 27 OCTOBER 1906, AGED 23.

David Wilson had no connection with Burnley FC but tragically collapsed and died immediately after playing for Leeds City against Burnley in their Second Division clash at Elland Road.

Wilson was born in Hebburn in 1883 and arrived at Leeds in 1905 via Dundee, Hearts and Hull City. Despite only playing 15 games he was City's top scorer in season 1905-06 with 13 goals, two of which came against Burnley at Turf Moor in March 1906. Whilst still a teenager he had also fought for his country in South Africa in the Boer War, hence his nickname. David Wilson left the field after about an hour of the match against Burnley complaining of chest pains. Against medical advice, he insisted on re-entering the fray after two Leeds players suffered injuries at the same time, but he was unable to complete the game. He left the field again only to collapse and had to be carried to the dressing rooms where attempts to revive him proved unsuccessful. At the subsequent inquest a verdict was returned that Wilson had died of heart failure.

RIP

In early February 1907 an eighteen year old goalkeeper was given a trial in a Burnley reserve game against St Helens Town at Turf Moor. He created a very favourable impression and after playing just three games was asked to sign a professional contract. The Burnley Express had been keeping a watchful eye on the teenager and revealed to its readers that he was a native of Holme-in-Cliviger and their verdict was "Burnley were wise in securing his signature. He has the makings of a fine custodian and has a future before him. If Burnley had not been 'struck' by this village blacksmith, other clubs certainly would have been." This future England international was the first of many legends who would go on to bring glory to Burnley FC but his own Turf Moor career would outlast them all.

The young man's name was Jerry Dawson.

Early in March 1907 a scheduled league fixture at Barnsley was postponed because the Tykes had an FA Cup tie with Woolwich to fulfill. A friendly match was arranged with Workington and Burnley sent a full strength team to Cumberland to play the Lancashire Combination team for the first time. Both Dick Smith and Jonathan Cretney had been born in Workington but neither they nor their team mates were made to feel especially welcome as the Cumbrians swept to a 4-1 victory. The Turfites' defeat was especially ironic as Workington played in the same League as Burnley reserves – who had already beaten them home and away that season!

Burnley-born Arthur Bell was by this time a regular choice in the Turfites' team, whenever he could fit football into his professional life as an architect. He had developed into a brilliant inside forward but, strictly an amateur throughout his football career, he quite often missed Burnley's away trips because of work commitments. He was also an accomplished cricketer at the 'other' Turf Moor and invariably chose to play for Burnley CC when the football and cricket seasons overlapped.

In April 1907 Bell was chosen to play in England's amateur international against Holland in The Hague. Among his team mates were full internationals Harold Hardman of Everton and Tottenham's Vivian Woodward, both of whom were professionals of the academic field rather than the football field. Like Bell, Woodward was an architect and Hardman was a solicitor. Arthur Bell, Burnley's first amateur international, had an excellent game and scored as England beat the Dutch 8-1.

Billy Green
regular goalkeeper but about to come up against stiff competion

Burnley's heavy defeat at Barnsley was the final appearance in the senior team of Joe Taylor, local boy made good, who had been at Turf Moor since 1893. Taylor had invariably performed with distinction on the Turf Moor stage and had been the first Turfite to top 300 league appearances. Taylor was retiring but also departing the Turf Moor scene was another local discovery, Arthur Dixon who, within days of Burnley's final league match, had been lured by the bright lights of London to join Tottenham, then in the Southern League but ambitious to progress to the Football League.

In the final weeks of the season Burnley once more overcame Blackburn Rovers on their way to retaining the East Lancashire Charity Cup even though Rovers had finished the season half way up the First Division. Burnley were too good for them, winning the Turf Moor semi final 3-1 before beating Lancashire Combination Accrington Stanley 1-0 in the final at Moorhead Park thanks to a penalty from Dick Smith.

Once again a subsidiary competition had been won and at least there was a trophy 'on the sideboard'. Once again however the real competition, the Second Division title, had always been well out of reach. In terms of final position it had been the best campaign for three years but, after seven seasons in Division Two, to the supporters, promotion seemed as far away as ever.

1906-07 - Second Division

		P	W	D	L	F	A	Pts
1	Nottingham F	38	28	4	6	74	36	60
2	Chelsea	38	26	5	7	80	34	57
3	Leicester F	38	20	8	10	62	39	48
4	West Bromwich A	38	21	5	12	83	45	47
5	Bradford C	38	21	5	12	70	53	47
6	Wolverhampton W	38	17	7	14	66	53	41
7	BURNLEY	38	17	6	15	62	47	40
8	Barnsley	38	15	8	15	73	55	38
9	Hull C	38	15	7	16	65	57	37
10	Leeds C	38	13	10	15	55	63	36
11	Grimsby T	38	16	3	19	57	62	35
12	Stockport C	38	12	11	15	42	52	35
13	Blackpool	38	11	11	16	33	51	33
14	Gainsborough T	38	14	5	19	45	72	33
15	Glossop	38	13	6	19	53	79	32
16	Burslem PV	38	12	7	19	60	83	31
17	Clapton O	38	11	8	19	45	67	30
18	Chesterfield	38	11	7	20	50	66	29
19	Lincoln C	38	12	4	22	46	73	28
20	Burton U	38	8	7	23	34	68	23

1906-07

Manager : Spen Whittaker

Division Two (7th)

	No	Date		h/a	Opponents	Result		h/t	Goalscorers/times	Opp. goal times
	1	Sep	1	h	WEST BROMWICH A	L	0-1	0-1		26
	2		3	h	BRADFORD C	L	0-1	0-1		19
Morrison's last game	3		8	a	Leicester F	L	0-2	0-1		35, 65
	4		15	h	NOTTINGHAM F	W	2-1	1-1	Whittaker (2) 30, 63	9
	5		22	a	Lincoln C	W	2-1	0-1	R.Smith 84, Cretney 87	20
	6		29	h	BURTON U	W	4-0	4-0	Bell (2) 13, 42, Moffat (2) 26, 37	
	7	Oct	6	a	Grimsby T	L	0-1	0-0		58p
	8		13	h	BURSLEM P V	W	6-0	3-0	R.Smith (3) 5, 32, 58, Bell 30, Taylor 63, A.Smith 77	
	9		20	a	Chesterfield	W	1-0	1-0	Whittaker 13	
	10		27	a	Leeds C	W	1-0	0-0	Bell 87	
	11	Nov	3	h	BARNSLEY	D	2-2	2-1	R.Smith 2, Bell 17	19, 69
	12		10	a	Chelsea	L	0-2	0-0		57, 60
	13		17	h	WOLVERHAMPTON W	W	3-0	2-0	Bell 17, Barron 24, Whittaker 50	
	14		24	a	Clapton O	L	1-2	0-1	R.Smith 65	35, 89
	15	Dec	1	h	GAINSBOROUGH T	W	1-0	1-0	R.Smith 40p	
	16		8	a	Stockport C	L	1-2	1-2	Whittaker 23	31, 44
	17		15	h	HULL C	W	4-2	2-0	Bell (2) 8, 35, Whittaker (2) 58, 84	50, 70
	18		22	a	Glossop	L	0-1	0-1		23
	19		25	h	BLACKPOOL	W	2-1	1-1	R.Smith 35, Whittaker 78	22
	20		29	a	West Bromwich A	L	2-3	1-3	R.Smith 10, Whittaker 65	25p, 30, 38
	21	Jan	1	a	Bradford C	L	1-3	0-3	Davidson 50	2, 4og, 43
	22		5	h	LEICESTER F	W	5-0	1-0	Whittaker (2) 5, 60, Ogden 50, R.Smith (2) 76, 78	
	23		19	a	Nottingham F	L	0-2	0-1		22, 64
	24		26	h	LINCOLN C	W	5-1	0-0	Bell 57, Whittaker 59, R.Smith (2) 65, 90, A.Smith 76	80
	25	Feb	2	a	Burton U	W	1-0	1-0	A.Smith 16	
	26		9	h	GRIMSBY T	W	2-0	2-0	Ogden (2) 1, 19	
	27		16	a	Burslem P V	D	4-4	4-2	Bell 1, Ogden 5, R.Smith (2) 12, 44	30, 32, 48, 60
	28		23	h	CHESTERFIELD	D	0-0	0-0		
	29	Mar	2	h	LEEDS C	L	1-2	0-0	Moffat 77p	50, 88
	30		16	h	CHELSEA	D	1-1	0-0	Bell 67	81
	31		23	a	Wolverhampton W	L	0-3	0-1		25, 80og, 88
	32		29	a	Blackpool	L	0-2	0-1		3, 60
	33		30	h	CLAPTON O	W	3-0	3-0	A.Smith (2) 6, 18, McFarlane 21	
	34	Apr	6	a	Gainsborough T	W	2-0	1-0	R.Smith 1, Ogden 52	
	35		13	h	STOCKPORT C	W	3-0	1-0	Whittaker 44, Bell 60, Moffat 67	
Joe Taylor's last game	36		18	a	Barnsley	L	0-5	0-3		3, 6, 8, 70, 90
	37		20	a	Hull C	D	1-1	0-0	Davidson 80	75
Dixon's last game	38		27	h	GLOSSOP	D	1-1	1-1	Davidson 35	17

FA Cup

No	Date		h/a	Opponents	Result		h/t	Goalscorers/times	Opp. goal times
1	Jan	12	h	ASTON VILLA	L	1-3	1-1	Whittaker 23	9, 75, 79

Final, Sheffield Wednesday 2-1 Everton, at Crystal Palace.

Other matches (friendlies and/or as detailed)

	Date		h/a	Opponents	Result		h/t	Goalscorers/times
Lancs Cup	Oct	1	a	Southport C	L	0-2		
	Mar	9	a	Workington	L	1-4		A.Smith
East Lancs Charity Cup semi	Apr	15	h	BLACKBURN R	W	3-1		R.Smith, Bell, Whittaker
East Lancs Charity Cup final		24	a	Accrington S	W	1-0	1-0	R.Smith 18p
		25	a	Failsworth	L	1-2		R.Smith

Att.	Pos	W Green	Barron	Dixon	Cawthorne	Cretney	Moffat	Trainer	A Davidson	R Smith	McFarlane	A Smith	Parker	J Taylor	Kenyon	Morrison	Whittaker	Bell	Goodwin	Ogden	Jon Dawson	Whiteley	Johnson	Whiteley	Jerry Dawson	Holden	
7,500		1	2	3	4	5	6	7	8	9	10	11															1
5,000		1	2	3		4			8	9	10	11	5	6	7												2
10,000		1	2	3	5	4	6			9	10	11			7	8											3
6,000	18	1	2	3		4	6			9		11		5	7		8	10									4
		1	2	3	5	4	6			9		11			7		8	10									5
5,500	8	1	2	3	5	4	6			9		11			7		8	10									6
4,000	12	1	2	3	5	4	6			10	9	11			7		8										7
4,000	8	1	2	3	5	4				9		11		6	7		8	10									8
4,000	6	1	2	3	5	4				9		11		6	7		8	10									9
14,000	6	1	2	3	5	4				9		11		6	7		8	10									10
10,000	5	1	2	3	5	4				9		11		6	7		8	10									11
10,000	8	1	2	3	5	4				9		11		6	7		8	10									12
4,000	6	1	2		5	4	3		6	9		11			7		8	10									13
5,000	10	1	2	3	5	4	6			9		11			7		8	10									14
6,000	7	1	2	3	5	4	6			9		11			7		8	10									15
2,000	10	1	2	3	5	4	6			9					7		8	10	11								16
6,000	7	1	2	3	5	4	6			9		11			7		8	10									17
		1	2		5	4	3		6	9		11			7		8	10									18
7,000	7	1	2		5	4	3		6	9		11			7		8	10									19
12,000		1	2		5		3		4	9		11		6			8			7	10						20
13,000	9	1	2		5		3		4	9		11		6	7		8			10							21
7,000	8	1	2	3		4	6		5	9		11			7		8			10							22
7,000	10	1	2	3			6		4	9		11	5		7		8			10							23
2,000	8	1	2	3		4	6			9		11	5		7		8	10									24
1,500	7	1	2	3		4	6			9		11	5		7		8			10							25
5,000	6	1	2	3		4	6			9		11	5					10		8		7					26
3,500	6	1	2	3			6			9		11	5		7			10		8			4				27
5,000	7	1	2	3		4	6			9		11	5		7			10		8							28
5,000	7	1	2	3	5	4	6					11			7		8	10		9							29
7,000	7	1	2	3		4	6			9		11	5		7		8	10									30
6,500	7	1	2	3		4	6	7		9		11	5				8	10									31
5,000		1	2	3		4	6			9	10	11	5		7		8										32
5,500		1	2	3		4	5			9	10	11			7		8							6			33
	7	1	2			4	3	7		9	5	11		6			8			10							34
3,000	7		2	6		4	3				5	11					8	10		9		7			1		35
1,500		1	2				3		10	9		11	5	6			8						4			7	36
7,000	7	1	2			4	3		10	9	5	11					8			7			6				37
2,500		1	2	6		4			10	9		11	5				8			7			3				38
Appearances		37	38	30	20	33	31	3	12	36	9	37	12	11	29	1	32	23	1	13	1	2	4	1	1	1	
Goals (62)			1			1	4		3	16	1	5		1			13	12		5							

Att.	Pos	W Green	Barron	Dixon	Cawthorne	Cretney	Moffat	Trainer	A Davidson	R Smith	McFarlane	A Smith	Parker	J Taylor	Kenyon	Morrison	Whittaker	Bell	Goodwin	Ogden	Jon Dawson	Whiteley	Johnson	Whiteley	Jerry Dawson	Holden	
16,242		1	2	3			6		4	9		11		5	7		8	10									1
Appearances		1	1	1			1		1	1		1		1	1		1	1									
Goals (1)																	1										

1907-08

For the coming season there was to be new look about the Burnley defence with the retirement of Joe Taylor and the transfer to Tottenham of Arthur Dixon. Both local boys, who had grown up at Turf Moor, they had played more than 500 senior games for Burnley between them and Taylor in particular had been almost part of the furniture at Turf Moor for over a decade. One of the new arrivals was half back Tom Wolstenholme who had struggled to make an impact at Bolton after impressing at Blackpool.

Another interesting newcomer was right winger William Bradshaw, top scorer at Burton United who had failed to gain re-election to the League after finishing at the very bottom. Bradshaw, who had been born in Burnley, was the son of former Turfites manager Harry Bradshaw and had played under his father at both Woolwich Arsenal and Fulham.

The supporters were confident that the campaign ahead would be a successful one and season ticket sales were the healthiest for a number of years. The local press was also upbeat with the Burnley Express of the opinion that the current squad of players was the best at Turf Moor for some years.

Alex Leake
experienced international signed from Aston Villa

For the fourth successive season Burnley started their league campaign against West Brom who did their best to deflate the Turfites' confidence with a 5-0 drubbing at the Hawthorns. It was Burnley's worst opening day defeat in twenty years of league football. Another new signing, Jonathon Beddows scored the Turfites' first two goals of the season in a win against Stoke with Dick Smith also weighing in with two in another victory against Bradford City. Burnley's problem, sheer inconsistency, became immediately apparent when, after the win against Bradford, who would finish as champions, they lost at home to Lincoln, who would finish bottom. The Lincoln defeat was a watershed in the Burnley careers of two fine goalkeepers, with William Green making way for the young pretender, Jerry Dawson. Dawson would be the man in possession for many years to come during which time he would see off challenges of dozens of rivals. Perhaps his best performance early on in a blossoming career was in Burnley's 3-2 win at Barnsley in October 1907 in which he produced save after magnificent save including a late penalty stop that had even the Barnsley fans applauding. One penalty Dawson didn't manage to save was Barnsley's late consolation goal in that game, smashed home by a young half back in only his second season of league football. He would go on captain Burnley to glory in the years ahead, and to play for his country.

His name was Tommy Boyle.

The Turfites' centre forward Dick Smith was also making a name for himself, scoring twelve goals in a twelve match spell including two in the last eight minutes to earn a point in a 2-2 draw at Leeds in November 1907.

In December 1907 there were definite signs of the ambitions of the Burnley directors when they announced the signing of defender Alex Leake from Aston Villa. Birmingham-born Leake had played more than 200 games for Small Heath, many as captain, before moving to Villa in 1902. He had appeared in almost 150 games for Villa and was in their FA Cup winning side of 1905 also winning five England caps. Even though Alex Leake was into his thirties, he was a natural leader and still had much to offer a Second Division team desperate to climb back into the top flight.

In the FA Cup first round of January 1908 Burnley were paired with Southampton, their first-ever meeting with the Saints, then playing in the Southern League. The supporters felt that here was a big chance to progress in the Cup and nearly 16,000 spectators, one of the biggest gates ever at Turf Moor, turned out to watch their heroes despatch the south coast upstarts. Not for the first time, or the last, disappointment lay in wait. Southampton scored early on, Arthur Bell raised the fans' hopes with an equaliser but the visitors booked their place in the next round with the winner in the last quarter.

In February 1908 Dick Smith, without a goal since Christmas Day, suddenly found his form again with hat-tricks in successive matches, against Barnsley and at Chesterfield. It was only the second time a Turfite had managed this since the foundation of the club more than a quarter of a century earlier, with Smith equalling the feat of Claude Lambie (Lambie the Leap) in 1890.

Smith's achievement was in the middle of an excellent run of form by the team, five successive victories, which lifted the supporters and really revived hopes of promotion. More history was made with the 1-0 win at Clapton Orient in March 1908, the first-ever victory in the capital by a Burnley team.

The winning run ended with a heavy defeat at Wolves but three more victories followed and after a 3-1 success at Stockport, Burnley were still fifth but only two points behind the league leaders. With four games to go including two clashes with promotion rivals Bradford City and Leicester Fosse, four victories would guarantee promotion, seven points might be enough.

OBITUARY
JAMES WILLIAM CRABTREE
DIED 18 JUNE 1908, AGED 37.

Former Burnley, Aston Villa and England star James Crabtree died at his home in Aston, Birmingham. He had had health problems for some time.

Crabtree was born in Sandygate, Burnley in 1870 and as a young man was soon recognised as a naturally gifted footballer. He played as an amateur in local football and for Burnley's reserves and appeared briefly in the Turfites' league side in 1889. After a spell away from Turf Moor he returned in 1892 and signed as a professional. It was the start of a very successful career and he won his first England cap against Ireland in Belfast in 1894, Burnley's first locally-born international. With three impressive Turf Moor seasons behind him it was time to move to a bigger stage and in 1895 "Crabby" was transferred to Aston Villa. In seven years at Villa he won four League Championship medals and was in the Villa side that won the League and Cup double in 1897, scoring the winner in an epic FA Cup final against Everton at the Crystal Palace. He won a total of 14 England caps and played nine times for the Football League. After playing non-league football and coaching at Plymouth he retired in 1906. Heavy drinking continued to contribute to increasing problems with his health and, two weeks after severely scalding himself, he developed pneumonia which led to his passing.

James Crabtree is almost certainly the most talented footballer ever born in Burnley and without doubt is among the very finest exponents of his art ever to have played the game.

RIP

The 0-1 defeat at strugglers Blackpool was a real anti-climax and the day's other results confirmed Second Division football at Turf Moor for at least another season. On the last day of the campaign at Leicester, Dick Smith scored his 24th league goal of the season to establish a new club record, easing in front of Jimmy Ross's previous record of 23 in the Second Division championship campaign of 1897-98.

Once again it had been a season that, at times, had promised so much but yet again the supporters had to settle for seventh place, on the face of it little better than a mid-table finish. At the end however, only six points separated the leading eight clubs and if just two defeats had been victories, Burnley could well have finished second and have been promoted back to the top flight. Points dropped against teams in the bottom six, including home points lost against both the bottom two, had been crucial. Ironically all the top three had been beaten at Turf Moor. On the plus side Burnley had, once again, won the East Lancashire Charity Cup and, as a bonus, Blackburn Rovers had been the Turfites' victims in the final.

Promotion was still to be some years away but at least Burnley still had a team in the Football League unlike the city of Stoke which had had two only a year earlier. Following Burslem Port Vale's demise in 1907, Stoke, who had finished mid-table in Division Two, suddenly resigned from the League because of financial difficulties. Lincoln City who had finished bottom and had failed to be re-elected, expected a reprieve but instead it was Southern League Tottenham Hotspur who took Stoke's place.

Burnley's reserves enjoyed their best season for some years when they finished as runners-up in Lancashire Combination Division Two to earn promotion. An unbeaten run since early February 1908, fifteen wins and one draw in sixteen games, had turned the campaign around, with Jonathon Beddows staking his claim for a first team place by scoring 19 goals in that sequence

A young Jerry Dawson
between the sticks at Turf Moor for the next two decades

1907-08 - Second Division

		P	W	D	L	F	A	Pts
1	Bradford C	38	24	6	8	90	42	54
2	Leicester F	38	21	10	7	72	47	52
3	Oldham A	38	22	6	10	76	42	50
4	Fulham	38	22	5	11	82	49	49
5	West Bromwich A	38	19	9	10	61	39	47
6	Derby C	38	21	4	13	77	45	46
7	BURNLEY	38	20	6	12	67	50	46
8	Hull C	38	21	4	13	73	62	46
9	Wolverhampton W	38	15	7	16	50	45	37
10	Stoke	38	16	5	17	57	52	37
11	Gainsborough T	38	14	7	17	47	71	35
12	Leeds C	38	12	8	18	53	65	32
13	Stockport C	38	12	8	18	48	67	32
14	Clapton O	38	11	10	17	40	65	32
15	Blackpool	38	11	9	18	51	58	31
16	Barnsley	38	12	6	20	54	68	30
17	Glossop	38	11	8	19	54	74	30
18	Grimsby T	38	11	8	19	43	71	30
19	Chesterfield	38	6	11	21	46	92	23
20	Lincoln C	38	9	3	26	46	83	21

1907-08

Manager : Spen Whittaker

Division Two (7th)

Note	No.	Date		Venue	Opponents	Result		h/t	Goalscorers/times	Opp. goal times
	1	Sep	7	a	West Bromwich A	L	0-5	0-1		11, 48, 60, 70, 80
	2		9	h	STOKE	W	3-1	0-0	Beddows (2) 51, 63, Whittaker 75	87
	3		14	h	BRADFORD C	W	2-1	1-0	R.Smith (2) 38p, 85	64
	4		16	h	LINCOLN C	L	1-2	0-2	R.Smith 82	29, 45
	5		21	a	Hull C	L	1-3	1-1	Valentine 35	25, 65, 85
	6		28	h	DERBY C	D	2-2	1-2	Bell 25, R.Smith 60	15, 36
	7	Oct	5	a	Lincoln C	W	3-1	2-1	R.Smith (2) 3, 82, Bell 35	8
	8		12	h	FULHAM	L	0-1	0-1		15
	9		19	a	Barnsley	W	3-2	2-1	Beddows (2) 18, 55, R.Smith 40	15, 85p
	10		26	h	CHESTERFIELD	D	1-1	0-1	Ogden 57	20
	11	Nov	2	h	GRIMSBY T	W	5-1	3-0	Beddows 4, R.Smith (2) 22p, 43, Bell (2) 49, 59	67
	12		9	a	Oldham A	D	1-1	1-1	Beddows 44	22
	13		16	h	CLAPTON O	W	3-0	0-0	A.Smith 50, R.Smith 52, Bradshaw 60	
	14		23	a	Leeds C	D	2-2	0-1	R.Smith (2) 82, 90	35, 80
	15		30	h	WOLVERHAMPTON W	W	1-0	1-0	Beddows 14	
	16	Dec	7	a	Gainsborough T	L	0-2	0-0		47, 80
	17		14	h	STOCKPORT C	W	4-0	2-0	Ogden 34, A.Smith 42, Moffat 65p, Bell 75	
	18		21	a	Glossop	L	1-3	1-2	R.Smith 36	12, 35, 88
	19		25	h	BLACKPOOL	W	2-1	1-0	A.Smith 43, R.Smith 51	80
	20		26	a	Stoke	D	0-0	0-0		
	21		28	h	LEICESTER F	W	4-1	3-0	Parker 3, A.Smith 23, Donaghey (2) 40, 70	74
	22	Jan	4	h	WEST BROMWICH A	D	1-1	1-0	A.Smith 2	65
	23		18	h	HULL C	W	5-0	4-0	McFarlane (2) 15, 45, Mayson 25, Cretney 42, A.Smith 88	
	24		25	a	Derby C	L	0-1	0-1		24
	25	Feb	8	a	Fulham	L	1-2	0-2	Leake 75	35, 40
	26		15	h	BARNSLEY	W	4-1	2-1	R.Smith (3) 1, 4, 60, Bell 55	25
	27		22	a	Chesterfield	W	4-2	2-1	R.Smith (3) 8, 12, 65, A.Smith 75	30, 80p
	28		29	a	Grimsby T	W	1-0	0-0	A.Smith 53	
	29	Mar	7	h	OLDHAM A	W	2-1	2-0	Mayson 10, Whittaker 15	68
	30		14	a	Clapton O	W	1-0	1-0	Whittaker 31	
	31		16	a	Wolverhampton W	L	1-5	0-3	R.Smith 70	10, 30, 38, 60, 80
	32		21	h	LEEDS C	W	1-0	1-0	R.Smith 43	
	33	Apr	4	h	GAINSBOROUGH T	W	2-0	1-0	A.Smith 5, Leake 52	
	34		11	a	Stockport C	W	3-1	2-0	R.Smith 30, Bell 43, Whittaker 46	75
	35		17	a	Blackpool	L	0-1	0-1		25
	36		18	h	GLOSSOP	W	1-0	1-0	A.Smith 21	
	37		20	a	Bradford C	L	0-2	0-1		12, 47
McFarlane's last game	38		25	a	Leicester F	L	1-3	1-1	R.Smith 35	10, 50, 80

FA Cup

No.	Date		Venue	Opponents	Result		h/t	Goalscorers/times	Opp. goal times
1	Jan	11	h	SOUTHAMPTON	L	1-2	0-1	Bell 59	2, 71

Final, Wolverhampton W 3-1 Newcastle U, at Crystal Palace.

Other matches (friendlies and/or as detailed)

Competition	Date		Venue	Opponents	Result		h/t	Goalscorers
Lancs Cup	Sep	30	a	Everton	W	4-1		Whittaker (3), A.Smith
Lancs Cup	Oct	14	h	LIVERPOOL	L	0-2		
ELCC semi, at Turf Moor	Feb	1	a	Darwen	D	1-1		Goreing
ELCC semi replay	Apr	28	h	DARWEN	W	1-0		R.Smith
East Lancs Charity Cup final		30	h	BLACKBURN R	W	4-2	3-0	R.Smith, Mayson (2)1p, McFarlane

Att.	Pos	W Green	Barron	Moffatt	Cretney	McFarlane	Wolstenholme	Bradshaw	Beddows	R Smith	Short	A Smith	Whittaker	Dawson	Wright	Valentine	Bell	Heys	Wilcox	Parker	Ogden	Smethams	Leake	Donaghey	Mayson	
16,032		1	2	3	4	5	6	7	8	9	10	11														1
10,500		1	2	3	4	5	6	7	8	9		11	10													2
8,000		1	2	3	4	5	6	7	8	9		11	10													3
4,500		1	2	3	4	5	6	7	8	9		11	10													4
8,000	13		2	3		5	6		8	9		11	10	1	4	7										5
10,000	13		2	3		5	6			9		11	8	1	4	7	10									6
3,000	10		2	3	4	5	6			9		11	8	1		7	10									7
8,000	15		2		4	5	6			9		11	8	1		7	10	3								8
5,000	12		2		4		6	7	8	9		11		1					3	5	10					9
6,000			2	3	4		6	7	8	9		11		1						5	10					10
4,000	8		2	3		4	6	7	8	9		11		1			10			5						11
14,000	9		2	3		4	6	7	8	9		11		1			10			5						12
7,500	7		2	3		4	6	7	8	9		11		1			10			5						13
7,000	8		2	3		4	6	7	8	9		11		1			10			5						14
5,000	6		2	3	4	5	6		8	9		11		1		7	10									15
4,000	7		2	3	4	5	6		8	9		11		1		7	10									16
6,000	7		2	3	4	5	6				8	11		1			10				9	7				17
	8		2	3	4		6			9		11		1							8	7	5	10		18
12,000			2	3	4		6			9		11		1			10					7	5	8		19
8,000	8		2	3	4		6			9		11		1								7	5	8	10	20
8,000	7			3	4		6			9		11		1			10			5		7	2	8		21
10,146	7		2	3	4		6			9		11		1			10					7	5	8		22
7,000	6		2	3	4	7	6			8		11		1			10						5		9	23
10,000	7		2	3	4	7	6			8		11		1			10						5		9	24
15,000	8		2	3	4	7	6			9		11	8	1			10						5			25
6,000	7		2	3		7	6			9			8	1			10				4	11	5			26
2,000	7		2	3	4	7	6			9		11	8	1									5		10	27
3,000	7		2	3	4	7	6			9		11	8	1									5		10	28
16,000	8		2	3	4	7	6					11	8	1			10						5		9	29
8,000			2	3	4	7	6			9		11	8	1			10						5			30
16,000	5		2	3	4	7	6			9		11	8	1			10						5			31
7,000	3		2	3	4	7	6			9		11	8	1			10						5			32
6,000	7		2	3	4	7	6			9		11	8	1			10						5			33
4,500	5		2	3	4	7	6			9		11	8	1			10						5			34
7,000	5		2	3	4	7	6			9		11	8	1			10						5			35
5,500			2		4		6	7		9		11	8	1			10			5			3			36
27,000	6		2		4	7	6			9		11	8	1			10			5			3			37
8,000			2	3	4	7	6			9	10	11	8	1									5			38
Appearances		4	37	34	31	30	38	11	13	36	3	37	21	34	2	6	26	1	1	9	5	7	21	5	6	
Goals (67)				1	1	2		1	7	24		10	4			1	7			1	2		2	2	2	

Att.	Pos	W Green	Barron	Moffatt	Cretney	McFarlane	Wolstenholme	Bradshaw	Beddows	R Smith	Short	A Smith	Whittaker	Dawson	Wright	Valentine	Bell	Heys	Wilcox	Parker	Ogden	Smethams	Leake	Donaghey	Mayson	
14,000			2	3	4		6			9		11		1			10				8	7	5			1
Appearances			1	1	1		1			1		1		1			1				1	1	1			
Goals (1)																	1									

1908-09

After eight years in Division Two and another season of false hopes, the Burnley fans were beginning to despair of the club ever regaining its former status in the top flight. However the campaign in store for the Turfites' faithful was to be one of the most memorable so far in the history of Burnley FC, with a series of epic FA Cup matches still talked about, and argued about, a century later.

The only ever-present of 1907-08, left half Tom Wolstenholme, moved on in the summer of 1908. He was transferred to Bradford Park Avenue, newly elected to the Football League and Bradford's ranks were also to include ex-Turfite Arthur Dixon who moved to Yorkshire after just one season in London with Tottenham. Spurs themselves had also won a place in the Football League and they were able to tempt another Turf Moor favourite to the capital when, after five years at Burnley, utility man Dugald McFarlane decided it was time to move on. The Burnley directors once more demonstrated their ambitions when they secured the services of Everton's powerful former England wing half or inside forward Walter Abbott.

Walter Abbott
England international signed from Everton

The start to the league season could best be described as inauspicious although an early highlight was Dick Smith's four goals in less than half an hour of Burnley's 5-2 demolition of Gainsborough in October 1908. It was the first four-goal haul of Smith's career and the fifth time he had registered a hat-trick in Burnley colours.

In November 1908 there was suddenly an exodus of players from Turf Moor with Albert Smith and Jonathan Parker being transferred to Bradford Park Avenue. They were closely followed by reserve goalkeeper William Green, who had given stalwart service to the Turf Moor cause but who was now very much in the shadow of the man of the moment, and indeed the man of the future, Jerry Dawson. With Arthur Dixon and Tom Wolstenholme already at Bradford, there were now five former Turfites playing for the league newcomers.

With only three wins since early October Burnley began the New Year in style with two successive victories at Glossop and at home to Stockport. Walter Abbott scored in both games, his first goals for the Tufites, and confidence was high for the trip to Bristol Rovers in the FA Cup. Arthur Ogden, after scoring twice against Stockport, hit three more against Rovers to book the Turfites' passage into the second round, another tie against another Southern League club, Crystal Palace to be played at the huge Crystal Palace Stadium, then of course the venue for the FA Cup final itself.

The official attendance for the tie was just over 17,000 but estimates were that there were many thousands more, as everybody who had paid to enter the Palace grounds before 1pm was able to watch the Cup tie free of charge.

The Burnley players were reported to have been somewhat overawed by the vastness of the ground but they played their part in what the Burnley Express described as "a typical, thunderous cup tie." At the end it was goalless so it was back to Turf Moor for the replay, an FA Cup encounter that would re-write the record books.

From the first whistle the Turfites tore into Palace as if their lives depended on it. Burnley hadn't been particularly prolific scorers that season, only 25 in 13 previous home matches, and that included five against both Gainsborough and Stockport. That total had been matched by half time against Palace, thanks to a couple from an unstoppable Dick Smith, screamers from Walter Abbott and Jonathan Cretney and one from a mercilessly pressured Palace defender. In the second half flying winger Charlie Smethams got in on the act, both Abbott and Cretney scored again with Smith smashing in a 20-yarder to complete his hat trick ten minutes from time. Final score Burnley 9-0 Crystal Palace.

It had been an absolutely spellbinding performance by the Turfites, in front of a crowd of over 12,000. Veterans with experience going back to the 1880's agreed that it ranked among the best-ever displays by a Burnley team.

There has inevitably been some debate over the years about the quality of an opposition that appeared to have let Burnley walk all over it and establish a record score that still stands a century later. In the Edwardian era the Southern League was certainly just as strong as the Second Division of the Football League. Palace themselves had collected some notable recent FA Cup scalps, including League Champions Newcastle in 1907 and, in the round before their clash with the Turfites, they had despatched the cup-holders Wolves, who, ironically had beaten Burnley easily 5-3 at Turf Moor earlier in the season!

The fact was that the Burnley players, to a man, had provided a phenomenal exhibition of football. The Burnley Express's verdict was that "in an embarrassingly one-sided game Palace were annihilated and on that day Burnley would have beaten any team, anywhere. Just as many chances were missed as were scored and the Palace goalkeeper had a fine game."

As if to portend what was to come five years hence, Gateshead's Herbert Bamlett had been the referee in both games against Palace, as he would be in Burnley's memorable FA Cup triumph in 1914!

There was another superlative goalkeeping performance to follow in the next game. It was the famous occasion when the Grimsby goalkeeper Walter Scott faced four Burnley penalties, saving three of them, although the Turfites managed to continue their unbeaten run with a 2-0 win.

The FA Cup third round was something of a replica of the second round. Drawn away against a London Club, a battling performance to earn a 0-0 draw and a replay back at Turf Moor. The Burnley players once again rose to the occasion and, in another scintillating cup tie, totally outplayed the Londoners with Abbott, Smith and Ogden scoring the goals in a 3-1 victory. Yet again it was breathtaking stuff for the Burnley fans who were loving every minute of their team's chance to bask in the limelight. After the Tottenham replay the Turfites were still unbeaten in ten games in 1909 and had lost only once since the league defeat at White Hart Lane in mid December. The players were on a high and the supporters were right up there with them.

Next it was to be league champions Manchester United in the quarter final and this time it was at Turf Moor. A huge attendance was forecast and workmen toiled night and day to increase Turf Moor's capacity. Earth bankings were increased substantially, a new enclosure was built and there were new barricades and turnstiles. One of the grandstands was even lengthened in an attempt to try to accommodate as many as 30,000 people.

Talk about best laid plans! During the night before the match it began to snow and, as kick off approached it was still snowing. The match kicked off on time but the awful weather had had its effect on the attendance, less than 16,000, still a huge Turf Moor crowd but well down on expectations. From the start Burnley continued as they had left off against both Palace and Tottenham. In atrocious weather and on a treacherous surface, the champions were simply outplayed by a Burnley team, yet again at the top of its form. Assisted by a strong wind in the first half, the Turfites took the lead on fifteen minutes with a goal from Arthur Ogden and, although their all round powerful play deserved more reward, it was still 1-0 at half time. In the second half the snow, now a blizzard, was in the faces of the Burnley players and United had much more of the game. The Turfites' defence was solid however, not too much got past them and when it did, Jerry Dawson looked unbeatable in goal.

Then it happened. The storm showed no signs of abating and after 72 minutes, the referee, Herbert Bamlett again, called the captains together to suggest the tie be abandoned. Alex Leake, naturally, thought the game should be played to its conclusion. United skipper Charlie Roberts was adamant that the game should never have been started at all as "the weather was not fit to turn a dog out". Mr Bamlett felt that the surface was becoming unsafe, was inclined to agree with Roberts, and called the teams off the pitch.

The Burnley supporters were bitterly disappointed but they felt that, having almost beaten the Reds once, their favourites could finish the job next time.

It was not to be, the chance had gone. Fred Barron was unfit for the replayed game, Burnley's first change in six FA Cup matches, and there was no doubt it affected the balance of the team. On a quagmire of a pitch the Turfites' display wasn't quite up to previous performances. It was still "a ding dong battle" but United played better than they had four days earlier and, in reality, could have won more convincingly than the eventual 3-2 scoreline. Arthur Ogden scored first and again near the end but, in between, the Reds played the more controlled football, and deserved their place in the semi final.

The FA Cup run was over but what memories the fans had to savour and, perhaps to soften the blow just a little, the aristocrats of Manchester United, First Division champions in 1908 remember, went on to lift the FA Cup themselves for the first time. As they paraded the trophy around Crystal Palace the Reds' players and supporters must have contemplated how close they had come to being dumped out of the competition on a snowy March afternoon at Turf Moor. Back in Burnley, fathers would soon begin educating sons and grandsons to educate their own sons and grandsons that, in future, whenever Manchester United came to town, they must strike up the immortal Turf Moor cry –

"Stop the game, it's snowing!"

Jonathan Morley
flying winger transfered from Sunderland

After narrow victories against Oldham and Clapton, the season that could have delivered so much finally ran out of steam. Burnley won only one of their last eight matches, against strugglers Barnsley, and scored just five goals, two of which were own goals! It had been a season of huge contrasts, Burnley's worst league campaign so far, apart from the near disaster in 1902-03, but far and away the best and most exciting FA Cup adventure in the club's history. The fans decided they liked success, relative though it had been, and they wanted more of it, more often. It would take time but success, huge success, would come their way.........eventually.

1908-09 - Second Division

		P	W	D	L	F	A	Pts
1	Bolton W	38	24	4	10	59	28	52
2	Tottenham H	38	20	11	7	67	32	51
3	West Bromwich A	38	19	13	6	56	27	51
4	Hull C	38	19	6	13	63	39	44
5	Derby C	38	16	11	11	55	41	43
6	Oldham A	38	17	6	15	55	43	40
7	Wolverhampton W	38	14	11	13	56	48	39
8	Glossop	38	15	8	15	57	53	38
9	Gainsborough T	38	15	8	15	49	70	38
10	Fulham	38	13	11	14	58	48	37
11	Birmingham	38	14	9	15	58	61	37
12	Leeds C	38	14	7	17	43	53	35
13	Grimsby T	38	14	7	17	41	54	35
14	BURNLEY	38	13	7	18	51	58	33
15	Clapton O	38	12	9	17	37	49	33
16	Bradford PA	38	13	6	19	51	59	32
17	Barnsley	38	11	10	17	48	57	32
18	Stockport C	38	14	3	21	39	71	31
19	Chesterfield	38	11	8	19	37	67	30
20	Blackpool	38	9	11	18	46	68	29

1908-09

Manager : Spen Whittaker

Division Two (14th)

	No.	Date			Opponents	Result		h/t	Goalscorers/times	Opp. goal times
	1	Sep	1	h	CHESTERFIELD	L	0-1	0-0		75p
	2		5	h	GLOSSOP	W	3-2	1-1	A.Smith 35, Morley 48, Whittaker 54	6, 80
	3		7	h	DERBY C	W	2-0	1-0	R.Smith 40p, Lindley 82	
	4		12	a	Stockport C	L	1-2	1-1	Lindley 1	40, 75
	5		19	h	WEST BROMWICH A	L	0-2	0-1		16, 79
	6		26	a	Birmingham	L	0-2	0-1		42, 70
	7	Oct	3	h	GAINSBOROUGH T	W	5-2	4-1	Morley 11, R.Smith (4) 26, 36, 38, 52	41, 65
	8		10	a	Grimsby T	W	1-0	0-0	Valentine 72	
William Green's last game	9		17	h	FULHAM	L	1-3	0-1	A.Smith 63	34p, 83, 88
	10		24	a	Bolton W	L	1-2	0-2	Morley 55	21, 45
	11		31	a	Bradford	W	3-2	1-2	R.Smith (2) 19, 75p, Whittaker 80	15, 17
Whittaker's last game	12	Nov	7	h	WOLVERHAMPTON W	L	3-5	0-4	Whittaker (2) 50, 53, R.Smith 75p	7, 12, 30, 40, 57
	13		14	a	Oldham A	L	1-4	0-3	Bell 65	7p, 26, 37, 67
Albert Smith's last game	14		21	h	CLAPTON O	L	0-1	0-0		55
	15		28	a	Leeds C	D	1-1	0-1	Watson 70og	25
	16	Dec	5	h	BARNSLEY	W	3-2	1-1	Mayson 40, Lindley 68, Bell 88	26, 90
	17		12	a	Tottenham H	L	2-4	1-3	Moffat 28, R.Smith 70	5, 25, 26, 75
	18		19	h	HULL C	W	1-0	1-0	Morley 15	
	19		25	h	BLACKPOOL	D	1-1	0-1	Morley 59	5
Bell's last game	20		26	a	Derby C	L	0-1	0-1		25
	21	Jan	2	a	Glossop	W	2-1	0-1	R.Smith 75, Abbott 80	15
	22		9	h	STOCKPORT C	W	5-1	0-1	Abbott 65, Cretney 67, Ogden (2) 84, 88, R.Smith 86	43
	23		23	a	West Bromwich A	D	0-0	0-0		
	24		30	h	BIRMINGHAM	D	1-1	0-0	Morley 86	50
	25	Feb	13	h	GRIMSBY T	W	2-0	2-0	Abbott (2) 16, 42p	
	26		27	h	BOLTON W	L	1-2	0-1	Mayson 85	10p, 75
	27	Mar	13	a	Wolverhampton W	L	1-2	0-1	Abbott 53	17, 68
	28		16	h	BRADFORD	D	3-3	1-2	Mayson (2) 40, 75, Ogden 60	30, 35, 50
	29		20	h	OLDHAM A	W	1-0	1-0	R.Smith 37p	
	30		27	a	Clapton O	W	1-0	0-0	Abbott 70	
	31		31	a	Fulham	L	0-3	0-3		15p, 30, 42
	32	Apr	3	h	LEEDS C	D	0-0	0-0		
	33		9	a	Blackpool	D	0-0	0-0		
	34		12	a	Chesterfield	L	0-1	0-0		65
	35		13	a	Barnsley	W	2-1	1-1	Little 30og, Morley 68	12
	36		14	a	Gainsborough T	L	0-1	0-0		85p
	37		17	h	TOTTENHAM H	L	1-2	0-2	Mayson 48	25, 43
	38		24	a	Hull C	L	2-3	2-0	R.Smith 10, Browell 16og	55, 60, 75

FA Cup

	Rd	Date			Opponents	Result		h/t	Goalscorers/times	Opp. goal times
	1	Jan	16	a	Bristol R	W	4-1	1-0	R.Smith 22, Ogden (3) 60, 63, 66	80
	2	Feb	6	a	Crystal P	D	0-0	0-0		
Dick Smith goals (3) 5, 20, 80	rep		10	h	CRYSTAL P	W	9-0	5-0	Collyer 23og, Abbott (2) 35, 66, Cretney (2) 44, 71, Smethams 68	
	3		20	a	Tottenham H	D	0-0	0-0		
	rep		24	h	TOTTENHAM H	W	3-1	1-0	Abbott 11, R.Smith 49, Ogden 51	78p
	4	Mar	10	h	MANCHESTER U	L	2-3	1-2	Ogden (2) 15, 85	24, 27, 59

Final, Manchester U 1-0 Bristol C, at Crystal Palace.

Other first team matches (friendlies and/or as detailed)

	Date			Opponents	Result		Goalscorers
Lancs Cup	Oct	12	a	Everton	L	1-4	Lindley
FA Cup tie aban 72m, blizzard	Mar	6	h	MANCHESTER U	aban	1-0	Ogden
East Lancs Charity Cup	Apr	27	h	BLACKBURN R	L	3-6	Morley, Mayson, Ogden

Att.	Pos	J Dawson	Barron	Moffatt	Cretney	Parker	Abbott	Morley	Brewis	R Smith	Mayson	A Smith	Whittaker	Howarth	Ogden	Lindley	Leake	Bell	Beddows	Green	Valentine	A Dawson	McLean	Cawthorne	Smethams	Wilcox	Woodward	Minion	Clarke	Watson	McLoughlin					
7,000		1	2	3	4	5	6	7	8	9	10	11																								1
8,000		1	2	3	4	5	6	7		9	10	11	8																							2
12,000		1	2			5	6	7		9		11	10	3	4	8																				3
6,000	7	1	2		4	5	6	7		9		11	10	3		8																				4
11,340	13	1	2		4		6	7		9		11	8	3			5	10																		5
20,000	14	1	2		4		6	7		8		11		3			5	10	9																	6
6,000	12	1	2		4		6	7		9		11		3		8	5	10																		7
4,000	10		2	3	4		6	7		9		11				8	5			1	10															8
7,000	13		2	3	4		6	7		9		11				8	5	10		1																9
8,000	13	1	2		4	5	6	7		9		8					3	10				11														10
14,000	12	1		3	4	5	6	7		9		11	8				2	10																		11
6,000	12	1	2		4	5	6	7		9		11	8				3	10																		12
10,000	15	1		3	4		6	7				11				8	5	10	9				2													13
7,000	16	1		6	4			7		9		11		2		8		10					3	5												14
14,000	15	1	2	6				7		9	10				4	8	5	11					3													15
5,000	13	1	2	6				7		9	10				4	8	5	11					3													16
10,000	16	1	2	6				7		9	10				4		5	11			8		3													17
7,000	13	1	2	6				7		9	10				4		5	11			8		3													18
12,000	13	1	2	6				7		9	10				4		5	11			8		3													19
12,000	15	1	2	6				7		9	10				4		5	11			8		3													20
3,000	15	1	2	6	4		10	7		9					8		5						3		11											21
6,000	11	1	2	6	4		10	7		9					8		5						3		11											22
18,220	12	1	2	6	4		10	7		9					8		5						3		11											23
8,000	10	1	2	6	4		10	7		9					8		5						3		11											24
8,000	10	1	2	6	4		10	7		9					8		5						3		11											25
7,000	12	1	2	6	4		10	7			9				8		5								11	3										26
7,500		1		6	4		10	7			9				8		5						3		11		2									27
2,500	13	1			4			7		9	10			2	8		5						3		11			6								28
7,000	13	1	2		4		10			9	7				8		5						3	6	11											29
	12	1			4		10			9	7			2	8		5						3		11			6								30
8,000	12	1			4		10			9				2	8		5						3	6	11				7							31
5,000	12	1	2	3	4		10	7		9					8		5								11					6						32
3,000		1	2	6	4		10			9	7					8	5								11	3										33
3,000		1	2	6			10	7		9	8						5						3		11						4					34
5,000	12	1	2	6			10	7		9	8						5						3		11						4					35
3,000	13	1	2	6				7	10	9	8						5						3		11						4					36
8,000	13	1	2	6			10	7		9	8						5						3		11						4					37
6,000		1	2	6			10	7		9	8						5						3		11						4					38
Appearances		36	31	27	26	7	29	34	2	35	19	14	6	9	19	10	33	15	2	2	5	1	23	3	18	2	1	2	1	1	5					
Goals (51)				1	1		6	7		13	5	2	4		3	3		2			1														3	ogs

Att.	J Dawson	Barron	Moffatt	Cretney	Parker	Abbott	Morley	Brewis	R Smith	Mayson	A Smith	Whittaker	Howarth	Ogden	Lindley	Leake	Bell	Beddows	Green	Valentine	A Dawson	McLean	Cawthorne	Smethams	Wilcox	Woodward	Minion	Clarke	Watson	McLoughlin					
6,000	1	2	6	4		10	7		9					8		5						3		11											1
17,076	1	2	6	4		10	7		9					8		5						3		11											2
14,000	1	2	6	4		10	7		9					8		5						3		11											rep
21,838	1	2	6	4		10	7		9					8		5						3		11											3
30,000	1	2	6	4		10	7		9					8		5						3		11											rep
16,850	1		6	4		10	7		9				2	8		5						3		11											4
Appearances	6	5	6	6		6	6		6				1	6		6						6		6											
Goals (18)				2		3			5							6								1										1	og

1909-10

There were no major signings at Turf Moor during the summer of 1909, the big news was the arrival of Birmingham's Benny Green during the first week of the new season. Green had been a steady rather than a prolific scorer in his six years with the Blues, averaging a goal in every four of his 200 games. A prominent name missing from future Burnley line-ups was to be Arthur Bell who had announced his retirement during the close season. Playing Lancashire League cricket during each summer, amateur international Bell had found all year round sport just too demanding, especially alongside his architect's practice.

After four games Burnley were bottom of the league with only one point and had scored just four goals, two of which were penalties from Walter Abbott. Before the end of September the expectations of many of the long-suffering Turfites' fans were already limited to not finishing in the bottom two.

Benny Green
top scorer in his first season at Turf Moor

In the first weeks of the season Burnley met Lancashire Combination side Accrington Stanley at Turf Moor in the East Lancashire Charity Cup. Stanley played well and dumped the Turfites out of the competition, winning 2-1, with even the Burnley consolation an own goal by an Accrington defender. The name of that defender was Harry Swift and, later in the season, he would feature again in the story of Burnley FC, this time in a much more significant way. He would be unwittingly involved in one of Turf Moor's saddest and most tragic episodes.

After their dismal start to the season Burnley rallied somewhat and after a 3-1 win against Grimsby at Turf Moor, they had risen to tenth, the high point of the league campaign. After a quiet opening to his Turf Moor career Benny Green scored his first Burnley goal in that match and it was just the kick-start he needed. Green went on to bag 19 in league and FA Cup, a total bettered only twice in the Turfites' league history up to that point. In December 1909 Burnley hit ten goals in successive home games against Leicester and Blackpool with Benny Green helping himself to five.

It was time for the FA Cup draw and the fates had decreed that the Turfites would get an early chance for revenge after their unfortunate exit in the fourth round of 1908-09. Manchester United were to visit Turf Moor for a re-match and the Burnley supporters could hardly wait.

When the day of the Cup-tie dawned, at least there was no snow but once again the conditions were against a bumper crowd. Heavy rain fell from early morning and an attendance that could have been way over 25,000 was less than 17,000, although still a huge crowd by normal Turf Moor standards. The Burnley fans immediately seized their opportunity to remind the opposition how fortunate they had been ten months earlier. As soon as the United players ran on to the pitch a tremendous cry rang out –

"Stop the game, it's snowing !"

Once again Second Division Burnley were too good for their illustrious opponents and this time the weather was on the side of the Turfites. They quickly mastered the sloppy conditions and Benny Green crashed in the first goal after just three minutes. Charlie Smethams sealed a 2-0 win with a second goal in the last quarter-hour but, in between, the Burnley players delivered their best performance of the season and they could and should have had more goals.

The Burnley fans had long since given up any ideas of promotion but when the second round draw paired the Turfites with Southern League Swindon Town, there were high hopes of another memorable FA Cup run. Alas it was not to be, a classic case of "after the Lord Mayor's Show". Swindon outplayed the Lancashire Lads as much as they themselves had outplayed Manchester United, even scoring their two goals at the same stages as Burnley had in the previous round.

On the pitch the season was more or less over before the end of February. There were to be happenings off the field however that would re-shape the club's future dramatically.

In March 1910 after Burnley had gone down 1-2 at Fulham, the players were returning to the railway station when Alex Leake was involved in a freak accident as he alighted from a bus. The other players suddenly spotted him lying unconscious in the road and in urgent need of hospital treatment. Leake didn't appear in the Burnley team again for some weeks and even then it was something of an emergency.

At the beginning of April the Turfites just managed to overcome strugglers Gainsborough Trinity 2-1 at Turf Moor thanks to two goals in the last ten minutes and a tremendous penalty save from Jerry Dawson, who yet again had been one of the successes of the season. It was only the fourth victory that the Burnley fans had seen at Turf Moor since New Year's Day and the excitement of the win against Manchester United seemed a long time ago. The attendance against Gainsborough was just 4,000, less than half the number of people that had seen each of Burnley reserves' last two matches at Turf Moor against local opposition.

New depths were plumbed at the beginning of April 1910 when Burnley visited bottom of the table Grimsby Town. The Turfites turned in an abysmal display and were five goals down before half time. There went on to be something of a recovery before the game ended 5-3 to Grimsby but it was another humiliating performance by a struggling team.

Burnley manager Spen Whittaker decided that a new centre half was the top of his priorities. Alex Leake had still not fully recovered from his accident in London and his deputy, JW Dollins had had a very poor game at Grimsby. Accrington's Harry Swift was the man Whittaker had earmarked for the heart of the Turfites' defence and he signed for Burnley on the evening of Friday 15 April. In order to ensure Swift's eligibility for Burnley's difficult looking game against Manchester City the following day, Spen Whittaker decided to take the overnight train to London to register his transfer with the Football League. It was a decision which would cost Spen Whittaker his life.

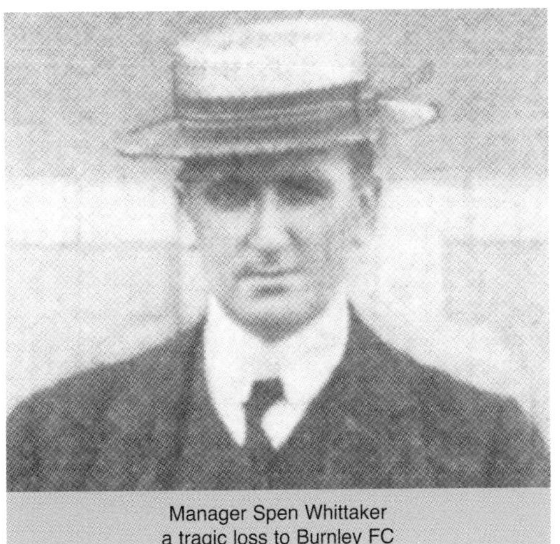

Manager Spen Whittaker
a tragic loss to Burnley FC

OBITUARY
SPENCER (SPEN) WHITTAKER
DIED 16 APRIL 1910, AGED 39.

The tragic passing of the Burnley FC secretary/manager left a widow and three orphaned children and robbed the football world of a young, energetic and very popular figure. Spen Whittaker was born in Oswaldtwistle in 1871 and as a young man played amateur football in and around Accrington before becoming Secretary of Oswaldtwistle Rovers FC. In 1899 he applied for the position of secretary/manager at Bristol City but was unsuccessful although he reached the final short list of two. In 1903 he was successful in his application to succeed Ernest Mangnall as Burnley secretary/manager and was then the youngest man in such a position in the Football League. He was in his seventh year at Turf Moor and would be sorely missed.

RIP

Some of the details are unclear, but a fellow-passenger in the same compartment as Whittaker was suddenly awakened in the early hours by a draught caused by the outside door swinging open. It was later thought that the Burnley manager had woken, got up to leave the compartment and had mistaken the outer door for the door to the train corridor. The alarm was raised immediately, the train was stopped midway between Crewe and Stafford and search parties began to walk up and down the line. Eventually poor Spen Whittaker was found, lying by the side of the track, having suffered terrible injuries. He died a few hours later.

Later that day, supporters arriving at Turf Moor for the eagerly awaited clash with league leaders Manchester City, were surprised to see the club's flag flying at half mast. News soon spread around the ground however of the tragic events during the night and as kick off approached the mood was very sombre.

Harry Swift did not make his first appearance for the Turfites on that day but Alex Leake insisted on turning out, his first game since his own unfortunate accident in London early in March. In the circumstances the Burnley players performed extremely well and led City 2-0 and 3-1 before being pegged back to 3-3 by the Second Division Champions-elect.

The following week a benefit match was played at Turf Moor for Spen Whittaker's wife and three young children. A Football League X1 was opposed by Manchester United and a crowd of 7,000 boosted the memorial fund that had been set up by £165. They witnessed an excellent game with the League X1, containing Burnley's Dawson, Cretney and Moffat, defeating Manchester United 4-1. United's inside right, making his second Turf Moor visit of the season, was John Picken, who would sign for Burnley a year later.

For the second successive season the Turfites had finished in fourteenth place and once again it had been a disappointing campaign, compounded by the tragic loss of the popular Spen Whittaker.

Changes would inevitably have to be made but there were more changes on the way than many imagined. By the time the 1910-11 season kicked off there would be a new King on the throne, a new manager at Turf Moor and brand new Burnley colours for the fans to identify with.

1909-10 - Second Division

		P	W	D	L	F	A	Pts
1	Manchester C	38	23	8	7	81	40	54
2	Oldham A	38	23	7	8	79	39	53
3	Hull C	38	23	7	8	80	46	53
4	Derby C	38	22	9	7	72	47	53
5	Leicester F	38	20	4	14	79	58	44
6	Glossop	38	18	7	13	64	57	43
7	Fulham	38	14	13	11	51	43	41
8	Wolverhampton W	38	17	6	15	64	63	40
9	Barnsley	38	16	7	15	62	59	39
10	Bradford PA	38	17	4	17	64	59	38
11	West Bromwich A	38	16	5	17	58	56	37
12	Blackpool	38	14	8	16	50	52	36
13	Stockport C	38	13	8	17	50	47	34
14	BURNLEY	38	14	6	18	62	61	34
15	Lincoln C	38	10	11	17	42	69	31
16	Clapton O	38	12	6	20	37	60	30
17	Leeds C	38	10	7	21	46	80	27
18	Gainsborough T	38	10	6	22	33	75	26
19	Grimsby T	38	9	6	23	50	77	24
20	Birmingham	38	8	7	23	42	78	23

1909-10

Manager : Spen Whittaker until April 1910, then R H Wadge (Director)

Division Two (14th)

Note	No	Date		Venue	Opponents	Result		h/t	Goalscorers/times	Opp. goal times
	1	Sep	4	a	Derby C	L	2-5	1-2	Abbott 30p, Lindley 75	8, 17, 60, 62, 89
	2		6	h	HULL C	L	0-1	0-0		54
	3		11	h	STOCKPORT C	D	2-2	1-1	Abbott 31p, Lomas 78	15, 73p
	4		18	a	Glossop	L	0-2	0-0		48, 63
	5		25	h	BIRMINGHAM	W	2-0	2-0	Ogden 8, Abbott 25p	
	6	Oct	2	a	West Bromwich A	W	2-1	2-0	Abbott 5, Ogden 41	62
	7		9	h	OLDHAM A	L	1-2	1-1	Abbott 10	25, 51
	8		16	a	Barnsley	D	0-0	0-0		
	9		23	h	FULHAM	W	2-0	1-0	Mayson 27, Morley 61	
	10		30	h	BRADFORD	W	1-0	1-0	Smethams 36	
	11	Nov	6	a	Leeds C	L	0-1	0-0		70
	12		13	h	WOLVERHAMPTON W	W	4-2	3-1	Abbott (3) 11, 23, 68p, Smethams 44	26, 65
	13		20	a	Gainsborough T	L	0-2	0-0		55, 70p
	14		27	h	GRIMSBY T	W	3-1	2-0	Green 6, Morley 15, opp 56og	74
	15	Dec	4	a	Manchester C	L	0-4	0-1		23, 47, 75, 85
	16		11	h	LEICESTER F	W	5-2	2-0	Green (2) 26, 37, Morley 48, Chadburn 77, Abbott 82	75, 90
	17		18	a	Lincoln C	D	0-0	0-0		
	18		25	h	BLACKPOOL	W	5-1	4-0	Green (3) 12, 31, 70, Chadburn (2) 22, 41	90
	19		27	a	Clapton O	L	1-2	1-0	Green 30	70, 80
	20	Jan	1	h	CLAPTON O	W	2-0	1-0	Morley 14, Chadburn 75	
	21		8	h	DERBY C	L	1-2	0-1	Green 61	3, 53
	22		22	a	Stockport C	D	1-1	1-1	Green 4	20
	23	Feb	12	h	WEST BROMWICH A	L	2-3	2-1	Green 8, R.Smith 33	30, 52, 72
	24		19	a	Oldham A	L	0-1	0-0		50
	25		26	h	BARNSLEY	W	2-0	1-0	Lomas 40, Smethams 90	
	26		28	a	Birmingham	L	1-2	1-1	R.Smith 15p	30, 67
	27	Mar	5	a	Fulham	L	1-2	1-0	Lomas 10	65, 80
Ogden's last game	28		12	a	Bradford	L	1-3	0-3	Lomas 65	10, 25, 41
	29		19	h	LEEDS C	W	3-0	0-0	Lomas (2) 61, 63, Green 73	
	30		25	a	Blackpool	W	3-2	1-1	Valentine 15, Green 70, Lomas 90	2, 55p
	31		26	a	Wolverhampton W	L	1-3	1-2	Lomas 20	28, 38, 70
	32		28	a	Hull C	L	2-3	1-1	Moffat 12, Green 82	23, 46, 80
	33	Apr	2	h	GAINSBOROUGH T	W	2-1	0-1	Moffat 80, Lomas 89	36
McLean's last game	34		9	a	Grimsby T	L	3-5	1-5	Green (2) 45, 86, Smethams 47	10p,15og,23,30,40
	35		16	h	MANCHESTER C	D	3-3	2-1	Lomas 23, Green (2) 33p, 48	35, 52, 70
	36		18	h	GLOSSOP	L	0-1	0-0		80
Abbott's last game	37		23	a	Leicester F	D	1-1	1-0	Lomas 15	80
last games for Dick Smith, Leake & Smethams	38		30	h	LINCOLN C	W	3-0	1-0	Green 42, Moffat 62, Morley 75	

FA Cup

No	Date		Venue	Opponents	Result		h/t	Goalscorers/times	Opp. goal times
1	Jan	15	h	MANCHESTER U	W	2-0	1-0	Green 3, Smethams 76	
2	Feb	5	a	Swindon T	L	0-2	0-1		2, 75

Final, Bradford C 1-0 Newcastle U, at Old Trafford, after a 0-0 draw, at Crystal Palace.

Other first team matches (friendlies and/or as detailed)

Competition	Date		Venue	Opponents	Result		Goalscorers
East Lancs Charity Cup semi	Sep	20	h	ACCRINGTON S	L	1-2	Swift og
Lancs Cup	Oct	13	a	Chorley	W	3-2	Lomas, Abbott (2)
Lancs Cup		25	a	Manchester C	L	1-4	Abbott p

Att.	Pos	Dawson	Barron	McLean	Cretney	Leake	Moffatt	Morley	Lindley	Lomas	Abbott	Smethams	Beddows	Watson	Clarke	B Green	R Smith	Mayson	Ogden	Valentine	Cawthorne	Tillotson	Chadburn	Weightman	Splitt	Dollins	Woodward	McLoughlin	Bamford	Boden	Dougan	Swift				
5,000		1	2	3	4	5	6	7	8	9	10	11																								1
7,000		1	2	3	4	5	6		8	9	10	11	7																							2
7,000		1	2	3	4	5				8	10	11		6	7	9																				3
4,000	20	1	2	3	4	5					10			6	7	8	9	11																		4
5,000	16	1	2	3	4	5	6		8	9	10	11							7																	5
15,175	13	1	2	3	4	5	6				10	11				8			9	7																6
9,000	15	1	2	3	4						10	11		6			9		8	7	5															7
5,000	16	1	2	3	4	5		7			10	11		6		8			9																	8
3,000	12	1	2	3	4	5	6	7			10	11				8		9																		9
8,500	11	1	2	3	4	5	6	7	8		10	11				9																				10
7,000	11	1	2	3	4	5	6	7			10	11				8		9																		11
6,000	10		2	3	4	5	6	7			10	11				8			9			1														12
	12		2	3	4	5	6	7			10	11				8			9			1														13
5,000	10	1	2	3	4	5	6	7			10	11				8							9													14
12,000	12	1	2	3	4	5	6	7			10	11				8								9												15
5,500	11	1	2		4	5	6	7			10	11				8							9		3											16
6,000	11	1	2		4		6	7			10					8				11			9		3	5										17
12,000		1	2		4	5	6	7			10	11				8							9		3											18
12,000	11	1	2			5	6	7			10	11				8			4				9		3											19
6,500	12	1	2		4	5	6	7			10	11				8							9		3											20
8,000	12	1	2		4	5	6	7			10	11				8							9		3											21
6,000		1	2		4	5	6	7			10	11				8	9										3									22
6,500	13	1	2		4	5	6	7			10	11				8	9								3											23
6,000	13	1	2		4	5	6	7			10	11				8	9								3											24
3,000			2		4		6	7		10		11				8	9					1			3	5										25
1,000	13	1	2		4	5	6	7		10		11				8	9								3											26
12,000	13	1	2			5	6	7		9	10	11				8									3			4								27
10,000	13	1			4		6	7		9	10	11				8			5						3		2									28
4,000	13	1	2	3	4		6	7		10		11				8	9									5										29
9,500	12	1			6		4			10		11				8				7				9		5			2	3						30
5,000		1			4		6			10		11				8				7				9		5			2	3						31
10,000	14	1			4		6			9	10					8				7						5			2	3	11					32
4,000	13	1		3	4		6			10		11				8				7			9			5			2							33
3,000	14	1		3	4		6			9		11				8							10			5			2	7						34
7,000		1			4	5	6	7		9		11				8		10							3				2							35
3,000	14	1			4		6			9		11				8		10							3				2	7		5				36
	14	1			4	5	6	7		9	10	11				8									3				2							37
2,000		1			4	5	6	7		9		11				8	10								3				2							38
Appearances		35	28	18	36	27	34	26	4	18	28	35	1	4	2	34	9	5	8	7	1	3	9	3	16	8	2	1	9	5	1	1				
Goals (62)							3	5	1	11	9	4				18	2	1	2	1			4												1	og

Att.	Pos	Dawson	Barron	McLean	Cretney	Leake	Moffatt	Morley	Lindley	Lomas	Abbott	Smethams	Beddows	Watson	Clarke	B Green	R Smith	Mayson	Ogden	Valentine	Cawthorne	Tillotson	Chadburn	Weightman	Splitt	Dollins	Woodward	McLoughlin	Bamford	Boden	Dougan	Swift				
16,628		1	2	3	4	5	6	7			10	11				8	9																			1
10,000		1	2	3	4	5	6	7			10	11				8	9																			2
Appearances		2	2	2	2	2	2	2			2	2				2	2																			
Goals (2)												1				1																				

1910-11

The summer of 1910 was dominated by the death of King Edward V11 and the accession to the throne of King George V. To some degree Turf Moor happenings mirrored those in royal circles with the sad passing of Burnley secretary/manager Spen Whittaker followed by the appointment of his successor. The new man was John Haworth, who like Whittaker, had been schooled in local football in and around Accrington and had been the secretary of Accrington Stanley for more than a decade. John Haworth would be the man to drive Burnley FC forward into a new decade, and into a new era of previously undreamed of success.

Haworth decided immediately that changes were needed and he reckoned that, to start with, it was time for a change in playing strip away from green. What better than to adopt the colours of the most successful team around, the League Champions of 1910, Aston Villa, who played in claret and blue.

"The Clarets" were born!

With a change of manager also came changes in the team. Veterans Alex Leake, Walter Abbott and Dick Smith all left Turf Moor, internationals Leake and Abbott had both brought their vast experience to the club and Dick Smith had scored goals regularly in his six years at Burnley. His total of 71 league goals was second only to Billy Bowes' 79 in the Turfites' history so far. With McLean, Smethams and Ogden also on their way out of Turf Moor, over half the side of the memorable FA Cup run of little more than a year ago, was surplus to requirements.

Max Seeburg
the first foreign player in the Football League

The main new arrival was full back Robert Reid from Cowdenbeath who would go on to take over from the long serving Fred Barron. There was also Charlie Bates, a young centre forward from Midland League football, whose main claim to Turf Moor fame would not be on the field but as the trainer to the 1921 League Championship side. An interesting new face at Turf Moor in 1910 was Max Seeburg who had played just one league game for Tottenham during 1909-10. Max Seeburg was born in Leipzig, Germany in 1884 and is generally accepted as the first "foreign" player, ie born outside the British Isles and Ireland, to appear in the Football League.

After two wins and a draw in the first three games Burnley sat at the top of the league, the best start to a season since the Second Division championship campaign of 1897-98. Unfortunately it didn't last and the Clarets, for the most part, played out the season in a position just outside the group of promotion hopefuls.

In December 1910, after nearly seven years at Turf Moor and well over 200 senior games for Burnley, defender Hugh Moffat was transferred to Oldham Athletic. A 20-year-old wing half called Willie Watson was now starting to make his presence felt and Moffat was no longer guaranteed a first team place. Hugh Moffat would be as consistent as ever in his time with the Latics and would go on to earn a well-deserved England cap.

In January 1911 the FA Cup came round again and Burnley were drawn away to Southern League Exeter City. The Clarets' directors soon became aware that there was a problem with the size of the pitch at Exeter's ground, St. James' Park, it was too short. Other clubs had protested and some recent ties, due to be played at Exeter, had been switched. As it happened the information provided didn't have to come very far, neighbours Nelson had been drawn at Exeter in the previous round and had successfully appealed to the FA, with their qualifying round match eventually being played at Seedhill.

The Exeter tie was indeed switched to Turf Moor and the Grecians were duly despatched 2-0. Barnsley were next, again beaten 2-0 and in the third round Burnley were drawn at home against Southern League Coventry City. In their wisdom the Burnley directors decided to double ticket prices to one shilling (5p) although fans were given the opportunity to buy Cup-tie tickets at the normal price at the previous home game against Fulham. The supporters voted on the price increase with their feet, the attendance inevitably suffered and, at under 12,000, was less than half the gate at the Barnsley match and probably a third of the crowd that would perhaps have been expected.

Burnley cruised into the next round with an overwhelming 5-0 victory, reaching the quarter final for the second time in three seasons. First Division Bradford City were waiting and, after the somewhat muted response in the last round Burnley was once again gripped by FA Cup fever. It was estimated that as many as 10,000 fans travelled to Bradford from Burnley, swelling the Valley Parade crowd to an official figure of 39,146. This was the largest number of people at any Burnley match in the club's history thus far and, a century later, is still the record attendance for Valley Parade and is the longest-standing ground attendance record of any League Club.

The Burnley players lived up to the occasion with a fine performance, particularly in defence. The only goal, when it came, was controversial with Jerry Dawson being barged as he went out to collect a high cross. The ball slipped out of his hands and squirmed into the net to send the City fans into raptures. As against Manchester United two seasons before, fortune had not favoured the Clarets and, as had been the case with Manchester United, their conquerors went on to lift the coveted trophy.

The following week, Stockport suffered the backlash of the Burnley's FA Cup exit when they were beaten 5-3 at Turf Moor, Charlie Bates scoring two of the goals. At that stage Burnley were sixth and still just about in touch with the Second Division leaders, with just one defeat, at Valley Parade, in the previous twelve games. With four of the leading contenders to play in the final nine games, promotion was still within the Clarets' reach.

Once again however the Clarets had flattered to deceive and in the next eight matches picked up just four points and scored only two goals. The promotion dream had been shattered yet again.

Burnley had not had a decent run in the Lancashire Cup for some years but after a replayed semi final against a strong Manchester United side, Blackburn Rovers were waiting in the final. It proved to be the most drawn out final on record, an epic four-game marathon, six and a half hours of football, before Rovers just edged out the Clarets 2-1 in the third replay at Ewood Park.

Fred Barron
400 League games for Burnley

In April 1911 stalwart defender Fred Barron played the last of his 400 League games for Burnley, against Barnsley at Turf Moor. He was still only 31 but planned to retire at the end of the season, having already taken over the licence of one of Burnley's town centre pubs. Barron had been a rock in the Burnley defence since 1898 and his Turf Moor career had spanned three decades and two centuries as well as three monarchs!

With just three games to go Burnley once more made their supporters sit up and take notice when they announced the arrival at Turf Moor of Everton and England centre forward Bert Freeman. Freeman was just 25 years old and had scored 61 League goals for Everton in only 86 games. His total included 36 in 1908-09 when he was the League's leading scorer with what was then the best-ever haul in First Division history.

Burnley had sprung some surprises in the past when they had managed to attract high profile, experienced players to Turf Moor, including Alex Leake, Walter Abbott and Benny Green. Bert Freeman however was still an established First Division star, arguably at the peak of his career, ostensibly with many goalscoring years at the top level in front of him. So it would prove and in the years ahead Bert Freeman would become a household name among Burnley fans as he helped to re-write the Turf Moor record books.

Freeman's arrival was one of the early indications that, after more than a decade of false hope and unfulfilled promise, Burnley FC were starting to build a team that was genuinely capable of challenging at the very top.

Exciting and successful times lay ahead.

OBITUARY
DANIEL (DANNIE) FRIEL
DIED JULY 1911.

Dannie Friel was undoubtedly the most influential and versatile Burnley player in the very earliest days of the club, before the advent of the Football League. Scotsman Friel came down from Vale of Leven in 1883 and first joined Accrington, although he was soon persuaded to transfer his allegiance to Turf Moor. He first donned the blue and white stripes of Burnley in November 1883 and was virtually a fixture in the team from then on, able to play equally proficiently in either defence or attack. Dannie Friel was Burnley's only ever present in the first season of league football, 1888-89, but it was his final campaign for the Turfites. After well over 300 hundred games, many as captain, he left Turf Moor, becoming a Burnley licensee, before eventually returning to Scotland. He later became a trainer to Glasgow Celtic.

RIP

1910-11 - Second Division

		P	W	D	L	F	A	Pts
1	West Bromwich A	38	22	9	7	67	41	53
2	Bolton W	38	21	9	8	69	40	51
3	Chelsea	38	20	9	9	71	35	49
4	Clapton O	38	19	7	12	44	35	45
5	Hull C	38	14	16	8	55	39	44
6	Derby C	38	17	8	13	73	52	42
7	Blackpool	38	16	10	12	49	38	42
8	BURNLEY	38	13	15	10	45	45	41
9	Wolverhampton W	38	15	8	15	51	52	38
10	Fulham	38	15	7	16	52	48	37
11	Leeds C	38	15	7	16	58	56	37
12	Bradford PA	38	14	9	15	53	55	37
13	Huddersfield T	38	13	8	17	57	58	34
14	Glossop	38	13	8	17	48	62	34
15	Leicester F	38	14	5	19	52	62	33
16	Birmingham	38	12	8	18	42	64	32
17	Stockport C	38	11	8	19	47	79	30
18	Gainsborough T	38	9	11	18	37	55	29
19	Barnsley	38	7	14	17	52	62	28
20	Lincoln C	38	7	10	21	28	72	24

1910-11

Manager : John Haworth

Division Two (8th)

Note	No.	Date		Venue	Opponents	Result		h/t	Goalscorers/times	Opp. goal times
	1	Sep	3	h	LINCOLN C	W	3-1	1-0	Lomas (2) 30, 65, Green 78	75
	2		5	h	GLOSSOP	D	0-0	0-0		
	3		10	a	Huddersfield T	W	1-0	0-0	Lomas 70	
	4		17	h	BIRMINGHAM	D	2-2	1-1	Green (2) 7, 80	9, 82
	5		24	a	West Bromwich A	L	1-2	1-1	Lomas 10	25, 55
	6	Oct	1	h	HULL C	D	0-0	0-0		
	7		8	a	Fulham	L	0-3	0-0		60, 65, 70
	8		15	h	BRADFORD	D	1-1	1-1	Green 40p	35
	9		22	a	Bolton W	D	1-1	0-1	Lomas 55	15
	10		29	a	Gainsborough T	W	2-1	1-0	Lomas (2) 20, 70	47
	11	Nov	5	h	LEEDS C	W	4-1	2-1	Mayson 21, Cretney 26, Lomas (2) 67, 71	41
	12		12	a	Stockport C	L	2-4	1-1	Green (2) 15, 80	17, 50, 54, 70
	13		19	h	DERBY C	W	2-1	1-1	Green 17, Mayson 55	26
	14		26	a	Barnsley	W	1-0	1-0	Mayson 35	
	15	Dec	3	h	LEICESTER F	W	2-1	0-1	Green 50, Watson 63p	5
Moffatt's last game	16		10	a	Wolverhampton W	L	0-1	0-1		35
Cretney's last game	17		17	h	CHELSEA	D	1-1	1-1	Morley 4	15
	18		24	a	Clapton O	W	2-0	1-0	Lomas 35, Morley 86	
	19		26	h	BLACKPOOL	D	1-1	1-1	Morley 28	7
	20		27	a	Hull C	L	0-3	0-0		50, 65, 85
	21		31	a	Lincoln C	L	0-1	0-1		35
	22	Jan	2	a	Glossop	D	1-1	0-0	Bates 55	70
	23		7	h	HUDDERSFIELD T	W	2-1	0-0	Bates (2) 53, 86p	85p
	24		21	a	Birmingham	D	1-1	1-1	Swift 11	4
	25		28	h	WEST BROMWICH A	W	2-0	1-0	Green (2) 19, 60	
	26	Feb	11	h	FULHAM	W	1-0	1-0	Newton 25	
	27		18	a	Bradford	D	1-1	1-0	Green 40	70
	28	Mar	4	h	GAINSBOROUGH T	D	1-1	0-0	Mayson 80p	82
	29		18	h	STOCKPORT C	W	5-3	3-1	Bates (2) 10, 44, Goodwin 25og, Mayson 51, Watson 55	35, 78, 87
	30		20	h	BOLTON W	L	1-3	1-2	Mayson 17	15, 27, 87
	31		25	a	Derby C	L	0-3	0-1		30, 55, 70p
	32		27	a	Leeds C	D	0-0	0-0		
Barron's last game	33	Apr	1	h	BARNSLEY	D	0-0	0-0		
	34		8	a	Leicester F	D	1-1	1-1	Newton 43	20
	35		14	a	Blackpool	L	0-1	0-0		80
	36		15	h	WOLVERHAMPTON W	D	1-1	1-0	Mountford 19	60
	37		22	a	Chelsea	L	0-3	0-0		61, 65, 80
Ben Green's last game	38		29	h	CLAPTON O	W	2-0	1-0	Bannister 27p, Mountford 63	

FA Cup

Note	No.	Date		Venue	Opponents	Result		h/t	Goalscorers/times	Opp. goal times
at Turf Moor	1	Jan	14	a	Exeter C	W	2-0	1-0	Mayson 32, Morley 58	
	2	Feb	4	h	BARNSLEY	W	2-0	2-0	Green 3, Morley 28	
	3		25	h	COVENTRY C	W	5-0	4-0	Green (2) 9, 45, Mayson (2) 20, 81, Watson 40	
	4	Mar	11	a	Bradford C	L	0-1	0-1		23

Final, Bradford C 1-0 Newcastle U, at Old Trafford, after a 0-0 draw, at Crystal Palace.

Other first team matches (friendlies and/or as detailed)

Note	Date		Venue	Opponents	Result		h/t	Goalscorers
East Lancs Charity Cup semi	Sep	12	a	Darwen	W	1-0		Green
Lancs Cup	Oct	7	h	ROCHDALE	W	1-0		P.Smith
Lancs Cup		24	h	ST HELENS	W	3-0		Harris, P.Smith (2)
East Lancs Charity Cup final	Nov	7	h	BLACKBURN R	L	0-1		
Lancs Cup semi, at Preston		21	n	Manchester U	D	0-0		
Lancs Cup semi rep, at Bury		30	n	Manchester U	W	2-1		Green, P.Smith
Lancs Cup final	Dec	12	a	Blackburn R	D	1-1	1-0	P.Smith
L. Cup final rep, aet, 1-1 at 90m	Jan	23	h	BLACKBURN R	D	2-2	1-1	Bates, Morley
L. Cup final 2nd rep, at Bolton	Apr	3	n	Blackburn R	D	0-0	0-0	
Lancs Cup final 3rd replay		18	a	Blackburn R	L	1-2	1-1	Bates

Att.	Pos	Dawson	Reid	Splitt	Cretney	Bannister	Moffatt	Morley	Green	Seeburg	Lomas	Mayson	Swift	P Smith	Watson	Harris	Bates	Dodd	Bamford	Barron	McCallum	McLaren	Newton	Tillotson	Woods	Lindley	B Freeman	Mountford		
8,000		1	2	3	4	5	6	7	8	9	10	11																		1
10,000		1	2	3	4	5	6	7	8	9	10	11																		2
7,371	top	1	2	3	4		6	7	8	9	10	11	5																	3
10,000	2	1	2	3	4		6	7	8		10	11	5	9																4
15,280	7	1	2	3	4		6	7	8		10	11	5	9																5
10,500	4	1	2	3	4			7	8		10	11	5	9	6															6
1,000	11	1	2	3	4		5	7	8		10			9	6	11														7
6,000	10	1	2	3	4			7	8			10	5	9	6	11														8
8,000	10	1	2	3	4				8	7	9	10	5		6	11														9
4,000	9	1	2	3	4				8	7	9	10	5		6	11														10
8,000	6	1	2	3	4				8	7	9	10	5		6	11														11
3,500	8	1	2	3	4				8	7	9	10	5		6	11														12
8,000	6	1	2	3	4				8	7	9	10	5		6	11														13
5,000	5	1	2	3	4				8	7	9	10	5		6	11														14
6,000	3	1	2	3			4		8	7			5	9	6	11	10													15
8,000	6	1	2	3			4		8	7			5	9	6	11	10													16
7,000	7	1	2	3	4			7	8		9		5		6	11	10													17
9,000		1	2	3				7	8		9	10	5		6	11		4												18
17,000		1	2	3				7	8		9	10	5		6	11		4												19
10,000	9	1	2					7	8		9	10	5		6	11		4	3											20
		1	2					7	8		9	10	5		6	11		4	3											21
	8	1	2					7	8	4		10	5		6		9			3	11									22
7,000	8	1	3					7	8	4		10	5		6	11	9			2										23
6,000	8	1	2	3				7	8				5		6	11	10					4	9							24
8,300	6		2					7	8	4		10	5			11			3			6	9	1						25
10,000	6	1	2					7	8			10	5		6	11			3			4	9							26
9,000	5	1	2					7	8				5		6	11	10		3			4	9							27
5,000	6		2						8	7		10	5		6				3		11	4	9	1						28
4,000		1	2					7	8			10	5		6	11	9		3			4								29
5,000	7		2			5		7	8			10			6	11			3			4		1	9					30
3,500		1		2				7	8			10	5		6	11	9		3			4								31
5,500	8							7	8			10	5		6	11	9		3	2		4		1						32
4,000	8								8	7		10	5		6		9		3	2	11	4		1						33
6,000	8			2						7		10	5		6				3		11	4	9	1		8				34
14,500		1		2				7	8			10	5		6		9	11	3			4								35
5,000	8	1		2				7	8			11	5		6				3			4					9	10		36
36,000	8	1		3				7	8			11	5		6		10		2			4					9			37
2,000		1	2	3		5		7	9			11			6							4				8		10		38
Appearances		32	31	26	15	4	8	27	37	17	18	32	33	7	32	24	13	5	15	4	4	15	6	6	1	2	2	2		
Goals (45)					1	1		3	11		10	6	1		2		5						2					2	1	og

Att.	Pos	Dawson	Reid	Splitt	Cretney	Bannister	Moffatt	Morley	Green	Seeburg	Lomas	Mayson	Swift	P Smith	Watson	Harris	Bates	Dodd	Bamford	Barron	McCallum	McLaren	Newton	Tillotson	Woods	Lindley	B Freeman	Mountford	
16,000		1	2	3				7	8	4	9	10	5		6	11													1
23,500		1	2					7	8			10	5		6	11			3			4	9						2
11,714		1	2					7	8			10	5		6	11			3			4	9						3
39,146		1	2					7	8			10	5		6	11			3			4	9						4
Appearances		4	4	1				4	4	1	1	4	4		4	4			3			3	3						
Goals (9)								2	3			3			1														

1911-12

The main departure from Turf Moor in the summer of 1911 was Benny Green. Green had been Burnley's top scorer in both his seasons with the club but with the arrival of Bert Freeman, it was decided that his future lay elsewhere and he was transferred to Preston. Bert Freeman was about to embark on a goalscoring journey with the Clarets that would put all previous records in the shade and his tally for the 1911-12 campaign has been exceeded just once, almost a century later.

Although Freeman had not scored in either of his two games for Burnley at the end of the previous season, he was soon on his way with a goal on the new campaign's opening day, a 3-1 victory at Glossop. The Clarets' other two goals were scored by Harry Mountford who had been signed from Everton at the same time as Freeman. The first four games were all won, Burnley's best ever start to a league season, and Bert Freeman scored in each game, as he also did in the next two.

Then came the news of the Clarets' latest signing, a player who would galvanise the Burnley team and go on to captain the side to all the game's domestic honours. Tommy Boyle's arrival from Barnsley was sensational news in Burnley, the supporters couldn't believe that a player of his stature had chosen to come to Turf Moor. It later emerged that Burnley had paid a record transfer fee of £1,150, a colossal sum in those days. Boyle made his Clarets' debut against his former Barnsley team mates in a 1-1 draw at Oakwell, with Bert Freeman not on the score sheet, the first time that had happened that season. He scored twice in the next game to make up for it! Another Burnley debutant in the Barnsley game had been Teddy Hodgson, newly arrived from Chorley. At the age of 25 Hodgson was a late arrival into league football, amazingly he had been playing in the Lancashire Combination since teenage and his potential had not been realised. Like Tommy Boyle he would play a key role in Burnley's success over the coming years, as indeed would Billy Nesbitt, signed from Portsmouth Rovers, initially as an amateur, during that significant week in September 1911.

Burnley's excellent start to the season continued and the goals kept on coming from the new hero of Turf Moor, Bert Freeman. He scored his first Clarets' hat-trick in an epic 4-3 win at Fulham, the first time Burnley had even picked up a point at Craven Cottage. Another hat-trick came in a 4-0 victory against Glossop at the turn of the year and at that stage Freeman had scored 23 goals in just 21 games. He was already only one short of the Burnley club record, held by Dick Smith, with half the season still to go!

The Clarets had been in the top two since the season began and it was not just Freeman's goals that were keeping them in the promotion places. Each member of the team was playing at the top of his form, with Tommy Boyle, by now club captain, beginning to exert his influence with his tremendous drive and ferocious will to win.

In December 1911 there was another significant arrival at Turf Moor, another addition to what was becoming a formidable squad, another name that was to become part of Turf Moor folklore. Left back David Taylor had been a key member of Bradford City's FA Cup winning side of 1911. City had knocked the Clarets out of the Cup that season of course and his commanding display, as well as his sheer pace, had made the Burnley manager and directors determined to see him in a Burnley shirt when the time was right. Another new signing was the experienced John Picken from Manchester United.

Bert Freeman
top scorer in his first season with 32 goals, a new record

January 1912 was a significant month in the push for promotion, with inside forward Richard Lindley, another emerging Turf Moor star, scoring his first Burnley hat-trick in a 5-1 demolition of Hull. There was also an injury to goal machine Bert Freeman, exit from the FA Cup at Fulham and two 0-1 league defeats, at Grimsby and crucially at Gainsborough, who were destined to finish at the very bottom of Division Two. Trinity would not win another home game at all that season and those two points dropped at Northolme would ultimately cost Burnley promotion. Significantly Bert Freeman missed the games against both Gainsborough and Grimsby!

It was back to winning ways again with a 1-0 success at Nottingham Forest, John Picken scoring a crucial goal, and a 3-0 home win against Barnsley, Bert Freeman on target again. Burnley were back on top of the league and seemed to have recovered their composure when they visited second in the table Chelsea. A crowd of 30,000 saw a polished, professional performance from the Clarets. Richard Lindley scored early on, then a crucial penalty save from the immaculate Jerry Dawson spurred the Burnley players on to raise their game to new heights. A goal from Bert Freeman finally clinched the points, with the Clarets full value for their 2-0 win.

Fulham were crushed 5-1 with yet another Freeman hat-trick in a magnificent team display, then Burnley came from behind to win 2-1 at Clapton, another of the promotion contenders. Burnley had now won six league games in a row, and were well clear at the top, and the supporters were already confident that promotion was as good as won.

The form of the Burnley team had been so outstanding that the international selectors had been to see for themselves. After his two games for England in 1909, Bert Freeman won three more full England caps in February and March 1912, scoring two goals and both Freeman and Tommy Boyle were chosen for the Football League against the Scottish League at Middlesbrough, with Freeman on target yet again.

A record Turf Moor crowd of 31,000 saw a goalless draw against fellow promotion hopefuls Derby, then came wins at Bristol City and against Stockport, yet another Burnley hat-trick, this time from Teddy Hodgson. At the start of the Easter weekend there were now only three teams in the race for promotion, Burnley were six points clear of Chelsea with Derby a further two points adrift. Crucially both Chelsea and Derby had played fewer games than the Clarets.

For the Good Friday game at Blackpool, Burnley were without Richard Lindley, and a poor game, a below par Clarets' performance, ended 0-0. Worse was to follow on Easter Saturday with a 0-4 hiding at mid-table Birmingham where Burnley, for just about the first time that season, were completely outplayed. A disastrous Easter weekend was completed with a 2-3 defeat at Leicester. Burnley were still on top but Derby and Chelsea had closed to within three points and both had two games in hand, although if Burnley won both their last two matches, their superior goal average would almost certainly guarantee promotion.

It was not to be. Huddersfield were beaten 3-0 in the last home game of the season but by then Derby had won their games in hand and were assured of the championship. Burnley were second best at Wolves in their final game and Chelsea won both their last two matches to edge Burnley out of the second promotion place by two points.

It had been a tremendous effort by the Burnley players and the Turf Moor fans had enjoyed some of the best football from their team in years. Bert Freeman had been awe-inspiring in front of goal, 32 in the league, including just one penalty, one more in a brief FA Cup run, and three hat-tricks. He had obliterated the Burnley goal scoring record and his 32 goals during that memorable campaign would only be exceeded on one occasion, and that by the peerless George Beel.

The hopes, indeed the expectations, of promotion back to the top flight had been shattered. The majority of Burnley fans however were not too downhearted, they knew full well that they now had a team to be proud of, a team to be reckoned with, a team going places. Their dream of First Division football at Turf Moor would just take a little longer but they were supremely confident that it would soon be realised.

They were absolutely right!

David Taylor
lightning quick full back signed from Bradford City

1911-12 - Second Division

		P	W	D	L	F	A	Pts
1	Derby C	38	23	8	7	74	28	54
2	Chelsea	38	24	6	8	64	34	54
3	BURNLEY	38	22	8	8	77	41	52
4	Clapton O	38	21	3	14	61	44	45
5	Wolverhampton W	38	16	10	12	57	33	42
6	Barnsley	38	15	12	11	45	42	42
7	Hull C	38	17	8	13	54	51	42
8	Fulham	38	16	7	15	66	58	39
9	Grimsby T	38	15	9	14	48	55	39
10	Leicester F	38	15	7	16	49	66	37
11	Bradford PA	38	13	9	16	44	45	35
12	Birmingham	38	14	6	18	55	59	34
13	Bristol C	38	14	6	18	41	60	34
14	Blackpool	38	13	8	17	32	52	34
15	Nottingham F	38	13	7	18	46	48	33
16	Stockport C	38	11	11	16	47	54	33
17	Huddersfield T	38	13	6	19	50	64	32
18	Glossop	38	8	12	18	42	56	28
19	Leeds C	38	10	8	20	50	78	28
20	Gainsborough T	38	5	13	20	30	64	23

1911-12

Manager : John Haworth

Division Two (3rd)

		Date			Opponents	Result		h/t	Goalscorers/times	Opp.goal times
	1	Sep	2	a	Glossop	W	3-1	2-0	Freeman 36, Mountford (2) 45, 65	49
	2		4	h	LEEDS C	W	4-2	2-1	Lindley 10, Freeman 31, Mountford (2) 60, 82	5, 74
	3		9	h	GAINSBOROUGH T	W	2-0	1-0	Lindley 16, Freeman 83	
	4		11	h	LEICESTER F	W	3-0	1-0	Mountford 30p, Freeman 56, Lindley 75	
	5		16	a	Hull C	L	1-4	1-2	Freeman 44	16, 25, 50, 75p
	6		23	h	GRIMSBY T	D	1-1	0-1	Freeman 70	14
	7		30	a	Barnsley	D	1-1	1-0	Mountford 25p	70
	8	Oct	7	h	NOTTINGHAM F	W	2-0	2-0	Freeman (2) 12, 23	
Mayson's last game	9		14	a	Bradford	L	1-2	0-1	Boyle 58	23, 60
	10		21	h	CHELSEA	D	2-2	1-0	Freeman 24, Harris 86	56, 59
	11		28	a	Fulham	W	4-3	2-0	Freeman (3) 25, 44, 62, Lindley 68	48p, 73, 85
	12	Nov	4	h	CLAPTON O	W	1-0	0-0	Freeman 65	
	13		18	h	BRISTOL C	W	4-2	2-1	Harris 20, Freeman (2) 45, 49p, Hodgson 74	40, 80
	14		25	a	Stockport C	W	1-0	0-0	Freeman 46	
	15	Dec	2	h	BIRMINGHAM	D	1-1	0-1	Freeman 65	42
	16		6	a	Derby C	L	0-2	0-2		30, 44
	17		9	a	Leeds C	W	5-1	2-0	Lindley 8, Freeman (2) 24, 65, Harris (2) 70, 80	90p
	18		16	a	Huddersfield T	D	1-1	1-1	Boyle 20	8
	19		23	h	WOLVERHAMPTON W	W	2-1	1-0	Freeman 42, Picken 49	57
	20		25	h	BLACKPOOL	D	1-1	0-1	Lindley 69	45
	21		30	h	GLOSSOP	W	4-0	1-0	Freeman (3) 20, 55, 60, Lindley 72	
Morley's last game	22	Jan	6	a	Gainsborough T	L	0-1	0-0		75p
	23		20	h	HULL C	W	5-1	1-0	Lindley (3) 43, 62, 70, Picken 49, Boyle 80	82p
	24		27	a	Grimsby T	L	0-1	0-0		65
	25	Feb	10	a	Nottingham F	W	1-0	1-0	Picken 5	
	26		12	h	BARNSLEY	W	3-0	1-0	Freeman 30, Hodgson (2) 57, 80	
Bannister's last game	27		17	h	BRADFORD	W	3-1	1-0	Lindley (2) 39, 84, Picken 79	77
	28		24	a	Chelsea	W	2-0	1-0	Lindley 20, Freeman 55	
	29	Mar	2	h	FULHAM	W	5-1	2-0	Freeman (3) 5, 13, 64, Lindley 51, Harris 61	59
	30		9	a	Clapton O	W	2-1	0-1	Freeman 61, Nesbitt 80	35
	31		16	h	DERBY C	D	0-0	0-0		
	32		23	a	Bristol C	W	3-0	2-0	Picken (2) 40, 75, Nesbitt 44	
	33		30	h	STOCKPORT C	W	4-1	3-0	Freeman 20, Hodgson (3) 25, 42, 87	70
	34	Apr	5	a	Blackpool	D	0-0	0-0		
	35		6	a	Birmingham	L	0-4	0-2		11, 40, 58, 67
Harris' last game	36		8	a	Leicester F	L	2-3	0-1	Freeman 70, Hodgson 80	44, 60, 76
	37		20	h	HUDDERSFIELD T	W	3-0	2-0	Freeman 13, Lindley 40, Boyle 70	
	38		27	a	Wolverhampton W	L	0-2	0-0		61, 70

FA Cup

1	Jan	13	a	Fulham	L	1-2	1-1	Freeman 20	35, 50

Final, Barnsley 1-0 West Bromwich A after extra time, at Bramall Lane, following a 0-0 draw, at Crystal Palace.

Other first team matches (friendlies and/or as detailed)

East Lancs Charity Cup semi	Oct	2	a	Accrington S	W	5-3		Goodison (3), Bates, Lindley	Bly Res
Lancs Cup		9	h	ST HELENS T	W	7-0		Freeman (4), Mayson (2), Lindley	
Lancs Cup		23	a	Oldham A	W	3-1		Lindley (2), Hodgson	
Lancs Cup semi	Nov	20	a	Blackburn R	W	3-1		Freeman (2) 1p, Lindley	
East Lancs Charity Cup final		27	h	BLACKBURN R	W	1-0	1-0	Hodgson	
Lancs Cup final	Dec	13	a	Bolton W	L	1-4	1-3	Bates	

Att.	Pos	Dawson	Reid	Bamford	McLaren	Swift	Watson	Morley	Lindley	B Freeman	Mountford	Mayson	Harris	Boyle	Hodgson	Snowden	Bates	Splitt	Goodison	D Taylor	Lowe	Picken	Woods	Bradshaw	Nesbitt	Bannister	Weightman	
2,000		1	2	3	4	5	6	7	8	9	10	11																1
15,000		1	2	3	4	5	6	7	8	9	10		11															2
10,000	top	1	2	3	4	5	6	7	8	9	10		11															3
9,000	top	1	2	3	4	5	6	7	8	9	10		11															4
10,000	top	1	2	3	4	5	6		8	9	10	11	7															5
11,000	top	1	2	3	4	5	6	7	8	9	10	11																6
8,000	top	1	2	3		4	6	7		9	10	11		5	8													7
17,833	top	1	2	3		4	6	7	8	9	10		11	5														8
25,000	2	1	2	3		4	6		8	9		10	11	5		7												9
12,000	2	1	2	3		4	6		8	9			11	5		7	10											10
16,000	2	1	2	3		4	6		8	9			11	5	10	7												11
16,000	top	1	2	3		4	6		8	9			11	5	10	7												12
11,000	top	1	2	3		4	6		8	9			11	5	10	7												13
8,000	top	1	2		4		6		8	9			11	5	10	7		3										14
13,000	top	1	2		4		6		8	9			11	5	10	7		3										15
12,000		1	2			4	6		8	9			11	5		7		3	10									16
10,000	top	1	2		4		6		8	9			11	5		7	10	3										17
8,000	top	1	2		4		6		8	9			10	5		7				3	11							18
7,000		1	2		4		6		8	9			11	5		7				3		10						19
26,500	2	1	2		4	5	6		8	9			11			7				3		10						20
11,000	2	1	2		4	5	6	7	8	9			11							3		10						21
2,000	3	1	2		4		6	7	8				10	5						3		9	11					22
10,000	2	1	2		4		6		8	9			11	5		7				3		10						23
3,000	3	1	2		4		6		8				11	5	10	7				3		9						24
9,000		1	2		4		6		8				7	5	9					3		10		11				25
8,000	top	1	2		4		6		8	9			11	5	10					3					7			26
14,000	top	1	2			4	6		8				11		10					3		9			7	5		27
30,000	top	1	2		4		6		8	9			11	5	10					3					7			28
16,000	top	1	2		4		6		8	9			11	5	10					3					7			29
17,000	top	1	2		4		6		8	9			11	5	10					3					7			30
30,000	top	1	2		4		6		8	9			11	5	10					3					7			31
10,000	top	1	2		4		6		8				11	5	10					3		9			7			32
12,500		1	2		4		6		8	9			11	5	10					3					7			33
15,000	top	1	2		4		6			9			11	5	8					3		10			7			34
35,000		1	2		4		6			9			11	5	8					3					7		10	35
	top	1	2		4		6			9			11	5	8					3		10			7			36
15,000	2	1	2		4		6		8	9	11			5	10					3					7			37
18,500		1	2		4		6		8	9	11			5						3		10			7			38
Appearances		38	38	13	29	17	38	9	34	33	10	5	33	29	20	14	2	4	1	21	1	12	1	1	13	1	1	
Goals (77)									15	32	6		5	4	7							6			2			

Att.	Pos	Dawson	Reid	Bamford	McLaren	Swift	Watson	Morley	Lindley	B Freeman	Mountford	Mayson	Harris	Boyle	Hodgson	Snowden	Bates	Splitt	Goodison	D Taylor	Lowe	Picken	Woods	Bradshaw	Nesbitt	Bannister	Weightman	
13,100		1	2		4		6		8	9		11			7				3		10	5						1
Appearances		1	1		1		1		1	1		1			1				1		1	1						
Goals (1)																												

1912-13

In the summer of 1912 there was just one significant arrival at Turf Moor, Edwin Mosscrop, a schoolmaster from Southport, who would go on to be a key part of the Turf Moor success story. Mosscrop made his debut in the opening match of the season, a 2-1 win against Glossop, but it was one of only two victories in the opening nine matches and, by mid-October Burnley were twelfth. The push for the long-awaited promotion seemed to have faltered and goal machine Bert Freeman had only scored twice.

Eddie Mosscrop
winger signed from Southport

Goalkeeper Jerry Dawson was dropped for the first time and a welcome 4-0 win against Huddersfield brought new signing James Bellamy his first Burnley goal. After a heavy defeat at Leeds the Clarets were back in mid table and a local overcoat specialist made the unique offer to provide a new coat to any Burnley player who scored two or more goals in a home match and also a coat to any spectator of that players' choice. The effect was almost instantaneous, Jerry Dawson was back to his brilliant best and the goals again started to flow from throughout the team, although Bert Freeman led the way once again. In his next 18 league and FA Cup games he scored an incredible 24 goals including four in a 5-1 demolition of Leicester Fosse at Turf Moor. Burnley reeled off eleven successive victories in league and FA Cup and a unique goalscoring sequence, beginning on Christmas Day, saw the team score at least three goals in ten successive matches. Promotion was very much back on track and from the turn of the year it looked like a three-horse race between Burnley, Preston and Birmingham for the two promotion places.

In January the FA Cup came round again and, after an abandonment at Leeds due to a snowy pitch, Burnley safely negotiated the replay to set up a Turf Moor meeting with Midland League Gainsborough Trinity. After giving their spirited visitors a goal start Burnley eventually turned on the power and emerged with a 4-1 victory but not until the last seven minutes were the Clarets fans able to relax. Within two hours of the final whistle, it was revealed that Burnley had signed Gainsborough's goalkeeper and both full backs! Trinity's captain Sam Gunton would not feature prominently in the Clarets' team but custodian Ronnie Sewell and left back Cliff Jones would both make their mark in Burnley's huge success to come.

Burnley were still on course for success on two fronts when promotion rivals Birmingham were swept aside 3-0 and First Division Middlesbrough were beaten 3-1 in the FA Cup, setting up a mouth watering confrontation with old adversaries Blackburn Rovers in the fourth round. Almost 43,000 people squeezed into Ewood Park to witness an epic encounter between two of football's oldest rivals, with the emerging force from Turf Moor proving just too strong for their First Division opponents, who of course, were the reigning league champions. Rovers performed well enough on the day but Burnley outplayed them with Jerry Dawson and Tommy Boyle in particular in magnificent form. Boyle it was who scored the winner, a thunderous header from an Eddie Mosscrop corner, a goal fit to win any match and it sent the thousands of Burnley supporters in the crowd into raptures. The Clarets had reached the semi finals of the FA Cup for the very first time.

Then, in March 1913, came the signing that was to complete the team re-building in that pre-war phase of the Turf Moor success story.

Bradford were persuaded to part with their Scottish right half back, a man who had earned himself a glowing reputation in two years at Park Avenue. On 15 March 1913, for a home match with Bury, the Turf Moor crowd enjoyed a 3-1 victory, a solid performance that kept Burnley in the promotion places. They were impressed with the display of the new man but they could not have realised that they were present on a historic day in Turf Moor history. The name of the new arrival was George Halley and the Burnley half back line that day, for the very first time, read Halley, Boyle and Watson.

In the FA Cup semi-final, to be played at Bramall Lane, Burnley were up against the best team in the country, Sunderland, who were the First Division leaders and who were confident of winning the first League and FA Cup double of the twentieth century. Very much the underdogs, the Clarets matched the Wearsiders all the way in an enthralling match, played in torrential rain throughout, with both teams adapting superbly to the dreadful conditions. The match finished goalless and the teams met again at St Andrews four days later. Once again Burnley refused to be overawed and, after Sunderland took an early lead, back they came with a penalty, crashed home by Tommy Boyle and a quite superb individual goal from the ever-reliable Bert Freeman. At half time Burnley were 2-1 in front and deservedly so, but after the interval it was a different story. The Clarets were under pressure for most of the second half with wave after wave of Sunderland attacks and, on the hour, the inevitable equaliser came from the penalty spot. Twelve minutes from time the Wearsiders' England forward George Holley beat Jerry Dawson with a blistering drive and it was all over. Sunderland could still win the coveted League and FA Cup double (although they didn't) and Burnley, who had proved they could live with the best, could concentrate on their main target, promotion back to Division One.

As it happened Burnley's new half back line did not play together much in that first season, both Tommy Boyle and Willie Watson missed the last six games of the campaign with injury. It mattered not, a win at Bradford, a point in a 1-1 draw at Champions-elect Preston and a comfortable 4-2 win at Turf Moor against Wolves saw the Clarets almost there.

Thirteen long years after Burnley had been relegated in 1900, promotion back to the top flight was finally clinched with a 3-2 victory at Filbert Street, Leicester. Teddy Hodgson was on target with two first half goals and although the Foxes hit back to equalise, yet again Bert Freeman was there with the winner with just 16 minutes to go. It was Freeman's 30th league goal of another memorable season for the England centre forward and his 35th in all in league and FA Cup. He had already surpassed his overall total of 33 in 1911-12 and with two league games to go he needed two to equal his own league record and three to establish a new one. There was also the question of the Second Division championship. Preston were three points in front with one game to play, Burnley had two matches left, both at home. Two wins coupled with a North End defeat would bring the title to Turf Moor for the second time.

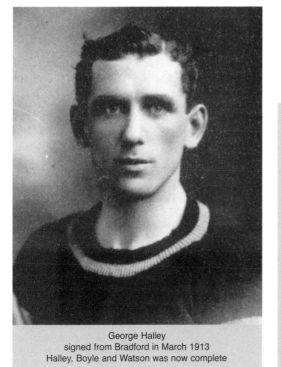

George Halley
signed from Bradford in March 1913
Halley, Boyle and Watson was now complete

It was not to be. Two lacklustre performances brought just two points and one goal for Bert Freeman. The Clarets had to settle for the runners up spot but, for the second season in succession they were the country's top scorers. Once again Bert Freeman had hit the thirty league goals mark and his totals of 32 in 1911-12 and 31 in 1912-13 still stand as second and third in Burnley history only to George Beel's phenomenal return of 35 in 1927-28.

To commemorate Burnley's return to the top flight, at the end of the Football League's twenty fifth year, the local MP Philip Morrell held a reception for the Burnley players, directors and officials. Supreme confidence was expressed in the Burnley team, it was felt that promotion was just the start and much more success was predicted for the club in the future.

That confidence was more than justified and no one who was present at that reception could possibly have imagined the success that Burnley Football Club was to enjoy in the years to come.

OVERCOAT WATCH

A total of eight overcoats were eventually presented to Burnley players, another eight going to their friends. Bert Freeman collected five of them for himself, politely declining a sixth for his third and fourth goals against Leicester Fosse. If the offer had been made at the start of the season and had covered all matches, 34 overcoats would have been given away, 20 of them to Bert Freeman or his friends!

1912-13 - Second Division

		P	W	D	L	F	A	Pts
1	Preston NE	38	19	15	4	56	33	53
2	BURNLEY	38	21	8	9	88	53	50
3	Birmingham	38	18	10	10	59	44	46
4	Barnsley	38	19	7	12	57	47	45
5	Huddersfield T	38	17	9	12	66	40	43
6	Leeds C	38	15	10	13	70	64	40
7	Grimsby T	38	15	10	13	51	50	40
8	Lincoln C	38	15	10	13	50	52	40
9	Fulham	38	17	5	16	65	55	39
10	Wolverhampton W	38	14	10	14	56	54	38
11	Bury	38	15	8	15	53	57	38
12	Hull C	38	15	6	17	60	56	36
13	Bradford PA	38	14	8	16	60	60	36
14	Clapton O	38	10	14	14	34	47	34
15	Leicester F	38	13	7	18	50	65	33
16	Bristol C	38	9	15	14	46	72	33
17	Nottingham F	38	12	8	18	58	59	32
18	Glossop	38	12	8	18	49	68	32
19	Stockport C	38	8	10	20	56	78	26
20	Blackpool	38	9	8	21	39	69	26

1912-13

Manager : John Haworth

Division Two (2nd)
Promoted

		Date			Opponents	Result		h/t	Goalscorers/times	Opp. goal times
	1	Sep	7	h	GLOSSOP	W	2-1	0-0	Mountford 66p, Taylor 84	72
	2		9	h	HULL C	D	0-0	0-0		
	3		14	a	Clapton O	L	0-2	0-2		2, 44
	4		16	h	PRESTON N E	D	2-2	2-1	Swift 6, Freeman 14	36, 69
	5		21	h	LINCOLN C	W	3-1	0-1	Freeman 52, Lindley (2) 85, 89	1
	6		26	a	Hull C	D	0-0	0-0		
	7		28	a	Nottingham F	L	1-2	1-2	Nesbitt 26	12, 44og
	8	Oct	5	h	BRISTOL C	D	2-2	0-1	Boyle 48, Husband 85	40, 81
Splitt's last game	9		12	a	Birmingham	L	0-3	0-2		25, 38, 90
	10		19	h	HUDDERSFIELD T	W	4-0	2-0	Husband 2, Bellamy 20, Freeman 51, Picken 83	
	11		26	a	Leeds C	L	1-4	0-1	Picken 52	18, 65, 79, 82
	12	Nov	2	h	GRIMSBY T	W	3-2	1-2	Watson 12, Freeman 61, Picken 64	14p, 20
	13		9	a	Bury	D	1-1	1-1	Picken 30	22
	14		16	h	FULHAM	W	5-0	2-0	Hodgson 35, Freeman (2) 43, 80, Watson 55, Husband 62	
	15		23	a	Barnsley	W	4-1	3-0	Husband 19, Freeman (2) 23, 40, Lindley 77	69
	16		30	h	BRADFORD	W	5-1	4-1	Freeman (2) 3, 33, Hodgson (2) 31, 38, Lindley 62	30
	17	Dec	7	a	Wolverhampton W	W	2-0	1-0	Hodgson 9, Boyle 80	
	18		14	h	LEICESTER F	W	5-1	3-0	Hodgson 13, Freeman (4) 22, 24, 51, 82	88p
	19		21	a	Stockport C	W	1-0	0-0	Freeman 86	
	20		25	h	BLACKPOOL	W	4-0	2-0	Husband 29, Hodgson (2) 22, 73, Bellamy 85	
	21		28	a	Glossop	W	3-1	2-0	Boyle 9p, Freeman 25, Hodgson 75	68
	22	Jan	4	h	CLAPTON O	W	5-0	3-0	Hodgson 6, Boyle 69, Lindley (3) 36, 43, 61	
	23		18	a	Lincoln C	W	3-1	1-1	Riley 35, Freeman (2) 56, 65	6
Swift's last game	24		25	h	NOTTINGHAM F	L	3-5	2-2	Freeman 24, Boyle 25p, Hodgson 90	10,12,55p,78,85
	25	Feb	8	a	Bristol C	D	3-3	1-2	Freeman (2) 28, 75, Mosscrop 87	7, 36, 56
	26		15	h	BIRMINGHAM	W	3-0	2-0	Lindley 33, Freeman (2) 38, 57	
	27		26	a	Huddersfield T	L	0-1	0-0		82p
	28	Mar	1	h	LEEDS C	D	2-2	1-0	Riley 45, Lindley 49	52, 80
	29		11	a	Grimsby T	L	0-2	0-2		30, 42
	30		15	h	BURY	W	3-1	3-1	Freeman (2) 35, 38, Boyle 42	4
	31		21	a	Blackpool	W	2-0	1-0	Mosscrop 43, Freeman 65	
	32		22	a	Fulham	L	2-4	0-4	Mosscrop 55, Freeman 70	5, 15, 17, 44
	33	Apr	5	a	Bradford	W	3-2	1-1	Husband (2) 36, 66, Freeman 55	4, 77
	34		10	a	Preston N E	D	1-1	0-1	Hodgson 49	7
	35		12	h	WOLVERHAMPTON W	W	4-2	1-1	Freeman 13, Halley 66p, Mosscrop 80, Hodgson 86	30, 63
	36		19	a	Leicester F	W	3-2	2-0	Hodgson (2) 37, 40, Freeman 74	54, 57
	37		23	h	BARNSLEY	L	0-1	0-1		41
	38		26	h	STOCKPORT C	W	3-2	2-0	Lindley 37, Hodgson 42, Freeman 75	47, 83

FA Cup

	1	Jan	15	a	Leeds C	W	3-2	1-1	Boyle 35p, Lindley 65, Freeman 82	15, 86
	2	Feb	1	h	GAINSBOROUGH T	W	4-1	0-1	Freeman 50, Hodgson (2) 65, 89, Boyle 83p	33
	3		22	h	MIDDLESBROUGH	W	3-1	1-1	Hodgson 35, Freeman (2) 58, 60	28
	4	Mar	8	a	Blackburn R	W	1-0	1-0	Boyle 33	
at Bramall Lane	semi		29	n	Sunderland	D	0-0	0-0		
at St Andrew's	rep	Apr	2	n	Sunderland	L	2-3	2-1	Boyle 12p, Freeman 17	6, 60p, 78

Final, Aston Villa 1-0 Sunderland, at Crystal Palace.

Other first team matches (friendlies and/or as detailed)

Lancs Cup	Oct	7	a	Bury	L	0-3	
FA Cup tie aban 50m, snow	Jan	11	a	Leeds C	aban	4-2	Hodgson, Boyle, Freeman (2)

Att.	Pos	Dawson	Reid	D Taylor	Bradshaw	Boyle	Watson	Mosscrop	Lindley	B Freeman	Picken	Mountford	Bamford	Swift	Nesbitt	Hodgson	McLaren	Husband	Splitt	Bellamy	Drabble	Riley	Sewell	Gunton	Jones	Halley	Charlton	
15,000		1	2	3	4	5	6	7	8	9	10	11																1
20,000	4	1	2	3			6		8	9		11	3	4	7	10												2
25,000		1	2	3			6			9		10		5	7	8	4	11										3
12,000	11	1	2	3		5	6			9		10		4	7	8		11										4
12,500	7	1	2	3		5	6		8	9		11		4	7	10												5
8,000		1	2	3		5	6		8	9		11		4	7	10												6
	7	1	2	3		5	6		8	9		11		4	7	10												7
15,000	6	1	2	3		5	6	7	8	9				4		10		11										8
15,000	12	1	2			5	6		8	9				4		10		11	3	7								9
13,000	7			3		5	6			9	10	8	2	4				11		7	1							10
10,000	11			3		5	6			9	10	8	2	4				11		7	1							11
12,000	8	1		3			6	7		9	10	8	2	4			5	11										12
12,000	8	1	2	5			6		8	9	10		3				4	11		7								13
13,000	8	1	2				6	7	8	9			3			10	5	11		4								14
7,000	6	1	2				6	7	8	9			3			10	5	11		4								15
13,000	3	1		3			6	7	8	9			2			10	5	11		4								16
6,000	2	1		3		5	6	7	8	9			2			10		11		4								17
15,000	top	1		3		5	6	7	8	9			2			10		11		4								18
8,000	top	1		3		5	6	7	8	9			2			10		11		4								19
25,000	top	1		3		5	6	7	8	9			2			10		11		4								20
5,000	top	1		3		5	6	7	8	9			2			10		11		4								21
13,000	2	1		3		5	6	7	8	9						10	2	11		4								22
	top	1		3		5	6		8	9				4	7		2	10				11						23
12,500	2	1		3		5	6		8	9			2	4	7	10						11						24
11,000	2					5	6	7	8	9						10	4	11					1	2	3			25
2,000	2			4			6		8	9		7	2			10	5	11					1		3			26
4,500						5	6		8		9	7	2			10	4	11					1		3			27
12,000	2			4			6		8	9			2		7	10	5					11	1		3			28
	2	1		3		5	6		8	9		7	2			10	4	11										29
13,000	2					5	6	7	8	9		11	2			10							1		3	4		30
13,000	2	1		3		5	6	7	8	9			2			10		11								4		31
25,000	2	1		3		5	6	7	8	9			2			10				4							11	32
15,000	2				6			7	8	9			2			10	5	11					1		3	4		33
18,000	2	1		3				7	8	9						10	5	11							2	4	6	34
5,000	2	1		3	6			7	8	9						10	5	11							2	4		35
		1		3	6			7	8	9						10		11		4					2	5		36
18,500	2	1		3	6			7	8	9			2			10		11		4						5		37
		1			6			7	8	9			3			10	2	11		4						5		38
Appearances		30	12	30	6	23	32	22	33	37	6	14	24	13	9	32	17	29	1	17	2	3	6	1	9	8	2	
Goals (88)				1		6	2	4	10	31	4	1		1	1	15		7		2		2				1		

Att.	Pos	Dawson	Reid	D Taylor	Bradshaw	Boyle	Watson	Mosscrop	Lindley	B Freeman	Picken	Mountford	Bamford	Swift	Nesbitt	Hodgson	McLaren	Husband	Splitt	Bellamy	Drabble	Riley	Sewell	Gunton	Jones	Halley	Charlton	
13,109		1		3		5	6	7	8	9			2			10	4	11										1
18,092		1		3		5	6	7	8	9			2			10	4	11										2
27,824		1		3		5	6		8	9		7	2			10	4	11										3
42,778		1		3		5	6	7	8	9			2			10	4	11										4
33,656		1		3		5	6	7	8	9			2			10	4	11										semi
30,000		1		3		5	6		8	9			2			10	4	11		7								rep
Appearances		6		6		6	6	4	6	6		1	6			6	6	6		1								
Goals (13)						4			1	5						3												

1913-14

There were no new signings at all in the summer of 1913, the team had done so well in their FA Cup clashes with First Division sides during the promotion season, the manager and directors decided the same players should be given a chance in Burnley's first top-flight campaign for thirteen years.

There were no victories in the first three games with the opening of the home campaign proving to be particularly disappointing. Blackburn Rovers were the visitors and a crowd of 38,000 turned up, the majority hoping that Rovers were to be put in their place. Bert Freeman scored in the first few minutes, his first ever Division One goal at Turf Moor, but Blackburn came back to take the points, an early reminder that a tough season lay ahead.

The Burnley players soon adapted to their new surroundings however. Chelsea were hit for six, thanks to a superb hat-trick from Teddy Hodgson, and there were comfortable wins against Sheffield Wednesday and Tottenham. By the end of October Burnley were eighth and looked to have settled in well amongst the country's football elite.

On the first day of November 1913 the Burnley Vice Chairman William Bracewell and Manager John Haworth visited St Helens to meet a talented young footballer then playing in the Lancashire Combination. Mr Bracewell had been watching the eighteen-year-old for a few weeks and reckoned he knew potential when he saw it. St Helens were asked not to play their young star in their FA Cup preliminary round match, a cheque for £275 was handed over, and the teenager was on his way to Turf Moor. That youngster left behind forever his life as a collier and went on to become arguably Burnley's greatest-ever player during the first half of the twentieth century and a key member of Turf Moor's legendary First Division Championship side less than eight years hence.

The young man's name was, of course, Bob Kelly.

At the turn of the year the Clarets travelled to Hillsborough for the first time to play Sheffield Wednesday, and thrashed the Owls 6-2. It was Burnley's first away win of the season and the first time they had ever scored six away from home in a First Division match. It set the team up perfectly for the FA Cup and South Shields, Derby and Bolton were all despatched at Turf Moor before the biggest test, an away tie at Sunderland. The Rokermen had beaten the Clarets in the semi final the previous year of course and the men from Turf Moor were out for revenge. An epic encounter with the reigning League Champions ended goalless and four days later the teams met again at Turf Moor. In front of a huge crowd of almost 50,000, dwarfing the previous Turf Moor record, both teams again served up a feast of football of the highest quality. This time however Burnley had the measure of their illustrious opponents and, as well as Sunderland played, the Clarets played better, goals from Teddy Hodgson and Richard Lindley earning a semi final place, with just a last minute consolation from the visitors.

After their two magnificent performances against Sunderland, who had been the favourites to progress, the Burnley Express was moved to write "if Burnley keep playing as they have been, no team on earth can stop them". However, the Clarets promptly went off the boil somewhat with four successive League defeats including a 0-5 hammering at Sheffield United, the third meeting in a week with the Blades. Burnley scored just once in these three games, but it was the goal that mattered, crashed in by skipper Tommy Boyle in the FA Cup semi final replay at Goodison Park. Almost 56,000 people had squeezed into Old Trafford for the first meeting and they had witnessed a disappointing goalless encounter, made even more disappointing for the Burnley contingent by an injury to Jerry Dawson. It transpired that Dawson, already carrying a groin injury, had torn a muscle and, although he completed the game, his movement was severely restricted and, unless he improved dramatically, his season appeared to be over.

Tommy Boyle
captain supreme with the FA Cup

Reserve keeper Ronnie Sewell stepped in to deputise in the lead-up to the final, with the Burnley trainer Ernest Edwards working constantly on Dawson to try to give him a fighting chance to take his place in the team on the big day. The week before the final it was decided to risk him in Burnley's penultimate league match at Manchester City. It was a costly error of judgement. Within ten minutes Dawson had been charged recklessly by the City centre forward and fifteen minutes later he hobbled off the field, obviously in great pain and unable to continue. A re-organised Burnley team, with David Taylor in goal, rather went through the motions for the remainder of the game, City winning 4-1.

Trainer Edwards continued his feverish treatment on Dawson during the last few days before Burnley's FA Cup final date with Liverpool, now given added significance with the announcement that King George V would be watching, the first time a reigning Monarch was to attend association football's most important occasion. The decision whether or not Jerry Dawson played was left until as late as possible on the very day of the final and, ultimately, was left to Dawson himself. Just an hour before kick off came the announcement of a change to Burnley's published line-up. Ronnie Sewell would replace Jerry Dawson in goal.

It has to be said that the final itself was not the most exciting. The day was far too sunny for football, and the ground was dry and hard. Both teams struggled with the heat and the first half was largely forgettable. The Burnley players knew that they were the better team and stepped up the pace in the second half. With almost an hour gone the Clarets had a throw in on the right, the ball was picked up by Billy Nesbitt who found Teddy Hodgson with a high cross. Hodgson beat Liverpool full back, Longworth, in the air and a precise header laid the ball into the path of Bert Freeman, steaming in to the penalty area. Freeman met the ball perfectly on the half volley and drove it into Liverpool's net beyond their despairing keeper. The Burnley section of the crowd erupted with joy, and from then until the final whistle, were in full voice. The Clarets' tails were now up and for the rest of the game piled on the pressure, Hodgson hit the post, Nesbitt stumbled with the goal at his mercy and Lindley shot wide with just the goalkeeper to beat. At last the final whistle blew and Burnley Football Club had won the FA Cup for the first time. After the cheering hordes had dispersed from the pitch Tommy Boyle was presented with the FA Cup by King George V, the very first time that a winning captain had received the famous old trophy from his Monarch.

Burnley supporters still wax lyrical about the team that played before the King and brought the FA Cup to Turf Moor for the first and so far only time.

Sewell, Bamford, Taylor, Halley, Boyle, Watson, Nesbitt, Lindley Freeman, Hodgson, Mosscrop.

It is perhaps a sobering thought to consider that that particular Burnley team played alongside each other on just four occasions altogether in League and FA Cup and, sadly, they were never to line up together again after that memorable and historic day all those years ago.

It was also the last act of the intimacy between the Crystal Palace Grounds and the FA Cup, the famous old Stadium would never again stage the FA Cup final.

On the Monday after the final, over 40,000 people turned up at Turf Moor for Burnley's last league game of the season against Bradford City. The result, a 2-2 draw confirming twelfth place didn't matter, what the fans had really come to see was the FA Cup, being paraded around their ground by their team. They all went home afterwards happy and content, already impatient for next season to start.

They could not have dreamt that, before another ball was kicked in Football League action, an assassin's bullet would set in motion a chain of events that would plunge their country, their continent, into the bloodiest conflict in history.

The Burnley team
leaving Rose Grove station with the FA Cup

1913-14 - First Division

		P	W	D	L	F	A	Pts
1	Blackburn R	38	20	11	7	78	42	51
2	Aston Villa	38	19	6	13	65	50	44
3	Middlesbrough	38	19	5	14	77	60	43
4	Oldham A	38	17	9	12	55	45	43
5	West Bromwich A	38	15	13	10	46	42	43
6	Bolton W	38	16	10	12	65	52	42
7	Sunderland	38	17	6	15	63	52	40
8	Chelsea	38	16	7	15	46	55	39
9	Bradford C	38	12	14	12	40	40	38
10	Sheffield U	38	16	5	17	63	60	37
11	Newcastle U	38	13	11	14	39	48	37
12	BURNLEY	38	12	12	14	61	53	36
13	Manchester C	38	14	8	16	51	53	36
14	Manchester U	38	15	6	17	52	62	36
15	Everton	38	12	11	15	46	55	35
16	Liverpool	38	14	7	17	46	62	35
17	Tottenham H	38	12	10	16	50	62	34
18	Sheffield W	38	13	8	17	53	70	34
19	Preston NE	38	12	6	20	52	69	30
20	Derby C	38	8	11	19	55	71	27

1913-14

Manager : John Haworth

Division One (12th)

		Date			Opponents	Result		h/t	Goalscorers/times	Opp. goal times
	1	Sep	1	a	Everton	D	1-1	0-0	Bellamy 71	83
	2		6	a	West Bromwich A	L	1-4	0-3	Freeman 56	5, 8, 10, 84
	3		8	h	BLACKBURN R	L	1-2	1-1	Freeman 4	35, 49
	4		13	h	SHEFFIELD W	W	3-0	0-0	Hodgson 65, Mountford 71, Freeman 79	
	5		20	a	Bolton W	D	0-0	0-0		
Chelsea goal 23m p	6		27	h	CHELSEA	W	6-1	3-1	Hodgson (3) 7, 69, 85, Halley 14, Freeman 30, Charlton 77	
	7	Oct	4	a	Oldham A	D	1-1	1-1	Boyle 23	10p
	8		11	h	MANCHESTER U	L	1-2	1-1	Freeman 36	28, 49
	9		18	h	TOTTENHAM H	W	3-1	1-1	Charlton (2) 16, 78, Boyle 52p	25
McLaren's last game	10		25	a	Preston N E	L	1-2	1-1	Hodgson 2	36, 83
	11	Nov	1	h	NEWCASTLE U	W	1-0	1-0	Lindley 35	
	12		8	a	Liverpool	D	1-1	1-1	Freeman 5	18
	13		15	h	ASTON VILLA	W	4-0	3-0	Lindley 5, Watson 23, Kelly 31, Freeman 87	
	14		22	a	Middlesbrough	L	1-2	1-2	Freeman 13	10, 43
	15		29	h	SHEFFIELD U	D	0-0	0-0		
	16	Dec	6	a	Derby C	L	1-3	1-1	Boyle 40p	30, 80, 87
	17		13	h	MANCHESTER C	W	2-0	1-0	Lindley 17, Hodgson 84	
	18		20	a	Bradford C	D	1-1	1-0	Freeman 8	75
	19		25	h	SUNDERLAND	L	0-1	0-0		69
	20		26	a	Sunderland	D	1-1	1-0	Hodgson 14	60
	21		27	h	WEST BROMWICH A	D	0-0	0-0		
	22	Jan	1	a	Blackburn R	D	0-0	0-0		
Wednesday goals 59m, 85m	23		3	a	Sheffield W	W	6-2	2-0	Halley 8, Hodgson 16, Nesbitt 46, Freeman 71, Lindley (2) 86, 89	
	24		17	h	BOLTON W	D	2-2	1-1	Hodgson (2) 9, 84	23, 47
	25		24	a	Chelsea	D	0-0	0-0		
	26	Feb	7	h	OLDHAM A	W	2-0	2-0	Hodgson 4, Lindley 44	
	27		14	a	Manchester U	W	1-0	1-0	Freeman 2	
	28		23	a	Tottenham H	L	0-2	0-0		80p, 83
	29		28	h	PRESTON N E	L	3-4	3-1	Boyle (2) 20p, 39, Mosscrop 44	15, 60, 76, 88
Liverpool goals 30m, 62m	30	Mar	14	h	LIVERPOOL	W	5-2	2-1	Lindley 2, Boyle 24p, Thorpe 75, Pickering 77, Mosscrop 89	
	31		18	a	Newcastle U	L	1-3	0-1	Nesbitt 61	24, 75, 84
Reid's last game	32		21	a	Aston Villa	L	0-1	0-1		29
	33	Apr	4	a	Sheffield U	L	0-5	0-2		21, 31, 52, 74, 77
	34		6	h	MIDDLESBROUGH	L	1-2	1-1	Freeman 15	24, 71
	35		10	h	EVERTON	W	2-0	1-0	Lindley 25, Freeman 48	
	36		11	h	DERBY C	W	5-1	2-1	Freeman (3) 10, 34, 65, Lindley (2) 70, 75	34
	37		18	a	Manchester C	L	1-4	0-2	Hodgson 65	15, 35, 76, 81
	38		27	h	BRADFORD C	D	2-2	0-2	Boyle 65p, Taylor 87	15, 30

FA Cup

	1	Jan	10	h	SOUTH SHIELDS	W	3-1	2-0	Lindley (2) 14, 16, Freeman 46	84
	2		31	h	DERBY C	W	3-2	1-0	Hodgson (3) 13, 78, 85	66, 82
	3	Feb	21	h	BOLTON W	W	3-0	1-0	Freeman 29, Hodgson 61, Halley 80	
	4	Mar	7	a	Sunderland	D	0-0	0-0		
	rep		11	h	SUNDERLAND	W	2-1	1-0	Hodgson 4, Lindley 66	90
at Old Trafford	semi		28	n	Sheffield U	D	0-0	0-0		
at Goodison Park	rep	Apr	1	n	Sheffield U	W	1-0	0-0	Boyle 75	
at Crystal Palace	Final		25	n	Liverpool	W	1-0	0-0	Freeman 58	

Other first team matches (friendlies and/or as detailed)

EL Charity Cup semi, 1912-13	Sep	22	a	Blackburn R	D	0-0	
Lancs Cup	Oct	6	h	BLACKBURN R	W	3-0	Lindley, Boyle p, Freeman
Lancs Cup		20	h	MANCHESTER C	L	1-2	Boyle p
ELCC semi rep, 1912-13	Jan	19	h	BLACKBURN R	L	2-4	Kelly, Robertson
East Lancs Charity Cup	Apr	15	a	Accrington S	L	0-3	
Charity match		29	a	Liverpool	L	0-1	
	May	17	a	Berlin Victoria	W	2-1	Lindley, Freeman
at Ferencvaros' ground		21	n	Celtic	D	1-1	Boyle p
		24	a	Ferencvaros	L	1-3	Lindley
at Ferencvaros' ground		27	a	Hungarian Am. XI	W	2-0	Freeman, Nesbitt
		31	a	Rapid Vienna	W	3-1	Freeman, Nesbitt, Kelly
at Rapid's ground	Jun	1	a	Austrian XI	L	0-3	

Att.	Pos	Dawson	Bamford	D Taylor	Halley	Boyle	Watson	Bellamy	Lindley	B Freeman	Hodgson	Husband	Nesbitt	Jones	Mosscrop	Mountford	McLaren	Charlton	Thorpe	Kelly	Milligan	Reid	Pickering	Bradshaw	Sewell	Tranter	
		1	2	3	4	5	6	7	8	9	10	11															1
27,014		1	2	3	4	5	6	7	8	9	10	11															2
36,000		1	2	3	4	5	6		8	9	10	11	7														3
23,000	10	1	2		4	5	6		8	9	10			3	7	11											4
33,000	12	1	2	3	4	5	6		8	9	10				7	11											5
30,000	9	1	2	3	4		6		8	9	10				7		5	11									6
20,000	6	1	2		4	5	6		8	9	10			3	7			11									7
30,000	10	1	2	3	4	5	6		8	9	10				7			11									8
22,000	7	1	2		4	5	6			9	10	11		3	7			8									9
27,000		1	2	3		5	6			9	10		11		7		4	8									10
25,000	8	1	2	3		5	6		8	9	10		11		7				4								11
18,000	8	1	2	3		5	6		8	9	10		11		7				4								12
20,000	6	1	2			5	6		8	9		11		3	7				4	10							13
15,800	9	1	2		4	5	6		8	9		11		3	7					10							14
23,000	8	1	2	3	4	5			8	9		11			7				6	10							15
12,000	10	1	2	3	4	5			8	9	10		11		7				6								16
20,000	8	1	2	3	4	5			8	9	10		11		7				6								17
16,000		1	2	3	4		6		8	9	10		11		7				5								18
25,000		1	2	3	4	5	6	7	8	9	10				11												19
35,000	11	1	2	3	4	9	6		8		10				7				5	11							20
15,000	8	1	2	3	4	9	6		8		10				7				5	11							21
48,000	8	1	2	3	4	5	6		8	9	10		7		11												22
	8	1	2	3	4	5	6		8	9	10		7		11												23
	9	1	2	3	4	5	6		8	9	10		7		11												24
35,000	9	1	2	3	4	5	6		8	9	10		7		11												25
20,000	5	1	2	3	4	5	6		8	9	10		7		11												26
35,000	5	1	2	3	4	5			8	9	10		7		11				6								27
15,000	7	1	2	3		5	6	11	8	9	10		7						4								28
	9	1	2	3	4	5	6		8	9			7		11						10						29
16,000	7	1	2		4	5			8		10		7		11				6			3	9				30
15,000	8	1	2		4						10	11	7						5		8	3	9	6			31
30,000	9		2		4		6					11	7						5	8		3	9		1	10	32
18,000			2	3	4	5	6		8		10	11	7												1	9	33
6,000	13		2	3	4		6		8	9			7						5	11					1	10	34
	11		2	3	4	5	6		8	9	10		7		11										1		35
18,000			2	3	4	5	6		8	9	10		7		11										1		36
18,000	12	1	2	3	4	5	6		8		10		7		11				9								37
40,000			2	3	4	5	11		8	9	10		7						6						1		38
Appearances		32	38	30	33	33	32	4	34	31	32	10	24	5	29	2	2	5	17	7	2	3	3	1	6	3	
Goals (61)				1	2	7	1	1	10	16	12		2		2	1		3	1	1			1				

Att.	Dawson	Bamford	D Taylor	Halley	Boyle	Watson	Bellamy	Lindley	B Freeman	Hodgson	Husband	Nesbitt	Jones	Mosscrop	Mountford	McLaren	Charlton	Thorpe	Kelly	Milligan	Reid	Pickering	Bradshaw	Sewell	Tranter	
18,000	1	2	3	4	5	6		8	9	10		7		11												1
30,000	1	2	3	4	5	6		8	9	10		7		11												2
32,734	1	2	3	4	5	6		8	9	10		7		11												3
34,581	1	2	3	4	5	6		8	9	10		7		11												4
49,737	1	2	3	4	5	6		8	9	10		7		11												rep
55,812	1	2	3	4	5	6		8	9	10		7		11												semi
27,000		2	3	4	5	6		8	9	10		7		11										1		rep
72,778		2	3	4	5	6		8	9	10		7		11										1		Final
Appearances	6	8	8	8	8	8		8	8	8		8		8										2		
Goals (13)				1	1			3	3	5																

1914-15

In the spring of 1914, following their FA Cup triumph, Burnley FC embarked on their first-ever continental tour and, less than three months before the clouds of war began to darken over Europe, the Clarets were playing football in Germany and in what was then Austria-Hungary. The club's first meeting with foreign opposition on foreign soil was against Berlin Victoria in May 1914 with goals from Richard Lindley and Bert Freeman ensuring a 2-1 victory. The tour took in matches against clubs famous today, Ferencvaros and Rapid Vienna, as well as a bad-tempered 1-1 draw against Celtic, also touring the continent.

Tom Bamford
an FA Cup winner in 1914, ever present in 1914-15

During the first week in August 1914, war was finally declared and for a time, it was uncertain whether or not the 1914-15 season would ever start. The Football Association met to consider suspending football at all levels but decided that, for the time being at least, the country's national game should continue but that "clubs having professional players are urged to give every facility for their temporary release".
The season began as the previous one had ended, with a home game against Bradford City. This time the world was a very different place and this time there was none of the excitement and sheer joy that had surrounded the Bantams' previous visit, the day the FA Cup had come to Turf Moor just four short months before. How long ago that now seemed. There was not too much for the Turf Moor faithful to enthuse about in the first few weeks of the new campaign although Tottenham were given a football lesson on their own ground, Bert Freeman leading the way to a 3-1 win with his first two goals of the season. Freeman hit one of his purple patches in October and November with a spell of eight goals in five games but, for the first time since his arrival at Turf Moor, he was destined not to finish the season as Burnley's leading scorer in the league. Teddy Hodgson would be the man to temporarily take over as the Clarets' leading marksman.
As the effects of the war began to bite more deeply into the Burnley economy, Turf Moor attendances were down, even though the club were able to reduce some admission prices. The arguments still raged about whether or not football should be played at all and indeed the War Office tried to persuade the clubs that all footballers should enlist in the Army. In response to this the Lancashire clubs met and decided that their players should all undergo military training. After discussion with the Players Union it was also decided that the wages of the players at the top clubs should be reduced with a fund set up to help out the smaller clubs.
When the FA Cup came round again, Burnley began their defence of the trophy with comfortable victories against Second Division Huddersfield and Southern League Southend, both at Turf Moor. Bolton were a different proposition however, especially at Burnden Park, and 43,000 people, by far the biggest crowd of the season to watch a Burnley match, saw the Clarets lose an epic encounter, and their hold on the famous old trophy, to a goal just seven minutes from the end of extra time.
As the season progressed, more and more families in Burnley and the surrounding area were affected by events across the Channel. News arrived almost on a daily basis of loved ones captured, wounded or, most tragically of all, never coming home. It was only a matter of time before the extended family that was, and is, Burnley Football Club began to be affected. Word arrived that assistant trainer Charlie Bates was a prisoner of war in Germany, then Henry Bowes, the soldier son of former Turfite Billy Bowes, was reported to have been killed. Then came the saddest news of all, for everyone at Turf Moor, the first Burnley footballer to be lost was reserve winger Alf Lorrimer.

OBITUARY
ALFRED (ALF) LORRIMER
DIED 1 FEB 1915, AGED 23

Alfred Lorrimer met his death in Egypt where he was serving his country as an RAMC reservist.
Born in Longridge in 1892, Alf Lorrimer was working as a tailor in Burnley and playing in the Burnley Tuesday League when he was given a trial in Burnley's reserve team in February 1914. He played his first Central League game on the right wing in Burnley's 2-1 win against Southport Central and impressed so much he was immediately offered a professional contract. He was fast, possessed excellent ball control and showed every sign of becoming a top professional player.
Immediately the news of his death reached Turf Moor, the club's flag was placed at half-mast.

RIP

As the league season approached its conclusion it became increasingly apparent that organised football could not and would not continue in its present form beyond the end of the current campaign. Ten thousand people turned up at Turf Moor for Burnley's last home league match, the last for some considerable time, a 2-1 win against Sunderland. It was fitting that the Clarets' last league goals of the season in front of their adoring fans should be scored by William Pickering and top-scorer Teddy Hodgson and both were cheered to the echo. Tragically, after the guns finally fell silent in 1918, neither player would be seen at Turf Moor in Football League action again.

Jerry Dawson (left) and Billy Nesbitt
Burnley stalwarts either side of the Great War

Following defeat at Bolton in March 1915, Burnley had ended a difficult season in some style, unbeaten in the final nine League matches with seven wins and two draws. After a goalless draw at Sheffield Wednesday on the season's final day Burnley had risen to fourth position, just three points behind Champions Everton, who had been beaten both home and away. With just a key extra point here and there Turf Moor could so easily have been celebrating its first-ever League title. Those celebrations however, as was surely the case at Goodison Park, would have been muted indeed.

The cup-winning habit had been continued however with the Lancashire Cup coming to Turf Moor for the first time in 25 years. Impressive wins over both Manchester United and Liverpool were followed by a gripping semi final against Blackburn, which Burnley just edged 2-1. The final was a comparatively straightforward 4-1 victory against Rochdale at Hyde Road, Manchester, where the Clarets came up against an old friend. Burnley-born Albert Smith had begun his senior career at Turf Moor in 1905 and had lit up many Turfites' performances with his electrifying pace along either wing.

As a bonus Burnley also won the East Lancashire Charity Cup, although the senior professional sides, Burnley included, were now beginning to field mainly reserve team players in the competition.

The final words of that final season of anything like football normality for four long years should be left with Lord Derby. His exhortation in front of the crowd of 70,000 at Old Trafford after presenting the FA Cup to Sheffield United captain George Utley, after the Blades' 3-0 victory over Chelsea was as follows –

"You have played with one another and against one another for the Cup. It is now the duty of everyone to join with one another, and play a sterner game - for England!"

1914-15 - First Division

		P	W	D	L	F	A	Pts
1	Everton	38	19	8	11	76	47	46
2	Oldham A	38	17	11	10	70	56	45
3	Blackburn R	38	18	7	13	83	61	43
4	BURNLEY	38	18	7	13	61	47	43
5	Manchester C	38	15	13	10	49	39	43
6	Sheffield U	38	15	13	10	49	41	43
7	Sheffield W	38	15	13	10	61	54	43
8	Sunderland	38	18	5	15	81	72	41
9	Bradford PA	38	17	7	14	69	65	41
10	West Bromwich A	38	15	10	13	49	43	40
11	Bradford C	38	13	14	11	55	49	40
12	Middlesbrough	38	13	12	13	62	74	38
13	Liverpool	38	14	9	15	65	75	37
14	Aston Villa	38	13	11	14	62	72	37
15	Newcastle U	38	11	10	17	46	48	32
16	Notts C	38	9	13	16	41	57	31
17	Bolton W	38	11	8	19	68	84	30
18	Manchester U	38	9	12	17	46	62	30
19	Chelsea	38	8	13	17	51	65	29
20	Tottenham H	38	8	12	18	57	90	28

1914-15

Manager : John Haworth

Division One (4th)

Note	No.	Date			Opponents	Result		h/t	Goalscorers/times	Opp. goal times
	1	Sep	5	h	BRADFORD C	L	0-1	0-0		61
	2		7	h	EVERTON	W	1-0	0-0	Thorpe 79	
	3		12	a	Manchester C	L	0-1	0-0		82p
	4		19	a	Tottenham H	W	3-1	1-0	Freeman (2) 30, 57, Hodgson 72	55
	5		26	h	NEWCASTLE U	W	2-0	1-0	Lindsay 4, Boyle 66	
	6	Oct	3	a	Middlesbrough	D	1-1	1-1	Lindsay 4	39
	7		10	h	SHEFFIELD U	L	1-2	0-0	Freeman 89	60, 86
	8		17	a	Aston Villa	D	3-3	2-1	Freeman (2) 11, 62, Lindsay 30	44p, 60, 68
	9		24	h	LIVERPOOL	W	3-0	2-0	Freeman (2) 24, 81, Hodgson 35	
	10		31	a	Bradford	D	2-2	1-1	Freeman (2) 15, 57	43, 50
	11	Nov	7	h	OLDHAM A	L	2-3	2-1	Freeman 27, Hodgson 34	43, 63, 83
	12		14	a	Manchester U	W	2-0	0-0	Hodgson (2) 63, 75	
	13		21	h	BOLTON W	W	5-0	1-0	Lindley (2) 37, 76, Hodgson 50, Kelly 60, Boyle 69p	
	14		28	a	Blackburn R	L	0-6	0-4		13,20,35,41,50og,84
	15	Dec	5	h	NOTTS C	D	0-0	0-0		
	16		12	a	Sunderland	L	1-2	0-2	Kelly 85	15, 38
	17		19	h	SHEFFIELD W	L	2-3	1-3	Hodgson 45, Lindsay 70	3, 5, 35
	18		25	h	WEST BROMWICH A	L	0-2	0-1		36, 75
	19		26	a	West Bromwich A	L	0-3	0-2		25, 35, 65
	20		28	a	Chelsea	W	4-1	2-0	Kelly 10, Hodgson 43, Freeman 60, Pickering 70	65
	21	Jan	2	a	Bradford C	D	0-0	0-0		
	22		18	h	MANCHESTER C	L	1-2	0-0	Hodgson 46	63, 80
	23		23	h	TOTTENHAM H	W	3-1	0-1	Kelly 67, Hodgson 78, Taylor 87	20
	24	Feb	6	h	MIDDLESBROUGH	W	4-0	0-0	Hodgson (2) 50, 75, Boyle 53, Kelly 65	
	25		13	a	Sheffield U	L	0-1	0-1		35
	26		22	h	ASTON VILLA	W	2-1	1-0	Kelly 43, Pickering 82	80
	27		27	a	Liverpool	L	0-3	0-2		16p, 29, 68
	28	Mar	6	h	BRADFORD	W	2-0	1-0	Thorpe 24, Hodgson 51	
	29		13	a	Bolton W	L	1-3	1-1	Hodgson 10	45, 53, 77
	30		20	h	MANCHESTER U	W	3-0	2-0	Pickering (2) 18, 44, Hodgson 85	
	31	Apr	2	a	Everton	W	2-0	1-0	Hodgson 25, Kelly 69	
	32		3	h	BLACKBURN R	W	3-2	1-0	Freeman 29, Hodgson 55, Mosscrop 70	52, 83p
	33		5	h	CHELSEA	W	2-0	1-0	Hodgson 40, Nesbitt 71	
	34		10	a	Notts C	D	0-0	0-0		
	35		14	a	Newcastle U	W	2-1	1-0	Boyle 20, Kelly 78	56
	36		17	h	SUNDERLAND	W	2-1	1-1	Pickering 10, Hodgson 86	55
	37		20	a	Oldham A	W	2-1	1-0	Kelly (2) 39, 75	80
last games for Hodgson & Bamford	38		24	a	Sheffield W	D	0-0	0-0		

FA Cup

Note	No.	Date			Opponents	Result		h/t	Goalscorers/times	Opp. goal times
	1	Jan	9	h	HUDDERSFIELD T	W	3-1	1-0	Freeman 22, Thorpe 47, Kelly 64	80
	2		30	h	SOUTHEND U	W	6-0	2-0	Freeman (2) 5, 65, Boyle 42p, Kelly 46, Thorpe 50, Watson 79	
After extra time, 1-1 at 90m	3	Feb	20	a	Bolton W	L	1-2	1-1	Hodgson 43	19, 113

Final, Sheffield Utd 3-0 Chelsea, at Old Trafford.

Other first team matches (friendlies and/or as detailed)

Note	Date			Opponents	Result		Goalscorers
	Aug	29	a	Blackpool	W	3-2	Boyle, Pickering (2)
"Buda Pesth Cup" match	Sep	1	h	CELTIC	L	1-2	Watson p
Lancs Cup	Oct	5	h	MANCHESTER U	W	5-0	Lindsay (3), Pickering, Hodgson
Lancs Cup		19	a	Liverpool	W	5-1	Grice, Thorpe, Hodgson (3)
Lancs Cup semi	Nov	9	h	BLACKBURN R	W	2-1	Hodgson, Kelly
Lancs Cup final at Man City	Dec	7	n	Rochdale	W	4-1	Pickering (2), Kelly, Hodgson
East Lancs Charity Cup	Jan	16	h	HASLINGDEN	W	6-1	Tranter, Barber, Lindsay (3), Pickering
East Lancs Charity Cup semi	Apr	12	h	PADIHAM	W	8-0	Lindsay, Mitton (4), Tranter, Jones (2) 1p
East Lancs Charity Cup final		24	h	BLACKBURN R	W	2-0	Tranter, Shaw
		28	a	Blackpool	L	3-6	Watson, Boyle p, Thorpe

Att.	Pos	Dawson	Bamford	D Taylor	Halley	Thorpe	Watson	Mosscrop	Lindley	B Freeman	Hodgson	Grice	Hampson	Lindsay	Boyle	Wilde	Kelly	Pickering	Nesbitt	Tranter	Sewell	C Jones	J Brown	Bolton	
10,000		1	2	3	4	5	6	7	8	9	10	11													1
12,000	9	1	2	3	4	5			8	9	10	11	6	7											2
10,000	17	1	2	3	7	4	6	11	8	9	10				5										3
25,000	10	1	2	3	7	4	6	11	8	9	10				5										4
15,000	6	1	2	3	7	4	6	11		9	10			8	5										5
15,000	5	1	2	3	7	4	6	11		9	10			8	5										6
18,000	10	1	2	3	7	4	6	11		9	10			8	5										7
16,000	9	1	2	3		4	6	11	7	9	10			8	5										8
18,000	9	1	2			4	6	11	7	9	10			8	5	3									9
9,000	8	1	2	3		4	6	11	7	9	10			8	5										10
15,000	11	1	2	3		4	6	11	7	9	10			8	5										11
12,000	10	1	2	3		4	6	11	8		10				5		7	9							12
12,000	9	1	2	3		4	6	11	8		10				5		7	9							13
21,700	9	1	2	3	4		6	11	8	9	10				5		7								14
9,500	8	1	2	3		4	6	11	8	9	10				5		7								15
2,000	10	1	2	3		4	6			9	10		5	8			7		11						16
9,000	12	1	2	3	4	5	6			9	10			8			7		11						17
10,000		1	2	3		4	6	11		9				8	5		7			10					18
15,853			2	3		4	6	11		8					5		7	9		10	1				19
20,000	12		2	3		4	6	11		9	10				5		7	8			1				20
15,000	12	1	2	3		4	6	11		9	10				5		7	8							21
8,000	13	1	2	3		4	6			9	10			8	5		7		11						22
4,000	12	1	2	5		4	6	11		9	10						8		7			3			23
9,000	11	1	2			4	6	11		9	10				5		8		7			3			24
5,000	13	1	2			4	6	11		9	10				5		8		7			3			25
8,000	12	1	2	3		4				11	10				5		8	9	7				6		26
22,000	13	1	2	3		4	6			11	10			8	5		9		7						27
12,000	12	1	2	3		4	6	11		9	10				5		8		7						28
	13	1	2		5	4	6	11		9	10						8		7			3			29
12,000		1	2	3			6	11			10		4		5		8	9	7						30
25,000	12	1	2	3			6	11		9	10		4		5		8		7						31
14,000		1	2	3		4	6	11		9	10				5		8		7						32
10,000	12	1	2	3		4	6	11		9	10				5		8		7						33
9,000	11	1	2	3		4	6	11		9	10				5		8		7						34
6,000	7	1	2	3		4	6			9	10				5		8		7					11	35
10,000		1	2	3		4	6		11		10				5		8	9	7						36
9,185	4	1	2	3		4	6		11		10				5		8	9	7						37
			2	3		4	6	11			10				5		8	9	7		1				38
Appearances		35	38	34	10	35	36	29	14	32	36	2	4	13	32	1	27	10	19	2	3	4	1	1	
Goals (61)				1		2		1	2	12	19			4	4		10	5	1						

Att.	Dawson	Bamford	D Taylor	Halley	Thorpe	Watson	Mosscrop	Lindley	B Freeman	Hodgson	Grice	Hampson	Lindsay	Boyle	Wilde	Kelly	Pickering	Nesbitt	Tranter	Sewell	C Jones	J Brown	Bolton	
14,423	1	2	3		4	6	11		9	10				5		7	8							1
	1	2	3		4	6	11		9	10				5		8		7						2
42,932	1	2	3		4	6	11		9	10				5		8		7						3
Appearances	3	3	3		3	3	3		3	3				3		3	1	2						
Goals (10)					2	1			3	1				1		2								

1915-16

As had been widely expected, at the Football League AGM in July 1915, it was decided that "at a time when our country comes first and sport second, the Football League competition will be suspended". Football was to be organised regionally with the senior professional clubs in the North West competing in the Lancashire Section. It was by no means unanimous, a number of clubs were of the view that there should be no organised football, or indeed organised sport of any kind, at all.

Most players, if they had not enlisted, were working for the War effort and, although they would still be registered with their own clubs, they would be free to appear for other clubs if that was more convenient. It was agreed by all that players would not receive any payment for appearing in football matches and gate receipts would be divided, as fairly as possible, between all the competing clubs, with a share going to various charities.

Most of Burnley's key players were still available for the Lancashire Section matches. Most played some part in that unreal season, very much a sideshow, performed alongside a far more brutal reality, being played out across the Channel. In addition the Clarets were able to call upon guest players, including a number from Blackburn Rovers, who had chosen not to compete in the Lancashire Section of 1915-16.

Burnley's opening match was at Turf Moor against Rochdale, and the modest number of Clarets' fans attending, were impressed with a 6-1 victory, their opening day welcome for Rovers' players Albert Walmsley and John Orr generous and sincere. Both had contributed to Blackburn's League Championship successes of 1912 and 1914, as had Arthur Cowell who was also later to exchange the blue and white for claret and blue. A fourth Rovers' stalwart who later appeared, to support the Turf Moor cause, again with two League Championship medals in his locker, was George Chapman.

Burnley were soon among the goals, 33 in the first nine games before the end of October 1915. Teddy Hodgson led the way with nine of them, including the season's first hat trick against Oldham. Manchester United were hit for seven at Old Trafford and from early on it was apparent that Burnley were sure to be challenging for honours.

In the return against Manchester United Burnley again scored seven with another hat trick from Teddy Hodgson with he and Billy Nesbitt leading the way in front of goal.

In January 1916, in the temporary absence of Jerry Dawson, a familiar figure appeared between the sticks for the first time in fourteen years, almost to the day. Jack Hillman had last donned the gloves behind Burnley's senior team in 1902 and, at the age of 45, here he was again, a little broader of beam but still more than capable.

Burnley eventually finished as runners-up to Manchester City in the Lancashire Section, Principal Competition which ran till the end of February 1916. The Lancashire Section was then divided again with the Northern Group of six clubs competing in their own subsidiary tournament, effectively extending the season until the end of April 1916. Although Burnley's unbeaten home record was then ended by Bury, the Clarets won eight games out of ten to win the subsidiary competition on goal average from Blackpool.

The first season under the new wartime conditions came to an end with a representative match at Goodison Park between the English soldiers and the Scottish soldiers. Burnley were well represented with Tommy Boyle captaining an English side that included Eddie Mosscrop and it was the Burnley winger who scored a late winner to edge out the Scots 4-3. A healthy crowd of 20,000 enjoyed an entertaining match that raised over £500 for the Lord Mayor of Liverpool's Roll of Honour fund.

Big Jack Hillman
in goal for Burnley again at the age of 45

1915-16

		Date			Opponents	Result		Goalscorers
	1	Sep	4	h	ROCHDALE	W	6-1	Nesbitt (2), Orr, Kelly, Mosscrop, Hodgson
	2		11	a	Preston N E	W	5-0	Freeman (2), Boyle, Kelly, Hodgson
	3		18	h	STOCKPORT C	D	1-1	Hodgson
	4		25	a	Liverpool	L	2-5	Nesbitt, Hodgson
	5	Oct	2	h	BURY	D	2-2	Boyle (2) 2p
	6		9	a	Manchester U	W	7-3	Lindley (2), Nesbitt (2), Hodgson, Mosscrop, Hampson
	7		16	h	BLACKPOOL	W	5-2	Nesbitt (2), Lindley, Taylor p, Hodgson
	8		23	a	Southport C	D	1-1	Nesbitt
	9		30	h	OLDHAM A	W	4-0	Hodgson (3), Lindley
	10	Nov	6	a	Everton	W	2-1	Hodgson, Freeman
	11		13	h	BOLTON W	W	3-0	Kelly, Nesbitt (2)
	12		20	a	Manchester C	L	0-1	
	13		27	h	STOKE	W	3-2	Lindley, Hodgson, Watson
	14	Dec	4	a	Rochdale	L	0-1	
	15		11	h	PRESTON N E	W	4-1	Kelly, Lindley, Nesbitt, Hodgson
	16		18	a	Stockport C	W	2-0	Freeman, Watson
	17		25	h	LIVERPOOL	D	3-3	Nesbitt, Hodgson, Walmsley
	18	Jan	1	a	Bury	L	0-3	
	19		8	h	MANCHESTER U	W	7-4	Hodgson (3), Mosscrop (2), Nesbitt, Boyle
	20		15	a	Blackpool	L	1-2	Nesbitt
	21		22	h	SOUTHPORT C	W	5-0	Boyle (2), Nesbitt (2), Lindley
	22		29	a	Oldham A	L	1-3	Hodgson
	23	Feb	5	h	EVERTON	W	2-1	Mosscrop, Nesbitt
	24		12	a	Bolton W	L	0-3	
	25		19	h	MANCHESTER C	W	3-1	Orr (2), Hodgson
	26		26	a	Stoke	D	2-2	Hodgson, Freeman
	27	Mar	4	h	BOLTON W	W	3-1	Halley, Hodgson, Watson p
	28		11	a	Blackpool	W	2-1	Hastie (2)
	29		18	h	BURY	L	1-2	Hastie
	30		25	h	SOUTHPORT C	W	6-1	Chapman (2), Lindley (3), Boyle
	31	Apr	1	a	Preston N E	W	2-1	Boyle p, Lindley
	32		8	a	Bolton W	L	0-2	
	33		15	h	BLACKPOOL	W	2-1	Hodgson, Chapman
	34		21	a	Preston N E	W	4-0	Kelly, Nesbitt, Hodgson, Ellis
	35		22	a	Bury	W	5-1	Lindley, Freeman, Hodgson, Watson, Kelly
	36		29	h	SOUTHPORT C	W	4-2	Kelly, Thorpe, Nesbitt, Lindley
War Charities match	37	May	6	a	Blackburn R	L	3-9	Hodgson, Lindley, Freeman

Matches 1 to 26 were in the Football League, Lancashire section, principal competition
Playing record P26 W15 D5 L7 F71 A43 Pts33, Burnley finished 2nd of 14 clubs

Matches 27 to 36 were in the Football League, Lancashire section, subsidiary competition
Playing record P10 W8 D0 L2 F29 A12 Pts16, Burnley finished 1st of 6 clubs

1916-17

The horrific events on the Somme in July 1916 made some British people again rethink their attitude to football being played in England.

However, after the first season of regionalised football had proved to be reasonably successful, and was what most people seemed to want, it was decided to adopt a similar format for 1916-17. The Lancashire Section was to be extended, with the inclusion of Blackburn and Port Vale.

During the course of 1916-17, at least 2 former Burnley players were reported killed in action. Bernard Donaghy played five games, scoring 2 goals, during season 1907-08 and Wilf Toman was a regular in the Turfites' Second Division Championship campaign of 1897-98. Altogether in his time at Turf Moor, Toman played 74 senior games for Burnley and scored 35 goals, also appearing once for the Football League in 1899.

RIP

By now all Burnley's registered players were either in the Army or were involved in munitions work but seven of them lined up for the opening match, at home to Oldham, which ended in a 3-2 victory. Burnley's first eight games produced 26 goals with ten of them scored by winger Billy Kellock, a Stockport lad who had played for Plymouth before the war.

At right back in Burnley's 2-1 win at Bury was William Cook, making his debut in Claret and Blue. Cook had strong Turf Moor connections, he had been Burnley Cricket Club's professional from 1906 until 1915 during which time Burnley had won the Lancashire League four times under the captaincy of Arthur Bell, the Burnley footballer. Cook was an Oldham player and something of a controversial character, having been suspended sine die for being sent off but refusing to leave the field in an Oldham match at Middlesbrough in 1915. His suspension had recently been lifted and he was now free to play for Burnley.

Richard Lindley
leading scorer in 1916-17

The Clarets scored plenty of goals during the first half of the season with Richard Lindley finding the net on a regular basis. He scored six of Burnley's eleven goals against Blackpool in a week over Christmas 1916 and ended the campaign as Burnley's leading scorer. Lindley was able to play in most of Burnley's games having been turned down by the Army, along with Jerry Dawson, for the time being at least they were surplus to the Forces' requirements, both having suffered broken bones during the course of their careers.

OBITUARY
PATRICK (PAT) GALLOCHER
DIED 1 DEC 1916, AGED 52

Pat Gallocher was the man who scored Burnley FC's first-ever League goal, in the Turfites' match against Preston at Deepdale on the opening day of League football in September 1888.

He was born in Johnston, Glasgow in 1864 and came south to join Padiham, then one of East Lancashire's leading clubs, in 1883. After occasionally appearing for Burnley as a guest player, Gallocher moved to Turf Moor in the summer of 1886 and was virtually an automatic choice in the Burnley team for the next three years. A very quick and tricky player with wonderful close ball control, Gallocher, nicknamed "the Artful Dodger", played 20 League matches for Burnley during that historic inaugural season of 1888-89 before leaving for Accrington in March 1889.

After his football career ended, Pat Gallocher joined the Army and served his country with distinction in South Africa during the Boer War.

RIP

The New Year began with a 4-1 win at Blackburn, but in the main the second half of the season was a struggle, as more and more players became unavailable and the team was chopped and changed on a regular basis.

The Clarets once again finished ahead of the other three clubs in their section of the subsidiary competition, although the official League table showed all 16 clubs with Burnley in third place.

The Turf Moor season ended with a match against a team of footballing soldiers of the 51st Training Reserve Battalion. The soldiers were captained by Burnley crowd favourite Lance Corporal Edward Hodgson and an entertaining encounter finished 3-2 to the Clarets, with the goals for the soldiers, "generous" penalties both, being wildly cheered by a good-humoured crowd.

1916-17

		Date			Opponents	Result		Goalscorers
	1	Sep	2	h	OLDHAM A	W	3-2	Freeman, Norman (2)
	2		9	a	Preston N E	W	5-4	Barber, Kellock (3), Kelly
	3		16	a	Blackpool	D	1-1	Kellock
	4		23	h	MANCHESTER U	W	7-1	Halley p, Kellock (2), Hancock (2), Lindley, Kelly
	5		30	a	Liverpool	D	0-0	
	6	Oct	7	h	STOCKPORT C	W	4-3	Kellock (2), Hodgson, Barber
	7		14	a	Bury	W	2-1	Freeman, Kelly
	8		21	h	STOKE	W	4-1	Lindley, Kellock (2), Halley
	9		28	a	Southport C	L	0-3	
	10	Nov	4	h	BLACKBURN R	W	2-0	Kelly, Lindley
	11		11	a	Manchester C	L	1-2	Lindley
	12		18	h	EVERTON	D	2-2	Halley, Johnson
	13		25	a	Rochdale	W	2-1	Kellock, Kelly
	14	Dec	2	h	BOLTON W	D	2-2	Hodgson, Mosscrop
	15		9	a	Port Vale	W	6-2	Johnson, Boyle, Kelly (2), Kellock, Cook p
	16		16	a	Oldham A	L	1-2	Lindley
	17		23	h	PRESTON N E	W	3-1	Kellock, Boyle (2) 1p
	18		25	h	BLACKPOOL	W	4-0	Kelly (2), Lindley (2)
	19		30	h	BLACKPOOL	W	7-0	Lindley (4), Yates, Joseph Wilde (2)
	20	Jan	1	a	Blackburn R	W	4-1	Hastie, Joseph Wilde (2), Lindley
	21		6	a	Manchester U	L	1-3	Lindley
	22		13	h	LIVERPOOL	L	0-1	
	23		20	a	Stockport C	L	0-1	
	24		27	h	BURY	L	3-4	Lindley (2), Kellock
	25	Feb	3	a	Stoke	L	0-6	
	26		10	h	SOUTHPORT C	W	7-0	Lawson, Roberts, Thomas, Lindley (2), Hastie, Lockett
	27		24	h	MANCHESTER C	L	0-1	
	28	Mar	3	a	Everton	L	0-5	
	29		10	h	ROCHDALE	W	4-3	Johnson, Hancock (2), Halley p
	30		17	a	Bolton W	L	1-3	Johnson
	31		24	h	PORT VALE	W	1-0	Hodgson
	32		31	a	Blackburn R	L	0-4	
	33	Apr	6	a	Blackpool	W	3-2	Hodgson (2), Nesbitt
	34		7	h	PRESTON N E	D	0-0	
	35		14	h	BLACKBURN R	W	4-1	Freeman, Woodward (2), Joseph Wilde
	36		21	a	Preston N E	W	3-2	Freeman (2), Woodward
Charity match	37		28	h	SOLDIERS/PLAYERS XI	W	3-2	Hancock, Lindley (2)

Matches 1 to 17 and 19 to 31 were in the Football League, Lancashire section, principal competition
Playing record P30 W15 D4 L11 F73 A56 Pts34, Burnley finished 6th of 16 clubs

Matches 18 and 32 to 36 were in the Football League, Lancashire section, subsidiary competition
Playing record P6 W4 D1 L1 F14 A9 Pts9, Burnley finished 3rd of 16 clubs, 1st in northern group of 4

1917-18

OBITUARY
JOHN (JACK) YATES
DIED 1 JUNE 1917, AGED 55

Burnley's first-ever international player, Jack Yates, passed away at his home in Burnley, after a long illness. Yates was born in Blackburn and was a cotton weaver, playing his early football with Blackburn Olympic. This team of working men astounded the football establishment in 1883 by not only reaching the FA Cup final, but beating the Cup holders, Old Etonians, to bring the famous old trophy to the North of England for the first time. After a spell at Accrington, Yates moved to Turf Moor ready for the advent of League football and took his place in the Burnley side on that historic day at Preston in September 1888. His form was inspired throughout that inaugural League campaign and his sheer consistency led to selection for the full England side to play Ireland at Anfield in March 1889. He scored three goals in a 6-1 victory, earning a unique place in Burnley FC history, but was never chosen for his country again. In later years he played as an amateur and became the licensee at one of the pubs in the shadow of Turf Moor.

RIP

For the new season football was to continue much as before, regional competitions with as little travelling as possible. More and more players were joining the forces but clubs and supporters were determined that football should still play its part in the fabric of English life.

One of Burnley's registered players, James Wilde, had established an unwanted record for himself in the Clarets' match at Blackpool in April 1917. He had been sent off for violent conduct, the first of only two Burnley players to be dismissed during the four seasons under Wartime conditions. As a result, although he had continued to play at the end of the previous campaign, the Football Authorities banned him from taking any part in organised football until October 1917. In the event he didn't appear at all for Burnley during the 1917-18 season.

The campaign began with a visit to Rochdale and, at the final whistle, it was already apparent that the season ahead was going to be a difficult one. Only one of Burnley's own players, captain Richard Lindley was able to turn out and the team around him was no match for a strong Rochdale side. 9-0 was the score and it rather established a pattern for the months ahead. Another nine goals were shipped at Everton, eight at Bolton, 7 at Liverpool, with only two victories before the turn of the year. A thoroughly miserable campaign brought just six wins in 36 competitive matches, all at Turf Moor, two of which were against Blackburn Rovers.

Although the Clarets' fans had not had much to cheer about, there were some supporters celebrating at Turf Moor in March 1917. With their 2-0 win at Burnley, Stoke clinched the Championship of the Lancashire Section, Principal Competition.

OBITUARY
WILLIAM PICKERING
KILLED IN ACTION
9 NOVEMBER 1917, AGED 23

William Pickering fell in Mesopotamia and was the only Burnley first team player to be killed in action during the Great War.

He was born in Glasgow in 1894 and joined Burnley from a Glasgow junior club in 1912. Pickering was a prolific scorer in Burnley's Reserve team in his first two seasons at Turf Moor and made his League debut against Liverpool in February 1914, scoring in a 5-2 victory. Altogether he appeared in 14 League and FA Cup games, scoring five goals, including one in the last League match to be played at Turf Moor before the suspension of the Football League, a 2-1 win against Sunderland in April 1915.

RIP

In Burnley's last match of that competition, yet another defeat, 0-1 at home to Blackpool, the Clarets' defence conceded its 100th goal of a woeful season. Only four victories since that tournament, none at all since January 1917, just 29 goals scored, eleven of which had come in just two matches. On the other 18 occasions that the opposition net had been found, one was from the penalty spot and two were own goals! There was a small crumb of comfort, Burnley were not bottom of the League. As bad as results and performances had been at Turf Moor, things had been even worse at Ewood Park, less points gained, less goals scored, more goals conceded and just two victories, one of which had been against Burnley.

In the overall scheme of things however, during that dark and uncertain period in history, how one's favourite football team performed on a Saturday was of minor importance. Many clubs, including Burnley, were obliged to use players that, in normal circumstances, would be nowhere near good enough for a first class football team. The supporters knew that it mattered little, they accepted that most of the professional players, strong, healthy, super-fit young men, were occupied elsewhere, engaged in a far more important, and dangerous game.

Bert Freeman
his hat-trick against Blackburn
one of the season's few highlights

1917-18

		Date			Opponents	Result		Goalscorers
	1	Sep	1	a	Rochdale	L	0-9	
	2		8	h	ROCHDALE	D	2-2	Hodgson, Nesbitt p
	3		15	a	Everton	L	0-9	
	4		22	h	EVERTON	L	0-5	
	5		29	a	Blackburn R	L	1-3	Kehoe
	6	Oct	6	h	BLACKBURN R	W	6-1	Freeman (3), Woodward, Heslop, Woods
	7		13	a	Port Vale	L	2-5	Freeman, Adamson
	8		20	h	PORT VALE	D	2-2	Woodward, Edwards
	9		27	h	BOLTON W	W	2-1	Woodward, Johnson
	10	Nov	3	a	Bolton W	L	0-8	
	11		10	h	PRESTON N E	L	1-2	Cornthwaite
	12		17	a	Preston N E	D	0-0	
	13		24	h	BLACKPOOL	W	3-1	Freeman, Heslop (2)
	14	Dec	1	a	Blackpool	L	1-5	Edwards
	15		8	h	MANCHESTER C	L	0-4	
	16		15	a	Manchester C	L	1-4	Freeman
	17		22	h	MANCHESTER U	L	0-5	
	18		25	h	BLACKPOOL	D	1-1	Booth og
	19		29	a	Manchester U	L	0-1	
	20	Jan	5	h	BURY	W	5-1	Edwards, Woods (2), Freeman, Whittaker
	21		12	a	Bury	L	1-2	Edwards
	22		19	h	SOUTHPORT C	W	1-0	Freeman
	23		26	a	Southport C	L	0-2	
	24	Feb	2	h	OLDHAM A	L	0-3	
	25		9	a	Oldham A	L	2-6	Thompson, Grundy og
	26		16	a	Liverpool	L	1-7	Cross
	27		23	h	LIVERPOOL	L	1-3	Adamson
	28	Mar	2	a	Stockport C	D	0-0	
	29		9	h	STOCKPORT C	L	0-2	
	30		16	a	Stoke	L	0-9	
	31		23	h	STOKE	L	0-2	
	32		29	a	Blackpool	L	0-1	
	33		30	a	Preston N E	L	1-2	W.Newton
	34	Apr	6	h	PRESTON N E	D	1-1	Freeman
	35		13	h	BLACKBURN R	W	3-0	Woods, Riley, Edwards
	36		20	a	Blackburn R	L	1-2	Briggs
friendly	37		27	h	COLLIERS XI	D	1-1	Stewart

Matches 1 to 12 and 15 to 32 were in the Football League, Lancashire section, principal competition
Playing record P30 W4 D5 L21 F29 A100 Pts13, Burnley finished 15th of 16 clubs

Matches 13 to 14 and 33 to 36 were in the Football League, Lancashire section, subsidiary competition
Playing record P6 W2 D1 L3 F10 A11 Pts5, Burnley finished 11th of 16 clubs

1918-19

In September 1918 football again kicked off for another season under wartime conditions. This time however, although the players and supporters could not have been aware of it, there was light at the end of the tunnel.

On the opening day of the new campaign, at home to Everton, Richard Lindley was again the only recognised first-teamer in the Burnley side that went down 0-6. Under Trainer Jack Hillman, who was in charge while regular Trainer Ernest Edwards recovered from a badly broken leg playing Army football, the Clarets made a depressing start to the season with ten defeats in the first eleven games. The only bright spot was a Bert Freeman hat trick in an exhilarating 4-3 victory at Ewood Park against a Blackburn side who were struggling as much as Burnley.

Then, from Compiegne, a small town in northern France, came the news that the world had been waiting for. Germany had finally admitted defeat and an armistice had been signed. After four long years of war, at the eleventh hour of the eleventh day of the eleventh month, the guns finally fell silent on the battlefields of Europe.

For Burnley's first home match after the end of hostilities, against Port Vale, a few crowd favourites were announced, David Taylor, Billy Nesbitt and Teddy Hodgson all appeared in the line-up, along with an earlier idol James Bellamy. Hodgson was soon into his stride with a hat trick in a 4-1 win. The crowd loved it, loved the euphoric atmosphere, the feeling of emerging from under a black cloud and at the end of the game, all the players, including the members of the Port Vale team, were cheered to the echo as they left the field.

On Christmas Day 1918, Burnley played host to traditional festive period opponents Blackpool in the first of the Subsidiary Competition matches and Richard Lindley and Teddy Hodgson each scored twice in a 5-1 victory. The Lancashire Football Association had decided to resurrect the Lancashire Cup and Burnley's matches in the Subsidiary Competition were also to act as group matches with each group winner to become a semi finalist. Burnley of course were the current holders of the Lancashire Cup, having won it after defeating Rochdale in 1915, since when the Trophy had been lodged in nearby Towneley Hall for safe keeping.

Over the next weeks and months, more of the established Burnley players began to appear on a regular basis, Jerry Dawson, Willie Watson, Bob Kelly, Eddie Mosscrop were all in the team by February 1919. Burnley's results, and attendances, were much better than they had been, but what really mattered was that the team was starting to look more like its old self again.

Then, for a home match with Stockport in March 1919, came the news that the Burnley supporters had been waiting for. After just one fleeting visit in two years, captain Tommy Boyle was back in town and in the Burnley side. 10,000 people applauded and cheered wildly as Boyle led his team out, his presence alone enough to convince his devoted fans that all, almost all, was right with the world. What those supporters could not have known however, was that Teddy Hodgson, a scorer that day in a 4-2 victory, tragically would never be seen at Turf Moor again.

By April 1919 results had long since ceased to matter but the quality of Burnley's performances had steadily improved. The season's competitive matches ended with home and away games against Blackburn Rovers with both Turf Moor and Ewood Park welcoming their biggest crowds of the season. Burnley won both encounters but the results were incidental. The last time the teams had met the world had been at war. Now both sets of supporters were just happy to have renewed their rivalry, knowing that football was important again.

Along with the cream of British manhood, the professional footballers, including many of the Burnley players, had played their part in making the world a better place. Sadly, not all would be coming back and of the ones that did return, not all would be taking up their careers again. For the ones that had come through the dark days however, it was time to show what they were really made of, at what they did best.

Real football was back.

Bob Kelly
playing and scoring again with hostilities at an end

1918-19

		Date			Opponents	Result		Goalscorers
	1	Sep	7	h	EVERTON	L	0-6	
	2		14	a	Everton	L	1-6	Freeman
	3		21	h	ROCHDALE	L	2-4	Freeman, Cliff
	4		28	a	Rochdale	L	1-2	Grant
	5	Oct	5	h	BLACKBURN R	L	0-1	
	6		12	a	Blackburn R	W	4-3	Freeman (3), Cunningham
	7		19	h	PRESTON N E	L	2-5	Lindley, Yates p
	8		26	a	Preston N E	L	2-4	Cunningham, Johnson
	9	Nov	2	a	Bolton W	L	1-2	Clarkson
	10		9	h	BOLTON W	L	0-4	
	11		16	a	Port Vale	L	2-4	Freeman, Lindley
	12		23	h	PORT VALE	W	4-1	Hodgson (3), A.Newton
	13		30	a	Manchester C	L	1-2	Broome
	14	Dec	7	h	MANCHESTER C	W	2-1	Freeman, Bellamy
	15		14	a	Oldham A	L	1-3	Freeman
	16		21	h	OLDHAM A	D	2-2	Freeman, Hodgson
also Lancs Cup	17		25	h	BLACKPOOL	W	5-1	Lindley (2), Hodgson (2), A.Newton
	18		28	a	Liverpool	L	0-7	
	19	Jan	11	a	Bury	D	0-0	
	20		18	h	BURY	W	2-1	Freeman, Hodgson
	21		25	a	Southport V	L	1-2	Johnson
	22	Feb	1	h	SOUTHPORT V	W	4-0	Brownhill, Nesbitt p, Kelly, Johnson
	23		8	a	Blackpool	D	1-1	Lindley
	24		15	h	BLACKPOOL	W	3-0	Freeman, Kelly, Hodgson
	25		22	h	MANCHESTER U	W	4-2	Hodgson, Freeman (2), Kelly
	26	Mar	1	a	Manchester U	L	0-4	
	27		8	h	STOCKPORT C	W	4-2	Freeman (3), Hodgson
	28		15	a	Stockport C	W	3-0	Freeman, Boyle, Kelly
	29		22	h	STOKE	L	1-2	Freeman
	30		29	a	Stoke	L	1-2	Kelly
also Lancs Cup	31	Apr	5	a	Preston N E	L	0-1	
	32		7	h	LIVERPOOL	W	5-3	Lindley, Kelly, S.Taylor (2), W.Taylor
also Lancs Cup	33		12	h	PRESTON N E	L	1-3	Freeman
also Lancs Cup	34		18	a	Blackpool	D	0-0	
also Lancs Cup	35		19	a	Blackburn R	W	4-2	Boyle, Kelly (2), Lindley
benefit for and at Nelson FC	36		21	n	Bob Crompton's XI	D	2-2	Freeman, Clarkson
also Lancs Cup	37		26	h	BLACKBURN R	W	5-1	Norris, Kelly (2), Clarkson, Nesbitt
friendly	38	May	9	h	BARNSLEY	W	5-2	Norris (4), Mosscrop
footballer's national war fund	39		24	h	BRADFORD C	D	2-2	Kelly, Norris

Matches 1 to 16, 18 to 30 and 32 were in the Football League, Lancashire section, principal competition
Playing record P30 W10 D3 L17 F54 A76 Pts23, Burnley finished 13th of 16 clubs

Matches 17, 31, 33 to 35 and 37 were in the Football League, Lancashire section, subsidiary competition, northern group
Playing record P6 W3 D1 L2 F15 A8 Pts7, Burnley finished 2nd of 4 clubs

Matches 17, 31, 33 to 35 and 37 also counted as Lancashire Cup ties

1919-20

At Turf Moor and around the country the build up to the new season was surrounded by mixed emotions. Euphoria and excitement in anticipation of the big kick-off and watching favourite teams and players again in League action, sadness because, for many players, their best football years had gone for ever and of course, a number had made the ultimate sacrifice.

Burnley had lost reserves Harry Langtree, William Johnson and Alfred Lorrimer as well as William Pickering who had broken into the first team just before war broke out. Still seriously ill were two of Turf Moor's FA Cup heroes of 1914, David Taylor and Teddy Hodgson. Taylor would eventually recover and wear the Claret and Blue again. For Teddy Hodgson the final whistle was about to sound.

OBITUARY
EDWARD (TEDDY) HODGSON
DIED 4 AUGUST 1919, AGED 33.

One of Burnley's most popular players, as well as one of the most influential, Teddy Hodgson was a late arrival into League football, moving to Turf Moor from Lancashire Combination Chorley in 1911 at the age of 25. He became a regular almost immediately and his intelligent inside forward play was a key factor in Burnley's promotion back to the First Division in 1913. He scored 17 goals during the Clarets' memorable 1913-14 campaign, including five in the FA Cup run that ended in glorious triumph and it was Teddy Hodgson who laid on Bert Freeman's match winner against Liverpool.

Hodgson's consistency led to selection for the Football League against the Scottish League but, as the clouds of war darkened over Europe, Teddy Hodgson joined the Army, although he turned out for Burnley whenever possible. His adoring fans at Turf Moor saw him play for the last time in March 1919 before he returned to Germany to serve with the Allied Army of occupation. Tragically, he developed kidney trouble from which he never recovered.

Edward Hodgson was always a perfect gentleman on and off the football field, his fans and his team mates loved him like a brother. The world was a poorer place for his passing.

RIP

Burnley's major new signing in the summer of 1919 had been right back Len Smelt who went into the first team immediately, replacing Tom Bamford. Other new arrivals who had to prove themselves at reserve team level were Alf Bassnett and Walter Weaver, both of whom, along with Smelt, would be part of the success story to come in 1920-21.

Although Burnley's first League game for more than four years was lost at Notts County, the players were soon into their stride and it was somehow fitting that captain Tommy Boyle should score the first goal to earn the first point in a 1-1 draw at Bolton. Five wins and a draw then saw the Clarets climb into second place and they were there to stay for more or less the entire season.

In September 1919, the Football League sent a representative team to Turf Moor to take on a Burnley side, including a few guests, in a benefit match for the family of Teddy Hodgson. The League X1 won 5-1, three of their goals being scored by the Bolton and England inside forward Joe Smith who had been one of the first to volunteer to play in the match. He had a particularly poignant reason to pay tribute to the sacrifice Teddy Hodgson had made during the Great War. His own brother Phil Smith, a former Burnley player, had been killed in action.

In October 1919 Willie Watson's excellent form was again noted by the international selectors and he played twice for England over successive weekends, in the Victory International against Wales at Stoke and then in the Home International against Ireland in Belfast.

Teddy Hodgson
a huge talent

The Clarets' results away from home had been excellent and Burnley were still mounting a determined challenge at the top of the League even though the team's home form had wavered. At the end of November 1919, after three successive victories, including a fine defensive performance in a 1-0 win at Old Trafford, the Clarets were back in second place. The Burnley supporters looked forward to the visit of mid table Bradford with some confidence, eagerly anticipating another two relatively easy points. Ably demonstrating the folly of underestimating the opposition, Bradford proceeded to teach Burnley a football lesson. The Yorkshiremen were two goals in front in no time, and went on to produce their best performance of the season, aided to some degree by a couple of howlers from the normally ultra reliable Jerry Dawson. Bradford won the match 6-2, Burnley's heaviest home defeat in the League for nearly thirty years. Predictably there were changes to the Burnley defence for the return fixture at Park Avenue the following week. George Halley, only recently demobbed, was back in the team, Tommy Boyle was fit again after injury and Burnley's half back line, once again, read Halley, Boyle and Watson, surprisingly the first time the three had appeared together since 1914!

The change was dramatic. Once again Burnley were solid in defence, once again Jerry Dawson was unbeatable in goal and a Billy Nesbitt strike was enough to bring the points back to Turf Moor. More club records had fallen, it was the Clarets' sixth successive victory on their travels and, significantly, after the matches played on Saturday 29 November 1919, Burnley Football Club sat at the top of the League for the first time ever. It was a historic moment and although the Clarets were deposed a week later, it was very much a sign of things to come in the not too distant future.

Burnley's home form improved considerably after the shambles against Bradford and the team remained unbeaten at Turf Moor for the rest of the season. The Clarets were fortunate in being able to call upon two fine goalkeepers in Jerry Dawson and his deputy Ronnie Sewell, who had, of course, replaced Dawson in Burnley's FA Cup final side of 1914. When Dawson suffered an injury in December 1920, up stepped Sewell again to perform superbly for a ten game spell between the Burnley posts. When Dawson was fit again however, Sewell immediately lost his place for a crucial FA Cup tie against Sunderland. Bitterly disappointed, Ronnie Sewell refused to play in Burnley's reserves and very soon he was on his way out of Turf Moor, eventually joining Blackburn Rovers. Another link with the FA Cup triumph had gone.

As the 1919-20 campaign entered its final month the Burnley Directors made two important signings, centre forward Joe Anderson from Clydebank and inside forward Benny Cross from Runcorn. Cross had appeared briefly for Burnley during the Great War, 'borrowed' from Liverpool's juniors, and he would make his mark during the epic season to come. Joe Anderson immediately went into the Burnley alongside Bert Freeman, although ultimately he would replace the man who had become a Turf Moor legend. Freeman had established many new scoring records in his time with Burnley, and his latest mark was his 100th League goal in a Burnley shirt, the first Claret to achieve this magnificent milestone. Ironically his 103rd League strike was alongside Joe Anderson on the occasion of the Scotsman's Burnley debut. It was in a 2-1 win against Sunderland at Turf Moor and how the crowd cheered as Freeman saluted his adoring fans. Sadly it would be the very last time that the name of Bert Freeman would appear as a Burnley goalscorer.

In April 1920 the inspirational Bob Kelly was at last chosen for the full England side to play Scotland at Hillsborough. Torrential rain and a heavy pitch could not prevent a classic match with Bob Kelly taking centre stage and scoring twice in a memorable 5-4 victory.

At the end of that important first season after the war that was supposed to end all wars, the Clarets had finished second and enjoyed their best League campaign ever in terms of First Division results. They had been in the top two positions for a good part of the season and had spent a week at the summit of the Football League, for the very first time in the history of the club. In truth however, West Brom had been the class act of that campaign and their sheer consistency had led to a fully deserved Championship success, the first time the League title had found its way to the Hawthorns.

At Turf Moor the supporters knew that, with just a little more consistency in their team, especially at home, their favourites were fully capable of mounting another, even more serious challenge at the top of the League.

Their confidence was fully justified, fine seeds had indeed been sown and a magnificent harvest was about to be reaped.

Joe Anderson
new signing from Clydebank,
a key factor in the success story to come

1919-20 - First Division

		P	W	D	L	F	A	Pts
1	West Bromwich A	42	28	4	10	104	47	60
2	BURNLEY	42	21	9	12	65	59	51
3	Chelsea	42	22	5	15	56	51	49
4	Liverpool	42	19	10	13	59	44	48
5	Sunderland	42	22	4	16	72	59	48
6	Bolton W	42	19	9	14	72	65	47
7	Manchester C	42	18	9	15	71	62	45
8	Newcastle U	42	17	9	16	44	39	43
9	Aston Villa	42	18	6	18	75	73	42
10	Arsenal	42	15	12	15	56	58	42
11	Bradford PA	42	15	12	15	60	63	42
12	Manchester U	42	13	14	15	54	50	40
13	Middlesbrough	42	15	10	17	61	65	40
14	Sheffield U	42	16	8	18	59	69	40
15	Bradford C	42	14	11	17	54	63	39
16	Everton	42	12	14	16	69	68	38
17	Oldham A	42	15	8	19	49	52	38
18	Derby C	42	13	12	17	47	57	38
19	Preston NE	42	14	10	18	57	73	38
20	Blackburn R	42	13	11	18	64	77	37
21	Notts C	42	12	12	18	56	74	36
22	Sheffield W	42	7	9	26	28	64	23

1919-20

Manager : John Haworth

Division One (2nd)

	No	Date		h/a	Opponents	Result		h/t	Goalscorers/times	Opp. goal times
	1	Aug	30	a	Notts C	L	0-2	0-1		30, 53
	2	Sep	1	a	Bolton W	D	1-1	0-1	Boyle 49p	35
	3		6	h	NOTTS C	W	2-1	0-1	Kelly 68, Freeman 87	5
	4		8	h	BRADFORD C	D	1-1	1-1	Nesbitt 14	43
	5		10	h	BOLTON W	W	2-1	1-1	Cragg 31, Nesbitt 55	28
	6		13	a	Blackburn R	W	3-2	2-2	Taylor 23, Boyle 44p, Mosscrop 83	17, 35og
	7		20	h	BLACKBURN R	W	3-1	1-1	Kelly 45, Freeman 65, Nesbitt 75	20
	8		27	a	Chelsea	W	1-0	1-0	Kelly 30	
	9	Oct	4	h	CHELSEA	L	2-3	2-2	Taylor 40p, Freeman 44	27, 35, 58
	10		11	h	SHEFFIELD U	D	2-2	1-1	Freeman 2, Boyle 83	40, 67
	11		18	a	Sheffield U	W	3-1	1-1	Kelly 25, Lindsay 47, Freeman 85	15
	12		25	h	LIVERPOOL	L	1-2	0-1	Lindsay 84	30, 80
	13	Nov	1	a	Liverpool	W	1-0	0-0	Freeman 65	
	14		8	h	MANCHESTER U	W	2-1	1-0	Watson 20, Cragg 74	70
	15		15	a	Manchester U	W	1-0	0-0	Nesbitt 68	
	16		22	h	BRADFORD	L	2-6	0-2	Cragg 55, Lindsay 75	13,17,65,70,80,85
	17		29	a	Bradford	W	1-0	0-0	Nesbitt 48	
	18	Dec	6	a	Oldham A	L	0-1	0-1		35
	19		13	h	OLDHAM A	W	2-1	1-1	Nesbitt 40, Boyle 55p	30
	20		20	a	Preston N E	W	1-0	1-0	Cragg 10	
	21		25	h	MIDDLESBROUGH	W	5-3	1-2	Mosscrop (2) 37, 48, Lindsay (2) 65, 75, Twiss 70	10, 35, 63
	22		26	a	Newcastle U	D	0-0	0-0		
	23		27	h	PRESTON N E	D	1-1	1-1	Freeman 30	4
	24	Jan	1	a	Middlesbrough	L	0-4	0-3		12p, 15, 20, 85
	25		3	a	Aston Villa	D	2-2	1-1	Cragg 30, Kelly 73	8, 60
	26		17	h	ASTON VILLA	D	0-0	0-0		
Sewell's last game	27		24	a	Sheffield W	L	1-3	0-1	Lindley 80	3, 69, 74
	28	Feb	7	a	Manchester C	L	1-3	0-1	Freeman 61	11, 77, 89
	29		14	h	MANCHESTER C	W	2-0	0-0	Kelly 57, Watson 88p	
	30		17	h	SHEFFIELD W	W	2-0	1-0	Watson (2) 30p, 73	
Thorpe's last game	31		21	a	Derby C	W	2-0	2-0	Kelly 10, Freeman 30	
	32		28	h	DERBY C	W	2-0	1-0	Bassnett 26, Freeman 80	
	33	Mar	6	h	WEST BROMWICH A	D	2-2	1-0	Boyle 19, Freeman 85	65, 68
Lindley's last game	34		13	a	West Bromwich A	L	1-4	1-2	Mosscrop 16	37, 45, 48, 70
	35		20	h	SUNDERLAND	W	2-1	1-1	Freeman 22, Lindsay 55	15
	36		27	a	Sunderland	L	0-3	0-1		25, 75, 80
	37	Apr	2	h	NEWCASTLE U	W	1-0	0-0	Kelly 61	
	38		3	h	ARSENAL	W	2-1	1-0	Weaver 5, Anderson 60	80
	39		10	a	Arsenal	L	0-2	0-1		40, 48
	40		17	h	EVERTON	W	5-0	1-0	Anderson (3) 15, 52, 57, Watson 65, Kelly 75	
	41		24	a	Everton	D	2-2	2-1	Anderson 6, Weaver 28	40, 65
	42	May	1	a	Bradford C	L	1-2	1-1	Anderson 38	18, 70

FA Cup

	Rd	Date		h/a	Opponents	Result		h/t	Goalscorers/times	Opp. goal times
at Fratton Park, Portsmouth	1	Jan	10	a	Thorneycrofts	D	0-0	0-0		
	rep		13	h	THORNEYCROFTS	W	5-0	3-0	Nesbitt 2, Lindsay (3) 17, 26, 79, Cragg 70	
	2		31	h	SUNDERLAND	D	1-1	0-0	Kelly 53	48
	rep	Feb	4	a	Sunderland	L	0-2	0-0		47, 76

Final, Aston Villa 1-0 Huddersfield T after extra time, at Stamford Bridge.

Other first team matches (friendlies and/or as detailed)

	Date		h/a	Opponents	Result		Goalscorers	
Teddy Hodgson benefit	Sep	22	h	FOOTBALL LEAGUE XI	L	1-5	Walden	Burnley XI with guests
East Lancs Charity Cup	May	3	h	BLACKBURN R	W	1-0	Lindsay	
East Lancs Charity Cup		6	a	Blackburn R	W	2-1	Cross, Watson p	
Lancs Cup		8	a	Manchester U	L	0-2		

Att.	Pos	Dawson	Smelt	C Jones	W Taylor	Boyle	Watson	Kelly	Lindsay	B Freeman	Norris	Mosscrop	Nesbitt	Cragg	Clarkson	Thorpe	Hastie	Lindley	Halley	Thompson	Sewell	Twiss	L Roberts	Gallocher	Bassnett	Jackson	Anderson	W Weaver	D Taylor	
13,000		1	2	3	4	5	6	7	8	9	10	11																		1
10,000		1	2	3	4	5	6	7	8	9	10	11																		2
13,000		1	2	3	4	5	6	8	10	9		11	7																	3
18,000	13	1	2	3	4	5	6	8		9			7	10	11															4
14,000		1	2	3	5		6	8		9			7	10	11	4														5
20,000	3	1	2	3	9	5	6	8	10			11	7			4														6
20,000	2	1	2	3		5	6	8	10	9		11	7			4														7
35,000	2	1	2	3	5		6	8	10	9		11	7			4														8
20,000	2	1	2	3	5		6	8	10	9		11	7			4														9
16,000	3	1	2			5	6	8	10	9		11	7			4	3													10
25,000	3	1	2	3	6	5		7	10	9		11				4		8												11
14,000	3	1	2	3		5		7	10	9		11				4		8	6											12
30,000	3	1	2	3			6		10	9		11	7	8		4				5										13
18,000	2	1	2	3			6	7	10			11	9	8		4				5										14
25,000	2	1	2	3			6	7	10			11	9	8		4				5										15
14,000	2	1	2	3			6	7	10	9			11	8		4				5										16
15,000	top	1	2	3		5	6	7	10			11	9	8					4											17
7,000	2	1	2	3		5	6	7	10			11	9	8		4														18
12,500	2	1	2			5	6	7	10			11	9	8			3		4											19
10,000	2		2			5	6	7	10			11	9	8			3		4		1									20
25,000			2			5	6	7	10			11		8			3		4		1	9								21
50,000			2			5	6	7	10			11		8			3		4		1	9								22
20,000	2		2			5	6	7	10	9		11		8			3		4		1									23
25,000	2		2			5	6	7	10			11		8			3		4		1	9								24
30,000	2		2			5	6	7	10	9			11	8		4			3		1									25
29,500	2		2			5	6	7	10			11	9			4		8	3		1									26
20,000	2		2			5	6	7	10			11	9			4		8	3		1									27
30,000	4	1	2		5		6	10		9		11	7			4		8	3											28
20,000	2	1	2				6	8				11	7			4			3	5			9	10						29
15,000	2	1	2		5		6	8				11	7			4			3			9		10						30
12,000	2	1	2		5		6	8		9		11	7			4			3					10						31
18,000		1	2		6	5		8		9		11	7						3					10	4					32
30,000	2	1	2			5	6	8		9		11	7						3						4	10				33
30,000		1	2	3		5	6	8		9		11	7					10	4											34
27,500	2	1	2			5	6		10	8		11	7						3						4		9			35
30,000	2	1	2			5	6		10	8			7						3						4		9	11		36
30,000		1	2		5		6	8		10			7						3						4		9	11		37
20,000	2	1	2		5		6	8	10	7									3						4		9	11		38
40,000	2	1	2			5	6		10	8			7						4								9	11	3	39
25,000	2	1	2			5	6	8	10	7									4								9	11	3	40
35,000	2	1	2			5	6	8	10	7									4								9	11	3	41
25,000	2	1	2	3		5	6	8	10	7									4								9	11		42
Appearances		34	42	19	15	29	39	38	32	28	2	31	30	15	2	20	7	6	26	5	8	4	1	4	6	1	8	7	3	
Goals (65)					2	5	5	9	6	12		4	6	5				1				1			1		6	2		

Att.	Pos	Dawson	Smelt	C Jones	W Taylor	Boyle	Watson	Kelly	Lindsay	B Freeman	Norris	Mosscrop	Nesbitt	Cragg	Clarkson	Thorpe	Hastie	Lindley	Halley	Thompson	Sewell	Twiss	L Roberts	Gallocher	Bassnett	Jackson	Anderson	W Weaver	D Taylor	
14,261			2			5	6	7	10	9			11	8		4			3		1									1
19,000			2			5	6	7	10	9			11	8		4			3		1									rep
33,222		1	2		5		6	8	10	9		11	7			4			3											2
44,618		1	2		5		6	8	10	9		11	7			4			3											rep
Appearances		2	4		2	2	4	4	4	4		2	4	2		4			4		2									
Goals (6)								1	3				1	1																

1920-21

After the Clarets had finished as runners-up to West Brom the mood around Turf Moor, and indeed around the town, during the summer of 1920 was not one of disappointment. There was a feeling of genuine anticipation that Burnley could go one better and bring the League Championship trophy home for the first time. During the lead up to the big kick off, the Burnley Express conducted an interview with captain supreme Tommy Boyle. In measured tones Boyle said how highly he valued his FA Cup winners medal, but he believed firmly that the true test of a team's greatness was to win the First Division Championship. He also believed that his team was good enough to do it. How prophetic!

Captain Tommy Boyle
full of confidence for the season ahead

The signs were not good in the opening game, indeed the opening 45 minutes, of the season against Bradford City at Turf Moor. By the time the referee blew his whistle for 'breathing time' the Clarets were four goals down and both Jerry Dawson and Tommy Boyle were injured. The game finished 4-1 to the Bantams and when the Burnley team trooped off the field the crowd were stunned. After such high expectations the heavy defeat was quite a shock but the supporters were still confident that the tide would turn. What they could not have known was that they had seen Bert Freeman for the last time at Turf Moor in a first team shirt.

Dawson and Boyle missed the next two games, both of which were lost, and after three matches, one goal and no points, the club's worst-ever start to a season, Burnley were bottom of the First Division.

The only way was up and it started with a 3-0 win in the return against Huddersfield at Turf Moor. For quite a time from then on the Burnley supporters were almost to forget what it was like to see their team lose.

In September 1920 another member of the FA Cup winning side left Turf Moor when Tom Bamford signed for Rochdale. Right back Bamford had not played any League games since before the War, he had been unlucky enough to be in competition with the tremendously consistent Len Smelt who had proved impossible to dislodge since his arrival in 1919.

In mid-November 1920 after a 2-2 draw at Oldham, just eleven weeks after they had been dumped at the foot of Division One, Burnley were at the top of the League for the first time. It was a position to which the Clarets would become accustomed.

To celebrate Burnley's new status Oldham were demolished 7-1 in the return at Turf Moor, Bob Kelly, at his imperious best, hitting four. The unbeaten run was now thirteen games and the Burnley Express was sufficiently impressed to write 'this team looks like beating a lot of records......!'

In December 1920 a win and a draw against Liverpool and a 2-0 victory against Preston at Turf Moor took the Clarets into the Christmas period three points clear at the top. It was now sixteen League games unbeaten, equalling the club record set during the Second Division Championship campaign of 1897-98. A new record was set on Christmas Day when the Turfites gave themselves and their fans the best possible present with a 6-0 crushing of Sheffield United. Joe Anderson was on target in the first minute, setting the scene for a ruthless display by the Burnley forwards. The United goalkeeper was in excellent form but just could not stop the goals going past him, Anderson helping himself to four.

Anderson got another four in a stunning 7-3 victory at Second Division Leicester in the FA Cup, the first time the Clarets had ever scored 7 goals away from home in League or FA Cup. Burnley FC were now big news and the 'Athletic News' described the team as the best in the country. Back in the First Division Burnley increased their lead at the top to six points with home and away victories against Blackburn Rovers. Almost 85,000 people saw the two clashes with Burnley, far too good for their closest rivals, winning 4-1 at Turf Moor and 3-1 at Ewood.

Further progress in the FA Cup at the expense of Queens Park Rangers, two more goals for Joe 'Andy', was followed by the visit of Aston Villa to Turf Moor. Villa were simply torn apart by a ferocious display of attacking from a rampant Burnley team, with Joe Anderson helping himself to five more goals. Anderson had now scored an incredible 19 goals in his last 9 games in League and Cup. Burnley did just enough at Villa Park the following week to earn a 0-0 draw, but the result established a new Football League record of 23 matches without defeat in a single season, edging out the 22 game runs of both Preston, in 1888-89 and Sheffield United in 1899-1900.

A home win against Derby looked like the prelude to what seemed an easy passage in the FA Cup at Second Division strugglers Hull. City had only won two games at home in nearly five months, and one of those had been against Western League Bath City in an earlier round of the FA Cup. Even though the Clarets were without the injured Joe Anderson and George Halley, who was ill, the Burnley public, and the football world as a whole, was staggered by Hull's 3-0 win against the runaway League leaders. The Tigers gave the Clarets a real mauling, thoroughly deserving their day of glory with one of those giant-killing feats that are the hallmark of the FA Cup.

Back to League action, Burnley scraped a 0-0 draw at Derby then collected six points in two epic battles with Bolton and two rather more dour encounters with Arsenal. It was now Easter 1921 and Burnley had not lost in 29 games of League football played since early September 1920, almost seven months before! On Good Friday the unbeaten run reached 30 games with a single goal victory against Manchester United at Turf Moor. How much longer could it go on?

Manchester City provided the answer on Easter Saturday with a thoroughly deserved 3-0 victory against the League leaders. With Championship aspirations themselves, the Blues overwhelmed the men from Turf Moor and, in some ways, took the pressure off. The unbeaten run was finally at an end, but the run in to the League title was still very much on!

It was back to Manchester on Easter Monday and a magnificent 3-0 victory in the Old Trafford mud swept away any doubts that might have appeared after the defeat at Hyde Road. City themselves were seen off 2-1 at Turf Moor and with just six games to go the Clarets were now a massive nine points clear at the top. Four more points would do it.

Two games against defending Champions West Brom only brought one point but other results meant that a draw at Goodison Park would secure the point necessary to bring the League Championship trophy to Turf Moor for the first time. Everton scored early and were the better team but the Clarets, with that characteristic grit of true Champions, equalised through Benny Cross and were then content to keep Everton at bay. When the final whistle blew the Burnley players hugged each other, the Everton players warmly congratulated their opponents and the Burnley fans in the crowd cheered their heroes loud and long.

A magnificent campaign then, although it ended a little disappointingly, as indeed it had begun. The first three games had all been lost, none of the last six games were won and sadly, the outstanding Jerry Dawson, who had missed the 1914 FA Cup triumph because of injury, also missed the last match of the season, a curtain call at Turf Moor against Sunderland when the League Championship trophy was presented.

There was another rather sad aspect to that magnificent campaign. At the end of it Bert Freeman was released after more than nine years at Turf Moor. He had become something of a hero among the Turf Moor fans, the first-ever Burnley player to score 100 League goals and had established a club record of 32 League goals in season 1911-12.

The Burnley newspapers waxed lyrical about the team's achievements and one scribe was sufficiently moved to write thus –

'We have been partners with the greatest team that ever was. We know full well that never in our lifetime will such a thing be accomplished again and we like to think that we live in an age that will be remembered when we personally are forgotten'

Burnley fans will never, ever, forget that magnificent achievement of all those years ago. The world was a different place, but football was essentially the same, simple game then, as it is now. It would be nearly 40 years before the League title came to Turf Moor again but it would be more than eighty years, and into the next millennium, before another team in the top flight of English football remained undefeated for more than 30 League games during a single season.

The greatest team that ever was ? Perhaps.

Benny Cross
a regular in his first season
the winner at Goodison Park to clinch the Championship

1920-21 - First Division

		P	W	D	L	F	A	Pts
1	BURNLEY	42	23	13	6	79	36	59
2	Manchester C	42	24	6	12	70	50	54
3	Bolton W	42	19	14	9	77	53	52
4	Liverpool	42	18	15	9	63	35	51
5	Newcastle U	42	20	10	12	66	45	50
6	Tottenham H	42	19	9	14	70	48	47
7	Everton	42	17	13	12	66	55	47
8	Middlesbrough	42	17	12	13	53	53	46
9	Arsenal	42	15	14	13	59	63	44
10	Aston Villa	42	18	7	17	63	70	43
11	Blackburn R	42	13	15	14	57	59	41
12	Sunderland	42	14	13	15	57	60	41
13	Manchester U	42	15	10	17	64	68	40
14	West Bromwich A	42	13	14	15	54	58	40
15	Bradford C	42	12	15	15	61	63	39
16	Preston NE	42	15	9	18	61	65	39
17	Huddersfield T	42	15	9	18	42	49	39
18	Chelsea	42	13	13	16	48	58	39
19	Oldham A	42	9	15	18	49	86	33
20	Sheffield U	42	6	18	18	42	68	30
21	Derby C	42	5	16	21	32	58	26
22	Bradford PA	42	8	8	26	43	76	24

1920-21

Manager : John Haworth

Division One Champions

Note	No	Date		h/a	Opponents	Result		h/t	Goalscorers/times	Opp. goal times
	1	Aug	28	h	BRADFORD C	L	1-4	0-4	Anderson 65	14, 25, 33, 45
	2		30	a	Huddersfield T	L	0-1	0-1		33
	3	Sep	4	a	Bradford C	L	0-2	0-1		12, 70
	4		6	h	HUDDERSFIELD T	W	3-0	2-0	Kelly 6, Boyle 10, Nesbitt 54	
	5		11	h	MIDDLESBROUGH	W	2-1	0-1	Cross 50, Anderson 62	39
	6		18	a	Middlesbrough	D	0-0	0-0		
	7		25	h	CHELSEA	W	4-0	0-0	Boyle 50p, Cross 62, Kelly 70, Nesbitt 87	
	8	Oct	2	a	Chelsea	D	1-1	0-0	Anderson 78	47
	9		9	a	Bradford	W	3-1	1-1	Kelly (2) 42, 73, Dickinson 55og	14
	10		16	h	BRADFORD	W	1-0	0-0	Anderson 52	
	11		23	a	Tottenham H	W	2-1	0-1	Anderson (2) 49, 53	20
	12		30	h	TOTTENHAM H	W	2-0	1-0	Kelly 4, Cross 75	
	13	Nov	6	a	Newcastle U	W	2-1	2-0	Boyle 36, Kelly 44	70
	14		13	h	NEWCASTLE U	W	3-1	2-1	Kelly 26, Cross 36, Boyle 48p	17
	15		20	a	Oldham A	D	2-2	2-0	Anderson 25, Weaver 39	57, 67
	16		27	h	OLDHAM A	W	7-1	4-0	Kelly (4) 15, 44, 75, 85, Cross (2) 29, 35, Boyle 64	59
	17	Dec	4	a	Liverpool	D	0-0	0-0		
	18		11	h	LIVERPOOL	W	1-0	1-0	Weaver 41	
	19		18	h	PRESTON N E	W	2-0	0-0	Anderson (2) 70, 73	
	20		25	h	SHEFFIELD U	W	6-0	2-0	Anderson (4) 1, 50, 60, 75, Cross 44, Kelly 82	
	21		27	a	Sheffield U	D	1-1	0-0	Kelly 62	50
	22	Jan	1	a	Preston N E	W	3-0	1-0	Cross 30, Kelly 55, Anderson 75	
	23		15	h	BLACKBURN R	W	4-1	2-1	Cross (2) 20, 71, Kelly 40, Boyle 77	38
	24		22	a	Blackburn R	W	3-1	2-1	Kelly 10, Mosscrop 42, Anderson 85	38
Villa goal 41m	25	Feb	5	h	ASTON VILLA	W	7-1	2-1	Watson 20p, Anderson (5) 37, 52, 60, 75, 77, Lindsay 55	
	26		9	a	Aston Villa	D	0-0	0-0		
	27		12	h	DERBY C	W	2-1	1-1	Anderson 25, Lindsay 83	28
	28		23	a	Derby C	D	0-0	0-0		
	29		26	h	BOLTON W	W	3-1	0-1	Kelly 53, Cross 55, Nesbitt 68	16
	30	Mar	5	a	Bolton W	D	1-1	1-0	Anderson 6	75
	31		12	h	ARSENAL	W	1-0	0-0	Watson 65p	
	32		19	a	Arsenal	D	1-1	0-1	Anderson 65	43p
	33		25	h	MANCHESTER U	W	1-0	0-0	Cross 72	
	34		26	a	Manchester C	L	0-3	0-1		5, 60, 85
	35		28	a	Manchester U	W	3-0	1-0	Boyle 42p, Kelly 70, Anderson 80	
	36	Apr	2	h	MANCHESTER C	W	2-1	0-1	Nesbitt 64, Anderson 66	4
	37		9	a	West Bromwich A	L	0-2	0-1		14, 75
	38		16	h	WEST BROMWICH A	D	1-1	0-1	Kelly 86	27
	39		23	a	Everton	D	1-1	1-1	Cross 18	15
	40		30	h	EVERTON	D	1-1	0-1	Cross 65	40
	41	May	2	a	Sunderland	L	0-1	0-1		36
	42		7	h	SUNDERLAND	D	2-2	1-2	Nesbitt 10, Kelly 65	30, 42

FA Cup

Note	Round	Date		h/a	Opponents	Result		h/t	Goalscorers/times	Opp. goal times
Leicester goals 42m, 65m, 75m	1	Jan	8	a	Leicester C	W	7-3	3-1	Anderson (4) 16, 30, 63, 65, King 20og, Kelly 52, Cross 62	
	2		29	h	QUEENS PARK R	W	4-2	3-1	Anderson (2) 15, 47, Kelly (2) 30, 45	28, 87
Freeman's last game	3	Feb	19	a	Hull C	L	0-3	0-1		44, 63, 77

Final, Tottenham H 1-0 Wolverhampton W, at Stamford Bridge.

Other first team matches (friendlies and/or as detailed)

Note	Date		h/a	Opponents	Result		Goalscorers
Opening of Peel Park, Accrington	Sep	22	n	Blackburn R XI	W	10-1	Anderson (7), Lindsay, Weaver, Jackson
East Lancs Charity Cup	Apr	18	h	BLACKBURN R	W	6-2	Kelly (3), Mosscrop, Cross, Anderson
East Lancs Charity Cup		27	a	Blackburn R	W	2-0	Anderson, Lindsay
Patsy Gallagher benefit	May	4	a	Scottish XI	W	2-1	Nesbitt, Kelly
Lancs Cup		9	a	Manchester C	L	0-2	
FA Charity Shield	May	16	a	Tottenham H	L	0-2	

Att	Pos	Dawson	Smelt	D Taylor	Halley	Boyle	Watson	B Freeman	Kelly	Anderson	Lindsay	Mosscrop	Birchenough	W Taylor	W Weaver	Nesbitt	Cross	McGrory	C Jones	Brophy	Bassnett	Douglas	Lane	Moorwood		
30,000		1	2	3	4	5	6	7	8	9	10	11														1
22,500			2	3	4		6	7	8	9	10		1	5	11											2
26,000	22		2	3	4		6	8		9	10		1	5	11	7										3
30,000	21	1	2	3	4	5	6		8	9					11	7	10									4
28,000	15	1	2	3	4	5	6		8	9					11	7	10									5
30,000	15	1	2	3	4	5	6		8	9					11	7	10									6
30,000	10	1	2	3	4	5	6		8	9					11	7	10									7
45,000	11	1		3	4	5	6		8	9					11	7	10	2								8
24,000	10	1		3	4	5	6		8	9					11	7	10	2								9
25,000	7	1			4	5	6		8	9					11	7	10	2	3							10
45,000	6	1	2	3	4	5	6			9	10				11	7	8									11
35,830	4	1	2		4	5	6		8	9					11	7	10		3							12
50,000	4	1	2		4	5	6		8	9					11	7	10		3							13
38,860	2	1	2		4	5	6		8	9					11	7	10		3							14
19,273	top	1	2		4	5	6		8	9					11	7	10		3							15
22,569	top	1	2		4	5	6		8	9					11	7	10		3							16
37,500	top	1	2		4	5	6		8	9					11	7	10		3							17
35,860	top	1	2		4	5	6		8	9					11	7	10		3							18
	top	1	2		4	5	6		8	9					11	7	10		3							19
35,912		1	2		4	5	6		8	9					11	7	10		3							20
50,000	top	1	2		4	5	6		8	9					11	7	10		3							21
32,000	top	1	2		4	5	6		8	9					11	7	10		3							22
41,534	top	1	2		4	5	6		8	9					11	7	10		3							23
43,000	top	1	2		4	5	6		8	9		11				7	10		3							24
40,000	top	1	2		4		6		8	9	10	11				7			3	5						25
40,000	top	1	2		4	5	6		8	9	10	11				7			3							26
30,000	top	1	2			5	6			9	8	11				7	10		3	4						27
17,000	top	1	2			5	6		8						11	7	10		3		4	9				28
42,653	top	1	2			5	6		8	9					11	7	10		3		4					29
57,000	top	1	2			5	6		8	9					11	7	10		3		4					30
30,000	top	1	2			5	6			9	8				11	7	10		3		4					31
45,000	top	1	2				6		8	9		11				7	10		3	5	4					32
40,000	top	1	2			5	6		8	9		11				7	10		3		4					33
42,000	top	1	2			5	6		8	9		11				7	10		3		4					34
30,000	top	1	2			5	6		8	9		11				7	10		3		4					35
37,000	top	1	2			5	6		8	9		11				7	10		3		4					36
16,000	top	1	2			5	6			9						7	10		3		4	11	8			37
26,422	top	1	2			5	6		8	9		11				7	10		3		4					38
40,000	top	1	2			5	6		8	9		11				7	10		3		4					39
22,066	top	1	2			5	6		8	9		11				7	10		3		4					40
20,000	top	1	2			5	6		8	9					11	7	10		3		4					41
22,000			2	3		5	6		8	9		11				7	10				4			1		42
Appearances		39	39	11	26	38	42	3	37	41	8	14	2	2	27	40	37	3	31	3	15	2	1	1		
Goals (79)						7	2		20	25	2	1			2	5	14								1	og

Att	Pos	Dawson	Smelt	D Taylor	Halley	Boyle	Watson	B Freeman	Kelly	Anderson	Lindsay	Mosscrop	Birchenough	W Taylor	W Weaver	Nesbitt	Cross	McGrory	C Jones	Brophy	Bassnett	Douglas	Lane	Moorwood		
29,149		1	2		4	5	6		8	9					11	7	10		3							1
41,007		1	2		4	5	6		8	9		11				7	10		3							2
30,000		1	2			5	6	9	8			7			11	4	10		3							3
Appearances		3	3		2	3	3	1	3	2		2			2	3	3		3							
Goals (11)									3	6							1								1	og

1921-22

OBITUARY
CLAUDE LAMBIE
DIED JULY 1921, AGED 53.

Born in Glasgow in 1868, Claude Lambie was a natural footballer and represented his country at junior level as a young teenager. He was a professional at Glasgow Thistle when Burnley's scouts North of the border spotted him and secured his signature in January 1890. Burnley were having a miserable season but Claude Lambie set about changing that and was an immediate inspiration to his new team mates. He was skilfull, strong on the ball and phenomenally good in the air. Not for nothing was his nickname "Lambie the Leap". He scored a hat trick in one of his early games, five goals altogether that season, and led the line superbly in the Turfites' famous victory against Blackburn in April 1890. Lambie hit 17 goals in just twenty matches in the following campaign before leaving to play for Clyde. He later joined the Highland Light Infantry, played for Burnley again briefly whilst on leave and then left for active service in South Africa. Sadly he next came to the public's attention when a body found on a railway line at Smethwick was eventually identified as Claude Lambie.

RIP

As the new season got under way the Football League Championship flag was delivered to Turf Moor. It obviously inspired the players, nine of the first eleven games were won and by the end of October the Clarets had established a two point lead at the top of the First Division. Burnley's hold on the League Championship trophy was not going to be relinquished lightly.

In early October 1921 both Jerry Dawson and Willie Watson were chosen to represent the Football League against the Irish League in Belfast. Watson was to be the captain and the Burnley connection was continued with Turf Moor assistant trainer Jack Hillman selected to be the trainer for the Football League camp. Dawson had last won a representative honour more than a decade earlier but his consistency and sheer dedication to his craft were, at last, to bring their just reward. Three weeks later Jerry Dawson, one-time Cliviger village blacksmith, stepped out on to the Windsor Park turf to win his first full England cap in a 1-1 draw against Ireland.

Back at Turf Moor, Burnley were still competing strongly at the top of the League but local newspaper comments were starting to appear to the effect that one or two of the Burnley players were showing their age and that "the Burnley coat was starting to wear a little thin in places".

In mid-December 1921 the Clarets met Huddersfield at Turf Moor and, after a titanic struggle, emerged as 1-0 winners, with Bob Kelly on target. Burnley were still top of the League at the end of that game and Huddersfield were second. It would be the last occasion for some time that the Clarets would sit at the top of the League. The two clubs met again in the FA Cup in January 1922 and Huddersfield got their revenge and progressed after a replay. It would not be very long before the Yorkshiremen would emerge as English football's dominant force.

On 11 February 1922 it was the end of a hugely significant Turf Moor era when the Burnley half back line read Halley, Boyle and Watson for the last time. It was ironic that the famous trio should bow out together for a 1-2 home defeat by Blackburn Rovers. It was Burnley's first defeat in the League at Turf Moor since August 1920 and the first time the old enemy had completed a League double over the Clarets since before the turn of the century. A page in the story of Burnley FC had turned and just a week later there was another significant final appearance. When the referee blew his whistle at the end of Burnley's 1-0 victory against Arsenal at Turf Moor, Tommy Boyle walked off the pitch at the end of a senior Burnley match for the last time. Although neither the crowd nor the Great Man himself knew it then, at the age of 34 Tommy Boyle's career in senior football was over.

Cliff Jones
a Championship winner in 1921

Jerry Dawson however, himself approaching 34, was playing as well as ever. His performance was breathtaking in Burnley's 1-0 win at Bolton, in February 1922, the first time the Clarets had ever brought back maximum points from Burnden Park and Wanderers' first home defeat to the men from Turf Moor since the very first week of League football in 1888!

On his 34th birthday, Dawson was again selected to play for the Football League, against the Scottish League at Ibrox. Bob Kelly was also in the side and at his majestic best, scoring in an emphatic 3-0 win for the English. Completing the Burnley connection was Cardiff City winger Billy Grimshaw, earning his only representative honour. Born in Burnley Lane, Grimshaw had appeared briefly in Burnley's reserve team during the 1910-11 season but was an example of "one that got away". After playing for Colne he was signed by Bradford City in 1912 but had come to prominence after being transferred to Cardiff in 1919, helping the Bluebirds to promotion to the top flight for the first time in 1921.

In March 1922 Liverpool were emerging as Burnley's likely successors as First Division Champions. The Reds were more consistent than their rivals and the Clarets' run-in was disappointing, only three victories in the final eleven games of the season. One of those wins was against the 1920 Champions West Brom, in which Burnley's young reserve centre forward George Richardson was selected for only his second League match, his first at Turf Moor. Richardson enjoyed centre stage, scoring a true hat trick in a 4-2 victory. Both Jerry Dawson and Bob Kelly were missing from the Burnley team that day. At the age of 34 Dawson had finally achieved his ultimate ambition when he played in his second full international, against Scotland at Villa Park. Kelly would gain more caps for England but Jerry Dawson's international career was over.

As in 1921, the destination of the 1922 League title was decided on Merseyside with three games to go, and once again Burnley were involved. In 1921 the Clarets had collected the point they needed in a 1-1 draw at Everton. This time it was Liverpool whose 2-1 victory against Burnley ensured they could not be caught by any of the other contenders, the Clarets among them. Ironically Burnley's last match of the 1921-22 season was at Everton and an insipid performance that ended in a 0-2 defeat was in marked contrast to the joyous scenes at Goodison Park just a year earlier, almost to the day. That game was George Halley's last senior appearance for Burnley, the farewell performance of another player who had contributed so much to the Turf Moor success story.

In five years of League football in peacetime, Burnley Football Club had won both the League Championship and the FA Cup and had finished in the top four in Division One in four successive campaigns. It had been an exciting few years for Clarets' supporters but alas it would be another quarter of a century before anything approaching comparable success would come again to Turf Moor.

Jerry Dawson
a second England cap at the age of 34

1921-22 - First Division

		P	W	D	L	F	A	Pts
1	Liverpool	42	22	13	7	63	36	57
2	Tottenham H	42	21	9	12	65	39	51
3	BURNLEY	42	22	5	15	72	54	49
4	Cardiff C	42	19	10	13	61	53	48
5	Aston Villa	42	22	3	17	74	55	47
6	Bolton W	42	20	7	15	68	59	47
7	Newcastle U	42	18	10	14	59	45	46
8	Middlesbrough	42	16	14	12	79	69	46
9	Chelsea	42	17	12	13	40	43	46
10	Manchester C	42	18	9	15	65	70	45
11	Sheffield U	42	15	10	17	59	54	40
12	Sunderland	42	16	8	18	60	62	40
13	West Bromwich A	42	15	10	17	51	63	40
14	Huddersfield T	42	15	9	18	53	54	39
15	Blackburn R	42	13	12	17	54	57	38
16	Preston NE	42	13	12	17	42	65	38
17	Arsenal	42	15	7	20	47	56	37
18	Birmingham	42	15	7	20	48	60	37
19	Oldham A	42	13	11	18	38	50	37
20	Everton	42	12	12	18	57	55	36
21	Bradford C	42	11	10	21	48	72	32
22	Manchester U	42	8	12	22	41	73	28

1921-22

Manager : John Haworth

Division One (3rd)

		Date			Opponents	Result		h/t	Goalscorers/times	Opp. goal times
	1	Aug	27	a	Birmingham	W	3-2	1-1	Boyle 40, Mosscrop 57, Anderson 59	34, 86
	2		31	a	Sunderland	L	2-3	1-2	Anderson 12, Kelly 70	21, 43, 85
	3	Sep	3	h	BIRMINGHAM	W	3-1	2-0	Boyle 5p, Anderson 18, Watson 75	76
	4		5	h	SUNDERLAND	W	2-0	1-0	Kelly 4, Cross 67	
	5		10	h	NEWCASTLE U	W	2-0	1-0	Anderson (2) 44, 65	
	6		17	a	Newcastle U	L	1-2	0-0	Cross 86	47, 70
	7		24	h	BRADFORD C	W	4-0	2-0	Kelly 42, Anderson 45, Mosscrop 55, Boyle 80p	
	8	Oct	1	a	Bradford C	W	4-0	2-0	Cross (2) 11, 64, Kelly 28, Anderson 49	
	9		8	h	SHEFFIELD U	W	2-1	2-1	Cross 32, Kelly 40	42
	10		15	a	Sheffield U	W	1-0	0-0	Kelly 60	
	11		22	h	CHELSEA	W	5-0	2-0	Kelly 38, Anderson (2) 42, 59, Cross (2) 65, 75	
	12		29	a	Chelsea	L	1-4	1-2	Anderson 8	5, 35, 63, 73
	13	Nov	5	h	PRESTON N E	D	3-3	1-0	Anderson (2) 28, 81, Cross 69	67, 76, 87
Jones' last game	14		12	a	Preston N E	L	1-2	1-1	Cross 22	29, 48
	15		19	a	Tottenham H	D	1-1	1-0	Anderson 26	80
	16		26	h	TOTTENHAM H	W	1-0	0-0	Kelly 85	
	17	Dec	3	a	Huddersfield T	L	0-1	0-1		7
	18		10	h	HUDDERSFIELD T	W	1-0	0-0	Kelly 48	
	19		17	a	Middlesbrough	L	1-4	0-3	Weaver 86	20, 23, 40, 70
	20		24	h	MIDDLESBROUGH	W	3-1	2-1	Kelly (3) 32, 44, 67	17
	21		26	a	Manchester U	W	1-0	0-0	Lindsay 50	
	22		27	h	MANCHESTER U	W	4-2	4-2	Mosscrop (2) 8, 22, Lindsay 16, Kelly 32	12, 44
	23		31	h	ASTON VILLA	W	2-1	0-0	Watson 55p, Mosscrop 70	75
	24	Jan	14	a	Aston Villa	L	0-2	0-0		60, 85
	25		21	a	Arsenal	D	0-0	0-0		
Burnley's 1000th League game	26	Feb	4	a	Blackburn R	L	2-3	2-2	Anderson (2) 5, 18	35, 40, 46
500th League game at Turf Moor	27		11	h	BLACKBURN R	L	1-2	0-1	Anderson 66	30, 71
	28		18	a	Bolton W	W	1-0	0-0	Anderson 55	
Boyle's last game	29		20	h	ARSENAL	W	1-0	1-0	Kelly 37	
Burnley's 500th 1st Division game	30		25	h	BOLTON W	W	2-0	1-0	Lindsay 4, Halley 62p	
	31	Mar	4	a	Oldham A	W	1-0	0-0	Kelly 85	
	32		11	h	OLDHAM A	L	0-1	0-0		75
	33		18	h	CARDIFF C	D	1-1	0-1	Anderson 67	9
	34		25	a	Cardiff C	L	2-4	1-2	Mosscrop 14, Bassnett 65	5, 17, 85, 88
	35	Apr	1	a	West Bromwich A	L	0-2	0-0		83, 86
	36		8	h	WEST BROMWICH A	W	4-2	1-0	Richardson (3) 13, 54, 66, Anderson 75	74, 77
	37		14	h	LIVERPOOL	D	1-1	1-0	Anderson 31	58
City goals 36m, 64m og	38		15	h	MANCHESTER C	W	5-2	2-1	Mosscrop 13, Fletcher 30og, Kelly 51, Fisher 87, Richardson 90	
	39		17	a	Liverpool	L	1-2	0-1	Richardson 62	22, 78
	40		22	a	Manchester C	L	0-2	0-1		28, 86
	41		29	h	EVERTON	W	2-0	2-0	Kelly 40, Fisher 43	
Halley's last game	42	May	6	a	Everton	L	0-2	0-0		78, 82

FA Cup

				Opponents	Result		h/t	Goalscorers/times	Opp. goal times
1	Jan	7	h	HUDDERSFIELD T	D	2-2	1-0	Mosscrop 45, Anderson 58	74, 88
rep		11	a	Huddersfield T	L	2-3	1-1	Kelly 30, Boyle 80	10, 67, 75

Final, Huddersfield T 1-0 Preston N E, at Stamford Bridge.

Other first team matches (friendlies and/or as detailed)

				Opponents	Result		Goalscorers
	Sep	20	h	CELTIC	W	3-0	Anderson (2), Weaver
East Lancs Charity Cup	Apr	24	h	BLACKBURN R	W	5-1	Crawley og,Weaver, Kelly, Richardson, Watson p
E Lancs Charity Cup, agg 6-3	May	1	a	Blackburn R	L	1-2	Weaver
Burnley Cricket Club benefit		4	h	FOOTBALL LEAGUE XI	W	3-0	Halley, Weaver, Bassnett
in Milan		25	n	Liverpool	W	1-0	Kelly
in Modena		28	n	Piedmontese XI	L	1-2	Kelly
in Padova	Jun	1	n	Venetian XI	W	3-1	unknown (3)
in Milan		4	n	Italian XI	W	3-1	unknown (3)
in Novara		5	n	Novara	W	2-1	unknown (2)

Att.	Pos	Dawson	Smelt	C Jones	Halley	Boyle	Watson	Nesbitt	Kelly	Anderson	Cross	Mosscrop	W Weaver	Morgan	Moorwood	Bassnett	D Taylor	Lindsay	Lane	Astin	Dobinson	Douglas	Emerson	Fisher	Richardson		
50,000		1	2	3	4	5	6	7	8	9	10	11															1
35,000		1	2	3	4	5	6	7	8	9	10		11														2
27,000		1	2	3	4	5	6	7	8	9	10	11															3
31,000	2	1	2	3	4	5	6	7	8	9	10	11															4
28,016	top	1	2	3	4	5	6	7	8	9	10	11															5
45,000	3	1	2	3	4	5	6	7	8	9	10	11															6
35,000	top	1	2	3	4	5	6	7	8	9	10	11															7
30,000	top		2	3	4	5		7	8	9	10	11		6	1												8
25,000	top	1	2	3	4	5	6	7	8	9	10	11															9
35,000	top	1	2	3	4	5	6	7	8	9	10	11															10
10,000	top		2	3	4	5	6	7	8	9	10	11			1												11
50,000	top	1	2	3	4	5		7	8	9	10	11		6													12
30,000	top	1	2	3	4		6	7	8	9	10	11				5											13
34,144	top	1	2	3	4		6	7	8	9	10	11				5											14
45,000	2	1	2		4			7	8	9		11		6		5	3	10									15
29,308	top	1	2		4	5	6	7	8	9		11					3		10								16
26,000	top	1	2		4	5	6	7	8	9	10	11					3										17
25,297	top	1			4	5	6	7	8	9	10		11				3			2							18
20,000	2	1	2		4	5	6	7	8	9	10		11				3										19
25,000		1	2		4	5	6	7	8	9		11					3	10									20
50,000		1	2		4	5	6	7	8	9		11					3	10									21
25,000	2	1	2		4	5	6	7	8	9		11					3	10									22
30,000	2	1	2		4	5	6	7	8	9		11					3	10									23
40,000	2	1	2			5	6	7	8			11				4	3	10			9						24
25,000	2	1	2			5	6	7	8			11				4	3	10			9						25
20,000	3	1	2			5	6	7	8	9	10	11				4	3										26
40,919	5	1	2		4	5	6	7	8	9	10		11				3										27
		1	2		4	5		7	8	9	10	11				6				3							28
16,000	2	1	2		4	5		7	8	9	10		11			6				3							29
29,412	2	1	2		4				8	9		11		6		5		10		3		7					30
17,436	2	1	2		4				8	9		11		6		5		10		3		7					31
20,438	2	1	2		4				8	9		11		6		5		10		3		7					32
30,000	2		2		4					9	10	11			1	5			8	3			6	7			33
30,000	2	1	2		4				8	9	10	11				5				3			6	7			34
15,000	4		2		4		6		8		10	11			1	5				3				7	9		35
12,000	3		2				6			10		11			1	5		8		3			4	7	9		36
30,000	3	1	2				6		8	10		11				5				3			4	7	9		37
16,000		1	2		4				8	10		11				5				3			6	7	9		38
50,000	3	1	2				6		8	10			11			5				3			4	7	9		39
25,000	3	1	2				6		8		10		11			5	3						4	7	9		40
	3	1	2				6		8			11				5	3	10					4	7	9		41
		1	2		3		6		8			11				5		10					4	7	9		42
Appearances		37	41	14	34	26	31	29	40	36	25	35	7	6	5	21	15	13	2	13	2	3	9	10	8		
Goals (72)					1	3	2	1	16	20	9	7	1			1		3						2	5	1	og

Att.	Pos	Dawson	Smelt	C Jones	Halley	Boyle	Watson	Nesbitt	Kelly	Anderson	Cross	Mosscrop	W Weaver	Morgan	Moorwood	Bassnett	D Taylor	Lindsay	Lane	Astin	Dobinson	Douglas	Emerson	Fisher	Richardson	
39,103		1	2		4	5	6	7	8	9		11					3	10								1
35,355		1	2		4	5	6	7	8		9	11					3	10								rep
Appearances		2	2		2	2	2	2	2	1	1	2					2	2								
Goals (4)						1			1	1		1														

1922-23

In the spring and early summer of 1922 the Burnley players and officials embarked on a tour of Italy. It was only the club's second such venture and the first since 1914 when Europe had been on the brink of war. This time of course the atmosphere was much more relaxed and the tour began with a match in Milan against League Champions Liverpool, beginning an Italian tour of their own. It was the first time Burnley had encountered another English club side on foreign soil and the Clarets emerged victorious thanks to a single goal from Bob Kelly. The two English teams then went their separate ways with Burnley winning three of their four encounters with various representative sides including a 3-1 victory, again in Milan, against what was billed as an Italian National XI.

For the coming season Burnley FC, after experimenting with a few friendlies, formally introduced a third team (Burnley 'A') and entered it in the North East Lancashire Combination. Home games were arranged to be played at Lowerhouse Mills Sports Field.

Tommy Boyle had reluctantly had to accept that 'anno domini', as well as his knee injury, had finally caught up with him. He had not been re-signed by Burnley as a Football League player but was intending to assist the club in the reserves and the new 'A' team whenever possible, and to use his vast experience as a coach. Willie Watson, one of only three members of the 1914 FA Cup winning side who were still regulars in the Burnley team, was appointed as the new Club Captain at Turf Moor.

The season began with a home game against West Brom and Benny Cross scored twice in a 3-0 victory, with Bob Kelly also on target. With the Clarets 2-0 in front skipper Willie Watson shot over the bar from a second half penalty, in the opinion of the vast majority of the crowd, very harshly awarded. After the match there were rumours that Watson had deliberately missed the penalty to even out the perceived injustice. It was never confirmed one way or the other.

In September 1922 it was announced that a substantial part of the extensive Thursby Estates was to be offered for sale by auction at the Mechanics Institute in Burnley. Lot 55 was described as 'a particularly valuable plot of land, occupying an area of about 8 acres, known as Turf Moor Football Ground'. Bidding was brisk with a number of interested parties and the gavel finally fell at £4500. There was an audible sigh of relief, as well as a ripple of applause, within the auction room when it became apparent that the purchaser was Burnley FC. Later in the sale, Turf Moor Cricket Ground was also bid for, and secured, by the Football Club.

On October 1922 two goals from Bob Kelly ensured a 2-0 victory at Newcastle and after nine games of the new season, Burnley were second, just a point behind Liverpool who had already been beaten at Turf Moor. Unfortunately that was as good as it got during that campaign.

In November 1922, newly promoted Nottingham Forest, the reigning Second Division Champions, came to Turf Moor for the first top flight clash between the clubs since the infamous encounter at the City Ground in April 1900. Burnley chose that day to turn on their most ferocious display of attacking power of the season, winning 8-2, the first time ten goals had ever been scored in a First Division game at Turf Moor. After just 15 minutes Benny Cross had claimed his first Burnley hat trick, Bob Kelly and Willie Watson both scored a couple with Walter Weaver also on target. The Clarets were now third but, ironically, the following week at the City Ground, it was very much a case of 'after the Lord Mayor's Show' when Forest took the points with a 1-0 win.

Len Smelt
a Championship winner in 1921,
still an ever present at right back

A season that had never really got going ended very disappointingly with only one victory and one draw in the last ten matches. Ironically the one win was against Sunderland at Turf Moor, who finished the campaign as runners up to Liverpool, who Burnley had also beaten at home earlier in the season. A little more consistency would have made a big difference but nevertheless fifteenth position was the Clarets' poorest finish since promotion to the First Division in 1913.

During the last week of the season Burnley signed a young goalscorer from Chesterfield who had scored 26 League and FA Cup goals in just one season at Saltergate. The Burnley Manager and Directors saw in the 23 year old an ability to score the goals that the Clarets had been lacking since the hey day of Bert Freeman. Joe Anderson had stepped into the breach and done his bit during the Championship campaign of 1920-21 but his output was no longer prolific. The newcomer would go on to fully justify the faith shown in him by breaking every single goalscoring record at Turf Moor, all of which still stand more than eight decades later. The name of the new arrival was, of course, George William Beel.

OBITUARY
ARTHUR BELL
DIED 22 APRIL 1923, AGED 40.

Arthur Bell remained a true amateur throughout his career as a League footballer as well as an accomplished Lancashire League cricketer.

Born in Burnley in 1882 he was educated at Burnley Grammar School, playing his early football with Burnley Belvedere. His real sporting passion however was cricket and he soon graduated through the ranks at the 'other' Turf Moor, going on to represent the senior team with distinction. Burnley Cricket Club were the dominant force in Lancashire League cricket around the turn of the century and Arthur Bell captained the side which captured three successive League titles between 1906 and 1908, winning five Championship medals altogether during his senior cricket career. A skilful inside forward, very comfortable on the ball he played 104 senior games for Burnley, scoring 30 goals. He was good enough to represent his country at amateur level on three occasions. After his retirement from football Arthur Bell maintained very close links with Burnley Football Club. His association continued when he was the principal architect behind the design and construction of Turf Moor's Brunshaw Road stand, built in the summer of 1911.

RIP

Just two weeks later there was another signing to fill another position that had become a problem. When anno domini had caught up with Tommy Boyle a huge gap, in fact a yawning chasm, had been left at the heart of Burnley's defence. His ability, his leadership and his sheer will to win had been sorely missed and the campaign just ended, the first one since Boyle's arrival at Turf Moor that had finished with nothing to play for, had proved how much the Burnley team had relied on his influence. Many top clubs had been admiring Plymouth Argyle's centre half and captain, a big strong Geordie who was billed as 'the tallest man in football'. Once again the Clarets were quickest off the mark to sign a man who was a born leader, a natural replacement for Tommy Boyle. The Burnley Directors had to pay a record £5000 transfer fee for their new signing, an England centre half of the future, Jack Hill.

In June 1923 Tommy Boyle himself joined Wrexham as player-coach. He had kept himself fit during his last season at Turf Moor and had played for the reserves and the newly-formed 'A' team, who he had helped to win the Championship of the North East Lancashire Combination.

Under Boyle's leadership the Clarets had won promotion, the FA Cup and the League Championship, but it was now time to look to the future for both Tommy Boyle and Burnley FC.

Willie Watson
still going strong after more than a dozen years at Turf Moor

George Beel
one era coming to a close
another one beginning

1922-23 - First Division

		P	W	D	L	F	A	Pts
1	Liverpool	42	26	8	8	70	31	60
2	Sunderland	42	22	10	10	72	54	54
3	Huddersfield T	42	21	11	10	60	32	53
4	Newcastle U	42	18	12	12	45	37	48
5	Everton	42	20	7	15	63	59	47
6	Aston Villa	42	18	10	14	64	51	46
7	West Bromwich A	42	17	11	14	58	49	45
8	Manchester C	42	17	11	14	50	49	45
9	Cardiff C	42	18	7	17	73	59	43
10	Sheffield U	42	16	10	16	68	64	42
11	Arsenal	42	16	10	16	61	62	42
12	Tottenham H	42	17	7	18	50	50	41
13	Bolton W	42	14	12	16	50	58	40
14	Blackburn R	42	14	12	16	47	62	40
15	BURNLEY	42	16	16	20	58	59	38
16	Preston NE	42	13	11	18	60	64	37
17	Birmingham	42	13	11	18	41	57	37
18	Middlesbrough	42	13	10	19	57	63	36
19	Chelsea	42	9	18	15	45	53	36
20	Nottingham F	42	13	8	21	41	70	34
21	Stoke	42	10	10	22	47	67	30
22	Oldham A	42	10	10	22	35	65	30

1922-23

Manager : John Haworth

Division One (15th)

		Date			Opponents	Result		h/t	Goalscorers/times	Opp. goal times
	1	Aug	26	h	WEST BROMWICH A	W	3-0	2-0	Kelly 11, Cross (2) 40, 88	
	2		28	a	Arsenal	D	1-1	0-0	Taylor 89	65
	3	Sep	2	a	West Bromwich A	L	1-2	1-2	Anderson 15	2, 25
	4		4	h	ARSENAL	W	4-1	2-0	Voysey 17og, Anderson (2) 22, 62, Kelly 89	83
	5		9	a	Tottenham H	W	3-1	2-0	Kelly 36, Watson 41, Cross 70	50
	6		16	h	TOTTENHAM H	L	0-1	0-1		15
	7		23	a	Liverpool	L	0-3	0-1		28, 49, 50
	8		30	h	LIVERPOOL	W	2-0	1-0	Weaver 43, Cross 67	
	9	Oct	7	a	Newcastle U	W	2-0	1-0	Kelly (2) 15, 80	
	10		14	h	NEWCASTLE U	D	0-0	0-0		
	11		21	h	BLACKBURN R	W	3-1	2-0	Kelly (2) 25p, 80, Cross 40	60
	12		28	a	Blackburn R	L	1-2	0-1	Anderson 80	30, 52
Forest goals 24m p, 80m	13	Nov	4	h	NOTTINGHAM F	W	8-2	5-1	Cross (3) 5, 13, 15, Kelly (2) 25p, 70, Watson (2) 44, 89, Weaver 60	
	14		11	a	Nottingham F	L	0-1	0-1		21p
	15		18	h	CHELSEA	W	1-0	0-0	Kelly 60	
Mosscrop's last game	16		25	a	Chelsea	W	1-0	0-0	Anderson 86	
	17	Dec	2	a	Middlesbrough	L	1-4	0-0	Kelly 69p	46, 49, 68, 82
	18		9	h	MIDDLESBROUGH	W	3-0	2-0	Kelly 1, Weaver 32, Cross 67	
	19		16	h	OLDHAM A	D	1-1	1-0	Weaver 5	70
	20		23	a	Oldham A	D	1-1	0-0	Cross 87	61
	21		25	h	ASTON VILLA	D	1-1	1-1	Watson 35	40
	22		26	a	Aston Villa	L	1-3	0-2	Cross 85	30, 45, 65
	23		30	a	Sheffield U	L	1-2	1-0	Anderson 30	48p, 75
	24	Jan	6	h	SHEFFIELD U	L	1-4	0-2	Bassnett 78	31, 33, 55, 88
	25		20	h	PRESTON N E	W	2-0	1-0	Bassnett 15, Anderson 68	
	26		27	a	Preston N E	L	1-3	0-0	Weaver 50	83, 84, 86
	27	Feb	10	a	Bolton W	L	1-2	0-2	Kelly 80	20, 26
	28		17	h	MANCHESTER C	W	2-0	2-0	Lindsay 14, Weaver 23	
	29		24	a	Manchester C	L	0-1	0-1		12
	30	Mar	3	h	STOKE	W	3-2	0-0	Fisher 50, Cross 53, Weaver 70	58, 68
	31		10	a	Stoke	W	1-0	0-0	Kelly 78	
	32		12	h	BOLTON W	W	2-1	1-1	Nesbitt 41, Anderson 48	4
	33		17	a	Huddersfield T	L	0-2	0-0		63, 90
	34		24	h	HUDDERSFIELD T	L	0-2	0-1		20og, 70
	35		30	h	CARDIFF C	L	1-5	0-2	Kelly 55	20, 29, 65, 66, 80
	36		31	a	Everton	L	0-1	0-0		65
Nesbitt's last game	37	Apr	2	a	Cardiff C	D	2-2	0-1	Lindsay 60, Kelly 75	27, 87
	38		7	h	EVERTON	L	0-1	0-0		88
	39		14	a	Sunderland	L	1-3	1-2	Lindsay 43	15, 25, 57
	40		21	h	SUNDERLAND	W	2-0	2-0	Kelly 22, Freeman 34	
	41		28	a	Birmingham	L	0-1	0-1		27
	42	May	5	h	BIRMINGHAM	L	0-2	0-1		20, 80

FA Cup

	Date			Opponents	Result		h/t	Goalscorers/times	Opp. goal times
1	Jan	13	a	Sunderland	L	1-3	0-1	Anderson 70	7, 62, 73

Final, Bolton W 2-0 West Ham U, first FA Cup final at Wembley.

Other first team matches (friendlies and/or as detailed)

	Date			Opponents	Result		Goalscorers	
Victoria Hospital benefit	Sep	5	h	RANGERS	W	3-0	Kelly, Anderson (2)	
Alex Archibald benefit		12	a	Rangers	L	0-2		
Whitehaven pit disaster fund	Oct	5	a	Cumberland XI	W	10-3	Kelly (5), Anderson (4), Richardson	at Workington
	Feb	3	a	Coventry C	D	2-2	Cross, Kelly p	
	Apr	3	a	Llanelli	W	3-1	Kelly (2), Lindsay	
East Lancs Charity Cup		23	a	Blackburn R	L	0-1		
E Lancs Charity Cup, agg 1-1	May	1	h	BLACKBURN R	W	1-0	Cross	
East Lancs Charity Cup replay		7	a	Blackburn R	L	0-2		

Att.	Pos	Dawson	Smelt	D Taylor	Emerson	Sims	Watson	Fisher	Kelly	Anderson	Cross	Mosscrop	Bassnett	W Weaver	Gee	Richardson	Nesbitt	Chambers	Pearson	Lindsay	Moorwood	Morgan	Lane	A Freeman	Waller	Evans	Greenhalgh	Beel		
24,472		1	2	3	4	5	6	7	8	9	10	11																		1
25,000		1	2	3	4	5	6	7	8	9	10	11																		2
23,561		1	2	3	4		6	7	8	9	10	11	5																	3
20,000	3	1	2	3	4		6	7	8	9	10	11	5																	4
40,000	3	1	2	3	4		6	7	8	9	10	11	5																	5
24,586	5	1	2	3	4		6	7	8	9	10	11	5																	6
40,000	9	1	2	3	6	5		7	8	9	10	11	4																	7
35,000	5	1	2	3	4		6		8	9	10	11	5	7																8
35,000	2	1	2	3	4		6		8	9	10	11	5	7																9
25,000	5	1	2	3	4		6		8	9	10	11	5	7																10
29,000	4	1	2	3			6		8	9	10	11	5	7	4															11
23,000	5	1	2	3	4		6		8	9	10	11	5	7																12
15,000	3	1	2	3	4		6		8	9	10	11	5	7																13
20,000	4	1	2	3	4		6		8	9	10	11	5	7																14
17,000	4	1	2	3	4		6	7	8		10	11	5			9														15
25,000	3	1	2	3	4		6	7	8	9	10	11	5																	16
25,000	4	1	2	3			6	7	8	9	10		5	11	4															17
15,000	3	1	2	3			6	7	8	9	10		5	11	4															18
12,000	4	1	2	3			6	7	8	9	10		5	11	4															19
9,162		1	2	3	4		6	7	8	9	10		5	11																20
27,000		1	2	3	4		6		8		10		5	11			7	9												21
40,000	6	1	2	3	4		6		8		10		5	11			7	9												22
20,000	9	1	2	3	4		6	7	8	9	10		5	11																23
18,000	9	1	2	3	4		6	7	8	9	10		5	11																24
16,033	8	1	2			5	6	7	8	9	10		4	11					3											25
21,000	11	1	2	3		5	6	7	8	9	10		4	11																26
	12	1	2	3	4	5	6	7	8	9	10			11																27
14,000	10	1	2	3	6	5	4	7	8		9			11						10										28
22,000	10	1	2	3	6	5	4	7	8		9			11						10										29
	10		2	3		5	6	7	8		10			11	4			9			1									30
20,000			2	3	4		6		8	9	10		5	11			7				1									31
	5		2	3	4		6		8	9	10		5	11			7				1									32
14,000	7		2	3	4		6		8		10		5	11			7	9			1									33
9,100	8		2	3	4		6		8	9	10		5	11			7				1									34
20,000	10	1	2	3	4		6		7	9	10		5	11						8										35
25,000			2	3	4				9		10		5	11			7			8	1	6								36
30,000	12		2	3			4		9		10		5	11			7			8	1	6								37
	13		2	3	4			7	9		10		5	11						8	1	6								38
20,000	14		2	3			4				10		5	11						8	1	6	7	9						39
12,000	14		2	3	6		4		8		10		5	11							1		7	9						40
19,400	15		2	3	6		4				10		5	11						8	1			9	7					41
8,000			2		6		4		8		10		5	11							1					3	7	9		42
Appearances		30	42	40	33	9	39	22	40	28	42	16	36	33	5	1	8	4	1	8	12	4	2	3	1	1	1	1		
Goals (58)				1			4	1	17	8	12		2	7			1			3				1					1	og

Att.	Pos	Dawson	Smelt	D Taylor	Emerson	Sims	Watson	Fisher	Kelly	Anderson	Cross	Mosscrop	Bassnett	W Weaver	
40,000		1	2	3	4		6	7	8	9	10		5	11	1
Appearances		1	1	1	1		1	1	1	1	1		1	1	
Goals (1)										1					

1923-24

Even after Burnley's worst season for some years, confidence at Turf Moor was still high for the coming campaign. The supporters were delighted that two of the best young prospects around, centre half Jack Hill and centre forward George Beel had recently been added to the playing strength and they were joined by Peter Bennie, a small but lightning quick winger from Albion Rovers.

George Beel scored his first Burnley goal at Notts County on the opening day but the season began disappointingly with just four points in the first six games, all from draws. Peter Bennie and Jack Hill both scored their first goals for their new club against Everton but after a heavy home defeat by Nottingham Forest the players and supporters knew that a difficult campaign lay ahead. Eleven games into the season, following a 2-1 defeat at Sheffield United the Clarets had dropped into the bottom two with just one victory, ironically a 2-0 success at Turf Moor against Champions Liverpool, thanks to two early goals from Joe Anderson, his last in a Burnley shirt.

George Waterfield
new signing from Mexborough, a stalwart for many years

In October 1923 another link with both the FA Cup winning triumph and the League Championship win was broken when Billy Nesbitt was transferred to Second Division Bristol City. Nesbitt had been one of the most prominent Burnley players in both those magnificent campaigns, his electric pace down the right wing and ability to cross a ball with pinpoint accuracy had contributed to many of the goals scored by Bert Freeman and Joe Anderson. Anderson himself was the next to leave Turf Moor, after much speculation about his Burnley future he returned to his former club Clydebank. Joe "Andy" had replaced Bert Freeman as the darling of the Turf Moor crowd and in his first season with the Clarets had top-scored with 31 goals in League and Cup as Burnley had swept to the Football League Championship in 1920-21. He had averaged better than a goal every two games in his Turf Moor career but with George Beel starting to demonstrate his ability in front of goal it was time for Joe Anderson to move on.

The Burnley Directors continued their team rebuilding with the signature of George Waterfield, a 22 year old left winger from Mexborough Town in the Midland League. Waterfield was another example of Burnley's excellent scouting network, a number of clubs had been watching the sturdy miner who played football part time but once again the Clarets were quickest off the mark, parting with a fee of £450 to bring the young man to Turf Moor. George Waterfield's early promise would be more than fulfilled but he would emerge as a natural full back, going on to play almost 400 games for the Clarets as well as representing his country.

In November 1923 Burnley celebrated only their third League win of the season with a thumping 5-1 success against West Ham at Turf Moor. It was the Hammers' first visit to Burnley in their first season in Division One and George Beel marked the occasion with a hat trick. It was his first for Burnley but it would certainly not be the last.

Around the turn of the year Burnley were still struggling and a heavy defeat at Preston, who were bottom of the League, did not inspire the fans with much confidence when the FA Cup came around again. The Clarets had not progressed beyond the third round since winning the trophy in 1914 and, in their first round tie, made heavy weather of beating Second Division South Shields 3-2 at Turf Moor.

OBITUARY
JONATHAN WALDERS
DIED 13 JANUARY 1924, AGED 42.

Born in Barrow in 1882 Jack Walders was playing for his home town team in the Lancashire Combination when he was transferred to Burnley in the summer of 1904. He joined his brother David who had taken the same route to Turf Moor a year earlier and the two lined up alongside each other in the Burnley defence for the opening game of the 1904-05 season. It was the first time brothers had played in the same Burnley team for a League game and that feat remained unique in Turf Moor history for over 75 years. Originally signed as a left back, Jack Walders had a wonderful turn of speed and he played many games for Burnley on the wing. In 1906 both brothers moved on to Oldham with Jack later playing for Luton. Jack Walders saw active service during the first World War before spending a long time as a prisoner of war. After the Armistice he moved back to Burnley to work in Bank Hall pit but for many years suffered with his health before he passed away at his Burnley home.

RIP

Victories home and away against West Brom lifted the Clarets to fourteenth place in the League, the highest of the whole season, and set the team up for a second round FA Cup tie at home to Fulham. The match was dreadful, described as one of the poorest seen at Turf Moor for many years. However the 0-0 draw at least kept Burnley in the hat and they duly won the replay 1-0 thanks to a Benny Cross goal in extra time.

The victory set up the Clarets for a third round clash with Huddersfield Town, then emerging as a real force in English football under their innovative Manager Herbert Chapman. Chapman had guided Huddersfield to their FA Cup success in 1922, incidentally after a semi final victory at Turf Moor, and in 1924 had designs on a League and FA Cup double, the first in English football since Aston Villa in 1897. Burnley had other ideas and, in their best performance of the season, outplayed and outlasted the Terriers, a first half goal from Walter Weaver clinching a memorable 1-0 victory. Jack Hill was inspired at centre half, his best display in a Burnley shirt, with Jerry Dawson, yet again, on top form. The Cup tie had caught the imagination of the Burnley people and, after a period when Turf Moor attendances were beginning to fall, they turned up in their thousands, well over 50,000 squeezing in to watch an epic encounter. The crowd that day was later confirmed at 54,775, setting a new record for Turf Moor that has never since been exceeded. Herbert Chapman's dreams of the coveted double for his team were over but Huddersfield lost only one more game from that day to the end of the season and emerged as Football League Champions for the first time, going on retain their title in 1925 and 1926. Meanwhile Burnley's notable FA Cup scalp had taken them into the last eight for the first time in ten years.

Jack Hill
huge boots to fill at centre half

The League form continued to be a worry and the Clarets were unable to find a victory from anywhere before their FA Cup quarter final with Swindon Town of the Third Division South. On the Wiltshire team's unique narrow pitch Walter Weaver's goal earned a 1-1 draw and George Beel scored twice in the replay at Turf Moor as Burnley eased through with a comfortable 3-1 victory. They would now come up against old rivals Aston Villa in the semi final at Bramall Lane. The next match, another home defeat in the League, this time by Sunderland, marked the last appearance in a senior Burnley match for a promising new local talent. The left half position had been filled with distinction since the Second Division days before the First World War by Billy Watson. Time however was finally catching up with the last of the famous half back trio and Burnley-born Billy Morgan was slowly but surely emerging as Watson's successor. Cruelly, Morgan's dreams were shattered when, after a shuddering collision with a Sunderland forward, he was carried off with what was subsequently found to be a badly broken leg. Billy Morgan never played senior football again. Morgan had played throughout Burnley's FA Cup run that season but Billy Watson stepped in for what would be his last FA Cup game for the Clarets, the semi final against Aston Villa at Bramall Lane. Burnley started promisingly but the fates had decreed it was not to be their day when Villa scored after 20 minutes against the run of play. Two goals late on, both due to misjudgements by Jerry Dawson, sealed it for Villa 3-0 and the Clarets were left to concentrate on their, very real, fight against relegation.

The drop was indeed avoided but Burnley managed just one victory in the last eight games of the season and the crowd of only 9,000 for the 4-1 win against Arsenal, Turf Moor's final League fixture, demonstrated the highs and lows of this season of contrasting fortunes. How long ago the pulsating throng of nearly 55000 people for the Cup tie against Huddersfield now seemed.

Another link with the glory days was gone when left back David Taylor announced he was leaving Turf Moor to take up the position as Manager of St Johnstone. After Jerry Dawson, Taylor had been the first member of the FA Cup winning team to establish himself and, in 15 years at Turf Moor, had appeared in almost 400 senior games for Burnley.

In May 1924 the Turf Moor curtain came down when Burnley's home staged its first schoolboy international, at under-14 level, Scotland beating England 2-1 in front of around 14,000 spectators.

1923-24 - First Division

		P	W	D	L	F	A	Pts
1	Huddersfield T	42	23	11	8	60	33	57
2	Cardiff C	42	22	13	7	61	34	57
3	Sunderland	42	22	9	11	71	54	53
4	Bolton W	42	18	14	10	68	34	50
5	Sheffield U	42	29	12	11	69	49	50
6	Aston Villa	42	18	13	11	52	37	49
7	Everton	42	18	13	11	62	53	49
8	Blackburn R	42	17	11	14	54	50	45
9	Newcastle U	42	17	10	15	60	54	44
10	Notts C	42	14	14	14	44	49	42
11	Manchester C	42	15	12	15	54	71	42
12	Liverpool	42	15	11	16	49	48	41
13	West Ham U	42	13	15	14	40	43	41
14	Birmingham	42	13	13	16	41	49	39
15	Tottenham H	42	12	14	16	50	56	38
16	West Bromwich A	42	12	14	16	51	62	38
17	BURNLEY	42	12	12	18	55	60	36
18	Preston NE	42	12	10	20	52	67	34
19	Arsenal	42	12	9	21	40	63	33
20	Nottingham F	42	10	12	20	42	64	32
21	Chelsea	42	9	14	19	31	53	32
22	Middlesbrough	42	7	8	27	37	60	22

1923-24

Manager : John Haworth

Division One (17th)

Note	No	Date		Venue	Opponents	Result		h/t	Goalscorers/times	Opp. goal times
	1	Aug	25	a	Notts C	L	1-2	0-2	Beel 46	38, 43
Emerson's last game	2		27	h	EVERTON	D	2-2	1-1	Bennie 37, Hill 70	2, 88
	3	Sep	1	h	NOTTS C	D	1-1	1-1	Beel 27	37
	4		3	a	Everton	D	3-3	1-1	Anderson (2) 28, 78, Kelly 75	3, 54, 58
	5		8	h	NOTTINGHAM F	L	2-4	2-1	Anderson 20, Freeman 24	22, 70, 72, 80
	6		15	a	Nottingham F	D	0-0	0-0		
	7		22	h	LIVERPOOL	W	2-0	2-0	Anderson (2) 24, 26	
	8		29	a	Liverpool	L	0-1	0-1		22
	9	Oct	6	h	ASTON VILLA	L	1-2	0-1	Cross 75p	20, 62
	10		13	a	Aston Villa	D	1-1	1-0	Moss 35og	65
Anderson's last game	11		20	a	Sheffield U	L	1-2	1-1	Bennie 35	30, 49
	12		27	h	SHEFFIELD U	W	2-0	0-0	Cross 51, Kelly 56p	
	13	Nov	3	a	Blackburn R	D	1-1	0-0	Kelly 85	89
	14		10	h	BLACKBURN R	L	1-2	1-0	Beel 17	49, 52
	15		17	h	WEST HAM U	W	5-1	2-0	Beel (3) 30, 55, 58, Bennie (2) 40, 65	48
	16		24	a	West Ham U	D	0-0	0-0		
	17	Dec	1	h	NEWCASTLE U	W	3-2	3-1	Hampson 10og, Beel (2) 20, 24	22, 89
	18		8	a	Newcastle U	L	0-2	0-1		9, 85
	19		15	h	CHELSEA	W	2-0	2-0	Bennie (2) 7, 22	
	20		22	a	Chelsea	L	2-3	1-2	Beel (2) 40, 65	9, 44, 47
	21		25	h	MIDDLESBROUGH	D	0-0	0-0		
	22		26	a	Middlesbrough	L	0-3	0-2		20, 44, 85
	23		29	h	PRESTON N E	W	1-0	1-0	Beel 32	
	24	Jan	5	a	Preston N E	L	0-5	0-4		15, 31, 43, 44, 71
	25		19	a	West Bromwich A	W	3-0	1-0	Beel 18, Cross 53, Hill 75	
	26		26	h	WEST BROMWICH A	W	4-0	0-0	Weaver (2) 52, 69, Bennie 80, Beel 88	
	27	Feb	9	h	BIRMINGHAM	L	1-2	0-1	Kelly 81p	14, 75
	28		16	a	Manchester C	D	2-2	0-0	Beel (2) 54, 84	74, 77
	29		27	a	Birmingham	L	1-2	1-1	Kelly 25	43, 65
	30	Mar	1	a	Bolton W	D	0-0	0-0		
	31		15	h	SUNDERLAND	L	0-3	0-2		14, 37, 84
	32		17	h	MANCHESTER C	W	3-2	3-2	Beel (2) 12, 41, Cross 17	43, 45
	33		22	a	Sunderland	W	1-0	0-0	Beel 67	
	34	Apr	1	h	BOLTON W	W	1-0	0-0	Taylor 63p	
	35		5	a	Arsenal	L	0-2	0-1		23, 57
	36		12	a	Cardiff C	L	0-2	0-1		30og, 85
	37		18	h	HUDDERSFIELD T	D	1-1	1-1	Waterfield 18	14
	38		19	h	CARDIFF C	L	1-2	1-1	Kelly 10	17, 78
	39		22	a	Huddersfield T	L	0-1	0-1		42
David Taylor's last game	40		26	h	TOTTENHAM H	D	2-2	1-1	Cross 23, Kelly 79	42, 65
	41		28	h	ARSENAL	W	4-1	3-0	Freeman (2) 18, 77, Kelly 20p, Beel 42	79
	42	May	3	a	Tottenham H	L	0-1	0-1		25

FA Cup

Note	Rd	Date		Venue	Opponents	Result		h/t	Goalscorers/times	Opp. goal times
	1	Jan	12	h	SOUTH SHIELDS	W	3-2	2-0	Cross 7, Kelly (2) 36, 76	81, 86
	2	Feb	2	h	FULHAM	D	0-0	0-0		
after extra time, 0-0 at 90m	rep		7	a	Fulham	W	1-0	0-0	Cross 92	
	3		23	h	HUDDERSFIELD T	W	1-0	1-0	Weaver 23	
	4	Mar	8	a	Swindon T	D	1-1	1-0	Weaver 15	77
	rep		12	h	SWINDON T	W	3-1	1-0	Beel (2) 18, 47, Weaver 58	66
at Bramall Lane	semi		29	n	Aston Villa	L	0-3	0-1		20, 78, 82

Final, Newcastle U 2-0 Aston Villa, at Wembley.

Other first team matches (friendlies and/or as detailed)

Competition	Date		Venue	Opponents	Result		Goalscorers	Notes
East Lancs Charity Cup	Sep	5	h	BLACKBURN R	W	2-0	Anderson, Cross	
E Lancs Charity Cup, agg 2-2		10	a	Blackburn R	L	0-2		
Lancs Cup		23	h	BOLTON W	W	2-0	Kelly, Anderson	
Lancs Cup	Oct	15	h	MANCHESTER C	D	2-2	Kelly, O'Beirne	
Lancs Cup replay		22	a	Manchester C	L	0-4		
East Lancs Charity Cup replay	Apr	23	a	Blackburn R	D	1-1	Beel	Cup shared

Att	Pos	Dawson	Smelt	D Taylor	Watson	Hill	Emerson	Bennie	Kelly	Beel	Cross	W Weaver	Morgan	Evans	Anderson	A Freeman	Bassnett	O'Beirne	Gillatt	Waterfield	Sims	S Page	Robinson	Parkin	Dixon	Wheelhouse	Greenhalgh		
18,000		1	2	3	4	5	6	7	8	9	10	11																	1
16,000		1	2	3	4	5	6	7	8	9	10	11																	2
17,000		1	2	3	4	5		7	8	9	10	11	6																3
25,000	17	1	2		4	5		7	8		11		6	3	9	10													4
15,000	18	1	2		4	5		7	8			11	6	3	9	10													5
20,000	17	1	2	3		5		7	8		11		6		9		4	10											6
17,765	15	1	2	3		5		7	8		11		6		9		4	10											7
40,000	19	1	2	3		5				8	11		6		9		4	10	7										8
17,000	20	1	2	3		5		7	8		11		6		9		4	10											9
20,000	19	1	2	3	11	5		7	8		10		6		9		4												10
15,000	21	1	2	3		5		7			10	11	6		9	8	4												11
12,000	18	1	2	3	6	5		7	8	9	10						4			11									12
20,000	18	1	2	3	6	5		7	8		10						4			11	9								13
30,000	18	1	2	3	6	5		7	8	9	10						4			11									14
9,000	16	1	2	3	6	5		7	8	9	10						4			11									15
20,000	17	1	2	3	6	5		7	8	9	10						4			11									16
8,000	15	1	2	3	6	5		7	8	9	10						4			11									17
25,000	16	1	2	3	6	5		7	8	9	10						4			11									18
15,000	15	1	2	3	6	5		7	8	9	10						4			11									19
17,500		1	2	3	6	5			8	9	10	7					4			11									20
25,000		1	2	3		5		7	8	9	10	11	6				4												21
20,000	15	1	2	3		5		7	8	9	10	11	6				4												22
12,000	14		2	3		5		7	8	9	10	11	6				4					1							23
15,000	16	1	2	3	6	5		7	8	9	10	11					4												24
8,527	14		2	3		5		7	8	9	10	11	6				4					1							25
15,000	14		2	3		5		7	8	9	10	11	6				4					1							26
10,000	15		2	3				7	8	9	10	11	6				4				5	1							27
25,000	15		2	3		5		7	8	9		11					4	10				1	6						28
14,500				2		5		7	8	9	10	11	6	3			4					1							29
10,000	15	1		2	6	5		7	8	9	10	11	6	3			4												30
14,000		1	2	3	6			7		8	10	11	6				5							4	9				31
12,000	15	1		2		5		7		8	10	11		3			4								9				32
30,000	15	1		2				7	8	9				3			5			11				4	10				33
		1		3	2	5		7	8	9	10	11					4							6		2			34
25,000	16	1	2			5			8	9	10	11		3			4			7				6					35
	17	1		3		5		7		9	10					8	4			11				6					36
25,000	16	1	2	3		5		7	8	9	10						4			11				6					37
	17	1		3		5		7	8	9	10						4			11				6		2			38
33,000		1		3		5		7	8	9	10									11			6	4		2			39
50,000		1		3		5			7	9	8						4			11				6		2	10		40
9,000	17	1				5			7	9	8					10	2			11			4	6		3			41
20,000		1				5			7	9	8	11				10	2						6	4		3			42
Appearances		36	31	37	19	39	2	36	37	34	39	21	18	7	8	6	36	5	1	17	2	6	4	11	3	6	1		
Goals (55)				1		2		7	8	19	5	2			5	3				1								2	ogs

Att	Pos	Dawson	Smelt	D Taylor	Watson	Hill	Emerson	Bennie	Kelly	Beel	Cross	W Weaver	Morgan	Evans	Anderson	A Freeman	Bassnett	O'Beirne	Gillatt	Waterfield	Sims	S Page	Robinson	Parkin	Dixon	Wheelhouse	Greenhalgh	
20,606		1	2	3		5		7	8	9	10	11	6				4											1
23,601			2	3		5		7	8	9	10	11	6				4					1						2
31,000			2	3		5		7	8	9	10	11	6				4					1						rep
54,775		1	2	3		5		7	8	9	10	11	6				4											3
22,210		1	2	3		5		7	8	9	10	11	6				4											4
34,089		1	2	3		5		7	8	9	10	11	6				4											rep
54,531		1	2	3	6	5		7	8	9	10	11					4											sf
Appearances		5	7	7	1	7		7	7	7	7	7	6				7					2						
Goals (9)									2	2	2	3																

1924-25

The season started slowly with Burnley's first two home matches both ending in goalless draws with a 2-0 win at Preston sandwiched in between. After three games the Clarets were fifth but the Turf Moor fans had not had a goal to either cheer or grumble about. It changed with a vengeance with the visit of Blackburn. After just sixteen minutes Burnley were three goals in front with the supporters relishing the prospect of a place in the top four at the final whistle. Seventy four minutes later everybody, except the Rovers players and fans, left the ground stunned after witnessing a capitulation by Burnley that was difficult to believe. The players had somehow managed to drag defeat from deep within the jaws of victory, allowing Rovers to storm back from being three goals down to win the game 5-3.

The depressing run continued and the Clarets did not win another match until early November 1924, by which time they had slipped into the bottom two. By the time of the welcome 2-1 success against Liverpool, the Turf Moor Directors had signed two former England internationals to try to arrest the slide down the table. Centre forward Tom Roberts from Preston and wing half Jack Tresadern from West Ham were both vastly experienced players who, co-incidentally, had both experienced recent FA Cup final disappointments. Roberts had been in the Preston side that had lost to Huddersfield at Stamford Bridge in 1922 and Tresadern had lined up for West Ham in the first historic Wembley final against Bolton in 1923.

Tom Roberts
top scorer even after a serious injury

Tom Roberts had scored well over 100 goals in his time at Deepdale and, even in a struggling Burnley team, was soon into his stride, scoring his first Clarets' hat trick in a much needed 4-0 victory against Bury in late November 1924. Jack Tresadern captained the side for the first time in this match.

In early December 1924 came the sad news that the Burnley Secretary/Manager John Haworth, who had been ill and away from his post for some months, had died of pneumonia at the comparatively young age of 48. The Turf Moor flag was immediately lowered to half mast and the Burnley players wore black armbands for the following match, a 3-3 draw at Manchester City.

In December 1924 another member of Burnley's League Championship side of 1920-21 left Turf Moor when Walter Weaver was transferred to Everton. Weaver had arrived from South Liverpool in 1919 and had won a place in Burnley's side on the left wing at the expense of Eddie Mosscrop, although both players had contributed magnificently to the Turf Moor cause.

Within a few short weeks Burnley Football Club has lost two men who were instrumental in shaping the club in its early days and then establishing it amongst the elite of English football.

OBITUARIES

HARRY BRADSHAW

DIED 28 SEPTEMBER 1924, AGED 71.

Born in Burnley in 1853, Harry Bradshaw played football for Burnley in the very earliest days of the association code, having already played rugby for the club's predecessor, Burnley Rovers. He was also actively involved in the running of the Club as a member of the Committee before being appointed as Honorary Secretary in 1891 and he was invited to become Team Manager in 1894. From 1897 he fulfilled both roles before accepting the position of Team Manager at Woolwich Arsenal in 1899, leaving for the same position at Fulham in 1904. In 1909 he accepted a new challenge as Secretary of the Southern League.

JOHN HAWORTH

DIED 4 DECEMBER 1924, AGED 48.

Born in Accrington in 1876, John Haworth came from a sporting family, his uncle was George Haworth, an England centre half in the 1880's. John Haworth played football as an amateur but soon realised his talents lay off the pitch and he was appointed Secretary of Accrington Stanley in 1897. Stanley had some Lancashire Combination success in the 1900's and it was from this background that John Haworth was appointed as Burnley's Secretary/Manager in 1910, following the tragic death of Spen Whittaker. At Haworth's suggestion, the Burnley colours were changed from green to claret and blue and the change was to bring a dramatic improvement in fortunes to Turf Moor. Promotion to Division One in 1913 was followed by a wonderful FA Cup triumph, in front of King George V, in 1914 and then the ultimate measure of club success, the Football League Championship, came to Turf Moor in 1921. The arrival of John Haworth at Turf Moor was the catalyst for Burnley Football Club to earn a place at the top table of English club football. His contribution to the Claret and Blue cause will never be forgotten.

RIP

Burnley's disastrous holiday games, two defeats by reigning Champions Huddersfield, including a 1-5 demolition at Turf Moor on Christmas Day, were followed by an early FA Cup exit at Everton. Suddenly however the team's form improved and from 20th place at the turn of the year, five successive League victories propelled the Clarets up the table. This perhaps unexpected, albeit short-lived, success was spearheaded by Tom Roberts, in a rich vein of form, with 9 goals in seven successive matches. From being relegation candidates, Burnley looked to be comfortable in mid-table when it all went wrong. Just seven minutes into the home match with Tottenham, Roberts was in collision with the Spurs goalkeeper Fred Hinton. Both players hit the ground heavily but Tom Roberts stayed down, obviously in great pain, before being carried off on a stretcher. He was immediately taken to hospital and a badly broken pelvis was diagnosed, he would not play again for the rest of the season and possibly his absence would be much longer.

Among the candidates for the position of Burnley's new Secretary/Manager was former crowd favourite Bert Freeman but the Directors' choice was one of their own, Albert Pickles, who had been a member of the Board since 1918. Burnley-born Pickles was a keen sportsman in his younger days, playing football for Burnley Belvedere and excelling on the running track. Albert Pickles wasted no time in demonstrating his knowledge of football talent, seeking out and signing the 21 year old Horwich RMI winger Jack Bruton, a youngster who had been under the scrutiny of many League clubs. Bruton fully justified the faith shown in him by the Clarets' new Manager, he became a regular in Burnley's League side for many years and went on to play for England.

Reserve centre forward John Williams stepped in initially to replace the stricken Tom Roberts and in his first senior match at Turf Moor scored twice in a remarkable 5-4 victory against West Ham. In one of the highest scoring matches ever at Turf Moor, the Clarets had opened up a 5-1 lead by half time but at the end were desperately hanging on to the points. Bob Kelly and Jack Hill missed this match, they were both in the England side that beat Wales 2-1 in Swansea, Hill deservedly winning his first full international cap.

After the excitement of the nine goal thriller with West Ham, the season rather drifted to a close, with just one more victory, 1-0 against Manchester City at Turf Moor on Easter Saturday. When Benny Cross scored a late equaliser to earn a 1-1 draw at Sunderland on the final day of the season, it was Burnley's first goal on their travels in three months, demonstrating the impact of the loss of Tom Roberts.

At the end of April 1925 a benefit match was played at Turf Moor between a Lancashire XI and a Yorkshire XI for the widow and family of Burnley's Secretary/Manager John Haworth. The Football Association sanctioned the game to be used as a test for the proposed new offside rule, two defending players beyond the attacker instead of three.

Billy Watson had appeared for the senior team just once during the season, playing mainly in Burnley's 'A' team and passing his vast experience on to the youngsters alongside him. He was released at the end of the season, severing yet another link with the glory days.

How long ago they now seemed.

Jack Bruton
lightning fast winger signed from Horwich RMI

1924-25 - First Division

		P	W	D	L	F	A	Pts
1	Huddersfield T	42	21	16	5	69	28	58
2	West Bromwich A	42	23	10	9	58	34	56
3	Bolton W	42	22	11	9	76	34	55
4	Liverpool	42	20	10	12	63	55	50
5	Bury	42	17	15	10	54	51	49
6	Newcastle U	42	16	16	10	61	42	48
7	Sunderland	42	19	10	13	64	51	48
8	Birmingham	42	17	12	13	49	53	46
9	Notts C	42	16	13	13	42	31	45
10	Manchester C	42	17	9	16	76	68	43
11	Cardiff C	42	16	11	15	56	51	43
12	Tottenham H	42	15	12	15	52	43	42
13	West Ham U	42	15	12	15	62	60	42
14	Sheffield U	42	13	13	16	55	63	39
15	Aston Villa	42	13	13	16	58	71	39
16	Blackburn R	42	11	13	18	53	66	35
17	Everton	42	12	11	19	40	60	35
18	Leeds U	42	11	12	19	46	59	34
19	BURNLEY	42	11	12	19	46	75	34
20	Arsenal	42	14	5	23	46	58	33
21	Preston NE	42	10	6	26	37	74	26
22	Nottingham F	42	6	12	24	29	65	24

1924-25

Manager : John Haworth until December 1924, then Albert Pickles from January 1925

Division One (19th)

		Date			Opponents	Result		h/t	Goalscorers/times	Opp. goal times
	1	Aug	30	h	CARDIFF C	D	0-0	0-0		
	2	Sep	6	a	Preston N E	W	2-0	1-0	Kelly 3, Parkin 85	
Watson's last game	3		8	h	EVERTON	D	0-0	0-0		
	4		13	h	BLACKBURN R	L	3-5	3-2	Hill (2) 11, 14, Freeman 16	20, 44, 54, 65, 75
	5		20	h	LEEDS U	D	1-1	1-1	Beel 32	3
	6		27	a	Birmingham	L	0-1	0-0		75
	7		29	h	SUNDERLAND	L	1-2	1-1	Beel 17	38, 73p
	8	Oct	4	h	WEST BROMWICH A	L	0-1	0-1		30
	9		11	a	Tottenham H	D	1-1	0-0	Roberts 60	47
	10		18	h	BOLTON W	D	0-0	0-0		
	11		25	a	West Ham U	L	0-2	0-1		37, 50
	12	Nov	1	h	SHEFFIELD U	D	1-1	1-1	Roberts 10	14p
	13		8	a	Newcastle U	L	0-3	0-0		49, 60, 85
	14		15	h	LIVERPOOL	W	2-1	0-0	Roberts 58, Beel 75	51
	15		22	a	Nottingham F	D	0-0	0-0		
	16		29	h	BURY	W	4-0	2-0	Roberts (3) 25, 35, 74, Weaver 86	
	17	Dec	6	a	Manchester C	D	3-3	0-1	Beel 46, Cross 50, Bassnett 63	26, 79, 81
	18		13	h	ARSENAL	W	1-0	0-0	Roberts 70	
Weaver 's last game	19		20	a	Aston Villa	L	0-3	0-0		50, 54p, 70
	20		25	h	HUDDERSFIELD T	L	1-5	0-2	Cross 70	32, 41, 56, 59, 73
	21		26	a	Huddersfield T	L	0-2	0-2		22, 27
	22	Jan	1	a	Everton	L	2-3	1-0	Roberts (2) 31, 85	57, 66, 68
	23		3	h	PRESTON N E	W	1-0	0-0	Roberts 65	
	24		17	a	Blackburn R	W	3-0	2-0	Roberts (2) 2, 63, Cross 42	
	25		24	a	Leeds U	W	2-0	1-0	Hill 15, Roberts 70	
	26	Feb	2	h	BIRMINGHAM	W	3-2	2-2	Tonner 1, Kelly 30, Roberts 78	8, 31
	27		7	a	West Bromwich A	W	4-1	2-1	Beel 9, Roberts 35, Tonner 60, Cross 62	20
	28		11	a	Cardiff C	L	0-4	0-1		5p, 67, 80, 85
	29		14	h	TOTTENHAM H	L	1-4	0-1	Beel 87	40p, 63, 68, 73
	30		21	a	Bolton W	L	0-5	0-3		6, 33, 40, 78, 89
	31		28	h	WEST HAM U	W	5-4	5-1	Williams (2) 5, 26, Beel (2) 10, 43, Cross 41	24, 52, 67, 83
	32	Mar	14	h	NEWCASTLE U	L	1-3	0-1	Bruton 77	29, 79, 81
	33		21	a	Liverpool	L	0-3	0-1		32, 48, 51
	34		28	h	NOTTINGHAM F	D	0-0	0-0		
	35	Apr	4	a	Bury	L	0-1	0-1		40
	36		6	a	Sheffield U	L	0-4	0-1		35, 60, 75, 85
	37		10	h	NOTTS C	D	1-1	0-0	Kelly 81	61
	38		11	h	MANCHESTER C	W	1-0	0-0	Beel 58	
	39		13	a	Notts C	L	0-2	0-1		41, 65
Smelt's last game	40		18	a	Arsenal	L	0-5	0-1		39, 49, 60, 70, 85
	41		25	h	ASTON VILLA	D	1-1	0-0	Cross 83	69
	42	May	2	a	Sunderland	D	1-1	1-0	Beel 17	52

FA Cup

	Date			Opponents	Result		h/t	Goalscorers/times	Opp. goal times
1	Jan	10	a	Everton	L	1-2	1-2	Roberts 41	27, 42

Final, Sheffield U 1-0 Cardiff C, at Wembley.

Other first team matches (friendlies and/or as detailed)

	Date			Opponents	Result	
Lancs Cup	Oct	15	a	Southport	L	0-1

Att.	Pos	Dawson	Smelt	Evans	Bassnett	Hill	Parkin	Kelly	Cross	Beel	Drummond	W Weaver	Watson	A Freeman	Waterfield	Armitage	Tonner	W T Roberts	Greenhalgh	Wheelhouse	Tresadern	Fergus	Lancaster	Williams	Hughes	Bruton	S Page	
20,000		1	2	3	4	5	6	7	8	9	10	11																1
22,000		1	2	3	4	5	6	7	8	9	10	11																2
20,172	7	1	2	3		5	4	7	8	9	10	11	6															3
16,000	15	1	2	3	4	5	6	7	8	9				10	11													4
23,000	15	1	2	3	4	5	6	7	10	9				8	11													5
20,000		1	2	3	4	5	6	8	10	9		7			11													6
10,000	18	1	2	3	4	5	6	8	10	9		7			11													7
30,000	19	1	2	3		5	6	8	10						11	4	7	9										8
30,000	18	1	2	3	4	5	6		10						11		7	9	8									9
	19	1	2		4		6	8	10						11	5	7	9		3								10
20,000	20	1	2		4		6	8	10			11				5	7	9		3								11
10,000	19	1	2	3	4			8	10			11				5	7	9			6							12
22,000	21	1	2	3		5	4	7	10	8					11			9			6							13
18,000	19	1	2		4			10		8					11	5	7	9		3	6							14
15,000	20	1	2		4			10		8					11	5	7	9		3	6							15
20,000	18	1	2		4			7	8	10		11				5		9		3	6							16
15,000	18	1	2		4			7	8	10		11				5		9		3	6							17
9,477	17	1	2		4			7	8	10		11				5		9			6	3						18
25,000	18	1	2		4			7	8	10		11				5		9			6	3						19
26,332		1	2		4				8						11	5	7	9	10		6	3						20
30,300	20	1	2		4	5			8	10					3		7	9			6		11					21
	20	1	2		4	5			8	10					3		7	9			6		11					22
17,988	20	1	2		4	5			8	10					11		7	9		3	6							23
20,000	20	1				4	6	7	8	10					3	5	11	9				2						24
15,000	18	1				4	6	7	8	10					3	5	11	9				2						25
7,636	15	1				4	6	7	8	10					3	5	11	9				2						26
24,000	13	1	3			4		7	8	10						5	11	9			6	2						27
5,000	13	1	3			4		7	8	10						5	11	9			6	2						28
20,000	17	1	3			4		7	8	10						5	11	9			6	2						29
20,000	17	1	3			4		7	8	10						5					6	2		9	11			30
10,000	15	1	3		4				8	10						5			7		6	2	11	9				31
9,000	17	1		3					8	10						5	11				6	2		9	4	7		32
25,000	18	1				4	6	7	8	9				10	3	5	11					2						33
10,000	16	1			5	4	6	7	8	9				10	3		11					2						34
15,000			2				4		8	9				10	3	5	11				6					7	1	35
7,000	18		2				4	7	8	9				10	3	5	11				6						1	36
13,000	17	1	2			4	6	7	8					10	3	5	11							9				37
13,000			2			4	6	7	8	10				9	3	5	11										1	38
8,000	17		2		4		6	7	8	10				9	3	5			11								1	39
20,000	20	1	2				4	7	8	10				9	3	5	11				6							40
7,500	19				4		5	8	10	9					3		7				6	2	11				1	41
7,000					4	5	6	7	10	9					3		11		8			2					1	42
Appearances		36	34	12	25	25	25	34	40	35	3	11	1	10	27	27	27	22	5	7	22	16	4	4	2	2	6	
Goals (46)					1	3	1	3	6	10		1		1			2	15						2		1		

Att.		Dawson	Smelt	Evans	Bassnett	Hill	Parkin	Kelly	Cross	Beel	Drummond	W Weaver	Watson	A Freeman	Waterfield	Armitage	Tonner	W T Roberts	Greenhalgh	Wheelhouse	Tresadern	Fergus	Lancaster	Williams	Hughes	Bruton	S Page	
28,315		1	2		4	5		7	11	10					3			9			6			8				1
Appearances		1	1		1	1		1	1	1					1			1			1			1				
Goals (1)																		1										

1925-26

Andy McCluggage
Burnley debut at Aston Villa
things could only get better

In the summer of 1925 there was a major change in the laws of football when the offside rule was amended. In future only two defending players, rather than three, would need to be nearer the opposition goal than the most forward attacking player. The new law had been much discussed before its implementation and, at the end of the previous season, a number of friendly matches had been used to try it out. One of these matches had been at Turf Moor in April 1925, a Lancashire XI against a Yorkshire XI, the benefit for Burnley Secretary/Manager John Haworth who had passed away in December 1924. Not for the first time, or the last, Burnley Football Club had played a key part in the continuing development of association football. It was a supreme irony then that, when the new season began with the new offside law in place, the players of Burnley FC seemed to have more difficulty adapting to it than any other team in the Football League!

Burnley's opening fixture was at Villa Park and, from the first whistle, Aston Villa, apparently comfortable with the new offside rules, were simply unstoppable. Within 30 seconds the Clarets were a goal behind, by half time they were four goals down and, when the referee blew to finally put the Burnley players and supporters out of their misery, Jerry Dawson's back must have been aching after picking the ball out of his net 10 (ten) times. Burnley's two new summer signings, Irish international full back Andy McCluggage and flying left winger Louis Page both made their debuts in this match. Both would go on to feature prominently for the Clarets but on that day they must have had their doubts.

A 4-0 success against Leicester seemed to steady the nerves but after conceding 14 goals in two visits to Manchester, Burnley had dropped into the bottom three. Amazingly, two days after their crushing 8-3 win against Burnley, City were themselves beaten 8-3 at Sheffield United!

After another heavy defeat, 3-5 at West Brom in November 1925, the great Bob Kelly bade farewell to Burnley FC, signing for Sunderland for a then record transfer fee estimated to be around £6500. Kelly had been at Turf Moor for over twelve years, had appeared in around 300 games, scored about 100 goals and was an established England international. He was undoubtedly a superstar of that bygone age and perhaps the one man who could genuinely compete with the Great Man, Jimmy McIlroy, as the best ever player to have worn the Claret and Blue of Burnley FC.

In December 1925 there was another fearful hammering for the Clarets, 1-8 at Bury, with an injury to Reserve goalkeeper Tommy Hampson thrown in for good measure. By Christmas Burnley were at the bottom of the League again, although a Louis Page hat trick in a 6-3 victory on Boxing Day against fellow strugglers Leeds, sent the Burnley supporters into the New Year in better spirits. After a surprise 3-1 victory at Newcastle on New Years Day, there was a depressing run of poor results and Burnley's First Division future was beginning to look decidedly uncertain.

In February 1926 Burnley's Scottish scouting network, ever on the lookout, unearthed a tough tackling wing half at Falkirk. The Burnley Directors accepted the recommendation that here was a player with a part to play in the Clarets' future, even though he was 30 years old, a transfer fee of £3000 was duly handed over and another Scot followed the well worn path to Turf Moor. That man had indeed a part to play in Burnley's future, he was still at Turf Moor forty years later, a legend alongside Harry Potts in the success story that was Burnley FC in the fifties and sixties. The name of the new arrival was Billy Dougall.

In March 1926, Blackburn completed the double over the Clarets with a 6-3 victory at Ewood. In a season of extraordinary matches, this one was up there with the most exciting with seven goals being scored in the last 15 minutes, with all Burnley's and two of Blackburn's hitting the net in the last 10! The defeat sent Burnley back to the bottom of the League and, with just nine games to go, relegation was looking a real possibility. With the next four matches all at Turf Moor however, the Burnley supporters had not yet given up all hope.

5-2 against second in the table Sunderland, Bob Kelly and all, was an excellent start and 1-0 against Newcastle meant a rise in the table to 20th position. Then over the Easter weekend of 1926, after West Brom came to Turf Moor and won 4-3, next it was second bottom Burnley against bottom of the table Manchester City. After conceding eight at Maine Road earlier in the season, the Burnley players were determined to make amends in front of their own supporters. Sadly it didn't happen. It was a poor game played between two poor teams and, on the day, Burnley took just one of their few chances, City took two of their even fewer chances, and won the game 2-1. With only five matches to go, three of which were away from home, the Clarets were rock bottom once again.

Then it happened, Saturday 10 April 1926, against Birmingham at St. Andrews. It would emerge as one of Burnley FC's most talked-about matches ever and as certainly the most celebrated individual achievement in a single game in the club's history. Jerry Dawson, George Waterfield and George Beel were all dropped as was centre forward Tom Roberts, with his place to be taken by left winger, and top scorer, Louis Page. As the players left the dressing room ready for the crucial encounter, Page received the good wishes of his team mates as he prepared for his first outing as leader of Burnley's attack. His facetious response to those good wishes was prophetic in the extreme, his exact words were said to have been -

"I'll score six goals and stop at that number!"

Louis Page
double hat-trick in a 7-1 victory at Birmingham

Incredibly that is precisely what Louis Page did in an awesome display of the goalscorers' art. Three goals in each half with one from Jack Bruton sandwiched in between, a true double hat trick. A consolation from the Blues four minutes from time made it 7-1. It was only the second time that Burnley had ever scored seven away from Turf Moor in a senior match and the very first time it had happened in a League game.

A 2-2 draw against Bury at Turf Moor was a point lost, then a crushing 1-6 defeat at Sheffield United left the Clarets still in the bottom two with just two games to go. A surprise 2-0 win at Tottenham in the penultimate match gave the Clarets a chance but even a victory on the final day of the season, at home to Cardiff, might not have been enough, depending on other results.

The Welshmen were duly despatched 4-1 but at the final whistle, Manchester City were still playing at Newcastle, losing 2-3 but a City equaliser would mean safety for them and relegation for Burnley. The news finally came that City had lost and been relegated, along with Notts County. Burnley were safe.

It had certainly been a season of ups and downs, more downs than ups perhaps but, at the end of it all, the Clarets had survived the dreaded drop by a single point, Burnley FC were still in the first Division.

1925-26 - First Division

		P	W	D	L	F	A	Pts
1	Huddersfield T	42	23	11	8	92	60	57
2	Arsenal	42	22	8	12	87	63	52
3	Sunderland	42	21	6	15	96	80	48
4	Bury	42	20	7	15	85	77	47
5	Sheffield U	42	19	8	15	102	82	46
6	Aston Villa	42	16	12	14	86	76	44
7	Liverpool	42	14	16	12	70	63	44
8	Bolton W	42	17	10	15	75	76	44
9	Manchester U	42	19	6	17	66	73	44
10	Newcastle U	42	16	10	16	84	75	42
11	Everton	42	12	18	12	72	70	42
12	Blackburn R	42	15	11	16	91	80	41
13	West Bromwich A	42	16	8	18	79	78	40
14	Birmingham	42	16	8	18	66	81	40
15	Tottenham H	42	15	9	18	66	79	39
16	Cardiff C	42	16	7	19	61	76	39
17	Leicester C	42	14	10	18	70	80	38
18	West Ham U	42	15	7	20	63	76	37
19	Leeds U	42	14	8	20	64	76	36
20	BURNLEY	42	13	10	19	85	108	36
21	Manchester C	42	12	11	19	89	100	35
22	Notts C	42	13	7	22	54	74	33

1925-26

Manager : Albert Pickles

Division One (20th)

	No.	Date			Opponents	Result		h/t	Goalscorers/times	Opp. goal times
	1	Aug	29	a	Aston Villa	L	0-10	0-4		1, 10, 15, 30, 50, 58, 64, 70, 80, 83
	2	Sep	5	h	LEICESTER C	W	4-0	2-0	Roberts (3) 13, 59, 88, Beel 23	
	3		7	h	NOTTS C	D	0-0	0-0		
	4		9	h	BOLTON W	D	1-1	0-0	Roberts 55	88
	5		12	a	West Ham U	L	0-2	0-1		33, 68p
	6		16	a	Bolton W	L	2-4	0-2	Pollard 50, Beel 63	7, 17, 78, 87
	7		19	h	ARSENAL	D	2-2	1-2	Page 15, Roberts 63	26, 37
	8		21	a	Notts C	W	1-0	1-0	Page 30	
	9		26	a	Manchester U	L	1-6	1-2	Beel 10	31,33,52,60p,77,87
	10	Oct	3	h	LIVERPOOL	W	2-1	2-0	Cross 1, Kelly 16	86
	11		10	a	Huddersfield T	L	1-2	1-2	McCluggage 10p	2, 17
	12		17	h	EVERTON	L	1-3	0-0	Roberts 55	57, 75, 80
	13		24	a	Manchester C	L	3-8	1-2	Hill 32, Kelly 76, Page 78	10,43,47,48,58p,68,88,90
	14		31	h	BLACKBURN R	L	1-3	0-0	Page 88	62, 84, 86
	15	Nov	7	a	Sunderland	D	2-2	1-2	Roberts 25, Kelly 80p	8, 36
	16		14	h	SHEFFIELD U	D	1-1	0-0	Page 74	56
Kelly's last game	17		21	a	West Bromwich A	L	3-5	2-2	Page 9, Roberts 23, Kelly 50	32,44,61,63,73
	18	Dec	7	h	BIRMINGHAM	W	3-1	0-1	Devine 47, Roberts 83, Bruton 84	27
	19		12	h	TOTTENHAM H	L	1-2	1-0	Page 13	60, 81
	20		16	a	Bury	L	1-8	1-3	Bruton 16	5,23,34,48,51,58,78,82
	21		19	a	Cardiff C	W	3-2	2-1	Hughes 30, Page (2) 43, 50	44, 58
	22		25	a	Leeds U	D	2-2	2-1	Page 9, Beel 43	7, 85
	23		26	h	LEEDS U	W	6-3	6-1	Beel 15, Page(3) 19, 30, 39, Cross 22, Hill 35	17, 49, 52
	24	Jan	1	a	Newcastle U	W	3-1	1-0	Beel (2) 32, 54, Armitage 84	67
	25		2	h	ASTON VILLA	L	2-3	1-1	Beel 2, Bruton 47	15, 65, 67
	26		16	a	Leicester C	L	2-3	1-3	Page 6, Roberts 65	9, 20, 31
	27		23	h	WEST HAM U	D	2-2	2-2	Devine 12, Roberts 14	5, 36
	28	Feb	3	a	Arsenal	W	2-1	1-1	Cross 2, Beel 75	15
	29		6	h	MANCHESTER U	L	0-1	0-0		77
	30		13	a	Liverpool	L	2-3	0-2	Page 56, Bruton 75	17, 19, 48
	31		2	h	HUDDERSFIELD T	D	1-1	1-0	Beel 7	62
	32		27	a	Everton	D	1-1	1-0	Richards 40	53
	33	Mar	13	a	Blackburn R	L	3-6	0-1	Richards (2) 80, 86, Bruton 85	30,58,75,76,82,88
	34		20	h	SUNDERLAND	W	5-2	3-1	Roberts (2) 16, 53, Page (2) 26, 30, Hargreaves 59	27, 74p
	35	Apr	2	h	NEWCASTLE U	W	1-0	1-0	McCluggage 25p	
	36		3	h	WEST BROMWICH A	L	3-4	1-4	McCluggage (2) 16p, 57p, Beel 88	19, 24, 37, 40
Roberts' last game	37		6	h	MANCHESTER C	L	1-2	0-0	Hill 72	52, 84
double hat-trick by Louis Page	38		10	a	Birmingham	W	7-1	3-0	Page (6) 22, 29, 44, 59, 60, 62, Bruton 58	86
	39		17	h	BURY	D	2-2	1-1	Parkin 19, Page 70	37, 48
	40		19	a	Sheffield U	L	1-6	1-3	Page 10	20,22,44,47,51p,75
	41		24	a	Tottenham H	W	2-0	0-0	McCluggage 47p, Beel 77	
	42	May	1	h	CARDIFF C	W	4-1	3-0	Bruton 22, Beel (2) 30, 38, Page 78	51

FA Cup

Round	Date			Opponents	Result		h/t	Goalscorers/times	Opp. goal times
3	Jan	9	a	Cardiff C	D	2-2	1-1	Beel (2) 25, 82	29, 70
rep		13	h	CARDIFF C	L	0-2	0-0		59, 84

Final, Bolton W 1-0 Manchester C, at Wembley.

Other first team matches (friendlies and/or as detailed)

	Date			Opponents	Result		Goalscorers
Bruton & Blinkhorn t/f match	Aug	31	a	Horwich RMI	W	7-0	Bruton (2), Chadwick (3), Beel, Freeman
Lancs Cup	Nov	11	a	Everton	L	0-2	
	Jan	30	a	Preston N E	L	0-3	
	Mar	6	h	MOTHERWELL	L	1-4	Richards
East Lancs Charity Cup	May	3	a	Blackburn R	L	1-2	Beel

Att.	Pos	Dawson	McCluggage	Waterfield	Bassnett	Hill	Parkin	Kelly	A Freeman	Roberts	Beel	L Page	Armitage	Hughes	Devine	Tonner	Pollard	Cross	Blinkhorn	Bruton	Fergus	Steel	Ashcroft	T Hampson	Spargo	Richards	W Dougall	Hargreaves	
37,025		1	2	3	4	5	6	7	8	9	10	11																	1
18,372		1	2	3		4		7		9	10	11	5	6	8														2
13,561	15	1	2	3		4		7		9	10	11	5	6	8														3
14,295	9	1	2	3		4		8		9	10	11	5	6		7													4
24,188	18	1	2	3		4		8		9	10	11	5	6		7													5
16,647	18	1	2	3		4		7		9	10	11	5	6			8												6
12,334		1	2	3	4			7		9	10	11	5	6			8												7
8,363	12	1	2	3	4			7		9	10	11	5	6			8												8
17,259	15	1	2	3		4		7		9	10	11	5	6			8												9
15,857	11	1	2	3		4	6	7		9	10	11	5					8											10
18,963	14	1	2	3		4	6	7		9	10	11	5					8											11
10,343	17	1	3			4	6	7		9	10	11	5					8	2										12
18,740	20	1	2	3		4	6	8			9	11	5					10		7									13
26,181	22	1	2	3	4	5		9			10	11		6				8		7									14
9,366	22	1		3	4	5		8		9		11		6				10		7	2								15
16,014	21	1		3		5		8		9		11		6				10		7	2	4							16
15,335	22	1		3		5		8		9		11		6				10		7	2	4							17
5,862	22		3	11		5				9				6	8			10		7	2	4	1						18
18,592	22		3			5				9		11		6	8			10		7	2	4		1					19
7,921			3			5				9		11		6	8			10		7	2	4		1					20
17,678	22	1		3		5					10	11	9	6	8			7			2	4							21
23,325		1		3		5					10	11	9	6	8					7	2	4							22
22,207	20	1		3		5					10	11	9	6				8		7	2	4							23
34,903	18	1		3		5					10	11	9	6				8		7	2	4							24
22,329	20	1		3		5					10	11	9	6				8		7	2	4							25
16,423	22	1	3			5				9	10	11		6				8		7	2	4							26
10,304	21	1		3		5	6			9	10	11			8					7	2	4							27
14,800	16	1	2	3		5				9	10	11		6				8		7		4							28
17,141	19	1	2	3		5				9	10	11		6				8		7		4							29
29,059	21	1	2	3							10	11		6		9		8		7		4			5				30
21,482	20	1	2	3		5					10	11		6				8		7		4				9			31
22,691	20	1	2	3		5					8	11		6						7		4				9	10		32
26,991	22	1	2	3						9	10	11								7		4			5	8	6		33
25,077	20	1	2	3		5				9	8	11				7						4					6	10	34
27,674	20	1	2			5				9	8	11				7			3			4					6	10	35
25,243		1	2	3		5				9	8	11				7						4					6	10	36
19,966	22	1	2	3		5				9	8	11				7						4					6	10	37
16,616	21		2			5						9				11		8	3	7		4		1			6	10	38
15,787			2				5					9				11		8	3	7		4		1			6	10	39
10,134	21		2			5						9				11		8	3	7		4		1			6	10	40
21,211	21	1	2		4	5					10	9			8				3	7							6	11	41
16,381			2		4	5					9	11						8	3	7				1			6	10	42
Appearances		35	33	32	7	37	7	17	1	27	33	41	17	26	9	10	4	24	7	25	13	25	1	6	2	3	11	9	
Goals (85)			5			3	1	4		13	14	26	1	1	2		1	3		7						3		1	

Att.	Pos	Dawson	McCluggage	Waterfield	Bassnett	Hill	Parkin	Kelly	A Freeman	Roberts	Beel	L Page	Armitage	Hughes	Devine	Tonner	Pollard	Cross	Blinkhorn	Bruton	Fergus	Steel	Ashcroft	T Hampson	Spargo	Richards	W Dougall	Hargreaves	
30,000		1		3		5			9		10	11		6				8		7	2	4							3
26,911		1		3		5			9		8	7		6				10		11	2	4							rep
Appearances		2		2		2			2		2	2		2				2		2	2	2							
Goals (2)											2																		

1926-27

In the summer of 1926 the Burnley Directors decided, perhaps reluctantly, that a new first choice goalkeeper was needed at Turf Moor. Jerry Dawson was now 38, still a consummate professional but with his best days undoubtedly behind him. The man with the unenviable task of replacing cult local hero Dawson was 25 year-old Scotsman George Sommerville, signed from Hamilton Academical, the only newcomer to the Burnley first team squad.

Joe Devine
9 goals from inside left

As the twenties had unfolded and the Championship side of 1920-21 continued to break up, the Clarets had descended, with alarming speed, from serious League title contenders to a side just making up the numbers in the top flight until relegation inevitably hit Turf Moor in 1930.

The 1926-27 campaign however was a veritable oasis of promise in an 8 year desert of mediocrity. Right from the season's opening day Burnley were always up there with the leaders, and spent much of the first half of the campaign at the very top, looking down on the rest.

Having beating Cardiff at Turf Moor in a 7 goal thriller, Burnley travelled to St James' Park for their first away match, and with a wonderful display of controlled football and lethal finishing, demolished the Magpies 5-1, George Beel the star of the show with a hat trick. After the match Hughie Gallacher, Newcastle's Scottish international centre forward, remarked to the waiting journalists - "Gentlemen, I think you've all seen the next Champions out there today". Gallacher was right, but it was Newcastle themselves who went on to lift the League title, losing just one more point at St James' Park all season!

The early promise could have evaporated after a 1-7 thrashing at Sunderland in early October 1926 but there was a new mood of determination amongst the players. Three successive victories, including 4-2 at Turf Moor against Sunderland, who had temporarily replaced Burnley at the top of the League, saw the Clarets back on top themselves. Four goals in the last nine minutes at Blackburn consolidated their position with a 5-1 success, Louis Page scoring twice in front of more than 42,000, Ewood's biggest crowd of the season.

There was more inconsistency with disappointing defeats at West Brom, who were bottom, and Birmingham, not much higher and Burnley were second when Tottenham, the new leaders, visited Turf Moor in November. For the Spurs it was one of those days when nothing went right from the kick off. By half time Walter Pollard and George Beel had scored to put Burnley two goals up, whilst Tottenham were two men down, one had gone off with an injury and one had developed a temperature and had had to retire. Both Pollard and Beel scored again early in the second half, Tottenham lost another man with an injury, leaving only eight, and then another Spur was hurt and hobbled on the wing for the rest of the game. Almost apologetically George Beel completed his hat trick, but the Spurs goalkeeper was then injured and received prolonged treatment. He recovered and continued between the sticks but the Burnley players, sympathetically, rather went through the motions for the rest of the game which ended 5-0 to the Clarets. After the match the Tottenham players and Management completely exonerated the Burnley team from blame for any of the incidents involving their players.

In November 1926 versatile defender Alf Bassnett was transferred to Lincoln City. Although he had been at Turf Moor since 1919 and had played his part in the epic Championship campaign of 1920-21, Bassnett was no longer a regular and had played just one League game during the current campaign.

December 1926 was an excellent month for the Clarets, four successive wins with two impressive victories over the Merseyside clubs, 5-1 against Everton and 4-0 against Liverpool on Christmas Day, George Beel scoring twice in each game. After coming from two goals down to draw 2-2 in the return at Anfield, Burnley once again sat proudly on top of the First Division going into the New Year.

George Beel was heading for his best-ever season in front of goal, 22 goals by the turn of the year, including three hat tricks. His output suddenly dried up however and he netted just twice in the League during the second half of the season. Beel's lethal finishing had been a key factor in Burnley's challenge at the top and, although his most prolific goalscoring feats for the Clarets were still to come, that particular campaign could have turned out so differently if his early season success had been maintained.

In early February 1927, Jerry Dawson completed 20 years with Burnley Football Club. He didn't appear at all for any of the Clarets' teams on the weekend of his anniversary but the following week lined up for Burnley Reserves against Derby Reserves at Turf Moor. He was cheered to the echo by the fans and, typical of the man, did his job quietly and efficiently with a clean sheet in a 2-0 victory. With an acute sense of history, the Burnley Directors chose that day for a young amateur outside left to be promoted from the "A" team to make his debut for the Reserves. His name was Arthur Dawson and he was the Great Man's nephew.

Jerry Dawson was involved in more Burnley FC history being made the following week when, for the first time, the Clarets fielded four teams in competitive action on the same day. The senior team bade farewell to the FA Cup with a 1-2 defeat in front of a massive 62,000 plus crowd at Chelsea. Meanwhile Burnley's Reserves, including Jerry, lost 1-5 at Sheffield United. Two "A" team fixtures, however, one at Turf Moor, were fulfilled simultaneously, both ending in victories for the Clarets' juniors.

Two of Burnley's players were rewarded for their consistency with their first England caps in the 3-3 draw against Wales at Wrexham. George Waterfield and Louis Page were both sorely missed as the Clarets lost 1-4 at Derby, dropping out of the top two for the first time since before Christmas. Burnley won just two more League games before Easter and two home defeats in less than a week, including a five goal hammering by Sheffield United, ended the last unbeaten home record in the top flight. The second home defeat, 0-2 against Birmingham, coincided with the absence of Big Jack Hill and Louis Page, representing England against Scotland at Hampden Park. Hill became the first Burnley player to captain his country, leading England to a famous 2-1 victory, the first time the English had been victorious north of the border for almost a quarter of a century.

There were three successive victories in April 1927, two against Leeds who were doomed to relegation but, in the end Burnley finished in fifth position, nine points adrift of Champions Newcastle. They had scored 91 goals, the most the Club had ever scored in a League season, and twelve more than when the Championship trophy had come to Turf Moor six years before. It was a season that had promised so much and with a little more consistency could even have delivered the ultimate prize again.

There were difficult times ahead for Turf Moor however and it was to be twenty years before the Clarets and their supporters would again experience comparable success.

Jerry Dawson
20 years at Turf Moor

1926-27 - First Division

		P	W	D	L	F	A	Pts
1	Newcastle U	42	25	6	11	96	58	56
2	Huddersfield T	42	17	17	8	76	60	51
3	Sunderland	42	21	7	14	98	70	49
4	Bolton W	42	19	10	13	84	62	48
5	BURNLEY	42	19	9	14	91	80	47
6	West Ham U	42	19	8	15	86	70	46
7	Leicester C	42	17	12	13	85	70	46
8	Sheffield U	42	17	10	15	74	86	44
9	Liverpool	42	18	7	17	69	61	43
10	Aston Villa	42	18	7	17	81	83	43
11	Arsenal	42	17	9	16	77	86	43
12	Derby C	42	17	7	18	86	73	41
13	Tottenham H	42	16	9	17	76	78	41
14	Cardiff C	42	16	9	17	55	65	41
15	Manchester U	42	13	14	15	52	64	40
16	Sheffield W	42	15	9	18	75	92	39
17	Birmingham	42	17	4	21	64	73	38
18	Blackburn R	42	15	8	19	77	96	38
19	Bury	42	12	12	18	68	77	36
20	Everton	42	12	10	20	64	90	34
21	Leeds U	42	11	8	23	69	88	30
22	West Bromwich A	42	11	8	23	65	86	30

1926-27

Manager : Albert Pickles

Division One (5th)

		Date			Opponents	Result		h/t	Goalscorers/times	Opp. goal times
	1	Aug	28	h	CARDIFF C	W	4-3	2-1	Hargreaves (2) 11, 86, Page 31, Beel 47	24, 65, 69
	2	Sep	1	a	Newcastle U	W	5-1	2-1	Beel (3) 15, 25, 60, Page 55, Bruton 70	30p
Bassnett's last game	3		4	a	Aston Villa	D	1-1	1-1	Beel 22	27
	4		6	h	NEWCASTLE U	D	3-3	0-2	Cross 48, Steel 80, Beel 88	3, 41, 70
	5		11	h	BOLTON W	W	4-3	3-2	Beel (3) 13, 27, 41, Hargreaves 55	7, 22, 53
	6		18	a	Manchester U	L	1-2	0-2	Cross 72	9, 21
	7		25	h	DERBY C	W	1-0	1-0	Bruton 20	
	8	Oct	2	a	Sheffield U	D	2-2	1-1	Beel 8, Steel 61	30, 52
	9		6	a	Sunderland	L	1-7	0-3	Page 63	20,30,43,47,61,71,78
	10		9	h	ARSENAL	W	2-0	0-0	Beel 57, Steel 60	
	11		12	h	SUNDERLAND	W	4-2	2-0	Cross (2) 34, 44, Steel 53, Freeman 54	50, 63
Blackburn goal 35m	12		16	a	Blackburn R	W	5-1	1-1	Cross 4, McCluggage 81p, Freeman 83, Page (2) 86, 89	
	13		23	h	HUDDERSFIELD T	D	2-2	1-0	Freeman 40, Beel 67	49, 73
	14		30	a	West Bromwich A	L	2-4	0-1	Beel 65, Devine 85	33, 47, 81, 86
	15	Nov	6	h	BURY	D	0-0	0-0		
	16		13	a	Birmingham	L	0-1	0-1		27
	17		20	h	TOTTENHAM H	W	5-0	2-0	Pollard (2) 5, 65, Beel (3) 28, 47, 74	
	18		27	a	West Ham U	L	1-2	1-0	Page 12	69, 88
	19	Dec	4	h	SHEFFIELD W	W	1-0	1-0	Page 31	
	20		11	a	Leicester C	W	3-0	1-0	Bruton 20, Page 52, Beel 72	
	21		18	h	EVERTON	W	5-1	2-0	Beel (2) 7, 48, Devine 9, Page 52, Freeman 81	58
	22		25	h	LIVERPOOL	W	4-0	1-0	Devine (2) 44, 71, Beel (2) 48, 70	
	23		27	a	Liverpool	D	2-2	0-2	Bruton 76, Beel 80	5, 44
	24	Jan	1	a	Everton	L	2-3	0-2	Freeman (2) 67, 82	26, 44, 57
	25		15	a	Cardiff C	D	0-0	0-0		
Villa goals 13m, 71m, 83m	26		22	h	ASTON VILLA	W	6-3	1-1	Beel 32, Cross 50, Devine 55, Bruton (2) 60, 73, Bowen 64og	
	27	Feb	5	h	MANCHESTER U	W	1-0	1-0	Bruton 44	
	28		12	a	Derby C	L	1-4	1-1	Devine 21	16, 59, 78, 85
	29		26	a	Arsenal	L	2-6	0-3	Hill 58, Devine 88	25,30,42,50,64,70
	30	Mar	5	h	BLACKBURN R	W	3-1	1-0	Beel 28, Cross 65, Page 71	49
	31		9	a	Bolton W	L	1-3	0-1	Page 77	29, 53, 87
	32		12	a	Huddersfield T	L	0-2	0-2		17, 32
	33		19	h	WEST BROMWICH A	W	2-1	0-1	Hargreaves 54, McCluggage 62p	1
	34		26	a	Bury	D	3-3	0-3	Page 67, Bruton 72, Devine 82	3, 12, 41
	35		29	h	SHEFFIELD U	L	2-5	1-2	Cross 2, Freeman 63	7, 43, 70, 73, 89
	36	Apr	2	h	BIRMINGHAM	L	0-2	0-1		35, 60
	37		9	a	Tottenham H	L	1-4	0-2	Richards 47	9, 35, 68, 84
	38		15	h	LEEDS U	W	3-2	1-0	Richards 42, Bruton 56, Devine 61	52, 64
	39		16	h	WEST HAM U	W	2-1	1-1	Steel 40, Richards 76	10
	40		19	a	Leeds U	W	2-0	1-0	Richards (2) 33, 78	
	41		23	a	Sheffield W	L	1-2	1-0	Earle 26	71, 80
	42		30	h	LEICESTER C	D	1-1	0-0	Page 48	51

FA Cup

				Opponents	Result		h/t	Goalscorers/times	Opp. goal times
3	Jan	8	h	GRIMSBY T	W	3-1	1-1	Bruton 28, Beel 52, Page 60	2
4		29	a	Fulham	W	4-0	1-0	Beel (2) 41, 69, Page 57, Bruton 85	
5	Feb	19	a	Chelsea	L	1-2	0-1	Cross 65	39, 47

Final, Cardiff C 1-0 Arsenal, at Wembley.

Other first team matches (friendlies and/or as detailed)

				Opponents	Result		Goalscorers
East Lancs Charity Cup	Sep	8	h	BLACKBURN R	L	1-3	Hill
Lancs Cup		28	h	ROCHDALE	W	1-0	McCluggage p
Lancs Cup	Nov	2	a	Bolton W	L	0-3	
Tom Scott (Falkirk) benefit	Apr	25	a	Falkirk	L	2-3	unknown (2)
W. Thomson (Ham'n) benefit		26	a	Hamilton A	W	2-1	Johnstone og, Dougall
E Lancs Charity Cup, agg 1-7	May	5	a	Blackburn R	L	0-4	
		14	a	Duisberg	W	4-2	Cross (2), Haddow, Devine
		17	a	Hamburg Victoria	W	10-4	Haddow (3), Beel (3), Bruton (3), Earle
in Berlin		21	a	Tennis Borussia	W	4-0	Devine, Dougall, Hargreaves, Haddow
in Dresden		22	a	Guts Muts	W	3-1	Richards (2), McCluggage p
		26	a	Nuremberg	L	2-4	Hargreaves (2)
		29	a	Enschede	W	7-2	Haddow (3), Devine, Hargreaves (2), Bruton

Att.	Pos	Sommerville	McCluggage	Blinkhorn	Steel	Hill	W Dougall	Bruton	Cross	Beel	Hargreaves	L Page	Bassnett	Parkin	Waterfield	A Freeman	Devine	Fergus	Burley	Pollard	Earle	Spargo	Reid	Richards	Dawson		
19,985		1	2	3	4	5	6	7	8	9	10	11															1
33,069		1	2	3	4	5	6	7	8	9	10	11															2
30,386		1	2	3		5	6	7	8	9	10	11	4														3
25,374	top	1	2	3	4	5		7	8	9	10	11		6													4
23,730	top	1	2	3	4	5	6	7	8	9	10	11															5
32,573	5	1	2	3	4	5	6	7	8	9	10	11															6
17,674	3	1	2	3	4	5	6	7	8	9	10	11															7
21,482	5	1	2	3	4	5	6	7	8	9	10	11															8
19,550	7	1	2		4	5	6	7	8	9	10	11			3												9
12,709		1	2		4		6	7	8	9		11		5	3	10											10
14,590	top	1	2		4	5		7	8	9		11		6	3	10											11
42,289	top	1	2		4	5	6	7	8	9		11			3	10											12
33,638	top	1	2		4		6	7	8	9		11		5	3	10											13
16,307	top	1	2		4		6	7		9		11		5	3	10	8										14
16,002	top	1			4	5	6	7	8	10		11			3			2	9								15
11,208	4	1	2		4	5	6	7	8	9		11			3		10										16
17,957	2	1	2		4	5	6	7		9		11			3		10			8							17
19,634	4	1	2		4	5	6	7		9		11			3		10			8							18
18,349	4	1			4	5	6	7		9		11			3		10	2		8							19
26,591	3	1			4	5	6	7		9		11			3	8	10	2									20
18,290	top	1			4	5	6	7		9		11			3	8	10	2									21
31,823		1			4	5	6	7		9		11			3	8	10	2									22
46,378	top	1			4	5	6	7		9		11			3	8	10	2									23
44,586	2	1			4	5	6	7		9		11			3	8	10	2									24
14,647	2	1	2			5	6	7		9		11		4	3	8	10										25
18,081	2	1	2			5	6	7	8	9		11		4	3		10										26
22,010	2	1	2		4	5		7	8	9		11		6	3		10										27
14,065	3	1	3		4		6	7	8	9				5			10	2			1						28
29,970	4	1			4	5	6	7	8	9		11			3		10	2									29
24,546	3	1	2		4	5	6	7	8	9		11			3		10										30
13,331	3	1	2		4	5	6	7	8	9		11			3		10										31
23,893	4	1	2		4	5	6	7	8	10		11			3				9								32
18,863	3	1	2		4	5	3	7		9	10	11		6		8											33
9,029		1	2		4	5	6	7	9			11			3	8	10										34
9,056	3	1	2		4		6	7	9					5	3	8	10				11						35
12,679	5	1	2		4			7	8	9	11			6	3		10					5					36
15,481	6	1			4			7	8		5	11		6	3		10						2	9			37
21,099	5	1	2		4	5	6	7	8			11			3		10							9			38
20,333			2		4	5	6	7	8		11				3		10							9	1		39
18,740	4	1	2		4	5	6	7		8	11				3		10							9			40
16,721	5	1	2		4	5	6	7							3		10			8	11			9			41
11,072		1	2			5	6	7	8	9		11		4	3		10										42
Appearances		41	33	8	38	35	37	42	29	36	14	36	1	14	32	14	26	9	2	4	3	1	1	5	1		
Goals (91)			2		5	1		9	8	24	4	13				7	9			2	1			5		1	og

Att.	Pos	Sommerville	McCluggage	Blinkhorn	Steel	Hill	W Dougall	Bruton	Cross	Beel	Hargreaves	L Page	Bassnett	Parkin	Waterfield	A Freeman	Devine	Fergus	Burley	Pollard	Earle	Spargo	Reid	Richards	Dawson		
19,556		1				5	6	7		9		11			3	8	10	2				4					3
23,562		1	2		4	5	6	7	8	9		11			3		10										4
62,238		1	2		4	5	6	7	8	9		11			3		10										5
Appearances		3	2		2	3	3	3	2	3		3			3	1	3	1				1					
Goals (8)								2	1	3		2															

1927-28

In the summer of 1927 Burnley embarked on another continental tour with matches in Germany and one in Holland. The Clarets achieved some impressive results, winning six of their seven games and scoring 30 goals, their only defeat coming against Nuremberg who were just about to clinch the Championship of the German First Division.

Confidence was high as the new season approached but that confidence soon evaporated after the first five games were all lost and, by mid September 1927, following a 2-5 thrashing at Sheffield United Burnley were rock bottom of Division One. It was the Clarets' worst-ever start to a League season.

The seemingly indestructible Jerry Dawson was still in Burnley's reserves deputising for regular keeper George Sommerville. Early in the season however the veteran suffered a broken wrist and became one of a number of Turf Moor casualties during that campaign. In November 1927 one of these casualties was Sommerville himself who emerged with a broken collarbone after a shuddering collision with Bolton's David Jack at Burnden Park. Sommerville was carried off, his season over, with first Jack Hill then Paddy Freeman taking over in goal. Bolton made the most of the situation with a 7-1 victory, Jack scoring a hat trick.

By this time Burnley had recovered somewhat from their poor start to the season and the Bolton defeat was only their second in eight games. Goalkeeper Billy Down, originally signed on trial from Doncaster to cover for Jerry Dawson in the Reserves, was now signed permanently as cover for George Sommerville in the First Division.

In November 1927 Turf Moor proudly staged its first full international fixture with England taking on Wales. Burnley were strongly represented in the England team with centre half Jack Hill captaining the side and Louis Page at outside left. In addition Clarets' Trainer Charlie Bates acted as the Trainer to the England team with one of the linesmen, Mr H.E.Hull, from the town. Huddersfield's George Brown (England) and Manchester United's Ray Bennion (Wales), both future Clarets, also took part in the match.

The game was not a huge success for England, who lost the game 1-2, or the Burnley players, with Hill heading Wales' second goal into his own net. Although Louis Page's corner was headed into his own net by the Wales captain for England's late consolation goal, Burnley's flying winger was generally unimpressive on his own ground and never played for his country again.

The Christmas fixtures pitted the Clarets against Leicester, home and away with Burnley at Leicester on Boxing Day. A 0-5 defeat was bad enough but Billy Dougall, just back from injury, was carried off after seriously damaging his knee. Sadly Billy Dougall never played for Burnley's senior team again but in later years he was to make a significant contribution to the club off the field.

The following day however, for the return with Leicester, the name Dougall was back on the Burnley team sheet. Billy's younger brother Peter stepped up from the Reserves to score on his debut in an impressive 5-1 victory, George Beel and Louis Page both scored twice. Both were on target again in a 3-1 New Years Eve victory against Blackburn at Turf Moor. It was Beel's twentieth of the season in just 21 games and he was well on the way to some important Burnley FC milestones.

After the turn of the year Burnley were in the top half of the table although League positions were rather meaningless with such a small number of points separating most of the clubs.

George Beel continued to knock in the goals with a hat trick in a 5-3 demolition of Sheffield United and another in a 3-0 win against Sunderland on a Turf Moor mud heap. His 25th in a thrilling 4-3 victory at Derby meant it was already his most prolific season in a Burnley shirt and there were still thirteen games to go!

Jack Hill
captain of Burnley and England

Amazingly, after a goalless draw at home to West Ham, Burnley were fifth and just four points off the top of the League. It was as good as it got however and the Easter games demonstrated just how unpredictable the 1927-28 season was and how fine was the line between success and failure. Following a 2-2 draw at home to Liverpool on Good Friday Burnley were eighth in the League, just eight points from the top. A day later, at the end of the Easter Saturday fixtures, following a 3-4 defeat at Old Trafford Burnley were fifteenth, only four points off the relegation zone!

The Clarets managed just one more crucial victory that

season, and what a vital 2 points it was. Burnley's game at Leeds Road against Huddersfield was scheduled for FA Cup final day with the Terriers going for the League and FA Cup double. It was re-arranged to take place during the following week and when Huddersfield lost to Blackburn at Wembley, the Burnley players knew they would be up against a deflated side. Sure enough the Clarets chose that day to perform at their very best and managed an excellent 2-1 victory against an admittedly tired team, with George Beel and Louis Page yet again both on target. Huddersfield's title hopes were now looking decidedly uncertain but more importantly for the Clarets and their fans, Burnley were just about safe from relegation. With his opener at Huddersfield, Beel had equalled Bert Freeman's Burnley club record of 32 League goals in a season. It was also his 99th First Division goal so Burnley's final home game of the season, against Everton, Dixie Dean and all, who were now favourites for the League Championship, promised to be a memorable occasion. It was certainly memorable for the Blues who won an epic encounter 5-3 to move closer to the First Division Title.

George Beel
top scorer in 1927-28 with 35 goals
will his total ever be beaten?

It was memorable too for Everton's centre forward Dixie Dean, a prodigious talent at 21, who crashed in his first goal after just thirty seconds and went on to hit four. However the lasting memories from a Burnley perspective belonged to George Beel. After ten minutes, against the best team in the land, Louis Page equalised Dean's early strike to make it 1-1. Then came the moment the Turf Moor crowd had waited for. On 15 minutes a corner from the left found Beel unmarked in the box and his bullet header flew past the Everton keeper to make the score 2-1 to Burnley. Five years to the day after his arrival at Turf Moor from Chesterfield, George Beel had written his own page in Burnley FC history with his 100th League goal, all scored in Division One It was also his 33rd of the season to establish a new club record. Beel scored again later in the game and both he and Louis Page scored in the last game at Cardiff, Beel's 35th of the season and Page's 22nd, the two having scored an impressive 57 of Burnley's 82 League goals between them.

The Clarets had ended the season in nineteenth place, a mere one point above the relegation zone but, in the closest finish ever seen in the top flight, they were also just five points off fourth position.

It had been a difficult campaign for all at Turf Moor but things were not about to get any easier.

THE WORLD OF FOOTBALL

Dixie Dean scored four goals in Everton's 5-3 victory at Turf Moor in April 1928. That brought his season's total to 57, just two short of the League record of 59, set by Middlesbrough's George Camsell in 1926-27. A week later Dean, still only 21, hit a hat-trick in Everton's final game to achieve his phenomenal record of 60 goals in a season.

1927-28 - First Division

		P	W	D	L	F	A	Pts
1	Everton	42	20	13	9	102	66	53
2	Huddersfield T	42	22	7	13	91	68	51
3	Leicester C	42	18	12	12	96	72	48
4	Derby C	42	17	10	15	96	83	44
5	Bury	42	20	4	18	80	80	44
6	Cardiff C	42	17	10	15	70	80	44
7	Bolton W	42	16	11	15	81	66	43
8	Aston Villa	42	17	9	16	78	73	43
9	Newcastle U	42	15	3	14	79	81	43
10	Arsenal	42	13	15	14	82	86	41
11	Birmingham	42	13	15	14	70	75	41
12	Blackburn R	42	16	9	17	66	78	41
13	Sheffield U	42	15	10	17	79	86	40
14	Sheffield W	42	13	13	16	81	67	39
15	Sunderland	42	15	9	18	74	76	39
16	Liverpool	42	13	13	16	84	87	39
17	West Ham U	42	14	11	17	81	88	39
18	Manchester U	42	16	7	19	72	80	39
19	BURNLEY	42	16	7	19	82	98	39
20	Portsmouth	42	16	7	19	66	90	39
21	Tottenham H	42	15	8	19	74	86	38
22	Middlesbrough	42	11	15	16	81	88	37

1927-28

Manager : Albert Pickles

Division One (19th)

		Date			Opponents	Result		h/t	Goalscorers/times	Opp. goal times
	1	Aug	27	a	Blackburn R	L	1-2	1-0	Hargreaves 33	64, 69
	2		31	a	Arsenal	L	1-4	0-1	Bruton 49	43, 62, 75, 85
	3	Sep	3	h	BURY	L	2-3	1-1	Freeman 41, Bruton 78	25, 58, 73
	4		5	h	ARSENAL	L	1-2	0-2	Beel 77	6, 24
	5		10	a	Sheffield U	L	2-5	1-2	Freeman 37, Beel 71	2, 38, 48, 57, 88
	6		17	h	ASTON VILLA	W	4-2	2-2	Beel (2) 22, 23, Hill 60, Page 66	30, 31
	7		24	a	Sunderland	W	3-2	3-1	Page (2) 26, 39, Hill 42	45, 58
	8	Oct	1	h	DERBY C	W	4-2	1-0	Freeman 15, Beel (3) 69, 85, 87	75, 88
	9		8	a	West Ham U	L	0-2	0-1		4, 79
	10		15	h	PORTSMOUTH	W	2-0	2-0	Beel 11, Page 30	
	11		22	a	Middlesbrough	W	3-2	3-0	Beel (2) 25, 40, Weston 32	57, 87
	12		29	h	SHEFFIELD W	W	3-1	1-0	Page (2) 42, 47, Beel 72	88p
	13	Nov	5	a	Bolton W	L	1-7	0-3	Page 53	25,30,32,46p,78,84,89
	14		12	h	BIRMINGHAM	W	2-1	2-0	Beel 2, Freeman 4	50
	15		19	a	Newcastle U	D	1-1	0-0	Beel 58	84
	16		26	h	MANCHESTER U	W	4-0	2-0	Beel (2) 5, 52, Hill 15, Devine 48	
	17	Dec	3	a	Tottenham H	L	0-5	0-2		15, 37, 60, 61, 85
	18		10	h	HUDDERSFIELD T	L	0-1	0-0		71
	19		17	a	Everton	L	1-4	0-1	Beel 73	36, 51, 71, 86
	20		24	h	CARDIFF C	W	2-1	0-0	W.Dougall 49, Beel 62	51
Billy Dougall's last game	21		26	a	Leicester C	L	0-5	0-3		25, 28, 35, 60, 75
	22		27	h	LEICESTER C	W	5-1	3-1	Page (2) 7, 75, Beel (2) 15, 21, P.Dougall 80	32og
	23		31	h	BLACKBURN R	W	3-1	2-0	Beel 17, Page 40, McCluggage 73p	47
	24	Jan	2	a	Liverpool	D	2-2	1-1	Page (2) 44, 46	43, 73
	25		7	a	Bury	L	0-2	0-1		16, 75
	26		21	h	SHEFFIELD U	W	5-3	2-1	Bruton (2) 21, 66, Beel (3) 38, 71, 81	31, 79, 83
	27	Feb	4	h	SUNDERLAND	W	3-0	1-0	Beel 36, Page (2) 49, 81	
	28		8	a	Aston Villa	L	1-3	0-2	Mantle 65	8, 43, 75
	29		11	a	Derby C	W	4-3	3-1	P.Dougall 10, Beel 19, Page 24, Freeman 70	28, 55, 80
	30		18	h	WEST HAM U	D	0-0	0-0		
	31		25	a	Portsmouth	L	0-1	0-0		51
	32	Mar	3	h	MIDDLESBROUGH	D	1-1	1-1	Beel 14	25
	33		10	a	Sheffield W	L	0-5	0-2		7, 31, 55, 65, 87
	34		17	h	BOLTON W	D	2-2	0-1	Page 48, Beel 79	32, 68
	35		24	a	Birmingham	L	0-4	0-3		17, 26, 41, 89
	36		31	h	NEWCASTLE U	W	5-1	4-1	Beel (2) 22, 28, Hill 40, Bruton 44, Page 52	20
	37	Apr	6	h	LIVERPOOL	D	2-2	2-0	Freeman 15, Pollard 22	80, 81
	38		7	a	Manchester U	L	3-4	2-1	Beel (2) 19, 30, Bruton 55	20, 46, 75, 90
	39		14	h	TOTTENHAM H	D	2-2	2-2	Page (2) 21, 26	7, 20
	40		25	a	Huddersfield T	W	2-1	1-1	Beel 21, Page 79	27
	41		28	h	EVERTON	L	3-5	2-3	Page 10, Beel (2) 15, 48	1, 24, 29, 60, 63
Cross' last game	42	May	5	a	Cardiff C	L	2-3	1-0	Beel 30, Page 57	55, 70, 80

FA Cup

	Date			Opponents	Result		h/t	Goalscorers/times	Opp. goal times
3	Jan	14	h	ASTON VILLA	L	0-2	0-0		69, 81

Final, Blackburn R 3-1 Huddersfield T, at Wembley.

Other first team matches (friendlies and/or as detailed)

	Date			Opponents	Result		Goalscorers	
Lancs Cup	Sep	27	h	BOLTON W	L	1-3	Devine	
East Lancs Charity Cup	Nov	17	a	Blackburn R	D	1-1	Devine	
E Lancs Charity Cup, agg 4-4		22	h	BLACKBURN R	D	3-3	Beel, Freeman, Bruton	Cup shared
	Jan	28	a	Grimsby T	D	4-4	Bruton, Beel (2), Pollard	
Nelson FC benefit, at Seedhill	Apr	23	n	Hamilton A	W	3-1	Earle, Freeman, Cross	
George Beel's benefit		30	h	FALKIRK	W	2-0	Beel (2)	

Att.	Pos	Sommerville	Reid	Waterfield	Parkin	Hill	W Dougall	Bruton	Devine	Haddow	Hargreaves	L Page	Pollard	Richards	Knox	A Freeman	Beel	Weston	J Brown	Steel	McCluggage	Forrest	Down	P Dougall	Burley	Heslop	Mantle	Cross	
32,441		1	2	3	4	5	6	7	8	9	10	11																	1
19,910		1	2	3	4	5	6	7	10			11	8	9															2
22,414		1		3	4	5	6	7	10			11			2	8	9												3
14,688	21	1		3	4	5	6	7			10	11			2	8	9												4
17,479	22	1		3	4	5		7			10	11			2	8	9	6											5
19,523	22	1		3	4	5	6	7	10			11			2	8	9												6
22,420	21	1		3	4	5	6	7	10			11			2	8	9												7
11,911	18	1		3	4	5	6	7	10			11			2	8	9												8
27,467	20	1		3	4		6	7	10			11			2	8	9		5										9
19,492	18	1		3	4	5	6	7	10			11			2	8	9												10
17,803	13	1		3	6			7	10						2	8	9	11	5	4									11
16,366	12	1		3	4			7	10			11				8	9		5		2	6							12
14,340	16	1		3	4	5		7	10			11				8	9		6		2								13
14,648	14			3	6	5		7	10			11				8	9		4		2		1						14
26,991	13			3	6	5		7	10			11				8	9		4		2		1						15
18,509				3	6	5		7	10			11				8	9		4		2		1						16
20,404	12			3	6	5		7	10			11				8	9		4		2		1						17
19,130	14			3	6	5		7	10			11				8	9			4	2		1						18
30,180	17			3	6	5	10	7				11	8				9			4	2		1						19
13,159				3	6	5	10	7				11				8	9			4	2		1						20
20,063				3	6	5	10	7				11				8	9			4	2		1						21
24,824	13			3	6			7				11				8	9		5	4	2		1	10					22
28,354				3	6	5		7				11				8	9			4	2		1	10					23
26,632	10			3	6	5		7				11				8	9			4	2		1	10					24
13,161	13			3	6	5		7				11				8	9			4	2		1		10				25
12,716	9			3	6	5		7				11	8			10	9			4	2		1						26
11,442				3	6	5		7				11	8		2	10	9			4			1						27
18,602	7			3	6	5						11				10			4		2		1		8	7	9		28
8,503	6			3	6	5		7				11				8	9			4	2		1	10					29
14,663	5			3	6	5		7				11				8	9			4	2		1	10					30
19,666	8			3	6	5		7				11	8		2		9			4			1	10					31
18,209	7			3	6	5		7				11	8			10	9			4	2		1						32
12,401	8			3	6			7				11	8			10	9		5	4	2		1						33
15,865	8			3	6	5		7				11				10	9		4	8	2		1						34
23,689	12			3	6	5		7				11				10	9		4	8	2		1						35
12,454	11			3	6	5		7				11	8			10	9			4	2		1						36
21,824	8			3	6	5		7				11	8			10	9			4	2		1						37
28,311	15			3	6	5		7	10			11				8	9			4	2		1						38
10,906	15			3	6	5		7				11	8			10	9			4	2		1						39
20,643	12			3	6	5		7				11	8			10	9			4	2		1						40
24,485	16			3		5		7				11	8			10	9		6	4	2		1						41
8,663				3	6	5		7				11				10	9			4	2		1					8	42
Appearances		13	2	42	41	37	12	41	17	1	3	41	12	1	11	38	39	2	14	25	29	1	29	6	2	1	1	1	
Goals (82)						4	1	6	1		1	22	1			6	35	1			1			2			1		

Att.	Pos	Sommerville	Reid	Waterfield	Parkin	Hill	W Dougall	Bruton	Devine	Haddow	Hargreaves	L Page	Pollard	Richards	Knox	A Freeman	Beel	Weston	J Brown	Steel	McCluggage	Forrest	Down	P Dougall	Burley	Heslop	Mantle	Cross	
26,150				3	6	5		7				11				8	9		10	4	2		1						3
Appearances				1	1	1		1				1				1	1		1	1	1		1						
Goals (0)																													

1928-29

The only major addition to the Burnley first team squad in the summer of 1928 was 25 year old inside forward Billy Stage from Bury. Scotsman Stage had played more than 200 senior games at Gigg Lane and was seen as a replacement for Benny Cross who was still suffering from the effects of a long term injury and had played just once during the previous campaign.

The Burnley Express, usually upbeat in its pre season comment about the club's prospects, was dubious about the quality and strength in depth of the squad, forecasting a difficult season ahead.

An opening day win against Sunderland followed by an astonishing 7-2 victory at Newcastle seemed to augur well for the new campaign although a 0-7 humiliation at Cardiff rather deflated the confused Turf Moor supporters. It was the Clarets' only defeat in the first six games however, after which they sat proudly at the top of the First Division.

Goalkeeper George Sommerville conceded 20 goals in four games

They were still top at the end of September 1928 but disturbing rumours began to circulate that centre half and captain Jack Hill was unsettled. Within weeks Hill, who had also captained England during his time at Turf Moor, was on his way to Newcastle for a record transfer fee of over £8,000. He would be teaming up with United's brilliant but flawed Scottish international centre forward Hughie Gallacher against whom Hill had had some violent and heated clashes in the past. Two of the most tempestuous had been earlier in the season when Burnley had put eleven goals past the Magpies in two games, five of them from George Beel!

Needless to say the Clarets' defence was never quite the same after the departure of Jack Hill, the nearest pivot in terms of ability and captaincy the club had had since the incomparable Tommy Boyle. Four goals were conceded at Derby, another seven at Huddersfield and the slide down the League table was under way. There were successes however, 6-3 at Birmingham was a timely reminder of the romp at St Andrews in 1926, Louis Page scored just twice this time, George Beel weighing in with a hat-trick.

OBITUARY

WALTER PLACE JUNIOR

DIED 11 DECEMBER 1928, AGED 56.

Born in Burnley in 1872, Walter Place junior joined his home town club from local football in 1893, and soon became a regular in Burnley's senior side, playing in a variety of forward positions. It was as a left winger that he excelled however with his speed and trickery down the flank invariably leading to accurate crosses, although he scored more than his share of goals himself. He was in top form during Burnley's Second Division Championship campaign of 1897-98, continuing to perform to a high standard back in the First Division. After Burnley's relegation in 1900 however he was lured to London by former Turfites' Manager Harry Bradshaw, now building a promotion team at Woolwich Arsenal. Place returned to Lancashire two years later, playing amateur football and working locally. Although Walter Place junior was almost six feet tall he was also known as "Little Walter" to distinguish him from his older, and bigger, cousin Walter Place senior (known as "Big Walter") also a prominent Burnley player and now a club Director.

During the early months of 1929, Burnley FC also lost two of the players who had been most prominent during the difficult years after the turn of the century. Locally born winger Albert Smith and defender David Walders, from Barrow, had each given sterling service to the Turf Moor cause after relegation to Division Two in 1900, both playing around 100 senior games for the club.

RIP

Over the weekend before Christmas 1928 goalkeeper Billy Down suffered an injury to his hand at Arsenal. On Christmas Day, for the match with Liverpool, the Turf Moor crowd was surprised and delighted to see an old friend striding out on to the field of play. 40 year old Jerry Dawson had been selected ahead of George Sommerville, still in the Reserves after sustaining a broken collar bone at Bolton more than a year earlier. Dawson was cheered to the echo as he took his place between the sticks and went on to perform competently enough as two goals from George Beel and one from Louis Page ensured a 3-2 victory over the men from Merseyside. However, Dawson had been around for over two decades and as the Burnley Express tactfully put it "now and again he demonstrated unmistakable evidence of the toll of years". The Burnley Directors and Manager thought so too, as indeed did the Great Man himself. At the final whistle he shook hands with his opponents, saluted the crowd, and walked off the Turf Moor pitch. Jerry Dawson's long career in League football was over.

George Sommerville stepped up for the return against Liverpool at Anfield on Boxing Day, after almost 14 months on the sidelines he was eager to demonstrate he was ready for First Division football again. Sommerville was welcomed back to the top flight by a Liverpool team in irresistible form and he had to pick the ball out of his net eight times. Liverpool also missed a penalty and had three goals disallowed.

Stan Bowsher
new signing from Newport County

There was even worse to come for Burnley and George Sommerville. Three games after the nightmare at Liverpool, the Clarets were at Bramall Lane against Sheffield United, just a week after the Blades had been despatched from the FA Cup, 2-1 at Turf Moor. A modest 2-0 in front at half time, the Yorkshiremen tore into the Clarets in the second half, racking up eight more goals, their 10-0 success equalling Burnley's worst-ever League defeat. It was a very poor performance all round from the Burnley team and there were a few letters of dissatisfaction to the Burnley Express, although some were obviously couched in language much too inelegant for Express readers. One letter "from an absolutely disgusted ticket holder" provoked the following editorial response "We cannot publish letters like yours without breaking the law of libel. We understand your feelings but why not send them direct to the Burnley FC Directors." Then rather mischievously, "They like reading such letters!"

At the end of February 1929, the Burnley Directors decided it was time to go into the transfer market again and gambled £3,000 plus on Derby's England international inside forward Harry Storer. Storer came from impressive sporting stock, he himself was also a county cricketer, his father had been a goalkeeper with Liverpool and Arsenal and his uncle had also played for Derby and had been an England Test cricketer.

Harry Storer seemed to have an immediate impact. On his debut against Leeds at Turf Moor, the Burnley team were inspired to a 5-0 victory with two goals from Louis Page and yet another hat-trick from George Beel.

By the last weekend of March 1929 however, after another poor performance and a 1-4 defeat at Manchester City, Burnley were 19th and just two points away from the relegation zone. The ten goal drubbing at Sheffield United in January had begun a ten-game sequence with only one win, the stroll against Leeds, and only four points being collected. The ship was steadied however and, although Burnley never managed to climb out of the bottom four, they suffered only one defeat in the final eight matches and finished seven points clear of relegation.

It had been another difficult season and, at the end of it, long serving stalwarts Benny Cross and Jerry Dawson were released. They had made just two League appearances between them during the two campaigns just ended but in the years before that both players had contributed to the considerable successes of Burnley Football Club. They were the final links with the glory days of the past, particularly Dawson, whose Turf Moor career had encompassed more than twenty years, promotion, an FA Cup triumph, a Football League Championship and a World War!

Dawson had been the first to arrive at the Turf Moor party and was now the last to leave.

1928-29 - First Division

		P	W	D	L	F	A	Pts
1	Sheffield W	42	21	10	11	86	62	52
2	Leicester C	42	21	9	12	96	67	52
3	Aston Villa	42	23	4	15	98	81	50
4	Sunderland	42	20	7	15	93	75	47
5	Liverpool	42	17	12	13	90	64	46
6	Derby C	42	18	10	14	86	71	46
7	Blackburn R	42	17	11	14	72	63	45
8	Manchester C	42	18	9	15	95	86	45
9	Arsenal	42	16	13	13	77	72	45
10	Newcastle U	42	19	6	17	70	72	44
11	Sheffield U	42	15	11	16	86	85	41
12	Manchester U	42	14	13	15	66	76	41
13	Leeds U	42	16	9	17	71	84	41
14	Bolton W	42	14	12	16	73	80	40
15	Birmingham	42	15	10	17	68	77	40
16	Huddersfield T	42	14	11	17	70	61	39
17	West Ham U	42	15	9	18	86	96	39
18	Everton	42	17	4	21	63	75	38
19	BURNLEY	42	15	8	19	81	103	38
20	Portsmouth	42	15	6	21	56	80	36
21	Bury	42	12	7	23	62	99	31
22	Cardiff C	42	8	13	21	43	59	29

1928-29

Manager : Albert Pickles

Division One (19th)

		Date			Opponents	Result		h/t	Goalscorers/times	Opp. goal times
	1	Aug	25	h	SUNDERLAND	W	3-1	1-0	Bruton (2) 11, 78, Devine 55	51
	2		29	a	Newcastle U	W	7-2	6-1	Bruton (2) 7, 22, Page (2) 10, 43, Beel (3) 19, 37, 64	25, 59
	3	Sep	1	a	Cardiff C	L	0-7	0-4		1,15,20,32,55,66,75
	4		3	h	WEST HAM U	D	3-3	2-2	Beel 20, Bruton 40, Page 49	30, 43, 71
	5		8	h	SHEFFIELD U	W	2-1	1-0	Bruton 29, McCluggage 82p	72
	6		10	h	NEWCASTLE U	W	4-3	0-0	Beel (2) 52, 75, Mantle 78, Page 81	48p, 63, 88p
	7		15	a	Bury	L	1-2	1-1	Beel 37	2, 83
	8		22	h	ASTON VILLA	W	4-1	4-0	McCluggage 10p, Devine 28, Beel (2) 31, 49	70
	9		29	a	Leicester C	D	1-1	1-0	Beel 16	67
	10	Oct	6	h	MANCHESTER U	L	3-4	2-4	McCluggage (2) 15p, 82p, Beel 26	5, 20, 34p, 43
	11		13	a	Leeds U	L	1-2	1-0	Fitton 5	75, 82
Hill's last game	12		20	h	BLACKBURN R	D	2-2	0-1	McCluggage 58p, Devine 80	32, 63
	13		27	a	Derby C	L	0-4	0-2		25, 26, 60, 75
	14	Nov	3	h	EVERTON	W	2-0	1-0	Devine 43, Bruton 62	
	15		10	a	Huddersfield T	L	1-7	0-4	Beel 87	4,6,30,44,74,81,89
	16		17	h	MANCHESTER C	L	2-3	1-3	Page (2) 32, 87	5, 14, 35
	17		24	a	Birmingham	W	6-3	2-1	Beel (3) 19, 64, 78, Page (2) 23, 55, Devine 75	39, 74, 89
	18	Dec	1	h	PORTSMOUTH	W	4-1	3-0	Beel (3) 2, 13, 29, Freeman 55	68
	19		8	a	Bolton W	W	1-0	0-0	Page 72	
	20		15	h	SHEFFIELD W	L	0-2	0-1		23, 86
	21		22	a	Arsenal	L	1-3	0-1	Page 73	29, 48, 70
Dawson's last game	22		25	h	LIVERPOOL	W	3-2	0-1	Beel (2) 47, 51, Page 79	29, 81
	23		26	a	Liverpool	L	0-8	0-3		15,25,35,50,60,70,75,80
	24		29	a	Sunderland	L	1-2	0-1	Beel 48	36, 67
	25	Jan	5	h	CARDIFF C	W	3-0	2-0	Beel (2) 36, 44, Bruton 68	
	26		19	a	Sheffield U	L	0-10	0-2		8,11,49,58,64,67,68,76,86,87
	27	Feb	2	a	Aston Villa	L	2-4	1-2	Wallace 10, Devine 86	23, 40, 46, 65
	28		9	h	LEICESTER C	L	0-1	0-1		23
	29		16	a	Manchester U	L	0-1	0-1		42
	30		18	h	BURY	D	0-0	0-0		
	31		23	h	LEEDS U	W	5-0	3-0	Page (2) 18, 29, Beel (3) 38, 59, 70	
	32	Mar	9	h	DERBY C	D	2-2	1-1	Page 32, Devine 54	17, 66
	33		16	a	Everton	L	0-2	0-1		15, 60
	34		29	a	West Ham U	L	0-4	0-3		30, 35, 40, 89
Albert Freeman's last game	35		30	a	Manchester C	L	1-4	1-1	Beel 31	19, 55, 65, 75
	36	Apr	6	h	BIRMINGHAM	W	4-0	2-0	Storer 9, Devine (2) 32, 63, Page 87	
	37		13	a	Portsmouth	L	1-3	1-1	Page 15	24, 52og, 88p
	38		16	h	HUDDERSFIELD T	W	3-2	2-2	Bruton 1, Page 30, Beel 68	36, 39
	39		20	h	BOLTON W	W	3-1	1-0	Beel 20, Brown 52, Devine 59	75
	40		27	a	Sheffield W	D	1-1	0-0	Storer 70	80
Parkin's last game	41	May	2	a	Blackburn R	D	1-1	0-1	Bruton 71	14
	42		4	h	ARSENAL	D	3-3	1-1	Beel 29, McCluggage 60p, Bruton 75	18, 61, 82

FA Cup

Round		Date		Opponents	Result		h/t	Goalscorers/times	Opp. goal times
3	Jan	12	h	SHEFFIELD U	W	2-1	2-1	Beel 3, Page 44	42
4		26	h	SWINDON T	D	3-3	1-3	Page 34, McCluggage 69p, Devine 71	1, 5, 29
rep		30	a	Swindon T	L	2-3	2-1	Beel 28, Devine 30	40p, 49, 58

Final, Bolton W 2-0 Portsmouth, at Wembley.

Other first team matches (friendlies and/or as detailed)

				Opponents	Result		Goalscorers
Lancs Cup	Sep	25	h	BLACKPOOL	L	1-3	Devine
East Lancs Charity Cup	Nov	15	a	Blackburn R	L	0-4	
E Lancs Charity Cup, agg 2-5	Apr	22	h	BLACKBURN R	W	2-1	Wallace, Steel

Att.	Pos	Down	McCluggage	Waterfield	Steel	Hill	Parkin	Bruton	Stage	Beel	Devine	L Page	Mantle	J Brown	Forrest	Heslop	A Freeman	Fitton	Knox	Hunt	Dawson	Sommerville	Wallace	Bowsher	Flack	Heap	Storer	T Conway	No.
21,448		1	2	3	4	5	6	7	8	9	10	11																	1
19,648		1	2	3	4	5	6	7	8	9	10	11																	2
20,174		1	2	3	4	5	6	7	8	9	10	11																	3
17,719	4	1	2	3	4	5	6	7		8	10	11	9																4
14,805		1	2	3	4		6	7		8	10	11	9	5															5
19,976	top	1	2	3	4	5	6	7		8	10	11	9																6
20,114	top	1	2	3	4	5	6	7	8	9	10	11																	7
19,147	top	1	2	3	4	5			8	9	10	11			6	7													8
26,506	top	1	2	3	4	5		7	8	9	10	11			6														9
17,693	4	1	2	3	4	5		7		9	10	11			6		8												10
29,565	7	1	2	3	4	5	6	7		9	10	11						8											11
35,694	9	1	2	3	4	5	6	7		9	10	11						8											12
13,091	10	1	2	3	4		5	7		9	10	11			6			8											13
25,959	7	1		3	4		5	7		9	10	11			6			8	2										14
12,645	8	1		3	4		5	7		9	10	11			6			8	2										15
14,021	11	1	2	3	4		5	7	8	9	10	11			6														16
13,071	8	1	2	3	4		6	7		9	10	11						8		5									17
17,525	7	1	2	3	4		6	7		9	10						11	8		5									18
17,222	5	1	2	3	4		6	7		9	10	11						8		5									19
16,173	7	1	2	3	4		6	7		9	10	11						8		5									20
14,990		1		3	4		6	7		9	10	11		5				8	2										21
25,361			2	3	4		5	7		9	10	11			6			8			1								22
42,449	13		2	3	4		5	7		9	10				6		11	8				1							23
23,678	12		2	3	4			7	8	9	10	11		5			6					1							24
10,966	11		2	3	4			7	8	9	10	11			6					5		1							25
23,280	12		2	3	4		6	7	8	9	10						11			5		1							26
21,277	15	1		3			4	7		9	10	11			6				2	5			8						27
14,879	17	1	2	3			4	7		9	10	11								5			8	6					28
12,516		1	2	3	4			7		9	10	11		5									8	6					29
6,238	17	1	2		4			7		10	8	11	9	5										6	3				30
13,506	14	1			4			7	8	9	10	11		5					2							3	6		31
19,979	16	1	2		4			7	8		10	11		5									9			3	6		32
17,810	18	1	2		4			7	8	9	10	11		5												3	6		33
20,926	19	1	2		4			7	8	9	10	11		5												3	6		34
33,166	19	1			4			7		9	10	11		5			8		2							3	6		35
13,730	19	1	2					7	8	9	10	11												5	3		6	4	36
23,031		1	2						8	9	10	11				7								5	3		6	4	37
15,426	19	1	3				4	7		9	10	11							2				8	5			6		38
14,584	19	1	3				4	7		9	10	11		5					2				8				6		39
33,314	19	1	3				4	7	8	9	10	11							2					5			6		40
5,461	19	1	3				4	7	8	9	10	11							2					5			6		41
7,400		1	3					7	8	9	10	11							2					5			6	4	42
Appearances		37	36	29	33	11	27	40	19	41	42	39	4	11	11	2	6	12	11	8	1	4	6	9	3	5	12	3	
Goals (81)			6					11		30	10	17	1	1			1	1					1				2		

Att.	Pos	Down	McCluggage	Waterfield	Steel	Hill	Parkin	Bruton	Stage	Beel	Devine	L Page	Mantle	J Brown	Forrest	Heslop	A Freeman	Fitton	Knox	Hunt	Dawson	Sommerville	Wallace	Bowsher	Flack	Heap	Storer	T Conway	No.
27,865			2	3	4		6	7	8	9	10	11								5		1							3
30,689			2	3				7	8	9	10	11			6					5		1						4	4
24,730		1	2	3			4	7	8	9	10	11			6					5									rep
Appearances		1	3	3	1		2	3	3	3	3	3			2					3		2						1	
Goals (7)			1							2	2	2																	

1929-30

Burnley made an encouraging start to the new season and after the first four matches were still unbeaten and in second position. That was very much as good as it got during that ultimately disappointing campaign and there was soon a rude awakening with a 1-6 hammering at Arsenal and a 1-4 home defeat by Aston Villa.

In September 1929 England international fullback Sam Wadsworth was signed from Huddersfield, even at 33 it was very much a coup for the Clarets to attract him to Turf Moor. Then Burnley's injuries began, first with Harry Storer, then Wadsworth himself after just three appearances, both later had to undergo knee operations. Wadsworth didn't play again that season and Storer was missing until the final match.

The tale of woe continued in early November 1929 when Burnley travelled to Ewood Park for the first of the season's fixtures with the old enemy. After half an hour, with score at 1-1, goalkeeper Billy Down was involved in a shuddering collision with Rovers' Bob Crompton. After a lengthy stoppage for treatment Down bravely carried on between the posts but was severely restricted in his movement. Rovers ruthlessly exploited their advantage, shooting from all angles and the game ended with an emphatic 8-3 victory to the Rovers. On the journey home Down collapsed and was rushed to hospital where he was found to have ruptured a kidney. His condition worsened, his wife was summoned to his bedside and for a time there were fears for his life. Thankfully Billy Down rallied and slowly improved but he never played for Burnley again.

Peter O'Dowd
continuing Burnley's knack
of introducing quality centre halves

The financial position at Turf Moor had been deteriorating for some time, with an inconsistent team performing in front of falling gates. After an attendance of just 6,600 for the home match with West Ham the Directors made the blunt announcement to the effect that offers would be considered for any of the Burnley players. There was certainly a defeatist tone and it was almost as if relegation had already been accepted as inevitable. "If the Burnley public will not maintain a First Division club, they will have to be satisfied with some other Division which provides the kind of football for which they are prepared to pay".

Within days Jack Bruton was on his way to Blackburn in return for a fee of £6,000 and Joe Devine played his last game for the Clarets at Christmas before his move to Newcastle.

In March 1930 Burnley at last signed a defender who looked as though he could be the answer to the Clarets' problems at centre half, a position that had never really been adequately filled since the departure of Jack Hill, eighteen months earlier. 22 year old Yorkshireman Peter O'Dowd arrived from Blackburn and ironically his Clarets' debut was against Newcastle, with Jack Hill at centre half! It was another feeble display against a team who were then bottom of the League, Hill and his fellow defenders comfortably held the Burnley attack at bay and another familiar name to Turf Moor fans, Joe Devine, scored one of the Magpies' goals in a 3-0 win.

In March 1930 there was a major change in the Turf Moor Boardroom when Chairman Harry Windle resigned after an association with Burnley FC stretching back almost 40 years. He had first worked for the club as an office junior in the 1890's before his election as a Director in 1907, becoming the club's Chairman in 1909. He now felt it was time to step aside and Vice Chairman William Bracewell, a Director since 1909, was appointed in his place.

Bracewell at least had the satisfaction of a victory for his first match as Burnley Chairman, an impressive 3-2 Turf Moor success against Blackburn. The Clarets had to come from 1-2 down with a penalty from Andy McCluggage and the winner from Peter O'Dowd, his first Burnley goal against his former club. On the Rovers side Jack Bruton was also facing the players who, until recently, had been his team mates. A poor performance in a 0-4 defeat at bottom of the table Grimsby was followed by an impressive 4-0 victory against Manchester United at Turf Moor and it was becoming difficult for the supporters to reconcile the up and down nature of their team's displays.

After two successive defeats at home to Huddersfield and at West Ham, Burnley played both the Merseyside clubs in a week and these two performances and results yet again epitomised a season of stark contrast in form. A hat trick from Louis Page in a 4-1 win against Liverpool at Turf Moor saw the best of Burnley, flowing energetic football against a team up near the top of the League. The following week, a miserable exhibition at Everton, and a 0-3 defeat, against a team who had been bottom of the League for most of the season and who won just one game at Goodison Park since early November 1929. As the Burnley Express put it, rather succinctly –"All teams are liable to slump, but Burnley have not slumped consistently!"

After a defeat at Middlesbrough in their penultimate fixture, the Clarets dropped into the bottom two for the first time but as other clubs caught up with outstanding fixtures, the situation at the bottom became extremely tense with just three points separating the bottom six.

On the last day of the season, to avoid relegation Burnley had to win their final match at Turf Moor, against Derby who were second. They also had to rely on at least one of the other four teams in trouble not winning. In the event the Clarets turned in one of their best performances of the season to thrash the Rams 6-2 with a hat-trick from Joe Mantle. The fans waited for other scores to come in, reasonably confident that their team had done enough. Amazingly, every single one of the bottom five picked up maximum points, with the final result from Newcastle, a 1-0 win for the home side against Sheffield United, confirming relegation for the Clarets. Had Newcastle not scored their single goal, they would have finished level on points with Burnley but would have been relegated with an inferior goal average. Ironically the Newcastle goal had been scored by none other than Joe Devine, a Turf Moor favourite just four months before.

After a number of years of struggle Burnley had at last succumbed to, what had perhaps seemed to some, the inevitability of relegation. Early season injuries to Harry Storer, goalkeeper Billy Down and new signing Sam Wadsworth, together with the departure of Jack Bruton and Joe Devine, had robbed the team of some genuine class.

After 17 years of First Division football, a period that had encompassed a World War and during which time all the top domestic honours had been won, the Clarets and their fans were contemplating life in Division Two. It was to be another 17 years, during which period another World War would be fought, before Turf Moor would stage top flight football once more.

Tommy Willighan
new signing from Irish club Willowfield

Louis Page
top scorer from the left wing

1929-30 - First Division

		P	W	D	L	F	A	Pts
1	Sheffield W	42	26	8	8	105	57	60
2	Derby C	42	21	8	13	90	82	50
3	Manchester C	42	19	9	14	91	81	47
4	Aston Villa	42	21	5	16	92	83	47
5	Leeds U	42	20	6	16	79	63	46
6	Blackburn R	42	19	7	16	99	93	45
7	West Ham U	42	19	5	18	86	79	43
8	Leicester C	42	17	9	16	86	90	43
9	Sunderland	42	18	7	17	76	80	43
10	Huddersfield T	42	17	9	16	63	69	43
11	Birmingham	42	16	9	17	67	62	41
12	Liverpool	42	16	9	17	63	79	41
13	Portsmouth	42	15	10	17	66	62	40
14	Arsenal	42	14	11	17	78	66	39
15	Bolton W	42	15	9	18	74	74	39
16	Middlesbrough	42	16	6	20	82	84	38
17	Manchester U	42	15	8	19	67	88	38
18	Grimsby T	42	15	7	20	73	89	37
19	Newcastle U	42	15	7	20	71	92	37
20	Sheffield U	42	15	6	21	91	96	36
21	BURNLEY	42	14	8	20	79	97	36
22	Everton	42	12	11	19	80	92	35

1929-30

Manager : Albert Pickles

Division One (21st)
Relegated

		Date			Opponents	Result		h/t	Goalscorers/times	Opp. goal times
	1	Aug	31	a	Manchester C	D	2-2	1-0	Fitton 10, Wallace 48	68, 75p
	2	Sep	2	h	EVERTON	D	1-1	0-1	Mantle 87	22
	3		7	h	PORTSMOUTH	W	4-0	1-0	Mantle 23, Page (2) 53, 72, Bruton 57	
	4		10	h	SUNDERLAND	W	2-0	0-0	McCluggage 58p, Bruton 68	
	5		14	a	Arsenal	L	1-6	0-4	Bruton 85	7, 8, 9, 20, 55, 58og
	6		21	h	ASTON VILLA	L	1-4	0-3	Page 88	4, 7, 10, 65
	7		25	a	Derby C	W	3-1	3-0	Mantle (2) 5, 43, Wallace 12	64
	8		28	a	Leeds U	L	0-3	0-1		31, 60, 84
	9	Oct	5	h	SHEFFIELD W	L	2-4	0-1	Beel 64, Walker 89og	27, 67, 77, 84
	10		12	a	Newcastle U	L	1-2	1-0	Wallace 17	62, 75
	11		19	h	SHEFFIELD U	W	5-0	1-0	Beel (2) 38, 78, Devine (2) 63, 83, Bruton 68	
	12		26	a	Huddersfield T	L	0-3	0-1		13, 78, 81
	13	Nov	2	h	BIRMINGHAM	W	3-1	2-0	Bruton 23, Devine 32, Page 56	52
Down's last game	14		9	a	Blackburn R	L	3-8	1-2	McCluggage (2) 32p, 85p, Page 66	23,37,50,54,58,68,71,88
	15		16	h	GRIMSBY T	W	3-1	0-0	Page 63, Bruton (2) 79, 87	53
	16		23	a	Manchester U	L	0-1	0-0		69
Bruton's last game	17		30	h	WEST HAM U	D	1-1	0-1	Bruton 60	20
	18	Dec	7	a	Liverpool	W	3-1	2-1	Beel (2) 15, 78, Page 26	10
	19		14	h	MIDDLESBROUGH	W	4-1	2-1	Devine 23, Heslop 32, Mantle 50, Hutchison 63	19
	20		21	a	Leicester C	L	3-4	1-2	Heslop 32, McCluggage 75p, Devine 85	13, 33, 61, 71
	21		25	a	Bolton W	D	1-1	1-0	Hutchison 18	65
Devine's last game	22		26	h	BOLTON W	D	2-2	2-1	McCluggage 7p, Beel 28	44, 65
	23		28	h	MANCHESTER C	W	4-2	3-1	Mantle (2) 23, 30, Wallace 42, Heslop 67	31, 80
	24	Jan	1	a	Sunderland	D	3-3	2-1	Wallace 15, Mantle (2) 43, 87	30, 60, 90
	25		4	a	Portsmouth	L	1-7	1-2	Mantle 15	25,35,60,80,82,84,88
	26		18	h	ARSENAL	D	2-2	2-1	Wallace 7, Mantle 35	25, 87
	27	Feb	1	h	LEEDS U	L	0-3	0-0		57, 78, 79
	28		5	a	Aston Villa	W	2-1	1-1	Heslop 27, Page 53	3
	29		8	a	Sheffield W	L	1-4	0-2	Page 83	21og, 39, 60, 88
	30		15	h	LEICESTER C	D	1-1	1-1	Page 31	2
	31		22	a	Sheffield U	L	1-3	0-1	Beel 85	3, 50, 60
	32	Mar	8	a	Birmingham	L	0-2	0-1		9, 90
	33		11	h	NEWCASTLE U	L	0-3	0-2		1, 26, 49
	34		15	h	BLACKBURN R	W	3-2	1-2	Binns 38og, McCluggage 47p, O'Dowd 49	34, 45
	35		22	a	Grimsby T	L	0-4	0-2		12, 41, 72, 75
	36		29	h	MANCHESTER U	W	4-0	3-0	Forrest 8p, Beel (2) 14, 87, O'Dowd 40	
	37	Apr	1	h	HUDDERSFIELD T	L	1-3	0-3	Page 83	7, 11, 15
	38		5	a	West Ham U	L	0-1	0-1		25
	39		12	h	LIVERPOOL	W	4-1	2-1	Page (3) 21, 40, 68, Stage 74	15
	40		18	a	Everton	L	0-3	0-1		36, 79, 80
	41		19	a	Middlesbrough	L	1-3	1-1	Beel 9	24, 60, 75
Derby goals 24m, 80m	42	May	3	h	DERBY C	W	6-2	3-1	O'Dowd 14, Mantle (3) 28, 35, 67, Page 56, Wallace 75	

FA Cup

				Opponents	Result		h/t	Goalscorers/times	Opp. goal times
3	Jan	11	a	Sheffield W	L	0-1	0-0		57

Final, Arsenal 2-0 Huddersfield T, at Wembley.

Other first team matches (friendlies and/or as detailed)

				Opponents	Result		Goalscorers
Jerry Dawson testimonial	Sep	16	h	INTERNATIONAL XI	D	6-6	Bruton (2), Beel, Brown, Page (2)
Lancs Cup	Oct	2	a	New Brighton	W	4-1	Wallace (2), Bruton, Page
Lancs Cup		28	a	Accrington S	D	2-2	Beel, Wallace
Lancs Cup	Nov	4	h	ACCRINGTON S	W	3-2	Whittaker og, Mantle (2)
Lancs Cup semi	Dec	4	a	Bury	W	3-1	Hunt, Wallace, Steel
East Lancs Cup semi	Apr	14	h	NELSON	D	2-2	Mantle, Fitton
East Lancs Cup semi replay		24	a	Nelson	L	2-4	Hutchison, Brown p
		26	h	ABERDEEN	W	9-5	Storer, McCluggage p, Wallace, Page, Pemberton, Prest (2), O'Dowd, Steel
Lancs Cup final	May	10	a	Manchester C	L	0-3	

Att.	Pos	Down	McCluggage	Waterfield	J Brown	Bowsher	Storer	Bruton	Wallace	Mantle	Devine	Fitton	Forrest	L Page	Beel	Wadsworth	Steel	R Henderson	Hutchison	Sommerville	Stage	Heslop	Knox	Prest	O'Dowd	Willighan	Chambers		
21,196		1	2	3	4	5	6	7	8	9	10	11																	1
17,704		1	2	3	4	5		7	8	9	10	11	6																2
15,094		1	2	3	4	5		7	8	9	10		6	11															3
19,691	2	1	2	3	4	5		7	8	9	10		6	11															4
38,556	7	1	2	3	4	5		7	8		10		6	11	9														5
14,062	13	1	2	3	4	5		7	8	9	10		6	11															6
14,413		1	2	11	4	5		7	8	9	10		6			3													7
26,676	14	1	2		4	5	6	7	8	9	10			11		3													8
17,294	18	1	2		4	5		7	8		10		6	11	9	3													9
33,306	19	1	2	3	4	5		7	8		10		11		9		6												10
12,569	16	1	2	3	4	5		7	8		10				9		6	11											11
15,644	18	1	2	3	4	5		7	8		10				9		6		11										12
11,068	15	1	2	3	4	5		7	8		10			11	9		6												13
22,647	17	1	2	3	4	5		7	8	9	10			11			6												14
11,660	14		2	3	4	5		7	8		10			11	9		6			1									15
9,060	16		2	3	4	5		7	8			10		11	9		6			1									16
6,640	14		2	3		5		7	10				6	11	9		4			1	8								17
15,210	13		2	3		5				9	10		6	11	8		4			1		7							18
8,671	10		2	3		5				9	10		6		8		4		11	1		7							19
16,188			2	3		5				9	10		6		8		4		11	1		7							20
21,533			2	3		5				9	10		6		8		4		11	1		7							21
27,515	13		2	3		5				9	10		6		8		4		11	1		7							22
20,239	11		2	3	4	5			10	9			6	11	8					1		7							23
28,615	8		2	3	4	5			10	9			6	11	8					1		7							24
20,366	13		2	3	4	5			10	9			6	11	8					1		7							25
22,566	13		2	3	5				10	9			6	11	8		4			1		7							26
12,505	13			3	4	5			10	9			6	11	8					1		7	2						27
13,378			2	3		5			10	9			6	11	8		4			1		7							28
23,864	15		2	3		5			10	9			6	11	8		4			1		7							29
10,717	15		2	3		5			10	9			6	11	8		4			1		7							30
18,066	16		2	3		5			10	9			6	11	8		4			1		7							31
19,485			2	3	4	5			10				6	11	9					1		7		8					32
12,487	17		2	3		4			8	9			6	11	10					1		7			5				33
16,673	17		2	3	4				10	7			6	11	9					1				8	5				34
11,262	19		2	3	4				8	9			6	11	10					1		7			5				35
11,659				3	4				10				6	11	9					1	8				5	2	7		36
9,418	17		2	3	4				10				6	11	9					1	8				5		7		37
12,092	19		2	3	4	6				9			10	11	8					1		7			5				38
12,693	16		2	3									6	11	9		4			1	8	7		10	5				39
47,897	17		2	3									6	11	9		4			1	8	7		10	5				40
5,370	21		2										6	11	9		4			1	8	7		10	5	2			41
18,328			2	3			10		7	9			6	11			4			1				8	5				42
Appearances		14	40	39	27	33	3	17	33	27	20	3	34	32	33	3	22	1	5	28	6	21	1	6	10	2	2		
Goals (79)			6					8	7	14	5	1	1	15	10				2		1	4			3			2	ogs

Att.	Pos	Down	McCluggage	Waterfield	J Brown	Bowsher	Storer	Bruton	Wallace	Mantle	Devine	Fitton	Forrest	L Page	Beel	Wadsworth	Steel	R Henderson	Hutchison	Sommerville	Stage	Heslop	Knox	Prest	O'Dowd	Willighan	Chambers		
31,794			2	3	5					9	10		6	11	8		4			1		7							3
Appearances			1	1	1					1	1		1	1	1		1			1		1							
Goals (0)																													

1930-31

During the summer of 1930, as Burnley Football Club prepared for life in the Second Division, there was precious little significant activity on the transfer front. Perhaps the one new arrival who would make any sort of impact at Turf Moor was Welshman Evan Jenkins, a right winger signed from Lincoln.

For Turf Moor's first League match in the second tier of English football for seventeen years, Burnley's opponents were Bury and the Shakers were comfortable 2-0 winners with a fast, robust and confident display. Two days later, Tottenham, one of the favourites for promotion, were next on the Clarets' fixture list. It was White Hart Lane where the message was really brought home to the Burnley players and their supporters that Second Division football would take some acclimatising to. The Clarets were outclassed from the first whistle, Spurs were quicker to the ball, far more energetic and aggressive and, above all, shot at goal on sight, cruising to an 8-1 victory. Lessons needed to be learned, and quickly.

Evan Jenkins
9 goals from the right wing

To the credit of the players, they did learn quickly. Peter O'Dowd's first goal of the season to earn the first point of the season at Southampton stopped the rot, then the recovery really began with two impressive home performances. First Nottingham Forest were crushed 5-2 then the debacle at Tottenham was well and truly exorcised by the Clarets with an eight goal spree of their own, with Reading the unfortunate victims.

Amazingly, and encouragingly, Burnley remained unbeaten until mid-November, by which time they had risen to third in the table and apparently with realistic promotion ambitions. It was not to be however, the Clarets were destined for a modest campaign and two results in seven days during the run up to Christmas demonstrated the main problem, that of inconsistency.

First came a Turf Moor clash with Everton, well clear at the top, destined to finish as Champions and with a young man called Dixie Dean leading their attack. With defender Stan Bowsher playing as Burnley's centre forward for the first time, the Clarets looked to be in trouble after just sixteen minutes with Everton two goals in front, although Dean was not on the scoresheet. From then on it was one way traffic, perhaps surprisingly towards the Everton goal! With Peter O'Dowd on top form and completely blotting out the Goodison goal machine, George Beel levelled the scores with two quick strikes, then Tom Prest put the Clarets ahead before half time. Louis Page and Harry Storer completed a remarkable turn around in the second half, Burnley emerging with a stunning 5-2 victory. It had been a superb performance from Burnley and it showed just what talent there was in the side. What a contrast just seven days later, the classic "after the Lord Mayor's Show". The Clarets visited Ninian Park to play Cardiff, rock bottom and destined to stay there. After a goalless first half the Bluebirds hit Burnley with four goals in thirty minutes and a very poor performance by the Clarets ended in a 0-4 defeat.

After another impressive display, this time a 3-0 victory in the FA Cup against First Division Manchester City, Burnley's hopes of a lucrative run were dashed with a 1-2 defeat at Bradford in the fourth round. The season seemed to be drifting along with no real prospects of promotion and reasonably safe from relegation when there was an announcement from the Turf Moor Directors to the effect that attendances were not sufficient to cover ordinary expenses and players may have to be sold. Then "owing to the club's financial position we are prepared to consider offers for any of our players".

At this particular time George Beel was in the middle of one of his regular deadly phases in front of goal. In a spell of 14 League games, Beel hit 13 goals, including a hat trick against promotion chasing Wolves. The fans feared the worst and that Burnley's most prolific goalscorer ever would soon be on his way. There was indeed an inevitable departure but it wasn't George Beel, it was centre forward Joe Mantle who left Turf Moor for Plymouth.

At Easter 1931 it was suddenly announced in the local, and national, press that Burnley captain Harry Storer had been appointed as Coventry City's Manager. Initially Storer himself proved to be somewhat elusive but the Burnley Directors confessed that they were "completely in the dark". Details slowly emerged that Storer, still a County cricketer with Derbyshire as well as a footballer with Burnley, would take up his appointment in August 1931. In the meantime he would play football for Burnley then cricket for Derbyshire in the summer. Harry Storer did carry on playing for Burnley until the match at Everton and he was included on Burnley's list of players retained, but he never donned the claret and blue shirt again.

With just four games to play, against the top three and bottom of the table Cardiff, Burnley were safe from relegation in mid-table but only three points off fourth place. West Brom, in third position, came to Turf Moor desperate for a victory to boost their promotion challenge. Although the Baggies scored early on, regular marksmen George Beel and Louis Page were both on target and the Clarets took the points with a 2-1 win. Next it was to Goodison Park to play Everton who had long since clinched the Second Division Championship and promotion. Everton won the encounter 3-2 but Burnley played their part to the full, reminding the Merseysiders that the men from Turf Moor had inflicted upon them their heaviest defeat of the season back in December 1930. After the match the Burnley players joined the rest of the Goodison Park crowd to applaud the Champions as the Second Division trophy was presented to Everton captain Ben Williams.

Jim Brown
solid defender for many years

Cardiff, already relegated, were seen off 1-0 then there was a very intriguing last match of the season, against Tottenham at Turf Moor. Spurs were third, a point behind West Brom, so to gain promotion, they needed to win at Turf Moor and hope the Baggies lost their last match, at home to Charlton. The Clarets were fired up for a battle, determined to avenge their humiliation at White Hart Lane in the first week of the season. In the event Tottenham never seemed up for the challenge and a late goal from George Beel decided a drab encounter in favour of the Clarets.

It had once again been a season of inconsistency, an eighth place finish but just two points from fourth place. All the top four had been beaten at least once, including a thrashing of the ultimate Champions, and yet every one of the bottom six had taken valuable points from the Clarets. There simply had to be much more consistency if Second Division football at Turf Moor was not to become the norm for the foreseeable future.

Off the field the supporters knew that money was tight, a very clear message had been delivered by the Directors. More people were needed through the turnstiles if the club was to enjoy sustained success, only time would tell when, if ever, that success would be forthcoming.

OBITUARY
WILLIAM MCFETRIDGE
DIED 9 MAY 1931, AGED 67.

A native of Ballymena, but brought up in Govan, Renfrewshire, Billy McFetridge first came south as a teenager to join Padiham, in the early 1880's the principal club in East Lancashire. He appeared as a guest player for Burnley on a number of occasions before moving permanently to Turf Moor in the summer of 1886. McFetridge was a hard, physical player and he soon established himself as a versatile member of Burnley's team, excelling both in attack and defence. He was a first team regular during the early days of League football and was also in the Burnley side that lifted the Lancashire Cup in 1890 after an epic final against Blackburn. After his final season at Turf Moor in 1892-93 he returned to his trade as a painter and decorator before becoming a publican, continuing to live and work in Burnley, his adopted town, until the end of his days.

RIP

1930-31 - Second Division

		P	W	D	L	F	A	Pts
1	Everton	42	28	5	9	121	66	61
2	West Bromwich A	42	22	10	10	83	49	54
3	Tottenham H	42	22	7	13	88	55	51
4	Wolverhampton W	42	21	5	16	84	67	47
5	Port Vale	42	21	5	16	67	61	47
6	Bradford PA	42	18	10	14	97	66	46
7	Preston NE	42	17	11	14	83	64	45
8	BURNLEY	42	17	11	14	81	77	45
9	Southampton	42	19	6	17	74	62	44
10	Bradford C	42	17	10	15	61	63	44
11	Stoke C	42	17	10	15	64	71	44
12	Oldham A	42	16	10	16	61	72	42
13	Bury	42	19	3	20	75	82	41
14	Millwall	42	16	7	19	71	80	39
15	Charlton A	42	15	9	18	59	86	39
16	Bristol C	42	15	8	19	54	82	38
17	Nottingham F	42	14	9	19	80	85	37
18	Plymouth A	42	14	8	20	76	84	36
19	Barnsley	42	13	9	20	59	79	35
20	Swansea T	42	12	10	20	51	74	34
21	Reading	42	12	6	24	72	96	30
22	Cardiff C	42	8	9	25	47	87	25

1930-31

Manager : Albert Pickles

Division Two (8th)

	No	Date		h/a	Opponents	Result		h/t	Goalscorers/times	Opp. goal times
	1	Aug	30	h	BURY	L	0-2	0-0		62, 72
Steel's last game	2	Sep	1	a	Tottenham H	L	1-8	1-4	Page 38	15,24,31,42,47,53,55,58
	3		6	a	Southampton	D	1-1	0-1	O'Dowd 52	30
Forest goals 54m, 62m	4		8	h	NOTTINGHAM F	W	5-2	4-0	Jenkins 12, Beel 21, Prest 30, Mantle 40, Page 75	
Reading goal 79m	5		13	h	READING	W	8-1	4-0	Prest 16, Brown 19, Page (2) 25, 82, Mantle (2) 39, 65, O'Dowd 68, Jenkins 85	
	6		17	a	Nottingham F	D	3-3	3-1	Page 7, Beel 19, Jenkins 21	1, 80, 88
	7		20	a	Wolverhampton W	W	4-2	2-0	Jenkins 15, O'Dowd 28, Page (2) 81, 82	51, 88
	8		27	h	BRADFORD	W	3-2	1-1	Jenkins 17, Beel 67, Prest 71	29, 57
	9	Oct	4	a	Stoke C	D	1-1	1-0	Mantle 2	73
	10		11	h	MILLWALL	W	2-1	1-1	Drinnan 11, Prest 90	22
	11		18	h	SWANSEA T	D	2-2	2-1	Page (2) 18, 21	13, 66
	12		25	a	Plymouth A	W	2-1	0-0	Mantle 50, Beel 60	46
	13	Nov	1	h	BRISTOL C	W	4-2	2-1	Prest (2) 8, 50, Storer 26, Beel 84	42, 51
	14		8	a	Barnsley	W	1-0	1-0	Prest 33	
	15		15	h	PORT VALE	L	1-2	1-1	Mantle 38	44, 75
	16		22	a	Bradford C	W	3-2	2-1	McCluggage 31p, Page 40, Beel 51	25, 85
	17		29	h	CHARLTON A	D	1-1	1-1	Prest 8	32
	18	Dec	6	a	West Bromwich A	L	0-2	0-2		1, 43
	19		13	h	EVERTON	W	5-2	3-2	Beel (2) 17, 31, Prest 43, Page 53, Storer 64	5, 16
	20		20	a	Cardiff C	L	0-4	0-0		57, 63, 64, 87
	21		25	h	PRESTON N E	W	1-0	1-0	Beel 6	
	22		26	a	Preston N E	L	0-2	0-1		44, 89
	23		27	a	Bury	L	1-2	0-1	Beel 71	11, 77
	24	Jan	3	h	SOUTHAMPTON	W	3-2	2-1	McCluggage 30p, Beel 44, Prest 51	20, 87
	25		17	a	Reading	L	1-3	1-2	Forster 40og	15, 30p, 65
	26		31	a	Bradford	L	1-4	0-3	Beel 60	22, 25, 40, 87
	27	Feb	3	h	WOLVERHAMPTON W	W	4-2	3-1	Beel (3) 13, 25, 42, Jenkins 75	17, 62
Mantle's last game	28		7	h	STOKE C	L	1-2	1-0	Beel 26	65, 68
	29		14	a	Millwall	L	1-2	0-1	Beel 88	27, 63
	30		21	a	Swansea T	D	1-1	1-1	Beel 16	21
	31		28	h	PLYMOUTH A	D	2-2	0-1	Jenkins 74, Drinnan 80	33, 61
	32	Mar	7	a	Bristol C	D	1-1	0-0	Beel 57	75
	33		14	h	BARNSLEY	D	2-2	1-1	Storer 15, Bowsher 51	10, 81
	34		21	a	Port Vale	D	0-0	0-0		
	35		28	h	BRADFORD C	D	1-1	1-1	Jenkins 25	40
Oldham goal 2m	36	Apr	3	h	OLDHAM A	W	6-1	4-1	Jenkins 17, Brown 25, Beel (2) 26, 43, Page 77, Jones 89	
	37		4	a	Charlton A	L	1-2	0-2	Kelly 89	3, 23
McCluggage's last game	38		6	a	Oldham A	L	1-3	1-3	Bowsher 35	4, 24, 34
	39		11	h	WEST BROMWICH A	W	2-1	1-1	Beel 23, Page 52	4
Storer's last game	40		18	a	Everton	L	2-3	1-3	Beel 9, Prest 65	4, 6, 30og
	41		25	h	CARDIFF C	W	1-0	1-0	Beel 38	
	42	May	2	h	TOTTENHAM H	W	1-0	0-0	Beel 82	

FA Cup

Rd	Date		h/a	Opponents	Result		h/t	Goalscorers/times	Opp. goal times
3	Jan	10	h	MANCHESTER C	W	3-0	2-0	McCluggage 31p, Prest 41, Jenkins 76	
4		24	a	Bradford	L	0-2	0-1		4, 63

Final, West Bromwich A 2-1 Birmingham, at Wembley.

Other first team matches (friendlies and/or as detailed)

	Date		h/a	Opponents	Result		Goalscorers
Lancs Cup	Oct	15	a	Accrington S	W	2-1	Drinnan, Mays
Lancs Cup	Nov	5	a	Liverpool	L	1-3	Hall

Att.	Pos	Sommerville	McCluggage	Waterfield	Steel	O'Dowd	Forrest	Jenkins	Mays	Mantle	Storer	L Page	Beel	Wadsworth	J Brown	Prest	H Conway	Drinnan	Hall	W Henderson	Bowsher	Weaver	Willighan	W H Wood	Jones	J Kelly		
13,842		1	2	3	4	5	6	7	8	9	10	11																1
23,518		1	2	3	4	5	6	7		9	10	11	8															2
13,045		1	2			5		7		9	6	11	8	3	4	10												3
10,393	16	1	2			5		7		9	6	11	8	3	4	10												4
9,861	11	1	2			5		7		9	6	11	8	3	4	10												5
3,824		1	2			5		7		9	6	11	8	3	4	10												6
18,504	7		2	3		5		7		9	6	11	8		4	10	1											7
13,132	6		2	3		5		7		9	6	11	8		4	10	1											8
13,140	7		2	3		5		7		9	6	11	8		4	10	1											9
12,440	6		2	3		5		7			6		9		4	8	1	10	11									10
11,624	5		2	3		5	6	7		9		11	8		4	10	1											11
18,494	4		3	2		5		7		9	6		8		4	10	1		11									12
10,207	3		2	3		5		7		9	6		8		4	10	1		11									13
9,427	3		2	3		5	4	7		9	6		8			10	1		11									14
12,277	4		2	3		5	4	7		9	6	11	8			10	1											15
12,886	2		2	3		5		7		9	6	11	8		4	10	1											16
11,021	4		2	3		5		7			6	11	9		4	10	1			8								17
17,050	5		2	3		5		7	9		6	11	8		4	10	1											18
17,849	5		2	3		5		7			6	11	8		4	10	1				9							19
7,485	6		2	3		5		7			6	11	8		4	10	1				9							20
31,000			2	3		5					6	11	8		4	10	1	9				7						21
28,682			2	3		5					6	11	8		4	10	1	9	7									22
13,295	6		2			5		7			6		8		4	10	1		11	9			3					23
10,712	6		3			5					6		8		4	10	1		11		9	7		2				24
8,141	7		2	3		5		7			6		8		4	10	1		11		9							25
7,954			2	3		5		7		9	6		8		4	10	1								11			26
8,652	6	1	2	3		5	6	7		9	11		8		4	10												27
10,517	7	1	2	3		5	6	7		9	11		8		4	10												28
15,417	7	1				5	6	7			3		9		4			10						2	11	8		29
10,906	9	1	3			5	6	7					9		4	8		10						2	11			30
4,986	8	1	2	3		5	6	7					9		4	8		10							11			31
8,940	9	1	2	3		5		8			6	11	9		4	7									10			32
7,877	9	1	2	3		5		7			6	11	8		4	10					9							33
9,185	9			3		5		7			6	11	8		4		1				9			2	10			34
7,082	9			3		5		7			6	11	8		4		1				9			2	10			35
11,563	5			3		5		7			6	11	8		4		1							2	10	9		36
12,688				3		5					6	11	8		4		1					7		2	10	9		37
12,346	11		2	3		5					6	11	8		4		1				9	7			10			38
12,109	11			3		5		7			6	11	9		4	10	1							2		8		39
19,144	11			3		5		7			6	11	9		4	10	1							2		8		40
4,125	11			3		5	6	7				11	9		4	8	1							2	10			41
10,077	8			3		5	6	7				11	9		4	8	1							2	10			42
Appearances		13	33	34	2	42	12	37	2	18	37	29	41	4	38	34	29	6	8	2	8	4	1	11	12	5		
Goals (81)			2			3		9		6	3	13	25		2	11		2			2				1	1	1	og
25,893			2	3		5		7			6		8		4	10	1		11		9							3
26,444			2	3		5		7		9	6		8		4	10	1		11									4
Appearances			2	2		2		2		1	2		2		2	2	2		2		1							
Goals (3)			1					1								1												

1931-32

OBITUARY
ALEXANDER (SANDY) MCLINTOCK
DIED 17 MAY 1931, AGED 77.

Sandy McLintock, perhaps the first in a long line of superb Burnley goalkeepers, originally came to prominence with the famous Vale of Leven club during the 1870's, helping them to three successive Scottish Cup victories in 1877, 1878 and 1879. By this time he was already a full Scottish international, winning three full caps, all against England. Amazingly all his football in Scotland had been played as a half back or a full back but it was as a goalkeeper that Burnley brought him to Turf Moor in the summer of 1884. McLintock excelled as the Turfites' last line of defence until he suffered a severe leg injury in a 4-4 draw with Preston in February 1885. Such was the strength of the man that he continued to play until he was forced to retire in December 1885. He became a publican in his adopted town before returning to his native Scotland to resume his original trade as a tinsmith.

RIP

For the second summer running there were no significant arrivals at Turf Moor, although the exit door had certainly been used. With the experienced Harry Storer having already departed to take up his first Managerial position at Third Division South Coventry, the Clarets' supporters were disappointed to learn that Andy McCluggage would also be leaving, after six years at Burnley and more than 200 senior games. Irish international full back McCluggage had felt unable to accept the terms that he had been offered and signed for Irish club Dundalk, although Burnley still held his registration. Unfortunately Andy McCluggage would not be the only high profile player to leave Turf Moor during the difficult campaign that lay ahead.

The season started with a heavy defeat at Southampton but Burnley more or less held their own during the early weeks with a victory against Stoke and at Charlton and Nottingham Forest together with a comfortable 2-0 win at Turf Moor against a Manchester United side described as "very poor indeed".

At the end of October 1931, after an impressive 3-1 success at Port Vale, the Clarets had sneaked into the top ten and then entertained Plymouth at Turf Moor. On the hour, with the Pilgrims ahead, Burnley were awarded a penalty when an Argyle defender handled a cross from the left. Up stepped captain George Waterfield but his well struck shot was brilliantly saved. However the referee decided that the keeper had moved too early and ordered the kick to be re-taken. A nervous Waterfield strode forward again and placed his shot ....outside the post. However the referee was still not satisfied, said that the keeper had moved again, and pointed to the spot for the third time. The Plymouth goalkeeper, and his defenders, were incensed and surrounded the referee, imploring him to change his decision. Needless to say he did no such thing and placed the ball on the spot. By this time Waterfield's nerves were completely shredded and he turned away, reluctant to try a third time. Peter O'Dowd, cool and unflappable as ever, stepped forward, smashed the ball into the Plymouth net, and walked purposefully back to the centre circle. The match ended 1-1 and the crowd applauded Peter O'Dowd, as they always did, such was his consistently high level of performance. Three days later the supporters were stunned when it was announced that O'Dowd had signed for Chelsea for a fee of £5,000. His many admirers at Turf Moor knew that Peter O'Dowd had a big future and, sure enough, five months later he was running out at Wembley, ready to face Scotland as a full England international.

After a heavy defeat at home by leaders Leeds, Burnley started to slide down the League table and a 5-3 victory against Barnsley at Turf Moor was the team's first success at home in two months. Eighteen goals were shipped in just four matches and the Directors decided a change was needed between the sticks. George Sommerville was rested and up stepped teenager Richard Twist, a colliery worker who had been spotted by a Burnley scout who had a good idea what to look for in a goalkeeper, Jerry Dawson! Twist was still an amateur and was the first non professional to appear in goal in a League match for Burnley for almost 30 years.

Amateur goalkeeper Richard Twist
Jerry Dawson was just about the hardest of acts to follow

There were changes behind the scenes in January 1932 when Chairman William Bracewell stepped down. He had been in the chair less than two years but had found the stress of Burnley's financial situation difficult to come to terms with. He was succeeded as Chairman by E J Tate who had been Vice Chairman for two years.

The gates at Turf Moor had been dwindling alarmingly during the course of the season but the all time low was reached with just 3,100 attending the match with Southampton in early January. This, and ironically the resignation of William Bracewell, was to prompt the formation of Burnley FC's first Supporters Club, which very quickly saw the light of day, and had the full backing of the Board.

Gates started to improve, a little, and then in February 1932, there was a victory to cheer at last when Bradford were beaten 3-2 at Turf Moor. A crowd of over 8,000 saw welcome goals from Evan Jenkins, new signing Sam Jennings and George Beel with his 179th League goal in a Burnley shirt. Sadly, it was the last time the net would billow from a shot by George Beel, a Turf Moor legend then, and still a legend eight decades later. Within a few days George Beel, a Turf Moor hero and a veritable goalscoring machine, had left Burnley after ten years to sign for his native Lincoln.

Just weeks later there was another blow for the supporters when it was announced that winger Louis Page had been transferred to Manchester United. Page had been another hero at Turf Moor, over 250 senior games, well over 100 goals and the scorer of still the only double hat-trick in Burnley FC history.

In the course of a little over three months the Clarets had lost three of their key players, Peter O'Dowd, George Beel and now Louis Page. The reaction was predictable, after the following match, a demoralising 0-4 defeat at Plymouth, the longest trip of the season, Burnley slipped into the bottom two for the first time. A home fixture on Good Friday with bottom club Bristol City should have been an incentive to attack constantly. It was, but a Burnley attack with little penetration met a stubborn Bristol defence who held out doggedly, City broke away twice, and scored twice, yet another defeat. After a 1-1 draw with Bradford City at Turf Moor on Easter Saturday Burnley had tasted victory just twice in nineteen League and FA Cup games since early December 1931 and were back in the bottom two.

Then came something of a tonic, the return Easter fixture with Bristol City at Ashton Gate saw the Clarets play some excellent football, with John Kelly helping himself to a hat-trick in a 6-1 victory. Strangely all the goals came in the second half but, no matter, Burnley were now out of the bottom two but, with just six games to play the men from Turf Moor probably needed to win three of them to guarantee safety.

A defeat at Leeds and a home win against Swansea set the Clarets up for a crucial clash with Barnsley at Oakwell. The Tykes were also in danger of relegation and the match, played in torrential rain and on a heavy pitch, was no place for the faint-hearted. A wonderful solo effort from winger John Hall, a long run and a left-foot piledriver, was enough to bring the points back to Turf Moor. Burnley now had three teams below them but still needed one more win to be absolutely safe.

Kelly scored again in a 1-1 draw with Notts County then, after a defeat at Millwall, Burnley were still two points clear of Port Vale and one clear of Barnsley with Bristol City already down. Then, someone from the Burnley Express, in an idle moment musing over the League tables, realised that, if Burnley lost their last game 0-2 and Port Vale won theirs 2-0, then Burnley and Port Vale would finish level on 33 points, both teams would have scored 58 goals and conceded 89. If Barnsley won their last match they would finish on 34 points above both Burnley and Port Vale, presumably leaving the Football League to untangle the conundrum.

Although Vale did indeed win 2-0 in their final game,

George Beel
farewell to a legend

Burnley awoke from such mathematical nightmares just in time and beat Nottingham Forest 1-0 in theirs, to guarantee that the club's Golden Jubilee year would not coincide with relegation.

Second Division football would again be played at Turf Moor in 1932-33.

1931-32 - Second Division

		P	W	D	L	F	A	Pts
1	Wolverhampton W	42	24	8	10	115	49	56
2	Leeds U	42	22	10	10	78	54	54
3	Stoke C	42	19	14	9	69	48	52
4	Plymouth A	42	20	9	13	100	66	49
5	Bury	42	21	7	14	70	58	49
6	Bradford PA	42	21	7	14	72	63	49
7	Bradford C	42	16	13	13	80	61	45
8	Tottenham H	42	16	11	15	87	78	43
9	Millwall	42	17	9	16	61	61	43
10	Charlton A	42	17	9	16	61	66	43
11	Nottingham F	42	16	10	16	77	72	42
12	Manchester U	42	17	8	17	71	72	42
13	Preston NE	42	16	10	16	75	77	42
14	Southampton	42	17	7	18	66	77	41
15	Swansea T	42	16	7	19	73	75	39
16	Notts C	42	13	12	17	75	75	38
17	Chesterfield	42	13	11	18	64	86	37
18	Oldham A	42	13	10	19	62	84	36
19	BURNLEY	42	13	9	20	59	87	35
20	Port Vale	42	13	7	22	58	89	33
21	Barnsley	42	12	9	21	55	91	33
22	Bristol C	42	6	11	25	39	78	23

1931-32

Manager : Albert Pickles

Division Two (19th)

		Date			Opponents	Result		h/t	Goalscorers/times	Opp. goal times
	1	Aug	29	a	Southampton	L	0-3	0-1		15, 59, 89
	2	Sep	5	h	STOKE C	W	3-0	2-0	Jones 9, Edwards 40, Prest 66	
	3		7	h	CHESTERFIELD	D	2-2	1-1	Brown 26, Waterfield 89p	12, 60
	4		12	a	Charlton A	W	1-0	1-0	Edwards 37	
	5		19	h	WOLVERHAMPTON W	L	1-3	1-0	Page 40	46, 72, 89
	6		26	a	Bradford	L	0-2	0-1		5, 64
	7	Oct	1	a	Nottingham F	W	2-1	1-1	Beel 43, Jenkins 46	2
	8		3	h	MANCHESTER U	W	2-0	1-0	Jones 8, Jenkins 63	
	9		10	a	Tottenham H	D	1-1	1-0	O'Dowd 15	48
	10		17	a	Oldham A	L	1-3	0-1	Beel 47	4, 53, 81
	11		24	h	BURY	D	2-2	1-2	Beel 44, Waterfield 78p	18, 35
	12		31	a	Port Vale	W	3-1	3-1	Page (2) 23, 30, Hall 38	42
O'Dowd's last game	13	Nov	7	h	PLYMOUTH A	D	1-1	0-1	O'Dowd 57p	34
	14		14	a	Bradford C	W	2-1	0-1	Page 66, Beel 83	44
	15		21	h	LEEDS U	L	0-5	0-3		2, 28, 33, 47, 85
	16		28	a	Swansea T	L	1-5	0-4	Page 65	11, 20, 30, 32, 82
	17	Dec	5	h	BARNSLEY	W	5-3	3-2	Hall 1, Brown 27p, Beel (2) 39, 65, Jones 75	10, 12, 88
	18		12	a	Notts C	L	0-5	0-0		52, 66, 72, 80, 87
	19		19	h	MILLWALL	D	1-1	1-0	Beel 43	47
	20		25	h	PRESTON N E	D	2-2	2-0	Beel (2) 34, 37	75, 90
	21		26	a	Preston N E	L	1-2	0-0	Beel 61	68, 87
	22	Jan	1	a	Chesterfield	L	1-5	0-4	Beel 70	9, 18, 25, 29, 60
	23		2	h	SOUTHAMPTON	L	1-3	1-1	Jenkins 16	42, 46, 81
	24		16	a	Stoke C	L	0-3	0-2		15, 37, 88
	25		23	h	CHARLTON A	L	0-1	0-1		26
	26		30	a	Wolverhampton W	L	1-3	1-2	Jones 43	14, 18, 53
Beel's last game	27	Feb	6	h	BRADFORD	W	3-2	1-0	Jennings 14, Beel 52, Jenkins 65	72, 77
	28		17	a	Manchester U	L	1-5	1-3	Jennings 32p	15, 22, 34, 72, 73
	29		20	h	TOTTENHAM H	W	2-0	0-0	Jones 49, Kelly 67	
Sommerville's last game	30		27	h	OLDHAM A	L	1-4	0-3	Smith 86	13, 41, 43, 90
	31	Mar	5	a	Bury	L	0-1	0-1		25
Page's last game	32		12	h	PORT VALE	D	2-2	2-1	Kelly (2) 18, 42	40, 50
	33		19	a	Plymouth A	L	0-4	0-2		10, 43p, 49, 85
	34		25	h	BRISTOL C	L	1-2	1-1	Hall 44	10, 58
	35		26	h	BRADFORD C	D	1-1	1-1	Jenkins 24	33
Bristol C goal 89m	36		28	a	Bristol C	W	6-1	0-0	Kelly (3) 50, 55, 71, Humpish 52og, Jenkins 65, Forrest 74	
	37	Apr	2	a	Leeds U	L	1-3	1-1	Jenkins 17	44, 57, 88
	38		9	h	SWANSEA T	W	4-1	1-0	Jones 10, Fairhurst 60p, Kelly 68, Harker 88	74
	39		16	a	Barnsley	W	1-0	0-0	Hall 46	
	40		23	h	NOTTS C	D	1-1	1-1	Kelly 41	40
	41		30	a	Millwall	L	0-2	0-1		44, 87
	42	May	7	h	NOTTINGHAM F	W	1-0	0-0	Kelly 75	

FA Cup

				Opponents			h/t	Goalscorers/times	Opp. goal times
3	Jan	9	h	DERBY C	L	0-4	0-2		16, 27, 72, 85

Final, Newcastle U 2-0 Arsenal, at Wembley.

Other first team matches (friendlies and/or as detailed)

Lancs Cup	Sep	22	h	BURY	W	3-2	Page, Jones, Edwards
Lancs Cup	Nov	4	a	Barrow	D	2-2	Edwards, Jones
Lancs Cup		17	h	BARROW	W	4-1	Page, Jenkins p, Hall, Beel
Lancs Cup semi	Apr	21	a	Manchester C	L	1-4	Harker

Att.	Pos	H Conway	W H Wood	Waterfield	J Brown	O'Dowd	Forrest	Jenkins	Prest	Beel	Jones	L Page	Sommerville	Edwards	Bowsher	Willighan	Hall	Merrick	Hughes	J Kelly	Twist	Whitty	Harker	Weaver	Jennings	Schofield	E Smith	Fairhurst								
14,293		1	2	3	4	5	6	7	8	9	10	11																								1
8,710			2	3	4	5	6	7	8		10	11	1	9																						2
9,207			2	3	4	5	6	7	8		10	11	1	9																						3
6,597	11		2	3	4	5	6	7		8	10	11	1	9																						4
11,286	16		2	3	4	5	6	7		8	10	11	1	9																						5
15,426	19		2	3	4	5		7		8	10	11	1	9	6																					6
7,175				3	4	5		7		8	10	11	1	9	6	2																				7
9,719	9			3	4	5		7		8	10	9	1		6	2	11																			8
28,877	8			3	4	5		7		8	10	9	1		6	2	11																			9
11,564	13			3	4	5		7		8	10	9	1		6	2	11																			10
12,590	13			3	4	5				8	10	7	1	9	6	2	11																			11
9,468	9			3	4	5		7			10	8	1	9	6	2	11																			12
9,461	8			3	4	5		7			10	8	1	9	6	2	11																			13
12,859	7			3	4			7		9	10	8	1		6	2	11	5																		14
12,767	10			3	4		6	8		9	10	7	1				11	5	2																	15
8,051	12			3	4			7		8	10	11	1		6	2		5		9																16
5,333	9		2	3	4				8	9	10	11	1		6		7	5																		17
13,198	12		2	3	4					9	8	11	1	10	6		7	5																		18
4,751	10		2	3	4				8	9	10	11			6		7	5			1															19
18,105			2	3	4				8	9		10			6		11	5			1	7														20
27,677	11		2		4					9	10	8			6	3	11	5			1	7														21
11,839			2		4		3			9		10			6		11	5			1		8	7												22
3,135	16		2		4		3	7		9		8		10	6		11	5			1															23
9,045	17			3	4		6	7		8	10			9	5	2	11				1															24
7,273	17			3	4			7		8	10				6	2	11	5			1				9											25
18,463	19			3	5			7		8	10	11			6	2					1				9	4										26
7,942	18			3	5			7		8	10	11			6	2					1				9	4										27
11,036				3	5			7			10	11			6	2					1				9	4	8									28
7,517	19			3	5		6				10	11	1			2	7			9						4	8									29
9,190	19			3	5		6				10	11	1			2	7			9						4	8									30
8,422	20	1		3	5		6				10	11				2	7			9						4	8									31
6,869	20	1		3			6				10	11				2	7			9					8	4		5								32
16,838	21	1		3	4		6	7			10					2	11			9					8			5								33
7,297	21	1			4		6		8		10				5	2	11		3	9				7												34
7,355		1			4			7			10				6	2	11		3	9			8					5								35
8,129	20	1		3	4		11	7			10				6	2				9			8					5								36
13,037	21	1		3	4		11	7			10				6	2				9			8					5								37
5,969	20	1		3	4		6	7			10					2	11			9			8					5								38
6,991	19	1		3	4		6		7		10					2	11			9			8					5								39
5,604	19	1		3	4		6	7			10					2	11			9			8					5								40
10,600	19	1		3	4		6	7			10					2	11			9			8					5								41
6,533	19	1		3	4		6	7			10				5	2	11			9			8													42
Appearances		13	13	37	41	13	22	29	8	23	39	30	19	12	27	29	29	11	3	15	10	2	9	2	6	7	4	9								
Goals (59)				2	2	2	1	7	1	12	6	5		2			4			9			1		2		1	1							1	og

Att.	Pos	H Conway	W H Wood	Waterfield	J Brown	O'Dowd	Forrest	Jenkins	Prest	Beel	Jones	L Page	Sommerville	Edwards	Bowsher	Willighan	Hall	Merrick	Hughes	J Kelly	Twist	Whitty	Harker	Weaver	Jennings	Schofield	E Smith	Fairhurst								
16,694				3	4		6	7		9	10	8			5	2	11				1															3
Appearances				1	1		1	1		1	1	1			1	1	1				1															
Goals (0)																																				

1932-33

After countless different players had appeared as Burnley's centre forward over recent seasons, the Burnley Directors made a significant signing in the summer of 1932 when Cecil Smith arrived from Stalybridge. Smith was a big, powerful Welshman who had scored goals at all his previous clubs before a season at Stalybridge in which he scored 77 goals, not surprisingly a record that still stands. A familiar face re-appeared at Turf Moor when Len Smelt, one of Burnley's League Championship winning side of 1920-21, was appointed as Assistant Trainer.

Cecil Smith
big powerful centre forward signed from Stalybridge

Just days before the start of the new season the Turf Moor camp was disrupted when Secretary/Manager Albert Pickles suddenly resigned. Pickles had taken over in 1924 after the death of John Haworth but had not enjoyed anything like the success of his predecessor and now felt it was time to step aside.

Pickles stayed on in a caretaker capacity until a successor was appointed and, after two impressive victories in the first four games, Burnley were sixth. It was something of a false dawn however with no more wins until well after the arrival of the new Manager, Tom Bromilow, former Liverpool half back and England international. Bromilow was the first Burnley Manager to have had previous experience of top class football and the appointment was warmly welcomed by Turf Moor supporters.

Bromilow's first games in charge were eventful to say the least, with plenty of goals, alas most of them at the wrong end. A 2-3 home defeat by Manchester United was followed by a 1-4 hammering at Tottenham and them came what looked like being a football lesson at Turf Moor against Fulham. Three goals down in less than an hour, Burnley appeared out of it until a remarkable fight back with three goals in the last fifteen minutes, including a last minute equaliser from Tom Jones made it 3-3. This was followed by yet another high scoring game at West Ham. Burnley led 2-0 and 3-2 but still had to come from behind to share the points in a 4-4 draw with Jones scoring all the Clarets' goals, the first time a Burnley player had ever scored four times and not finished on the winning side. There was yet another new face between the Burnley posts for this encounter, local boy Charlie Hillam replacing Herman Conway.

In December 1932 Burnley's young full back Tommy Willighan won his first full international cap when he was selected for Ireland against Wales at Wrexham. Willighan had been at Turf Moor since 1928 but had not found it easy to establish himself, eventually taking over the right back spot from his fellow countryman Andy McCluggage.

Still without a win since his arrival Tom Bromilow decided it was time to bring in some new faces, particularly in defence. Centre half George Bellis was signed from Wolves, together with a 36 year old Welsh international wing half from Manchester United. The newcomer would finish his playing career at Turf Moor but would go on to become a coach and play his part in some of Burnley's greatest successes in the years to come. His name was Ray Bennion.

OBITUARY
LEONARD SMELT
DIED 8 FEBRUARY 1933, AGED 42.

A native of Rotherham, Len Smelt first played League football for Gainsborough in the years before the First World War. After guesting for a number of clubs during the war, including Burnley, he was signed by the Clarets in March 1919 immediately making the right back position his own. A solidly built defender, Smelt scarcely missed a game during the Turf Moor glory years after hostilities ended, forming a durable full back partnership with David Taylor. Len Smelt was a key member of the Clarets' side which had established that remarkable unbeaten League record during 1920-21 as Burnley won the League Championship for the first time. After almost 250 senior appearances Len Smelt played his final League game for the Clarets in April 1925 then spent a season coaching whilst playing in Burnley's "A" team. His playing career finished in the lower leagues before he returned to Turf Moor in the summer of 1932 as Assistant Trainer to Charlie Bates.

RIP

Both new arrivals made their Clarets' debuts in the home match with Southampton, a welcome 2-0 win, Bromilow's first victory as Burnley Manager. Three more defeats followed before home and away victories over Grimsby at Christmas 1932 temporarily lifted the Clarets out of the bottom four. They were soon back in it however after a 0-6 capitulation at

Ray Bennion
the beginning of a long association with Burnley FC

relegation-bound Chesterfield, a performance described by the Burnley Express as "deplorable".

In January 1933 it was time for the FA Cup again with a tricky looking tie at old rivals Third Division South Swindon. Burnley had played at the County Ground three times before in the FA Cup without success, but this time came away with a hard earned 2-1 victory to set up a home tie with First Division Sheffield United. Two goals from George Mee and one from Cecil Smith gave the Clarets a well-deserved 3-1 win and a passage into the fifth round for the first time since 1927. Struggling Chesterfield were to be Burnley's next opponents but events off the field took a tragic turn with the sudden death, after a short illness, of Assistant Trainer Len Smelt.

Although Burnley overcame Chesterfield 1-0 in the FA Cup fifth round, League success was proving rather more difficult and by the time of the sixth round tie with Manchester City at Turf Moor, the Clarets had won only one League game since Christmas, alongside three FA Cup victories. Nearly 49,000 people turned up at Turf Moor for the City Cup tie, Burnley's largest gate for some years, but the majority were to go away disappointed as City eased into the semi final with a 1-0 victory that was just about deserved.

It was a case of bouncing back and in the next home match Cecil Smith recorded his first Burnley hat-trick in an impressive 4-0 win against West Ham at Turf Moor but it was not enough to stop the Clarets slipping into the bottom two for the first time. Other results during the following week conspired to dump Burnley at the very bottom but the team rose to the occasion with a 4-1 victory at Lincoln. Points were gathered slowly as the season approached its conclusion and, although the Clarets had been in the bottom four virtually every week since the turn of the year, the poor form of others was to save them from relegation. An exciting 1-1 draw against promotion chasing Tottenham suited both clubs and with two games to go Burnley were just about safe although it was another 1-0 win, against Bury, on the final day of the campaign that finally saw relegation mathematically avoided, by just two points.

It had been yet another disappointing season but at least Second Division football would still be seen at Turf Moor. The glory days of the early twenties were a distant memory and future glory was still a dream.

1932-33 - Second Division

		P	W	D	L	F	A	Pts
1	Stoke C	42	25	6	11	78	39	56
2	Tottenham H	42	20	15	7	96	51	55
3	Fulham	42	20	10	12	78	65	50
4	Bury	42	20	9	13	84	59	49
5	Nottingham F	42	17	15	10	67	59	49
6	Manchester U	42	15	13	14	71	68	43
7	Millwall	42	16	11	15	59	57	43
8	Bradford PA	42	17	8	17	77	71	42
9	Preston NE	42	16	10	16	74	70	42
10	Swansea T	42	19	4	19	50	54	42
11	Bradford C	42	14	13	15	65	61	41
12	Southampton	42	18	5	19	66	66	41
13	Grimsby T	42	14	13	15	79	84	41
14	Plymouth A	42	16	9	17	63	67	41
15	Notts C	42	15	10	17	67	78	40
16	Oldham A	42	15	8	19	67	80	38
17	Port Vale	42	14	10	18	66	79	38
18	Lincoln C	42	12	13	17	72	87	37
19	BURNLEY	42	11	14	17	67	79	36
20	West Ham U	42	13	9	20	75	93	35
21	Chesterfield	42	12	10	20	61	84	34
22	Charlton A	42	12	7	23	60	91	31

1932-33

Managed by Club Directors until October 1932, then Tom Bromilow

Division Two (19th)

	No.	Date			Opponents	Result		h/t	Goalscorers/times	Opp. goal times
	1	Aug	27	h	CHESTERFIELD	D	1-1	1-1	Forrest 17	2
	2		30	a	Preston N E	L	1-6	0-5	Crompton 90	16,27,28,30,43,72
	3	Sep	3	a	Bradford	W	4-0	3-0	Harker 20, Kelly (2) 25, 37, Mee 86	
	4		5	h	PRESTON N E	W	4-0	1-0	C.Smith (2) 20, 90, Jones 71, Mee 85	
	5		10	h	PLYMOUTH A	D	1-1	0-1	Fairhurst 80p	39
	6		17	a	Nottingham F	D	1-1	0-0	Harker 59	88
	7		24	h	CHARLTON A	L	0-1	0-0		68
	8	Oct	1	a	Stoke C	L	0-3	0-2		22, 32, 65
	9		8	h	MANCHESTER U	L	2-3	1-1	Prest 12, Forrest 78p	28, 48, 67
	10		15	a	Tottenham H	L	1-4	0-2	Prest 55	20, 30, 70, 80
	11		22	h	FULHAM	D	3-3	0-2	Mee 75, Fairhurst 77, Jones 89	9, 13, 51
	12		29	a	West Ham U	D	4-4	2-1	Jones (4) 25, 42, 60, 87	44, 46, 50, 72
	13	Nov	5	h	LINCOLN C	D	0-0	0-0		
	14		12	a	Bradford C	L	1-2	0-1	Bicknell 81og	31, 47
	15		19	h	PORT VALE	D	1-1	0-0	Edwards 49	89
	16		26	a	Millwall	L	1-4	0-2	Edwards 85	38, 39, 70, 86
	17	Dec	3	h	SOUTHAMPTON	W	2-0	2-0	Jones 4, Edwards 41	
	18		10	a	Notts C	L	2-4	0-1	Crompton (2) 48, 50	16, 62, 87, 89
	19		17	h	SWANSEA T	L	1-2	1-0	Jones 17	54, 80
	20		24	a	Bury	L	3-5	2-1	Crompton 2, Reynolds 43, Jones 84	19, 50, 57, 66, 75
	21		26	a	Grimsby T	W	2-1	2-1	Harker 7, Reynolds 28	2
	22		27	h	GRIMSBY T	W	2-0	2-0	Harker (2) 22, 34	
	23		31	a	Chesterfield	L	0-6	0-2		17,19,49,57,72,78
	24	Jan	7	h	BRADFORD	W	2-0	1-0	C.Smith 28, Jones 52	
	25		21	a	Plymouth A	L	0-4	0-3		3, 18, 40, 76
	26		31	h	NOTTINGHAM F	D	3-3	2-3	C.Smith 11, Crompton (2) 35, 66	33, 44, 45
	27	Feb	4	a	Charlton A	D	2-2	0-1	Crompton 50, Richmond 61	42, 51
Bowsher's last game	28		11	h	STOKE C	L	1-2	1-1	C.Smith 13	43, 59
Forrest's last game	29		22	a	Manchester U	L	1-2	1-2	C.Smith 34	29, 36
	30	Mar	8	a	Fulham	L	1-2	0-2	Jones 60	1, 4og
	31		11	h	WEST HAM U	W	4-0	1-0	C.Smith (3) 26, 63, 64, Hancock 85	
	32		18	a	Lincoln C	W	4-1	1-0	C.Smith 1, Mustard 57, Jones (2) 77, 88	79
	33		25	h	BRADFORD C	D	0-0	0-0		
	34	Apr	1	a	Port Vale	D	1-1	0-1	C.Smith 75	4og
	35		8	h	MILLWALL	W	3-0	2-0	C.Smith 27, Mustard 40, Jones 57	
	36		14	h	OLDHAM A	D	1-1	0-1	Mustard 64p	45
	37		15	a	Southampton	L	1-3	0-2	C.Smith 59	11, 27, 70
	38		17	a	Oldham A	D	2-2	0-1	Hancock 75, C.Smith 89	8, 52
	39		22	h	NOTTS C	W	2-1	1-0	Hancock 22, Reynolds 72	81
	40		24	h	TOTTENHAM H	D	1-1	0-0	Jones 67	69
	41		29	a	Swansea T	L	0-2	0-0		81og, 89
	42	May	6	h	BURY	W	1-0	0-0	Jones 67	

FA Cup

	Rd	Date			Opponents	Result		h/t	Goalscorers/times	Opp. goal times
	3	Jan	14	a	Swindon T	W	2-1	2-1	Harker 17, C.Smith 37	19
	4		28	h	SHEFFIELD U	W	3-1	1-0	Mee (2) 11, 74, C.Smith 72	54
	5	Feb	18	h	CHESTERFIELD	W	1-0	1-0	Hancock 29	
Jenkins' last game	6	Mar	4	h	MANCHESTER C	L	0-1	0-1		13

Final, Everton 3-0 Manchester C, at Wembley.

Other first team matches (friendlies and/or as detailed)

	Date			Opponents	Result		Goalscorers
Lancs Cup	Sep	28	a	Everton	L	1-6	C.Smith

Att.	Pos	H Conway	Willighan	Waterfield	J Brown	Fairhurst	Forrest	Crompton	Prest	C Smith	T Jones	Hall	Richmond	J Kelly	Harker	Mee	W H Wood	Manns	Reynolds	Bowsher	Hillam	Schofield	Edwards	Merrick	Jeavons	Bennion	Bellis	E Smith	Hancock	Mustard	W Wood	Jenkins				
8,935		1	2	3	4	5	6	7	8	9	10	11																								1
12,732		1	2		4	5	6	7	10	9	11		3	8																						2
11,020		1	2	3	4	5	6	7			10			9	8	11																				3
14,271	6	1	3			5	6	7		9	10				8	11	2	4																		4
12,438	8	1	2	3	4	5	6	7			10			9	8	11																				5
9,736	5	1	2	3		5	6	7			10			9	8	11		4																		6
10,657	9	1	2	3		5	6	7			10			9	8	11		4																		7
13,056	13	1	2	3		5	6	11		9	10				8			4	7																	8
5,314	17	1	2	3			6		8		10			9		11		4	7	5																9
26,097	19	1		3		5	6		8		10			9		11	2	4	7																	10
6,603	19	1		3		5	6		8	9	10		2			11		4	7																	11
12,009	19			3		5	6		8	9	10		2			11		4	7		1															12
9,046	17			3		5	6		8	9	10		2			11		4	7		1															13
11,378	19			3		5	6	11	8	9	10		2					4	7		1															14
7,940	17		2	3		5	6	11	8		10								7		1	4	9													15
10,865	19		2	3			6	11			10				8						1	4	9	5	7											16
7,139	19		2	3			6	11	7		10										1		9			4	5	8								17
8,216	20		2	3			6	11	7		10										1		9			4	5	8								18
6,637	20	1	2	3	4		6	11	7		10			9													5	8								19
7,789		1	2	3	4		6	11		9	10								7				8				5									20
11,186		1	2	3			6	11			10				8				7				9			4	5									21
13,602	18		2	3			6	11			10			9	8				7		1					4	5									22
8,403	20		2	3			6	11			10			9	8				7		1					4	5									23
7,640	19	1	2				6	11		9	10		3		8				7							4	5									24
11,529	20	1	2					11		9	10		3		8				7	6						4	5									25
4,845	19	1		3			6	7		9	10		2		8	11				5						4										26
7,777	18	1	2				6	7		9	10		3			11				5						4			8							27
12,228	19		2				6	7		9	10		3			11				5	1					4			8							28
18,533				3			6			9	10		2		8	11			7		1					4	5									29
11,506				3	6			11		9	10		2						7		1					4	5		8							30
10,771	21			3	6			11		9	10		2		7						1					4	5		8							31
8,617	21			3	6					9	10		2								1					4	5		8	7	11					32
12,228	20			3	6					9	10		2								1					4	5		8	7	11					33
7,221	19			3	6					9	10		2								1					4	5		8	7	11					34
8,691	19			3	6					9	10		2								1					4	5		8	7	11					35
13,787	19			3	6					9	10		2								1					4	5		8	7	11					36
7,302				3	6					9	10		2								1					4	5		8	7	11					37
13,501	19	1		3	6				10	9			2						7							4	5		8		11					38
7,665		1		3	6				10	9			2			11			7							4	5		8							39
11,353	19	1		3	6					9	10		2			11										4	5		8	7						40
3,843	20	1		3	6					9	10		2			11										4	5		8	7						41
5,697		1		3	6						10		2			11			7							4	5		8	9						42
Appearances		23	22	36	19	14	28	25	14	27	40	1	24	10	15	18	2	10	19	5	19	2	6	1	1	24	23	3	15	9	7					
Goals (67)						2	2	7	2	14	16		1	2	5	3			3				3						3	3					1	og

Att.		H Conway	Willighan	Waterfield	J Brown	Fairhurst	Forrest	Crompton	Prest	C Smith	T Jones	Hall	Richmond	J Kelly	Harker	Mee	W H Wood	Manns	Reynolds	Bowsher	Hillam	Schofield	Edwards	Merrick	Jeavons	Bennion	Bellis	E Smith	Hancock	Mustard	W Wood	Jenkins				
		1	2				6	11		9	10		3		8				7							4	5									3
25,380		1		3			6	7		9	10		2		8	11				5						4										4
31,699				3			6	7		9	10		2			11					1					4	5		8							5
48,717				3			6			9	10		2			11					1					4	5		8			7				6
Appearances		2	1	3			4	3		4	4		4		2	3			1	1	2					4	3		2			1				
Goals (6)										2					1	2													1							

1933-34

In the summer of 1933 regular defenders Stan Bowsher and Alex Forrest both left Turf Moor along with locally born goalkeeper Charlie Hillam. Among the new arrivals was a towering young goalkeeper, Bob Scott from Liverpool and another huge defender, centre half Tom Wallace from Sunderland. There was also Sydney Chedgzoy, son of the former Everton and England winger Sam Chedgzoy, and the first player to welcome the newcomer to Turf Moor was Wilf Crompton, himself in the giant shadow of a famous father, the legendary Bob Crompton of Blackburn and England.

Tommy Wallace
towering centre half signed from Sunderland

Defeats in the first two games, at Grimsby and Preston the two clubs who would go on to be promoted, were followed by a scrappy win at home to Nottingham Forest and a very poor performance in the return against Preston at Turf Moor. The Clarets were struggling already and the mood of the supporters was not improved by another departure, the previous season's top scorer, Tom Jones, who was transferred to Blackpool. Moving in the opposite direction, from Bloomfield Road to Turf Moor, were full back Wilf Smith and inside forward Tom Douglas who was to become a regular in the Clarets' senior team. Douglas scored after just eight minutes of his debut at Manchester United, with Ray Bennion captaining the side for the first time against his former club, but Burnley ended up on the wrong end of a 5-2 scoreline, also losing right back Tommy Willighan with a serious leg injury. Willighan never played for the Clarets again.

After Burnley were outfought and outclassed in a 1-3 home defeat by League leaders Bolton, leaving them in the relegation zone, the Directors decided it was time for another gamble in the transfer market to try to bring in some quality. Their target was 27 year old wing half Alick Robinson who had been at Bury for eight years but, with the Shakers in an even worse financial situation than Burnley, an offer of £2,500 was too much for them to resist. Although the Clarets lost heavily, 2-5 at Brentford, on his debut, Robinson would go on to serve his new club well, spending the rest of his career at Turf Moor.

Cecil Smith scored twice in a 2-1 win against Fulham at Turf Moor then Burnley came from behind to take the points in a thrilling 3-2 victory against Blackpool at Turf Moor. Teddy Hancock got two in a 3-1 win against Swansea then another the season's newcomers Harry O'Grady scored the season's only hat-trick, inside eighteen minutes, in a 3-1 win against Lincoln.

In the 1930's, West Indians in East Lancashire were not a common sight and the only ones that most people had seen were cricketers in the Lancashire League. The pioneer was the best and most famous of all, Learie Constantine, who had been the professional at Nelson since 1929. In November 1933 another page in Burnley FC history was written when Alfred Charles was signed. Charles was a promising player from Trinidad and, with no professional football at all in the West Indies, he had decided to try his luck in England, coming over with his friend Edwin St Hill, who had been the professional at Lowerhouse. Alf Charles did become a regular in Burnley's Reserves but he was never quite able to break into the first team and was released at the end of the season.

After a disappointing Christmas with home and away defeats against Oldham, Burnley saw out the old year with their best performance of the season against League leaders Grimsby. Goals from Tom Douglas and Alick Robinson earned the points against a team who went on to win the Second Division Championship very comfortably.

Two breakaway goals from Harry O'Grady and a stout rearguard action clinched a 2-0 success at Nottingham Forest before an FA Cup third round clash with Bury ended 0-0. There was to be no lucrative Cup run with Bury edging home 3-2 in the replay at Gigg Lane.

Another new signing, inside forward Arthur Warburton, scored his first Burnley goal in an excellent 4-2 victory against West Ham at Turf Moor. After the Clarets were beaten 0-1 at Plymouth, Manchester United came to Turf Moor on the back of a run of nine defeats and two draws in eleven games and next to bottom of Division Two. After Arthur Warburton scored inside two minutes Burnley were overwhelmed by United, the Burnley Express describing the subsequent capitulation and 1-4 defeat as "a deplorable exhibition of football".

For the next match at Bolton there was a new face between

the sticks, Thomas Hetherington, who had been signed earlier in the season from Walker Celtic in the North Eastern League. Although Hetherington performed well enough on his debut, Burnley were again well beaten and were once more hovering just above the relegation zone. Within less than a minute of Brentford's first ever visit to Turf Moor, Burnley were a goal behind but came back to take the points with goals from Cecil Smith (2) and Teddy Hancock. Another new signing, left winger Thomas Weale, scored his first Clarets' goal to earn a point at Fulham then Teddy Hancock got two more in a 2-1 victory against Southampton at Turf Moor. A 1-1 draw at Blackpool was followed by an excellent display in a 4-2 victory at Turf Moor against Bradford City before Cecil Smith scored twice to earn the points in a "smash and grab" 2-0 win at Port Vale.

Charlie Bates
services suddenley dispensed with

After a 1-0 win against Bradford at Turf Moor on Good Friday, courtesy of a first minute goal from Teddy Hancock, Burnley crept into the top half of the League for the first time that season. A day later another single goal victory followed, this time against Notts County with Tom Douglas on target. The Clarets had now gone eight games unbeaten and had won their last three matches without conceding a goal and some of the more fanciful Burnley supporters even began to have dreams of a late push for promotion. Realism hit home on Easter Monday however with a 0-5 drubbing in the return at Bradford but the Clarets had shown some quite decent form since the turn of the year, albeit in patches, and had certainly recovered after a period early in the season when relegation had looked a distinct possibility. Although Bury won 2-1 in Turf Moor's final League match, the Clarets ended the season on something of a high with a Cecil Smith goal enough to bring the points back from Hull after a 1-0 victory. Burnley's fourth successive season in Division Two had ended in mid-table, but for the first time in three years, any fears of relegation had been banished well before the end of the campaign.

As was usually the case after the final matches had been played, a number of players were released but it was behind the scenes where the major surprise came when it was announced that Trainer Charlie Bates was not being retained. Bates had been at Turf Moor since 1910, initially as a player, and had been Burnley's senior Trainer since 1919, his tenure of course including the magnificent League Championship success of 1920-21. After a number of years in the doldrums however the Burnley Directors "were of the opinion that it was to the advantage of Burnley FC to have a change of Trainer and of training methods".

1933-34 - Second Division

		P	W	D	L	F	A	Pts
1	Grimsby T	42	27	5	10	103	59	59
2	Preston NE	42	23	6	13	71	52	52
3	Bolton W	42	21	9	12	79	55	51
4	Brentford	42	22	7	13	85	60	51
5	Bradford PA	42	23	3	16	86	67	49
6	Bradford C	42	20	6	16	73	67	46
7	West Ham U	42	17	11	14	78	70	45
8	Port Vale	42	19	7	16	60	55	45
9	Oldham A	42	17	10	15	72	60	44
10	Plymouth A	42	15	13	14	69	70	43
11	Blackpool	42	15	13	14	62	64	43
12	Bury	42	17	9	16	70	73	43
13	BURNLEY	42	18	6	18	60	72	42
14	Southampton	42	15	8	19	54	58	38
15	Hull C	42	13	12	17	52	68	38
16	Fulham	42	15	7	20	48	67	37
17	Nottingham F	42	13	9	20	73	74	35
18	Notts C	42	12	11	19	53	62	35
19	Swansea T	42	10	15	17	51	60	35
20	Manchester U	42	14	6	22	59	85	34
21	Millwall	42	11	11	20	39	68	33
22	Lincoln C	42	9	8	25	44	75	26

1933-34

o

Manager : Tom Bromilow

Division Two (13th)

		Date			Opponents	Result		h/t	Goalscorers/times	Opp. goal times
	1	Aug	26	a	Grimsby T	L	0-1	0-0		60
	2		28	a	Preston N E	L	2-3	0-1	C.Smith 73, Miller 85	15, 49, 58
Jones' last game	3	Sep	2	h	NOTTINGHAM F	W	1-0	0-0	Jones 89	
	4		4	h	PRESTON N E	L	1-4	1-3	Sellars 33	30, 36, 42, 57
	5		9	a	West Ham U	W	2-1	2-1	C.Smith 10, Hancock 30	2
	6		16	h	PLYMOUTH A	D	2-2	1-0	Sellars 29, C.Smith 76	66, 73
Willighan's last game	7		23	a	Manchester U	L	2-5	1-1	Douglas 8, Mustard 82p	32, 51, 60, 71, 75
	8		30	h	BOLTON W	L	1-3	1-2	C.Smith 40	12, 13, 85
	9	Oct	7	a	Brentford	L	2-5	0-1	C.Smith 67, Douglas 80	20, 46, 57, 78, 86
	10		14	h	FULHAM	W	2-1	1-1	C.Smith (2) 3, 61	36
	11		21	a	Southampton	L	1-2	1-2	C.Smith 29	2, 40
	12		28	h	BLACKPOOL	W	3-2	0-1	Crompton 50, Hancock 57, Robinson 87	3, 70
	13	Nov	4	a	Bradford C	L	1-2	0-1	C.Smith 60	15, 47
	14		11	h	PORT VALE	D	0-0	0-0		
	15		18	a	Notts C	L	1-3	1-2	O'Grady 32	15, 44, 75
	16		25	h	SWANSEA T	W	3-1	2-1	Prest 30, Hancock (2) 40, 53	33
	17	Dec	2	a	Millwall	D	0-0	0-0		
	18		9	h	LINCOLN C	W	3-1	2-0	O'Grady (3) 33, 41, 51	67
	19		16	a	Bury	D	1-1	1-0	Hancock 17	68
	20		23	h	HULL C	W	3-1	2-0	O'Grady 20, Maddison 25og, Waterfield 65	89
	21		25	h	OLDHAM A	L	0-1	0-0		89
	22		26	a	Oldham A	L	0-1	0-1		44
	23		30	h	GRIMSBY T	W	2-0	1-0	Douglas 25, Robinson 77	
	24	Jan	6	a	Nottingham F	W	2-0	0-0	O'Grady (2) 63, 65	
	25		20	h	WEST HAM U	W	4-2	1-1	Douglas 21, Warburton 47, C.Smith 48, 63	44, 83p
	26		27	a	Plymouth A	L	0-1	0-1		43
Herman Conway's last game	27	Feb	3	h	MANCHESTER U	L	1-4	1-2	Warburton 2	32, 41, 51, 62
	28		10	a	Bolton W	L	1-4	1-3	Warburton 30	10, 24, 39, 77
	29		17	h	BRENTFORD	W	3-1	2-1	C.Smith (2) 25, 58, Hancock 37	1
	30		24	a	Fulham	D	1-1	0-0	Weale 68	59
Bennion's last game	31	Mar	3	h	SOUTHAMPTON	W	2-1	2-1	Hancock (2) 39, 41	45
	32		10	a	Blackpool	D	1-1	0-0	Douglas 78	68
	33		17	h	BRADFORD C	W	4-2	1-0	Waterfield 12, C.Smith 50, Hancock 76, Warburton 78	81, 83
	34		24	a	Port Vale	W	2-0	0-0	C.Smith (2) 72, 75	
	35		30	h	BRADFORD	W	1-0	1-0	Hancock 1	
	36		31	h	NOTTS C	W	1-0	0-0	Douglas 67	
	37	Apr	2	a	Bradford	L	0-5	0-1		44, 46, 65, 70, 82
	38		7	a	Swansea T	L	0-3	0-2		2, 35, 65
	39		14	h	MILLWALL	W	2-1	0-0	Chedgzoy 83, Weale 87	52
	40		21	a	Lincoln C	L	0-4	0-3		30, 35, 37, 62
	41		28	h	BURY	L	1-2	0-1	Douglas 48	31, 67
	42	May	5	a	Hull C	W	1-0	0-0	C.Smith 52	

FA Cup

				Opponents			h/t	Goalscorers/times	Opp. goal times
3	Jan	13	h	BURY	D	0-0	0-0		
rep		17	a	Bury	L	2-3	1-1	Richmond 8, C.Smith 85	30, 62, 87

Final, Manchester C 2-1 Portsmouth, at Wembley.

Other first team matches (friendlies and/or as detailed)

Lancs Cup	Sep	20	a	Bolton W	L	0-3

Att.	Pos	H Conway	Richmond	Waterfield	Bennion	Bellis	J Brown	Sellars	Hancock	Meechan	T Jones	T Miller	Willighan	C Smith	Chedgzoy	O'Grady	Scott	Mustard	Douglas	Robinson	Prest	Crompton	W H Wood	Warburton	Graham	Wallace	W Smith	Hetherington	Weale							
10,501		1	2	3	4	5	6	7	8	9	10	11																								1
18,950		1		3	4	5	6	7	8		10	11	2	9																						2
11,219		1	3		4	5	6	7	8		10	11	2	9																						3
13,543	19	1		3		5	6	7	8	9		11	2		4	10																				4
22,087	15			3	4	5	6	7	8				2	9		10	1	11																		5
11,609	17		2	3	4	5	6	7	8					9		10	1	11																		6
18,411	21			3	4	5	6	7	8				2	9			1	11	10																	7
12,672	21		2	3		5	6	7	8					9		4	1	11	10																	8
14,797	21		2	3		5	4	7	8			11		9			1		10	6																9
9,878	20	1	2	3		5	4		8					9					10	6	7	11														10
10,404	20	1	2	3		5	4	7	8					9					10	6		11														11
18,150	19	1	2	3		5	4	7	8					9					10	6		11														12
10,594	19	1	2	3		5	4	7	8					9				11	10	6																13
13,445	19	1	2	3		5	4		8					9				11	10	6	7															14
7,938	19	1	2	3		5	4	11						9		8			10	6	7															15
8,708	19		3			5	4		7					9		8	1		10	6	11		2													16
8,686	18		3			5	4		7								1		10	6	11		2	8	9											17
7,993	18		3			5	4		7							9	1		10	6	11		2	8												18
7,510	18		3			5	4		7							9	1		10	6	11		2	8												19
10,246			2	3		5	6		7							9	1		10		11			8		4										20
19,394			3			6	4		7							9	1		10		11		2	8		5										21
15,259	19	1	3			6	4		7							9			10		11		2	8		5										22
9,598	18	1	2			6	4	7								9			10	3		11		8		5										23
8,452	16	1	2				4	7								9			10	6		11		8		5	3									24
9,655	13	1	2			6	4		7					9					10	11				8		5	3									25
13,952	14	1	2			6	4		7					9					10	11				8		5	3									26
9,906	17	1	2			5	4	11	7					9					10	6				8			3									27
13,214	18		2			5	4		7					9					10	6				8			3	1	11							28
11,666	17		2			3	4		7					9					10	6				8		5		1	11							29
15,059	17		2			6	4		7					9					10					8		5	3	1	11							30
9,177	14				2	6	4		7					9					10					8		5	3	1	11							31
13,278	15			3		6	4		7					9					10					8		5	2	1	11							32
8,624	14		2	11		3	4		7					9					10	6				8		5		1								33
7,367	14		2	11		3	4		7					9					10	6				8		5		1								34
18,721	11		2	11		3	4		7					9					10	6				8		5		1								35
13,971			2			3	4	7						9					10	6				8		5		1	11							36
15,360			2			3	4							9					10	6		7		8		5		1	11							37
7,146	13		2			3	4	7						9					10	6				8		5		1	11							38
7,157			2			3	4							9	7				10	6				8		5		1	11							39
3,483	13		2			3	4							9	7				10	6				8		5		1	11							40
4,125	13		2			3		7						9	4				10	6				8		5		1	11							41
3,784			2	3		6								9	7				10	4	8					5		1	11							42
Appearances		16	36	20	7	41	40	19	32	2	3	5	5	32	5	13	11	6	36	28	11	6	6	25	1	21	8	15	12							
Goals (60)				2				2	10		1	1		17	1	7		1	7	2	1	1		4					2						1	og
37,379		1	2			6	4	7								9			10	3		11		8		5										3
20,169		1	2			3	4		7					9		8			10	6				11		5										rep
Appearances		2	2			2	2	1	1					1		2			2	2		1		2		2										
Goals (2)			1											1																						

1934-35

New players for the approaching season included left winger Percy Downes from Stockport, who would become a regular in Burnley's senior team, together with Manchester City forwards Robert Syme and Malcolm Comrie. This was also the period in Burnley's history when players would start appearing whose careers would continue on into the late thirties and would span the Second World War, and the very first of these arrived at Turf Moor in the summer of 1934. Inside forward or winger Ronnie Hornby had just celebrated his 20th birthday when he was signed from Cheshire League Stalybridge Celtic. Hornby would certainly play his part in the progress of Burnley Football Club in the years to come but, as with countless players the length and breadth of the country, he would be robbed of many of the best years of his career because of the War.

Some of the most significant changes at Turf Moor came off the field when Billy Dougall was the man chosen to replace Charlie Bates as Burnley's senior Trainer. Ray Bennion had not been retained on the senior playing staff but was offered the position as Player/coach to the club's newly resurrected "A" team. Turf Moor's backroom team was completed with the appointment of former Newcastle and England full back Frank Hudspeth as assistant Trainer. There were also changes in the Boardroom when EJ Tate stood down as the Clarets' Chairman, to be replaced by Vice Chairman Tom Clegg.

As far as the fans were concerned however, the most noticeable change of the summer was to the players' shirts, when it was suddenly announced that claret and blue was to be replaced by light blue with claret collars and cuffs.

The new campaign began well with five victories and a draw in the first seven games, after which the Clarets were third. The Directors obviously felt that promotion was definitely on the cards and decided to invest in some more experience for Burnley's front line. The arrival of George Brown from Aston Villa was greeted with tremendous enthusiasm by the Burnley fans, here was a goalscorer with a proven track record who had found the net at the highest level. Brown had been prolific in his days at Huddersfield after being spotted by the legendary Herbert Chapman and had been a key member of the Terriers' three consecutive League Championship campaigns. He had continued to find the net on a regular basis at Villa Park and it had been a shrewd piece of business by Burnley Manager Tom Bromilow to bring him to Turf Moor for a fee of around £2,000. George Brown scored on his Clarets' debut, albeit in a home defeat by Manchester United, and hit a hat-trick in only his fifth outing in what was now blue and claret, a 3-1 victory at Hull. Following a 1-6 drubbing at Champions-to-be Brentford, the Clarets enjoyed a 3-1 victory at Turf Moor against Fulham, then managed by former Turfite Jimmy Hogan. Hogan's playing career in England had been relatively modest but he had gone on to forge a coaching career for himself on the Continent where he was far more successful, and well known, than in his own country.

Inconsistent as ever, Burnley lost at home to Plymouth, won 3-2 on their first ever visit to Norwich, lost heavily at home to Newcastle then beat high-riding Bolton 2-1 on Christmas Day in front of Turf Moor's biggest League crowd of the season, over 26,000. Through it all George Brown kept finding the net and when he scored twice in a 4-0 win against Notts County early in January 1935, he had netted 14 in his first 16 games for Burnley, a better return than George Beel! At the turn of the year the Clarets were still in the top ten in Division Two but perhaps ambitions of League success had already evaporated. As always the FA Cup, given a kind draw and reasonable luck, represented a real chance of success as well as much-needed income.

Burnley's FA Cup campaign began with a hard-won 4-2 victory against Division Three North Mansfield. On a bumpy, snow-covered pitch, the result was in doubt until George Brown notched the Clarets' fourth goal just two minutes from time, after strikes from Teddy Hancock (2) and Cecil Smith. Smith, Hancock and Brown all scored again in the fourth round, a 3-1 win against Luton, again at Turf Moor, to set up a fifth round meeting with Nottingham Forest at the City Ground. A heroic defensive performance, especially from goalkeeper Bob Scott, earned the Clarets a 0-0 draw and Forest were despatched 3-0 in the replay, with Hancock and Brown yet again on target, this time after an early goal from skipper Alick Robinson.

George Brown
ex England star and prolific goalscorer
signed from Aston Villa

Burnley were now in the FA Cup quarter final, the stage they had reached just two years earlier when they had been knocked out at Turf Moor by first Division Manchester City. Once again they were drawn at home, once again it was a First Division club, and once again football fever gripped the town.

This time it was Birmingham, conquerors of Blackburn in

the fifth round, who were waiting. Had it been the old enemy who were to visit instead, there is no doubt that a new record attendance at the Turf Moor would have been set, such was the excitement and anticipation as the day of the match approached. As it was more than 47,000 people turned up eager for another thrilling Cup tie and hopefully another upset and progress to the semi final.

The majority were not disappointed. The Blues, showing First Division class from the first whistle, stormed into a 2-0 lead inside half an hour. They also had two goals disallowed for offside, both marginal, both hotly contested. At half time Manager Tom Bromilow simply told his players that the Birmingham team thought the game was already won, they would be totally unprepared for any kind of fight back. Whatever was instilled into those players before they left the dressing room, the second half of that quarter final has gone down in Burnley FC history. A totally different team kicked off and tore into the Birmingham players from the start. Seven minutes in Ronnie Hornby smashed in Burnley's first and the crowd erupted. After another seven minutes Teddy Hancock equalised from close in, crashing into the post as he did so. The Burnley supporters in the crowd were delirious, they just knew a famous victory was on the cards. Sure enough, with just eleven minutes to go Ronnie Hornby was there again to sweep in the winner and the Clarets were in the semi final for the first time in 11 years. The crowd was ecstatic, hats were thrown in the air by the thousand and many fans were already planning a trip to the famous Wembley Stadium.

Alas the Clarets had peaked too early. Against Sheffield Wednesday at Villa Park they never really looked like reaching the level of performance they had delivered against Birmingham. Wednesday scored early on and, although Burnley threatened occasionally, they were never really able to master their faster, bigger and younger opponents, especially left winger Ellis Rimmer who scored twice and was almost unplayable. It was a small crumb of comfort that Wednesday went on to lift the famous old trophy by beating West Brom 4-2 at Wembley, Rimmer scoring twice more!

Another momentous FA Cup run was over but with such utter concentration on a possible lucrative trip to Wembley, the Clarets' League form had suffered during the Cup campaign, with just a single victory in Division Two, 3-0 at Turf Moor against lowly Swansea. That particular day, 23 February 1935, was a significant date in the history of Burnley FC and indeed the history of English football in general.

Burnley's "A" team won 3-2 against a team from Lancaster in a West Lancashire League fixture. Two of Burnley's goals that day were scored by a young boy from Bolton, only fifteen years old, playing his very first game in Burnley's colours. That boy very quickly became a man and went on to become one of the most prolific goalscorers ever in English football and arguably the most gifted all-round centre forward the game has ever seen.

The name of that boy, of course, was Tommy Lawton.

Burnley finished that campaign in mid table but the attendance of less than 4,000 at the last home match of the season, a 1-0 success against Norwich, was in sharp contrast to the 47,000 plus who had squeezed into Turf Moor for the epic FA Cup quarter final triumph against Birmingham. The Norwich game also proved to be the last occasion that the Burnley fans would see two durable and popular defenders. George Waterfield and Jim Brown had appeared in more than 600 senior games for Burnley between them with Waterfield having been a fixture in the Clarets' defence for almost a dozen years. With Tom Prest also leaving Turf Moor, the final playing links with First Division days only five years before, had now gone.

Captain Alick Robinson (left) and Birmingham's Joe Bradford before the epic FA Cup quarter final at Turf Moor

1934-35 - Second Division

		P	W	D	L	F	A	Pts
1	Brentford	42	26	9	7	93	48	61
2	Bolton W	42	26	4	12	96	48	56
3	West Ham U	42	26	4	12	80	63	56
4	Blackpool	42	21	11	10	79	57	53
5	Manchester U	42	23	4	15	76	55	50
6	Newcastle U	42	22	4	16	89	68	48
7	Fulham	42	17	12	13	76	56	46
8	Plymouth A	42	19	8	15	75	64	46
9	Nottingham F	42	17	8	17	76	70	42
10	Bury	42	19	4	19	62	73	42
11	Sheffield U	42	16	9	17	79	70	41
12	BURNLEY	42	16	9	17	63	73	41
13	Hull C	42	16	8	18	63	74	40
14	Norwich C	42	14	11	17	71	61	39
15	Bradford PA	42	11	16	15	55	63	38
16	Barnsley	42	13	12	17	60	83	38
17	Swansea T	42	14	8	20	56	67	36
18	Port Vale	42	11	12	19	55	74	34
19	Southampton	42	11	12	19	46	75	34
20	Bradford C	42	12	8	22	50	68	32
21	Oldham A	42	10	6	26	56	95	26
22	Notts C	42	9	7	26	46	97	25

1934-35

Manager : Tom Bromilow

Division Two (12th)

Notes	No	Date		h/a	Opponents	Result		h/t	Goalscorers/times	Opp. goal times
	1	Aug	25	h	SOUTHAMPTON	W	3-0	2-0	Robinson (2) 20, 29p, Douglas 78	
	2		27	a	West Ham U	W	2-1	1-1	Walker 25og, Douglas 60	29
	3	Sep	1	a	Notts C	L	0-1	0-1		10
West Ham goals 14m, 89m,	4		3	h	WEST HAM U	W	5-2	1-1	Wallace 25, Douglas (2) 51, 82, C.Smith 53, Robinson 57p	
	5		8	h	BRADFORD C	W	2-0	1-0	Douglas 5, C.Smith 65	
	6		15	a	Sheffield U	D	0-0	0-0		
	7		22	h	BARNSLEY	W	4-1	1-0	Robinson 35p, Downes (2) 50, 85, Alderman 73	70p
	8		29	a	Port Vale	L	1-3	1-2	Downes 13p	1, 21, 67
	9	Oct	6	h	MANCHESTER U	L	1-2	1-0	G.Brown 35	51, 68
	10		13	a	Swansea T	L	0-2	0-0		60, 84
	11		20	a	Blackpool	L	0-1	0-0		87
	12		27	h	BURY	D	3-3	3-2	Hancock 5, G.Brown 16, Graham 41	35, 40, 50
	13	Nov	3	a	Hull C	W	3-1	3-0	G.Brown (3) 15, 19, 30	72p
	14		10	h	NOTTINGHAM F	W	2-1	1-0	Robinson 34p, Hancock 54	78
	15		17	a	Brentford	L	1-6	0-2	G.Brown 75	27,40,58,59,72,88
	16		24	h	FULHAM	W	3-1	2-0	Prest 31, G.Brown 34, Alderman 58	51
	17	Dec	1	a	Bradford	D	1-1	1-1	G.Brown 3	10
	18		8	h	PLYMOUTH A	L	1-2	1-2	G.Brown 27	20, 43p
	19		15	a	Norwich C	W	3-2	3-0	C.Smith 14, G.Brown (2) 25, 40	65, 80
	20		22	h	NEWCASTLE U	L	0-3	0-1		12, 85, 89
	21		25	h	BOLTON W	W	2-1	2-0	C.Smith 29, G.Brown 31	70
	22		29	a	Southampton	D	0-0			
	23	Jan	2	a	Bolton W	L	0-7	0-3		14,25,35,47,54,59,87
	24		5	h	NOTTS C	W	4-0	1-0	G.Brown (2) 37, 77, Downes 63, C.Smith 79	
	25		19	a	Bradford C	D	1-1	0-1	C.Smith 86	38
	26		28	h	SHEFFIELD U	L	0-2	0-1		17, 50
	27	Feb	2	a	Barnsley	D	0-0			
	28		9	h	PORT VALE	D	2-2	2-0	G.Brown 1, Vickers 17og	50, 56
	29		23	h	SWANSEA T	W	3-0	1-0	Hancock (2) 15, 53, C.Smith 86	
	30	Mar	5	h	BLACKPOOL	L	1-2	0-1	Clacher 49	30, 51
	31		9	a	Bury	D	0-0			
	32		19	h	HULL C	L	1-3	0-1	Graham 72	28, 51, 61
	33		23	a	Nottingham F	L	0-5	0-3		8, 39, 43, 62, 72
	34		27	a	Manchester U	W	4-3	0-0	G.Brown (2) 53, 58, Hornby 72, Rayner 80	70, 75, 89
	35		30	h	BRENTFORD	L	0-3	0-1		43, 59, 81
Prest's last game	36	Apr	6	a	Fulham	L	0-2	0-0		60, 75
	37		13	h	BRADFORD	L	1-2	1-0	G.Brown 37	50, 81
	38		19	h	OLDHAM A	W	4-2	3-2	G.Brown (2) 14, 47, Rayner 18, Douglas 34	1, 16
	39		20	a	Plymouth A	D	2-2	2-0	Rayner 8, Robinson 20	65, 75
	40		22	a	Oldham A	W	2-1	2-1	Rayner 10, Downes 40	2
Bellis' last game	41		27	h	NORWICH C	W	1-0	1-0	G.Brown 25	
last games for Waterfield & James Brown	42	May	4	a	Newcastle U	L	0-2	0-2		40, 43

FA Cup

Notes	Rd	Date		h/a	Opponents	Result		h/t	Goalscorers/times	Opp. goal times
	3	Jan	12	h	MANSFIELD T	W	4-2	2-1	Hancock (2) 16, 21, C.Smith 55, G.Brown 88	37p, 53
	4		26	h	LUTON T	W	3-1	1-1	C.Smith 7, Hancock 55, G.Brown 65	11
	5	Feb	16	a	Nottingham F	D	0-0	0-0		
	rep		19	h	NOTTINGHAM F	W	3-0	2-0	Robinson 3, Hancock 25, G.Brown 62	
	6	Mar	2	h	BIRMINGHAM	W	3-2	0-2	Hornby 52, 79, Hancock 59	18, 25
at Villa Park	semi		16	n	Sheffield W	L	0-3	0-1		6, 59, 80

Final, Sheffield W 4-2 West Bromwich A, at Wembley.

Other first team matches (friendlies and/or as detailed)

Notes	Date		h/a	Opponents	Result		Goalscorers
Lancs Cup	Sep	11	a	Rossendale U	D	3-3	Howarth, Weale, Schofield
Lancs Cup		18	h	ROSSENDALE U	L	0-1	
John Clacher transfer match	Sep	19	a	Altrincham	D	3-3	Syme (2), Comrie
Charlie Bates benefit		24	h	BLACKBURN R XI	L	3-6	C.Smith, Downes, Alderman
	Apr	8	h	CLIFTONVILLE	W	2-0	Briton, Rayner
George Waterfield benefit		24	h	HAMILTON A	L	2-3	G.Brown, Rayner

Att.	Pos	Scott	Richmond	Bellis	J Brown	Wallace	Robinson	Hancock	Comrie	Syme	Douglas	Downes	Alderman	C Smith	Waterfield	W Smith	G Brown	Hetherington	Readett	Prest	Graham	Clacher	Hornby	Johnson	Weale	Rayner		
12,995		1	2	3	4	5	6	7	8	9	10	11																1
18,070		1	2	3	4	5	6	7	8	9	10	11																2
15,363		1	2	3	4	5	6		8	9	10	11	7															3
13,562	3	1	2	3	4	5	6		8		10	11	7	9														4
14,325	3	1	2	3	4	5	6		8		10	11	7	9														5
14,040	3	1	2	3	4	5	6			7	10	11	8	9														6
9,424	3	1	2	3	4	5	6	7		9	10	11	8															7
7,311	3	1	2	6	4			7		9	10	11	8		3	5												8
16,757	4	1	2	6	4	5		7			10	11	8		3		9											9
10,076	7			6	4			7				11	8	9	3	5	10	1	2									10
22,096	11			3	4		6	7				11	8			5	9	1	2	10								11
10,715	11			3	4	5	6	8				11	7				9	1	2		10							12
5,896	9				4	5	6	7			10	11			3	2	9	1			8							13
12,373	7				4	5	6	7			10	11	8		3	2	9	1										14
15,459	9	1		5	4		6	7			10	11	8		3	2	9											15
11,263	7	1			4	5	6	7				11	8		3	2	9			10								16
8,803	8	1			4	5	6	7				11	8		3	2	9			10								17
11,072	9	1			4	5	6	7				11	8		3	2	9			10								18
10,634	9	1			4	5	6			7		11		9	3	2	8			10								19
14,792		1			4	5	6			7		11		9	3	2	8			10								20
26,518		1	3		4	5		7				11		9		2	8					6	10					21
11,257	9	1	3		4	5					10	11	7	9		2	8					6						22
19,354		1	3		4	5					10	11	7	9		2	8					6						23
10,409	9	1			4		6			7		11		9	3	2	8						10	5				24
12,048	9	1	2				6	7				11		9	3	5	8					4	10					25
4,974		1	2				6	7				11		9	3	5	8					4	10					26
5,924	9	1	2				6					11	7	9	3	5	8					4	10					27
9,830	9	1	2		4		6	7				11		9	3	5	8						10					28
9,452	8	1	2			5	6	7	8					9	3							4	10		11			29
8,992	11	1	2		4	5		7	8			11		9	3							6	10					30
8,151	11	1	2	5	4				8			11	7		3		9					6	10					31
4,256	12	1	2		4	5	6	7				11			3		9				8		10					32
5,366	13	1	2		4	5	6	7				11		9	3		8						10					33
10,247			2	3	4		10	7									9	1				6	11	5		8		34
11,206	11		2	3	4	5	6	7						9				1					10		11	8		35
14,173	14		2	3	4		6									5	9	1		7			10		11	8		36
5,833	15		3	2	4		6				10	11				5	9	1			7					8		37
4,813	14		2	5	4		6	7			10	11			3		9	1								8		38
11,929				2	4	5	6	7			10	11			3		9	1								8		39
6,857	11			2	4	5	6	7			10	11			3		9	1								8		40
3,765	10			2	4	5	6	7			10	11			3		9	1								8		41
7,718			2		4	5	6	7				11			3		9	1					10			8		42
Appearances		28	27	22	38	28	34	29	8	9	19	38	19	18	26	21	31	14	3	7	4	10	15	2	3	9		
Goals (63)						1	6	4			6	5	2	7			21			1	2	1	1			4	2	ogs

Att.	Pos	Scott	Richmond	Bellis	J Brown	Wallace	Robinson	Hancock	Comrie	Syme	Douglas	Downes	Alderman	C Smith	Waterfield	W Smith	G Brown	Hetherington	Readett	Prest	Graham	Clacher	Hornby	Johnson	Weale	Rayner		
20,790		1	2		4		6	7				11		9	3	5	8						10					3
26,605		1	2		4		6	7				11		9	3	5	8						10					4
34,180		1	2		4	5	6	7				11		9	3		8						10					5
29,520		1	2		4	5	6	7				11		9	3		8						10					rep
47,670		1	2		4	5	6	7				11		9	3		8						10					6
56,625		1	2		4	5	6	7				11		9	3		8						10					semi
Appearances		6	6		6	4	6	6				6		6	6	2	6						6					
Goals (13)							1	5						2			3						2					

1935-36

Following the departure of James Brown to Manchester United, veteran George Waterfield was signed by Crystal Palace, then in the Third Division South and at the time managed by former Claret Jack Tresadern. Waterfield's move seemed to trigger a number of links with Palace who then signed Burnley's full back Wilfred Smith. Then, within days it was announced that Tresadern had left Palace and been appointed as Manager of Tottenham and that Burnley's Manager Tom Bromilow had accepted the position of Manager of Crystal Palace. For the time being the Burnley Board decided not to appoint a successor to Bromilow, Secretary Alf Boland would take on any additional duties.

On the field the Clarets' only newcomer for the opening match of the season at Charlton was full back George Nevin, signed from Sheffield Wednesday, although new defenders John Hindmarsh and Harry Hubbick were waiting in the wings. Charlton, newly promoted as Champions of the Third Division North, were far too good for the Clarets, winning comfortably 4-0 and already on their way to a second successive promotion. Burnley managed their first point of the season in a 1-1 draw at Port Vale with George Brown on target, as he was in home victories against Hull and Port Vale, and apparently continuing his rich vein of form in front of goal. Suddenly, however, he was gone, First Division strugglers Leeds having stepped in with an offer impossible to resist for the Burnley Board. The town was aghast, Brown had really made an impact in his short time at Turf Moor, 27 goals in just 41 games in League and Cup, but this was the harsh reality of a Second Division team that was almost permanently struggling. The dependable Cecil Smith was left as Burnley's main goalscoring threat although he was to have a number of partners before the end of the campaign.

The Burnley supporters were by this time coming to terms with yet another change of strip and for the first time since 1910 there was no claret to be seen. The blue and claret shirts of 1934-35 had now given way to white jerseys with black collars and cuffs.

In November 1935 Smith and Teddy Hancock both scored twice in a 5-2 success against Swansea at Turf Moor but it was one of the season's few highlights, most of it being spent in the bottom four. Blackpool were beaten 3-2 in an exciting Christmas Day fixture at Turf Moor and another newcomer, Stephen Kilcar, scored twice in Burnley's first away win of the season, 2-1 at bottom of the table Hull, as 1936 got under way.

Hopes of another lucrative FA Cup run were quickly dashed by Sheffield United in the third round before Cecil Smith scored Burnley's only hat-trick of the season in a one-sided 3-0 victory against Barnsley at a snow-covered Turf Moor.

In February 1936 there was another departure from Turf Moor when goalkeeper Bob Scott was transferred to Wolves for a substantial fee, described as 'highly satisfactory' by the Burnley Directors. The money received was immediately used when goalkeeper Ted Adams was signed from Southport and winger Charles Fletcher was secured from Brentford. The spending had not finished and in March 1936 the Burnley Directors made another of their astute signings when inside forward Bob Brocklebank was secured from Aston Villa. Still only 27, Brocklebank had spent his entire professional career at Villa Park but had never really established himself as a regular. Brocklebank played his first game for Burnley at Southampton, a 0-1 defeat, but it was in the following match, at home to Doncaster, that a debut was made by a Burnley player that really stole the headlines, and made Turf Moor history into the bargain.

Winger Teddy Hancock

The Burnley Directors announced that Tommy Lawton was to lead the attack at the age of 16 years and 163 days, still the club's youngest ever player in League football. Lawton had been a prolific scorer for Burnley's "A" team but had played only a handful of games for the Reserves. It was unfortunate that Lawton's debut, the talk of Burnley during the week before, took place in such a poor match. The Burnley Express described it as "a puerile display, the worst for a long time, an inept performance by the forwards", although they did add that "Lawton was no worse than his colleagues"! In the event Burnley did pick up a point in a 1-1 draw, Charlie Fletcher scoring his first goal for the Turfites, a late equaliser from the penalty spot.

It was the good people of Swansea who were to witness the first League goals by the young pretender. In an impressive performance, unrecognisable from the shambles against Doncaster, an unchanged Burnley team cruised to a 3-1 victory against the Swans, with two second half strikes from Lawton, following another penalty from Fletcher. A new Burnley record had been established by Tommy Lawton, the club's youngest ever scorer in League football, and a brilliant career of success in front of goal had begun. After his third game, this time unproductive, Lawton picked up a slight injury but returned to the side to score another two goals in a comfortable 4-0 victory at Bury. It was only Burnley's second win since February but with three games to go, the two points were enough to banish any fears of relegation. The season ended abruptly for centre half Bob Johnson who broke his leg after just six minutes of the re-arranged match against Tottenham at Turf Moor. Johnson has impressed after stepping up to replace Tommy Wallace, who had himself been injured at Norwich earlier in the campaign. Wallace never returned to Burnley's senior side but Bob Johnson would be part of the Turf Moor scene for many years to come. Lawton scored his first goal in front of the Turf Moor fans in the 2-2 draw with Leicester but, as usual, typical end of season fare did not attract many fans. It was Burnley's sixth successive draw at home but the campaign ended disappointingly with a poor performance against Fulham, less than 4,000 people bothering to turn up to watch the Turfites stumble to a 0-2 defeat.

Tommy Lawton
a star is born

OBITUARY
THOMAS WILLIGHAN
DIED 7 JULY 1936, AGED 33.

Tommy Willighan was born in East Belfast in 1903 and played his early football with Willowfield, a Belfast junior club, whilst working on the docks in Belfast. He was 24 when he joined Burnley as a professional in March 1928 and although he soon became a regular in the Clarets' junior teams he took some time to make an impact at first team level. He made his League debut in March 1930, replacing fellow Irishman Andy McCluggage at right back in Burnley's 4-0 victory against Manchester United at Turf Moor, but in the main it was McCluggage's consistency that kept Tommy Willighan in reserve. A strong robust full back, Willighan at last became a regular after Andy McCluggage left Turf Moor and his pairing with England international left back George Waterfield was solid enough. Tommy Willighan was selected for his country twice, first against Wales at Wrexham in December 1932 and in an historic 2-1 victory for the Irish against Scotland at Celtic Park in September 1933. Just a week later Tommy Willighan suffered a serious knee injury in a League game at Old Trafford and his senior career was at an end. He later returned to Ireland where he worked as a coach before he became ill.

RIP

1935-36 - Second Division

		P	W	D	L	F	A	Pts
1	Manchester U	42	22	12	8	85	43	56
2	Charlton A	42	22	11	9	85	58	55
3	Sheffield U	42	20	12	10	79	50	52
4	West Ham U	42	22	8	12	90	68	52
5	Tottenham H	42	18	13	11	91	55	49
6	Leicester C	42	19	10	13	79	57	48
7	Plymouth A	42	20	8	14	71	57	48
8	Newcastle U	42	20	6	16	88	79	46
9	Fulham	42	15	14	13	76	52	44
10	Blackpool	42	18	7	17	93	72	43
11	Norwich C	42	17	9	16	72	65	43
12	Bradford C	42	15	13	14	55	65	43
13	Swansea T	42	15	9	18	67	76	39
14	Bury	42	13	12	17	66	84	38
15	BURNLEY	42	12	13	17	50	59	37
16	Bradford PA	42	14	9	19	62	84	37
17	Southampton	42	14	9	19	47	65	37
18	Doncaster R	42	14	9	19	51	71	37
19	Nottingham F	42	12	11	19	69	76	35
20	Barnsley	42	12	9	21	54	80	33
21	Port Vale	42	12	8	22	56	106	32
22	Hull C	42	5	10	27	47	111	20

1935-36

Managed by Selection Committee

Division Two (15th)

		Date			Opponents	Result		h/t	Goalscorers/times	Opp. goal times
	1	Aug	31	a	Charlton A	L	0-4	0-3		1, 16, 44, 90
	2	Sep	2	a	Port Vale	D	1-1	0-1	Brown 65	30
	3		7	h	HULL C	W	2-0	1-0	Brown 34, Smith 65	
George Brown's last game	4		9	h	PORT VALE	W	5-1	1-0	Smith 28, Hancock (2) 53, 78, Brown 76, Hornby 84	88
	5		14	a	Barnsley	L	1-3	0-2	Kilcar 57	1, 40, 75
	6		18	a	Fulham	D	2-2	2-1	Smith 12, Downes 44	45, 65
	7		21	h	PLYMOUTH A	L	0-1	0-1		42
	8		28	a	Bradford C	D	0-0	0-0		
	9	Oct	5	h	NEWCASTLE U	L	1-2	0-1	Kilcar 70	9, 60
	10		12	a	Tottenham H	L	1-5	1-1	Smith 10	5, 47, 49, 77, 83
	11		19	h	NOTTINGHAM F	W	1-0	1-0	Hancock 25	
Wallace's last game	12		26	a	Norwich C	L	0-2	0-1		10, 80
	13	Nov	2	h	SOUTHAMPTON	W	2-0	1-0	Hancock 24, Hornby 67	
	14		9	a	Sheffield U	L	0-2	0-1		30, 75
	15		16	h	BRADFORD	D	1-1	0-0	Liggins 89	75p
	16		23	a	Doncaster R	L	0-1	0-1		12
	17		30	h	SWANSEA T	W	5-2	1-1	Smith (2) 30, 63, Hancock (2) 52, 87, Kilcar 82	13, 61
	18	Dec	14	h	BURY	D	1-1	1-1	Kilcar 30	40
	19		21	a	Leicester C	L	0-2	0-0		55, 77
	20		25	h	BLACKPOOL	W	3-2	1-1	Hindmarsh 33, Smith 55, Storey 60	23, 86
	21		26	a	Blackpool	L	0-2	0-0		80, 85p
	22		28	h	CHARLTON A	L	0-2	0-1		25, 78
	23	Jan	4	a	Hull C	W	2-1	0-0	Kilcar (2) 49, 66	50
	24		18	h	BARNSLEY	W	3-0	2-0	Smith (3) 20, 40, 57	
	25		29	a	Plymouth A	L	0-2	0-1		44og, 65
	26	Feb	1	h	BRADFORD C	W	3-0	2-0	Hancock 15, Cowan 44og, Storey 60	
Scott's last game	27		3	a	West Ham U	D	0-0	0-0		
	28		8	a	Newcastle U	D	1-1	1-0	Hornby 12	86
	29		22	a	Nottingham F	L	0-2	0-0		80, 87
	30		29	h	WEST HAM U	W	1-0	0-0	Hornby 60	
	31	Mar	7	a	Bradford	L	0-2	0-0		51, 67
	32		14	h	SHEFFIELD U	D	1-1	0-0	Kilcar 81	65
	33		21	a	Southampton	L	0-1	0-0		84
	34		28	h	DONCASTER R	D	1-1	0-0	Fletcher 78p	67
	35	Apr	4	a	Swansea T	W	3-1	1-0	Fletcher 25p, T.Lawton (2) 47, 73	84
	36		10	h	MANCHESTER U	D	2-2	1-2	Fletcher 42, Hubbick 58	10, 26
	37		11	h	NORWICH C	D	1-1	0-1	Fletcher 52p	28
Cecil Smith's last game	38		13	a	Manchester U	L	0-4	0-3		15, 25, 34, 65
	39		18	a	Bury	W	4-0	1-0	T.Lawton (2) 35, 79, Fletcher 78, Brocklebank 81	
	40		20	h	TOTTENHAM H	D	0-0	0-0		
Douglas' last game	41		25	h	LEICESTER C	D	2-2	1-0	T.Lawton 12, Brocklebank 73	66, 75
Downes' last game	42	May	2	h	FULHAM	L	0-2	0-2		42, 45

FA Cup

				Opponents	Result		h/t	Goalscorers/times	Opp. goal times
3	Jan	11	h	SHEFFIELD U	D	0-0	0-0		
rep		16	a	Sheffield U	L	1-2	1-2	Hancock 16	14, 43

Final, Arsenal 1-0 Sheffield U, at Wembley.

Other first team matches (friendlies and/or as detailed)

				Opponents	Result	
Lancs Cup	Sep	30	a	Blackburn R	L	0-1

Att.	Pos	Hetherington	Nevin	Richmond	Clacher	Wallace	Robinson	Hancock	Rayner	G Brown	Hornby	Downes	C Smith	Kilcar	Hindmarsh	Scott	Douglas	Hubbick	Johnson	Liggins	Nisbet	Storey	Adams	Fletcher	Brocklebank	T Lawton	Ashbridge	J Lawton	J Oliver		
20,681		1	2	3	4	5	6	7	8	9	10	11																			1
9,450		1	2	3	4	5	6	7	8	9	10	11																			2
10,082		1	2	3	4	5	6	7		8	10	11	9																		3
11,268		1	2	3	4	5	6	7		8	10	11	9																		4
10,921	11	1	2	3	4	5	6	7			10	11	9	8																	5
10,188		1	2	3	4	5	6	7			8	11	9	10																	6
10,631	16	1	2	3	4	5	6	7			8	11	9	10																	7
7,419	19	1	2	3		5	6	7			8	11	9	10	4																8
10,765	19	1	2	3		5	6		7		8	11	9	10	4																9
34,483	19		2	3		5	6	7				11	9	10	4	1	8														10
5,226	17		2			5	6	7				11	9	10	4	1	8	3													11
18,030	18		2			5	6	7	8		11		9	10	4	1		3													12
8,524	15		2				6	7	8		11		9	10	4	1		3	5												13
11,825			2				6	7	8		11			10	4	1		3	5	9											14
10,047	19			2			6	7	8		11			10	4	1		3	5	9											15
12,999	19			2				7						11	4	1	10	3	5	9	6	8									16
6,823	18			2				7				11	9	8	4	1	10	3	5		6										17
8,906	19			2			6	7				11	9	8	4	1	10	3	5												18
9,042				2			6	7			10	11	9	8	4	1		3	5												19
19,367				2			6				10	11	9	8	4	1		3	5			7									20
15,779	18			2			6				10	11	9	8	4	1		3	5			7									21
11,572				2			6	7	8			11	9		4	1	10	3	5												22
5,811	19			2			6				10	11	9	8	4	1		3	5			7									23
6,757	19			2			6	8			10	11	9		4	1		3	5			7									24
8,566				2			6	8			10	11	9		4	1		3	5			7									25
8,808				2			6	8			10	11	9		4	1		3	5			7									26
12,212	16		2				6	8			10	11	9		4	1		3	5			7									27
17,487	15	1	2				6	8	11		10		9		4			3	5			7									28
7,513	17	1	2				6	8	11		10		9		4			3	5			7									29
7,614	16		2				6	8			10		9		4			3	5			7	1	11							30
5,120	18		2				6	8			10		9		4			3	5			7	1	11							31
12,920	18			2			6				10			8	4			3	5	9		7	1	11							32
5,095	19			2			6				10		9		4			3	5			7	1	11	8						33
12,350	19			2			6	7			10				4			3	5				1	11	8	9					34
5,890	18			2			6	7			10				4			3	5				1	11	8	9					35
27,245	19			2			6	7			10				4			3	5				1	11	8	9					36
10,651				2			6	7			10		9		4			3	5				1	11	8						37
39,855	19			2			6	7			10		9		4			3	5					11	8		1				38
7,093				2			6		4					10				3	5				1	11	8	9		7			39
8,567	17			2			6		4								10	3	5				1	11	8	9		7			40
5,543	15		2				5	7	4						6		10	3					1	11	8	9					41
4,764			2				6		4		10	11						3					1		8	9		7	5		42
Appearances		11	21	31	7	12	40	33	14	4	33	23	29	20	32	18	8	32	28	4	2	14	12	12	10	7	1	3	1		
Goals (50)								7		3	4	1	10	7	1			1		1		2		5	2	5				1	og

Att.	Pos	Hetherington	Nevin	Richmond	Clacher	Wallace	Robinson	Hancock	Rayner	G Brown	Hornby	Downes	C Smith	Kilcar	Hindmarsh	Scott	Douglas	Hubbick	Johnson	Liggins	Nisbet	Storey	Adams	Fletcher	Brocklebank	T Lawton	Ashbridge	J Lawton	J Oliver		
25,444				2			6	7			10	11	9	8	4	1		3	5												3
12,802				2			6	7			10	11	9	8	4	1		3	5												rep
Appearances				2			2	2			2	2	2	2	2	2		2	2												
Goals (1)								1																							

1936-37

There was still no Team Manager at Turf Moor for the new season, according to the Chairman Tom Clegg "team selection would be under the direct control of the Board".

Perhaps the most significant new arrival in the summer of 1936 was a 23 year old defender who would very soon make a big impact at Turf Moor and go on to become part of Burnley's famous "Iron Curtain" defence in the 1940's, Arthur Woodruff.

Tommy Lawton was soon into his stride as the new campaign got under way with two goals on the opening day in a 3-0 victory against Nottingham Forest. He scored again at Chesterfield but was then injured and replaced by a young schoolteacher from Bacup who did his best to fill Lawton's boots whilst the boy wonder was on the sidelines. John Gastall scored after just four minutes of his debut and helped himself to 4 goals altogether in his first three League outings.

Early in October 1936 the Burnley Directors once more decided to bring some more quality and experience to Turf Moor with Scots Willie "Golden" Miller and Jimmy Stein arriving from Everton. Jimmy Stein in particular was to make his mark with Burnley FC, in years to come he would operate a talent scout for the club in Scotland, responsible for a number of young discoveries, including Andy Lochhead, Harry Thomson and Willie Morgan.

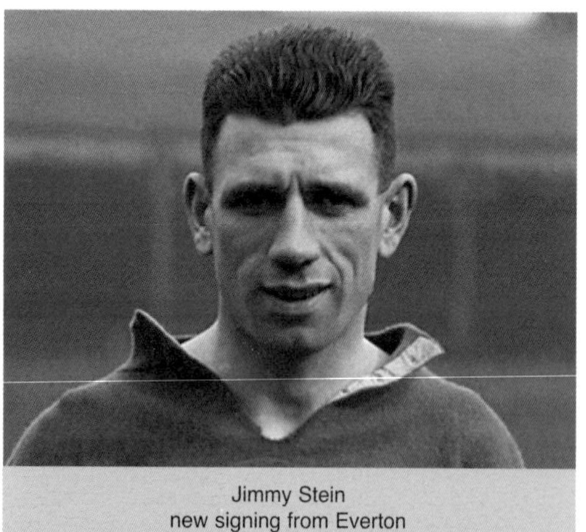

Jimmy Stein
new signing from Everton
Turf Moor talent scout in the years to come

Miller and Stein both made their Burnley debuts in a 1-1 draw at Southampton. Lawton returned to lead the attack with John Gastall retaining his place in the team but moving to the right wing. Two days later Tommy Lawton celebrated his 17th birthday and was asked to come in to see the Burnley Chairman Tom Clegg and Secretary Alf Boland. He was invited to sign the professional form that had been prepared for him almost from his first day at Burnley as a hugely talented 15 year old. After a few days to think it over with his family, Lawton signed. Even then there had been speculation that it would only be a matter of time before the young star would be on his way to a bigger club. For now however Turf Moor was Tommy Lawton's stage and Tottenham were to be the opposition for his first game as a professional.

Lawton chose that particular day, important enough in itself, not only to proudly announce his arrival in the professional ranks, but to positively bellow it from the rooftops. His direct opponent in Tottenham's defence was Arthur Rowe, a full England international, but Lawton, not for the first time, or the last, demonstrated a scant regard for reputations. Just 30 seconds into his professional career, he was on the end of a flowing move to put Burnley ahead with a low drive. Before the interval he had scored again, a far post header crashed into the net from a John Gastall corner. Three minutes into the second half the man of the moment (but really still a boy) took a fiercely driven pass from Gastall in his stride, powered past Rowe and smashed the ball past the Tottenham keeper to complete a hat-trick he could only have dreamt of, as well as putting the finishing touches to a script that would have been rejected as far too fanciful by a Hollywood film producer!

Lawton kept on scoring and adding to his reputation, as well as to his value when the inevitable transfer came. When he got the only goal in a victory against Sheffield United just before Christmas 1936 however, his admirers in the Turf Moor crowd could not have known it was to be his last goal in a Burnley shirt. He made his final appearance in front of his adoring fans in a 3-0 win against Doncaster on Christmas Day 1936. His League debut had also been at Turf Moor against Doncaster just 10 months earlier and strangely his last game for Burnley would also be against Doncaster, this time at Belle Vue.

As Burnley supporters awakened after celebrating the dawn of a brand new year, they were soon to realise that 1937 would start without Tommy Lawton in their team. The fans had known for some time that the big clubs were coveting their talented young discovery but it was Everton, who had moved in as the New Year approached, with a bid speculated to be around £7,000, far too much for a club like Burnley to resist. Lawton was a rising star who had appeared all too briefly in the Turf Moor sky. All at Burnley however could be justly proud of their contribution to the early development of a player who would go on to become one the game's true legends.

Life without Lawton began well enough with a 3-1 win against Chesterfield at Turf Moor, with young centre forward Arthur Richardson scoring after just eight minutes of his debut. Aston Villa were beaten at Villa Park as another FA Cup campaign began, Jimmy Stein scored his first Burnley goal as Bradford City were overcome 3-0 at Turf Moor then Bury were despatched 4-1 in the FA Cup fourth round. At that point Burnley were eighth in the Second Division, in touch with the leaders and definite contenders for promotion back to the top flight. There was also the mouth watering prospect of a fifth round FA Cup tie at Turf Moor against the team everybody wanted to see, and beat, Arsenal. The Gunners were the FA Cup holders although they had only finished sixth in the First Division in 1936 after winning the Championship in each of the three previous campaigns. Unfortunately Burnley chose the weeks leading up to the Arsenal tie to produce their worst form of the season, with three defeats, at home to Southampton, Saints' only away win of the season, and at Swansea and Tottenham, conceding three goals each time. It was definitely not the ideal preparation to face household names of the calibre of Alf Kirchen, Ted Drake, Cliff Bastin and Alex James!

The crowds flocked to Turf Moor in their thousands to see "the costliest team ever to play in Burnley", the majority, as ever, confident of a victory for their favourites.

After just eleven minutes, with the score still 0-0, a shot from Bob Brocklebank was kicked off the line by Eddie Hapgood. Afterwards fans and even photographers who were close by assured everyone who would listen that the ball was a foot over the line. The referee ignored the pleas from the home fans, waved play on and Turf Moor hopes were dashed. Within another eleven minutes Burnley were four goals down and just about out of the FA Cup for another season. Although Arthur Richardson pulled one back, Arsenal were simply unstoppable with Ted Drake helping himself to four goals in a 7-1 victory. The Burnley players had given their all but it simply wasn't enough in the face of "a wonderful exhibition of football that no team in England could have lived with".

Within days another of Burnley's young stars was on his way out of Turf Moor, full back Harry Hubbick signing for Bolton for another substantial fee.

In the coming weeks there were varied fortunes against the clubs heading for promotion to Division One, Blackpool and Leicester, with Burnley scoring three goals in each case. The Seasiders were comfortably beaten at Turf Moor but it was a different story at Filbert Street with Champions-elect Leicester winning 7-3, the second time in just three weeks that the hard-pressed Burnley defence had conceded seven!

Burnley's next game, against West Ham at Turf Moor, was a sombre affair, after the club received the news that former Trainer Charlie Bates had passed away that morning in hospital in Manchester. The Turf Moor flag was flown at half mast and both sets of players wore black arm bands.

OBITUARY

CHARLES BATES

DIED 20 MARCH 1937, AGED 52.

A native of West Bromwich, Charlie Bates had been playing junior football in the Birmingham Leagues when he was signed by Burnley in May 1910. He managed only a handful of Second Division games before an injury ended his playing career but, in the years before the First World War, he was then taken on as the Clarets' assistant trainer. In 1919 he succeeded Ernest Edwards as senior trainer and played his part to the full as Burnley finished as First Division runners up at the end of his first season. In 1920-21 Burnley FC took their place as England's premier club with Charlie Bates again a key member of the team behind the team. A qualified chiropodist, Bates' career also included acting as trainer to the full England side when Turf Moor hosted the international fixture against Wales in 1927.

Charlie Bates suddenly left Turf Moor in 1934, later joining Newport County as trainer before he returned to live in Burnley where he remained for the rest of his days.

RIP

The season finished with a victory at Plymouth, with three unbeaten games, unusual in itself and with the team in mid-table. League attendances had been much better than in recent campaigns but the three games in the FA Cup, particularly the huge crowd against Arsenal, the second biggest gate ever at Turf Moor, with record receipts, had significantly helped the club's financial situation, as of course had the sale of Tommy Lawton and Harry Hubbick.

Charlie Fletcher
top scorer from the left wing

1936-37 - Second Division

		P	W	D	L	F	A	Pts
1	Leicester C	42	24	8	10	89	57	56
2	Blackpool	42	24	7	11	88	53	55
3	Bury	42	22	8	12	74	55	52
4	Newcastle U	42	22	5	15	80	56	49
5	Plymouth A	42	18	13	11	71	53	49
6	West Ham U	42	19	11	12	73	55	49
7	Sheffield U	42	18	10	14	66	54	46
8	Coventry C	42	17	11	14	66	54	45
9	Aston Villa	42	16	12	14	82	70	44
10	Tottenham H	42	17	9	16	88	66	43
11	Fulham	42	15	13	14	71	61	43
12	Blackburn R	42	16	10	16	70	62	42
13	BURNLEY	42	16	10	16	57	61	42
14	Barnsley	42	16	9	17	50	64	41
15	Chesterfield	42	16	8	18	84	89	40
16	Swansea T	42	15	7	20	50	65	37
17	Norwich C	42	14	8	20	63	71	36
18	Nottingham F	42	12	10	20	68	90	34
19	Southampton	42	11	12	19	53	77	34
20	Bradford PA	42	12	9	21	52	88	33
21	Bradford C	42	9	12	21	54	94	30
22	Doncaster R	42	7	10	25	30	84	24

1936-37

Managed by Selection Committee

Division Two (13th)

		Date			Opponents	Result		h/t	Goalscorers/times	Opp. goal times
	1	Aug	29	h	NOTTINGHAM F	W	3-0	0-0	Fletcher 50, Lawton (2) 62, 70	
	2	Sep	5	a	Chesterfield	L	1-4	1-1	Lawton 8	41, 48, 63, 79
	3		7	h	FULHAM	L	0-2	0-0		68, 89
	4		12	h	ASTON VILLA	L	1-2	1-2	Gastall 4	27, 42
	5		14	h	PLYMOUTH A	W	2-0	0-0	Gastall 55, Brocklebank 67	
	6		19	a	Bradford C	W	3-1	1-0	Fletcher 43, Gastall (2) 48, 78	72
	7		21	a	Fulham	L	0-2	0-1		44, 83
	8		26	h	SWANSEA T	D	0-0	0-0		
	9	Oct	3	a	Southampton	D	1-1	1-0	Brocklebank 16	88
	10		10	h	TOTTENHAM H	W	3-1	2-0	Lawton (3) 1, 25, 48	70
	11		17	a	Blackpool	L	0-2	0-1		17, 59
	12		24	h	BLACKBURN R	D	0-0	0-0		
	13		31	a	Bury	L	1-3	0-2	Gastall 78	38, 40, 73
Hancock's last game	14	Nov	7	h	LEICESTER C	D	0-0	0-0		
	15		14	a	West Ham U	W	2-0	0-0	Lawton (2) 59, 78	
	16		21	h	NORWICH C	W	3-0	2-0	Toll (2) 3, 83, Lawton 30	
	17		28	a	Newcastle U	L	0-3	0-1		2, 49, 53
	18	Dec	5	h	BRADFORD	D	2-2	2-0	Toll 1, Lawton 30	57, 59
	19		12	a	Barnsley	D	1-1	1-0	Fletcher 43	87
	20		19	h	SHEFFIELD U	W	1-0	0-0	Lawton 55	
	21		25	h	DONCASTER R	W	3-0	1-0	Fletcher 34p, Miller (2) 75, 82	
	22		26	a	Nottingham F	W	2-1	1-0	Brocklebank 44, Fletcher 57	58
Tommy Lawton's last game	23		28	a	Doncaster R	L	0-2	0-1		16, 65
	24	Jan	2	h	CHESTERFIELD	W	3-1	2-1	Richardson 8, Fletcher 30, Toll 87	42
	25		9	a	Aston Villa	D	0-0	0-0		
	26		23	h	BRADFORD C	W	3-0	2-0	Fletcher 21p, Mackie 43og, Stein 75	
	27	Feb	6	h	SOUTHAMPTON	L	1-3	1-2	Toll 11	14, 41og, 67
	28		11	a	Swansea T	L	0-3	0-1		42, 50, 69
	29		13	a	Tottenham H	L	0-3	0-2		22, 35, 65
	30		24	h	BLACKPOOL	W	3-0	0-0	Fletcher (2) 50, 87p, Stein 54	
	31		27	a	Blackburn R	L	1-3	1-1	Stein 16	33, 64, 88
	32	Mar	6	h	BURY	L	1-2	1-1	Brocklebank 44	5, 67
	33		13	a	Leicester C	L	3-7	1-2	Gastall 35, Brocklebank 81, Fletcher 87	15,36,60,65,71,74,75
	34		20	h	WEST HAM U	W	2-1	1-1	Fletcher 10, Toll 48	20
	35		26	h	COVENTRY C	D	3-3	2-2	Toll (2) 2, 48, Fletcher 38	8, 22, 68
	36		27	a	Norwich C	D	2-2	1-2	Pake 35, Toll 78	7, 30
	37		30	a	Coventry C	W	1-0	1-0	Brocklebank 16	
	38	Apr	3	h	NEWCASTLE U	L	0-3	0-2		15, 30, 85
	39		10	a	Bradford	L	0-2	0-1		30, 54
	40		17	h	BARNSLEY	W	3-0	2-0	Brocklebank (2) 4, 38, Rayner 69	
	41		24	a	Sheffield U	D	1-1	1-0	Brocklebank 29	65
	42	May	1	a	Plymouth A	W	1-0	1-0	Miller 5	

FA Cup

	3	Jan	16	a	Aston Villa	W	3-2	2-1	Toll (2) 12, 32, Brocklebank 51	44, 69
	4		30	h	BURY	W	4-1	2-1	Fletcher 12, Stein 25, Brocklebank 59, Toll 68	16p
Hubbick's last game	5	Feb	20	h	ARSENAL	L	1-7	1-4	Richardson 26	13,15,20,22,56,63,87

Final, Sunderland 3-1 Preston N E, at Wembley.

Other first team matches (friendlies and/or as detailed)

				Opponents			Goalscorers	
Lancs Cup	Sep	16	a	Manchester U	L	4-5	Kilcar (2), Fletcher, Pake	1st team !

Att.	Pos	Hetherington	Richmond	Hubbick	Hindmarsh	Johnson	Robinson	Carson	Brocklebank	T Lawton	Kilcar	Fletcher	Hancock	Gastall	Woodruff	Hornby	Rayner	Storey	Pinkerton	Clacher	W Miller	Stein	W S Smith	Toll	J Oliver	Richardson	Adams	Nevin	Pake	Fisher	Chester					
11,498		1	2	3	4	5	6	7	8	9	10	11																								1
14,762		1	2	3	4	5	6	7	8	9	10	11																								2
9,998		1	2	3	4	5	6	7	8	9	10	11																								3
16,098		1	2	3	4	5	6		8		10	11	7	9																						4
8,725	16	1	2	3	4		6		8			11	7	9	5	10																				5
10,221		1	2	3			6		8			11		9	5	10	4	7																		6
9,967	15	1	2	3			6		8			11		9	5	10	4	7																		7
12,131	16	1	2	3			6		8			11		9	5		4	7	10																	8
16,066	15	1	2	3			4		8	9				7	5					6	10	11														9
20,447	12	1	2	3			4		8	9				7	5					6	10	11														10
22,529	14	1	2	3			4		8	9				7	5					6	10	11														11
32,567	13	1	2	3	4		6		8	9				7	5						10	11														12
21,721	16	1	2	3			4		8	9				7	5						10	11	6													13
10,208	18	1	2	3			4		8	9		11	7		5						10		6													14
19,464	14	1	2	3			6			9		11		7	5		4				10			8												15
9,352	9	1	2	3			6			9		11		7	5		4				10			8												16
27,465	12	1	2	3			6			9		11		7	5		4				10			8												17
7,360	11	1	2				6	7		9		11			5		4				10			8	3											18
7,086	10	1	2	3				7		9		11			5		4			6	10			8												19
10,905	10	1	2	3				7	10	9		11			5		4			6				8												20
21,295		1	2	3					8	9		11			5		4			6	10	7														21
21,340		1	2	3					8	9		11			5		4			6	10	7														22
8,140	9	1	2	3					8	9		11			5		4			6	10	7														23
8,476	9	1	2	3			6		10			11			5		4					7		8		9										24
37,691	9		2	3			6		10			11			5		4					7		8		9	1									25
8,461	8		2	3			6		10			11			5		4					7		8		9	1									26
13,345	9		2	3			6		10			11			5		4					7		8		9	1									27
6,018	10		3									11			5		4				10	7	6	8		9	1	2								28
30,288	11		2			5	6		10			11									4	7		8			1	3	9							29
9,051	10		2				3					11		9	5		4				10	7	6				1			8						30
18,240	12		2				3					11		9	5		4				10	7	6				1			8						31
9,006	13	1	2				6		10			11			5		4					7			3	9				8						32
19,747	14	1	3						10			11		9	5		4			6		7								8	2					33
8,455	14		3				6		10			11			5		4					7		8		9	1				2					34
9,982	14		3						10			11			5		4			6		7		8			1		9		2					35
15,792			3									11			5		4			6	10	7		8			1		9		2					36
20,240	13		3						10			11			5		4			6		7		8			1	2	9							37
10,574	14		3						10			11			5		4			6		7		8			1	2	9							38
9,697	14		3		6							11			5		4				10	7		9			1	2		8						39
4,919	14		3				2		9			11			5	10	4				8	7	6				1									40
12,412	14		3				2		9			11			5	10	4				8	7	6				1									41
9,915			3				2		9			11			5	10	4				8	7	6				1									42
Appearances		26	42	26	7	5	30	6	32	18	4	37	3	16	37	6	30	3	1	13	23	27	8	18	2	7	16	5	5	5	4					
Goals (57)									9	11		12		6			1				3	3		9		1			1						1	og

Att.	Pos	Hetherington	Richmond	Hubbick	Hindmarsh	Johnson	Robinson	Carson	Brocklebank	T Lawton	Kilcar	Fletcher	Hancock	Gastall	Woodruff	Hornby	Rayner	Storey	Pinkerton	Clacher	W Miller	Stein	W S Smith	Toll	J Oliver	Richardson	Adams	Nevin	Pake	Fisher	Chester					
44,000			2	3			6		10			11			5		4					7		8		9	1									3
28,404			2	3			6		10			11			5		4					7		8		9	1									4
54,445			2	3			6		10			11			5		4					7		8		9	1									5
Appearances			3	3			3		3			3			3		3					3		3		3	3									
Goals (8)									2			1										1		3		1										

1937-38

Transfer activity was fairly subdued in the summer of 1937, although former England winger Arthur Cunliffe was signed from Middlesbrough. Another new arrival was a 17 year old inside forward from the North East who, in the years ahead, was destined to become one of the giants of Burnley FC in the glory days to come at Turf Moor, a man who would lead the Clarets to the ultimate prize in English club football, the League Championship.

The name of that young man was Harry Potts.

Newcomer Harry Potts
a young man with a big future at Turf Moor

The season began with, in the main, promising displays and results at Turf Moor but poor performances away from home. The campaign's first away victory, 3-2 at bottom club Plymouth in mid-October, was immediately followed by the first home defeat, a shambolic display against Chesterfield. Changes were needed and following the surprise transfer of goalscoring winger Charles Fletcher to Plymouth, two 17 year olds were promoted, demonstrating that the future of Burnley FC lay very much in the hands of the youngsters. First Len Martindale at half back then Fred Taylor on the right wing more than held their own at senior level, indeed Taylor became only the second Burnley player in nearly fifty years to score twice on his League debut in a 3-0 victory against Norwich.

Jimmy Stein hit a hat-trick in a 4-0 success at Turf Moor against Southampton but the only other victory of 1937 for the fans to cheer was a scrambled 1-0 win against Fulham on Christmas Day, with another new signing, William Robson from Stoke, on target.

The New Year began with a crushing defeat at Bury, with the Burnley Express describing Burnley's 'amazing mediocrity' as 'too bad to be true'. The Turfites then demonstrated their infuriating inconsistency with a deserved 1-1 draw at Sheffield Wednesday in the FA Cup, easily overcoming the Tykes 3-1 in the replay, Bob Brocklebank scoring twice. High riding Coventry were beaten 2-0 at Turf Moor before a visit to Chesterfield in the FA Cup fourth round. A bright start and a penalty from Willie Miller had the travelling fans singing but it was another false dawn, the Spirites scored three times, a last minute goal from Robson was mere consolation and a visit to Wembley would have to wait for another year.

The disappointment of the FA Cup exit was soon forgotten after a hard earned point at Nottingham Forest and a thoroughly deserved 2-1 win against Newcastle at Turf Moor. At the end of January 1938 the Turfites were still in the top six and just perhaps in with a slim chance of promotion.

A 1-3 defeat at Luton came next however, plenty of decent approach play but little punch up front. A late goal from William Robson just about clinched the points against Barnsley and with a trip to struggling Stockport to come followed by a visit from bottom club Plymouth the fans were certain there were four more points to be won.

Unfortunately the Burnley players chose the next two games to perform at their very worst. Stockport, managed by former Turf Moor idol Bob Kelly, swept aside a feeble Turfites' team, almost strolling to a 3-1 victory, with Bob Brocklebank's late goal a mere consolation. If that was bad the display against Plymouth was even worse, described by the Burnley Express as 'an exhibition that this time did not even bear the stamp of mediocrity'. Not for the first time a struggling club easily overcame Burnley on their own ground, winning 2-0, both goals coming from Charles Fletcher who, only weeks before had been a firm favourite amongst the Turf Moor faithful.

Older fans of both Burnley and Aston Villa were saddened to learn of the death of Alex Leake over the weekend that, but for Villa's appearance in the FA Cup semi final, the clubs would have met at Turf Moor.

OBITUARY
ALEXANDER LEAKE
DIED 29 MARCH 1938, AGED 66.

The transfer of Alex Leake from Aston Villa to Burnley in 1907 was a major coup for a side then struggling in Division Two. Born in Small Heath in 1871, Leake had played over 350 games for both Birmingham clubs, earning five full England caps and collecting an FA Cup winners medal with Villa in 1905. He was 36 when he moved to Turf Moor but still supremely fit and a natural leader, soon assuming the Burnley captaincy. Mild-mannered, articulate and always a perfect gentleman, Alex Leake was a wonderful influence on and off the field during his time at Turf Moor which ended in 1910 when he returned to the Midlands to begin a coaching career. After some years in the doldrums, the end of the Edwardian decade was to see a dramatic improvement in the fortunes of Burnley FC. Although he left Turf Moor before the real glory days arrived, Alex Leake' contribution to the club's future success was enormous and his arrival in East Lancashire was certainly one of the real milestones in Burnley FC history.

RIP

The postponed match against League leaders Villa was re-arranged for the following midweek and the performance of the Burnley team, as if in tribute to a departed hero, was as exhilarating as it had been woeful just a few short weeks before against Plymouth. On a wet and slippery pitch Villa, destined to be promoted as Champions, were swept aside after the tonic of an early goal from Willie Miller. Miller later helped himself to a second goal and Bob Brocklebank finished it off with a fine solo effort two minutes from time.

Immediately after the clash with Villa there was another new arrival at Turf Moor when former England wing half Tommy Gardner was signed. Gardner had been at Villa Park since 1934 but had not been a regular in the Villa side for some time and the Burnley Directors had kept in touch with their Villa counterparts for over a year. Tommy Gardner had a reputation as a long throw expert and, in fact, had won competitions amongst footballers with his huge throws. It was only after Gardner arrived at Turf Moor that Burnley were told that they couldn't play him in any of the season's remaining matches. Even though promotion was only a remote possibility there was still a chance that the Turfites could finish in the top four and qualify for talent money. New rules stipulated that players signed after the transfer deadline were not eligible in these circumstances so, for the time being, it was Reserve team football for Tommy Gardner.

Bob Brocklebank
ever present and top scorer

Without Gardner, West Ham and Manchester United, another team on its way back to the top flight, were both beaten at Turf Moor although three days later, United had their revenge, handing out a 4-0 walloping to the Turfites at Old Trafford.

The curtain came down at Turf Moor with Burnley's fifth successive home victory, a comfortable 3-1 win against Blackburn, good enough to finally banish the memory of the debacle against Plymouth, which in fairness, was one of only two home defeats that season.

Even after a rather disappointing end to the campaign, three defeats in the last four games, the Burnley fans had still enjoyed their best season since relegation to the Second Division in 1930. Not only was the sixth place finish the highest in eight years, the supporters had seen some quality football, particularly against the better sides in the Division. The victory against eventual Champions Aston Villa was reckoned to be Burnley's best performance for years and both Manchester United and Sheffield United, who finished just behind Villa, were also beaten at Turf Moor. The inconsistency was still there however and, in truth, the Turfites were never quite up with the real pacesetters, although eight points dropped against the bottom three clubs didn't help! Bob Brocklebank and Willie Miller had been very much the main goalscorers and in fact had scored exactly half of the season's League and FA Cup goals between them.

The fans were confident that better times were ahead and with more young players ready to emerge the Turf Moor future looked bright.

1937-38 - Second Division

		P	W	D	L	F	A	Pts
1	Aston Villa	42	25	7	10	73	35	57
2	Manchester U	42	22	9	11	82	50	53
3	Sheffield U	42	22	9	11	73	56	53
4	Coventry C	42	20	12	10	66	45	52
5	Tottenham H	42	19	6	17	76	54	44
6	BURNLEY	42	17	10	15	54	54	44
7	Bradford PA	42	17	9	16	69	56	43
8	Fulham	42	16	11	15	61	57	43
9	West Ham U	42	14	14	14	53	52	42
10	Bury	42	18	5	19	63	60	41
11	Chesterfield	42	16	9	17	63	63	41
12	Luton T	42	15	10	17	89	86	40
13	Plymouth A	42	14	12	16	57	65	40
14	Norwich C	42	14	11	17	56	75	39
15	Southampton	42	15	9	18	55	77	39
16	Blackburn R	42	14	10	18	71	80	38
17	Sheffield W	42	14	10	18	49	56	38
18	Swansea T	42	13	12	17	45	73	38
19	Newcastle U	42	14	8	20	51	58	36
20	Nottingham F	42	14	8	20	47	60	36
21	Barnsley	42	11	14	17	50	64	36
22	Stockport C	42	11	9	22	43	70	31

1937-38

Managed by Selection Committee

Division Two (6th)

		Date			Opponents	Result		h/t	Goalscorers/times	Opp. goal times
	1	Aug	28	h	BURY	W	2-0	2-0	Fletcher 7, Brocklebank 40	
	2		30	a	Tottenham H	L	0-4	0-2		20, 43, 43, 75p
	3	Sep	4	a	Coventry C	L	0-1	0-0		77
	4		6	h	TOTTENHAM H	W	2-1	0-0	Fletcher 58p, Richardson 82	75
	5		11	h	NOTTINGHAM F	D	0-0	0-0		
	6		13	h	SHEFFIELD U	W	2-0	2-0	Fisher 33, Miller 44	
	7		18	a	Newcastle U	D	2-2	2-0	Fisher 5, Brocklebank 12	47p, 79
	8		20	a	Sheffield U	L	1-2	0-1	Fletcher 79	32, 47
	9		25	h	LUTON T	W	3-2	1-1	Fletcher 16p, Hornby 59, Brocklebank 83	37, 75
	10	Oct	2	a	Barnsley	D	2-2	1-0	Storey 38, Miller 72	75, 79
	11		9	h	STOCKPORT C	D	0-0	0-0		
	12		16	a	Plymouth A	W	3-2	2-1	Miller 4, Brocklebank (2) 7, 67	17, 51
	13		23	h	CHESTERFIELD	L	0-2	0-1		42, 82
Fletcher's last game	14		30	a	Swansea T	L	1-3	0-2	Brocklebank 86	12, 14, 70
	15	Nov	6	h	NORWICH C	W	3-0	1-0	Taylor (2) 42, 53, Gastall 87	
	16		13	a	Aston Villa	D	0-0	0-0		
	17		20	h	SOUTHAMPTON	W	4-0	0-0	Stein (3) 49, 67, 89, Miller 63	
	18		27	a	West Ham U	L	0-1	0-0		75
Hetherington's last game	19	Dec	4	h	BRADFORD	D	1-1	1-1	Chester 30	10
	20		11	a	Blackburn R	D	3-3	1-0	Miller 28, Stein 55p, Storey 81	49, 71, 84
	21		18	h	SHEFFIELD W	D	1-1	1-0	Storey 4	70
	22		25	h	FULHAM	W	1-0	0-0	Robson 59	
	23		27	a	Fulham	L	1-2	1-1	Miller 44	4, 82
	24	Jan	1	a	Bury	L	0-4	0-1		44, 55, 63, 89
	25		15	h	COVENTRY C	W	2-0	1-0	Miller 43p, Storey 67	
	26		26	a	Nottingham F	D	1-1	0-0	Miller 73	70
	27		29	h	NEWCASTLE U	W	2-1	1-0	Miller 9, Hornby 64	85
	28	Feb	5	a	Luton T	L	1-3	0-1	Miller 62p	4, 50, 58
	29		12	h	BARNSLEY	W	1-0	0-0	Robson 82	
	30		19	a	Stockport C	L	1-3	0-3	Brocklebank 78	15og, 17, 38
	31		26	h	PLYMOUTH A	L	0-2	0-2		18, 34
	32	Mar	5	a	Chesterfield	W	1-0	1-0	Brocklebank 39	
	33		12	h	SWANSEA T	W	2-0	1-0	Taylor 3, Miller 85p	
	34		19	a	Norwich C	L	0-1	0-1		35
	35	Apr	2	a	Southampton	D	0-0	0-0		
	36		5	h	ASTON VILLA	W	3-0	1-0	Miller (2) 7, 72, Brocklebank 88	
	37		9	h	WEST HAM U	W	2-0	1-0	Hornby 20, Brocklebank 57	
	38		15	h	MANCHESTER U	W	1-0	0-0	Brocklebank 58	
	39		16	a	Bradford	L	1-3	0-2	Brocklebank 87	4p, 23, 48
	40		18	a	Manchester U	L	0-4	0-0		47, 77, 86, 88
Stein's last game	41		23	h	BLACKBURN R	W	3-1	1-0	Brocklebank (2) 21, 75, Stein 53	78
	42		30	a	Sheffield W	L	1-2	1-2	Storey 8	3, 22p

FA Cup

	Date			Opponents	Result		h/t	Goalscorers/times	Opp. goal times
3	Jan	8	a	Sheffield W	D	1-1	1-0	Stein 38	89
rep		11	h	SHEFFIELD W	W	3-1	2-1	Brocklebank (2) 31, 33, Hornby 62	12
4		22	a	Chesterfield	L	2-3	1-1	Miller 16p, Robson 90	39, 48, 71

Final, Preston N E 1-0 Huddersfield T after extra time, at Wembley.

Other first team matches (friendlies and/or as detailed)

	Date			Opponents	Result		Goalscorers
Lancs Cup	Apr	25	h	BLACKPOOL	W	2-0	Richardson, Bray
Lancs Cup	May	2	a	Everton	W	2-1	Martindale (2)
Lancs Cup semi		11	a	Southport	L	1-2	Brocklebank

Att.	Pos	Adams	Robinson	Richmond	Rayner	Woodruff	W S Smith	Cunliffe	Toll	Brocklebank	W Miller	Fletcher	Richardson	Johnson	Lumsden	Fisher	Storey	Hornby	Stein	Pinkerton	Chester	Martindale	F Taylor	Gastall	Hetherington	Robson	
16,221		1	2	3	4	5	6	7	8	9	10	11															1
13,766		1	2	3	4	5	6	7	8	9	10	11															2
25,608		1	2	3	4	5	6	7		8	10	11	9														3
11,287	13	1	2	3	4	5	6	7		8	10	11	9														4
11,161		1	2	3	4	5	6	7		10	8	11	9														5
7,847	13	1		3	4	2	6			9	10	11		5	7	8											6
14,982		1	2	3	4	5	6			9						8	7	10	11								7
8,270	10	1	2	3	4	5				9		11				8	7	10		6							8
14,073	9	1	2	3	4	5	6			9	8	11					7	10									9
15,358	9	1	2		4	5	6			9	8	11					7	10			3						10
16,423	9	1	2		4	5	6	7		9	8	11						10			3						11
15,417	8	1	2		4	5	6	7		9	8	11						10			3						12
9,329	8	1	2		4	5	6	7		9	8	11						10			3						13
10,111	10	1	2			5	6			9	8	11					7	10			3	4					14
11,073	7	1	2				6			10	8			5					11		3	4	7	9			15
37,167	8	1	2				6			10	8			5					11		3	4	7	9			16
11,717	6	1	2				6			10	8			5					11		3	4	7	9			17
21,607	8	1	2				6			10	8			5					11		3	4	7	9			18
9,453	8		2				6			10	8			5					11		3	4	7	9	1		19
15,136	8	1	2				6			10	8			5			7		11		3	4				9	20
13,722	6	1	2				6			10	8			5			7		11		3	4				9	21
27,584		1	2				6			10	8			5					11		3	4	7			9	22
18,008	7	1		2			6			9	8			5			7		11	10	3	4					23
21,717	8	1	2		4		6			10	8		9	5			7		11		3						24
9,821	6	1	2				6			10	8			5			7	11			3	4				9	25
5,761	6	1	2			5	6			10	8							11	7		3	4				9	26
10,550	6	1	2			5	6			10	8							11	7		3	4				9	27
14,957	7	1	2			5	6			10	8							11	7		3	4				9	28
12,178	6	1	2			5	6	7		10	8							11			3	4				9	29
14,097	7	1	2		4	5	6			10	8						7	11			3					9	30
9,315	9	1	2	3		5	6			10	8						7	11				4				9	31
12,208	7	1	2				6			9	8			5		10		11			3	4	7				32
9,050	6	1	2				6			9	8			5		10		11			3	4	7				33
10,072	7	1	2				6			9	8			5		10		11			3	4	7				34
15,113		1	2				6			9	8			5		10	7	11			3	4					35
16,704	6	1	2				6			9	8			5		10	7	11			3	4					36
11,173	6	1	2				6			9	8			5		10	7	11			3	4					37
28,459	6	1	2				6			9	8			5		10		11			3	4	7				38
10,180		1	2		6					9	8			5		10		11			3	4	7				39
35,808	6	1	2		6	4				9	8			5		10	11				3	7					40
14,139	6	1	2		6					9	8			5		10	7		11		3	4					41
19,571		1	2		6					9	8			5		10	7	11			3	4					42
Appearances		41	40	11	19	21	37	9	2	42	40	13	4	23	1	14	18	24	15	2	32	27	11	5	1	10	
Goals (54)										14	13	4	1			2	5	3	5		1		3	1		2	

Att.	Pos	Adams	Robinson	Richmond	Rayner	Woodruff	W S Smith	Cunliffe	Toll	Brocklebank	W Miller	Fletcher	Richardson	Johnson	Lumsden	Fisher	Storey	Hornby	Stein	Pinkerton	Chester	Martindale	F Taylor	Gastall	Hetherington	Robson	
33,006		1	2				6			10	8		9	5				11	7		3	4					3
25,933		1	2				6			10	8			5				11	7		3	4				9	rep
21,620		1	2				6			10	8			5			7	11			3	4				9	4
Appearances		3	3				3			3	3		1	3			1	3	2		3	3				2	
Goals (6)										2	1							1	1							1	

1938-39

In July 1938 Burnley FC lost one of its most influential supporters with the death of 61 year old former Chairman Harry Windle whilst on holiday in Bournemouth. Windle's 23 year association with the club had included Turf Moor's finest achievements and he had been instrumental in Burnley's rise from Second Division obscurity to one of the most powerful clubs in the land.

Joe Taylor, another dedicated Burnley FC servant, also passed away as the new season was about to kick off.

OBITUARY
JOSEPH TAYLOR
DIED 21 AUGUST 1938, AGED 64.

Joe Taylor was born in Burnley in 1874, played all his professional football for his home town club and was the first Burnley player to top 300 League appearances.

A prolific scorer in local football, Taylor was converted to a half back after he joined Burnley as a professional in 1893. He made his League debut in January 1895 and very soon became a virtual fixture in the Burnley side. A hard-tackling defender, Joe Taylor was one of the quickest players in the team with very few opposing wingers able to beat him for speed. He experienced relegation in 1897 but played in every game at centre half as Burnley swept to the Second Division Championship in 1897-98 and were promoted back to the top flight.

After over 350 senior games Joe Taylor retired in 1907 but retained his connection with Burnley, for many years assisting the Turf Moor groundsman.

RIP

After a draw at Coventry on the new season's opening day and three successive victories at Turf Moor, Burnley sat proudly at the top of the Second Division table. It had been the best start to a campaign for 27 years and the supporters soon began dreaming of First Division football. Alas it didn't last, following four games unbeaten it was four games without a win and after a 0-4 drubbing at Norwich, themselves relegation-bound, the Turfites were back in tenth place.

19 year old wing half George Bray made his first senior appearance as Luton were beaten 3-2 at Turf Moor then, in mid-October 1938, Burnley added to their growing ex-Aston Villa contingent with the signing of centre forward James Clayton for a fee estimated to be around £3,500. Clayton immediately endeared himself to the Turf Moor faithful with two goals on his home debut in an enthralling local derby against Blackburn. In front of Turf Moor's biggest crowd of the campaign, Clayton scored twice inside 16 minutes only for Rovers to pull it back to 2-2 with a quarter of an hour to go. Then, with just eight minutes left, Ronnie Hornby took advantage of a defensive mix-up to slot home the winner against the team who would be crowned as Second Division Champions at the end of the season. There was a depressing run to come for the Burnley fans, with only one more victory to cheer before the Christmas period. That was against bottom club Tranmere at Turf Moor and once again James Clayton took centre stage with a hat-trick in a 3-1 victory. An interesting debutant in the Tranmere side was Willie Miller, who had been signed from Burnley just days earlier. On Christmas Eve 1938 Coventry were beaten 1-0 at Turf Moor with James Clayton again on target. This time however he also made headlines for the wrong reasons after he was sent off along with Coventry's centre half George Mason after the two were involved in a violent confrontation. Over the Christmas period, another of Turf Moor's post war stars, Jack Billingham, made his League debut at Tottenham. Billingham had been signed in the summer from Bristol City and was soon to make his mark in front of goal. He was followed into Burnley's Second Division side by Billy Morris, a 20 year old inside forward from Llandudno Town who was also destined to be part of the Turf Moor success story in the years to come.

Ronnie Hornby
regular left winger in 1938-39

After Turf Moor interest in the FA Cup was very quickly ended at Notts County, Burnley found some form with Newcastle and Norwich both beaten at Turf Moor. Jack Billingham was on target in both games and he scored again in a 2-1 victory at West Brom, the Turfites' first away win in almost a year. Burnley were now eighth, just five points from the top of a very congested League table. With a little consistency there could just have been a genuine promotion push but it was not to be. There were only two more victories until April 1939 and the chance, if it was ever a reality, had gone.

Doomed Tranmere were beaten 3-0 in Burnley's first-ever match at Prenton Park then, on Easter Saturday 1939, West Ham were the visitors to Turf Moor. The Hammers were beaten by the only goal of the match from Bob Brocklebank in what would be Burnley's last League victory for more than seven years.

Two weeks later the curtain came down on another Turf Moor season after another goal from Bob Brocklebank had not been enough to beat Sheffield Wednesday who won 2-1. As the players trooped off the Turf Moor pitch after the final whistle to the applause of the fans little did anyone realise that Turf Moor would not be staging another Football League match until August 1946.

It had been a disappointing end to the season, the final three matches all lost and just one victory at Turf Moor since February. However the Burnley fans were confident that the future of their club appeared to be in the safe hands, or feet, of the most promising crop of young players for years. During the latter part of the campaign Burnley's first team had been liberally sprinkled with teenagers, who had graduated from the "A" team under the watchful eye of Ray Bennion. There were many more waiting for their chance, including Harry Potts, still only 18, who had had his first taste of success during 1938-39 as Burnley's "A" team had won the Championship of the West Lancashire League.

Jack Billingham
signed from Bristol City

Sadly Potts and the rest of the Turf Moor youngsters would have to wait rather longer than they expected for their first taste of League football and many of the players who appeared in the final matches of the 1938-39 League programme would never again don a Burnley shirt in Football League action.

Just twenty years after the Football League had kicked off again following the War that had been supposed to end all Wars, clouds of conflict were once again about to darken over Europe.

Ted Adams
ever present in goal

1938-39 - Second Division

		P	W	D	L	F	A	Pts
1	Blackburn R	42	25	5	12	94	60	55
2	Sheffield U	42	20	14	8	69	41	54
3	Sheffield W	42	21	11	10	88	59	53
4	Coventry C	42	21	8	13	62	45	50
5	Manchester C	42	21	7	14	96	72	49
6	Chesterfield	42	20	9	13	69	52	49
7	Luton T	42	22	5	15	82	66	49
8	Tottenham H	42	19	9	14	67	62	47
9	Newcastle U	42	18	10	14	61	48	46
10	West Bromwich A	42	18	9	15	89	72	45
11	West Ham U	42	17	10	15	70	52	44
12	Fulham	42	17	10	15	61	55	44
13	Millwall	42	14	14	14	64	53	42
14	BURNLEY	42	15	9	18	50	56	39
15	Plymouth A	42	15	8	19	49	55	38
16	Bury	42	12	13	17	65	74	37
17	Bradford PA	42	12	11	19	61	82	35
18	Southampton	42	13	9	20	56	82	35
19	Swansea T	42	11	12	19	50	83	34
20	Nottingham F	42	10	11	21	49	82	31
21	Norwich C	42	13	5	24	50	91	31
22	Tranmere R	42	6	5	31	39	99	17

1938-39

Managed by Selection Committee

Division Two (14th)

	No	Date			Opponents	Result		h/t	Goalscorers/times	Opp. goal times
	1	Aug	27	a	Coventry C	D	1-1	0-1	Hornby 65	6og
	2		30	h	SOUTHAMPTON	W	2-1	0-0	F.Taylor 50, Brocklebank 86	57
	3	Sep	3	h	NOTTINGHAM F	W	2-1	1-1	Martindale 18, Hornby 49	25
	4		5	h	FULHAM	W	2-0	0-0	Gardner 57, Brocklebank 68	
	5		10	a	Newcastle U	L	2-3	1-3	Hornby 25, Martindale 73	4, 29, 34
	6		12	a	Fulham	D	0-0	0-0		
	7		17	h	WEST BROMWICH A	L	0-3	0-1		22, 46, 80
	8		24	a	Norwich C	L	0-4	0-2		3, 37, 75, 77
	9	Oct	1	h	LUTON T	W	3-2	2-1	Miller 23, Hornby 40, Rayner 85	20, 80
	10		8	a	Plymouth A	L	0-1	0-1		28
	11		15	h	BLACKBURN R	W	3-2	2-0	Clayton (2) 2, 16, Hornby 82	51, 75
	12		22	a	Millwall	D	1-1	0-0	Hornby 59	48
	13		29	h	BURY	L	0-1	0-0		67
	14	Nov	5	a	Bradford	D	2-2	2-2	F.Taylor 10, Clayton 28	22, 38
	15		12	h	SWANSEA T	D	1-1	0-0	F.Taylor 46	70
Willie Miller's last game	16		19	a	Chesterfield	L	2-3	0-1	Miller 65p, F.Taylor 80	23, 57, 88
	17		26	h	TRANMERE R	W	3-1	2-1	Clayton (3) 13, 23p, 75	21
	18	Dec	3	a	West Ham U	L	0-1	0-1		30
	19		10	h	MANCHESTER C	D	1-1	1-0	Gardner 21	73
	20		17	a	Sheffield W	L	1-4	0-1	Clayton 60	19og, 58, 75, 79p
	21		24	h	COVENTRY C	W	1-0	1-0	Clayton 12	
	22		26	h	TOTTENHAM H	W	1-0	1-0	A.Taylor 12	
	23		27	a	Tottenham H	L	0-1	0-1		42
	24		31	a	Nottingham F	D	2-2	1-2	Rayner 11, Clayton 88	39, 40
Rayner's last game	25	Jan	2	a	Sheffield U	D	1-1	0-1	Billingham 54	30
	26		14	h	NEWCASTLE U	W	2-0	1-0	Billingham 17, Dryden 60	
	27		28	h	NORWICH C	W	3-0	2-0	Brocklebank 20, Billingham 43, Hornby 48	
	28	Feb	1	a	West Bromwich A	W	2-1	1-1	Billingham 35, Gardner 60	22
	29		4	a	Luton T	L	0-1	0-0		51og
	30		11	h	PLYMOUTH A	W	1-0	1-0	Billingham 40	
	31		18	a	Blackburn R	L	0-1	0-1		25
	32		25	h	MILLWALL	W	2-0	1-0	Brocklebank (2) 31, 56	
	33	Mar	4	a	Bury	L	0-1	0-0		82
	34		11	h	BRADFORD	D	0-0	0-0		
Richmond's last game	35		18	a	Swansea T	L	0-4	0-4		16, 17, 30, 40
	36		25	h	CHESTERFIELD	L	1-2	1-2	Brocklebank 44	9, 42
	37	Apr	1	a	Tranmere R	W	3-0	3-0	Knight 9, Dryden 11, Billingham 20	
	38		7	h	SHEFFIELD U	L	2-3	1-1	Knight 7, Billingham 55	14, 68, 81
Chester's last game	39		8	h	WEST HAM U	W	1-0	0-0	Brocklebank 53	
	40		15	a	Manchester C	L	0-2	0-0		47, 51
Alick Robinson's last game	41		22	h	SHEFFIELD W	L	1-2	1-2	Brocklebank 11	19, 43
last games for Adams, Gardner & Brocklebank	42		29	a	Southampton	L	1-2	1-0	Clayton 17	57, 79

FA Cup

Rd	Date			Opponents	Result		h/t	Goalscorers/times	Opp. goal times
3	Jan	7	a	Notts C	L	1-3	0-2	Brocklebank 75	37, 39, 59

Final, Portsmouth 4-1 Wolverhampton W, at Wembley.

Other first team matches (friendlies and/or as detailed)

	Date			Opponents	Result		Goalscorers
Football League Jubilee match	Aug	20	a	Blackburn R	L	2-3	Dryden, Miller
Lancs Cup	Sep	21	a	Everton	L	1-6	Brocklebank

Att.	Pos	Adams	Richmond	Chester	Gardner	Johnson	W Smith	F Taylor	W Miller	Brocklebank	Fisher	Hornby	Woodruff	Martindale	Rayner	Marshall	Robinson	Bray	Clayton	A Taylor	Billingham	Dryden	Morris	G Knight	
25,830		1	2	3	4	5	6	7	8	9	10	11													1
13,334		1	2	3	4	5	6	7	8	9	10	11													2
11,534		1		3	4	5	6	7	8	9		11	2	10											3
13,892	top	1		3	4	5	6	7	10	9		11	2	8											4
30,824		1		3	4	5	6	7	10	9		11	2	8											5
11,966	4	1		3	4	5	6	7		9		11	2	10	8										6
15,990	8	1		3	4	5	6	7		9	10	11	2	8											7
13,345	10	1			4	5	6	7		9		11	2	10	8	3									8
11,699	7	1		3	4	5		7	10	9		11			8		2	6							9
16,996	11	1		3	4	5		7	10	8		11					2	6	9						10
29,254	10	1		3	4	5		7	8	10		11					2	6	9						11
33,975	10	1		3	4			7	10	8		11	5				2	6	9						12
17,719	12	1		3	4			7	10	8		11	5				2	6	9						13
12,408	12	1		3	8			7				11	5	4			2	6	9	10					14
12,128	13	1		3	8			7				11	5	4			2	6	9	10					15
13,780	14	1			8			7	10			11	5	4		3	2	6	9						16
9,354	13	1			8			7		10		11	5	4		3	2	6	9						17
18,759	16	1			8			7		10		11	5	4		3	2	6	9						18
24,096	14	1			8			7		10		11	5	4		3	2	6	9						19
12,251	16	1			8			7		10		11	5	4		3	2	6	9						20
12,382		1			8			7		10		11	5	4		3	2	6	9						21
15,629		1			8					10		11	5		4	3	2	6	9	7					22
30,276	14	1			8					10		11	5		4	3	2	6	9		7				23
11,456		1			8						10	11	5		4	3	2	6	9		7				24
20,958	13	1			8			7		10		11	5		4	3	2	6			9				25
12,745	11	1			8			7		10			5	4		3	2	6			9	11			26
10,345	11	1			4			7		10		11	5			3	2	6			9		8		27
7,831	8	1			4			7		10		11	5			3	2	6			9		8		28
13,547	10	1			4			7		10		11	5			3	2	6			9		8		29
12,893	8	1			4			7		10			5			3	2	6			9	11	8		30
30,223	10	1			4			7		10		11	5			3	2	6			9		8		31
10,312	9	1						7		9		11	5	4		3	2	6					8	10	32
13,950	11	1	3		9			7				11	5	4			2	6					8	10	33
8,473	11	1	3					7		9		11	5	4			2	6					8	10	34
10,357	11	1	3					7		9		11	5	4			2	6					8	10	35
8,095	12	1			8			7		9		11	5	4		3	2	6						10	36
6,759	12	1			4					8		11	5			3	2	6			9	7		10	37
18,104	12	1			4					8		11	5			3	2	6			9	7		10	38
10,420	12	1		2	4			7		8		11	5			3		6			9			10	39
19,230	14	1			4			7		10		11	5			3	2	6			9		8		40
9,953	14	1			4			7		10		11	5			3	2	6			9		8		41
4,169	14	1			2			7		10		11	5	4		3		6	9				8		42
Appearances		42	5	15	39	11	8	37	11	37	4	40	37	21	7	25	32	34	16	3	14	4	12	8	
Goals (50)					3			4	2	8		7		2	2				10	1	7	2		2	

Att.	Pos	Adams	Richmond	Chester	Gardner	Johnson	W Smith	F Taylor	W Miller	Brocklebank	Fisher	Hornby	Woodruff	Martindale	Rayner	Marshall	Robinson	Bray	Clayton	A Taylor	Billingham	Dryden	Morris	G Knight	
14,500		1			8			7		10		11	5		4	3	2	6			9				3
Appearances		1			1			1		1		1	1		1	1	1	1			1				
Goals (1)										1															

1939-40

With the approach of the new season overshadowed by the tense situation in Europe, plans were being laid at Turf Moor for yet another determined push for promotion back to the top flight. Defender Joe Loughran was signed from Luton, as was Tom Smith, who was actually a native of Higham. Jack Hays arrived from Bradford and 30-year-old goalkeeper Harry Morton was transferred from Everton.

Jack Hays
Burnley career on hold

Once again the ever-optimistic Burnley fans were confident of Turf Moor success and were looking forward to seeing the players appearing in numbered shirts for the first time. The numbering experiment had first been tried in an international trial match at Turf Moor in 1937 and had now been sanctioned for use in Football League matches.

Ronnie Hornby opened Burnley's account for the new campaign in a 1-1 draw with Coventry at Turf Moor. However even as the Turfites' match in Birmingham was taking place on the second Saturday of the season, German troops had already invaded Poland. The following morning, on 3 September 1939, War was declared. Just two weekends of league football had been possible before the competition was suspended after the Government banned all sports gatherings where crowds would congregate.

Within two weeks however some football grounds "in neutral areas" were allowed to re-open and the Burnley directors very quickly arranged a friendly fixture with Accrington. It was the first game to be played under wartime conditions and, although all players' contracts had been cancelled, both teams were able to field more or less full-strength sides, even though most of the players had been working full time, many on shifts.

Early in October 1939 the Football League announced the introduction of regional leagues, to minimise travelling, with Burnley to play in a 12-club North West section. Although points would be played for, there would be no promotion or relegation, nor would there be trophies or medals.

As time went on, more and more players were joining the forces. Clubs quite often found it difficult to fulfil fixtures with full strength teams, sometimes borrowing players from other clubs and even recruiting surplus players from their opponents. At Christmas 1939 Burnley played Barnsley at Turf Moor on Christmas Day, losing 2-3 with a strong team. For the return fixture, at Oakwell on Boxing Day, Burnley had to borrow two Blackburn players and use a Barnsley reserve called Allison who had played against Burnley the day before! Our friend Allison scored the Turfites' only goal in a 1-5 defeat.

In March 1940 the announcement of a Football League War Cup competition was well received. In the early stages ties were to be played over two legs, with aggregate scores determining the winners, and ties drawn over two legs going to a replay. Although the concept of away goals being of additional value was still a long way off, there were certainly plans for an early version of "sudden death extra time" if teams were still level at the end of extra time in a replay.

OBITUARY
THOMAS WILKINSON BOYLE
DIED JANUARY 1940, AGED 51.

Tommy Boyle was arguably the most influential player ever to pull on a Burnley FC shirt, captaining the team in the golden years at Turf Moor either side of World War One.

Boyle was born in Barnsley in 1888 and was signed by his home-town team in 1904. He very quickly made a huge impact at Oakwell, one of the shining stars in a galaxy of talent uncovered in that dour Yorkshire mining area during the Edwardian era. He led Barnsley to the FA Cup final of 1910 before he was seen by the Burnley Directors as the man they needed to help bring success to Turf Moor. Tommy Boyle was undoubtedly the fulcrum around which the great Burnley sides of the next dozen years would revolve. Soon after his arrival in 1911 he was appointed club captain and in 1913, following the signing of George Halley, a page of Burnley FC history was written "Halley, Boyle and Watson". Boyle led the Clarets to FA Cup triumph in 1914, accepting the famous old trophy from King George V before the clouds of War darkened over Europe. In 1920 Burnley finished as runners-up in Division One then, in 1921, Tommy Boyle led the Clarets to the League Championship, the ultimate measure of achievement in club football. Although Boyle left Turf Moor in 1922 his legacy lives on and he is still the only Claret ever to lead his team to both League Championship and FA Cup glory.

Tommy Boyle – Captain supreme!

RIP

No extra time or replays were needed in Burnley's cup matches as Chester were beaten easily in the first round and Blackpool, almost as easily, were the Turfites' conquerors in the second round. Burnley finished their North West Regional League fixtures with a comfortable 7-0 victory against Accrington at Turf Moor, their third win in four games, to finish sixth of twelve. The football authorities had done their best to organise a competitive programme under difficult conditions understandably imposed by a Government with far more serious issues than football to address. At the end of that first wartime season it has to be said that supporters had, in general, demonstrated a lukewarm response to regional football. Along with the rest of the population the fans were impatient for things to return to normal.

They would come to realise that normality was still some way in the future.

1939-40

		Date			Opponents	Result		Goalscorers
Football League Jubilee match	1	Aug	19	h	BLACKBURN R	W	3-1	Clayton, Dryden, Hornby
Div 2 fixture, later voided	2		26	h	COVENTRY C	D	1-1	Hornby
Div 2 fixture, later voided	3	Sep	2	a	Birmingham	L	0-2	
friendly	4		16	h	ACCRINGTON S	W	2-1	Clayton, Bray
friendly	5		23	a	Bradford C	W	4-1	Woodruff, Brocklebank (3)
friendly	6		30	h	BURY	L	1-3	Martindale
friendly	7	Oct	7	a	Bury	L	2-4	Brocklebank (2)
friendly	8		14	a	Everton	L	0-4	
	9		21	h	BOLTON W	D	1-1	Brocklebank
	10		28	a	Preston N E	L	1-2	Taylor
Lancs Cup	11	Nov	4	h	EVERTON	L	2-3	Knight, Jackson og
	12		11	a	Bury	L	0-5	
	13		18	h	CARLISLE U	W	8-0	Knight (2), Clayton (4), Brocklebank, Taylor
	14		25	a	Oldham A	L	1-3	Brocklebank
	15	Dec	2	h	ROCHDALE	W	3-1	Clayton, Knight (2)
	16		9	a	Blackburn R	L	0-1	
friendly	17		16	h	MANCHESTER C	L	0-2	
	18		23	h	BLACKPOOL	D	1-1	Knight
friendly	19		25	h	BARNSLEY	L	2-3	Dryden p, Brocklebank
friendly	20		26	a	Barnsley	L	1-5	Allison
	21	Jan	6	a	Barrow	L	2-5	Knight, Moir
	22		20	h	SOUTHPORT	W	7-3	Brocklebank (2), Taylor, Hornby (2)1p, Knight (2)
	23	Feb	24	h	PRESTON N E	W	1-0	Taylor
friendly	24	Mar	2	a	Manchester C	L	1-3	Wood
	25		9	h	BURY	L	1-2	Wood
	26		16	a	Carlisle U	W	4-3	Wood (2), Brocklebank, Hornby
friendly	27		22	h	HUDDERSFIELD T	L	2-3	Hornby (2) 1p
	28		23	h	OLDHAM A	W	4-3	Wood (2), Taylor, Brocklebank
	29		30	a	Rochdale	D	1-1	Wood
	30	Apr	6	h	BLACKBURN R	D	0-0	
	31		10	a	Bolton W	L	1-5	Hornby
	32		13	a	Blackpool	L	0-5	
Football League War Cup	33		20	a	Chester	W	3-1	Morris (2), Hornby
FL War Cup, agg 6-1	34		27	h	CHESTER	W	3-0	Brocklebank, Hornby (2)
Football League War Cup	35	May	4	h	BLACKPOOL	L	1-2	Morris
FL War Cup, agg 1-5	36		11	a	Blackpool	L	1-3	Billingham
	37		21	h	BARROW	W	2-0	Hornby (2)
	38		25	a	Southport	D	1-1	Knight
	39		29	a	Accrington S	W	2-1	Knight (2)
	40	Jun	1	h	ACCRINGTON S	W	7-0	Hornby (2), Nuttall (2), Knight p, Brocklebank, Gardner

Matches 9 to 10, 12 to 16, 18, 21 to 23, 25 to 26, 28 to 32 and 37 to 40 were in the North West Regional League
Playing record P22 W9 D5 L8 F48 A43 Pts 23, Burnley finished 6th of 12 clubs

1940-41

For the second season under wartime conditions, clubs were again to play in geographical sections but this time the division was just between North and South. Clubs were invited, as far as possible, to arrange their own fixtures, not necessarily playing every other club in their section home and away. No points were at stake and, after each round of matches, league tables would be prepared showing teams in order of goal average only.

The campaign began on the last day of August with a 2-1 victory against the old enemy thanks to goals from Ronnie Hornby and Bob Brocklebank. In the Burnley side was 18-year old Neil Dougall, son of trainer Billy, who would go on to play for Scotland but whose league career would flourish away from Turf Moor after the war. One of the Clarets' post war stars, Peter Kippax, also 18, was another youngster about to make his mark. Kippax had already played for Burnley's first team in May 1940 but really announced his arrival with twelve goals in just nine games, including a hat trick at Southport and all four in an enthralling 4-3 victory against Bury at Turf Moor.

Taking centre stage at Turf Moor in Burnley's Lancashire Cup-tie against Everton in January 1941 was another youngster, this time one who had left Burnley behind. Tommy Lawton was making his first Turf Moor appearance since leaving for Everton in 1937 and scored twice in a 3-2 win for the Merseysiders.

By now a familiar face was back between the sticks at Turf Moor. Herman Conway had left Burnley for West Ham in 1934, becoming the regular custodian at Upton Park, and he had helped the Hammers to win the first Football League War Cup in June 1940, Blackburn being beaten 1-0 in the Wembley final. Conway was now back in Burnley as the Depot Superintendent of the local ARP Headquarters.

Another familiar face to re-appear was Alick Robinson, still registered as a Burnley player, but who had been working in Bury and turning out for the Shakers on a regular basis. Robinson had now been recalled by Burnley, following Jack Marshall's call-up by the RAF, and soon showed he had lost none of his versatility when he played two games in Burnley's goal when no regular custodians were available.

The second leg of Burnley's Lancashire Cup quarter final against Everton at Goodison Park finally took place in early May, more than three months after the original scheduled date. The Turfites were 2-3 down from the first leg and were not expected to progress but an early goal from youngster Frank Coates made the aggregate score 3-3. At the end of 90 minutes the teams were still level and, after an extra time period of thirty minutes, it was still 3-3. The Lancashire FA had decided they would follow the lead of the Football Association and introduce "sudden death extra time" with the game continuing until the next goal was scored. After 129 minutes of an historic cup-tie, it was Coates again who got the ball into Everton's net to bring the game to an abrupt end, Burnley winning 4-3 on aggregate.

In the semi final the Turfites were up against Blackpool and an end-to-end game was decided by two second half penalties. Herman Conway produced a brilliant save to deny Blackpool the lead, then Bob Brocklebank stroked his spot kick into the Seasiders' net just eleven minutes from time to earn Burnley a place in the final. The Blackpool goalkeeper on that day was a man who would go on to become a huge Turf Moor favourite in the years to come, becoming almost a permanent fixture in the Burnley team and establishing his own unique appearance record. The man in question was of course Jimmy Strong, then a Walsall player but stationed in Blackpool with the RAF.

Burnley went into the Turf Moor final against Manchester United bang in form, with five successive victories behind them and unbeaten in their last nine games. Almost 10,000 people turned up, most of them confident that the Turfites could lift the trophy for the first time in 26 years, and only the second time in the club's history. For the second successive match, and Lancashire Cup tie, Burnley came up against a goalkeeper who would go on to appear for them, Jack Breedon played in the Turfites' FA Cup campaign of 1945-46.

As against Blackpool, Bob Brocklebank had the chance to score from the spot, but Breedon was equal to his weak effort. United were already 1-0 in front and Burnley's chance, the nearest they got to collecting silverware during the war, had gone.

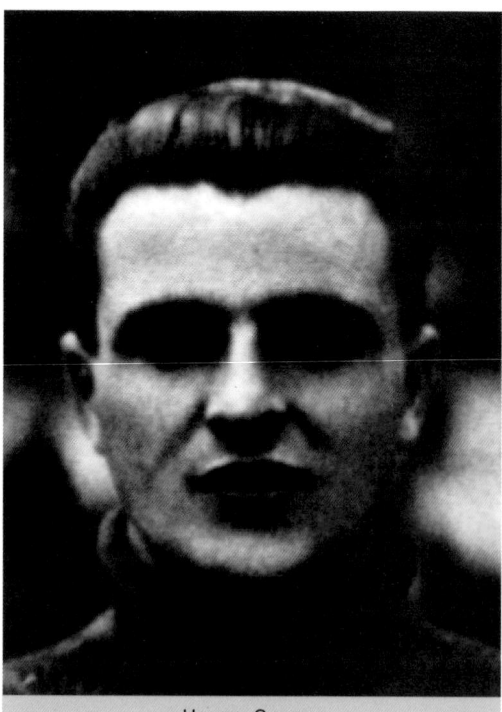

Herman Conway
back in goal for Burnley after nearly seven years

1940-41

Note	No.	Date			Opponents	Result		Goalscorers
	1	Aug	31	h	BLACKBURN R	W	2-1	Hornby, Brocklebank
	2	Sep	7	a	Rochdale	W	2-1	Cooke, Brocklebank
	3		14	a	Bury	D	0-0	
	4		21	h	CREWE A	W	5-1	Cooke (3), Brocklebank, Martindale
	5		28	a	Preston N E	L	2-6	Martindale, Brocklebank p
	6	Oct	5	h	STOCKPORT C	D	2-2	Wilkinson (2)
	7		12	h	MANCHESTER U	L	0-1	
	8		19	a	Oldham A	L	1-6	Hornby
	9		26	h	OLDHAM A	W	2-1	Brocklebank, Kippax
	10	Nov	2	a	Manchester U	L	1-4	Kippax
	11		9	a	Blackburn R	D	1-1	Gardner
	12		16	a	Chester	D	0-0	
	13		23	a	Rochdale	L	0-1	
	14		30	h	BURY	W	4-3	Kippax (4)
	15	Dec	7	a	Stockport C	L	0-1	
	16		14	a	Chester	W	4-3	Kippax (2), Brocklebank (2)
	17		21	a	Southport	W	3-1	Kippax (3)
	18		25	h	MANCHESTER C	D	2-2	Brocklebank p, Kippax
	19		28	h	PRESTON N E	W	2-0	Knight, Brocklebank
also Lancs Cup	20	Jan	25	h	EVERTON	L	2-3	Brocklebank (2)
	21	Feb	1	h	BLACKBURN R	W	2-1	Knight, Bright
Football League War Cup	22		15	a	Bolton W	L	1-3	Brocklebank
FL War Cup, agg 3-5	23		22	h	BOLTON W	D	2-2	Hornby, Bright
	24	Mar	1	a	Oldham A	L	0-2	
	25		8	h	OLDHAM A	W	4-0	Knight (2), Brocklebank (2)
	26		15	a	Blackburn R	L	2-3	Knight (2)
	27		22	a	Halifax T	D	2-2	Coates, Bright
	28		29	a	Sheffield W	W	2-0	Bright, Hornby
	29	Apr	5	h	SHEFFIELD W	W	2-0	Bright, Kippax
	30		12	h	BOLTON W	D	2-2	Kippax, Coates
	31		14	a	Bolton W	W	2-0	Hornby, Coates
	32		19	h	HALIFAX T	W	3-1	Bright, Kippax, Brocklebank
	33		26	a	Huddersfield T	W	3-0	Brocklebank, Coates, Kippax
also Lancs Cup, aet, agg 4-3	34	May	3	a	Everton	W	2-0	Coates (2)
also Lancs Cup semi	35		10	h	BLACKPOOL	W	1-0	Brocklebank p
also Lancs Cup final	36		17	h	MANCHESTER U	L	0-1	
	37		24	a	Blackpool	L	0-3	

Matches 1 to 21 and 24 to 37 were in the North Regional League
Playing record P35 W17 D7 L11 F62 A53, points were not awarded, positions were decided on goal average only
Burnley finished 14th of 36 clubs

Matches 20 and 34 to 36 also counted as Lancashire Cup ties

1941-42

For the new season clubs were once again to play in geographical sections but this time with two separate competitions, one up to, and one after, Christmas 1941. The first competition was to be decided on points won after 18 games, home and away against nine selected opponents, while the second competition was also to incorporate the Football League War Cup.

Burnley began the new season with an excellent 3-2 victory at Halifax thanks to two goals from Peter Kippax and one from Bob Brocklebank, the club's two leading marksmen in 1940-41. In goal for Burnley, as he had been for a few games during the previous season, was Preston's England international Harry Holdcroft.

OBITUARY
GEORGE HALLEY
DIED 18 DECEMBER 1941, AGED 54.

Born in Ayrshire in 1887, George Halley joined Kilmarnock from junior football in 1907 before treading the well-worn path to England in 1911, when he was transferred to Bradford. After less than two seasons at Park Avenue he was seen by Burnley manager John Haworth as the player to complete a magnificent team and, on 15 March 1913, Burnley's half back line, for the very first time, read Halley, Boyle and Watson. After playing in all the Clarets' FA Cup games when the famous old trophy came to Turf Moor in 1914 Halley was still a regular in the Burnley team after the Great War. He was an ever-present as the Burnley juggernaut carried all before it in the triumphant League Championship campaign of 1920-21, until he developed pneumonia in February 1921 and missed the rest of the campaign. His illness also cost George Halley the chance of a richly-deserved Scottish international cap. He left Turf Moor in 1922 to join Southend but eventually settled in Burnley, his adopted town, where he will always be remembered as a member of one of the greatest half-back lines of all time, Halley, Boyle and Watson.

Burnley FC Director Harry Duckworth, a Board Member since 1926 and one of very few Directors to have previously played for the club, passed away on 30 December 1941.
RIP

At the end of October Burnley came up against Bury and, a week after a 3-3 draw at Gigg Lane, the Shakers came to Turf Moor for the return. Bury started well with two goals in the first three minutes but then they were hit by a devastating performance from the Turfites who were 7-2 in front by half time. There was a hat-trick from Bob Brocklebank and two goals from Peter Kippax as Burnley eventually ran out 9-3 winners, the club's highest score in wartime football. Just weeks later it was Burnley's turn to be on the wrong end of a hammering, Blackpool crushing the Turfites 9-0 at Bloomfield Road. The Seasiders went on to finish at the top of the first competition in the North Regional League, with Burnley in 19th place.

For the second competition Burnley were placed in a qualifying group with five other clubs who would be played home and away. Other clubs were in similar groups and at the end of those group matches the leading 32 clubs in the North would go forward to the knockout stages of the Football League War Cup.

Burnley's cup campaign got off to a bad start with a 1-5 defeat at Bradford City but after their ten games in the qualifying competition, and goal average boosted by a 6-0 win against Stockport, they just about squeezed into the knockout stages, finishing 31st out of 32. Before the knockout stage began, a number of other matches had been arranged, including two against Blackpool and the Seasiders continued where they had left off earlier in the season, racking up 19 more goals against the luckless Harry Holdcroft.

After Blackburn ended Burnley's interest in the Lancashire Cup, Liverpool put paid to any Football League War Cup glory with a 7-1 aggregate win in the first knockout round.

For the Turfites' last game of their season, at Preston, goalkeeper Gordon Bentley was home on leave but with Harry Holdcroft also available, Bentley was selected at centre forward. He was the eighth different player to lead the attack during the campaign but it was not a fairy tale end to the season for Bentley or Burnley, North End winning 2-0.

Although Burnley had now finished their fixture programme, some of Burnley's players decided to make themselves available to other clubs whose seasons had not yet come to an end. Arthur Woodruff and Tommy Gardner, both of whom had played in all but one of Burnley's games during the season, appeared in Blackburn's Lancashire Cup semi final at Liverpool, Gardner scoring in a 3-2 victory. Gardner also played in the final, at Blackpool, but, as in the 1941 final, he was in the losing camp, Rovers going down 1-7 to a strong Blackpool side that included Stan Mortensen and a certain Stanley Matthews!

Winger Peter Kippax
again amongst the goals

1941-42

		Date			Opponents	Result		Goalscorers
	1	Aug	30	a	Halifax T	W	3-2	Brocklebank, Kippax (2)
	2	Sep	6	h	HALIFAX T	L	0-1	
	3		13	h	ROCHDALE	W	3-1	Gardner, Kippax, Whalley
	4		20	a	Rochdale	D	1-1	Brocklebank
	5		27	a	Preston N E	L	1-2	Kippax
	6	Oct	4	h	PRESTON N E	W	1-0	Brocklebank
	7		11	h	SOUTHPORT	W	4-2	Kippax, Brocklebank (2), Gardner
	8		18	a	Southport	D	1-1	Brocklebank
	9		25	a	Bury	D	3-3	Whalley, Brocklebank, Hornby
	10	Nov	1	h	BURY	W	9-3	Salmon, Kippax (2), Whalley (2), Hornby, Brocklebank (3)
	11		8	h	BOLTON W	W	2-1	Hornby, Brocklebank p
	12		15	a	Bolton W	L	1-3	Gardner
	13		22	a	Blackburn R	L	2-3	Kippax (2)
	14		29	h	BLACKBURN R	D	0-0	
	15	Dec	6	h	BLACKPOOL	D	2-2	Clayton, Gardner
	16		13	a	Blackpool	L	0-9	
	17		20	a	Oldham A	L	2-5	Gardner, Kippax
	18		25	h	OLDHAM A	D	1-1	Waddington
also Football League War Cup	19		27	a	Bradford C	L	1-5	Hornby
also Football League War Cup	20	Jan	3	h	BRADFORD C	W	3-1	Jackson, Brocklebank p, Bright
also Football League War Cup	21		10	h	MANCHESTER C	L	1-2	Hornby
also Football League War Cup	22		17	a	Manchester C	L	0-5	
also Football League War Cup	23		24	h	STOCKPORT C	W	6-0	Gardner (2), Jackson, Brocklebank (2), Kippax
also Football League War Cup	24		31	a	Stockport C	D	0-0	
also Football League War Cup	25	Feb	7	a	Everton	L	2-3	Gardner, Kippax
also Football League War Cup	26		14	h	EVERTON	W	1-0	Gardner
also Football League War Cup	27		21	a	Sheffield W	L	1-3	Gardner
also Football League War Cup	28		28	h	SHEFFIELD W	W	3-0	Brocklebank, Kippax, Millership og
	29	Mar	7	a	Blackpool	L	0-13	
also Lancs Cup	30		14	a	Blackburn R	L	2-6	Brocklebank (2)
	31		21	h	BLACKPOOL	L	0-6	
also Lancs Cup, agg 4-6	32		28	h	BLACKBURN R	W	2-0	Jackson, Brocklebank
also FL War Cup, KO	33	Apr	4	h	LIVERPOOL	L	0-3	
also FL War Cup, KO, agg 1-7	34		6	a	Liverpool	L	1-4	Gutteridge og
	35		11	h	HUDDERSFIELD T	W	3-0	Waddington (2), Brocklebank
	36		25	h	PRESTON N E	W	3-0	Bright, Jackson (2)
	37	May	2	a	Preston N E	L	0-2	

Matches 1 to 18 were in the North Regional League, first competition
Playing record P18 W6 D6 L6 F36 A40 Pts18, Burnley finished 19th of 38 clubs

Matches 19 to 37 were in the North Regional League, second competition
Playing record P19 W7 D1 L11 F29 A53 Pts15, Burnley finished 20th of 22 clubs

Matches 19 to 28 also counted in the Football League War Cup, qualifying competition
Matches 33 to 34 also counted in the Football League War Cup, knockout competition

Matches 30 and 32 also counted as Lancashire Cup ties

1942-43

OBITUARY
WILLIAM BANNISTER
DIED 25 MARCH 1942, AGED 53.

A native of Burnley Lane, Billy Bannister was a pit worker at Barden Colliery when, as a 20-year-old, he was given a trial at Turf Moor in 1899. He impressed enough to be immediately signed as a professional and within months he was in Burnley's First Division side. Bannister's progress was remarkably swift and he very soon made the centre half position his own. At the end of only his first full season he was chosen for his country and in March 1901 lined up alongside James Crabtree, Steve Bloomer and other famous names in England's 6-0 demolition of Wales at St. James' Park. Turf Moor finances dictated a transfer to Bolton for Billy Bannister in 1901, and he later played for Woolwich Arsenal and Leicester before returning for another brief spell at Turf Moor. After retirement he became a publican in Leicester.

RIP

Arrangements for the new season were similar to 1941-42, two separate competitions taking place, with the second embracing the qualifying stages of the Football League War Cup. Burnley began the campaign with two matches against Blackburn, sharing six goals with Rovers at Ewood Park on the opening day. The Turfites' first goal of the season was scored by newcomer Hugh O'Donnell who was a Blackpool player and a physical training instructor in the RAF. Born in Fifeshire, O'Donnell, who had also appeared for Preston, had begun his professional career with Celtic and had been a member of the Celts' Scottish Cup winning side of 1933.

After three wins and a draw, and ten goals in the first four matches, a successful season seemed to be beckoning. However it was something of a false dawn with only two more victories registered before February and only five more all season!

Harry Jackson hit the only hat-trick of the season in a 5-0 victory against Rochdale at Turf Moor, before Blackpool, the strongest team around in 1942, were Burnley's opponents in late November. Goals from local youngster Waddington, Tommy Gardner and Ronnie Hornby gave the Turfites an astonishing 3-0 lead, also going 4-1 ahead before the Seasiders rallied to share the points at 4-4. Liverpool, also very strong, were beaten 3-1 in Burnley's next home match but, a week later, exacted their revenge with a 9-2 victory at Anfield.

A 1-1 draw against Halifax at Turf Moor on Christmas Day ended the first competition with Burnley in 32nd place out of 48 clubs who competed. Leading the way again were Blackpool who had dropped just three points, one of them at Burnley in the 4-4 draw when the Turfites had been so impressive. Liverpool were second, one of only three defeats suffered by them was at Burnley early in December.

No victories, two draws and just two goals in the first six qualifying matches virtually put paid to Turf Moor hopes of progress in the Football League War Cup. Burnley's only victory in that round of qualifying matches was out of context with a depressing run of performances, an exciting 5-4 success against Southport at Turf Moor in February 1943. Only Burnley's second win since early December 1942 came in a 4-1 victory against Bolton at Turf Moor, with Peter Kippax scoring twice in one of his very few games for Burnley that season. In the Lancashire Cup the Turfites were drawn against Blackpool Services, a team of footballers of varying abilities stationed in Blackpool. They were too good for Burnley however and the men from Turf Moor went down 3-5 on aggregate.

Burnley ended the second league competition with a welcome 2-0 win against Rochdale at Turf Moor thanks to a penalty from Tommy Gardner and a goal from Alick Robinson, playing at centre forward for the first time. The curtain came down on what had been a very disappointing campaign with a 0-3 defeat in a friendly at Preston with Burnley having to borrow two North End juniors.

Although there was no success for Burnley's first team the reserves brought back some silverware to the town after a 6-3 win against Farnworth team Moss Rovers in the final of the Lancashire FA Junior Shield. The final took place at Bolton's Burnden Park ground and the young Turfites had to come back from two goals down to earn a well-deserved victory. None of the youngsters in that team made it to football's professional ranks after the war but the goalkeeper, Maurice Tate, became a well-known steeplejack in Burnley and a prominent local councillor.

The Burnley youngsters with the Lancashire FA Junior Shield

1942-43

		Date			Opponents	Result		Goalscorers
	1	Aug	29	a	Blackburn R	D	3-3	O'Donnell, Bright, Brocklebank
	2	Sep	5	h	BLACKBURN R	W	1-0	Taylor og
	3		12	h	OLDHAM A	W	3-0	Gardner (2), Bright
	4		19	a	Oldham A	W	3-1	Waddington, O'Donnell, Bright
	5		26	a	Everton	L	1-2	Jackson
	6	Oct	3	h	EVERTON	L	1-4	Waddington
	7		10	h	STOCKPORT C	D	0-0	
	8		17	a	Stockport C	L	1-4	O'Donnell
	9		24	a	Bolton W	L	4-7	Brocklebank, Bright, Kippax, O'Donnell
	10		31	h	BOLTON W	L	1-2	Bright
	11	Nov	7	h	ROCHDALE	W	5-0	Waddington (2), Jackson (3)
	12		14	a	Rochdale	L	1-2	Waddington
	13		21	h	BLACKPOOL	D	4-4	Waddington, Gardner, Hornby, Webster
	14		28	a	Blackpool	L	1-5	Bright
	15	Dec	5	h	LIVERPOOL	W	3-1	McEwan (2), Hornby
	16		12	a	Liverpool	L	2-9	Bright, Jackson
	17		19	a	Halifax T	D	0-0	
	18		25	h	HALIFAX T	D	1-1	Bright
also Football League War Cup	19		26	a	Blackburn R	L	1-3	Gardner
also Football League War Cup	20	Jan	2	h	BLACKBURN R	D	0-0	
also Football League War Cup	21		9	h	BURY	D	0-0	
also Football League War Cup	22		16	a	Bury	L	0-3	
also Football League War Cup	23		23	a	Bolton W	L	1-4	Jackson
also Football League War Cup	24		30	h	BOLTON W	L	0-1	
also Football League War Cup	25	Feb	6	h	SOUTHPORT	W	5-4	Manning, Robinson (2), Crawshaw, Gardner p
also Football League War Cup	26		13	a	Southport	L	0-2	
also Football League War Cup	27		20	a	Rochdale	L	2-4	Crawshaw, Manning
also Football League War Cup	28		27	h	ROCHDALE	D	1-1	Crawshaw
	29	Mar	6	a	Bolton W	L	1-4	Crawshaw
	30		13	h	BOLTON W	W	4-1	Brindle, Gardner, Kippax (2)
Lancs Cup	31		20	a	Blackpool Services	L	1-3	Martindale
Lancs Cup, agg 3-5	32		27	h	BLACKPOOL SERVICES	D	2-2	Jackson (2)
	33	Apr	3	a	Rochdale	L	0-4	
	34		10	h	ROCHDALE	W	2-0	Gardner p, Robinson
friendly	35		17	a	Preston N E	L	0-3	

Matches 1 to 18 were in the North Regional League, first competition
Playing record P18 W5 D5 L8 F35 A45 Pts15, Burnley finished 32nd of 48 clubs

Matches 19 to 30 and 33 to 34 were in the North Regional League, second competition
Playing record P14 W3 D3 L8 F17 A31 Pts9, Burnley finished 51st of 54 clubs

Matches 19 to 28 also counted in the Football League War Cup, qualifying competition
Burnley failed to qualify for the knockout stages

1943-44

A welcome return to Turf Moor for Tommy Lawton

Before the start of the new season there was a challenge match at Turf between a Burnley Xl and a National Police and Civil Defence Xl. Tommy Lawton and Stanley Matthews were originally chosen to boost the Burnley team against strong opposition which included Bob Brocklebank who was a member of Burnley's Police Force. In the event Matthews was unable to turn out but the Burnley crowd were more than happy to welcome one of their own, Tommy Lawton, who was still a big favourite at Turf Moor. All admission monies were for the benefit of Police Charities and a healthy crowd enjoyed an exciting game, which finished 5-2 to the Services team. The "Tommies" Gardner and Lawton scored Burnley's goals but the real star of the day was Preston's Scottish international Jimmy Dougall, brother of the Burnley trainer and Neil Dougall's uncle, of course. Jimmy Dougall scored four goals, giving a hard time to the Turfites' centre half, no mean performer himself but second best on the day, Arthur Woodruff. In goal for Burnley that day was Jimmy Strong who had played a few games for the Turfites as a guest but was now to become a regular in the team.....for a further nine years!

Bob Brocklebank was back in the Burnley team for the opening match of the season, scoring twice as Bolton were beaten 4-0 at Turf Moor. Peter Kippax and an own goal from ex Claret Harry Hubbick secured the points in the return at Burnden Park. When Bury were beaten 5-1 at Turf Moor, three victories and eleven goals in the three opening games of the season represented the best start for Burnley in any of the wartime campaigns. Unfortunately it didn't really last and the goals dried up, as did the points.

Oldham were beaten at Turf Moor thanks to a single goal from Alick Robinson and goals from Brocklebank and Barney Reid, a regular guest player from Queens Park Rangers, gave the Turfites a 2-0 win against Rochdale. In November 1944 Blackpool came calling and, as usual, were expected to give the Turfites a hiding. The Seasiders had won the League's first competition in each of the previous two campaigns, and were destined to do so again. However the Burnley players were determined to make an impression and at half time were holding their own at 0-0. Then amazingly, amid wild cheers from the Turf Moor fans, the Turfites were 3-0 ahead inside fifteen minutes of the second half thanks to goals from Reid, Gardner and Tottenham guest Fred Sargent. The Blackpool team however simply took the setbacks in its stride, roared back and scored five times to win the match 5-3. Stanley Matthews, Stan Mortensen, Jock Dodds and Harry Johnston were all on target, aided by a superb exhibition of wing play from Hugh O'Donnell, who had appeared for Burnley in 1942-43.

On Christmas Day 1944 Burnley lost at home to Halifax in their final match in the first competition, to finish 24th out of 50 teams, with Blackpool, as usual, finishing at the top.

Burnley managed four victories in ten matches in the qualifying stages of the War Cup to squeeze into the knockout stages in 32nd place, out of 32, on goal average. Surprisingly two of the wins were against Blackpool but it was Bob Brocklebank's goals that made the difference in this stage of the season. Brocklebank hit a hat-trick in another big win against Bolton and four more in a 5-1 victory against Blackburn at Turf Moor. Also on the scoresheet against Bolton there was the name of a young man with a big future at Turf Moor, Harry Potts was on target with his very first senior goal for Burnley.

It was Rochdale who ended Burnley's interest in the War Cup, the Turfites going down 4-5 on aggregate in the first knockout round. Blackburn then took their own revenge with a 4-3 aggregate victory in the Lancashire Cup.

Harry Jackson scored five goals in a week in home and away victories against Bury before two high-scoring games against Manchester United brought the season to a close. Fifteen goals were scored altogether, unfortunately twelve of them found Jimmy Strong's net!

OBITUARY

HARRY CULPAN

DIED 22 AUGUST 1943, AGED 84.

Burnley-born Harry Culpan was one of the pioneers of football in the town and one of the most versatile of Burnley's early players. He was the reserve team's regular goalkeeper in the very earliest days but soon gained a first team place as a half back. He was Burnley's centre half in the club's historic victory in the very first Hospital Cup final in June 1883. Harry Culpan worked for the railways but his first love, even above football, was music and he was a member of Burnley Parish Church choir for more than 50 years.

RIP

1943-44

		Date			Opponents	Result		Goalscorers
	1	Aug	28	h	BOLTON W	W	4-0	Brocklebank (2), Gardner p, Robinson
	2	Sep	4	a	Bolton W	W	2-0	Kippax, Hubbick og
	3		11	h	BURY	W	5-1	Snowden (2), Hornby, Hart og, Rudman
	4		18	a	Bury	D	1-1	Brocklebank
	5		25	h	EVERTON	D	0-0	
	6	Oct	2	a	Everton	D	0-0	
	7		9	a	Oldham A	L	2-4	Hornby, Gardner
	8		16	h	OLDHAM A	W	1-0	Robinson
	9		23	a	Stockport C	D	1-1	Reid
	10		30	h	STOCKPORT C	D	0-0	
	11	Nov	6	a	Rochdale	L	1-3	McFarlane
	12		13	h	ROCHDALE	W	2-0	Brocklebank, Reid
	13		20	a	Blackpool	L	0-3	
	14		27	h	BLACKPOOL	L	3-5	Reid, Sargent, Gardner
	15	Dec	4	h	LIVERPOOL	L	0-1	
	16		11	a	Liverpool	D	1-1	Jackson
	17		18	a	Halifax T	D	1-1	Brocklebank
	18		25	h	HALIFAX T	L	0-1	
also Football League War Cup	19		26	h	SOUTHPORT	D	2-2	Gardner, Rudman
also Football League War Cup	20	Jan	1	a	Southport	L	1-4	Brocklebank
also Football League War Cup	21		8	a	Bolton W	L	1-2	Brocklebank
also Football League War Cup	22		15	h	BOLTON W	W	5-1	Brocklebank (3), Potts, Gardner
also Football League War Cup	23		22	h	ROCHDALE	D	2-2	Gardner, Sargent
also Football League War Cup	24		29	a	Rochdale	L	1-3	Jackson
also Football League War Cup	25	Feb	5	h	BLACKPOOL	W	2-1	Robinson, Brocklebank
also Football League War Cup	26		12	a	Blackpool	W	3-1	Potts, Watson (2)
also Football League War Cup	27		19	h	BLACKBURN R	W	5-1	Brocklebank (4), Watson
also Football League War Cup	28		26	a	Blackburn R	L	0-2	
also FL War Cup, KO	29	Mar	4	h	ROCHDALE	D	3-3	Gardner p, Brocklebank, Watson
also FLW Cup KO, aet, agg 4-5	30		11	a	Rochdale	L	1-2	Gardner
also Lancs Cup	31		18	a	Blackburn R	L	1-2	Burns
also Lancs Cup, agg 3-4	32		25	h	BLACKBURN R	D	2-2	Gardner (2)
	33	Apr	1	a	Bury	W	4-2	Jackson (3), Gardner
	34		8	h	BURY	W	3-1	Jackson (2), Watson
friendly	35		10	a	Blackpool Services	L	1-4	Jackson
	36		15	a	Manchester U	L	0-9	
	37		22	h	MANCHESTER U	D	3-3	Bright (2), Gardner

Matches 1 to 18 were in the North Regional League, first competition
Playing record P18 W5 D7 L6 F24 A22 Pts17, Burnley finished 24th of 50 clubs

Matches 19 to 34 and 36 to 37 were in the North Regional League, second competition
Playing record P18 W6 D6 L6 F39 A42 Pts18, Burnley finished 37th of 56 clubs

Matches 19 to 28 also counted in the Football League War Cup, qualifying competition
Matches 29 to 30 also counted in the Football League War Cup, knockout competition

Matches 31 to 32 also counted as Lancashire Cup ties

1944-45

OBITUARY
THOMAS BAMFORD
DIED 9 AUGUST 1944, AGED 57.

Born in Horwich in 1887, Tom Bamford signed for Burnley from Darwen in the summer of 1909. He eventually replaced the veteran Fred Barron as the Turfites' regular right back although he was equally as comfortable on the left flank. Following Burnley's promotion back to the top flight in 1913, Bamford was an ever-present in League and Cup until the outbreak of World War One and he was a key member of the magnificent Burnley side that brought the FA Cup back to Turf Moor in 1914. He was into his thirties by the time league football began again in 1919 and was unable to win back his first team place from Len Smelt. After more than 150 senior games for Burnley Tom Bamford signed for Rochdale in 1920, just as the Clarets' momentous unbeaten League run was beginning.

RIP

For the opening game of the season, against Blackburn at Turf Moor, Burnley had two Liverpool players in their ranks. Winger Bill Kinghorn who was a Scottish amateur international, and George Paterson, a Scottish junior international would both play their part in Burnley's most successful campaign of the wartime period. After a draw against Blackburn, Kinghorn and Harry Potts scored in a 2-0 victory in the Ewood Park return before Kinghorn got two more goals in a 3-1 win against Southport at Turf Moor. Newcomer William Brooks, from Wigan, scored a hat-trick as Bolton were overcome 6-3, Kinghorn on target with two more.

The season really began to take off in late November with a 5-0 victory at Accrington, Paterson and Bob Brocklebank each scoring twice. It was the start of a prolific spell in front of goal for Brocklebank who scored five goals in four days at Christmas 1944. His run included two at Ewood Park in a 4-2 victory on Christmas Day in the first game of the qualifying stages of the War Cup. Jack Dryden scored twice in his first Burnley game since 1939, in a 4-1 win in the return against Blackburn then Brooks and Oliver Burns were on target in a 2-0 success against Blackpool. Burnley had now won their last five games and were unbeaten since early November. After a 0-4 defeat at Blackpool the Turfites reeled off four more victories with thirteen goals scored and none conceded, Harry Jackson netting four in that spell.

Burnley qualified easily from the preliminary stages of the War Cup but were unfortunate enough to come up against Manchester United in the knockout stage. A crowd of nearly 14,000 at Turf Moor saw a valiant effort in the first leg but United were too strong, winning 3-2, and going though 7-2 on aggregate.

There were high hopes in the Lancashire Cup and Oldham were beaten home and away before a surprise exit at the hands of Accrington put paid to any aspirations of silverware for another season.

The war in Europe officially came to an end in the first week of May 1945 and Germany's formal surrender came in the city of Reims in northern France. Just fifteen years later the Champagne city was to become a significant part of Burnley's first European adventure. There were joyous celebrations all over Burnley and the Turfites quickly arranged a VE (victory in Europe) friendly match against Blackburn Rovers. Len Martindale put away the first Burnley goal in peacetime since war had been declared on Germany nearly seven years before and further goals from Harold Rudman and Martindale again gave the Turfites a 3-1 win.

Within days of the end of hostilities the Burnley Board made the appointment of the manager who would be charged with leading the revival at Turf Moor after many years of struggle. Cliff Britton was a Bristolian who had made his name with Everton and England in the 1930's.

The curtain came down on another Turf Moor campaign with a 5-1 victory against Tranmere and the Burnley supporters streamed away from the ground content with their football and life in general. After the final game at Preston, Burnley had finished fourth in the League's second competition, by far Turf Moor's most successful campaign since the start of the war. The fans were already eager for next season to begin.

Alick Robinson
retiring from senior football
after almost 12 years at Turf Moor

1944-45

		Date			Opponents	Result		Goalscorers
	1	Aug	26	h	BLACKBURN R	D	1-1	Reid
	2	Sep	2	a	Blackburn R	W	2-0	Potts, Kinghorn
	3		9	a	Southport	L	2-3	Gardner p, Potts
	4		16	h	SOUTHPORT	W	3-1	Kinghorn (2), Brocklebank
	5		23	h	ROCHDALE	D	2-2	Wyles, Gardner p
	6		30	a	Rochdale	L	1-3	Jackson
	7	Oct	7	a	Oldham A	L	1-3	Gardner p
	8		14	h	OLDHAM A	W	1-0	Jackson
	9		21	h	BOLTON W	W	6-3	Burns, Brooks (3), Kinghorn (2)
	10		28	a	Bolton W	L	0-4	
	11	Nov	4	a	Halifax T	L	1-2	Mignot
	12		11	h	HALIFAX T	L	1-2	Brocklebank
	13		18	h	ACCRINGTON S	D	0-0	
	14		25	a	Accrington S	W	5-0	Brocklebank (2), Patterson (2), Brooks
	15	Dec	2	a	Blackpool	W	2-0	Brooks, Potts
	16		9	h	BLACKPOOL	W	5-1	Jackson (2), Gardner, Brocklebank, Webster
	17		16	a	Preston N E	D	1-1	Gardner
	18		23	h	PRESTON N E	W	5-1	Brocklebank, Kippax, Brooks (2), Martindale
also Football League War Cup	19		25	a	Blackburn R	W	4-2	Gardner, Brocklebank (2), Kippax
	20		26	h	BRADFORD	W	4-2	Brocklebank (2), Gardner p, Bright
also Football League War Cup	21		30	h	BLACKBURN R	W	4-1	Dryden (2), Brocklebank, Gardner
also Football League War Cup	22	Jan	6	h	BLACKPOOL	W	2-0	Burns, Brooks
also Football League War Cup	23		13	a	Blackpool	L	0-4	
also Football League War Cup	24		20	a	Accrington S	W	4-0	Jackson (2), Gardner (2)
also Football League War Cup	25		27	h	ACCRINGTON S	W	3-0	Gardner, Patterson, Brocklebank
also Football League War Cup	26	Feb	3	h	ROCHDALE	W	2-0	Patterson (2)
also Football League War Cup	27		10	a	Rochdale	W	4-0	Jackson (2), Dryden (2)
also Football League War Cup	28		17	a	Preston N E	L	1-2	Gardner
also Football League War Cup	29		24	h	PRESTON N E	D	1-1	Patterson
	30	Mar	3	h	BARNSLEY	W	4-0	Patterson, Brocklebank, Brooks, Kinghorn
	31		10	a	Barnsley	L	0-2	
also Lancs Cup	32		17	a	Oldham A	W	2-1	Martindale, Patterson
also FL War Cup, KO	33		24	h	MANCHESTER U	L	2-3	Gardner, Jackson
also Lancs Cup, agg 5-2	34		29	h	OLDHAM A	W	3-1	Gardner (2), Brocklebank
also FL War Cup, KO, agg 2-7	35		31	a	Manchester U	L	0-4	
also Lancs Cup	36	Apr	7	h	ACCRINGTON S	W	1-0	Martindale
also Lancs Cup, agg 1-4	37		14	a	Accrington S	L	0-4	
	38		21	h	SHEFFIELD U	W	2-0	Brooks (2)
	39		28	a	Sheffield U	D	1-1	Smith
at Turf Moor	40	May	5	a	Bradford	D	1-1	Drury
'Victory in Europe' celebration	41		9	h	BLACKBURN R	W	3-1	Martindale (2), Rudman
	42		12	a	Tranmere R	L	2-3	Martindale (2)
	43		19	h	TRANMERE R	W	5-1	Rudman (2), Salmon, Martindale, Drury
	44		26	a	Preston N E	L	1-2	Martindale

Matches 1 to 18 were in the North Regional League, first competition
Playing record P18 W8 D4 L6 F39 A27, Burnley finished 20th of 54 clubs

Matches 19 to 44 were in the North Regional League, second competition
Playing record P26 W15 D3 L8 F56 A36, Burnley finished 4th of 60 clubs

Matches 19 and 21 to 29 also counted in the Football League War Cup, qualifying competition
Matches 33 and 35 also counted in the Football League War Cup, knockout competition

Matches 32, 34 and 36 to 37 also counted as Lancashire Cup ties

1945-46

In the weeks before the new campaign started, events in Hiroshima and Nagasaki finally brought seven years of hostilities to a total conclusion. Although football would still take some time to get completely back to normal, fans around the country knew that their teams would start to get stronger as their players began to be demobbed from the Forces.

For the new season the clubs were still to play in regional leagues, the First and Second Division clubs being divided into North and South, with 22 clubs in each Division. For the first time since 1939 the FA Cup was to be competed for as normal although there was some regionalisation in the early rounds. For this season only, the ties would be played over two legs.

In August 1945 Burnley stalwart Alick Robinson announced his retirement from professional football at the age of 39. Bob Brocklebank, another long-standing and popular Turfite, was also leaving, following his appointment as manager of Chesterfield.

William Brooks scored Burnley's first league goal of the new season but it was only a consolation in a disappointing 1-3 home defeat by Liverpool on the opening day. The Turfites then turned the tables with a 3-2 victory at Anfield with two goals from Aldershot's Oscar Hold on his Burnley debut. There was a single goal victory at Newcastle but, on the whole it was a disappointing start to the season, although Blackpool were beaten home and away in the first round of the Lancashire Cup. When Burnley won at Leeds on the first Saturday in November, it was only the third victory of the season in the the North Regional League, but the fans at Turf Moor hadn't seen a single one! The following week, at home to Leeds, there was another new face in the Turf Moor ranks, a young West Ham wing half, then appearing as a guest, but who would go on to become one of Turf Moor's favourite sons of the postwar period. His name of course was Reg Attwell.

There was at last a home victory to cheer when Bradford were beaten with goals from Billy Morris and Harry Jackson. It was Morris' first goal on his first Turf Moor appearance since 1940 and the Welshman was to be another star of the Burnley success story to come.

After a hectic Christmas programme it was time for Burnley's first FA Cup tie for seven years, a two-legged affair against Stoke. It was a short-lived run however, the Clarets going down 3-4 on aggregate. There were 16 goals in a week for the Clarets' fans to savour at Turf Moor when Huddersfield were beaten 4-3, then Middlesbrough were walloped 8-1 with a hat-trick from Harry Jackson.

At the end of February 1946 manager Cliff Britton made arguably his most significant signing when centre half Alan Brown arrived from Huddersfield. Brown was to be the lynchpin of the "Iron Curtain" defence that would carry the Turfites to postwar success and, for his first game, a friendly against the Polish RAF team, the Burnley half-back line read, for the first time "Attwell, Brown and Bray". Ironically it was Alan Brown's only game of the season for Burnley, he fell in the snow and suffered ligament damage!

The season was rather drifting to a close, with players and supporters already eagerly anticipating the return of the Football League proper. Chesterfield were beaten 3-1 at Turf Moor, Billy Morris got the only goal against Stoke and Chester were beaten in both legs of the Lancashire Cup quarter final. In the semi final, Liverpool were beaten at Anfield, an exciting tie being won 3-2 in extra time thanks to a late goal from Jack Knight.

It was a slightly disappointing end to the campaign with Sheffield United winning 1-0 as the curtain came down at Turf Moor and over 36,000 fans turning up at Maine Road for the Lancashire Cup final. Burnley were edged out again 1-0 by Manchester United but the thousands of Turfites' fans wending their way home from Manchester were not downhearted. They knew that within a few short months the Football League, the real thing, would be starting up again.

In June 1946 Burnley responded to many calls for a return to tradition by re-registering the club's colours as claret and blue, not used on a regular basis since 1935. Huge and unprecedented success had followed the original introduction of the famous old colours during the Edwardian era. Time would reveal that there was more success to come, another golden age was ahead for Burnley Football Club.

Bob Brocklebank
stalwart in peacetime and in war time

1945-46

		Date			Opponents	Result		Goalscorers
Lancs Cup	1	Aug	16	h	BLACKPOOL	W	1-0	Kippax
	2		25	h	LIVERPOOL	L	1-3	Brooks
	3	Sep	1	a	Liverpool	W	3-2	Hold (2), Kippax p
	4		8	a	Bolton W	L	0-2	
	5		12	a	Newcastle U	W	1-0	Drury
	6		15	h	BOLTON W	D	2-2	Drury, Crowther
Lancs Cup, agg 3-0	7		17	a	Blackpool	W	2-0	Crowther, Drury
	8		22	h	BURY	L	2-3	Crowther, Hays
	9		29	a	Bury	L	0-1	
	10	Oct	6	a	Preston N E	L	0-4	
	11		13	h	PRESTON N E	D	0-0	
	12		20	a	Blackburn R	L	2-4	Hays (2)
	13		27	h	BLACKBURN R	L	1-4	Hold
	14	Nov	3	a	Leeds U	W	2-1	Hold, Hays
	15		10	h	LEEDS U	L	2-3	Jackson, Kippax
	16		17	a	Bradford	L	0-7	
	17		24	h	BRADFORD	W	2-1	Morris, Jackson
	18	Dec	1	a	Manchester U	D	3-3	Jackson (2), Morris
	19		8	h	MANCHESTER U	D	2-2	Hays, Morris
	20		15	h	MANCHESTER C	W	1-0	Haigh
	21		22	a	Manchester C	W	2-1	Jackson, Morris
	22		25	a	Sunderland	D	1-1	Hornby
	23		26	h	SUNDERLAND	L	2-3	Chew, Jackson
	24		29	h	NEWCASTLE U	W	3-2	Morris, Jackson (2) 1p
	25	Jan	1	a	Sheffield U	l	1-5	Jackson
FA Cup round 3	26		5	a	Stoke C	L	1-3	Morris
FA Cup, round 3 replay, agg 3-4	27		7	h	STOKE C	W	2-1	Jackson, Kippax p
	28		12	h	SHEFFIELD W	D	2-2	Jackson, Morris
	29		19	a	Sheffield W	D	1-1	Kippax
	30		26	h	HUDDERSFIELD T	W	4-3	Jackson, Morris (2), Kippax
	31	Feb	2	h	MIDDLESBROUGH	W	8-1	Hays (2), Morris, Jackson (3), Kippax, Douglas og
	32		16	a	Huddersfield T	L	2-4	Attwell, Kippax p
	33		23	a	Stoke C	D	0-0	
friendly	34	Mar	2	h	POLISH RAF XI	W	6-1	Jackson (2), Kippax, Morris, Haigh (2)
	35		9	a	Chesterfield	L	0-3	
Lancs Cup	36		11	h	CHESTER	W	2-1	Burns, Jackson
	37		16	h	CHESTERFIELD	W	3-1	Hays, Chew, Jackson
Lancs Cup, agg 4-1	38		20	a	Chester	W	2-0	Jackson, Kippax
	39		23	a	Grimsby T	D	1-1	Jackson
LC semi, aet, 2-2 at 90m	40		27	a	Liverpool	W	3-2	Morris, Jackson, J.Knight
	41		30	h	GRIMSBY T	L	1-2	Morris
	42	Apr	1	h	STOKE C	W	1-0	Morris
	43		6	a	Barnsley	L	0-3	
	44		10	a	Middlesbrough	L	1-2	Morris
	45		13	h	BARNSLEY	W	3-2	Kippax, Jackson, Pallister og
	46		19	h	BLACKPOOL	D	1-1	Kippax
	47		20	a	Everton	L	0-2	
	48		27	h	EVERTON	W	1-0	Jackson
	49		29	a	Blackpool	L	1-2	Kippax
	50	May	4	h	SHEFFIELD U	L	0-1	
LC final, at Maine Road	51		11	n	Manchester U	L	0-1	

All matches not marked otherwise were in the Football League North
Playing record P42 W13 D10 L19 F63 A84 Pts36, Burnley finished 16th of 22 clubs

1946-47

After organised football's lost years during World War II, followed by the partial return to normal service with the 1945-46 F.A. Cup competition, it was back to League action on 31 August 1946. The fixtures for the new season were those that had originally been set for the aborted 1939-40 campaign, thus Burnley resumed Second Division action with a home game against Coventry City. In common with most other League clubs following the long enforced break, Burnley embarked on the new season with a sense of high expectation from their supporters. 1,300 season tickets had been sold, a club record, and for the first time there was a manager at the club whose remit was totally on the playing side. Cliff Britton, former Everton and England left-half, had been appointed in May 1945 and brought with him new ideas in training and tactics. In Billy Dougall and Ray Bennion, both time-served Turf Moor men, Britton had assistants who knew the club and knew the job they had to do. Burnley's support had slumped during the thirties, with home gates at the end of the final pre-war season struggling to reach 10,000, but the attendance for the Coventry game was a healthy 18,427. The team on view included four players, right-back Arthur Woodruff, left-half George Bray, inside-right Billy Morris and centre-forward Jack Billingham, who had played League football for Burnley before the war, while goalkeeper Jimmy Strong, left-back Harold Mather, right-half Harold Spencer, the wingers Jackie Chew and Peter Kippax, and inside-left Harry Potts, had all appeared for the club in the wartime competitions. The one completely new face was centre-half and captain Alan Brown, who was to prove a key figure in the season ahead.

Peter Kippax became Burnley's first scorer of the post-war era as Coventry took a point away from the Turf with a 1-1 draw. Amateur players were relatively rare at League level even in 1946, but Kippax was one of the best of that breed, as well as being a fine local league cricketer and successful businessman. The Clarets, restored to their traditional colours and wearing shirts bought with supporters' clothing coupons, registered their first win of the new era a week later as Birmingham were beaten 2-0 at St. Andrews. A 3-2 home win against Newport then maintained the fine start, with Gordon Haigh, another player who had made his mark at Turf Moor in the war years, on target on his League debut.

Two defeats followed, but Burnley then proceeded to show their mettle with a sixteen-game unbeaten run. Notable debutants during this run were centre-forward Ray Harrison, left-winger Jack Hays and a player who had made a big impression in the final wartime season. Cultured wing-half Reg Attwell was signed from West Ham in October 1946, a much-welcomed piece of business by Cliff Britton, and made his debut on 9th November in the home game against Luton, when the renowned half-back line of Attwell, Brown and Bray appeared together for the first time.

By this time, Burnley had to be taken seriously as promotion challengers. A 2-2 draw at Bury the previous week, watched by over 26,000 at Gigg Lane, put the Clarets on top of the Second Division. They lost the position with a sequence of five drawn games, but soon afterwards embarked upon an extraordinary run when only two goals were conceded in fourteen League fixtures. Not for nothing did Burnley's defence of the early postwar years become known as the Iron Curtain. Alan Brown was the lynchpin of that defence. Already 31 when he joined Burnley in February 1946, and possessed of relatively little pre-war League experience, his leadership qualities were recognised by manager Britton and he proved a true iron man in the Clarets' rearguard. He was ably assisted by two solid full-backs in Woodruff and Mather and a most reliable presence in goal in Jimmy Strong.

Billy Morris became Burnley's first hat-trick scorer of the post-war era when he registered all three in a victory at Coventry just after Christmas. The diminutive Morris, whose right-wing partnership with Jackie Chew was a major asset for the side, would win his first full Welsh cap before the end of the season. The first game of 1947 brought Birmingham, one of the teams in contention with Burnley in a tightly-packed top end of the table, to Turf Moor. A crowd of 36,000 saw Harry Potts score the only goal to keep up the pressure on leaders Manchester City.

Captain Alan Brown
the iron man of Burnley's defence

Even that gate was topped the following Saturday as Burnley's F.A. Cup campaign opened with a third round home tie against Aston Villa. The First Division side started as favourites, but they were no match on the day as the Clarets ran riot, Villa's goal a mere late consolation as they were beaten 5-1. Morris and Ray Harrison scored two apiece, with Harry Potts completing the nap hand. It proved to be Burnley's biggest win of the season so far, and surely proved that they were ready once again to compete with the best.

League gates at Turf Moor by now were regularly into the high 20,000s, and such a crowd saw another notable victory when Newcastle were crushed 3-0 at the end of January to strengthen Burnley's hold on second place. By this time, one of the harshest winters in memory had set in, but conditions leading to postponements had to be far worse then than today, and games were often played on pitches covered with snow or frost. It didn't seem to do Burnley any harm, and they continued on their hard-to-beat way, piling up League points, remaining as mean as ever at the back, and progressing in the Cup. Victories over fellow Second Divisioners Coventry and Luton (with Ray Harrison scoring a hat-trick in the replay against the latter) set up a quarter-final tie against Middlesbrough from the top flight. A 1-1 draw at Ayresome Park brought Boro back to the Turf, and the ground's biggest gathering for ten years, over 49,000, saw the Clarets reach the semi-finals, Billy Morris scoring the only goal early in extra-time. The harsh weather wasn't affecting the side's performances, but the Cup run was contributing to a backlog of fixtures in the League.

Champions-elect Liverpool were the semi-final opponents, and on 29th March 1947 there were 53,000 at Ewood Park to see Alan Brown once again towering in defence as Burnley held on for a goalless draw. Seven days later, a bitterly cold Easter Saturday saw Chesterfield at Turf Moor in a game which saw the conditions get the better of several of the players, Burnley finishing with nine men and three of the Chesterfield players collapsing at the final whistle. Seven days later again, Maine Road was the venue for the semi-final replay; the 72,000 crowd included Bert Freeman and Billy Watson from the Cup-winning side of 33 years earlier, and they saw Ray Harrison score with a superb shot to ensure Burnley's first-ever trip to Wembley Stadium.

There was only one League match between the semi-final and final, an innocuous-looking home game against Bradford Park Avenue. Perhaps the excitement had been too much... the Clarets went down to only their second defeat in 38 matches in League and Cup, causing fears that they might fall between the two stools of Cup and promotion. But soon came the big date, 26th April 1947, and a crowd of 98,215 at Wembley for Burnley of the Second Division versus Charlton Athletic of the First... the F.A. Cup final.

Sadly, it was not a classic. More sadly still, Burnley were the losers, despite having the better of the play for much of the ninety minutes of normal time and despite Harry Potts hitting the crossbar. All looked set fair when it was still goalless at full-time, the Clarets after all having proved themselves masters of the defensive art, even against the soon-to-be League champions. But it was not to be, and Charlton's little left-winger Chris Duffy struck the decisive blow seven minutes from the end of extra-time to take the Cup to the Valley. It had, though, been a magnificent effort by a Burnley side whose names belong in any Turf Moor hall of fame... Strong, Woodruff, Mather, Attwell, Brown, Bray, Chew, Morris, Harrison, Potts and Kippax.

There were still seven League games left to play, and much still to play for. The Second Division's match of the season took place on 10th May when Burnley returned to the scene of their semi-final triumph, but this time it was Manchester City who were celebrating as their 1-0 win ensured their promotion. Defeat at Fulham a week later saw the Clarets slip out of the top two, but crucially they still had games in hand on Birmingham, the team that had taken their place.

A 4-1 win at Leicester and a 1-1 home draw against Bury left Burnley third, but level on points with Birmingham, who had completed their fixtures. Just one point was needed from the two remaining games. The first of those was at West Ham, and the Clarets made no mistake, registering their biggest win of the season, with Harry Potts on target twice and Jackie Chew, Billy Morris and Jack Hays once each as the Hammers were "hammered" 5-0. Burnley were back among the elite after ten seasons and seventeen years in the Second Division. The final game was academic, but for the record the 1-1 draw at home to Millwall remains to this day the only League game Burnley have ever played in the month of June.

The fans pay tribute as the Wembley team return home now for promotion!

It had been a truly extraordinary season. The Iron Curtain defence was undoubtedly the "star" of the side, conceding only 29 goals in the League, as good a goals-per-game ratio as the club has ever achieved. Burnley had shown not only by their promotion but by their performances against some of the best in the land in the Cup that they were more than ready to compete once again amongst the elite. The good times, for sure, were back at Turf Moor.

1946-47 - Second Division

		P	W	D	L	F	A	Pts
1	Manchester C	42	26	10	6	78	35	62
2	BURNLEY	42	22	14	6	65	29	58
3	Birmingham	42	25	5	12	74	33	55
4	Chesterfield	42	18	14	10	58	44	50
5	Newcastle U	42	19	10	13	95	62	48
6	Tottenham H	42	17	14	11	65	53	48
7	West Bromwich A	42	20	8	14	88	75	48
8	Coventry C	42	16	13	13	66	59	45
9	Leicester C	42	18	7	17	69	64	43
10	Barnsley	42	17	8	17	84	86	42
11	Nottingham F	42	15	10	17	69	74	40
12	West Ham U	42	16	8	18	70	76	40
13	Luton T	42	16	7	19	71	73	39
14	Southampton	42	15	9	18	69	76	39
15	Fulham	42	15	9	18	63	74	39
16	Bradford PA	42	14	11	17	65	77	39
17	Bury	42	12	12	18	80	78	36
18	Millwall	42	14	8	20	56	79	36
19	Plymouth A	42	14	5	23	79	96	33
20	Sheffield W	42	12	8	22	67	88	32
21	Swansea T	42	11	7	24	55	83	29
22	Newport C	42	10	3	29	61	133	23

1946-47

Manager : Cliff Britton

Division Two (2nd)
Promoted

		Date			Opponents	Result		h/t	Goalscorers/times	Opp. goal times
	1	Aug	31	h	COVENTRY C	D	1-1	1-1	Kippax 10	31
	2	Sep	7	a	Birmingham C	W	2-0	0-0	Spencer 55p, Billingham 80	
	3		9	h	NEWPORT C	W	3-2	1-0	Chew 14, Billingham 50, Haigh 75	60, 70
Fred Taylor's last game	4		14	h	WEST BROMWICH A	L	0-2	0-2		12, 23
	5		16	a	Barnsley	L	0-1	0-1		42
	6		21	a	Newcastle U	W	2-1	2-0	Potts (2) 21, 30	90
	7		28	h	SWANSEA T	W	1-0	1-0	Harrison 37	
	8		30	h	BARNSLEY	D	2-2	0-0	Harrison 66, Bray 88	63og, 82
	9	Oct	5	a	Tottenham H	D	1-1	0-1	Kippax 69p	10
	10		12	h	WEST HAM U	W	2-1	1-0	Billingham 1, Kippax 89p	65
	11		19	a	Sheffield W	W	2-1	2-0	Chew 9, Billingham 30	67
	12		26	h	FULHAM	W	2-0	2-0	Bray 7p, Billingham 35	
	13	Nov	2	a	Bury	D	2-2	1-0	Billingham 9, Potts 79	78, 87
	14		9	h	LUTON T	D	1-1	1-1	Billingham 26	15
	15		16	a	Plymouth A	D	2-2	0-2	Billingham 63, Morris 78	15, 25
	16		23	h	LEICESTER C	D	0-0	0-0		
	17		30	a	Chesterfield	D	0-0	0-0		
	18	Dec	7	h	MILLWALL	W	3-0	1-0	Billingham 35, Kippax 47, Potts 70	
	19		14	a	Bradford	W	1-0	1-0	Morris 16	
	20		21	h	MANCHESTER C	D	0-0	0-0		
	21		25	h	NOTTINGHAM F	W	3-0	1-0	Chew (2) 20, 52, Kippax 85	
	22		26	a	Nottingham F	L	0-1	0-0		70
	23		28	a	Coventry C	W	3-0	1-0	Morris (3) 18, 49, 71	
	24	Jan	4	h	BIRMINGHAM C	W	1-0	0-0	Potts 80	
	25		18	a	West Bromwich A	D	1-1	1-0	Chew 40	84
	26		28	h	NEWCASTLE U	W	3-0	2-0	Chew 18, Potts (2) 30, 53	
	27	Feb	1	a	Swansea T	W	2-0	0-0	Chew 77, Harrison 85	
	28		18	h	TOTTENHAM H	D	0-0	0-0		
	29		22	h	SHEFFIELD W	W	2-0	1-0	Harrison 30, Morris 55	
	30	Mar	15	a	Luton T	W	3-1	1-0	Potts (2), 34, 76, Harrison 88	68
	31		22	h	PLYMOUTH A	W	2-1	0-1	Chew 46, Potts 90	44
	32	Apr	4	h	SOUTHAMPTON	W	1-0	1-0	Kippax 35	
	33		5	h	CHESTERFIELD	D	1-1	0-1	Potts 57	42
	34		7	a	Southampton	W	1-0	0-0	J.Knight 75	
	35		19	h	BRADFORD	L	1-2	1-1	Potts 7	30, 68
	36	May	3	a	Newport C	W	3-0	2-0	Hays 3, Morris 35, Potts 80	
	37		10	a	Manchester C	L	0-1	0-0		83
	38		17	a	Fulham	L	0-1	0-0		77
	39		24	a	Leicester C	W	4-1	3-0	Billingham (2) 4, 5, Hays (2) 13, 77	71
	40		26	h	BURY	D	1-1	1-0	Billingham 41	65
	41		31	a	West Bromwich A	W	5-0	3-0	Chew 17, Morris 38, Potts (2) 43, 55, Hays 60	
	42	Jun	7	a	Millwall	D	1-1	0-1	Morris 47	15p

FA Cup

	3	Jan	11	h	ASTON VILLA	W	5-1	2-0	Morris (2) 8, 23, Potts 70, Harrison (2) 78, 79	87
	4		25	h	COVENTRY C	W	2-0	1-0	Chew 31, Potts 85	
	5	Feb	8	a	Luton T	D	0-0	0-0		
	rep		11	h	LUTON T	W	3-0	0-0	Harrison (3) 51, 68, 83	
	6	Mar	1	a	Middlesbrough	D	1-1	0-1	Morris 80	44
after extra time	rep		4	h	MIDDLESBROUGH	W	1-0	0-0	Morris 94	
at Ewood Park, after extra time	semi		29	n	Liverpool	D	0-0	0-0		
at Maine Road	rep	Apr	12	n	Liverpool	W	1-0	0-0	Harrison 79	
at Wembley, after extra time	Final		26	n	Charlton A	L	0-1	0-0		113

Other first team matches (friendlies and/or as detailed)

Lancs Cup	Oct	9	a	Accrington S	D	0-0	
Lancs Cup, agg 3-0		21	h	ACCRINGTON S	W	3-0	Burns (3)
Lancs Cup, at Maine Road	Nov	20	a	Manchester U	L	3-4	Harrison, Haigh, Hornby
Lancs Cup aet, agg 5-4	Dec	3	h	MANCHESTER U	W	2-0	Moran og, Harrison
Lancs Cup semi	May	21	a	Liverpool	L	0-1	

Att.	Pos	Strong	Woodruff	Mather	H Spencer	Brown	Bray	Chew	Morris	Billingham	Potts	Kippax	Haigh	F Taylor	Rudman	G Knight	Harrison	J Hays	Attwell	Marshall	Loughran	Hornby	J Knight	
18,427		1	2	3	4	5	6	7	8	9	10	11												1
42,309	9	1	2	3	4	5	6	7	8	9	10	11												2
18,008	9	1	2	3	4	5	6	7		9	10	11	8											3
22,252	9	1	2	3	4	5	6			9	10	11	8	7										4
26,247		1	2	3		5	6		8	9		11	10		4	7								5
61,255	9	1	2	3		5	6			8	8		10		4		9	11						6
19,968	7	1	2	3		5	6			8	8		10		4		9	11						7
24,959		1	2	3		5	6	10		8	8	11			4		9							8
44,351	6	1	2	3		5	6	7		10	8	11			4		9							9
22,233	7	1	2	3		5	6	7		10	8	11			4		9							10
22,083	3	1	2	3		5	6	7		10	8	11			4		9							11
26,905	2	1	2	3		5	6	7	8	9	10	11			4									12
26,167	top	1	2	3		5	6	7	8	9	10	11			4									13
26,007	3	1	2	3		5	6	7	8	9	10	11							4					14
30,032	2	1	2	3		5	6	7	8	9	10	11							4	2				15
19,062	3	1		3		5	6	7	8	10		11					9		4		2			16
16,570	4	1		3		5	6	7	8		10						9	11			4			17
17,968	3	1	2	3		5	6	7	8	9	10	11									4			18
10,731	top	1	2	3		5	6	7	8	9	10							11			4			19
31,210	3	1	2	3		5	6	7	8	9	10	11							4					20
21,036		1	2	3		5	6	7	8	9	10	11							4					21
31,484	3	1	2	3		5		7			10	11	8				9		4		6			22
26,944	3	1	2	3		5	6	7	8	9	10							11			4			23
36,281	2	1	2	3		5	6	7	8	9	10	11							4					24
43,427		1	2	3		5	6	7	8		10	11					9		4					25
26,877		1	2	3		5	6	7	8		10	11					9				4			26
18,247	2	1	2	3		5	6	7	8		10						9				4	11		27
28,462		1	2	3		5	6	7	8		10						9	11	4					28
26,651	2	1	2	3		5	6	7	8		10	11					9		4					29
18,462	2	1	2	3		5	6	7	8		10						9	11	4					30
28,287	2	1	2	3		5	6	7	8		10	11					9		4					31
31,713		1	2	3		5	6	7	8		10	11					9		4					32
23,719	2	1	2	3		5	6			9	8	11						7	4				10	33
20,330		1	2	3		5	6			7	8						9	11			4		10	34
32,905	2	1	2	3		5	6		8	7	10	11					9		4					35
14,751		1	2	3		5	6	7	8		10						9	11	4					36
69,463	2	1	2	3		5	6	7	8		10						9	11	4					37
25,432	3	1	2	3		5	6	7	8		10						9	11	4					38
21,626	2	1	2	3		5	6	7	8	9	10							11	4					39
40,145		1	2	3		5	6	7	8	9	10							11	4					40
20,198	2	1	2	3		5	6	7	8	9	10							11	4					41
15,684	2	1	2	3		5	6	7	8		10						9	11	4					42
Appearances		42	40	42	4	42	41	35	31	28	40	26	6	1	9	1	23	16	22	1	9	1	2	
Goals (65)					1		2	9	9	12	15	6	1				5	4					1	

Att.	Strong	Woodruff	Mather	H Spencer	Brown	Bray	Chew	Morris	Billingham	Potts	Kippax	Haigh	F Taylor	Rudman	G Knight	Harrison	J Hays	Attwell	Marshall	Loughran	Hornby	J Knight	
38,532	1	2	3		5	6	7	8		10	11					9		4					3
39,796	1	2	3		5	6	7	8		10	11					9				4			4
22,640	1	2	3		5	6	7	8		10	11					9				4			5
28,330	1	2	3		5	6	7	8		10	11					9				4			rep
53,025	1	2	3		5	6	7	8		10	11					9		4					6
49,244	1	2	3		5	6	7	8		10	11					9		4					rep
53,000	1	2	3		5	6	7	8		10	11					9		4					semi
72,000	1	2	3		5	6		8	7	10	11					9		4					rep
98,215	1	2	3		5	6	7	8		10	11					9		4					Final
Appearances	9	9	9		9	9	8	9	1	9	9					9		6		3			
Goals (13)							1	4		2						6							

1947-48

These days, promotion to the top flight of English football usually signals the start of frantic activity in the transfer market. It wasn't so in 1947, when the financial implications of promotion, or more particularly failure to sustain life at the higher level, were in no way comparable to the situation six decades on. So it was that Burnley began life back in the First Division, where they had last played seventeen years earlier, with manager Cliff Britton keeping faith with the men who had served the club so well in the previous campaign.

The start could hardly have been better. Two minutes into the opening match at Fratton Park, Portsmouth, Harry Potts gave the Clarets the lead, and, in keeping with their performances of the previous campaign, they duly held on for the remaining 88 minutes to put the first two points on the board. Reality hit home on the following Tuesday, however, as Turf Moor staged its first top-flight game for too long. Derby were the visitors, there was an expectant crowd of 43,067, and two goals in a minute gave the Rams victory. The Burnley side for these first two games, and indeed for the next five, saw two changes from the Cup final line-up of a few months earlier, with Jack Billingham restored to the centre-forward role in place of Ray Harrison, and Jack Hays replacing Peter Kippax on the left wing. Kippax had not in fact played since the big day at Wembley, illness ruling him out not only of Burnley's promotion run-in but what would have been a full England debut, a rare honour indeed for an amateur player.

The team soon recovered from the Derby setback, registering a home win four days later against Bolton and then taking a point from the return game at the Baseball Ground. Draws at Liverpool and at home to Manchester United, against the League's top two of the previous season, showed that Burnley were to be taken seriously as a First Division side, with the "Iron Curtain" as solid as ever. And this was to prove just the start of a fine run going right through to Christmas, as the Clarets lost only one League game out of twenty in that four-month spell.

Throughout this time, the side remained virtually unchanged. Captain Alan Brown missed two games, including that solitary defeat, at home against Arsenal, the side destined to take the title the following May. Jackie Chew's brief absence saw a switch to the right side for Jack Heys and a return on the left for Peter Kippax; and Jack Knight enjoyed his one spell as a first-team regular, stepping in for the injured Billy Morris between November and March. Otherwise, it was very much business as usual as Burnley proved the equal or better of most of what the First Division had to offer. Harry Potts enjoyed a particularly prolific spell between November and Christmas, scoring in six consecutive games including two double strikes, while Jack Billingham was not far behind in the goal stakes, averaging well over one in two games during the same spell. The biggest win of the period was a 4-0 thrashing of Sunderland in late November, with the Jacks, Knight and Billingham adding to Potts' pair in a victory that lifted Burnley to the lofty heights of second in the League, although still with some work to do to catch Arsenal.

All over the country, football crowds were booming, and Turf Moor benefited as much as anywhere from the unprecedented interest in the game. The gate against Blackpool on 11th October, when Harry Potts scored the only goal of the game, was 52,869, the highest ever recorded for a League game at the ground. The Arsenal game also drew a bumper crowd of almost 48,000, as the Burnley public revelled in their team's success.

A hat-trick from Billingham saw off Portsmouth on the Saturday before Christmas, then came a festive double-header against Preston. Another fine turnout, 44,645, saw Potts again the match-winner on Christmas Day to cement the Clarets' hold on second place, but the season's first real blip was around the corner. The Boxing Day return fixture at Deepdale brought the first loss since the end of September, Preston's 3-2 victory taking them to within two points of Burnley in the final League table of 1947. It was the first time the Clarets had conceded three since the post-war resumption, but worse was to follow on New Year's Day at Maine Road, as Manchester United (still in the temporary home following the wartime damage to Old Trafford) breached the Iron Curtain five times. It was a bad day all round, with Potts missing a penalty and Brown being booked, an event by no means as commonplace in those days as now.

Manager Cliff Britton (right) holding court with (left to right) Billy Morris, Harold Mather and Ray Harrison

It seemed likely that some relief was around the corner as Burnley began their quest to return to Wembley following the previous season's heroics. The third round opposition was modest, Swindon Town of the Third Division (South) being notable mainly for the presence in the manager's chair of a Burnley hero from pre-war, the free-scoring winger Louis Page. He had played when the clubs met in the F.A. Cup back in 1929, when Swindon upset the odds with victory in a fourth round replay. This time they only needed one attempt, their 2-0 victory, fully deserved on the day, consigned the Clarets to the role of "giants killed", and left them to concentrate on the League.

Harry Potts
top scorer in 1947-48

Happily, there was no sign of any Cup hangover the following week as reigning champions Liverpool came to the Turf and were seen off 3-0. Victory at Middlesbrough confirmed that things were back on track, but Valentine's Day brought the season's sternest test, with a visit to long-time leaders Arsenal. It was not quite a massacre, but Burnley were well beaten by three clear goals to leave them eight points adrift and clearly now with a tough uphill battle if they were to entertain serious hopes of the League title.

The first week in March 1948 brought Blackburn Rovers to Turf Moor for what would be their last League visit for ten years. Rovers were facing relegation, and that may have ensured that the Blackpool record gate stayed unbroken; the result, a goalless draw, did neither side any favours, and the following week proved that Maine Road was not a happy hunting ground for the Clarets as Manchester City coasted to a 4-1 win. A season that had been so full of promise was now looking in danger of flattering to deceive.

There had been few team changes in the first two thirds of the season, but Cliff Britton, perhaps in an effort to revive the Clarets' flagging fortunes, made some alterations in the latter stages. Joe Loughran became a regular in the side as both the full-backs Woodruff and Mather had spells on the sidelines, Ray Harrison was in at centre-forward in place of Billingham, and even veteran Ronnie Hornby, whose best days had been in the pre-war side, was given a handful of starts on the left wing. Hornby scored one of the goals in a 4-1 win against Grimsby; admittedly it was against a side bound for Division Two at the end of the season, but it at least ended the barren spell.

The Easter programme began well, with a 4-0 Good Friday hammering of Stoke, Harrison showing that he still had the magic touch in front of goal by scoring two, as did Jackie Chew. But the Potters almost reversed the scoreline at the Victoria Ground on Easter Monday, hitting three without reply. Arsenal were by now well out of sight, and second place was looking increasingly unlikely unless form picked up. It did, and Burnley won four of their last six games, but just missed out on runners-up spot on goal average to Manchester United who had emerged from mid-table with a fine New Year run which also ended with them taking the F.A. Cup.

Any disappointment at missing out on the runners-up spot, though, was surely misplaced. Third place was an excellent effort in Burnley's first season back among the elite, and equalled their best position since their 1920-21 championship season. The momentum from the promotion season had been maintained far beyond most people's expectations, and the average home League gate of 33,621 was 30 per cent up on 1946-47 and the highest ever recorded by the club. The team was not getting any younger, but in the reserves and "A" team there were players whose promise would be fulfilled in the seasons ahead. As Turf Moor shut up shop for the summer of '48 there was plenty of cause for optimism.

1947-48 - First Division

		P	W	D	L	F	A	Pts
1	Arsenal	42	23	13	6	81	32	59
2	Manchester U	42	19	14	9	81	48	52
3	BURNLEY	42	20	12	10	56	43	52
4	Derby C	42	19	12	11	77	57	50
5	Wolverhampton W	42	19	9	14	83	70	47
6	Aston Villa	42	19	9	14	65	57	47
7	Preston NE	42	20	7	15	67	68	47
8	Portsmouth	42	19	7	16	68	50	45
9	Blackpool	42	17	10	15	57	41	44
10	Manchester C	42	15	12	15	52	47	42
11	Liverpool	42	16	10	16	65	61	42
12	Sheffield U	42	16	10	16	65	70	42
13	Charlton A	42	17	6	19	57	66	40
14	Everton	42	17	6	19	52	66	40
15	Stoke C	42	14	10	18	41	55	38
16	Middlesbrough	42	14	9	19	71	73	37
17	Bolton W	42	16	5	21	46	58	37
18	Chelsea	42	14	9	19	53	71	37
19	Huddersfield T	42	12	12	18	51	60	36
20	Sunderland	42	13	10	19	56	67	36
21	Blackburn R	42	11	10	21	54	72	32
22	Grimsby T	42	8	6	28	45	111	22

1947-48

Manager : Cliff Britton

Division One (3rd)

Note	No	Date		Venue	Opponents	Result		h/t	Goalscorers/times	Opp. goal times
1st League goal anywhere	1	Aug	23	a	Portsmouth	W	1-0	1-0	Potts 2	
	2		26	h	DERBY C	L	0-2	0-0		46, 47
	3		30	h	BOLTON W	W	2-0	2-0	Potts 18, Morris 38	
	4	Sep	3	a	Derby C	D	1-1	0-1	Bray 86	4
	5		6	a	Liverpool	D	1-1	0-1	Hays 67	31
	6		8	h	MANCHESTER U	D	0-0	0-0		
	7		11	h	MIDDLESBROUGH	W	3-0	3-0	Hays 2, Potts 37, Chew 40	
	8		20	a	Charlton A	D	1-1	0-0	Billingham 80	65
	9		27	h	ARSENAL	L	0-1	0-1		37
	10	Oct	4	a	Sheffield U	D	1-1	1-1	Billingham 16	7
	11		11	h	BLACKPOOL	W	1-0	0-0	Potts 79	
	12		18	a	Blackburn R	W	2-1	1-0	Tomlinson 5og, Morris 55	63
	13		25	h	MANCHESTER C	D	1-1	0-0	Hays 64	90
	14	Nov	1	a	Grimsby T	W	2-1	1-1	Billingham (2) 36, 65	43
	15		8	h	WOLVERHAMPTON W	D	1-1	1-1	Potts 43	37
	16		15	a	Everton	W	3-0	1-0	Knight 40, Billingham 57, Potts 70	
	17		22	h	SUNDERLAND	W	4-0	1-0	Billingham 24, Potts (2) 67, 69p, Knight 71	
	18		29	a	Aston Villa	D	2-2	2-0	Potts (2) 7, 34	73, 82
	19	Dec	6	h	CHELSEA	W	1-0	1-0	Potts 14	
	20		13	a	Huddersfield T	W	1-0	0-0	Potts 84p	
	21		20	h	PORTSMOUTH	W	3-2	2-2	Billingham (3) 2, 10, 61	1, 37
	22		25	h	PRESTON N E	W	1-0	0-0	Potts 90	
	23		26	a	Preston N E	L	2-3	1-1	Billingham 35, Bray 80	5, 65, 70
	24	Jan	1	a	Manchester U	L	0-5	0-3		10, 21, 40, 68, 72
	25		3	a	Bolton W	D	1-1	1-1	Harrison 30	8
	26		17	h	LIVERPOOL	W	3-0	0-0	Billingham (2) 52, 88, Knight 69	
	27		31	a	Middlesbrough	W	2-1	1-0	Chew 38, Potts 61	80
	28	Feb	14	a	Arsenal	L	0-3	0-1		14, 47, 63
	29		21	h	SHEFFIELD U	D	0-0	0-0		
	30	Mar	6	h	BLACKBURN R	D	0-0	0-0		
	31		13	a	Manchester C	L	1-4	1-1	Westwood 13og	42, 50, 78, 84
	32		20	h	GRIMSBY T	W	4-1	2-0	Haigh 9, Harrison (2) 39, 69, Hornby 87	82
	33		26	h	STOKE C	W	4-0	2-0	Harrison (2) 15, 75, Chew (2) 30, 60	
	34		27	a	Wolverhampton W	D	1-1	0-0	Morris 76	60
	35		29	a	Stoke C	L	0-3	0-1		25, 48, 65
	36	Apr	3	h	EVERTON	L	0-1	0-0		81
Hornby's last game	37		7	a	Blackpool	W	1-0	1-0	Morris 30	
	38		10	a	Sunderland	L	0-2	0-1		33, 60
	39		17	h	ASTON VILLA	W	1-0	1-0	Harrison 44	
	40		20	h	CHARLTON A	L	0-2	0-0		46, 48
	41		24	a	Chelsea	W	2-0	0-0	Billingham 65, Attwell 79	
Kippax's last game	42	May	1	h	HUDDERSFIELD T	W	2-1	0-1	Bray 61, Harrison 64	3

FA Cup

Round	Date		Venue	Opponents	Result		h/t	Goalscorers/times	Opp. goal times
3	Jan	10	h	SWINDON T	L	0-2	0-2		2, 43

Final, Manchester U 4-2 Blackpool, at Wembley.

Other first team matches (friendlies and/or as detailed)

Note	Date		Venue	Opponents	Result		Goalscorers
Lancs Cup	Oct	15	a	Blackpool	L	0-1	
	Feb	7	h	LEEDS U	W	5-3	Bray (2), Billingham, Chew (2)
		28	a	Swansea T	W	3-1	J.Knight, Potts, Bray
	Apr	26	a	Cornwall XI	W	3-0	unknown
	May	11	a	Norkopping	L	1-3	Chew
in Copenhagen		14	a	Danish Olympic XI	L	2-3	Billingham, Opponent og
in Copenhagen		18	a	Danish 'B' XI	L	1-2	unknown
in Copenhagen		20	a	Udvalgt Dansk Hold	L	1-4	Morris
		25	a	Malmo	L	1-2	unknown

Att.	Pos	Strong	Woodruff	Mather	Attwell	Brown	Bray	Chew	Morris	Billingham	Potts	J Hays	Butterfield	Johnson	Kippax	J Knight	Harrison	Loughran	Haigh	Hornby	
33,967		1	2	3	4	5	6	7	8	9	10	11									1
43,067		1	2	3	4	5	6	7	8	9	10	11									2
35,835	5	1	2	3	4	5	6	7	8	9	10	11									3
32,565		1	2	3	4	5	6	7	8	9	10	11									4
56,074	9	1	2	3	4	5	6	7	8	9	10	11									5
38,517		1	2	3	4	5	6	7	8	9	10	11									6
34,944	4	1	2	3	4	5	6	7	8	9	10	11									7
37,588	6	1		3	4	5	6	7	8	9	10	11	2								8
47,958	7	1	2	3	4		6	7	8	9	10	11		5							9
40,930	8	1	2	3	4		6	7	8	9	10	11		5							10
52,869	6	1	2	3	4	5	6	7	8	9	10	11									11
41,635	4	1	2	3	4	5	6	7	8	9	10	11									12
41,454	4	1	2	3	4	5	6	7	8	9	10	11									13
17,697	4	1	2	3	4	5	6		8	9	10	7			11						14
38,356	4	1	2	3	4	5	6		8	9	10	7			11						15
49,442	3	1	2	3	4	5	6			9	8	7			11	10					16
21,939	2	1	2	3	4	5	6	7		9	8	11				10					17
56,595	2	1	2	3	4	5	6	7		9	8	11				10					18
30,865	2	1	2	3	4	5	6	7		9	8	11				10					19
36,375	2	1	2	3	4	5	6	7		9	8				11	10					20
30,131	2	1	2	3	4	5	6	7		9	8	11				10					21
44,645		1	2	3	4	5	6	7		9	8	11				10					22
39,400	2	1	2	3	4	5	6	7		9	8	11				10					23
61,100		1	2	3	4	5	6	7		9	8	11				10					24
43,442	3	1	2	3	4	5	6			7	8	11				10	9				25
31,470	2	1		3	4	5	6			9	10	7	2		11	8					26
36,208	2	1		3		5	6	7		9	10	11	2			8		4			27
62,125	2	1		3	4	5	6	7		9	10	11				8		2			28
20,667	2	1		3	4	5	6	7		9	10	11				8		2			29
44,240	2	1		3	4	5	6	11		9	10	7				8		2			30
32,213	3	1		3	4	5	6	11		9	10	7						2	8		31
19,522	3	1	2	3		5	6			7	8						9	4	10	11	32
28,989		1	2	3		5	6	7			8						9	4	10	11	33
38,360	2	1	2	3	4	5	6	7	8	9	10	11									34
33,014		1	2	3		5	6			7	8						9	4	10	11	35
23,933	3	1	2		4	5	6	7	8		10	11					9	3			36
16,732	3	1	2		4	5	6	7	8		10						9	3		11	37
47,003	3	1	2		4	5	6	7	8		10	11					9	3			38
25,671	3	1	2	3	10		6	7	8			11		5			9	4			39
26,627		1	2	3	10		6	7	8			11		5			9	4			40
33,390	3	1	2	3	10		6	7	8	9		11		5				4			41
25,443	3	1	2		4		6		8			7		5	11	10	9	3			42
Appearances		42	35	38	38	36	42	34	23	35	38	37	3	6	6	16	10	15	4	4	
Goals (56)					1		3	4	4	13	14	3				3	7		1	1	2 ogs

Att.	Pos	Strong	Woodruff	Mather	Attwell	Brown	Bray	Chew	Morris	Billingham	Potts	J Hays	Butterfield	Johnson	Kippax	J Knight	Harrison	Loughran	Haigh	Hornby	
34,229		1	2	3	4	5	6			7	8	11				10	9				3
Appearances		1	1	1	1	1	1			1	1	1				1	1				
Goals (0)																					

1948-49

OBITUARY
WALTER PLACE SENIOR
DIED 21 JUNE 1948, AGED 78.

Born in Burnley in 1870, Walter Place was almost certainly the most complete all-round sportsman the town has ever produced. He first appeared for the Turfites as a 16-year-old in 1886 and, although he preferred to play as a half back, he was equally comfortable in any position on the field. On two occasions in 1893, in the absence of a regular custodian, he played in goal and, as he invariably did, performed with style and confidence. He retired from professional football in 1900 going on to captain Burnley Belvedere as an amateur. Walter Place senior, known as Big Walter, to differentiate him from his cousin Walter Place junior (Little Walter), was also a roller-skater, a skilful snooker player and an accomplished athlete, specialising in sprinting backwards!. He was an expert crown green bowler, played cricket to a high standard and was a crackshot with a rifle. He was also an extremely strong swimmer and is reported to have saved both human and canine life in the canal running through the town. He also bred and flew homing pigeons but by way of contrast, took on and almost defeated a touring Russian wrestling champion, who immediately declared his opponent to be England's best wrestler. In the 1920's Walter Place spent a number of years as a director at Burnley FC, his vast sporting experience and knowledge proving to be invaluable.

RIP

There were changes in personnel at Turf Moor in the summer of 1948, but none to disturb the established order as the season kicked off with a home game against Manchester City. Of the previous season's regular line-up, only Harry Potts was absent, with Jack Knight occupying the number ten shirt as the new campaign saw Burnley getting off to a winning start with Jack Billingham scoring the only goal of the game, watched by a crowd of nearly 34,000.

One of the new arrivals, Ian Wilson, a winger signed from Preston, made his debut on the left in place of Jack Hays in the season's third game, a one-goal defeat at Portsmouth, which also saw the return of Potts. That game marked the start of something of a goal famine for the Clarets, and the side continued to struggle to score until mid-September when a 3-0 trouncing of Preston at Deepdale brought some relief. Only Jackie Chew was prolific in this spell, as he registered five goals in the first twelve games, surpassing his total for the whole of the previous season.

There were two significant departures from the Turf around this time. Manager Cliff Britton, the man who had introduced true football management to the club, left at the end of September to return to the scene of his playing glory days, Everton. He was to remain at Goodison Park for eight years without ever achieving the success he had at Burnley. A week later, the player who had arguably been Britton's best signing, captain Alan Brown, was transferred to Third Division South high-fliers Notts County. Having lost many of his best years to the war, Brown undoubtedly saw his playing career peak with the Clarets. The fee of £12,500 was surprisingly high for a 34-year-old, and reflected Brown's standing in the game.

The next month saw little immediate improvement in the team's fortunes, although they did at least manage to score in all the games in October. Brown's initial successor at centre-half was 36-year-old veteran Bob Johnson, who had first appeared in the pre-war side, but Arthur Woodruff, himself only a year younger, took over the role as Joe Loughran, a comparative youngster of 33, enjoyed an extended run in the side at right-back. Jack Hays meanwhile took over on the left wing as Ian Wilson was dropped to the reserves.

Arriving late in October, Cliff Britton's successor in the manager's chair was Frank Hill, a member of the legendary Arsenal side that had won three consecutive League titles in the 1930s, for whom the move to Burnley was a big step up from Third Division Crewe, where he had cut his managerial teeth. His first full month in charge brought two wins and two defeats, the highlight being a Ray Harrison hat-trick in a 3-0 win against Bolton.

Reg Attwell
one of the all-time greats in claret and blue

Hill's first moves in the transfer market came in December 1948, when Jack Knight moved to Preston in exchange for centre-forward Andy McLaren, while another front man, Alf Clarke, arrived from the manager's old club Crewe. But the most significant newcomer to the first team around this time was undoubtedly Tommy Cummings. The 20-year-old centre-half had an outstanding debut in a 2-2 draw at

Manchester City a week before Christmas, and would soon make the number five shirt his own. Meanwhile, another of the 1947 Cup side bowed out, with Peter Kippax moving to Liverpool in January 1949. He was only to make one appearance for the Reds, his final game in League football.

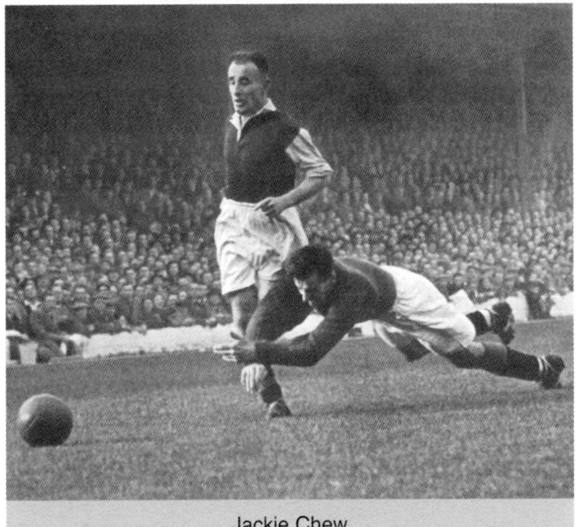

Jackie Chew
top scorer from the right wing

Two defeats against Stoke ensured a less than festive Christmas, then January as ever brought the Cup. The third round brought the chance for revenge against the Clarets' 1947 Wembley nemesis, Charlton, and the chance was duly taken as newcomers McLaren and Clarke scored the goals that gave Burnley a 2-1 victory after extra time. The reward was an away tie at Third Division high-fliers Rotherham, where Jack Spencer, a player who had come through the Turf Moor ranks, scored the only goal of the game. Burnley's opponents in the last sixteen were Brentford, and it was there that the dream ended, despite rare strikes from both Reg Attwell and George Bray, it was the Second Division side that went through by 4-2 at Griffin Park.

Tommy Cummings was making a big impression, notably with a fine display against Jackie Milburn in a 1 -1 draw at Newcastle, and, with Joe Loughran holding down the right-back role, there was no place in the side for Arthur Woodruff in the early months of 1949. Otherwise, though, the old guard was still holding on, but the age of the side was beginning to take its toll and League form was indifferent. There were occasional high spots, such as a 3-0 win against Chelsea in February, but away from Turf Moor the team struggled badly for results, and it was not until the end of March that they registered only the second away win of the season, ever-reliable Jackie Chew notching the only goal of the game at Bolton.

There were then eight games left, with the best that Burnley could reasonably hope for being a place in the top half of the table. It wasn't to be, and the season fizzled out disappointingly, with only one further victory, 3-1 against Derby, and that followed by four consecutive games without scoring. The final home game, against Liverpool of all clubs, attracted only 17,693 to the Turf as supporter interest ebbed away, and the final position of fifteenth felt like failure after the triumphs of the two previous campaigns.

Disruption had played its part in the side's disappointing showing. Several players had suffered with injuries, and the captain's armband never found a regular wearer after Alan Brown's departure, with Bob Johnson, Harry Potts, George Bray, Joe Loughran and Harold Mather all leading the side out at some stage of the season. Andy McLaren's stay at the club proved very brief, as he moved on to Sheffield United after only three months after failing to settle in the area. And of course, the old guard were not getting any younger, not that Burnley were the only club with this problem in the years immediately following the war.

There was good news in 1948-49, however. The average home crowd of 30,290, while down on the previous season's record-breaking level, remained healthy. Although, Tommy Cummings apart, no young player at the club had seriously challenged for a regular first-team spot, the promise for the future was evident as Burnley Reserves won the Central League title for the first time, their best previous showing in that competition being third place.

Reg Attwell was selected for the Football League side, following in the footsteps of Arthur Woodruff, Peter Kippax and Alan Brown over the previous two seasons. Attwell seemed the best bet for a full England cap, but sadly he never quite made that breakthrough, and Welshman Billy Morris remained the only full international on Burnley's books.

So there was no cause for despondency as the end of the decade approached. Burnley had survived their second season back among the elite, and the good times were in fact only just beginning.

1948-49 - First Division

		P	W	D	L	F	A	Pts
1	Portsmouth	42	25	8	9	84	42	58
2	Manchester U	42	21	11	10	77	44	53
3	Derby C	42	22	9	11	74	55	53
4	Newcastle U	42	20	12	10	70	56	52
5	Arsenal	42	18	13	11	74	44	49
6	Wolverhampton W	42	17	12	13	79	66	46
7	Manchester C	42	15	15	12	47	51	45
8	Sunderland	42	13	17	12	49	58	43
9	Charlton A	42	15	12	15	63	67	42
10	Aston Villa	42	16	10	16	60	76	42
11	Stoke C	42	16	9	17	66	68	41
12	Liverpool	42	13	14	15	53	43	40
13	Chelsea	42	12	14	16	69	68	38
14	Bolton W	42	14	10	18	59	68	38
15	BURNLEY	42	12	14	16	43	50	38
16	Blackpool	42	11	16	15	54	67	38
17	Birmingham C	42	11	15	16	36	38	37
18	Everton	42	13	11	18	41	63	37
19	Middlesbrough	42	11	12	19	46	57	34
20	Huddersfield T	42	12	10	20	40	69	34
21	Preston NE	42	11	11	20	62	75	33
22	Sheffield U	42	11	11	20	57	78	33

1948-49

Manager : Cliff Britton until September 1948, then Frank Hill

Division One (15th)

Note	No	Date			Opponents	Result		h/t	Goalscorers/times	Opp. goal times
	1	Aug	21	h	MANCHESTER C	W	1-0	0-0	Billingham 60	
	2		25	a	Charlton A	L	1-3	1-1	Chew 14	8, 70, 87
	3		28	a	Portsmouth	L	0-1	0-1		15
	4		31	h	CHARLTON A	D	0-0	0-0		
	5	Sep	4	h	NEWCASTLE U	L	0-3	0-2		8, 34, 81
	6		6	h	PRESTON N E	W	1-0	1-0	Chew 20	
	7		11	a	Middlesbrough	L	1-4	0-1	Potts 54	30, 47, 82, 85
	8		15	a	Preston N E	W	3-0	1-0	Chew 18, Bray 60p, Billingham 75	
	9		18	h	BIRMINGHAM C	D	2-2	0-1	Chew 59, Potts 80	1, 69
	10		25	a	Chelsea	L	0-1	0-0		88
Alan Brown's last game	11	Oct	2	h	EVERTON	W	1-0	0-0	Wilson 62	
	12		9	a	Arsenal	L	1-3	1-1	Chew 30	38, 60, 87
	13		16	h	HUDDERSFIELD T	L	1-2	1-0	Billingham 34	66, 89
	14		23	a	Manchester U	D	1-1	0-0	Billingham 85	84
	15		30	h	SHEFFIELD U	W	2-0	1-0	Chew 36, Knight 60	
	16	Nov	6	a	Aston Villa	L	1-3	1-1	Haigh 34	24, 57, 68
	17		13	h	SUNDERLAND	W	3-1	1-1	Chew 27, Hays 57, Attwell 76p	15
	18		20	a	Wolverhampton W	L	0-3	0-2		31, 45, 70
	19		27	h	BOLTON W	W	3-0	1-0	Harrison (3) 12, 65, 86	
	20	Dec	4	a	Liverpool	D	1-1	0-0	Potts 74	79
	21		11	h	BLACKPOOL	W	2-0	1-0	Harrison 8, Morris 61	
	22		18	a	Manchester C	D	2-2	0-1	Harrison 53, Attwell 65p	40og, 85
	23		25	h	STOKE C	L	1-3	0-2	Potts 70	15, 38, 80
	24		27	a	Stoke C	L	1-2	1-0	Chew 31	60, 75
Billingham's last game	25	Jan	1	h	PORTSMOUTH	W	2-1	1-1	Chew 13, McLaren 70	20og
	26		15	a	Newcastle U	D	1-1	1-0	Morris 26	84
	27		22	h	MIDDLESBROUGH	D	0-0	0-0		
	28	Feb	5	a	Birmingham C	D	0-0	0-0		
	29		19	h	CHELSEA	W	3-0	1-0	Attwell 38p, Morris 60, Harrison 82	
	30		26	a	Everton	L	1-2	0-2	Attwell 60p	5, 31
	31	Mar	5	h	ARSENAL	D	1-1	1-0	Potts 4	90
	32		12	a	Huddersfield T	L	0-1	0-1		8
	33		19	h	WOLVERHAMPTON W	D	0-0	0-0		
	34		26	a	Bolton W	W	1-0	1-0	Chew 8	
	35	Apr	2	h	ASTON VILLA	D	1-1	1-1	Chew 28	25
	36		9	a	Sunderland	D	0-0	0-0		
	37		15	h	DERBY C	W	3-1	0-1	Potts 76, Hays 84, Harrison 88	43
	38		16	h	MANCHESTER U	L	0-2	0-0		56, 71
	39		18	a	Derby C	L	0-2	0-2		12, 19
	40		23	a	Sheffield U	D	0-0	0-0		
	41		30	h	LIVERPOOL	L	0-2	0-0		83, 85
	42	May	7	a	Blackpool	D	1-1	1-0	Potts 8	67

FA Cup

Note	Rd	Date			Opponents	Result		h/t	Goalscorers/times	Opp. goal times
after extra time, 1-1 at 90 mins	3	Jan	8	h	CHARLTON A	W	2-1	0-0	McLaren 63, Clarke 102	74
	4		29	a	Rotherham U	W	1-0	0-0	Spencer 53	
	5	Feb	12	a	Brentford	L	2-4	0-1	Bray 57, Attwell 63	1, 58, 74, 79

Final, Wolverhampton W 3-1 Leicester C, at Wembley.

Other first team matches (friendlies and/or as detailed)

Note	Date			Opponents	Result		Goalscorers
Lancs Cup	Sep	28	h	SOUTHPORT	W	3-0	Chew, J.Knight (2)
Lancs Cup	Nov	10	a	Manchester C	D	1-1	Spencer
Lancs Cup, aet, 1-1 at 90m		16	h	MANCHESTER C	L	1-2	Hays
	May	15	a	Real Madrid XI	D	0-0	
		22	a	Deportivo La Coruna	L	2-3	Attwell p, Morris
at Les Corts Stadium		26	a	Barcelona	W	1-0	Morris
at Les Corts Stadium		28	a	Barcelona	L	0-1	

Att.	Pos	Strong	Woodruff	Mather	Attwell	Brown	Bray	Chew	Morris	Billingham	Knight	Hays	Potts	Wilson	Loughran	Harrison	Johnson	Haigh	Cummings	Martindale	McLaren	Clarke	Kirkham	J Spencer	
33,621		1	2	3	4	5	6	7	8	9	10	11													1
29,397		1	2	3	4	5	6	7	8	9	10	11													2
37,846	18	1	2	3	4	5	6	7	8	9			10	11											3
18,926		1	2	3		5	6	7			8		10	11	4	9									4
32,826	19	1	2	3	4	5					8	7	10	11	6	9									5
35,665		1		3	4	5	6	7	8				10	11	2	9									6
28,903	20	1		3	4	5	6	7	8				10	11	2	9									7
33,032		1		3	4	5	6	7	8	9			10	11	2										8
34,081	15	1		3	4	5	6	7	8	9			10	11	2										9
53,193	17	1		3	4		6	7	8	9	10			11	2		5								10
31,341	15	1		3	4	5	6	7	8	9			10	11	2										11
53,647	16	1	2	3			6	7	8	9			10	11	4		5								12
28,976	17	1	2	3			6	7	8	9			10	11	4		5								13
49,919	17	1	5	3	4		6	7		9	8			11	2			10							14
26,216	16	1	5	3	4		6	7		9	8	11			2			10							15
43,323	17	1	5	3	4		6	7		9	8	11			2			10							16
18,939	16	1	5	3	4		6	7		9		11	8		2			10							17
37,096	16	1	5	3	4		6	7		9		11	8		2			10							18
37,291	16	1	5	3	4		6	7	8			11	10		2	9									19
41,001	15	1	5	3	4		6	7	8			11	10		2	9									20
37,969	15	1	5	3	4		6	7	8			11	10		2	9									21
26,849	14	1		3	4		6	7	8			11	10		2	9			5						22
39,262		1	5	3	4		6	7	8			11	10		2	9									23
39,583	15	1	5	3	4			7				11	10		2					6	8	9			24
31,045	15	1	5	3	4		6	7		9		11	10		2						8				25
33,439	14	1		3	4			7	8			11	10		2				5	6		9			26
36,506	14	1		3	4		6	7				11	10		2	9			5		8				27
34,003	13	1			4		6	7	8			11	10		2				5				3	9	28
28,754	12	1		3	4		6	7	8			11	10		2	9			5						29
34,568	14	1		3	4		6	7	8			11	10		2	9			5						30
20,810	12	1		3	4		6	7	8			11	10		2	9			5						31
23,136	14	1	2	3	4		6	7	8	9		11	10						5						32
31,804	14	1		3	4		6	7	8			11	10		2	9			5						33
26,593	12	1		3	4		6	7	8			11	10		2	9			5						34
24,709	10	1		3	4		6	7	8			11	10		2	9			5						35
34,410	11	1		3	4		6	7	8			11	10		2	9			5						36
30,966		1		3	4		6	7	8			11	10		2	9			5						37
38,682	10	1		3	4		6	7	8			11	10		2	9			5						38
26,095	12	1		3			4					7	10	11	2	9		8	5	6					39
33,508	13	1		3			6	7	8			11	10		2	9			5	4					40
17,693	13	1		3			6	7	8			11	10		2	9			5	4					41
21,626	15	1		3			6	7	8				10	11	2	9			5	4					42
Appearances		42	19	41	35	10	39	40	31	16	8	30	36	14	38	23	3	6	18	6	3	2	1	1	
Goals (43)					4		1	11	3	4	1	2	7	1		7		1			1				

Att.	Strong	Woodruff	Mather	Attwell	Brown	Bray	Chew	Morris	Billingham	Knight	Hays	Potts	Wilson	Loughran	Harrison	Johnson	Haigh	Cummings	Martindale	McLaren	Clarke	Kirkham	J Spencer	
37,000	1	5	3	4		6	7				11	10		2						8	9			3
22,000	1		3	4		6	7				11	10		2				5			9		8	4
34,000	1			4		6	7				11	10		2				5			9	3	8	5
Appearances	3	1	2	3		3	3				3	3		3				2		1	3	1	2	
Goals (5)				1		1														1	1		1	

1949-50

OBITUARY
DAVID TAYLOR
DIED 6 AUGUST 1949, AGED 65

Widely acknowledged as the fastest full-back in the Football League, Scotsman David Taylor had a reputation as a sprinter on both sides of the border. He was signed from Bradford City in 1911 to fill Burnley's left-back spot. Whilst at Valley Parade he had collected an FA Cup winners medal, the Bantams beating Burnley on the way to lifting the famous old trophy in 1911. Taylor had started his playing career with Motherwell and also played for Glasgow Rangers before heading south. A regular in the Burnley side before the Great War, he won his second FA Cup winner's medal on that famous day at the Crystal Palace in 1914. After the war, however, he was unable to command a regular place in the first team but managed to re-establish himself in 1922 and only missed five games over the following two seasons. He decided to end his playing career and returned to Scotland to manage St Johnstone and later had a brief spell as a coach with Blackburn Rovers. He returned to the management scene for two years at Carlisle United before eventually retiring from the game and returning once again to Scotland.
RIP

Frank Hill began his first full term in charge at Turf Moor with much the same personnel as he had at the end of the previous season. The only relatively unfamiliar name in the line-up for the opening game, away at Arsenal, was Len Martindale, most of whose first-team experience had come as a teenager in the pre-war era. Billy Morris scored the only goal of that game, and Burnley maintained this fine start, picking up nine points from the first six games, the only side to take anything from them in this spell being a resurgent Sunderland. This opening spell, which saw the Clarets briefly lead the First Division, brought the return of Arthur Woodruff in his familiar right-back slot. The player who had taken his place there for most of the previous season, Joe Loughran, moved to Southend in September following his appointment as an advisor to Kent Education Authority in his capacity as a PE instructor, and went on to enjoy four further years of League football before retiring from the game.

Another player to leave the club around this time was Jack Billingham, whose prominent role in the 1946-47 promotion side was sometimes overlooked as Ray Harrison had been preferred for that season's Cup Final. Billingham had been a fine servant to the Clarets since before the war, but younger centre-forwards were keeping him out of the first-team picture and he moved to Third Division Carlisle.

Burnley's ageing side could not keep up the pace at the top of the table and fell away somewhat, winning only two of their next nine games and scoring only five goals in the process. The defence still retained something of the "Iron Curtain" quality, but up front Burnley often fell short. Changes were made up front in the attempt to rectify this failing, with Harrison being replaced by Alf Clarke, who in turn gave way to Jack Spencer, but the killer goal touch continued to elude the team. In League table terms, fortunately, it never mattered too much, 1949-50 saw one of the most closely-contested First Division campaigns, and Burnley were one of many clubs who stayed in contention not too far from the top.

November brought a revival of form with three wins, including one over reigning champions and the side destined to retain the title, Portsmouth, and a very creditable goalless draw at Molineux against Wolves. Then the first week in December 1949 saw a rare goal feast at Turf Moor as Everton were thrashed 5-1, with Harry Potts scoring his only hat-trick for the club. There was a settled side at this stage, and it included eight of the team who had played at Wembley three seasons earlier, the only exceptions being Tommy Cummings at centre-half, Jack Spencer at centre-forward and Jack Hays on the left wing.

That side played together for ten consecutive games until, just after Christmas, a new face appeared in the line-up. It was Les Shannon, who had recently signed from Liverpool for £6,000. A perpetual reserve at Anfield, Shannon had impressed playing for a representative Central League side against Burnley Reserves, the previous season's Champions. His debut, against Blackpool, was on the right wing in place of Jackie Chew, but his impact was less than immediate and his best days as a Claret still lay some way ahead.

George Bray
player, coach and kit man
during a Burnley career of over 50 years

By Christmas 1949, the improved form had come to an end, and after the Christmas Eve victory at Bolton, the Clarets went ten League games without a further win, the "goals for" column as ever illustrating the root of the problem. The only good news around this time came in the FA Cup. The third round brought a trip to Notts County, the side who dominated that season's Third Division South and who had among their ranks a very distinguished ex-Claret in Tommy Lawton. It seems incredible these days that a player of his stature should have been playing Third Division football, still aged only 30. However, Tommy Cummings was more than a match for Turf Moor's one-time boy wonder, and Burnley eased into the fourth round with a 4-1 win. Another Third Division side, Port Vale, were next, and amazingly nearly 50,000 packed the Turf for this tie; the magic of the Cup was plainly very much intact in 1950. Burnley won 2-1 to qualify for a fifth round trip to Highbury, where Arsenal won 2-0 on their way to an eventual Wembley triumph.

Arthur Woodruff
almost 300 Burnley games either side of World War 2

The long run without a League win finally ended in March 1950 when Les Shannon's first senior Burnley goal proved enough to beat Huddersfield at Turf Moor. The following week, Harry Potts scored the only goal of the game to beat Aston Villa, and at this stage Burnley were only seven points behind the First Division leaders. 1949-50 was surely a season of "if only", if only there had been more consistency, more firepower up front, the Clarets could have been serious contenders.

Easter 1950 brought two more newcomers into the side. Scottish defender Jock Aird had been at the club for nearly two years before he got his chance, replacing Arthur Woodruff at right-back, although the veteran would not be finished for a while yet. He performed well against Billy Liddell in a 0-2 home defeat against Liverpool on Good Friday, while on Easter Monday the return trip to Anfield saw a first team bow for 18-year-old winger Roy Stephenson as Burnley took revenge with Alf Clarke scoring in a 1-0 win. Clarke in fact was arguably the star performer at the end of the season, scoring in each of the last four games, three of which Burnley won. They rounded off the campaign with a 3-2 home win against Middlesbrough, when one of the other scorers was Harry Potts, cementing his position as Burnley's leading scorer for the third time since the war. That proved to be Potts' last goal for the Clarets. The team's final position was tenth, just eight points behind champions Portsmouth. Only Pompey and Blackpool conceded fewer goals than Burnley's 40, but conversely only relegated Manchester City and Birmingham registered less than the 40 scored by the Clarets. Even so, there had been a definite improvement over the season before.

The Central League title was not retained, but Burnley finished a very creditable third in the reserves' competition, and unlike their senior counterparts the second string were a free-scoring outfit, averaging nearly two goals a game. Several of the reserves were starting to press their claim for first-team recognition and could not be denied for much longer. Shannon, Aird and Stephenson had already broken through and names such as Bill Holden and Jimmy Adamson were ones that would soon become much better-known with the Burnley public. Most significant of all there was also a teenager from Northern Ireland whose time was not too far away.

1949-50 - First Division

		P	W	D	L	F	A	Pts
1	Portsmouth	42	22	9	11	74	38	53
2	Wolverhampton W	42	20	13	9	76	49	53
3	Sunderland	42	21	10	11	83	62	52
4	Manchester U	42	18	14	10	69	44	50
5	Newcastle U	42	19	12	11	77	55	50
6	Arsenal	42	19	11	12	79	55	49
7	Blackpool	42	17	15	10	46	35	49
8	Liverpool	42	17	14	11	64	54	48
9	Middlesbrough	42	20	7	15	59	48	47
10	BURNLEY	42	16	13	13	40	40	45
11	Derby C	42	17	10	15	69	61	44
12	Aston Villa	42	15	12	15	61	61	42
13	Chelsea	42	12	16	14	58	65	40
14	West Bromwich A	42	14	12	16	47	53	40
15	Huddersfield T	42	14	9	19	52	73	37
16	Bolton W	42	10	14	18	45	59	34
17	Fulham	42	10	14	18	41	54	34
18	Everton	42	10	14	18	42	66	34
19	Stoke C	42	11	12	19	45	75	34
20	Charlton A	42	13	6	23	53	65	32
21	Manchester C	42	8	13	21	36	68	29
22	Birmingham C	42	7	14	21	31	67	28

1949-50

Manager : Frank Hill

Division One (10th)

	No.	Date			Opponents	Result		h/t	Goalscorers/times	Opp. goal times
	1	Aug	20	a	Arsenal	W	1-0	1-0	Morris 13	
	2		23	h	SUNDERLAND	D	2-2	2-2	Harrison 8, Attwell 44p	15, 33
Loughran's last game	3		27	h	BOLTON W	W	2-1	1-0	Potts 17, Chew 54	53
	4		31	a	Sunderland	L	1-2	1-1	Clarke 22	16, 84p
	5	Sep	3	a	Birmingham C	W	1-0	1-0	Clarke 14	
	6		5	h	STOKE C	W	2-1	1-0	Potts (2) 23, 48	70
	7		10	h	DERBY C	L	0-1	0-1		28
	8		12	a	Stoke C	D	1-1	1-1	Attwell 30p	1
	9		17	a	West Bromwich A	L	0-3	0-3		11, 27, 41
	10		24	h	MANCHESTER U	W	1-0	1-0	Spencer 7	
	11	Oct	1	a	Chelsea	W	1-0	0-0	Spencer 63	
	12		8	h	NEWCASTLE U	L	1-2	0-1	Attwell 85p	37, 46
	13		15	a	Fulham	L	0-1	0-1		33
Harrison's last game	14		22	h	MANCHESTER C	D	0-0	0-0		
	15		29	a	Charlton A	D	1-1	0-1	Chew 86	23
	16	Nov	5	h	ASTON VILLA	W	1-0	1-0	Spencer 13	
	17		12	a	Wolverhampton W	D	0-0	0-0		
	18		19	h	PORTSMOUTH	W	2-1	1-0	Morris 19, Potts 62	67
	19		26	a	Huddersfield T	W	2-1	1-1	Chew 33, Bray 88	2
	20	Dec	3	h	EVERTON	W	5-1	3-1	Potts (3) 8, 31, 41, Hays 68, Spencer 86	21
	21		10	a	Middlesbrough	L	1-4	0-2	Hays 50	16, 31, 53, 56
	22		17	h	ARSENAL	D	0-0	0-0		
	23		24	a	Bolton W	W	1-0	0-0	Chew 57	
	24		26	h	BLACKPOOL	D	0-0	0-0		
	25		27	a	Blackpool	L	0-2	0-0		68, 78
	26		31	h	BIRMINGHAM C	D	1-1	0-1	Chew 67	7
	27	Jan	14	a	Derby C	D	1-1	0-1	Potts 50	38og
	28		21	h	WEST BROMWICH A	D	0-0	0-0		
	29	Feb	4	a	Manchester U	L	2-3	0-0	Potts 59, Carey 87og	49, 65, 77
	30		18	h	CHELSEA	L	1-2	0-1	Spencer 86	12, 63og
	31		25	a	Newcastle U	D	0-0	0-0		
	32	Mar	4	h	FULHAM	D	0-0	0-0		
	33		11	a	Portsmouth	L	1-2	0-2	Spencer 82	1, 25
	34		18	h	HUDDERSFIELD T	W	1-0	1-0	Shannon 45	
	35		25	a	Aston Villa	W	1-0	0-0	Potts 79	
	36	Apr	1	h	WOLVERHAMPTON W	L	0-1	0-1		2
	37		7	h	LIVERPOOL	L	0-2	0-0		47, 51
	38		8	a	Manchester C	L	0-1	0-1		16
	39		10	a	Liverpool	W	1-0	1-0	Clarke 44	
	40		15	h	CHARLTON A	W	1-0	0-0	Clarke 59	
	41		22	a	Everton	D	1-1	1-1	Clarke 22	44
	42		29	h	MIDDLESBROUGH	W	3-2	2-0	Spencer 7, Clarke 40, Potts 60	69, 79

FA Cup

Rd	Date			Opponents	Result		h/t	Goalscorers/times	Opp. goal times
3	Jan	7	a	Notts C	W	4-1	1-1	Attwell 43p, Potts 78, Wilson 86, Spencer 87	17
4		28	h	PORT VALE	W	2-1	1-0	Hays 16, Spencer 48	90
5	Feb	11	a	Arsenal	L	0-2	0-2		13, 39

Final, Arsenal 2-0 Liverpool, at Wembley.

Other first team matches (friendlies and/or as detailed)

	Date			Opponents	Result		Goalscorers
Lancs Cup	Oct	18	h	BURY	W	4-0	Spencer (2), Henderson, Wilson
Lancs Cup	Nov	29	h	CHESTER	D	4-4	Chew, Clarke, Wilson (2)
Lancs Cup	Jan	18	a	Chester	W	4-3	Samuels, O'Neill (3)
Lancs Cup	Apr	18	a	Rochdale	W	2-1	Potts, Chew
Lancs Cup final	May	6	h	LIVERPOOL	W	3-0	Spencer, Attwell p, Clarke
		10	a	Stuttgart	L	1-2	Stephenson
		14	a	Nuremburg	W	2-1	Attwell, Stephenson
in Frankfurt		18	a	South German XI	L	3-4	Clarke (2), Hays
		20	a	Wiesbaden	W	5-0	unknown (5)

Att.	Pos	Strong	Loughran	Mather	Attwell	Cummings	Martindale	Chew	Morris	Harrison	Potts	J Hays	Woodruff	Clarke	Wilson	Henderson	J Spencer	Bray	Shannon	Kirkham	W Hayes	Haigh	Aird	Stephenson		
47,794		1	2	3	4	5	6	7	8	9	10	11														1
35,599		1	2	3	4	5	6	7	8	9	10	11														2
31,581	5	1	2	3	4	5	6	7	8	9	10	11														3
53,032		1		3	4	5	6	7	8		10	11	2	9												4
36,341	4	1		3	4	5	6	7	8		10	11	2	9												5
22,575		1		3	4	5	6	7	8		10	11	2	9												6
34,600	4	1		3	4	5	6		8		10	11	2	9	7											7
25,004		1		3	4	5	6		8		10	11	2	9		7										8
37,091	6	1		3	4	5	6		8		10	11	2	9			7									9
41,262	4	1		3	4	5			7		10	11	2	9			8	6								10
54,574	3	1		3	4	5			7		10	11	2	9			8	6								11
37,268	5	1		3	4	5			7		10	11	2	9			8	6								12
34,313	7	1		3		5	4				10	11	2	9		7	8	6								13
25,063	6	1		3	4	5		7		9	10	11	2				8	6								14
29,195	7	1		3	4	5		7	8		10	11	2				9	6								15
24,030	6	1		3	4	5		7	8		10	11	2				9	6								16
40,216	7	1		3	4	5		7	8		10	11	2				9	6								17
28,541	5	1		3	4	5		7	8		10	11	2				9	6								18
19,154	5	1		3	4	5		7	8		10	11	2				9	6								19
19,961	5	1		3	4	5		7	8		10	11	2				9	6								20
26,369	5	1		3	4	5		7	8		10	11	2				9	6								21
25,651	6	1		3	4	5		7	8		10	11	2				9	6								22
34,461	5	1		3	4	5		7	8		10	11	2				9	6								23
49,815		1		3	4	5		7	8		10	11	2				9	6								24
31,074		1		3	4	5			8		10	11	2				9	6	7							25
25,473	6	1		3	4	5		7	8		10		2		11		9	6								26
32,464	7	1		3	4	5		7	8		10		2	9	11			6								27
26,129	8	1		3	4	5		7	8		10		2		11		9	6								28
48,528	7	1			4	5		7	8		10		2		11		9	6		3						29
23,446	8	1			4	5		7	8		10	11					9	6		3	2					30
30,032	9	1			4	5		7	8		10	11	2				9	6			3					31
19,858	8	1			4	5					10	11	2	9			8	6	7		3					32
26,344	9	1			4	5			8		10	11	2				9	6	7		3					33
19,960	8	1			4	5			8		10	11	2				9	6	7		3					34
29,923	8	1				5			8		10	11	2				9	6	7		3	4				35
23,171	10	1		3	4				8		10	11	5				9	6	7	2						36
33,025		1		3	4	5		11			10						9	6	7			8	2			37
31,298	13	1			4	5		11	8		10			9				6	7	3			2			38
43,716		1		3	4	5	10				8	11		9				6					2	7		39
20,867	10	1		3	4	5	10				8	11		9				6					2	7		40
35,784	10	1		3	4	5	10				8	11		9				6					2	7		41
12,367	10	1		3	4	5					8	11		9			10	6		2				7		42
Appearances		42	3	34	40	41	13	25	34	4	42	36	32	17	5	2	29	33	8	5	6	2	5	4		
Goals (40)					3			5	2	1	11	2		6			7	1	1						1	og

Att.		Strong	Loughran	Mather	Attwell	Cummings	Martindale	Chew	Morris	Harrison	Potts	J Hays	Woodruff	Clarke	Wilson	Henderson	J Spencer	Bray	Shannon	Kirkham	W Hayes	Haigh	Aird	Stephenson		
43,482		1		3	4	5		7	8		10		2		11		9	6								3
49,692		1		3	4	5		7	8		10	11	2				9	6								4
55,458		1			4	5		7	8		10		2		11		9	6		3						5
Appearances		3		2	3	3		3	3		3	1	3		2		3	3		1						
Goals (6)					1						1	1			1		2									

1950-51

This was to be the season when the Clarets' first team line-up finally began to take on a much different look from the heroes of 1946-47. There were no new faces in the side that took the field for the opening game, which for the second season running was against Arsenal, but the inclusion of Roy Stephenson on the left wing was perhaps a sign of the changes to come. The Gunners reversed the previous season's opening day scoreline by winning 1-0.

Jimmy Strong
more than 200 consecutive games in goal

Burnley were soon off the mark, however, registering two away wins over the following week, as old stagers Billy Morris, who scored both at Blackpool, and Jackie Chew, with the only goal at Sheffield Wednesday, ensured a good showing in the first published League table of the new campaign. Stephenson opened his Clarets scoring account on the third Saturday with a brace in the 3-1 Turf Moor victory against Middlesbrough, a game which also marked the debut of Bill Holden. A product of Bolton's famed Folds Road School, Holden had initially joined Burnley as an amateur in September 1949 before becoming a relatively late starter, aged 22, to the professional ranks at the start of this season. He quickly established himself as Burnley's first choice centre-forward, filling the void left after the departures of Billingham and Harrison as Alf Clarke and Jack Spencer had not quite managed to do.

October saw another of the stalwarts of the momentous 1946-47 leave Turf Moor. Harry Potts had been unsettled at the club, and he rejoined his former manager Cliff Britton at Everton, the fee of £20,000 setting a new Burnley record. In fact, Potts' best days as a player were already almost over, and although he would remain at Goodison for six years, his first-team appearances grew fewer as he moved more and more on to the coaching side. It was perhaps the first sign of greater things to come from a man whose most significant impact on Burnley F.C. was still to be seen.

Potts' final game was a 5-1 win against Charlton which brought Bill Holden's first two League goals. Holden scored again the following week in a 1-1 draw at Sunderland, but that game was much more notable for the debut of the player who took over Potts' number ten shirt. Manager Frank Hill had signed Jimmy McIlroy from the Northern Irish club Glentoran in March 1950 for £8,000, which may have seemed a large fee for a relatively unknown teenager, but it was soon clear that this was no gamble. "Mac" was four days short of his nineteenth birthday when he made his Burnley bow, and he was immediately the automatic choice in the inside-left position.

Six games had passed without a win before the Charlton game, which had also marked Reg Attwell's first appearance of the season following injury, but the Clarets embarked on a better run up to the end of November, a run which included McIlroy's first goal in a Burnley shirt, in a 2-0 home win against Wolves on 11 November 1950. They might have been in closer contention with the front-runners had it not been for some indifferent away results, a trend emphasised with a 1-4 defeat at lowly Fulham on the first Saturday in December.

Better news followed, with three wins and three clean sheets including a revenge win at Highbury, where Bill Holden scored the only goal. Christmas was disappointing, with only one point out of four against the side that would finish bottom at the end of the season, Everton, but the Clarets saw 1950 out in good style, pulling back from three goals down to draw 3-3 at Ayresome Park against League leaders Middlesbrough.

January, as ever, brought the third round of the F.A. Cup, and a trip to Villa Park. The last time Burnley had met Villa in the Cup had been four years earlier when a memorable victory set the Clarets on the road to Wembley, but there was to be no such joy this time as the "other" side in claret and blue ran out 2-0 winners. Villa Park was to become a place Burnley sides dreaded visiting in the fifties and this was the first of no less than ten defeats there in League and Cup during that decade.

10 February 1951 brought a trip to Bolton and another notable first team debut. Jimmy Adamson had already been at the club for four years and had seemed to be stuck in the reserves, never really showing his true potential as an inside forward and, once converted to wing-half, unable to displace Reg Attwell or George Bray as first choice. But at nearly 22 years old, he finally got his chance, taking over Attwell's number four shirt and performing so well that he kept his

place right through to the end of the season. Although Burnley's second golden era was still nearly a decade away, the nucleus of that side was already in place, with Cummings, McIlroy and now Adamson all first-team regulars by early 1951.

For all this, League form remained patchy. Jackie Chew scored both goals as Tottenham, destined to be League champions in their first season after promotion, were overcome at the Turf at the end of February, but this was the only victory in thirteen games in League and Cup between Christmas and Easter 1951. One player with something to celebrate, however, was goalkeeper Jimmy Strong, who completed a run of 200 consecutive League appearances, going right back to the post-war resumption, on 3 March 1951. Already 30 years old at the time of his Burnley debut, Strong had become Mr. Dependable as the Clarets' last line, and his record of goals conceded per game certainly stands comparison with most.

Bill Holden
top scorer in his first Turf Moor season

Good Friday brought an end to the poor run of results, when Bill Holden scored both goals as Chelsea were beaten 2-1, but this game also saw an end to Strong's remarkable unbroken run after he was injured in a clash with Bobby Smith, a centre-forward of the old school who would go on to feature in many clashes between Burnley and Tottenham a few years hence. Strong's record of 203 straight League appearances, though, stands as a Burnley record to this day, and it's difficult to see it being surpassed in the foreseeable future. Patient reserve Joe McNulty stepped in for the two remaining Easter games, a 1-2 defeat at Old Trafford and a 2-0 win at Stamford Bridge to complete the double over Chelsea.

Apart from Adamson's emergence, the two major changes in the side towards the end of the season were on the wings. Jackie Chew made way for Roy Stephenson on the right, and Stephenson proved his worth with two goals over Easter, while on the opposite wing Jack Hays' long run as first choice number eleven finally ended as the speedy Terry Lyons was promoted from the reserves. Lyons was the scorer in consecutive 1-0 wins against Wolves and Derby, but his time in the Turf Moor limelight was destined to be brief.

A season plagued by inconsistency fizzled out with three consecutive defeats, leaving Burnley in tenth place, the same position as the previous season but with three points fewer. The reserves had done well again however, this time finishing as runners-up in the Central League, while first-team gates actually showed a small improvement on the previous campaign with an average of 28,296. So, despite a lack of tangible rewards, 1950-51 was a season that maintained Burnley's steady progress as a side now firmly established in the First Division.

1950-51 - First Division

		P	W	D	L	F	A	Pts
1	Tottenham H	42	25	10	7	82	44	60
2	Manchester U	42	24	8	10	74	40	56
3	Blackpool	42	20	10	12	79	53	50
4	Newcastle U	42	18	13	11	62	53	49
5	Arsenal	42	19	9	14	73	56	47
6	Middlesbrough	42	18	11	13	76	65	47
7	Portsmouth	42	16	15	11	71	68	47
8	Bolton W	42	19	7	16	64	61	45
9	Liverpool	42	16	11	15	53	59	43
10	BURNLEY	42	14	14	14	48	43	42
11	Derby C	42	16	8	18	81	75	40
12	Sunderland	42	12	16	14	63	73	40
13	Stoke C	42	13	14	15	50	59	40
14	Wolverhampton W	42	15	8	19	74	61	38
15	Aston Villa	42	12	13	17	66	68	37
16	West Bromwich A	42	13	11	18	53	61	37
17	Charlton A	42	14	9	19	63	80	37
18	Fulham	42	13	11	18	52	68	37
19	Huddersfield T	42	15	6	21	64	92	36
20	Chelsea	42	12	8	22	53	65	32
21	Sheffield W	42	12	8	22	64	83	32
22	Everton	42	12	8	22	48	86	32

1950-51

Manager : Frank Hill

Division One (10th)

		Date			Opponents	Result		h/t	Goalscorers/times	Opp. goal times
	1	Aug	19	h	ARSENAL	L	0-1	0-0		87
Martindale's last game	2		21	a	Blackpool	W	2-1	0-1	Morris (2) 81, 89	15
	3		26	a	Sheffield W	W	1-0	1-0	Chew 37	
	4		29	h	BLACKPOOL	D	0-0	0-0		
	5	Sep	2	h	MIDDLESBROUGH	W	3-1	0-1	Stephenson (2) 57, 75, Morris 73	41
	6		4	h	PORTSMOUTH	D	1-1	0-0	Kirkham 80	75
	7		9	a	Huddersfield T	L	1-3	1-1	Stephenson 7	4og, 57p, 75
	8		16	h	NEWCASTLE U	D	1-1	1-0	Bray 35	65
	9		23	a	West Bromwich A	L	1-2	0-1	Spencer 59	41, 88
	10		30	h	STOKE C	D	1-1	0-0	Lyons 58	57
	11	Oct	7	a	Tottenham H	L	0-1	0-0		50
Potts' last game	12		14	h	CHARLTON A	W	5-1	0-1	Stephenson 61, Hays 68, Holden (2) 72, 88, Morris 86	25
	13		21	a	Sunderland	D	1-1	1-1	Holden 10	40p
	14		28	h	ASTON VILLA	W	2-0	1-0	Holden 28, Attwell 57	
	15	Nov	4	a	Manchester U	D	1-1	1-0	Holden 35	61
	16		11	h	WOLVERHAMPTON W	W	2-0	1-0	McIlroy 30, Holden 79	
	17		18	a	Derby C	D	1-1	1-0	Morris 30	48
	18		25	h	LIVERPOOL	D	1-1	0-1	Chew 82	12
	19	Dec	2	a	Fulham	L	1-4	0-2	O'Neill 65	30, 35og, 59, 75
	20		9	h	BOLTON W	W	2-0	1-0	McIlroy 42, Holden 84	
	21		16	a	Arsenal	W	1-0	1-0	Holden 25	
	22		23	h	SHEFFIELD W	W	1-0	0-0	Morris 48	
	23		25	a	Everton	L	0-1	0-0		75
	24		26	h	EVERTON	D	1-1	1-1	McIlroy 10	30
	25		30	a	Middlesbrough	D	3-3	1-3	Chew 35, McIlroy 50, Morris 86	7, 10, 25
	26	Jan	13	h	HUDDERSFIELD T	L	0-1	0-1		11og
	27		20	a	Newcastle U	L	1-2	0-2	Morris 57	7, 31
	28	Feb	3	h	WEST BROMWICH A	L	0-1	0-1		26
	29		10	a	Bolton W	D	1-1	1-0	Holden 7	86p
Hays' last game	30		17	a	Stoke C	D	0-0	0-0		
	31		24	h	TOTTENHAM H	W	2-0	1-0	Chew (2) 27, 55p	
	32	Mar	3	a	Charlton A	D	0-0	0-0		
	33		10	h	SUNDERLAND	D	1-1	0-1	McIlroy 76	18
	34		17	a	Aston Villa	L	2-3	2-2	Holden 35, Morris 43	18, 26, 82
	35		23	h	CHELSEA	W	2-1	1-0	Holden (2) 29, 80	60p
	36		24	h	MANCHESTER U	L	1-2	1-1	Stephenson 23	18, 59
	37		26	a	Chelsea	W	2-0	1-0	Stephenson 20, Morris 75	
	38		31	a	Wolverhampton W	W	1-0	0-0	Lyons 87	
	39	Apr	7	h	DERBY C	W	1-0	1-0	Lyons 26	
	40		14	a	Liverpool	L	0-1	0-1		43
	41		21	h	FULHAM	L	0-2	0-0		47, 79
	42	May	5	a	Portsmouth	L	1-2	1-2	Morris 17	8og, 39og

FA Cup

Rd	Month	Day		Opponents		Result	h/t	Goalscorers/times	Opp. goal times
3	Jan	6	a	Aston Villa	L	0-2	0-1		9, 63

Final, Newcastle U 2-0 Blackpool, at Wembley.

Other first team matches (friendlies and/or as detailed)

	Month	Day		Opponents		Result	Goalscorers
Lancs Cup	Oct	24	h	BLACKBURN R	W	3-1	McIlroy, Lyons. Morris
Lancs Cup	Jan	23	a	Oldham A	W	4-1	Clarke (2), Holden (2)
		27	h	BLACKBURN R	D	1-1	Lyons
	Apr	16	h	HAMILTON A	D	1-1	Holden
Lancs Cup semi		24	a	Bury	L	0-2	
		26	h	HAMBURG	L	1-3	Shannon
exhibition match at Kendal	May	1	n	Blackburn R	D	0-0	
in Ankara		13	a	Demispor	W	3-1	Samuels (2), Clarke
in Ankara		19	a	Ankaragucu	W	3-1	Samuels, McIlroy, Holden
		20	a	Besiktas	D	0-0	
		26	a	Galatasaray	D	0-0	
		27	a	Fenerbahce	W	3-2	Martindale (2), Shannon
		30	a	Besiktas	D	0-0	

Att.	Pos	Strong	Woodruff	Mather	Martindale	Cummings	Bray	Chew	Morris	Clarke	Potts	Stephenson	J Spencer	J Hays	Kirkham	Holden	Samuels	W Hayes	Rudman	Lyons	Attwell	McIlroy	O'Neill	Aird	Adamson	McNulty	
32,706		1	2	3	4	5	6	7	8	9	10	11															1
33,161		1	2	3	4	5	6	7	8	9			10	11													2
40,754	6	1	2	3		5	6	7	8		10		9	11	4												3
38,688		1	2	3		5	6	7	8		10		9	11	4												4
29,779	3	1	2	3		5	6		8			7	10	11	4	9											5
30,670		1	2	3		5	6				8	7		11	4	9	10										6
30,664	9	1	2	3		5	6		8		10	7		11	4	9											7
33,283	9	1	2	3		5	6		8		10	7		11	4	9											8
32,058	13	1	2			5	6		8			7	10	11	4	9		3									9
23,776	13	1	2			5	6				8	7	10			9		3	4	11							10
46,518	18	1	2	3			6	11	8		10	7				9		2	4								11
20,008	11	1	2	3		5	6		8		10	7		11		9					4						12
38,982	12	1	2	3		5	6		8			7		11		9					4	10					13
26,471	7	1	2	3		5	6	7	8					11		9					4	10					14
41,244	8	1	2	3		5	6	7	8					11		9					4	10					15
36,157	6	1	2	3		5	6	7	8					11		9					4	10					16
21,418	6	1	2	3		5	6	7	8					11		9					4	10					17
31,901	7	1	2	3		5	6	7	8					11		9					4	10					18
25,250	9	1	2	3		5	6	7						11		9					4	10	8				19
31,124	8	1	2	3		5	6	7	8					11		9					4	10					20
32,374	7	1	2	3		5	6	7	8					11		9					4	10					21
21,272	6	1	2	3		5	6	7	8					11		9					4	10					22
40,864		1	2	3		5	6	7	8					11		9					4	10					23
38,444		1	2	3		5	6	9	8			7		11							4	10					24
34,349	6	1		3		5	6	7	8				9	11				2			4	10					25
22,168	8	1		3		5	6	7	8					11		9		2			4	10					26
40,658	9	1		3		5	6	7	8					11		9		2			4	10					27
19,101	11	1		3		5	6	7	8					11		9					4	10		2			28
35,540	11	1		3		5	6	7	8					11		9						10		2	4		29
20,823	10	1	2	3		5	6	7	8					11		9						10			4		30
33,047	9	1	2	3		5	6	7	8							9				11		10			4		31
30,491	9	1	2	3		5	6	7	8							9				11		10			4		32
25,065	9	1	2	3		5	6	7	8							9				11		10			4		33
26,347	10	1	2	3		5	6	7	8							9				11		10			4		34
22,266		1	2	3		5	6	7	8							9				11		10			4		35
36,656	9		2	3		5	6		8			7				9				11		10			4	1	36
23,723			2	3		5	6		8			7				9				11		10			4	1	37
20,572	7	1	2	3		5	6		8			7				9				11		10			4		38
21,714	6	1	2	3		5	6		8			7				9				11		10			4		39
24,118	7	1	2	3		5	6		8			7				9				11		10			4		40
19,929	9	1	2	3		5	6					7				9	8			11		10			4		41
22,510	10	1	2	3		5	6	11	8	9		7										10			4		42
Appearances		40	37	40	2	41	42	28	38	3	9	18	7	27	7	35	2	6	2	12	17	30	1	2	14	2	
Goals (48)							1	5	11			6	1	1	1	12				3	1	5	1				

Att.	Pos	Strong	Woodruff	Mather	Martindale	Cummings	Bray	Chew	Morris	Clarke	Potts	Stephenson	J Spencer	J Hays	Kirkham	Holden	Samuels	W Hayes	Rudman	Lyons	Attwell	McIlroy	O'Neill	Aird	Adamson	McNulty	
38,833		1	2	3		5	6	7	8				9	11							4	10					3
Appearances		1	1	1		1	1	1	1				1	1							1	1					
Goals (0)																											

1951-52

It was a familiar-looking line-up at Charlton on the opening day of the new season. There were a couple of players in roles not normally associated with them, with Jock Aird, still not a first-team regular, at left-back, and Les Shannon, who had not made a single appearance during 1950-51, on the left wing. The normal order was soon restored when Harold Mather returned to the number three shirt, but the left wing was to provide the big story of the early part of the season.

The previous campaign's two mainstays on the left both left Turf Moor in September 1951, Jack Hays going to Bury and Terry Lyons to Bradford Park Avenue. Lyons' transfer was as a makeweight in the deal that brought in the new number eleven, and Burnley's record signing at £25,000, 26-year-old Billy Elliott had impressed with the Yorkshire side over the previous few seasons and soon became a favourite of the Burnley supporters with his speed and crossing ability. Unusually for a winger, Elliott was also a notoriously tough competitor whose battles with opposing defenders became the stuff of Turf Moor legend.

Despite this activity, it was a poor start to the season for the Clarets. The opening match was lost 0-1, and the first six games brought only one win, three goals and three points. Elliott's debut was in unpromising circumstances, a 0-5 hammering at Middlesbrough which also saw the first appearance of Tony Hapgood, son of the Arsenal legend Eddie. Hapgood had been a patient reserve for several years before getting his first team chance, and he scored on his second appearance, a 1-1 home draw against reigning champions Tottenham.

It looked like the season was finally taking off when, in early September, West Bromwich Albion came to the Turf and were trounced 6-1, with Billy Morris becoming the first Claret in nearly twenty years to score four goals in one game. But it proved a false dawn, as a week later Newcastle's George Robledo emulated Morris's feat when the Magpies thrashed Burnley 7-1 at St. James' Park. There was good news on the international front around this time, however. Morris's fine form for Burnley brought a recall to the Welsh side at the age of 33, while at the other end of the age scale, Jimmy McIlroy won his first cap for Northern Ireland, appearing against Scotland in Belfast shortly before his twentieth birthday. It was to be the start of a long and distinguished career for his country.

Morris was enjoying an Indian summer to his career, scoring more freely than ever before, while one of his 1946-47 colleagues, George Bray, was coming to the end of his days as a first-teamer. Something of an unsung hero in the post-war Burnley side, Bray had missed only a handful of games in the previous five seasons, but a defeat at Stoke at the end of September proved to be his final game, his place as captain of the side being taken by Tommy Cummings. His service to the Clarets was far from over however, he joined the coaching staff soon afterwards and remained with the club, eventually as first-team trainer, until 1974 when he retired. Even then he couldn't stay away, and his service at first team kit man lasted until the early 90s.

Still the results wouldn't come, though and after the West Brom triumph, the next eight games brought only one win, and the team's struggles were reflected in lower gates. It took until late November 1951 before the first away win of the season was registered, a 3-1 victory against relegation-bound Huddersfield being notable for Billy Elliott's first Burnley goal. By that time the Clarets were much too close to the bottom of the First Division table for comfort.

November and December brought some improvement, however, as Bill Holden found the shooting boots he had been lacking up to then, scoring in four successive games and then hitting a hat-trick on the last Saturday of the year as revenge was fully extracted against Middlesbrough. The ever-reliable Morris also notched three as Boro were beaten 7-1, Burnley's biggest win since the war up to that date. Four days earlier, on Christmas Day, Burnley had entertained Preston; they were beaten 2-0, but the game was most notable for a running battle between Billy Elliott and North End's own hard man, right-back Willie Cunningham. Cunningham was moved to the left side after several bruising encounters with the Burnley winger.

Billy Elliott
record signing from Bradford

The new year began with a 2-1 revenge victory against Preston at Deepdale, then soon afterwards came the start of another F.A. Cup campaign. It said a great deal for the esteem in which the Cup was held that Turf Moor saw a gate of well over 38,000, the best of the season so far, for the third round visit of Hartlepools United, perennial also-rans in the Third Division North. Les Shannon scored the only goal of a surprisingly close encounter to take the Clarets through to a home tie against Second Division Coventry, which brought an even bigger crowd and a 2-0 victory. Burnley were at this time enjoying their best spell of the season, and a 2-1 win against Newcastle on 19 January1925 saw what has gone down in Turf Moor history as the best goal ever scored on the ground. The unlikely marksman was Tommy Cummings, whose run took him from the edge of his own penalty area and past numerous hapless Magpies before firing with aplomb, left-footed, to give Burnley a 2-1 win.

Tommy Cummings
the greatest-ever goal at Turf Moor?

The next two League games saw a 4-1 win at Bolton followed by a 4-0 home trouncing of Stoke. Goals were coming from all parts of the team, with Billy Elliott on target three times over the two games, and the still-young midfield pairing of Jimmy Adamson and Jimmy McIlroy contributing two of the goals against Stoke. All was nicely set up for the fifth round Cup tie against Liverpool, and the Burnley populace responded accordingly, as Turf Moor saw its biggest crowd since the war (54,031). The team didn't let them down either, as Morris and Shannon's goals took the Clarets to their first FA Cup quarter-final since the Wembley year of 1947.

Sadly, that marked the high point of the season. Losing to mid-table Second Division opposition in the sixth round was bad enough, but to make matters worse it was Blackburn Rovers who were the victors, 3-1 at Ewood Park, after Jackie Chew had given Burnley the lead. The next League game was notable on two counts, Burnley's 1-0 win at Maine Road was their first away win against Manchester City in 21 League attempts, and a Claret was sent off for the only time in the first nineteen seasons of post-war League football. The "sinner" in question was Billy Elliott, and his crime, bizarrely, was "a look of intent", an incident, and a phrase, that had become part of Turf Moor folklore.

Good news was thin on the ground from then on, with six of the last nine games ending in defeat, including a 1-6 hammering at Old Trafford and a home defeat against Sunderland which saw Turf Moor's lowest post-war gate to that time, only 11,618. As if that were not bad enough, Bill Holden missed the end of the season after suffering a broken leg in a 1-4 defeat at Aston Villa. A notable playing career with Burnley came to an end in the season's penultimate game, a 1-4 defeat at Chelsea, when Arthur Woodruff played his 292nd and last game, more than fifteen years after his debut for the club. Jock Aird had been the regular number two for much of the 1951-52 season, but Woodruff actually replaced his long-time full-back partner Harold Mather for that match. A doughty defender, Woodruff would almost certainly have been among Burnley's leading appearance-makers had it not been for the war; as it was, he was, at 39 years and 7 days, up to then the second oldest player to appear for the Clarets, younger only than the legendary Jerry Dawson.

Time moves on however, and youth moves in. 17-year-old local lad Albert Cheesebrough was the scorer in that Chelsea defeat, playing on the right wing, having made his debut a week earlier on the left. Burnley were a team in transition, and 14th place was a disappointing finish after the promise of December and January. It would be a long, long time before they finished so far down the table again.

OBITUARY
HUGH MOFFAT
DIED 14 NOVEMBER 1952, AGED 67

Sadly for Hugh Moffat, his best-remembered contribution to Burnley FC's history nowadays is the occasion when, on 26 November 1904, he missed his train connection to the match at Chesterfield, resulting in the one occasion when the club has had to field a ten-man team. This is a shame, as Moffat was a consistent defender who gave sterling service to the club in the years just before its first golden era.

He joined Burnley from hometown club Congleton Town in 1904, and over the next six years was generally a regular in the side, featuring either at left-back or left-half. He was one of the relatively few players of that era to pass 200 League appearances for the club, and also weighed in with his share of goals.

He left Burnley for Oldham in 1910 and, after winning his only full international cap in 1913, came tantalisingly close to a League championship medal in 1915 when the Latics finished runners-up to Everton. He played on for a short time after the war with Chesterfield, then back at Congleton Town. He died close to his roots, in Macclesfield.

RIP

1951-52 - First Division

		P	W	D	L	F	A	Pts
1	Manchester U	42	23	11	8	95	52	57
2	Tottenham H	42	22	9	11	76	51	53
3	Arsenal	42	21	11	10	80	61	53
4	Portsmouth	42	20	8	14	68	58	48
5	Bolton W	42	19	10	13	65	61	48
6	Aston Villa	42	19	9	14	79	70	47
7	Preston NE	42	17	12	13	74	54	46
8	Newcastle U	42	18	9	15	98	73	45
9	Blackpool	42	18	9	15	64	64	45
10	Charlton A	42	17	10	15	68	63	44
11	Liverpool	42	12	19	11	57	61	43
12	Sunderland	42	15	12	15	70	61	42
13	West Bromwich A	42	14	13	15	74	77	41
14	BURNLEY	42	15	10	17	56	63	40
15	Manchester C	42	13	13	16	58	61	39
16	Wolverhampton W	42	12	14	16	73	73	38
17	Derby C	42	15	7	20	63	80	37
18	Middlesbrough	42	15	6	21	64	88	36
19	Chelsea	42	14	8	20	52	72	36
20	Stoke C	42	12	7	23	49	88	31
21	Huddersfield T	42	10	8	24	49	82	28
22	Fulham	42	8	11	23	58	77	27

1951-52

Manager : Frank Hill

Division One (14th)

	No.	Date			Opponents	Result		h/t	Goalscorers/times	Opp. goal times
	1	Aug	18	a	Charlton A	L	0-1	0-0		64
	2		21	h	LIVERPOOL	D	0-0	0-0		
	3		25	h	FULHAM	W	1-0	1-0	Holden 6	
	4		29	a	Liverpool	L	1-3	1-2	Morris 25	12, 44, 86
	5	Sep	1	a	Middlesbrough	L	0-5	0-2		37,40,55og,59,72
	6		3	h	TOTTENHAM H	D	1-1	0-1	Hapgood 79	35
	7		8	h	WEST BROMWICH A	W	6-1	4-0	Hapgood 7, Holden 15, Morris (4) 27, 33, 79, 82	78
	8		10	a	Tottenham H	D	1-1	1-0	McIlroy 25	90p
	9		15	a	Newcastle U	L	1-7	1-4	Morris 19	21,26,28,43,58,69,82
	10		22	h	BOLTON W	L	1-3	1-1	Morris 32	15, 69, 71
Bray's last game	11		29	a	Stoke C	L	1-2	1-2	Holden 42	2, 26
	12	Oct	6	h	BLACKPOOL	W	2-0	0-0	Shannon 52, Morris 60	
	13		13	a	Arsenal	L	0-1	0-1		33
	14		20	h	MANCHESTER C	D	0-0	0-0		
	15		27	a	Derby C	L	0-1	0-0		46
	16	Nov	3	h	ASTON VILLA	W	2-1	1-0	Morris (2) 15, 79	65
	17		10	a	Sunderland	D	0-0	0-0		
	18		17	h	WOLVERHAMPTON W	D	2-2	1-0	McIlroy 20, Cummings 85	49, 60
	19		24	a	Huddersfield T	W	3-1	0-0	Holden 46, Elliott 57, Shannon 78	61og
	20	Dec	1	h	CHELSEA	D	1-1	0-1	Holden 65	5og
	21		8	a	Portsmouth	D	2-2	2-1	Shannon 15, Holden 32	10p, 63
	22		15	h	CHARLTON A	W	1-0	0-0	Holden 77	
	23		22	a	Fulham	W	2-1	2-0	Shannon 5, Adamson 38	80
	24		25	h	PRESTON N E	L	0-2	0-1		13, 89
	25		29	h	MIDDLESBROUGH	W	7-1	4-1	Holden (3) 2, 4, 14, Morris (3) 26, 68, 86, Shannon 59	24
	26	Jan	1	a	Preston N E	W	2-1	1-1	Morris 15, Chew 75	19
	27		5	a	West Bromwich A	D	1-1	1-1	Morris 41	36
	28		19	h	NEWCASTLE U	W	2-1	1-0	Morris 10, Cummings 84	75
	29		26	a	Bolton W	W	4-1	2-0	Elliott 3, Holden (2) 44, 89, Morris 60	83
	30	Feb	9	h	STOKE C	W	4-0	2-0	Elliott (2) 27, 49, Adamson 43, McIlroy 76	
	31		16	a	Blackpool	L	0-1	0-1		44
	32	Mar	1	h	ARSENAL	L	0-1	0-1		31
	33		12	a	Manchester C	W	1-0	1-0	Shannon 20	
	34		15	h	DERBY C	L	0-1	0-1		31
	35		22	a	Aston Villa	L	1-4	0-2	Shannon 64	6, 32, 72, 89
	36		29	h	SUNDERLAND	L	0-1	0-1		26
	37	Apr	5	a	Wolverhampton W	W	2-1	0-1	Shannon 72, McIlroy 86	30
	38		11	h	MANCHESTER U	D	1-1	0-1	Shannon 85	30
	39		12	h	HUDDERSFIELD T	L	0-2	0-0		53, 86
	40		14	a	Manchester U	L	1-6	0-0	Morris 79	51,54,57,62,73,84
Woodruff's last game	41		19	a	Chelsea	L	1-4	0-3	Cheesebrough 54	6, 27, 34, 73
	42		26	h	PORTSMOUTH	W	1-0	0-0	Elliott 71	

FA Cup

Rd	Date			Opponents	Result		h/t	Goalscorers/times	Opp. goal times
3	Jan	12	h	HARTLEPOOLS U	W	1-0	1-0	Shannon 40	
4	Feb	2	h	COVENTRY C	W	2-0	2-0	Holden 30, Elliott 40	
5		23	h	LIVERPOOL	W	2-0	2-0	Morris 2, Shannon 44	
6	Mar	8	a	Blackburn R	L	1-3	1-1	Chew 38	44, 57, 82

Final, Newcastle U 1-0 Arsenal, at Wembley.

Other first team matches (friendlies and/or as detailed)

	Date			Opponents	Result		Goalscorers
	Aug	4	a	Hamburg	L	1-2	McIlroy
no details		5	a	Werder Bremen			
opening of Spandau stadium		8	a	Spandauer SV	W	4-0	Holden (2), Shannon (2)
Lancs Cup	Oct	16	a	Bury	W	1-0	Morris
Lancs Cup	Feb	20	h	BOLTON W	W	2-1	Unknown (2)
Lancs Cup semi	Apr	24	h	BLACKBURN R	W	1-0	Elliott
		29	h	HAMBURG	W	5-1	Shannon (2), Cheesebrough (2), Elliott
Lancs Cup final	May	10	a	Barrow	W	1-0	Cheesebrough

Att.	Pos	Strong	Woodruff	Aird	Adamson	Cummings	Attwell	Stephenson	Morris	Holden	McIlroy	Shannon	Mather	Bray	Hapgood	Elliott	Chew	McNulty	Clarke	Cheesebrough	Corr	
21,453		1	2	3	4	5	6	7	8	9	10	11										1
25,162		1	2		4	5		7	8	9	10	11	3	6								2
18,797	14	1	2		4	5		7	8	9	10	11	3	6								3
32,857		1	2		4	5		7	8	9	10	11	3	6								4
31,711	19	1	2		4	5		7	8	9			3	6	10	11						5
27,045		1	2		4	5			8	9	10		3	6	7	11						6
23,868		1	2			5	4		8	9	10		3	6	7	11						7
35,948	14	1		2		5	4		8	9	10		3	6	7	11						8
51,278	15	1			6	5	4		8	9	10		3	2	7	11						9
37,196	18	1	2			5	4		8	9	10		3	6	7	11						10
28,577	21	1	2			5	4		8	9	10		3	6	7	11						11
34,355	16	1	2		4	5	6	7	8			10	3			9	11					12
45,531	18	1	2		4	5	6	7	8			10	3			9	11					13
30,977	18	1		2	4	5	6		8		9	10	3			11	7					14
21,147	19	1	2		4	5	6		8	9	10		3			11	7					15
17,680	17	1		2	4	5	6		8	9	10		3			11	7					16
33,139	18	1		2	4	5	6		8	9	10		3			11	7					17
22,881	17	1		2	4	5	6		8	9	10		3			11	7					18
14,882	16	1		2	4	5	6		8	9		10	3			11	7					19
21,772	16	1		2	4	5	6		8	9		10	3			11	7					20
23,648	16	1		2	4	5	6		8	9	7	10	3			11						21
16,841	14	1		2	4	5	6		8	9	7	10	3			11						22
20,102	14	1		2	4	5	6		8	9	7	10	3			11						23
36,468		1		2	4	5	6		8	9	7	10	3			11						24
26,057	15	1		2	4	5	6		8	9		10	3			11	7					25
34,097		1		2	4	5	6		8	9		10	3			11	7					26
25,977	14	1		2	4	5	6		8	9		10	3			11	7					27
33,719	12	1		2	4	5	6		8	9		10	3			11	7					28
38,149	9	1		2	4	5	6		8	9		10	3			11	7					29
29,714	7	1		2	4	5	6		8		10	9	3			11	7					30
26,079	10			2	4	5	6		8	9		10	3			11	7	1				31
41,040	12	1		2	4	5	6		8	9		10	3			11	7					32
20,223		1		2	4	5	6		8	9		10	3			11	7					33
25,129	11	1		2	4	5	6			9	8	10	3			11	7					34
31,128	14			2	4	5	6		8	9		10	3			11	7	1				35
11,618	14	1		2	4	5	6				8	10	3			11	7		9			36
16,737	14			2	4	5	6		8		10	9	3			11	7	1				37
38,907				2	4	5	6		8		10	9	3				7	1		11		38
23,081	13			2	4	5	6		8		10	9	3				7	1		11		39
46,339	14			2	4	5	6		8		10		3			11		1		7	9	40
26,349	15	1	2	3	4	5	6		8		10	9				11				7		41
16,790	14	1		2	4	5	6				8	10	3			11			9	7		42
Appearances		36	13	30	38	42	37	7	39	31	28	30	40	10	7	36	24	6	2	5	1	
Goals (56)					2	2			18	12	4	9			2	5	1			1		

Att.	Strong	Woodruff	Aird	Adamson	Cummings	Attwell	Stephenson	Morris	Holden	McIlroy	Shannon	Mather	Bray	Hapgood	Elliott	Chew	
38,508	1		2	4	5	6		8	9		10	3			11	7	3
40,696	1		2	4	5	6		8	9		10	3			11	7	4
54,031	1		2	4	5	6		8	9		10	3			11	7	5
53,000	1		2	4	5	6		8	9		10	3			11	7	6
Appearances	4		4	4	4	4		4	4		4	4			4	4	
Goals (6)								1	1		2				1	1	

1952-53

There was again a familiar look to the Burnley side that started the season with a home game against Middlesbrough, although two of the mainstays, Jackie Chew and Jimmy McIlroy, were missing. That opener was lost 0-1, but, with the two absentees back at the expense of Albert Cheesebrough and Billy Morris, the next five matches were all won, to put the Clarets top of the First Division. These victories included two away from home, at West Brom and Stoke, and encouragingly the twelve goals scored were shared between five different players, McIlroy and Les Shannon leading the way with three apiece.

Jock Aird
regular at right back in 1952-53

Three draws followed, to maintain this fine start, before there was another team change. It came about whilst Billy Elliott, who had made his England debut in the close season, was on duty for the Football League. Into his place came 19-year-old left-winger Brian Pilkington, who performed impressively against England right-back Alf Ramsey although he was unable to prevent the side going down to defeat at White Hart Lane against Tottenham, whose winner came in the final minute. Two further defeats followed, but it was a temporary blip, as a 3-1 victory against reigning champions Manchester United at Old Trafford heralded a run of four victories. Bill Holden was especially prolific in front of goal around this time, scoring in eight of the ten games up to Christmas Day. The home game against Arsenal in mid-December 1952, a 1-1 draw, was notable in several respects. Reg Attwell failed to notify manager Frank Hill after he stayed behind to care for his sick mother after his father's funeral, and didn't turn up for the game. Two of the side that did play, however, had been colleagues of Attwell in the great 1946-47 side and were making their final appearances for the Clarets. Goalkeeper Jimmy Strong had been consistency itself and had missed only eight games since the postwar resumption, but at 36 he finally gave way to new signing Des Thompson, one of a family of goalkeepers, who had just arrived from York City. Billy Morris, the previous season's leading scorer, also bowed out due to age although he would remain on the Turf Moor staff for a further eight years as coach to the "A" team.

Two other newcomers to the side around this time were Joe Brown, who would achieve more behind the scenes in years to come than he ever did as a player in Burnley's colours, and full-back Doug "Jock" Winton. The regular line-up was seldom disturbed however, with Jock Aird now well-established as Harold Mather's full-back partner, Tommy Cummings at centre-half, Jimmy Adamson and Atwell the other half-backs, and Chew, McIlroy, Holden, Shannon and Elliott holding down the forward positions. It was a settled line-up that was getting good results and bringing increased crowds to the Turf. Seventeen League games between mid-October and the end of February brought only one defeat, at Sunderland, as the Clarets kept up the pressure near the top of the table. A return of three points out of four against Liverpool over Christmas 1952 was followed by a fine start to 1953, with Shannon scoring a hat-trick as West Brom were over-run 5-0 at Turf Moor. Albion, like Burnley at that stage, still entertained reasonable hopes of the League title.

OBITUARY
JOHN (JACK) HILLMAN
DIED 16 DECEMBER 1952, AGED 82

Banned for a complete season in 1900 after attempting to bribe Nottingham Forest players to throw a match so that the Clarets would not be relegated, the 'Burly One' is one of the great characters in Turf Moor history. Born in Devon he moved to Burnley with his family as a child and was spotted playing junior football in the town. A spell in the reserves led to promotion to the first team where he made over 100 appearances before being transferred to Everton and then Dundee. He returned to Burnley in 1898 but, 50 appearances and an England cap later, he was out for a season following the bribery scandal. He later won a Second Division Championship medal and an FA Cup winners medal with Manchester City and ended his playing career with Millwall before returning to Burnley when he became a trainer until the mid-1920s. He later ran a corner shop in his adopted home town, close to Turf Moor

RIP

The draw for the third round of the F.A. Cup presented the Clarets with a tricky task, a visit to Portsmouth who, while not the force they had been a few years earlier when they won successive League titles, remained a strong First Division side. Burnley proved equal to the task as Roy Stephenson, making his first appearance of the season, scored in a 1-1 draw, and then the replay at Turf Moor was won 3-1. There was more top-class opposition to follow, Sunderland were overcome by two Bill Holden goals in round four, but Arsenal, en route to their second post-war League title, proved too strong in the last sixteen, winning 2-0 at Turf Moor. Both the Sunderland and Arsenal games attracted crowds of over 50,000 as the FA Cup continued to be the competition that everyone wanted to watch.

Burnley by this time stood second in the League table, just a point behind leaders West Brom with a game in hand. Undeterred by the Cup defeat, they went on three days later to defeat Tottenham 3-2 thanks to Les Shannon's second hat-trick of the year, and moved into top place. Amazingly, this game was watched by less than 14000 spectators, three-quarters of the Cup crowd inexplicably staying away! Victory at struggling Derby on the following Saturday kept the Clarets in pole position, and it seemed like a first League title for 32 years could really be on the cards. It was a particularly tightly-fought First Division that season, though, and there was no room for slip-ups.

March 1953 began with Blackpool's visit to the Turf. Their 1-0 win saw an end to the unbeaten League run as the Seasiders became the only side to do the "double" over Burnley that season. Wins against Chelsea and Manchester United suggested that this was only a blip in form, but sadly that proved not to be the case as the rest of the season proved a sad anti-climax. A last-minute goal at Fratton Park enabled Portsmouth to take revenge for their F.A. Cup exit, and a run of five games yielding only one point saw the Clarets sliding out of contention by the time Easter was over. Changes were made for the next game, with Roy Stephenson and Joe Brown returning to the side and Jock Winton beginning his first run in the side, stepping in for Harold Mather at left-back. The hero of the day, though, was Bill Holden, who scored four in the 5-1 demolition of Sunderland.

Holden was on target again a week later, but this time Burnley were on the wrong end of a 5-1 scoreline against Wolves at Molineux. The season was fizzling out, and Burnley's chief contribution to the end of the season was as Arsenal's opponents on the final day, when the Gunners' 3-2 victory at Highbury clinched the League title that many had believed might be on its way to Turf Moor not that long before. Sixth place, then, was ultimately a disappointing finish, particularly as just seven extra points would have secured Burnley the championship. But there were lots of plus points to the 1952-53 campaign. The Clarets were combining success with truly entertaining, attacking football for the first time in years, although this is not to take anything away from the achievements of the "Iron Curtain" side. Some of the younger players were already established as first-team regulars, by the end of the season, McIlroy was still only 21, Adamson and Cummings 24, and Holden 25. Roy Stephenson and Brian Pilkington, both 20, and Albert Cheesebrough, 18, were on the fringes of the first eleven. Bill Holden became the first Burnley player to exceed twenty League goals in a season since the war, and Les Shannon's fifteen goals was an exceptional return for an inside-forward. The average Turf Moor gate of 28,480 was the best for four years at a time when the post-war attendance boom was starting to fade.

Billy Elliott had become an England regular, scoring three goals in his five appearances for the national side, while Jimmy McIlroy was by now firmly established in the Northern Ireland side. It was clear that the club was on the right lines, and as they "broke up" for the summer of 1953, there were plenty of grounds for optimism.

Jimmy McIlroy
the greatest of them all

1952-53 - First Division

		P	W	D	L	F	A	Pts
1	Arsenal	42	21	12	9	97	64	54
2	Preston NE	42	21	12	9	85	60	54
3	Wolverhampton W	42	19	13	10	86	63	51
4	West Bromwich A	42	21	8	13	66	60	50
5	Charlton A	42	19	11	12	77	63	49
6	BURNLEY	42	18	12	12	67	52	48
7	Blackpool	42	19	9	14	71	70	47
8	Manchester U	42	18	10	14	69	72	46
9	Sunderland	42	15	13	14	68	82	43
10	Tottenham H	42	15	11	16	78	69	41
11	Aston Villa	42	14	13	15	63	61	41
12	Cardiff C	42	14	12	16	54	46	40
13	Middlesbrough	42	14	11	17	70	77	39
14	Bolton W	42	15	9	18	61	69	39
15	Portsmouth	42	14	10	18	74	83	38
16	Newcastle U	42	14	9	19	59	70	37
17	Liverpool	42	14	8	20	61	82	36
18	Sheffield W	42	12	11	19	62	72	35
19	Chelsea	42	12	11	19	56	66	35
20	Manchester C	42	14	7	21	72	87	35
21	Stoke C	42	12	10	20	53	66	34
22	Derby C	42	11	10	21	59	74	32

1952-53

Manager : Frank Hill

Division One (6th)

	No.	Date			Opponents	Result		h/t	Goalscorers/times	Opp. goal times
	1	Aug	23	h	MIDDLESBROUGH	L	0-1	0-0		89
	2		26	h	STOKE C	W	3-2	1-2	Shannon (2) 3, 87, McIlroy 85	9, 11
	3		30	a	West Bromwich A	W	2-1	1-1	Chew 27, Elliott 65p	23
	4	Sep	1	a	Stoke C	W	3-1	1-1	McIlroy (2) 35, 89, Elliott 60	20
	5		6	h	NEWCASTLE U	W	2-1	1-1	Chew 10, Holden 50	36
	6		8	h	MANCHESTER C	W	2-1	1-1	Holden 40, Shannon 75	30
	7		13	a	Cardiff C	D	0-0	0-0		
	8		17	a	Manchester C	D	0-0	0-0		
	9		20	h	SHEFFIELD W	D	1-1	0-0	Shannon 60	56
	10		27	a	Tottenham H	L	1-2	0-0	Holden 70	50, 89
	11	Oct	4	h	DERBY C	L	1-2	1-0	Neilson 26og	80, 83
	12		11	a	Blackpool	L	2-4	0-1	Elliott 62p, Shannon 72	33, 60, 70, 82p
	13		18	h	CHELSEA	D	1-1	1-1	Holden 30	43
	14		25	a	Manchester U	W	3-1	2-1	McIlroy (2) 25, 36, Holden 81	4
	15	Nov	1	h	PORTSMOUTH	W	3-2	1-2	Holden 43, Shannon 68, Adamson 88	27, 40
	16		8	a	Bolton W	W	2-1	1-0	Barrass 7og, Holden 81	87
	17		15	h	ASTON VILLA	W	1-0	1-0	Elliott 30	
Burnley's 2000th League game	18		22	a	Sunderland	L	1-2	0-1	Holden 61	7, 83
	19		29	h	WOLVERHAMPTON W	D	0-0	0-0		
last games for Morris and Strong	20	Dec	13	h	ARSENAL	D	1-1	1-1	Holden 1	42
	21		20	a	Middlesbrough	D	2-2	0-1	Holden 46, Elliott 66	19, 72
	22		25	h	LIVERPOOL	W	2-0	2-0	McIlroy 12, Holden 19	
	23		26	a	Liverpool	D	1-1	0-1	Adamson 60	31p
	24	Jan	3	h	WEST BROMWICH A	W	5-0	1-0	McIlroy 32, Shannon (3) 52, 73, 84, Elliott 89	
	25		17	a	Newcastle U	D	0-0	0-0		
	26		24	h	CARDIFF C	D	0-0	0-0		
	27	Feb	7	a	Sheffield W	W	4-2	2-1	Holden (2) 2, 52, Shannon 28, McIlroy 76	1, 83p
	28		17	h	TOTTENHAM H	W	3-2	2-1	Shannon (3) 11, 30, 88	40, 51
	29		21	a	Derby C	W	3-1	2-1	Elliott 29, McIlroy 33, Chew 53	44
	30	Mar	3	h	BLACKPOOL	L	0-1	0-0		65
	31		7	a	Chelsea	W	2-0	1-0	Holden (2) 17, 70	
	32		14	h	MANCHESTER U	W	2-1	0-0	Chew 71, Holden 74	80p
	33		21	a	Portsmouth	L	1-2	1-1	Shannon 16	24, 88
	34		28	h	BOLTON W	L	0-1	0-0		56
	35	Apr	3	h	PRESTON N E	D	2-2	1-0	McIlroy 25, Elliott 82p	67, 72
	36		4	a	Aston Villa	L	0-2	0-1		22, 76
	37		6	a	Preston N E	L	1-2	1-0	McIlroy 20	55, 75p
	38		11	h	SUNDERLAND	W	5-1	1-0	Holden (4) 16, 46, 47, 75, Adamson 61	83
	39		18	a	Wolverhampton W	L	1-5	1-1	Holden 24	19, 66, 75, 81, 84
	40		22	a	Charlton A	D	0-0	0-0		
	41		25	h	CHARLTON A	W	2-0	0-0	Holden 65, Shannon 77	
Elliott's last game	42	May	1	a	Arsenal	L	2-3	1-3	Stephenson 8, Elliott 74	9, 13, 26

FA Cup

Round	Date			Opponents	Result		h/t	Goalscorers/times	Opp. goal times
3	Jan	10	a	Portsmouth	D	1-1	0-0	Stephenson 67	66
rep		13	h	PORTSMOUTH	W	3-1	1-0	McIlroy 8, Shannon 48, Elliott 80p	70
4		31	h	SUNDERLAND	W	2-0	2-0	Holden (2) 10, 28	
5	Feb	14	h	ARSENAL	L	0-2	0-0		59, 62

Final, Blackpool 4-3 Bolton W, at Wembley.

Other first team matches (friendlies and/or as detailed)

	Date			Opponents	Result		Goalscorers
Lancs Cup	Oct	28	h	PRESTON N E	L	0-1	
	Dec	30	a	Distillery	W	3-2	Adamson, Holden, Shannon
	Feb	28	a	Liverpool	L	2-3	Holden (2)
	May	9	a	Offenbach K	W	2-1	McIlroy, Elliott
		13	a	Schalke 04	L	1-3	Holden
		14	a	Bayern Munich XI	W	5-1	Shannon (2), Pilkington, Stephenson, Elliott
		17	a	Augsburg	W	1-0	Stephenson

Att.	Pos	Strong	Aird	Mather	Adamson	Cummings	Attwell	Cheesebrough	Morris	Holden	Shannon	Elliott	Chew	McIlroy	Pilkington	J Brown	Binns	Winton	Thompson	Rudman	Stephenson		
27,386		1	2	3	4	5	6	7	8	9	10	11											1
20,847		1	2	3	4	5	6			9	10	11	7	8									2
31,400	7	1	2	3	4	5	6			9	10	11	7	8									3
26,287		1	2	3	4	5	6			9	10	11	7	8									4
35,068	2	1	2	3	4	5	6			9	10	11	7	8									5
27,083		1	2	3	4	5	6			9	10	11	7	8									6
45,182	2	1	2	3	4	5	6			9	10	11	7	8									7
25,094		1	2	3	4	5	6			9	10	11	7	8									8
33,049	3	1	2	3	4	5	6			9	10	11	7	8									9
43,031	5	1	2	3	4	5	6			9	10		7	8	11								10
26,248	6	1	2	3	4	5	6		8	9	10		7		11								11
35,671	8	1	2	3	4	5	6			9	10	11	7	8									12
27,692	11	1	2	3	4	5				9	10	11	7	8		6							13
38,754	7	1	2	3	4	5	6			9	10	11	7	8									14
28,273	6	1	2	3	4	5	6			9	10	11	7	8									15
37,604	3	1	2	3	4	5	6			9	10	11	7	8									16
24,750	2	1		3	4	5	6			9	10	11	7	8			2						17
40,225	4	1		3	4	5	6			9	10	11	7	8			2						18
30,808	5	1		3	4	5	6			9	10	11	7	8				2					19
32,753	6	1	2	3	4	5			7	9	10	11	6	8									20
19,155	6		2	3	4	5	6			9	10	11	7	8					1				21
35,878			2	3	4	5	6			9	10	11	7	8					1				22
46,589			2	3	4	5	6			9	10	11	7	8					1				23
35,680	3		2	3	4	5	6			9	10	11	7	8					1				24
49,366	3		2	3	4	5	6			9	10	11	7	8					1				25
29,491	3		2	3	4	5				9	10	11	7	8					1	6			26
41,262	2		2	3	4	5	6			9	10		7	8	11				1				27
13,771	top		2	3	4	5	6			9	10	11	7	8					1				28
19,646	top		2	3	4	5	6			9	10	11	7	8					1				29
20,874			2	3	4	5	6			9	10	11	7	8					1				30
39,214	top		2	3	4	5	6			9	10	11		8					1		7		31
45,422	top		2	3	4	5	6			9	10	11	7	8					1				32
33,413	2		2	3	4	5	6			9	10	11	7	8					1				33
20,392	4		2	3	4	5	6			9	10	11	7	8					1				34
41,685			2	3	4	5	6			9	10	11	7	8					1				35
32,404	5			3	4	5	6			9	10	11	7	8			2		1				36
39,741	7		2		4	5	6			9	10	11		8	7				1	3			37
21,252	4		2		4	5				9	10	11		8		6		3	1		7		38
33,474	7		2			5				9	10	11		8		6		3	1	4	7		39
19,303			2		4	5				9	10	11	8			6		3	1		7		40
19,673	5		2		4	5				9	10		8		11	6		3	1		7		41
51,586	6		2		4	5				9	10	11		8		6		3	1		7		42
Appearances		20	38	36	41	42	34	1	3	42	42	38	36	38	5	6	3	6	22	3	6		
Goals (67)					3					22	15	9	4	11							1	2	ogs

Att.	Strong	Aird	Mather	Adamson	Cummings	Attwell	Cheesebrough	Morris	Holden	Shannon	Elliott	Chew	McIlroy	Pilkington	J Brown	Binns	Winton	Thompson	Rudman	Stephenson	
40,532		2	3	4	5	6			9	10	11	7						1		8	3
39,385		2	3	4	5	6			9	10	11	7	8					1			rep
53,105		2	3	4	5	6			9	10	11	7	8					1			4
51,025		2	3	4	5	6			9	10	11	7	8					1			5
Appearances		4	4	4	4	4			4	4	4	4	3					4		1	
Goals (6)																					

1953-54

The main news coming out of Turf Moor in the summer of 1953 was the sale of Billy Elliott to Sunderland. The left-winger had become a hugely popular player since his arrival at Burnley less than two years earlier, and his transfer came as something of a shock, only partially cushioned by the fact that the club made a £1,000 profit on him, the fee of £26,000 breaking the club record. Sunderland were at that time regarded as the "Bank of England" club, but their big spending brought little in terms of sustained League or Cup success. Elliott went on to become a regular at Roker Park over the next six seasons, but was never again capped for England after he left Turf Moor.

There was a ready-made replacement for Elliott in the Burnley side in the shape of Brian Pilkington, but manager Frank Hill ensured that the transfer funds were well used by spending £16,000 on Billy Gray, a right-winger who had been a fixture in Chelsea's side for the previous four years.

Both Gray and Pilkington were in the line-up as Burnley faced Wolves on the opening day, and Pilkington opened his scoring account for the club in an impressive 4-1 win, the victory coming after Wolves had gone in front in the first minute. The result would look even more impressive eight months later when the men from Molineux were crowned champions, and it signalled a solid start to the campaign for the Clarets, who went on to win five of their first seven games, scoring a fine tally of eighteen goals in the process. Unexpectedly leading the scoring charts was Gray, who notched six in those seven games including a hat-trick in a 4-2 home win against Tottenham.

Although three of the next four games were lost, Burnley quickly recovered ground with four more straight wins, the goals continuing to flow freely with all the forwards chipping in, including a hat-trick from Bill Holden in a notable 5-2 victory at Highbury against defending champions Arsenal. The team was largely settled in these early stages of the season, although Harold Mather regained his left-back slot at the expense of Doug Winton, and another member of the immediate post-war side, Jackie Chew, whose favoured right-wing position had been taken over by Gray, played his last game for the first team in a 2-1 win at Old Trafford at the beginning of October. That game also saw the debut of Bobby Seith, a Scot who had been a patient reserve for the previous few seasons, although still only 21 at the time of his first-team bow. Seith came into the side at right-half, with Jimmy Adamson moving over to the left and Reg Atwell making way.

A sequence of home wins and away defeats followed before another four-game winning run in December. There were five different scorers for the Clarets as Sunderland were trounced 5-1, then the following week two from Bill Holden proved enough to complete the double over Wolves, a feat only achieved by Burnley that season. Christmas 1953 brought the then regular double header against Preston, each side registering a 2-1 win, then in the opening game of 1954 Sheffield Wednesday became the first side in sixteen games to keep a clean sheet against the Clarets.

Brian Pilkington
the latest in a series of flying Burnley wingers

The F.A. Cup brought a plum third round draw, at home to Manchester United, and what an occasion it proved to be! There was the expected bumper crowd, almost 53000, but many had still not taken their places in the stand and on the terraces by the time the score was 2-2 after just six minutes! Burnley were two ahead in half that time, Les Shannon and Holden doing the damage, but United were very quickly back on terms through Dennis Viollet and a Jock Aird own goal. Shannon put the Clarets back in front before half-time, but United were back level again soon after through Tommy Taylor. It was to be Burnley's day, though, as Jimmy McIlroy and Billy Gray took the final score to 5-3 in a game that would be talked about for years ahead.

Another nap hand followed a week later as the prolific Gray scored his second hat-trick of the campaign in a 5-0 hammering of Middlesbrough. By this time, Burnley's League record showed seventeen wins, ten defeats and no draws! A goalless stalemate at West Bromwich in late January 1954 brought the first one point return of the season, and there was another draw the following Saturday when Newcastle were the visitors in the fourth round of the Cup. Again there was a 50,000-plus gate, but there was to be no repeat of the fireworks of the United game, and Burnley went down to a penalty in the replay at St. James' Park. Younger fans may be amazed to note that the crowd was smaller for the replay than that for the original tie at Turf Moor!

Manchester United were back at the Turf in mid-February, and a 2-0 Burnley win, with two more goals from Gray, put them fourth in the First Division table, but as in the previous two seasons the run-in was poor. There were wins against Arsenal, Manchester City and Huddersfield, who finished the season in third place, but not too much else to cheer despite the goals continuing to flow more regularly than had been the case in earlier years. The worst result of all was a 1-5 defeat at Burnley's least favourite away ground, Villa Park, but that game did see a notable debutant, with Colin McDonald making his first appearance in goal. He had originally joined Burnley as a 17-year-old amateur in 1948 and had had a long wait for first-team recognition In the four years since his debut for the Reserves, McDonald had appeared in the Southern League for Headington United, later Oxford United, prior to signing professional terms at Turf Moor in the summer of 1952. Despite his long wait and conceding five goals on his debut, he was in the side to stay and was destined to become one of Burnley's finest-ever keepers, and arguably the best of them all.

The season ended with Burnley in seventh position, one place and two points worse off than in 1952-53. On the plus side, they had established Turf Moor as something of a fortress, winning sixteen of their 21 home games to give them the best home record in the First Division. The final return of 78 goals scored was by far the best since the days of George Beel and Louis Page. Billy Gray had confounded expectations with his return of nineteen in the League, well in excess of his entire career total at Chelsea, while Jimmy McIlroy, only two behind, registered the best scoring season of his career. Amazingly, apart from an own goal, the 78 goals were shared between only seven players, the five forwards, plus Roy Stephenson and Jimmy Adamson.

On the down side, only two teams in the First Division lost more away games than Burnley, and 67 goals conceded was the club's worst figure since the war. Even so, the side had performed better than many would have expected following the sale of one of their star players, and Burnley were now becoming established not just among the top flight, but as one of the most consistent teams in it.

Billy Gray
ever present on the right wing
and top scorer in his first season

1953-54 - First Division

		P	W	D	L	F	A	Pts
1	Wolverhampton W	42	25	7	10	96	56	57
2	West Bromwich A	42	22	9	11	86	63	53
3	Huddersfield T	42	20	11	11	78	61	51
4	Manchester U	42	18	12	12	73	58	48
5	Bolton W	42	18	12	12	75	60	48
6	Blackpool	42	19	10	13	80	69	48
7	BURNLEY	42	21	4	17	78	67	46
8	Chelsea	42	16	12	14	74	68	44
9	Charlton A	42	19	6	17	75	77	44
10	Cardiff C	42	18	8	16	51	71	44
11	Preston NE	42	19	5	18	87	58	43
12	Arsenal	42	15	13	14	75	73	43
13	Aston Villa	42	16	9	17	70	68	41
14	Portsmouth	42	14	11	17	81	89	39
15	Newcastle U	42	14	10	18	72	77	38
16	Tottenham H	42	16	5	21	65	76	37
17	Manchester C	42	14	9	19	62	77	37
18	Sunderland	42	14	8	20	81	89	36
19	Sheffield W	42	15	6	21	70	91	36
20	Sheffield U	42	11	11	20	69	90	33
21	Middlesbrough	42	10	10	22	60	91	30
22	Liverpool	42	9	10	23	68	97	28

1953-54

Manager : Frank Hill

Division One (7th)

Note	No	Date		h/a	Opponents	Result		h/t	Goalscorers/times	Opp. goal times
	1	Aug	19	h	WOLVERHAMPTON W	W	4-1	0-1	Shannon (2) 63, 82, Holden 67, Pilkington 71	3
	2		22	a	Charlton A	L	1-3	0-0	McIlroy 53	59, 62, 83
	3		25	h	BLACKPOOL	W	2-1	2-0	Pilkington 10, Shimwell 33og	60
	4		29	h	SHEFFIELD W	W	4-1	4-1	Pilkington (2) 18, 32, Gray (2) 20, 28p	24
	5		31	a	Blackpool	L	0-2	0-0		58, 62
	6	Sep	5	a	Middlesbrough	W	3-1	1-0	Holden 8, Stephenson 53, Gray 73	70
	7		7	h	TOTTENHAM H	W	4-2	3-0	McIlroy 1, Gray (3) 8, 33, 84	65, 70
	8		12	h	WEST BROMWICH A	L	1-4	0-2	Stephenson 62	24, 35, 75, 84
	9		16	a	Tottenham H	W	3-2	1-2	McIlroy (2) 30, 65, Gray 78	11, 20
	10		19	a	Liverpool	L	0-4	0-4		2, 6, 22, 44
	11		26	h	NEWCASTLE U	L	1-2	0-0	Holden 54	56, 84
Chew's last game	12	Oct	3	a	Manchester U	W	2-1	2-1	Stephenson 13, Gray 35	43
	13		10	h	PORTSMOUTH	W	1-0	1-0	McIlroy 35	
	14		17	a	Arsenal	W	5-2	3-2	Holden (3) 15, 39, 81, Stephenson (2) 20, 87	5, 28
	15		24	h	CARDIFF C	W	3-0	1-0	McIlroy 32, Gray 69, Pilkington 73	
	16		31	a	Manchester C	L	2-3	0-1	Adamson 57, Gray 67	41, 61, 79
	17	Nov	7	h	SHEFFIELD U	W	2-1	1-0	McIlroy (2) 7, 58	70
	18		14	a	Chelsea	L	1-2	1-2	Stephenson 36	38, 42
	19		21	h	ASTON VILLA	W	3-2	2-1	Stephenson 24, Gray 37, McIlroy 50	44, 89
	20		28	a	Huddersfield T	L	1-3	1-2	Shannon 24	11, 31, 60
Sunderland goal 4m	21	Dec	5	h	SUNDERLAND	W	5-1	2-1	Shannon 34, Gray 36, Holden 48, Adamson 83, McIlroy 86	
	22		12	a	Wolverhampton W	W	2-1	1-0	Holden (2) 23, 54	85
	23		19	h	CHARLTON A	W	2-0	1-0	Shannon 31, McIlroy 59	
	24		25	h	PRESTON N E	W	2-1	0-1	Pilkington 60, Shannon 75	32
	25		26	a	Preston N E	L	1-2	1-0	McIlroy 25	65, 70
	26	Jan	2	a	Sheffield W	L	0-2	0-2		35og, 44
	27		16	h	MIDDLESBROUGH	W	5-0	2-0	Holden 3, Gray (3) 5, 53, 75, McIlroy 57	
	28		23	a	West Bromwich A	D	0-0	0-0		
	29	Feb	6	h	LIVERPOOL	D	1-1	1-0	Pilkington 19	81
	30		13	a	Newcastle U	L	1-3	1-1	McIlroy 13	6, 55, 83
	31		20	h	MANCHESTER U	W	2-0	1-0	Gray (2) 11, 89	
	32		27	a	Portsmouth	L	2-3	2-0	McIlroy 13, Adamson 38	57, 61, 85
	33	Mar	6	h	ARSENAL	W	2-1	1-1	Holden 19, Shannon 80	30
	34		13	a	Cardiff C	L	0-1	0-0		89
	35		20	h	MANCHESTER C	W	3-1	0-1	Holden 48, Gray 73, McIlroy 78	9
	36		27	a	Sheffield U	L	1-2	1-0	McIlroy 17	63, 64
	37	Apr	3	h	CHELSEA	L	1-2	1-1	Gray 30	29, 75
	38		10	a	Aston Villa	L	1-5	0-2	Holden 70	8, 42, 63, 66, 72
	39		16	a	Bolton W	D	0-0	0-0		
	40		17	h	HUDDERSFIELD T	W	2-1	1-0	Pilkington 2, Adamson 67	54
	41		19	h	BOLTON W	D	1-1	1-0	Holden 35	70
	42		24	a	Sunderland	L	1-2	1-2	Adamson 4	19, 24

FA Cup

Rd	Date		h/a	Opponents	Result		h/t	Goalscorers/times	Opp. goal times
3	Jan	9	h	MANCHESTER U	W	5-3	3-2	Shannon (2) 1, 18, Holden 5, McIlroy 67, Gray 70	6, 7og, 51
4		30	h	NEWCASTLE U	D	1-1	1-0	Pilkington 42	49
rep	Feb	3	a	Newcastle U	L	0-1	0-0		85p

Final, West Bromwich A 3-2 Preston N E, at Wembley.

Other first team matches (friendlies and/or as detailed)

Note	Date		h/a	Opponents	Result		Goalscorers
	Oct	13	a	Grimsby T	L	0-1	
Lancs Cup		28	a	Blackpool	L	0-6	
in Madagascar	May	9	a	Tananarive	W	14-1	Holden (6), McIlroy (4), Shannon (3), Stephenson
		13	a	Mauritius XI	W	4-0	Holden (3), McIlroy
		15	a	Mauritius XI	W	7-1	Cargill p, Holden (2), Shannon (2), McIlroy (2)
		20	a	Mauritius XI	W	8-1	unknown (8)
		23	a	Mauritius XI	W	3-0	Holden, Shannon, Seith
		27	a	Mauritius XI	W	6-0	unknown (6)
		30	a	Mauritius XI	W	6-0	unknown (6)

Att.	Pos	Thompson	Aird	Winton	Adamson	Cummings	Rudman	Gray	McIlroy	Holden	Shannon	Pilkington	Attwell	Chew	Stephenson	Binns	Mather	Cargill	Seith	Milner	McDonald		
32,822		1	2	3	4	5	6	7	8	9	10	11											1
24,802	7	1	2	3	4	5	6	7	8	9	10	11											2
41,574		1	2	3	4	5		7	8	9	10	11	6										3
25,813	3	1	2	3	4	5		7	8	9		11	6	10									4
18,113		1	2	3	4	5		7	8	9		11	6	10									5
32,597	3	1	2	3	4	5		7	8	9		11	6		10								6
34,280		1	2	3	4	5		7	8	9		11	6		10								7
38,948	3	1	2	3	4	5		7	8	9		11	6		10								8
30,472	4	1			4	5		7	8	9	10		6			2	3	11					9
36,643	7	1			4	5		7	8	9	10		6			2	3	11					10
33,688	7	1	2		4	5		7	8	9	10	11	6				3						11
39,550	6	1	2		6	5		7		9		11		10	8		3		4				12
28,142	5	1	2		6			7	10	9		11			8	5	3		4				13
47,353	5	1	2		6			7	10	9		11			8	5	3		4				14
29,539	4	1	2		6			7	10	9		11			8	5	3		4				15
32,353	4	1	2		6			7	10	9		11			8	5	3		4				16
15,846	4	1	2		6			7	10	9		11			8	5	3		4				17
39,731	4	1	2		6			7	10	9		11			8	5	3		4				18
26,868	4	1	2		6	5		11	10	9	8				7		3		4				19
34,666	4	1	2		4	5		7	10		9	11					3		6	8			20
27,839	4	1	2		4	5		7	8	9	10	11					3		6				21
35,043	4	1	2		4	5		7	8	9	10	11	6				3						22
25,369	4	1	2		4	5		7	8	9	10	11	6				3						23
33,398		1	2		4	5		7	8	9	10	11	6				3						24
32,416		1	2			5		7	8	9	10	11	6				3		4				25
33,061	4	1	2			5		7	8	9	10	11	6				3		4				26
23,481	3	1	2		4	5		7	8	9	10	11	6				3						27
42,644	3	1	2		4	5		7		9	10	11	6		8		3						28
24,025	4	1	2		4	5		7	10		9	11	6		8		3						29
29,114	5	1	2	9	4	5		7	8		10	11	6				3						30
31,402	4	1	2			5		7	8	9	10	11	6				3		4				31
24,155	4	1	2		4	5		7	8	9	10	11	6				3						32
22,726	4	1	2	3	4	5		7	8	9	10	11							6				33
33,413	4	1	2	3	4	5		7	8	9	10	11							6				34
23,061	4	1	2	3	4	5		7	8	9	10	11							6				35
22,784	4	1	2	3	4	5		7	8	9	10	11							6				36
20,312	5	1	2	3	4	5		7	8	9	10	11							6				37
23,043	6		2	3	4			7	8	9	10	11				5			6		1		38
34,394			2	3	4	5		7	8	9	10	11							6		1		39
26,180	6		2	3	4	5		7	8	9	10	11							6		1		40
25,857			2	3	4	5		7	8	9	10	11							6		1		41
28,014	7		2	3	4	5		7	8	9	10	11							6		1		42
Appearances		37	40	19	39	35	2	42	40	39	30	39	20	3	13	9	24	2	23	1	5		
Goals (78)					5			19	17	14	7	8			7							1	og

Att.	Pos	Thompson	Aird	Winton	Adamson	Cummings	Rudman	Gray	McIlroy	Holden	Shannon	Pilkington	Attwell	Chew	Stephenson	Binns	Mather	Cargill	Seith	Milner	McDonald	
52,847		1	2		4	5		7	8	9	10	11	6				3					3
52,011		1	2		4	5		7	8	9	10	11	6				3					4
48,284		1	2		4	5		7	8	9	10	11	6				3					rep
Appearances		3	3		3	3		3	3	3	3	3	3				3					
Goals (6)								1	1	1	2	1										

1954-55

There were two significant changes at Turf Moor during the close season of 1954. One was the first major structural alteration for many years to the ground itself, as the terrace facing the main stand, in later years to be immortalised as the Longside, was roofed over at a cost of £20,000. The other was a change of Manager. Shortly before the start of the new season, Frank Hill moved to Preston where, earlier in his career he had worked as a trainer. His tenure at the Turf, nearly six years, had seen the gradual break-up of the famous post-war side and the emergence of a new team including several fine players brought in by Hill, most notably of course Jimmy McIlroy. Under his management, the side had also shaken off its reputation as a dour defensive outfit to rank high among the First Division's entertainers.

Into the hot seat came a man well known to Burnley fans, the captain of that "Iron Curtain" side, Alan Brown. It was his first managerial role, having previously acquired coaching experience at Sheffield Wednesday, and his appointment marked the beginning of the club's reliance on ex-Clarets in the Manager's chair. It would be nearly thirty years before Burnley would have another manager without previous Turf Moor playing connections.

OBITUARY
ANDREW (ANDY) MCCLUGGAGE
DIED 14 OCTOBER 1954, AGED 54

As a defender, Andy McCluggage's debut was hardly an auspicious start as the Clarets lost 0-10 at Aston Villa on the opening day of the 1925-26 season. But Burnley knew they had the right man for the job after capturing the Irish international from Bradford and for the next six seasons he made the right-back position his own. Signed as a replacement for Championship winner Len Smelt, McCluggage's polished performances were to keep him in the Northern Ireland set-up throughout his Turf Moor career which saw more than 200 appearances. He left for Irish club Dundalk in 1931, before signing for Preston, and he made his debut for the Lilywhites in a 2-2 Christmas Day draw at Turf Moor. He left League football the following season and played for Morecambe before hanging up his boots and working as a maintenance man at Huncoat Pit.

RIP

For the opening game against Cardiff, it was the same line-up as had ended the previous season apart from veteran Harold Mather's return at left-back in place of Jock Winton. Les Shannon scored the only goal of the game, but goals were in short supply in the early stages of the season, with only two in the first five matches. In an attempt to rectify the situation, Brown introduced Peter McKay, signed in May from Dundee United, a player small in stature but great in goalscoring reputation, in 237 games at Tannadice, he had scored an amazing 202 goals. His impact at Burnley was not immediate, though, and he soon reverted to the reserves where he was a prolific scorer.

The last two playing survivors of the 1946-47 side made their first-team exits in September 1954. Reg Attwell, now 34, could no longer compete with Jimmy Adamson or Bobby Seith for his usual midfield role, and he bowed out in a 0-2 home defeat against Everton, soon afterwards to be transferred to Bradford City. Just two days later, the Turf Moor faithful saw the last of Harold Mather, just a year younger, in a 3-1 home victory against Leicester, with Winton going on to take over the number three shirt on a regular basis.

Colin McDonald
now established in the Burnley goal
an England star of the future

The influence of Alan Brown soon became apparent, with Burnley reverting to the style of the side he had captained, the emphasis being on solid defence. Results were slow in coming however, after the opening day victory, only one of the next nine games was won, and that against a Leicester side destined for the shortest possible stay in the top flight. It was October before a reasonable run was strung together, as Roy Stephenson, a player who had never quite managed to achieve "regular" status, scored in four successive games to contribute to the side's improved standing. November soon brought a harsh return to earth, though, with a 0-5 hammering at Molineux. Colin McDonald lost his place in goal after that defeat, but only briefly. Right-back Jock Aird, now a full Scottish international, was a more long-term casualty, his somewhat unlikely replacement being Harold Rudman, who had been at Turf Moor since 1942 but had seen little first-team action since the war.

Aird was not the only Claret to make an international debut in 1954. Brian Pilkington was still only 21 when, in October, he took Tom Finney's place in the England side for a 2-0 win against Northern Ireland in Belfast. All seemed set for a long international career, but despite years of consistency on Burnley's left wing, Pilkington was never capped again.

By the end of the year, the goals were flowing more freely, with Bill Holden rediscovering his scoring touch and Billy Gray doing the same without ever threatening to repeat his heroics of the previous ampaign. At least by Christmas 1954, the Clarets had climbed to a mid-table position in the First Division, and in one of the most tightly-fought of top flight seasons, a good run in the new year could still see them challenging for honours.

There were to be no honours in the F.A. Cup. For the second time in three seasons, Burnley were drawn against Sunderland, but this time it was in the third round and at Roker Park, and Billy Elliott was on the opposing side. Elliott it was who scored the only goal of the game five minutes from the end to kill off the Cup dreams of his former team-mates.

The best run of the season followed shortly afterwards, with five wins from seven games and only two goals conceded in that spell. The run began with the return of another former Claret, Tommy Lawton, now nearing the end of his playing career. His Arsenal side was well beaten, 3-0, and Charlton fell by the same score a fortnight later, when there was a new name on the scoresheet in John Walton, who had come into the side at inside-forward a few weeks earlier. By the end of the run, Burnley had risen to fourth place in the table, and it seemed that Alan Brown's side was finally getting it right at both ends of the pitch.

But, as was becoming habitual, the Clarets faded away at the end of the season, and finished tenth after taking only five points from their last seven games. Jock Aird made his final appearance for the side in a 0-1 defeat at Blackpool, and shortly afterwards emigrated to New Zealand. There was a new face in the number two shirt for the next game as Dave Smith, yet another "patient reserve" who had been at the club for nearly five years already, was given his chance, while a fellow-Scot, right-winger Doug Newlands, recently acquired from Aberdeen, made his bow in the final game of the season, a 1-0 win at Bolton.

The 1954-55 season saw Burnley's average home gate drop by over 3,000 to 25,094. Although the immediate post-war boom had passed, there was some cause for concern as, despite their mid-table finish, the side had been in contention for honours for most of the season, such was the close-fought nature of the First Division, runners up Wolves ended with only 48 points, just five more than the Clarets. Maybe a factor was the lack of goals on view, as Burnley both scored and conceded the fewest of all the sides in the top flight.

The Reserves had another good season, with Peter McKay scoring 36 of their 94 goals, but, despite constant rumours about a possible transfer, Bill Holden had held down his first team place and was top scorer for the third time, taking his total to 75 League goals, making him comfortably Burnley's most prolific postwar marksman up to that time. Brian Pilkington also reached double figures for the season, as did Roy Stephenson, although for him the breakthrough to a regular first-team slot seemed as distant as ever. Alan Brown's change of tactics may have been responsible for the relatively poor goal returns of Mcllroy and Shannon, but both remained automatic choices for the side, and while the final position was disappointing, there was really no cause for concern among the faithful.

Harold Rudman
more than ten years at Turf Moor

1954-55 - First Division

		P	W	D	L	F	A	Pts
1	Chelsea	42	20	12	10	81	57	52
2	Wolverhampton W	42	19	10	13	89	70	48
3	Portsmouth	42	18	12	12	74	62	48
4	Sunderland	42	15	18	9	64	54	48
5	Manchester U	42	20	7	15	84	74	47
6	Aston Villa	42	20	7	15	72	73	47
7	Manchester C	42	18	10	14	76	69	46
8	Newcastle U	42	17	9	16	89	77	43
9	Arsenal	42	17	9	16	69	63	43
10	BURNLEY	42	17	9	16	51	48	43
11	Everton	42	16	10	16	62	68	42
12	Huddersfield T	42	14	13	15	63	68	41
13	Sheffield W	42	17	7	18	70	86	41
14	Preston NE	42	16	8	18	83	64	40
15	Charlton A	42	15	10	17	76	75	40
16	Tottenham H	42	16	8	18	72	73	40
17	West Bromwich A	42	16	8	18	76	96	40
18	Bolton W	42	13	13	16	62	69	39
19	Blackpool	42	14	10	18	60	64	38
20	Cardiff C	42	13	11	18	62	76	37
21	Leicester C	42	12	11	19	74	86	35
22	Sheffield W	42	8	10	24	63	100	26

1954-55

Manager : Alan Brown

Division One (10th)

		Date			Opponents	Result		h/t	Goalscorers/times	Opp. goal times
	1	Aug	21	h	CARDIFF C	W	1-0	1-0	Shannon 2	
	2		23	a	Chelsea	L	0-1	0-0		75
	3		28	a	Manchester C	D	0-0	0-0		
	4		31	h	CHELSEA	D	1-1	0-0	Pilkington 88	60
Attwell's last game	5	Sep	4	h	EVERTON	L	0-2	0-1		34, 55
Mather's last game	6		9	h	LEICESTER C	W	3-1	2-0	Holden 9, Gray 21, Stephenson 65	78
	7		11	a	Newcastle U	L	1-2	0-1	Stephenson 60	25, 66
	8		13	a	Leicester C	D	2-2	0-1	Stephenson 62, Pilkington 65	30, 71
	9		18	h	WEST BROMWICH A	L	0-2	0-1		32, 85
	10		25	a	Arsenal	L	0-4	0-3		22, 31, 38, 47
	11	Oct	2	h	SHEFFIELD U	W	2-1	1-1	Holden 19, Gray 58p	21
	12		9	a	Charlton A	L	1-3	0-2	Stephenson 82	14, 28, 57
	13		16	h	BOLTON W	W	2-0	0-0	Stephenson 55, McIlroy 89	
	14		23	a	Sheffield W	D	1-1	0-1	Stephenson 64	19
	15		30	h	PORTSMOUTH	W	1-0	1-0	Stephenson 34	
	16	Nov	6	a	Wolverhampton W	L	0-5	0-4		13, 24, 34, 38, 72p
	17		13	h	ASTON VILLA	W	2-0	2-0	Holden (2) 24, 36	
	18		20	a	Sunderland	D	2-2	0-1	Holden 62, Pilkington 71	11, 46
Thompson's last game	19		27	h	TOTTENHAM H	L	1-2	0-1	McIlroy 68	29, 73
	20	Dec	4	a	Huddersfield T	W	1-0	0-0	Holden 88	
	21		11	h	MANCHESTER U	L	2-4	1-0	Gibson 15og, Gray 78	49, 55, 84, 89
	22		18	a	Cardiff C	W	3-0	1-0	Sherwood 41og, Stephenson 61, Holden 67	
	23		25	h	PRESTON N E	D	2-2	2-2	Gray (2) 27, 33	38, 42
	24		27	a	Preston N E	W	1-0	1-0	Holden 25	
	25	Jan	1	h	MANCHESTER C	W	2-0	1-0	Stephenson (2) 30, 63	
	26		15	a	Everton	D	1-1	0-1	McIlroy 52p	7
	27		22	h	NEWCASTLE U	L	0-1	0-0		62
	28	Feb	3	a	West Bromwich A	D	2-2	0-2	Pilkington (2) 48, 80	14, 18
	29		12	h	ARSENAL	W	3-0	2-0	Gray (2) 2, 14, Holden 55	
	30		19	a	Sheffield U	L	0-1	0-0		64
	31		26	h	CHARLTON A	W	3-0	1-0	Pilkington 10, Gray 54, Walton 65	
	32	Mar	3	a	Manchester U	L	0-1	0-0		66
	33		12	h	SHEFFIELD W	W	2-0	0-0	Holden (2) 50, 88	
	34		19	a	Portsmouth	W	2-0	0-0	Holden 64, Pilkington 65	
	35		26	h	WOLVERHAMPTON W	W	1-0	0-0	Walton 56	
	36	Apr	2	a	Aston Villa	L	1-3	1-2	Pilkington 16	6, 41, 71
	37		8	h	BLACKPOOL	L	0-1	0-0		46
	38		9	h	HUDDERSFIELD T	D	1-1	0-0	Pilkington 56	59og
Aird's last game	39		11	a	Blackpool	L	0-1	0-0		64
	40		16	a	Tottenham H	W	3-0	2-0	Holden (2) 26, 43, Pilkington 54	
	41		23	h	SUNDERLAND	L	0-1	0-1		14
	42		30	a	Bolton W	W	1-0	0-0	Pilkington 85	

FA Cup

				Opponents	Result		h/t	Goalscorers/times	Opp. goal times
3	Jan	8	a	Sunderland	L	0-1	0-0		85

Final, Newcastle U 3-1 Manchester C, at Wembley.

Other first team matches (friendlies and/or as detailed)

				Opponents	Result		Goalscorers
	Oct	4	a	Dundee U	W	4-0	Stephenson (2), McKay (2)
Lancs Cup		26	h	BLACKPOOL	W	4-1	McKay (2), Cheesebrough, Cargill
	Jan	29	a	Hull C	W	2-1	McIlroy, Pilkington
Lancs Cup	Feb	14	a	Rochdale	L	1-2	Scott

Att.	Pos	McDonald	Aird	Mather	Adamson	Cummings	Seith	Gray	McIlroy	Holden	Shannon	Pilkington	McKay	Attwell	Stephenson	Winton	Cargill	Thompson	Rudman	Cheesebrough	Walton	Scott	D Smith	Binns	Newlands	
27,836		1	2	3	4	5	6	7	8	9	10	11														1
30,239		1	2	3	4	5	6	7	8	9	10	11														2
38,201	11	1	2	3	4	5	6	7	8	9	10	11														3
28,472		1	2	3	4	5		7	8	9	6	11	10													4
31,963	17	1	2	3		5		7	8	9	6	11	10	4												5
20,602		1	2	3		5	4	7	10	9	6	11			8											6
47,346	13	1	2			5	4	7	10		6	11	9		8	3										7
26,413		1	2		4	5	6	7	10		9	11			8	3										8
29,727	14	1	2		4	5	6	7	10		9	11			8	3										9
46,190	16	1	2		4	5	6	7	8	9	10	11				3										10
22,237	16	1	2		4	5	6	7		9	10				8	3	11									11
21,883	16	1	2		4	5	6		8	9	10	11			7	3										12
30,016	16	1	2		4	5		7	10	9	6	11			8	3										13
28,960	15	1	2		4	5		7	10	9	6	11			8	3										14
23,815	13	1	2		4	5		7	10	9	6	11			8	3										15
27,524	15	1	2		4	5		7	10	9	6	11			8	3										16
19,186	14				4	5		7	10	9	6	11			8	3		1	2							17
42,305	14				4	5		7	10	9	6	11			8	3		1	2							18
21,973	14				4	5		7	10	9	6	11			8	3		1	2							19
17,372	14	1				5	4	7	10	9	6	11				3			2	8						20
24,967	15	1				5	4	7	10	9	6	11				3			2	8						21
22,035	15	1			4	5		7	10	9	6				8	3			2	11						22
29,758		1				5	4	7	10	9	6				8	3			2	11						23
38,525		1			4	5		7	10	9	6				8	3			2	11						24
28,825	11	1			4	5		7	10	9	6				8	3			2	11						25
29,520	10	1			4	5		7	10		6		9		8	3			2	11						26
23,467	11	1			4	5		7	10	9	6	11				3			2		8					27
22,749	11	1			4	5		7	8	9	6	11				3			2		10					28
24,940	9	1			4	5		7	8	9	6	11				3			2		10					29
22,111	9	1			4	5		7	8	9	6	11				3			2		10					30
19,289	9	1			4	5		7	8	9	6	11				3			2		10					31
33,577	9	1			4	5		7	8	9	6					3			2		10	11				32
20,082	9	1			4	5		7	8	9	6	11				3			2		10					33
21,755	7	1			4	5		7		9	6	11			8	3			2		10					34
23,157	7	1			4	5		7	8	9	6	11				3			2		10					35
19,950	8	1			4	5		7	8	9	6	11				3			2		10					36
35,212		1			4	5		7	8	9	6	11				3			2		10					37
22,214	9	1			4	5		7	8	9	6	11			10	3			2							38
32,881		1	2		4	5		7	8	9	6	11			10	3										39
23,555	8	1			4			7	8	9	6	11				3					10		2	5		40
19,227	10	1			4			7	8	9	6	11			10	3							2	5		41
20,671	10	1			4				8	9	6	11				3					10		2	5	7	42
Appearances		39	17	6	36	39	13	40	40	38	42	35	4	1	22	36	1	3	22	7	13	1	3	3	1	
Goals (51)								8	3	14	1	11			10						2					2 ogs
50,107		1			4	5		7	10	9	6				8	3			2	11						3
Appearances		1			1	1		1	1	1	1				1	1			1	1						
Goals (0)																										

1955-56

OBITUARY
BERTRAM (BERT) FREEMAN
DIED 11 AUGUST 1955, AGED 69

The first Burnley player to score 100 league goals, Bert Freeman remains the only Claret to have scored the winning goal in an FA Cup Final. A proven goalscorer at Everton, Burnley must have been amazed when Goodison Park officials decided he was surplus to requirements in 1911 and Freeman became part of the success story being written at Turf Moor. In four seasons before the outbreak of the Great War he became the club's all-time leading scorer. In that short time he scored 91 league goals and 12 in the FA Cup, most notable of which was the winner against Liverpool at the Crystal Palace, in 1914. Another top player who saw his progress halted by the war, Freeman returned after the conflict to indelibly carve his name in Turf Moor folklore with a goal against Derby in February 1920 which took his tally to 100. He added three more goals that season, but the writing was on the wall for the FA Cup hero when Burnley signed Joe Anderson. Freeman played only three league games in the following campaign as Burnley went on to lift the Championship and his final Burnley appearance was, appropriately, in the FA Cup. He joined Wigan Borough at the end of the season and later moved to Kettering Town before retiring.

RIP

The side that started the season contained no new faces, and was substantially the side recognised as the first eleven at the end of the previous campaign, including the resurgent Harold Rudman at right-back and John Walton in the number ten shirt. It was a fine start for the Clarets, with Brian Pilkington scoring the only goal to earn victory at White Hart Lane against Tottenham.

Failure to win any of the next four games, however, brought a significant change to the line-up. Bill Holden had actually lost his place already, with Jimmy McIlroy seeing brief service in an unfamiliar centre-forward role, but the claims of Peter McKay, such a prolific scorer in the reserves, could no longer be denied, and he duly announced his return to the side with a hat-trick as First Division newcomers Luton Town were beaten 3-1 at Turf Moor. Retaining his place for the following Saturday, he scored again as Birmingham were overcome 3-2 at the Turf. Burnley's forward line at this time consisted of Billy Gray at 5' 6", McIlroy (5' 8", McKay, 5' 6", Albert Cheesebrough, 5' 7", and Pilkington, 5' 6", surely one of the smallest front lines ever to turn out in the Football League.

Cheesebrough, who had struggled to secure a regular place since his debut as a 17-year-old, was now, at 20, considered ready for regular First Division football, and John Walton was the unfortunate player to drop out. Another player to lose his place, albeit temporarily, around this time was Jimmy Adamson, who made way for the return in the number four shirt of Bobby Seith, absent from the first team for most of the previous year. The side settled into a good run of form, staying unbeaten for eleven games from October until early December1955. The player making the headlines at this stage was undoubtedly that man McKay, who averaged a goal a game during the unbeaten run, his tally includmg a hat-trick against Portsmouth following double strikes against Aston Villa and in a memorable 4-4 draw against League leaders Sunderland at Roker Park. Sadly, this game saw McIlroy suffer a bad ankle ligament injury, which would keep him out of the side for three months, his first absence of any length since he had made his first impact five years earlier.

Albert Cheesebrough
Burnley-born inside forward

The great man's absence did not, however, have any immediate adverse effect on results. Victory at Arsenal on the last Saturday in November took Burnley up to third place, just a point behind Blackpool and Manchester United. But although the goals continued to flow, December was a disappointing month, culminating in defeats on successive days against regular Christmas opponents Preston. Christmas also saw the departure from Turf Moor of Bill Holden, transferred to Sunderland for £12,000. At 27, Holden should have been at the peak of his career, but he was unable to dislodge McKay, who was three years older, from the first eleven, and he also struggled to make much impression at Roker Park. Within a year, he had moved down to the Third

Division with Stockport, and the rest of his League career, which lasted until 1963, was spent in the lower divisions.

1956 dawned with the start of another F.A. Cup campaign, and a third round derby game at Bury, then in the Second Division. An eventful afternoon saw the Clarets two up by half-time, but Bury came back to equalise before the thickening fog forced the referee to abandon the game after 65 minutes. Three days later, Burnley visited Gigg Lane again, and this time a goal from Billy Gray was enough to decide the issue and set up a home fourth round tie against Chelsea, reigning League champions but with no chance of retaining their title. It looked a tie that the Clarets should be capable of winning.

No-one would have predicted the course the tie would take, as over the course of nineteen days the sides went on to meet five times before a winner emerged. It nearly wasn't so, in the first game at Turf Moor, Burnley came within five minutes of victory before Chelsea stole a late equaliser. The replay at Stamford Bridge saw a new face in the Clarets line-up, a 19-year-old left-half from Hapton called Brian Miller of whom much more would be heard. Another 1-1 draw, after extra time, meant a toss-up for choice of ground, which Burnley won, and the second replay took place at St. Andrew's Birmingham in front of a more than respectable "neutral" crowd of over 21,000. Extra time again couldn't separate the sides, it ended 2-2, and the saga moved on to Highbury, clearly Chelsea's choice of venue. No goals this time, so just two days later London staged its third meeting of this marathon, and at White Hart Lane Burnley finally bowed out, beaten 0-2. In all, nine hours of football had been played in front of crowds totalling over 160,000, an epic Cup-tie the like of which, perhaps sadly, will not be seen again.

Back with League matters, still at that time considered very much the bread-and-butter, Burnley hit a bad patch, registering only one point in six games, that from a 1-1 home draw with Sheffield United which was notable for Brian Miller's first goal for the club. McIlroy had returned by this time, so the run could hardly be blamed on his absence, but the demands of the Cup marathon may well have played their part. With no lack of irony, a resounding end was brought to the depressing run with a 5-0 win against, who else, Chelsea, with Brian Pilkington scoring a hat-trick. 'Pilky' was a regular marksman from his left-wing position, and it was perhaps surprising that he had failed to add to his single England cap. The loss of points between late January and early March 1956 had all but taken away Burnley's chance of glory for the 1955-56 season, a First Division campaign eventually dominated by the Busby Babes of Manchester United. There was little to choose, though, between the sides in the chasing pack, and better form towards the end of season kept the Clarets not too far from the summit. A fortnight after the Chelsea triumph, they beat Sunderland 4-0 at the Turf, a new name on the scoresheet being that of Doug Newlands, being given his first run in the senior side at the expense of Billy Gray. Peter McKay, whose early-season heroics seemed to have faded away after the New Year, was also back to finding the net, and seven goals in the season's final ten games took his tally to 25, as well as two in the FA Cup, comfortably the best by any Claret so far in the post-war era.

The last three away games were all won, McKay taking his tally against Luton to five with a pair in the final game, a 3-2 victory at Kenilworth Road. It took Burney to a final position of seventh, just five points adrift of runners-up Blackpool (yes, the 1950s was a good decade for football in Lancashire). Yet again, it was a case of so near yet so far, but Alan Brown was clearly doing plenty that was right, and the talent emerging through the ranks suggested that the best was yet to come.

Peter McKay
top scorer with 25 goals
in his only season as a first team regular

1955-56 - First Division

		P	W	D	L	F	A	Pts
1	Manchester U	42	25	10	7	83	51	60
2	Blackpool	42	20	9	13	86	62	49
3	Wolverhampton W	42	20	9	13	89	65	49
4	Manchester C	42	18	10	14	82	69	46
5	Arsenal	42	18	10	14	60	61	46
6	Birmingham C	42	18	9	15	75	57	45
7	BURNLEY	42	18	8	16	64	54	44
8	Bolton W	42	18	7	17	71	58	43
9	Sunderland	42	17	9	16	80	95	43
10	Luton T	42	17	8	17	66	64	42
11	Newcastle U	42	17	7	18	85	70	41
12	Portsmouth	42	16	9	17	78	85	41
13	West Bromwich A	42	18	5	19	58	70	41
14	Charlton A	42	17	6	19	75	81	40
15	Everton	42	15	10	17	55	69	40
16	Chelsea	42	14	11	17	64	77	39
17	Cardiff C	42	15	9	18	55	69	39
18	Tottenham H	42	15	7	20	61	71	37
19	Preston NE	42	14	8	20	73	72	36
20	Aston Villa	42	12	13	18	52	69	35
21	Huddersfield T	42	14	7	21	54	83	35
22	Sheffield U	42	12	9	21	63	77	33

1955-56

Manager : Alan Brown

Division One (7th)

	No	Date			Opponents	Result		h/t	Goalscorers/times	Opp. goal times
	1	Aug	20	a	Tottenham H	W	1-0	0-0	Pilkington 52	
Holden's last game	2		22	h	BLACKPOOL	L	0-2	0-1		40, 87
	3		27	h	EVERTON	L	0-1	0-1		6p
	4		29	a	Blackpool	D	1-1	1-0	Pilkington 43	65
	5	Sep	3	a	Newcastle U	L	1-3	0-3	Pilkington 67	8, 31, 35
	6		5	h	LUTON T	W	3-1	1-1	McKay (3) 38, 64, 75	25
	7		10	h	BIRMINGHAM C	W	3-2	3-0	Pilkington 12, Cheesebrough 22, McKay 42	59, 68
	8		17	a	West Bromwich A	L	0-1	0-1		33
	9		24	h	MANCHESTER U	D	0-0	0-0		
	10	Oct	1	a	Sheffield U	W	2-1	0-0	Cheesebrough 46, Burke 70	54
	11		8	h	HUDDERSFIELD T	W	2-0	0-0	McKay 84, Gray 89	
	12		15	a	Cardiff C	D	2-2	1-2	Cheesebrough 28, McKay 54	4, 36
	13		22	h	BOLTON W	W	2-0	1-0	McKay 13, McIlroy 55	
	14		29	a	Chelsea	D	0-0	0-0		
	15	Nov	5	h	ASTON VILLA	W	2-0	0-0	McKay (2) 62, 74	
	16		12	a	Sunderland	D	4-4	3-2	McIlroy 1, Hedley 4og, McKay (2) 37, 78	33, 36, 60, 81
	17		19	h	PORTSMOUTH	W	3-0	2-0	McKay (3) 3, 28, 75	
	18		26	a	Arsenal	W	1-0	0-0	Cheesebrough 83	
	19	Dec	3	h	MANCHESTER C	D	2-2	1-0	McKay 20p, Stephenson 87	52, 74
	20		10	a	Wolverhampton W	L	1-3	0-3	McKay 51	26, 27, 41
	21		17	h	TOTTENHAM H	W	2-0	2-0	McKay 2, Shannon 24	
	22		24	a	Everton	D	1-1	1-1	Pilkington 11	38
	23		26	h	PRESTON N E	L	1-2	0-2	Stephenson 53	28, 36
	24		27	a	Preston N E	L	2-4	0-1	Winton 51p, Shannon 80	30p, 48, 54og, 60
	25		31	h	NEWCASTLE U	W	3-1	2-1	Pilkington (2) 15, 41, Gray 61	39
	26	Jan	14	a	Birmingham C	W	2-1	2-0	McKay 35, Burke 36	67
	27		21	h	WEST BROMWICH A	L	1-2	1-1	Burke 10	6, 57
	28	Feb	4	a	Manchester U	L	0-2	0-0		46, 64
	29		11	h	SHEFFIELD U	D	1-1	0-0	Miller 68	88
	30		18	a	Huddersfield T	L	0-1	0-0		60
	31		25	h	CARDIFF C	L	0-2	0-1		40, 71
Stephenson's last game	32	Mar	3	a	Portsmouth	L	1-3	0-1	Stephenson 82	27, 77, 86
	33		10	h	CHELSEA	W	5-0	1-0	Cheesebrough 30, Pilkington (3) 47, 65, 76, McKay 74	
	34		19	a	Aston Villa	L	0-2	0-2		25, 35
	35		24	h	SUNDERLAND	W	4-0	0-0	Cheesebrough 60, Newlands 64, Pilkington 81, McKay 89	
	36		30	a	Charlton A	L	1-2	1-0	McKay 20	65, 70
	37		31	a	Bolton W	W	1-0	0-0	Burke 57	
	38	Apr	2	h	CHARLTON A	W	2-1	1-1	McKay 20, Burke 78	30
	39		7	h	ARSENAL	L	0-1	0-1		14
	40		14	a	Manchester C	W	3-1	2-0	McKay 5, McIlroy (2) 39, 58	60
	41		21	h	WOLVERHAMPTON W	L	1-2	1-2	Newlands 31	25, 35
	42		28	a	Luton T	W	3-2	1-2	Pilkington 22, McKay (2) 63p, 72	24, 39

FA Cup

	Rd	Date			Opponents	Result		h/t	Goalscorers/times	Opp. goal times
	3	Jan	10	a	Bury	W	1-0	1-0	Gray 43	
	4		28	h	CHELSEA	D	1-1	1-0	McKay 5	84
after extra time, 1-1 at 90 mins	rep	Feb	1	a	Chelsea	D	1-1	0-0	Pilkington 70	60
at St Andrews, aet, 2-2 at 90 mins	2rep		6	n	Chelsea	D	2-2	1-1	McKay 18, McIlroy 48	33p, 76
at Highbury, after extra time	3rep		13	n	Chelsea	D	0-0	0-0		
at White Hart Lane	4rep		15	n	Chelsea	L	0-2	0-1		37, 81

Final, Manchester C 3-1 Birmingham C, at Wembley.

Other first team matches (friendlies and/or as detailed)

		Date			Opponents	Result		Goalscorers	
		Sep	13	h	FIRST VIENNA	D	2-2	McKay (2)	
		Oct	10	a	Coventry C	W	2-1	McKay, Cheesebrough	
		Nov	24	a	Kilmarnock	W	2-1	Cheesebrough (2)	
Lancs Cup		Dec	14	a	Manchester C	D	2-2	Walton, Cargill	
Lancs Cup, at Maine Road	rep		19	h	MANCHESTER C	L	3-4	Holden (2), Milner	
FA Cup tie aban 65m - fog		Jan	7	a	Bury	aban	2-2	McKay (2)	
		Mar	3	a	Southampton	D	2-2	Gray, McKay p	
behind closed doors		Apr	11	h	ENGLAND XI	W	1-0	Pilkington	25 mins each way
			17	h	BOTAFOGO	L	1-2	McKay	
		May	2	a	Rouen	D	0-0		
			6	a	Arras	W	3-1	McKay, Cheesebrough, Newlands	
in Caen			8	n	Rampla Juns (Montevideo)		3-4	unknown (3)	
			12	a	Fortuna Dusseldorf	W	1-0	unknown	
			16	a	Nuremburg	D	1-1	unknown	

Att.	Pos	McDonald	Rudman	Winton	Adamson	Cummings	Shannon	Gray	McIlroy	Holden	Walton	Pilkington	Stephenson	Cheesebrough	McKay	Burke	Seith	D Smith	Miller	Cargill	Newlands		
33,178		1	2	3	4	5	6	7	8	9	10	11											1
35,226		1	2	3	4	5	6	7	8	9	10	11											2
22,482	17	1	2	3	4	5	6	7	9			11	8	10									3
25,774		1	2	3	4	5	6	7	9			11	8	10									4
41,272	20	1	2	3	4	5	6	7	9			11	8	10									5
19,350		1	2	3	4	5	6	7	8			11		10	9								6
22,808	11	1	2	3	4	5	6	7	8			11		10	9								7
23,362	15	1	2	3	4	5	6	7				11		10	9	8							8
26,723	15	1	2	3		5	6	7	9			11		10		8	4						9
22,559	13	1	2	3		5	6	7	8			11		9		10	4						10
22,109	9	1	2	3		5	6	7				11		10	9	8	4						11
24,338	11	1	2	3		5	6	7	8			11		10	9		4						12
23,839	9	1	2	3		5	6	7	8			11		10	9		4						13
39,069	8	1	2	3		5	6	7	8			11		10	9		4						14
20,592	7	1	2	3		5	6	7	8			11		10	9		4						15
39,787	5	1	2			5	6	7	8			11		10	9		4	3					16
20,575	4	1	2			5	6	7				11		10	9	8	4	3					17
37,583	3	1	2			5	6	7				11		10	9	8	4	3					18
26,217	3	1	2			5	6	7				11	8	10	9		4	3					19
24,276	4	1	2			5	6	7				11	8	10	9		4	3					20
20,346	3	1	2			5	6	7				11		10	9	8	4	3					21
35,406	3	1	2	3		5	6	7				11		10	9	8	4						22
31,006		1	2	3		5	6	7				11	8	10	9		4						23
29,524		1	2	3		5	6	7			8	11	9	10			4						24
29,302	4	1	2	3		5	6	7			8	11		10	9		4						25
27,388	3	1	2	3		5	6	7				11		10	9	8	4						26
23,749	4	1	2	3		5	6	7				11		10	9	8	4						27
27,542	5	1		3	5	2		7			10				9	8	4		6	11			28
19,017	5	1	2	3		5	6	7	8						9	10			4	11			29
16,243	5	1	2	3		5	6	7	8			11		10	9		4						30
18,549	10	1		3	5	2	6	7				11		10	9	8	4						31
19,279	12	1			5	2	6					11	7	10	9	8	4	3					32
18,670	9	1		3	5	2	6		8			11		10	9		4				7		33
15,120		1	2	3	5		6		8			11		10	9		4				7		34
23,782	8	1		3	5	2	6		8			11		10	9		4				7		35
22,119	10	1		3	5	2	6		8			11		10	9		4				7		36
29,488	6	1		3	5	2	6		8			11			9	10	4				7		37
20,274		1		3	5	2	6		8			11			9	10	4				7		38
24,393	9	1		3	5	2	6		8			11			9	10	4				7		39
29,087	7	1	2	3	5		6		8			11		10	9		4				7		40
22,322	9	1		3	5	2	6					11		10	9	8	4				7		41
15,999	7	1		3	5	2	6					11		10	9	8	4				7		42
Appearances		42	31	35	21	40	41	31	24	2	5	40	8	35	34	19	33	7	2	2	10		
Goals (64)				1			2	2	4			12	3	6	25	5			1		2	1	og
18,346		1	2	3		5	6	7				11		10	9	8	4						3
44,857		1	2	3	6	5		7	8			11		10	9		4						4
26,661		1		3	5	2		7	8			11		10	9		4		6				rep
21,921		1		3	5	2		7	8			11		10	9		4		6				2nd rep
42,757		1		3	5	2	6	7	8			11		10	9		4						3rd rep
27,210		1	2	3		5	6	7	8			11		10	9		4						4th rep
Appearances		6	3	6	4	6	3	6	5			6		6	6	1	6		2				
Goals (5)								1	1			1			2								

1956-57

OBITUARY
WILLIAM (BILLY) WATSON
DIED 1 SEPTEMBER 1955, AGED 64

The first outfield player to establish himself in the side that went on to win the FA Cup in 1914, Billy Watson was a member of what is arguably the greatest half-back line in Burnley history – Halley, Boyle and Watson. Signed in 1909 from Southport Central, it took him two seasons to carve out a place in the first team, but from then on he was a vital cog in the Clarets' defence. His consistency was unequalled during his time with the Clarets and, had the Great War not intervened just months after the FA Cup success of 1914 against Liverpool he would, surely, have won more than three England caps. When domestic football resumed after the hostilities, Burnley announced their arrival on the big stage by finishing in second place. The following season Watson was the only ever-present as the Clarets won the league title for the first time and enjoyed a 30-match unbeaten run in the process. He retired from league football in 1925 and coached at Accrington and Blackburn, captaining the A team at Ewood Park, before returning to his native Southport and entering politics as a local councillor.

RIP

The new season started with a sense of familiarity. The Burnley side on view was pretty much the one considered the strongest eleven at the end of the previous campaign, with Tommy Cummings lining up at right-back to accommodate a half-back line of Seith, Adamson and Shannon. Possibly the only surprise was the return of Billy Gray on the right wing, although Doug Newlands would soon reassert his right to the number seven shirt. The opponents at Turf Moor were also very familiar, Chelsea having lined up against the Clarets seven times in just over six months! Goals from Jimmy McIlroy and Albert Cheesebrough saw the season off to a promising start with a 2-0 win.

The right-back position was to prove something of a problem in the early stages of the season. Cummings was injured in the opening game, and was destined to miss almost the whole of the season, and the veteran Harold Rudman returned for what would be his final two first-team appearances before Dave Smith was given his first extended run in the side. The home game against Everton early in September saw Smith move to left-back, from which position he scored, as Burnley used their fourth number two of the infant season. John Angus, just turned 18, would go on to make the shirt his own.

That Everton game was the sixth of the season, and the Clarets had won four of them, with Peter McKay carrying on where he had left off the season before. The little Scot took his goal tally to seven from seven by scoring both in a 2-2 draw at West Bromwich, and three weeks later he added another pair as Sheffield Wednesday were beaten 4-1 at the Turf. Yet as it turned out, there was not much more to come from this prolific marksman. McKay was a striker in the purest sense of the word, a goal poacher, and contributed little else to the side. When Alan Brown decided that a fuller contribution was expected from all of his players, McKay was the one who suffered with the loss of his place, and by mid-season he had returned to his native land to play for St. Mirren.

Bobby Seith
as solid as they come at half back

An earlier departure from Turf Moor was that of Roy Stephenson, who joined Rotherham in September, his chance of regular first-team football with Burnley seemingly having passed. His best was yet to come, however, as Burnley would discover to their cost a few years down the line.

1956-57 was certainly a season when youth was given its chance, and the home game against Blackpool in early October saw a scoring debut from another of the promising teenagers at the club, Jimmy Robson. Like Angus and the longer-established Cummings and Adamson, Robson was from the North-East, an area which was increasingly providing Burnley with some exceptional young talent. Robson's chance arose through Jimmy McIlroy being on Northern Ireland international duty, but despite his goal, his time had to wait.

Results, meanwhile, had been rather disappointing after the season's fine start. Only two games out of eleven were won between early September and mid-November, and December brought a further setback when Colin McDonald suffered an ankle injury in the away game at Chelsea. So ended an unbroken run of appearances stretching back almost exactly two years, and into McDonald's shoes stepped 19-year-old Scot Adam Blacklaw. He made his debut on the same day that John Angus began his first extended run in the side, a foggy Saturday afternoon when Burnley thrashed relegation-bound Cardiff 6-2. That was also the game when Peter McKay dropped out, his unlikely replacement in the number nine shirt being Les Shannon.

The usual Christmas double-header against Preston brought only one point, and it was with some relief that attention turned to the F.A. Cup. The third round opponents were Chesterfield of the Third Division North, and in came yet another teenage debutant, and what a debut it proved to be for 17-year-old Ian Lawson. The Spireites were hammered 7-0 and Lawson scored four of the goals to record arguably the most spectacular arrival ever in the Clarets' first eleven. As if to prove it was no fluke, he hit a hat-trick in the fourth round as non-League New Brighton were put to the sword by nine clear goals, equalling Burnley's record score, with Jock Winton also missing a penalty!. Jimmy McIlroy also scored three in that game, his first hat-trick for the club.

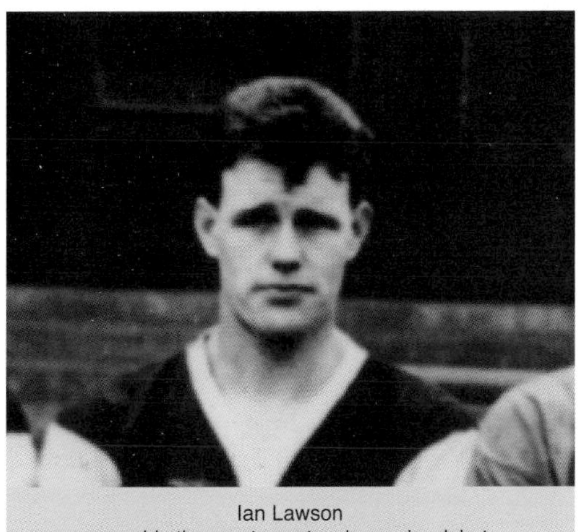

Ian Lawson
arguably the most spectacular senior debut
in Turf Moor history

Over 55,000 assembled at Leeds Road, Huddersfield, for Burnley's fifth round match, and the new wonder boy was on target again as the Clarets won 2-1 to reach the last eight. Lawson, though, was to prove something of a nine-day wonder, and quite soon he was back in the reserves where he would remain for most of the remainder of his Turf Moor career, a victim of the sheer volume of attacking talent on the club's books around that time. He did play in the quarter-final game against Aston Villa, a 1-1 draw, but lost his place for the Villa Park replay to yet another newcomer, Padiham-born Alan Shackleton. Villa lived up to their bogey-team reputation by winning the replay 2-0.

So again it was back to the League, and, with McDonald restored to fitness and back in goal, Burnley embarked on their best run of the season, with six wins and a draw from the next seven games. Shackleton was the top scorer during this run, with five, including two in a revenge win over Villa. But whereas nearly 50,000 had turned out to see the Cup quarter-final, only a third of that number attended the League game. Despite their fine run of form, not to mention the fact that they were still unbeaten at home, the Burnley public realised there was no realistic prospect of League honours and many were staying away. The Busby Babes were again pre-eminent in 1956-57, and it was United who became the first visitors to triumph at Turf Moor when they won 3-1 on Good Friday. To compound a miserable Easter, their City neighbours, down at the opposite end of the table, came to the Turf and won 3-0 a day later, then United completed the double on Easter Monday at Old Trafford.

The end of the season saw yet more unfamiliar names appearing in the Clarets line-up. One, who had appeared briefly during the good run in March, was an 18-year-old left-winger named John Connelly. Seldom if ever had there been a season when youth had emerged on this scale, and few at the time would have realised the potential some of the young players possessed.

Seventh place for the second successive season was a creditable enough achievement, and but for a poor away record, Burnley were winless on their travels between October 1956 and March 1957, it might have been even better. This season however would be seen in retrospect as the dawn of Burnley's second golden era, as the club's youth scheme, soon to be envied throughout the football world, really began to bear fruit.

1956-57 - First Division

		P	W	D	L	F	A	Pts
1	Manchester U	42	28	8	6	103	54	64
2	Tottenham H	42	22	12	8	104	56	56
3	Preston NE	42	23	10	9	84	56	56
4	Blackpool	42	22	9	11	93	65	53
5	Arsenal	42	21	8	13	85	69	50
6	Wolverhampton W	42	20	8	14	94	70	48
7	BURNLEY	42	18	10	14	56	50	46
8	Leeds U	42	15	14	13	72	63	44
9	Bolton W	42	16	12	14	65	65	44
10	Aston Villa	42	14	15	13	65	55	43
11	West Bromwich A	42	14	14	14	59	61	42
12	Chelsea	42	13	13	16	73	73	39
13	Birmingham C	42	15	9	18	69	69	39
14	Sheffield W	42	16	6	20	82	88	38
15	Everton	42	14	10	18	61	79	38
16	Luton T	42	14	9	19	58	76	37
17	Newcastle U	42	14	8	20	67	87	36
18	Manchester C	42	13	9	20	78	88	35
19	Portsmouth	42	10	13	19	62	92	33
20	Sunderland	42	12	8	22	67	88	32
21	Cardiff C	42	10	9	23	53	88	29
22	Charlton A	42	9	4	29	62	120	22

1956-57

Manager : Alan Brown

Division One (7th)

		Date			Opponents	Result		h/t	Goalscorers/times	Opp. goal times
	1	Aug	18	h	CHELSEA	W	2-0	1-0	Cheesebrough 33, McIlroy 61	
	2		21	a	Arsenal	L	0-2	0-0		47, 60
Rudman's last game	3		25	a	Cardiff C	D	3-3	1-3	McKay (2) 11, 73p, McIlroy 80	2, 7, 20
	4		28	h	ARSENAL	W	3-1	1-0	McIlroy (2) 20, 84, McKay 52	65
	5	Sep	1	h	BIRMINGHAM C	W	2-0	1-0	McKay (2) 35, 59	
	6		3	h	EVERTON	W	2-1	0-0	Pilkington 55, Smith 70	78
	7		8	a	West Bromwich A	D	2-2	0-1	McKay (2) 49, 87	34, 63
	8		12	a	Everton	L	0-1	0-0		68p
	9		15	h	PORTSMOUTH	D	1-1	0-1	Pilkington 46	29
	10		22	a	Newcastle U	D	1-1	1-1	Pilkington 2	24
	11		29	h	SHEFFIELD W	W	4-1	3-0	McKay (2) 7, 47, McIlroy (2) 22, 27	65
	12	Oct	6	h	BLACKPOOL	D	2-2	1-2	Cheesebrough 7, Robson 80	3, 11
	13		13	a	Manchester C	W	1-0	1-0	Gray 40	
	14		20	h	LEEDS U	D	0-0	0-0		
	15		27	a	Tottenham H	L	0-2	0-1		34p, 79
	16	Nov	3	h	LUTON T	D	1-1	0-1	Seith 47	13og
	17		10	a	Aston Villa	L	0-1	0-1		7
	18		17	h	WOLVERHAMPTON W	W	3-0	1-0	Cheesebrough 34, McKay 49, Pilkington 73	
	19		24	a	Bolton W	L	0-3	0-0		79, 80, 82
	20	Dec	1	h	CHARLTON A	W	2-1	1-0	McKay 38, McIlroy 55	77
	21		8	a	Sunderland	L	1-2	1-2	McIlroy 9	15, 27
McKay's last game	22		15	a	Chelsea	L	0-2	0-1		2, 62
Cardiff goals 6m, 58m	23		22	h	CARDIFF C	W	6-2	3-1	McIlroy (2) 12, 65, Newlands (2) 14, 32, Shannon 47, Cheesebrough 80	
	24		25	h	PRESTON N E	D	2-2	1-0	Shannon 25, Cheesebrough 66	83, 87
	25		26	a	Preston N E	L	0-1	0-0		80og
	26		29	a	Birmingham C	L	0-2	0-1		36, 72
	27	Jan	12	h	WEST BROMWICH A	W	1-0	0-0	Cheesebrough 67	
	28		19	a	Portsmouth	L	0-1	0-0		86
	29	Feb	2	h	NEWCASTLE U	W	3-2	0-1	Pilkington 52, Newlands 55, Lawson 67	31, 82
	30		9	a	Sheffield W	D	0-0	0-0		
	31	Mar	9	h	SUNDERLAND	W	2-0	0-0	Newlands 70, McIlroy 87	
	32		11	a	Leeds U	D	1-1	0-0	Newlands 65	82
	33		16	a	Luton T	W	2-0	1-0	Shackleton 23, Cheesebrough 88	
	34		30	a	Wolverhampton W	W	2-1	2-1	Newlands 9, Cheesebrough 33	17
	35	Apr	6	h	BOLTON W	W	1-0	0-0	Shackleton 75	
	36		13	a	Charlton A	W	2-1	2-0	McIlroy 3, Shackleton 44	67
	37		15	h	ASTON VILLA	W	2-1	2-1	Shackleton (2) 31, 33	45
	38		19	h	MANCHESTER U	L	1-3	1-2	McIlroy 36	17, 43, 70
	39		20	h	MANCHESTER C	L	0-3	0-2		18, 25, 57
	40		22	a	Manchester U	L	0-2	0-0		65, 85
	41		29	h	TOTTENHAM H	W	1-0	0-0	Lawson 70	
Gray's last game	42	May	1	a	Blackpool	L	0-1	0-1		14

FA Cup

	3	Jan	5	h	CHESTERFIELD	W	7-0	2-0	Lawson (4) 7, 54, 81, 86, Pilkington 33, Cheesebrough (2) 75, 88	
Lawson's goals (3) 7, 60, 78	4		26	h	NEW BRIGHTON	W	9-0	5-0	McIlroy (3) 25, 41, 53, Cheesebrough 34, Newlands 44, Pilkington 77	
	5	Feb	16	a	Huddersfield T	W	2-1	0-1	Cheesebrough 56, Lawson 68	31
	6	Mar	2	h	ASTON VILLA	D	1-1	1-0	Aldis 30og	64
	rep		6	a	Aston Villa	L	0-2	0-1		30, 65

Final, Aston Villa 2-1 Manchester U, at Wembley.

Other first team matches (friendlies and/or as detailed)

	Sep	18	h	F DUSSELDORF	D	2-2	McIlroy, McKay	
	Oct	1	a	Coventry C	D	1-1	Curtis og	
	Nov	5	a	Accrington S	L	0-2		
Lancs Cup	Feb	5	h	BLACKPOOL	W	4-0	Shackleton (4)	
	Apr	1	a	Charleroi Olympique	L	0-1		
Lancs Cup		9	a	Bury	W	2-1	Wilson, Grey	
Lancs Cup semi		17	h	SOUTHPORT	W	1-0	Lawson	Final played Oct 57
in Caen	May	8	a	Reims	D	1-1	McIlroy	
		14	a	Charleroi Olympique	W	4-1	Cheesebrough (3), McIlroy	
in Essen		16	a	German XI	W	4-0	Cheesebrough (2), McIlroy, Robson	
		20	a	Servette Geneve	D	1-1	Robson	
no details		28	a	Metz				
		30	a	Athletic Bilbao	W	5-1	McIlroy (3), unknown (2)	

Att.	Pos	McDonald	Cummings	Winton	Seith	Adamson	Shannon	Gray	McIlroy	McKay	Cheesebrough	Pilkington	Rudman	Newlands	D Smith	Angus	Robson	Miller	Blacklaw	Lancaster	Lawson	Shackleton	Connelly	Wilson	Appleby		
21,960		1	2	3	4	5	6	7	8	9	10	11															1
38,321		1		3	4	5	6	7	8	9	10	11	2														2
30,769	12	1		3	4	5	6		8	9	10	11	2	7													3
19,049		1	2	3	4	5	6		8	9	10	11		7													4
25,531	5	1		3	4	5	6		8	9	10	11		7	2												5
24,185		1			4	5	6		8	9	10	11		7	3	2											6
23,611	3	1			4	5	6		8	9	10	11		7	3	2											7
27,591		1			4	5	6		8	9	10	11		7	3	2											8
22,756	5	1		3	4	5	6		8	9	10	11		7	2												9
36,790	6	1		3	4	5	6		8	9	10	11		7	2												10
23,559	5	1		3	4	5	6		8	9	10	11		7	2												11
27,694	5	1		3	4	5	6			9	10	11		7	2		8										12
35,981	5	1		3	4	5	6	7	8	9	10	11			2												13
26,440	4	1		3	4	5	6	7	8	9	10	11			2												14
49,154	4	1		3	4	5		7	8	9	10			11	2			6									15
22,891	5	1		3	4	5	6	7	8	9	10	11			2												16
22,420	7	1		3	4	5			8	9		11		7	2		10	6									17
25,776	5	1		3	4	5			8	9	10	11		7	2			6									18
26,062	7	1		3	4	5			8	9	10	11		7	2			6									19
18,348	6	1		3	4	5			8	9	10	11		7	2			6									20
29,588	8	1		3	4	5			8	9	10	11		7	2			6									21
18,371	10	1		3	4	5			8	9	10	11		7	2			6									22
10,118	7			3	4	5	9		8		10	11		7		2		6	1								23
23,737				3	4	5	9		8		10	11		7		2		6	1								24
19,265				3	4	5	9		8		10	11		7		2		6	1								25
31,733	10			3	4	5	9		8		10			7		2		6	1	11							26
24,299	10			3	4	5			8		10	11		7		2		6	1		9						27
22,057	10			3	4	5			8		10	11		7		2		6	1		9						28
26,778	10			3	4	5			8		10	11		7		2		6	1		9						29
29,583	10			3	4	5			8		10	11		7		2		6	1		9						30
21,892	9	1		3	4		6		8		10	11		7		2		5				9					31
31,956		1		3	4		6		8		10			7		2		5				9	11				32
16,420	9	1		3	4		6		8		10	11		7		2		5				9					33
25,462	9	1		3	4		6		8		10	11		7		2		5				9					34
23,250	9	1		3	4		6		8		10	11		7		2		5				9					35
13,334	8	1		3	4	5			8		10	11		7		2		6				9					36
17,381		1		3	4	5			8		10	11		7		2		6				9					37
37,823	7	1		3	4	5			8		10	11		7		2		6				9					38
16,746	7	1		3	4	5			8		10	11		7		2		6				9					39
41,540	8	1		3	4	5			8		10	11		7		2		6			9						40
12,048		1		3	4	5	6		8					7		2	10				9		11				41
13,919	7	1					6	7			8				3	2	10				9		11	4	5		42
Appearances		34	2	38	41	36	26	7	40	22	40	37	2	36	19	23	4	25	8	1	7	9	3	1	1		
Goals (56)					1		2	1	13	11	8	5		6	1		1				2	5					

Att.	Pos	McDonald	Cummings	Winton	Seith	Adamson	Shannon	Gray	McIlroy	McKay	Cheesebrough	Pilkington	Rudman	Newlands	D Smith	Angus	Robson	Miller	Blacklaw	Lancaster	Lawson	Shackleton	Connelly	Wilson	Appleby		
27,608				3	4	5			8		10	11		7		2		6	1		9						3
41,453				3	4	5			8		10	11		7		2		6	1		9						4
55,168				3	4	5			8		10	11		7		2		6	1		9						5
49,436				3	4	5			8		10	11		7		2		6	1		9						6
46,182				3	4		6		8		10	11		7		2		5	1			9					rep
Appearances				5	5	4	1		5		5	5		5		5		5	5		4	1					
Goals (19)									3		4	2		1							8					1	og

1957-58

Alan Brown's tenure as Burnley's Manager ended in July 1957 when he took the well-trodden path to Roker Park, Sunderland. His time in charge had seen the club consolidate as a top-half First Division side, and the Turf Moor youth scheme had really started to blossom under his management. An ex-Claret of an earlier vintage took over, Billy Dougall, who had played for the club back in the 1920s before embarking on a long spell on the coaching staff, rising to the position of first-team trainer in 1934. He and reserve coach Ray Bennion were key men behind the scenes for many years before Dougall, at the age of 61, finally gained promotion to the manager's chair.

Another summer departure was that of right-winger Billy Gray, who moved to Nottingham Forest where he was converted to an inside-forward role and went on to enjoy six more years of First Division football before moving into management. Doug Newlands' success in the number seven shirt had reduced Gray to something of a bit-player in his last season at Burnley.

The new season began with the long trip to Portsmouth. Of the teenagers who had emerged during the previous campaign, only John Angus was in the side, while Alan Shackleton was preferred to Ian Lawson at centre-forward. A goalless draw at Fratton Park was followed by a 2-0 home win against Preston, with Shackleton scoring both goals. Overall, it was a moderate start to the season, notable mainly for a brief return to first-team duty by Tommy Cummings, but things went badly wrong in September when thirteen goals were conceded in two away games, with a seven goal hammering at Nottingham Forest on a Wednesday being followed by a 1-6 drubbing at Chelsea the following Saturday.

Two more defeats followed; the second of these, at Luton, saw a change at centre-forward with the first appearance of Ray Pointer. A relatively late starter in League football, Pointer was just short of 21 on his debut, but he very quickly became a crowd favourite with his distinctive blond hair, all-action style, and not least his eye for goal. He was on target on his home debut a week later, as the Clarets' poor run ended in style with a 6-0 victory over Sunderland. Goals were very much the currency of the time, a month later Leicester came to the Turf and were humbled 7-3, with both Jimmy McIlroy and Albert Cheesebrough registering hat-tricks. Although Pointer scored in that game, he lost his place to Shackleton the following week, and the local boy duly weighed in with two in a 4-2 win at Blackpool.

Clearly there was plenty of entertainment on offer, but Burnley were struggling to achieve real consistency and remained somewhat porous at the back, where Dave Smith had resumed in place of Angus. Although comfortably placed by Christmas 1957, this weakness raised its head again as visits to Manchester City and West Brom saw a total of nine goals conceded.

Just before the festive period came a landmark occasion, when the Turf Moor floodlights were officially switched on for a friendly game against Blackburn Rovers with the two clubs not having met in the League for almost a decade. The following Saturday, the home game against Portsmouth saw the first use of the lights for a League game, and the Clarets marked the event with a 3-1 win.

Early in the new year, Billy Dougall resigned. He had been hospitalised in November, at which point Ray Bennion took over first-team duties, and finally took medical advice and quit the job in January. He was immediately appointed as physiotherapist, and remained in that role for a further seven years until his retirement.

Another ex-Claret took over the reins, in what was surely one of the wisest appointments ever made by the club. In the seven years or so since his departure from Turf Moor as a player, Harry Potts had begun his coaching career at Everton as his first-team opportunities grew fewer. He then moved briefly to Wolves as a coach before taking up his first managerial appointment at Shrewsbury in the summer of 1957. He had therefore served only a brief apprenticeship as a manager, and was still relatively young at 37, when he moved into the Burnley hot seat. Dougall and Bennion were well-known to Potts from his playing days at the Turf, and both were to remain as trusted assistants on his return in his new role.

Harry Potts signs on the dotted line, watched by Bob Lord another golden era begins at Turf Moor

The F.A. Cup brought disappointment. Second Division Swansea were comfortably beaten 4-2 in the third round, and further progress looked likely after a 2-2 draw at Eastville against another Second Division side, Bristol Rovers. But despite leading twice, Burnley were beaten 2-3 in the replay at Turf Moor, a game which incidentally drew the biggest home crowd of the season, over 41,000.

Alan Shackleton
ten goals from inside forward

In the League, the goals continued to flow at both ends, with all five forwards chipping in. The number nine shirt reverted to Ray Pointer for the middle period of the season, while Jimmy Robson and John Connelly were both given further first-team experience. The mainstays up front, though, were Doug Newlands and Brian Pilkington on the wings, and Jimmy McIlroy and Albert Cheesebrough in the inside-forward positions, and as long as the goals kept going in there seemed little reason to change. Brian Miller had a good run in the side at the expense of Bobby Seith, while John Angus was struggling to displace Dave Smith on a regular basis in the number two shirt.

Chairman Bob Lord, who had taken over the position three years earlier, was already making a name for himself through his outspokenness. He attracted much controversy with his comments following the Munich air disaster to the effect that Burnley would not be one of the clubs willing to help out the stricken Manchester United side by providing players, on a permanent basis or otherwise. United visited Turf Moor some six weeks after the tragedy, with only two of the players who had faced Burnley at Old Trafford earlier in the season. Burnley won 3-0, but there was bad feeling between the players and, after the match, club officials as well, a sad state of affairs.

The average Turf Moor crowd during 1957-58 was 22,251, the lowest since the war, and, as had tended to be the case over the last few years, gates fell off in the latter stages as it became clear that there was no chance of honours. It was a shame, as the entertainment value was clearly high. Five players reached double figures in League goals, McIlroy leading the way with sixteen, and the 80 goals scored and 74 conceded both set new post-war benchmarks. Defence seemed to be a foreign concept all over the First Division that season, Manchester City, in finishing fifth, both scored and conceded a century. Even Leicester, who only avoided relegation by a point, scored 91, five of them coming against the Clarets at Filbert Street on Easter Saturday 1958.

Sixth place in the final table meant another solid season at Turf Moor. Perhaps the Burnley public was becoming blase as the side continued to do well without quite breaking through to the next stage, but almost all of the players who would make that breakthrough were by now at the club, and it was only a matter of time.

1957-58 - First Division

		P	W	D	L	F	A	Pts
1	Wolverhampton W	42	28	8	6	103	47	64
2	Preston NE	42	26	7	9	100	51	59
3	Tottenham H	42	21	9	12	93	77	51
4	West Bromwich A	42	18	14	10	92	70	50
5	Manchester C	42	22	5	15	104	100	49
6	BURNLEY	42	21	5	16	80	74	47
7	Blackpool	42	19	6	17	80	67	44
8	Luton T	42	19	6	17	69	63	44
9	Manchester U	42	16	11	15	85	75	43
10	Nottingham F	42	16	10	16	69	63	42
11	Chelsea	42	15	12	15	83	79	42
12	Arsenal	42	16	7	19	73	85	39
13	Birmingham C	42	14	11	17	76	89	39
14	Aston Villa	42	16	7	19	73	86	39
15	Bolton W	42	14	10	18	65	87	38
16	Everton	42	13	11	18	65	75	37
17	Leeds U	42	14	9	19	51	63	37
18	Leicester C	42	14	5	23	91	112	33
19	Newcastle U	42	12	8	22	73	81	32
20	Portsmouth	42	12	8	22	73	88	32
21	Sunderland	42	10	12	20	54	97	32
22	Sheffield W	42	12	7	23	69	92	31

1957-58

Manager : Billy Dougall until January 1958 then Harry Potts

Division One (6th)

	No.	Date		Venue	Opponents	Result		h/t	Goalscorers/times	Opp. goal times
	1	Aug	24	a	Portsmouth	D	0-0	0-0		
	2		27	h	PRESTON N E	W	2-0	0-0	Shackleton (2) 48, 78	
	3		31	h	WEST BROMWICH A	D	2-2	1-2	Cheesebrough 43, Shackleton 68	19, 25
	4	Sep	4	a	Preston N E	L	1-2	0-1	McIlroy 82p	43, 60
	5		7	a	Tottenham H	L	1-3	0-2	Cheesebrough 75	26, 44, 53
	6		9	h	NOTTINGHAM F	W	3-1	2-1	Shackleton (2) 12, 30, Pilkington 73	43
	7		14	h	BIRMINGHAM C	W	3-1	3-0	Pilkington 6, Cheesebrough 34, Shackleton 38	82
	8		18	a	Nottingham F	L	0-7	0-4		2,10,17,24,55,65,75
	9		21	a	Chelsea	L	1-6	0-3	Cheesebrough 79	3,13,20,47,55,89
	10		28	h	NEWCASTLE U	L	0-2	0-1		11, 59
	11	Oct	5	a	Luton T	L	2-3	0-2	Pilkington (2) 68, 75	18, 36, 61
	12		12	h	SUNDERLAND	W	6-0	2-0	Newlands (2) 9p, 80, Cheesebrough 19, Shannon (2) 55, 83, Pointer 67	
	13		19	a	Everton	D	1-1	0-0	Cheesebrough 47	56
	14		26	h	ASTON VILLA	W	3-0	1-0	Pilkington (2) 30, 55, Newlands 82	
	15	Nov	2	a	Manchester U	L	0-1	0-0		51
Leicester goals 1m, 24m, 80m	16		9	h	LEICESTER C	W	7-3	3-2	McIlroy (3) 17, 83, 89, Cheesebrough (3) 33, 35, 56, Pointer 85	
	17		16	a	Blackpool	W	4-2	3-0	Cheesebrough 3, Shackleton (2) 6, 29, Pilkington 68	86, 89
	18		23	h	LEEDS U	W	3-1	2-1	McIlroy 4, Pilkington 37, Shackleton 84	44p
	19		30	a	Wolverhampton W	L	1-2	0-1	McIlroy 62	8, 48
	20	Dec	7	h	ARSENAL	W	2-1	1-0	Newlands 6, Cheesebrough 79	84
	21		14	a	Bolton W	L	1-2	0-1	Newlands 89	36, 59
	22		21	h	PORTSMOUTH	W	3-1	0-0	Pointer 51, Newlands (2) 55, 70	87
	23		25	h	MANCHESTER C	W	2-1	0-0	Pilkington 68, Cheesebrough 79	57
	24		26	a	Manchester C	L	1-4	0-1	Pointer 67	44, 58, 69, 85
	25		28	a	West Bromwich A	L	1-5	1-0	Pilkington 18	54, 75, 78, 81, 84
	26	Jan	11	h	TOTTENHAM H	W	2-0	1-0	McIlroy (2) 19, 88	
	27		18	a	Birmingham C	W	3-2	1-1	White (2) 25, 79, Pilkington 59	13, 69
	28	Feb	1	h	CHELSEA	W	2-1	2-1	Pilkington 11, McIlroy 12	5
	29		15	h	LUTON T	L	1-2	1-1	Pointer 39	35, 66
	30		22	a	Sunderland	W	3-2	2-0	Robson (2) 7, 74, Pointer 43	48, 84
	31	Mar	1	h	EVERTON	L	0-2	0-1		11, 54
	32		8	a	Aston Villa	L	0-3	0-2		26p, 36, 86
	33		15	h	MANCHESTER U	W	3-0	0-0	McIlroy 47, Shackleton 74, Cheesebrough 75	
	34		22	a	Leeds U	L	0-1	0-1		44
	35		29	h	BLACKPOOL	W	2-1	1-1	McIlroy 34, Pilkington 83	25
	36	Apr	4	h	SHEFFIELD W	W	2-0	1-0	McIlroy 11, Newlands 75	
	37		5	a	Leicester C	L	3-5	2-4	Miller 40, McIlroy (2) 44, 69	18, 19, 39, 41, 55
	38		7	a	Sheffield W	W	2-1	1-1	Pointer 21, Newlands 55	15
	39		12	h	WOLVERHAMPTON W	D	1-1	0-1	Newlands 53	13
	40		19	a	Arsenal	D	0-0	0-0		
	41		26	h	BOLTON W	W	3-1	2-0	McIlroy (2) 7, 65, Seith 34	58
	42		28	a	Newcastle U	W	3-1	1-0	Newlands 14, Pointer 60, Seith 78	81

FA Cup

Round	Date		Venue	Opponents	Result		h/t	Goalscorers/times	Opp. goal times
3	Jan	4	h	SWANSEA T	W	4-2	3-0	Newlands 35, Cheesebrough 39, McIlroy (2) 42, 47	62, 80
4		25	a	Bristol R	D	2-2	0-1	Connelly 60, Pointer 61	25, 65og
rep		28	h	BRISTOL R	L	2-3	1-0	McIlroy 5, Pointer 63	50, 72, 80

Final, Bolton W 2-0 Manchester U, at Wembley.

Other first team matches (friendlies and/or as detailed)

	Date		Venue	Opponents	Result		Goalscorers
opening of Nou Camp, Barcelona	Sep	25	n	Flamengo (Brazil)	L	0-4	
Lancs Cup final (1956-57)	Oct	2	a	Chester	L	0-1	
		20	h	LODSKI CLUB SPORTOWY	W	6-0	Cheesebrough (2), Pilkington (2), McIlroy (2)
Lancs Cup	Nov	12	h	BLACKBURN R	W	4-0	Robson, Connelly (2), Shackleton
new Turf Moor floodlights	Dec	16	h	BLACKBURN R	L	0-1	
	Feb	17	h	OFFENBACH K	W	1-0	Pointer
Lancs Cup	Mar	18	h	LIVERPOOL	L	2-3	Pointer, Wilson
in Brno	May	14	a	Czech XI	L	0-3	
in Prague		15	a	Czech XI	L	1-2	Pilkington
in Vienna		21	a	Austrian XI	L	0-3	
		24	a	Lodski Club Sportowy	W	1-0	Shannon

Att.	Pos	McDonald	Angus	Winton	Seith	Adamson	Shannon	Newlands	McIlroy	Shackleton	Cheesebrough	Pilkington	D Smith	Cummings	Miller	Wilson	Blacklaw	Robson	Pointer	White	Connelly	
30,134		1	2	3	4	5	6	7	8	9	10	11										1
27,804		1	2	3	4	5	6	7	8	9	10	11										2
24,428	5	1		3	4	5	6	7	8	9	10	11	2									3
31,267		1			4	5	6	7	8	9	10	11	3	2								4
40,108	12	1			4	5	6	7	8	9	10	11	3	2								5
15,818		1			4	5	6	7	8	9	10	11	3	2								6
20,522	7	1	2	3	4		6	7	8	9	10	11			5							7
26,842		1	2	3			6	7	8	9	10	11			5	4						8
42,449	14		2	3	4	5		7	8	9	10	11			6		1					9
18,465	18		2	3	4	5		7	8	9	10	11			6		1					10
15,179	19		2	3	4	5		7			10	11			6		1	8	9			11
22,868	15	1		3	4	5	6	7			10	11	2					8	9			12
45,024	14	1		3	4	5	6	7	8		10	11	2						9			13
20,860	13	1		3	4	5	6	7	8		10	11	2						9			14
49,689	13	1		3	4	5	6	7	8		10	11	2						9			15
20,978	12	1		3	4	5	6	7	8		10	11	2						9			16
21,641	12	1		3	4	5	6	7	8	9	10	11	2									17
24,144	11	1		3	4	5	6	7	8	9	10	11	2									18
32,888	13	1		3	4	5	6	7	8	9	10	11	2									19
18,563	10	1		3	4	5	6	7	8		10	11	2					9				20
20,197	14	1		3	4	5	6	7	8	9	10	11	2									21
19,761	11	1		3	4	5	6	7	8		10	11	2						9			22
27,666		1		3	4	5	6	7	8		10	11	2						9			23
47,285	9	1		3	4		6	7	8		10	11	2		5				9			24
38,183	11	1	3	6	4			7			10	11	2		5				9	8		25
25,927	9	1		3	4	5	6	7	8		10	11	2						9			26
22,281	9	1	2	3	4	5			8			11			6				9	7	10	27
20,599	8	1		3	4	5	6	7	8			11	2						9		10	28
16,869	10	1		3	4	5	6	7	8		10	11	2						9			29
30,595		1	2	3	4	5	6	7			10	11						8	9			30
19,657	8	1	2	3		5	6	7			10	11			4				9		8	31
25,679	11	1	2	3		5	4	7			10	11			6				9	8		32
37,447	9	1		3		5	4	7	8	9	10	11	2		6							33
24,994	10	1		3		5	4	7	8	9	10	11	2		6							34
20,781	9	1		3		5	4	7	8	9	10	11	2		6							35
18,165		1		3		5	4	7	8	9	10	11	2		6							36
26,150		1		3		5	4	7	8	9	10	11	2		6							37
22,417		1		3			4	7	8		10	11	2	5	6				9			38
28,539	8	1		3		5	4	7	8		10	11	2		6				9			39
31,440		1		3	4	5		7	8		10	11	2		6				9			40
17,419		1		3	4			7	8		10	11	2	5	6				9			41
21,610	6	1		3	4	5	6	7	8		10	11		2					9			42
Appearances		39	12	39	32	36	35	41	36	19	40	42	30	6	19	1	3	4	22	3	3	
Goals (80)					2		2	11	16	10	13	13			1			2	8	2		

Att.	Pos	McDonald	Angus	Winton	Seith	Adamson	Shannon	Newlands	McIlroy	Shackleton	Cheesebrough	Pilkington	D Smith	Cummings	Miller	Wilson	Blacklaw	Robson	Pointer	White	Connelly	
26,193		1		3	4		6	7	8		10	11	2		5				9			3
35,088		1		3	4	5	6		8			11	2						9	7	10	4
41,113		1		3	4	5	6		8		10	11	2						9		7	rep
Appearances		3		3	3	2	3	1	3		2	3	3		1				3	1	2	
Goals (8)								1	3		1								2		1	

1958-59

The big footballing event of the summer of 1958 was the World Cup in Sweden, when, for the first and so far only time, all four home countries qualified. Burnley had two representatives at the finals. One, needless to say, was Jimmy McIlroy, a key member of the Northern Ireland side which confounded expectations by reaching the quarter-finals. The other, by now established as England's premier goalkeeper, was Colin McDonald. He had made his international debut in May 1958, and went on to play in all four of England's games in Sweden. Such was McDonald's excellence, particularly in a goalless draw against eventual world champions Brazil, that he was voted the best keeper of the tournament.

Back on home territory, Harry Potts' first full season in charge began with Manchester City's visit to Turf Moor. Tommy Cummings, who had returned near the end of the previous season after practically two years on the sidelines, lined up at right-back, and Ray Pointer was chosen to lead the forward line, but otherwise the team selection was predictable. The match, however, was anything but, Pointer scored twice and Brian Pilkington once, to get Burnley's season off to a flier, 3-0 up at half-time. By the final whistle however, they had been beaten 4-3 and it looked as if the high scoring at both ends of the field, such a feature of 1957-58, was about to continue in.

The line-up soon took on a more youthful look. For the third game, Pointer, John Connelly and Jimmy Robson appeared together for the first time, and Robson scored the goal to earn a 1-1 draw at Leeds and earn the Clarets' first point of the season. It was a hesitant start, though, with four of the first seven games being lost, and Potts was not averse to making changes to the side, only McDonald, Cummings, Bobby Seith and Brian Pilkington played in all of those seven games.

Alan Shackleton was sold to Leeds in October. He had averaged better than a goal every two games in his brief time as a first-teamer at Turf Moor, but it was clear that with Pointer's emergence he would be surplus to requirements. Doug Newlands and Albert Cheesebrough became occasionals rather than regulars as Connelly and Robson moved up the ranks, while the new regular half-back line became Seith, Cummings and Jimmy Adamson. The man making way in that department was Les Shannon, who played the last of his 262 League games for Burnley on 20 September 1958. His role had changed several times over the years, but he had been a stalwart of the side throughout most of the decade now nearing its close.

Despite these changes, the Clarets' season struggled to take off until a good run of results towards the end of the year. The run coincided with the first real indication of the potency of Pointer, who scored twelve times in eight games between late November and mid-January. Connelly was also proving prolific in this spell, and by the end of December Burnley had risen from the bottom half of the First Division table on the back of this improved form. Two players whose best days still lay a few years ahead, John Talbut and Gordon Harris, made their first team debuts around this time, while Doug Winton, whose left-back spot had been lost to Dave Smith, was sold to Aston Villa.

1959 began with a comfortable 3-1 home win against Leeds which saw the return to favour of Brian Miller. He was to remain in the side for good this time, initially appearing at centre-half with Cummings back out to the right. Next came the start to another F.A. Cup campaign, and Third Division Stockport were edged out in round three, setting up a meeting with Blackburn at Ewood Park. Rovers had just returned to the top flight and were having a decent first season, but goals from Robson and Jimmy Mac took the Clarets through to the last sixteen.

John Angus
Burnley's finest ever right back?

February 1959 was a month of mixed fortunes. In the League, a 6-2 defeat at Luton was followed by a first senior hat-trick for Jimmy Robson as Chelsea were beaten 3-1 at Stamford Bridge. In the FA Cup, a single goal was enough to see off Portsmouth, taking the Clarets to a quarter-final against their 50's nemesis, Aston Villa, at Villa Park. For once, that ground's jinx failed to strike and a goalless draw brought Villa back to Turf Moor, where the jinx was usually on them. They had been beaten on each of their last ten League visits, and they were, at the time of the game, bottom of the First Division. Past form is sometimes no guide however and this time it was Villa who took their place in the last four with a 2-0 win.

Another jolt to the system followed with a 1-4 defeat at Ewood Park, but then came a magnificent run of seven consecutive victories, the best winning sequence since the war. Nineteen goals were scored, with Pointer, who else, leading the way with nine of them. West Brom away, Manchester United, at home and Preston away were all hit for four. But in the midst of the celebrations came bad news, much worse than was realised at the time. On 17 March 1959, Colin McDonald broke his leg playing for the Football League against the League of Ireland in Dublin. Complications arose, and, although he recovered sufficiently to play for the reserves in the following season, this superb goalkeeper would never play senior football again, his career effectively ended at the age of 28. It was a huge loss to both club and country.

The tail-end of the season saw Albert Cheesebrough return to the side and remind the fans of his own goal knack with doubles at both Wolves and Tottenham. John Angus finally established himself at right-back, and Adam Blacklaw became the unwitting beneficiary of McDonald's injury as he finally saw an extended run of first-team action. Despite none of the last three games being won, it had been a fine end to the season, and though Burnley slipped down a place to seventh from the previous year, their record was actually slightly better, with 81 goals scored setting another post-war record. This had been the season when Burnley's young talent had fully blossomed, none more so than Ray Pointer, whose 27 League goals was the best tally by a Claret since the days of George Beel. Connelly and Robson also reached double figures. At the end of the season, they were both 20 years old, as was John Angus; Blacklaw was 21, Pointer and Miller 22. Coming through the ranks were Talbut and Harris, both 18, and other youngsters yet to make their first-team mark. In the summer of 1959, Turf Moor's exceptional collection of young talent was still a relatively well-kept secret, although not for much longer.

Ray Pointer
top scorer in 1958-59
the Clarets' leading marksman in post-war football

OBITUARY
SAMUEL CLIFFORD (CLIFF) JONES
DIED 5 APRIL 1959, AGED 69

Burnley's run to the semi-final of the FA Cup in 1913 included a second round victory against Gainsborough Trinity, a club that had dropped out of the League at the end of the previous season. Although Trinity conceded four goals that day, Burnley were sufficiently impressed to sign their goalkeeper and both full-backs. The one destined to make the biggest impact at Turf Moor was the left-back, Cliff Jones. Struggling at first to displace the established David Taylor in the side, Jones did not really make his mark until after the war, and by the 1920-21 season he was finally established as first choice in the number three shirt. He was a regular throughout most of that season's record-breaking run of 30 unbeaten First Division games and played at Everton in the match in April 1921 when the League title was clinched.

He started the following campaign as the regular left-back in the side, but lost out again to Taylor when the team's form faltered. He moved to Accrington Stanley in December 1922.

RIP

1958-59 - First Division

		P	W	D	L	F	A	Pts
1	Wolverhampton W	42	28	5	9	110	49	61
2	Manchester U	42	24	7	11	103	66	55
3	Arsenal	42	21	8	13	88	68	50
4	Bolton W	42	20	10	12	79	66	50
5	West Bromwich A	42	18	13	11	88	68	49
6	West Ham U	42	21	6	15	85	70	48
7	BURNLEY	42	19	10	13	81	70	48
8	Blackpool	42	18	11	13	66	49	47
9	Birmingham C	42	20	6	16	84	68	46
10	Blackburn R	42	17	10	15	76	70	44
11	Newcastle U	42	17	7	18	80	80	41
12	Preston NE	42	17	7	18	70	77	41
13	Nottingham F	42	17	6	19	71	74	40
14	Chelsea	42	18	4	20	77	98	40
15	Leeds U	42	15	9	18	57	74	39
16	Everton	42	17	4	21	71	87	38
17	Luton T	42	12	13	17	68	71	37
18	Tottenham H	42	13	10	19	85	95	36
19	Leicester C	42	11	10	21	67	98	32
20	Manchester C	42	11	9	22	64	95	31
21	Aston Villa	42	11	8	23	58	87	30
22	Portsmouth	42	6	9	27	64	112	21

1958-59

Manager : Harry Potts

Division One (7th)

	No	Date		h/a	Opponents	Result		h/t	Goalscorers/times	Opp. goal times
	1	Aug	23	h	MANCHESTER C	L	3-4	3-0	Pointer (2) 2, 20, Pilkington 42	49, 71, 81, 90
	2		26	a	Arsenal	L	0-3	0-0		54, 59, 66
	3		30	a	Leeds U	D	1-1	1-0	Robson 15	85
	4	Sep	2	h	ARSENAL	W	3-1	2-0	Connelly 20, Robson 35, Pilkington 70	50
	5		6	h	WEST BROMWICH A	L	1-3	0-1	Shackleton 75	5, 80, 88
	6		9	h	EVERTON	W	3-1	2-0	Shackleton (2) 24, 35, Pilkington 88	65
	7		13	a	Birmingham C	L	1-2	1-0	Robson 34	52, 59
	8		17	a	Everton	W	2-1	1-1	McIlroy 35p, Pilkington 75	30
Shannon's last game	9		20	h	LUTON T	D	2-2	1-2	Newlands 29, Seith 87	2, 16
	10		27	a	Bolton W	W	2-1	1-1	Pointer 27, Seith 65	29
	11	Oct	4	h	CHELSEA	W	4-0	1-0	Cheesebrough 25, Adamson 48p, Pilkington 53, Robson 69	
	12		11	a	Blackpool	D	1-1	0-1	Newlands 68	43
	13		18	h	BLACKBURN R	D	0-0	0-0		
	14		25	a	West Ham U	L	0-1	0-1		30
	15	Nov	1	h	NOTTINGHAM F	L	0-2	0-1		32, 57
	16		8	a	Manchester U	W	3-1	2-0	McIlroy 23p, Pointer (2) 30, 80	87
Winton's last game	17		15	h	WOLVERHAMPTON W	L	0-2	0-1		30, 89
	18		22	a	Portsmouth	L	2-4	1-2	Connelly (2) 40, 52	15, 21, 71, 87
	19		29	h	ASTON VILLA	W	3-1	0-0	Connelly 57, McIlroy 60p, Pointer 88	64
	20	Dec	6	a	Newcastle U	L	2-5	1-3	Pointer (2) 44, 58	4p,26,33,55,76
	21		13	h	TOTTENHAM H	W	3-1	1-1	Pointer 9, Connelly 59, Robson 77	27
	22		20	a	Manchester C	W	4-1	3-1	Connelly 2, Pointer (2) 24, 32, Robson 81	1
	23		26	a	Leicester C	D	1-1	1-0	Pointer 37	75
Newlands' last game	24		27	h	LEICESTER C	D	3-3	1-1	Pointer (2) 29, 72, Connelly 78	28og, 67, 89
	25	Jan	3	h	LEEDS U	W	3-1	1-0	McIlroy 32, Pointer 59, Harris 81	61
	26		31	h	BIRMINGHAM C	L	0-1	0-0		55
	27	Feb	7	a	Luton T	L	2-6	1-3	Connelly 16, Miller 83	19,21,35,47,60,76
	28		21	a	Chelsea	W	3-1	1-0	Robson (3) 2, 59, 67	70
	29	Mar	7	a	Blackburn R	L	1-4	1-2	Pointer 20	25, 35, 77, 86
	30		11	a	West Bromwich A	W	4-2	1-0	Pointer (2) 5, 64, McIlroy 74p, Connelly 75	72, 81
McDonald's last game	31		14	h	WEST HAM U	W	1-0	0-0	Connelly 89	
	32		17	h	BLACKPOOL	W	3-1	1-0	Pointer (2) 30, 60, Robson 74	90
	33		21	a	Nottingham F	W	2-1	2-0	Connelly 4, Pointer 40	80
	34		27	h	PRESTON N E	W	1-0	1-0	Connelly 3	
	35		28	h	MANCHESTER U	W	4-2	2-1	Pilkington 14, Seith 24, Pointer (2) 67, 71	35, 86
	36		30	a	Preston N E	W	4-0	2-0	McIlroy 18, Cheesebrough 32, Pointer (2) 63, 69	
	37	Apr	4	a	Wolverhampton W	D	3-3	2-1	Pointer 16, Cheesebrough (2) 36, 46	19, 67, 78
	38		8	a	Tottenham H	D	2-2	1-0	Cheesebrough (2) 30, 89	65, 70
	39		11	h	PORTSMOUTH	W	2-1	0-0	Pointer 55, Pilkington 78	74
	40		14	h	BOLTON W	L	0-1	0-1		27
	41		18	a	Aston Villa	D	0-0	0-0		
Cheesebrough's last game	42		25	h	NEWCASTLE U	D	2-2	1-1	Pilkington 1, Cheesebrough 75	14, 74

FA Cup

Round	Date		h/a	Opponents	Result		h/t	Goalscorers/times	Opp. goal times
3	Jan	14	a	Stockport C	W	3-1	1-1	Pilkington 10, Pointer (2) 51, 84	30
4		28	a	Blackburn R	W	2-1	0-1	McIlroy 62, Robson 88	10
5	Feb	14	h	PORTSMOUTH	W	1-0	1-0	Adamson 9	
6		28	a	Aston Villa	D	0-0	0-0		
rep	Mar	3	h	ASTON VILLA	L	0-2	0-0		53, 65

Final, Nottingham F 2-1 Luton T, at Wembley.

Other first team matches (friendlies and/or as detailed)

	Date		h/a	Opponents	Result		Goalscorers
Billy Dougall testimonial	Oct	14	h	INTERNATIONAL XI	W	4-2	Cheesebrough (3), Pointer
		20	h	PRAGUE DYNAMO	D	0-0	
Lancs Cup		28	h	ACCRINGTON S	W	4-1	Pilkington, Shackleton, Robson, Newlands
Lancs Cup	Dec	16	h	EVERTON	L	0-2	
FA Cup tie aban 45m - frost	Jan	24	a	Blackburn R	aban	0-0	

Att.	Pos	McDonald	Cummings	Winton	Seith	Adamson	Shannon	Newlands	McIlroy	Pointer	Cheesebrough	Pilkington	Robson	D Smith	Connelly	Shackleton	Angus	Blacklaw	Talbut	Miller	Harris	
31,371		1	2	3	4	5	6	7	8	9	10	11										1
41,298		1	2	3	4	5	6	7	8		10	11	9									2
22,739	19	1	5	3	4		6		8	9		11	10	2	7							3
28,444		1	5	3	4		6		8	9		11	10	2	7							4
23,589	17	1	5	3	4		6		8			11	10	2	7	9						5
23,050		1	5	3	4		6		8			11	10	2	7	9						6
23,926	19	1	2		4	5	6	7			10	11	8	3		9						7
50,457		1	5	3	4	6		7	10	9		11	8	2								8
23,760	14	1	5	3	4		6	7	10	9		11	8	2								9
32,359	12	1	5		4	6		7	8	9		11	10	3			2					10
22,902	8		5		4	6		7		9	10	11	8	3			2	1				11
31,744	8	1	5		4	6		7	8	9		11	10	3			2					12
41,961	9	1	5		4	6		7	8	9		11	10	3			2					13
29,387	12	1	5		4	6			8		10	11	9	3	7		2					14
22,644	14	1	5		4	6			7	9	10	11	8	3			2					15
48,509	13	1	5	3	4	6			8	9		11	10	2	7							16
23,067	13	1	5	3	4	6			8	9		11	10	2	7							17
17,320	15	1	5		4	6			8	9		11	10	3	7		2					18
14,923	13	1	5		4	6			8	9		11	10	3	7		2					19
42,561	15	1	5		4	6			8	9		11	10	3	7		2					20
17,047	13	1	5		4	6			8	9		11	10	3	7		2					21
22,328	10	1	5		4	6			8	9		11	10	3	7		2					22
32,182		1			4	6			8	9		11	10	3	7		2		5			23
24,468	11	1			4	6		7	8	9			10	3	11		2		5			24
26,013	11	1			4	6			8	9			10	3	7		2			5	11	25
22,101	12	1	2		4	6			8	9		11	10	3	7					5		26
15,753	13		5		4				8	9	10	11		3	7		2	1		6		27
27,564	12	1	2		4	6			8	9		11	10	3	7					5		28
27,071	13		2		4	6			8	9		11	10	3	7			1		5		29
18,164			2		4	6			8	9		11	10	3	7			1		5		30
17,311	11	1	2		4	6			8	9			10	3	7					5	11	31
15,881	11		2		4	6			8	9		11	10	3	7			1		5		32
27,811	9		2		4	6			8	9		11	10	3	7			1		5		33
18,322			2		4	6			8	9		11	10	3	7			1		5		34
44,577	7		5		4				8	9		11	10	3	7		2	1		6		35
17,357			5		4				8	9	10	11		3	7		2	1		6		36
39,810	5		5		4				8	9	10	11		3	7		2	1		6		37
32,296			5		4				8	9	10	11		3	7		2	1		6		38
18,174	3		5		4				8	9	10	11		3	7		2	1		6		39
23,664			5		4	6			8	9	10	11		3	7		2	1				40
27,097	4		2		4	5			8	9	10	11			7		3	1		6		41
15,132			3		4	5			8	9	10	11			7		2	1		6		42
Appearances		27	39	10	42	31	8	10	40	37	14	39	33	38	32	3	23	15	2	17	2	
Goals (81)					3	1		2	6	27	7	8	10		12	3				1	1	

Att.		McDonald	Cummings	Winton	Seith	Adamson	Shannon	Newlands	McIlroy	Pointer	Cheesebrough	Pilkington	Robson	D Smith	Connelly	Shackleton	Angus	Blacklaw	Talbut	Miller	Harris	
23,147		1	5		4	6			8	9		11	10	3	7		2					3
43,752		1	2		4	6			8	9		11	10	3	7					5		4
32,055		1	5		4	6			8	9		11	10	3	7		2					5
53,511		1	5		4	6			8	9	10	11		3	7		2					6
38,931		1	2		4	6			8	9	10	11		3	7					5		rep
Appearances		5	5		5	5			5	5	2	5	3	5	5		3			2		
Goals (6)						1			1	2		1	1									

1959-60

Two players who had been prominent over Burnley's last few seasons moved on in the summer of 1959. In June, Albert Cheesebrough was transferred to Leicester for £20,000, he was still only 24, and went to enjoy several good seasons at Filbert Street including an F.A. Cup final appearance at Wembley. The following month saw Doug Newlands leave for Stoke for a fee of £12,000, a year later, he would return to his native Scotland.

The new season got off to a fine start. A 3-2 win at Leeds, with Tommy Cummings in an unfamiliar left-back role and Brian Miller at centre-half, was followed by an excellent 5-2 victory against Everton as Turf Moor opened its turnstiles once more. It was rather hit-and-miss for the next few weeks, though, with three of the next six being won and three lost. The last of those games saw the first changes to the side, with Cummings moving back to number five and Miller to left-half, and a new face coming in at left-back. This was 18-year-old Alex Elder, who had been signed the previous January from Glentoran, the Irish League side who had previously provided Burnley with Jimmy McIlroy. Elder cost £5,000, and it would be another eight years before Burnley again paid out a transfer fee. His debut was at Preston, and although the Clarets were beaten 1-0, the teenager acquitted himself well against Tom Finney, and was in the side to stay.

> OBITUARY
> RICHARD (DICK) SMITH
> DIED 10 DECEMBER 1959, AGED 82
>
> One of Burnley's leading scorers of the pre-World War I era, Dick Smith's 24 League goals in the 1907-08 season set a new club record. Although a team-mate of Jerry Dawson and Billy Watson, Smith had left the club by the time Burnley's first golden era began in 1911.
>
> A Cumbrian by birth, he joined Burnley from Workington in 1904 and soon established himself in the first team, although his first two seasons brought only modest goalscoring returns. His partnership with the amateur Arthur Bell reaped rich rewards in 1906-07 and 1907-08, though, and despite being less prolific in 1908-09 he was still Burnley's top scorer and was rewarded with selection for the Football League squad, although he travelled but did not play.
>
> The following season saw him struggle to hold down a first team place, with age catching up, and in 1910 he returned to Workington where he worked as a publican. Something of an unrecognised hero these days, his goal ratio nevertheless still stands among the best in the club's history.
>
> RIP

Wins in the next two games took Burnley into the top four, just a point behind leaders Tottenham and it was already looking as if the championship race of 1959-60 was going to be a close one. After ten games, Burnley had scored 22 goals, every one of them coming from the prolific forward line of Connelly, McIlroy, Pointer, Robson and Pilkington. Leaders Tottenham were the next opponents, and the result was a very creditable draw, with the first goal of the season from a non-forward, Brian Miller.

Inconsistency was still a failing, though, as was the side's seeming inability to hold a lead. October 1959 brought defeats against Blackpool, 1-4 at home, and at Blackburn. Connelly missed the Blackburn game as he was on England duty for the first time and he would go on to become Burnley's second most-capped England international after Bob Kelly. November, though, was better. It began with a 4-1 win against Wolves, champions of the previous two seasons, and two weeks later Nottingham Forest came to Turf Moor and were thrashed 8-0, still Burnley's biggest League win of the post-war era. Jimmy Robson became the first Claret to score five in a match for over thirty years, with Pointer (2) and Pilkington completing the rout. It was a less than happy return to the Turf for Billy Gray, who was Forest's captain for the day. Yet almost predictably, this was followed by a single-goal defeat the following week at newly-promoted Fulham.

That proved only a temporary setback, though, and the next two games brought eight goals, with Connelly scoring a hat-trick in a memorable 4-2 win at Highbury after Arsenal had gone two goals ahead. McIlroy's performance in that game received rave reports despite the fact that he had effectively played with only one good leg after an early injury. But yet again Burnley looked to have flattered to deceive, when Leeds, the bottom club, came to the Turf a week later and went away with both points. The Clarets began the Christmas period in fourth place, three points behind Tottenham at the top. Victory against Manchester United at Old Trafford on Boxing Day, with Ian Lawson returning to the side for the first time since his exploits three seasons earlier, was followed by a 1-4 drubbing against United at home two days later. The Turf Moor fans, it seemed, just never knew what was coming next.

The new decade began in style, however, with a 5-2 win at West Ham, themselves riding high in the First Division table. The first two F.A. Cup opponents, Lincoln and Swansea, both of the Second Division, were both overcome in home replays, and Burnley rose to second place in the table by the end of January. No team was showing real consistency, the Clarets on their day were clearly a match for anyone, and the feeling was growing that this might just be their season at last. The fifth round Cup opponents were Bradford City, a Third Division side not expected to cause too many problems. But with ten minutes to go at Valley Parade and the Clarets two goals down, a shock looked on the cards. John Connelly proved the saviour, eventually equalising in the very last minute, and the tie certainly caught the imagination of the Burnley public, who turned out in unprecedented numbers for the replay. The official gate was 52,850, but it seems certain that many more got into Turf Moor without paying, and thousands were locked out. This time no mistake was made, as the Clarets ran out 5-0 winners to set up a second Cup meeting in consecutive seasons with arch-rivals Blackburn Rovers.

March 1960 began with a vital home game against League leaders Tottenham, which Burnley won 2-0 to leave themselves still three points adrift, but with two games in hand. Before the Rovers Cup tie came a Turf Moor "rehearsal" in the League, and the omens looked good as Blackburn were beaten 1-0. They looked even better a week later when, with 75 minutes of the quarter-final tie gone, Burnley led 3-0. But then it all went wrong, the ball hit Alex Elder's arm, the referee decreed handball, and Bryan Douglas scored from the spot. It gave Rovers new impetus, and they came back to draw 3-3. In the replay on the following Wednesday evening, Burnley unaccountably failed to play anywhere near their capabilities and were beaten 0-2. Both games had been watched by crowds of over 50,000, but that was little consolation to the Turf Moor faithful.

So it was "concentrate on the League", and soon came another crunch game, this time against Wolves, who had overtaken Burnley to go second, at Molineux. Although the Clarets still had those two games in hand against both the teams above them, title hopes looked to have been severely dented when Wolves ran out as 6-1 winners. Soon afterwards, there was discord in the camp when Bobby Seith, who had been in possession of the number four shirt for most of the season, was put on the transfer list, apparently following a dispute with chairman Bob Lord when he lost his place in the side. The home game against Sheffield Wednesday on 2 April 1960 proved to be the Scot's last of 211 League appearances for Burnley. Jimmy Adamson took over the right-half spot, with Tommy Cummings, who had missed the middle third of the season, returning at centre-half and Brian Miller, still ever-present, moving to number six.

Three victories followed, but at a cost. John Connelly was injured during the 1-0 victory against Leicester, although he still managed score the winning goal, his 20th in the League that season, and he was out for the remainder of the campaign. Into his place came the relatively unknown Trevor Meredith, who soon showed that he could score a goal or two himself, starting in the return game at Leicester, which unfortunately ended in defeat.

At this stage, Wolves were clear favourites to retain the title and were also strongly fancied to achieve the first League and Cup double of the twentieth century. But Tottenham's victory at Molineux ensured that the race was not over yet and, with three games still to play compared to their rivals' one, Burnley were still very much in that race. The first of the games in hand was at Birmingham, and a late goal from Brian Pilkington took the Clarets second, now behind Wolves only on goal average and a point ahead of Spurs.

The season's final home game was against Fulham, not too testing on paper, but Burnley still refused to do things the easy way and could only manage a goalless draw. Their rivals both ended their seasons with victories, leaving Wolves top on 54 points, followed by Tottenham and Burnley on 53. But the Clarets still had that game in hand! It took place on 2 May 1960 at Maine Road in front of almost 66000 spectators including, it seemed, most of the population of Burnley. Brian Pilkington sent them wild with a goal after just four minutes, but Manchester City refused to be sacrificial lambs and were soon level. Burnley were back in front before half-time, though, through Trevor Meredith. The next hour was just about as tense as it gets, but at the end of it the Clarets had held on to win 2-1. Champions!

Burnley had never led the First Division table at any stage of the season until the very end, but the only table that matters is the final one. For the first time in 39 years, the Football League championship had come to Turf Moor, and it been won by a team mostly made up of young players who, it could reasonably be assumed, still had their best years to come. In League and Cup, exactly 100 goals had been scored, with Connelly, Pointer and Robson all passing the twenty mark. In McIlroy and captain Jimmy Adamson, Burnley had two true masters of their craft. And the late emergence of Meredith showed that Burnley still had aces up their sleeve.

Perhaps most of all, though, the title was a triumph for Harry Potts, who had led Burnley to the pinnacle only two years after his arrival as manager. With him in charge, the sky seemed the limit.

The Burnley fans welcome home the Champions

1959-60 - First Division

		P	W	D	L	F	A	Pts
1	BURNLEY	42	24	7	11	85	61	55
2	Wolverhampton W	42	24	6	12	106	67	54
3	Tottenham H	42	21	11	10	86	50	53
4	West Bromwich A	42	19	11	12	83	57	49
5	Sheffield W	42	19	11	12	80	59	49
6	Bolton W	42	20	8	14	59	51	48
7	Manchester U	42	19	7	16	102	80	45
8	Newcastle U	42	18	8	16	82	78	44
9	Preston NE	42	26	12	14	79	76	44
10	Fulham	42	17	10	15	73	80	44
11	Blackpool	42	15	10	17	59	71	40
12	Leicester C	42	13	13	16	66	75	39
13	Arsenal	42	15	9	18	68	80	39
14	West Ham U	42	16	6	20	75	91	38
15	Everton	42	13	11	18	73	78	37
16	Manchester C	42	17	3	22	78	84	37
17	Blackburn R	42	16	5	21	60	70	37
18	Chelsea	42	14	9	19	76	91	37
19	Birmingham C	42	13	10	19	63	80	36
20	Nottingham F	42	13	9	20	50	74	35
21	Leeds U	42	12	10	20	65	92	34
22	Luton T	42	9	12	21	50	73	30

1959-60

Manager : Harry Potts

Division One (1st)
Champions

Note	No.	Month	Day	Venue	Opponents	Result	Score	h/t	Goalscorers/times	Opp. goal times
	1	Aug	22	a	Leeds U	W	3-2	2-0	Pilkington 23, Connelly 34, Pointer 84	65p, 86
Everton goals 35m, 78m	2		25	h	EVERTON	W	5-2	3-1	Connelly (2) 14, 87, Pilkington 18, Pointer 20, Robson 72	
	3		29	h	WEST HAM U	L	1-3	1-1	Connelly 3	9, 63, 76
	4	Sep	2	a	Everton	W	2-1	1-1	Pointer (2) 36, 86	20
	5		5	a	Chelsea	L	1-4	1-2	Connelly 21	34, 40, 61, 67
	6		8	h	PRESTON N E	W	2-1	0-1	Pointer 71, Robson 84	15
	7		12	h	WEST BROMWICH A	W	2-1	0-1	Robson 55, Pilkington 64	44
	8		15	a	Preston N E	L	0-1	0-1		6
	9		19	a	Newcastle U	W	3-1	1-1	McIlroy 33, Connelly (2) 47, 85	27
	10		26	h	BIRMINGHAM C	W	3-1	1-0	Pointer 9, McIlroy 69, Connelly 89	57
	11	Oct	3	a	Tottenham H	D	1-1	0-1	Miller 87	7
	12		10	h	BLACKPOOL	L	1-4	1-2	Robson 5	11, 13, 48, 73
	13		17	a	Blackburn R	L	2-3	1-2	Pilkington 14, Douglas 48og	2, 27, 81
	14		24	h	MANCHESTER C	W	4-3	2-0	Pilkington 15, Pointer 18, White (2) 85, 86	78, 87, 88
	15		31	a	Luton T	D	1-1	1-1	Pointer 25	9
	16	Nov	7	h	WOLVERHAMPTON W	W	4-1	3-1	Pointer (2) 22, 44, Robson 25, Connelly 72	23
	17		14	a	Sheffield W	D	1-1	1-1	Robson 14	3
	18		21	h	NOTTINGHAM F	W	8-0	5-0	Robson (5) 3, 35, 40, 44, 60, Pilkington 13, Pointer (2) 53, 82	
	19		28	a	Fulham	L	0-1	0-1		32
	20	Dec	5	h	BOLTON W	W	4-0	1-0	Pointer 22, Connelly 53, McIlroy (2) 74, 89	
	21		12	a	Arsenal	W	4-2	0-2	Adamson 67p, Connelly (3) 72, 78, 88	38, 43
	22		19	h	LEEDS U	L	0-1	0-1		39
	23		26	a	Manchester U	W	2-1	2-0	Robson 22, Lawson 35	65
	24		28	h	MANCHESTER U	L	1-4	1-1	Robson 28	20, 58, 84, 87
	25	Jan	2	a	West Ham U	W	5-2	3-1	Lawson (2) 11, 75, Pilkington 32, Connelly (2) 44, 89	12, 78p
	26		16	h	CHELSEA	W	2-1	1-0	Robson (2) 38, 64	52
	27		23	a	West Bromwich A	D	0-0	0-0		
	28	Feb	6	h	NEWCASTLE U	W	2-1	1-0	Robson 4, Pointer 67	55
	29		27	a	Bolton W	L	1-2	1-1	Connelly 10	2, 51
	30	Mar	1	h	TOTTENHAM H	W	2-0	0-0	Pointer 62, Connelly 70	
	31		5	h	BLACKBURN R	W	1-0	1-0	Robson 27	
	32		19	h	ARSENAL	W	3-2	1-0	Pointer 7, Miller 54, Connelly 75	48, 85
	33		30	a	Wolverhampton W	L	1-6	1-4	Pointer 15	13,14,18,36,65,70
Seith's last game	34	Apr	2	h	SHEFFIELD W	D	3-3	0-1	Connelly 55, McIlroy 78p, Miller 88	2, 56, 77
	35		9	a	Nottingham F	W	1-0	0-0	Pointer 61	
	36		15	h	LEICESTER C	W	1-0	1-0	Connelly 8	
	37		16	h	LUTON T	W	3-0	2-0	Pointer 16, Robson 33, McIlroy 63p	
	38		18	a	Leicester C	L	1-2	0-2	Meredith 74	29, 37
	39		23	a	Blackpool	D	1-1	1-0	Meredith 32	84
	40		27	a	Birmingham C	W	1-0	0-0	Pilkington 81	
	41		30	h	FULHAM	D	0-0	0-0		
	42	May	2	a	Manchester C	W	2-1	2-1	Pilkington 4, Meredith 31	18

FA Cup

Note	Round	Month	Day	Venue	Opponents	Result	Score	h/t	Goalscorers/times	Opp. goal times
	3	Jan	9	a	Lincoln C	D	1-1	1-0	Pointer 29	65
	rep		12	h	LINCOLN C	W	2-0	2-0	McIlroy 26p, Pilkington 37	
	4		30	a	Swansea T	D	0-0	0-0		
	rep	Feb	2	h	SWANSEA T	W	2-1	1-0	Robson (2) 28, 47	83
	5		20	a	Bradford C	D	2-2	0-0	Connelly (2) 78, 89	55, 75
	rep		23	h	BRADFORD C	W	5-0	2-0	Pointer (2) 5, 63, Robson (2) 8, 70, Connelly 64	
	6	Mar	12	h	BLACKBURN R	D	3-3	0-0	Pilkington 48, Pointer 57, Connelly 61	75p, 79, 86
after extra time, 0-0 at 90 mins	rep		16	a	Blackburn R	L	0-2	0-0		103, 114

Final, Wolverhampton W 3-0 Blackburn R, at Wembley.

Details of other first team games elsewhere.

Att.	Pos	Blacklaw	Angus	Cummings	Seith	Miller	Adamson	Connelly	McIlroy	Pointer	Robson	Pilkington	Elder	White	Harris	Lawson	Marshall	Meredith	Furnell		
20,233		1	2	3	4	5	6	7	8	9	10	11									1
29,165		1	2	3	4	5	6	7	8	9	10	11									2
26,756	5	1	2	3	4	5	6	7	8	9	10	11									3
39,416		1	2	3	4	5	6	7	8	9	10	11									4
36,023	5	1	2	3	4	5	6	7	8	9	10	11									5
29,195		1	2	3	4	5	6	7	8	9	10	11									6
23,907	3	1	2	3	4	5	6	7	8	9	10	11									7
27,299		1	2	5		6	4	7		9	10	11	3	8							8
38,576	4	1	2	5		6	4	7	8	9	10	11	3								9
23,848	4	1	2	5		6	4	7	8	9	10	11	3								10
42,717	3	1	2	5		6	4	7		9	10	11	3	8							11
28,104	4	1	2	5		6	4	7	8	9	10	11	3								12
33,316	7	1	2		4	6	5		8	9		7	3	10	11						13
28,653	6	1	2		4	5	6	7	8	9		11	3	10							14
15,638	7	1	2		4	5	6	7	8	9		11	3	10							15
27,793	5	1	2		4	5	6	7	8	9	10	11	3								16
18,420	6	1	2		4	5	6	7	8	9	10	11	3								17
24,349	4	1	2		4	5	6	7	8	9	10	11	3								18
29,582	6	1	2		4	5	6	7	8	9	10	11	3								19
26,510	6	1	2		4	5	6	7	8	9	10	11	3								20
26,056	3	1	2		4	5	6	7	8	9	10	11	3								21
17,398	4	1	2		4	5	6	7		9	10	11	3	8							22
62,673		1	2		4	5	6	7		9	10	11	3			8					23
47,696		1	2		4	5	6	7	8	9	10	11	3								24
25,752	2	1	2		4	5	6	7		9	10	11	3			8					25
21,916	2	1	2		4	5	6	7		9	10	11	3			8					26
23,512	2	1	2		4	5	6	7		9	10		3		11	8					27
26,998	2	1	2		4	5	6	7		9	10	11	3			8					28
28,772	4	1	2	5		6	4	7	8	9		11	3			10					29
32,992		1	2	5		6	4	7	8	9	10	11	3								30
32,331	3	1	2		4	5	6	7	8	9	10	11	3								31
20,327	3	1	2		4	6	5	7		9	10	11	3			8					32
33,953		1		2	4	5	6	7	8	9	10	11	3								33
23,123	3	1	2		4	6	5	7	8	9	10	11	3								34
24,640	4	1	2	5		6	4		8	9	10	11					3	7			35
23,777		1	2	5		6	4	7	8	9	10	11	3								36
20,893	3	1	2	5		6	4		8	9	10	11	3					7			37
24,429		1	2	5		6	4		8	9	10	11	3					7			38
23,753	3		2	5		6	4		8	9	10	11	3					7	1		39
37,032		1	2	5		6	4		8	9	10	11	3					7			40
30,807	3	1	2	5		6	4			9	10	11	3			8		7			41
65,981	top	1	2	5		6	4		8	9	10	11	3					7			42
Appearances		41	41	23	27	42	42	34	32	42	38	41	34	6	2	8	1	7	1		
Goals (85)						3	1	20	6	19	18	9		2		3		3		1	og

Att.	Pos	Blacklaw	Angus	Cummings	Seith	Miller	Adamson	Connelly	McIlroy	Pointer	Robson	Pilkington	Elder	White	Harris	Lawson	Marshall	Meredith	Furnell	
21,693		1	2		4	5	6	7		9	10	11	3			8				3
35,456		1	2		4	5	6	7	8	9	10	11	3							rep
29,976		1	2		4	5	6	7	8	9	10	11	3							4
37,040		1	2		4	5	6	7		9	10	11	3	8						rep
26,244		1	2		4	5	6	7	8	9	10	11	3							5
52,850		1	2		4	5	6	7	8	9	10	11	3							rep
51,501		1	2		4	5	6	7	8	9	10	11	3							6
53,892		1	2		4	5	6	7	8	9	10	11	3							rep
Appearances		8	8		8	8	8	8	6	8	8	8	8	1		1				
Goals (15)								4	1	4	4	2								

1960-61

Following the championship triumph, 1960 was a busy summer for Burnley's players, as they travelled to the USA to take part in the New York soccer tournament along with, among others, Bayern Munich, Sampdoria, Red Star Belgrade and Kilmarnock. It was not a happy trip, however, and any thoughts that Burnley might be involved in some kind of pioneering exercise for soccer across the Atlantic proved sadly misguided.

Bobby Seith was transferred to Dundee during the summer. His fall-out with the chairman had been the one sour note of Burnley's title-winning season, and he was denied the Championship medal to which his 27 League appearances had entitled him. It was an injustice eventually rectified some 40 years later when he returned to Turf Moor to be presented with a medal. Seith went on to success with Dundee, who two years later won the Scottish League title for the only time in their history, and he later enjoyed some success as a manager.

The 1960-61 season was to be the busiest in Burnley's history, as they competed for honours on no fewer than five fronts. First up was the F.A. Charity Shield, the traditional Champions v FA Cup winners curtain-raiser to the season. Turf Moor was the venue, Wolves the opposition, and the game was drawn 2-2, a result that entitled each club to hold the trophy for six months.

League action began with a 3-2 home win against Arsenal, but it was to prove a hesitant start to the season, with three of the first five games being lost, two of them against Manchester City, on whose patch of course the title had been claimed a few months earlier. Walter Joyce was a debutant in the game at Maine Road, while in the return game a week later there was a first appearance for 19-year-old Scottish forward Andy Lochhead, standing in for Ray Pointer. Trevor Meredith also had another run of first-team action, as before following an injury to John Connelly.

September 1960 saw the Clarets get into their stride, and to some tune, as they began a run of eight wins from nine. Jimmy Robson was on fire in this spell, scoring twelve goals, including hat-tricks against Preston and Fulham at home, both 5-0 wins, and Chelsea away, 6-2. In all, the team registered 33 goals, an average of nearly four a game, in the process of rising to third place in the table. Yet even at this stage, it was clear that retaining the title was going to be a very tall order, as Bill Nicholson's mighty Tottenham side had only dropped one point and were already looking uncatchable.

Burnley made their debut in the Football League's new competition, the League Cup, on 24 October 1960. Against top-flight opposition at Cardiff, Harry Potts anticipated much more recent thinking by fielding a line-up well below full strength. It was one of the reserves, Gordon Harris, who led the charge, scoring a hat-trick in a 4-0 win. In the next round, against Third Division Brentford, the team on show was to all intents the Central League side. Only Harris was retained from the League line-up of the previous Saturday, and Andy Lochhead scored his first Clarets goal in a 1-1 draw. The regulars returned for the replay, which Burnley won 2-1 .

The week before the first Brentford game brought a milestone in Turf Moor history, as French champions Reims came to Turf Moor in the second round of the European Cup, Burnley having been given a bye in the first. Reims were formidable opponents who had reached the final of the previous year's competition, and contained in their ranks such notables as Raymond Kopa and Just Fontaine. But goals from Jimmy Robson and Jimmy McIlroy gave the Clarets a two-goal cushion for the second leg, which proved vital as Reims won 3-2 to almost level the tie. It was a fraught occasion, with crowd disturbances and play-acting from the French side upsetting Harry Potts so much that his protests on the pitch got him into trouble with the authorities, again anticipating more modern management techniques!

The League, meanwhile, was providing the fans with some superb entertainment. In the period leading up to Christmas, four out of five games were won and 22 goals scored. The victories included 5-3 scorelines at home to arch-rivals Wolves and at Bolton, and 5-2 at Arsenal, with Ray Pointer hitting a hat-trick at Highbury. The match that wasn't won, though, was the best of them all. It took place on 3 December 1960 at White Hart Lane against the runaway First Division leaders Tottenham in dreadful mudbath conditions before a crowd of nearly 60,000 The reasons for Spurs' domination of the League were there for all to see as they raced to a 4-0 lead well before the interval The Burnley side of 1960 were nobody's pushovers however, and amazingly they fought back to draw 4-4 in one of the greatest matches in which the club has ever been. Involved.

Christmas 1960 brought a double-header against an Everton side nearing their own peak. Burnley were beaten at Turf Moor on Boxing Day, but ran out 3-0 winners at Goodison Park the day afterwards in front of a gate of almost 75000, the biggest League crowd ever to watch the Clarets. New Year's Eve brought a fitting end to an amazing year, with yet another 5-3 win, this time at home to Newcastle. By this time, 24 League games had been played, and Jimmy Robson was averaging a goal a game, while the side as a whole had notched 72 goals, not a bad total for a whole season!

Alex Elder
invariably immaculate at left back

The early part of 1961 brought something of a slump in League form, with only one win in eight, but there was action on three other fronts to keep the fans happy. The next two rounds of the League Cup were comfortably dealt with, as Nottingham Forest and Second Division Southampton were beaten, to take Burnley into the semi-finals. By mid-February, they were also in the last eight of the F.A. Cup as three lower division sides, including Swansea for the third season in four, were overcome. Perhaps most significantly, the first leg of the European Cup quarter-final brought a fine victory at Turf Moor against the German champions SV Hamburg, the 3-1 scoreline setting Burnley up nicely for the second leg, which would not be played until two months later.

John Connelly (left) and Gordon Harris crowd Tottenham keeper Bill Brown

Brian Pilkington scored two of the goals against Hamburg, but a few weeks later he had left Turf Moor, transferred to Bolton for £25,000. The little number eleven had been at the club for ten years and played in exactly 300 League games, scoring 67 goals, a fine return for a winger. He was still only 28, but Gordon Harris's claim for a regular first-team spot was too strong to resist and so "Pilky" was on his way He was the first to leave Turf Moor of the team that had clinched the League title on that epic night at Maine Road just a few short months before.

March 1961 began with the F.A. Cup sixth round game at Sheffield Wednesday, where Adam Blacklaw was the star in a goalless draw. The replay brought Turf Moor's biggest crowd of the season, almost 49,000, more than both European Cup games, and they saw the Clarets reach their first semi-final since 1947 with a 2-0 win. The semi-final game was only eleven days away, and the second leg against Hamburg only eight, so for the next League game, at home to Chelsea, Harry Potts took the opportunity to rest most of his first-choice players, with only Tommy Cummings and Gordon Harris of the regular League side lining up for the match. A 4-4 draw thanks to two goals each from Harris and Andy Lochhead, showed the strength in depth that Burnley had at this time, but the decision to field a weakened side cost the club a £1,000 fine.

The week that followed saw Burnley's interest in two competitions come to an end. The return game in Hamburg, televised live in the UK, brought massive disappointment as the Germans, inspired by their star Uwe Seeler, overturned the Clarets' lead, winning 4-1 to take the tie 5-4 on aggregate. Perhaps there had been a touch of complacency brought on by the first leg result, Jimmy McIlroy's shot that hit the post in the last minute only added to the gloom. Then came the F.A. Cup semi-final against Tottenham at Burnley's least-loved venue, Villa Park, and Spurs stayed on course for the double with a comfortable 3-0 victory.

With no realistic chance of retaining the League title, it seemed that a season that had provided so much excitement was destined to end in disappointment. April was the kind of month to test the best, with eleven games, nine in the League and both legs of the League Cup semi-final. The new competition was Burnley's last hope of silverware from the 1960-61 campaign, and by the end of two poorly-attended drawn games against Aston Villa, surely the last side the Clarets would have chosen for the opposition, that matter remained unresolved. There was a stirring finale to the League season, though, as, in the final home game, Tottenham, by now crowned as worthy successors to Burnley as champions, were beaten 4-2. The last two away games were also won, to earn a final position of fourth. After League hostilities ended, a third League Cup game against Villa was played at Old Trafford, watched by a meagre crowd of less than 8,000. The new competition had yet to win over the fans and was several years from providing the incentive of a Wembley final, let alone a place in Europe. Burnley missed out on a place in its first final, the old hoodoo striking yet again as Villa won 2-1 .

Fourth in the League, semi-finalists in both domestic Cups, quarter-finalists in Europe, scorers of a club record 102 goals. Hardly a poor season, yet in the end a disappointment, all the promise of 1960 seeming to have evaporated after the new year. For this to be regarded as failure however surely showed just how far the club had come.

1960-61 - First Division

		P	W	D	L	F	A	Pts
1	Tottenham H	42	31	4	7	115	55	66
2	Sheffield W	42	23	12	7	78	47	58
3	Wolverhampton W	42	25	7	10	103	75	57
4	BURNLEY	42	22	7	13	102	77	51
5	Everton	42	22	6	14	87	69	50
6	Leicester C	42	18	9	15	87	70	45
7	Manchester U	42	18	9	15	88	76	45
8	Blackburn R	42	15	13	14	77	76	43
9	Aston Villa	42	17	9	16	78	77	43
10	West Bromwich A	42	18	5	19	67	71	41
11	Arsenal	42	15	11	16	77	85	41
12	Chelsea	42	15	7	20	98	100	37
13	Manchester C	42	13	11	18	79	90	37
14	Nottingham F	42	14	9	19	62	78	37
15	Cardiff C	42	13	11	18	60	85	37
16	West Ham U	42	13	10	19	77	88	36
17	Fulham	42	14	8	20	72	95	36
18	Bolton W	42	12	11	19	58	73	35
19	Birmingham C	42	14	6	22	62	84	34
20	Blackpool	42	12	9	21	68	73	33
21	Newcastle U	42	11	10	21	86	109	32
22	Preston NE	42	10	10	22	43	71	30

1960-61

Manager : Harry Potts

Division One (4th)

Note	No	Date		Venue	Opponents	Result		h/t	Goalscorers/times	Opp. goal times
	1	Aug	20	h	ARSENAL	W	3-2	1-1	Willis 13og, Pointer 77, Connelly 81	39, 47
	2		24	a	Manchester C	L	1-2	1-1	Robson 5	44, 78
	3		27	a	Newcastle U	W	1-0	0-0	Robson 85	
	4		30	h	MANCHESTER C	L	1-3	0-0	Meredith 60	61, 65, 77
	5	Sep	3	h	CARDIFF C	L	1-2	0-1	Robson 66	40, 88
	6		6	h	PRESTON N E	W	5-0	3-0	Robson (3) 14, 39, 63, Meredith 36, Pointer 73	
	7		10	a	West Bromwich A	W	2-0	0-0	Pointer 53, Miller 86	
	8		13	a	Preston N E	W	3-2	1-1	Harris (2) 28, 62, Pointer 86	17, 72
	9		17	h	BIRMINGHAM C	W	2-1	2-0	Robson 2, Meredith 44	49og
	10		24	a	Sheffield W	L	1-3	1-3	Robson 30	2, 15, 31
	11	Oct	1	h	FULHAM	W	5-0	2-0	Robson (3) 24, 35, 67, Pointer (2) 73, 88	
	12		8	a	Blackburn R	W	4-1	2-1	Connelly (2) 20, 43, Adamson 80p, Robson 86	28
	13		15	h	MANCHESTER U	W	5-3	3-2	Pointer 10, Connelly (2) 32, 50, Joyce 37, McIlroy 86	29, 41, 82
	14		22	a	Chelsea	W	6-2	4-2	Robson (3) 22, 52, 70, Miller 25, McIlroy (2) 35, 44	6, 28
	15		29	h	BLACKPOOL	L	1-2	1-1	McIlroy 7	30, 47
	16	Nov	5	a	Aston Villa	L	0-2	0-1		35, 46
	17		12	h	WOLVERHAMPTON W	W	5-3	3-3	Pointer (2) 13, 44, Robson 42, McIlroy 67, Pilkington 70	2, 10, 35
	18		19	a	Bolton W	W	5-3	3-1	Connelly (2) 15, 37, Pointer (2) 38, 60, Robson 49	24, 70, 83
	19	Dec	3	a	Tottenham H	D	4-4	1-4	Connelly (2) 37, 72, Robson 56, Pointer 58	18, 19, 21, 35
	20		10	h	LEICESTER C	W	3-2	2-1	Robson 34, Pointer 43, Connelly 62	41, 84
	21		17	a	Arsenal	W	5-2	0-0	Pointer (3) 48, 64, 83, McIlroy 66, Robson 84	55, 89
	22		26	h	EVERTON	L	1-3	1-2	Pointer 35	15, 25, 75
	23		27	a	Everton	W	3-0	1-0	Robson (2) 33, 73, Connelly 67	
	24		31	h	NEWCASTLE U	W	5-3	2-2	McIlroy 18, Robson (2) 35, 59, Harris 46, Miller 50	17, 38, 61
	25	Jan	14	a	Cardiff C	L	1-2	1-2	Pointer 2	11, 35
	26		21	h	WEST BROMWICH A	L	0-1	0-1		33
	27	Feb	11	h	SHEFFIELD W	L	3-4	2-3	Adamson 23p, Connelly 30, Pointer 64	3, 20, 32, 71p
	28		22	a	Fulham	W	1-0	0-0	Harris 73	
	29		25	h	BLACKBURN R	D	1-1	0-0	Miller 60	62
	30	Mar	11	h	CHELSEA	D	4-4	3-1	Harris (2) 9, 36, Lochhead (2) 20, 72	15, 67, 76, 89
	31		23	a	Blackpool	D	0-0	0-0		
	32		25	h	ASTON VILLA	D	1-1	0-0	Lawson 80	62
	33		31	h	NOTTINGHAM F	W	4-1	2-1	Connelly 1, Miller 44, Pointer 47, McIlroy 72p	7
	34	Apr	1	a	Leicester C	D	2-2	1-2	Connelly 36, McIlroy 70	16, 19
	35		3	a	Nottingham F	L	1-3	1-2	Lochhead 12	7, 9, 68
	36		8	h	BOLTON W	W	2-0	0-0	Pointer 62, Fenton 64	
David Smith's last game	37		12	a	Manchester U	L	0-6	0-2		30,43,49,61,72,80
	38		15	a	Wolverhampton W	L	1-2	0-1	Harris 50	18, 63
	39		18	h	WEST HAM U	D	2-2	0-0	Connelly 50, Pointer 70	71, 79
	40		22	h	TOTTENHAM H	W	4-2	0-2	Harris (2) 50, 84, McIlroy 67, Robson 85	19, 40
	41		27	a	Birmingham C	W	1-0	0-0	Adamson 56p	
	42		29	a	West Ham U	W	2-1	0-1	Lawson 75, Harris 88	12

FA Cup

Note	Rd	Date		Venue	Opponents	Result		h/t	Goalscorers/times	Opp. goal times
	3	Jan	7	h	BOURNEMOUTH & B A	W	1-0	0-0	Connelly 78	
	4		28	a	Brighton & H A	D	3-3	1-1	Miller 25, Carolan 52og, Robson 73	43, 59, 66
	rep		31	h	BRIGHTON & H A	W	2-0	1-0	Miller 36, Robson 75	
Pilkington's last game	5	Feb	18	h	SWANSEA T	W	4-0	3-0	Connelly 14, Robson (2) 42, 73, Pointer 44	
	6	Mar	4	a	Sheffield W	D	0-0	0-0		
	rep		7	h	SHEFFIELD W	W	2-0	0-0	Robson 58, McIlroy 70	
at Villa Park	semi		18	n	Tottenham H	L	0-3	0-1		30, 49, 89

Final, Tottenham H 2-0 Leicester C, at Wembley.

League Cup

Note	Rd	Date		Venue	Opponents	Result		h/t	Goalscorers/times	Opp. goal times
	2	Oct	24	a	Cardiff C	W	4-0	1-0	Harris (3) 35, 49, 89, Connelly 78	
	3	Nov	22	a	Brentford	D	1-1	0-0	Lochhead 83	58
	rep	Dec	6	h	BRENTFORD	W	2-1	0-1	Pointer 68, Robson 88	17
	4	Jan	10	h	NOTTINGHAM F	W	2-1	1-0	Robson 15, Connelly 88	75
	5	Feb	6	a	Southampton	W	4-2	2-0	Pilkington 4, Pointer 20, Fenton (2) 52, 76	58, 69
	semi	Apr	10	h	ASTON VILLA	D	1-1	1-1	Miller 28	30
after extra time, 2-2 at 90 mins	2nd leg		26	a	Aston Villa	D	2-2	0-2	Robson 60, McIlroy 75	28, 34
at Old Trafford	rep	May	2	n	Aston Villa	L	1-2	0-0	Robson 71	69p, 87

Final, Aston Villa 3-2 Rotherham U, on aggregate.

Details of other first team games elsewhere.

Att.	Pos	Blacklaw	Angus	Elder	Adamson	Cummings	Miller	Connelly	McIlroy	Pointer	Robson	Pilkington	Joyce	Lawson	Meredith	Harris	Lochhead	Marshall	Walker	Fenton	Furnell	D Smith	Scott	Talbut	Towers	White	
24,553		1	2	3	4	5	6	7	8	9	10	11															1
26,941		1	2	3	4		5	7	8		10	11	6	9													2
35,485	8	1	2	3	4	5	6		8		10			9	7	11											3
29,547		1	2	3	4	5	6		8		10	11			7		9										4
19,695	15	1	2	3	4	5	6		8	9	10	11			7												5
19,443		1	2	3	4	5	6		8	9	10	11			7												6
26,407	6	1	2	3	4	5	6		8	9	10	11			7												7
25,604		1	2	3	4	5	6		8	9		11			7	10											8
20,749	3	1	2	3	4	5	6		8	9	10	11			7												9
35,829	7	1	2	3	4	5	6		8	9	10	11			7												10
19,965	4	1	2	3	5		6	7	8	9	10	11	4														11
26,223	4	1	2		6	5		7		9	8	11	4			10		3									12
33,611	4	1	2	3	5		6	7	8	9	10	11	4														13
29,080	3	1	2	3	5		6	7	8	9	10		4			11											14
29,689	5	1	2	3	5		6	7	8	9	10		4			11											15
35,923	5	1	2	3	5		6	7	8	9	10	11	4														16
26,813	4	1		3	5		6	7	8	9	10	11	4					2									17
23,830	3	1	2			5	6	7	8	9	10	11	4					3									18
58,737	4	1	2	3		5	6	7	8	9	10	11	4														19
20,640	5	1	2	3		5	6	7	8	9	10	11	4														20
37,042	4	1	2	3	5		6	7	8	9	10	11	4														21
44,232		1	2	3	5		6	7	8	9	10	11	4														22
74,867		1	2	3	5		6	7	8	9	10		4			11											23
24,972	3	1	2	3	5		6	7	8	9	10		4			11											24
25,670	4	1	2	3		5	6	7		9	10	11	4	8													25
15,005	4	1	2	3		5	6	7		9	10	11		8					4								26
25,542	4	1	2	3	5		6	7		9	10	11	4							8							27
13,139		1		3	5		6	7	8	9	10		4			11		2									28
26,492	4	1	2	3	5		6	7	8	9	10		4			11											29
19,435	4					5								8	7	11	9	3	4	10	1	2	6				30
19,391		1	2	3	5		6	11	8	9			4		7					10							31
17,726	4	1	2	3		5	6	7	8		10		4	9		11											32
18,650		1	2	3	5		6	7	8	9	10		4			11											33
27,838	4	1	2	3	4	5	6	7	8	9	10					11											34
27,965		1	2	3	4	5		7	8		10		6			11	9										35
22,998	4	1	2	3		5	6	7	8	9			4			11				10							36
24,616		1	2			5		11					4		7	10	9			8		2	6				37
25,558	5	1	2	3		5		11		9	8		6		7	10			4								38
11,609		1	2	3		5	6	7	8	9	10		4			11											39
28,991	5	1	2	3		5	6	7	8	9	10		4			11											40
15,015		1	2		6								3	8		11	9		4	10				5	7		41
18,759	4	1	2		6	3		7		9	10		4	8		11								5			42
Appearances		41	39	36	30	25	35	32	33	34	36	22	30	8	12	21	5	5	4	6	1	2	2	2	1		
Goals(102)					3		5	15	10	22	25	1	1	2	3	10	3			1							1 og

Att.	Pos	Blacklaw	Angus	Elder	Adamson	Cummings	Miller	Connelly	McIlroy	Pointer	Robson	Pilkington	Joyce	Lawson	Meredith	Harris	Lochhead	Marshall	Walker	Fenton	Furnell	D Smith	Scott	Talbut	Towers	White	
24,817		1	2	3		5	6	7	8	9	10		4			11											3
28,672		1	2	3	5		6	7	8	9	10	11	4														4
22,726		1	2	3	5		6	7	8	9	10	11	4														rep
30,977		1	2	3	5		6	7	8	9	10	11	4														5
55,000		1	2	3	5		6	7	8	9	10		4			11											6
48,894		1	2	3		5	6	7	8	9	10		4			11											rep
70,000		1	2	3	5		6	7	8	9	10		4			11											semi
Appearances		7	7	7	5	2	7	7	7	7	7	3	7			4											
Goals (12)							2	2	1	1	5																1 og

Att.	Pos	Blacklaw	Angus	Elder	Adamson	Cummings	Miller	Connelly	McIlroy	Pointer	Robson	Pilkington	Joyce	Lawson	Meredith	Harris	Lochhead	Marshall	Walker	Fenton	Furnell	D Smith	Scott	Talbut	Towers	White	
8,110		1	2			5		7		9	10		4			11		3		8			6				2
9,890															7	11	9	3	4	10	1	2	6	5		8	3
12,787		1	2	3		5	6	7	8	9	10	11	4														rep
12,489		1	2	3		5	6	7		9	10	11	4	8													4
26,535		1		3	5		6	7		9	10	11	4					2		8							5
15,908		1	2	3		5	6	7	8	9			4			11				10							semi
23,077		1	2	3	4	5		7	8	9	10		6			11											2nd leg
7,593		1	2		4	5	6	7		9	10		3	8		11											rep
Appearances		7	6	5	3	6	5	7	3	7	6	3	7	2	1	5	1	3	1	4	1	1	2	1		1	
Goals (17)							1	2	1	2	4	1				3	1			2							

1961-62

A season of high expectation began with a trip to Highbury and a 2-2 draw against Arsenal. The line-up for Burnley lacked only John Angus of the regular first eleven, although his replacement at right-back, Walter Joyce, had in fact played in well over half of the previous season's games. The same eleven featured in the first home game, which brought newly-promoted Ipswich Town to Turf Moor for the first time. It was a closer encounter than many had expected, the Clarets narrowly winning by 4-3, but it gave little indication of what was to come at Portman Road a week later. The unfancied East Anglians trounced Burnley 6-2 and in the Ipswich side was Roy Stephenson, who had left the Turf some five years earlier.

This was to prove little more than an early season blip, however. Indeed, September 1961 was to prove one of the most remarkable months in Burnley's history, with all seven League games won and an amazing 27 goals scored. Their form on the road was nothing short of sensational, a 6-2 win at Birmingham was followed four days later by a trip to Leicester and another victory by the same score. Another ten days on, and Fulham were beaten 5-3 at Craven Cottage. All five forwards were scoring prolifically, with hat-tricks for Ray Pointer at St. Andrew's and John Connelly at Fulham. By the end of the month, with nine victories from eleven, the Clarets were riding high at the top of the First Division, and at this stage they were looking well-nigh unstoppable.

A mini-slump followed, with only two wins from the next six, but by the end of the year they were well and truly back on course, having put four past Manchester United, at Old Trafford, and Sheffield United on successive Saturdays, and four more past Sheffield Wednesday on Boxing Day 1961. With just over half the season gone, Burnley had scored 65 goals in the League, and only once failed to find the net. Clean sheets were rare, but given the entertainment on offer and the results, did anyone really care?

The team line-up had stayed virtually unchanged throughout that first half of the season, and Burnley's success was reaping its rewards in international recognition for the players. Jimmy McIlroy was of course long established as a fixture in the Northern Ireland side, and Alex Elder was usually in there alongside him. John Connelly was featuring quite regularly on the right wing for England, although the form of Bryan Douglas down the road at Blackburn ensured that Connelly's selection was less than automatic. Ray Pointer's goal-scoring exploits earned him three England caps in September and October 1961, and he scored on his debut against Luxembourg and again against Portugal. John Angus and Brian Miller had both made their England debuts in May in Austria, but neither would add to their single international cap. Gordon Harris was already being included in England squads but it would be some time before he would actually line up for his country.

1962 began with no let-up. With Burnley having opted out of entering the League Cup, in common with several of the major clubs of the day, the F.A. Cup was the sole knockout interest, and the first Saturday of the new year was third round day. Third Division Q.P.R. unsurprisingly, were no match for the rampant Clarets who ran out 6-1 winners. There were another half-dozen goals for the Turf Moor faithful to savour a week later, when Manchester City were on the wrong end of a 6-3 scoreline. There was a surprise in the next round of the Cup when Leyton Orient, soon to be promoted to the top flight for the only time in their history, came within seven minutes of a shock win at the Turf, but a late equaliser saved the Clarets, who duly went on to thrash Birmingham 7-1 in the League, making it thirteen goals against the Blues that season, before scraping through in the replay at Brisbane Road.

Brian Miller
Turf Moor stalwart for more than 40 years
the start of a dynasty

Although gates were up at Turf Moor, the average for the season would go on to top 27,000, it still took the FA Cup to fill the ground to anything like capacity. The biggest crowd of the season, over 50,000, was for the fifth round tie against Everton, a side themselves approaching greatness. Coming back from a goal behind, the Clarets won 3-1 to reach the last eight, where Bramall Lane saw an even larger gathering as Ray Pointer scored the only goal of the game to beat Sheffield United. A week later, Burnley scored six yet again, West Ham this time being the lambs to the slaughter.

Top of the League with games in hand, and into the semi-finals of the F.A. Cup, it was not surprising that by this time there was talk of Burnley emulating Tottenham's feat of 1960-61 and achieving the coveted "double". Yet from around mid-March, doubts began to set in. The team's free-scoring style suddenly seemed to desert them, lesser teams were getting results against Burnley that they could only have dreamed of a few months earlier, and threats were emerging from the chasing pack. Tottenham's challenge was expected, far less so was the emergence of Alf Ramsey's First Division newcomers, the Ipswich team that had given Burnley such a jolt back in August. But for now, Burnley remained in pole position, and they still had those vital games in hand.

April 1962 was a month that was always going to be crucial, with Burnley having no fewer than eleven games to play. The Cup semi-final against Fulham, then staging their annual battle against relegation, had been played on the last day of March, and, on the Clarets' bogey ground of Villa Park, and in a snowstorm, the Clarets needed a huge performance from Adam Blacklaw in goal before John Connelly's equaliser earned a replay. On a Monday night at Leicester's Filbert Street, two goals from Jimmy Robson took Burnley to a 2-1 victory and, fifteen years on from the last time, a return to Wembley. The double was still on!

Sadly, that replay win was one of only two victories recorded by Burnley in April. While the Clarets failed to take advantage of their games in hand, and often inexplicably struggled even to score, Ipswich carried on getting the results to keep them nagging at the Clarets' heels. Easter brought defeat at Sheffield United and only a draw at Blackpool, and the final Saturday dawned with Ipswich now two points ahead. All was not lost however, Burnley still had one extra game to play, just as two years earlier, had the superior goal average, and looked to have a straightforward task against a Chelsea side bound for Division Two. But, although the players were the same, this was not the Clarets side that had taken the football world by storm back in September 1961. Chelsea went away from Turf Moor with a 1-1 draw, whilst Ipswich beat Aston Villa and were crowned champions. From a seemingly unassailable position, Burnley had missed out on the League title.

The Cup still offered possible consolation, and on 5 May 1962 a Wembley crowd of 100,000 gathered for another epic confrontation between the country's two finest sides of the early sixties, Burnley and Tottenham Hotspur. League disappointment was put to one side, and when Jimmy Robson scored soon after half-time to equalise Jimmy Greaves' early opener for Spurs, hopes ran high. They were very soon dashed, though, when Bobby Smith put Tottenham back in front, and a late penalty from Danny Blanchflower ensured that the Cup remained at White Hart Lane. It had been a classic final, but that counted for little at the time. After looking possible, even probable, double-winners only a few weeks earlier, Burnley had ended the season with nothing.

Failure, however, is relative. Burnley had finished second in both major competitions. Their captain, Jimmy Adamson, was voted Footballer of the Year, with Jimmy McIlroy as runner-up. For the second season running, they had scored a century of League goals, in the process playing some of the finest attacking football ever witnessed in this country. The Reserves, few of whom were able to experience even the briefest taste of first-team action during 1961-62, stormed to the Central League title with 67 points and 113 goals.

Some of those reserves were to become big Turf Moor names in the years ahead, as Burnley continued to grace the top flight of English football. But their second golden era, in truth, was already coming to an end.

Wembley 1962
a classic final but not Burnley's day

1961-62 - First Division

		P	W	D	L	F	A	Pts
1	Ipswich T	42	24	8	10	93	67	56
2	BURNLEY	42	21	11	10	101	67	53
3	Tottenham H	42	21	10	11	88	69	52
4	Everton	42	20	11	11	88	54	51
5	Sheffield U	42	19	9	14	61	69	47
6	Sheffield W	42	20	6	16	72	58	46
7	Aston Villa	42	18	8	16	65	56	44
8	West Ham U	42	17	10	15	76	82	44
9	West Bromwich A	42	15	13	14	83	67	43
10	Arsenal	42	16	11	15	71	72	43
11	Bolton W	42	16	10	16	62	66	42
12	Manchester C	42	17	7	28	78	81	41
13	Blackpool	42	15	11	16	70	75	41
14	Leicester C	42	17	6	19	72	71	40
15	Manchester U	42	15	9	18	72	75	39
16	Blackburn R	42	14	11	17	50	58	39
17	Birmingham C	42	14	10	18	65	81	38
18	Wolverhampton W	42	13	10	19	73	86	36
19	Nottingham F	42	13	10	19	63	79	36
20	Fulham	42	13	7	22	66	74	33
21	Cardiff C	42	9	14	19	50	81	32
22	Chelsea	42	9	10	23	63	94	28

1961-62

Manager : Harry Potts

Division One (2nd)

		Date			Opponents	Result		h/t	Goalscorers/times	Opp. goal times
	1	Aug	19	a	Arsenal	D	2-2	1-2	McIlroy 16, Harris 78	31, 40
	2		22	h	IPSWICH T	W	4-3	2-1	Pointer 23, Harris 42, Miller 64, McIlroy 77	30, 52, 73
	3		26	h	BOLTON W	W	3-1	2-0	Pointer (2) 3, 80, Robson 25	62
	4		29	a	Ipswich T	L	2-6	1-3	McIlroy 11, Elsworthy 86og	3,12,21,49,66,73
	5	Sep	2	a	Manchester C	W	3-1	2-1	Harris 8, McIlroy (2) 13, 63	15
	6		5	h	LEICESTER C	W	2-0	1-0	Appleton 3og, King 85og	
	7		9	h	WEST BROMWICH A	W	3-1	2-1	Pointer (2) 4, 60, Connelly 6	27
	8		16	a	Birmingham C	W	6-2	4-0	Pointer (3) 13, 29, 70, Robson 16, McIlroy 44, Harris 64	79, 80
Leicester goals 34m, 80m	9		20	a	Leicester C	W	6-2	4-1	Harris 19, Connelly (2) 23, 28, Robson (2) 33, 69, Pointer 49	
	10		23	h	EVERTON	W	2-1	1-0	Pointer (2) 27, 70	80
	11		30	a	Fulham	W	5-3	3-2	Pointer 15, Connelly (3) 21, 29, 47, McIlroy 60p	12, 35, 77
	12	Oct	14	a	West Ham U	L	1-2	1-2	Harris 26	3, 6
	13		21	h	CARDIFF C	W	2-1	1-0	Harris 13, Robson 64	59
	14		28	a	Tottenham H	L	2-4	2-3	Pointer (2) 10, 14	16, 25, 39, 85
	15	Nov	4	h	ASTON VILLA	W	3-0	2-0	Connelly 2, Robson 23, Deakin 66og	
	16		11	a	Nottingham F	L	2-3	1-3	Adamson 44, Miller 48	17og, 19, 43
	17		18	h	WOLVERHAMPTON W	D	3-3	1-1	Connelly (2) 17, 89, Harris 50	20, 72, 78
	18		25	a	Manchester U	W	4-1	1-1	Harris 36, Robson 61, Pointer 69, Connelly 89	6
	19	Dec	2	h	SHEFFIELD U	W	4-2	2-1	Robson 7, Richardson 20og, Pointer 62, Connelly 82	17og, 77
	20		9	a	Chelsea	W	2-1	0-1	Harris 70, Pointer 79	30
	21		16	h	ARSENAL	L	0-2	0-0		52, 57
	22		26	h	SHEFFIELD W	W	4-0	0-0	Robson 63, Connelly (2) 70, 86, McIlroy 83p	
City goals 20m, 35m, 82m	23	Jan	13	h	MANCHESTER C	W	6-3	4-2	McIlroy (2) 14, 41, Harris 19, Robson (2) 36, 80, Sear 55og	
	24		20	a	West Bromwich A	D	1-1	0-0	McIlroy 84	74
Birmingham goal 75m	25	Feb	3	h	BIRMINGHAM C	W	7-1	3-0	Harris 20, Robson 32, Connelly 41, Pointer (2) 65, 72, Adamson 70, McIlroy 87	
	26		10	a	Everton	D	2-2	0-1	McIlroy 46, Pointer 53	15, 69
	27		20	h	FULHAM	W	2-1	1-0	Pointer 34, Connelly 63	80
	28		24	a	Blackburn R	L	1-2	1-0	Pointer 27	46, 62
	29	Mar	3	h	WEST HAM U	W	6-0	3-0	Robson (2) 1, 76, Towers (2) 24, 74, Pointer 43, McIlroy 85	
	30		14	a	Cardiff C	D	1-1	0-0	Miller 46	49
	31		17	h	TOTTENHAM H	D	2-2	1-0	Harris 39, Robson 59	49, 88
	32		24	a	Aston Villa	W	2-0	1-0	Connelly 7, Harris 88	
	33	Apr	3	h	NOTTINGHAM F	D	0-0	0-0		
	34		7	a	Wolverhampton W	D	1-1	0-0	Pointer 69	49
	35		11	a	Bolton W	D	0-0	0-0		
	36		14	h	MANCHESTER U	L	1-3	0-1	Pointer 66	40, 64p, 88
	37		17	h	BLACKBURN R	L	0-1	0-1		31
	38		20	h	BLACKPOOL	W	2-0	2-0	Connelly 20, Cummings 36	
	39		21	a	Sheffield U	L	0-2	0-1		29, 52p
	40		23	a	Blackpool	D	1-1	1-1	McIlroy 27p	36
	41		28	h	CHELSEA	D	1-1	1-0	Towers 29	69
	42		30	a	Sheffield W	L	0-4	0-1		12, 53, 58, 67

FA Cup

QPR's goal 74m	3	Jan	6	h	QUEENS PARK R	W	6-1	1-0	Connelly 6, McIlroy 55p, Ingham 61og, Elder 70, Harris (2) 82, 85	
	4		30	h	LEYTON O	D	1-1	0-0	Harris 83	57
	rep	Feb	6	a	Leyton O	W	1-0	0-0	Miller 60	
	5		17	h	EVERTON	W	3-1	0-1	Miller 46, Connelly 60, Robson 69	35
	6	Mar	10	a	Sheffield U	W	1-0	0-0	Pointer 52	
at Villa Park	semi		31	n	Fulham	D	1-1	0-1	Connelly 50	27
at Filbert Street, Leicester	rep	Apr	9	n	Fulham	W	2-1	1-0	Robson (2) 31, 80	89
at Wembley	Final	May	5	n	Tottenham H	L	1-3	0-1	Robson 49	3, 50, 82p

Details of other first team games elsewhere.

Att.	Pos	Blacklaw	Joyce	Elder	Adamson	Cummings	Miller	Connelly	McIlroy	Pointer	Robson	Harris	Angus	Towers	Lochhead	Fenton	Meredith	Talbut	Walker	Simpson	
42,856		1	2	3	4	5	6	7	8	9	10	11									1
24,577		1	2	3	4	5	6	7	8	9	10	11									2
24,167	5	1		3	4	5	6	7	8	9	10		2	11							3
23,835	7	1		3	4	5	6	7	8	9	10		2	11							4
38,171		1		3	4	5	6	7	8	9	10	11	2								5
22,339	top	1		3	4	5	6	7	8	9	10	11	2								6
22,001	top	1		3	4	5	6	7	8	9	10	11	2								7
18,764	top	1		3	4	5	6	7	8	9	10	11	2								8
25,567	top	1		3	4	5	6	7	8	9	10	11	2								9
35,776	top	1		3	4	5	6	7	8	9	10	11	2								10
30,665	top	1		3	4	5	6	7	8	9	10	11	2								11
32,238	top	1		3	4	5	6		8		10	11	2	7	9						12
22,765	top	1	3		4	5	6	7		9	10	11	2			8					13
56,772	top	1	4	3		5	6	7	8	9	10	11	2								14
22,487	top	1	4	3		5	6	7	8	9	10	11	2								15
26,409	top	1	2	3	4	5	6	7	8	9	10	11									16
25,904	top	1	2	3	4	5	6	7	8	9	10	11									17
41,029	top	1		3	4	5	6	7	8	9	10	11	2								18
21,526	top	1		3	4	5	6	7	8	9	10	11	2								19
33,296	top	1		3	4	5	6	7	8	9	10	11	2								20
22,887	top	1	4	3		5	6	7	8	9	10	11	2								21
28,966	top	1	4	3		5	6	7	8	9	10	11	2								22
22,728	top	1		3	4	5	6	7	8	9	10	11	2								23
22,141	top	1		3	4	5	6	7	8	9	10	11	2								24
24,047	top	1		3	4	5	6	7	8	9	10	11	2								25
54,369	top	1	6	3	4	5		7	8	9	10	11	2								26
25,605	top	1		3	4	5	6	7	8	9	10	11	2								27
33,914	top	1		3	4	5	6	7	8	9	10		2	11							28
24,379	top	1		3	4	5	6	7	8	9	10		2	11							29
15,416	top	1		3	4	5	6	7	8	9	10	11	2								30
46,810	top	1		3	4	5	6	7	8	9	10	11	2								31
36,864	2	1		3	4	5	6	7	8	9		11	2			10					32
23,217	2	1		3	4	5	6			9	8	11	2			10	7				33
26,001	top	1	4	3		5	6			9	8	11	2			10	7				34
26,615		1	4	3				7		9	8	11	2			10		5	6		35
36,240	2	1	6	3		5		7		9	10	11	2	8					4		36
29,997	2	1	6	3	4			7	8	9	10		2	11				5			37
34,132		1		3	4	5	6	7	8	9	10		2	11							38
25,003		1		3	4	5	6	7	8	9	10	11	2								39
31,660	2	1		3	4	5	6	7	8	9	10		2	11							40
29,078	2	1		3	4	5	6	7	8	9	10		2	11							41
19,684		1	4	3			6				10	11	2		9		7	5		8	42
Appearances		42	15	41	34	39	38	38	36	40	41	34	38	10	2	5	3	3	2	1	
Goals (101)					2	1	3	17	15	25	15	14		3							6 ogs

Att.	Blacklaw	Joyce	Elder	Adamson	Cummings	Miller	Connelly	McIlroy	Pointer	Robson	Harris	Angus	
29,238	1		3	4	5	6	7	8	9	10	11	2	3
37,830	1		3	4	5	6	7	8	9	10	11	2	4
31,090	1		3	4	5	6	7	8	9	10	11	2	rep
50,514	1		3	4	5	6	7	8	9	10	11	2	5
54,628	1		3	4	5	6	7	8	9	10	11	2	6
59,989	1		3	4	5	6	7	8	9	10	11	2	semi
31,000	1	6	3	4		5	7	8	9	10	11	2	rep
100,000	1		3	4	5	6	7	8	9	10	11	2	Final
Appearances	8	1	8	8	7	8	8	8	8	8	8	8	
Goals (16)			1			2	3	1	1	4	3		1 og

1962-63

There can be few doubts about the biggest headline of the 1962-63 season.

The date was 27 February, 1963, and the headline read "MAC: ANGRY FANS WANT TO KNOW WHY!"

The shock news was that legendary international inside-forward Jimmy McIlroy had been placed on the transfer list. For 13 seasons he had been the darling of the Turf Moor crowd, the most-capped player in the club's history, the biggest crowd pleaser of all time.

The previous summer the club had turned down an offer of around £30,000 from Italian club Sampdoria. But as the big freeze of 1963 took its grip - the Clarets went without a league game for two months – the FA Cup departure at the end of February was immediately followed by the shock announcement that McIlroy was on the transfer list.

Angry fans raised petitions and on the door of chairman Bob Lord's Lowerhouse warehouse, daubed in white letters nine inches tall, the message could not have been clearer. "We Want McIlroy. Sack Potts" summed up the mood in town.

Lord set a target price of £40,000 and several clubs were immediately in the reckoning. Burnley Express reporter Keith McNee went to see McIlroy who simply said: "I suppose you want to know what this is all about. Well so do I!"

Lord told the Express there was no chance of a change of heart and nine days after the shock news first broke McIlroy was sold to Stoke for £25,000-plus.

Manager Harry Potts reacted to it all by issuing a statement that read: "The only person responsible is Jimmy himself. I am perfectly sure that Burnley Football Club have done all they possibly could for Jimmy McIlroy during the time he has been with the club. Unfortunately he has not reciprocated on all occasions on the field."

McIlroy himself refused to be drawn into a slanging match and simply replied: "Have I not been good to them too?"

Some fans called for a boycott, others in the letters pages of the Burnley Express asked: "Do you support Jimmy McIlroy or Burnley Football Club?" Some simply said they would never go to Turf Moor again. Some never did.

A draw with West Ham on March 9th was the first home league match of 1963 and then the Clarets faced the prospect of 17 games in 55 days to try and get back into the race for the Championship. Another era came to an end when Tommy Cummings left after 15 years to become manager of Aston Villa.

A draw and a defeat saw a change of team and Arthur Bellamy scored a debut goal as Manchester City were thrashed 5-2 at Maine Road with McIlroy an interested spectator.

Andy Lochhead scored for the third successive game in a 1-1 draw with Spurs and then Gordon Harris got the only goal of the game as Blackburn Rovers were beaten. That game saw the 65th consecutive appearance of the defensive trio of Adam Blacklaw, Alex Elder and John Angus. But that post-War record run came to an end as Elder sustained a hamstring injury.

Big wins against Villa and Fulham followed, but then the good run came to a juddering halt at Molineux as the Clarets were thrashed 7-2. They had been in front thanks to a seventh minute strike from Lochhead, but they were 6-1 behind before Pointer struck again.

With eight games to go the title was still a mathematical possibility, but really nothing less than eight straight wins would do.

A goalless draw at Nottingham Forest was not the ideal start to that run and for the trip to Sheffield Wednesday Willie Morgan was drafted into the team and the average age was just 22.

Defeat at Ipswich finally ended the title dream, but there was still the chance of a place in European football the following season.

A mixed bag of results between then and the end of the season resulted in the Clarets claiming third place in the table as the Reserves won the Central League title with Jimmy Robson leading the line.

In the run in to the end of the season Brian O'Neil made his debut, Alex Elder scored his first goal for the club and McIlroy opened a ladies' and gents' outfitters in Colne Road.

The season ended with a cruise of the Mediterranean as the Clarets were rewarded for providing top class entertainment in a season where they won 22 of their 42 league games and drew 10 others.

But what of the first half of the season, the months before the shock February headlines?

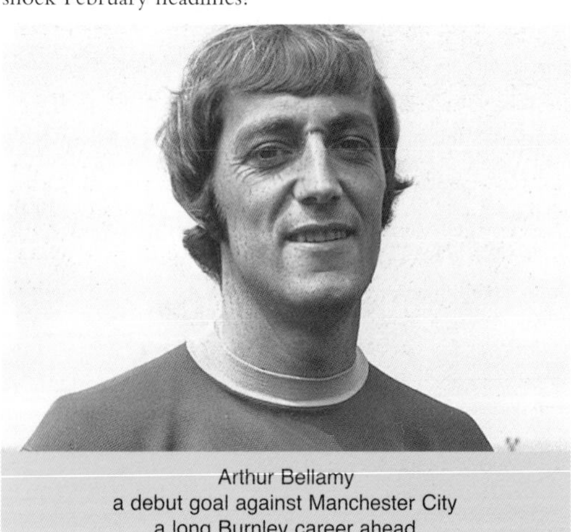

Arthur Bellamy
a debut goal against Manchester City
a long Burnley career ahead

Four weeks before the start of the season a new gymnasium was opened for the players at Turf Moor and a row was brewing over Burnley's nomination for the Inter-Cities Fairs Cup as the town was not a city and did not have a trade fair. Just 11 weeks after their Wembley defeat, the Clarets were back in training and the Fairs Cup committee ruled against Burnley. The Football League and FA promised to support Burnley and Lord returned from a holiday in Canada to pronounce himself disappointed with the decision.

Skipper Jimmy Adamson had spent the summer in Chile as England manager Walter Winterbottom's assistant in the World Cup. When Winterbottom resigned, Footballer of the Year Adamson ruled himself out of the running to replace him as he did not have the relevant experience.

The Clarets beat a combined Hearts and Hibs side 4-2 in a charity match at Tynecastle and then McIlroy, according to

McNee, was at his "critic-shattering" best in a 3-3 draw at Bradford City.

The season opened with a disappointing defeat at home to Everton as the club ran out of season ticket books and a fluke goal at Burnden Park gave Bolton a draw. McIlroy's international career was under threat following a pay dispute with the Irish FA but the inside forward was honoured with the Burnley captaincy as Adamson was forced to sit out the start of the season with a back injury.

Andy Lochhead
top scorer in his first full season

A win at West Bromwich Albion featured an unusual incident as a whistle sounded as McIlroy had the goal at his mercy. Play stopped, but the whistle had been in the crowd and a policeman was dispatched to find the culprit.

A win over Arsenal and a draw with Leicester saw Burnley handily placed in sixth and their first four home games had been watched by a combined total of 114,000 fans, an increase of 27,000 on the previous season and season ticket sales stood at a club record £34,000.

Cinderella side Leyton Orient were beaten 2-0 as McNee opined: "When Jimmy McIlroy plays, Burnley play" in the Burnley Express and the next game witnessed a John Connelly hat-trick against Manchester United. It was the first Clarets' hat-trick for almost exactly 12 months. The previous one was also scored by Connelly, this time at Fulham.

Adamson returned to the side for a 3-2 win at Ewood Park and when the Clarets travelled to Portsmouth for the official switch-on of the Fratton Park floodlights, McIlroy and Elder were further afield playing for Northern Ireland in Katowice. Those midweek travels did no harm and everyone returned for a 5-1 demolition of Sheffield Wednesday where Lochhead bagged a second successive brace to take his tally to eight goals in six games.

Adamson made his 400th league appearance in a 1-1 draw at Upton Park and then nearly 17,000 supporters turned out for a benefit match for Colin McDonald. The former Burnley and England keeper featured in an all-star team alongside the likes of Jimmy Armfield, Roger Hunt, Nat Lofthouse and Tom Finney as the Clarets put out their first choice team in honour of one of the finest keepers ever to represent the club.

McIlroy was back in the headlines as he won his 50th international cap in a 5-1 defeat in Glasgow and then a win at Liverpool saw the Clarets up to third in the table.

Lord responded to suggestions that Ipswich Town were to approach Adamson to replace Alf Ramsey as manager by saying: "If any request regarding Adamson comes to me by letter, it will find it's way to one place – the fire!"

Wolves were beaten 2-0 as McIlroy scored with a header for the first time in 61 league and cup matches and in late November there can have been few thoughts of his departure as his understudy, Ron Fenton, was sold to West Brom for £17,000.

The first 10 games at Turf Moor attracted a total crowd of just under 300,000, up by an average of almost 2,700 a game on the previous season and there was much cause for optimism as at the halfway stage in the season the Clarets were second in the table just two points behind Everton.

Everton were the next opponents and they completed the double of the Clarets who then signed off the year with a 4-0 win over Sheffield Wednesday on a pitch like an ice rink.

Twice postponed, the Clarets finally got their chance to avenge their FA Cup Final defeat of the previous season when they beat Spurs 3-1 at White Hart Lane. After the game, McIlroy said: "A team can only take so much and no more. We decided we had taken enough from Spurs. That's the way it was with us this afternoon!"

More league postponements followed, the fourth round date with Liverpool at Turf Moor ended 1-1 as Connelly grabbed an equaliser but the replay was postponed three times before a Ronnie Moran penalty late in the day handed Liverpool a 2-1 win.

Up until that point in the season, the weather apart, things seemed to be going well for the Clarets.

But the following week saw the headline that stunned everyone and ended a golden era at Turf Moor.

1962-63 - First Division

		P	W	D	L	F	A	Pts
1	Everton	42	25	11	6	84	42	61
2	Tottenham H	42	23	9	10	111	62	55
3	BURNLEY	42	22	10	10	78	57	54
4	Leicester C	42	20	12	10	79	53	52
5	Wolverhampton W	42	20	10	12	93	65	50
6	Sheffield W	42	19	10	13	77	63	48
7	Arsenal	42	18	10	14	86	77	46
8	Liverpool	42	17	10	15	71	59	44
9	Nottingham F	42	17	10	15	67	69	44
10	Sheffield U	42	16	12	14	58	60	44
11	Blackburn R	42	15	12	15	79	71	42
12	West Ham U	42	14	12	26	73	69	40
13	Blackpool	42	13	14	15	58	64	40
14	West Bromwich A	42	16	7	19	71	79	39
15	Aston Villa	42	15	8	19	62	68	38
16	Fulham	42	14	10	18	50	71	38
17	Ipswich T	42	12	11	19	59	78	35
18	Bolton W	42	15	5	22	55	75	35
19	Manchester U	42	12	10	20	67	81	34
20	Birmingham C	42	10	13	19	63	90	33
21	Manchester C	42	10	11	21	58	102	31
22	Leyton O	42	6	9	27	37	81	21

1962-63

Manager : Harry Potts

Division One (3rd)

Note	No	Month	Day		Opponents	Result		h/t	Goalscorers/times	Opp. goal times
	1	Aug	18	h	EVERTON	L	1-3	1-1	Pointer 10	20, 62, 75
Cummings' last game	2		22	a	Bolton W	D	2-2	2-0	Connelly 31, Joyce 41	54, 82
	3		25	a	West Bromwich A	W	2-1	0-0	Miller 55, Pointer 69	89
	4		28	h	BOLTON W	W	2-1	0-1	Connelly 68, McIlroy 74p	34
	5	Sep	1	h	ARSENAL	W	2-1	0-0	Miller 80, Connelly 82	68
	6		4	h	LEICESTER C	D	1-1	0-1	Robson 63	4
	7		8	a	Birmingham C	L	1-5	0-3	Pointer 89	6, 8, 19, 60, 88
	8		15	h	LEYTON O	W	2-0	1-0	McIlroy 41, Lochhead 57	
	9		19	a	Leicester C	D	3-3	2-1	Pointer 12, Lochhead 41, McIlroy 87p	8, 62, 69
	10		22	a	Manchester U	W	5-2	3-0	Lochhead 5, Connelly (3) 35, 66, 84, McIlroy 42	59, 65
	11		29	h	BLACKPOOL	W	2-0	1-0	Connelly 40, Lochhead 84	
	12	Oct	6	a	Blackburn R	W	3-2	2-1	Harris 35, Lochhead (2) 37, 63	22, 49p
	13		13	h	SHEFFIELD U	W	5-1	3-0	Lochhead (2) 21, 51, Harris 35, Connelly 37, Miller 71	79
	14		22	a	West Ham U	D	1-1	1-1	Robson 40	1
	15		27	h	MANCHESTER C	D	0-0	0-0		
	16	Nov	3	a	Liverpool	W	2-1	1-0	Pointer 35, Lochhead 67	49
	17		10	h	WOLVERHAMPTON W	W	2-0	2-0	McIlroy 16, Lochhead 18	
	18		17	a	Aston Villa	L	1-2	1-2	Connelly 18	7, 20
	19		24	h	TOTTENHAM H	W	2-1	0-1	Connelly 57, Pointer 80	40
	20	Dec	1	a	Nottingham F	L	1-2	0-1	Pointer 51	36, 68
	21		8	h	IPSWICH T	W	3-1	1-0	Lochhead 3, Miller (2) 66, 71	65
	22		15	a	Everton	L	1-3	0-3	McIlroy 58	18, 20, 24
	23		29	h	SHEFFIELD W	W	4-0	2-0	Miller 24, Pointer (2) 26, 86, Harris 79	
	24	Mar	2	a	Sheffield U	L	0-1	0-1		2
	25		9	h	WEST HAM U	D	1-1	0-0	Pointer 60	86
	26		20	a	Blackpool	D	0-0	0-0		
	27		23	h	LIVERPOOL	L	1-3	0-1	Lochhead 55	24, 75, 89
	28		26	a	Manchester C	W	5-2	3-1	Lochhead 4, Harris (2) 12, 24, Pointer 49, Bellamy 52	20, 84
	29		30	a	Tottenham H	D	1-1	0-1	Lochhead 50	19
	30	Apr	2	h	BLACKBURN R	W	1-0	1-0	Harris 37p	
	31		6	h	ASTON VILLA	W	3-1	2-1	Lochhead 2, Harris 8, Pointer 46	19
	32		12	h	FULHAM	W	4-0	2-0	Bellamy 2, Lochhead (2) 43, 58, Pointer 66	
	33		13	a	Wolverhampton W	L	2-7	1-2	Lochhead 7, Pointer 80	31,33,58,62,73og,78,86
	34		15	a	Fulham	D	1-1	0-1	Connelly 67	38
	35		20	h	NOTTINGHAM F	D	0-0	0-0		
	36		23	a	Sheffield W	W	1-0	1-0	Johnson 38og	
	37		27	a	Ipswich T	L	1-2	0-0	Connelly 66	60, 67
	38		30	h	WEST BROMWICH A	W	2-1	1-0	Lochhead 32, Connelly 88	70
	39	May	4	h	MANCHESTER U	L	0-1	0-0		70
	40		7	a	Leyton O	W	1-0	1-0	Towers 20	
	41		11	a	Arsenal	W	3-2	1-2	Irvine 20, Elder 63p, Towers 80	23, 33
	42		14	h	BIRMINGHAM C	W	3-1	1-0	Irvine (3) 15, 58, 75	72

FA Cup

Note	Rd	Month	Day		Opponents	Result		h/t	Goalscorers/times	Opp. goal times
	3	Jan	16	a	Tottenham H	W	3-0	1-0	Harris 40, Connelly 47, Lochhead 55	
	4		26	h	LIVERPOOL	D	1-1	0-1	Connelly 50	25
McIlroy's last game (aet)	rep	Feb	20	a	Liverpool	L	1-2	1-1	Elder 24	45, 120

Final, Manchester U 3-1 Leicester C, at Wembley.

Details of other first team games elsewhere.

Att.	Pos	Blacklaw	Angus	Elder	Joyce	Cummings	Miller	Connelly	McIlroy	Pointer	Robson	Harris	Talbut	Walker	Lochhead	Adamson	Towers	Meredith	Bellamy	Buxton	Morgan	O'Neil	Simpson	Irvine	
37,100		1	2	3	4	5	6	7	8	9	10	11													1
28,897		1	2	3	4	5	6	7	8	9	10	11													2
23,812		1	2	3	4		6	7	8	9	10	11	5												3
27,529		1	2	3	4		6	7	8	9	10	11	5												4
26,131	7	1	2	3	4		6	7	8	9	10	11	5												5
23,876		1	2	3	4		6	7	8	9	10	11	5												6
24,463	7	1	2	3	4		6	7	8	9	10	11	5												7
24,778	8	1	2	3			6	7	10	8		11	5	4	9										8
26,692		1	2	3			6	7	10	8		11	5	4	9										9
46,176	5	1	2	3			6	7	10	8		11	5	4	9										10
28,351	4	1	2	3			6	7	10	8		11	5	4	9										11
26,626	3	1	2	3			6	7	10	8		11	5		9	4									12
27,560	3	1	2	3			6	7	10	8		11	5		9	4									13
34,612	2	1	2	3			6	7		8	10	11	5			4	9								14
30,504	3	1	2	3			6	7	10	8		11	5		9	4									15
43,870	3	1	2	3			6	7	10	8		11	5		9	4									16
27,824	3	1	2	3			6	7	10	8		11	5		9	4									17
32,380	3	1	2	3			6	7	10	8		11	5		9	4									18
44,478	3	1	2	3			6	7	10	8		11	5		9	4									19
34,171	3	1	2	3			6	7	10	8		11	5		9	4									20
19,498	2	1	2	3			6	7	10	8		11	5		9	4									21
48,443	3	1	2	3			6	7	10	8		11	5		9	4									22
20,853	3	1	2	3			6	7	10	8		11	5		9	4									23
26,939	4	1	2	3			6	7		8	10	11	5		9	4									24
17,197	5	1	2	3			6	7		8	10	11	5		9	4									25
16,445		1	2	3			6	11		8	10		5		9	4		7							26
28,500	6	1	2	3			6	7		8	10	11	5	4	9										27
21,985		1	2	3			6	7		8		11	5	4	9				10						28
46,536	4	1	2	3			6	7		8		11	5	4	9				10						29
25,746		1	2				6	7		8		11	5	4	9				10	3					30
19,605	4	1	2	3			6	7		8		11	5	4	9				10						31
22,405		1	2	3			6	7		8		11	5	4	9				10						32
21,562	4	1	2	3			6	7		8		11	5	4	9				10						33
25,869		1	2	3			6	7		8		11	5	4	9				10						34
16,253	5	1	2	3			6	7		8		11	5	4	9				10						35
24,649		1	2	3			6	11			8		5	4	9				10		7				36
18,645		1	2	3			6	7			8	11	5	4	9				10						37
15,981		1	2	3			6	7			8	11	5		9							4	10		38
30,226	4	1	2	3			6	7			8	11	5		9							4	10		39
10,095		1	2	3			6					11	5		9	4	10	7	8						40
23,526	4	1	2	3			6	7				11	5			4	10		8					9	41
14,350	3	1	2	3			6	11				10	5			4			8		7			9	42
Appearances		42	42	41	7	2	42	41	22	35	16	40	40	15	32	18	3	2	13	1	2	2	2	2	
Goals (78)				1	1		6	13	6	14	2	7			19		2		2					4	1 og

Att.	Pos	Blacklaw	Angus	Elder	Joyce	Cummings	Miller	Connelly	McIlroy	Pointer	Robson	Harris	Talbut	Walker	Lochhead	Adamson	Towers	Meredith	Bellamy	Buxton	Morgan	O'Neil	Simpson	Irvine	
32,756		1	2	3			6	7	10		8	11	5		9	4									3
49,827		1	2	3			6	7	10		8	11	5		9	4									4
57,906		1	2	3			6	7	10	8		11	5		9	4									rep
Appearances		3	3	3			3	3	3	1	2	3	3		3	3									
Goals (5)				1				2				1			1										

1963-64

A Chairman hitting out at the club's annual meeting; a Manager blasting match officials; players asking for transfers; the sale of a fans' favourite; dismal form on their travels for the Clarets; a crippling injury list and even the manager and several first team players leaping from the team bus to apprehend teenagers who had pelted it with stones! Could this really be the story of the 1963-64 season?

It was a season in which the Clarets kept up an admirable run of finishing in the top half of the table. They also reached the quarter-finals of the FA Cup. But there was no League Cup success as Burnley chose not to play in the competition.

The season started with club secretary Albert Maddox reporting a heavy demand for season tickets, Ian Towers asking for a transfer – just two months after signing a new contract – as he wanted more first team football and full back Alex Elder expected to be out for up to three months having broken an ankle in a pre-season practice game at Gawthorpe.

As the build-up to the season continued, inside-forward Peter Simpson was sold to Bury, but bids of £14,000, £20,000 and later £23,000 from Stoke for Towers were rejected.

Ray Pointer was also set to miss the start of the season following a badly bruised shin at Nottingham Forest towards the end of the previous season. Manager Harry Potts denied that Pointer's injury could end his career and also rejected popular local opinion that a "big name" signing was needed to fire the local imagination and ensure that the Clarets finished in the top four for the fifth successive season.

As Burnley opened their season with a defeat at Ipswich, Pointer proved his manager right by playing for the reserves. He was promoted back to the senior line-up for the first home game of the season, a goalless draw with Chelsea, as Gordon Harris made his 100th league appearance for the club. John Talbut, the rising star of the team, made his 50th appearance as the Clarets claimed their first victory of the season by beating Sheffield Wednesday.

And chairman Bob Lord made his first major headline of the season in early September following a stormy annual meeting. Questioned about the sale of Jimmy McIlroy he simply said: "When you only have one customer you have got to take a bad price. We had only one customer and yet got a good price, and time will prove it." Lord also admitted that the team was in a stage of transition and asked supporters to allow time for that to take place.

Although champions Everton were beaten 4-3 at Goodison largely due to Arthur Bellamy's first league hat-trick, the poorest start to the season for five years saw just nine points claimed from the first 10 game. Harry Potts pointed to the mounting injury list and the fact that he had been forced to use 16 players in those 10 matches.

Blackburn were beaten in a bad-tempered match at Turf Moor in which Mike England was sent-off for a challenge that sent Andy Lochhead reeling, two away draws followed and Potts was again back in the headlines for seeking an abolition of the off-side rule.

The injury list in the build-up to the return at Ewood saw 10 senior players on the treatment table. They all missed the game but John Connelly netted twice to earn the points. Unfortunately, the Clarets did not win another away game until their final trip of the season.

Talbut was selected to captain the England Under 23 side and Jimmy Adamson was linked with the vacant managerial position with the US national side but claimed he had another three seasons of first team football to look forward to.

All roads then led to Stoke as Jimmy McIlroy lined-up against the Clarets for the first time. Burnley came from 3-0 and 4-1 down to earn a 4-4 draw.

And there were plenty of goals, 20 in fact, as an All Stars team featuring the likes of Bert Trautmann, Ray Wilson, Tom Finney, Roger Hunt and Bobby Charlton drew with the Clarets in Tommy Cummings' testimonial game.

Harry Potts was back on the front pages after protesting about rough play. He claimed that until certain managers and players changed their ways, there would be nothing referees could do to stamp out the sort of play he believed should have seen Spurs' first two goals in a 3-2 win over the Clarets at White Hart Lane ruled out.

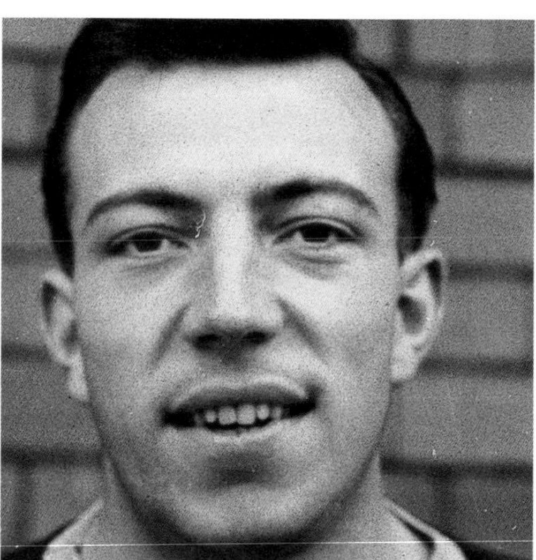

John Talbut
another talented defender
off the Turf Moor production line

By the end of November there was another setback as Connelly was rushed to hospital for an emergency appendectomy, news that brought the number of senior players who had been ruled out at some stage so far in the campaign to 22.

The lowest crowd at Turf Moor since 1961, saw Jackie Price score his first goal for the Clarets in a 2-0 win against Aston Villa. In the next game John Angus was severely hampered with a side injury as Liverpool won 2-0 at Anfield to send the Clarets down to ninth in the table. It was where they were destined to finish the campaign.

New England manager Alf Ramsey visited Turf Moor for the clash with Nottingham Forest but did not learn much as Angus failed a fitness test and neither Talbut nor Harris played well.

In the last game before the holiday schedule, Alex Elder made his first appearance of the season and there was more good news as Jimmy Adamson and Connelly returned to training well ahead of their Christmas schedule.

Manchester United were humbled 6-1 on Boxing Day as Andy Lochhead hit four and Keith McNee in the Burnley Express gave the man-of-the-match honours to Willie-The-Wisp-Morgan, but United had their revenge two days later with a 5-1 win at Old Trafford.

Adam Blacklaw stopped Second Division Rotherham United scoring an FA Cup upset as a Frank Casper equaliser earned the Millers a replay. But despite leading 2-1, Rotherham eventually went out to a Towers winner four minutes from time.

Even Everton manager Harry Catterick admitted that a handball decision against Brian Miller was "harsh", but it helped defending champions Everton battle back from 2-0 down to win 3-2 at Turf Moor and the refereeing was again under the spotlight as the Clarets drew 0-0 at St Andrew's. Burnley hit the back of the net four times, but each "goal" was disallowed. Potts slammed referee Raymond Aldous and was later fined £50, a sum put into perspective by the fact that later in the season, Althams Travel offered fans the chance to fly to London for a match for less than £8.

The FA Cup fourth round saw the Clarets up against Fourth Division opponents for the first time in their history but Newport County won a lot of admiration for their display in a 2-1 defeat at Turf Moor.

The start of February saw Bod Lord back in the headlines by claiming there was no crisis at Turf Moor. It was popularly suggested at the time that clubs like Burnley were on the brink of financial collapse, but Lord was not having any of it! Another £13,000 came into the coffers as Walter Joyce turned down a transfer to Scunthorpe United and moved to Ewood Park; George Bray was promoted from reserve team coach to first team coach following the retirement of Ray Bennion and Elder was star man as Huddersfield were beaten 3-1 to get the Clarets into the quarter-finals of the FA Cup for the sixth time in seven years.

West Ham United were their opponents and Adamson was ruled out with a back injury. But the Clarets left Upton Park beaten 3-2 with chairman, manager and captain Brian Miller all fuming over the Hammers' third goal as Johnny Byrne appeared to foul Miller and was off-side when he received the ball.

Revenge was immediate as West Ham lost a midweek date at Turf Moor but more away misfortune came Burnley's way before all eyes were again on Turf Moor, this time for the visit of Stoke City.

In the build-up to the game McIlroy said in the Burnley Express: "I was asked if I wanted to play at Turf Moor or give it a miss in view of the Easter programme. My reply to our manager was that I did want to play or they would call me a coward."

In the end, McIlroy's Turf Moor return resulted in a 1-0 win for Burnley as the Clarets picked-up three points from three games over Easter.

With three games to go, the Clarets needed points to make sure they finished in the top half of the table for the 12th successive season but it started badly as they lost 3-0 at home to Liverpool. Then came the shock news that John Connelly had been sold to Manchester United for £50,000 and for the first time the words "sell to survive" were used in a Burnley Express headline. Connelly himself said that Matt Busby convinced him he had good prospects at Old Trafford but added that he would miss Burnley.

The last away game of the season saw Burnley win at Forest and make more headlines as the team bus was stoned by home fans. Potts, Talbut, Elder, Miller and Blacklaw were among those who leapt from the bus to apprehend the culprits until the police arrived.

The youngest team of the season then brought the curtain down on the season by denying Spurs runners-up spot by beating them 7-2 at Turf Moor and then another chapter ended with the announcement of the retained list as Trevor Meredith, a goalscoring hero of that magical 1960 night at Maine Road, was sold to Shrewsbury for a "small fee".

OBITUARY

JAMES PETER O'DOWD

DIED 8 MAY 1964, AGED 56

One of the very few players to claim an ever-present record throughout his stay at Turf Moor, Peter O'Dowd's Burnley career was admittedly brief, but he achieved greater fame, and indeed England recognition, after leaving the club.

Born in Halifax in 1908, his first League experience came with Blackburn Rovers, from whom he joined Burnley for £2,500 in March 1930. A tall and skilful centre-half, he settled quickly into the role for the Clarets, but was unable to prevent relegation at the end of that season. Playing in all 42 League games the following season, he was often the star man in a defence that was by no means the tightest around, and his performances on an FA tour of Canada after the end of the season enhanced his reputation further.

Plainly a player destined for better things than the Second Division, he moved to Chelsea for £5,000 in November 1931, and it was at Stamford Bridge that he won his three England caps. Unusually for a player of his era, he decided at the peak of his career to move abroad, joining the French club Valenciennes in 1934. He ended his playing career with Torquay, and settled in the South of England, living in Bournemouth at the time of his premature death.

RIP

1963-64 - First Division

		P	W	D	L	F	A	Pts
1	Liverpool	42	26	5	11	92	45	57
2	Manchester U	42	23	7	12	90	62	53
3	Everton	42	21	10	11	84	64	52
4	Tottenham H	42	22	7	13	97	81	51
5	Chelsea	42	20	10	12	72	56	50
6	Sheffield W	42	19	11	12	84	67	49
7	Blackburn R	42	18	10	14	89	65	46
8	Arsenal	42	17	11	14	90	82	45
9	BURNLEY	42	17	10	15	71	64	44
10	West Bromwich A	42	16	11	15	70	61	43
11	Leicester C	42	16	11	15	61	58	43
12	Sheffield U	42	16	11	15	61	64	43
13	Nottingham F	42	16	9	17	64	68	41
14	West Ham U	42	14	12	16	69	74	40
15	Fulham	42	13	13	16	58	65	39
16	Wolverhampton W	42	12	15	15	70	80	39
17	Stoke C	42	14	10	18	77	78	38
18	Blackpool	42	13	9	20	52	73	35
19	Aston Villa	42	11	12	19	62	71	34
20	Birmingham C	42	11	7	24	54	92	29
21	Bolton W	42	10	8	24	48	80	28
22	Ipswich T	42	9	7	26	56	121	25

1963-64

Manager : Harry Potts

Division One (9th)

Note	No.	Date		Venue	Opponents	Result		h/t	Goalscorers/times	Opp. goal times
	1	Aug	24	a	Ipswich T	L	1-3	0-2	Miller 68	26, 34, 78
	2		27	h	CHELSEA	D	0-0	0-0		
	3		31	h	SHEFFIELD W	W	3-1	2-0	Miller 16, Robson 35, Pointer 50	57
	4	Sep	4	a	Chelsea	L	0-2	0-1		13p, 89
	5		7	a	Everton	W	4-3	4-1	Bellamy (3) 4, 35, 44, Miller 33	10, 51, 64
	6		10	h	FULHAM	W	4-1	2-0	Connelly 35, Robson 44, Harris 68, Meredith 89	67
	7		14	h	BIRMINGHAM C	W	2-1	0-0	Bellamy 53, Harris 89	81
	8		18	a	Fulham	L	1-2	1-1	Meredith 27	36, 54
	9		21	a	West Bromwich A	D	0-0	0-0		
	10		28	h	ARSENAL	L	0-3	0-2		7og, 12, 50
	11	Oct	1	h	BLACKBURN R	W	3-0	1-0	Bellamy (2) 15, 63, Joyce 78	
	12		5	a	Leicester C	D	0-0	0-0		
	13		7	a	West Ham U	D	1-1	1-0	Harris 17	62
	14		12	h	BLACKPOOL	W	1-0	0-0	Harris 50	
	15		19	a	Blackburn R	W	2-1	0-1	Connelly (2) 58, 83	19
	16		26	h	SHEFFIELD U	L	1-2	0-2	Robson 86	1, 9
	17	Nov	2	a	Stoke C	D	4-4	0-3	Lochhead 55, Allen 56og, Harris (2) 84, 88	20, 27, 44, 81
	18		9	h	WOLVERHAMPTON W	W	1-0	0-0	Connelly 85	
	19		16	a	Tottenham H	L	2-3	0-2	Harris 67, Lochhead 82	4, 26, 59
	20		23	h	ASTON VILLA	W	2-0	1-0	Robson 38, Price 69	
Meredith's last game	21		30	a	Liverpool	L	0-2	0-0		70, 86p
Walter Joyce's last game	22	Dec	7	h	NOTTINGHAM F	D	1-1	0-0	Pointer 57	71
	23		14	h	IPSWICH T	W	3-1	2-1	Lochhead 4, Miller (2) 21, 83	44
	24		21	a	Sheffield W	L	1-3	0-1	Miller 62	30, 77, 86
	25		26	h	MANCHESTER U	W	6-1	2-1	Lochhead (4) 6, 43, 73, 88, Morgan (2) 66, 83	29
	26		28	a	Manchester U	L	1-5	0-3	Lochhead 88	12, 14, 24, 68, 72
	27	Jan	11	h	EVERTON	L	2-3	2-1	Connelly (2) 23, 41	44, 58, 62
	28		18	a	Birmingham C	D	0-0	0-0		
	29	Feb	1	h	WEST BROMWICH A	W	3-2	2-1	Towers 16, Connelly (2) 27, 62	44, 48
	30		8	a	Arsenal	L	2-3	2-2	Lochhead 26, Towers 36	12, 42, 65
Adamson's last game	31		22	a	Blackpool	D	1-1	0-0	Morgan 80	74
	32	Mar	3	h	WEST HAM U	W	3-1	2-0	Harris 4, Robson (2) 39, 46	86
	33		7	a	Sheffield U	L	0-2	0-2		14, 39
	34		10	h	LEICESTER C	W	2-0	1-0	Morgan 30, Bellamy 47	
	35		21	a	Wolverhampton W	D	1-1	0-0	Lochhead 76	65
	36		28	h	STOKE C	W	1-0	0-0	Elder 64	
	37		30	a	Bolton W	L	1-2	1-2	Irvine 35	18, 27
	38		31	h	BOLTON W	D	1-1	0-0	Bellamy 81	58
	39	Apr	4	a	Aston Villa	L	0-2	0-0		53, 59
Connelly's last game	40		14	h	LIVERPOOL	L	0-3	0-1		20, 52, 60
	41		18	a	Nottingham F	W	3-1	2-0	Towers (2) 14, 71, Irvine 17	65
Tottenham goals 54m, 68m	42		21	h	TOTTENHAM H	W	7-2	4-0	Harris (2) 7,14, Irvine (2) 21,52, O'Neil (2) 40,50, Lochhead 70	

FA Cup

Round	Date		Venue	Opponents	Result		h/t	Goalscorers/times	Opp. goal times
3	Jan	4	h	ROTHERHAM U	D	1-1	1-1	Lochhead 20	36
rep		7	a	Rotherham U	W	3-2	1-0	Connelly 20, Lochhead 77, Towers 86	47, 57
4		25	h	NEWPORT C	W	2-1	1-1	Morgan 33, Connelly 55	38
5	Feb	15	h	HUDDERSFIELD T	W	3-0	1-0	Pointer 2, Lochhead 55, Atkins 89og	
6		29	a	West Ham U	L	2-3	1-0	Connelly 16, Pointer 80	54, 58, 68

Final, West Ham U 3-2 Preston N E, at Wembley.

Details of other first team games elsewhere.

Att.	Pos	Blacklaw	Angus	Joyce	Adamson	Talbut	Miller	Connelly	Lochhead	Irvine	Robson	Harris	Pointer	Walker	Morgan	Meredith	Bellamy	O'Neil	Price	Buxton	F Smith	Elder	Towers	Todd		
23,000		1	2	3	4	5	6	7	8	9	10	11														1
19,674		1	2	3	4	5	6	7	8		10	11	9													2
20,238	9	1	2	3		5	6	11			8	10	9	4	7											3
31,881		1	2	3		5	6	11			8	10	9	4	7											4
54,409	12	1	2	3	4	5	6	11			9	10				7	8									5
19,349		1	2	3	4	5	6	11			9	10				7	8									6
20,350	5	1	2	3	4	5	6	11			9	10				7	8									7
17,282		1	2	3	4	5	6	11			9	10				7	8									8
24,591	8	1	2	3	4	5	6	11	9		8	10			7											9
20,628	9	1	2	3	4	5	6	11	9		8	10			7											10
24,345		1	2	3		5	6	11	9		10					7	8	4								11
26,310	9	1	2	3		5	6	11	9		8	10				7		4								12
21,372		1	2	3	4	5	6	11	9			10					8		7							13
20,025	8	1	2			5	6	11	9		8	10						4	7	3						14
26,740	4	1	2			5	6	11	9			10				7	8	4		3						15
21,345	7	1	2			5	6	11	9		10					7	8	4		3						16
36,924	8	1	2			5	6	11	8		9	10				7		4			3					17
19,775	7	1	2	3		5	6	11	8		9	10				7		4								18
42,222	8	1	2	3		5	6	11	8		9	10				7		4								19
13,606	7	1	2	3		5	6		9		8	10				7		4	11							20
42,968	9	1	2	3		5	6				8	10	9			7		4	11							21
15,304	9	1		3		5	6					10	9		7		8	4	11		2					22
10,558	7	1	3			5	6		9			10	8		7			4	11		2					23
18,603	9	1	2			5	6		9			10	8		7			4	11			3				24
35,766		1	2			5	6		9			10	8		7			4				3	11			25
48,035	9	1	2			5	6		9		10		8		7			4	11			3				26
23,082	11	1	2			5	6	11	9			10			7		8	4				3				27
15,917	12	1				5	6	11	9		10				7			4			2	3	8			28
15,840	9	1	2			5	6	11	9		10				7			4				3	8			29
30,863		1	2			5	6	11	9		10				7			4				3	8			30
12,938	11	1	2		6	5		11	9			10	8		7			4				3				31
14,428		1	2			5	6	11	9		8	10			7			4				3				32
15,880	12	1				5	6		9		8	10			7			4			2	3	11			33
12,664		1	2			5	6	11	9			10			7		8	4				3				34
18,082	11	1	2				5	11	9			10		4	7		8	6				3				35
26,868	9	1	2			5		11	9					4	7		10	6				3	8			36
14,112		1	2			5	6	11	9	8				4	7		10					3				37
12,554		1	2			5	6	11	9	8					7		10	4				3				38
12,296	12	1				5	6	11	9	8					7		10	4			2	3				39
34,804		1				5	6	11		9		10			7		8	4			2	3				40
19,005	12	1				5	6		8	9		10			7			4			2	3	11			41
16,660	9	1				5	6		8	9		10			7			4				3	11	2		42
Appearances		42	35	18	10	41	40	32	33	7	25	32	10	5	25	13	17	30	8	3	8	19	8	1		
Goals (71)				1			6	8	11	4	6	10	2		4	2	8	2	1			1	4		1	og

Att.	Pos	Blacklaw	Angus	Joyce	Adamson	Talbut	Miller	Connelly	Lochhead	Irvine	Robson	Harris	Pointer	Walker	Morgan	Meredith	Bellamy	O'Neil	Price	Buxton	F Smith	Elder	Towers	Todd		
24,948		1	2			5	6	11	9			10	8		7			4				3				3
23,813		1	2			5	6	11	9			10			7			4				3	8			rep
23,027		1	2			5	6	11	9			10			7			4				3	8			4
39,326		1	2		6	5		11	9			10	8		7			4				3				5
36,681		1	2			5	6	11	9			10	8		7			4				3				6
Appearances		5	5		1	5	4	5	5			5	3		5			5				5	2			
Goals (11)								3	3				2		1								1		1	og

1964-65

After years of title challenges, cup runs and drama, 1964-65 was by any standards an average season. In 42 league games, the Clarets won 16 and lost 16. They scored 70 goals and conceded 70 goals. The FA Cup run ended in the fifth round and Burnley again chose to ignore the League Cup.

But it was not an average season that could ever be classed as boring. A dreadful start led to no wins in the first eight games and the word relegation was even muttered in some quarters.

But it was the season that saw the birth of the Willie Irvine-Andy Lochhead strike partnership that would yield 118 league goals in three seasons.

And was it ever possible to have a "boring" season while Bob Lord remained as chairman?

On the eve of the new season the club reported a loss – around £7,000 – for only the third time since the War and Keith McNee in the Burnley Express reported a mystery-in-triplicate.

The first surrounded captain Jimmy Adamson who, it was suggested, might leave to become a manager elsewhere.

The second was the future of pay-rebel Alex Elder who had twice had requests to go on the transfer list turned down.

And the third was the future of injury-jinxed Ray Pointer who appeared to be at a crossroads in his career.

The annual meeting in early September heard that plans for a new 17,000 main stand had been shelved.

And quizzed about the playing strength of the club the chairman also said: "We have not been in the habit of buying players over the last 10 years, but, should circumstances compel us to change our policy, then it will be changed."

Two draws and two defeats meant the start to the season was the worst since the War and two more draws followed to make it no wins in six.

Both manager Harry Potts and skipper Adamson were approached by Sunderland over their managerial vacancy with Lord threatening to report the Weirsiders to the League for a "flagrant breach" of league rules as Adamson was immediately elevated to the role of player-coach.

Things got worse on the field with two more defeats although McNee reported that the Clarets were not playing anything like as badly as the results suggested.

The first win of the season came at West Ham United but was immediately followed by a 5-1 thumping at Hillsborough and just one win had been chalked up in the first 10 games.

Irvine bagged both goals at The Hawthorns to hand the Clarets their first away win of the season and at the start of October the Football League announced a commission of enquiry into the Sunderland-Adamson affair. It later decided to take no action.

John Connelly came back to Turf Moor with his new club but Adam Blacklaw, on his 150th consecutive league appearance, shut out the former Claret and his strike colleagues in a 0-0 draw and the next game saw the recent unbeaten run against Blackburn Rovers extended in a 1-1 draw.

The next game saw the club's London jinx strike again as Arsenal won 3-2 at Highbury, although Burnley's second half performance deserved at least a draw, the poor start continued with a 1-0 home defeat against Leeds United but then the Clarets surprised everyone by beating league leaders Chelsea at Stamford Bridge with Irvine scoring the only goal.

Elder was made captain for the game against Leicester City in honour of him accepting a similar role with Ireland and he scored one of the goals in a 2-1 success.

But it was back to the same routine in the next game, described by McNee as a "tragedy of missed chances" as a 3-2 reverse was suffered at Roker Park. Elder and Irvine both missed the game as they were in Switzerland on World Cup qualification duty with Ireland.

Brian O'Neil, the Bedlington Terrier revered at Turf Moor

The 19th game of the season brought the seventh draw as the Clarets were held 1-1 by Wolves as a succession of chances went begging, incredibly only three more draws followed in the remaining 23 matches, but it was the same old story at Villa Park as the team suffered its eighth away defeat.

Burnley Football Club was back on the front pages as the Board refused the transfer of 100 shares to businessman Eric Cookson who asked: "Are they afraid of opposition?"

That rumpus was followed by a 5-1 thumping by champions Liverpool but in their next game the Clarets looked anything other than relegation candidates as Lochhead hit a hat-trick in a 4-2 win at Blackpool. There had been four changes to the line-up that day and, incredibly, by the half-way stage in the season there had been 53 changes, although in the days of a strict 2-3-5 formation a share of those had been positional.

Ralph Coates made his debut in a 3-1 win against Sheffield United and it was a very happy Clarets' Christmas as Fulham were beaten twice to make it four straight wins. Irvine bagged seven goals in those four games, including a Boxing Day hat-trick.The run came to an end with defeat at Everton in the first game of 1965.

The players prepared for their FA Cup opener against Brentford by sweating it out in the 250°F heat of a Finnish sauna in Darwen. A 1-1 Turf Moor draw was followed by a 2-0 win in the replay as Irvine scored with two perfect headers.

For the first time all season there were no players on the injured list as winning ways returned in the league with a 2-0 defeat of Birmingham and then shares were back on the front page.

Former vice-chairman Luther Wilkinson, father-in-law of Jimmy McIlroy, again tried to transfer 100 shares, but was again refused permission. On this occasion the prospective purchaser was a 33-year-old company director from Brinscall near Chorley called Kenneth Bates!

A 3-2 defeat at West Ham United was followed by a 1-1 draw at Reading in the FA Cup. Lochhead won the replay with a goal six minutes from time to earn Burnley the right to play Manchester United at Old Trafford in the fifth round.

Burnley had all the possession but none of the goals as they slipped back into the old routine with defeat at home to West Bromwich Albion and Les Latcham made his senior debut in the 3-2 defeat at Old Trafford which was a dress rehearsal for the following weekend's cup clash.

The players warmed up for that cup date with a return to the Darwen sauna and a game of golf at Clitheroe, but it did not work. As McNee summed it up in the Burnley Express it was a bad day for the Clarets: "For sensational, bitter, sickening defeat there never has been anything to compare with the way the Clarets bit the fifth round dust at Old Trafford." It is easy to see his point as Burnley had been within five minutes of the quarter-finals before United scored twice to knock them out.

Irvine took his tally to 18 goals in 23 games with a double in a niggardly match at Ewood which saw Burnley win 4-1 and wins against Arsenal and Sheffield Wednesday followed.

Near neighbours Nelson suffered a blow in March. They had been trying to get enough money together to get McIlroy as player-manager for the following season but the former Turf favourite opted to stay in first class football for another season.

After 194 consecutive league and cup appearances, Blacklaw missed the game at Leicester after sustaining a rib injury in the 5-1 mauling at Leeds. Harry Thomson saved a penalty as Burnley won 1-0 and kept his place for the remainder of the season.

Burnley finished the season with an unbeaten run of eight games to sit 12th in the table. It was the first time since 1952 they had finished outside the top half of the table but they at least signed off in style as Lochhead hit five in the 6-2 drubbing of Chelsea.

Lochhead finished with 21 goals in 36 games, Irvine 22 in 32 and both scored three in the FA Cup. It was a partnership that was starting to make people sit up and pay attention.

Both were, of course, products of the club's youth system. And that system also earned a reward as the FA chose Burnley to represent England in an under-21 international tournament in West Germany.

Willie Irvine (9) and Willie Morgan
celebrate a goal by the Irishman at Ewood Park

Wins over Ajax, Auswahl Marl and Juventus saw Burnley through to the final where they lost to Red Star Belgrade.

Jimmy Robson had been sold to Blackpool in the latter stages of the season and there was more money in the bank as David Walker went to Southampton and John Price to Stockport County.

But Gordon Harris had a transfer request turned down and was hit by another blow as he heard he would be banned for the first two weeks of the new season as he had been cautioned twice in the 1964-65 campaign!

1964-65 - First Division

		P	W	D	L	F	A	Pts
1	Manchester U	42	26	9	7	89	39	61
2	Leeds U	42	26	9	7	83	52	61
3	Chelsea	42	24	8	10	89	54	56
4	Everton	42	17	15	10	69	60	49
5	Nottingham F	42	17	13	12	71	67	47
6	Tottenham H	42	19	7	16	87	71	45
7	Liverpool	42	17	10	15	67	73	44
8	Sheffield W	42	16	11	15	57	55	43
9	West Ham U	42	19	4	19	82	71	42
10	Blackburn R	42	16	10	16	83	79	42
11	Stoke C	42	16	10	16	67	66	42
12	BURNLEY	42	16	10	16	70	70	42
13	Arsenal	42	17	7	18	69	75	41
14	West Bromwich A	42	13	13	16	70	65	39
15	Sunderland	42	14	9	19	64	74	37
16	Aston Villa	42	16	5	21	57	82	37
17	Blackpool	42	12	11	19	67	78	35
18	Leicester C	42	11	13	18	69	85	35
19	Sheffield U	42	12	11	19	50	64	35
20	Fulham	42	11	12	19	60	78	34
21	Wolverhampton W	42	13	4	25	59	89	30
22	Birmingham C	42	8	11	23	64	96	27

1964-65

Manager : Harry Potts

Division One (12th)

		Date			Opponents	Result		h/t	Goalscorers/times	Opp. goal times
	1	Aug	22	h	BLACKPOOL	D	2-2	2-1	Lochhead 21, Irvine 34	12, 80
	2		25	h	TOTTENHAM H	D	2-2	2-1	Irvine 8, Towers 29	37, 63
	3		29	a	Sheffield U	L	0-2	0-1		32, 77
	4	Sep	2	a	Tottenham H	L	1-4	1-2	Towers 40	20, 34, 52, 82
	5		5	h	EVERTON	D	1-1	1-0	O'Neil 29p	47
	6		8	h	NOTTINGHAM F	D	2-2	1-1	Irvine 1, Bellamy 89	24, 84
	7		12	a	Birmingham C	L	1-2	0-2	Morgan 50	12, 22p
	8		15	a	Nottingham F	L	1-3	1-2	Lochhead 41p	5, 37, 88
	9		19	h	WEST HAM U	W	3-2	2-1	Pointer 15, Lochhead 34, Towers 78	20, 79
	10		23	a	Sheffield W	L	1-5	0-5	Lochhead 53	26, 35, 36, 37, 45
	11		26	a	West Bromwich A	W	2-1	1-0	Irvine (2) 12, 66	81
	12	Oct	6	h	MANCHESTER U	D	0-0	0-0		
	13		10	h	BLACKBURN R	D	1-1	0-0	Lochhead 86p	82p
Burnley's 2500th League game	14		17	a	Arsenal	L	2-3	0-2	Angus (2) 60, 65	3, 23, 67
	15		24	h	LEEDS U	L	0-1	0-1		25
	16		31	a	Chelsea	W	1-0	0-0	Irvine 51	
	17	Nov	7	h	LEICESTER C	W	2-1	2-0	Elder 17, Miller 30	65
Pointer's last game	18		14	a	Sunderland	L	2-3	1-2	Lochhead 6, Bellamy 73	41, 43, 60
	19		21	h	WOLVERHAMPTON W	D	1-1	1-1	Lochhead 43	34
	20		28	a	Aston Villa	L	0-1	0-0		49
	21	Dec	5	h	LIVERPOOL	L	1-5	0-1	Price 53	34, 72, 77, 85, 89
	22		12	a	Blackpool	W	4-2	2-1	Lochhead (3) 6, 55, 61, Irvine 35	25, 89
	23		19	h	SHEFFIELD U	W	3-1	1-1	Elder 40p, Irvine (2) 75, 80	18
	24		26	h	FULHAM	W	4-0	1-0	Irvine (3) 44, 50, 76, Todd 89	
	25		28	a	Fulham	W	1-0	1-0	Irvine 12	
	26	Jan	2	a	Everton	L	1-2	0-2	Harris 79	23, 36
	27		16	h	BIRMINGHAM C	W	2-0	1-0	Irvine 42, Harris 68	
	28		23	a	West Ham U	L	2-3	2-2	Lochhead 32, Irvine 38	17, 44, 60
Robson's last game	29	Feb	6	h	WEST BROMWICH A	L	0-1	0-1		26
	30		13	a	Manchester U	L	2-3	0-2	Walker 46, Irvine 88	8, 32, 51
	31		24	a	Blackburn R	W	4-1	2-0	Irvine (2) 40, 89, Elder 44, O'Neil 80	85
	32		27	h	ARSENAL	W	2-1	2-0	Bellamy 15, O'Neil 19	64
	33	Mar	13	h	SHEFFIELD W	W	4-1	2-0	Lochhead (2) 9, 69, Irvine 28, Morgan 51	76
	34		15	a	Leeds U	L	1-5	1-1	Morgan 24	37, 51, 65, 76, 87
	35		20	a	Leicester C	W	2-0	2-0	Coates 5, Irvine 10	
	36		27	h	SUNDERLAND	D	0-0	0-0		
	37	Apr	3	a	Wolverhampton W	W	2-1	1-1	Lochhead 6, Latcham 72	38
	38		10	h	ASTON VILLA	D	2-2	1-1	Elder 7p, Lochhead 71	8, 86
	39		17	a	Liverpool	D	1-1	0-0	Lochhead 46	52
	40		19	a	Stoke C	L	0-2	0-0		60, 70
	41		20	h	STOKE C	W	1-0	0-0	Irvine 78	
	42		24	h	CHELSEA	W	6-2	4-1	Lochhead (5) 1, 16, 44, 67, 89, Irvine 19	34, 86

FA Cup

				Opponents	Result		h/t	Goalscorers/times	Opp. goal times
3	Jan	9	h	BRENTFORD	D	1-1	0-0	Irvine 57	62
rep		12	a	Brentford	W	2-0	1-0	Irvine (2) 12, 83	
4		30	a	Reading	D	1-1	1-0	Lochhead 14	75
rep	Feb	2	h	READING	W	1-0	0-0	Lochhead 84	
5		20	a	Manchester U	L	1-2	1-0	Lochhead 17	84, 85

Final, Liverpool 2-1 Leeds U, after extra time, at Wembley.

Details of other first team games elsewhere.

Att.	Pos	Blacklaw	Angus	Elder	O'Neil	Talbut	Miller	Morgan	Lochhead	Irvine	Harris	Towers	Walker	F Smith	Robson	Price	Bellamy	Pointer	Todd	Buxton	Coates	Latcham	H Thomson	Merrington	
15,773		1	2	3	4	5	6	7	8	9	10	11													1
21,661		1	2		6	5	3	7	8	9	10	11	4												2
13,831	14	1	2		4	5	6	7		9	10			3	8	11									3
42,326		1	2		6	5	3	7	8	9	10	11	4												4
23,703	18	1	2		6	5	3	7	8	9	10	11	4												5
13,420		1	2	3	6	5		7		9	10	11	4				8								6
16,890	18	1	2	3	6	5		7	9		10	11	4				8								7
27,331		1	2	3	6	5		7	9		10	11	4				8								8
13,541	17	1	2	3	6		5	7	9			11	4		10			8							9
16,604		1	2	3	6		5	7	9			11	4		10			8							10
15,863	15	1	2	3		5	6	7	9	8		11					10		4						11
31,056		1	2	3		5	6	7	9	8		11					10		4						12
21,199	17	1	2	3		5	6	7	9	8		10				11			4						13
24,962	18	1	2			5	6	7	9	8						11	10		4	3					14
24,371	18	1		3		5	6	7	9	8				2		11	10		4						15
29,040	17	1		3		5	6	7	8	9			4	2		11	10								16
13,780	17	1		3		5	6	7	8	9			4	2		11	10								17
36,102	18	1			4	5	6	7	8					2		11	10	9		3					18
13,651	16	1	2	3	4	5	6	7	8	9	11						10								19
18,177	18	1	2	3	4	5	6	7	8		11				9		10								20
12,479	18	1	2	3	4	5	6	7	9		10					11	8								21
11,000	18	1		3	6		5		8	9	10	7		2		11			4						22
10,295	17	1		3	6		5			9		7		2		11	10		4		8				23
15,602		1		3	6		5		8	9	10	7		2		11			4						24
10,162		1		3	6		5		8	9	10			2		11	7		4						25
42,177	15	1		3	6		5		8	9	10	7		2		11			4						26
9,971	13	1		3	4	5	6	7	8	9	10			2			11								27
25,490	14	1	3		4	5	6	7	8	9	10	11		2											28
12,902	14	1	2	3	4	5	6	7	8		10				9		11								29
39,135	15	1		3	4		5			9	10	7	6	2			8					11			30
15,340		1	2	3	4	5	6		8	9		7					10					11			31
12,744	13	1	2		4	5	6	7	8	9							10			3		11			32
12,362	13	1	2	3	4	5	6	7	8	9	11						10								33
38,506		1		3	10	5	6	7	8	9			4						2		11				34
11,929	12			3	4	5	6	7	8	9							10		2		11		1		35
13,303	12			3	4	5	6	7	8	9	11						10		2				1		36
16,481	11			3	4	5	6	7	8		10								2		9	11	1		37
10,105	11			3	4	5	6	7	8	9	10								2		11		1		38
30,004	12			3	4	5	6	7	8	9	10	11		2									1		39
19,801				3	6		5	7	8	9	10	11		2					4				1		40
13,398				3	6		5	7	8	9	10			2					4		11		1		41
15,213	12			2	4		6	7	8	9	10									3	11		1	5	42
Appearances		34	22	34	35	31	39	35	38	33	27	21	12	16	5	13	23	3	17	4	7	4	8	1	
Goals (70)			2	4	3		1	3	21	22	2	3	1			1	3	1	1		1	1			

Att.	Pos	Blacklaw	Angus	Elder	O'Neil	Talbut	Miller	Morgan	Lochhead	Irvine	Harris	Towers	Walker	F Smith	Robson	Price	Bellamy	Pointer	Todd	Buxton	Coates	Latcham	H Thomson	Merrington	
15,100		1		3	6		5		8	9	10	7	4	2		11									3
30,448		1		3	4	5	6		8	9	10	7		2			11								rep
17,872		1		3	4	5	6		8	9	10	7		2			11								4
20,591		1		3	4	5	6	7	8		10	11		2	9										rep
54,000		1		3	4	5	6		8	9	10			2			7					11			5
Appearances		5		5	5	4	5	1	5	4	5	4	1	5	1	1	3					1			
Goals (6)											3	3													

1965-66

The 1965-66 season was one that promised much. On face value it did not live up to expectations. But it was a season to yield a firm place in the history books and produce some statistics that have yet to be repeated.

Willie Irvine set a new post-War goalscoring record of 29 league goals. No-one was to hit 20 in a season for 26 years until Michael Conroy swept all before him as the Clarets won the Fourth Division in 1992.

Irvine scored four hat-tricks in the season. Even the legendary George Beel never managed more than three.

Irvine became the first Claret to ever score a hat-trick in an away tie in the FA Cup and Andy Lochhead scored five in a different FA Cup tie, no Burnley player had ever gone nap in that competition and he was the club's first player to ever score five in two games.

Burnley were up for the cup in two competitions. Having boycotted the competition for four seasons, they were back in the League Cup and chairman Bob Lord even suggested that the League should make entry compulsory!

In the end, however, the season was to end in disappointment as the league campaign tailed off to see the Clarets finish third and neither cup brought much joy.

They did, however, do enough to earn a place in the Inter-Cities Fairs Cup the following season. That, in itself, was reward for a team that many at the time actually rated as better than the First Division champions of six years earlier.

Five weeks before the start of the new campaign, Harry Potts welcomed the decision to allow one named substitute to be used in each game to replace an injured player. "The idea is a good one in theory. I just hope that it is not abused, and I don't think it will be," he told the Burnley Express.

Before the season kicked off Alex Elder was named as skipper in place of Brian Miller, the first team returned undefeated from a summer trip to Austria and Switzerland and a profit of £33,000 was recorded on the previous 12 months.

A draw at Chelsea was followed by a 3-1 win over Blackpool in which Irvine got his record-breaking run underway. The 2-2 draw against Arsenal saw Ian Towers as the first substitute ever used in league action and Irvine added two more to his tally as Blackpool were again beaten 3-1 to leave the Clarets second in the table on goal average behind Leeds.

Blackpool captain Jimmy Armfield paid the Clarets the following tribute after the double defeat: "Burnley's scouting system must be the best in the country; their coaching of players seems to have very little wrong with it. All in all a perfect set up for here is a club that has got to the top the hard way."

Ray Pointer had hardly been in the team for the previous two seasons and following a transfer to Bury he proved he still knew where the target was by banging a hat-trick in against Derby County while the share-transfer saga of the previous year rumbled on at the club's annual meeting. It was to raise its head again later in the season when construction company chief Eric Cookson threatened legal action but Lord said: "The directors will not lose a minute's sleep."

Goodison witnessed the first defeat of the season, but the Clarets bounced back with a 4-1 win over Northampton as Irvine got his first treble of the season. Unfortunately, plain clothes police officers were on duty on the terraces to try and catch "match hooligans" who had thrown things on to the pitch during the Arsenal game and the next home game saw Manchester United supporters cause a rumpus after their side lost 3-0. Seven appeared in court.

A thunderous, unstoppable volley from Elder sealed a 2-1 win at Northampton and with 12 points from eight games Burnley were top by a point from Leeds, Stoke, West Brom and Sheffield United.

Gordon 'Bomber' Harris
over 300 senior games in claret and blue

They lost 3-2 against Newcastle in a game which had Lord fuming over the Geordies' "rough house" tactics but the return to League Cup action was more profitable as Andy Lochhead hit a hat-trick and Doncaster were swept aside.

West Brom had taken over at the top but lost 2-0 at the Turf. It was Irvine's 50th league appearance and he had netted 37 goals in those games, but then the Clarets lost top spot themselves when their recent good run against Blackburn ended in a miserable 4-1 defeat on home soil.

The last 16 of the League Cup beckoned after a 3-2 win over Southampton and winning ways returned in the league with success over Leicester and Sheffield United. Next up was a trip to Elland Road. The 1-1 scoreline did not reflect the quality of a game that had everything and even referee Keith Howley joined in the applause at the end!

When Burnley beat West Ham 3-1 they went back to the top of the table after 15 games. Irvine and Lochhead got the goals between them and by that stage of the season had 23 of the team's 36 senior goals. Incredibly, it was the first time they had both appeared on the same scoresheet!

Stoke were next to taste defeat in the League Cup and following a 4-0 win over Sunderland at Roker Park Keith McNee in the Burnley Express was compelled to write: "I will go down on record as saying that this is already a better Burnley team than the McIlroy-Adamson inspired outfit which won the Championship in 1960."

The first major setback of the season saw the Clarets dumped out of the League Cup at Peterborough but they were back on song in the league by beating Aston Villa to set up a showdown with leaders Liverpool, but they struggled with injuries at Anfield and lost 2-1. The build-up to that game saw a 1-1 draw at Chorley in the Lancashire Senior Cup in a game only notable for a goal from goalkeeper Harry Thomson with a near gale at his back. Burnley went on to win the competition for the fifth time in seven years.

At the half-way stage in the season, Burnley had 30 points from 21 games and trailed Liverpool by two with a game in hand. Irvine was half-way to the record with 14 league goals. They suffered defeat against Stoke and then avenged it over Christmas and started the New Year with a 2-0 win over Blackburn at Ewood during which Willie Morgan was sent off for aiming a flying kick at centre forward Mike England. He was the first Claret for almost 14 years to be sent off, the last one being Billy Elliott for the infamous "look of intent" at Maine Road in March 1952.

Mixed results followed in the league and then the FA Cup campaign started at Dean Court with Field Marshal Viscount Montgomery an interested spectator. That game finished 1-1, skipper Elder received a letter from the war hero before the replay telling him to hit the Cherries for six and they went one better with a 7-0 win that saw Lochhead hit five.

After two league defeats, the rot was stopped with a draw at Arsenal, but the return to London the following week was not as fruitful as they lost 4-3 in the FA Cup at Tottenham despite Irvine's hat-trick.

It was the same old story in the league as the Clarets led against Everton but failed to press home the advantage and drew 1-1 to leave themselves nine points behind Liverpool with two games in hand. Things got worse following a 4-2 defeat at Old Trafford but then Adam Blacklaw had his best game of the season as the Clarets scored twice in 90 seconds to win at The Hawthorns.

Irvine's fourth hat-trick of the season came in the 4-1 win over Nottingham Forest and he scored a late equaliser against West Ham in what was Brian O'Neil's 100th league appearance.

Irvine then scored the only goal of the game as Sunderland were beaten again and then Pointer's post-War record was equalled as he bagged both in a 2-1 win over Sheffield Wednesday. The record was all his as he scored in the defeat at Aston Villa and he added his last goal of the season in the 2-0 win over Liverpool.

The season ended with a win at Spurs, a home defeat against Leeds, Montgomery again an interested observer, and victory at Hillsborough. It was all good enough for third place and the Clarets were confirmed as one of the English teams to partake in the following season's Fairs Cup. They were originally drawn to play Hanover who, interestingly, they had already agreed to meet in a pre-season game.

David Merrington
valuable member of the Clarets' squad

The campaign ended with an under-21s team again on the continent for an international tournament and this time they went one better. Having beaten Fortuna Dusseldorf (3-1), Cologne (3-0) and Inter Milan (1-0) they then beat Barcelona (2-1) in the final.

1965-66 - First Division

		P	W	D	L	F	A	Pts
1	Liverpool	42	26	9	7	79	34	61
2	Leeds U	42	23	9	10	79	38	55
3	BURNLEY	42	24	7	11	79	47	55
4	Manchester U	42	18	15	9	84	59	51
5	Chelsea	42	22	7	13	65	53	51
6	West Bromwich A	42	19	12	11	91	69	50
7	Leicester C	42	21	7	14	80	65	49
8	Tottenham H	42	16	12	14	75	66	44
9	Sheffield U	42	16	11	15	56	59	43
10	Stoke C	42	15	12	15	65	64	42
11	Everton	42	15	11	16	56	62	41
12	West Ham U	42	15	9	18	70	83	39
13	Blackpool	42	14	9	19	55	65	37
14	Arsenal	42	12	13	17	62	75	37
15	Newcastle U	42	14	9	19	50	63	37
16	Aston Villa	42	15	6	21	69	80	36
17	Sheffield W	42	14	8	20	56	66	36
18	Nottingham F	42	14	8	20	56	72	36
19	Sunderland	42	14	8	20	51	72	36
20	Fulham	42	14	7	21	67	85	35
21	Northampton T	42	10	13	19	55	92	33
22	Blackburn R	42	8	4	30	57	88	20

1965-66

Manager : Harry Potts

Division One (3rd)

No	Date		Venue	Opponents	Result		h/t	Goalscorers/times	Opp. goal times
1	Aug	21	a	Chelsea	D	1-1	0-1	Bellamy 46	39
2		24	h	BLACKPOOL	W	3-1	3-0	Lochhead 22, Bellamy 24, Irvine 33	73
3		28	h	ARSENAL	D	2-2	2-1	Elder 19, Lochhead 24	33, 75
4		30	a	Blackpool	W	3-1	3-1	Irvine (2) 16, 40, O'Neil 27	34
5	Sep	4	a	Everton	L	0-1	0-0		60
6		7	h	NORTHAMPTON T	W	4-1	1-0	Foley 18og, Irvine (3) 58, 81, 89	65
7		11	h	MANCHESTER U	W	3-0	1-0	Harris (2) 6, 47, Elder 89p	
8		15	a	Northampton T	W	2-1	0-0	Irvine 55, Elder 86	52
9		18	a	Newcastle U	L	2-3	1-1	Lochhead (2) 14, 82	8, 70, 76
10		25	h	WEST BROMWICH A	W	2-0	1-0	Lochhead 33, O'Neil 58	
11	Oct	9	h	BLACKBURN	L	1-4	1-3	Lochhead 28	16, 18, 30, 69
12		16	a	Leicester C	W	1-0	0-0	Morgan 51	
13		23	h	SHEFFIELD U	W	2-0	1-0	Harris 36, Lochhead 88	
14		30	a	Leeds U	D	1-1	0-0	Irvine 48	47
15	Nov	6	h	WEST HAM U	W	3-1	1-1	Irvine (2) 37, 85, Lochhead 74	40
16		11	a	Sunderland	W	4-0	2-0	Harris 27, Coates (2) 43, 83, Irvine 59	
17		20	h	ASTON VILLA	W	3-1	0-1	Lochhead (2) 63, 84, Irvine 64	36
18		27	a	Liverpool	L	1-2	0-1	Irvine 76	45, 62
19	Dec	4	h	TOTTENHAM H	D	1-1	1-0	Irvine 39	63
20		11	a	Fulham	W	5-2	2-1	Irvine (3) 13, 40, 55, O'Neil 57, Miller 84p	26og, 75
21		18	h	LEICESTER C	W	4-2	1-1	Lochhead (2) 7, 82, Elder 70p, Miller 80	22, 52
22		27	a	Stoke C	L	1-3	1-0	Coates 5	70, 73, 81
23		28	h	STOKE C	W	4-1	0-1	Irvine 47, Harris 55, O'Neil 66, Bellamy 77	14
24	Jan	1	a	Blackburn R	W	2-0	1-0	Irvine 19, Harris 69	
25		8	h	FULHAM	W	1-0	1-0	Angus 37	
26		15	a	Sheffield U	L	1-2	0-0	Bellamy 79	51, 61
27		29	h	CHELSEA	L	1-2	1-1	Angus 44	45, 54
28	Feb	5	a	Arsenal	D	1-1	0-1	Latcham 70	17
29		19	h	EVERTON	D	1-1	0-0	Elder 55p	86
30		26	a	Manchester U	L	2-4	1-2	Lochhead 8, Irvine 50	3, 41, 63, 66
31	Mar	8	a	Nottingham F	L	0-1	0-0		82
32		12	h	NEWCASTLE U	W	1-0	0-0	Morgan 55	
33		19	a	West Bromwich A	W	2-1	0-1	Elder 67, Harris 68	25
34		26	h	NOTTINGHAM F	W	4-1	2-1	Irvine (3) 1, 24, 50, Lochhead 82	15
35	Apr	2	a	West Ham U	D	1-1	0-0	Irvine 74	60
36		9	h	SUNDERLAND	W	1-0	1-0	Irvine 45	
37		11	h	SHEFFIELD W	W	2-1	0-1	Irvine (2) 59, 72	30
38		16	a	Aston Villa	L	1-2	1-1	Irvine 3	24, 59
39		23	h	LIVERPOOL	W	2-0	1-0	Irvine 7, Coates 49	
40		30	a	Tottenham H	W	1-0	0-0	Lochhead 79	
41	May	7	h	LEEDS U	L	0-1	0-0		60og
42		9	a	Sheffield W	W	2-0	0-0	Coates 49, Latcham 63	

FA Cup

Rd	Date		Venue	Opponents	Result		h/t	Goalscorers/times	Opp. goal times
3	Jan	22	a	Bournemouth & B A	D	1-1	1-0	Irvine 18	76
rep		25	h	BOURNEMOUTH & B A	W	7-0	5-0	Lochhead (5) 13, 19, 29, 44, 58, Irvine 22, Harris 86	
4	Feb	12	a	Tottenham H	L	3-4	2-1	Irvine (3) 1, 5, 58	35, 50, 71, 87

Final, Everton 3-2 Sheffield W, at Wembley.

League Cup

Note	Rd	Date		Venue	Opponents	Result		h/t	Goalscorers/times	Opp. goal times
Towers' last game	2	Sep	22	a	Doncaster R	W	4-0	4-0	Lochhead (3) 24, 38, 40, Towers 45	
	3	Oct	13	h	SOUTHAMPTON	W	3-2	1-0	Irvine (2) 6, 79, Harris 82	75, 85
	4	Nov	3	a	Stoke C	D	0-0	0-0		
after extra time, 1-1 at 90m	rep		9	h	STOKE C	W	2-1	0-0	Coates 69, Irvine 92	89
	5		17	a	Peterborough U	L	0-4			56, 65, 72og, 79

Final, West Bromwich A 5-3 West Ham U, on aggregate.

Att.	Pos	H Thomson	Angus	Elder	O'Neil	Talbut	Miller	Morgan	Lochhead	Irvine	Bellamy	Coates	Latcham	Towers	Harris	Merrington	Blacklaw	Buxton	Todd	Kinsella	F Smith		
34,067		1	2	3	4	5	6	7	8	9	10	11											1
15,208		1	2	3	4	5	6		8	9	10	7	11										2
16,741	2	1	2	3	4	5	6	7	8	9*	10	11		S*									3
17,723		1	2	3	4	5	6	7	8	9	S*	11*			10								4
44,633	7	1	2	3	4	5	6	7		9	8	11			10								5
14,792		1	2	3	4	5	6	7	8	9	10				11								6
30,137	top	1	2	3	4	5	6	7	8	9			11		10								7
19,336		1	2	3	4	5	6	7	8	9	11				10								8
35,883	3	1	2	3	4	5	6	7	8	9	11				10								9
20,487	top	1	2	3	4	5	6	7	8	9	11				10								10
23,198	5	1	2	3	4	5	6	7	8	9	11				10								11
17,978	4	1	2	3	4	5	6	7	8	9		11			10								12
20,693	2	1	2	3	4		6	7	8	9		11			10	5							13
41,628	2		2	3	4		6	7		9	8	11			10	5	1						14
17,100	top		2	3	4		6	7	8	9		11			10	5	1						15
38,224	top		2		4		6	7	8	9		11			10	5	1	3					16
14,281	2		2*	3	4		5	7	8	9		11			10		1		6	S*			17
50,282	2			3	4		5	7		9	8	11*			10		1		6	S*	2		18
19,509	2		2		4		6	7	8	9		11			10	5	1	3					19
12,092	2		2	3*	4		6	7	8	9		11			10	5	1		S*				20
13,837	2		2	3	4		6	7	8	9		11			10	5	1						21
35,946			2	3	4		6	7	8	9		11			10	5	1						22
23,214			2	3	4		5	7		9	8	11			10		1		6				23
28,013	2		2	3	4		5	7		9	8	11			10		1		6				24
17,202	2		2	3	4*		5	7	S*	9	8	11			10		1		6				25
16,072	2		2	3	4		5	7	8	9	11				10		1		6				26
23,825	2		2	3		4	6	7	8	9		11			10	5	1						27
28,652	2		2	3			5		8	9	6	11	7		10	4	1						28
19,670	2	1	2	3	4		5	7	8	9		11			10	6							29
50,188	4	1	2		4		5	7	8	9		11			10	6		3					30
28,246			2	3	4		5		8	9		7*	11		10	6	1		S*				31
16,259	3		2	3	4		5	7		9		8	11		10		1		6				32
18,747	2		2	3	4		5	7	8	9		11			10		1		6				33
10,027	2		2	3	4		5	7	8	9		11			10		1		6				34
17,665	2		2	3	4		5	7	8	9		11			10		1		6				35
15,699	2			3	4		5	7	8	9		11			10		1		6		2		36
17,874				3	4		5	7	8	9*		11			10		1		6	S*	2		37
14,100	2		2	3	4		5	7	8	9		11			10		1		6				38
36,530	2		2	3	4		5	7	8	9		11			10		1		6				39
29,337	2		2	3	4		5	7	8	9		11			10		1		6				40
33,035	2		2	3	4		5	7	8	9		11			10		1		6				41
20,348	3		2	3			5	7*		9	4	11	8		10		1		6	S*			42
Appearances		15	39	39	39	13	42	39	34	42	17	35	6		39	13	27	3	17		3		
Apps as sub									1		1			1					2	4			
Goals (79)			2	6	4		2	2	15	29	4	5	2		7							1	og

Att.	Pos	H Thomson	Angus	Elder	O'Neil	Talbut	Miller	Morgan	Lochhead	Irvine	Bellamy	Coates	Latcham	Towers	Harris	Merrington	Blacklaw	Buxton	Todd	Kinsella	F Smith	
16,082			2	3	4		6	7	8	9		11			10	5	1					3
21,743			2	3		4	6	7	8	9		11			10	5	1					rep
50,611			2	3	4	5	6	7	8	9		11			10		1					4
Appearances			3	3	2	2	3	3	3	3		3			3	2	3					
Goals (11)									5	5					1							

Att.	Pos	H Thomson	Angus	Elder	O'Neil	Talbut	Miller	Morgan	Lochhead	Irvine	Bellamy	Coates	Latcham	Towers	Harris	Merrington	Blacklaw	Buxton	Todd	Kinsella	F Smith	
24,988		1	2	3	4	5	6	7	9		10		11	8								2
10,868		1	2	3	4	5	6	7	8	9		11			10							3
14,400			2	3	4		6	7		9	8	11			10	5	1					4
13,666			2	3	4		6	7	8	9		11			10	5	1					rep
14,796			2		4		6	7	8	9		11			10	5	1	3				5
Appearances		2	5	4	5	2	5	5	4	4	2	4	1	1	4	3	3	1				
Goals (9)									3	3		1		1	1							

1966-67

8 February 1967, should go down in Burnley FC folklore as a night to remember for goalkeeper Harry Thomson. In Napoli's San Paulo Stadium he made 13 breathtaking saves, one from the penalty spot, as the Clarets drew 0-0 to protect their 3-0 lead from the first leg.

Afterwards he was described in the Daily Express as 'a god in a green jersey', but the action on the pitch is barely remembered.

This Inter-Cities Fairs Cup clash remains The Battle of Naples in the memory of all those who witnessed it.

The first leg at Turf Moor had been X-certificate stuff and Napoli's Dino Panzanato was dismissed.

Ralph Coates had given Burnley the lead after just two minutes and they never looked back. In the end they should have won more convincingly.

In the three weeks between the two legs the Italian press whipped up Fairs Cup fever with sentiments like 'from Lancashire where studs are made out of rose petals ... to Naples where visiting players are put through a mincing machine at the end of the game and their remains are roasted on a spit'.

The game was a nightmare for the Burnley players, but they stood tall. An accidental clash left Les Latcham with a nasty head wound. His sentiments to trainer George Bray were simply 'hurry up, I want to get back out there'.

Things got ugly towards the end of the game. Omar Sivori, still seething from being left out of the first leg, elbowed Dave Merrington in the stomach and then left the ball to have a go at Latcham.

At the end of the game Thomson, after enjoying in his finest hour, offered a friendly handshake to Orlando who promptly spat in his face. Substitute goalkeeper Adam Blacklaw leapt in to split them up and was pounced on by a dozen men. They kicked and hacked at him; he managed to throw one down the stairs and escape but was then approached by another man who revealed a gun under his coat.

In the end an armoured lorry, nine jeep-loads of militia and a dozen police motor-cyclists formed a protective convoy to get the team coach to the airport. The visiting press were whisked away in taxis with police outriders to make sure they got out alive!

Having experienced European football after their 1959-60 title and then been denied Fairs Cup action subsequently, Burnley had pined for a return to the top club stage. This was hardly the headlines they had been looking for.

And it was all a far cry from the start of the season.

The annual meeting took place before the big kick-off and chairman Bob Lord revealed plans to turn Turf Moor into a sports, social and recreation centre. "Burnley FC will not only entertain people on the field, but in many other aspects as well," he said.

Fans were keen to see the team back in action and before the start of the new campaign the club had sold five times as many season tickets as it had at the same point in 1965. Lord then revealed plans to demolish the Bee Hole End and replace it with a stand housing a social centre. Those plans were to be replaced later in the season following an agreement to buy a strip of land of the neighbouring cricket club and replace a terrace with a stand.

The Fairs Cup committee decided to disallow Hannover's entry and they were replaced as Burnley's first round opponents by VFB Stuttgart and on the eve of the season Lord summed up the feeling within the club by saying: "We think we have come out of a three-year period of transition. We believe our potential is now as good as any other First Division club."

Gordon Harris scored a hat-trick as Sheffield United were beaten on the opening day and away wins followed at The Hawthorns and Craven Cottage before the Clarets dropped their first point of the season in a stalemate at home to Fulham.

A 1-1 draw against Leeds, described by Keith McNee in the Burnley Express as 'bitter, bad-tempered and sometimes brutal', led to manager Harry Potts challenging his Leeds counterpart Don Revie to a TV debate about his tactics and following draws against Everton and Manchester United, unbeaten Burnley were joint top after seven games.

Sammy Todd
classy Irish defender

More draws, including the first leg in Stuttgart followed before the Clarets suffered their first defeat of the season in a 4-1 reverse at Old Trafford, but the return to winning ways came in two cups. Stuttgart were despatched 2-0 and then Shrewsbury were 5-0 victims in the League Cup, but Sheffield United avenged their opening day defeat by disposing of the Clarets in the next round.

The news that Ralph Coates had been called up to the England Under 23s meant the club had 11 internationals on their books – Blacklaw, Angus, Elder, Miller, Todd, Irvine and Harris at full international level and Talbut, O'Neil, Lochhead and Coates in the Under 23s.

Coates scored one as Wales were beaten 8-0 and was then one of five different Burnley goalscorers as Leicester bit the Turf Moor dust.

Three headed goals won the day as Burnley triumphed 3-1 in the Stade Olympique against Lausanne and they were safely through to the next round following a 5-0 home win.

The Clarets then came back down to earth with a bump with three straight defeats and Arthur Bellamy broke his leg in the third of those games at Anfield.

More mixed results followed, but the Clarets were still handily placed, fifth in the table five points behind Manchester United, but a double defeat at the hands of Stoke over Christmas saw things starting to slip.

John Talbut was sold to West Brom for £32,000, and his New Year's Eve debut against the Clarets could not have been worse as he scored an own goal and his new side lost 1-5.

Defeats to Leeds and Newcastle were hardly the ideal preparation for the home leg against Naples, but when the Lira-laden Italian giants arrived at Turf Moor Coates scored after just two minutes and Burnley never looked back.

Another league defeat followed, this time at Spurs, and after a home draw, Burnley bowed out of the FA Cup to holders Everton 2-1, goalscorer Willie Irvine breaking his shin at Goodison Park.

On the eve of the trip to Italy, Burnley drew 1-1 at Old Trafford to slip to 12th in the table, but they were back in the top half when Colin Blant scored both goals in a win at Bloomfield Road.

Following a defeat at home to Chelsea, manager Tommy Docherty asked if Burnley would sign his 16-year-old son as an apprentice. Lord described the news as: "One of the finest compliments Burnley Football Club has even been paid."

March, despite witnessing a win over champions Liverpool, saw the end of the line for the Clarets in the race for a European place. Four defeats out of five games meant their only hope was an Inter-Cities Fairs Cup win.

The plane taking the official party to Eintracht Frankfurt for the first leg was struck by lightning over West Germany, but Brian Miller scored in a 1-1 draw and hopes were high of a semi-final place.

But by the middle of April the dream was over. McNee described Burnley as 'lost in a tactical bog' and with 18 minutes to go they were 2-0 down. They needed three to go through, Miller scored once but it was too little to late.

The season was over and when they lost 7-0 at Hillsborough it was their heaviest defeat in a decade.

They finished with a 1-1 draw at Everton, but Harry Potts missed the game as he went to watch Rotherham play Bury at Millmoor. His target at the time, although not officially known, was believed to be inside-forward Frank Casper.

And it looked as though there could be big changes ahead as Alex Elder went on the transfer list at his own request and Potts said that offers would be considered for Blacklaw.

Their busiest and most strenuous season ever saw 55 senior games and the senior squad was again heavily hit by injuries. Things went well in the first half of the season, but in the final 21 games they picked-up just 14 points and finished 14th.

As everyone began to reflect on a season in which Burnley had looked capable of challenging on four fronts, there was another major headline.

Frank Casper arrived and Burnley actually paid out a transfer fee for him. The Turf Moor chequebook had been locked away for a decade, but Casper cost them £27,000. Lord, as ever, was philosophical. Quizzed if the club could afford transfer fees and wages he simply said: "What we can't afford is to go into the Second Division."

Harry Thomson
immortalised as 'a god in a green jersey'

1966-67 - First Division

		P	W	D	L	F	A	Pts
1	Manchester U	42	24	12	6	84	45	60
2	Nottingham F	42	23	10	9	64	41	56
3	Tottenham H	42	24	8	10	71	48	56
4	Leeds U	42	22	11	9	62	42	55
5	Liverpool	42	19	13	10	64	47	51
6	Everton	42	19	10	13	65	46	48
7	Arsenal	42	16	14	12	58	47	46
8	Leicester C	42	18	8	16	78	71	44
9	Chelsea	42	15	14	13	67	62	44
10	Sheffield U	42	16	10	16	52	59	42
11	Sheffield W	42	14	13	15	56	47	41
12	Stoke C	42	17	7	18	63	58	41
13	West Bromwich A	42	16	7	19	77	73	39
14	BURNLEY	42	15	9	18	66	76	39
15	Manchester C	42	12	15	15	43	52	39
16	West Ham U	42	14	8	20	80	84	36
17	Sunderland	42	14	8	20	58	72	36
18	Fulham	42	11	12	19	71	83	34
19	Southampton	42	14	6	22	74	92	34
20	Newcastle U	42	12	9	21	39	81	33
21	Aston Villa	42	11	7	24	54	85	29
22	Blackpool	42	6	9	27	41	76	21

1966-67

Manager : Harry Potts

Division One (14th)

		Date			Opponents	Result		h/t	Goalscorers/times	Opp. goal times
	1	Aug	20	h	SHEFFIELD U	W	4-0	0-0	Harris (3) 55, 79, 85p, Irvine 58	
	2		23	h	FULHAM	W	3-0	1-0	Lochhead 27, Irvine 60, Elder 75p	
	3		27	a	West Bromwich A	W	2-1	1-1	O'Neil (2) 2, 85	35
	4		29	a	Fulham	D	0-0	0-0		
	5	Sep	3	h	LEEDS U	D	1-1	0-1	Harris 46	17
	6		6	a	Everton	D	1-1	0-1	Lochhead 52	30
	7		10	a	Newcastle U	D	1-1	1-1	Harris 24	26
	8		17	h	TOTTENHAM H	D	2-2	2-2	Lochhead (2) 32, 44	28, 38
	9		24	a	Manchester U	L	1-4	1-1	Lochhead 44	39, 50, 87, 89
	10	Oct	1	h	BLACKPOOL	W	1-0	1-0	Irvine 18	
	11		8	a	Chelsea	W	3-1	2-1	Lochhead (2) 3, 43, Morgan 84	19
	12		15	h	LEICESTER C	W	5-2	3-0	Harris 21, Lochhead 31, Irvine 33, Coates 67, Elder 75	58, 82
	13		29	h	MANCHESTER C	L	2-3	0-1	Irvine 59, Morgan 84	34, 70, 87
Talbut's last game	14	Nov	5	a	Leicester C	L	1-5	0-2	Elder 59	4,44,49,67,88
	15		9	a	Liverpool	L	0-2	0-1		4, 90
	16		12	h	SOUTHAMPTON	W	4-1	1-0	Harris (2) 1, 87, Lochhead (2) 47, 65	80
	17		19	a	Sunderland	L	3-4	1-1	Irvine (2) 28, 58, Lochhead 47	44, 65, 76, 79
	18		26	h	ASTON VILLA	W	4-2	0-1	Lochhead (4) 58, 62, 80, 85	22, 79
	19	Dec	3	a	Arsenal	D	0-0	0-0		
	20		10	h	WEST HAM U	W	4-2	2-2	Irvine (2) 9, 77, O'Neil 12, Lochhead 58	21, 43
	21		17	a	Sheffield U	D	1-1	0-1	Irvine 62	27
	22		26	h	STOKE C	L	0-2	0-0		63, 77
Blacklaw's last game	23		27	a	Stoke C	L	3-4	2-2	Irvine 12, Harris (2) 34, 90p	5, 20, 47, 75
	24		31	h	WEST BROMWICH A	W	5-1	4-0	Talbut 4og, Irvine (2) 14, 72, Lochhead (2) 37, 40	81
	25	Jan	7	a	Leeds U	L	1-3	0-0	Coates 86	57, 66, 69
	26		14	h	NEWCASTLE U	L	0-2	0-1		18, 67
	27		21	a	Tottenham H	L	0-2	0-2		43, 44
	28	Feb	4	h	MANCHESTER U	D	1-1	0-1	Harris 89p	33
	29		11	a	Blackpool	W	2-0	0-0	Blant (2) 52, 66	
	30		25	h	CHELSEA	L	1-2	0-1	Blant 82	41, 48
	31	Mar	4	a	Manchester C	L	0-1	0-0		89
	32		18	h	LIVERPOOL	W	1-0	0-0	Latcham 86	
	33		25	a	West Ham U	L	2-3	1-1	Morgan 11, O'Neil 59	13, 63, 68
	34		27	a	Nottingham F	L	1-4	0-2	Latcham 62	1, 40, 70, 80
	35		28	h	NOTTINGHAM F	L	0-2	0-1		22, 81
	36	Apr	1	h	SHEFFIELD W	W	2-0	0-0	Latcham 54, Harris 76	
	37		8	a	Southampton	L	0-4	0-2		37, 38, 54, 86
	38		15	h	SUNDERLAND	W	1-0	1-0	Harris 24	
Miller's last game	39		22	a	Aston Villa	W	1-0	1-0	Withers 12og	
	40		29	h	ARSENAL	L	1-4	1-3	F.Smith 40	18, 32, 43, 61
	41	May	6	a	Sheffield W	L	0-7	0-2		38,44,46,48,54,61,77
Elder's last game	42		13	h	EVERTON	D	1-1	0-0	Blant 72	83p

FA Cup

				Opponents	Result		h/t	Goalscorers/times	Opp. goal times
3	Jan	28	h	EVERTON	D	0-0	0-0		
rep		31	a	Everton	L	1-2	1-1	Irvine 38	20, 75

Final, Tottenham H 2-1 Chelsea, at Wembley.

League Cup

				Opponents	Result		h/t	Goalscorers/times	Opp. goal times
2	Sep	14	a	Shrewsbury T	D	1-1	0-0	Morgan 74	85
rep		29	h	SHREWSBURY T	W	5-0	4-0	Lochhead 3, Talbut 10p, Wood 23og, Hemsley 45og, France 52	
3	Oct	5	a	Sheffield U	L	0-2	0-0		77, 84og

Final, Queens Park R 3-2 West Bromwich A, first League Cup final at Wembley.

Details of other first team games elsewhere.

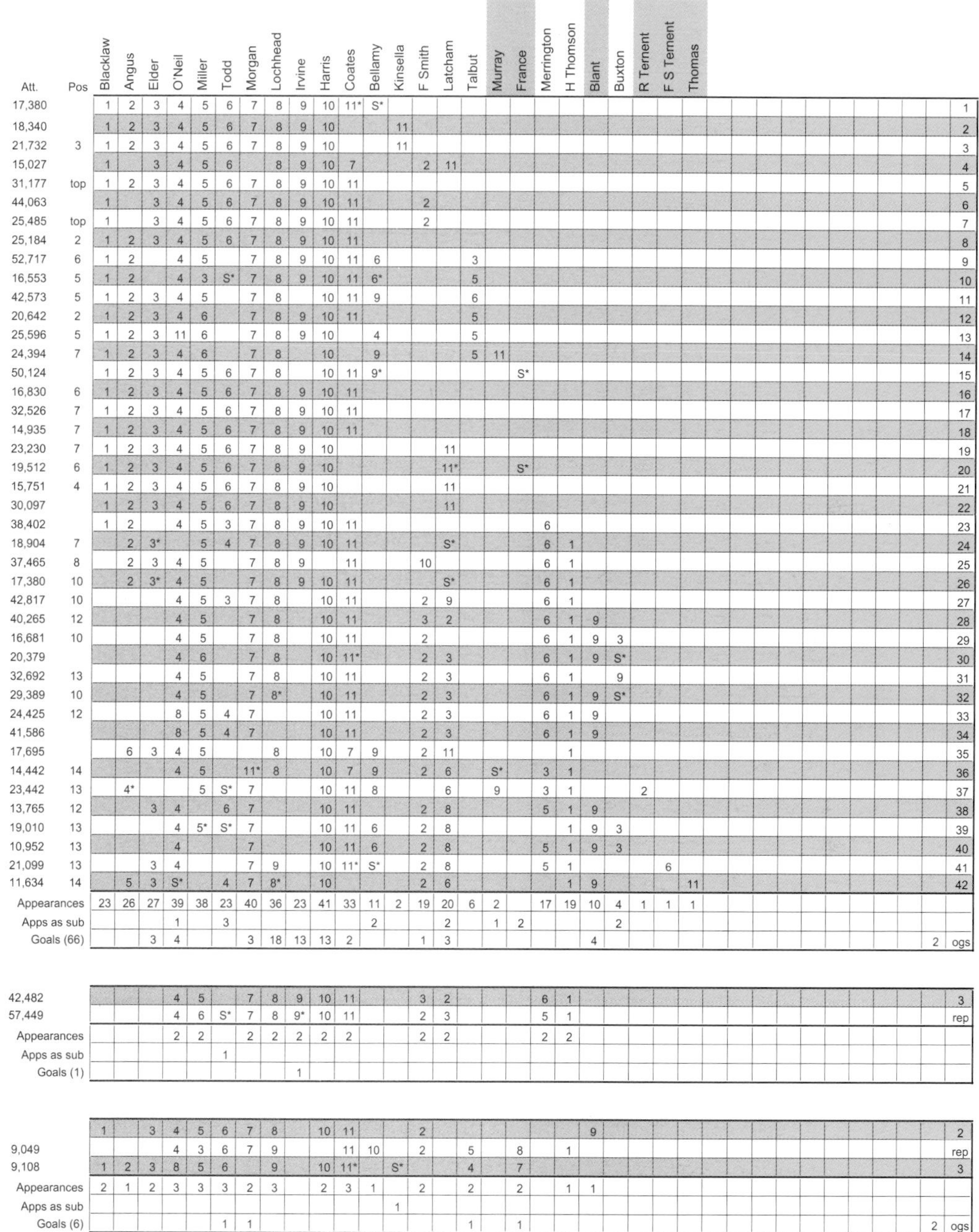

Att.	Pos	Blacklaw	Angus	Elder	O'Neil	Miller	Todd	Morgan	Lochhead	Irvine	Harris	Coates	Bellamy	Kinsella	F Smith	Latcham	Talbut	Murray	France	Merrington	H Thomson	Blant	Buxton	R Ternent	F S Ternent	Thomas		
17,380		1	2	3	4	5	6	7	8	9	10	11*	S*															1
18,340		1	2	3	4	5	6	7	8	9	10			11														2
21,732	3	1	2	3	4	5	6	7	8	9	10			11														3
15,027		1		3	4	5	6		8	9	10	7			2	11												4
31,177	top	1	2	3	4	5	6	7	8	9	10	11																5
44,063		1		3	4	5	6	7	8	9	10	11			2													6
25,485	top	1		3	4	5	6	7	8	9	10	11			2													7
25,184	2	1	2	3	4	5	6	7	8	9	10	11																8
52,717	6	1	2		4	5		7	8	9	10	11	6				3											9
16,553	5	1	2		4	3	S*	7	8	9	10	11	6*				5											10
42,573	5	1	2	3	4	5		7	8		10	11	9				6											11
20,642	2	1	2	3	4	6		7	8	9	10	11					5											12
25,596	5	1	2	3	11	6		7	8	9	10		4				5											13
24,394	7	1	2	3	4	6		7	8		10		9				5	11										14
50,124		1	2	3	4	5	6	7	8		10	11	9*						S*									15
16,830	6	1	2	3	4	5	6	7	8	9	10	11																16
32,526	7	1	2	3	4	5	6	7	8	9	10	11																17
14,935	7	1	2	3	4	5	6	7	8	9	10	11																18
23,230	7	1	2	3	4	5	6	7	8	9	10					11												19
19,512	6	1	2	3	4	5	6	7	8	9	10					11*			S*									20
15,751	4	1	2	3	4	5	6	7	8	9	10					11												21
30,097		1	2	3	4	5	6	7	8	9	10					11												22
38,402		1	2		4	5	3	7	8	9	10	11								6								23
18,904	7		2	3*		5	4	7	8	9	10	11				S*				6	1							24
37,465	8		2	3	4	5		7	8	9		11			10					6	1							25
17,380	10		2	3*	4	5		7	8	9	10	11				S*				6	1							26
42,817	10				4	5	3	7	8		10	11			2	9				6	1							27
40,265	12				4	5		7	8		10	11			3	2				6	1	9						28
16,681	10				4	5		7	8		10	11			2					6	1	9	3					29
20,379					4	6		7	8		10	11*			2	3				6	1	9	S*					30
32,692	13				4	5		7	8		10	11			2	3				6	1		9					31
29,389	10				4	5		7	8*		10	11			2	3				6	1	9	S*					32
24,425	12				8	5	4	7			10	11			2	3				6	1	9						33
41,586					8	5	4	7			10	11			2	3				6	1	9						34
17,695			6	3	4	5			8		10	7	9		2	11					1							35
14,442	14				4	5		11*	8		10	7	9		2	6		S*		3	1							36
23,442	13		4*			5	S*	7			10	11	8			6		9		3	1			2				37
13,765	12			3	4		6	7			10	11			2	8				5	1	9						38
19,010	13				4	5*	S*	7			10	11	6		2	8					1	9	3					39
10,952	13				4			7			10	11	6		2	8				5	1	9	3					40
21,099	13			3	4			7	9		10	11*	S*		2	8				5	1				6			41
11,634	14		5	3	S*		4	7	8*		10				2	6					1	9				11		42
Appearances		23	26	27	39	38	23	40	36	23	41	33	11	2	19	20	6	2		17	19	10	4	1	1	1		
Apps as sub					1		3						2			2		1	2				2					
Goals (66)				3	4			3	18	13	13	2			1	3						4					2	ogs

Att.	Pos	Blacklaw	Angus	Elder	O'Neil	Miller	Todd	Morgan	Lochhead	Irvine	Harris	Coates	Bellamy	Kinsella	F Smith	Latcham	Talbut	Murray	France	Merrington	H Thomson	Blant	Buxton	R Ternent	F S Ternent	Thomas		
42,482					4	5		7	8	9	10	11			3	2				6	1							3
57,449					4	6	S*	7	8	9*	10	11			2	3				5	1							rep
Appearances					2	2		2	2	2	2	2			2	2				2	2							
Apps as sub							1																					
Goals (1)										1																		

Att.	Pos	Blacklaw	Angus	Elder	O'Neil	Miller	Todd	Morgan	Lochhead	Irvine	Harris	Coates	Bellamy	Kinsella	F Smith	Latcham	Talbut	Murray	France	Merrington	H Thomson	Blant	Buxton	R Ternent	F S Ternent	Thomas		
		1		3	4	5	6	7	8		10	11			2							9						2
9,049					4	3	6	7	9			11	10		2		5		8		1							rep
9,108		1	2	3	8	5	6		9		10	11*		S*			4		7									3
Appearances		2	1	2	3	3	3	2	3		2	3	1		2		2		2		1	1						
Apps as sub														1														
Goals (6)							1	1									1		1								2	ogs

1967-68

The 1967-68 season brought Cup glory to Turf Moor again, this time in the shape of the FA Youth Cup.

But that was just one of the major headlines of a season that saw Andy Lochhead join the 100 Club by scoring his 100th league goal for the club on the last day of the season; the sale of big names like Willie Irvine, Adam Blacklaw, Alex Elder and Gordon Harris and the first phase of the redevelopment of Turf Moor.

The FA Youth Cup caught the imagination at the end of a season which had seen the word relegation used seriously for the first time in many years.

Having had a first round bye, the young Clarets started their campaign against the highly-regarded Yorkshire Amateurs who were swept aside 7-0 to set up a trip to Maine Road.

Former rugby player Steve Kindon made his Youth Cup debut against Manchester City and immediately caught the imagination. He scored twice and prompted the Burnley Express to report: "As for his speed, there is only one word for it ... phenomenal. He bounds along with huge powerful strides, eating up ground, like a kangaroo, at an astonishing rate." Skippy was born!

The Clarets were back in Manchester for the next round and a goal-less draw against United at Old Trafford set up a 2-1 win at Turf Moor and then victory over Sheffield United at Bramall Lane handed them a two-legged semi-final with Everton.

Burnley did the hard work by drawing 0-0 at Goodison and a 3-2 win in the second leg gave Burnley an end-of-season date with Coventry City in the final. The first leg at Highfield Road finished 2-1 to the Sky Blues, but David Hartley – injured for the first leg – grabbed the second leg by the scruff of the neck, scored twice in a 2-0 victory and the cup was Burnley's.

Before the season kicked-off there was a big increase in the price of season tickets and the most expensive had risen to £10 for the first time.

As the players reported back for training, there was no Blacklaw as he had been sold to Blackburn Rovers for £15,000 and Harris was named skipper in place of the transfer-listed Elder who was sold to Stoke for £50,000 on the eve of the season. Chairman Bob Lord told the team: "Competition will be even more intense this season, but keep at it and your efforts will bring rewards."

Manager Harry Potts dismissed rumours that Lochhead was on the transfer list and at the annual meeting the spiralling cost of First Division football was reflected in a 16% increase on the wage bill and a loss of £3,700. At the meeting Lord revealed that the club was to spend anything up to £500,000 on the ground and work on the new Cricket Field Stand got underway midway through the season.

When the season started, Frank Casper immediately started repaying his £27,000 transfer fee with a goal in the win over promoted Coventry. He bagged again in the defeat at West Ham and maintained his goal-a-game ratio as the Clarets lost at Hillsborough. Away defeats were to dog Burnley all season and they ended the season with the worst away record in the division.

Following a high-scoring draw at home to West Ham, Lochhead got the ball rolling after just 25 seconds in the next home game, Casper got another two and the Burnley Express screamed "Super Spurs Shattered" after the 5-1 scoreline.

Cardiff were accounted for in the League Cup and the first artist's impressions of the new stand were unveiled in September. Despite the fact that the changing rooms in that stand were described as "temporary" at the time, they are still in use to this day.

Home form remained reliable and a 3-0 success against Sunderland lifted the Clarets to eighth in the table but key injuries to strikers Irvine, Lochhead and Ralph Coates saw them lose to Leeds and when that was followed with a 3-2 defeat at Wolves they were back in the bottom half of the table. Harry Potts was not at the game and his scouting mission was to bear fruit shortly afterwards.

Willie Morgan
ever present on the right wing and a first Scottish cap

After nine game, Burnley were the divisions top scorers with 21 goals, but had conceded 18. It was not difficult to see where the problem lay. When they beat Fulham 2-0 they were 10th in the table with 10 points from 10 games, a 1-1 draw with Forest was followed by a win over the same opposition in the League Cup and when they won 2-0 at Stoke "Burnley were again recognisable as Burnley" according to the Daily Express.

Entertainments manager Jack Butterfield launched an October competition to provide the club with a mascot similar to World Cup Willie of the previous year. Among the leading contenders was Burnley Bertie!

When Brian Miller went back into hospital for a second cartilage operation, Colin Waldron was unveiled as the new £30,000 signing from Chelsea. Add that fee to the £27,000 spent on Casper and the Clarets had spent more in four months that they had in the last decade.

Draws against Liverpool and Southampton saw the club maintain the record as the only club in the top flight to have scored in every match and when Martin Chivers missed a penalty at the Dell, Harry Thomson stretched his run to having conceded only one penalty in eight tries.

Queens Park Rangers were beaten in the League Cup to set up a quarter-final showdown with Arsenal and the unbeaten run was stretched to eight games with a 1-1 draw against Chelsea. By this stage Casper had seven goals, more than he hit in 25 games for Rotherham the previous year in Division Two.

But the unbeaten run came to a crashing end as the worst defeat for 37 years saw the Clarets lose 8-1 at the Hawthorns.

Mixed results in the league were followed by three games against Arsenal, a 3-3 draw in the League Cup, a 1-0 win in the league and than a replay defeat at Highbury. Having netted in the previous 19 league and five League Cup games, Burnley's scoring run came to an end with a 1-0 defeat at Bramall Lane.

When the Clarets lost 5-1 at Highfield Road, Keith McNee described them in the Burnley Express as the Turfy Topplers and suggested that the warning signs of relegation were everywhere. They responded with two wins and one defeat over Christmas to take some of the pressure off.

Harris became the club's biggest ever sale when he went to Sunderland for £70,000 but when the Clarets were knocked out of the FA Cup in the third round by West Ham United they had 17 games to go and only pride to play for.

The start of February saw Irvine ask for a transfer. "I'm very glad my request has been granted, my future clearly lies elsewhere," he told the Burnley Express.

Leaders Manchester United were beaten 2-1 as the Clarets climbed up to 11th in the table, but when they lost at Nottingham Forest it was their 11th defeat in 15 away games. It was followed by a similar 1-0 score at home to Manchester City, their first double-blank in more than a year,

Irvine finally departed for Deepdale for £45,000 in March but defeat at Anfield saw them drop to 11th in the table, just five points ahead of the relegation places. Brian O'Neil starred in a 2-0 success against Southampton but when that was followed by a 5-0 drubbing by Spurs they were down to 13th with only a four-point cushion.

In the following month Miller's persistent knee injury saw him finally retire as a player and join the coaching staff and a win, two draws and one defeat saw the Clarets edge closer to safety.

A 4-2 win against Stoke eased relegation fears and despite defeats to Chelsea and Arsenal, they had done enough.

One of the worst displays of the season was reserved for the penultimate game, a 2-0 home defeat by Sheffield United but then Lochhead produced another major headline by scoring his 100th league goal as the Clarets signed off with a 3-0 win over Leeds United.

At the end of the season Stan Ternent was sold to Carlisle United for £4,000 and first team players Gary France and Mick Buxton were both placed on the transfer list.

Burnley had finished 14th for the second successive season, but this time around did not have the strains of the Fairs Cup to blame, just a shambolic run of results away from home.

OBITUARY
RAYMOND (RAY) BENNION
DIED 12 MAY 1968, AGED 71

Arriving at Turf Moor at the tail-end of a successful playing career, Ray Bennion was to remain at the club for well over thirty years and become a key component of the club's backroom staff during the glory years of the late 50s and early 60s.

Born in Wrexham in 1896, he had already won ten international caps for Wales when he joined Burnley from Manchester United in November 1932. He was a regular at right-half for the remainder of that season, but age was catching up and he retired from playing in the close season of 1934, moving on to the Turf Moor coaching staff. Initially "A" team trainer, he moved up to coaching the reserves and was in charge when the second string won their first Central League championship in 1949.

His career at Burnley was inextricably linked with that of Billy Dougall, and Bennion took over as first-team trainer during Dougall's brief stint as manager in the 1957-58 season. When Harry Potts took over in February 1958, both Bennion and Dougall were retained on the coaching staff and they made vital contributions as the Clarets enjoyed some of their finest years with Potts at the helm.

Ray Bennion retired in 1965 and died three years later, his work with Burnley's youngsters still being carried on by, among others, Joe Brown and bearing fruit with the winning of the FA Youth Cup just two days before his death.

RIP

1967-68 - First Division

		P	W	D	L	F	A	Pts
1	Manchester C	42	26	6	10	86	43	58
2	Manchester U	42	24	8	10	89	55	56
3	Liverpool	42	22	11	9	71	40	55
4	Leeds U	42	22	9	11	71	41	53
5	Everton	42	23	6	13	67	40	52
6	Chelsea	42	18	12	12	62	68	48
7	Tottenham H	42	19	9	14	70	59	47
8	West Bromwich A	42	17	12	13	75	62	46
9	Arsenal	42	17	10	15	60	56	44
10	Newcastle U	42	13	15	14	54	67	41
11	Nottingham F	42	14	11	17	52	64	39
12	West Ham U	42	14	10	18	73	69	38
13	Leicester C	42	13	12	17	64	69	38
14	BURNLEY	42	14	10	18	64	71	38
15	Sunderland	42	13	11	18	51	61	37
16	Southampton	42	13	11	18	66	83	37
17	Wolverhampton W	42	14	8	20	66	75	36
18	Stoke C	42	14	7	21	50	73	35
19	Sheffield W	42	11	12	19	51	63	34
20	Coventry C	42	9	15	18	51	71	33
21	Sheffield U	42	11	10	21	49	70	32
22	Fulham	42	10	7	25	56	98	27

1967-68

Manager : Harry Potts

Division One (14th)

	Date				Opponents	Result		h/t	Goalscorers/times	Opp. goal times
	1	Aug	19	h	COVENTRY C	W	2-1	1-0	Casper 32, Irvine 63	82og
	2		21	a	West Ham U	L	2-4	1-0	Irvine 26, Casper 64	53, 55, 65, 80
	3		26	a	Sheffield W	L	1-2	0-2	Casper 80	10, 15
	4		29	h	WEST HAM U	D	3-3	1-1	Lochhead 44, Bellamy 46, Harris 73p	8, 61, 80
	5	Sep	2	h	TOTTENHAM H	W	5-1	3-1	Lochhead (2) 2, 56, Casper (2) 39, 42, Coates 78	11
	6		9	a	Manchester U	D	2-2	1-0	Lochhead (2) 44, 61	86, 89
	7		16	h	SUNDERLAND	W	3-0	2-0	Lochhead 11, Coates 13, Morgan 69	
	8		20	a	Leeds U	L	1-2	1-1	Irvine 17	35, 77
	9		23	a	Wolverhampton W	L	2-3	1-1	Harris (2) 27p, 85p	17, 53, 87
	10		30	h	FULHAM	W	2-0	0-0	Casper 59, Coates 81	
	11	Oct	7	h	NOTTINGHAM F	D	1-1	0-0	Irvine 80	47
	12		14	a	Stoke C	W	2-0	2-0	O'Neil 26, Irvine 28	
	13		24	h	LIVERPOOL	D	1-1	0-0	O'Neil 50	82
	14		28	a	Southampton	D	2-2	1-1	Casper 38, Irvine 58	20, 49
	15	Nov	4	h	CHELSEA	D	1-1	0-0	Morgan 89	82
	16		11	a	West Bromwich A	L	1-8	0-5	Bellamy 85	16,20,24,36,44,59,68,75
	17		18	h	NEWCASTLE U	W	2-0	0-0	Harris 49, Lochhead 64	
	18		25	a	Manchester C	L	2-4	0-3	Casper 58, Morgan 89	1, 7, 44, 52
	19	Dec	2	h	ARSENAL	W	1-0	0-0	Harris 62	
	20		9	a	Sheffield U	L	0-1	0-0		49
	21		16	a	Coventry C	L	1-5	0-2	Lochhead 76	11, 44, 53, 63, 88
	22		23	h	SHEFFIELD W	W	2-1	2-1	Casper 19, Lochhead 43	2p
	23		26	a	Everton	L	0-2	0-1		21, 75
Harris' last game	24		30	h	EVERTON	W	2-1	1-1	Morgan 40, Latcham 81	44
	25	Jan	20	a	Sunderland	D	2-2	1-1	Casper 43, Coates 73	19, 52og
	26	Feb	3	h	WOLVERHAMPTON W	D	1-1	0-0	Casper 74	48
	27		10	a	Fulham	L	3-4	0-1	Lochhead 60, Casper 62, Dempsey 90og	19, 73, 80, 89
	28		17	h	MANCHESTER U	W	2-1	0-1	O'Neil 62, Dobson 67	9
	29		24	a	Nottingham F	L	0-1	0-1		44
	30	Mar	2	h	MANCHESTER C	L	0-1	0-0		65p
	31		16	a	Liverpool	L	2-3	1-1	Coates (2) 22, 84	32, 63, 75
	32		23	h	SOUTHAMPTON	W	2-0	1-0	Morgan 43, O'Neil 84	
	33		30	a	Tottenham H	L	0-5	0-2		28,31,54,66,74
	34	Apr	6	h	WEST BROMWICH A	D	0-0	0-0		
	35		13	a	Newcastle U	L	0-1	0-0		72
	36		15	h	LEICESTER C	D	1-1	0-0	Lochhead 71	89p
	37		16	a	Leicester C	W	2-0	2-0	Casper 3, Dobson 29	
	38		20	h	STOKE C	W	4-0	1-0	Morgan (2) 24, 63, Lochhead 51, Casper 65	
	39		22	a	Chelsea	L	1-2	0-2	Lochhead 88	1, 14
	40		27	a	Arsenal	L	0-2	0-0		72, 89
	41	May	4	h	SHEFFIELD U	L	0-2	0-0		74, 88
	42		11	h	LEEDS U	W	3-0	1-0	O'Neil 23p, Lochhead 65, Dobson 89	

FA Cup

Irvine's last game	3	Jan	27	h	WEST HAM U	L	1-3	1-1	Casper 14	23, 50, 55

Final, West Bromwich A 1-0 Everton after extra time, at Wembley.

League Cup

2	Sep	12	h	CARDIFF C	W	2-1	0-0	Harris 87p, Casper 89	72
3	Oct	10	h	NOTTINGHAM F	W	3-0	2-0	Irvine (2) 4, 56, Lochhead 13	
4		31	a	Queens Park R	W	2-1	1-0	Irvine 15, Casper 69	51
5	Nov	29	h	ARSENAL	D	3-3	2-3	Lochhead 2, O'Neil 8, Irvine 87	31, 34, 39
rep	Dec	5	a	Arsenal	L	1-2	0-1	Irvine 59	29, 57

Final, Leeds U 1-0 Arsenal, at Wembley.

Details of other first team games elsewhere.

Att.	Pos	H Thomson	Angus	Latcham	O'Neil	Merrington	Todd	Morgan	Bellamy	Irvine	Harris	Casper	Blant	Kinsella	Buxton	Lochhead	F Smith	Coates	F S Ternent	Dobson	Waldron	Thomas	France	R Ternent	R Jones		
21,483		1	2	3	4	5	6	7	8	9	10	11															1
30,414		1	2	3	4	5	6	7	8	9	10	11															2
29,517	14	1	2	3	4	5*		7	6	9	10	11	8	S*													3
16,625		1	5	2	4			7	6	9	10	11			3	8											4
23,337	8	1	5	3	4			7	6		10	8				9	2	11									5
55,809	14	1	5	3	4			7	6		10	8				9	2	11									6
19,414	8	1	5	3	4			7	6		10	8				9	2	11									7
32,944		1	5	3	4	S*		7	6	11*	10	8				9	2										8
28,151	12	1		3	4			7	6		10	8					2	11	5	9							9
14,227	10	1		3	4			7	6	S*	10	8					2*	11	5	9							10
18,400	10	1	2	3	4			7	6	S*	10	11				8			5	9*							11
19,538	8	1	2	3	4	5		7	6	8	10	11				9											12
29,763		1	2	3	4	5		7	6	9	10	11				8											13
22,696	9	1	2		4	5		7		9	6	11				8			10		3						14
17,651	9	1		3	4	5		7	10	9	6	8*						11		S*	2						15
18,952	11	1	2	3	4			7	10	9	6					8					5	11					16
15,447	9	1	2	3	4			7	10	9	6	11				8					5						17
37,098	13	1	2	3	4	6		7	10			11	S*			9					5		8*				18
15,381	10	1		3	4			7			6	11	9			8	2	10			5						19
14,363	10	1		3	4			7		9	6	10				8	2	11			5						20
28,560	12	1		3	4	6		7	10	9		S*				8	2*				5	11					21
13,050	12	1		3	4	6		7	10	9		11				8					5			2			22
54,324		1		3	4	6		7*	10	9		11				8		S*			5			2			23
22,592	11	1		3	4			7	10	9	6	S*				8*		11			5			2			24
27,860	12	1		3		6		7	10			4	5			8		11		9				2			25
12,643	11	1		3			4	7	10			9	6			8		11			5			2			26
15,317	12		2				4	7				9	6			8		11		10	5			3	1		27
32,165	11	1	2	3	10	6	4	7				9				8*		11		S*	5						28
26,110	11	1	2*	3	10	6	4	7		8		9	S*					11			5						29
23,486	12	1		3	10	6	4	7				9				8		11			5			2			30
41,114	12	1		3	4	6	10	7	8								2	11		9	5						31
9,405	12	1		3	4		6	7	10							8	2	11		9	5						32
26,494	13	1		3	4	10	6	7*				9				8	2	11		S*	5						33
11,918	12	1		3	4		10	7	6			9				8	2	10			5						34
27,229	14	1		3	4		10	7	6			9				8	2	10			5						35
12,570		1	2	3	4	5	6	7	10							8		11		9							36
20,032		1	2	3			10	7	6*			9	S*	5		8				4		11					37
13,187	11	1	2	3			4	7	10			9		6		8		11			5						38
23,494		1	2	3			6	7	10			9		5		8		11		4							39
15,278	13	1	2	3		6	4	7	10			9		S*		8		11*			5						40
10,244	15	1	2	3	4	6	10	7				9				8		11			5						41
13,142	14	1	2	3	4	5	6	7	10			11*				8		S*		9							42
Appearances		41	25	40	35	21	19	42	33	17	20	36	5	3	1	34	14	25	4	11	24	3	1	7	1		
Apps as sub						1				2		2	3	2				2		3							
Goals (64)				2	5			7	2	6	5	14				13		6		3						1	og

Att.	Pos	H Thomson	Angus	Latcham	O'Neil	Merrington	Todd	Morgan	Bellamy	Irvine	Harris	Casper	Blant	Kinsella	Buxton	Lochhead	F Smith	Coates	F S Ternent	Dobson	Waldron	Thomas	France	R Ternent	R Jones		
23,452		1		3	4	6		7	10*	S*		9				8		11			5			2			3
Appearances		1		1	1	1		1	1			1				1		1			1			1			
Apps as sub										1																	
Goals (1)												1															

Att.	Pos	H Thomson	Angus	Latcham	O'Neil	Merrington	Todd	Morgan	Bellamy	Irvine	Harris	Casper	Blant	Kinsella	Buxton	Lochhead	F Smith	Coates	F S Ternent	Dobson	Waldron	Thomas	France	R Ternent	R Jones		
11,731		1	2	3	4			7	6	S*	10	8				9	2	11*									2
14,421		1	2	3	4	5		7	6	8	10	11				9											3
24,213		1	2	3	4	5		7	6	9	10	11				8*		S*									4
16,032		1	2	3	4	5		7	10*	9	6	11				8		S*									5
36,570		1	2*	3	4	5		7		9	6	11				8	S*	10									rep
Appearances		5	5	5	5	4		5	4	4	5	5				5	1	2									
Apps as sub										1							1	2									
Goals (11)					1					5	1	2				2											

1968-69

For six weeks of the 1968-69 season the "Burnley Babes" ruled English football. They were fearless. They banged goals in for fun. They looked set to conquer the domestic game.

Burnley, on the back of six straight league wins, climbed the table after the horrors of their 4-0 defeat against Liverpool.

They also progressed through two rounds of the League Cup. Everyone was starting to pay attention to a team with an average age of less than 22 skippered by a 20-year-old who had not even been at the club at the start of the previous season

Having won the FA Youth Cup the previous season it was little wonder that pre-season hype suggested that Burnley would pin their hopes on their youngsters.

Of the senior squad, the average age was 21, but Keith McNee in the Burnley Express stuck his neck out by saying: "With so many city slickers around, First Division survival can be the only real aim for Burnley this time around."

As the season neared, chairman Bob Lord sought a change in league rules to stop big city clubs dominating the game. In 1961 he had predicted that by 1968 there would be only one small town Lancashire club left in the top flight. By 1968 he was right, and he was determined to keep Burnley there.

The club reported a profit of £1,500, but had the burgeoning Development Association not pumped £92,000 into the club it would have been a far different story.

The season started with a 2-2 draw at Nottingham Forest and immediately Scottish international winger Willie Morgan asked for a transfer. Leeds United were immediately interested and Manchester United were "watching the position".

Following a 3-0 defeat at Leeds, the Clarets missed a host of chances but still beat Manchester United 1-0 and followed that with a 3-0 success against Southampton.

The Old Trafford club wrote a cheque for £117,000 to take Morgan and Burnley followed his departure by suffering defeats against West Bromwich Albion and West Ham United, the latter game witnessing Steve Kindon's senior debut.

When the annual meeting came around, Lord promised that no more players would be sold, but the following month an offer from Leicester City was just too tempting and 100 Club striker Andy Lochhead was on his way.

Lord also summed up how difficult life was for the club in the wake of the abolition of the maximum wage. "We are embroiled in a pure and simple rat race of the first magnitude. Having experienced 22 years of advancements in First Division football no other club in the world has such as record as Burnley," he told shareholders.

Things got tougher on the field with a 7-0 hammering at Spurs and 20 goals had been conceded in the first five away games. It was a trend that recurred throughout the season, but back at Turf Moor Grimsby Town were put to the sword 6-0 in a League Cup replay.

Les Latcham, not for the first time, snuffed out the threat of George Best as a Brian O'Neil wonder goal beat United 1-0 and the Clarets had eight points from their first nine games.

Defeat at Hillsborough was followed by the signings of Doug Collins for £30,000 from Grimsby and Jim Thomson for a club record £40,000 from Chelsea. That joint expenditure in two weeks was more than had been spent on incoming transfers in the previous nine years.

More League Cup success came against Workington and the best display of the season to date saw Chelsea beaten 2-1 at Turf Moor. But the injuries were piling up and with eight senior players sidelined the first home defeat came when Liverpool put four unanswered goals into the Turf Moor nets.

Three members of the Youth Cup winning team were in action against West Ham and the Burnley Babes won in fine style. It was their youngest-ever team and three of the players were under 20.

Leicester were next and they were beaten 4-0 in the League Cup. The draw for the quarter-finals was made at Turf Moor and Burnley were paired with Crystal Palace.

League leaders Leeds were the next test for Burnley's brave young battlers and the result was a sensation. Their title hopes looked flimsy as the floodgates opened and Burnley won 5-1. In 13 previous games they had conceded 10 goals and the Daily Mirror recorded: "The best defence in the country was thrown into confusion by players who have not yet achieved the status of household names in Burnley never mind the country."

Frank Casper
top scorer in each of his first two seasons

When Leicester were beaten in the league the Clarets were in the top half of the table, but there was a shock when Andy Lochhead was sold to Filbert Street for £70,000, but League Cup progress continued as Burnley beat Palace 2-0 to reach the semi-finals.

It was seven straight wins in the space of 25 days when Ipswich were beaten 1-0 and in that run 20 goals had been scored against just three conceded.

QPR were next to fall to the Clarets and they were fifth in

the table but then the fairy tale run of eight victories was over as they crunched to a halt against Wolves' brick wall defence and drew 1-1.

The first leg of the League Cup semi-final saw a 2-1 defeat against Third Division Swindon and that was followed by two league defeats as injuries mounted. The second leg of the semi-final went to the Clarets and a replay was needed but by the time Burnley arrived at the Hawthorns they had been cut down to size by Manchester City in another seven-goal hammering and drawn with Stoke.

The replay ended in heartache for the second time for the Clarets having suffered a similar fate in 1960-61. Burnley have reached that stage in the competition just once in the years since and the League Cup remains the only senior trophy to evade the club.

Back in the league and Leeds avenged their earlier defeat with a 6-1 triumph and Christmas results were indifferent as the efforts of the young Clarets faded.

The FA Cup was next on the agenda and the 3-1 win over Derby was branded as the day brutality took over. Burnley's reward was a trip to Liverpool where they lost 2-1 with Frank Casper having a good "goal" disallowed for off-side and seeing another effort crash into the woodwork.

With 14 games to go there was nothing left to play for. It would have taken a remarkable run for them to qualify for Europe and it did not materialise.

In February the plans for the new Turf Moor were finally unveiled. With the Cricket Field Stand due to open the following season the rest of the redevelopment was on display for the first time. It included a new stand on Brunshaw Road, a cabaret room for 1,750 people, a ballroom and banqueting suite for 860, a theatre for 550, a restaurant for 300, a cafeteria for 225, a club shop and a leisure centre for snooker, darts and table tennis. Although it was given planning approval by the council, most of it never left the drawing board.

Harry Thomson played in the 2-0 defeat at Arsenal despite having been involved in a car crash with Freddie Smith the previous day and the month ended with John Murray, a nine-goal hero of the Burnley Babes' run, asking for a transfer just two days after his 21st birthday.

Casper scored after just 62 seconds to get the ball rolling in a 3-1 win over Forest, David Merrington scored his first senior goal in a win over champions Manchester City and following a 1-0 defeat at Newcastle Sammy Todd and O'Neil joined Murray on the list.

West Brom did their best to gift Burnley victory but the game ended in a 2-2 draw and with eight games to go the Clarets were eighth in the table.

Lord suggested that Spurs should have been beaten 6-1, but the game ended 2-2 and then Chelsea were beaten 3-2 at Stamford Bridge to give Burnley their first away win in the league for five months.

A 5-1 defeat at the Dell followed and it was the seventh time in the season the Clarets had conceded four or more. Defeat followed against Everton and hopes of the Fairs Cup evaporated.

April saw O'Neil off the transfer list but when the season finished with two further defeats the statistics summed up the season.

Burnley had conceded 82 goals and 57 of them had been in away games. Of 18 defeats, 14 were on their travels and for the third successive season the final table saw Burnley in 14th place.

In May Youth Cup goal heroes Willie Brown and David Hartley were given free transfers and as the players prepared for their summer break there was time for one more sensation.

Harry Thomson, having missed just nine games in two seasons, was sacked. Manager Harry Potts said it was a "domestic matter" and refused to comment further and Thomson simply appealed to the Football League to have his registration released.

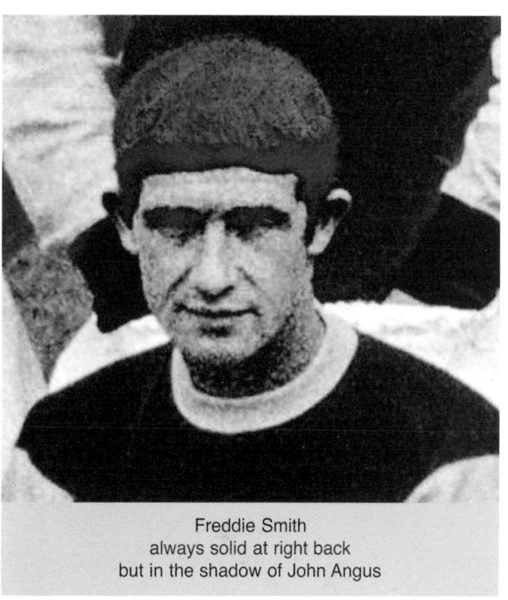

Freddie Smith
always solid at right back
but in the shadow of John Angus

1968-69 - First Division

		P	W	D	L	F	A	Pts
1	Leeds U	42	27	13	2	66	26	67
2	Liverpool	42	25	11	6	63	24	61
3	Everton	42	21	15	6	77	36	57
4	Arsenal	42	22	12	8	56	27	56
5	Chelsea	42	20	10	12	73	53	50
6	Tottenham H	42	14	17	11	61	51	45
7	Southampton	42	16	13	13	57	48	45
8	West Ham U	42	13	18	11	66	50	44
9	Newcastle U	42	15	14	13	61	55	44
10	West Bromwich A	42	16	11	15	64	67	43
11	Manchester U	42	15	12	15	57	53	42
12	Ipswich T	42	15	11	16	59	60	41
13	Manchester C	42	15	10	17	64	55	40
14	BURNLEY	42	15	9	18	55	82	39
15	Sheffield W	42	10	16	16	41	54	36
16	Wolverhampton W	42	10	15	17	41	58	35
17	Sunderland	42	11	12	19	43	57	34
18	Nottingham F	42	10	13	19	45	57	33
19	Stoke C	42	9	15	18	40	63	33
20	Coventry C	42	10	11	21	46	64	31
21	Leicester C	42	9	12	21	39	68	30
22	Queens Park R	42	4	10	28	39	95	18

1968-69

Manager : Harry Potts

Division One (14th)

	No.	Date		Venue	Opponents	Result		h/t	Goalscorers/times	Opp. goal times
	1	Aug	10	a	Nottingham F	D	2-2	0-0	Waldron 81, Casper 86	61, 72
	2		13	a	Everton	L	0-3	0-2		27, 37, 70
	3		17	h	NEWCASTLE U	W	1-0	1-0	McNamee 23og	
	4		20	h	SOUTHAMPTON	W	3-1	2-0	Casper (2) 24, 26, Bellamy 67	87
	5		24	a	West Bromwich A	L	2-3	0-2	Casper 87, Lochhead 89	43, 44, 82
	6		26	a	West Ham U	L	0-5	0-4		17, 20, 31, 44, 59
	7		31	h	COVENTRY C	D	1-1	0-1	Waldron 59	15
	8	Sep	7	a	Tottenham H	L	0-7	0-4		10, 21, 28p, 44, 52, 66, 87
	9		14	h	MANCHESTER U	W	1-0	0-0	O'Neil 88	
	10		21	a	Sheffield W	L	0-1	0-1		37
	11		28	h	CHELSEA	W	2-1	1-0	Thomas (2) 44, 48	62
Lochhead's last game	12	Oct	5	h	LIVERPOOL	L	0-4	0-2		20, 35, 52, 87
	13		8	h	WEST HAM U	W	3-1	2-0	Murray 8, Kindon 25, Dobson 58	60
	14		12	a	Stoke C	W	3-1	1-0	Blant 12, Murray 77, Coates 82	86
	15		19	h	LEEDS U	W	5-1	2-1	Coates 19, Casper (2) 21, 80, Murray 46, Kindon 78	23
	16		26	a	Leicester C	W	2-0	1-0	Casper 44p, Murray 46	
	17	Nov	2	h	IPSWICH T	W	1-0	0-0	Blant 62	
	18		9	a	Queens Park R	W	2-0	1-0	Murray 24, Casper 77	
	19		16	h	WOLVERHAMPTON W	D	1-1	1-1	Casper 20	43
	20		23	a	Sunderland	L	0-2	0-2		13, 20
	21		30	h	ARSENAL	L	0-1	0-1		32
	22	Dec	7	a	Manchester C	L	0-7	0-3		2, 23, 39, 50, 65, 77, 85
	23		14	h	STOKE C	D	1-1	1-1	Casper 34	29
	24		21	a	Leeds U	L	1-6	0-4	Coates 60	2,25,33,37,75,88
	25		26	a	Liverpool	D	1-1	1-1	Casper 28	43
	26		28	h	LEICESTER C	W	2-1	1-1	Collins 24, Kindon 74	7
	27	Jan	11	a	Ipswich T	L	0-2	0-1		16, 89
	28		18	h	QUEENS PARK R	D	2-2	2-0	Latcham 17, Kindon 23	54, 70
	29	Feb	1	a	Wolverhampton W	D	1-1	1-1	Collins 36	31
	30		15	a	Arsenal	L	0-2	0-0		53, 88
	31	Mar	1	h	NOTTINGHAM F	W	3-1	1-1	Casper 1, Dobson (2) 49, 73	4
	32		4	h	MANCHESTER C	W	2-1	1-1	Thomas 45, Merrington 66	30
	33		8	a	Newcastle U	L	0-1	0-1		18
	34		15	h	WEST BROMWICH A	D	2-2	2-1	Dobson 4, Latcham 15	22, 72
	35		22	a	Coventry C	L	1-4	0-0	Collins 78	56, 59, 75, 83
	36		29	h	TOTTENHAM H	D	2-2	2-1	Probert 7, Coates 43	38, 73
	37	Apr	5	a	Chelsea	W	3-2	1-1	Thomas 31, Collins (2) 60, 63	21, 51
	38		7	a	Southampton	L	1-5	0-3	Blant 84	15, 20, 26, 67p, 70
	39		8	h	EVERTON	L	1-2	0-2	Coates 50	28, 39
	40		12	h	SHEFFIELD W	W	2-0	2-0	Collins 22, Casper 24	
	41		19	a	Manchester U	L	0-2	0-0		57, 60og
Harry Thomson's last game	42		23	h	SUNDERLAND	L	1-2	1-2	Probert 44	32, 43

FA Cup

Round	Date		Venue	Opponents	Result		h/t	Goalscorers/times	Opp. goal times
3	Jan	4	h	DERBY C	W	3-1	2-0	Blant 8, Casper (2) 44, 53	84
4		25	a	Liverpool	L	1-2	1-2	Latcham 35	13p, 23

Final, Manchester C 1-0 Leicester C, at Wembley.

League Cup

	Round	Date		Venue	Opponents	Result		h/t	Goalscorers/times	Opp. goal times
	2	Sep	4	a	Grimsby T	D	1-1	0-0	Lochhead 84	78
	rep		10	h	GRIMSBY T	W	6-0	3-0	Casper (2) 25, 84, Lochhead (2) 29, 80, Thomas 30, Murray 86	
	3		25	a	Workington	W	1-0	1-0	Blant 26	
	4	Oct	16	h	LEICESTER C	W	4-0	2-0	Thomas 15, Murray (2) 33, 46, Casper 81	
	5		30	h	CRYSTAL P	W	2-0	2-0	Casper 38p, Murray 44	
	semi	Nov	20	h	SWINDON T	L	1-2	0-1	Coates 63	44, 65
agg 3-3		Dec	4	a	Swindon T	W	2-1	0-0	Casper 50, Kindon 52,	57
at The Hawthorns, aet, 1-1 at 90m	rep		18	n	Swindon T	L	2-3	0-1	Thomas 90, Casper 91	9, 104og, 109

Final, Swindon T 3-1 Arsenal, at Wembley.

Details of other first team games elsewhere.

Att.	Pos	H Thomson	Angus	Latcham	O'Neil	Waldron	Merrington	Coates	Lochhead	Casper	Bellamy	Thomas	P Jones	F Smith	Todd	Dobson	W Brown	Kindon	Blant	Murray	J Thomson	Collins	R Jones	Wrigley	Probert	Docherty	Kinsella		[match]
30,298		1	2	3	4	5	6	7	8	9	10	11																	1
48,903		1		3	4	5	6	7	8	9	10	11	2																2
13,579	12	1		3	4	5	6	7	8	9	10	11		2															3
12,170		1		3	4	5		7*	8	9	10	11		2	6	S*													4
21,882	8	1		3	4	5		7	8	9	10	11*		2	6		S*												5
28,340		1		3	4	5		7	8	9	6	11		2				10											6
12,939	15	1	2	3	4*	5	6	7	8	9	10	11							S*										7
30,167	15	1	2	3	4	5	6	7	8	9	10	11																	8
32,935	9	1		3	4	5	6	7	8	9	10*	11							S*	2									9
23,270	17	1		3	4	5	6	7	8*	9		11				10			S*	2									10
14,762	13	1		3	4	5	6*	7		9		11			10				8	S*		2							11
26,418	15	1		3	4	5		8*	10	9		7			6				S*		2	11							12
13,799	12	1		3		5				9		7		2	4	10		11	6	8									13
14,168	11	1		3		5		4		9		7		2		10		11	6	8									14
26,434	10	1		3		5		10		9		7		2		4		11	6	8									15
21,307	9	1		3		5		4		9		7		2		10		11	6	8									16
14,721	8	1		3		5		10		9		7*		2		4		11	6	8		S*							17
22,572	6	1		3		5		10		9		7		2		4		11*	6	8		S*							18
20,848	7	1		3		5		10		9		7*		2		4		11	6	8		S*							19
19,607	8				3					9	8	7		2		4		11	6			10	1	5					20
16,264	9						3			9	8			2		10			6	11*	S*	7	1	5	4				21
31,009	9			3	4					9	8	7*		2		10		11	6			S*	1	5					22
10,465	9	1		3			2			9					10	8			6		5	7				4	11		23
31,409	10	1		3				10		9		7		2				11	6			8		5		4			24
52,477		1		3		5	4	10		9	8	7		2				11	6										25
15,594	8	1		3		5		8		9	4	7		2				11	6			10							26
18,858	8	1		3		5	4	8		9	10	7		2					6			11							27
12,674	9	1		3		5	6	8		9	4	7		2				11				10							28
27,733	10	1		3		5		10		9	4	7		2					6		11	8							29
27,614	10	1		3		5		8		9	4	7*			S*	2			6		11	10							30
11,884	9			3		5		8		9	4	7		2		10			6			11	1						31
18,360				3		5	4	8		9		S*		2*		10			6		7	11	1						32
32,460	8			3		5	4	8		9	S*	7*				10			6		2	11	1						33
12,218	8			3		5	4	8		9		S*				10		7*	6		2	11	1						34
26,584	9			3		5	4	8		9	S*	7				10			6	2		11	1*						35
14,547	9	1	2	3		5		8		9		7				4			6			11			10				36
30,266	10	1	2	3	S*	5		8		9		7				4*			6			11			10				37
19,551		1	2	3	4	5		8		9		7							6			11*			10	S*			38
17,144		1		3	4	5		8			9							10	6	7		11				2			39
9,597	9	1	2	3		5		8		9		7				4*			6			11			10	S*			40
52,626	12	1		3		5	2	8		9		7							6			11			10	4			41
10,181	14	1		S*		5	2	8		9		7				3			6*			11			10	4			42
Appearances		34	7	39	16	37	19	37	11	41	20	37	1	22	6	22		16	30	12	7	23	8	4	7	5	1		
Apps as sub				1	1						2	2			1	1	1		4	1	1	4				2			
Goals (55)				2	1	2	1	5	1	13	1	4				4		4	3	5		6			2			1	og

Att.	H Thomson	Angus	Latcham	O'Neil	Waldron	Merrington	Coates	Lochhead	Casper	Bellamy	Thomas	P Jones	F Smith	Todd	Dobson	W Brown	Kindon	Blant	Murray	J Thomson	Collins	R Jones	Wrigley	Probert	Docherty	Kinsella	[round]
22,842	1		3		5	4	8		9	10	7		2					6			11						3
53,667	1		3		5		8		9	4*	7		2				S*	6		11	10						4
Appearances	2		2		2	1	2		2	2	2		2					2		1	2						
Apps as sub																	1										
Goals (4)			1						2									1									

Att.	H Thomson	Angus	Latcham	O'Neil	Waldron	Merrington	Coates	Lochhead	Casper	Bellamy	Thomas	P Jones	F Smith	Todd	Dobson	W Brown	Kindon	Blant	Murray	J Thomson	Collins	R Jones	Wrigley	Probert	Docherty	Kinsella	[round]
8,762	1	2	3	4	5	6	7	8	9	10	11																2
5,928	1	2	3	4	5	6	7	8	9	10*	11								S*								rep
9,664	1		3	4	5	6	7		9		11			10				8	2								3
11,486	1		3		5		10		9		7*		2	S*	4		11	6	8								4
17,879	1		3		5		10		9		7		2		4		11	6	8								5
25,755	1		3	S*	5*		10		9		7		2		4		11	6	8								semi
28,000			S*	4		3*			9	7	10		2		8		11	6				1	5				2nd leg
20,000	1		3				8		9	10	7		2				11	6		4*			5		S*		rep
Appearances	7	2	7	4	6	4	7	2	8	4	8		5	1	4		5	6	4	1		1	2				
Apps as sub			1	1										1					1						1		
Goals (19)							1	3	6		3						1	1	4								

1969-70

The 1969-70 season saw the end of the greatest managerial career in Burnley's history – and it also saw the death of one of the few players able to rival Jimmy McIlroy for the title of "Greatest Claret of All Time".

OBITUARY
ROBERT (BOB) KELLY
22 SEPTEMBER 1969, AGED 74

Bob Kelly remains the Clarets' most-capped Englishman. But there is another title many are keen to bestow upon him and it will take more than facts and figures to settle the argument. There are those, who learned football from their father or grandfather, who will tell you that he was the greatest-ever Claret, the only man capable of wresting that accolade from Jimmy McIlroy. Although signed before the Great War, he did not really have much chance to shine until after it, as the Clarets finished as runners-up. The next season, the epic first Championship campaign, saw his mercurial skills take centre stage as he scored 20 goals from the inside-right position. Along with Tommy Boyle, Kelly was a major influence on that side and his sheer genius in terms of ball control coupled with the ability to avoid the fiercest of tackles and hit a thunderbolt of a shot made him a Turf Moor legend. Third place the following year was followed by a decline in fortunes and he was sold to Sunderland for £6.500. Spells with Huddersfield, Preston, Carlisle and Stockport followed before Kelly left football for good and became a publican in the Blackpool area.

RIP

In February 1970, with the Clarets still not out of the relegation woods, Harry Potts was made general manager with Jimmy Adamson elevated to the position of first team manager. It happened almost 12 years to the day from Potts' original appointment – and what a 12 years that had been in the club's history – and it was news that came out of the blue.

There had been no hint in the weeks building up to the decision that Potts was to relinquish a role that had seen him bring the Championship to Turf Moor for the first time in almost four decades; bring the Clarets their first – and as yet, only – forays into European club competitions and their last FA Cup final appearance to date.

As the Clarets prepared for a season which, at one stage saw them bottom of the table, there was nothing to suggest the drama to follow.

Olympic athlete Malcolm Yardley was drafted in to help with speed and stamina training and Harry Thomson moved on, first to Bacup Borough and 13 days later to Blackpool for a four-figure fee.

Innovations for the new season included pitch-side advertising and a new strip which no longer bore the town's coat of arms, in its place an italicised BFC.

A pre-season game against Middlesbrough saw Lord Rhodes, the Lord Lieutenant of Lancashire, officially open the £200,000 Cricket Field Stand and the Brunshaw Road Stand, was closed to prepare for demolition and reconstruction later in the season.

As the season approached, Keith McNee in the Burnley Express reflected: "Survival as a First Division club must surely be the main objective and, despite the cynics, they should attain that goal with something to spare." He was right on both counts.

The season started with a goal-less draw at Derby County during which new keeper Peter Mellor dislocated a finger. He played a few days later at "White Hurt Lane" as the Clarets were beaten 4-0, a result which brought the recent run at Spurs to four straight defeats during which the Clarets conceded 18 goals.

A 3-0 win over Sunderland was followed by a home defeat at the hands of Spurs and Burnley faced a long, hard winter. It was still only August!

But they bounced back with a 3-3 draw at Anfield and then Mellor really caught the headlines by making nine top class saves in the second half as Leeds were held 1-1 at Turf Moor. Draws against Manchester City and Southampton sandwiched a League Cup win at Stoke and were followed by a defeat against Arsenal during which 18-year-old David Thomas made his 50th full appearance.

A loss at Chelsea was followed by draws at Wolves and Rotherham, the latter in the League Cup, and before the replay, which the Clarets won 2-0, an unusually calm annual meeting saw the Clarets report a profit of £42,000 and chairman Bob Lord, when quizzed about the future of stars such as Ralph Coates, Brian O'Neil and David Thomas, said: "Get one thing straight, Burnley Football Club has no intention of selling out to Manchester United or any other club."

Goalkeeper Peter Mellor
plucked from non league football, an excellent first season

Lord also fired a broadside at the Press, several of whom had already had facilities withdrawn from them, by saying: "They grab all the hospitality you can offer, drink you out of the place and eat everything on the table." The local branch of the National Union of Journalists sought a public condemnation of the chairman from the Football League and the Football Association. Lord's answer was simple: "If the cap fits, wear it."

The sixth defeat of the season came at West Ham United and Burnley, joint bottom of the table, were without a league win in 10 matches. The pressure was eased with a 1-0 win at Roker Park, where Coates scored the only goal, and a 4-2 home success against Crystal Palace.

A League Cup draw with Manchester United preceded a game which saw three goals in four minutes sink Sheffield Wednesday as the Clarets headed back towards the top half of the table.

The League Cup run came to an end with a 1-0 defeat at Old Trafford where Arthur Bellamy hit the post late on with Alex Stepney stranded and in the next game a late goal denied Burnley victory at Nottingham Forest.

Things started to go wrong as the "bad luck bogey" and "same old story" hit Burnley against Newcastle and Stoke and they were back down to 17th in the table, four points above the relegation zone.

And they stayed in that position following draws against Coventry and Manchester United and a defeat at Everton despite taking the lead. They moved up two places with a win at The Hawthorns, but slipped back again following defeat at Arsenal.

Following a disappointing Christmas, Burnley started the new decade in style when three goals in ten minutes sank Wolves in the FA Cup. They were then unlucky to return from Maine Road with only one point before Wolves avenged their cup exit with a 3-1 success at Turf Moor – 20 points from 27 games was their worst return since promotion in 1947.

Frank Casper and Sammy Todd both made their 100th appearances at Ipswich as Casper scored the only goal, but dreams of FA Cup glory ended in replay defeat at the hands of Chelsea. Coates gave them the lead, but Burnley went out in extra-time.

The League now needed their full attention. There was a third of the season to go and they needed points.

The first came with a 3-2 win at West Ham United after which England World Cup winning captain Bobby Moore said: "David Thomas is the future."

And there was a third win in a row when Burnley visited Selhurst Park for the first time and returned with a 2-1 win.

The Valentine's Day clash saw both Burnley and Derby County have a goal disallowed on their way to a 1-1 draw. (This was my first visit to Turf Moor, as a birthday treat. Why could my parents not have waited a week?) Then Forest were beaten 5-0 and Steve Kindon scored his first senior hat-trick!

The following week saw Potts move "upstairs" and 40-year-old Adamson take over. "Without doubt he is the right man for the job," said Potts. With 12 games to go, Burnley were 10 points clear of trouble but they lost at Hillsborough and at home to Everton.

When John Murray was sold to Blackpool for £10,000, Burnley had banked £800,000 in 20 years. Their next match was a tough test at Old Trafford and, for the first time in 64 games, they were without Coates who was on duty for the Football League against the Scottish League. Thomas scored twice; the game ended 3-3 and Burnley were a point nearer safety.

The 10th win of the season saw West Brom beaten 2-1 and a draw with Southampton meant that just one point was needed from the final five games.

The Easter programme of three games in four days could not have gone better. Before the game with Stoke, Coates was applauded on to the pitch to mark his call up for the England squad as Sir Alf Ramsey prepared for Mexico '70. At 23, he was the oldest player in the Burnley line-up that drew 1-1, a scoreline repeated against Coventry before Newcastle were beaten 1-0.

John Angus was skipper for the day to mark his 400th appearance. But the trip to Leeds United ended, as usual, in defeat and then – following a 3-1 win over Chelsea in their final game – the end-of-season table saw Burnley in 14th spot for the fourth consecutive season.

Coates had a hand in each of the three England goals on his full debut against Northern Ireland, but his summer was to end in disappointment. Taken to Mexico as part of the initial 28-man squad, he was one of the six axed for the final line-up and returned "choked and baffled".

O'Neil became the second biggest sale when he went to Southampton for £75,000 and it was also the end of the Turf Moor line for Todd (Sheffield Wednesday, £40,000) and Freddie Smith (Portsmouth, £10,000).

Despite his close-season elevation to the post of Vice-President of the Football League, there was nothing Bob Lord could do to prevent a price hike for the following season that saw the most expensive season ticket jump by more than a third to £16 and the summer also saw the appointment of entertainments manager Jack Butterfield as the club's first-ever commercial manager.

David Thomas
prodigious talent, the youngest Claret in post-war football

1969-70 - First Division

		P	W	D	L	F	A	Pts
1	Everton	42	29	8	5	72	34	66
2	Leeds U	42	21	15	6	84	49	57
3	Chelsea	42	21	13	8	70	50	55
4	Derby C	42	22	9	11	64	37	53
5	Liverpool	42	20	11	11	65	42	51
6	Coventry C	42	19	11	12	58	48	49
7	Newcastle U	42	17	13	12	57	35	47
8	Manchester U	42	14	17	11	66	61	45
9	Stoke C	42	15	15	12	56	52	45
10	Manchester C	42	16	11	15	55	48	43
11	Tottenham H	42	17	9	16	54	55	43
12	Arsenal	42	12	18	12	51	49	42
13	Wolverhampton W	42	12	16	14	55	57	40
14	BURNLEY	42	12	15	15	56	61	39
15	Nottingham F	42	10	18	14	50	71	38
16	West Bromwich A	42	14	9	19	58	66	37
17	West Ham U	42	12	12	18	51	60	36
18	Ipswich T	42	10	11	21	40	63	31
19	Southampton	42	6	17	19	46	67	29
20	Crystal P	42	6	15	21	34	68	27
21	Sunderland	42	6	14	22	30	68	26
22	Sheffield W	42	8	9	25	40	71	25

1969-70

Manager : Harry Potts until February 1970, then Jimmy Adamson

Division One (14th)

Note	No	Date		Venue	Opponents	Result		h/t	Goalscorers/times	Opp. goal times
	1	Aug	9	a	Derby C	D	0-0	0-0		
	2		13	a	Tottenham H	L	0-4	0-2		2, 42, 51, 58
	3		16	h	SUNDERLAND	W	3-0	3-0	Casper (2) 8, 28, Kindon 44	
	4		19	h	TOTTENHAM H	L	0-2	0-2		15, 25
	5		23	a	Liverpool	D	3-3	0-1	Thomas 55, Casper 60, Dobson 68	36p, 49, 80
	6		26	h	LEEDS U	D	1-1	1-1	O'Neil 10	32
	7		30	h	MANCHESTER C	D	1-1	1-1	Dobson 1	3
	8	Sep	6	a	Southampton	D	1-1	1-0	O'Neil 6	56
	9		13	h	ARSENAL	L	0-1	0-0		83
	10		17	a	Chelsea	L	0-2	0-0		58, 89
	11		20	a	Wolverhampton W	D	1-1	1-1	Casper 22	26
	12		27	h	IPSWICH T	L	0-1	0-0		74
	13	Oct	4	a	West Ham U	L	1-3	0-2	Kindon 80	11, 14, 62
	14		8	a	Sunderland	W	1-0	0-0	Coates 58	
	15		11	h	CRYSTAL P	W	4-2	1-2	Dobson 36, Wrigley 47, Casper 51, Coates 71	2, 34
	16		18	h	SHEFFIELD W	W	4-2	0-1	Murray 57p, Collins 60, Dobson 62, Kindon 88	14, 51
	17		25	a	Nottingham F	D	1-1	0-0	Kindon 51	88
	18	Nov	1	h	NEWCASTLE U	L	0-1	0-0		73
	19		8	a	Stoke C	L	1-2	1-0	Casper 23	60, 77
Blant's last game	20		15	h	COVENTRY C	D	0-0	0-0		
	21		22	a	Everton	L	1-2	1-1	Coates 43	14, 56
	22		29	h	MANCHESTER U	D	1-1	1-1	Nulty 42	5
	23	Dec	6	a	West Bromwich A	W	1-0	1-0	Kindon 12	
	24		13	a	Arsenal	L	2-3	1-2	Kindon 22, Storey 46og	33, 43, 77
	25		26	h	LIVERPOOL	L	1-5	0-3	O'Neil 86	26,38,43,52,60
	26	Jan	6	a	Manchester C	D	1-1	0-1	Dobson 86	43
Fred Smith's last game	27		10	h	WOLVERHAMPTON W	L	1-3	0-2	Coates 53	2, 43, 74p
	28		17	a	Ipswich T	W	1-0	0-0	Casper 66	
	29		31	h	WEST HAM U	W	3-2	2-0	Thomas 23, Kindon 43, Coates 73	50, 82
	30	Feb	11	a	Crystal P	W	2-1	0-0	Loughlan 28og, Kindon 89	55
	31		14	h	DERBY C	D	1-1	1-1	Casper 22	24
	32		21	h	NOTTINGHAM F	W	5-0	2-0	Kindon (3) 30, 41, 84, Chapman 48og, Bellamy 59	
	33		28	a	Sheffield W	L	0-2	0-1		30, 84
	34	Mar	7	h	EVERTON	L	1-2	1-2	Kindon 15	14, 40
	35		17	a	Manchester U	D	3-3	3-1	Kindon 2, Thomas (2) 5, 30	24, 70, 87
	36		21	h	WEST BROMWICH A	W	2-1	1-1	Kindon 36, Bellamy 85	21
	37		24	h	SOUTHAMPTON	D	1-1	0-0	Bellamy 54	80
	38		27	h	STOKE C	D	1-1	1-0	Probert 3	83
	39		28	a	Coventry C	D	1-1	0-1	Kindon 65	33p
	40		30	a	Newcastle U	W	1-0	1-0	Moncur 31og	
last games for O'Neil & Todd	41	Apr	4	a	Leeds U	L	1-2	1-1	Faulkner 26og	10, 71
	42		15	h	CHELSEA	W	3-1	2-1	Dobson 10, Kindon (2) 15, 71	16

FA Cup

Note	Rd	Date		Venue	Opponents	Result		h/t	Goalscorers/times	Opp. goal times
	3	Jan	3	h	WOLVERHAMPTON W	W	3-0	0-0	Dobson 73, Casper 78, O'Neil 83	
	4		24	a	Chelsea	D	2-2	0-0	Dobson (2) 80, 87	65, 68
after extra time, 1-1 at 90 mins	rep		27	h	CHELSEA	L	1-3	1-0	Coates 35	73, 92, 116

Final, Chelsea 2-1 Leeds U after extra time, at Old Trafford, after a 2-2 draw after extra time, at Wembley.

League Cup

Rd	Date		Venue	Opponents	Result		h/t	Goalscorers/times	Opp. goal times
2	Sep	3	a	Stoke C	W	2-0	0-0	Thomas 57, Kindon 73	
3		24	a	Rotherham U	D	1-1	1-0	Dobson 34	90
rep		30	h	ROTHERHAM U	W	2-0	0-0	Nulty 63, Dobson 80	
4	Oct	15	h	MANCHESTER U	D	0-0	0-0		
rep		20	a	Manchester U	L	0-1	0-0		54p

Final, Manchester C 2-1 West Bromwich A, at Wembley.

Details of other first team games elsewhere.

Att.	Pos	Mellor	Angus	Latcham	O'Neil	Waldron	Todd	Thomas	Coates	Casper	Docherty	Kindon	Probert	Nulty	Collins	Bellamy	Merrington	Dobson	D Wilson	Wrigley	Murray	P Jones	Blant	J Thomson	F Smith	R Ternent	West	Kinsella	
29,451		1*	2	3	4	5	6	7	8	9	10	11	S*																1
35,920		1	2	3	4	5	6	7	8	9	10	11																	2
13,409	11	1		3	4	5	6	7*	8	9	2	11	10	S*															3
19,485		1		3	4	5	6	7	8	9	2	11			10*	S*													4
51,113	12	1	2	3	4		6	7	8	9		11					5	10											5
28,141		1	2	3	4		6	7	8	9		11					5	10											6
26,342	14	1	2	3	4		6	7	8	9		11					5	10											7
19,339	14	1	2	3	4		6	7*	8	9		11				S*	5	10											8
14,721	16	1	2	3	4	5	6	7*	8	9		11						10	S*										9
24,904	16	1	2	3	4	5	6	7*	8	9		11	S*					10											10
27,556		1	2	3	4	5	6	7	8	9		11						10											11
12,366		1	2	3	4	5	6	7*	8	9		11		S*				10											12
26,445	20	1	2	3	4		6	7	8	9		11					5	10											13
20,311	18	1	2	3				7	8	9		11	6			4	5	10											14
12,661	16	1	2	3					8	9		11	6*		S*	4		10		5	7								15
13,202	13	1		3	S*	5		7*	8	9		11			10			6			4	2							16
19,771	13	1		3	7		6		8	9	2	11			10	4		5											17
16,444	14	1		3	4		6		8	9	2	11			7	10		5											18
18,437	17	1	3		4	5	6	7	8	9	2	11				10													19
11,428	15	1	3	2	4	5		S*	8	9		11*	7			10							6						20
46,380	17	1	3*	6	4			7	8		2	11	9			10		5						S*					21
23,770	17	1		3	4			7*	8		2	11		9		10		5	S*		6								22
18,512	15	1		6	4			7	8		2	11		9			3	5			10								23
21,404	16	1		3	4			7	8		2	11		9		S*	6	5			10*								24
22,954		1		3	4			10	8	S*	2	11		9			6	5			7*								25
22,074	17	1			4				8	7		11				10	6	5	9					3	2				26
13,193	17	1			4			S*	8	7		11*				10	6	5	9					3	2				27
17,801	17	1	2		4		6		8	7		11				10		5	9					3					28
14,494	16	1	2		4			10	8	7		11					6	5	9					3					29
20,857		1	2		4				8	7		11				10	6	5	9					3					30
18,470	16	1	2		4		S*	10	8	7		11					6*	5	9					3					31
11,185	16	1	2		4		6	10	8	7		11				9		5						3					32
23,102	16	1	2		4		6	10	8	7		11				9		5						3					33
21,114	16	1	2		4		6	10	8	7		11				9		5						3					34
38,337		1	2		6		4	7		9		11				8	5	10						3					35
12,801	16	1	2		4		6	10	8	7		11				9		5						3					36
11,166		1	2		4		6	10	8	7		11				9		5						3					37
16,109		1						7	8		2	11	10	9				5		4						3	6		38
24,713	15	1			4	6	S*	10	8	7	2	11	9					5						3*					39
33,264		1	2			4	6	10	8	7	3	11	9					5											40
24,671	15	1	2		S*	4	6	10		7	3	11	9			8*		5											41
12,033		1	2			4		7		9		11	10		8			5								3		6	42
Appearances		42	29	24	35	15	25	34	39	36	16	42	10	5	5	19	15	36	6	2	6	1	1	13	2	2	1	1	
Apps as sub					2		2	2		1			2	2	1	3			2					1					
Goals (56)					3			4	5	8		17	1	1	1	3		6		1	1								5 ogs

Att.	Pos	Mellor	Angus	Latcham	O'Neil	Waldron	Todd	Thomas	Coates	Casper	Docherty	Kindon	Probert	Nulty	Collins	Bellamy	Merrington	Dobson	D Wilson	Wrigley	Murray	P Jones	Blant	J Thomson	F Smith	R Ternent	West	Kinsella	
19,397		1			4				8	7		11				10	6	5	9					3	2				3
48,282		1	2		4				8	7		11				10	6	5	9					3					4
32,000		1	2	S*	4				8	7		11				10	6	5	9*					3					rep
Appearances		3	2		3				3	3		3				3	3	3	3					3	1				
Apps as sub				1																									
Goals (6)					1				1	1								3											

Att.	Pos	Mellor	Angus	Latcham	O'Neil	Waldron	Todd	Thomas	Coates	Casper	Docherty	Kindon	Probert	Nulty	Collins	Bellamy	Merrington	Dobson	D Wilson	Wrigley	Murray	P Jones	Blant	J Thomson	F Smith	R Ternent	West	Kinsella	
19,294		1	2	3	4		6	7	8	9		11					5	10											2
10,969		1	2	3	4	5	6	7	8	9		11						10											3
10,319		1	2	3	4		6		7	9		11		8			5	10											rep
27,959		1	2	3				7	8	9		11			10	4		5				6							4
50,275		1	2*	3	7				8	9	S*	11			10	4		5				6							rep
Appearances		5	5	5	4	1	3	3	5	5		5		1	2	2	2	5				2							
Apps as sub											1																		
Goals (5)								1				1		1				2											

1970-71

OBITUARY
JEREMIAH (JERRY) DAWSON
DIED 8 AUGUST 1970, AGED 82

Many footballers are remembered for one match. Jerry Dawson is an exception as he is remembered for one he did not play in. At the peak of his considerable powers, Dawson was injured in the FA Cup semi-final against Sheffield United and missed the replay. Ronnie Sewell deputised in that game and the next four league games before Dawson returned, only to be injured again. Thus Sewell walked out at the Crystal Palace for the Final against Liverpool in 1914 as Dawson selflessly ruled himself out and missed out on one of the most famous days in Clarets history. But Dawson made up for that absence in so many ways. He signed as a full-time professional as a teenager and by the time he was 20 he had made almost 30 appearances. The Great War halted his career, but he was back in goal by the time domestic football resumed and, of course, earned a Champions' medal in 1920-21. Dawson remained first choice stopper for the next five seasons as he built up 522 league appearances and a total of 569 which remains a record to this day. He made his final appearance on Christmas Day 1928 before joining the coaching staff, also playing Lancashire League cricket at the adjoining Burnley Cricket Club while continuing to live in Cliviger.

RIP

Burnley fans of a certain vintage remember the "team of the seventies" quote by manager Jimmy Adamson with a shiver in the spine.

After finishing 14th for four successive seasons, Adamson looked forward to the new campaign full of confidence and told a pre-season press conference: "Burnley will be the team of the seventies. We are building one of the finest stadiums in the country and we have a great young team to go with it. In the next few years we will win the championship not once, but several times. Everything looks good and we are ready to go."

After four games they were joint bottom of the table, they never climbed out of the bottom two and, after 24 years in the top flight, they were relegated!

It was a season of injury and injustice. Time and time again, opposing managers said Burnley were too good to be relegated. It did not save them.

The summer had seen the start of redevelopment work on the Bee Hole End terrace so that it could accommodate 20,000 fans and plans were in place for two new stands and a capacity of around 40,000.

Adamson returned from holiday to dismiss rumours linking star striker Ralph Coates with a £200,000 transfer to Arsenal. He played more league games than anyone as the sorry season unfolded, but five days after it was finished he departed for a British record transfer fee of £190,000, the move to Spurs concluded on a Staffordshire hotel car park.

Before the season started, chairman Bob Lord, never far from the headlines, hit out at the Professional Footballers' Association by labelling them "nothing more than a bunch of socialists" and claiming that the abolition of the maximum wage had seen top players taking too much out of the game and "not caring one iota" for players in the lower divisions.

Despite the signing of former Liverpool keeper Tony Waiters, already in his 30s, as player-coach, Burnley prepared for the season with their youngest-ever squad and an average age of just 21. Waiters was signed as cover for Peter Mellor and as a coach to all the keepers at the club, but injury to Mellor led to him playing 35 times.

Another keeper was also, sadly, in the headlines as the death of Jerry Dawson was announced. A record-breaker in every sense at Turf Moor he made over 800 appearances for the first team, the reserves, in wartime games, friendlies and various county cup competitions.

Lord told shareholders not to lose any sleep over a £46,000 loss, but fans were concerned when Martin Dobson broke his leg in a pre-season friendly, Peter Mellor needed surgery for a dislocated shoulder and Frank Casper was set to miss the start of the season with illness.

An opening day defeat against Liverpool was followed by draws against Everton and Manchester City, but Burnley were joint bottom after home defeats to Manchester United and Leeds United.

Another draw followed against Chelsea, but when Burnley were beaten 3-0 by bottom club Ipswich, they went bottom themselves. "It is a cause for concern but not a crisis," insisted Adamson, adding that the club was not thinking of making any signings.

Defeats in the League Cup to Aston Villa and Arsenal in the League prompted Gunners' goalkeeper Bob Wilson to say: "They seem to be in a false position but confidence will come when they get their first win."

That win came in the new Texaco Cup when they beat Hearts 3-0, but they lost the second leg 4-1 and went out. But the confidence did not come and they suffered two more defeats to find themselves cut adrift at the foot of the table.

A fifth straight defeat came against West Ham United and the players took the unprecedented step of writing to the Burnley Express. Skipper Dave Merrington, writing on behalf of the entire playing squad, wrote: "The players are 100% behind Jimmy Adamson. Anyone saying different is definitely wrong. We want people to know we have great respect for Mr Adamson. He commands our admiration and loyalty, as always."

The first league win of the season remained elusive and after 12 games they had four points and just six goals to their name. It prompted Keith McNee to write in the Burnley Express: "Relegation is written all over the current Turf Moor scene in large, ugly black letters. They must surely buy someone before long."

It was an outburst that prompted Coates to again deny asking for a transfer and reports from within Turf Moor to suggest that the manager had the unprecedented sum of £100,000 to spend.

But following a 2-0 defeat at Southampton Lord had his own thoughts. "We are not prepared to make the rat race any bigger. There will be no panic buys."

The first win came in the 15th game with success against Crystal Palace but it was swiftly followed by more pain at White Hart Lane and a 4-0 defeat. At this stage in the season the Clarets had scored just eight goals in 16 games, conceding 29 in the process. Defeat at home to Huddersfield made life even tougher for the Turf Moor team, but then teenager Leighton James enjoyed a wonderful debut as Nottingham Forest were dragged back into the relegation mire as the Clarets won 2-1. Mellor and Dobson were back in the fold after seven months out, but hopes of a pre-Christmas revival faded with defeat at the hands of Newcastle United.

In December, Merrington asked to be relieved of the captaincy as he believed it was affecting his performances and Dobson took over. His first game as skipper was a 1-1 draw with West Brom and after 13 weeks, Burnley were off the foot of the table. It was a momentary respite and a draw with Stoke saw them back at the bottom. The year ended with more disappointing results and as 1971 started, they were still bottom, three points from safety.

Oxford United, featuring a certain Ron Atkinson, sent the Clarets reeling in the FA Cup with a 3-0 win and when Dave Thomas made his 100th league appearance in a 1-1 draw with Newcastle, United manager Joe Harvey said: "They are too good to be where they are in the table."

Time was really starting to run out following a defeat at the hands of West Brom. With 15 games to go they were a point shy of safety, but West Ham United had two games in hand. The next game was against their relegation rivals from the East End and when the Hammers won it, the writing really was on the wall.

A defeat at Forest was followed by a draw with Stoke and a first away win of the season as the Clarets completed a "double" over Crystal Palace. It was only their third win of the season and Burnley were in the final third of a troubled campaign.

With 12 games to go the Clarets broke their incoming transfer record by signing Paul Fletcher from Bolton Wanderers for £60,000. But his arrival was followed by an eighth home defeat and after 31 games; Burnley had scored in only 16.

A brief fightback started with a 1-0 win at Huddersfield and draws against Spurs and Ipswich, but a heavy defeat against Leeds saw them cast six points adrift of safety with just seven games to go.

Easter saw wins over relegation rivals Blackpool – Fletcher scoring his first goal – and West Ham, but relegation was almost a certainty after a 3-0 defeat against Coventry.

That near-certainty became a reality with defeat at Arsenal – they went on to do the double that season – and Adamson said: "I accept the whole blame."

The final game brought the 22nd defeat of the season and the Clarets failed to score for the 20th time. With just seven victories all season the Clarets had failed to get their wins column into double figures for to first time ever in a 42-game season. It was to happen on two further occasions in the next decade.

The dust had barely had chance to settle and fans had little enough opportunity to come to terms with relegation before news of the Ralph Coates transfer broke.

As Lord promised to back Adamson, the manager said: "We did not want to sell him (Coates), we had to sell him. If we are going to remain a first class club, we have got to offer our players first class contracts."

Lord described it as: "One of the finest pieces of business enterprise ever pulled off by a football club." And more space was created in the ranks by the departures of Merrington (Bristol City), Les Latcham (Plymouth Argyle) and Ray Ternent (Southend United).

As the players headed away for the summer, fans were divided on prospects of an immediate return but the general consensus of opinion remained that this relegation was only a temporary blip and that things would come good within the not too distant future.

Ralph Coates and Wednesday keeper Peter Springett
Coates bows out after a memorable Turf Moor career

1970-71 - First Division

		P	W	D	L	F	A	Pts
1	Arsenal	42	29	7	6	71	29	65
2	Leeds U	42	27	10	5	72	30	64
3	Tottenham H	42	19	14	9	54	33	52
4	Wolverhampton W	42	22	8	12	64	54	52
5	Liverpool	42	17	17	8	42	24	51
6	Chelsea	42	18	15	9	52	42	51
7	Southampton	42	17	12	13	56	44	46
8	Manchester U	42	16	11	15	65	66	43
9	Derby C	42	16	10	16	56	54	42
10	Coventry C	42	16	10	16	37	38	42
11	Manchester C	42	12	17	13	47	42	41
12	Newcastle U	42	14	13	15	44	46	41
13	Stoke C	42	12	13	17	44	48	37
14	Everton	42	12	13	17	54	60	37
15	Huddersfield T	42	11	14	17	40	49	36
16	Nottingham F	42	14	8	20	42	61	36
17	West Bromwich A	42	10	15	17	58	75	35
18	Crystal P	42	12	11	19	39	57	35
19	Ipswich T	42	12	10	20	42	48	34
20	West Ham U	42	10	14	18	47	60	34
21	BURNLEY	42	7	13	22	29	63	27
22	Blackpool	42	4	15	23	34	66	23

1970-71

Manager : Jimmy Adamson

Division One (21st)
Relegated

Note	No.	Month	Day	Venue	Opponents	Result	Score	h/t	Goalscorers/times	Opp. goal times
	1	Aug	15	h	LIVERPOOL	L	1-2	1-1	Thomas 41	19, 77
	2		18	a	Everton	D	1-1	1-0	Thomas 8	50
	3		22	a	Manchester C	D	0-0	0-0		
	4		25	h	MANCHESTER U	L	0-2	0-0		75, 82
	5		29	h	LEEDS U	L	0-3	0-3		1, 8, 38
	6	Sep	1	h	CHELSEA	D	0-0	0-0		
	7		5	a	Ipswich T	L	0-3	0-2		5, 44, 51p
	8		12	h	ARSENAL	L	1-2	1-1	Roberts 29og	4, 79
	9		19	a	Derby C	L	0-1	0-1		6
	10		26	h	WOLVERHAMPTON W	L	2-3	0-1	Thomas 49p, Waldron 65	42, 60, 78
	11	Oct	3	a	West Ham U	L	1-3	0-2	Coates 82	37, 39, 80
	12		10	h	COVENTRY	D	0-0	0-0		
	13		17	a	Liverpool	L	0-2	0-1		44, 51
	14		24	a	Southampton	L	0-2	0-1		44, 90
	15		31	h	CRYSTAL P	W	2-1	2-0	Probert (2) 21, 26	76
	16	Nov	7	a	Tottenham H	L	0-4	0-1		15, 55, 60, 70
	17		14	h	HUDDERSFIELD T	L	2-3	1-1	West 25, Kindon 87	12, 66, 74
	18		21	h	NOTTINGHAM F	W	2-1	1-0	Nulty 34, Probert 46	52
	19		28	a	Newcastle U	L	1-3	1-1	Probert 24	6, 70, 89
	20	Dec	5	h	WEST BROMWICH A	D	1-1	0-0	Kindon 54	70
	21		12	a	Stoke C	D	0-0	0-0		
	22		19	h	MANCHESTER C	L	0-4	0-2		25, 35, 49, 61
	23		26	a	Blackpool	D	1-1	0-1	Casper 65	9
	24	Jan	9	h	EVERTON	D	2-2	1-0	Casper 6, Dobson 79	53, 56
Merrington's last game	25		16	a	Manchester U	D	1-1	0-0	Dobson 74	46
	26		30	a	Newcastle U	D	1-1	1-0	Probert 20	84
	27	Feb	6	a	West Bromwich A	L	0-1	0-1		44
	28		20	a	Nottingham F	L	0-1	0-1		29
	29		23	h	STOKE C	D	1-1	0-1	Dobson 66	13
	30		27	a	Crystal P	W	2-0	2-0	Coates 6, Dobson 26	
	31	Mar	6	h	SOUTHAMPTON	L	0-1	0-0		82
	32		13	a	Huddersfield T	W	1-0	1-0	Waldron 26	
	33		20	h	TOTTENHAM H	D	0-0	0-0		
	34		27	h	IPSWICH T	D	2-2	0-0	Casper 54, Nulty 90	70, 80
	35	Apr	3	a	Leeds U	L	0-4	0-2		8, 42, 71, 82
	36		10	h	BLACKPOOL	W	1-0	0-0	Fletcher 80	
	37		13	h	WEST HAM U	W	1-0	0-0	Nulty 67	
	38		17	a	Coventry C	L	0-3	0-0		53, 86, 90
	39		20	a	Arsenal	L	0-1	0-1		25p
Latcham's last game	40		24	h	DERBY C	L	1-2	1-0	Casper 29	58, 81
	41		26	a	Chelsea	W	1-0	0-0	Kindon 50	
Coates' last game	42	May	1	a	Wolverhampton W	L	0-1	0-0		66

FA Cup

Round	Month	Day	Venue	Opponents	Result	Score	h/t	Goalscorers/times	Opp. goal times
3	Jan	11	a	Oxford U	L	0-3	0-1		28, 74, 89

Final, Arsenal 2-1 Liverpool after extra time, at Wembley.

League Cup

Round	Month	Day	Venue	Opponents	Result	Score	h/t	Goalscorers/times	Opp. goal times
2	Sep	9	a	Aston Villa	L	0-2	0-0		65, 77

Final, Tottenham H 2-0 Aston Villa, at Wembley.

Details of other first team games elsewhere.

Att.	Pos	Waiters	Angus	Latcham	Bellamy	Waldron	J Thomson	Thomas	Coates	Nulty	Collins	Kindon	Merrington	Probert	Docherty	R Ternent	Casper	West	D Wilson	Cliff	Mellor	Dobson	James	Welch	Fletcher	H Wilson		
25,783		1	2	3	4	5	6	7	8	9	10	11																1
44,717		1	2		4	5	6	7	8			11	3	9	10													2
36,599	15	1	2		4	5	6	7	8			11	3	9	10													3
29,442		1	2		4*	5	6	7	8		S*	11	3	9	10													4
26,057	20	1	2		4	5	6	7	8			11	3	9	10													5
14,580		1	2			5	6	7	8			11		10	4	3	9											6
15,993	22	1	2		S*	5	6	7	8			11		10	4	3	9*											7
12,710	22	1	2			5	6	7	8		10	11	3		4		9											8
26,749	22	1	2			5	6	7	8	11	10		3		4		9											9
13,056	22	1	2*			5	6	7	8	11	10		3		4		9	S*										10
23,295	22	1	2			5		7	8	S*			3	6*	4		9	11	10									11
12,549	22	1	2		11	5	3	7	8						4		9	6	10									12
40,804	22	1			11	5	3		8	2		7			4		9	6	10									13
19,709	22	1			4	5		7	8	6		11		9	2			10		3								14
12,870	22	1			4	5		7	8	6		11		9	2			10		3								15
30,524	22	1		S*	4	5		7	8	6		11		9	2*			10		3								16
18,150	22	1				5		7	8	6		11		9		2	4	10		3								17
13,013	22		2			5		7	8	3				9	4			10			1	6	11					18
20,994	22		2			5		7		8	11		3	9	4			10			1	6						19
12,477	22		2			5		7		3	10	8		9	4						1	6	11					20
13,300	22		2			5		7		3	10	8*		9	4			11			1	6	S*					21
19,917	22		2			5		7	8	3	10			9	4			S*			1	6	11*					22
28,371		1	2			5		7	8	3				9	4		11	10				6						23
17,512	22	1	2			5		7	8	3			S*	9	4		11*	10				6						24
38,796	22	1	2			5		7	8			10	3	9	4		11*		S*			6						25
12,553	22	1	2	3		5		7	8	9		11		10								6		4				26
16,982	22	1	2	3	4	5			8	9		11		10	S*		7*					6						27
20,873	22	1	2	3	9	5		7	8			11		10	4							6						28
12,243	21	1	2	3	9	5		7	8			11		10	4							6						29
20,436	21	1	2	3	9	5		7	8	4		11		10								6						30
15,786	21	1	2	3	7	5			8	4		11		10								6			9			31
18,793	21	1	2	3	10	5		7	8	4		11										6			9			32
16,376	21	1	2	3	10	5		7*	8	4	S*	11										6			9			33
13,479	21	1	2*	3	10	5			8	4	S*	11					7					6			9			34
31,192	21	1		3	10				8	4		11		5	2		7					6			9			35
14,539		1	2	3	4			7*	8	6		11			S*		10					5			9			36
15,841	21	1	2	3	10				8	6	11				4		7					5			9			37
18,365	21	1	2	3	10				8	6	11			S*	4		7*					5			9			38
47,591	21		S*	3	10	2		7		6	8			11	4*						1	5			9			39
10,373	21		2	3	8				7	6	11			4			10		9		1	5						40
14,356	21	1	2					7	8	6	10	11		4			9					5				3		41
19,612	21	1	2					7	8	6	11	10		4			9					5				3		42
Appearances		35	35	16	24	35	12	34	38	30	14	29	10	30	29	3	21	12	4	4	7	25	3	1	9	2		
Apps as sub			1	1	1					1	3		1	1	2			2	1				1					
Goals (29)						2		3	2	3		3		5			4	1				4			1		1	og

Att.	Pos	Waiters	Angus	Latcham	Bellamy	Waldron	J Thomson	Thomas	Coates	Nulty	Collins	Kindon	Merrington	Probert	Docherty	R Ternent	Casper	West	D Wilson	Cliff	Mellor	Dobson	James	Welch	Fletcher	H Wilson		
17,010		1	2			5		7	8	3			S*	9	4			10				6	11*					3
Appearances		1	1			1		1	1	1				1	1			1				1	1					
Apps as sub													1															
Goals (0)																												

Att.	Pos	Waiters	Angus	Latcham	Bellamy	Waldron	J Thomson	Thomas	Coates	Nulty	Collins	Kindon	Merrington	Probert	Docherty	R Ternent	Casper	West	D Wilson	Cliff	Mellor	Dobson	James	Welch	Fletcher	H Wilson		
28,389		1	2		9	5	6	7	8		S*	11		10*	4	3												2
Appearances		1	1		1	1	1	1	1			1		1	1	1												
Apps as sub											1																	
Goals (0)																												

1971-72

The prospects of an automatic return to the top flight produced mixed feelings within the Turf Moor camp. Fans, almost unanimously, demanded it. But there was more caution from officials of the club.

The players certainly had an incentive. In July, manager Jimmy Adamson made it quite clear when he said: "The structure of payments to players has been revised. The emphasis is now on incentive money to get us back in the First Division as soon as possible."

And as the players returned for pre-season training he added: "A lot of people seem keen to warn us that it will be tougher physically in the Second Division. How will we fare? I would say just this. We may not be everybody's idea of promotion favourites, but we must have a good chance."

Relegation had off-the-field effects on the club as well. For the sixth time since the war the balance sheet revealed a loss, this time totalling £27,000, while ambitious plans for an entertainment centre and new main stand in Brunshaw Road were shelved. Despite that, chairman Bob Lord told shareholders at the annual meeting that the club would be doing everything it could to earn promotion at the first attempt.

The season started with a confidence-boosting away draw at Cardiff City followed by a home success against Luton Town. But just a few short months after their FA Cup third round exit at the Manor Ground, the Clarets returned to Oxford and lost again, recovering from that setback with a derby day 3-1 success against Preston North End.

Sidelined for the Deepdale game, Tony Waiters went on the transfer list at his own request, but the early season signs continued to look good with a draw against high-riding Bristol City and a League Cup success against First Division Coventry City that set up a mouth-watering clash with Manchester United.

Wins over Fulham and Queens Park Rangers saw the Clarets climb to third in the table, just one point behind leaders Norwich City.

But they were followed by a defeat at Charlton after which Adamson hit out at Charlton Athletic following reports of a £180,000 bid for Steve Kindon. "It is a deliberate attempt to sabotage Burnley Football Club and its ambitions," said the manager.

Mixed fortunes continued with a 6-1 demolition of Orient followed by a 1-0 defeat against Sunderland after which manager and former Claret Alan Brown said: "We have just beaten the best side in the Second Division."

Leighton James gave Burnley the lead and Paul Fletcher hit the post before Manchester United fought back to force a League Cup replay. That replay saw another great display from Burnley but they lost 1-0.

The Clarets won the first-ever league clash with Carlisle United to climb back up to fourth in the table, but they then lost against leaders Norwich City at Carrow Road before bouncing back with a win over Cardiff City.

The signs were still promising that promotion could be achieved, but it was certainly not proving to be a stroll back to the top flight.

Burnley were certainly enjoying their away games – something Adamson would comment on later in the season – and scored their fifth away win with success at Hull City. Frank Casper scored from the penalty spot to earn a draw with Birmingham City and after 15 games the Clarets remained fourth, four points behind the leaders.

Keith McNee in the Burnley Express believed they were in danger of losing touch with the promotion pack after a 2-1 defeat at Hillsborough saw them slip to six points off the pace, but they remained the goal kings of the division when a 5-2 win over Middlesbrough took their tally to 33 in 17 games. By the end of the season, no-one had scored more Second Division goals than the Clarets who bagged a total of 70. But they let in 55 and only one team in the top half of the table conceded more.

At just 18, Jeff Parton became the Clarets' youngest post-War keeper in the defeat at Watford and when Burnley lost to Swindon in their next game, McNee was prompted to get realistic and write: "Promotion at the first attempt ? Not on this form!"

In December the club revealed that work on a new cantilever stand in Brunshaw Road was already underway and would cost a total of £500,000, the first phase accounting for around £150,000 of that.

Centre forward Paul Fletcher
ever present in his first full season at Turf Moor
a big future in football both on and off the field

Burnley's next game saw them draw 1-1 at Millwall in an X-certificate game and after Waiters left to take up a coaching role at Coventry City, another defeat followed, this time at home to Portsmouth. At the half-way stage Burnley had 22 points from 21 games and were 10 points behind the leaders. The year drew to a close with a win at Ashton Gate and a Boxing Day success against Blackpool in which Steve Kindon equalised before Martin Dobson headed the winner. And having looked set to retire through persistent injury, John Angus returned to training during the festive period.

The New Year started with another away defeat, a 3-1 reverse at Loftus Road. But no-one could really believe that the Clarets had lost and England manager Sir Alf Ramsey, an interested spectator, said afterwards that it was "daylight robbery". Phil Parkes had one of the best games of his career in the Rangers' goal that day and when Oxford United visited Turf Moor for the next match, Mick Kearns followed suit to help his side to a 1-1 draw.

OBITUARY
WILLIAM (BILLY) NESBITT
DIED 11 JANUARY 1972, AGED 80

Billy Nesbitt played a major role in the greatest of times at Turf Moor as a member of both the FA Cup winning side of 1914 and as a league champion in 1920-21. Joining Burnley from Portsmouth Rovers in 1911, he failed to establish himself in his first two seasons. But by the time the FA Cup bandwagon was rolling, he had made the right-wing berth his own and played in each of the eight games that eventually saw the Clarets lift the famous old trophy. He was on the verge of international honours at the outbreak of the Great War, and when domestic football resumed afterwards he remained in the Burnley starting line-up. The 1920-21 season saw him miss just the first two games and his right wing partnership with Bob Kelly was one of the keys to Burnley's success. Two years later he was transferred to Bristol City but eventually succumbed to persistent injury and retired.

RIP

Burnley crashed out of the FA Cup at the first hurdle when a shambolic defensive display allowed First Division Huddersfield Town to beat them 1-0.

That reverse prompted Adamson to splash out £50,000 on England Under 23 international keeper Alan Stevenson, but his debut ended in a 1-0 defeat against Orient.

"Clarets want a new badge" was the big headline in the Burnley Express as commercial manager Jack Butterfield said that they wanted to get away from the borough badge so that they could copyright it. A prize of £50 was on offer and entries flooded in. Two months later John Jolleys of Ashton-in-Ribble was named as the winner. Although not on display as the badge had not been copyrighted, the design was said to include two lions, two red roses, a shuttle, a bee, the hand of friendship and the year 1882. Fans had to wait until the summer of 1973 to finally see the crest which is still in use to this day.

Casper netted another crucial goal as his penalty earned victory over leaders Norwich but cries of "Adamson out, Adamson out" rang round Turf Moor after Hull shook off relegation fears to chalk up a 2-0 win.

A third successive defeat followed against promotion favourites Birmingham, Peter Mellor was sold to Fulham for £25,000 and the losing run was over when Sheffield Wednesday suffered a 10th successive Turf Moor defeat, this time 5-3.

After 34 league and cup appearances, ever-present Dave Thomas missed the trip to Middlesbrough, but Dobson must have wished he'd been the absentee. On his previous visit to Ayresome Park he returned with a broken leg. This time he scored the only goal of the game, unfortunately in his own goal.

Carlisle were beaten for the second time, but defeat at Luton was followed by a 1-1 draw at home to Fulham. Adamson had heard enough of the barracking and hit out at the fans. He described remarks aimed at him as "like water off a duck's back" but stressed that he felt his team were often better away from home where there were not as many Burnley fans to harangue them. He substituted teenager Harry Wilson and said after the game: "He is only a youngster and yet they expect him to play like Terry Cooper. Look at Peter Mellor, a confident, composed goalkeeper – because he was playing for Fulham. He got so much stick here we had to sell him. There is a message there, surely?"

A poor Easter run saw the promotion dream evaporate and although they were to finish with six straight wins, it was too little, too late. The lowest post-War crowd for a league game, less than 9,000, witnessed a great display as relegated Watford went down 3-0. As the Second Division campaign ended with a 2-1 win at Fratton Park, Turf Moor played host to a schoolboy international match which England won 5-2 against Scotland.

In May and after over 500 senior appearances, Angus asked to be released from his contract so he could start a business in his native North-East and there was still plenty of news to come from Turf Moor.

Harry Wilson led a young Clarets team to victory in an international youth tournament in Sunderland. After group success against Sheffield United, Offenbach Kickers and Standard Liege they beat the hosts 1-0 in the final.

Whilst that was going on, teenager Paul Bradshaw was helping England win the "Little World Cup" in Spain. He played a prominent part in all the games leading up to the final against West Germany in Barcelona where he laid on both goals in a 2-0 win.

As the town prepared for the annual holidays, there was more good news as Keith Newton, a member of the England squad in both 1966 and 1970, signed on. But then there was a shock for everyone as Steve Kindon departed for Wolves for a six-figure fee. The 21-year-old had played in 105 league games and scored 25 goals.

1971-72 - Second Division

		P	W	D	L	F	A	Pts
1	Norwich C	42	21	15	6	60	36	57
2	Birmingham C	42	19	18	5	60	31	56
3	Millwall	42	19	17	6	64	46	55
4	Queens Park R	42	20	14	8	57	28	54
5	Sunderland	42	17	16	9	67	57	50
6	Blackpool	42	20	7	15	70	50	47
7	BURNLEY	42	20	6	16	70	55	46
8	Bristol C	42	18	10	14	61	49	46
9	Middlesbrough	42	19	8	15	50	48	46
10	Carlisle U	42	17	9	16	61	57	43
11	Swindon T	42	15	12	15	47	47	42
12	Hull C	42	14	10	18	49	53	38
13	Luton T	42	10	18	14	43	48	38
14	Sheffield W	42	13	12	17	51	58	38
15	Oxford U	42	12	14	16	43	55	38
16	Portsmouth	42	12	13	17	59	68	37
17	Orient	42	14	9	19	50	61	37
18	Preston NE	42	12	12	18	52	58	36
19	Cardiff C	42	10	14	28	56	69	34
20	Fulham	42	12	10	20	45	68	34
21	Charlton A	42	12	9	21	55	77	33
22	Watford	42	5	9	28	24	75	19

1971-72

Manager : Jimmy Adamson

Division Two (7th)

		Date			Opponents	Result		h/t	Goalscorers/times	Opp. goal times
	1	Aug	14	a	Cardiff C	D	2-2	0-2	Casper 65, Dobson 82	9, 36
Angus' last game	2		21	h	LUTON T	W	2-1	0-0	Casper 55, Kindon 57	65
Waiters' last game	3		28	a	Oxford U	L	1-2	0-1	Casper 58	14, 51
	4		30	a	Preston N E	W	3-1	1-0	Kindon 44, Casper 48, Waldron 60p	69p
	5	Sep	4	h	BRISTOL C	D	1-1	0-0	Bellamy 47	49
	6		11	a	Fulham	W	2-0	1-0	James (2) 45, 87	
	7		18	h	QUEENS PARK R	W	1-0	1-0	Bellamy 2	
	8		25	a	Charlton A	L	0-2	0-0		60p, 80
	9		28	h	ORIENT	W	6-1	3-0	Bellamy (3) 6, 87, 88, Thomas 21, Fletcher 45, James 48	55
	10	Oct	2	h	SUNDERLAND	L	0-1	0-0		86
	11		9	a	Carlisle U	W	3-0	0-0	Casper (2) 66, 70, James 86	
	12		13	a	Norwich C	L	0-3	0-2		20, 24, 52
	13		16	h	CARDIFF C	W	3-0	1-0	Casper (2) 40, 64, Thomas 87	
	14		23	a	Hull C	W	2-1	1-0	Fletcher 40, James 68	60
	15		30	h	BIRMINGHAM C	D	1-1	1-0	Casper 40p	49
	16	Nov	6	a	Sheffield W	L	1-2	0-2	West 67	11, 33
	17		13	h	MIDDLESBROUGH	W	5-2	1-1	Bellamy 15, James (2) 60, 88, Nulty 69, Dobson 73	28, 62
	18		20	a	Watford	L	1-2	0-0	Casper 87	61, 84
	19		27	h	SWINDON T	L	1-2	0-2	Dobson 66	42, 44
	20	Dec	4	a	Millwall	D	1-1	1-0	West 8	87
	21		11	h	PORTSMOUTH	L	1-3	1-1	Waldron 19	37og, 65, 82
	22		18	a	Bristol C	W	2-0	0-0	Fletcher (2) 58, 90	
	23		27	h	BLACKPOOL	W	2-1	0-1	Kindon 63, Dobson 83	21
	24	Jan	1	a	Queens Park R	L	1-3	0-1	Fletcher 88	9, 75, 78
	25		8	h	OXFORD U	D	1-1	1-1	Kindon 16	19og
	26		22	a	Orient	L	0-1	0-0		88
	27		29	h	NORWICH C	W	1-0	0-0	Casper 62p	
	28	Feb	12	h	HULL C	L	0-2	0-0		47, 89
	29		19	a	Birmingham C	L	0-2	0-1		32, 86
	30		26	h	SHEFFIELD W	W	5-3	2-2	Fletcher (2) 11, 66, Thomas 35, Casper 47, James 56	12, 34, 88p
	31	Mar	4	a	Middlesbrough	L	0-1	0-0		75
	32		11	h	CARLISLE U	W	3-1	1-0	Thomas 32, Fletcher 55, Collins 90	84
	33		18	a	Luton T	L	0-1	0-1		36
	34		25	h	FULHAM	D	1-1	0-1	Collins 53	38
	35	Apr	1	a	Blackpool	L	2-4	0-4	Casper (2) 46, 83p	2, 5, 36, 44
Bellamy's last game	36		3	a	Sunderland	L	3-4	2-1	Probert 42, Dobson 44, Casper 57	39, 77, 78, 80
	37		4	h	CHARLTON A	W	3-1	1-0	Casper (2) 28, 73, Fletcher 50	78
	38		8	h	WATFORD	W	3-0	2-0	Dobson (2) 29, 71, Casper 31	
	39		15	a	Swindon T	W	1-0	0-0	Probert 76	
	40		22	h	MILLWALL	W	2-0	0-0	Fletcher 53, Dobson 57	
	41		25	h	PRESTON N E	W	1-0	0-0	Probert 51	
	42		29	a	Portsmouth	W	2-1	1-0	Dobson 34, Thomson 75	60

FA Cup

Mellor's last game	3	Jan	15	h	HUDDERSFIELD T	L	0-1	0-0		77

Final, Leeds U 1-0 Arsenal, at Wembley.

League Cup

2	Sep	7	a	Coventry C	W	1-0	0-0	Casper 61	
3	Oct	6	a	Manchester U	D	1-1	1-1	James 32	44
rep		18	h	MANCHESTER U	L	0-1	0-0		79

Final, Stoke C 2-1 Chelsea, at Wembley.

Details of other first team games elsewhere.

Att.	Pos	Waiters	Angus	H Wilson	Bellamy	Waldron	Dobson	Thomas	West	Fletcher	Casper	Kindon	Docherty	Cliff	Collins	Mellor	James	Probert	Nulty	Parton	Thomson	Stevenson	Ingham	Rodaway	
23,004		1	2	3	4	5	6	7	8	9	10	11													1
13,365		1	2	3	4	5	6	7	8	9	10	11													2
8,978	10	1			4	5	6	7	8*	9	10	11	2	3	S*										3
27,284					4	5	6	7	8	9	10	11	2	3		1									4
13,634	7				4*	5	6	7	8	9	10	11	2	3	S*	1									5
10,395	6				4	5	6	7	8	9	10		2	3		1	11								6
13,795	3				4	5	6	7	8	9	10	S*	2	3		1	11*								7
8,920					4	5	6	7	8	9*	10	S*	2	3		1	11								8
12,433					4	5	6	7	8	9	10		2	3		1	11								9
16,496	6				4	5	6	7	8	9	10	S*	2	3		1	11*								10
11,625	4				4	5	6	7	8	9	10		2	3		1	11								11
24,356	4				4*	5	6	7	8	9	10	S*	2	3		1	11								12
12,494	4				4	5	6	7	8	9	10		2	3		1	11								13
15,469	5				4	5	6	7	8	9	10		2	3		1	11								14
17,170	5				4	5	6	7	8	9	10		2	3		1	11								15
23,398	6				4	5	6	7	8	9*	10		2	3		1	11	S*							16
15,720	4				4*	5	6	7	8	9	10	S*	2			1	11		3						17
11,538	5				S*	5	6	7		9	10	8	2				11	4*	3	1					18
12,329	6				S*	5	6	7	4	9	10	11*	2				8		3	1					19
14,747	5				4	5	6	7	8	9	10		2			1	11		3						20
11,381	8				4	5	6	7	8	9	10		2			1	11		3						21
12,909	6				4	5	6	7	8	9		10	2			1	11				3				22
22,015	6				4*	5	6	7	8	9	S*	10	2			1	11				3				23
14,614	7				S*	5	6	7*	4	9	8	10	2			1	11				3				24
10,971	8					5	6	7	4	9	8	10	2			1	11				3				25
9,231	8					5	6	7	4	9	8	10	2				11				3	1			26
13,713	8					5	6	7	4	9	8	10	2				11				3	1			27
11,751	9					5	6	7	4*	9	8	10	2				11				3	1	S*		28
32,035	10			3	S*	5	6	7	4*	9	8		2				11	10				1			29
10,617	9			3	4	5	6	7*		9	8		2		S*		11	10				1			30
17,069	9			3*	4	5	6			9	8	S*	2		7		11	10				1			31
10,346	8			3	4	5	6	7*		9	8		2		S*		11	10				1			32
8,490	9			3	4	5	6	7*		9	8		2		S*		11	10				1			33
10,107	9			3*	4	5	6			9		7	2		8		11	10				1	S*		34
15,931	10			3		5	6	7		9	4		2		8		11	10				1			35
14,034				3	4	5	6			9	8		2					10			11	1	7		36
9,385						5	6			9	8		2				11	10	3		4	1	7		37
8,695	10					5	4			9	8*	S*	2				11	10	3		6	1	7		38
11,818	10					5	4			9	8		2				11	10	3		6	1	7		39
11,271	9					5	4			9	8		2				11	10	3		6	1	7		40
13,067							4			9	8		2				11	10	3		5	1	7	6	41
5,885	7						4			9	8		2				11	10	3		5	1	7	6	42
Appearances		3	2	10	27	40	42	33	28	42	39	15	40	14	3	20	36	15	11	2	14	17	7	2	
Apps as sub					4						1	7			5			1					2		
Goals (70)					6	2	9	4	2	10	18	4			2		8	3	1		1				

Att.	Pos	Waiters	Angus	H Wilson	Bellamy	Waldron	Dobson	Thomas	West	Fletcher	Casper	Kindon	Docherty	Cliff	Collins	Mellor	James	Probert	Nulty	Parton	Thomson	Stevenson	Ingham	Rodaway	
21,563						5	6	7	4	9	8	10	2			1	11				3				3
Appearances						1	1	1	1	1	1	1	1			1	1				1				
Apps as sub																									
Goals (0)																									

Att.	Pos	Waiters	Angus	H Wilson	Bellamy	Waldron	Dobson	Thomas	West	Fletcher	Casper	Kindon	Docherty	Cliff	Collins	Mellor	James	Probert	Nulty	Parton	Thomson	Stevenson	Ingham	Rodaway	
15,413					4	5	6	7	8	9	10		2	3		1	11								2
44,600					4	5	6	7*	8	9	10	S*	2	3		1	11								3
27,511						5	6	7	8	9	10		2	3		1	11	4							rep
Appearances					2	3	3	3	3	3	3		3	3		3	3	1							
Apps as sub												1													
Goals (2)											1						1								

1972-73

OBITUARY
JOHN HENRY (JACK) HILL
DIED APRIL 1972, AGED 75

Ranking third among the players most often capped by England while with Burnley, Jack Hill's place in Turf Moor folklore is perhaps less than he deserves because his time at the club coincided with a decline in its fortunes.

He was born at Hetton-le-Hole, a uniquely rich source of fine players for Burnley, in 1897. The fee paid by Burnley to Plymouth for his signature in May 1923, £6,000, was a club record, and Hill very quickly lived up to his billing. Tommy Boyle, centre-half and captain of the side that had won the League title two years earlier, was a supremely tough act to follow, but Hill filled both roles to perfection over the next five years. Tall and strongly built, he was a stopper of the old school and remained a stalwart in a Clarets' defence that was not noticeably watertight in that period.

First capped for his country in 1925, he went on to make eight England appearances while at Turf Moor, a total topped only by Bob Kelly and John Connelly. One of those appearances was as the England captain in the only full international staged at the Turf, but it was not Hill's finest day as he put through his own goal as Wales beat England 2-1.

He was sold to Newcastle for £8,000 in October 1928, becoming captain there and winning further England caps. He subsequently played for Bradford City and Hull where he was later appointed manager.

RIP

One of the key reasons for Burnley's failure to bounce straight back in the 1971-72 season was a lack of consistency in team selection. Only two players were ever-present, four goalkeepers were used and injuries to key players had resulted in a stop-start season.

But 1972-73 was a different story. Six players – Alan Stevenson, Keith Newton, Colin Waldron, Jim Thomson, Frank Casper and Leighton James – featured in all 42 games, skipper Martin Dobson missed just one and Paul Fletcher played in 40.

They provided a successful spine to the team and after a consistent campaign in which only four games were lost, they were champions of the Second Division for the first time since 1898.

In July when the players reported back for training, chairman Bob Lord told them: "Let's try to get back to the First Division. But for one bad patch at the start of the year, we might be there now."

And manager Jimmy Adamson added: "We were apprehensive last year but now we know what to expect and we also feel better equipped than last year. The signings of Alan Stevenson and Keith Newton will strengthen the defensive part of the game and I don't expect to give away the vital goals that we were conceding last season."

Pre-season games in Wales resulted in a win at Swansea and a draw at Newport County. At the end of July, Burnley made their debut in the Watney Cup and beat Lincoln City before losing to Bristol Rovers. A friendly defeat at Blackpool did not make for good reading and Adamson admitted: "We looked a bit lethargic, now we've got a week to sharpen up both physically and mentally.

Whatever happened in that week did the trick as the Clarets opened the season with a 16-match unbeaten run.

Lord stressed at the annual meeting of shareholders that promotion was going to be the focus of the entire club, but just before the season kicked off Preston North End manager Alan Ball said: "Burnley are a bit of a mystery to me, but they should not be dismissed despite their slump last season and their pre-season failings this time."

By the end of August he was to find out just how good the Clarets were. Draws against Carlisle and Fulham, Peter Mellor conceding his first goal at Craven Cottage in his 10th appearance there, were followed by a 4-1 thumping of Aston Villa.

Preston were next up, Burnley won 2-0 and Adamson was manager-of-the-month for August.

A 2-0 win at Portsmouth saw Burnley on top of the table with eight points from five games and they were never out of the top three for the remainder of the season.

Following a 4-0 League Cup exit at the hands of Leeds United, Burnley showed great resilience to come from behind to draw with QPR, Hull and Orient, but when they went 4-0 up against Blackpool things nearly went horribly wrong and the Clarets battled hard to hold out for a 4-3 win.

They remained unbeaten after 10 games but the draw against Middlesbrough was a goalless bore according to Peter Higgs in the Burnley Express.

Leighton James then gave the Clarets the lead after three minutes at Luton, but had to come up with a late equaliser to salvage a point. That draw saw them slip off the top of the table, but Dobson grabbed a winner against Swindon to send them straight back to the summit.

Dave Thomas was withdrawn after 30 minutes of the Luton game, suspended by the club for two weeks following an internal hearing and before that suspension was over he was sold to QPR for £165,000 – a fee that broke the Loftus Road record of £110,000 they had spent on Stan Bowles. At that stage QPR did not appear to be among the main promotion rivals, but by the end of the season it had become a two-horse race.

Fletcher scored his first league hat-trick as Cardiff were beaten 3-0 and after a third of the season, Burnley were top with 21 points from 14 games.

Fletcher bagged an equaliser at Millwall in Dobson's 150th league appearance and, according to Higgs, Burnley committed floodlight robbery to score twice in the last 10 minutes and earn a 3-3 draw at Ayresome Park.

Despite sitting on top of the table, Burnley were attracting 2,000 less fans for their home games than they had the previous season and fans started a campaign to get more people to Turf Moor. Adamson welcomed the initiative by saying: "The Turf Moor crowd has helped us on several occasions already this season. The more there are the better it will be."

The 17th game of the season brought the first defeat as Orient won 2-1 at Turf Moor, but Burnley bounced back immediately as Dobson scored the only goal of the game at the Goldstone Ground and their position at the top of the table was cemented with a win over Forest.

The run of 1-0 wins continued at Roker Park and Ashton Gate and when the Clarets signed off 1972 with a win over Blackpool - Harry Potts had recently returned to management by taking over from Bob Stokoe at Bloomfield Road – and draws against Oxford and Fulham, all roads appeared to lead back to the First Division.

As 1973 started with a 3-0 win at Villa Park, Higgs asked "Who can stop Burnley now?" to which Adamson replied "We're not taking promotion for granted."

The Second Division leaders were paired with First Division toppers Liverpool in the FA Cup. The Turf Moor date ended in a 0-0 stalemate, but Liverpool went on to win the replay 3-0, although the Clarets were far from disgraced. With 17 games to go, all that now mattered was the chase for promotion. The next game was a top-versus-second clash at Loftus Road. Rangers won 2-0, but Burnley still led by a point after their 14th away game of the season had resulted in their first away defeat.

Wins over Huddersfield and Hull were followed by a draw at Carlisle and a similar result at home to Bristol City and with nine weeks to go Burnley and QPR had pulled well clear of the chasing pack.

Swindon asked for their game at the County Ground to be switched to Friday evening so that it did not clash with the following day's League Cup Final. Burnley won 1-0 and then the squad headed to London to watch former team-mate Ralph Coates come off the bench to score the only goal as Spurs beat Norwich.

The title hopes took a knock when Wednesday ended years of Turf Moor misery by chalking up a 1-0 win. But once again, Burnley went straight back to the top with a win at Cardiff followed by success against both Portsmouth and Millwall.

With seven games to go, Burnley were 11 points clear of the third place team and within touching distance of the top flight. They were also three clear of QPR, but the Londoners had a game in hand.

A 3-0 reverse against Forest, their heaviest defeat of the season, put the champagne on hold, but when QPR lost at Oxford the Clarets were a point clear and on level games.

Promotion was assured with four games to go as Huddersfield and Sunderland were both beaten 2-0 and the race was on for the title.

Easter brought a first-ever win over Oxford and further success against Brighton and Luton and with one game to go, a point was all that was needed to bring the title to Turf Moor.

But what would football be without a twist in the tale? The last game was at Preston and North End needed a point to stay up! The home side applauded Burnley on to the pitch and after a dull opening, took the lead two minutes before the interval. Waldron equalised and everyone had what they wanted. Adamson, however, would have none of the suggestions that it was a contrived result. "Some people will say it was a fix, but you only had to see the game to realise it was nothing of the kind. If we could have scored five, we would have done."

It had taken a season longer than many had hoped for Burnley to return to the promised land, but they had done it in style. Fletcher led the way with 15 goals, but Burnley were not totally reliant on one man and Dobson, Casper and James all reached double figures.

If there was one disappointment it was the level of support. Four days after the title was confirmed, 16,000 turned out for the John Angus testimonial evening and that was 2,000 up on the average league attendance.

The evening itself was a fitting tribute to a true one-club man. An Old Stars team played the young Clarets and then the champions took on a Millionaires team largely made up of players Burnley had sold.

Willie Irvine returned to Turf Moor and proved that Angus meant so much to his former team-mates by missing a relegation battle for his new club, Halifax, at Walsall – a decision which cost him a £100 fine!

Adamson was named manager-of-the-year, Dobson was Granada TV's player-of-the-year despite opposition from First Division players in the region and Jimmy Robson returned to the club as a youth development player.

As the first team squad enjoyed a celebratory holiday in Majorca, Ray Hankin headed for Italy for the Little World Cup. Striker Hankin had made his Burnley debut in the penultimate game of the season and featured in every game as England went on to beat East Germany in the final, scoring one of the goals in a 3-2 success.

Martin Dobson
led the Clarets to the Second Division Championship

1972-73 - Second Division

		P	W	D	L	F	A	Pts
1	BURNLEY	42	24	14	4	72	35	62
2	Queens Park R	42	24	13	5	81	37	61
3	Aston Villa	42	18	14	10	51	47	50
4	Middlesbrough	42	17	13	12	46	43	47
5	Bristol C	42	17	12	13	63	51	46
6	Sunderland	42	17	12	13	59	49	46
7	Blackpool	42	18	10	14	56	51	46
8	Oxford U	42	19	7	15	52	43	45
9	Fulham	42	16	12	14	58	49	44
10	Sheffield W	42	17	10	15	59	55	44
11	Millwall	42	16	10	16	55	47	42
12	Luton T	42	15	11	16	44	53	41
13	Hull C	42	14	12	16	64	59	40
14	Nottingham F	42	14	12	16	47	52	40
15	Orient	42	12	12	18	49	53	36
16	Swindon T	42	10	16	16	46	60	36
17	Portsmouth	42	12	11	19	42	59	35
18	Carlisle U	42	11	12	19	50	52	34
19	Preston NE	42	11	12	19	37	64	34
20	Cardiff C	42	11	11	20	43	58	33
21	Huddersfield T	42	8	17	17	36	56	33
22	Brighton & HA	42	8	13	21	46	83	29

1972-73

Manager : Jimmy Adamson

Division Two (1st)
Champions

			Date		Opponents	Result		h/t	Goalscorers/times	Opp. goal times
	1	Aug	12	h	CARLISLE U	D	2-2	0-1	James 49, Thomas 76	29, 64
	2		19	a	Fulham	D	1-1	1-0	James 2	50
	3		26	h	ASTON VILLA	W	4-1	3-1	Collins 3, Fletcher 28, Dobson 32, Casper 76	15
	4		29	h	PRESTON N E	W	2-0	1-0	James 35, Thomas 55	
	5	Sep	2	a	Portsmouth	W	2-0	1-0	Fletcher 7, Thomas 63	
	6		9	h	QUEENS PARK R	D	1-1	1-1	Casper 38	35
	7		16	a	Hull C	D	1-1	0-1	James 84	30
	8		18	a	Orient	D	1-1	0-1	Casper 87	7
	9		23	h	BLACKPOOL	W	4-3	2-0	Waldron 16, Dobson 30, James 59, Thomas 63	66, 83, 86
	10		26	h	MIDDLESBROUGH	D	0-0	0-0		
Thomas' last game	11		30	a	Luton T	D	2-2	1-1	James (2) 3, 89	16p, 54
	12	Oct	7	h	SWINDON T	W	2-1	1-0	Fletcher 31, Dobson 80	68
	13		14	a	Sheffield W	W	1-0	0-0	James 53	
	14		21	h	CARDIFF C	W	3-0	1-0	Fletcher (3) 30, 64, 83p	
	15		28	a	Millwall	D	1-1	0-1	Fletcher 56	37
	16	Nov	4	a	Middlesbrough	D	3-3	1-1	Waldron 21, Fletcher 80, Dobson 87	37, 47, 78
West's last game	17		11	h	ORIENT	L	1-2	1-0	Dobson 9	70, 87
	18		18	a	Brighton & H A	W	1-0	0-0	Dobson 46	
	19		25	h	NOTTINGHAM F	W	1-0	0-0	Fletcher 57	
	20	Dec	2	a	Sunderland	W	1-0	0-0	Fletcher 70	
	21		16	a	Bristol C	W	1-0	1-0	Dobson 4	
	22		23	h	OXFORD U	D	1-1	1-0	Waldron 44	73
	23		26	a	Blackpool	W	2-1	1-1	Casper (2) 10, 78	22
	24		30	h	FULHAM	D	2-2	1-1	Nulty 36, Pentecost 72og	5, 88
	25	Jan	6	a	Aston Villa	W	3-0	2-0	Newton 7, Nulty 23, Ingham 48	
	26		27	a	Queens Park R	L	0-2	0-2		15, 20
	27	Feb	3	h	HUDDERSFIELD T	W	2-1	0-0	Nulty 66, Ingham 87	90
	28		10	h	HULL C	W	4-1	1-0	Casper 31, Nulty 51, Ingham 56, Dobson 77	50
	29		17	a	Carlisle U	D	1-1	1-0	Dobson 45	85
	30		24	h	BRISTOL C	D	1-1	1-0	Dobson 7	65
	31	Mar	2	a	Swindon T	W	1-0	1-0	Fletcher 6	
	32		10	h	SHEFFIELD W	L	0-1	0-0		74
	33		17	a	Cardiff C	W	1-0	1-0	Casper 3	
Probert's last game	34		20	h	PORTSMOUTH	W	4-0	4-0	Nulty 15, Casper (2) 17, 36, Fletcher 29	
	35		24	h	MILLWALL	W	2-1	2-1	Dobson 42, Nulty 44	24
	36		31	a	Nottingham F	L	0-3	0-2		5, 26, 73
	37	Apr	14	a	Huddersfield T	W	2-0	0-0	Casper 61, Fletcher 74	
	38		16	h	SUNDERLAND	W	2-0	1-0	Fletcher (2) 27, 89	
	39		20	a	Oxford U	W	2-0	1-0	Casper 43, Ingham 80	
	40		21	h	BRIGHTON & H A	W	3-0	1-0	James 38, Casper 72, Dobson 82	
	41		24	h	LUTON T	W	3-0	0-0	James 62, Thomson 67, Collins 72	
	42		28	a	Preston N E	D	1-1	0-1	Waldron 53	43

FA Cup

					Result		h/t	Goalscorers/times	Opp. goal times
3	Jan	13	h	LIVERPOOL	D	0-0	0-0		
rep		16	a	Liverpool	L	0-3	0-1		36, 49, 74

Final, Sunderland 1-0 Leeds U, at Wembley.

League Cup

					Result		h/t	Goalscorers/times	Opp. goal times
2	Sep	6	a	Leeds U	L	0-4	0-0		47, 52, 57, 75

Final, Tottenham H 1-0 Norwich C, at Wembley.

Details of other first team games elsewhere.

Att.	Pos	Stevenson	Docherty	Newton	Dobson	Waldron	J Thomson	Ingham	Casper	Fletcher	Thomas	James	West	Collins	Nulty	Cliff	Probert	Hankin		
9,834		1	2	3	4	5	6	7*	8	9	10	11	S*							1
10,285	10	1	2	3	4	5	6		8	9	7	11		10						2
14,941	6	1	2	3	4	5	6	S*	8	9	7	11*		10						3
13,205	2	1	2	3	4	5	6		8	9	7	11		10						4
11,701	top	1	2	3	4	5	6		8	9	7	11		10						5
10,896	2	1	2	3	4	5	6		8	9	7	11		10						6
8,921	3	1	2	3	4	5	6		8	9	7	11		10						7
4,924		1	2	3	4	5	6		8	9	7*	11		10	S*					8
14,625	top	1	2	3	4	5	6		8	9	7	11		10*	S*					9
12,398		1	2	3		5	6	10	8	9	7	11			4					10
12,197	3	1	2	3	4	5	6		8	9	7*	11		10	S*					11
11,434	top	1	2	3	4	5	6		8	9		11		10	7					12
30,394	top	1	2	3	4	5	6		8	9		11		10	7					13
13,442	top	1	2	3	4	5	6		8	9		11		10	7					14
11,622	top	1	2	3	4	5	6		8	9		11		10	7					15
18,127	top	1	2	3	4	5	6		8	9		11		10	7					16
12,090	top	1	2	3	4*	5	6		8	9		11	S*	10	7					17
17,470	top	1	2	3	4	5	6		8	9		11		10	7					18
12,095	top	1	2	3	4	5	6		8	9		11		10	7					19
16,812	top	1	2	3	4	5	6		8	9		11		10	7					20
15,334	top	1	2	3	4	5	6		8	9		11		10	7					21
12,808	top	1	2	3	4	5	6		8	9		11		10	7					22
25,277	top	1	2	3	4	5	6		8	9		11		10	7					23
15,512	top	1	2	3	4	5	6		8	9		11		10	7					24
38,637	top	1	2	3	4	5	6	10	8	9		11			7					25
22,518	top	1	2	3	4	5	6	S*	8	9		11		10*	7					26
14,589	top	1	2	3	4	5	6	S*	8	9*		11		10	7					27
13,760	top	1	2	3	4	5	6	9	8			11		10	7					28
17,840	top	1		3	4	5	6	9	8			11		10	7	2				29
13,630	top	1		3	4	5	6		8	9		11		10	7	2				30
12,730	top	1	2	3	4	5	6		8	9		11		10	7					31
16,968	2	1	2	3	4	5	6	S*	8	9		11		10*	7					32
11,343	top	1	2	3	4	5	6	10	8	9		11			7					33
13,610		1	2	3*	4	5	6		8	9		11		10	7		S*			34
13,656	top	1	2	3	4	5	6	S*	8	9		11		10*	7					35
12,552	top	1	2	3	4	5	6	S*	8	9		11		10*	7					36
13,437	top	1	2*	3	4	5	6	S*	8	9		11		10	7					37
22,852		1		3	4	5	6	2	8	9		11		10	7					38
13,740		1		3	4	5	6	10	8	9		11			7	2				39
15,968	top	1		3	4	5	6	2	8	9		11		10	7					40
17,708		1		3	4	5	6	2	8*	9		11		10	7			S*		41
21,550	top	1		3	4	5	6	2	8	9		11		10	7					42
Appearances		42	35	42	41	42	42	11	42	40	11	42		37	32	3				
Apps as sub								7					2		3		1	1		
Goals (72)				1	12	4	1	4	12	15	4	10		2	6				1	og

Att.	Pos	Stevenson	Docherty	Newton	Dobson	Waldron	J Thomson	Ingham	Casper	Fletcher	Thomas	James	West	Collins	Nulty	Cliff	Probert	Hankin		
35,730		1	2	3	4	5	6	10	8	9		11			7					3
56,124		1	2	3	4	5	6	S*	8	9		11		10*	7					rep
Appearances		2	2	2	2	2	2	1	2	2		2		1	2					
Apps as sub								1												
Goals (0)																				

Att.	Pos	Stevenson	Docherty	Newton	Dobson	Waldron	J Thomson	Ingham	Casper	Fletcher	Thomas	James	West	Collins	Nulty	Cliff	Probert	Hankin		
20,857		1	2	3	4*	5	6		8	9	7	11		10	S*					2
Appearances		1	1	1	1	1	1		1	1	1	1		1						
Apps as sub															1					
Goals (0)																				

1973-74

Two games seven days apart on the other side of the Pennines created some of the biggest headlines of the 1973-74 season. Malcolm Macdonald scored twice at Hillsborough to deny the Clarets a place at Wembley in the FA Cup Final as Burnley looked to put the icing on the cake of a stunning return to the top flight.

But their chances had been hindered by events at Elland Road the previous weekend.

Leeds United already had one hand on the Championship trophy by the time the Burnley squad made the trip to Yorkshire. But by the time the Clarets had won 4-1 in front of almost 40,000 fans one of their talismen was struggling to make the date with Newcastle.

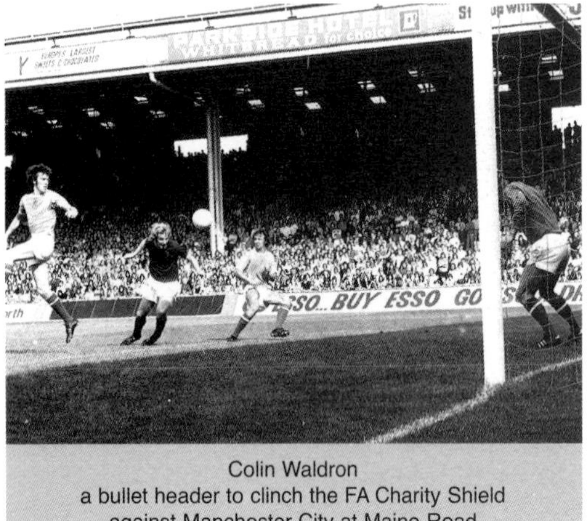

Colin Waldron
a bullet header to clinch the FA Charity Shield against Manchester City at Maine Road

The scoreline caught the public imagination. Paul Fletcher's stunning overhead kick was talked about for years afterwards. But the injury to Frank Casper, inflicted off the ball by Norman Hunter, made the following week's FA Cup semi-final an even tougher task for the Clarets and also curtailed Casper's career.

Fletcher headed the Clarets into the lead, but Allan Clarke equalised. Almost immediately came the goal that had Clarets' fans drooling. A Peter Noble centre was flicked up by Geoff Nulty for Fletcher. With his back to goal, he leapt into the air and bicycle-kicked his volley beyond a bemused David Harvey.

Seventeen minutes after the restart Martin Dobson tackled Paul Madeley in midfield and left Leeds exposed. Casper passed to Fletcher and he swung the ball to Dougie Collins who placed the perfect lob over Harvey and the result was beyond doubt.

With 20 minutes to go Collins floated the ball over to Colin Waldron who headed across the face of goal and Nulty got down on all fours to head the ball home.

Leeds were humbled. Casper had prompted and probed and Hunter had had enough. With just eight minutes to go Hunter fouled Casper. The ball was yards away and Casper was on the running track that surrounded the Elland Road pitch. Although Casper did play again for the Clarets, it was a tackle that effectively ended his career as he never fully rediscovered his form.

He did play at Hillsborough, but it was a patched-up Casper who tried to help his team against Newcastle and in the end they suffered the agony of semi-final defeat.

Both those games came towards the end of a season in which Burnley raised more than a few eyebrows.

The summer had seen the departure of Eddie Cliff and Eric Probert to Notts County for a combined fee of £35,000, an amount re-invested in the purchase of Peter Noble from Swindon Town.

The Second Division champions kicked off the season with a Charity Shield victory at Maine Road when Colin Waldron scored the only goal of the game.

Manchester City winger Mike Summerbee, a Claret himself two years later, was fulsome in his praise: "This could be one of the greatest teams. The big name First Division sides are going to get some shocks this season. Once Burnley have settled in the top flight they could easily become the team of the 70s."

On the eve of the season the club unveiled a new crest that had been two years in the making and is still in use today.

Chairman Bob Lord threatened to resign from the League Management Committee if he did not get his own way in a crucial vote of other chairman over payments made from both Football Pools and television companies.

The Clarets certainly started the season in fine style, unbeaten in the first seven games with wins on the road at Sheffield United – 'Back with a Bang' screamed the headline in the Burnley Express - Tottenham Hotspur and Wolverhampton Wanderers, Turf Moor success against Chelsea and draws with Coventry, Spurs and Derby County.

In the absence of the injured Mick Docherty, stretchered off at Bramall Lane on the opening day of the season, new recruit Noble had his chance. Originally signed as striker or attacking midfielder, he was forced into action at right back and missed only one game in the remainder of the season.

Casper started the season alongside Fletcher, but after six games he made way for Ray Hankin, a winner with England during the summer in the Little World Cup competition in Italy.

Casper had pulled the strings in the win at White Hart Lane. Six days later in the Turf Moor return he was carried off after just 12 minutes, targeted for some rough treatment by the Spurs defence.

A 7-0 thrashing of East Fife in the Texaco Cup which saw Fletcher grab a hat-trick was followed by the first defeat of the season at Ipswich where the Clarets lost 3-2. "It was a bad result but a good performance," said Adamson afterwards.

But they bounced back immediately and three more wins followed.

Burnley were attracting a lot of attention and not all of it was welcome. Adamson went on record as saying that he had instructed his players to wear shin pads in every game and highlighted that Keith Newton had avoided serious injury following a challenge by Mike Summerbee as the Clarets beat City 3-0.

Burnley played their 10th game of the season at Upton Park, winning 1-0 to sit second in the table behind Leeds United

despite being tipped for relegation by most bookmakers.
Colin Waldron was sent off in the 2-2 draw at Cardiff in the League Cup. He was the first Claret to be dismissed for more than five years, Waldron himself being the last following a clash with Allan Clarke at Leicester City.
During the summer England Under 23 midfielder Alan West had been rumoured to be on his way. A bid from Manchester United was turned down, he was "sold" to Sunderland for £75,000 but then failed a medical and then departed to Second Division Luton Town for £100,000, becoming the fifth Burnley player to leave the club for a six-figure sum.
The Texaco Cup paired the Clarets with Hearts and for the first time fans were given the chance to catch a charter flight. It was well supported and the fans were rewarded with a 3-0 win against a side managed by 1959/60 Championship winner Bobby Seith.
In the last 32 of the League Cup, Burnley were tipped to go all the way but crashed out 2-1 to Plymouth with Argyle boss Tony Waiters criticising Burnley fans for slow hand-clapping their team in the second half.
There were no goals, but Burnley gave leaders Leeds a fright in front of over 37,000 fans, the biggest attendance at Turf Moor for more than seven years and the third biggest of the day in the First Division.

OBITUARY
JAMES (JIMMY) HOGAN
DIED 30 JANUARY 1974, AGED 91

Jimmy Hogan's Burnley career was fairly brief, but much later in life he became something of a legend in the game for his pioneering work as a coach in Europe.
Born in Nelson in 1882, his first professional club was his home town team. He arrived at Turf Moor via Rochdale in 1903 and made 50 League appearances for Burnley as an inside-forward over the next two years but moved to Fulham after a dispute with the club. He later appeared for Swindon and Bolton but never really broke through to greatness as a player.
Once his playing days were over, though, it was a different story. His first coaching appointment was with the Dutch FA in 1910 and he also worked in Austria, Hungary and various other European countries during the 1920s and 30s. He returned to England in 1934 to manage first Fulham and then Aston Villa, who he led to the Second Division title in 1938.
The peak of his career, though, came after the war when he coached the famous Hungarian side Honved, who contributed much to the Hungary team which thrashed England twice in the 1953-54 season, in the process destroying the myth of English football infallibility. In all, Hogan's football career lasted 66 years and he was given much of the credit for the advances made in playing techniques in Europe. He died in hospital in Burnley, the town he always looked on as home.
RIP

By mid-November kick-off times were being rearranged to accommodate the power cuts during the miners' strike and an off key side lost to Leicester before recovering with wins against Stoke and Norwich to stand third in the table behind Leeds and Liverpool.
Norwich were beaten home and away for a 5-2 aggregate win and a place in the Texaco Cup final, before Arsenal were beaten 2-1 at Turf Moor.
The Clarets signed off the year with victory over Liverpool, defeat at Maine Road and a draw with Wolves before starting the New Year with another draw, this time with Coventry.
Grimsby were despatched in the third round of the FA Cup but then Burnley conceded five for the first time in more than four years as Derby County beat them 5-1.
The miners' strike brought another change for the Clarets. Most kick-off times had been altered to avoid the use of floodlight, but Bob Lord spent £30,000 on a generator and Burnley lost 2-1 to Sheffield United in a game that kicked-off at 7 p.m. on a Saturday.
The FA Cup campaign continued with a 4-1 win over Oldham and in the next game, a 1-1 draw at Arsenal, Brian Flynn made his debut.
Going well in the FA Cup and with a place in the Texaco Cup final to look forward to, the Clarets could not win a league game and were slipping down the table.
Aston Villa were despatched in the FA Cup as the new Brunshaw Road Stand was used for the first time and they eventually claimed a league victory, 3-1 win at Everton, on 16 March, the eve of a momentous run for the club. The FA Cup was dangling in their faces and the UEFA Cup still beckoned.
The 4-1 win at Elland Road was one of the biggest headlines of the season, but it was a patched-up Casper who came closest to scoring at Hillsborough the following weekend as the cup dream died.
Seventh in the table, they had nine games to climb to fourth and a definite place in Europe, or fifth and hope for things to go in their favour.
But too many draws and a heavy defeat against Stoke eventually saw them finish sixth and miss out on goal difference.
They lost the Texaco Cup final in extra-time at St James's Park but finished the season by winning the FA Cup third place play-off match at Filbert Street.

1973-74 - First Division

		P	W	D	L	F	A	Pts
1	Leeds U	42	24	14	4	66	31	62
2	Liverpool	42	22	13	7	52	31	57
3	Derby C	42	17	14	11	52	42	48
4	Ipswich T	42	18	11	13	67	58	47
5	Stoke C	42	15	16	11	54	42	46
6	BURNLEY	42	16	14	12	56	53	46
7	Everton	42	16	12	14	50	48	44
8	Queens Park R	42	13	17	12	56	52	43
9	Leicester C	42	13	16	13	51	41	42
10	Arsenal	42	14	14	14	49	51	42
11	Tottenham H	42	14	14	14	45	50	42
12	Wolverhampton W	42	13	15	14	49	49	41
13	Sheffield U	42	14	12	16	44	49	40
14	Manchester C	42	14	12	16	39	46	40
15	Newcastle U	42	13	12	17	49	48	38
16	Coventry C	42	14	10	18	43	54	38
17	Chelsea	42	12	13	17	56	60	37
18	West Ham U	42	11	15	16	55	60	37
19	Birmingham C	42	12	13	17	52	64	37
20	Southampton	42	11	14	17	47	68	36
21	Manchester U	42	10	12	20	38	48	32
22	Norwich C	42	7	15	20	37	62	29

1973-74

Manager : Jimmy Adamson

Division One (6th)

	Date			Opponents	Result		h/t	Goalscorers/times	Opp. goal times
1	Aug	25	a	Sheffield U	W	2-0	2-0	Collins 32, Dobson 42	
2		28	h	CHELSEA	W	1-0	0-0	Casper 80	
3	Sep	1	h	COVENTRY C	D	2-2	1-1	Fletcher 29, Dobson 75	33, 54
4		5	a	Tottenham H	W	3-2	1-2	James 11, Casper 82p, Collins 85	16, 44
5		8	a	Wolverhampton W	W	2-0	0-0	Casper 48, Nulty 82	
6		11	h	TOTTENHAM H	D	2-2	2-1	Nulty 27, Waldron 34	45, 51
7		15	h	DERBY C	D	1-1	0-1	Hankin 73	32
8		22	a	Ipswich T	L	2-3	1-2	James 44, Collins 77	29, 35, 60
9		29	h	MANCHESTER C	W	3-0	2-0	Fletcher (2) 3, 49, Dobson 37	
10	Oct	6	a	West Ham U	W	1-0	0-0	Waldron 65	
11		13	h	QUEENS PARK R	W	2-1	1-0	Nulty 43, Hankin 67	63
12		20	a	Everton	L	0-1	0-1		27
13		27	h	MANCHESTER U	D	0-0	0-0		
14	Nov	3	a	Southampton	D	2-2	2-1	Fletcher 8, Hankin 18	2, 82
15		10	h	LEEDS U	D	0-0	0-0		
16		17	a	Leicester C	L	0-2	0-1		27, 48
17		24	h	STOKE C	W	1-0	1-0	Fletcher 3	
18	Dec	8	h	NORWICH C	W	1-0	0-0	Ingham 62	
19		15	h	ARSENAL	W	2-1	0-1	Hankin 62, Waldron 78	7
20		22	a	Manchester C	L	0-2	0-1		38, 70
21		26	h	LIVERPOOL	W	2-1	1-0	Fletcher 3, Hankin 85	84
22		29	h	WOLVERHAMPTON W	D	1-1	0-0	Fletcher 55	50
23	Jan	1	a	Coventry C	D	1-1	1-1	Nulty 18	25
24		12	a	Derby C	L	1-5	0-2	James 85	11,32,48,60,87
25		19	h	SHEFFIELD U	L	1-2	0-1	Hankin 52	3, 73
26	Feb	2	a	Arsenal	D	1-1	0-1	Brady 88og	16
27		9	h	IPSWICH T	L	0-1	0-1		39
28		23	h	WEST HAM U	D	1-1	1-0	Nulty 34	55
29		27	a	Queens Park R	L	1-2	1-1	Casper 42	40, 66
30	Mar	2	a	Liverpool	L	0-1	0-0		89
31		13	a	Chelsea	L	0-3	0-0		70, 73, 81
32		16	h	EVERTON	W	3-1	0-1	Waldron 76, Nulty 78, James 79	24
33		23	a	Leeds U	W	4-1	2-1	Fletcher (2) 16, 40, Collins 62, Nulty 70	39
34	Apr	3	a	Manchester U	D	3-3	1-1	Fletcher 16, James (2) 68p, 81p	1, 66, 85
35		6	a	Stoke C	L	0-4	0-2		27, 31, 77, 80
36		10	a	Newcastle U	W	2-1	2-1	Nulty 17, Dobson 40	45
37		12	h	BIRMINGHAM C	W	2-1	1-1	Hankin (2) 15, 50	23
38		13	h	LEICESTER C	D	0-0	0-0		
39		16	a	Birmingham C	D	2-2	1-0	Ingham 31, Fletcher 73	65, 78
40		20	a	Norwich C	L	0-1	0-1		2p
41		22	h	SOUTHAMPTON	W	3-0	1-0	Fletcher 37, James 76, Nulty 85	
42		27	h	NEWCASTLE U	D	1-1	1-1	Fletcher 20	18

FA Cup

	3	Jan	5	a	Grimsby T	W	2-0	2-0	Newton 8, Hankin 31	
	4		26	a	Oldham A	W	4-1	2-0	Dobson (2) 4, 87, Fletcher 6, James 75	89
	5	Feb	16	h	ASTON VILLA	W	1-0	1-0	Fletcher 10	
	6	Mar	9	h	WREXHAM	W	1-0	0-0	Casper 58	
at Hillsborough	semi		30	n	Newcastle U	L	0-2	0-0		52, 77
3rd place play off		May	9	a	Leicester C	W	1-0	1-0	Hankin 43	

Final, Liverpool 3-0 Newcastle U, at Wembley.

League Cup

	2	Oct	10	a	Cardiff C	D	2-2	1-0	James (2) 34, 65	57, 90
after extra time, 1-1 at 90m	rep		16	h	CARDIFF C	W	3-2	0-0	Hankin 69, James (2) 91p, 110	76, 93p
	3		30	h	PLYMOUTH A	L	1-2	1-1	Hankin 16	33, 87

Final, Wolverhampton W 2-1 Manchester C, at Wembley.

Details of other first team games elsewhere.

Att.	Pos	Stevenson	Docherty	Newton	Dobson	Waldron	Thomson	Nulty	Casper	Fletcher	Collins	James	Noble	Ingham	Hankin	Rodaway	Flynn	Finn	Parton	Brennan	Flavell	
25,803		1	2*	3	4	5	6	7	8	9	10	11	S*									1
23,899		1		3	4	5	6	7	8	9	10	11	2									2
20,683	3	1		3	4	5	6	7	8	9*	10	11	2	S*								3
25,543	2	1		3	4	5	6	7	8		10	11	2		9							4
25,382	2	1		3	4	5	6	7	8	9	10	11	2									5
25,158	2	1		3	4	5	6	7	8*		10	11	2	S*	9							6
24,493	2	1		3	4	5	6	7		9	10	11	2		8							7
19,126	6	1		3	4	5	6	7		9	10	11	2		8							8
24,147	3	1		3	4	5	6	7		9	10	11	2		8							9
23,604	2	1		3	4	5	6	7		9	10	11	2		8							10
18,349	2	1		3	4	5	6	7		9	10	11*	2	S*	8							11
41,018	2	1		3	4		5	7		9	10	11	2		8	6						12
31,810	3	1		3	4		5	7		9	10	11	2		8	6						13
21,541	4	1		3	4	5	6	7		9	10	11	2		8							14
40,087	2	1		3	4	5	6	7		9	10	11	2	S*	8*							15
21,761	5	1		3	4	5	6	7		9	10	11	2	S*	8*							16
14,550	3	1		3	4	5	6	7		9	10	11	2		8							17
13,246	3	1		3	4	5	6*	7		9	10	11	2	8	S*							18
13,169	3	1		3	4	5		7		9	10	11	2	6	8							19
28,114	3	1		3	4	5		7		9	10	11	2	6	8							20
24,000	3	1		3	4	5		7		9	10	11	2	6	8							21
20,196	3	1		3	4	5		7		9	10	11	2	6	8							22
24,876	3	1		3	4	5		7		9	10	11	2	6	8							23
24,948	3	1		3	4	5		7		9	10	11	2	6	8							24
18,878	3	1		3	4	5	6	7		9	10	11	2		8							25
20,910	4	1		3	4	5	6	7		9	10		2	11			8					26
15,497	6	1		3	4	5	6	7*	S*	9	10		2	11	8							27
18,258	6	1		3	4	5	6	7		9	10	11	2		8							28
21,306		1		3	4	5	6	7	8	9		11	2	10								29
42,562	8	1		3	4	5	6	7	8	9	10	11	2									30
8,171				3	4	5	6	7	8		S*	11		2	9		10*	1				31
19,365	8	1		3*	4	5	6	7	8		10	11	2	S*	9							32
39,453	7	1		3	4	5	6	7	8	9	10*	11	2	S*								33
33,336				3		5	6	7		9	10	11	2	4	8				1			34
19,253	7	1			4	5	6	7		9	10	11	2		8					3		35
30,168		1		3	4	5		7		9		11	2	10	8	6						36
17,038		1		3	4	5		7		9	10	11	2		8	6						37
18,115	5	1		3	4	5		7		9	S*	11*	2	10	8	6						38
36,548		1		3	4	5		7		9	10*	11	2	S*	8	6						39
17,782	5	1			4	5	3	7		9		11	2	10	8	6						40
15,222		1			4	5	3	7		9	10	11	2		8	6						41
17,145	5	1		3		5		7		9	4	11	2	10	8	6						42
Appearances		40	1	39	40	40	31	42	11	38	37	40	40	16	33	9	2	1	1	1		
Apps as sub									1		2		1	8	1							
Goals (56)					4	4		9	4	13	4	7		2	8							1 og

Att.	Pos	Stevenson	Docherty	Newton	Dobson	Waldron	Thomson	Nulty	Casper	Fletcher	Collins	James	Noble	Ingham	Hankin	Rodaway	Flynn	Finn	Parton	Brennan	Flavell	
14,152		1		3	4	5		7		9	10	11	2	6	8							3
26,000		1		3	4	5	6	7		9	10	11	2		8							4
29,301		1		3	4	5	6	7		9	10*	11	2	S*	8							5
35,500		1		3	4	5	6	7	8	9	10	11		2								6
55,000		1		3	4	5	6	7	8	9	10	11	2									semi
4,432				2			5	7					9	4	8	6	11	1		3	10	3rd place play off
Appearances		5		6	5	5	5	6	2	5	5	5	5	3	4	1	1	1		1	1	
Apps as sub														1								
Goals (9)				1	2				1	2		1			2							

Att.	Pos	Stevenson	Docherty	Newton	Dobson	Waldron	Thomson	Nulty	Casper	Fletcher	Collins	James	Noble	Ingham	Hankin	Rodaway	Flynn	Finn	Parton	Brennan	Flavell	
8,775		1			4	5	6	7		9	10	11	2	3	8							2
12,397		1		3	4	5	6	7		9	10	11	2		8							rep
11,167		1		3	4	5	6	7		9	10	11	2		8							3
Appearances		3		2	3	3	3	3		3	3	3	3	1	3							
Apps as sub																						
Goals (6)												4			2							

1974-75

"Hang your heads in shame after this defeat, Burnley. The match they said was a 'free pass' into the next round of the FA Cup provided arguably the most humiliating result in the history of Burnley FC." So wrote Peter Higgs in the Burnley Express in early 1975 after a game which sent many a schoolboy home in floods of tears.

Wimbledon, cup winners themselves not much more than a decade later, tore the form book to shreds in this third round encounter.

Never, since the Football League was reorganised in the early 1920s, had a non-League team visited the home of a First Division club in the premier knockout competition and walked away with victory.

Burnley were, according to the bookmakers, fifth favourites for the cup. But they went behind four minutes after the interval, resorted to long ball tactics and saw everything they could throw at the Wimbledon goal blocked by the irrepressible Dickie Guy.

But should this season be remembered for that one game? Probably not. It should probably be remembered as the season the Clarets threw away their last realistic chance to repeat the championship of 1959-60.

Having come so close to FA Cup glory the previous season, the Wimbledon defeat was doubly hard to swallow.

Having come within a point of a place in the UEFA Cup the previous season, they saw their odds slashed to 20/1 and were sixth favourites for the title.

Before the season kicked-off, long-term injury victims Mick Docherty and Frank Casper were some way short of fitness, Dave Merrington returned as reserve team trainer and the balance sheet showed a loss of £224,000 with the wage bill showing no fewer than 11 players topping £10,000 a year for the first time in Turf Moor history.

Manager Jimmy Adamson told shareholders at the annual meeting that Burnley would "fight to win every match and fight to win the championship."

In a pre-season press conference he added that he believed Burnley to be one of six or seven clubs capable of lifting the title but added: "We cannot afford to spend £250,000 or anything like that on a player. It is a great disadvantage not to be able to go and buy big players like the city clubs."

As the finishing touches were put to the new stand in Brunshaw Road, director Dr David Iven revealed that it was to be named the Bob Lord Stand. The chairman, it was reported, had played no part in the decision and said: "This came as a complete surprise to me. It was all decided without my knowledge and I must say it makes me extremely proud."

The opening game saw a 2-1 home defeat against Wolves, Burnley then battled back from 3-0 down to draw 3-3 at Chelsea but a strong performance against Ipswich went unrewarded.

The next game was a home clash with Chelsea, but where was skipper Martin Dobson? On his way to Goodison Park in exchange for a club record £300,000. There was uproar from supporters, many of whom claimed the captain had only been sold to pay for the new stand.

Lord replied: "It will cost us £450,000 to run the club this season and we could not turn down £300,000. Four years ago people were fed up with a three-sided ground and wanted a new stand, so we built one."

Adamson missed the 3-0 win over Coventry amid rumours of a scouting mission and admitted: "I'm the only person who knows the identity of the player and I'm not saying anything." But the mission bore no fruit and no new players were added to the squad until after the season finished.

Peter Noble, so often deployed in defence in the past, had moved into midfield for the Coventry match as Ian Brennan was promoted to the first team. Noble scored that day and then scored the only goal of the game at Highbury as the early-season form took a turn for the better, a fact highlighted with League Cup success against Hull.

There was no shortage of headlines when Leeds visited Turf Moor in September. Former Prime Minister Ted Heath officially opened the new stand, Peter Lorimer gave Leeds the lead before Paul Fletcher equalised and Leighton James grabbed the winner from the penalty spot. Ray Hankin and Gordon McQueen were dismissed for fighting in the centre circle and afterwards Adamson revealed that Fletcher would have had his leg broken by a McQueen tackle had he not been wearing shinguards.

Peter Noble
superb Turf Moor servant who could play just about anywhere

Defeat at the hands of eventual champions Derby was followed by a game which created more headlines. Brennan had, before the game, told everyone he was being encouraged to get forward as often as possible. At Anfield he got within 30 yards of goal and unleashed a cannonball that rifled into the net to hand Burnley victory.

Alan Stevenson held his hand up after a 5-3 defeat against West Ham United and then Higgs commented "It's goals all the way with Burnley" following a 3-2 win at White Hart Lane in which James grabbed a last-minute winner.

Reading were next to go in the League Cup, Manchester City were beaten 2-1 and a seventh league win in nine games came

when Fletcher scored the only goal against Ipswich at Turf Moor. When that run of results came to an end with defeat at Stoke, Burnley were seventh in the table and only four points off the top. The next game was against leaders Everton at Turf Moor and Hankin scored an equaliser to leave things the same at the top. Dobson later apologised for his goal celebrations by saying: "I'm terribly disappointed if I upset anyone at Turf Moor."
Everything was right except the result as Leicester beat the Clarets 1-0, but things looked good when a Hankin double put Burnley well on top against Birmingham, only for City to hit back and earn a draw.
The Clarets twice took the lead at Old Trafford in the League Cup, but they dipped in the second half, United hit back and grabbed a late winner. But in their next match, it was Burnley who snatched something as they twice came from behind to earn a draw at Bramall Lane.
Burnley then gained sweet revenge for their FA Cup exit of the previous season by beating Newcastle United 4-1. Noble scored a hat-trick and one of them, a flying header from the edge of the area, was a genuine goal-of-the-season contender. Hankin hit another double at Luton. It was his 50th league appearance and he had 16 league goals to his credit ... not a bad return for an 18-year-old!
The first half of the season ended with a 3-0 win over QPR and the Clarets were third, three points off the top.
The second half of the season started with a 4-2 defeat at Wolves. Burnley remained the division's top scorers with 40 goals, but they had conceded 36.
Draws with Middlesbrough and Leeds preceded the £120,000 sale of Geoff Nulty to Newcastle United. "We have no plans to buy anyone at the present time," commented Adamson, adding: "But if we get any injuries we will reconsider the situation."
The old year ended with victory over Carlisle United and, following the Wimbledon debacle, the new one started with Hankin scoring his 10th goal of the season to secure victory at Loftus Road. Billy Ingham scored the only goal of the game at Luton and Burnley, with 14 points from nine games, were third in the table, one point behind Everton.
A draw at Birmingham saw the Clarets play their best football for many weeks and another First Division defence, this time Leicester, found 22-year-old James too hot to handle as Burnley won 2-0 on his 150th league appearance.
Burnley then missed the chance to go top when Malcolm Macdonald bagged another double to send them to a 3-0 defeat at Newcastle and although the Clarets won the next two the writing was already on the wall.
Injuries and suspensions to key players, especially among the forwards, blighted the last 10 games, only one of which the Clarets won.
They went from genuine title contenders, to UEFA Cup hopefuls, to also-rans.
It was a depressing end to a season which had promised so much glory.
With eight games to go, Burnley were three points off the top and level in second place with Ipswich. Middlesbrough, Stoke and Liverpool were a further point adrift and Derby seemed out of it.
Burnley were not the only team to lose their heads, Derby steamed through the pack to take the title and Burnley – the end was written for them when they lost three out of four Easter games – finally finished 10th in the table, eight points behind the new champions.
As the season drew to a close, Bob Lord had had enough of football hooliganism and called for the reintroduction of the birch to deal with them, while Adamson revealed he wanted at least two new players before the start of the next campaign.
The first to come in was goalkeeper Gerry Peyton signed from non-League Atherstone. But big names loomed on the horizon and before the Clarets headed off for an end-of-season trip to Madeira, Willie Morgan and Mike Summerbee had been signed for a combined total of £57,000.

Ian Brennan
more than 200 games but remembered
for one game and one goal, Anfield 1974

1974-75 - First Division

		P	W	D	L	F	A	Pts
1	Derby C	42	21	11	10	67	49	53
2	Liverpool	42	20	11	11	60	39	51
3	Ipswich T	42	23	5	14	66	44	51
4	Everton	42	16	18	8	56	42	50
5	Stoke C	42	17	15	10	64	48	49
6	Sheffield U	42	18	13	11	58	51	49
7	Middlesbrough	42	18	12	12	54	40	48
8	Manchester C	42	18	10	14	54	54	46
9	Leeds U	42	16	13	13	57	49	45
10	BURNLEY	42	17	11	14	68	67	45
11	Queens Park R	42	16	10	16	54	54	42
12	Wolverhampton W	42	14	11	17	57	54	39
13	West Ham U	42	13	13	16	58	59	39
14	Coventry C	42	12	15	15	51	62	39
15	Newcastle U	42	15	9	18	59	72	39
16	Arsenal	42	13	11	18	47	49	37
17	Birmingham C	42	14	9	19	53	61	37
18	Leicester C	42	12	12	18	46	60	36
19	Tottenham H	42	13	8	21	52	63	34
20	Luton T	42	11	11	20	47	65	33
21	Chelsea	42	9	15	18	42	72	33
22	Carlisle U	42	12	5	25	43	59	29

1974-75

Manager : Jimmy Adamson

Division One (10th)

	No	Date		h/a	Opponents	Result		h/t	Goalscorers/times	Opp. goal times
	1	Aug	17	h	WOLVERHAMPTON W	L	1-2	1-2	Hankin 32	6, 40
	2		21	a	Chelsea	D	3-3	0-3	Hankin 54, Dobson 60, Fletcher 81	5, 20, 44
	3		24	a	Ipswich T	L	0-2	0-1		35p, 57
	4		27	h	CHELSEA	L	1-2	0-0	James 57p	73, 84
	5		31	h	COVENTRY C	W	3-0	1-0	Hankin 5, Noble 50, James 89	
	6	Sep	7	a	Arsenal	W	1-0	0-0	Noble 78	
Bob Lord Stand opened	7		14	h	LEEDS U	W	2-1	0-1	Fletcher 57, James 69p	42
	8		21	a	Derby C	L	2-3	1-0	Todd 19og, Daniel 88og	46, 54, 65
	9		24	a	Liverpool	W	1-0	1-0	Brennan 37	
	10		28	h	WEST HAM U	L	3-5	1-1	Fletcher (2) 3, 87, Noble 57	18, 54, 65, 71, 83
	11	Oct	5	a	Tottenham H	W	3-2	2-0	England (2ogs) 7og, 17og, James 89	78, 80
	12		12	h	MANCHESTER C	W	2-1	1-1	Fletcher 14, Clarke 60og	39p
	13		15	h	IPSWICH T	W	1-0	1-0	Fletcher 45	
	14		19	a	Stoke C	L	0-2	0-2		13, 30
	15		26	h	EVERTON	D	1-1	1-1	Hankin 39	36
	16	Nov	2	a	Leicester C	L	0-1	0-0		49
	17		9	h	BIRMINGHAM C	D	2-2	1-1	Hankin (2) 20, 63	19, 55og
	18		16	a	Sheffield U	D	2-2	1-1	Rodaway 14, Fletcher 79	30, 49
	19		23	h	NEWCASTLE U	W	4-1	1-0	James 12, Noble (3) 49, 82, 83	90
	20		30	a	Luton T	W	3-2	1-1	Hankin (2) 31, 53, James 49	37, 51
	21	Dec	7	h	QUEENS PARK R	W	3-0	2-0	Clement 20og, Collins 33, Waldron 80	
Nulty's last game	22		14	a	Wolverhampton W	L	2-4	2-2	James (2) 22, 44p	9, 37, 50, 65
	23		21	h	MIDDLESBROUGH	D	1-1	1-0	Fletcher 15	90
	24		26	a	Leeds U	D	2-2	1-1	James (2) 21, 85	13, 68
	25		28	h	CARLISLE U	W	2-1	0-1	James 50, Collins 88	16
	26	Jan	11	a	Queens Park R	W	1-0	0-0	Hankin 59	
	27		18	h	LUTON T	W	1-0	1-0	Ingham 34	
	28	Feb	1	a	Birmingham C	D	1-1	1-1	Hankin 44	22
	29		8	h	LEICESTER C	W	2-0	0-0	Hankin 53, Newton 87	
	30		15	a	Newcastle U	L	0-3	0-2		14, 32, 87
	31		22	h	SHEFFIELD U	W	2-1	0-0	Noble 77, Fletcher 85	89
	32	Mar	1	a	Coventry C	W	3-0	1-0	James 38, Noble 51, Fletcher 88	
	33		8	h	LIVERPOOL	D	1-1	1-0	Hankin 33	73
	34		15	a	West Ham U	L	1-2	1-0	Collins 43	66, 76
	35		22	h	ARSENAL	D	3-3	1-2	Noble 10, Hankin 50, James 85p	14, 30, 52
	36		29	a	Middlesbrough	L	0-2	0-0		54, 60
	37		31	h	DERBY C	L	2-5	1-3	Hankin 18, James 66p	1, 20, 29, 78, 90
	38	Apr	1	a	Carlisle U	L	2-4	1-2	Parker 38, James 59p	27, 37, 88, 89
	39		4	a	Everton	D	1-1	0-0	Noble 79	57
	40		12	h	TOTTENHAM H	W	3-2	2-0	Noble (2) 4, 22, James 66p	57, 64
	41		19	a	Manchester C	L	0-2	0-1		26, 72
	42		26	h	STOKE C	D	0-0	0-0		

FA Cup

Rd	Date		h/a	Opponents	Result		h/t	Goalscorers/times	Opp. goal times
3	Jan	4	h	WIMBLEDON	L	0-1	0-0		49

Final, West Ham U 2-0 Fulham, at Wembley.

League Cup

Rd	Date		h/a	Opponents	Result		h/t	Goalscorers/times	Opp. goal times
2	Sep	11	a	Hull C	W	2-1	0-0	James 80, Ingham 87	52
3	Oct	9	a	Reading	W	2-1	0-0	Noble 70, Newton 76	55
4	Nov	13	a	Manchester U	L	2-3	2-1	Noble 22, Hankin 32	30, 49, 87

Final, Aston Villa 1-0 Norwich C, at Wembley.

Details of other first team games elsewhere.

Att.	Pos	Stevenson	Noble	Newton	Dobson	Thomson	Rodaway	Nulty	Hankin	Fletcher	Collins	James	Waldron	Ingham	Brennan	Flynn	Docherty	Morris	Bradshaw	Parker	Finn	Dixey	Scott		
20,187		1	2	3	4	5	6	7	8	9	10	11													1
23,745		1	2	3	4		6	7	8	9	10	11	5												2
22,361	18	1	2	3	4		6	7	8	9	10	11	5												3
17,441		1	2	3			6		8	9	10	11	5	4	7										4
14,644	16	1	7	2			6		8	9	10	11	5	4	3										5
23,546	13	1	7	2			6		8	9	10	11	5	4	3										6
25,384	11	1	7	2			6		8	9	10	11	5	4	3										7
21,377	12	1	7	2			6		8	9	10	11*	5	4	3	S*									8
44,639		1	7	2			6			9	10	11	5	4	3	8									9
17,644	13	1	7	2			6			9	10	11	5	4	3	8									10
18,441	10	1	7	2			6			9	10	11	5	4	3	8									11
23,512	11	1	7	2			6		8	9	10	11	5		3	4									12
18,011		1	7	2			6		8	9	10	11	5		3	4									13
23,561	8	1	7	2			6		8	9	10	11	5		3	4									14
22,599	8	1	7	2			6		8	9	10	11	5		3	4									15
19,981	12	1	7	2			6		8	9	10*	11	5	S*	3	4									16
16,075	13	1	7	2			6		8	9		11	5	10	3	4									17
20,784	12	1	7				6		8	9	10	11	5	S*	3	4*	2								18
19,513	11	1	7	2			6		8	9	10	11	5	4	3										19
11,816	9	1	7	2			6		8	9	10	11	5	4	3										20
16,522	7	1	7	2			6		8	9	10	11	5	4	3										21
17,945	8	1	7	2			6*	S*	8	9	10	11	5	4	3										22
17,637	8	1	7	2			6		8	9	10*	11	5	4	3	S*									23
34,724	8	1	6	2					8	9	10	11	5	4	3	7									24
19,729	7	1	7	2					8	9	10	11	5	4	3	6									25
19,539	5	1	3	2		5	6		8	9	10	11		4				7							26
17,237	3	1	4	3		5	6		8	9	10	11		2	7										27
24,990	4	1	7	2		6			8	9	10	11	5	4	3										28
16,352	3	1	4	2		6			8	9	10	11	5	7	3										29
40,602	3	1	4	2		6			8	9	10	11	5	7	3										30
18,567	2	1	4	2		6			8	9	10	11	5	7	3*	S*									31
17,358	2	1	4	2		6			8	9	10	11	5	7		3									32
32,111	2	1	4	3		6			8	9	10	11	5	2		7									33
28,830	2	1	4	3		6	S*		8	9	10	11	5	2		7*									34
17,800	6	1	4	3		6	9		8		10	11	5	2		7*			S*						35
28,922	7	1	4	2		6			9		10*	11	5	8	3	7				S*					36
24,317		1	4	2		6			9			11	5	8	3	7				10					37
12,783			4	2					8			11	5	9	3	7				10	1	6			38
46,882	7		4	3		S*			8		10	11	5	9	2	7*					1	6			39
17,865	7		9	2							10	11	5	4	3	7				8	1	6			40
30,723	9	1	9				6				10	11	5	4	3	7		S*		8*			2		41
19,322	10	1	9				6		8		10	11	5	4	3	7							2		42
Appearances		39	42	39	3	13	28	3	37	34	39	42	39	33	34	23	1	1		4	3	3	2		
Apps as sub						1	1	1						2		3		1	1	1					
Goals (68)			12	1	1		1		14	10	3	16	1	1	1					1				6	ogs

Att.	Pos	Stevenson	Noble	Newton	Dobson	Thomson	Rodaway	Nulty	Hankin	Fletcher	Collins	James	Waldron	Ingham	Brennan	Flynn	Docherty	Morris	Bradshaw	Parker	Finn	Dixey	Scott		
19,683		1	6	2		3*			8	9	10	11	5	4		7		S*							3
Appearances		1	1	1		1			1	1	1	1	1	1		1									
Apps as sub																		1							
Goals (0)																									

Att.	Pos	Stevenson	Noble	Newton	Dobson	Thomson	Rodaway	Nulty	Hankin	Fletcher	Collins	James	Waldron	Ingham	Brennan	Flynn	Docherty	Morris	Bradshaw	Parker	Finn	Dixey	Scott		
7,544		1	7	2			6		8	9	10	11	5	4	3										2
14,258		1	7	2			6		8	9	10	11	5	4*	3	S*									3
46,275		1	7	2			6		8	9	10	11	5		3	4									4
Appearances		3	3	3			3		3	3	3	3	3	2	3	1									
Apps as sub																1									
Goals (6)			2	1					1			1		1											

1975-76

The near-miss season of 1974-75 had seen four players responsible for the majority of Burnley's goals. Peter Noble, Leighton James, Ray Hankin and Paul Fletcher fired the Clarets to the top of the First Division goalscoring charts with 52 of the team's 68 league goals.

The relegation season of 1975-76 saw just 43 goals in 42 games. The "big four" of the previous season did not feature in the same game at any time in a troubled campaign.

But that was not the only reason Burnley dropped from the top flight. More than three decades later they are still waiting to get back.

James left for a club record £310,000, manager Jimmy Adamson was asked to resign at a crucial stage in the season and the Clarets were victims of injuries, suspensions and some of the worst refereeing decisions in living memory.

With Willie Morgan and Mike Summerbee signed the prospects looked good.

Commercial manager Jack Butterfield was asked to raise £250,000 through his department's efforts so that players would not have to be sold and for the first time match and matchball sponsorship was available and plans for Turf Moor's first-ever pop concerts were in the pipeline.

As the players reported back for training, season ticket sales topped £100,000 for the first time in the club's history and chairman Bob Lord told them he was sure that with "a fair run of the ball" they could compete for honours. A fair run of the ball seemed to completely desert them all season!

The new "V for Victory" strip was unveiled and, after a mixed run of pre-season fixtures which culminated in a win over Blackburn Rovers, the season started with draws against both Arsenal and Everton in which Summerbee made his debut and Mick Docherty returned from 28 months in the injury wilderness.

There was a sign of things to come at Upton Park where the Clarets went ahead, had four cleared off the line and another hit the post before going down 3-2, but they battled bravely for a point at Portman Road.

Noble, no longer shackled to a defensive role, hit a hat-trick in the victory over Middlesbrough, the Clarets played badly for the first time all season in a 3-0 defeat at the hands of champions Derby and Brian Flynn scored his first senior goals in a 4-1 League Cup victory at Hereford.

Noble was back in the goals again as he hit all four in the 4-4 draw with Norwich City – becoming only the second Claret ever to hit four in a game and not end up on the winning side, repeating the feat performed by Tommy Jones at Upton Park in 1932.

The 4-0 defeat at Birmingham was a double disaster for the Clarets as Doug Collins broke his leg in the game and Ian Brennan broke his in a road accident afterwards. James was also stretchered from the field but his injury was not as bad as was first thought.

Back in action and Burnley did everything but win as they lost at Bramall Lane and then bad luck coupled with a liberal pressing of the self-destruct button saw them go down to Leeds. Those results left them one point clear of the Blades who were bottom of the stack.

Leighton James scored the winner at Highfield Road and again Adamson insisted that he was not for sale and then came a mini-revival as great displays brought a 1-1 draw at Liverpool in the League Cup, a goalless outcome at Maine Road and Noble scoring his 13th goal of the season to send Burnley through to the fourth round.

Frank Casper, after solid Central League performances, was back in the team for the visit of league leaders QPR and some of the gloom lifted as he drilled home a free kick in the 87th minute to hand Burnley victory. It was his 100th and final Football League goal. The unlucky Casper featured only briefly again that season but his playing days were already numbered.

The revival continued with a 1-1 draw at Villa Park with Noble scoring at both ends and the problem was obvious. Burnley had 16 league goals to their name after 14 games. Noble had 10 of them and only three other players had hit the target.

Two games later Noble injured his groin scoring a penalty at Leicester and the rot set in.

Although the Foxes were beaten a few days later to move Burnley into the fifth round of the League Cup, the Clarets suffered a horrible defeat in their next game as Wolves tore them apart. Ahead after just 15 seconds, Wolves won 5-1, had three further "goals" disallowed and also had two cleared off the line!

Midfield maestro Doug Collins

More unbelievable refereeing cost them a point at QPR and top clubs started to circle around Turf Moor as James handed in a transfer request. Derby County won the race and parted with £310,000 for the 22-year-old who became Burnley's record sale in the process. In the Burnley Express, Peter Higgs summed up how big a loss it was to the Clarets by writing: "Apart from George Best and Jimmy Greaves, he is the best player I have seen in the last 10 years."

Both Morgan and Collins limped out of the defeat at White Hart Lane, leaving the Clarets to battle with ten men for half the game, but there was something new to cheer as goalkeeper Gerry Peyton made a remarkable debut in the goalless Turf Moor date with Liverpool.

The first half of the season closed with Kevin Kennerley bagging his first senior goal in the 2-0 win over West Ham and Burnley had just 15 points from their first 21 games.
There was more capital punishment for the Clarets as they were beaten 1-0 at Arsenal, their fourth London defeat of the season, and having been left out of the side again, Alan Stevenson handed in a transfer request.
Newcastle won the Boxing Day clash at Turf Moor with a late penalty although the Clarets should have had a spot kick of their own seconds later and the miserable year of 1975 ended with a 2-1 defeat at Old Trafford when they deserved at least a point from what was Keith Newton's 500th League appearance.
If Burnley were hoping for a better year in 1976, it certainly did not start well as they lost in the FA Cup at Blackpool with Ray Hankin sent off and skipper Colin Waldron having a late "goal" disallowed.
Adamson resigned almost immediately afterwards saying: "I am resigning for the good of the club. I am the one who had to be responsible when things started to go wrong. It is wrong for anybody to blame anyone but the manager."
Joe Brown was promoted to the manager's role, but his term started badly with a 3-1 defeat at Norwich and with 17 games to go a dramatic turn around in fortunes was definitely required if Burnley were to stay in the top flight.
But it did not come as, for the third time in four games, they went down to a debatable goal in the 88th minute when James returned to Turf Moor with Derby. "Nothing, it appears, can change their ill-fated progress," wrote Higgs in the Burnley Express before firing a broadside at James for complaining in the national Press about constant booing from Burnley supporters.
They desperately needed a win and got it at Everton as Brian Flynn and Derek Scott both scored their first League goals in a 3-2 success. Tony Morley signed for a club record £100,000 from Preston after turning down to a move to Arsenal, but he could not prevent the Clarets from suffering a 1-0 defeat against Ipswich.
Hankin scored an equaliser at Ayresome Park as the Clarets sent in the heavy brigade and they climbed out of the relegation zone with a Newton winner against Leicester – but then they were back in the bottom two following defeat at Molineux.
More points were accumulated as bottom club Sheffield United were beaten 3-1 and Villa, despite taking a 2-0 lead, were held as Flynn scored twice.
But a 4-2 defeat at Stoke left them in serious trouble with eight games to go.
Morgan departed for Bolton on a free transfer on deadline day and manager Brown summed up the entire situation by commenting: "Think of something that can possibly go wrong – and it will happen to Burnley!"
That did not appear to be the case in the next game when Manchester City were held 0-0 despite having two penalties. The first was saved by Peyton, the second went in but was retaken because of encroachment and the third attempt hit the base of the post.
Another late goal consigned them to defeat against Spurs, super-sub David Fairclough hit a double at Anfield and their fate was almost sealed with defeat at Elland Road.
Birmingham and Newcastle were both beaten by the odd goal, but it was too late for the Clarets and their destiny was finally sealed as they lost at home to Manchester United.
That left the last rites of a defeat by Coventry at Turf Moor, and Burnley, after three seasons of stark contrast, were back in the Second Division.
Waldron (Manchester United), Docherty (Manchester City), Collins (Plymouth), Kennerley, Mick Finn and Richard Dixey were all given free transfer and Paul Bradshaw was made available for transfer in the close season as Joe Brown set about the task of rebuilding a team that would be capable of climbing back into the First Division.

Keith Newton
oozed class throughout his career

1975-76 - First Division

		P	W	D	L	F	A	Pts
1	Liverpool	42	23	14	5	66	31	60
2	Queens Park R	42	24	11	7	67	33	59
3	Manchester U	42	23	10	9	68	42	56
4	Derby C	42	21	11	10	75	58	53
5	Leeds U	42	21	9	12	65	46	51
6	Ipswich T	42	16	14	12	54	48	46
7	Leicester C	42	13	19	10	48	51	45
8	Manchester C	42	16	11	15	64	46	43
9	Tottenham H	42	14	15	13	63	63	43
10	Norwich C	42	16	10	16	58	58	42
11	Everton	42	15	12	15	60	66	42
12	Stoke C	42	15	11	16	48	50	41
13	Middlesbrough	42	15	10	17	46	45	40
14	Coventry C	42	13	14	15	47	57	40
15	Newcastle U	42	15	9	18	71	62	39
16	Aston Villa	42	11	17	14	51	59	39
17	Arsenal	42	13	10	19	47	53	36
18	West Ham U	42	13	10	19	48	71	36
19	Birmingham C	42	13	7	22	57	75	33
20	Wolverhampton W	42	10	10	22	51	68	30
21	BURNLEY	42	9	10	23	43	66	28
22	Sheffield U	42	6	10	26	33	82	22

1975-76

Manager : Jimmy Adamson until January 1976, then Joe Brown

Division One (21st)
Relegated

Note	No	Month	Date	Venue	Opponents	Result	Score	h/t	Goalscorers/times	Opp. goal times
	1	Aug	16	h	ARSENAL	D	0-0	0-0		
	2		19	h	EVERTON	D	1-1	0-0	Hankin 55	60
	3		23	a	West Ham U	L	2-3	1-0	James 31, Noble 64	60, 77, 80
	4		26	a	Ipswich T	D	0-0	0-0		
	5		30	h	MIDDLESBROUGH	W	4-1	2-1	Noble (3) 15, 26, 54, Hankin 75	6
	6	Sep	6	a	Derby C	L	0-3	0-2		5, 20, 48
	7		13	h	NORWICH C	D	4-4	3-1	Noble (4) 1, 26p, 43p, 87	31, 66, 76, 90
	8		20	a	Birmingham C	L	0-4	0-0		51, 53, 67, 78
	9		23	a	Sheffield U	L	1-2	1-1	Noble 13	35, 87
	10		27	h	LEEDS U	L	0-1	0-1		24
	11	Oct	4	a	Coventry C	W	2-1	0-0	Hankin 54, James 89	69
	12		11	a	Manchester C	D	0-0	0-0		
	13		18	h	QUEENS PARK R	W	1-0	0-0	Casper 87	
	14		25	a	Aston Villa	D	1-1	0-0	Noble 50	78og
	15	Nov	1	h	STOKE C	L	0-1	0-0		55
	16		8	a	Leicester C	L	2-3	1-2	Noble 15p, James 60	5, 36, 73
	17		15	h	WOLVERHAMPTON W	L	1-5	0-3	Hankin 48	1, 12, 43, 59, 70
	18		22	a	Queens Park R	L	0-1	0-0		55
	19		29	a	Tottenham H	L	1-2	1-0	Hankin 25	63, 75
	20	Dec	6	h	LIVERPOOL	D	0-0	0-0		
	21		13	h	WEST HAM U	W	2-0	2-0	Hankin 19, Kennerley 35	
	22		20	a	Arsenal	L	0-1	0-0		88
	23		26	h	NEWCASTLE U	L	0-1	0-0		88
	24		27	a	Manchester U	L	1-2	1-0	Hankin 34	51, 80
last games for Casper & Docherty	25	Jan	10	a	Norwich C	L	1-3	0-2	Newton 64	35, 40, 59
	26		17	h	DERBY C	L	1-2	0-1	Fletcher 47	22, 88
	27		31	a	Everton	W	3-2	1-0	Noble 41, Flynn 73, Scott 87	47, 89
	28	Feb	7	h	IPSWICH T	L	0-1	0-0		57
	29		14	a	Middlesbrough	D	1-1	1-1	Hankin 24	9
	30		17	h	LEICESTER C	W	1-0	1-0	Newton 36	
	31		21	a	Wolverhampton W	L	2-3	0-1	Fletcher 54, Hankin 88	24, 70, 72
	32		24	h	SHEFFIELD U	W	3-1	1-1	Hankin 45, Scott 71, Flynn 85	41
	33		28	h	ASTON VILLA	D	2-2	1-2	Flynn (2) 40, 47	17, 20
	34	Mar	6	a	Stoke C	L	1-4	1-3	Hankin 37	17, 24, 31, 74
	35		13	h	MANCHESTER C	D	0-0	0-0		
Collins' last game	36		20	h	TOTTENHAM H	L	1-2	0-0	Waldron 83	58, 87
Waldron's last game	37		27	a	Liverpool	L	0-2	0-1		40, 61
	38	Apr	3	a	Leeds U	L	1-2	1-1	Hankin 40	20, 72
	39		10	h	BIRMINGHAM C	W	1-0	0-0	Hankin 48	
	40		17	a	Newcastle U	W	1-0	1-0	Noble 10	
	41		19	h	MANCHESTER U	L	0-1	0-0		58
	42		24	h	COVENTRY C	L	1-3	1-0	Parker 6	48, 85, 87

FA Cup

Note	Rd	Month	Date	Venue	Opponents	Result	Score	h/t	Goalscorers/times	Opp. goal times
Morgan's last game	3	Jan	3	a	Blackpool	L	0-1	0-0		56

Final, Southampton 1-0 Manchester U, at Wembley.

League Cup

Rd	Month	Date	Venue	Opponents	Result	Score	h/t	Goalscorers/times	Opp. goal times
2	Sep	10	a	Hereford U	W	4-1	1-0	Flynn (2) 35, 64, Noble (2) 47, 78	50
3	Oct	7	a	Liverpool	D	1-1	0-0	Noble 48	81
rep		14	h	LIVERPOOL	W	1-0	1-0	Noble 44p	
4	Nov	11	h	LEICESTER C	W	2-0	0-0	Morgan 61p, Hankin 78	
5	Dec	3	h	MIDDLESBROUGH	L	0-2	0-1		2, 80

Final, Manchester C 2-1 Newcastle U, at Wembley.

Details of other first team games elsewhere.

Att.	Pos	Stevenson	Docherty	Newton	Noble	Waldron	Thomson	Morgan	Hankin	Summerbee	Collins	James	Flynn	Brennan	Ingham	Casper	Fletcher	Bradshaw	Peyton	Kennerley	Loggie	Scott	Morris	Rodaway	Morley	Pashley	Jakub	Parker	
18,831		1	2	3	4*	5	6	7	8	9	10	11	S*																1
20,069		1	2	3	4	5	6		8	9	10*	11	7	S*															2
28,048	15	1	2	3	4	5	6	S*	8	9	10*	11	7																3
23,579		1	2	3	4	5	6		8	9	10	11	7																4
17,066	10	1	2	3	4	5	6	7	8	9	10	11																	5
24,026	14	1	2	3	4	5	6	7	8	9	10	11																	6
15,513	16	1		3	4	5	6		8	9	10	11	7	2															7
25,830	17	1		3	4	5	6		8	9	10*	11	7	2	S*														8
21,477		1	2	3	4	5	6		8	9		11	7		10														9
23,045	19	1	2	3		5	6	7	8	9		11	4		10														10
15,432	18	1	2	3	4	5	6	7	8*	9		11	10		S*														11
35,003	17	1	2	3	4	5	6	7	8	9		11	10																12
20,378	17	1		3	4	5	6	7		9		11	10		2	8													13
35,204	17	1	2	3	4	5	6			9		11	10			8	7												14
18,326	18	1	2	3	4	5	6			7		11	10			8	9												15
18,344	18	1	2	3	4*	5	6	8	9	7		11	10		S*														16
14,530	20	1	2	3		5	6	7	9*	8	10	11	4			S*													17
17,390	20	1	2	3		5	6	7	9	8	10		4					11											18
21,222	20	1	2	3		5	6	7	9	8	10*		4				11	S*											19
18,524	21		2	3		5	6		9	7			10		4			11	1	8									20
14,942	19		2	3		5	6		9	7			10		4			11	1	8									21
16,459	20		2	3		5	6		9	7			10		4			11	1	8									22
22,736	20		2	3	S*	5	6		9	7			10		4*			11	1	8									23
59,726	20		2	3		5	6	8	9	7	4*		10			S*		11	1										24
17,473	21	1	2	3		5	6						8		4	11		7		9	10								25
21,088	21			3	11	5	6						8		4		10	7	1	9		2							26
21,389	21			3	11	5	6						8		4		10		1			2	7	9					27
17,536	21			3	11	5	6			9			8		4		10		1			2			7				28
17,856	21			3	11*	5	6		8	9			S*				10		1			2		4	7				29
13,542				3		5	6		8	11			10		9				1			2		4	7				30
19,390	21			3		5	6		9	11			8*		S*		10		1			2		4	7				31
14,623		1		3		5	6		8	11			10				9					2	7	4					32
17,174	20	1		3		5	6		8	11			10				9					2	7	4					33
16,065	20			3		5	6		8	11			10				9		1			2	7	4*	S*				34
24,329	21			3			5		9	6	11		8				10		1			2		4	7				35
15,490	21			3		5			9	4	11		8				10		1			2		6	7				36
36,708	21			3	4	5			9	11			8				10		1			2		6	7				37
25,384	21			3*	4		5		9	11			8		S*		10		1			2	7	6					38
13,679	21				4		5		9	11			8				10		1			2	7	6		3			39
24,897	21			3	4		5		9	11			8		10				1			2	7	6					40
27,418				3	4		5		9*	11			8		S*		10		1			2	7	6					41
11,675	21			3	9		5			11					4				1			2		6	7		8	10	42
Appearances		22	22	41	25	36	40	12	34	39	14	17	37	2	14	4	17	8	20	6	1	17	8	15	8	1	1	1	
Apps as sub					1			1					2	1	6	2		1							1				
Goals (43)				2	13	1			13			3	4			1	2			1		2						1	

Att.	Pos	Stevenson	Docherty	Newton	Noble	Waldron	Thomson	Morgan	Hankin	Summerbee	Collins	James	Flynn	Brennan	Ingham	Casper	Fletcher	Bradshaw	Peyton	Kennerley	Loggie	Scott	Morris	Rodaway	Morley	Pashley	Jakub	Parker	
20,573			2	3		5	6	8*	9	7			10		4			11	1		S*								3
Appearances			1	1		1	1	1	1	1			1		1			1	1										
Apps as sub																					1								
Goals (0)																													

Att.	Pos	Stevenson	Docherty	Newton	Noble	Waldron	Thomson	Morgan	Hankin	Summerbee	Collins	James	Flynn	Brennan	Ingham	Casper	Fletcher	Bradshaw	Peyton	Kennerley	Loggie	Scott	Morris	Rodaway	Morley	Pashley	Jakub	Parker	
11,360		1		3	4	5	6		8	9	10	11	7	2															2
24,607		1	2	3	4	5	6	7	8	9		11	10																3
20,022		1	2	3	4	5	6	7	8*	9		11	10		S*														rep
15,019		1	2			5	6	7	10	8	3	11	4				9												4
15,431		1	2	3	4	5	6		9	8	10*		11					7			S*								5
Appearances		5	4	4	4	5	5	3	5	5	3	4	5	1			1	1											
Apps as sub															1						1								
Goals (8)					4			1	1				2																

1976-77

Off the field the 1976-77 season created just about every headline. The manager was sacked, fans called for the chairman's resignation, a pools winner offered to buy a player, another promising player departed for a big fee ... the list was almost endless.

On the field it was a struggle, often a dour struggle, and relegation to the Third Division for the first time in the club's history was only avoided with two games to go.

When the players reported back for pre-season training they found Frank Casper on the coaching staff and a new chief scout, Harry Potts replacing David Blakey who had resigned following the wholesale dismantling of the scouting network. Chairman Bob Lord told the players he hoped for promotion at the first attempt, but the signs were not good when the group games in the Anglo-Scottish Cup produced a win, a draw and a defeat and no place in the knockout stages.

The balance sheet revealed that relegation had cost the club a loss of £147,000. A huge drop in transfer income was partly to blame and Lord told shareholders at the annual meeting that players had only been released on free transfers because no-one was willing to pay a fee for them.

The season itself kicked-off with a goalless draw at Wolves and the weather was so hot that the 11 Burnley players lost almost 60lbs between them! Fulham were beaten 3-1 as the early signs were promising, but three defeats followed including a disastrous League Cup exit at the hands of Torquay United.

Tony Morley stole the show as up-for-sale Ray Hankin and Peter Noble scored in the 2-0 success against FA Cup holders Southampton and then on-loan striker Malcolm Smith scored as missed chances proved costly and the Clarets lost 2-1 to Carlisle United.

In the lead up to the goalless draw with Hull in which Smith hit the crossbar with minutes to go, Ray Hankin (£180,000) and Paul Bradshaw (£20,000) were sold to Leeds United and Sheffield Wednesday respectively, and the Clarets looked anything other than promotion prospects when they lost 1-0 to Sheffield United.

Terry Cochrane's on-off transfer saga ended when he finally joined from Coleraine for £15,000 and he scored on his debut against Orient. Burnley had gone behind in that game before leading 3-1. They were eventually pegged back to 3-3.

And if that had been remarkable, it was nothing compared with their Turf Moor date with Charlton. The 3,000th League game played by the Clarets saw them go 1-0 behind before Smith equalised. With 18 minutes to go they were 4-1 down, but goals from Noble, Paul Fletcher and Cochrane sealed a dramatic fightback.

Burnley had played an attacking 4-2-4 formation for those games, but it backfired in a 5-2 defeat at Nottingham Forest and the Clarets found themselves in the relegation zone.

That prompted an unofficial fans group to launch a bid to oust Lord. But the chairman simply replied: "These people can do what they like but there will be no new regime and I will not be resigning."

Manager Joe Brown swung the axe and made five changes for the trip to Home Park. Smith scored the only goal and Burnley, back in a 4-3-3 formation, were out of the bottom three.

The club then revealed that it was over £400,000 in the red and losing £4,000 a week. The Smith signing looked in jeopardy, despite five goals in seven games, and pools winner Danny Carr offered to put up the required £25,000.

Skipper Noble scored the only goal of the game as Oldham were beaten 1-0, but despite another Smith strike the Clarets lost 2-1 at Burnden Park. Smith was signed immediately afterwards and the club revealed that Carr's money had not been used for the transfer.

In November, John Jackson joined the board and the Clarets found themselves 17th in the table after 15 games, a situation that was to worsen following defeat against league-leaders Chelsea during which Ian Britton scored the first goal of the game.

As Gerry Peyton was sold to Fulham for £40,000, former boss Jimmy Adamson was appointed manager of Sunderland and before too long he was joined by Dave Merrington, appointed deputy team manager, Mick Docherty, who arrived at Roker as skipper, and commercial manager Jack Butterfield.

Jim Thomson
more than 350 senior appearances
in a Turf Moor career spanning three decades

Following a 0-0 draw at home to Cardiff in a game described as a "pantomime on ice" and a 3-1 defeat at the hands of Millwall, Lord issued the following ultimatum to Brown: "He has got to get better results or there will be changes. It's no good putting blinkers on ... it's staring everyone in the face." Peter Noble took over as captain and Mike Summerbee was given a free transfer to Blackpool.

Boxing Day brought a stirring fightback at Ewood Park as the Clarets scored through Noble and Ian Brennan to earn a draw, but the dull, goalless draw against Blackpool left the Clarets hovering just above the relegation zone as the old year came to an end.

1977 did not get off to the start everyone hoped for as Plymouth won 2-0 at Turf Moor and relegation loomed large at the half-way stage as the Clarets were 20th in the division at the half-way stage with just 16 points.

Brown again rang the changes for the FA Cup clash with Lincoln City which ended 2-2 before Alan Stevenson made three vital saves and Fletcher netted the only goal in the Sincil Bank replay.

Burnley did enough to give everyone hope with draws against Fulham and Wolves and Bob Lord spelt out his vision of the future in the News of the World by saying that clubs like championship-chasing Ipswich Town and former champions Burnley would have no place in football's elite within 10 years.

He added of such clubs: "Their main function will be to groom players and sell them to bigger and more powerful clubs. I am a realist. You won't recognise the Football League in the 1980s. An economic blast will blow through the League and it is my belief that many of our clubs – lots of them with proud traditions – are being thrown on the road to ruin."

There was more heartache with an FA Cup exit at Vale Park, Alan Stevenson had an excellent game but could not prevent a 2-0 defeat at Luton, Noble grabbed an equaliser against bottom club Hereford and there was another dismal chapter in the sorry story with a 3-1 defeat at Oldham.

The defeat at Southampton was the final straw, Joe Brown was dismissed and Harry Potts was back behind the manager's desk he had vacated almost seven years before.

Brown had been in the job for less than 14 months, the team was 21st in the Second Division and his 45-match League tenure had yielded just nine wins.

Potts needed to make an instant impression and he reverted to the 4-2-4 formation as Carlisle were beaten 2-0.

But he had no such luck against Notts County when a series of baffling refereeing decisions helped the home side win 5-1, or at Hull, where the Tigers won 4-1. With 12 games to go the Clarets were in serious trouble and several of the clubs around them had games in hand.

Things took a definite turn for the better with wins over Sheffield United and Orient, Brennan crashing in a 30-yarder at Brisbane Road, but the Clarets were dumped back into the bottom three when results went against them during a blank weekend for the Clarets, a situation compounded by defeat against promotion-chasing Forest.

Easter brought four much-needed points from three games. Smith, Noble and Peter Robinson were the goalscoring heroes of the derby win over Blackburn, Smith scored again in the draw at Blackpool and a goalless draw with Bolton saw them two points clear of trouble with six games to go.

Noble hit the target again in a drawn match at Eastville and the home game against fancied Chelsea ended 1-0 to the Clarets as Billy Ingham scored an 85th minute scorcher. "All I can remember is getting the ball on the edge of the area, flicking it over a defender and then just hitting it," said Ingham who instantly earned the nickname "Ginger Pele".

Billy Rodaway
a ten year Burnley career
then a return for a swansong in 1986-87

Despite a 5-2 defeat at Charlton, the Clarets were almost safe and confirmed their place in the Second Division when Noble led by example in the relegation battle at Cardiff and scored the only goal.

The last home game saw Morley again on top form to score twice in the 3-1 win against Notts County and, although the season ended with a disappointing defeat at Millwall, Harry Potts had worked something of a miracle and taken the Clarets from 21st to 16th.

The entire playing staff was named on the retained list as Potts set his stall out for the following season, but following persistent rumours all season it seemed only a matter of time before Welsh international midfielder Brian Flynn joined the big-money Turf exodus.

1976-77 - Second Division

		P	W	D	L	F	A	Pts
1	Wolverhampton W	42	22	13	7	84	45	57
2	Chelsea	42	21	13	8	73	53	55
3	Nottingham F	42	21	10	11	77	43	52
4	Bolton W	42	20	11	11	75	54	51
5	Blackpool	42	17	17	8	58	42	51
6	Luton T	42	21	6	15	67	48	48
7	Charlton A	42	16	16	10	71	58	48
8	Notts C	42	19	10	13	65	60	48
9	Southampton	42	17	10	15	72	67	44
10	Millwall	42	15	13	14	57	53	43
11	Sheffield U	42	14	12	16	54	63	40
12	Blackburn R	42	15	9	18	42	54	39
13	Oldham A	42	14	10	18	52	64	38
14	Hull C	42	10	17	15	45	53	37
15	Bristol R	42	12	13	17	53	68	37
16	BURNLEY	42	11	14	17	46	64	36
17	Fulham	42	11	13	18	54	61	35
18	Cardiff C	42	12	10	20	56	67	34
19	Orient	42	9	16	17	37	55	34
20	Carlisle U	42	11	12	19	49	75	34
21	Plymouth A	42	8	16	18	46	65	32
22	Hereford U	42	8	15	19	57	78	31

1976-77

Manager : Joe Brown until February 1977, then Harry Potts

Division Two (16th)

		Date			Opponents	Result		h/t	Goalscorers/times	Opp. goal times
	1	Aug	21	a	Wolverhampton W	D	0-0	0-0		
	2		24	h	FULHAM	W	3-1	2-1	Hankin 17, Bradshaw 27, Noble 58p	43
	3		28	h	LUTON T	L	1-2	1-1	Bradshaw 36	41, 79
	4	Sep	4	a	Hereford U	L	0-3	0-1		44, 72, 90
	5		11	h	SOUTHAMPTON	W	2-0	1-0	Hankin 20, Noble 63	
Hankin's last game	6		18	a	Carlisle U	L	1-2	0-1	Smith 71	21, 84
	7		25	h	HULL C	D	0-0	0-0		
	8	Oct	2	a	Sheffield U	L	0-1	0-0		58
	9		9	h	ORIENT	D	3-3	2-1	Fletcher 23, Cochrane 37, Smith 48	10, 49, 65
Burnley's 3000th league game	10		16	h	CHARLTON A	D	4-4	1-2	Smith 12, Noble 72, Fletcher 74, Cochrane 85	2p, 24, 46, 54
	11		23	a	Nottingham F	L	2-5	1-1	Flynn 19, Smith 48	3, 50p, 54, 76, 80
	12		30	a	Plymouth A	W	1-0	0-0	Smith 58	
	13	Nov	6	h	OLDHAM A	W	1-0	0-0	Noble 59p	
	14		9	a	Bolton W	L	1-2	1-1	Smith 1	38, 77
	15		20	h	BRISTOL R	D	1-1	1-1	Noble 10	39
	16		27	a	Chelsea	L	1-2	0-2	Noble 77	15, 44p
	17	Dec	4	h	CARDIFF C	D	0-0	0-0		
Summerbee's last game	18		18	h	MILLWALL	L	1-3	1-2	Cochrane 31	15, 36, 79
	19		27	a	Blackburn R	D	2-2	0-0	Noble 80, Brennan 88	54, 63
	20		28	h	BLACKPOOL	D	0-0	0-0		
	21	Jan	3	h	PLYMOUTH A	L	0-2	0-1		45, 84
	22		15	a	Fulham	D	2-2	2-1	Noble 24p, Fletcher 30	15, 88
	23		22	h	WOLVERHAMPTON W	D	0-0	0-0		
	24	Feb	5	a	Luton T	L	0-2	0-1		12, 82
	25		12	h	HEREFORD U	D	1-1	0-1	Noble 54	29og
	26		15	a	Oldham A	L	1-3	1-1	Flynn 20	8p, 65, 75
	27		19	a	Southampton	L	0-2	0-1		30p, 47
	28		26	h	CARLISLE U	W	2-0	0-0	Cochrane 54, Noble 67p	
	29	Mar	2	a	Notts C	L	1-5	0-2	Smith 70	35p,42p,59og,73,89
	30		5	a	Hull C	L	1-4	1-3	Smith 4	3, 23, 44, 83
	31		12	h	SHEFFIELD U	W	1-0	0-0	Smith 67	
	32		19	a	Orient	W	1-0	1-0	Brennan 9	
	33	Apr	2	h	NOTTINGHAM F	L	0-1	0-0		65
	34		8	h	BLACKBURN R	W	3-1	1-1	Smith 6, Noble 63, Robson 82	45
	35		9	a	Blackpool	D	1-1	1-0	Smith 32	48
	36		12	h	BOLTON W	D	0-0	0-0		
	37		16	a	Bristol R	D	1-1	0-1	Noble 64	17
	38		23	h	CHELSEA	W	1-0	0-0	Ingham 85	
	39		26	a	Charlton A	L	2-5	1-2	Newton 24, Ingham 83	39, 42p, 63, 80, 84
	40		30	a	Cardiff C	W	1-0	1-0	Noble 6	
	41	May	7	h	NOTTS C	W	3-1	2-1	Morley (2) 9, 85, Fletcher 27	10
	42		14	a	Millwall	L	0-2	0-1		27, 75

FA Cup

				Opponents	Result		h/t	Goalscorers/times	Opp. goal times
3	Jan	8	h	LINCOLN C	D	2-2	1-1	Noble 11, Fletcher 58	7, 64
rep		12	a	Lincoln C	W	1-0	0-0	Fletcher 70	
4		29	a	Port Vale	L	1-2	0-1	Flynn 89p	37, 56

Final, Manchester U 2-1 Liverpool, at Wembley.

League Cup

				Opponents	Result		h/t	Goalscorers/times	Opp. goal times
2	Sep	1	a	Torquay U	L	0-1	0-1		25

Final, Aston Villa 3-2 Everton (aet) at Old Trafford in a 2nd replay, following a 1-1 draw (aet) at Hillsborough after a 0-0 draw, at Wembley.

Details of other first team games elsewhere.

Att.	Pos	Peyton	Scott	Pashley	Noble	Thomson	Rodaway	Bradshaw	Ingham	Hankin	Flynn	Summerbee	Newton	Morley	Jakub	M Smith	Fletcher	Loggie	Stevenson	Cochrane	Brennan	P Robinson	
19,480		1	2	3	4	5	6	7	8	9	10	11											1
11,506		1	2	3	4	5	6	7	8	9	10	11											2
12,262	10	1	2	3	4	5	6	7	8	9	10	11											3
9,548	16	1	2		4	5	6			9	10	11	3	7	8								4
9,142	12	1	2	3	4	5	6			9	10	11		7	8								5
8,969	16	1	2	3	4	5	6		S*	9	10			7	8	11*							6
10,320	16	1	2	3	4	5	6				10			7	8	11*	9	S*					7
16,082	17	1	2	3	4	5	6				10			7	8	11	9						8
10,228	18		2	3	4	5	6				10			11		8	9		1	7			9
10,601	19	1	2	3	4	5	6				10			11		8	9			7			10
15,279	20	1	2	3	4	5	6				10			11		8	9			7			11
14,704	17				4	5	6		7		10	11	2			8	9		1		3		12
14,305	15				4	5	6		7		10	11	2			8	9		1		3		13
21,737	19				4		6		7		10	11	2	9		8			1		3	5	14
10,371	17				4	5	6		7*		10	11	2	S*		8	9		1		3		15
28,595	16				4	5	6		7		10	11	2	S*		8	9*		1		3		16
8,967	17				4		6				10	11	2	7		8	9		1		3	5	17
8,427	19				4		6				10	11	2	9		8*	S*		1	7	3	5	18
22,189	19				4	5	6		11		10		2	S*		8	9*		1	7	3		19
19,682					4	5	6		11		10		2	9		8			1	7	3		20
10,406			2		4	5	6		11		10			9		8			1	7	3		21
8,815	20				4	5	6		S*		10		2			11*	9		1	7	3	8	22
13,638	19				4	5	6		11		10		2				9		1	7	3	8	23
8,638	19				4	5	6				10		2			11	9		1	7	3	8	24
8,748	19				4	5	6				10		2	11			9		1	7	3	8	25
12,438					4	5	6				10		2	11			9		1	7	3	8	26
17,981	21				4	5	6		8		10		2	11			9	7	1		3		27
10,834	18				4	5	6		S*		10		2	11		8	9		1	7*	3		28
8,492			2		4	5	6				10			11		8	9		1	7	3		29
6,636	20				4	5	6		10				2	11		8	9		1	7	3		30
10,608	19				4		6				10		2	11		8	9		1	7	3	5	31
5,610	18		S*		4		6		7		10*		2	11		8	9		1		3	5	32
11,112	20				4		6		7*		10		2	11		8	9		1	S*	3	5	33
17,372					4		6				10		2	11		8	9		1	7	3	5	34
14,526	18			S*	4		6		7		10		2	11		8	9*		1		3	5	35
20,433					4		6		7		10		2	11		8		9	1		3	5	36
6,375	18				4		6		7		10		2	11		8		9	1		3	5	37
14,977	16				4		6		7		10		2	11		8	9		1		3	5	38
6,592	16				4		6		7		10		2	11		8	9		1		3	5	39
11,247	15				4		6		7		10		2	11			9		1	8	3	5	40
11,699	15				4		6		7		10		2	11			9		1	8	3	5	41
6,833	16				4		6		7		10		2	11			9		1	8	3	5	42
Appearances		10	13	10	42	27	42	3	24	6	41	12	30	31	5	30	30	3	32	20	31	20	
Apps as sub			1	1					3					3			1	1		1			
Goals (46)					13			2	2	2	2		1	2		11	4			4	2	1	

Att.	Pos	Peyton	Scott	Pashley	Noble	Thomson	Rodaway	Bradshaw	Ingham	Hankin	Flynn	Summerbee	Newton	Morley	Jakub	M Smith	Fletcher	Loggie	Stevenson	Cochrane	Brennan	P Robinson	
11,583			3		4	5	6		11		10		2	S*			9		1	7*		8	3
11,414					4	5	6				10		2			11	9		1	7	3	8	rep
18,068					4	5	6		11		10		2			7	9		1	S*	3	8	4
Appearances			1		3	3	3		2		3		3			2	3		3	2	2	3	
Apps as sub														1						1			
Goals (4)					1						1						2						

Att.	Pos	Peyton	Scott	Pashley	Noble	Thomson	Rodaway	Bradshaw	Ingham	Hankin	Flynn	Summerbee	Newton	Morley	Jakub	M Smith	Fletcher	Loggie	Stevenson	Cochrane	Brennan	P Robinson	
7,084		1	2		4	5	6	7*	8	9	10	11	3	S*									2
Appearances		1	1		1	1	1	1	1	1	1	1	1										
Apps as sub														1									
Goals (0)																							

1977-78

Of all football's clichés, "a game of two halves" is probably the most overused.

But for Burnley in 1977-78 it was not so much a game of two halves as a season of starkly contrasting halves.

Having said that, it was probably more a season that could be split into distinct thirds.

The first third yielded just one win and the Clarets were in danger of being cut adrift at the foot of the Second Division. The second segment heralded the return of crowd favourite Steve Kindon and five wins which lifted the team off the bottom of the table.

And the third produced no fewer than 21 points – in the days of two points for a win that was championship form – and although safety was not a mathematical certainty until the final week, Burnley finished in the top half of the table.

Before the season started, the Clarets met with their usual mixed fortunes in the group stages of the Anglo-Scottish Cup but then successfully dealt with Chester over two legs to reach the second round of the League Cup.

The league programme started with a defeat at home to Bolton Wanderers which the Clarets could easily have won if they had converted a string of chances.

That was followed by a 3-0 defeat at Roker Park and a 2-1 reverse against Stoke City – Peter Shilton made a string of fine saves to deny them – before the Clarets collected their first point with a Turf Moor draw against Crystal Palace.

In between those two games Tony Morley and Terry Cochrane were in inspired form as First Division Norwich City were dispatched in the League Cup, but the Clarets were already at the foot of the table and worse was to follow with defeat against Southampton, a draw with Brighton and successive defeats against Mansfield, Millwall and Fulham. A "ludicrous" goal also saw them exit the League Cup at the hands of Ipswich Town.

Sandwiched in the middle of the run of misery, the stars turned out at Turf Moor for Frank Casper's testimonial game. Casper played in his own select side which featured the likes of Martin Dobson, Mike Summerbee, Francis Lee, Ray Hankin, Dave Thomas, Willie Irvine and Stuart Pearson. Over 5,000 turned out for the game and Casper bagged his last Turf Moor goal in a 4-2 win.

The 10th game of the season brought the first victory, a 3-1 win over Bristol Rovers, but the Clarets stayed bottom and there was more bad news for the club when the balance sheet revealed a loss of more than £80,000 despite the Turf Moor Development Association contributing a six-figure sum for the first time.

Three defeats in the next four games – the Clarets had just five points from 14 games – demanded drastic action. And manager Harry Potts delivered it by signing Brian Hall for £25,000 from Plymouth Argyle and Kindon for £80,000 from Wolves.

Brian Flynn financed those transfers following his £175,000 move to Leeds United, He had looked all set to move to Queens Park Rangers for £200,000, but stalled too long over his answer, Rangers' interest cooled and Leeds stepped in.

Kindon made an immediate impact and scored on his second debut as Notts County were beaten 3-1. But as important to the Clarets was the fact that Paul Fletcher was now fully restored to the starting line-up and missed only one game in the remainder of the season.

An eighth away game brought an eighth away defeat as Cardiff City grabbed the winner from the penalty spot and Burnley were four points away from the next-bottom club. Orient somehow escaped from Turf Moor with a point from a ridiculously one-sided match, but the second away win followed at Luton Town as Kindon rounded off a stylish display with a winning goal.

Tony Morley
wonderful talent, but made his name away from Turf Moor

Kindon then scored the only goal of the match against Charlton Athletic at Turf Moor, but the mini-revival ended when Burnley lost 3-0 at Notts County.

They went into the four-match holiday programme bottom of the table and desperately in need of some points. What they got were defeats at the hands of Blackburn Rovers and Oldham Athletic and a draw with Sunderland before man-of-the-match Ian Brennan fired a double, one of them the goal of the season, in a 2-1 success at Bolton Wanderers.

The FA Cup saw former keeper Gerry Peyton back at Turf Moor and he performed heroics to shut out his former team-mates until Fletcher struck in the 86th minute to secure a 1-0 win over Fulham.

The return to league action saw Kindon strike against Stoke City and, for the first time all season, Burnley were off the foot of the table. They added a point from a brave battle in the Selhurst Park mud but then crashed out of the FA Cup at Stamford Bridge. Brilliant going forward, they took the lead through Fletcher. Shambolic at the back they were 6-1 down before Kindon struck a late consolation.

With 16 games to go they had climbed to 20th in the table and needed points quickly. But despite leading 2-0 and 3-1 they had to settle for a draw against Southampton and then lost out to promotion-chasing Brighton and Hove Albion after conceding their 11th penalty of the season, Goldstone boss Alan Mullery admitting to relief at the eventual outcome.

The Clarets started the final third of the season still deep in trouble.

They came out of it looking like a side to be reckoned with in the season to come.

Having not won three games in succession for three years, they embarked on a 10-match unbeaten run.

Draws at Millwall and Bristol Rovers – Kindon hit a double at Eastville – preceded a stunning display against Sheffield United where Cochrane got two and the Clarets won 4-1.

Goalscorer Fletcher was sent-off for fighting at the end of the 2-0 win at Mansfield Town, but the goals continued to flow as Hull City were beaten 3-1.

The Christmas holiday fixtures had been something of a nightmare, but the Clarets – now 17th in the table – could not afford for the same thing to happen over Easter. It didn't!

Cochrane scored another double as Oldham Athletic were beaten 4-1 and he then produced an exquisite finish to silence Ewood Park with the only goal of the game. The last Easter game was a trip to Blackpool where Malcolm Smith scored in a 1-1 draw and the Clarets had gone from relegation certainties to a team with a bright future.

As Keith Newton announced he was to retire at the end of the season, Burnley knew they still had work to do and their next Turf Moor opponents were promotion-chasing Tottenham Hotspur who were unbeaten in 19 games. But Burnley were the other form team of the division at that stage and Billy Ingham was outstanding and scored one of the goals as the Clarets won 2-1.

Potts was named manager-of-the-month for March and, after an enforced rest due to opponents' cup commitments, Burnley returned to action with another Kindon double as Cardiff City were beaten 4-1 at Turf Moor.

In 23 games since rejoining the club, Kindon had scored 13 goals in leading the charge towards safety. Although Burnley were up to 14th, they were still not safe and their 10-match unbeaten run ended with defeats at Orient and Charlton Athletic.

With two games to go they could still finish in the top half of the table, get relegated or sit anywhere in between.

But Fletcher and Noble slammed the relegation trapdoor firmly shut with goals against Fulham and the Clarets then signed off in style with another win, this time against Luton Town, to finish in 11th position.

Bolton won the division with 58 points, Southampton had 57 and Spurs 56. Burnley finished 11th with 40 – but had they come up with the same form over the first two-thirds of the season as they produced in the final 14 games, they would have walked it with 63 points.

Kindon was the catalyst, Stevenson got somewhere near his best form of earlier seasons and was the only ever-present while Morley and Cochrane both lit up games at various stages in the season.

In the end, however, it was sheer blood, guts and determination that kept them up and every one of the senior players was retained with Jim Thomson offered a new deal despite having been on the transfer list all season.

Burnley had finished the season in style and now everyone was looking forward to a spirited push for promotion next time around.

Over 250 senior games for Billy Ingham
a loyal Turf Moor servant

1977-78 - Second Division

		P	W	D	L	F	A	Pts
1	Bolton W	42	24	10	8	63	33	58
2	Southampton	42	22	13	7	70	39	57
3	Tottenham H	42	20	16	6	83	49	56
4	Brighton & HA	42	22	12	8	63	38	56
5	Blackburn R	42	16	13	13	56	60	45
6	Sunderland	42	14	16	12	67	59	44
7	Stoke C	42	16	10	16	53	49	42
8	Oldham A	42	13	16	13	54	58	42
9	Crystal P	42	13	15	14	50	47	41
10	Fulham	42	14	13	15	49	49	41
11	BURNLEY	42	15	10	17	56	64	40
12	Sheffield U	42	16	8	18	62	73	40
13	Luton T	42	14	10	18	54	52	38
14	Orient	42	10	18	14	43	49	38
15	Notts C	42	11	16	15	54	62	38
16	Millwall	42	12	14	16	49	57	38
17	Charlton A	42	13	12	17	55	68	38
18	Bristol R	42	13	12	17	61	77	38
19	Cardiff C	42	13	12	17	51	71	38
20	Blackpool	42	12	13	17	59	60	37
21	Mansfield T	42	10	11	21	49	69	31
22	Hull C	42	8	12	22	34	52	28

1977-78

Manager : Harry Potts

Division Two (11th)

		Date			Opponents	Result		h/t	Goalscorers/times	Opp. goal times
	1	Aug	20	h	BOLTON W	L	0-1	0-0		51
	2		23	a	Sunderland	L	0-3	0-2		7, 30, 65og
	3		27	a	Stoke C	L	1-2	0-1	Burke 82	9p, 62
	4	Sep	3	h	CRYSTAL P	D	1-1	1-1	Nicholas 15og	23
	5		10	a	Southampton	L	0-3	0-2		34, 41, 72p
	6		17	h	BRIGHTON & H A	D	0-0	0-0		
	7		24	a	Mansfield T	L	1-4	1-1	Brennan 25	9, 60, 63p, 83
	8	Oct	1	h	MILLWALL	L	0-2	0-2		2, 5
	9		4	a	Fulham	L	1-4	0-1	Flynn 88	22, 51, 65, 79
	10		8	h	BRISTOL R	W	3-1	1-0	Smith 35, Cochrane 75, Robinson 79	83
	11		15	a	Sheffield U	L	1-2	0-0	Noble 75	52, 61
	12		22	h	HULL C	D	1-1	1-0	Flynn 38	52
	13		29	h	BLACKPOOL	L	0-1	0-0		58
	14	Nov	5	a	Tottenham H	L	0-3	0-2		14, 45, 47
	15		12	h	NOTTS C	W	3-1	2-0	Fletcher (2) 16, 80, Kindon 27	57p
	16		19	a	Cardiff C	L	1-2	1-1	Fletcher 26	2, 68p
	17		26	h	ORIENT	D	0-0	0-0		
	18	Dec	3	a	Luton T	W	2-1	1-0	Hall 29, Kindon 50	79
	19		10	h	CHARLTON A	W	1-0	1-0	Kindon 17	
	20		17	a	Notts C	L	0-3	0-3		14, 20og, 41
	21		26	h	BLACKBURN R	L	2-3	0-3	Morley 64, Noble 89p	3, 29, 40
	22		27	a	Oldham A	L	0-2	0-1		33, 83p
	23		31	h	SUNDERLAND	D	0-0	0-0		
	24	Jan	2	a	Bolton W	W	2-1	1-0	Brennan (2) 11, 47	89
	25		14	h	STOKE C	W	1-0	0-0	Kindon 70	
	26		21	a	Crystal P	D	1-1	1-1	Noble 24	38
	27	Feb	4	h	SOUTHAMPTON	D	3-3	2-0	Kindon (2) 5, 56, Cochrane 29	46, 83, 90
Newton's last game	28		11	a	Brighton & H A	L	1-2	0-1	Scott 50	45, 75
	29		25	a	Millwall	D	1-1	0-1	Noble 64p	41
	30	Mar	4	a	Bristol R	D	2-2	1-1	Kindon (2) 37, 83	44, 90
	31		11	h	SHEFFIELD U	W	4-1	0-1	Cochrane (2) 55, 89, Noble 71p, Ingham 85	40
	32		14	h	MANSFIELD T	W	2-0	1-0	Fletcher 43, Kindon 48	
	33		18	a	Hull C	W	3-1	1-1	Fletcher 27, Ingham 70, Noble 78p	37
	34		25	h	OLDHAM A	W	4-1	1-0	Cochrane (2) 32, 71, Kindon 56, Brennan 82	61p
	35		27	a	Blackburn R	W	1-0	1-0	Cochrane 20	
	36		28	a	Blackpool	D	1-1	1-1	Smith 5	34
	37	Apr	1	h	TOTTENHAM H	W	2-1	1-1	Ingham 27, Noble 52	19
	38		15	h	CARDIFF C	W	4-2	2-2	Ingham 19, Kindon (2) 37, 62, Fletcher 82	8, 44
	39		18	a	Orient	L	0-3	0-1		35, 84, 89
	40		22	a	Charlton A	L	2-3	1-2	Cochrane 1, Smith 60	36, 45, 74
	41		25	h	FULHAM	W	2-0	0-0	Fletcher 61, Noble 70	
	42		29	h	LUTON T	W	2-1	1-1	P.Futcher 37og, Smith 54	35

FA Cup

				Opponents	Result		h/t	Goalscorers/times	Opp. goal times
3	Jan	7	h	FULHAM	W	1-0	0-0	Fletcher 86	
4		31	a	Chelsea	L	2-6	1-3	Fletcher 1, Kindon 79	4,17,26,68,74,75

Final, Ipswich T 1-0 Arsenal, at Wembley.

League Cup

				Opponents	Result		h/t	Goalscorers/times	Opp. goal times
1	Aug	13	h	CHESTER	W	2-0	1-0	Cochrane (2) 23, 51	
		17	a	Chester	L	0-1	0-1		42
2		30	h	NORWICH C	W	3-1	2-0	Morley 24, Noble 29, Ingham 88	58p
3	Oct	25	h	IPSWICH T	L	1-2	1-1	Fletcher 4	16, 48

Final, Nottingham F 1-0 Liverpool, at Old Trafford, after a 0-0 draw after extra time, at Wembley.

Details of other first team games elsewhere.

Att.	Pos	Stevenson	Newton	Brennan	Burke	P Robinson	Rodaway	Morley	Ingham	Loggie	Flynn	Cochrane	M Smith	Scott	Noble	Pashley	Higgins	Fletcher	Thomson	R Overson	Hall	Kindon	
14,732		1	2	3	4	5	6	7	8	9*	10	11	S*										1
31,450		1	2	3	4	5	6	11	8		10	7	9										2
12,835	22	1		3	S*	5	6	8	7		10	11	9*	2	4								3
10,460	22	1		3	4	5	6	11	8		10	7		2	9								4
17,412	22	1		3		5	6	11	8		10	7	9	2	4								5
9,227	22	1		3		9	6	11	8*		10	7	S*		4	2	5						6
8,274	22	1		3		9	6	11*	S*		10	7			4	2	5	8					7
7,242	22	1	2	3		5	6*		8	9	11	7	10		4	S*							8
6,895		1	2	3		5			8		10	7	11		4		6	9					9
7,253	22	1	2	3		5		11			10	7	8		4			9	6				10
14,151	22	1	2	3		5		S*	11		10	7*	8		4			9	6				11
8,592	22	1	2	3				11	7		10		8		4			9	6	5			12
11,243	22	1			10	S*	5	11				7	8*	2	4	3		9	6				13
30,634	22	1	11		10		5					7	8	2	4	3		9	6				14
9,734	22	1	2	3			6	11				7			4			9	5		8	10	15
7,069	22	1	2	5			4	11				S*			6	8*		9	3		7	10	16
8,525	22	1	2	3			6	11				7			4			9	5		8	10	17
6,921	22	1	2	3			6	11	7						4			9	5		8	10	18
9,478	22	1	2	3			6	11				7			4			9	5		8	10	19
7,639	22	1	2	3			6	11	7			S*			4			9*	5		8	10	20
27,427		1	2	3			6	11	7*			S*			4			9	5		8	10	21
15,172		1		3	7*		6	11				S*		2	4			9	5		8	10	22
12,726	22	1		3			6	11				7	S*	2	4			9	5		8*	10	23
28,232		1		3		10	6	11	7			8		2	4			9	5				24
11,101	21	1		3			6	11	8			7		2	4			9	5			10	25
15,367	20	1	11	3			6		8			7		2	4			9	5			10	26
10,592	20	1	6	3				11	8			7		2	4			9	5			10	27
22,694	20	1	6	3				11	8			7		2	4			9	5			10	28
7,166	21	1		3			6	11	8			7	9	2	4				5			10	29
7,520	21	1		3			6	11	8			7		2	4			9	5			10	30
11,801	20	1		3			6	11	8			7		2	4			9	5			10	31
9,893		1		3			6	11	8			7		2	4			9	5			10	32
5,936	17	1		3			6		8			7	11	2	4			9	5			10	33
13,529	17	1		3			6	S*	8			7	11	2	4			9	5			10*	34
24,379		1		3			6		8			7	11	2	4			9	5			10	35
13,393		1		3			6		8			7	11	2	4			9	5			10	36
16,916	14	1		3			6		8			7	11	2	4			9	5			10	37
11,610	14	1		3		5	6		8			7	11	2	4			9				10	38
5,795		1		3		5	6*		8			7	11	2	4			9			S*	10	39
6,511	16	1		3		5			8			7	11	2	4			9	6			10	40
9,465		1		3		6			8			7	11	2	4			9	5			10	41
11,648	11	1		3		6			8			7	11	2	4			9	5			10	42
Appearances		42	18	40	6	17	33	27	32	2	12	36	21	26	40	5	3	34	31	1	9	27	
Apps as sub					1	1		2	1			4	3			1					1		
Goals (56)				4	1	1		1	4		2	8	4	1	8			7			1	12	2 ogs

Att.	Stevenson	Newton	Brennan	Burke	P Robinson	Rodaway	Morley	Ingham	Loggie	Flynn	Cochrane	M Smith	Scott	Noble	Pashley	Higgins	Fletcher	Thomson	R Overson	Hall	Kindon	
10,984	1		3			6	11	8			7	S*	2	4			9*	5			10	3
32,168	1	11*	3			6	S*	8			7		2	4			9	5			10	4
Appearances	2	1	2			2	1	2			2		2	2			2	2			2	
Apps as sub							1					1										
Goals (3)																	2				1	

Att.	Stevenson	Newton	Brennan	Burke	P Robinson	Rodaway	Morley	Ingham	Loggie	Flynn	Cochrane	M Smith	Scott	Noble	Pashley	Higgins	Fletcher	Thomson	R Overson	Hall	Kindon	
4,792	1	2	3		5	6		7		10	11	8		4			9					1
4,097	1	2	3	S*	5	6*		7		10	11	8		4			9					2nd leg
6,492	1		3	4	5	6	11	8		10	7		2	9								2
9,581	1	2	3			5	11			10	7	8		4			9	6				3
Appearances	4	3	4	1	3	4	2	3		4	4	3	1	4			3	1				
Apps as sub				1																		
Goals (6)							1	1			2			1			1					

1978-79

The 1978-79 campaign was, for more than two decades, Burnley's best chance to get back into the top flight of domestic football. But the fixture pile-up caused by a long, hard winter and the inability to close out the campaign saw the Clarets finish a disappointing 13th in the Second Division table. But it was also a season which brought an incredible Anglo-Scottish Cup triumph and a game against Celtic that created enough headlines on the field ... and too many off it.

The summer had seen Terry Pashley sold to Blackpool for £30,000, the return of Ray Pointer as youth team coach and speculation surrounding the possible return of Geoff Nulty end when he signed for Everton.

Pre-season activity saw wins over Preston and Blackpool and a draw with Blackburn in the group stages of the Anglo-Scottish Cup and Burnley were handed a plum draw against Celtic to be played over two legs in September.

While many derided the competition because of possible fixture implications, manager Harry Potts came out with the prophetic: "I'm glad we're still in it. Nothing succeeds like success. It brings extra interest for players and fans and I hope we do as well as we can in the competition."

The league campaign started with three draws, two of which saw the Clarets have seemingly good "goals" disallowed. Another draw followed in the League Cup against Fourth Division Bradford City, but the first win of the campaign was not far away and, following a penalty spot equaliser from skipper Peter Noble, it duly arrived as Ian Brennan beat Notts County with a 25-yard stunner.

Trailing 2-0 in the League Cup replay, Burnley mounted a second half fightback to go through and new signing Leighton James, a £165,000 capture from QPR, watched as Burnley again came from 2-0 down to win via a Jim Thomson header against West Ham United.

Amid terrible scenes of crowd violence – 60 fans were injured as cans, bottles, stones and even iron railings were hurled – Burnley took the first leg of their Celtic showdown with Steve Kindon notching the only goal of the game as James returned to the Turf Moor fold. Celtic had eight straight Scottish Premier League wins under their belts and the Burnley win was a shock. The violence was even more shocking and prompted an FA commission of enquiry.

That game was followed by the first defeat of the season as Burnley were blown away 4-0 by Sheffield United. And the next Turf Moor date was a humbling 2-1 defeat against Sunderland who had two men sent off. It was a crunching encounter in which Gary Rowell scored twice for the Rokerites before Tony Morley pulled one back.

After successive defeats, Burnley were certainly not favourites when they arrived at Parkhead. But James got everything right on the night. Brennan scored a scorching free kick and Kindon rounded off the tie 2-1 with a fine solo goal.

Brilliant defence and well-executed counter-attack brought a 2-0 win at Millwall and despite plenty of pressure there was only one goal as Malcolm Smith scored a late winner against Oldham Athletic. In between those two league games, Burnley were beaten 3-1 in the League Cup by Brighton and Hove Albion.

Despite claims that Burnley were building for the future and not intent on selling their players, Terry Cochrane went to Middlesbrough for £210,00 with Burnley handing over a quarter of it as a sell-on clause which was part of his original deal from Coleraine.

Burnley bounced back from a 3-1 defeat against leaders Stoke City by beating fancied Brighton 3-1 with Billy Ingham bagging a brace and with a quarter of the season gone, the Clarets were riding high just one point out of the promotion places.

Having been held 2-2 at Deepdale, Burnley returned to cup action and Peter Higgs wrote in the Burnley Express: "Burnley's 2-1 win in the first leg of the Anglo-Scottish Cup semi-final at Mansfield has to go down as one of the greatest acts of soccer robbery." They had gone behind, but Kindon was certainly enjoying this competition and both he and James scored to get one foot in the final.

More deserved was the 2-1 win which followed over Crystal Palace, but the second leg of the semi-final was a tense affair. Mansfield won it 1-0, the game went to penalties and the Clarets eventually prevailed 8-7!

At this stage in the season, mounting brave fightbacks was certainly not unusual. Trailing 2-0 at Filbert Street, Ingham pulled one back, but there was to be no equaliser on this occasion. It was a different story when Fulham took the lead at Turf Moor. Burnley responded brilliantly and won 5-3 with Noble scoring his fourth league hat-trick for the club.

Following draws against Notts County and Cambridge United, the Clarets were fifth in the table, Harry Potts was manager-of-the-month for November and all eyes turned to the Anglo-Scottish Cup final.

Steve Kindon
a welcome return to Turf Moor,
almost certainly the fastest Claret of all time

On a Boundary Park pitch more like an ice rink, most of the Burnley players wore training shoes rather than studded boots and won 4-1. Kindon had the night of his life with a goal in the first minute and another later on. Noble and Thomson also scored and, although Oldham won the return leg 1-0 at Turf Moor, the cup was presented to Burnley skipper Noble.

December started with defeat against Orient and the year closed with a great individual performance from Billy Ingham against Bristol City, a day of missed chances against

Newcastle, a fine 2-1 Boxing Day win against Blackburn and a goalless draw against Cardiff.

By this stage, Burnley were one game into the second half of the season and had suffered just one postponement.

The New Year started with another and the only game in January was the FA Cup win over Birmingham. Before the season was over, the Clarets suffered a total of 20 postponements including eight against Sunderland in the FA Cup. In the league most of the postponements were due to snow and ice but one was due to gastric flu at Oldham and another due to too much sun thawing the ice and flooding the pitch at Selhurst Park!

The first league game of 1979, at Roker Park in February, saw a clash that summed up Burnley's season to date. They lost 3-1 and had a miserable return of one away win from 12 attempts. At home, on the other hand, they had lost just once in 11 games.

Alan Stevenson
well over 500 senior games
in more than ten years at Turf Moor

When the FA Cup clash with Sunderland was finally played, the fixture pile-up got worse as a replay was needed after a Thomson header.

Before it could be played, the Clarets lost 3-0 against Stoke. And that scoreline was to be repeated in the next two games as Ingham, Fletcher and Kindon crowned an FA Cup night to remember at Roker Park to earn a date at Anfield just two days later.

Every schoolboy in the land knew the names of every Liverpool player. But the European champions had to thank Ray Clemence for shutting the Clarets out three times in the early exchanges before the Reds finally won 3-0.

Defeat against Brighton followed and Burnley, having played only three league games since Christmas, were down to 15th with bags of games in hand, but fixture congestion looming large.

Whilst everyone was looking at a good run to the end of the season and the prospect of promotion, the worrying fact was that a draw with Sheffield United left the Clarets only six points above the relegation zone.

But the panic was over as they climbed back up to ninth following a draw with Preston and wins against Luton Town and Wrexham.

Derek Scott scored with a vicious 25-yard shot 90 seconds from time to earn a victory over Charlton that saw Burnley up to seventh and, following a 1-1 draw with Cambridge, Potts insisted that promotion was very much still on the cards. At the time, Burnley were 10 points behind the promotion places, but with 11 games to go they had games in hand on everyone but West Ham United.

Having gone 2-0 behind after just seven minutes against Luton, they had no chance of recovery and lost 4-1, but wins over Newcastle United, courtesy of a Brian Hall strike, and Blackburn Rovers, thanks to Morley and Hall, meant the dream was still alive.

It remained alive, however, for just two more games. A goalless draw against Wrexham was followed by a defeat against Bristol Rovers and the only thing that could do the trick was a winning run until the end of the season. They did not win another game and finished 13th!

West Ham won 3-1 at Upton Park, Orient contrived a win despite having only 20% of the possession and Kindon scored in the draw at Ninian Park.

The last home game of the season was a flop against bottom club Millwall, Crystal Palace had a club record crowd of over 51,000 as they clinched promotion by winning 2-0 and the Clarets signed off by losing 2-0 against Oldham.

After 58 games which had promised so much, the Clarets had the Anglo-Scottish Cup and some memorable FA Cup games to show for their efforts.

All 29 players were retained, but just two weeks after the end of the season Morley was sold to Aston Villa for £220,000 to take the post-War transfer income to more than £3,000,000.

As the players went off for a hard-earned summer break, rumours again suggested that Nulty could be on his way back to Turf Moor from Everton, along with Martin Dobson.

1978-79 - Second Division

		P	W	D	L	F	A	Pts
1	Crystal P	42	19	19	4	51	24	57
2	Brighton & HA	42	23	10	9	72	39	56
3	Stoke C	42	20	16	6	58	31	56
4	Sunderland	42	22	11	9	70	44	55
5	West Ham U	42	18	14	10	70	39	50
6	Notts C	42	14	16	12	48	60	44
7	Preston NE	42	12	18	12	59	57	42
8	Newcastle U	42	17	8	17	51	55	42
9	Cardiff C	42	16	10	16	56	70	42
10	Fulham	42	13	15	14	50	47	41
11	Orient	42	15	10	17	51	51	40
12	Cambridge U	42	12	16	14	44	52	40
13	BURNLEY	42	14	12	16	51	62	40
14	Oldham A	42	13	13	16	52	61	39
15	Wrexham	42	12	14	16	45	42	38
16	Bristol R	42	14	10	18	48	60	38
17	Leicester C	42	10	17	15	43	52	37
18	Luton T	42	13	10	19	60	57	36
19	Charlton A	42	11	13	18	60	69	35
20	Sheffield U	42	11	12	19	52	69	34
21	Millwall	42	11	10	21	42	61	32
22	Blackburn R	42	10	10	22	41	72	30

1978-79

Manager : Harry Potts

Division Two (13th)

	Date			Opponents	Result		h/t	Goalscorers/times	Opp. goal times
1	Aug	19	h	LEICESTER C	D	2-2	0-1	Fletcher 46, Noble 69p	2p, 56
2		22	a	Charlton A	D	1-1	1-1	Cochrane 22	31
3		26	a	Fulham	D	0-0	0-0		
4	Sep	2	h	NOTTS C	W	2-1	1-1	Noble 11p, Brennan 69	9
5		9	h	WEST HAM U	W	3-2	1-2	Brennan 37, Fletcher 50, Thomson 81	32, 35
6		16	a	Sheffield U	L	0-4	0-3		15p, 17, 19, 48
7		23	h	SUNDERLAND	L	1-2	0-0	Morley 75	60, 69p
8		30	a	Millwall	W	2-0	1-0	Fletcher 23, Noble 64	
9	Oct	7	h	OLDHAM A	W	1-0	0-0	Smith 85	
10		14	a	Stoke C	L	1-3	1-2	Ingham 17	15, 30, 55
11		21	h	BRIGHTON & H A	W	3-0	0-0	Ingham (2) 57, 75, Brennan 71	
12		28	a	Preston N E	D	2-2	1-2	Kindon 18, Noble 67p	7, 27
13	Nov	4	h	CRYSTAL P	W	2-1	1-0	Brennan 16, Fletcher 48	66p
14		11	a	Leicester C	L	1-2	0-0	Ingham 88	64, 75
15		18	h	FULHAM	W	5-3	2-2	Noble (3) 20p, 26p, 83, James 46, Kindon 85	15, 30, 54
16		21	a	Notts C	D	1-1	0-0	Ingham 76	52
17		25	a	Cambridge U	D	2-2	1-2	Ingham 42, Fletcher 61	4, 23
18	Dec	9	a	Orient	L	1-2	1-0	Fletcher 40	79, 81
19		16	h	BRISTOL R	W	2-0	1-0	Ingham (2) 30, 80	
20		23	a	Newcastle U	L	1-3	0-2	Noble 86	25, 29, 53
21		26	h	BLACKBURN R	W	2-1	2-0	Fletcher 5, Noble 43	57
22		30	h	CARDIFF C	D	0-0	0-0		
23	Feb	3	a	Sunderland	L	1-3	1-0	James 44	51, 65, 87
24		24	h	STOKE C	L	0-3	0-0		63, 75, 89
25	Mar	3	a	Brighton & H A	L	1-2	0-0	Ingham 51	50p, 69
26		6	h	SHEFFIELD U	D	1-1	1-1	Fletcher 32	7
27		10	h	PRESTON N E	D	1-1	0-0	Noble 51	56
28		13	h	LUTON T	W	2-1	1-0	Noble (2) 42p, 54	60
29		21	a	Wrexham	W	1-0	1-0	Fletcher 38	
30		24	h	CHARLTON A	W	2-1	1-1	James 14, Scott 89	32
31		31	h	CAMBRIDGE U	D	1-1	1-0	Robinson 18	87
32	Apr	7	a	Luton T	L	1-4	0-2	Noble 58p	2, 7, 66, 88
33		10	h	NEWCASTLE U	W	1-0	1-0	Hall 10	
34		14	a	Blackburn R	W	2-1	0-1	Morley 46, Hall 71	26
35		16	h	WREXHAM	D	0-0	0-0		
36		21	a	Bristol R	L	0-2	0-1		35, 52
37		24	a	West Ham U	L	1-3	1-2	Noble 1	4, 10, 53
38		28	h	ORIENT	L	0-1	0-0		49
39	May	5	a	Cardiff C	D	1-1	1-0	Kindon 41	53
40		8	h	MILLWALL	L	0-1	0-1		24
41		11	a	Crystal P	L	0-2	0-0		77, 83
42		14	a	Oldham A	L	0-2	0-1		15, 66

FA Cup

3	Jan	9	a	Birmingham C	W	2-0	1-0	Morley 1, James 85	
4	Feb	21	h	SUNDERLAND	D	1-1	1-0	Thomson 28	65
rep		26	a	Sunderland	W	3-0	2-0	Fletcher 5, Ingham 20, Kindon 88	
5		28	a	Liverpool	L	0-3	0-1		43, 59, 61

Final, Arsenal 3-2 Manchester U, at Wembley.

League Cup

	2	Aug	29	h	BRADFORD C	D	1-1	0-1	Cochrane 75	25
	rep	Sep	5	a	Bradford C	W	3-2	0-2	Noble 47, Cochrane 75, Ingham 86	24p, 45
Cochrane's last game	3	Oct	3	h	BRIGHTON & H A	L	1-3	0-1	Brennan 64	5, 46, 76

Final, Nottingham F 3-2 Southampton, at Wembley.

Details of other first team games elsewhere.

Att.	Pos	Stevenson	Scott	Brennan	Noble	Thomson	Rodaway	Cochrane	Ingham	Fletcher	Kindon	M Smith	Hall	James	Morley	P Robinson	Arins	Jakub	Young	Robertson	
12,048		1	2	3	4	5	6	7	8	9	10	11									1
8,580		1	2	3	4	5	6	7	8	9	10	11									2
6,135	11	1	2	3	4	5	6	7	8	9	10*	11	S*								3
9,787	6	1	2	3	4	5	6	7	8	9	10	11									4
12,392	4	1	2	3	4	5	6	7		9	10	11	8								5
15,355	8	1	2	3	4	5	6	7		9	10		8	11							6
13,368	13	1	2		4	5	6		3		10	9	8	11	7						7
5,389	9	1	2	3	4	5	6		8	9	10	7		11							8
11,835	7	1	2	3	4	5	6		8	9	10	7		11							9
18,434	11	1	2	3	4	5	6		8	9	10	7		11							10
10,321	7	1	2	3	4	5	6		8	9	10		7	11							11
14,975	7	1	2	3	4	5	6		8	9	10		7	11							12
11,129	7	1	2	3		5	6		8	9	10		7	11		4					13
12,842	8	1	2	3	4	5	6		8	9	10		7	11							14
10,566	5	1		3	4	5	6		8	9	10*		7	11		S*	2				15
8,520		1		3	4	5	6		8	9	10		7	11			2				16
6,502	5	1		3	4	5	6		8	9	10		7*	11		S*	2				17
4,754	11	1		3	4	5	6		8	9	10*		7	11		S*	2				18
9,257	8	1		3	4	5	6		8	9	10		7	11			2				19
23,639	8	1	2	3	4	5	6		8	9	10		7	11*		S*					20
23,133		1	2	3	4	5	6		8	9	10		7	11*	S*						21
9,821	7	1	2*	3	4	5	6		8	9	10		7	11	S*						22
23,030	9	1	2	3	4	5	6		9		10		8	11	7						23
13,890	13	1	2	3	4	5	6		8	9	10			11		7					24
19,379	15	1	2	3	4	5	6		8	9	10		7	11							25
8,208		1	2	3	4	5	6		8	9*	10			11	S*			7			26
15,270	14	1	2	3	4	5	6		8*	9	10			11	S*			7			27
7,691		1	2	3	4	5	6			9	10		S*	11		8*		7			28
8,840		1	2	3	4	5	6		8	9	10			11				7			29
8,560	7	1	2	3	4	5	6		8	9				11	10			7			30
8,234	9	1	2	3	4	5			8	9	10*			11	S*	6		7			31
6,466	9	1	2	3	4	5			8	9	S*			11	10	6		7*			32
7,771		1	2		4	5	6		8	9*	10		7	11	S*			3			33
14,761	7	1			4	5	6		8	9	10*		7	11	S*		2	3			34
9,401		1			4	5	6			9			7	11	10		2	3	8*	S*	35
5,947	7	1	2	3	4	5	6		8	9*			7	11	10	S*					36
24,139		1	2	3	4	5	6		8				S*	11	10	9		7*			37
7,195	9	1	2	3	4		6				9		8	11	10	5		7			38
10,254	10	1	2	3	4	5	6		8		9		7	11	10						39
5,837		1	2	3	4	5	6		8	S*	9		7*	11	10						40
51,482		1	2	3	4	5	6		8		9		7	11	10						41
6,791	13	1	2	3	4	5			8		9			11	10	6		7			42
Appearances		42	35	38	41	41	39	6	37	34	37	9	25	37	12	8	7	13	1		
Apps as sub										1	1		3		7	5				1	
Goals (51)			1	4	14	1		1	9	9	3	1	2	3	2	1					

Att.	Pos	Stevenson	Scott	Brennan	Noble	Thomson	Rodaway	Cochrane	Ingham	Fletcher	Kindon	M Smith	Hall	James	Morley	P Robinson	Arins	Jakub	Young	Robertson	
15,535		1	2	3	4	5	6		8		10		7	11	9						3
20,852		1	2	3	4	5	6		8	S*	10		7	11	9*						4
37,507		1	2	3	4	5	6		8	9	10			11		7					rep
47,161		1	2	3	4	5	6		7	9	10		8	11							5
Appearances		4	4	4	4	4	4		4	2	4		3	4	2	1					
Apps as sub										1											
Goals (6)						1			1	1	1			1	1						

Att.	Pos	Stevenson	Scott	Brennan	Noble	Thomson	Rodaway	Cochrane	Ingham	Fletcher	Kindon	M Smith	Hall	James	Morley	P Robinson	Arins	Jakub	Young	Robertson	
9,185		1	2	3	4	5	6	7	8	9		11			10						2
9,192		1	2	3	4	5	6	7	8	9	10	11									rep
9,076		1	2	3	4	5	6	7	8	9	10			11							3
Appearances		3	3	3	3	3	3	3	3	3	2	2		1	1						
Apps as sub																					
Goals (5)				1	1			2	1												

1979-80

Can the 1979-80 season be classed as the worst-ever in Clarets' history? Certainly in terms of wins it could be as Burnley recorded their lowest-ever number of wins – six – in a 42-game season. And it is the season which carries with it the stigma of being the one that led to relegation to Division Three for the first time in almost 100 years of the club's fine traditions.

So what went wrong? This was more than just the usual combination of injury crises, woeful refereeing and the inability to win away from home.

This was just the inability to win anywhere – all six wins came in a 10-game burst midway through the season – coupled with a change of manager and the sale of experienced players while relying on a crop of younger talents to try and save the day.

But it was also a season with notable highlights. It saw the return of Martin Dobson and the arrival of Turf Moor legend Billy Hamilton.

Also back at Turf Moor, as Ladbrokes quoted Burnley at 25/1 for the title, was Arthur Bellamy as coach in charge of the resurrected 'B' team. Michael Phelan was among the new crop of apprentices and the new season also saw the end of the V for Victory strip, replaced by a more traditional claret and blue affair.

With only one draw to show from their group games, Burnley's defence of the Anglo-Scottish Cup ended before it had really started and Peter Higgs predicted in the Burnley Express: "Testing times ahead for the Clarets. It is hard to see Burnley as one of the main promotion contenders."

Burnley's season opened at Brisbane Road with Ralph Coates scoring a double for new-look Orient with Leighton James the Clarets' saviour, setting-up goals for himself and Steve Kindon.

A defeat at the hands of Notts County was followed by a 1-1 draw with Wolves in the first leg of their League Cup clash, but there was no justice as they were beaten 2-1 at Swansea and then crashed out of the cup as Wolves hit them with two long-range shots.

Skipper Peter Noble was in and out of the team with injury whilst early-season knocks also deprived the Clarets of the services of Paul Fletcher and Kindon. The return to league action saw a 1-1 draw with Oldham, but poor finishing consigned them to a 3-1 defeat against Fulham.

The better side, Burnley had to settle for a share of the spoils against Sunderland and then they lost against both West Ham United – despite taking the lead – and Chelsea, having rattled the woodwork and seen two goal-bound efforts cleared off the line.

The Clarets finally found the scoring touch in their match at The Valley, but had to settle for a draw. Defeat in the next game, against Cardiff at Turf Moor, led to Harry Potts resigning and Brian Miller taking over, with Frank Casper as his assistant.

Miller's first act was to recall Malcolm Smith and try and sort out an escalating contract dispute. And as he looked to try and work a Turf Moor miracle he said: "The slate is wiped clean. Everything that has happened in the past is now forgotten."

But he could not work the oracle instantly and Burnley lost 3-2 at Deepdale. After 127 successive games, Alan Stevenson did not make the trip to QPR and young stand-in Billy O'Rourke had a horror debut in front of the Match of the Day cameras as Rangers rattled in seven unanswered goals. In truth, O'Rourke got little protection from his defence and there was little he could have done with any of the goals.

It was Burnley's worst defeat in more than a decade and prompted chairman Bob Lord to say: "These players are among the best paid in the Second Division and they are simply not doing their job."

Defeat against Orient – Richard Overson came on as a substitute and joined younger brother Vince on the pitch to become the first pair of brothers to play in the same Burnley team since Jack and David Walders in the early 1900s – meant that Burnley were bottom of the table after a third of the season and the only team in the Football League without a single win.

That was followed by a 1-1 draw at Filbert Street. Leicester should have won as they were awarded an 88th minute penalty, but the spot kick hit the upright and Gary Lineker put the rebound straight at the returning Stevenson. Another draw followed against league leaders Luton Town.

More than 350 senior games for Derek Scott in a ten year Turf Moor career

And then came the long-awaited win. Smith re-signed for the club and the Clarets thrashed Cambridge United 5-3 and there was more good news as Hamilton signed from QPR for £55,000. His arrival put Fletcher's future in doubt as he had failed to score in 23 games, and Hamilton almost made the perfect start, only to see his early "goal" at Eastville ruled-out and the game finish 0-0.

Bob Lord created the next headlines with another outspoken attack on the local Press at the annual general meeting. "They are trying to hound me out of the club," he claimed.

But back on the field there was a more positive outcome as Marshall Burke scored the only goal of the game and Watford boss Graham Taylor said: "I think Burnley will get out of trouble. They have got over their bad spell and I can see them gaining plenty of points."

But Birmingham's £1m. defence was too strong for them as new-signing Frank Worthington scored his first two goals for City. With a packed Christmas programme looming, Burnley were three points adrift and needed points. And they got them as Wrexham were beaten 1-0, Newcastle United 3-2 and Notts County 3-2, the latter game seeing a Phil Cavener double and the first away win of the season.

On the back of those four wins in five games, Miller was named manager-of-the-month for December, but the Clarets then lost on a frozen pitch at Shrewsbury before raising more than a few eyebrows by dumping First Division Stoke City out of the FA Cup courtesy of a Martin Dobson penalty.

A lifeless, goalless draw against Swansea was followed by the shock news that Noble had been sold for a bargain fee of £5,000 to Blackpool and, having been knocked out of the cup by Third Division Bury, they beat Fulham 2-1 in Stevenson's 300th league appearance for the Clarets.

That left Burnley with 17 games in 12 weeks to get themselves out of trouble. What they needed was a final third of the season like the one experienced in the previous campaign. What they got was a sequence of no wins in the final 17 games.

Having turned down a £15,000 offer for Fletcher, Miller accepted £30,000 from Blackpool and the next game was a humbling 5-0 defeat at Roker Park. The Clarets found themselves a point adrift of safety after defeat against promotion-chasing West Ham and a third successive defeat followed with a 2-1 reverse at Ninian Park.

Leighton James was placed on the transfer list as Miller tried to generate funds to strengthen the squad and striker Martyn Busby was signed on loan from QPR.

Paul Dixon scored a late equaliser against Preston North End, but relegation loomed large following defeats against Oldham and QPR. With 10 games to go, the Clarets were four points from safety.

Chelsea went back to the top of the Second Division as they beat the Clarets 2-1 despite Busby's opener and the relegation trapdoor was staring wide open as promotion-chasing Leicester won by the same 2-1 scoreline.

Having missed the last four games, Dobson was ruled-out for the remainder of the season with Achilles' tendon damage in both ankles and the squad was further weakened as Busby returned to Loftus Road having refused a second month's loan.

Billy Hamilton gave Burnley the lead against Luton, but they were held 1-1 and a Christmas-like points return was needed from the Easter programme.

Wrexham ended a 127-year wait for a win against Burnley with a 1-0 success at the Racecourse and when draws followed against both Shrewsbury and Newcastle, Burnley's only hope of survival was four straight wins to sign off the season.

But a 1-1 draw at home to Bristol Rovers ended the fight and in five years the Clarets had plummeted from 10th in the First Division to the Third Division.

Brian Miller summed it up by saying: "It is a bitter disappointment and, of course, it is a terrible blow for the fans. People must realise that football is not the same now as it was when we were a force in the First Division. It is also worth recalling that we are the last of the small town clubs in Lancashire to taste life in the Third Division."

The three final games yielded just one more point and Burnley finished 21st in the division.

James was sold to Swansea for £130,000; Smith, Brian Hall and Burke were among the 11 players given free transfers and Stevenson, Billy Rodaway and Ian Brennan refused the new deals on offer to them.

Miller made it clear that he wanted to rebuild for the challenges that lay head. After 525 league appearances for Oldham Athletic, Ian Wood signed on a free transfer, but Preston's Eric Potts turned down a move after the clubs had agreed a fee while the chase was on to try and lure Tommy Cassidy from Newcastle United.

OBITUARY

EDWIN (EDDIE) MOSSCROP

DIED 14 MARCH 1980, AGED 87

Eddie Mosscrop was the last survivor of Burnley's FA Cup winning side of 1914 and championship-winning team of 1921. Born in Southport in 1892, he had played for the same junior club as another member of that great team, Billy Watson.

He joined Burnley from Southport Central in 1912 and was initially played on the right-wing, but in his second season at Turf Moor, 1913-14, he switched to the number eleven shirt and it was on the left that he appeared in that season's FA Cup final when Liverpool were beaten 1-0; he did in fact play in every game of the Cup run that season. His fine form was recognised with two England caps against Wales and Scotland towards the end of that campaign.

Still only 22 when League football was suspended for World War I, Mosscrop served in Salonika during the hostilities, then returned to Turf Moor to resume duty on the left wing. Towards the end of the 1919-20 season, he lost his place to Walt Weaver, and he was only an occasional choice during the championship campaign. Back to first choice in 1921-22, he retired from football soon afterwards following a serious illness, eventually returning to Southport where he continued is career as a teacher.

RIP

1979-80 - Second Division

		P	W	D	L	F	A	Pts
1	Leicester C	42	21	13	8	58	38	55
2	Sunderland	42	21	12	9	69	42	54
3	Birmingham C	42	21	11	10	58	38	53
4	Chelsea	42	23	7	12	66	52	53
5	Queens Park R	42	18	13	11	75	53	49
6	Luton T	42	16	17	9	66	45	49
7	West Ham U	42	20	7	15	54	43	47
8	Cambridge U	42	14	16	12	61	53	44
9	Newcastle U	42	15	14	13	53	49	44
10	Preston NE	42	12	19	11	56	52	43
11	Oldham A	42	16	11	15	49	53	43
12	Swansea C	42	17	9	16	48	53	43
13	Shrewsbury T	42	18	5	19	60	53	41
14	Orient	42	12	17	13	48	54	41
15	Cardiff C	42	16	8	18	41	48	40
16	Wrexham	42	16	6	20	40	49	38
17	Notts C	42	11	15	16	51	52	37
18	Watford	42	12	13	17	39	46	37
19	Bristol R	42	11	13	18	50	64	35
20	Fulham	42	11	7	24	42	74	29
21	BURNLEY	42	6	15	21	39	73	27
22	Charlton A	42	6	10	26	39	78	22

1979-80

Manager : Harry Potts until October 1979, then Brian Miller

Division Three (21st)
Relegated

		Date			Opponents	Result		h/t	Goalscorers/times	Opp. goal times
	1	Aug	18	a	Orient	D	2-2	1-1	James 37, Kindon 76	4, 61
	2		21	h	CHARLTON A	D	1-1	0-0	Kindon 47	86
	3		25	h	NOTTS C	L	0-1	0-1		39
	4	Sep	1	a	Swansea C	L	1-2	1-1	Noble 7	28, 75
	5		8	h	OLDHAM A	D	1-1	0-1	Kindon 84	9
	6		15	a	Fulham	L	1-3	1-1	Noble 36p	33, 84, 85
	7		22	h	SUNDERLAND	D	1-1	0-1	Dobson 48	26
	8		29	a	West Ham U	L	1-2	1-0	Scott 40	67p, 70
	9	Oct	6	h	CHELSEA	L	0-1	0-0		48
	10		9	a	Charlton A	D	3-3	0-1	Dobson 63, James 64, Noble 75	30, 72, 87
Hall's last game	11		13	h	CARDIFF C	L	0-2	0-1		41, 50
	12		20	a	Preston N E	L	2-3	1-2	Dobson 25, James 77	3, 45, 79
	13		27	a	Queens Park R	L	0-7	0-4		19, 26, 41, 44, 48, 73, 89
last games for Noble & Kindon	14	Nov	3	h	ORIENT	L	1-2	0-1	Arins 70	30, 54
	15		10	a	Leicester C	D	1-1	0-0	James 65	79
	16		17	h	LUTON T	D	0-0	0-0		
Fletcher's last game	17		24	h	CAMBRIDGE U	W	5-3	2-2	Burke 12, Dobson 42, Biley 67og, James 86, Tate 89	15, 20, 69
	18	Dec	1	a	Bristol R	D	0-0	0-0		
	19		8	h	WATFORD	W	1-0	1-0	Burke 40	
	20		15	a	Birmingham C	L	0-2	0-1		37, 57
	21		21	h	WREXHAM	W	1-0	0-0	Burke 67	
	22		26	h	NEWCASTLE U	W	3-2	1-1	Hamilton 35, Smith 47, Dobson 74p	40, 89
	23		29	a	Notts C	W	3-2	2-1	Cavener (2) 18, 74, Hamilton 24	35, 86
	24	Jan	1	a	Shrewsbury T	L	0-2	0-1		12, 62
	25		12	h	SWANSEA C	D	0-0	0-0		
	26	Feb	2	h	FULHAM	W	2-1	0-0	Burke 48, James 83	58
	27		9	a	Sunderland	L	0-5	0-2		17,28,58,78,82
	28		19	h	WEST HAM U	L	0-1	0-1		18
	29		23	a	Cardiff C	L	1-2	0-1	Hamilton 50	16, 80
	30	Mar	1	h	PRESTON N E	D	1-1	0-1	Dixon 85	40
	31		4	a	Oldham A	L	1-2	1-1	Arins 21	16, 54
	32		8	h	QUEENS PARK R	L	0-3	0-2		3, 35, 88
	33		15	a	Chelsea	L	1-2	1-0	Busby 25	50, 77
Peter Robinson's last game	34		22	h	LEICESTER C	L	1-2	0-1	Scott 83	20, 69
	35		29	a	Luton T	D	1-1	0-0	Hamilton 60	67
	36	Apr	4	a	Wrexham	L	0-1	0-0		54
Brennan's last game	37		5	h	SHREWSBURY T	D	0-0	0-0		
	38		7	a	Newcastle U	D	1-1	0-1	Hamilton 72	26
	39		12	h	BRISTOL R	D	1-1	0-1	Hamilton 87	41
	40		19	a	Cambridge U	L	1-3	1-0	Hamilton 15	54, 76, 86
Malcolm Smith's last game	41		26	h	BIRMINGHAM C	D	0-0	0-0		
Ingham's last game	42	May	3	a	Watford	L	0-4	0-4		29, 38, 40, 45

FA Cup

3	Jan	5	h	STOKE C	W	1-0	0-0	Dobson 76p	
4		26	a	Bury	L	0-1	0-1		20

Final, West Ham U 1-0 Arsenal, at Wembley.

League Cup

	2	Aug	26	h	WOLVERHAMPTON W	D	1-1	1-0	Dobson 38	66
agg 1-3		Sep	4	a	Wolverhampton W	L	0-2	0-1		21, 64

Final, Wolverhampton W 1-0 Nottingham F, at Wembley.

Details of other first team games elsewhere.

Att.	Pos	Stevenson	Scott	Brennan	Noble	Thomson	Rodaway	Ingham	Dobson	Fletcher	Kindon	James	Jakub	Arins	P Robinson	Hall	Young	Tate	O'Rourke	V Overson	Cavener	R Overson	P Dixon	Burke	Hamilton	M Smith	Busby	Robertson	McAdam	Laws		
6,151		1	2	3	4	5	6	7	8	9	10	11																				1
6,924		1	2	3	4	5	6	7	8	9	10	11																				2
7,005	13	1	2	3	4	5	6	7	8		10	11	9																			3
16,670	19	1	2	3	4*	5	6	7	8			11	9	10	S*																	4
6,974	18	1	2	3*		5	6	7	8	10	S*	11	9	4																		5
6,633	20	1	2		4	5	6	7	8	9	10	11	3																			6
8,872	20	1	2			5	6		8	9	10	11	3			4	7															7
18,327	21	1	2	S*		5	6		8	9	10	11	3			4	7*															8
8,458	21	1	2		4*	5	6	S*	8	9		11	3			7	10															9
5,279		1	2		4	5	6		8			11	3			7	10	9														10
6,450	22	1	2		4	5	6		8		S*	11	3			7	10	9*														11
12,323	22	1	2	3	4	5	6		8	9	11	7					10															12
11,261	22		2	3	4	5	6		8	9	11	7					10		1													13
6,777	22				4	5*			8	9	11	10		2			3		1	6	7	S*										14
17,191	22	1		3			S*		8	9		7		2			10	11		5		4	6*									15
7,119	22	1		3					8	9		7		2			10	11		5		4*	6	S*								16
6,873	22	1		3					8	9*		7		2			10	11		5	S*		6	4								17
5,373	22	1		3					8			7		2			10			5			6	4	9	11						18
8,608	22	1	S*	3					8			7		2			10			5			6*	4	9	11						19
13,997	22	1		3			6		8			7		2			10			5		11		4	9							20
7,042	22	1		3			6		8			7		2			10			5				4	9	11						21
16,634	20	1		3			6		8			7*		2			10			5	S*			4	9	11						22
7,596	18	1	2	3			6		8								10			5	7			4	9	11						23
10,504	19	1	2	3			6		8								10			5	7			4	9	11						24
8,853	20	1	2				6		8			7					10*			5	S*		3	4	9	11						25
6,977	20	1	2				6		8			7	3							5	10			4	9	11						26
21,855		1	2				6		8			7	3							5	10			4	9	11						27
9,030	20	1		3					8			7		2			10			5	S*		6	4*	9	11						28
6,342	20	1		3			5					7		2	8		10						6	4	9	11						29
11,046	20	1		3					8			7		2			10*			5	S*		6		9	11	4					30
9,519	20	1		3								7	10	2	8					5	S*		6		9	11	4*					31
7,579	20	1		3								7	10	2						5	8	4	6		9	11						32
16,519	20	1		3								7	10	2						5	8		6		9	11	4					33
7,173	20	1	4	3								7	11	2	8					5			6		9		10					34
8,507	20	1	4	3								7	10	2						5			6		9	11		8				35
6,605		1	4	3								7	10	2						5			6		9	11		8				36
6,333	20	1	2	3		5	6					7	10				S*							4	9	11*		8				37
18,863		1	2			5	6					7	10											4	9	11		8	3			38
5,353	20	1	2			5	6					7	10				S*							4*	9	11		8	3			39
4,727	21	1	4			5	6					7	10	2											9	11		8	3			40
10,388	21	1	4			5	6					7	10	2											9	11		8	3			41
11,931	21	1	4			5*	6	11					10				S*				7				9			8	3	2		42
Appearances		40	27	27	11	20	28	7	29	13	9	39	23	22	3	5	22	5	2	22	8	4	15	16	25	22	4	8	5	1		
Apps as sub			1	1			1	1			2				1		3				6	1		1								
Goals (39)			2		3				5		3	6		2				1			2		1	4	7	1	1				1	og

Att.	Pos	Stevenson	Scott	Brennan	Noble	Thomson	Rodaway	Ingham	Dobson	Fletcher	Kindon	James	Jakub	Arins	P Robinson	Hall	Young	Tate	O'Rourke	V Overson	Cavener	R Overson	P Dixon	Burke	Hamilton	M Smith	Busby	Robertson	McAdam	Laws		
13,478		1	2				6		8								10			5	7		3	4	9	11						3
17,722		1	2	3			6		8			7					10*			5	S*			4	9	11						4
Appearances		2	2	1			2		2			1					2			2	1		1	2	2	2						
Apps as sub																					1											
Goals (1)									1																							

Att.	Pos	Stevenson	Scott	Brennan	Noble	Thomson	Rodaway	Ingham	Dobson	Fletcher	Kindon	James	Jakub	Arins	P Robinson	Hall	Young	Tate	O'Rourke	V Overson	Cavener	R Overson	P Dixon	Burke	Hamilton	M Smith	Busby	Robertson	McAdam	Laws		
6,163		1	2	3	4	5	6	7	8		10	11	9																			2
17,411		1	2	3		5	6	7	8	10	S*	11	9*	4																		2nd leg
Appearances		2	2	2	1	2	2	2	2	1	1	2	2	1																		
Apps as sub											1																					
Goals (1)									1																							

1980-81

Burnley dipped their collective toes in the water of the Third Division for the first time in the 1980-81 season and whatever they were expecting, they never really threatened to go straight back to Division Two despite being on the fringes for three-quarters of the season.

Manager Brian Miller wanted nothing less than an automatic return to Division Two. And on the eve of the new campaign he said: "Our aim for the season is nothing less than promotion. If we do quite well and finish among the leading group, but fail to make the top three, I will not be satisfied. We want to go back to the Second Division as soon as possible"

Peter Higgs of the Burnley Express was certain that good things were just around the corner and boldly stated that if Burnley did not finish in the top six he would walk to the first away game of the following season. Brave words indeed, and an offer that would come back to haunt him.

Before the ink had dried on the obituaries of the previous season, Miller had moved to bring in Ian Wood on a free transfer from Oldham Athletic.

Whilst enjoying his summer break, moves were afoot to bring in midfielder Tommy Cassidy from Newcastle United and he eventually signed for a tribunal-fixed fee of £30,000.

Also on the way into Turf Moor was Oldham's other full back, David Holt, along with Mansfield Town striker Steve Taylor. Between them they cost a further £80,000 and some of that money was recouped when Peter Robinson went to Sparta Rotterdam for £35,000.

Martin Dobson returned to training in a search for full fitness having missed the final 12 games of the relegation season and as William Hill's quoted the Clarets at odds of 7/1 for the title, the skipper denied any interest in the player-manager's job at Bury.

The first competitive action was again the Anglo-Scottish Cup and the Clarets once again proved it was an all-or-nothing competition. This time it was nothing as they lost to Bury, beat Oldham and drew with Shrewsbury.

Once again the League Cup was a curtain-raiser to the season and Burnley beat Wrexham, who for the first time in their history were a division higher than the Clarets, 3-1 at Turf Moor before winning the second leg 2-1.

Before the league campaign started, Billy Ingham – a veteran of some 12 seasons at Turf Moor – was sold to Bradford City for £30,000.

The Clarets' old frailties of giving away needless goals and spurning chances were there for all to see as they drew their first game 1-1 with Newport County at Turf Moor before losing 3-1 at Fellows Park.

There was another taste of things to come as Dobson scored the only goal of the game from the penalty spot as Chesterfield were beaten at Turf Moor. Holt and Chesterfield's Alan Birch were dismissed following a 62nd minute brawl to start a trend for early baths as the season continued.

A 2-0 defeat at Charlton saw the Clarets in the wrong half of the table after just four games and more defeats followed as West Ham claimed a 6-0 aggregate win, the eventual scoreline regarded as more than a little unfair on the Clarets. Billy Hamilton, fast becoming a big crowd favourite, scored the decisive goal as Colchester were beaten and Miller was linked with a move for former striker Ray Hankin, although the £150,000 fee sought by Vancouver Whitecaps was a major stumbling block.

OBITUARY
GEORGE WILLIAM BEEL
DIED 30 DECEMBER 1980, AGED 80

Of all the goalscoring sons of Turf Moor, George Beel still holds most of the records.

In a nine-year spell in the 1920s and 30s, he ripped up all the old records and posted a host of new ones. He arrived at Turf Moor from Chesterfield in 1923 and scored more than 180 senior goals at a ratio of better than a goal every other game in a team invariably struggling at the wrong end of the First Division. His tally included 11 hat-tricks and he was top scorer in six of his nine seasons as a first team regular. In the tightest ever First Division campaign – the 1927-28 season saw just five points separate fourth place from bottom and the Clarets beat the drop by just one point – he simply could not stop scoring and hit the net 35 times in 39 appearances. That was followed by another 30 the following season, but the spectre of relegation loomed large and when it happened he was transferred to his home town club, Lincoln City. A season at Rochdale was to follow and he was then appointed player-manager at Tunbridge Wells and settled in Kent.

RIP

A goalless draw against top-scorers Exeter City saw Burnley back in touch with the leaders as they were just three points off the pace after six games and, as the Hankin speculation died down, Eric Potts looked set for a move from Deepdale, out of the reckoning at Preston, he finally made the short trip to Turf Moor for £30,000 less than the fee originally agreed.

Kevin Young scored his first league goal as Burnley climbed into the top 10 on the back of a 2-0 win over Hull and despite a goalless outcome at Sealand Road, the Clarets were emerging as a team of considerable potential.

Taylor scored a hat-trick as Burnley rattled up their biggest win in nine years by beating Millwall 5-0 and a 0-0 draw at Boothferry Park saw them equal a record run of six games without conceding. The achievement of the 1946-47 promotion team was finally eclipsed as Burnley won 2-0 at Fulham to climb to fourth in the table.

Taylor hit a double in a thrilling 3-2 win over Sheffield United that saw Burnley climb to third and a 1-1 draw with Rotherham followed. Brian Miller was displeased with Rotherham's tactics – Jimmy Mullen was sent off and there was a rash of bookings – and said: "Rotherham are without doubt the most physical side we have played. They did not allow us to display our skill."

The unbeaten run of nine games ended when they went 3-0 down after 25 minutes at Fratton Park. Derek Scott scored twice to launch a fightback, but there was no late goal on this occasion. Once again a 0-0 scoreline did not reflect the quality of Burnley's play – they "oozed class" according to Higgs – at Huddersfield and after 15 games, the Clarets were sixth in the table and just a point out of the promotion places. Wins followed over Brentford and Swindon and, as the balance sheet showed a profit of over £37,000, Miller denied rumours of a bid to sign Jimmy Greenhoff from Manchester United.

Burnley had to mount a defensive battle for the final 30 minutes to shut out Sheffield United as another clean sheet was added to the burgeoning collection, but there was no saving them against Reading. All three goals were scored by players who would end their careers with international honours to their credit. Hamilton gave Burnley the lead, but Reading won courtesy of strikes from Kerry Dixon and Neil Webb. It was only their second defeat in 14 games and Burnley slipped to seventh in the table when they drew 0-0 in their next match, a home clash with Walsall.

Hamilton scored a great goal to beat Mark Kendall at Newport and he was on the scoresheet again as Scarborough were accounted for in the first round of the FA Cup.

Burnley were back up to sixth in the table after a 3-2 success against Gillingham, but they missed the chance to go second when they lost 1-0 at home to Barnsley. They did climb to fourth in the table following a 2-0 win over Oxford, Ian Brennan was sold to Bolton for £25,000, and then the attention switched back to the FA Cup.

The Clarets were held 1-1 at Turf Moor by Port Vale who then belied that status near the foot of the Fourth Division by chalking up a 2-0 success at Vale Park in the replay.

Leading scorer Taylor got both goals as Burnley climbed to third in the table following a 2-1 victory over promotion rivals Plymouth Argyle. But Christmas did not initially go according to plan as they found themselves 3-0 down against Carlisle – Peter Beardsley among the scorers. They hit back to score twice and almost snatch a point and continued the form of the second half of the game into their 4-1 win over Blackpool.

Alan Stevenson was sent off in that game and Billy O'Rourke deputised in the goalless game against Brentford.

The Christmas holidays also saw the death of Clarets legend and record goalscorer George Beel at the age of 80.

The next three games were postponed for different reasons – a flu epidemic, a waterlogged pitch and FA Cup involvement – and the three-week lay-off hit the Clarets as they suffered a major setback with a 3-1 defeat at the hands of Portsmouth.

Another defeat followed, 3-0 against promotion rivals Chesterfield, and with 16 games to go Burnley were six points outside the promotion race.

Miller made five changes for the game against Exeter, England youth international Michael Phelan was handed a debut and Dobson scored the only goal of the game, but the next game saw Vince Overson dismissed as the Clarets lost 2-1 on their first-ever visit to Colchester United.

There were further setbacks with defeat against Charlton and a draw against Millwall and Miller was forced to deny rumours suggesting that impressive full back Brian Laws – the find of the season – was on his way to the First Division for £300,000.

Wins over Chester and Fulham saw Burnley back to within three points of promotion, three more postponements left the situation the same, but a fixture pile-up was looming.

Phelan scored his first goal for the club at Barnsley, but Burnley lost 3-2 to a late, debatable goal and Rotherham stayed second in the table by making Burnley's job harder following a 1-0 win at Millmoor.

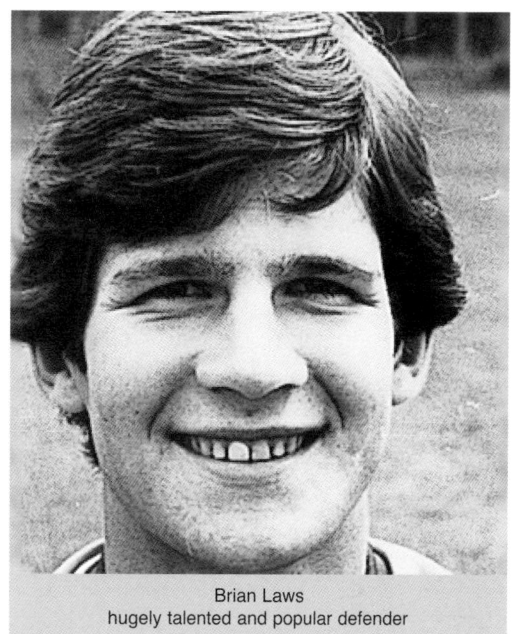

Brian Laws
hugely talented and popular defender

Goalless draws against Swindon and Gillingham saw them drop out of the promotion race and not even wins over Reading and Huddersfield could get them back into it.

Miller labelled it a "season of progress" but added "we need to strengthen the team to mount a serious challenge next season". He had the defence sorted out as a new record of 21 clean sheets was created. But the Clarets missed out by losing vital games and failing to turn solid chances into promotion-winning goals.

1980-81 - Third Division

		P	W	D	L	F	A	Pts
1	Rotherham U	46	24	13	9	62	32	61
2	Barnsley	46	21	17	8	72	45	59
3	Charlton A	46	25	9	12	63	44	59
4	Huddersfield T	46	21	14	11	71	40	56
5	Chesterfield	46	23	10	13	72	48	56
6	Portsmouth	46	22	9	15	55	47	53
7	Plymouth A	46	19	14	13	56	44	52
8	BURNLEY	46	18	14	14	60	48	50
9	Brentford	46	14	19	13	52	49	47
10	Reading	46	18	10	18	62	62	46
11	Exeter C	46	16	13	17	62	66	45
12	Newport C	46	15	13	18	64	61	43
13	Fulham	46	15	13	18	57	64	43
14	Oxford U	46	13	17	16	39	47	43
15	Gillingham	46	12	18	16	48	58	42
16	Millwall	46	14	14	18	43	60	42
17	Swindon T	46	13	15	18	51	56	41
18	Chester	46	15	11	20	38	48	41
19	Carlisle U	46	14	13	19	56	70	41
20	Walsall	46	13	15	18	59	74	41
21	Sheffield U	46	14	12	20	65	63	40
22	Colchester U	46	14	11	21	45	65	39
23	Blackpool	46	9	14	23	45	75	32
24	Hull C	46	8	16	22	40	71	32

1980-81

Manager : Brian Miller

Division Three (8th)

	Date			Opponents	Result		h/t	Goalscorers/times	Opp. goal times
1	Aug	16	h	NEWPORT C	D	1-1	1-1	Cassidy 12	22
2		20	a	Walsall	L	1-3	0-0	Taylor 84	68, 72, 82
3		23	h	CHESTERFIELD	W	1-0	1-0	Dobson 21p	
4		30	a	Charlton A	L	0-2	0-0		54, 68
5	Sep	6	h	COLCHESTER U	W	1-0	1-0	Hamilton 25	
6		13	a	Exeter C	D	0-0	0-0		
7		16	h	HULL C	W	2-0	0-0	Young 72, Taylor 88	
8		20	a	Chester	D	0-0	0-0		
9		27	h	MILLWALL	W	5-0	1-0	Hamilton 12, Dobson 55, Taylor (3) 57, 85, 88	
10		30	a	Hull C	D	0-0	0-0		
11	Oct	4	a	Fulham	W	2-0	1-0	Laws 34, Potts 85	
12		7	h	SHEFFIELD U	W	3-2	2-1	Taylor (2) 31, 85, Hamillton 38	23, 60
13		11	h	ROTHERHAM U	D	1-1	0-0	Dobson 48	68
14		18	a	Portsmouth	L	2-4	1-3	Scott (2) 37, 76	2, 17, 25, 89
15		21	a	Huddersfield T	D	0-0	0-0		
16		25	h	BRENTFORD	W	2-0	1-0	Dobson 42p, Cavener 67	
17	Nov	1	a	Swindon T	W	3-0	1-0	Carter 21og, Scott (2) 80, 90	
18		4	a	Sheffield U	D	0-0	0-0		
19		8	h	READING	L	1-2	1-1	Hamilton 11	44, 77
20		11	h	WALSALL	D	0-0	0-0		
21		15	a	Newport C	W	2-1	2-0	Hamilton 42, Taylor 44	87
22		29	h	GILLINGHAM	W	3-2	2-0	Scott 18, Taylor 40, Weatherly 56og	48, 63
23	Dec	2	h	BARNSLEY	L	0-1	0-0		60
24		6	a	Oxford U	W	2-0	1-0	Scott 13, Young 47	
25		20	h	PLYMOUTH A	W	2-1	1-0	Taylor (2) 13, 49	67
26		26	a	Carlisle U	L	2-3	0-3	Scott 66, Taylor 78	12, 17, 27
27		27	h	BLACKPOOL	W	4-1	2-0	Taylor 14, Potts 44, Laws 67, Holt 87	89
28	Jan	3	a	Brentford	D	0-0	0-0		
29		27	h	PORTSMOUTH	L	1-3	1-1	Hamilton 7	41, 71, 83
30		31	a	Chesterfield	L	0-3	0-2		32, 38, 47
31	Feb	7	h	EXETER C	W	1-0	1-0	Dobson 42p	
32		14	a	Colchester U	L	1-2	0-1	Hamilton 79	25, 65
33		17	h	CHARLTON A	L	0-1	0-1		19
34		21	a	Millwall	D	2-2	0-0	Taylor 63, Hamilton 73	57, 62
35		28	h	CHESTER	W	1-0	0-0	Young 80	
36	Mar	7	h	FULHAM	W	3-0	2-0	Hamilton 9, Dobson (2) 27, 73	
37		28	a	Barnsley	L	2-3	2-1	Phelan 16, Scott 35	13, 58, 88
38		31	a	Rotherham U	L	0-1	0-0		67
39	Apr	4	h	SWINDON T	D	0-0	0-0		
40		7	a	Gillingham	D	0-0	0-0		
41		11	a	Reading	W	3-1	1-0	Taylor (2) 30, 76, Phelan 50	58og
42		14	h	HUDDERSFIELD T	W	4-2	3-1	Brown 16og, Scott 39, Overson 45, Potts 57	5, 56
43		18	a	Blackpool	D	0-0	0-0		
44		21	h	CARLISLE U	L	0-3	0-1		23, 54, 58
45		25	a	Plymouth A	L	1-2	0-1	Cavener 89	26, 71
46	May	2	h	OXFORD U	D	1-1	1-0	Potts 20	50

FA Cup

1	Nov	22	h	SCARBOROUGH	W	1-0	0-0	Hamilton 77	
2	Dec	13	h	PORT VALE	D	1-1	0-0	Potts 61	48
rep		16	a	Port Vale	L	0-2	0-2		12, 18

Final, Tottenham H 3-2 Manchester C, at Wembley, after a 1-1 draw after extra time, also at Wembley.

League Cup

	1	Aug	9	a	Wrexham	W	3-1	1-1	Davis 36og, Cassidy 61, Thomson 70	21
agg 5-2			12	h	WREXHAM	W	2-1	1-1	Scott 12, Dobson 85p	24
Jim Thomson's last game	2		26	h	WEST HAM U	L	0-2	0-2		14, 21
agg 0-6		Sep	2	a	West Ham U	L	0-4	0-1		34, 67, 75og, 83

Final, Liverpool 2-1 West Ham U, at Villa Park, after a 1-1 draw after extra time, at Wembley.

Details of other first team games elsewhere.

Att.	Pos	Stevenson	Wood	Holt	Scott	Thomson	Rodaway	Cassidy	Dobson	Hamilton	S Taylor	Cavener	Young	Laws	V Overson	Robertson	Potts	Anderson	Wharton	O'Rourke	Phelan	Steven	Wardrobe	og	No.
6,733		1	2	3	4	5	6	7	8	9	10	11													1
4,714		1	2	3	4	5	6	7	8	9	10	11													2
5,880	13	1	2	3	4	5	6		8	9	10	11	7												3
5,445	20	1		3	4			7	6	9	10	11	8	2	5										4
4,436	18	1		3				7	6	9	10	11	8	2	5	4									5
4,534	14	1		3	4			7	6	9	10	11	8	2	5										6
4,933		1	S*	3	4			7	6	9*	10	11	8	2	5										7
3,660	12	1		3	4			7	6	9	10	11		2	5		8								8
5,620	5	1		3	4			7	6	9	10	11		2	5		8								9
5,497		1		3	4			7	6	9	10	11		2	5		8								10
4,673	4	1		3	4*			7	6	9	10	11		2	5		8	S*							11
7,308	3	1		3	4			7	6	9	10	11		2	5		8								12
9,352	3	1	S*	3*	4			7	6	9	10	11		2	5		8								13
13,449	5	1	3		4			7	6	9	10	11		2	5		8								14
15,741	6	1	3		4			7	6	9	10	11		2	5		8								15
7,324	4	1	3		4			7	6	9	10	11		2	5		8								16
6,436		1		3	4			7	6	9	10	11		2	5		8								17
14,585	5	1		3	4			7	6	9	10	11		2	5		8								18
6,925	7	1		3	4			7	6	9	10	11		2	5		8								19
5,573	7	1		3				7	6	9	10	11	4	2	5		8								20
5,370	6	1		3	4			7	6	9	10	11		2	5		8								21
5,797	6	1			4				6	9	10	11	7	2	5		8		3						22
9,109	6	1			4				6	9	10	11	7	2	5		8		3						23
3,513	4	1			4				6	9	10	11	7	2	5		8		3						24
5,695	3	1		3	4			7	6	9	10	11		2	5		8								25
7,136	5	1		3	4			7	6	9	10	11		2	5		8								26
10,782	4	1		3	4*			7	6	9	10	11	S*	2	5		8								27
6,379	4			3				7	6	9	10	11	4	2	5		8			1					28
6,689	6		4	3			5		6	9	10	11	7	2			8			1					29
7,637	7	1	4	3			5		6	9	10*		7	2			8	11			S*				30
5,496	6	1	4	3					6	9		11	7	2		10	8				5				31
3,082	7	1		3					6	9	S*	11	7	8	5	10*			2		4				32
5,786	7	1		3					6	9	10	11	7	4		8			2		5				33
4,691	7	1		3					6	9	10	11	7	2	4	8					5				34
4,997	7	1		3					6	9	10	11	7	2	4	8					5				35
5,472	7	1		3	10				6	9		11*	7	2	4	8	S*				5				36
13,689	8	1		3	10				6	9		S*	7		5	8	11		2		4*				37
9,762	8	1		3					6	9	10		7	2	5	8	11				4				38
4,736	8	1		3					6	9	10	S*	7	2	5	8	11*				4				39
4,412		1		3					6	9	10	4	7	2	5	8	11								40
3,977	7	1	S*	3*					6	9	10		7	2	5	8	11				4				41
11,075		1	2		10*				6	9			7	3	5	8	11				4	S*			42
7,198	7	1	2		10				6	9			7	3	5	8	11				4				43
5,126	8	1	2					10	6	9			7*	3	5	8	11				4		S*		44
4,331	8	1	2					10	6	9		S*	7	3	5	8	11				4*				45
3,947		1	3*					4	6	9		S*	7	2	5	8	11				10				46
Appearances		44	14	35	29	3	5	27	46	46	37	36	28	42	39	17	34	1	6	2	15				
Apps as sub			3								1	4	1				1	1			1	1	1		
Goals (60)				1	9			1	7	9	16	2	3	2	1		4				2			3	ogs

Att.	Pos	Stevenson	Wood	Holt	Scott	Thomson	Rodaway	Cassidy	Dobson	Hamilton	S Taylor	Cavener	Young	Laws	V Overson	Robertson	Potts	Anderson	Wharton	O'Rourke	Phelan	Steven	Wardrobe	og	No.
7,789		1		3	4				6	9	10	11	7	2	5		8*		S*						1
7,497		1		3	4				6	9		11	7	2	5		8						10		2
7,684		1		3	4			7	6	9	10*	11	S*	2	5		8								rep
Appearances		3		3	3			1	3	3	2	3	2	3	3		3						1		
Apps as sub													1						1						
Goals (2)										1							1								

Att.	Pos	Stevenson	Wood	Holt	Scott	Thomson	Rodaway	Cassidy	Dobson	Hamilton	S Taylor	Cavener	Young	Laws	V Overson	Robertson	Potts	Anderson	Wharton	O'Rourke	Phelan	Steven	Wardrobe	og	No.
5,126		1	2	3	4	5	6	7	8	9	10	11													1
4,448		1		3	4	5	6		8	9	10	11	7	2											2nd leg
6,673		1	2		4	5	6	7*	8	9	10	11	S*	3											2
15,216		1	S*	3	4*			7	6	9	10	11	8	2	5										2nd leg
Appearances		4	2	3	4	3	3	3	4	4	4	4	2	3	1										
Apps as sub			1										1												
Goals (5)					1	1		1	1															1	og

1981-82

OBITUARY
JOHN (JACK) BILLINGHAM
DIED 7 OCTOBER 1981, AGED 66.

Jack Billingham was Burnley's first-choice centre-forward for much of the first post-war season which ended with the Clarets promoted to the First Division and at Wembley for the first time. He arrived at Turf Moor from Bristol City in May 1938. His Burnley debut came at Christmas that year at Tottenham, and after two games on the right wing he moved to centre-forward, where he scored in each of his first four games. He ended that season with seven goals from fourteen games. He served in the RAF during the war, but was back at Turf Moor when the League resumed in August 1946. He played in most of the games over the next two years as Burnley first reached and then prospered in the top flight, and was second top scorer behind Harry Potts in both seasons. Billingham was transferred to Carlisle in September 1949, and remained a League player until he was 40, ending in the Third Division North with Southport.

A key player during one of the finest seasons in the Clarets' history, Jack Billingham was one of many whose careers could have been so much greater had it not been for World War II.

RIP

On the field, the 1981-82 season brought another title to Turf Moor and seemed to herald a new beginning.

Off the field it truly did bring the end of an era with the resignation, and subsequent death, of chairman Bob Lord after more than a quarter of a century at the helm.

Having put the majority of his shares up for sale in September, a consortium including directors Dr David Iven and John Jackson bought almost 3,000 of them to take control of the club.

Lord retained 100 shares and managed to stay on as chairman for three weeks before Jackson took over saying: "I don't suppose there is a football chairman in this country who didn't always want, from his earliest days as a young supporter, to become chairman. I am no different to the others."

Jackson immediately started to make changes. He helped set up an official supporters' club and also announced a review of match admission prices.

In December Bob Lord died and the Burnley Express, which had campaigned for two seasons for his resignation, said: "The death of Bob Lord on Tuesday this week robbed the town of its best-known character, a man who was larger than life."

He had not always been football's favourite son, but he was widely mourned by the game and a roll-call of the sport's biggest names turned out for his funeral.

Lord's departure as chairman came at a time when a Third Division championship looked anything other than on the cards. Relegation was a more likely possibility.

Manager Brian Miller attempted to strengthen the squad and had discussions with West Ham's former England striker Stuart Pearson. He admitted that bringing in free transfers was proving difficult as likely targets wanted high wages, but offered a trial to Newport's John Aldridge despite the club wanting £100,000 for him.

Stalwart defenders Jim Thompson (Morecambe) and Billy Rodaway (Peterborough) were given free transfers and Peter Higgs of the Burnley Express prepared to stick to his promise of walking to the first away game of the season, never dreaming it would be a 270-mile trek to Gillingham.

Miller had to prepare for new challenge as league rules switched to three points for a win. Before the big kick-off he said: "I am sure it will affect our approach to matches. It means that when a match is there to be won we know it is more important than ever that we win it. We cannot say that a point will do when we are playing an inferior team." The full impact of the new rule was highlighted with a five-match unbeaten run later in the season. Burnley won one and drew four for seven points out of 15. The previous season they would have claimed six out of 10. But at the end of the season none of the promotion places was actually affected by the new set-up.

The new season started at the Priestfield Stadium and after a 3-1 defeat Miller issued an "improve or else" warning to his team. Tranmere scored a 4-2 win in the first leg of the League Cup tie, a Martin Dobson penalty brought victory against Plymouth but, despite a remarkable debut from Trevor Steven, defeat was the order of the day at Eastville.

Any hope of salvaging their League Cup campaign died when they went 2-0 down in the first five minutes of the second leg and the game eventually ended 3-3 with Burnley beaten 7-5 on aggregate.

The Clarets' plight at the bottom of the table worsened with a 4-3 defeat at Millwall. Trailing 2-1, they led 3-2 but could not hold on for a precious victory and then one lapse against Carlisle led to another defeat and Burnley were in the bottom three despite the fact that everyone could see they were better than that.

Draws at home to Exeter and away at Preston left them in trouble, but the signs were good and the unbeaten run continued with a 2-2 draw against Fulham.

Another draw, 0-0 with Brentford, saw them continue to avoid defeat, but the Clarets really needed to score wins and a Tommy Cassidy goal saw them beat Chester – another of the struggling sides.

Striker Paul McGee signed on a two-month loan from Deepdale, Vince Overson equalised to salvage a point against Wimbledon and more changes to the line-up saw 20-year-old Brian Laws the oldest of four defenders on duty as Burnley drew 1-1 with Reading. A McGee double brought replay success in the FA Cup against Runcorn and he scored another brace to seal victory over Bristol City.

That took the unbeaten run to 11 games in league and cup, the best run for nine seasons.

Hamilton scored a late winner against high-riding Oxford United as Miller aimed to make it into the top half of the table by the end of the year and there was a pre-Christmas surprise as David Holt scored a late winner against Watford to see Burnley into the quarter-finals of the Group Cup.

A big freeze then saw the Clarets with no action for almost four weeks and the fixture congestion worsened when the Gigg Lane FA Cup clash ended 1-1 before Steven scored a great winner to see them through to the third round.

Despite going 15 games without defeat, Burnley started 1982 in 19th place with 22 points from 18 games.

But they continued to gather points as Plymouth were held 1-1 and Newport County beaten 2-1.

The FA Cup odyssey continued with a 6-1 win over Altrincham – Hamilton bagging a hat-trick – but ended with a 1-0 defeat against Shrewsbury.

With 26 games to go in the league, Burnley were still in the wrong half of the table but only nine points off the promotion places.

But McGee was back at Deepdale with new Deepdale boss Gordon Lee refusing to honour a Tommy Docherty agreement that he would sign for £25,000 when the loan was over.

Steve Taylor scored a double at Leeds Road to secure a victory which Huddersfield manager Mick Buxton said "should set Burnley up for the rest of the season" and a 1-0 win over Gillingham moved them seven places up the table to ninth.

Burnley finally finished the first half of the season in early February with a 4-0 win over Bristol Rovers and they were up to eighth in the table.

The unbeaten run in the league was extended to 16 matches when they won 1-0 at Doncaster and a new post-War unbeaten run in the league was created with a 2-1 win over Swindon – a sixth straight victory.

The Group Cup campaign ended with a 5-0 defeat at the hands of Wimbledon, but after a 1-1 draw with Millwall, Miller finally started talking about promotion. "It would be a tragedy if this team did not get promoted," he added after a 3-0 win against Portsmouth and they climbed to fourth in the table with a draw against Walsall.

The unbeaten run finally ended at Exeter, Brian Flynn signed on loan from Leeds and Burnley earned a good point against leaders Fulham. A win against Chester saw Burnley two points off the promotion places with 15 games to go and McGee returned on the eve of the transfer deadline to bolster the attack following an injury to Taylor.

Draws followed against Wimbledon and new leaders Lincoln and with 12 games to go, Burnley were right in the hunt and had the luxury of 12 home games to look forward to.

Hamilton scored after three minutes to set up a 3-0 win over second-placed Reading and he scored the only goal of the game to beat Lincoln in front of nearly 11,000 fans.

Chesterfield were the Easter Monday victims and it really was pick any three from five in the run in to the end of the season.

A goalless draw at Oxford was followed by a horrific 5-3 defeat at Turf Moor at the hands of Southend, but a win and a draw saw the Clarets back in the hunt. With five games to go, however, they were nine points behind leaders Carlisle.

But they came good when it mattered and McGee scored the winner against Carlisle before Walsall were beaten 2-1.

With three games to go, seven points would assure them of promotion, but could they claim the title?

A Hamilton double, the second coming at the end of a trademark 60-yard run, saw off Preston and with results elsewhere going their way, Burnley knew they would be promoted if they could win at Southend. McGee scored another double and Burnley were back in the Second Division courtesy of a 4-1 success.

The last game, at home to Chesterfield, was drawn 1-1 and the following night, Carlisle had to beat Chester by seven goals to steal the title from the Clarets.

They managed just a single goal victory and Burnley were Champions, writing another page of club history, now having won every Division in which they had played.

Billy Hamilton
top scorer in the Third Division Championship campaign

1981-82 - Third Division

		P	W	D	L	F	A	Pts
1	BURNLEY	46	21	17	8	66	45	80
2	Carlisle U	46	23	11	12	65	50	80
3	Fulham	46	21	15	10	77	51	78
4	Lincoln C	46	21	14	11	66	40	77
5	Oxford U	46	19	14	13	63	49	71
6	Gillingham	46	20	11	15	64	56	71
7	Southend U	46	18	15	13	63	51	69
8	Brentford	46	19	11	16	56	47	68
9	Millwall	46	18	13	15	62	62	67
10	Plymouth A	46	18	11	17	64	56	65
11	Chesterfield	46	18	10	18	57	58	64
12	Reading	46	17	11	18	67	75	62
13	Portsmouth	46	14	19	13	56	51	61
14	Preston NE	46	16	13	17	50	56	61
15	Bristol R	46	18	9	19	58	65	61
16	Newport C	46	14	16	16	54	54	58
17	Huddersfield T	46	15	12	19	64	59	57
18	Exeter C	46	16	9	21	71	84	57
19	Doncaster R	46	13	17	16	55	68	56
20	Walsall	46	13	14	19	51	55	53
21	Wimbledon	46	14	11	21	61	75	53
22	Swindon T	46	13	13	20	55	71	52
23	Bristol C	46	11	13	22	40	65	46
24	Chester	46	7	11	28	36	78	32

1981-82

Manager : Brian Miller

Division Three (1st)
Champions

Note	No.	Date		h/a	Opponents	Result		h/t	Goalscorers/times	Opp. goal times
	1	Aug	29	a	Gillingham	L	1-3	0-1	Taylor 61	15, 51, 52
	2	Sep	5	h	PLYMOUTH A	W	1-0	0-0	Dobson 78p	
	3		12	a	Bristol R	L	1-2	0-1	Kite 69og	23, 78
	4		19	h	HUDDERSFIELD T	D	0-0	0-0		
	5		22	h	DONCASTER R	L	0-1	0-0		78
	6		26	a	Millwall	L	3-4	3-2	Laws 23, Potts 42, Overson 44	9, 35, 55, 68
	7		29	a	Carlisle U	L	0-1	0-0		66
	8	Oct	3	h	SWINDON T	L	0-2	0-2		16, 37
	9		10	a	Portsmouth	W	2-1	1-0	Young 12, Wharton 61	47p
	10		17	h	EXETER C	D	3-3	1-2	Taylor 10, Overson 49, Laws 62p	25, 34, 87
	11		20	a	Preston N E	D	1-1	0-0	Wharton 61	57
	12		24	h	FULHAM	D	2-2	2-0	Hamilton 7, Taylor 18	53, 83
	13		31	a	Brentford	D	0-0	0-0		
	14	Nov	3	h	CHESTER	W	1-0	0-0	Cassidy 74	
	15		7	h	WIMBLEDON	D	2-2	1-0	Hamilton 27, Overson 82	55, 81
	16		14	a	Reading	D	1-1	0-1	Steven 62	43
	17		28	a	Bristol C	W	3-2	1-1	Young 3, McGee (2) 77, 89	14, 52
	18	Dec	5	h	OXFORD U	W	2-1	0-0	Cassidy 58, Hamilton 84	49
	19	Jan	9	h	PLYMOUTH A	D	1-1	0-0	Young 47	74
	20		16	h	NEWPORT C	W	2-1	0-1	Taylor 52, Overson 57	8
	21		30	a	Huddersfield T	W	2-1	0-0	Taylor (2) 46, 63	90
	22	Feb	2	h	GILLINGHAM	W	1-0	0-0	Wharton 60	
	23		6	h	BRISTOL R	W	4-0	2-0	Hamilton 5, Mabbutt 32og, Scott 56, Taylor 84	
	24		9	a	Doncaster R	W	1-0	0-0	Wharton 71	
	25		13	a	Swindon T	W	2-1	2-1	Taylor 15, Cassidy 43	40
	26		20	h	MILLWALL	D	1-1	1-0	Hamilton 40	71
	27		27	h	PORTSMOUTH	W	3-0	1-0	Taylor 10, Phelan 57, Scott 67	
	28	Mar	2	a	Walsall	D	1-1	0-0	Hamilton 70	65
	29		6	a	Exeter C	L	1-2	0-0	Allen 88	83, 87
	30		13	a	Fulham	D	1-1	1-1	Young 43	18
	31		17	a	Chester	W	1-0	1-0	Laws 28p	
	32		20	h	BRENTFORD	D	0-0	0-0		
	33		27	a	Wimbledon	D	0-0	0-0		
	34		31	a	Lincoln C	D	1-1	0-0	Steven 88	69
Burnley's 500th league goal (3m)	35	Apr	3	h	READING	W	3-0	2-0	Hamilton (2) 3, 13, Young 89	
	36		10	h	LINCOLN C	W	1-0	0-0	Hamilton 70	
	37		12	a	Chesterfield	W	2-1	2-1	Laws 27, Dobson 39	43
	38		17	a	Oxford U	D	0-0	0-0		
	39		20	h	SOUTHEND U	L	3-5	2-2	McGee 30, Steven 41, Otulakowski 71og	8, 14, 46, 52p, 61
	40		24	h	BRISTOL C	W	2-0	0-0	Laws 59, Dobson 80	
	41	May	1	a	Newport C	D	0-0	0-0		
	42		4	h	CARLISLE U	W	1-0	0-0	McGee 71	
Eric Potts' last game	43		8	h	WALSALL	W	2-1	1-0	McGee 1, Young 50	46
	44		11	h	PRESTON N E	W	2-0	0-0	Hamilton (2) 52, 84	
	45		14	a	Southend U	W	4-1	2-1	Wharton 32, McGee (2) 40, 83, Laws 88	45
	46		18	h	CHESTERFIELD	D	1-1	0-1	Young 48	43

FA Cup

Note	Rd	Date		h/a	Opponents	Result		h/t	Goalscorers/times	Opp. goal times
	1	Nov	21	h	RUNCORN	D	0-0	0-0		
	rep		24	a	Runcorn	W	2-1	1-1	McGee (2) 12, 78	32
	2	Jan	2	a	Bury	D	1-1	0-0	Taylor 46	89
after extra time, 1-1 at 90m	rep		4	h	BURY	W	2-1	1-0	Hamilton 43, Steven 101	54
	3		18	h	ALTRINCHAM	W	6-1	1-0	Taylor (2) 23, 67, Steven 47, Hamilton (3) 60, 70, 78	74
	4		23	a	Shrewsbury T	L	0-1	0-0		75

Final, Tottenham H 1-0 Queens Park R, at Wembley, after a 1-1 draw after extra time, also at Wembley.

League Cup

Note	Rd	Date		h/a	Opponents	Result		h/t	Goalscorers/times	Opp. goal times
	1	Sep	1	a	Tranmere R	L	2-4	0-1	Potts 58, Hamilton 72	14, 73, 76, 81
agg 5-7			15	h	TRANMERE R	D	3-3	2-3	Holt (2) 19, 22, Cassidy 89	4, 5, 20

Final, Liverpool 3-1 Tottenham H after extra time, at Wembley.

Details of other first team games elsewhere.

Att.	Pos	Stevenson	Laws	Holt	Scott	Phelan	Dobson	Cavener	S Taylor	Hamilton	Cassidy	Potts	Young	V Overson	Steven	Robertson	P Dixon	Wharton	Anderson	McGee	Allen	Flynn	
4,663		1	2	3	4*	5	6	7	8	9	10	11	S*										1
3,476		1	2	3			6	7	8	9	10	11	4	5									2
5,083	16	1	2	3	4		6	7*	8	9		11		5	10	S*							3
6,524	15	1	2	3	4		6	7		9	10			5	8	11							4
3,799	21	1	2	3	4		6		S*	9	10*	7		5	8	11							5
4,796	22	1	2	3	4		6		10	9*		7		5	8	11	S*						6
3,983	22	1	2		4	9	6		10			7		5	8	11		3					7
3,377	22	1	2		4	9	6		10			7	S*	5	8	11*		3					8
9,891	21	1	2		4*	7	6		10	9		S*	11	5	8			3					9
3,982	21	1	2		4	7	6		10	9			11	5	8			3					10
7,521	21	1	2		9	3	4		11	10			7	5	6			8					11
4,124	21	1	2		4	7	6		10	9			11	5	8			3					12
6,929	21	1	2		4*	7	6		10	9			11	5	8			3	S*				13
3,484	20	1	2			7	6		10	9	4	S*	11*	5	8			3					14
4,242	20	1	2			6				9	4	7	11	5	8			3		10			15
4,337	20	1	2			6				9	4	7	11	5	8			3		10			16
5,255	20	1	2			6	7			9	4	S*	11	5	8*			3		10			17
4,380	18	1	2			6	7			9	4		11	5	8			3		10			18
5,065	19	1	2				6		10	9	8		11	5	7		4	3					19
4,730	18	1	2				6		10	9	7		11	5	8		4	3					20
10,269	15	1	2	6	S*		7		10	9	4		11	5	8*			3					21
5,848		1	2	6	8		7		10	9	4		11	5				3					22
5,784	8	1	2	6	8		7		10	9	4		11	5				3					23
5,638	7	1	2	6	8	S*	7		10	9	4		11	5*				3					24
5,296	5	1	2	6	8	5*	7	S*	10	9	4	11						3					25
7,081	5	1	2	6	8	5	7		10	9	4		11					3					26
7,013	4	1	2	6	8	5	7		10*	9	4	S*	11					3					27
4,196	4	1	2	6	8	5	7			9	4	10	11					3*			S*		28
3,136	7	1	2	6	8*	5	7			9	4	10	11	3							S*		29
7,214		1	2	3	4	6	7			9			11	5	8							10	30
3,509	6	1	2	3	4	6	7			9		S*	11	5	8							10*	31
7,906	6	1	2	3	4	6	7			9			11	5	8					10			32
2,641	6	1	2		4	6*	7			9		S*	11	5	8				3	10			33
6,188	6	1	2				7			9		4	11	5	8		6	3		10			34
6,661	5	1	2	6			7	4		9			11	5*	8			3	S*	10			35
10,911		1	2	6	4		7	S*		9			11		8		5	3*		10			36
7,732	5	1	2	6			7	4		9			11		8		5		3	10			37
10,407	5	1	2	6	4		7			9			11		8		5	3		10			38
8,171	5	1	2	6	4		7	S*		9			11		8		5	3*		10			39
7,063	5	1	2	6			7			9	4		11	5	8			3		10			40
4,094	6	1		6	2		7			9	4	11		5	8			3		10			41
9,760	5	1	2	6			7			9	4		11	5	8			3		10			42
8,537	4	1		6	2*		7			9	4	S*	11	5	8			3		10			43
13,911	2	1	2	6			7			9	4		11	5	8			3		10			44
5,123		1	2	6			7			9	4		11	5	8			3		10			45
18,711	1	1	2	6			7			9	4		11		8		5	3		10			46
Appearances		46	44	30	29	22	44	6	21	44	27	14	37	36	36	5	8	34	2	19		2	
Apps as sub					1	1		3	1			7	2			1	1		2		2		
Goals (66)			6		2	1	3		9	11	3	1	7	4	3			5		7	1		3 ogs

Att.	Pos	Stevenson	Laws	Holt	Scott	Phelan	Dobson	Cavener	S Taylor	Hamilton	Cassidy	Potts	Young	V Overson	Steven	Robertson	P Dixon	Wharton	Anderson	McGee	Allen	Flynn	
6,112		1	2			6				9	4	7	11	5	8			3		10			1
5,500		1	2			6	7			9	4		11	5	8			3		10			rep
9,200		1	2				7		10	9	4		11	5	8		6	3					2
9,108		1	2				7		10	9	4		11	5	8		6	3					rep
10,174		1	2				7		10	9	4		11	5	8		6	3					3
7,679		1	2				7		10	9	4	S*	11	5	8		6*	3					4
Appearances		6	6			2	5		4	6	6	1	6	6	6		4	6		2			
Apps as sub												1											
Goals (11)									3	4					2					2			

Att.	Pos	Stevenson	Laws	Holt	Scott	Phelan	Dobson	Cavener	S Taylor	Hamilton	Cassidy	Potts	Young	V Overson	Steven	Robertson	P Dixon	Wharton	Anderson	McGee	Allen	Flynn	
2,034		1	2	3		5	6	7	8	9	10	11	4										2
2,363		1	2	3*	4		6	S*		9	10	7		5	8	11							2nd leg
Appearances		2	2	2	1	1	2	1	1	2	2	2	1	1	1	1							
Apps as sub								1															
Goals (5)				2						1	1	1											

1982-83

Wildly contrasting League and Cup campaigns defined Burnley's first season back in Division Two.

While the Clarets struggled to make an impact at a higher level, they defeated almost all before them to come within a whisker of a Wembley cup final.

The summer of 1982 was one of celebration, and for Burnley striker Billy Hamilton – crowned Player of the Year - came international, as well as double domestic glory.

The Northern Ireland striker became the first Burnley player ever to score in the World Cup finals when he found the net twice against Austria in Madrid.

Hamilton, who also played a starring role in Ireland's famous 1-0 victory over hosts Spain, later said: "It was a match that will stay with me for the rest of my life."

Back in Burnley, as the new season approached, Hamilton agreed a new two-year deal with the Clarets, signing up along with out of contract quintet Derek Scott, Steve Taylor, David Holt, Paul Dixon and Billy O'Rourke.

Young stars Vince Overson, Brian Laws, Trevor Steven, Michael Phelan and Andy Wharton also signed two-year deals to protect some of the club's biggest assets.

All this backed up Clarets' manager Brian Miller's claim that he was placing his faith in the players who earned the club promotion.

Ultimately, it was to be faith misplaced.

There was little to bemoan as Burnley began the season in style, following up an opening day stalemate with Bolton with successive 4-1 wins against Middlesbrough and Carlisle.

Returning hero Hamilton hit the ground running, notching a hat-trick against the Cumbrians to add to his goal at 'Boro four days earlier.

Sandwiched between was another goal-fest, this time a 5-3 Milk Cup first round, first leg victory at Bury.

Thirteen goals in three games should have been a catalyst.

Yet four straight league defeats brought a startling reality check and stopped the Clarets in their tracks.

A 4-3 aggregate Milk Cup victory over Middlesbrough helped to lighten the mood somewhat, along with a Martin Dobson-inspired win over Crystal Palace to get a welcome three points on the board.

However, the clouds continued to darken menacingly over Turf Moor, with five straight league defeats hinting at a bleak winter ahead.

Cup form was seemingly keeping spirits high and as November dawned the Clarets celebrated their first ever trip to an all-seater stadium by beating First Division Coventry City 2-1 in the Milk Cup third round.

League form also showed flickering signs of improvement. The arrival of Scottish international Willie Donachie from American outfit Portland Timbers and the protracted return of Welsh midfielder Brian Flynn for £60,000, five years after he quit Turf Moor for Leeds United, sparked an upturn in fortunes.

Two Steve Taylor goals earned a crucial win against Cambridge and back-to-back draws at Sheffield Wednesday and at home to Derby hinted at a revival.

Sadly, it was another false dawn and despite Birmingham becoming the latest First Division side to be swept aside by Burnley in the Milk Cup, another five league defeats in a row - including one to bitter rivals Blackburn Rovers at Christmas - left Burnley ending the year next to bottom in Division Two.

Under-pressure manager Miller missed the first of those damaging defeats, at Chelsea, to take in a spying mission across London on Milk Cup quarter final opponents Tottenham Hotspur.

But he could never have anticipated what happened next.

A gutless 0-3 league defeat at Bolton four days before the trip to White Hart Lane proved to be the last straw and the manager was relieved of his duties, to be replaced by Frank Casper on the very eve of the quarter final tie.

Just 24 hours later, the Burnley Express proudly trumpeted 'The Result of the Century' as Casper's Clarets thumped Spurs 4-1 on their own patch.

Starting as 100/1 outsiders, those odds multiplied after Keith Burkinshaw's side took the lead at the start of the second half.

Cue outrageous scenes as Burnley proceeded to take apart a star-studded Spurs team unbeaten on their own turf for three seasons.

Graham Roberts' fortuitous 65th minute own-goal set the ball rolling and Billy Hamilton sent the travelling fans into dreamland soon after with a close-range tap-in.

The hapless Roberts' doubled his own own-goal tally five minutes from time, deflecting in Steve Taylor's cross and Hamilton sealed an incredible, against-all-odds victory with the goal of the game from 20 yards in the dying minutes.

A postscript to an amazing night was that physiotherapist Jimmy Holland missed the team's triumph after infamously crashing into the roof of the visiting dug out during the first half.

Trevor Steven
another Turf Moor gem who went on to sparkle elswhere

A two-legged semi final tie with Liverpool was to be Burnley's reward for their heroics, and that lip-smacking prospect inspired the team as they earned four wins and a draw from their next five league outings, including a 7-1 thumping of nine-man Charlton that saw Hamilton and Taylor both net hat-tricks – the first time that had happened in more than a quarter of a century.

Progress to the fifth round 25 years on was also quietly secured at Swindon Town's expense, leading to more cup fever sweeping the town!

However it was the eagerly-awaited 'David v Goliath' Milk Cup semi-final with the Liverpudlians, sitting pretty 12 points clear at the top of the First Division, which was always likely to grab the hearts and minds.

Ahead of the first leg at Anfield, where Burnley were roared

on by 7,000 supporters, Casper was officially named as permanent manager – the sixth in a row to be promoted from within at Turf Moor.
But the current cup holders, fresh from eight successive victories, mounted an unassailable 3-0 lead to fatally crush the Clarets' hopes.
Reds' manager Bob Paisley later claimed Burnley had given the hosts as much trouble as any First Division side, while in the Burnley Express Peter Higgs proudly wrote: "On Tuesday evening at Anfield I was privileged to watch a talented team play superb, quality football. Liverpool weren't bad either!"
That result made the second leg, a week later, a formality. But on a night many still talk about, Burnley gained revenge over the Reds with a performance to make the town proud.
Derek Scott's volleyed second half goal was the all-important statistic, but with Trevor Steven clipping a post and Mark Lawrenson forced into a desperate goal line clearance, the 0-3 first leg deficit was tantalisingly close to being bridged.

OBITUARY
ARTHUR WOODRUFF
DIED 5 JANUARY 1983, AGED 69.

Had it not been for the Second World War, Arthur Woodruff would almost certainly be near the top of Burnley's appearances records. As it was, he stayed around long enough to become, for many years, the oldest Claret player of the post-war era.
An archetypal Yorkshireman and no-nonsense defender, he joined the club in July 1936. He quickly made his mark at Turf Moor, and was Burnley's first choice centre-half for most of the period up to the outbreak of hostilities. It was after the war, though, that his reputation was really made. Moved to right-back, he was an integral part of the "Iron Curtain" defence that took the Clarets into the top flight in 1947 and established them there over the next few seasons. He appeared twice for the Football League in 1947, but never quite made it to the full England side. He remained the more or less automatic choice in the number two shirt until early in the 1951-52 season, making his final appearance just after his 39th birthday near the end of that campaign. He moved to Workington that summer, and later returned to live and run a newsagent's shop in Burnley.
RIP

In defeat, the Clarets had at least gained the taste for glory. Although along with the distraction of an assault on a second cup, there remained the ongoing battle to avoid an embarrassing relegation.
Casper lifted his players immediately for the FA Cup fifth round goalless draw at Crystal Palace, which led to a replay 10 days later and a controversially re-taken Taylor penalty, which secured a quarter final meeting with Second Division rivals Sheffield Wednesday.
But it was another Taylor penalty that arguably proved to be the decisive factor in determining Burnley's FA Cup fate.
The striker had taken over spot kick duties from Laws, but his fifth minute attempt in front of a packed Turf Moor was saved by Wednesday stopper Bob Bolder and the Clarets needed a rare headed goal from midfielder Tommy Cassidy to rescue a replay following a 1-1 draw.
How close the Clarets had come to a second cup semi-final, this time against fellow outsiders Brighton!
Yet how far it proved as the re-match proved to be a one-sided affair; the Owls earning a showdown with the Seagulls in a 0-5 Hillsborough thumping.
With cup fever cured for another year, the league was now all that mattered. Following the heartbreak of that FA Cup exit, five successive reversals cast Burnley adrift at the foot of the table and plunged them into a fifth relegation fight in eight seasons.
The low point of that run was unquestionably an Easter Monday riot at Ewood Park, sparking some of the most disgraceful scenes ever involving Burnley supporters, which led to a 15-minute match delay and 33 arrests.
When the dust had settled Casper's rallying call to the players ahead of the final seven games was for five wins to secure a great escape.
Relegation rivals Chelsea were dispatched 3-0 in the first, renewing hope.
Defeat at Derby was followed by a Micky Phelan-inspired victory at Shrewsbury to leave the Clarets four points from safety with as many games remaining.
It was nail-biting stuff and four points from successive home games, against Grimsby and QPR respectively, further notched up the tension.
The safety margin with two games remaining was now down to two points and a creditable draw at high-flying Leicester led the Burnley Express to preview the final showdown away to Crystal Palace as a 'Date with Destiny'
Only victory for Burnley in their last game would save them: in turn condemning Palace – once described as "The Team of the Eighties" to relegation.
"Agatha Christie at her most imaginative could not have produced a more spell binding drama," wrote an excitable Higgs.
Sadly, the script did not live up to the hype and Burnley went down with a whimper, losing 1-0 on a night when a whole season went up in smoke.
All that remained were the memories of a roller-coaster ride.
The exhilarating highs of those fabulous cup runs; the gut-wrenching lows of relegation back to Division Three.
Did the cup runs distract the Clarets?
Who knows, but the battle was now on to rebuild and bounce back.

1982-83 - Second Division

		P	W	D	L	F	A	Pts
1	Queens Park R	42	26	7	9	77	36	85
2	Wolverhampton W	42	20	15	7	68	44	75
3	Leicester C	42	20	10	12	72	44	70
4	Fulham	42	20	9	13	64	47	69
5	Newcastle U	42	18	13	11	75	53	67
6	Sheffield W	42	16	15	11	60	47	63
7	Oldham A	42	14	9	9	64	47	61
8	Leeds U	42	13	21	8	51	46	60
9	Shrewsbury T	42	15	14	13	48	48	59
10	Barnsley	42	14	15	13	57	55	57
11	Blackburn R	42	15	12	15	58	58	57
12	Cambridge U	42	13	12	17	42	60	51
13	Derby	42	10	19	13	49	58	49
14	Carlisle U	42	12	12	18	68	70	48
15	Crystal P	42	12	12	18	43	52	48
16	Middlesbrough	42	11	15	16	46	67	48
17	Charlton A	42	13	9	20	63	86	48
18	Chelsea	42	11	14	17	51	61	47
19	Grimsby T	42	12	11	19	45	70	47
20	Rotherham U	42	10	15	17	45	68	45
21	BURNLEY	42	12	8	22	56	66	44
22	Bolton W	42	11	11	20	42	61	44

1982-83

Manager : Brian Miller until January 1983, then Frank Casper

Division Two (21st)
Relegated

Note	No	Date			Opponents	Result		h/t	Goalscorers/times	Opp. goal times
	1	Aug	28	h	BOLTON W	D	0-0	0-0		
	2	Sep	4	a	Middlesbrough	W	4-1	3-0	Dobson 12, Laws 30, Young 32, Hamilton 59	77
	3		7	h	CARLISLE U	W	4-1	3-0	Hamilton (3) 13, 18, 68p, McGee 33	88
	4		11	h	ROTHERHAM U	L	1-2	0-1	Steven 47	1, 65
	5		18	a	Barnsley	L	0-3	0-2		26, 37, 79
	6		25	h	SHREWSBURY T	L	1-2	1-1	Wharton 36	26, 85
	7	Oct	2	a	Queens Park R	L	2-3	2-0	Steven (2) 17, 44	48, 56, 65
	8		9	h	CRYSTAL P	W	2-1	0-1	Taylor 60, Hamilton 87	27
	9		16	a	Charlton A	L	1-2	1-1	Phelan 19	5, 56
	10		20	a	Leeds U	L	1-3	1-2	Muir 30	5, 14, 71
	11		23	a	Fulham	L	1-3	1-1	Laws 40p	5, 74, 85
	12		30	h	OLDHAM A	L	1-2	1-0	Hamilton 23	50, 82
	13	Nov	6	a	Newcastle U	L	0-3	0-1		19, 64, 85
	14		13	h	CAMBRIDGE U	W	2-1	1-0	Taylor (2) 15, 74	51
	15		20	a	Sheffield W	D	1-1	1-1	Steven 28	33
	16		27	h	DERBY C	D	1-1	1-0	McGee 37	81
	17	Dec	4	a	Chelsea	L	1-2	1-2	Laws 45p	10, 26
	18		11	h	LEICESTER C	L	2-4	1-1	Steven 11, Taylor 50	40, 55, 70, 74
	19		18	a	Grimsby T	L	2-3	2-2	Laws 35p, Moore 45og	7, 17, 90
	20		27	h	BLACKBURN R	L	0-1	0-1		33
	21		28	a	Wolverhampton W	L	0-2	0-0		70, 89
	22	Jan	1	h	SHEFFIELD W	W	4-1	2-0	Taylor (3) 19, 20, 89, Hamilton 59	70
	23		3	h	MIDDLESBROUGH	D	1-1	1-0	Scott 45	64
Holt's last game	24		15	a	Bolton W	L	0-3	0-2		15, 31, 79
	25		22	h	BARNSLEY	W	3-1	2-0	Hamilton 1, Steven 34, Taylor 88p	73
	26	Feb	5	a	Rotherham U	D	1-1	1-0	Taylor 44	50
Charlton goal 41m	27		26	h	CHARLTON A	W	7-1	2-1	Taylor (3) 25, 80, 84, Hamilton (3) 27, 77, 89, Steven 87	
	28	Mar	5	h	FULHAM	W	1-0	1-0	Flynn 22	
	29		19	h	NEWCASTLE U	W	1-0	0-0	Donovan 71	
	30		26	a	Cambridge U	L	0-2	0-0		46, 54
	31	Apr	2	h	WOLVERHAMPTON W	L	0-1	0-1		7
	32		4	a	Blackburn R	L	1-2	0-0	Scott 85	59, 78
	33		9	h	LEEDS U	L	1-2	1-1	Steven 5	21, 80
	34		12	a	Oldham A	L	0-3	0-2		39, 42, 54
	35		16	a	Carlisle U	D	1-1	0-0	Phelan 70	85
	36		23	h	CHELSEA	W	3-0	1-0	Hamilton (2) 24, 82, Donovan 65p	
Stevenson's last game	37		30	a	Derby C	L	0-2	0-2		3, 38
	38	May	3	a	Shrewsbury T	W	2-1	0-0	Phelan 49, Donovan 52	65
last games for Laws & Cassidy	39		7	h	GRIMSBY T	D	1-1	1-1	Donovan 17p	30
	40		10	h	QUEENS PARK R	W	2-1	2-0	Donovan (2) 12, 33	59
	41		14	a	Leicester C	D	0-0	0-0		
Steven's last game	42		17	a	Crystal P	L	0-1	0-0		63

FA Cup

Note	Rd	Date			Opponents	Result		h/t	Goalscorers/times	Opp. goal times
	3	Jan	8	a	Carlisle U	D	2-2	1-1	Taylor 1, Wharton 87	9, 46
	rep		11	h	CARLISLE U	W	3-1	1-0	Flynn 16, Steven 80, Laws 89p	51
Cavener's last game	4		29	h	SWINDON T	W	3-1	2-0	Hamilton (2) 16, 78, Steven 42	50
	5	Feb	19	a	Crystal P	D	0-0	0-0		
	rep		28	h	CRYSTAL P	W	1-0	0-0	Taylor 83p	
	6	Mar	12	h	SHEFFIELD W	D	1-1	0-1	Cassidy 46	37
	rep		15	a	Sheffield W	L	0-5	0-3		19,29,42p,56,84

Final, Manchester U 4-0 Brighton & H A, at Wembley, after a 2-2 draw after extra time, also at Wembley.

League Cup

Note	Rd	Date			Opponents	Result		h/t	Goalscorers/times	Opp. goal times
Bury goals 1m, 34m, 60m	1	Aug	31	a	Bury	W	5-3	2-2	Scott 26, Wharton 36, Phelan 62, Steven 78, McGee 84	
agg 8-4		Sep	14	h	BURY	W	3-1	1-0	Cruickshank 44og, Laws 76p, Hamilton 84	60
	2	Oct	5	h	MIDDLESBROUGH	W	3-2	1-1	Hamilton 32, Phelan 54, Young 61	41, 48
agg 4-3			26	a	Middlesbrough	D	1-1	0-1	Laws 79p	7
	3	Nov	9	a	Coventry C	W	2-1	1-1	McGee (2) 43, 69	5
	4		30	h	BIRMINGHAM C	W	3-2	2-0	McGee 12, Taylor 35, Brazier 73og	61, 62
	5	Jan	19	a	Tottenham H	W	4-1	0-0	Roberts (2ogs) 65, 85, Hamilton (2) 75, 89	46
	semi	Feb	8	a	Liverpool	L	0-3	0-1		41, 72, 80
agg 1-3			15	h	LIVERPOOL	W	1-0	0-0	Scott 55	

Final, Liverpool 2-1 Manchester U after extra time, at Wembley.

Details of other first team games elsewhere.

Att.	Pos	Stevenson	Laws	Ray	Scott	Phelan	Holt	Dobson	Steven	Hamilton	McGee	Young	Wharton	S Taylor	Cassidy	Cavener	Muir	Donachie	Flynn	O'Rourke	Walsh	Miller	Donovan	V Overson	L Dixon	
10,562		1	2	3	4	5	6	7	8	9	10	11														1
8,036	6	1	2		4	5	6	7	8	9	10	11	3													2
7,703	5	1	2		4	5	6	7	8	9	10	11	3													3
9,169	10	1	2		4*	5	6	7	8	9	10	11	3	S*												4
11,938	12	1	2		4	5	6	7	8	9	10*		3	S*	11											5
6,480	14	1	2		4	5	6	7	8	9	10		3	S*	11*											6
9,165	18	1	2		4	5	6	7	8	9		11	3	10												7
6,480	14	1	2		4	5	6	7		9		11	3	10		8										8
5,940	17	1	2		4	5	6	7*		9		11	3	10		8	S*									9
13,827		1	2		4	5	6	7		9		11	3			8	10									10
9,040	18	1	2		4*	5	6	7	S*	9		11	3	10		8										11
7,265	19	1	2		10	5	6	7*	8	9	4	11	3			S*										12
20,961	20	1	2		6	4	5	7	8	9	10	11	3													13
6,039	20	1	2		6	5		7	8		10	11		9	4			3								14
16,329	19	1	2		S*	5		7	8	9	11			10	4			3*	6							15
7,513	19	1	2			5		7	8	9	11		3	10	4				6							16
8,184	19	1	2		S*	5*		7	8	9	11		3	10	4				6							17
6,503	20	1	2			5	3	7	8	9	11			10	4				6							18
5,448	21	1	2			5	3	7	8	9	11			10	4				6							19
20,439	21		2			5	3	7	8	9				10	4				6	1	11					20
21,961	22		2		11	5	3	7	8	9				10	4				6	1						21
9,548	21		2		11*	5		7	8	9				10				3	6	1	4	S*				22
9,205	21		2		11	5	7		8	9				10				3	6	1	4					23
8,894	21		2		7	5	4		8	9		11	S*	10*				3	6	1						24
10,358	21	1			2	4		5	8*	9		11	S*	10		7		3	6							25
6,079	21	1	2		7	4		5	8	9		11*		10	S*			3	6							26
7,040	21	1	2		7	4		5	8	9		11		10				3	6							27
8,774	19	1	2			4		5	8	9		11		10	7			3	6*				S*			28
14,069	21	1	2		7	4		5	8	9		11						3	6				10			29
3,549	22	1	2		7	4		5	8			11		9				3	6				10			30
9,643	22	1	2		7	4		5	8			11*		9				3	6				10	S*		31
13,434	22	1	2		7	4		5	8	9		11		10				3	6							32
12,205	22	1	2		7	4		5	8	9		11*			S*			3	6				10			33
6,126	22	1	2		7*	4		5	8	9				S*				3	6				10	11		34
5,081	22	1	2			4		5	8	9			11		7			3	6				10			35
7,452	22	1	2		11	4		5	8	9					7			3	6				10			36
14,674	22	1	2		11	4		5	8	9					7			3	6				10			37
3,573	22		2		11	4		5	8	9					7*			3	6	1			10	S*		38
7,136	22		2		11	4		5	8	9					7*			3	6	1			10	S*		39
7,215	22				11	4			8	9	S*	7*						3	6	1			10	5	2	40
29,453	21				11	4		5	8	9		7						3	6	1			10		2	41
22,743	21				11	4		5*	8	9			7					3	6	1			10	S*	2	42
Appearances		32	38	1	34	42	19	39	38	39	14	24	16	22	16	5	1	23	28	10	3		13	2	3	
Apps as sub					2				1		1		2	4	2	1	1					1	1	4		
Goals (56)			4		2	3		1	8	13	2	1	1	12			1		1				6			1 og

Att.	Pos	Stevenson	Laws	Ray	Scott	Phelan	Holt	Dobson	Steven	Hamilton	McGee	Young	Wharton	S Taylor	Cassidy	Cavener	Muir	Donachie	Flynn	O'Rourke	Walsh	Miller	Donovan	V Overson	L Dixon	
6,998			2		7	4	5		8	9		11	S*	10				3	6*	1						3
9,439			2		7*	5	4		8	9		11	S*	10				3	6	1						rep
9,786		1			2	4		5	8	9		11		10	S*	7*		3	6							4
14,949		1	2		7	4		5	8	9		11		10				3	6							5
16,240		1	2		7	4		5	8	9		11		10				3	6							rep
23,134		1	2			4		5	8	9		11*		10	7			3	6				S*			6
41,731		1	2		7	4		5*	8	9		11		10				3	6				S*			rep
Appearances		5	6		6	7	2	5	7	7		7		7	1	1		7	7	2						
Apps as sub													2		1								2			
Goals (10)			1						2	2			1	2	1				1							

Att.	Pos	Stevenson	Laws	Ray	Scott	Phelan	Holt	Dobson	Steven	Hamilton	McGee	Young	Wharton	S Taylor	Cassidy	Cavener	Muir	Donachie	Flynn	O'Rourke	Walsh	Miller	Donovan	V Overson	L Dixon	
3,111		1	2		4*	5	6	7	8	9	10	11	3	S*												1
3,714		1	2		4	5	6	7	8	9	10*		3	S*	11											2nd leg
3,909		1	2		4	5	6	7	8*	9		11	3	10	S*											2
10,328		1	2			5	6	7	8	9	4	11	3			10										2nd leg
7,437		1	2		6	4	5	7	8		10	11		9	3											3
10,726		1	2			5		7	8	9	11		3	10	4				6							4
30,771		1	2		7	5		4	8	9		11		10				3	6							5
33,520		1	2		7	4		5	8	9		11		10				3	6							semi
22,228		1	2		7	4		5	8	9		11		10*	S*			3	6							2nd leg
Appearances		9	9		7	9	5	9	9	8	5	7	5	6	3	1		3	4							
Apps as sub														2	2											
Goals (22)			2		2	2			1	4	4	1	1	1												4 ogs

1983-84

"The name's Bond ... John Bond".
It's highly unlikely that formed the basis of the former Manchester City manager's introductory pitch to the Burnley board after he emerged as an early frontrunner in a shortlist of six to succeed outgoing caretaker Frank Casper.
But a break with tradition was soon on the cards as 'outsider' Bond, 50, strode into Turf Moor in June 1983 as the first manager in 31 years not to have prior connections with the club. It was a decision that would ultimately backfire on several levels.
John Benson was immediately appointed as assistant manager, while Casper left ignominiously by the back door following 16 years' service.
Bond, whose appointment generated hostility from some fans, immediately announced: "If my record at other clubs is anything to go by, it shouldn't take long to put things right."
The new broom also hinted that he may have to sweep clean in order to strengthen a relegated team.
That comment reverberated all the way to Goodison Park. And it took less than a week for long-time admirers Everton, who had been granted first refusal on Trevor Steven, to pounce with a £350,000 offer for the midfield starlet and England youth international.
So, despite making only 76 Football League appearances, Steven became Burnley's record sale, smashing the £310,000 received from Derby for Leighton James eight years earlier.
Along with the £50,000 sale of Brian Laws, the Clarets' new management team suddenly found their means of financing a Turf Moor revolution.
Former £1m striker Kevin Reeves, veteran winger Tommy Hutchison and goalkeeper Roger Hansbury - a replacement for the released Alan Stevenson after the legendary goalkeeper amassed a post-war record of 438 League appearances - were the first names snapped up.
A third former Manchester City old boy, Gerry Gow, soon followed and even before a ball had been kicked in anger, Bond's inimitable management style was being called into question.
Having no affinity to the club undoubtedly made Bond a target for a section of support who had grown accustomed to familiar faces at the helm.
Quickly stripping Martin Dobson of the captaincy and handing it to Hutchison further angered the dissenting voices.
However, accusations of being a "short-term" manager who would bankrupt the club with ageing signings and inflated waged were swiftly rebuked by the ebullient manager.
"I haven't come here to destroy Burnley Football Club or to be a failure as a manager," boomed Bond at a hastily arranged Q&A session with supporters.
"I have never been sacked as a manager and all I want is a chance. But I have felt less wanted at this club than any other and that disappoints me."
A 1-4 opening day defeat at Hull did little to appease the critics. However, the fledgling strike partnership of Billy Hamilton and new boy Reeves was proving a bright spot.
Four league games into the campaign they had already amassed eight goals and looked capable of igniting a promotion push for the runaway title favourites.
Bond, meanwhile, remained on the hunt for players to strengthen a squad he believed was no better than a mid-table team.
And he soon announced a deal that sounded too good to be true; the signing of Steve Daley – the most expensive player in British soccer history four years earlier – on a free transfer from the North American Soccer League!
It took two long months for the protracted deal for the 30-year-old midfielder to finally materialise, but after several rounds of bureaucratic wrangling Burnley finally had two £1m men among their ranks.
Back on the field, inconsistent form was setting the tone for the season. With away wins proving hard to come by, seven home wins in eight games was proving the bedrock of Bond's belief. And more home comfort arrived with November's 7-0 thumping of bottom club Port Vale, which included Reeves' first hat-trick for the club.
The Clarets, who embarrassingly lost to Crewe in the Milk Cup first round just a year after reaching the semi-finals, also survived an FA Cup banana skin by overcoming Northern Premier League Hyde United 2-0 in a game switched to Turf Moor.
It needed a replay to overcome Chesterfield in round two, which came in the same December week that finally saw the Clarets notch up their first away win of the league season at Wimbledon.

Vince Overson
swashbuckling defender

The season of goodwill had truly arrived and at the club's annual meeting, Bond, who had been working without a contract, finally agreed a three-year deal.
He celebrated by taking his Turf Moor tally to seven full internationals with the signing of 34-year-old Dennis Tueart. And the latest arrival with Manchester City connections made a New Year's Eve debut as the Clarets ended a troubled year on a high with a 5-0 victory over Scunthorpe.
A feelgood factor finally appeared to have taken residence at Turf Moor.

The goals were flowing and Reeves was proving a class act with 15 goals to his name, the same as strike partner Hamilton. It would not last.

An FA Cup third round replay defeat away to Oxford left the eighth-placed Clarets concentrating solely on promotion.

Reeves had, seemingly insignificantly, limped off with a hip injury with 18 minutes of the Manor Ground tie remaining.

His injury was initially overshadowed by Hull City's failure to turn up at Turf Moor days later and fulfil a league fixture. Hull cited heavy snowfall as the reason, infuriating Burnley officials who had to postpone the game an hour before kick off.

But as the temperatures plummeted, anger soon turned to bone-numbing disbelief with the news that Reeves had suffered a stress fracture of the hip and would miss the remainder of the season.

As it transpired, the talisman striker would not play professional football again and he retired from the game the following summer, aged just 26.

With such a huge void to fill, Bond shrugged off the massive blow to seek a replacement in 22-year-old Matlock Town hitman Wayne Biggins, the Northern Premier League's top goalscorer.

And Biggins wasted no time making his mark, scoring his debut goal in the 4-0 defeat of Exeter and further establishing his credentials with a hat-trick against his former league employers, Lincoln City.

While Biggins was stealing the headlines, small print in the local media chronicled the February departures of Billy O'Rourke, Andy Wharton and a 19-year-old full back by the name of Lee Dixon.

Bond revealed the decision was made to give the youngsters a better chance of finding a club in mid-season, rather than competing with the flood of players released elsewhere that summer. Dixon would go on to play over 600 games for Arsenal and earn 22 England caps!

March dawned with the Clarets in eighth spot, 11 points behind league leaders and FA Cup conquerors Oxford.

But another distraction lay just around the corner. Dobson had just celebrated his 400th appearance in his second spell with the Clarets with the offer of a 12-month contract extension.

But out of the blue, managerless Bury pounced with an audacious attempt to land Dobson as their new player/boss.

Bond initially refused Bury permission, but quickly changed his mind so as not to deny his 36-year-old defender the opportunity to move into management.

An eventful week later, Dobson was Gigg Lane bound.

Biggins softened the blow, signing a new two-year deal and scoring his sixth goal in eight league games to earn a crucial victory over Millwall.

The former non-league marksman repeated the trick a week later with the only goal at Gillingham to take Burnley up to seventh place with 12 games remaining.

However, the Clarets would win just one more game all season; a Steve Daley hat-trick seeing off Walsall.

John Bond was clear as to the reasons why Burnley's promotion push ultimately failed to materialise.

"Biggins has done really well for us, but the loss of Reeves has been a bitter blow to us," he lamented.

Yet Hamilton too was a casualty of Reeves' untimely injury. The prolific Irishman scored just five goals in the second half of the season following the loss of his strike partner.

Mike Phelan
locally born star groomed at Turf Moor

Bond, meanwhile, took the unusual step of missing Burnley's meaningless end to the season after embarking on a recruitment drive for next season.

He was subsequently absent for an amazing final match at Turf Moor, which saw THREE sets of supporters witness the game with Hull City. Sheffield United brought several hundred fans over the Pennines to cheer on the Clarets and stop City scoring the 3-0 victory that would ensure they pipped the Blades to promotion.

In contrast, six points from a possible 36 was the Clarets' sad epitaph.

The clear-out was instant ... and Bond soon followed in dramatic circumstances.

1983-84 - Third Division

		P	W	D	L	F	A	Pts
1	Oxford U	46	28	11	7	91	50	95
2	Wimbledon	46	26	9	11	97	76	87
3	Sheffield U	46	24	11	11	86	53	83
4	Hull C	46	23	14	9	71	38	83
5	Bristol R	46	22	13	11	68	54	79
6	Walsall	46	22	9	15	68	61	75
7	Bradford C	46	20	11	15	73	65	71
8	Gillingham	46	20	10	16	74	69	70
9	Millwall	46	18	13	15	71	65	67
10	Bolton W	46	18	10	18	56	60	64
11	Orient	46	18	9	19	71	81	63
12	BURNLEY	46	16	14	16	76	61	62
13	Newport C	46	16	14	16	58	75	62
14	Lincoln C	46	17	10	19	59	62	61
15	Wigan A	46	16	13	17	46	56	61
16	Preston NE	46	15	11	20	66	66	56
17	Bournemouth	46	16	7	23	63	73	55
18	Rotherham U	46	15	9	22	57	64	54
19	Plymouth A	46	13	12	21	56	62	51
20	Brentford	46	11	16	19	69	79	49
21	Scunthorpe U	46	9	19	18	54	73	46
22	Southend U	46	10	14	22	55	76	44
23	Port Vale	46	11	10	25	51	83	43
24	Exeter C	46	6	15	25	50	84	33

1983-84

Manager : John Bond

Division Three (12th)

		Date			Opponents	Result		h/t	Goalscorers/times	Opp. goal times
	1	Aug	27	a	Hull C	L	1-4	1-2	Reeves 19	11, 15, 47, 77
	2	Sep	3	h	BOURNEMOUTH	W	5-1	4-1	Dobson 2, Reeves 20, Hamilton (3) 33, 45, 59	23
	3		6	h	NEWPORT C	W	2-0	0-0	Reeves 75, Hamilton 89	
	4		10	a	Oxford U	D	2-2	0-0	Hamilton 76, Flynn 89	46, 65
Young's last game	5		24	a	Brentford	D	0-0	0-0		
	6		27	a	Bolton W	D	0-0	0-0		
	7	Oct	1	h	PLYMOUTH A	W	2-1	0-1	Hamilton 65, Scott 88	21
Wharton's last game	8		9	a	Millwall	L	0-2	0-1		26, 64
	9		13	h	GILLINGHAM	L	2-3	0-0	Dobson 75, Hamilton 80	48, 64, 85
	10		18	h	SOUTHEND U	W	3-0	1-0	Hamilton 25, Miller 58, Reeves 70	
	11		22	a	Lincoln C	L	1-3	1-1	Hamilton 20	37, 80, 89
	12		29	h	WIGAN A	W	3-0	2-0	Flynn 36, Hutchison 42, Reeves 89	
	13	Nov	2	a	Exeter C	D	1-1	1-1	Flynn 16	35
	14		5	h	PRESTON N E	W	2-1	2-0	Reeves 19, Hamilton 42	86
	15		8	h	SHEFFIELD U	W	2-1	1-0	Dobson 2, Donachie 59	61
	16		12	a	Bristol R	L	1-2	1-2	Reeves 42	3, 38p
	17		26	h	PORT VALE	W	7-0	6-0	Hamilton 4, Reeves (3) 13p, 45, 49, Hutchison 19, Flynn 24, Donachie 27	
	18	Dec	3	a	Rotherham U	D	1-1	1-1	Flynn 9	30
	19		17	a	Wimbledon	W	4-1	3-1	Reeves 22, Hamilton 25, Scott (2) 43, 63	23
	20		26	h	BRADFORD C	L	1-2	1-0	Jackson 4og	81, 85
	21		27	a	Walsall	D	1-1	0-0	Hamilton 70	65
	22		31	h	SCUNTHORPE U	W	5-0	3-0	Flynn 5, Hutchison 22, Dobson 37, Reeves 55p, Tueart 89	
	23	Jan	2	a	Orient	W	2-1	1-1	Flynn 34, Hamilton 75	32
	24		21	a	Sheffield U	D	0-0	0-0		
	25	Feb	4	a	Plymouth A	D	1-1	0-0	Tueart 57	63
	26		11	h	BRENTFORD	D	2-2	2-0	Hamilton 36, Tueart 42	55, 67
	27		14	h	EXETER C	W	4-0	1-0	Tueart 17p, Flynn 66, Phelan 80, Biggins 83	
	28		18	a	Wigan A	L	0-1	0-1		39
	29		25	h	LINCOLN C	W	4-0	2-0	Biggins (3) 12, 24, 59, Flynn 62	
	30	Mar	2	a	Southend U	D	2-2	1-1	Hutchison 20, Hamilton 90	40, 72
	31		6	a	Preston N E	L	2-4	1-1	Donachie 40, Tueart 89	8, 48, 64, 67
Dobson's last game	32		10	h	BRISTOL R	D	0-0	0-0		
	33		17	h	MILLWALL	W	1-0	1-0	Biggins 33	
	34		24	a	Gillingham	W	1-0	0-0	Biggins 79	
	35		27	h	OXFORD U	D	1-1	1-0	Daley 20p	50
	36		31	h	BOLTON W	D	2-2	1-1	Hamilton 45, Miller 89	1, 77
	37	Apr	7	a	Newport C	L	0-1	0-0		84
	38		9	a	Bournemouth	L	0-1	0-1		30
	39		14	h	ROTHERHAM U	D	2-2	1-2	Biggins 29, Scott 55	2, 10
	40		21	a	Bradford C	L	1-2	1-1	Biggins 27	39, 53
	41		23	h	WALSALL	L	0-2	0-1		42, 47
	42		28	a	Port Vale	W	3-2	1-1	Daley (3) 25, 68, 80	12, 63
	43	May	5	h	ORIENT	L	2-3	2-1	Hamilton 1, Phelan 7	31, 51, 60
	44		7	a	Scunthorpe U	L	0-4	0-2		26, 31, 73, 82
	45		12	h	WIMBLEDON	L	0-2	0-2		21, 26
last games for Hamilton & Donachie	46		15	h	HULL C	L	0-2	0-1		2, 65

FA Cup

at Turf Moor	1	Nov	19	a	Hyde U	W	2-0	1-0	Waldron 44, Reeves 85p	
	2	Dec	10	a	Chesterfield	D	2-2	2-1	Dobson 20, Reeves 43	34, 54p
	rep		19	h	CHESTERFIELD	W	3-2	2-1	Reeves 6, Hamilton (2) 14, 83	15p, 65
	3	Jan	7	h	OXFORD U	D	0-0	0-0		
Kevin Reeves' last game	rep		11	a	Oxford U	L	1-2	0-1	Hamilton 48	6, 70

Final, Everton 2-0 Watford, at Wembley.

League Cup

	1	Aug	30	a	Crewe A	L	0-1	0-0		47
agg 3-5		Sep	13	h	CREWE A	L	3-4	1-4	Flynn (2) 11, 54p, Wharton 71	7, 21, 30p, 45

Final, Liverpool 1-0 Everton, at Maine Road, after a 0-0 draw after extra time, at Wembley.

Details of other first team games elsewhere.

Att.	Pos	Hansbury	Dixon	Donachie	Phelan	Gallagher	Flynn	Scott	K Reeves	Hamilton	Young	Hutchison	Wharton	V Overson	Dobson	Gow	Donovan	Miller	M Waldron	Daley	Tueart	Kennedy	Biggins	Baker	Glendon	Malley		
8,394		1	2	3	4	5	6	7	8	9	10	11																1
5,525	11	1			4		6	2	8	9		11	3*	5	7	10	S*											2
6,755		1		2	4		6		8	9		11	3	5	7	10												3
5,824	9	1		2	4		6	S*	8	9		11	3*	5	7	10												4
8,042	13	1			4		6	2		9	11*	7	3	5	8	10		S*										5
9,709		1			4		6	2		9		11	3	5	7	8			10									6
6,845	8	1			4		6	2	S*	9		11	3	5	7	8			10*									7
6,707	11	1			4		6	2	8	9		7	3		11	10			5									8
5,590	15	1		3	4		6	S*	8	9		7		5*	11	10			2									9
5,307		1		3	4		6		8	9		7		5	11			10	2									10
3,793	15	1		3	4		6	2	8	9		7		5	11	S*		10*										11
7,458	13	1		3	4		6	2	8	9		7		5	11			10										12
3,714		1		3	4		6	2	8	9		7		5				10	11									13
8,095	11	1		3	4		6	2	8	9		7		5	11				10									14
9,574		1		3	4		6	2	8	9		11		5	10				7									15
7,021	10	1		3	4		6	2	8	9		7		5	11*				10	S*								16
6,385	6	1		3	4		6	2	8	9		7		5	11*				10	S*								17
5,544	10	1		3	4		6	2	8	9		7		5					11	10								18
2,883	7	1		3	4			2	8	9		7		5	11				6	10								19
12,327	10	1		3	4		6	2	8	9		7		5					11	10								20
8,131	10	1		3	4		6	2	8	9		7		5	11					10								21
7,668	8	1		3*	4		6	2	8	9		7		5	11				10		S*							22
4,457	6	1			3		6		8	9		7		4	5				2	10	11							23
13,892	7	1		3			6	2		9		7		5	11					8	10	4						24
5,104	8	1		3	4		6	2		9		11		5	8					10	7							25
7,027	8	1		3	4		6	2		9		11		5	8						7		10					26
5,968		1		3	4		6	2		9		11		5	8						7		10					27
7,509	8	1		3	4		6*	2		9		11		5	8				7	S*			10					28
6,652	8	1		3	4		6	8		9		11			5					7			10	2				29
2,864	8	1		3	4		6*	8		9		11			5			S*		7			10	2				30
8,813		1		3	4			8		9		11			5					6	7		10	2				31
6,306	9	1		3	4		6	8		9		11			5					7			10	2				32
5,088	8	1		3	4		6	8*		9		11		5				7			S*		10	2				33
4,319	8	1		3	4		6*			9		11		5				8		7	S*		10	2				34
8,058		1		3	4		6			9		11		5				8*		7	S*		10	2				35
8,350	7	1		3	4		6			9		11		5				8		7*	S*		10	2				36
2,306	7	1		3	4		6*	8		9		11		5							S*		10	2	7			37
4,113		1		3				8		9		11		5				6			7	4	10	2				38
4,676	7	1		3	4		6	8		9		11		5						7		2	10					39
5,578	11	1		3*	4		6	2		9		11		5				8			S*	7	10					40
3,948		1		3	4		6*	8		9		11						5			7	2	10			S*		41
3,061	8	1			4		6	8		9		11						5		7		2	10		3			42
3,301	11	1			4		6	2		9		11		5				8		7		10			3			43
2,720	12	1			4		6	2		9		11		5				8		7			10		3			44
3,382	12	1		3	4		6	2		9		11		5				8		7			10					45
8,051	12	1		3	4		6	2		9		11		5						7			10			8		46
Appearances		46	1	37	44	1	43	38	20	46	2	46	7	38	28	8		15	16	20	8	7	20	10	4	1		
Apps as sub								2	1							1	1	2		3	7					1		
Goals (76)				3	2		9	4	12	18		4			4			2		4	5		8				1	og

Att.	Pos	Hansbury	Dixon	Donachie	Phelan	Gallagher	Flynn	Scott	K Reeves	Hamilton	Young	Hutchison	Wharton	V Overson	Dobson	Gow	Donovan	Miller	M Waldron	Daley	Tueart	Kennedy	Biggins	Baker	Glendon	Malley		
7,723		1		3	4		6	2	8	9		7		5	11				10									1
5,788		1		3	4		6	2	8	9		7		5	11					10								2
8,286		1		3	4		6	2	8	9		7		5					11	10								rep
11,672		1		3	4*		6	2	8	9		7		5	11					S*	10							3
10,497		1		3			6	2	8*	9		7		5	11				4	S*	10							rep
Appearances		5		5	4		5	5	5	5		5		5	4				3	2	2							
Apps as sub																				2								
Goals (8)									3	3					1				1									

Att.	Pos	Hansbury	Dixon	Donachie	Phelan	Gallagher	Flynn	Scott	K Reeves	Hamilton	Young	Hutchison	Wharton	V Overson	Dobson	Gow	Donovan	Miller	M Waldron	Daley	Tueart	Kennedy	Biggins	Baker	Glendon	Malley		
3,043		1	2*		4		6	7	8	9		11	3	5	10		S*											1
5,659		1		2	4	5	6	7	8*	9		11	3			10						S*						2nd leg
Appearances		2	1	1	2	1	2	2	2	2		2	2	1	1	1												
Apps as sub																	1					1						
Goals (3)							2						1															

1984-85

Life under John Bond had rarely been rosy.
But life after would become much worse.
The months before Bond's sudden and acrimonious departure certainly lived up to expectations.
The final weeks of the previous season were spent ignoring first team affairs and instead searching far and wide for fresh blood.
Stoke defender Peter Hampton, Blackburn Rovers striker Peter Devine and Gillingham winger Neil Grewcock, whose contribution would later go down in Burnley folklore, were soon unveiled by the manger, who admitted "two-thirds" of the blame for a season that left supporters angrier than ever.
Alan Taylor, a former FA Cup winner with West Ham and former Leeds and Blackburn Rovers defender Kevin Hird soon joined the beleaguered Clarets.
Meanwhile, out went a clutch of veterans who had followed former Manchester City pied piper Bond into Turf Moor less than 12 months previously.
Steve Daley, Dennis Tueart and Gerry Gow all quit the club and former Scottish international Willie Donachie was the biggest name of seven players released.
"To a Burnley public which, season after season got used to seeing the same squad with the addition of another 'find' coming through a seemingly never-ending youth policy, the personnel changes are being made almost too fast to sink in," noted the Burnley Express.
No sooner had the ink dried on those words than striker Billy Hamilton, whose 18 league goals had proved a highlight of a dismal first season in Division Three, joined the exodus.
The out-of-contract Northern Ireland international joined Oxford United after four unforgettable years with the Clarets that brought a total of 77 goals.
Hamilton was virtually an ever-present in his last four campaigns, missing just nine games.
A true legend!
If that left Burnley fans reeling, what came next was astonishing as the bombshell of Bond's exit overshadowed everything on the eve of the new season.
A power struggle in the Turf Moor boardroom led Bond to warn that his job was becoming untenable, given an uncertain resolution.
Five days before the season kicked off against Plymouth Argyle, matters came to a head when it emerged that either chairman John Jackson or the man he appointed just 12 months previously would have to go.
There was only one winner and, as Bond sped off into the Burnley night after hearing his contract had been terminated, the three-man board appointed assistant John Benson as the club's fourth manager in just 20 months.
The official post-mortem was that Bond was far too hasty in deciding where the strengths lay within his current squad, before plunging for players living on past reputations.
Yet the epitaph to his successor's solitary season in charge was a campaign of yet more turmoil and a new low point in the history of a proud football club.
How could a team constantly ranked among the favourites for promotion sink two divisions in three years to end up in the Fourth Division?
It was almost beyond comprehension.
It was shameful.
The season began brightly enough, a two-legged Milk Cup victory over Crewe earning a crack at the mighty Manchester United in round two.
The reality check of a 0-7 aggregate defeat was an ominous sign of things to come.
Benson's Burnley won just two of their first 11 league games, away to Orient and at home to Newport.
Player of the Year Derek Scott fractured his right leg in the 3-2 defeat to Rotherham and a first league home defeat of the season followed to Lincoln in mid-October.
The ghost of Bond also continued to hang around as the former manager announced he was to sue the club, alleging breach of contract and claiming damages for wrongful dismissal.
He would ultimately have his revenge ... but not in court.
The writing was on the wall and, with firepower a glaring problem and precious little money to solve it, the Clarets lay a lowly 15th in a dreadfully poor division with a quarter of the season played.
Brian Flynn, the Clarets' Welsh international, was made available for transfer at his own request and a 5-1 hammering at Reading was the final straw for one Clarets' fan who, in an emotional letter to the Burnley Express, moaned: "When you have been brought up on caviar, you cannot expect to watch tripe!"

Wayne Biggins
top scorer in his only full season at Turf Moor

Defending his corner, Benson argued that a good side had not become bad overnight.
The results, however, begged to differ.
A victory over Brentford was an all-too brief respite, before six defeats in seven games before the turn of the year poured oil on the troubled waters of a reported "self-induced" £300,000 club debt, blamed by the board on Bond's disastrous transfer dealings.
Even a club-record equalling 9-0 FA Cup victory over non-league Penrith, courtesy of hat-tricks for Wayne Biggins and

Taylor, failed to lighten the mood.

The cup was an unwelcome distraction and, following a 3-1 second round success over Halifax, it was a blessed relief when Wimbledon ended the Clarets' interest in the competition in round three and left them with the not inconsiderable task of avoiding relegation.

Such was the growing concern, former Clarets star Jimmy McIlroy penned a front page leader in the Burnley Express following two humiliating Christmas defeats - 0-4 away to York and Bristol City respectively.

"To believe that things can only get better is to believe in miracles. I have to concede that nothing short of a miracle can stop the rot and the unthinkable – Fourth Division football at Turf Moor next season," insisted the Turf Moor legend.

In Burnley, miracles were in short supply.

Off the pitch, 1985 dawned with the news that Lancashire cricketer Jack Simmons and local businessman Frank Teasdale would take the board of directors' numbers up to six.

On it, Burnley started the year with another home defeat to Wigan that left them with one point from 21 and clinging to a perilous 20th spot.

Amazingly, that was the only league game in January as the icy winter accentuated the shakes that supporters were already suffering.

The month-long hiatus saw a fit-again Scott take over the club captaincy from Hutchison, while the enforced mid-winter break initially appeared to benefit the team.

Burnley returned to league action with a convincing 7-0 win over Rotherham at joyous Turf Moor and back to back wins over Lancashire rivals Preston and Bolton made it just one defeat in five games as the sunshine of spring replaced deep winter.

A month of postponements, however, handed Benson's men a punishing schedule of two games a week throughout March and April – and this had a devastating effect on the players.

One win in 15 games, a welcome 2-0 home win over Cambridge United, saw the crisis deepen.

Burnley slipped into the dreaded bottom four following a home defeat to Bournemouth that 'attracted' just 2,655 fans.

Looming large was now an end-of-season decider with Swansea, ironically now managed by John Bond!

The Swans were in a handful of teams fighting to avoid the drop, along with already doomed Cambridge, Preston, Orient and, regrettably, the Clarets.

Only one team could escape and the date with the Welsh side therefore took on extra significance, with just three games remaining.

Taylor's goal allowed Turf Moor to breath again in a dramatic 1-0 win at Vetch Field but, two days later, a dreadful home defeat to Bristol City by the same scoreline, undid all that hard work and kept the nerves jangling.

An emergency board meeting 48 hours before a trip to Walsall that would decide Burnley's fate – at which chairman John Jackson announced he was to stand down, but retain his place on the board - only served to heighten the tension.

And despite a heroic 3-2 win in the Midlands, there was to be an anxious six-day wait until Swansea, of all teams, finished their own fixtures to clear up the final relegation picture.

Tommy Hutchison
ever present in a depressing campaign

Burnley held its collective breath, knowing Bond's side needed just one point from their home game against fourth placed Bristol City.

But the blackest week in the club's history (so far) was confirmed when the game in South Wales ended in a goalless draw to seal the Clarets' inevitable and utterly avoidable fate.

Fourth Division football was the punishment for a season of startling underachievement.

The immediate aftermath saw Benson fall on his sword, while Teasdale took over the chairmanship just four months after being appointed onto the board of directors.

It was one more new dawn.

Was it to be another false one?

1984-85 - Third Division

		P	W	D	L	F	A	Pts
1	Bradford C	46	28	10	8	77	45	94
2	Millwall	46	26	12	8	73	42	90
3	Hull C	46	25	12	9	78	49	87
4	Gillingham	46	25	8	13	80	62	83
5	Bristol C	46	24	9	13	74	47	81
6	Bristol R	46	21	12	13	66	48	75
7	Derby C	46	19	13	14	65	54	70
8	York C	46	20	9	17	70	57	69
9	Reading	46	19	12	15	68	62	69
10	Bournemouth	46	19	11	16	57	46	68
11	Walsall	46	18	13	15	58	52	67
12	Rotherham U	46	18	11	17	55	55	65
13	Brentford	46	16	14	16	62	64	62
14	Doncaster R	46	17	8	21	72	74	59
15	Plymouth A	46	15	14	17	62	65	59
16	Wigan A	46	15	14	17	60	64	59
17	Bolton W	46	16	6	24	69	75	54
18	Newport C	46	13	13	20	55	67	52
19	Lincoln C	46	11	18	17	50	51	51
20	Swansea C	46	12	11	23	53	80	47
21	BURNLEY	46	11	13	22	60	73	46
22	Orient	46	11	13	22	51	76	46
23	Preston NE	46	13	7	26	51	100	46
24	Cambridge U	46	4	9	33	37	95	21

1984-85

Manager : John Benson

Division Three (21st)
Relegated

Notes	No	Date		h/a	Opponents	Result		h/t	Goalscorers/times	Opp. goal times
	1	Aug	25	h	PLYMOUTH A	D	1-1	0-1	Taylor 82	32
	2		31	a	Doncaster R	L	0-2	0-1		41, 83
	3	Sep	8	h	BRISTOL R	D	0-0	0-0		
	4		15	a	Derby C	D	2-2	1-2	Biggins 38, Hird 76	16, 41
	5		18	a	Orient	W	2-0	0-0	Foster 48og, Taylor 75	
	6		22	h	HULL C	D	1-1	0-1	Biggins 61	13p
	7		29	a	Rotherham U	L	2-3	1-1	Biggins (2) 44, 80	43, 81, 90p
	8	Oct	2	h	NEWPORT C	W	2-0	0-0	Flynn 47, Grewcock 72	
	9		6	a	Bournemouth	D	1-1	1-1	Hird 22	24
	10		13	h	LINCOLN C	L	1-2	1-0	Hird 31p	59, 87
	11		20	a	Reading	L	1-5	1-0	Biggins 16	54, 56, 78, 79, 85
	12		23	h	BRENTFORD	W	3-1	2-1	Hird 15p, Biggins 42, Roberts 65og	40og
	13		27	h	BOLTON W	W	3-2	2-1	Hird 1, Grewcock 33, Miller 75	26, 56
Flynn's last game	14	Nov	3	a	Preston N E	D	3-3	2-2	Biggins (2) 11, 20, Whatmore 61	6, 14, 88
	15		6	h	GILLINGHAM	L	0-1	0-0		50
	16		10	a	Cambridge U	W	3-2	0-2	Biggins 47, Grewcock 78, Hird 85	30, 44og
	17		24	h	BRADFORD C	L	1-2	1-2	Biggins 39	9, 11
	18	Dec	1	a	Millwall	L	1-2	0-1	Hird 68	27, 54
	19		15	h	SWANSEA C	D	1-1	0-0	Lawrence 65	80
	20		22	h	WALSALL	L	1-2	1-1	Hird 5	28, 65
	21		26	a	York C	L	0-4	0-3		8, 14, 38, 84
	22		29	a	Bristol C	L	0-1	0-0		90
	23	Jan	1	h	WIGAN A	L	1-2	0-1	Biggins 68	44, 52
	24	Feb	2	h	ROTHERHAM U	W	7-0	2-0	Devine 38, Hird (3) 40, 55p, 63, Biggins (2) 50, 81, Lawrence 90	
	25		9	a	Hull C	L	0-2	0-0		74, 76
	26		16	h	ORIENT	D	1-1	1-1	Hird 45	8
	27		23	h	PRESTON N E	W	2-0	0-0	Scott 47, Biggins 48	
	28	Mar	2	a	Bolton W	W	3-1	2-1	Devine 1, Grewcock 15, Hampton 80	3
	29		5	a	Brentford	L	1-2	0-0	Hird 73	82, 88
	30		9	h	READING	L	0-2	0-0		51, 71
	31		12	h	DONCASTER R	L	0-1	0-0		80
	32		16	a	Lincoln C	L	1-3	1-1	Hird 22	21, 76, 79
	33		23	h	BOURNEMOUTH	D	1-1	0-1	Biggins 74	38
	34		26	a	Plymouth A	D	2-2	1-2	Biggins 24, Hird 77p	9, 21
	35		29	a	Gillingham	D	1-1	0-0	Biggins 49	71
	36	Apr	2	a	Newport C	L	1-2	0-2	Grewcock 59	33, 41
	37		6	h	YORK C	D	1-1	0-0	Phelan 53	66
	38		8	a	Wigan A	L	0-2	0-0		66, 84
	39		13	h	CAMBRIDGE U	W	2-0	1-0	Taylor (2) 2, 53	
	40		16	a	Bristol R	L	0-4	0-3		15, 29, 44, 51
	41		20	a	Bradford C	L	2-3	0-0	Grewcock 82, Biggins 85	61, 65, 87
	42		23	h	DERBY C	L	0-1	0-1		38
	43		27	h	MILLWALL	D	1-1	1-0	Overson 1	85
	44	May	4	a	Swansea C	W	1-0	1-0	Taylor 36	
Scott's last game	45		6	h	BRISTOL C	L	0-1	0-0		76
last games for Phelan,	46		11	a	Walsall	W	3-2	1-1	Taylor (2) 14, 56, Hird 51	30, 58

Hutchison & Hansbury

FA Cup

Round	Date		h/a	Opponents	Result		h/t	Goalscorers/times	Opp. goal times
1	Nov	17	a	Penrith	W	9-0	2-0	Hird (3) 7p, 44, 48, Taylor (3) 53, 62, 85, Grewcock 71, Powell (2) 78, 88	
2	Dec	8	h	HALIFAX T	W	3-1	1-1	Hird 27, Devine 60, Biggins 80	36
3	Jan	5	a	Wimbledon	L	1-3	0-1	Devine 89	27, 77, 85p

Final, Manchester U 1-0 Everton, at Wembley.

League Cup

Notes	Round	Date		h/a	Opponents	Result		h/t	Goalscorers/times	Opp. goal times
	1	Aug	23	h	CREWE A	L	1-2	1-2	Grewcock 27	10, 25
agg 4-2		Sep	4	a	Crewe A	W	3-0	0-0	Overson 52, Hird 65, Grewcock 80	
	2		26	a	Manchester U	L	0-4	0-2		1, 18, 55, 74
agg 0-7		Oct	9	h	MANCHESTER U	L	0-3	0-0		46, 78, 86

Final, Norwich C 1-0 Sunderland, at Wembley.

Details of other first team games elsewhere.

Att.	Pos	Hansbury	Scott	Hampton	Phelan	V Overson	Hird	Grewcock	Powell	A Taylor	Biggins	Hutchison	Flynn	Miller	Kennedy	Whatmore	Malley	Gallagher	Devine	Palmer	Lawrence	Neenan	Rhodes	Chilton		
4,644		1	2	3	4	5	6	7	8	9	10	11														1
3,368	22	1	2	3	4	5	6	7	8*	9	10	11	S*													2
4,573	20	1	2	3	4	5	6	7		9	10	11		8												3
11,755	18	1	2	3	4	5	6	7	S*	9	10	11		8*												4
2,359		1	2	3	4	5	6	7	8	9	10	11														5
5,526	14	1	2	3	4	5	6	7	8	9*	10	11	S*													6
4,646	17	1	2*	3	4	5	6	7	8	S*	10	11	9													7
3,666	13	1		3	4	5	6	7			10	11	8		2	9										8
3,180	13	1		3	4	5	6	7			10	11	8	S*	2*	9										9
4,315	16	1		3	4	5	6	7		S*	10	11	8	2		9*										10
4,024	19	1		3*	4	5	6	7	S*		10	11	8	2		9										11
2,916	15	1		3	4	5	6	7			10	11	S*	8*		9	2									12
6,501	15	1		3	4	5	6	7			10	11		8		9	2									13
4,995	15	1		3		5	6	7			10	11*	S*	8		9	2	4								14
3,595	17	1		3		5	6	7		S*	10	11		8		9	2	4*								15
2,505	16	1		3		5	6	7	4	9*	10	11		8	2				S*							16
7,060	16	1		3	4	5	6	7	8		10	11								2	9					17
5,376	17	1		3	4		6	7	8		10	11			5					2	9					18
3,798	19	1		3	4	5	6	7	8		10	11								2	9					19
3,350	20	1		3	4	5	6	7			10	11		8						2	9					20
6,397	20	1		3	4	5	6	7			10	11		8						2	9					21
8,282	20	1		3	4		6	7			10	11			5		8		S*	2	9*					22
5,235	20	1		3*	4		6	7			10	11			5		8	S*	9	2						23
3,907	20			3*	4	5	6	7			10	11			8				9	2	S*	1				24
6,478	20		S*	3	4	5	6	7			10	11			8*				9	2		1				25
3,744	20		8	3	4	5	6	7			10	11							9	2		1				26
4,768	20		8	3	4		6	7			10	11						5	9	2		1				27
6,468	20		8	3	4	5	6	7			10	11							9	2		1				28
3,267	20		8	3	4	5	6	7			10	11							9	2		1				29
3,955	20		8	3	4	5	6	7			10	11							9	2		1				30
3,020	20		8	3	4	5	6	7			10	11							9*	2	S*	1				31
2,137	20		8	3	4	5	6	7			10	11						9		2*	S*	1				32
2,784	21	1	8	3	4	5	6	7			10	11							9	2						33
3,165	20	1	8	3	4	5	6	7*			10	11							9	2	S*					34
5,935	21	1	8	3	4	5	6	7			10	11							9	2						35
1,689	21	1	8	3	4	5	6	7			10	11							9	2						36
3,844	22	1	8	3	4	5	6	7		9	10	11								2						37
3,517	22	1	8	3*	4	5	6	S*		9	10	11								2			7			38
2,843	21	1	8		4	5		7		9	10	11					2						6	3		39
4,866	21	1	8*	S*	4	5		7		9	10	11		2			3						6			40
8,156	21	1	2	3	4	5	6	S*		8*	10	11							9				7			41
3,873	21	1	2	3*	4	5	6	7		9	10	11							S*				8			42
3,586	23	1	2	3	4	5	6	7			10	11					S*		9*				8			43
5,221	21	1	2	3	4	5	6	7		9	10	11											8			44
4,570	21	1	2	3	4	5	6	7*		9	10	11		S*									8			45
3,396	21	1		3	4	5	6	7		9	10*	11							S*	2			8			46
Appearances		37	27	44	43	42	44	44	9	16	46	46	5	12	8	8	8	4	15	23	6	9	9	1		
Apps as sub			1	1				2	2	3			4	2			1	1	4		4					
Goals (60)			1	1	1	1	16	6		7	18		1	1		1			2		2				2	ogs

Att.	Hansbury	Scott	Hampton	Phelan	V Overson	Hird	Grewcock	Powell	A Taylor	Biggins	Hutchison	Flynn	Miller	Kennedy	Whatmore	Malley	Gallagher	Devine	Palmer	Lawrence	Neenan	Rhodes	Chilton	
1,813	1		3	4	5*	6	7	8	9	10	11		2	S*										1
5,543	1		3	4	5	6	7	8		10	11							9	2					2
3,381	1		3	4	8	6	7			10	11			5				9	2					3
Appearances	3		3	3	3	3	3	2	1	3	3		1	1				2	2					
Apps as sub														1										
Goals (13)						4	1	2	3	1								2						

Att.	Hansbury	Scott	Hampton	Phelan	V Overson	Hird	Grewcock	Powell	A Taylor	Biggins	Hutchison	Flynn	Miller	Kennedy	Whatmore	Malley	Gallagher	Devine	Palmer	Lawrence	Neenan	Rhodes	Chilton	
3,043	1	2	3	4	5	6	7	8	9	10	11													1
3,067	1	2	3	4	5	6	7		9	10	11		8											2nd leg
28,383	1	2	3	4	5	6	7	8	9*	10	11	S*												2
12,690	1		3	4	5	6	7			10	11	8	2		9									2nd leg
Appearances	4	3	4	4	4	4	4	2	3	4	4	1	2		1									
Apps as sub												1												
Goals (4)					1	1	2																	

1985-86

Reflecting their standing as a fallen giant, sixty-two applications were received in the close season to succeed John Benson as the Clarets' 12th post-war manager.

Player of the Year Tommy Hutchison, fresh from a second successive ever-present season at the age of 37, was the name at the top of that list as player/manager.

So it was a huge shock when, out of the blue, former Scotland and Manchester United defender Martin Buchan, a man with no managerial experience, was unveiled.

The equally stunned Hutchison was immediately sounded out for assistant manager, but chose instead to leave the club.

And in keeping with recent campaigns Turf Moor was thrown into more chaos within four months when Buchan suddenly threw in the towel and followed.

Optimism had been high, with Liverpool visiting Turf Moor for a pre-season friendly and the Clarets installed as firm favourites for promotion.

But with little or no money to spend - in a close season that saw Derek Scott quit Burnley after a decade to join Bolton and Michael Phelan join Norwich - things started badly and quickly fell away.

Back-to-back home defeats at the start of the campaign, in front of successive sub-4,000 crowds, were an ominous precursor.

A first round Milk Cup exit at the hands of Bury was a further warning sign.

And things reached farcical proportions when the visit of cricketing legend Ian Botham - spotted at Turf Moor watching close friend Joe Neenan - sparked wild rumours that the England all-rounder may even be drafted in to help beef up Burnley!

Eight games in, however, there was a glimmer of hope with the Clarets bowling along in eighth place, handily placed for the long winter ahead.

But a fractured jaw suffered by new summer signing Neenan, coinciding with a dismal run of results, proved too much for one man.

And following the 0-1 defeat at Chester in early October, described by the manager as "suicidal", Buchan tendered his shock resignation.

Unbelievably, the Scot had become the fifth manager to leave the club in two and a half seasons, admitting: "I could not make the transition from dressing room to management.

"There are certain aspects of the job that I honestly just could not handle.

"Football management is a job I can't cope with and I do not see any future for me in the game."

It was a brutally honest assessment that did little to help Burnley's general malaise.

And the sale of Wayne Biggins to Norwich City following a third straight defeat led to angry demonstrations by supporters, concerned at the alarming tailspin.

The ageing Tommy Cavanagh, who had been drafted in by Buchan to help out in pre-season, immediately took the pilot's seat, insisting: "This club has got to get down to some straight talking. It (the club) needs stability and credibility."

And after an inauspicious beginning Cavanagh seemed to have found the magic formula as the club ended yet another turbulent year with five victories and just one defeat in nine games.

Kevin Hird scored in three successive wins to kick-start the run, including the Bonfire Night winner against league leaders Mansfield that raised spirits on the field and in the stands.

A 4-0 romp away to Cambridge - hauling the Clarets back into the comforts of mid-table, was another relative 'highlight', as was the avoidance of FA Cup first round humiliation with a last minute 3-2 victory over non-league Nuneaton.

Off the field though, the situation remained perilous and the annual balance sheet, showing growing losses of over £250,000, bank debts of £410,000 and a further £240,000 owed to creditors, did little to alleviate the fears of concerned fans, some of who had already instigated the 'Save Our Club' group.

Kevin Hird
equally at home in defence or midfield

And if ever a reminder of the overall pattern was needed, a second round defeat away to Rotherham confirmed the fact that Burnley Football Club would not be contesting the FA Cup third round.

The 5-2 New Year's Day victory over Wrexham proved to be an antidote to thousands of hangovers, as was a 3-2 success at Southend 48 hours later that lifted the Clarets up to ninth place in the table.

Following a fifth successive home victory over Hereford, there appeared to be light at the end of a long and particularly dark tunnel.

All that hard work was undone however, when Cavanagh's Clarets entered another trough of form that brought just one victory in nine league games.

Five points from 27 – including a gut-wrenching 0-2 defeat away to the club lying 92nd, Torquay United – was more ammunition for the supporters, whose off-field fight for change was gathering more and more momentum.

Former chairman John Jackson, against whom much of the fans' fury had been vented in recent months, had already buckled and announced that he was selling the majority of his shares to current chairman Frank Teasdale, initially retaining just enough to keep his membership of the board of directors.

But in mid-February, Jackson finally caved in to the personal abuse he had been subjected to and resigned from the board. There had been consistent calls for the barrister to resign, from the moment he took the chairmanship in 1981 and beyond his resignation of the post four years later.

Individual casualties may have left many feeling better, but they were hollow victories in the bigger picture. Teasdale emphasised this by calling an extraordinary meeting soon after to emphasise the desperate cash plight facing the club; insisting a new shares issue - raising the share capital from £8,000 to £50,000 - was the only way to avoid liquidation and guarantee the club's future.

Alan Taylor
top scorer in 1985-86

Meanwhile, the icy mood off the field was matched by the biting and unrelenting winter, which forced ten postponements throughout January and February.

It was 29 March before the Clarets finally got back to winning ways, a winner against Wrexham from 18-year-old birthday boy Ashley Hoskin - who broke his leg earlier in the season - unable to alter the equally painful fact that Fourth Division football beckoned for a second season.

It all culminated in less than 2000 supporters attending the April clash with Crewe to register another lowest post-war gate at Turf Moor.

Two weeks later, following a disappointing take-up, the deadline for potential investors to the new shares issue was hastily extended, with directors warning that Burnley Football Club had just days to "fold or survive."

The club even took steps to increase the number of matchday programmes for the final home game of the season against Scunthorpe, in case it became a collector's item ... the last ever!

A positive response to the appeal - an approach by a group of Burnley businessmen - forced another extension until May as attention turned from a pitiful end to the season to Burnley's well publicised financial crisis.

Finally, after a nervy few weeks, came the news everyone hoped for as the club's bankers, TSB, stepped in to secure the future of the club for another 12 months.

It had undoubtedly been the worst season in Burnley Football Club's history, on and off the field.

Summing things up in his own epitaph of what he described as a "dreadful season", Burnley Express reporter Granville Shackleton added that another failure next season could put a founder member of the Football League into the Gola League.

How close those words came to becoming a prophesy.

1985-86 - Fourth Division

		P	W	D	L	F	A	Pts
1	Swindon T	46	32	6	8	82	43	102
2	Chester C	46	23	15	8	83	50	84
3	Mansfield T	46	23	12	11	74	47	81
4	Port Vale	46	21	16	9	67	37	79
5	Orient	46	20	12	14	79	64	72
6	Colchester U	46	19	13	14	88	63	70
7	Hartlepool U	46	20	10	16	68	67	70
8	Northampton T	46	18	10	18	79	58	64
9	Southend U	46	18	10	18	69	67	64
10	Hereford U	46	18	10	18	74	73	64
11	Stockport C	46	17	13	16	63	71	64
12	Crewe A	46	18	9	19	54	61	63
13	Wrexham	46	17	9	20	68	80	60
14	BURNLEY	46	16	11	19	60	65	59
15	Scunthorpe U	46	15	14	17	50	55	59
16	Aldershot	46	17	7	22	66	74	58
17	Peterborough U	46	13	17	16	52	64	56
18	Rochdale	46	14	13	19	57	77	55
19	Tranmere R	46	15	9	22	74	73	54
20	Halifax T	46	14	12	20	60	71	54
21	Exeter C	46	13	15	18	47	59	54
22	Cambridge U	46	15	9	22	65	80	54
23	Preston NE	46	11	10	25	54	89	43
24	Torquay U	46	9	10	27	43	88	37

1985-86

Manager : Martin Buchan until October 1985, then Tommy Cavanagh

Division Four (14th)

		Date			Opponents	Result		h/t	Goalscorers/times	Opp. goal times
	1	Aug	17	h	NORTHAMPTON T	W	3-2	3-0	Hird 12, Biggins (2) 28, 44	49, 86
	2		23	h	STOCKPORT C	L	0-1	0-0		77
	3		26	h	PORT VALE	L	1-2	1-1	Taylor 23	25, 50
	4		31	a	Aldershot	W	2-0	0-0	Taylor (2) 62, 68	
	5	Sep	7	h	HARTLEPOOL U	W	2-0	1-0	Biggins 37, Heggarty 89	
	6		14	a	Hereford U	D	2-2	1-0	Malley 18, Hird 65p	57, 88
	7		17	a	Preston N E	L	0-1	0-1		3
	8		21	h	ROCHDALE	W	1-0	1-0	Biggins 1	
	9		28	a	Peterborough U	D	0-0	0-0		
	10	Oct	1	h	COLCHESTER U	L	0-2	0-0		46, 60
	11		5	a	Chester C	L	0-4	0-2		16, 20, 60, 88
Biggins' last game	12		12	h	SWINDON T	L	0-2	0-1		10, 49
	13		19	a	Crewe A	L	1-3	0-2	Taylor 48	20, 31, 63
	14		22	h	TORQUAY U	W	3-0	2-0	Hird 14p, Taylor (2) 31, 88	
	15		26	a	Halifax T	D	2-2	1-0	Parker 19, Grewcock 86	55, 57
	16	Nov	2	h	SOUTHEND U	L	1-3	1-0	Robinson 44	73, 76, 89
	17		5	h	MANSFIELD T	W	2-1	1-0	Taylor 44, Hird 67	46
	18		9	a	Cambridge U	W	4-0	4-0	Hird 1, Parker 28, Devine 29, Taylor 35	
	19		23	h	EXETER C	W	3-1	1-0	McNichol 14og, Hird (2) 50p, 81p	79
	20		30	a	Scunthorpe U	D	1-1	1-0	Hoskin 8	63
	21	Dec	14	h	ORIENT	W	1-0	1-0	Taylor 23	
	22		20	a	Stockport C	D	1-1	0-0	Heesom 79	81
	23		26	a	Tranmere R	L	1-2	1-0	Taylor 44	52, 80
	24	Jan	1	h	WREXHAM	W	5-2	2-2	Taylor 27, Deakin 32, Grewcock 50, Parker (2) 58, 75	7, 21
	25		3	a	Southend U	W	3-2	0-1	Taylor (2) 65, 77, Deakin 66	11, 67
	26		18	a	Northampton T	L	0-2	0-1		35, 88
	27		25	h	HEREFORD U	W	3-2	1-2	Taylor (2) 5, 56, Lawrence 72	27, 33
	28	Feb	1	a	Hartlepool U	L	1-3	0-0	Lawrence 56	62, 69, 74
	29		4	a	Torquay U	L	0-2	0-1		41, 74
	30		24	a	Port Vale	D	1-1	0-1	Lawrence 86	15
	31	Mar	1	h	PETERBOROUGH U	D	1-1	0-0	Paris 50og	52
	32		8	h	CHESTER C	W	1-0	0-0	Lawrence 70	
	33		11	h	ALDERSHOT	L	1-2	1-0	Grewcock 19	51, 70
	34		15	a	Swindon T	L	1-3	1-1	Lawrence 44	35, 54, 85
	35		18	a	Rochdale	L	0-1	0-0		61
	36		22	h	HALIFAX T	L	1-3	1-2	Hampton 15	19, 27, 80
	37		29	a	Wrexham	W	1-0	1-0	Hoskin 41	
	38		31	h	TRANMERE R	W	3-1	1-1	Grewcock (2) 34, 89, Malley 67	20
	39	Apr	5	a	Mansfield T	D	0-0	0-0		
	40		12	h	CAMBRIDGE U	D	1-1	0-1	Grewcock 87	24
	41		15	h	CREWE A	L	0-1	0-0		71
	42		19	a	Exeter C	W	2-0	1-0	Taylor 20, Parker 47	
	43		22	h	PRESTON N E	D	1-1	0-0	Deakin 49	83
	44		26	h	SCUNTHORPE U	L	1-2	1-1	Grewcock 20	11, 78
	45	May	3	a	Orient	L	0-3	0-1		42, 46, 63
last games for Alan Taylor, Hird & Devine	46		6	a	Colchester U	D	2-2	0-1	Lawrence 62, Devine 89	44, 80

FA Cup

					Opponents	Result		h/t	Goalscorers/times	Opp. goal times
	1	Nov	16	a	Nuneaton B	W	3-2	2-0	Malley 15, Devine (2) 44, 89	75, 82
	2	Dec	7	a	Rotherham U	L	1-4	0-1	Parker 47	35, 78, 85, 89

Final, Liverpool 3-1 Everton, at Wembley.

League Cup

					Opponents	Result		h/t	Goalscorers/times	Opp. goal times
	1	Aug	20	h	BURY	W	2-1	1-1	Taylor 10, Biggins 82	13
agg 5-6		Sep	3	a	Bury	L	3-5	2-2	Taylor (2) 25, 85, Hird 40	20, 34, 46, 62, 90

Final, Oxford U 3-0 Queens Park R, at Wembley.

Details of other first team games elsewhere.

Att.	Pos	Neenan	Palmer	Hampton	Heggarty	V Overson	Deakin	Hird	Malley	A Taylor	Biggins	Grewcock	Chippendale	Devine	Peacock	Rhodes	A Robinson	Parker	Heesom	Hoskin	Harrington	Edwards	Lawrence	Kilner	Haddock	Holden		
4,279		1	2	3	4	5	6	7	8	9	10	11																1
3,909		1	2	3	6	5	11	4	8	9	10	7																2
3,995	14	1	2	3	6	5	11	4	8	9	10	7*	S*															3
1,744	9	1	2	3	6	5	11	4	8	9*	10	7		S*														4
3,175	7	1	2	3	6	5	11	4	8	9	10*		7	S*														5
3,411	8	1	2	3	6	5	11	4	8	9	10		7															6
5,585		1	2	3	6	5	11	4	8	9*	10		7	S*														7
4,241	8	1	2	3	6	5	11	4	8		10	7*	S*	9														8
3,700	8		2	3	6		5		8	9*	10	7	4	S*	1	11												9
3,424			2	3	6		5		8	S*	10	7	4*	9	1	11												10
2,974	12		2	3	6		5	4	8	9	10		7*	S*	1	11												11
3,022	14			3	5		6	4*	2	9	10			11	1	S*	7	8										12
1,998	17			2	6		5	4	10*	9		S*		11	1		7	8	3									13
2,295				2	5		6	4	8	9				11	1		7	10	3									14
2,334	16			2	5		6	4*	8	9		S*		11	1		7	10	3									15
2,673	18				5*		6	2	8	9		4		11	1		7	10	3	S*								16
2,020				2	5		6	4*	8	9		7		11				10	3	S*	1							17
1,917	12				5		6	2	8	9		7		4				10	3	11*	1	S*						18
2,893	11	1			5		6	2	8	9*		7		4				10	3	11			S*					19
2,001	13	1			5		6	2	8	9		7		4				10	3	11								20
3,007	10	1		S*		5	6	2	8	9		7		4				10	3	11*								21
3,472		1		11		5	6	2	8	9		7		4				10	3									22
3,188	12	1		11*	4	5	6	2	8	9		7						10	3				S*					23
4,106	11	1			4	5	6	2	8	9		7		11*				10	3					S*				24
2,619		1			4	5	6	2		9		7		8				10	3					11				25
3,095	11	1		4		5	6	2		9		7		8				10*	3				S*	11				26
3,936	8	1		11		5	6	2	4	9		7		8					3				10					27
3,359	9	1		11		5	6	2	4	9		7		8					3*				10	S*				28
1,335	12	1		11		5	6	2	4	9*		7		8					3				10	S*				29
3,030		1		11		5	6	2	4	9		7		8					3				10					30
2,676	10	1		11		5	6	2	4	9		7		8					3				10					31
3,742	9	1		11	S*	5	6	2	4	9		7		8*					3				10					32
2,675		1		11	S*	5	6	2	4	9		7		8*					3				10					33
7,311	10	1		3	6	5	8	2	4	9		7								11			10					34
2,406		1		3	6	5	8	2	4*	9				7					S*	11			10					35
3,326	12	1		3	6	5	8	2	4	9*		7		S*						11			10					36
2,057	11	1		3			6	2	4	9		7		8						11			10		5			37
3,132	9	1		3			6	2*	4	9		7		8					S*	11			10		5			38
3,678	10	1		2	4		6			9		7		8					3	11			10		5			39
2,796	11	1		2	S*		6		4	9		7		8					3*	11			10		5			40
1,988	13	1		3	2	6	8		4	9				7*				10		11			S*		5			41
2,019	13	1		3	2	6	8		4	9		7						10		11					5			42
3,835		1		3	2	6	8		4	9		7						10		11					5			43
2,542	14	1		3	6	5*	8	2	4	9		7						10		11			S*					44
1,955	15	1		3	5		6	2	4	9		7		8						11*			10			S*		45
2,726		1		3	5		6	2	4	9		7		8						11			10					46
Appearances		36	11	39	33	28	46	39	43	44	12	36	6	31	8	3	5	19	23	17	2		16	2	7			
Apps as sub				1	3					1		2	2	6		1			2	2		1	5	3		1		
Goals (60)				1	1		3	7	2	16	4	7		2			1	5	1	2			6				2	ogs

Att.	Pos	Neenan	Palmer	Hampton	Heggarty	V Overson	Deakin	Hird	Malley	A Taylor	Biggins	Grewcock	Chippendale	Devine	Peacock	Rhodes	A Robinson	Parker	Heesom	Hoskin	Harrington	Edwards	Lawrence	Kilner	Haddock	Holden	
4,500		1			5		6	2	8	9		7		4				10	3	11							1
4,264		1	2		5		6	4	8	9		7						10	3	11							2
Appearances		2	1		2		2	2	2	2		2		1				2	2	2							
Apps as sub																											
Goals (4)									1					2				1									

Att.	Pos	Neenan	Palmer	Hampton	Heggarty	V Overson	Deakin	Hird	Malley	A Taylor	Biggins	Grewcock	Chippendale	Devine	Peacock	Rhodes	A Robinson	Parker	Heesom	Hoskin	Harrington	Edwards	Lawrence	Kilner	Haddock	Holden	
3,303		1	2	3	6	5	11	4	8	9	10	7															1
3,762		1	2	3	6	5	11	4	8	9	10*	7		S*													2nd leg
Appearances		2	2	2	2	2	2	2	2	2	2	2															
Apps as sub														1													
Goals (4)								1		3	1																

1986-87

OBITUARY
REGINALD FREDERICK (REG) ATTWELL
DIED 1 DECEMBER 1986, AGED 66.

Reg Attwell first made his mark for Burnley as a wartime guest player. Unable to gain a regular place at West Ham, he was signed by Cliff Britton in October 1946 and went on to provide notable service to the Clarets in the early post-war period.
The son of a footballer, he became an indispensable member of the side that re-established Burnley as a force in the First Division. A class act at wing-half, he was arguably the most skilful footballer in that fine side that achieved promotion and reached the Cup final in 1947, a superb passer of the ball who always seemed to have time to think. There were certainly many who believed he deserved an England call-up, but he had to be satisfied with just one appearance for the Football League, in 1949.
Attwell remained in the first team picture longer than most of his immediate post-war colleagues, making his final appearance in September 1954. As with many from that 1947 side, his post-Burnley career was brief, little more than half a season at Bradford City before he retired, and, again like so many of them, returned to live in the town.

RIP

Miracles do happen.
At least that's what Burnley fans were left believing after the worst season in the club's history ended in the most dramatic circumstances imaginable.
All seemed lost as the Clarets, now under the leadership of Brian Miller for the second time following manager Tommy Cavanagh's summer resignation through ill health, entered the final week of the campaign with their fate out of their hands.
The history books now show that the Clarets survived and went on to rebuild and recover. But scratch beneath the surface and what is revealed is the almost fictional tale of an unforgettable, never-to-be-forgotten ten months in the history of Burnley Football Club.
Prodigal son Leighton James, 33, returned in the summer for a third spell with the Clarets who, under the management of Miller, resorted back to the tried and tested method of employing those with a close affinity to the club.
Former Chelsea and Blackpool midfielder Ian Britton followed – initially on loan – and would soon earn his own place in Clarets' folklore.
One defeat in the opening seven league games offered not the merest hint of the unfolding drama.
But all too soon the realisation grew that Burnley were locked into a devastating downward spiral with an unimaginable ending.
Five losses in six subsequent games were as painful as they were unexpected and, from fifth place, the Clarets' season imploded.
Cash-strapped Miller's struggle to improve the quality of his squad left little room for manoeuvre and despite a mini-revival in early November, the seeds were already sown.
Between the end of that month and early March, just one victory in 15 matches sent the Clarets plummeting down the fourth division.
A demoralising 0-6 home defeat to Hereford United established another record low post-war attendance for a Burnley home match in the Football League.
Away from the supposed sanctuary of Turf Moor, things arguably got worse. Eight straight defeats highlighted an alarming lack of resilience and among them, a humiliating 0-3 FA Cup first round defeat at Conference side Telford was a massive blow, both to financial hopes and, crucially, morale.
Contrasting results at Christmas – a 4-0 thrashing of Crewe immediately offset by a 0-3 home defeat to Rochdale - showed consistency also was an all-too evident concern.
And by the time the club had slumped to four straight defeats in late April and early May, deepening the crisis, club stalwart Miller, a man with over 30 years of club service, openly declared: "This club is now facing the most important month of its history."
The month gradually became weeks and weeks dragged into endless days until, on 9 May 1987, just 90 minutes was all that separated Burnley FC from footballing oblivion.
The countdown to the Orient game, so often overlooked, is worthy of note itself.

Ray Deakin
a date with destiny

Following those damaging four defeats, the Clarets answered their manager's rallying call and a last gasp Leighton James penalty salvaged a point from the home game with Torquay.
Despite shocking home form, that took Burnley two points clear of rock bottom Rochdale – the next opponents at Spotland.
A 2-0 victory ignited wild celebrations and widened the gap, while one more valuable point in the subsequent game at home to Wrexham took the Clarets five clear of the drop.
Defeats to Cardiff and Scunthorpe though piled on the pressure and, as relegation rivals fought their own fight and May dawned with Burnley sitting rock bottom of the Football League, one point adrift of both Rochdale and Torquay.
Just three games remained for a proud club to avoid the unthinkable and become the first league side ever to suffer automatic expulsion to the Conference.
Ninety nine years of history was slipping away before our very

eyes and even a gutsy recovery from a goal down to beat Southend 2-1 - in turn registering only the second Turf Moor success in 11 games - was soon forgotten as controversy and fury surrounded defeat at Crewe 48 hours later.
Another dreadful performance and a 0-1 defeat was overshadowed by the allegation that referee Ken Lupton blew for full time nearly three minutes early.
Clutching at any straw, Clarets' chairman Frank Teasdale launched an impassioned and immediate appeal for an investigation into the premature end to a game on which the club's very survival hinged.
But the appeal was predictably laughed out and so it came down to one nail-biting day in May 1987.
Burnley's grave situation was now clear.
The Clarets knew that even if they beat Orient their main rivals in distress, Lincoln and Torquay, both needed to drop points to ensure survival.
Orient, in contrast, were acutely aware that three points would catapult them into play off contention.
The scene was set for the most dramatic act in the history of Burnley Football Club.
National newspaper journalists came from far and wide to write the epitaph of a club they had followed into Europe only two decades earlier.
Messages and well-wishes poured into the club from almost every other league ground.
Supporters answered the call to arms in huge numbers to flood to Turf Moor in one last show of united support.
The players responded.
After a 15-minute delay due to crowd congestion and, in electric surroundings, Burnley set about their mammoth task.
It took until first half stoppage time for Turf Moor to erupt, as Neil Grewcock cut in from the right flank and crucially found the bottom corner from 20 yards.
Three minutes into the second half, with positive news flooding in from elsewhere, Ian Britton – the smallest player on the pitch – somehow rose highest to head home Grewcock's right wing free kick to double the lead.
Orient responded with a 56th minute goal that sent nerves jangling again and as Frank Clark's side laid siege to the Burnley goal, the fight for survival became even more intense.
Torture ensued until referee George Courtney finally blew for time to signal mass hysteria.
The 'great escape' had been achieved and Lincoln City slipped through the trap door instead.
Yet all the tears being shed inside Turf Moor were of pure relief.
The Sunday Times proclaimed: "It was not morbid curiosity that brought everyone to Turf Moor. It was the dilemma of either seeing a dramatic, last-gasp escape from oblivion or paying last respects to a great club which 99 years ago had been a founder member of the Football League and which, in the 1960s had, with great class and culture, ruled as champions and taken on and beaten the finest in Europe."
It may not have been the same, but to almost 16,000 people, it certainly felt like it.
"This must never happen again," was the instant and oft-repeated mantra coming from all four sides of a rocking Turf Moor in the aftermath of an unforgettable day.
Miller, who willingly stepped into the breach when his club called, was confirmed as manager, with the club's scouting system hurriedly re-introduced.
A club statement, also urging fans to back various fund-raising schemes, concluded: "If a lesson is to be learned from last season, it is that the future must depend on the continued support of every fan.
"Let us never forget 9 May 1987."
Amen to that!

Ian Britton
carried shoulder high after the Great Escape

1986-87 - Fourth Division

		P	W	D	L	F	A	Pts
1	Northampton T	46	30	9	7	103	53	99
2	Preston NE	46	26	12	8	72	47	90
3	Southend U	46	25	5	16	68	55	80
4	Wolverhampton W	46	24	7	15	69	50	79
5	Colchester U	46	21	7	18	64	56	70
6	Aldershot	46	20	10	16	64	57	70
7	Orient	46	20	9	17	64	61	69
8	Scunthorpe U	46	18	12	16	73	57	66
9	Wrexham	46	15	20	11	70	51	65
10	Peterborough U	46	17	14	15	57	50	65
11	Cambridge U	46	17	11	18	60	62	62
12	Swansea C	46	17	11	18	56	61	62
13	Cardiff C	46	15	16	15	48	50	61
14	Exeter C	46	11	23	12	53	49	56
15	Halifax T	46	15	10	21	59	74	55
16	Hereford U	46	14	11	21	60	61	53
17	Crewe A	46	13	14	19	70	72	53
18	Hartlepool U	46	11	18	17	44	65	51
19	Stockport C	46	13	12	21	40	69	51
20	Tranmere R	46	11	17	18	54	72	50
21	Rochdale	46	11	17	18	54	73	50
22	BURNLEY	46	12	13	21	53	74	49
23	Torquay U	46	10	18	18	56	72	48
24	Lincoln C	46	12	12	22	45	65	48

1986-87

Manager : Brian Miller

Division Four (22nd)

		Date			Opponents	Result		h/t	Goalscorers/times	Opp. goal times
	1	Aug	23	a	Torquay U	D	1-1	0-0	Parker 80	86
	2		30	h	SCUNTHORPE U	W	1-0	1-0	James 25p	
	3	Sep	6	a	Hereford U	L	0-2	0-0		71, 82
	4		13	h	HARTLEPOOL U	D	1-1	0-0	Entwistle 71	69
	5		16	h	SWANSEA C	D	1-1	1-1	Entwistle 13	2
	6		20	a	Wolverhampton W	W	1-0	1-0	Grewcock 30	
	7		27	h	HALIFAX T	W	3-0	0-0	Parker (2) 47, 69, Hoskin 49	
	8		30	a	Tranmere R	L	1-2	0-0	Britton 75	54, 70
	9	Oct	4	h	PRESTON N E	L	1-4	0-2	James 88p	32, 39, 63, 77
	10		11	a	Aldershot	L	0-2	0-1		2, 81
	11		18	h	STOCKPORT C	W	2-0	1-0	Matthewson 19og, Regis 85	
	12		22	a	Northampton T	L	2-4	0-3	James 60, Hoskin 84	29, 37, 43, 61
	13		25	a	Exeter C	L	0-3	0-1		28, 54, 77
	14	Nov	1	h	PETERBOROUGH U	D	0-0	0-0		
	15		4	h	COLCHESTER U	W	2-1	2-0	Grewcock 29, Hoskin 43	84
	16		8	a	Cambridge U	L	1-3	0-1	James 62p	23, 46, 84
	17		22	h	LINCOLN C	W	3-1	2-1	James 11, Rodaway 43, Murphy 61	30
	18		28	a	Southend U	L	1-2	1-2	Gallagher 44	21, 35
	19	Dec	13	a	Orient	L	0-2	0-0		79, 89
	20		19	h	CARDIFF C	L	1-3	0-0	Hoskin 65	57, 58, 79
	21		26	a	Wrexham	D	2-2	0-0	Parker 64, Murphy 71	58, 80
	22		27	h	CREWE A	W	4-0	1-0	Murphy 16, Hoskin 47, James 67, Malley 76	
	23	Jan	1	h	ROCHDALE	L	0-3	0-1		37, 49, 60
	24		3	a	Lincoln C	L	1-2	1-1	Murphy 15	30, 67
	25		24	h	HEREFORD U	L	0-6	0-2		17,24,57,72,81,84
	26		31	a	Hartlepool U	D	2-2	2-0	Malley 10, Grewcock 40	78, 90
	27	Feb	6	a	Swansea C	D	2-2	1-1	Murphy 29, Hoskin 58	12, 86
	28		14	h	WOLVERHAMPTON W	L	2-5	2-1	James 15, Grewcock 22	9, 48, 50, 79, 81
	29		21	a	Halifax T	D	2-2	0-0	James 62, Grewcock 81	61, 64
	30		28	h	TRANMERE R	D	2-2	2-0	Grewcock 33, Rodaway 40	50, 81
	31	Mar	4	a	Peterborough U	D	1-1	0-1	Grewcock 60	30
	32		7	h	EXETER C	D	0-0	0-0		
	33		13	a	Stockport C	W	1-0	1-0	Hoskin 16	
	34		17	h	NORTHAMPTON T	W	2-1	1-1	Hoskin 39, Gallagher 70	16
	35		21	h	ALDERSHOT	L	0-1	0-0		54
	36		28	a	Preston N E	L	1-2	0-0	Parker 75	55, 58
	37	Apr	4	h	CAMBRIDGE U	L	0-2	0-1		5, 81
	38		10	a	Colchester U	L	0-1	0-1		29
Parker's last game	39		14	h	TORQUAY U	D	2-2	0-1	Britton 63, James 90p	14, 50
	40		18	a	Rochdale	W	2-0	1-0	Devaney 13, Gallagher 53	
	41		20	h	WREXHAM	D	0-0	0-0		
	42		25	a	Cardiff C	L	0-1	0-0		64
	43		28	a	Scunthorpe U	L	1-2	1-0	Malley 4	47, 49
	44	May	2	h	SOUTHEND U	W	2-1	1-1	James 29, Grewcock 50	19
	45		4	a	Crewe A	L	0-1	0-1		5
last games for Rodaway, Neenan, Hampton & Gallagher	46		9	h	ORIENT	W	2-1	1-0	Grewcock 45, Britton 48	56

FA Cup

	1	Nov	15	a	Telford U	L	0-3	0-2		19, 33, 50

Final, Coventry C 3-2 Tottenham H, at Wembley.

League Cup

	1	Aug	26	a	Rochdale	D	1-1	1-0	James 12	75
agg 2-4		Sep	2	h	ROCHDALE	L	1-3	0-1	James 70p	31, 51, 76

Final, Arsenal 2-1 Liverpool, at Wembley.

Details of other first team games elsewhere.

Att.	Pos	Neenan	Malley	Hampton	Rodaway	Gallagher	Deakin	Britton	Parker	Entwistle	James	Hoskin	Grewcock	Kennedy	Regis	Leebrook	Heesom	Harris	Murphy	Woodworth	Caughey	Devaney	Hardy		
2,144		1	2	3	4	5	6	7	8	9	10	11													1
3,008	5	1	2	3	4	5	6	7	8		10	11	9												2
2,796	13	1	2	3	4	5	6	7*	8	S*	10	11	9												3
2,465	11	1	2*	3	4	5	6	8	9	S*	10	11	7												4
2,775		1		3	2	5	6	4	8	9	10	11	7												5
5,786	9	1		3	2	5	6	4	8	9	10	11	7												6
3,296	5	1		3	2	5	6	4	8	9	10	11	7												7
2,017		1		3	2	5	6	4	8	9	10	11	7												8
5,974	11	1		3	2	5	6	4	8	9	10	11	7												9
2,061	16	1	2	3	4	5	6	8	9		10	11	7												10
2,410	12	1	2*	3	4	5	6	7			10	11	9	8	S*										11
5,718		1		3	2	5	6	8	9		10	11	7	4											12
3,198	17	1		3	4	5	6	7	8		10	11	9	2											13
2,229	19	1	2	3	4	5	6	7			10	11	9		8										14
1,696		1	2	3	4	5	6	7			10	11	9		8										15
2,572	15	1	2	3	4	5	6	7			10	11	9		8										16
2,177	13	1			4	5	6				10	11	9			2	3	7	8						17
3,309		1			4	5	6				10	11	7			2	3	8	9						18
2,413	19	1			4	5	6				10	11	9			2	3	7	8						19
1,717		1			4	5	6	7			10	11				2	3	8	9						20
4,568	19	1			4	5	6	7	8		10	11				2	3		9						21
2,560	16	1	5		4		6	7	8		10	11				2	3		9						22
4,217	17	1	5		4		6	7	8		10	11				2	3		9						23
2,343	19	1	5		4		6		8		10	11	7			2	3		9						24
1,961	21		5		4		6	S*	8		10	11	7			2	3		9*	1					25
1,506	21	1	5		4		6		8		10	11	7			2	3		9						26
6,015		1	5			4	6	S*	8		10*	11	7			2	3		9						27
2,947	21	1	5			4	6		8		10	11	7			2	3		9						28
1,735	21	1			5	4	6	8			10	11	7			2	3				9				29
2,394	21	1	11	3	4	5	6	8			10		7			2					9				30
4,304		1	11	3	4	5	6	8			10		7			2					9				31
1,792	21	1	11	3	4	5	6	8			10		7			2			S*		9*				32
2,500		1	8	3	4	5	6	11				10	7			2					9				33
2,691		1	11	3	4	5	6	8				10	7			2					9				34
2,690	20	1	8	3*	4	5	6	10				11				2					9	7	S*		35
10,716	20	1	8	3	4*	5	6	10	7			11				2			S*		9				36
1,874	21	1	8	3	4	5	6	7	9*		10	11				2			S*						37
2,635	23	1	8	3	4	5	6	10	9		11	S*	7*			2									38
2,718		1	8	3	4	5	6	7	9*		10	11				2						S*			39
5,739	22	1	8	3	4	5	6	10			9	11				2						7			40
4,090	22	1	8	3	4	5	6	9*			10	11	S*			2						7			41
2,003	22	1	8	3	4	5	6	9*			10	S*	11			2						7			42
1,770		1	8	3	4	5	6				9	11	7			2						10			43
3,991	23	1	8	3	4	5	6	11			10		7			2						9			44
4,175	24	1	8	3	4	5	6	11			9		7			2						10			45
15,696	22	1	8	3	4	5	6	11			9		7			2						10			46
Appearances		45	33	33	44	41	46	37	24	6	42	38	35	3	3	30	13	4	12	1	8	8			
Apps as sub								2		2		2	1		1				3			1	1		
Goals (53)			3		2	3		3	5	2	10	8	9		1				5			1		1	og

Att.	Neenan	Malley	Hampton	Rodaway	Gallagher	Deakin	Britton	Parker	Entwistle	James	Hoskin	Grewcock	Kennedy	Regis	Leebrook	Heesom	
4,145	1	2	3**	4	5	6	7*	9		10	11	8		S*		S**	1
Appearances	1	1	1	1	1	1	1	1		1	1	1					
Apps as sub														1		1	
Goals (0)																	

Att.	Neenan	Malley	Hampton	Rodaway	Gallagher	Deakin	Britton	Parker	Entwistle	James	Hoskin	Grewcock	
1,937	1	2	3	4	5	6	7	8	9	10	11		1
2,605	1	2	3	4	5	6	7*	8	S*	10	11	9	2nd leg
Appearances	2	2	2	2	2	2	2	2	1	2	2	1	
Apps as sub									1				
Goals (2)										2			

1987-88

OBITUARY
(FREDERICK) PETER KIPPAX
DIED 21 SEPTEMBER 1987, AGED 65.

Peter Kippax's League career at Turf Moor was very brief, but he left an indelible impression as the regular left-winger in the side that won promotion in 1946-47 and was ever-present in the Cup run that year that ended at Wembley.

Burnley-born Kippax numbered football as just one of many sporting activities at which he excelled. He was also a successful businessman, and remained an amateur throughout his football career. Even though football was arguably not his main sporting interest, he was good enough to win three caps for the Great Britain side at the 1948 Olympics, held in London.

The 1947 Cup final should have marked the peak of his Turf Moor career, but he was taken ill the day before and played well below his best. His League career at the club, which he had joined in 1940, was already almost over, and he seldom featured the following season, eventually being transferred to Liverpool early in 1949.

He continued to be a mainstay of Burnley's Lancashire League cricket side for many years after the end of his football career, and retired, still relatively young, to St. Annes, which was where he died.

RIP

Who would have believed that just 12 months after stepping back from the abyss, Burnley would celebrate the anniversary of their survival with a walk down Wembley Way?

Yet that was the Clarets handsome 'reward' for a season where the often ridiculed Sherpa Van Trophy, a competition designed to offer lower league sides one shot at glory, overshadowed a thankfully less traumatic league season.

There had been much speculation what might have happened in the summer of 1987 if the fairy tale had had a much different ending.

Those rumours have carried weight for 20 years, with many of today's supporters still believing their club would have folded after 99 years but for salvation of 'The Orient Game'.

Fans in 1987 certainly had plenty of optimism. Incredibly, season tickets actually rose in anticipation of a Lazarus-style recovery.

The biggest summer clear-out of the professional playing staff since World War Two, with only seven players retained, must have helped as Brian Miller cleared out the dead wood.

Leighton James, one of the biggest casualties announced in the wake of a nightmare campaign, later took up the role of youth coach as the club sought to build new foundations.

Goalkeeper Chris Pearce and outfield players George Oghani, Paul Comstive, Peter Daniel, Andy Farrell and Steve Taylor were among the nine replacements – all signed for less than £20,000!

And Manx Cup victory over bitter rivals Blackburn Rovers, where Ian Britton added to his historic strike against Orient months earlier with another 'celebrated' winner, was the perfect curtain raiser to the new season.

The balloon was well and truly burst with an opening day 0-3 home defeat to Colchester, but lift-off came a week later at Newport as Oghani opened his account in a debut season that would see the striker harvest 19 goals.

On-fire Oghani, who scored three times in the opening five league games, also netted early goals against Wrexham and First Division Norwich in the Littlewoods Cup, where the Canaries eventually edged past the Clarets 2-1 on aggregate in round two.

At this time, the announcement of the preliminary draw for the Sherpa Van Trophy was little more than a space filler in the local newspapers.

News of group games against Tranmere Rovers and Rochdale hardly drove Clarets' fans wild with excitement.

Instead, a hat-trick of Division Four victories, all won 1-0, had them deliriously dreaming of a much bigger route to glory - promotion.

The Clarets even went top of the table after beating Tranmere away, completing the treble with a home win over Wrexham.

Gates had almost trebled from the previous season and optimism was high that this could be the start of a new era.

But as any Burnley fan can testify, false dawns have been aplenty and the wheels immediately fell off with three straight defeats and one goal scored in four miserable games ahead of October.

Crucially, ahead of the Sherpa Van group games, a five-game unbeaten league run that coincided with Steve Davis arriving from Crewe – initially on loan - restored damaged confidence and lifted Miller's men back up to third.

It provided the platform for a tournament where Burnley kicked off at Tranmere watched by just 1,800 fans.

Seven months later, the Clarets could walk tall at Wembley Stadium in front of over 80,000. Remarkable.

Goals from Oghani and Neil Grewcock saw off Rovers to guarantee progress from the preliminary stage to the last 16, sealed in style with a 3-2 win against Rochdale in late November.

Chris Pearce
hugely popular keeper, ever present in his first season

By now, another disappointing run of league form had been ended with the first win in a month over Lancashire rivals Bolton, following an FA Cup first round defeat to Wanderers a week earlier that was overshadowed by riots before and after the Turf Moor game.

A 0-5 thrashing at Peterborough followed and December brought equally fluctuating fortunes and an incredible 17 goals in three games.

When the dust finally settled on a draining four games in eight days Burnley began the New Year and the second half of the campaign in a disappointing 14th place.

But it wasn't all bad news.

The club's annual report trumpeted the healthiest financial position of the decade, with losses being slashed by over £100,000 to a manageable £40,000.

Third Division Chester were soon defeated 1-0 in the Sherpa Van Trophy, earning a meeting with Bury in round two.

By the time that Gigg Lane game came around, the roller-coaster campaign was back on again as Burnley rose to eighth in the league.

And a merited victory just down the M66, courtesy of Comstive's clinical penalty that secured a Northern area semi-final, started rumblings of success on two fronts.

Aiming to capitalise on the feel-good factor that February brought, the Clarets board announced a radical fund-raiser aimed at boosting Brian Miller's transfer kitty.

Every Clarets' fan was offered the chance to pay double the admission price for home games against Scarborough and Exeter.

The optional increase, from £2.50 to £5 was to be treated as a donation and 7,841 fans responded for the first of those games, which typically saw bang in-form Burnley, by now up to fifth, stumble to a first home defeat since September!

Undeterred, steely back-to-back wins maintained the promotion push and the Clarets were up to fourth when they hosted Halifax in the Sherpa Van Trophy northern semi-final.

After 120 goalless minutes in front of over 10,000 supporters, it all came down to spot kicks and Ray Deakin, Ashley Hoskin, Ian Britton, Oghani and the reliable Comstive all found the net to earn Burnley a dramatic shoot-out success and a two-legged Northern final clash with Preston.

As so often happens when cup success beckons, the league form suffers and any lingering hopes Miller had of steering Burnley to a two pronged assault on honours fell flat following four losses in five games leading up to April's showdown with North End.

With five of their last eight games at Turf Moor, sixth-placed Burnley still should have been ideally placed to overhaul their Fourth Division play-off rivals.

But Easter brought a painful 0-3 reversal at home to runaway leaders Wolves – an ominous sign of things to come – and defeat at Bolton 48 hours later was another fatal blow.

Round one against North End left visiting fans heading back to Deepdale dreaming of the Twin Towers.

The Lilywhites side earned a 0-0 draw at Turf Moor and many thought the hard work was done with a draw away to a lower league side.

But as Miller pointed out: "We have now played three Third Division sides in this competition and we haven't conceded a goal against any of them."

What was now needed was a performance to back up those words. And on Preston's controversial artificial pitch a week later, Burnley delivered.

Oghani struck first before Brazil sent a pulsating game into extra time with a second half equaliser.

Three minutes into the first period, Hoskin scored at the second attempt and as firm favourites North End became increasingly desperate, Comstive wrapped things up three minutes from the end.

For Burnley fans, it was unconfined joy.

For Miller it was payback time.

In 1962, this intensely loyal one-club man proudly walked out as a member of the Burnley FA Cup final side to face the mighty Spurs.

As a Burney manager Miller had later been sacrificed at the alter of a wild, impossible dream that in the mid 1980s an 'outside' manager was right for the Clarets. In 1987 he was called back to sort out what he described as a "shambles".

Now the wheel had come full circle and 25 years later Mr Burnley would be walking his team out at Wembley.

Back in Division Four, in a tight play-off battle, the Clarets crumbled.

Echoing previous occasions, cup highs were followed by league misery and three games without a victory sent Burnley to 13th, their lowest league placing of the year and out of contention.

An emotionally-charged campaign of over 60 matches had finally taken its toll and amid chaotic scenes and two pitch invasions, Cardiff's final day 2-1 victory at Turf Moor proved meaningless as results elsewhere condemned the Clarets to another season in the basement league.

All that remained was the 'celebration' of Wembley in front of what remains a record attendance between two Fourth Division teams.

And in the Football League's Centenary year, it was perhaps fitting that two founder members reached the final.

Alas, it was Wolves who took the trophy to seal a league and cup double, following a hard-fought 2-0 victory.

But this was about so much more than the result for the supporters who made the exodus south from Turf Moor.

It was all about the re-birth of a club on its death bed just 12 months earlier.

Suddenly, Clarets fans' could smile again.

1987-88 - Fourth Division

		P	W	D	L	F	A	Pts
1	Wolverhampton W	46	27	9	10	82	43	90
2	Cardiff C	46	24	13	9	66	41	85
3	Bolton W	46	22	12	12	66	42	78
4	Scunthorpe U	46	20	17	9	76	51	77
5	Torquay U	46	21	14	11	66	41	77
6	Swansea C	46	20	10	16	62	56	70
7	Peterborough U	46	20	10	16	52	53	70
8	Leyton O	46	19	12	15	85	63	69
9	Colchester U	46	19	10	17	47	51	67
10	BURNLEY	46	20	7	19	57	62	67
11	Wrexham	46	20	6	20	69	58	66
12	Scarborough	46	17	14	15	56	48	65
13	Darlington	46	18	11	17	71	69	65
14	Tranmere R	46	19	9	18	61	53	64
15	Cambridge U	46	16	13	17	50	52	61
16	Hartlepool U	46	15	14	17	50	57	59
17	Crewe A	46	13	19	14	57	53	58
18	Halifax T	46	14	14	18	54	59	55
19	Hereford U	46	14	12	20	41	59	54
20	Stockport C	46	12	15	19	44	58	51
21	Rochdale	46	11	15	20	47	76	48
22	Exeter C	46	11	13	22	53	68	46
23	Carlisle U	46	12	8	26	57	86	44
24	Newport C	46	6	7	33	35	105	25

*** - Tranmere Rovers deducted 2 points for failing to fulfil fixture**
*** - Halifax Town deducted 1 point for fielding an ineligible player**

1987-88

Manager : Brian Miller

Division Four (10th)

Note		Date			Opponents	Result		h/t	Goalscorers/times	Opp. goal times
	1	Aug	15	h	COLCHESTER U	L	0-3	0-2		24, 31, 75
	2		22	a	Newport C	W	1-0	0-0	Oghani 65	
	3		29	h	CARLISLE U	W	4-3	3-1	Zelem 3, Oghani 5, Deakin 30, Taylor 75	23, 64, 84
	4	Sep	1	a	Leyton O	L	1-4	0-1	Farrell 80	25, 48, 74, 78
	5		5	h	SWANSEA C	W	1-0	0-0	Oghani 90	
	6		11	a	Tranmere R	W	1-0	0-0	Comstive 90	
	7		15	h	WREXHAM	W	1-0	0-0	Farrell 75	
	8		19	h	CAMBRIDGE U	L	0-2	0-2		9, 39
	9		26	a	Rochdale	L	1-2	0-1	Oghani 60	13, 69
	10		29	h	CREWE A	D	0-0	0-0		
	11	Oct	3	a	Scarborough	L	0-1	0-1		42
	12		10	h	HARTLEPOOL U	W	1-0	0-0	Comstive 52	
	13		17	a	Exeter C	W	2-1	1-1	Oghani (2) 22p, 54	9
	14		20	h	SCUNTHORPE U	D	1-1	0-0	Taylor 57	88
	15		24	a	Torquay U	W	3-1	1-0	Britton 36, Comstive 54, Taylor 76	90
	16		31	h	STOCKPORT C	D	1-1	1-1	Davis 43	16
	17	Nov	3	a	Halifax T	L	1-2	1-1	Taylor 22	11, 80
	18		7	a	Wolverhampton W	L	0-3	0-0		73, 78, 87
	19		21	h	BOLTON W	W	2-1	0-0	Britton 53, Reeves 68	70
	20		28	a	Peterborough U	L	0-5	0-3		6, 28, 43, 74, 81
	21	Dec	12	h	HEREFORD U	D	0-0	0-0		
	22		19	a	Cardiff C	L	1-2	0-0	Davis 47	79, 81
	23		26	h	ROCHDALE	W	4-0	3-0	Oghani 10, Farrell 43, Comstive 44, Britton 67	
Burnley's 3500th League game	24		28	a	Darlington	L	2-4	1-1	Reeves (2) 3, 59	44, 54, 70, 81
	25	Jan	1	a	Carlisle U	W	4-3	2-2	Oghani 18, Wright 45og, Deakin 51, Davis 59	11, 22, 58
	26		2	h	TRANMERE R	D	1-1	0-1	Comstive 88	34
	27		9	h	NEWPORT C	W	2-0	0-0	Reeves 51, Comstive 87	
	28		16	a	Cambridge U	L	0-2	0-0		57, 58
	29	Feb	2	a	Wrexham	W	3-1	0-0	Bowden 67og, Hoskin 78, Oghani 90	65
	30		6	a	Swansea C	D	0-0	0-0		
	31		13	h	DARLINGTON	W	2-1	1-0	Reeves (2) 13, 89	88
	32		19	a	Colchester U	W	1-0	1-0	Reeves 32	
	33		27	h	SCARBOROUGH	L	0-1	0-0		84
	34	Mar	1	a	Crewe A	W	1-0	0-0	Gage 88og	
	35		5	h	EXETER C	W	3-0	1-0	Davis 35, Reeves 57, Taylor 74	
	36		12	a	Hartlepool U	L	1-2	0-2	Oghani 64	18, 22
	37		18	a	Stockport C	L	0-2	0-1		30, 63
	38		22	h	LEYTON O	W	2-0	1-0	Oghani (2) 14p, 63	
	39	Apr	2	h	WOLVERHAMPTON W	L	0-3	0-1		10, 61, 88
Leebrook's last game	40		4	a	Bolton W	L	1-2	1-1	Oghani 35	37, 46
	41		8	h	HALIFAX T	W	3-1	1-1	Davis 44, Comstive 58, Taylor 66	40
	42		23	a	Scunthorpe U	D	1-1	0-0	Britton 76	87
Malley's last game	43		30	h	PETERBOROUGH U	L	1-2	1-0	Comstive 29p	71, 76
	44	May	2	a	Hereford U	L	1-2	1-1	Deakin 7	34, 76
	45		4	h	TORQUAY U	W	1-0	1-0	McGrory 7	
	46		7	h	CARDIFF C	L	1-2	0-0	Oghani 84	72, 89

FA Cup

	Date			Opponents	Result		h/t	Goalscorers/times	Opp. goal times
1	Nov	14	h	BOLTON W	L	0-1	0-0		72p

Final, Wimbledon 1-0 Liverpool, at Wembley.

League Cup

Note		Date			Opponents	Result		h/t	Goalscorers/times	Opp. goal times
	1	Aug	18	a	Wrexham	L	0-1	0-0		63
agg 3-1			25	h	WREXHAM	W	3-0	0-0	Comstive 76, Oghani 80p, Farrell 89	
	2	Sep	22	h	NORWICH C	D	1-1	1-1	Oghani 7	15
agg 1-2		Oct	7	a	Norwich C	L	0-1	0-0		49

Final, Luton T 3-2 Arsenal, at Wembley.

Details of other first team games elsewhere.

Att.	Pos	Pearce	Leebrook	McGrory	Daniel	Zelem	Deakin	Grewcock	Farrell	Oghani	Comstive	Britton	Hoskin	Gardner	S Taylor	James	Malley	S Davis (1)	D Reeves	Devaney		
5,419		1	2	3**	4	5	6	7	8	9	10	11*	S*	S**								1
2,016	14	1	2		4	5	3	7	8	9	10			6	11							2
5,781	4	1	2		4	5	3	7	8	9	10			6	11							3
3,560		1	2		4	5	3	7	8	9	10*		S*	6	11							4
4,787	6	1	2		4	5	3	8	7	9	10			6	11							5
4,209	4	1	2		4		3	8	7	9	10			6	11	5						6
5,650		1	2		4		3	8	7	9	10			6	11	5						7
5,789	3	1	2		4		3	8	7	9	10			6	11	5						8
4,655	7	1	2*				3	8	7	9	10		S*	6	11	5	4					9
5,408		1	2**		S*		3*	8	7	9	10		S**	6	11	5	4					10
4,782	10	1	2					8	7	9	10		S*	6	11	3	4*	5				11
5,216	6	1	2	3				8	7	9	10			6	11	4		5				12
2,780	4	1		3	2			8	7	9	10			6	11	4		5				13
6,353		1		3	2			8	7	9	10			6	11	4		5				14
2,836	3	1		3*	2			8	7		10	9		6	11	4	S*	5				15
6,642	8	1			2	S**		8	7**	9	10	S*		6	11	4	3*	5				16
3,419		1			2			8	7	9	10			6	11	4	3	5				17
10,002	10	1			2		3	8	7*	9	10	S*		6	11	4		5				18
7,544	9	1				5	3	8	2		10	7		6	11			4	9			19
3,394	10	1				5*	3	8	2		10	7	S*	6	11			4	9			20
4,217	12	1			2		3	8	7	9*	10	S**		6	S*	4**		5	11			21
3,401	15	1	2				3		7	9	10	4	11	6				5	8			22
7,013	9	1	2				3	8	7**	9	10	4	S*	6	S**			5	11*			23
3,325	14	1	2				3	8	7	9*	10	4		6	S*			5	11			24
4,260	9	1	2				3	8	7	9	10	4		6				5	11			25
7,401	10	1	2			6	3	8	7	9**	10	4*	S*		S**			5	11			26
5,256	9	1	2*			6	3	8	7		10	4	S*		9			5	11			27
2,146	9	1					3	8	2		10	4	7	6	9			5	11			28
1,821		1		10	2		3		7	9		4	11	6	8			5				29
3,498	8	1			2		3		7	9*	10	4	11	6				5	8	S*		30
6,440	5	1			2		3	S*	7		10	4	11*	6	9			5	8			31
2,520		1			2*		3	S*	7		10	4	11	6	9			5	8			32
7,645	7	1		3	2			S*	7*	S**	10	4	11	6	9**	5			8			33
3,720		1		3	2			S*	7		10	4	11*	6	9	5			8			34
6,052	4	1			2		3	11	7		10	4		6	9			5	8			35
2,893	6	1	2	3			10		7	8		4	11		9	6		5				36
4,423		1		2			3		7	8*	10	4	11	6	9			5		S*		37
5,842		1	2				3		7	8	10	4	11	6	9			5				38
10,386	7	1	2*				3		7	8	10	4	11	6	9			5		S*		39
9,921	9	1	2				3		7	8	10	4		6	9	11		5				40
5,833		1		2			3		7	8	10	4	11	6	9			5				41
5,347	8	1		3	2		6			8	10	4	11		9		7	5				42
6,315	11	1		2			3		7*	8**	10	4	11	6	9		S**	5		S*		43
2,304	13	1		3	2		6		7	8	10	11		4	9			5				44
5,075		1		11	2		3		7	8	10	4		6	9			5				45
8,421	10	1		11	2		3		7	8	10	4		6	9	5						46
Appearances		46	22	16	26	9	37	28	45	36	44	29	15	41	38	19	6	33	16			
Apps as sub					1	1		4		1		3	9	1	4		2			4		
Goals (57)				1		1	3		3	14	8	4	1		6			5	8		3	ogs

Att.	Pearce	Leebrook	McGrory	Daniel	Zelem	Deakin	Grewcock	Farrell	Oghani	Comstive	Britton	Hoskin	Gardner	S Taylor	James	Malley	S Davis (1)	D Reeves	Devaney	
10,788	1			2*	5	3	8	7	9**	10	S*	S**	6	11	4					1
Appearances	1			1	1	1	1	1	1	1			1	1	1					
Apps as sub											1	1								
Goals (0)																				

Att.	Pearce	Leebrook	McGrory	Daniel	Zelem	Deakin	Grewcock	Farrell	Oghani	Comstive	Britton	Hoskin	Gardner	S Taylor	James	Malley	S Davis (1)	D Reeves	Devaney	
2,301	1	2	3	4	5	6	7	8	9*	10	11	S*								1
3,788	1	2		4	5	3	7	8	9	10			6	11						2nd leg
7,912	1	2				3	8	7	9	10			6	11	5	4				2
6,168	1	2	3				8	7	9	10			6	11	4		5			2nd leg
Appearances	4	4	2	2	2	3	4	4	4	4	1		3	3	2	1	1			
Apps as sub												1								
Goals (4)								1	2	1										

1988-89

OBITUARY
GEORGE SMITH WATERFIELD
DIED OCTOBER 1988, AGED 87.

George Waterfield made more League appearances for Burnley (371) in the period between the two world wars than any other player. He was an England international, but, having played just after the club's first golden age, is a relatively unsung hero today.
He joined Burnley from Mexborough Town in 1923 and started out as a left-winger, but it was his move to left-back during the 1924-25 season that saw him really established in the side. His partnership with Irish right-back Andy McCluggage went on to become as much a fixture in the Burnley line-up as the Angus-Elder full-back pairing of a later era. A consistency effective performer at a time when defences in general, and Burnley's more than most, were struggling to come to terms with the change in the offside law, he won his one international cap in February 1927 in a 3-3 draw against Wales at Wrexham.
By the time he left Turf Moor in the close season of 1935, he stood third in the table of Burnley appearances, behind only Jerry Dawson and Fred Barron. After just one season at Crystal Palace, he retired from League football in 1936.

RIP

Following two seasons at totally opposite ends of the spectrum, the Clarets lurched towards the end of the decade amid more upheaval and turmoil.
The managerial merry-go-round of several years ago had seemingly been ended with the return to Turf Moor of Brian Miller who, following a desperate plight in his first season back at the helm, took Burnley back to Wembley for the first time in a quarter of a century.
Football has little room for sentiment, however, and Miller would last just half of his third full season in charge before history repeated itself and Frank Casper replaced him in a year of transition.
The summer saw far less activity than the clear out 12 months earlier. Brendan O'Connell was the first new face as Miller looked to add firepower to the side that had narrowly missed out on the Fourth Division play offs.
Oldham midfielder Paul Atkinson soon followed the former Exeter striker on a free transfer, leading to some criticism from fans that cash raised in the previous campaign was not being spent where it was needed most.
Chairman Frank Teasdale immediately launched an impassioned defence and then, before the first ball had been kicked in anger, backed those words with actions by handing Miller a new two-year contract as rewards for his efforts the previous season.
There was a proviso though and Teasdale left no-one in doubt as to his own expectations for the season.
Riding the wave of the Clarets' trip to Wembley in May, he announced that the number one priority was promotion.
Having raised the bar, the players responded by flying out of the traps. Four goals from Paul Comstive and a lightening start from O'Connell contributed to three successive league victories over Rochdale, Halifax and the coup de grace, a 6-0 thrashing of York that emphatically confirmed the best winning start to a post-war season since 1966.
The 100% record, went at the fourth time of asking in a stalemate at Stockport, but after nine league games all the signs were good as table-topping Clarets registered six wins and lost just once, at Torquay.
Rochdale suffered again as the Clarets' two-legged victory earned a crack at Littlewoods Cup holders Luton Town in the second round.
And even the First Division side were caught up in Burnley's whirlwind start as Miller's men earned a fantastic draw on the plastic pitch to go into the second leg on level terms.
Supporters bought into the growing optimism and already Burnley's average home crowds were dwarfing all of their Fourth Division rivals.
Over 9,000 flocked to see league leaders Rotherham defeated 1-0 and when Exeter went the same way at Turf Moor four days later, a fifth successive home win propelled Burnley back to the top of the table.
October's bumper crowd of over 14,000 saw Luton dent that home record to end hopes of a cup run – a fluke goal proving just enough despite battling Burnley making a mockery of the three division gap between the two teams.
But few could have predicted the slump that would immediately set in to wreck another season and ultimately cost Miller his job.
Between that Littlewoods Cup exit on 11 October and New Year's Eve, pacesetters Burnley would win just one league game in 11 attempts.

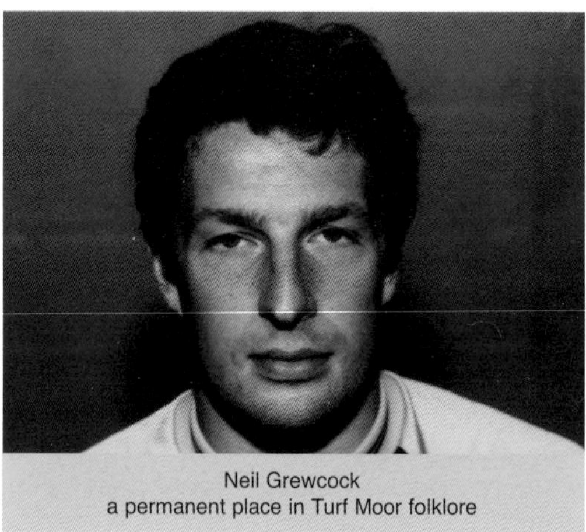

Neil Grewcock
a permanent place in Turf Moor folklore

Yet more misery came in the FA Cup first round defeat, 0-2 at home to Chester City.
There had been mitigating circumstances. Neil Grewcock had not featured for six months since two operations on a knee injured in March and skipper Ray Deakin was another notable absentee.
Yet despite the loss of such key players the squad had seemingly coped admirably. And the ensuing signings of winger Winston White and defender Ian Measham were seen as a welcome loosening of the purse strings that had been overflowing due to impressive crowds.
Indeed, the road to Wembley had paved the way for the club's

annual report to headline a healthy £210,000 annual profit – the first for over a decade.

But in a results orientated business, the cold hard facts were that Burnley's unforeseen slump threatened to kill, stone dead, the main aim of the season and it was therefore no surprise when Miller effectively ended his own reign in January 1989.

He said: "It is the right time for me, it is the right time for the club and it is the right time for the fans who, I believe wanted it this way."

Miller immediately accepted the role of chief scout while Teasdale, who weeks earlier had rebuked a "laughable" proposal by former Colne Dynamoes chief Graham White to takeover the football club, now had a more serious problem on his hands.

And in an eerie echo of yesteryear, Casper was the familiar face the club turned to in their hour of need.

Starting from 14th place following a disastrous few months Casper, who quit his job as assistant manager to Martin Dobson at Bury to come "home", insisted promotion was not yet out of the question.

But after the initial honeymoon period enjoyed by so many managers – three wins in four league games and a leap to eighth place reviving ill-placed hope – the marriage made in heaven quickly turned sour.

Another 11 game winless sequence came out of the blue and following an explosive goalscoring start to the campaign, led by triumvirate of Comstive, Oghani and O'Connell, the goals had now almost slowed to a trickle.

One win in 20 away games highlighted the slide as yet another season fizzled out in disappointment and a certain amount of anger on the terraces.

"Some of the players here are just not good enough and there is a lot of work to be done," was Casper's response to the growing criticism.

Burnley Express sportswriter Granville Shackleton went one better, insisting: "Unless I am reading it totally wrong, some players appear to think that Turf Moor is some sort of holiday camp, providing your credentials from the past are good."

That dig was aimed fairly and squarely at some of the more experienced players in the camp, who were now accused of shirking responsibility as what was once a promotion charge degenerated into an unthinkable second survival act in three seasons.

Colne Dynamoes' White even tried to ride the growing groundswell for change at the top, launching a blueprint for the club's future through the media after seeing a second takeover bid thrown out.

April dawned and finally, Burnley woke up to their shocking league predicament.

Sitting 18th with nine games remaining, and memories of the Orient game still fresh in everyone's memories, a long overdue first win in two months and four points from two home games eased the pressure.

However within days, yet another bombshell hit the club as ever-present goalkeeper Chris Pearce underwent surgery for a broken nose and fractured cheekbone following an alleged training ground bust-up that ended with striker Oghani being sacked following an internal enquiry.

Brendan O'Connell
top scorer in 1988-89

By now, everyone just wanted the season to end and Burnley were finally mathematically safe from the dreaded drop by early May, following successive victories over Doncaster and the first away win in eight months at Lincoln.

The last rites were delivered with a final day home defeat to Scarborough, leading to ugly scenes as fans invaded the pitch demanding changes at the top.

Inside and outside Turf Moor, chants of "Sack the Board" became the soundtrack to the season.

The frustrations of not only the past ten months, but the past few years, were evident in the demonstrations.

The supporters would take some placating and it all meant another tough summer for those in charge of restoring the club to former glories.

1988-89 - Fourth Division

		P	W	D	L	F	A	Pts
1	Rotherham U	46	22	16	8	76	35	82
2	Tranmere R	46	21	17	8	62	43	80
3	Crewe A	46	21	15	10	67	48	78
4	Scunthorpe U	46	21	14	11	77	57	77
5	Scarborough	46	21	14	11	67	52	77
6	Leyton O	46	21	12	13	86	50	75
7	Wrexham	46	19	14	13	77	63	71
8	Cambridge U	46	18	14	14	71	62	68
9	Grimsby T	46	17	15	14	65	59	66
10	Lincoln C	46	18	10	18	64	60	64
11	York C	46	17	13	16	62	63	64
12	Carlisle U	46	15	15	16	53	52	60
13	Exeter C	46	18	6	22	65	68	60
14	Torquay U	46	17	8	21	45	60	59
15	Hereford U	46	14	16	16	66	72	58
16	BURNLEY	46	14	13	19	52	61	55
17	Peterborough U	46	14	12	20	52	74	54
18	Rochdale	46	13	14	19	56	82	53
19	Hartlepool U	46	14	10	22	50	78	52
20	Stockport C	46	10	21	15	54	52	51
21	Halifax T	46	13	11	22	69	75	50
22	Colchester U	46	12	14	20	60	78	50
23	Doncaster R	46	13	10	23	49	78	49
24	Darlington	46	8	18	20	53	76	42

1988-89

Manager : Brian Miller until January 1989, then Frank Casper

Division Four (16th)

		Date			Opponents	Result		h/t	Goalscorers/times	Opp. goal times
	1	Aug	27	h	ROCHDALE	W	2-1	1-0	Comstive 15, Farrell 46	47
	2	Sep	3	a	Halifax T	W	2-1	1-0	Comstive 33, O'Connell 76	88
	3		10	h	YORK C	W	6-0	2-0	Atkinson 17, Britton 24, Comstive (2) 47p, 87, Oghani 56, O'Connell 70	
	4		16	a	Stockport C	D	0-0	0-0		
	5		20	a	Torquay U	L	0-2	0-1		27, 46
	6		24	h	COLCHESTER U	W	2-0	1-0	Rowell 43, O'Connell 53	
	7	Oct	1	a	Darlington	D	1-1	0-0	O'Connell 84	81
	8		4	h	ROTHERHAM U	W	1-0	0-0	Oghani 74	
	9		8	h	EXETER C	W	3-0	1-0	Oghani 32, Zelem 71, O'Connell 88	
	10		15	a	Peterborough U	L	0-3	0-1		9, 55, 76
	11		22	h	LEYTON O	D	2-2	0-1	Comstive 61p, O'Connell 70	9, 60
	12		25	a	Carlisle U	D	0-0	0-0		
	13		29	h	CAMBRIDGE U	W	2-0	1-0	Oghani 9, O'Connell 83	
Daniel's last game	14	Nov	5	a	Scunthorpe U	L	1-2	0-0	O'Connell 81	69, 72
	15		8	h	LINCOLN C	L	1-4	1-1	Comstive 30p	25, 46, 49, 83
	16		12	a	Scarborough	L	0-1	0-0		79
Morley's last game	17		26	a	Doncaster R	L	0-1	0-0		84
	18	Dec	3	h	HARTLEPOOL U	D	0-0	0-0		
	19		17	a	Hereford U	D	0-0	0-0		
	20		26	h	WREXHAM	L	1-3	1-1	O'Connell 39	14, 74, 87
	21		31	h	GRIMSBY T	W	1-0	0-0	Oghani 88	
Steve Taylor's last game	22	Jan	2	a	Tranmere R	L	1-2	0-1	Britton 79	9, 63
	23		14	h	HALIFAX T	W	2-1	1-0	Oghani (2) 9, 67	89
	24		21	a	Rochdale	L	1-2	1-0	Farrell 40	53, 58
	25		28	h	STOCKPORT C	W	1-0	0-0	Britton 64	
Hoskin's last game	26	Feb	4	h	TORQUAY U	W	1-0	0-0	O'Connell 79	
	27		10	a	Colchester U	D	2-2	2-0	White (2) 13, 15p	62, 75
	28		18	a	Exeter C	L	0-3	0-1		5, 65, 83
	29		25	h	PETERBOROUGH U	D	1-1	0-0	Measham 73	64
	30	Mar	4	a	Leyton O	L	0-3	0-0		68, 82, 88
David Miller's last game	31		11	h	SCUNTHORPE U	L	0-1	0-1		38
	32		14	a	Cambridge U	L	1-2	0-1	White 63	45, 81
	33		18	a	York C	D	0-0	0-0		
	34		21	h	CARLISLE U	D	0-0	0-0		
	35		25	h	TRANMERE R	D	2-2	0-1	Comstive (2) 56, 90	28, 63
	36		27	a	Wrexham	L	2-4	1-2	Grewcock 5, McGrory 68	37, 42, 50, 78
	37	Apr	1	h	HEREFORD U	D	3-3	1-1	James (2) 12p, 72p, Monington 85	2, 66, 82
Oghani's last game	38		4	h	CREWE A	W	1-0	1-0	Hardy 33	
	39		8	a	Grimsby T	L	0-1	0-0		78
	40		15	h	DARLINGTON	L	0-1	0-0		80
	41		22	a	Rotherham U	L	1-3	1-3	Farrell 31	32, 39, 44
	42		29	h	DONCASTER R	W	3-0	1-0	O'Connell (2) 7, 85, Comstive 88	
	43	May	1	a	Lincoln C	W	3-2	2-0	White (2) 26, 73, O'Connell 40	83, 89
	44		6	a	Hartlepool U	D	2-2	1-0	Farrell 8, James 75p	65, 86
Comstive's last game	45		9	a	Crewe A	L	0-4	0-1		14, 49, 62, 75
last games for James & Britton	46		13	h	SCARBOROUGH	L	0-1	0-0		60

FA Cup

				Opponents	Result		h/t	Goalscorers/times	Opp. goal times
1	Nov	19	h	CHESTER C	L	0-2	0-0		49, 71

Final, Liverpool 3-2 Everton after extra time, at Wembley.

League Cup

					Opponents	Result		h/t	Goalscorers/times	Opp. goal times
	1	Aug	30	a	Rochdale	D	3-3	1-1	O'Connell 19, Comstive 54p, Oghani 80	45, 68, 84
agg 5-4		Sep	6	h	ROCHDALE	W	2-1	1-0	O'Connell (2) 16, 53	60
	2		27	a	Luton T	D	1-1	1-1	Comstive 42p	38
agg 1-2		Oct	11	h	LUTON T	L	0-1	0-0		55

Final, Nottingham F 3-1 Luton T, at Wembley.

Details of other first team games elsewhere.

Att.	Pos	Pearce	Daniel	Deakin	Farrell	S Davis (1)	Gardner	Britton	Oghani	Rowell	Comstive	James	O'Connell	Atkinson	S Taylor	Zelem	White	McGrory	Hoskin	Morley	Measham	Miller	D Jones	Hardy	Monington	Grewcock	Williams	Hooper	
7,511		1	2	3	4	5	6	7	8	9*	10	11	S*																1
4,071	3	1	2	3	4	5	6	7	8		10		9	11															2
7,258	top	1	2	3	4	5	6	7	8		10		9	11															3
6,676		1	2	3	4	5	6	7	8		10		9	11															4
3,021		1	2	3	4	5	6	7	8		10		9	11															5
7,177	3	1	2	3*	4	5	6	7	8	S*	10		9	11															6
3,409	4	1	2		3	5	6	7	8	4	10		9	11*	S*														7
9,290		1	2		3		6	7	8	4	10		9	11		5													8
7,894	top	1	2		3		6	7	8	4	10		9	11		5													9
5,023	top	1	2		3		6	7	8	4	10		9	11		5													10
8,503	2	1	2		4	6	3	11*	8	S*	10		9			5	7												11
4,543		1	2		4	6			8	11*	10		9			5	7	3	S*										12
8,669	top	1	2		4		6		8		10		9			5	7	3		11									13
6,358	4	1	2		4		6		8		10		9			5	7	3		11									14
8,445		1			4	6	2*		8	S*	10		9			5	7	3		11									15
5,258	5	1			4	5	6		8		10		9				7	3		11	2								16
2,724	9	1			3	5	6	4	8*	S*	10		9	11**			S**			7	2								17
6,289	9	1			3	5	6	4	8*	S**	10		9	11**	S*		7				2								18
2,442	9	1			3	5	6	4	8		10		9	11			7				2								19
9,174	12	1			3	5	6	4	8		10		9	11*			7		S*		2								20
7,367	10	1			3	5	6	4	8		10		9				7	S*	11		2*								21
7,974	13	1			2	5	6	4	8		10		9		S*		7	3	11*										22
8,298	12	1			3	5	6	4	8		10*	11	9			S*	7				2								23
5,812	13	1			3	5	6	4	8		10	11*	9				7	S*			2								24
8,942	9	1			3	5	6	4	8		10	11	9				7				2								25
6,626	8	1			3	5	6	4	8		10	11*	9				7**	S**	S*		2								26
3,831		1		11	3*	5	6	4	8	S*	10		9				7				2								27
3,672	10	1		11	S**	5		4	8	S*	10*		9				7	3**			2	6							28
6,853	9	1		11		5	3	4	8	10*		S*	9				7				2	6							29
3,944	11	1			3	5	10	4	8**	S*		11					7*				2	6	9	S**					30
6,813	14	1			7	5	6	4	8			11		S**			S*				2	10*	9**	3					31
2,555		1				5	6	4	8**	S**	10*	S*	9				7				2			3	11				32
3,164	18	1				5	6	4	8		10		9				7*				2			3	11	S*			33
5,283		1					6	4	8*	S*	10		9				7				2			3	5	11			34
6,839	15	1					6	4	8		10		9				7				2			3	5	11			35
3,956	17	1					6	4*		8	10	S**	9				7**	S*			2			3	5	11			36
5,534	18	1					6**	4	8		10*	11	9				S**	S*			2			3	5	7			37
5,677		1				5	6	4	8			11	9					10			2			3		7			38
4,856	17					5	6	4				11	9				S*	10			2		8*	3		7	1		39
5,577	17					5	6	4				11*	9				S*	10			2		8**	3	S**	7	1		40
5,726	17				4	5	6	S*				11	9				8	10*			2			3		7**	1	S**	41
4,211	16			11	4	5	6				S*		9				8	10*			2			3		7	1		42
3,594	16			11	4	5	6				10		9				8				2			3		7	1		43
2,038	16			11	4	5	6				10	9					8				2			3		7	1		44
3,597				11	4*	5	6				10**	S*	9				8	S**			2			3		7	1		45
6,206	16	1		11	4	5	6	10*				7**	9				8	S*			2			3	S**				46
Appearances		39	14	14	35	37	44	36	37	8	37	14	42	13		8	30	12	2	5	30	4	4	16	6	12	7		
Apps as sub					1			1		10	1	4	1	1	3	1	5	7	3					1	2	1		1	
Goals (52)					4			3	7	1	9	3	13	1		1	5	1			1			1	1	1			

Att.	Pos	Pearce	Daniel	Deakin	Farrell	S Davis (1)	Gardner	Britton	Oghani	Rowell	Comstive	James	O'Connell	Atkinson	S Taylor	Zelem	White	McGrory	Hoskin	Morley	Measham	Miller	D Jones	Hardy	Monington	Grewcock	Williams	Hooper	
8,474		1			4*	5	6	S*	8		10		9	11			7	3			2								1
Appearances		1			1	1	1		1		1		1	1			1	1			1								
Apps as sub								1																					
Goals (0)																													

Att.	Pos	Pearce	Daniel	Deakin	Farrell	S Davis (1)	Gardner	Britton	Oghani	Rowell	Comstive	James	O'Connell	Atkinson	S Taylor	Zelem	White	McGrory	Hoskin	Morley	Measham	Miller	D Jones	Hardy	Monington	Grewcock	Williams	Hooper	
3,669		1	2	3	4	5	6	7	8		10	11	9																1
6,674		1	2	3	4	5	6	7	8		10		9	11															2nd leg
6,282		1	2		3	5	6	7	8	4	10		9	11															2
14,036		1	2		3		6	7	8	2	10		9	11		5													2nd leg
Appearances		4	4	2	4	3	4	4	4	2	4	1	4	3		1													
Apps as sub																													
Goals (6)									1		2		3																

1989-90

OBITUARY
GEORGE JAMES (JIMMY) STRONG
DIED 11 OCTOBER 1989, AGED 73.

Records are there to be beaten, but one Burnley record that has stood firm for well over fifty years is held by goalkeeper Jimmy Strong. His 203 consecutive League appearances, starting from the first match of the post-war era, is a mark that will take some equalling.

Born in Morpeth, he was amazingly already 30 when the run began. He had played League football, most notably for Portsmouth, before the war, but it was not until he came to Turf Moor, signing in January 1946 after appearing as a wartime guest player, that he really established himself as a top-flight keeper. He was the last line of the famous "Iron Curtain" defence that won promotion and reached Wembley in 1947, and was consistency itself over the next six years or so as the Clarets consolidated their First Division status.

Injury brought his long tenure in the side to an end at Easter 1951, but he remained the first choice in the number one shirt until December 1952, by which time age was catching up. He continued to live in Burnley, for some time running a poultry farm, right up to his death.

RIP

Frank Casper wasted little time rebuilding ahead of his first full season back in charge, signing no less than six players, including Roger Eli, John Deary, Peter Mumby, Tony Hancock and former Claret Joe Jakub.

Midfielder Andy Farrell brought his manager more good news by signing a new contract after indicating, earlier in the summer that he wanted to leave.

Behind the scenes, former Manchester United manager Tommy Docherty lent his vast experience to scouting staff at Turf Moor, his recruitment no doubt smoothed by having son Michael operating as Casper's right hand man.

Long-suffering Burnley supporters had suffered their share of false dawns at the start of recent campaigns.

And unfortunately, this was to be more of the same.

Hopes were raised in August and September as the club put the absence of key central defenders Steve Davis (knee) and Steve Gardner (broken leg) behind them to grind out five wins and three draws in the first nine league games.

The solitary defeat came on the opening day at Rochdale, where a huge travelling support watched as an own goal sealed Burnley's fate.

A Littlewoods Cup exit to a Blackpool side managed by Jimmy Mullen only added to the general fear among supporters that the club was once again in decline.

But with their backs to the wall, Burnley suddenly shook off that early series of setbacks to knuckle down to the task at hand.

There were even ironic chants of "Teasdale In" at the end of the first victory away to Chesterfield!

And following successive wins following the long trips to Torquay and Maidstone, Casper's Clarets really had the fans on their side as they leapt to joint fourth in the Division Four table.

The unbeaten run stretched to nine league games by early October, helped by that encouraging away form and a grand total of six clean sheets.

Hancock in particular had wowed the crowds with a series of impressive performances in a confident start to his Burnley career.

But with no goal to his name, the striker's barren run was symptomatic of a general lack of clinical firepower that was to eat away at that promising start.

Opponents knew that by packing their defence and waiting for their opportunities, points could be plundered from Turf Moor and one point from home games against rock bottom Hartlepool and Peterborough not only ended the unbeaten run but clearly emphasised Burnley's attacking frailties.

They were not lost on Casper either and the search began immediately for a frontman to provide the polish.

Twelve games in, a fourth away win of the season – double the previous campaign – put the busy manager just two points behind his 24-point target.

But as in previous seasons, the wheels were about to fall off in spectacular fashion.

That 3-2 win at Doncaster was the only three point haul in ten games that brought only seven measly goals.

Roger Eli
cult hero, celebrating with the fans

Ron Futcher, 33, was the answer to the goalscoring conundrum and, following protracted talks, the Port Vale striker, who had also played for Manchester City, Luton and Oldham, in a well travelled career, joined his eighth English club in a £65,000 move to Turf Moor.

The newcomer wasted precious little time making his mark.

The FA Cup had been kind to Burnley, offering up a home tie in the first round for the third successive year.

The veteran striker made his debut in the 1-1 draw with Stockport, and announced his arrival with a goal in the Edgeley Park replay to set up a second round tie at Scunthorpe.

The first time in four seasons that Burnley had progressed past the first round was cause for celebration in itself, especially as a welcome distraction to the Autumn slump.

December brought an interesting aside when the Clarets team included two Steve Davis's!

Davis Mk II (Stephen) had been on the fringe of breaking through at First Division Southampton and joined his namesake Steve for the home game with Grimsby.

Few fans knew it at the time, but a true club legend had started a long and fruitful association with the Clarets.

The FA Cup second round brought another quirk as, following two draws, Casper won the coin toss to host a second replay, which saw Futcher and Eli both score twice in a 5-0 thrashing of Scunthorpe.

It was the perfect Christmas present for fans who had waited three long months for a home win at a ground that had become a haven for visitors.

And wouldn't you know it, a second victory followed six days later with a heartening 2-1 Boxing Day win over league leaders Carlisle.

With the good times rolling – relatively speaking – the year ended with renewed challenges to the existing hierarchy at Burnley.

Colne Dynamoes supreme Graham White, who had seen two takeover bids thrown out the previous year, came up with a new £1m plan to share Turf Moor with his rapidly rising, Conference-bound non-league club.

In tandem, a wealthy shareholder was demanding that 35,000 un-issued shares go on sale at £30 each to bring in a further £1m.

The prospect of a £2m cash windfall must have been seriously tempting to Teasdale and his board of directors.

But preliminary talks had failed to reach a resolution by late January, when the disappointment of a third round FA Cup exit to Lancashire rivals Blackpool was offset by four straight wins either side of the New Year, which hoisted the Clarets up twelve places to 5th and right back into play off contention.

Capitalising on growing crowds and rising stock, both on and off the pitch, Casper swooped to splash out £90,000 on Sheffield United striker John Francis.

In a surprise move, over half of that fee was raised by offloading Hancock to Preston just six months after he arrived at Burnley with great hopes.

As torrential rain caused a host of postponements throughout late January and into February, it was soon the turn of chairman Teasdale to pour cold water on the plans for a proposed new shares issue.

After rejecting the plans outright, Teasdale also hit out at his critics, insisting: "Three years ago Burnley FC was down, almost out and in a very precarious financial position.

"Few assets, debts in the region of £850,000 and staff who were not certain of next week's wages.

"I and my colleagues would appreciate a bit less knocking from those in privileged positions and a bit less of the takeover nonsense.

"We will examine everything, but please get off our backs and let us get on with the job."

When Burnley finally did get back into action, they were playing catch up. Only three games had been managed in the whole of February and when Scarborough gained revenge for their defeat at Turf Moor with a 4-2 victory, a fifth defeat in six games meant all forward momentum had screeched to a sudden halt.

Twenty league games now had to be packed into two months, and although games in hand dangled a carrot, it was the stick that painfully prevailed.

Negotiations over a ground share with Colne Dynamoes collapsed when White pulled out in early March.

The Burnley team followed suit.

Between 13 March and the curtain call on 5 May, the Clarets won once in 15 games.

Demonstrations outside Turf Moor once again surfaced, with the numbers growing to over 500 at one stage, as supporters demanded a change of, in no particular preference, chairman, board and manager!

Teasdale again came out fighting. "We understand patience has been sorely tested and we have got the message," he said. "But we will not succumb to the foul abuse hurled at us by a uninformed and disruptive minority."

Teasdale rightly explained that stability had been achieved on his watch, but that frequent changes to the team through injury had a "considerable disrupting effect."

Supporters wondered if, fit or not, the squad was good enough to ever get out of the basement division.

Casper too vowed to fight on despite the prospect of a sixth season in Division Four.

Undoubtedly key injuries, especially to defensive personnel throughout the season, hampered the manager.

And surveying the wreckage of a turbulent season, he insisted: "It takes a couple of years to sort out who you want at the club and who you do not want.

"We have got those we do not want out and in the next 12 months we will be sorted completely."

It was a clear plea for time.

Casper would get his wish.

1989-90 - Fourth Division

		P	W	D	L	F	A	Pts
1	Exeter C	46	28	5	13	83	48	89
2	Grimsby T	46	22	13	11	70	47	79
3	Southend U	46	22	9	15	61	48	75
4	Stockport C	46	21	11	14	68	62	74
5	Maidstone U	46	22	7	17	77	61	73
6	Cambridge U	46	21	10	15	76	66	73
7	Chesterfield	46	19	14	13	63	50	71
8	Carlisle U	46	21	8	17	61	60	71
9	Peterborough U	46	17	17	12	59	46	68
10	Lincoln C	46	18	14	14	48	48	68
11	Scunthorpe U	46	17	15	14	69	54	66
12	Rochdale	46	20	6	20	52	55	66
13	York C	46	16	16	14	55	53	64
14	Gillingham	46	17	11	18	46	48	62
15	Torquay U	46	15	12	19	53	66	57
16	BURNLEY	46	14	14	18	45	55	56
17	Hereford U	46	15	10	21	56	62	55
18	Scarborough	46	15	10	21	60	73	55
19	Hartlepool U	46	15	10	21	66	88	55
20	Doncaster R	46	14	9	23	53	60	51
21	Wrexham	46	13	12	21	51	67	51
22	Aldershot	46	12	14	20	49	69	50
23	Halifax T	46	12	13	21	57	65	49
24	Colchester U	46	11	10	25	48	75	43

1989-90

Manager : Frank Casper

Division Four (16th)

	No.	Date			Opponents	Result		h/t	Goalscorers/times	Opp. goal times
	1	Aug	19	a	Rochdale	L	1-2	1-1	White 28p	14, 74
	2		26	h	STOCKPORT C	D	0-0	0-0		
	3	Sep	2	a	Chesterfield	W	1-0	0-0	Mumby 51	
	4		9	h	EXETER C	W	1-0	1-0	White 44p	
	5		16	a	Gillingham	D	0-0	0-0		
	6		23	h	HEREFORD U	W	3-1	2-1	Mumby 21, O'Connell (2) 36, 73	14
	7		26	h	YORK C	D	1-1	1-0	Mumby 27	66
	8		30	a	Torquay U	W	1-0	0-0	Grewcock 63	
	9	Oct	7	a	Maidstone U	W	2-1	1-1	O'Connell 14, Deary 81	42
	10		14	h	HARTLEPOOL U	D	0-0	0-0		
	11		17	h	PETERBOROUGH U	L	1-2	0-1	Grewcock 73	37, 83
	12		21	a	Doncaster R	W	3-2	3-1	White 13p, Davis 42, Jakub 44	2, 78
	13		28	h	ALDERSHOT	D	0-0	0-0		
	14		31	a	Southend U	L	2-3	2-2	Farrell 30, O'Connell 35	8, 15, 55
	15	Nov	4	h	COLCHESTER U	D	0-0	0-0		
	16		11	a	Scunthorpe U	L	0-3	0-3		10, 17, 38
	17		25	a	Lincoln C	L	0-1	0-1		37
	18	Dec	2	h	GRIMSBY T	D	1-1	1-0	Jakub 14	71
	19		26	h	CARLISLE U	W	2-1	1-1	Futcher 35, Jakub 80	30
	20		30	h	HALIFAX T	W	1-0	1-0	Futcher 35	
	21	Jan	1	a	Cambridge U	W	1-0	0-0	Bent 54	
	22		9	h	SCARBOROUGH	W	3-0	1-0	Futcher 43, Bent (2) 68, 82	
	23		13	a	Stockport C	L	1-3	1-0	White 34	76, 78, 85
	24		20	h	ROCHDALE	L	0-1	0-1		40
	25	Feb	10	h	GILLINGHAM	L	i-2	1-1	Walker 18og	19, 90
	26		17	a	Grimsby T	L	2-4	1-1	Francis (2) 16, 89	41, 55, 72, 74
	27		24	h	LINCOLN C	D	0-0	0-0		
	28	Mar	3	a	Scarborough	L	2-4	0-3	Futcher (2) 53, 67	1, 35, 45, 67
	29		6	h	TORQUAY U	W	1-0	1-0	Farrell 12	
	30		10	a	York C	W	3-1	2-0	White (2) 1p, 39, Deary 77	81
	31		13	a	Wrexham	L	0-1	0-1		14
	32		17	h	MAIDSTONE U	D	1-1	1-0	Golley 2og	47
O'Connell's last game	33		20	a	Hartlepool U	L	0-3	0-2		12, 23, 87
	34		24	a	Peterborough U	L	1-4	0-2	Futcher 61p	14, 31, 67, 72
	35		28	a	Hereford U	W	1-0	0-0	Francis 66	
	36		31	h	DONCASTER R	L	0-1	0-1		13
	37	Apr	3	h	CHESTERFIELD	D	0-0	0-0		
	38		6	a	Aldershot	D	1-1	1-1	Jakub 8	13
	39		10	h	SOUTHEND U	D	0-0	0-0		
Gardner's last game	40		14	h	CAMBRIDGE U	L	1-3	0-2	Futcher 89p	8, 26, 68
	41		16	a	Carlisle U	D	1-1	0-0	Saddington 83og	70
	42		21	h	WREXHAM	L	2-3	0-2	Jakub 72, Mumby 89	28, 35, 74
	43		24	a	Halifax T	D	0-0	0-0		
	44		28	h	SCUNTHORPE U	L	0-1	0-1		17
	45	May	1	a	Exeter C	L	1-2	1-0	Francis 25	48, 59
McGrory's last game	46		5	a	Colchester U	W	2-1	1-1	Taylor 39og, White 65p	17

FA Cup

	Rd	Date			Opponents	Result		h/t	Goalscorers/times	Opp. goal times
	1	Nov	18	h	STOCKPORT C	D	1-1	0-0	White 59p	55
	rep		22	a	Stockport C	W	2-1	0-0	Futcher 70, O'Connell 75	57
	2	Dec	9	a	Scunthorpe U	D	2-2	1-1	Mumby 34, Deary 59	12, 62
after extra time, 1-1 at 90m	rep		12	h	SCUNTHORPE U	D	1-1	1-0	Eli 26	61
	2rep		18	h	SCUNTHORPE U	W	5-0	2-0	Eli (2) 18, 48, Futcher (2) 44, 46, Hardy 78	
	3	Jan	6	a	Blackpool	L	0-1	0-0		78

Final, Manchester U 1-0 Crystal P, at Wembley, after a 3-3 draw after extra time, also at Wembley.

League Cup

	Rd	Date			Opponents	Result		h/t	Goalscorers/times	Opp. goal times
	1	Aug	22	a	Blackpool	D	2-2	1-1	Mumby 37, White 80	23, 47
agg 2-3			29	h	BLACKPOOL	L	0-1	0-0		69

Final, Nottingham F 1-0 Oldham A, at Wembley.

Details of other first team games elsewhere.

Att.	Pos	Pearce	Measham	Deakin	Eli	Monington	Harris	White	Mumby	O'Connell	Jakub	Farrell	Hancock	Deary	Grewcock	S Davis (1)	Hardy	McGrory	Atkinson	Futcher	S Davis (2)	Bent	McKay	Francis	Gardner	N Smith	Rowell	Buckley	Williams	Howarth	
5,420		1	2	3	4*	5	6	7	8**	9	10	11	S**	S*																	1
6,537	18	1	2	3*	4	5	6	7	8**	9	10	11	S**	S*																	2
4,061	10	1	2	3		5	6	7	8		10		9	4	11																3
5,431	10	1	2	3		5	6	7	8		10		9	4	11																4
3,853	10	1	2	3		5		7	8	S*	10		9*	4		6	11														5
5,828	5	1	2	3		5		7	8	11	10		9	4		6															6
7,205		1	2	3	S*	5		7	8	11	10		9*	4		6															7
2,214	7	1	2	3		5		7	8	11	10		9*	4	S*	6															8
3,769	5	1	2	3	S**	5		7	8*	11	10		9**	4	S*	6															9
7,450	6	1	2	3	5			7	8	11	10		9*	4	S*	6															10
7,189		1	2	3		5		7	8*	9	10		S*	4	11	6															11
2,900	7	1	2	3	S*	5		7	8**	9	10			4	11*	6		S**													12
6,451	7	1	2	3		5		7	8**	9	10	11*	S*	4		6	S**														13
3,765		1	2		S*	5**		7	8	9	10	11	S**	4		6	3*														14
6,145	8	1	2		5			7*	8	9	10	11	S*	4		6	3														15
4,745	13	1	2		5			7	8*	9	10	11	S*			6	3		4												16
4,079	13	1	2					7	S**	9	10	4	6**				3	5	11*	8	S*										17
5,647	14	1	2					7	8		10	4				5	3*	S*		9	6	11									18
12,277	14	1	2		8			7			10	5		4		6	3		11*	9	S*										19
9,109	12	1	2		8**			7			10	5		4		6	3*			9	11	S**	S*								20
3,738	10	1	2					7**			10	5		4		6	3*	S*		9	11	8	S**								21
7,330		1	2*		S*			7			10	5		4		6	3			9	11	8									22
5,210	8	1			2			7*			10	5	S*	4		6	3**		S**	9	11	8									23
8,174	9	1			2			7			10	5		4		6		3*	S*	9	11	8									24
7,274	13	1			2			7			10	5				6	3*			9	4	8	S*	11							25
5,973	15	1		3	2			7			10	5				6			8*	9		S*	4**	11	S**						26
5,897	15	1		3	2						10	5		8						9		7	4	11	6						27
2,961	17	1		3	8*			S*		7	10	5		4						9			2	11	6						28
4,533		1		3				S*		7	10	5		4				8*		9			2	11	6						29
3,216	15	1		3				9		7	10	5		4				8					2*	11	6	S*					30
4,346		1		3				9	S*	7	10	5		4				8*					2**	11	6	S**					31
5,050	15	1		3	8*			9		7	10	5		4						S**			2**	11	6	S*					32
3,187		1		3	2			9		7	10*	5		4						8				11	6		S*				33
3,841	15	1	2	3	8						10	5		4		7				9				11				6			34
2,391			2	3	8			7			10	5		4		6				9				11					1		35
5,066	14		2	3				7**	S*		10	5		4		6	11*			9						S**		8	1		36
3,959			2	3*	8			7			10	5		4		6	S*			9								11	1		37
2,325			2		11			7			10	5		4		6	3			9								8	1		38
3,967			2	6	11			7			10	5		4			3*			9				S*				8	1		39
3,975	16		2	S*	8			7*			10	5**		4			3			9				11	6	S**			1		40
6,738	16	1	2	6	8				S*		10	5		4			3**	S**		9*				11		7					41
4,513	17	1	2	3	8				S*		10	5		4		6	S**	11*						9		7**					42
2,556		1	2	3	8				7*		10	5		4		6	11						S*	9							43
4,098	17	1	2	3					8		10	5		4		6	11*		S**				7**	9		S*					44
7,544		1	2	3				S*	8		10	5		4		6	11							9		7*					45
2,788	16		2	3				7			10	5		4		6		S*	11*					9		8**			1	S**	46
Appearances		39	35	32	24	13	4	37	20	20	46	36	9	39	4	31	20	6	5	22	7	7	8	18	8	4		5	7		
Apps as sub				1	5			3	5	1			8	2	3		3	5	3	1	2	2	4	1	1	6	1			1	
Goals (45)								7	4	4	5	2		2	2	1				7		3		4							4 ogs

Att.	Pearce	Measham	Deakin	Eli	Monington	Harris	White	Mumby	O'Connell	Jakub	Farrell	Hancock	Deary	Grewcock	S Davis (1)	Hardy	McGrory	Atkinson	Futcher	S Davis (2)	Bent	McKay	
8,030	1	2		5*			7		9	10	4	S*			6	3		11	8				1
6,257	1	2					7	S*	9	10	4	6*				3	5	11	8				rep
5,698	1	2					7	3		10	4		8		6		5	11	9				2
7,682	1	2		S*			7	8*		10	5		4		6	S**	3	11**	9				rep
7,429	1	2		8**			7			10	5		4		6	S*	3*	11	9			S**	2nd rep
7,790	1	2		8			7			10	5	S*	4		6	3			9			11*	3
Appearances	6	6		3			6	2	2	6	6	1	4		5	3	4	5	6			1	
Apps as sub				1				1				2				2						1	
Goals (11)				3			1	1	1				1			1			3				

Att.	Pearce	Measham	Deakin	Eli	Monington	Harris	White	Mumby	O'Connell	Jakub	Farrell	Hancock	Deary	Grewcock	
4,540	1	2	3	4	5*	6	7	8	9	10	11		S*		1
6,085	1		3	2	5	6	7	8**	9	10	4*	S**	11	S*	2nd leg
Appearances	2	1	2	2	2	2	2	2	2	2	2		1		
Apps as sub												1	1	1	
Goals (2)							1	1							

1990-91

Having your promotion hopes dashed in the final throes of a nail-biting season is bad enough.

Watching the drama unfold on a giant 48 sq metre screen only adds to the pain.

Yet that was the stark choice facing Burnley supporters as a ten-months of hard work was effectively killed stone dead in Devon on a sunny Sunday in May 1991.

Back in August, every Burnley fan would happily have grabbed a play-off place with both hands as a sixth season in Division Four was severely testing the patience.

The pressure had intensified on manager Frank Casper who, following another dreadfully disappointing campaign, suffered a further blow before a ball had been kicked in anger.

Assistant manager Mick Docherty suddenly announced he was joining Stan Ternent at Hull, leaving a void that needed filling urgently.

Casper had already released seven players, focusing all his attentions on attracting a higher standard of player to improve the club's chances of climbing out of the basement league.

Now he had double trouble.

The answer would soon have huge ramifications on Burnley's future and the man he turned to was Jimmy Mullen.

Sacked by Blackpool earlier in the year, Mullen jumped at the chance to join his old pal and was immediately appointed as Casper's right hand man.

Attention immediately turned back to new recruits, but the only significant signing ahead of the opening day 2-2 draw with Lincoln City was experienced midfielder David Hamilton.

The 1990-91 campaign brought much tighter restrictions on clubs following the Hillsborough disaster in April of 1989.

The recommendations of the resulting Taylor Report into stadiums meant that Turf Moor faced a much reduced ground capacity.

New safety measures meant the Long Side and Cricket Field Stand capacities were reduced and the addition of segregation brought the overall capacity down from 19,000, leaving club officials fearing serious financial implications if the Clarets enjoyed early league success.

'Fat chance' might have been the supporters' response following a 1-3 defeat in the first away game at Darlington.

But a two-legged Rumbelows Cup victory over Stockport soon had the club dreaming of a full house when cup holders Nottingham Forest were drawn as the second round opponents.

Burnley finally got their season up and running at the third time of asking, defeating Scarborough 2-1 and building on the three points by announcing that Bristol City defender John Pender had signed, initially on loan.

Pender would prove to be a very useful acquisition when he later signed for £70,000 and took the strongest squad in the division to a top-heavy 27 professionals.

Enjoying such strength in numbers, and revelling in better support alongside John Francis, veteran striker Ron Futcher made it four goals in as many league games with a double at Stockport.

Indeed, the free-scoring Clarets had bagged sixteen goals in just eight league games by the time Northampton were cast aside 3-0 in early October.

Forest's class had told in the cup, however, and a 1-4 reversal in the first leg at the City Ground killed off hopes of a Clarets' shock in front of over 11,000 Turf Moor fans two weeks later.

A seven-game unbeaten league run finally came to an end at Hereford, but soon after five more wins in six matches sent optimism in the Clarets camp sky high.

The only defeat in that rise to third place came at The Bescot Stadium, the league's newest ground and home to Walsall.

But Burnley put that blip behind them in more unfamiliar settings the following week, avoiding an embarrassing banana skin by beating Conference side Stafford Rangers 3-1 in the FA Cup first round, including an own goal by a certain Stan Collymore!

Third Division Stoke City were swept aside in round two, leading to a glamour tie at Turf Moor against First Division Manchester City.

Like the country, busy celebrating the downfall of Margaret Thatcher following her ill-fated Poll Tax plans, Clarets' fans suddenly sensed a wind of change.

Even the Russians were coming; at least in the guise of Dynamo Brest, who visited Turf Moor in late December for a strangely timed friendly that Burnley won 1-0.

Meanwhile £50,000 spent on ground improvements since the Taylor Report recommendations looked like being well spent, as permission was given in the nick of time to increase the Turf Moor ground capacity from around 13,000 to 20,900 in time for Manchester City's FA Cup third round visit.

A packed crowd saw Burnley give as good as they got against top-flight City, only to finally go down fighting 0-1.

Impressive home form continued to underpin the drive for the number one aim - promotion.

Ron Futcher
top scorer with 18 goals

And back-to-back victories over Stockport and Walsall in early February took the unbeaten run to 14 league matches.

In contrast, the form away from 'fortress' Turf Moor was all that held Burnley back.

Only eight points had been gleaned on the road in the first half of the campaign, forcing Casper to demand an improvement.

It came in the Leyland DAF Trophy, where January wins at Stockport (after extra time) and Bradford had supporters dreaming of another visit to Wembley.

The Valley Parade game was especially memorable as

goalkeeper Chris Pearce turned in arguably his greatest ever performance in a Burnley shirt, constantly thwarting everything the Bantams threw at him, including a penalty save, to earn the Clarets a Northern Area semi final date with old foes Preston.

Burnley headed to Deepdale's plastic pitch in fine spirits after putting a frustrating series of postponements behind them to further bury their away hoodoo at Halifax.

But the cup dreams were in ruins 90 minutes later as Casper's side conceded six goals for the first time under his tenure.

The league was now all that mattered and Burnley were handily placed in third after bouncing back to beat Walsall at Turf Moor.

But the Clarets had clearly not got that pummelling at Preston out of their system and three costly away defeats in eight crucial days at Doncaster, Cardiff and Chesterfield widened the gap at the top.

Now reliant on an unblemished home record, it took two equalisers against Gillingham to keep the Clarets in the hunt in sixth place.

The unbeaten run reached 17 with home wins over Carlisle and Hereford - true grit earning maximum points after the hosts fell behind in both games.

But at struggling York, Burnley undid all that hard work by losing 0-2 to slip from third back to sixth.

"Some fans may be getting anxious about our away form but the wheels are not going to come off our challenge and I believe we will be there at the end of the season," roared a defiant Casper.

True to his word, Burnley claimed their fourth away win of the season at Scarborough as a hectic March came to an end.

But wouldn't you know it, that proud unbeaten home record was blown out of the water in the very next game as Chesterfield became the first team all season to march away with the spoils.

Undeterred, a six-game unbeaten run in April was exactly what was required.

Converted striker Roger Eli and top scorer Ron Futcher chose precisely the right time to hit a rich vein of form, bagging 11 goals between them as four straight victories put the Clarets within touching distance.

Never in their Fourth Division years had the Clarets been in better shape. And convincing back-to-back home wins over high-riding Peterborough and play-off rivals Blackpool – the latter attracting over 18,000 fans – cemented Burnley into the third of four automatic promotion spots.

A shock 0-1 defeat at Maidstone threw a spanner in the works but Futcher's last gasp headed winner against Doncaster kept the pot boiling.

Typically, in keeping with the season, a slip-up at Rochdale in the penultimate game left Burnley's slim chances of automatic promotion hanging by a thread and dependent on others.

A 2-0 win over Wrexham was not enough and unbelievably, a 79-point haul was not enough to secure a top four spot.

And so, two points shy of what was needed, the play-offs beckoned.

Torquay were the opponents and with only 700 tickets made available for the first leg in Devon, a big screen was erected at Turf Moor to allow fans to watch the action.

Despite controlling long periods of the game, it made for painful viewing though as United clocked up a two-goal lead to protect.

Steve Davis (1)
ever present at the heart of the Clarets' defence

And protect it they did, defying a constant barrage in the second leg and even teasing Burnley by conceding a last minute own goal before the final whistle ended the Clarets' dream.

The prospect of a seventh season in the basement was almost too much to bear and almost immediately speculation mounted over Casper's Turf Moor future.

The response from the boardroom was swift.

Casper was offered one more year to get the club out of the Fourth Division.

It would be a season no-one would forget in a hurry.

1990-91 - Fourth Division

		P	W	D	L	F	A	Pts
1	Darlington	46	22	17	7	68	38	83
2	Stockport C	46	23	13	10	84	47	82
3	Hartlepool U	46	24	10	12	67	48	82
4	Peterborough U	46	21	17	8	67	45	80
5	Blackpool	46	23	10	13	78	47	79
6	BURNLEY	46	23	10	13	70	51	79
7	Torquay U	46	18	18	10	64	47	72
8	Scunthorpe U	46	20	11	15	71	62	71
9	Scarborough	46	19	12	15	59	56	69
10	Northampton T	46	18	13	15	57	58	67
11	Doncaster R	46	17	14	15	56	46	65
12	Rochdale	46	15	17	14	50	53	62
13	Cardiff C	46	15	15	16	43	54	60
14	Lincoln C	46	14	17	15	50	61	59
15	Gillingham	46	12	18	16	57	60	54
16	Walsall	46	12	17	17	48	51	53
17	Hereford U	46	13	14	19	53	58	53
18	Chesterfield	46	13	14	19	47	62	53
19	Maidstone U	46	13	12	21	66	71	51
20	Carlisle U	46	13	9	24	47	89	48
21	York C	46	11	13	22	45	57	46
22	Halifax T	46	12	10	24	59	79	46
23	Aldershot	46	10	11	25	61	101	41
24	Wrexham	46	10	10	26	48	74	40

1990-91

Manager : Frank Casper

Division Four (6th)

Note	No	Date			Opponents	Result		h/t	Goalscorers/times	Opp. goal times
	1	Aug	25	h	LINCOLN C	D	2-2	1-1	Deary 22, Jakub 77	34, 57
	2	Sep	1	a	Darlington	L	1-3	1-2	Futcher 36	27p, 44, 55
	3		8	h	SCARBOROUGH	W	2-1	0-1	Futcher 67, Grewcock 69	5
	4		14	a	Stockport C	D	2-2	2-0	Futcher (2) 14, 32p	47, 72
	5		18	a	Blackpool	W	2-1	2-0	Mumby 10, Deary 23	50
	6		22	h	ALDERSHOT	W	3-0	2-0	Jakub 39, Mumby 43, Francis 83p	
	7		28	a	Carlisle U	D	1-1	0-1	Edwards 49og	27
	8	Oct	2	h	NORTHAMPTON T	W	3-0	0-0	Francis (2) 67, 80, Eli 88	
	9		6	h	YORK C	D	0-0	0-0		
	10		13	a	Hereford U	L	0-3	0-0		55, 62, 77
	11		20	a	Peterborough U	L	2-3	2-3	Futcher (2) 30, 44	11, 13, 45
	12		23	h	MAIDSTONE U	W	2-1	2-0	Davis 3, Futcher 32	47
	13		27	h	ROCHDALE	W	1-0	1-0	White 45	
	14	Nov	3	a	Wrexham	W	4-2	1-0	Jakub 28, Francis 53, Mumby (2) 60, 77	67, 78
	15		10	a	Walsall	L	0-1	0-0		63
	16		24	h	HALIFAX T	W	2-1	0-0	Mumby 48, Francis 53	86
	17	Dec	1	h	CARDIFF C	W	2-0	0-0	Deary 56, Francis 59	
	18		15	a	Gillingham	L	2-3	0-3	Deary 51, Futcher 57p	15, 20, 28
	19		22	h	HARTLEPOOL U	W	4-0	2-0	Francis (2) 28, 43, Deary 53, Davis 55	
	20		29	a	Torquay U	L	0-2	0-1		23, 55
	21	Jan	1	h	SCUNTHORPE U	D	1-1	1-0	Francis 30	72
	22		12	h	DARLINGTON	W	3-1	2-0	Davis 10, Futcher 25, Francis 70	77
	23		19	a	Lincoln C	L	0-1	0-0		89
	24		26	h	STOCKPORT C	W	3-2	2-1	Deary 40, Futcher 44, Eli 63	8, 73
	25	Feb	16	a	Halifax T	W	2-1	0-1	Francis (2) 69, 71p	11
	26		23	h	WALSALL	W	2-0	0-0	Grewcock 49, Eli 84	
	27		26	a	Doncaster R	L	1-2	1-0	Deary 44	77, 80
	28	Mar	1	a	Cardiff C	L	0-3	0-3		6, 32p, 37
	29		5	a	Chesterfield	L	1-2	0-1	White 62	43, 54
	30		9	h	GILLINGHAM	D	2-2	0-1	Futcher 47p, Davis 59	23, 55
	31		12	a	Northampton T	D	0-0	0-0		
	32		16	h	CARLISLE U	W	2-1	0-1	Farrell (2) 68, 80	25
	33		19	h	HEREFORD U	W	2-1	0-1	Futcher 46, Eli 49	16
	34		23	a	York C	L	0-2	0-2		15, 18
White's last game	35		26	a	Scarborough	W	1-0	1-0	Francis 4	
	36		30	h	CHESTERFIELD	L	0-1	0-0		85
	37	Apr	1	a	Hartlepool U	D	0-0	0-0		
Deakin's last league game	38		6	h	TORQUAY U	D	1-1	0-0	Futcher 58p	50
	39		13	a	Scunthorpe U	W	3-1	0-0	Futcher 50, Eli 52, Davis 86	65
	40		16	a	Aldershot	W	2-1	0-0	Eli (2) 63, 77	68
	41		20	h	PETERBOROUGH U	W	4-1	4-1	Eli (2) 19, 39, Futcher (2) 20, 30p	32
	42		23	h	BLACKPOOL	W	2-0	0-0	Eli 65, Futcher 75	
	43		27	a	Maidstone U	L	0-1	0-1		42p
	44		30	h	DONCASTER R	W	1-0	0-0	Futcher 90	
Futcher's last game	45	May	4	a	Rochdale	D	0-0	0-0		
last games for Grewcock and Davis (1)	46		11	h	WREXHAM	W	2-0	1-0	Francis (2) 31, 83	

FA Cup

Rd	Date			Opponents	Result		h/t	Goalscorers/times	Opp. goal times
1	Nov	17	a	Stafford R	W	3-1	3-0	Collymore 17og, Mumby 20, White 32	72
2	Dec	12	h	STOKE C	W	2-0	0-0	Francis 72, White 88	
3	Jan	6	h	MANCHESTER C	L	0-1	0-0		52

Final, Tottenham H 2-1 Nottingham F, at Wembley.

League Cup

Note	Rd	Date			Opponents	Result		h/t	Goalscorers/times	Opp. goal times
	1	Aug	27	a	Stockport C	W	2-0	1-0	Hamilton 41, Futcher 54	
agg 2-1		Sep	4	h	STOCKPORT C	L	0-1	0-1		30
	2		26	a	Nottingham F	L	1-4	0-1	Mumby 51	23, 71, 74, 82
agg 1-5		Oct	10	h	NOTTINGHAM F	L	0-1	0-0		86

Final, Sheffield W 1-0 Manchester U, at Wembley.

Details of other first team games elsewhere.

Att.	Pos	Pearce	France	Bray	Deary	Farrell	S Davis (1)	Mumby	Futcher	Francis	Jakub	Grewcock	Hamilton	White	Deakin	Measham	Pender	Eli	Williams	N Smith	Sonner	Lancashire	
6,106		1	2*	3	4	5	6	7**	8	9	10	11	S*	S**									1
3,671	19	1		3*	4	5	6	S**	9	8	10		2	7**	11	S*							2
4,723	14	1			4	5	6	7	8	9	10*	S*	11		3	2							3
3,523		1			4	S**	6	7**	8*	9	10	S*	11		3	2	5						4
4,737		1			4	S*	6	8		9	10		11	7*	3	2	5						5
5,517	3	1			4		6	8		9	10		11	7*	3	2	5	S*					6
5,205		1			4	11	6	8		9	10			7	3	2	5						7
6,271		1			4	11	6	8		9	10			7	3	2	5*	S*					8
6,808	2	1			4	5	6	8*	S**	9	10	S*		7	3	2		11**					9
3,688	9	1			4	11*	6	8	S**	9	10	S*		7**	3	2	5						10
5,102	9	1			4	11	6		8	9	10			7*	3	2	5	S*					11
5,567		1			4		6	S*	8	9	10	11*		7	3	2	5						12
7,971	6	1			4		6	S*	8*	9	10	11		7	3	2	5						13
3,997	2	1			4		6	8		9	10	11		7	3	2	5						14
5,710	3	1			4		6	9		8	10	11*		7	3	2	5	S*					15
6,620	3	1			4	S*	6	8		9	10	11		7	3	2	5*						16
6,348	3	1			4	S*	6	8	S**	9	10	11		7**	3	2	5*						17
3,679	4	1			4	5	6		8	9	10	11		7	3	2							18
8,514	2	1			4	S*	6	S**	8	9	10	11**		7	3	2	5*						19
4,210	5				4		6		8	9	10	11		7*	3	2	5	S*	1				20
8,557	5	1			4	S*	6		8	9	10	11		7*	3	2	5						21
8,491	6	1				4	6		8	9	10			7	3	2	5	S*		11*			22
4,167	6	1				4	6		8	9	10	11			3	2	5	S*		7*			23
8,946	5	1			4	7	6		8		10	11			3	2	5	9					24
4,755	4				4	7	6			9	10	11			3	2	5	8	1				25
7,883	3				4	5	6			8	10	11		7	3	2		9	1				26
3,080		1	S*		4	7	6			8	10	11**		S**	3	2	5*	9					27
3,591	6	1			4	7**	6		S*	8	10	11		S**	3	2	5	9*					28
4,022		1			4		6		8	9	10	S*	11*	7	3	2	5						29
6,459	6	1			4		6		8*	9	10	11		7	3	2	5	S*					30
3,710		1			4		6		8	9	10		11	7	3	2	5						31
6,635	6	1			4	S**	6		8	9	10	11**		7*	3	2	5	S*					32
5,716		1			4	7	6		8	9	10				3	2	5	11					33
4,407	6	1			4	7	6	S*		9	10			8*	3	2	5	11					34
2,373		1			4	7	6		8	9	10			11	3	2	5						35
8,373	5	1			4	7	6	11*	8	9	10				3	2	5	S*					36
4,967	4	1			4	7	6	11*	8	9	10	S*			3	2	5						37
6,661	7	1		S**	4	7	6		8	9	10	11*			3**	2	5	S*					38
4,449	7	1		3	4	7	6		8	9*	10					2	5	11			S*		39
2,473		1		3	4	7	6		8	9	10					2	5	11					40
10,018	6	1		3	4	7	6		8*	9	10	S*	S**			2	5**	11					41
18,395		1		3	4	7	6		8	9	10					2	5	11					42
3,130	6	1		3*	4	7	6		8	9	10	S*				2	5	11					43
10,410		1		3	4	7	6		8	9	10					2	5	11					44
7,344	6	1		3	4**	7	6		8	9*	10	S*	S**			2	5	11					45
10,161	6	1		3		7	6			9	10	8	4*			2	5				11	S*	46
Appearances		43	1	10	43	30	46	15	30	45	46	21	8	26	37	44	40	15	3	2	1		
Apps as sub			1	1		7		5	4			9	3	3		1		11			1	1	
Goals (70)					7	2	5	5	18	15	3	2		2				10					1 og

Att.	Pearce	France	Bray	Deary	Farrell	S Davis (1)	Mumby	Futcher	Francis	Jakub	Grewcock	Hamilton	White	Deakin	Measham	Pender	Eli	
4,117	1			4		6	8*	S*	9	10	11		7	3	2	5		1
12,949	1			4	S*	6	S**	8**	9	10	11		7	3	2	5*		2
20,331	1			4	S**	6		8	9	10	11**	S*	7*	3	2	5		3
Appearances	3			3		3	1	2	3	3	3		3	3	3	3		
Apps as sub					2		1	1				1						
Goals (4)							1		1				2					1 og

Att.	Pearce	France	Bray	Deary	Farrell	S Davis (1)	Mumby	Futcher	Francis	Jakub	Grewcock	Hamilton	White	Deakin	Measham	Pender	Eli	
2,786	1		3	4	5	6		9	8	10		2	7	11				1
3,912	1		3	4	5	6		9	8	10		2	7	11				2nd leg
17,897	1			4	S*	6	8**		9	10		11*	7	3	2	5	S**	2
11,399	1			4	5		7		9	10*	11		8	3	2	6	S*	2nd leg
Appearances	4		2	4	3	3	2	2	4	4	1	3	4	4	2	2		
Apps as sub					1												2	
Goals (3)							1	1				1						

1991-92

On a balmy night in April 1992, York was added to the list of venues where Burnley fans celebrated success.
Ending a seven year stay in Division Four may not rank up there with the champagne moment that vintage Clarets enjoyed at Maine Road, Manchester nigh on four decades earlier.
Preston North End's Deepdale in 1973, when Burnley hauled themselves back into the First Division, was another momentous day in the club's history.
But after suffering years of sad, sorry decline, this was finally payback time for the loyal band of Burnley fans who had followed their team through thick - and plenty of thin.
And no man was going to stop the Bootham Crescent party!
An unforgettable season began with Ray Deakin and Neil Grewcock - the last playing links to 'The Orient Game' four years earlier - both being released.
However, it was something of a shock when top scorer Ron Futcher, who scored 19 goals the previous season, had his contract terminated by mutual consent.
Player of the year Steve Davis, who refused new terms, also left to join Barnsley for a fee of £180,000.
Cut-price replacements arrived to redress the balance. Barely a week later Glasgow-born Mike Conroy was signed as a replacement from Third Division Reading for just £35,000 – a fee he would repay many times over.
Joined by new arrival Steve Harper, the re-shaped Burnley team prepared for the season by jetting off to Russia for a tour arranged following the visit to Lancashire of Dynamo Brest 12 months earlier.
The Clarets ground out two 1-1 draws behind the former Iron Curtain - and on their return to England, Conroy celebrated his first senior competitive goal for the Clarets on his home debut in the 1-1 Manx Cup draw with Blackburn Rovers.
A week later, on the eve of the new season, Casper played his joker and Burnley awoke to the news that Steve Davis MK II, who had impressed in nine games on loan from Southampton the previous season, joined the Clarets for a snip £60,000.
Now nobody was regretting his MK I namesake leaving for Oakwell less than a month earlier.
Burnley were ready for action, but their early optimism was promptly punctured by an opening day defeat at Rotherham.
The promotion drive was up and running a week later with Aldershot the Turf Moor victims.
A first round Rumbelows Cup defeat to Wigan failed to dampen enthusiasm - and back-to-back league wins over Doncaster and Chesterfield – the latter courtesy of a Roger Eli hat-trick - immediately put everything into perspective.
Casper had made promotion his only priority and the team duly responded. At least in the short term.
A series of setbacks, including red cards for David Hamilton and John Francis and a broken arm suffered by Harper in training, preceded a trio of league defeats that proved the final straw for a proud man.
Facing mounting criticism yet again from the terraces, Casper finally buckled and resigned seven games into the season.
Assistant Jimmy Mullen, appointed little over 12 months previously, took charge in a caretaker capacity.

And Mullen enjoyed the kind of honeymoon period every manager must dream of.
Victory over Carlisle in his first game in charge was welcome.
Graham Lancashire's first half hat-trick in the 6-2 demolition of Wrexham at Racecourse Ground was a handy follow-up.
The Burnley board had seen enough to convince them and Mullen was immediately handed the role full time.
Incredibly the wins just kept on coming.
Walsall, Lincoln, Halifax, York and league leaders Mansfield were all knocked over in successive league games and Mullen made it eight straight wins in all competitions with an Autoglass Trophy win at Blackpool.
It was now officially the best ever start by a Burnley manager and with 24 goals scored in that blistering spell –a healthy average of three a game – the Clarets were officially on a roll!
Even Burnley's cups runneth over and, in the space of 11 days in November, Doncaster were beaten in both the FA Cup and Autoglass Trophy as the charge for honours entered three fronts.
Away wins at Maidstone and Northampton made it an amazing nine straight league wins since Mullen had taken charge.
And even the end of Nottingham Forest goalkeeper Andy Marriott's successful three-month loan spell at Turf Moor failed to dampen spirits.
Mullen was the only candidate in the running as he predictably landed the 'Manager of the Month' trophy for November.
The dreaded curse of the award duly struck and, following a hard-fought FA Cup second round victory over Rotherham, the winning league run came to a sticky end.
First Scunthorpe earned a battling point at Turf Moor and then, on Boxing Day, Rotherham landed a sucker punch to defeat the new league leaders.

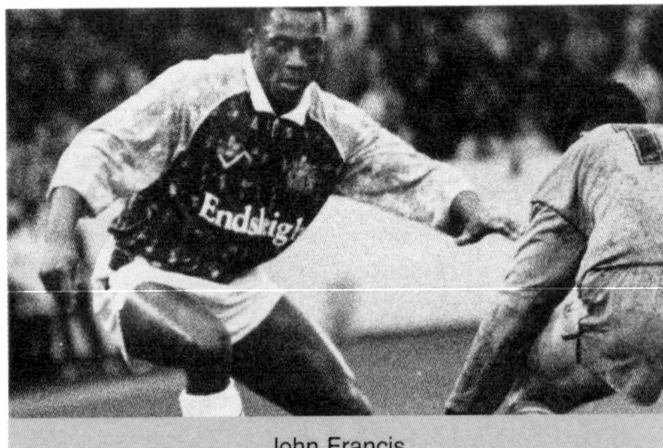

John Francis
the winner on a never to be forgotten night at York

Burnley had gone top just days earlier, after completing the double over Aldershot 2-1 at the Recreation Ground.
However as the season reached its climax this result, and the three points collected back in August's Turf Moor curtain raiser, would be expunged from Football League records as the Shots resigned from the league.
As the New Year celebrations died down, Burnley increased their lead at the top of the Fourth Division at Chesterfield.
Another convincing victory at Saltergate was the seventh in succession, breaking a club record stretching back to 1919.
Almost 19,000 fans saw the Clarets take Second Division Derby to a replay in the FA Cup third round.

The replay would provide another golden memory for anyone who travelled to the Baseball Ground.
Heavy fog forced abandonment at the first time of trying, with Burnley two goals down.
Undeterred, thousands made the same journey later in the month to witness a fervent show of unity and support arguably unmatched in recent times.
Two goals down yet again and with the tie effectively over, the massed ranks in the visiting enclosure began a chant of "Jimmy Mullen's Claret and Blue Army" that grew louder by the minute and continued long after both teams had left the field.
Mullen was eventually asked to appease those fans with an appearance and, clearly choked with emotion, he later said: "In 23 years of football I have never seen anything like that."
February's 5-0 battering of Northampton, with five different players on target, made it three wins in four games as Burnley returned to Division Four action to turn the screw on their promotion rivals
An Autoglass Trophy (Northern) semi final was also secured following a penalty shoot out at Rotherham, where Chris Pearce made two crucial saves just weeks after coming off the transfer list after losing his place for the second time to on-loan Mark Kendall.
That didn't stop Mullen swooping for Nicky Walker, the fourth goalkeeper to don the green jersey that season.
And the Scot made his debut against Blackpool in front of over 18,000 fans at Turf Moor, where the Clarets remained top on goal difference following a 1-1 draw.
There was tragedy on 10 March 1990 when apprentice Ben Lee tragically died after falling from the Longside roof.
Burnley's game at York that evening was immediately called off as a mark of respect.
The Clarets would later make the journey a fitting one in memory of the promising teenager.
Back in action a week later, Huddersfield could not stop the Burnley juggernaut progressing to the Autoglass Trophy Northern Final.
And with Mansfield beaten in a howling gale at Field Mill days later, Burnley leapfrogged the Stags into second place in the league table.
The games were now coming thick and fast and on deadline day, Mullen spent a princely £25,000 on Robbie Painter to strengthen his squad for the run in.
And the day ended with Burnley going back to the top of the league without kicking a ball as Aldershot's demise – and the wiping of their league record – took them back to the summit.
Further wins over Painter's former club Maidstone and Hereford strengthened the position, and in hindsight perhaps it was a blessing when Stockport County ended the Clarets hopes of a Wembley return by winning both legs of their Autoglass Trophy Northern final.
It left minds fully focused on ending seven seasons among the dead men.
The finishing line was in sight and just seven points were needed from the final five games to end the barren years.
Three came in the Turf Moor victory over Cardiff, in which Painter opened his account with a goal after just 16 seconds.
And a share of the spoils at Carlisle - where 8,000 Clarets' fans travelled in hope, many in fancy dress - put the champagne on ice.
Cue Bootham Crescent on Tuesday 28 April. York tried to spoil the party by talking the lead just before half time, while thousands of Burnley fans were still trying to get into the ground!
But roared on by the travelling army, John Deary equalised on the hour and in the final minutes John Francis converted Mike Conroy's cross for the promotion winning goal.
The rest of the season was a blur for Burnley fans. Inevitable defeat at home to Wrexham, where the real focus for over 21,000 fans was the presentation of the Fourth Division championship trophy to John Pender, was followed by normal service being resumed in the 3-1 win at play-off chasing Rochdale, including Conroy's 30th goal of a truly prolific season.
Bermuda-bound, following a pledge by club sponsors, Mullen and his players jetted off to enjoy a hard-earned break.
They left behind a town rejuvenated. Four years earlier the Clarets had survived by the skin of their teeth.
Twelve months later they were at Wembley.
Now the swirling waters of Fourth Division football were a thing of the past. Burnley were back!

24-goal Mike Conroy
first Claret with over 20 since England's World Cup win!

1991-92 - Fourth Division

		P	W	D	L	F	A	Pts
1	BURNLEY	42	25	8	9	79	43	83
2	Rotherham U	42	22	11	9	70	37	77
3	Mansfield T	42	23	8	11	75	53	77
4	Blackpool	42	22	10	10	71	45	76
5	Scunthorpe U	42	21	9	12	64	59	72
6	Crewe A	42	20	10	12	66	51	70
7	Barnet	42	21	6	15	81	61	69
8	Rochdale	42	18	13	11	57	53	67
9	Cardiff C	42	17	15	10	66	53	66
10	Lincoln C	42	17	11	14	50	44	62
11	Gillingham	42	15	12	15	63	53	57
12	Scarborough	42	15	12	15	64	68	57
13	Chesterfield	42	14	11	17	49	61	53
14	Wrexham	42	14	9	19	52	73	51
15	Walsall	42	12	13	17	48	58	49
16	Northampton T	42	11	13	18	46	57	46
17	Hereford U	42	12	8	22	44	57	44
18	Maidstone U	42	8	18	16	45	56	42
19	York C	42	8	16	18	42	58	40
20	Halifax T	42	10	8	24	34	75	38
21	Doncaster R	42	9	8	25	40	65	35
22	Carlisle U	42	7	13	22	41	67	34

*** - Aldershot resigned mid-season, record expunged**

1991-92

Manager : Frank Casper until October 1991, then Jimmy Mullen

Division Four (1st) Champions

Note	No.	Date		Venue	Opponents	Result		h/t	Goalscorers/times	Opp. goal times
	1	Aug	17	a	Rotherham U	L	1-2	1-0	Conroy 39	73, 78
	2		31	a	Doncaster R	W	4-1	1-1	Conroy 1p, 85, Harper 73, Yates 77	27
	3	Sep	3	h	CHESTERFIELD	W	3-0	1-0	Eli (3) 26, 54, 74	
	4		7	h	CREWE A	D	1-1	0-0	Francis 52	54
	5		14	a	Hereford U	L	0-2	0-1		28, 56
	6		21	h	ROCHDALE	L	0-1	0-0		70
Mumby's last game	7		28	a	Scarborough	L	1-3	1-2	Lancashire 17	16, 20, 69
	8	Oct	5	h	CARLISLE U	W	2-0	1-0	Pender 23, Lancashire 57	
	9		12	a	Wrexham	W	6-2	4-2	Lancashire (3) 3, 27, 29, Harper 4, Davis 57, Eli 89	2, 38
	10		19	h	WALSALL	W	2-0	2-0	Davis 20p, Lancashire 23	
	11		26	a	Lincoln C	W	3-0	1-0	Francis 39, Conroy 75p, Lancashire 83	
	12	Nov	2	a	Halifax T	W	2-0	0-0	Deary 55, Farrell 87	
	13		5	h	YORK C	W	3-1	2-1	Conroy 10, Deary 16, Lancashire 82	25
	14		9	h	MANSFIELD T	W	3-2	1-1	Conroy 7p, Davis 55, Pender 83	29, 60
	15		23	a	Maidstone U	W	1-0	1-0	Conroy 28p	
	16		30	a	Northampton T	W	2-1	1-0	Conroy (2) 20, 86	85
	17	Dec	14	h	SCUNTHORPE U	D	1-1	1-0	Farrell 34	72
	18		26	h	ROTHERHAM U	L	1-2	0-0	Francis 70	46, 78
	19		28	h	DONCASTER R	W	2-1	2-0	Conroy 6, Eli 25	78
	20	Jan	1	a	Chesterfield	W	2-0	2-0	Deary 2, Francis 25	
	21		11	a	Blackpool	L	2-5	0-2	Conroy 63, Francis 70	16, 38, 66, 73, 89
	22		18	h	GILLINGHAM	W	4-1	1-1	Conroy (3) 8, 65, 83, Randall 66	19
	23	Feb	1	a	Walsall	D	2-2	0-1	Eli 69, Conroy 83	5, 47
	24		8	h	LINCOLN C	W	1-0	1-0	Conroy 45	
	25		11	h	NORTHAMPTON T	W	5-0	1-0	Deary 35, Eli 50, Conroy 56, Harper 68, Francis 78	
	26		15	a	Scunthorpe U	D	2-2	0-2	Conroy 46p, Davis 90	30, 37
	27		22	h	BLACKPOOL	D	1-1	1-1	Eli 30	31
	28		29	a	Cardiff C	W	2-0	0-0	Randall 85, Conroy 89	
	29	Mar	3	a	Gillingham	L	0-3	0-1		1, 65, 71
	30		7	h	BARNET	W	3-0	1-0	Davis 10, Barnett 52og, Deary 61	
	31		14	h	HALIFAX T	W	1-0	0-0	Pender 70	
	32		21	a	Mansfield T	W	1-0	1-0	Conroy 41	
	33		24	a	Barnet	D	0-0	0-0		
	34		28	h	MAIDSTONE U	W	2-1	0-0	Davis 77, Eli 87	46
	35		31	h	HEREFORD U	W	2-0	2-0	Monington 25, Conroy 30	
	36	Apr	4	a	Crewe A	L	0-1	0-0		85
Pearce's last game	37		20	h	SCARBOROUGH	D	1-1	1-1	Eli 9	34
	38		22	h	CARDIFF C	W	3-1	1-1	Painter 1, Farrell 60, Conroy 63	29
	39		25	a	Carlisle U	D	1-1	1-0	Francis 43	79
	40		28	a	York C	W	2-1	0-1	Deary 60, Francis 90	43
	41	May	2	h	WREXHAM	L	1-2	1-0	Conroy 33	62, 78
	42		5	a	Rochdale	W	3-1	2-1	Measham 30, Conroy 41, Painter 67	15

FA Cup

Round	Date		Venue	Opponents	Result		h/t	Goalscorers/times	Opp. goal times
1	Nov	16	h	DONCASTER R	D	1-1	0-0	Davis 66	65
rep		27	a	Doncaster R	W	3-1	1-1	Harper (2) 38, 50, Eli 86	45
2	Dec	7	h	ROTHERHAM U	W	2-0	0-0	Conroy 59, Lancashire 83	
3	Jan	4	h	DERBY C	D	2-2	1-1	Harper 6, Eli 84	1, 78
rep		25	a	Derby C	L	0-2	0-0		53, 65

Final, Liverpool 2-0 Sunderland, at Wembley.

League Cup

Note	Round	Date		Venue	Opponents	Result		h/t	Goalscorers/times	Opp. goal times
	1	Aug	20	a	Wigan A	L	1-3	1-1	Conroy 8	4, 52, 82
agg 3-6			27	h	WIGAN A	L	2-3	0-0	Patterson 47og, Davis 79	46, 63, 85

Final, Manchester U 1-0 Nottingham F, at Wembley.

Details of other first team games elsewhere.

Att.	Pos	Pearce	Measham	Jakub	Deary	Pender	Monington	Farrell	S Davis (2)	Francis	Conroy	S Harper	Hardy	Lancashire	Marriott	France	Bray	Yates	Eli	Hamilton	Sonner	Mumby	Randall	Kendall	Walker	Painter	Williams	McKenzie		
6,042		1	2	3	4	5	6	7	8	9*	10	11**	S**	S*																1
2,940	3				8	5	6		4	9	10	S*			1	2**	3*	7	11	S**										2
6,647					8	5	6		4	9	10	3			1			11	7	2										3
9,657	2				8*	5	6	S*	4	9	10	3			1			11	7	2										4
4,400	8			S*		5	6	11	4	9	10	3			1		S**	8**	7	2*										5
8,633	10			11	8	5	6	2		9	10		4		1		3*	7**	S*		S**									6
2,596	11		2	10	8	5	S**	6	4				3	9*	1			S*	11			7**								7
6,157	11		2	10**	8	5		6	4			7		9*	1		3	S**	11		S*									8
3,181	8			10	8	5	S*	6	4			7		9*	1	2	3		11											9
7,289	7			10	8	5		6	4	S*		7		9	1	2	3*		11											10
3,235	7		2	3	8	5		6	4	9	10	7		S*	1				11*											11
4,491	3			3	8	5		6	4	9	10	7		S*	1	2			11*											12
7,389				3	8	5		6	4	9	10*	7		11	1	2					S*									13
11,848	3			3	8	5		6	4	9*	10	7		11	1	2			S*											14
2,375	3		2	3	8	5		6	4	9	10	7			1				11											15
4,020	2		2	3	8			6	4	9	10	7		S*	1			5	11*											16
8,419	2	1	2	3	8*	5		6	4	9	10	7		S**				S*	11**											17
13,812	top	1	2	3	8	5		6**	4	9	10	7		11*					S*				S**							18
9,605	top	1	2	3	8	5		6	4	9	10			S**				S*	11**				7*							19
7,789	top		2	3	8	5		6	4	9	10*			S*					11				7	1						20
8,007	2		2	3	8	5		6	4	9	10	7*							11				S*	1						21
8,908	top	1	2	3	8	5		6*	4	9	10	7		11**				S**					S*							22
5,287	top	1	2	3	8	5		6*	4	9	10	S*		S**					11**				7							23
9,748	top	1	2	3	8	5		6	4	9	10	7		S*					11*											24
8,825		1	2	3	8	5		6*	4	9	10	7		S**					11**				S*							25
5,303	top	1	2	3	8	5		6*	4	9	10	7							11				S*							26
18,183	top		2	3	8	5		6*	4	9	10	7**		S**					11				S*		1					27
16,030	top		2	3	8			5	4	9	10	7		S*					11*				6		1					28
3,729			2	3	8			5	4	9	10	7*		S*				S**	11				6**		1					29
12,018	top		2	3	8	5		6	4*	9	10	7							11				S*		1					30
10,903	3		2	3	8	5	S*	4		9	10	7*		11									6		1					31
8,336	2			3	8	5		2	4	9	10	7							11				6		1					32
4,881		1		3	8	5		2	4	9	10	7		S*					11*				6							33
10,986	top	1		3	8	5		2	4	9*	10	7**						S**	S*				6			11				34
10,578		1		3		5	6	2	4		10			S*				8	11*				7			9				35
5,530	top	1		3	8	5	6	2	4		10*			S*				7	11							9				36
12,312	top	1	2	3	8	5		6	4	9	10	S*							11*							7				37
12,408			2	3	8	5		6	4	9	10	S*											11*			7	1			38
10,000	top		2	3	8	5		6	4	9	10	11*														7	1	S*		39
7,620	top		2	3	8	5		6	4	9	10	11*														7	1	S*		40
21,216	top		2	3	8	5	S**	6*	4	9	10							S*								7	1	11**		41
8,175	top		2	3	8	5			4	9	10	11						6								7*	1	S*		42
Appearances		14	27	38	40	39	8	38	40	36	38	31	2	9	15	6	5	9	29	3		1	11	2	6	9	5	1		
Apps as sub				1			4	1		1		4	1	16			1	8	4	1	3		7					3		
Goals (79)			1		6	3	1	3	6	8	24	3		8				1	10				2			2			1	og

Att.	Pos	Pearce	Measham	Jakub	Deary	Pender	Monington	Farrell	S Davis (2)	Francis	Conroy	S Harper	Hardy	Lancashire	Marriott	France	Bray	Yates	Eli	Hamilton	Sonner	Mumby	Randall	Kendall	Walker	Painter	Williams	McKenzie		
7,076		1		3	8	5		6	4	9	10	7		11*		2			S*											1
4,207		1	2	3	8	5*		6	4	9	10	7						S*	11											rep
9,775		1	2	3	8	5		6	4	9	10	7		S*					11*											2
18,772			2	3	8	5		6	4	9*	10	7		S*					11					1						3
18,374		1	2	3	8	5		6	4	9	10	7*		11**				S**	S*											rep
Appearances		4	4	5	5	5		5	5	5	5	5		2		1			3					1						
Apps as sub														2				2	2											
Goals (8)									1		1	3		1					2											

Att.	Pos	Pearce	Measham	Jakub	Deary	Pender	Monington	Farrell	S Davis (2)	Francis	Conroy	S Harper	Hardy	Lancashire	Marriott	France	Bray	Yates	Eli	Hamilton	Sonner	Mumby	Randall	Kendall	Walker	Painter	Williams	McKenzie		
2,826		1	2	11*	8	5	6	S**	4	9	10	S*					3		7**											1
3,876		1			8	5	6	S*	4	9	10	S**				2	3**		7	11*										2nd leg
Appearances		2	1	1	2	2	2		2	2	2					1	2		2	1										
Apps as sub								2				2																		
Goals (3)									1		1																		1	og

1992-93

After seemingly a lifetime getting out of football's basement, the last thing Burnley wanted was a swift return.

The seven years spent in English football's wilderness wanted to be consigned to the history books as quickly as possible.

Immediate relegation from whence they came would have been heartbreaking.

But that never happened, and the slow and steady progress back up the pyramid could begin.

The Clarets would go on to consolidate in their first season in the new-look Second Division, following the introduction of the Premiership.

No-one in Claret and Blue thought it would be easy, but a gritty determination and will to succeed brought them their aim of safety.

And despite it being a team effort, two players in particular would stand up above the crowds more than anyone.

After using five goalkeepers during the Fourth Division Championship campaign, there was far more consistency between the sticks when Marlon Beresford arrived from Sheffield Wednesday early in the season and went on to steal the show.

So much so, that by the season's end, he would be chosen by his peers to receive a PFA award, and be named the Goalkeeper of the Year for the division.

Beresford travelled to Turf Moor from Hillsborough in search of first team football, and that's exactly what he got.

However, his success was more than merited, as he became a virtual ever-present, bar the first two games of the season.

And it's not as if Burnley didn't have an able replacement, with David Williams, one of the five used in the previous campaign, restricted to keeping the bench warm.

A few games in particular stood out as Beresford's highlights, including his debut against Rotherham, the long trip to Plymouth, and a 1-1 draw at Huddersfield.

But one stood out more than any, a 2-1 win over West Brom on the first weekend in October.

Burnley went into the game with no hope at all, against a side top of the table, and managed by Ossie Ardiles with his "total football" style.

But the Baggies hadn't banked on Burnley, who were given the dream start when Steve Harper fired in one of the goals of the season in the opening minute.

West Brom threw everything at their hosts, with wave after wave of attacks.

But one thing always stood in their way, and that was the immovable force of Beresford.

Mike Conroy added a second after the interval, and despite West Brom pulling one back through old adversary Simon Garner, Burnley held on for the win.

Beresford was the hero, undoubtedly, and he would go on producing performance after performance inbetween the posts.

By that stage in the season, Burnley were holding their own, after Swansea had been accounted for on the opening day.

Five games without a win after that point dampened the spirits slightly, but a victory over Mansfield and draws against Wigan and Plymouth restored the pride.

The West Brom win was soon followed by two more against Fulham and Blackpool.

But this good start to the campaign was also helped on its way by another new signing, who turned out to be the other star of the season.

Adrian Heath was brought to Turf Moor after two and a half years at Manchester City, and netted on his debut in the Clarets' first away game of the season at Stockport.

And from that point on, he didn't stop scoring.

Tap-ins, long shots, volleys, headers, scrappy goals, outstanding goals and even penalties, Heath notched the lot throughout the course of the campaign.

He went on to pass 100 league goals in an illustrious career, and join a select band of Clarets to pass 20 for a league season.

This was to be his most prolific campaign ever in terms of goal scoring, but he only got what he deserved.

His boundless energy and never-ending enthusiasm saw him lead the line in all but three games over the course of the season.

And he waited until the final home game of the season to reach that magical 20 mark, netting against Blackpool in a 2-2 draw.

The continued efforts of both Heath and Beresford brought attention from across the country.

Nobody could argue that these two were major successes at Turf Moor, and nobody could deny them a place in the hearts of the fans.

Those wins over Fulham and Blackpool yielded eight goals

Winger Steve Harper in full flow

from the Clarets, with Heath netting the fourth in a 5-2 demolition of the former.

That was to be only his second goal in the first 15 league games, but he soon put that right with a brace in a 2-2 draw at Exeter.

By this stage of the season, Burnley had already crashed out of the Coca Cola Cup at the first hurdle, losing 5-2 on aggregate to Carlisle.

But they had experienced success in the FA Cup, seeing off Scarborough and Shrewsbury to set up a third round tie in the new year with Sheffield United.

Back in the league, and that point at Exeter, after a home success over Leyton Orient, had elevated Burnley to tenth in the table.

But successive 3-0 defeats at Brighton and Port Vale, plus a solitary goal reversal at home to Wigan, brought the Clarets back down the earth with a bump.

Sheffield United proceeded to dump them out of the FA Cup, beaten 4-2 in a replay at home after a gritty 2-2 draw at Bramall Lane.

But that only served as a catalyst for the Clarets, as they embarked on a league run of eight games without defeat.

Another Heath penalty accounted for Rotherham at Millmoor, while Chester, who would go on to finish rock bottom of the pile, were hit for five at Turf Moor without reply.

Goals from Andy Farrell and another from Heath accounted for Preston in February's local derby.

And a 2-1 win at Plymouth, thanks to two goals from John Pender, was enough to send Burnley seventh, with Beresford again proving his worth with a penalty save.

So good was the result that it was Plymouth's first home defeat of the season fourteen matches in.

And it put Burnley just two points behind Rotherham in the final play-off place.

But just one win in their next eight outings cost them dear, as only Hull were accounted for, 2-0 at Turf Moor.

Heath was on target again in that one, but he was joined on the scoresheet by loan man Steve Slawson.

A run of four games without a win was ended at home to Hartlepool, where Steve Davis added his name alongside two more goals from Heath in a 3-0 success.

That came in the middle of a purple patch for Heath, who netted eight goals in eight games towards the back end of the campaign.

A brace at Leyton Orient in a 3-2 defeat was matched in a 3-1 success at home to Exeter.

But by that time, the Clarets only had pride on their minds, as safety was assured, and the play-offs had long gone.

That win over Exeter proved to be their last of the season, as the Clarets only proceeded to pick up two points from their remaining three outings.

A 1-1 draw at Stoke on the final day of the season saw the home side presented with the Second Division title.

Burnley even led in that game thanks to Adrian Randall, and visions of Wrexham spoiling their championship party exactly 12 months earlier came to the fore.

But the fact that the Clarets were one of only six sides to take anything from the Victoria Ground during that campaign told its own story.

Burnley had consolidated and there were even happier times ahead.

Joe Jakub in action
with Graham Lancashire in support

1992-93 - Second Division

		P	W	D	L	F	A	Pts
1	Stoke C	46	27	12	7	73	34	93
2	Bolton W	46	27	9	10	80	41	90
3	Port Vale	46	26	11	9	79	44	89
4	West Bromwich A	46	25	10	11	88	54	85
5	Swansea C	46	20	13	13	65	47	73
6	Stockport C	46	19	15	12	81	57	72
7	Leyton O	46	21	9	16	69	53	72
8	Reading	46	18	15	13	66	51	69
9	Brighton & HA	46	20	9	17	63	59	69
10	Bradford C	46	18	14	14	69	67	68
11	Rotherham U	46	17	14	15	60	60	65
12	Fulham	46	16	17	13	57	55	65
13	BURNLEY	46	15	16	15	57	59	61
14	Plymouth A	46	16	12	18	59	64	60
15	Huddersfield T	46	17	9	20	54	61	60
16	Hartlepool U	46	14	12	20	42	60	54
17	Bournemouth	46	12	17	17	45	52	53
18	Blackpool	46	12	15	19	63	75	51
19	Exeter C	46	11	17	18	54	69	50
20	Hull C	46	13	11	22	46	69	50
21	Preston NE	46	13	8	25	65	94	47
22	Mansfield T	46	11	11	24	52	80	44
23	Wigan A	46	10	11	25	43	72	41
24	Chester C	46	8	5	33	49	102	29

1992-93

Manager : Jimmy Mullen

New Division Two (13th)

Note	No	Date		Venue	Opponents	Result		h/t	Goalscorers/times	Opp. goal times
	1	Aug	15	h	SWANSEA C	W	1-0	0-0	Penney 67	
	2		22	a	Stockport C	L	1-2	0-1	Heath 71	27, 89
	3		29	h	ROTHERHAM U	D	1-1	0-0	Deary 85	73
	4	Sep	5	a	Chester C	L	0-3	0-2		11, 23, 66
	5		12	a	Preston N E	L	0-2	0-0		54, 79
	6		15	h	PORT VALE	D	1-1	0-0	Monington 90	69
	7		19	h	MANSFIELD T	W	1-0	1-0	Monington 32	
	8		26	a	Wigan A	D	1-1	0-0	Deary 89	66
	9		29	h	PLYMOUTH A	D	0-0	0-0		
	10	Oct	3	h	WEST BROMWICH A	W	2-1	1-0	Harper 1, Conroy 53	62
	11		11	a	Bradford C	L	0-1	0-1		45
	12		17	h	FULHAM	W	5-2	4-1	Harper 12, Farrell 19, Penney 32, Heath 45, Conroy 46	2, 53
	13		24	a	Blackpool	W	3-1	3-1	Harper 15, Farrell 28, Penney 44	25
	14		31	h	STOKE C	L	0-2	0-2		21, 36
	15	Nov	3	h	READING	D	1-1	1-1	Harper 8	28
	16		7	a	Hull C	W	2-0	1-0	Heath (2) 45, 88	
	17		21	h	HUDDERSFIELD T	W	2-1	2-1	Deary 22, Clayton 45	30
	18		28	a	Bolton W	L	0-4	0-2		25, 35, 55, 61
	19	Dec	12	h	LEYTON O	W	2-0	1-0	Bellamy 39og, Heath 81	
	20		19	a	Exeter C	D	2-2	2-1	Heath (2) 8, 43	28, 90og
	21		26	a	Brighton & H A	L	0-3	0-1		19, 51, 56
	22	Jan	9	a	Port Vale	L	0-3	0-1		26, 58, 67
	23		16	h	WIGAN A	L	0-1	0-0		52
Eli's last game	24		23	a	Mansfield T	D	1-1	1-0	Pender 23	88
	25		26	a	Rotherham U	W	1-0	0-0	Heath 78p	
	26		30	h	STOCKPORT C	D	1-1	0-0	Conroy 49	63
	27	Feb	5	a	Swansea C	D	1-1	0-1	Farrell 66	22
	28		13	h	CHESTER C	W	5-0	4-0	Conroy (2) 5, 20, Heath 21, Pender 45, Harper 79	
	29		16	h	PRESTON N E	W	2-0	1-0	Heath (2) 45, 67	
	30		20	a	Plymouth A	W	2-1	1-1	Pender (2) 4, 86	23
	31		27	h	BRADFORD C	D	2-2	1-2	Slawson 22, McCarthy 90og	2, 42
	32	Mar	6	a	West Bromwich A	L	0-2	0-1		3, 71
	33		9	a	Hartlepool U	D	0-0	0-0		
	34		13	h	HULL C	W	2-0	1-0	Heath 42, Slawson 79	
	35		16	h	BOURNEMOUTH	D	1-1	1-1	Conroy 14	5
	36		20	a	Reading	L	0-1	0-0		79
	37		23	h	BOLTON W	L	0-1	0-0		81
	38		27	a	Huddersfield T	D	1-1	1-0	Heath 13	64
	39	Apr	3	h	HARTLEPOOL U	W	3-0	1-0	Heath (2) 14, 53, Davis 81	
	40		6	a	Leyton O	L	2-3	1-3	Heath (2) 34p, 82	9, 13, 37
	41		10	h	BRIGHTON & H A	L	1-3	1-2	Conroy 29	9, 31, 81
	42		13	a	Bournemouth	D	1-1	0-1	Davis 68	27
Jakub's last game	43		17	h	EXETER C	W	3-1	1-0	Heath (2) 45, 86, Daniels 65og	58
	44		24	a	Fulham	W	0-4	0-1		45, 51, 66, 76
	45	May	1	h	BLACKPOOL	D	2-2	1-0	Heath 28, Francis 47	54, 85
last games for Conroy and Steve Harper	46		8	a	Stoke C	D	1-1	1-0	Randall 39	64

FA Cup

Round	Date		Venue	Opponents	Result		h/t	Goalscorers/times	Opp. goal times
1	Nov	14	h	SCARBOROUGH	W	2-1	1-0	Conroy 26, Curran 55og	79
2	Dec	5	h	SHREWSBURY T	D	1-1	0-0	Conroy 69	62
rep		15	a	Shrewsbury T	W	2-1	0-0	Pender 87, Conroy 90	74
3	Jan	2	a	Sheffield U	D	2-2	2-0	Heath (2) 18, 39	81, 89
rep		12	h	SHEFFIELD U	L	2-4	1-3	Heath 17, Monington 67	19, 27, 45, 59

Final, Arsenal 2-1 Sheffield W after extra time, at Wembley, after a 1-1 draw after extra time, also at Wembley.

League Cup

Note	Round	Date		Venue	Opponents	Result		h/t	Goalscorers/times	Opp. goal times
	1	Aug	18	a	Carlisle U	L	1-4	0-2	Sonner 85	1, 41, 59, 78
agg 2-5			25	h	CARLISLE U	D	1-1	0-1	Pender 51	32

Final, Arsenal 2-1 Sheffield W, at Wembley.

Details of other first team games elsewhere.

Att.	Pos	Williams	Measham	Jakub	Randall	Pender	Farrell	Penney	Deary	Painter	Conroy	S Harper	Monington	Heath	Clayton	L Thompson	Beresford	Lancashire	Mooney	S Davis (2)	Sonner	Palin	Eli	Donowa	Yates	Wilson	Slawson	Campbell	Pickering	Francis	
10,913		1	2	3	4	5	6	7	8	9	10	11																			1
4,953	15	1	2	3	4	5			8	S*	10		6	7	9	11*															2
9,684	16		2	3	4	5*	S*		8	7		11	6	10			1	9													3
4,981	19		2	3	4	5			8	7		11	6	10		S*	1	9*													4
7,209	21		2	3	4	5	10*		8			S*	6	9		11	1		7												5
8,556			2	3	4	5	10		8				6	9			1		7	11*	S*										6
8,613	20		2	3	6	5			8			11	9	10			1		7	4											7
4,032	18		2	3	6	5			8		S*	11	9*	10			1		7	4											8
8,676			2	3	6	5	8				10	11		9			1		7	4											9
14,796	16		2	3	6	5	7				10	11	9	8			1			4											10
10,235			2	3		5	6				10	11		8			1		7*	4		9	S*								11
9,881	14		2	3		5	6	7	8		10**	11	S**	9*			1			4			S*								12
7,942	13		2	3		5	6	7	8		10	11*		9			1			4			S*								13
16,667	14		2	3			6	7*	8		10	11	5	9			1			4			S*								14
8,382			2	3			6	7*	8	S*	10**	11	5	9			1			4			S**								15
5,751	13		2	3		5	6	7	8		10	11		9			1			4											16
10,615	10		2	3		5	6	7	8			11		9	10*		1			4			S*								17
11,438	14		2	3		5	6	7	8			11		9	10*		1			4			S*								18
8,882	10		2	3	6	5	S*	7*	8		10	11		9			1			4**			S**								19
3,179	10		2	3		5	6	7*	8		10	11	S*	9			1			4											20
8,741	13		2	3		5	6*	S*	8	S**	10		7	9			1			4			11**								21
8,815	14		2	3	8	5	6			7*	10	11		9			1			4			S*								22
9,154	15		2	3	8	5	6				10	11	9*				1	S*		4				7							23
3,991	13		2	3	8	5	4		6	S*	10	11					1						9*	7**	S**						24
4,989			2	3		5	8		6		10	11		9			1			4				7							25
11,229	13		2	3		5	8		6		10	11		9			1			4				7							26
4,973			2	7		5	8		6		10*	11	S*	9			1			4						3					27
9,434	10		2			5	8		6		10	7		9			1			4						3	11				28
12,648			2			5	8*		6		10	7	S*	9			1			4						3	11				29
5,905	7					5	8		6	S*	10	7	2	9			1			4						3	11*				30
13,262	9		2			5	8		6		10	7	S*	9			1			4						3	11*				31
15,722	9		2	S**		5	8		6	11	10	7*	S*	9			1			4**						3					32
3,021			2	6	11	5	8**			S**	10		S*	9			1			4*						3		7			33
9,974	10		2		6	5	8*			7	10		4	9			1									3	11	S*			34
8,601			2	7	S*	5	8*			11	10		4	9			1									3		6			35
6,398	12		2	6	S*	5	8			S**	10		11*	9			1			4						3		7**			36
15,085			2		7	5	8			S*	10			9			1			4						3		6*	11		37
9,411	11		2**		S**	5	8				10*		S*	9			1			4						3		6	11	7	38
8,226	12					5	8				10		2	9			1			4						3		6	11	7	39
4,236					S*	5	8			S**	10		2	9			1			4						3		6*	11**	7	40
9,424	12				6	5	8				10	11	2	9			1			4						3				7	41
4,456						5	8		6		10	11	2	9			1			4						3				7	42
7,332	12			6		5	8		11		10		2	9			1			4						3				7	43
5,531	13		2			5	8		6		10	11		9			1			4						3				7	44
12,475	13		2			5	8		6		10	11	S*	9*			1			4						3				7	45
21,840	13				8	5	2		6	S*	10	11	4	9			1*									3				7	46
Appearances		2	39	31	19	44	40	10	32	7	38	33	22	43	3	2	44	2	6	37		1	2	4		20	5	7	4	9	
Apps as sub				1	4		2	1		10	1	1	9			1		1			1		9		1			1			
Goals (57)					1	4	3	3	3		7	5	2	20	1					2							2			1	3 ogs

Att.	Williams	Measham	Jakub	Randall	Pender	Farrell	Penney	Deary	Painter	Conroy	S Harper	Monington	Heath	Clayton	L Thompson	Beresford	Lancashire	Mooney	S Davis (2)	Sonner	Palin	Eli	Donowa	Yates	
8,359		2	3		5	6	7	8		10	11		9			1			4						1
10,038		2	3	S**	5	6*	7	8		S*	11		9**			1			4			10			2
5,671		2	3**		5	6*	7	8		10	11	S**	9			1			4			S*			rep
23,041		2	3	8	5	6			7	10	11		9			1			4						3
19,061		2	3	8	5	6*				10	11	7	9			1			4			S*			rep
Appearances		5	5	2	5	5	3	3	1	4	5	1	5			5			5			1			
Apps as sub				1						1		1										2			
Goals (9)					1					3		1	3												1 og

Att.	Williams	Measham	Jakub	Randall	Pender	Farrell	Penney	Deary	Painter	Conroy	S Harper	Monington	Heath	Clayton	L Thompson	Beresford	Lancashire	Mooney	S Davis (2)	Sonner	Palin	Eli	Donowa	Yates	
4,066	1	2	3	4	5	6	7		9*	10	11									S*				8	1
5,524	1	2	3	4	5	6	7**	8	11	10			S*	9*	S**										2nd leg
Appearances	2	2	2	2	2	2	2	1	2	2	1			1										1	
Apps as sub													1		1					1					
Goals (2)					1															1					

1993-94

Wembley.
Just uttering the word is enough to send shivers down a football fan's spine.
Those privileged enough to attend this magnificent stadium, before refurbishment, will always remember it.
That was the thing about Wembley, you would fondly remember it in the face of either victory or defeat.
Not every club graced the hallowed turf, but Burnley did it twice in six seasons before the inevitable facelift.
And that second occasion will forever live on as one of the greatest experiences in the lives of countless Clarets' supporters.
Ironically, it was exactly six years to the day since their last visit, in the Sherpa Van Trophy final of 1988.
But this time, the winning dressing room was painted Claret.
No word of a lie, the 44,806 that were packed inside that famous old venue were predominantly Burnley supporters.
It seemed like the entire population of Lancashire had travelled down to roar on Jimmy Mullen's side, with just a small contingent of Stockport County supporters tucked away behind one of the goals.
It was like a home game!
But while the tension and anticipation was unbearable, it got worse just two minutes in.
Chris Beaumont rose highest to head in David Frain's free kick, and all of a sudden, Claret hearts sank.
There were no other words for it apart from utter dejection.
To make matters worse, John Francis limped off with a knee injury soon after.
But a moment of stupidity from County's Michael Wallace saw him spit at Ted McMinn, and he was handed his marching orders from referee David Elleray.
And within minutes, the Claret hordes were jubilant as David Eyres picked up Adrian Heath's pass and bent an exquisite effort beyond John Keeley.
Eyres hit the bar in first half stoppage time, but just after the hour, County were reduced to nine men when goal hero Beaumont was dismissed for stamping on Les Thompson.
And the turn around was complete when Gary Parkinson's toe poke bobbled over Keeley and rolled over the line.
That was it as far as Burnley were concerned. They were in the ascendancy, and against nine men, what could go wrong?
And so it proved, as skipper John Pender bound his way up the 39 steps to hold the Second Division play-off trophy aloft.
It was a victory that arrived through adversity, but there was no question that it was richly deserved.
And that came through in abundance at Home Park just 11 days earlier, where the Clarets beat the odds to put Plymouth to the sword in their own back yard.
A goalless draw at Turf Moor in the first leg of the semi-final had seemingly put the Pilgrims firmly in the box seat.
After all, they had ended the season in third place, 12 points ahead of Burnley and just three points behind an automatic spot.
But despite having been beaten there earlier in the season, and falling behind here, two goals from John Francis and one from Warren Joyce made sure it was the visitors who would be booking the coaches to Wembley.
The season had started with the Clarets far from promotion favourites.
Kevin Russell, Joyce and Eyres all arrived in the summer, and they were all to have major impacts in the season ahead.
None more so than Joyce, who cracked a debut brace to seal a 2-1 win on the opening day of the season against Port Vale.
But the Claret faithful were to bid a fond farewell to a hero, as Mike Conroy travelled across Lancashire to join Preston, just two days after Burnley had won 2-1 at Deepdale in the first leg of the Coca Cola Cup first round.
The second leg was won 4-1 at Turf Moor to seal an emphatic aggregate win, but that was after their first defeat of the campaign at Reading.
Turf Moor was becoming something of a fortress, with Burnley's first six home games in league and cup all producing victories.
That run was ended with a 1-1 draw against Huddersfield, with Eyres notching a late penalty to maintain his side's place in the top six.
From that point on, Burnley never once dropped out of the top seven.
But prior to that Huddersfield clash, Burnley put in a superb display to hold Tottenham to a goalless draw at Turf Moor in the first leg of the Coca Cola Cup second round, only to lose out 3-1 on aggregate.
The FA Cup first round saw York beaten 3-2 in a replay at Bootham Crescent, while a 2-1 home league win over the same opposition put Burnley third in the table.
Whilst Burnley were not stringing wins together in sequence, they were arriving at regular intervals, and the

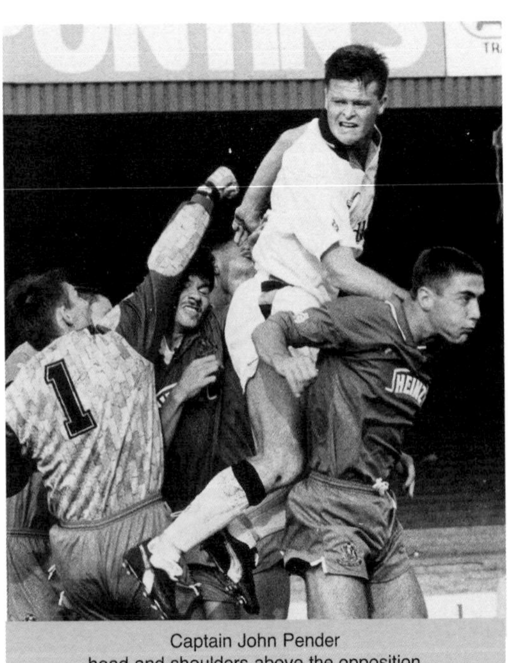
Captain John Pender
head and shoulders above the opposition

Midfield dynamo John Deary

Clarets also looked to have unearthed a goalscorer extraordinaire in David Eyres.
His double in the win over York took him to 10 for the campaign, and he was on target again in a 3-2 home success over Exeter.
Rochdale were thrashed 4-1 in the FA Cup second round tie at Turf Moor, but the game was marred by three sendings off, one of which was Clarets' defender Mark Monington.
John Mullin notched his first senior goal for the club in a 1-1 draw at Port Vale, before the largest Turf Moor crowd of the season saw the Clarets come from behind to beat a spirited Wrexham side 2-1, thanks to a thunderous volley from Steve Davis.
Back to back defeats came in the form of Bradford at Turf Moor and Plymouth at Home Park.
But little would anyone involved with Burnley know that they would more than exact their revenge on the Devon side when it really mattered.
Three successive home wins over Cambridge, Cardiff and Bournemouth, all emphatic and all without conceding, put Burnley's promotion bandwagon back on the rails.
But a run of four games without a win, starting with a 2-1 loss at Cardiff, sent momentary panic through the Claret camp that their spot in the playoff shake-up was slipping away from them.
McMinn, who had spent time on loan at Burnley, signed a two-year deal that saw him join from Birmingham City.
And he was to prove to be the missing piece of the promotion puzzle as far as Burnley were concerned.
The 'Tin Man', as he was affectionately known, notched on his home debut as his new side came from behind to share the spoils with Stockport, but the two dropped points meant Burnley slipped out of the top six for the first time since December.
But after conceding a late equaliser at Brighton, Tony Philliskirk, Adrian Heath and McMinn again were all on target in a 3-1 home success over promotion rivals Bristol Rovers.
But disaster struck at Hartlepool, as John Pender and Heath were both sent off in a 4-1 defeat, before a solitary goal reverse at Wrexham on Easter Monday.
Were Burnley really about to throw away their hopes of a place in the end of season lottery, after such an impressive campaign?
The simple answer was - no.
Those suspicions were quashed with four wins in their next six outings, including a 5-0 hammering of Barnet that saw a 22-minute hat-trick in the second half from Tony Philliskirk.
Victory at Blackpool followed, while a 4-1 win over Brentford in their final home game of the season sealed a play-off place.
But so much for ideal preparations, as they were thumped by the same scoreline at already-relegated Exeter in their final match.
That meant the Clarets had only taken one point from four away matches against the four teams who ended up being relegated.
Their best performances on the road came against the top sides and what a great omen that proved to be.

Andy Farrell
first Claret to play twice for Burnley at Wembley

1993-94 - Second Division

		P	W	D	L	F	A	Pts
1	Reading	46	26	11	9	81	44	89
2	Port Vale	46	26	10	10	79	46	88
3	Plymouth A	46	25	10	11	88	56	85
4	Stockport C	46	24	13	9	74	44	85
5	York C	46	21	12	13	64	40	75
6	BURNLEY	46	21	10	15	79	58	73
7	Bradford C	46	19	13	14	61	53	70
8	Bristol R	46	20	10	16	60	59	70
9	Hull C	46	18	14	14	62	54	68
10	Cambridge U	46	19	9	18	79	73	66
11	Huddersfield T	46	17	14	15	58	61	65
12	Wrexham	46	17	11	18	66	77	62
13	Swansea C	46	16	12	18	56	58	60
14	Brighton & HA	46	15	14	17	60	67	59
15	Rotherham U	46	15	13	18	63	60	58
16	Brentford	46	13	19	14	57	55	58
17	Bournemouth	46	14	15	17	51	59	57
18	Leyton O	46	14	14	18	57	71	56
19	Cardiff C	46	13	15	18	66	79	54
20	Blackpool	46	16	5	25	63	75	53
21	Fulham	46	14	10	22	50	63	52
22	Exeter C	46	11	12	23	52	83	45
23	Hartlepool U	46	9	9	28	41	87	36
24	Barnet	46	5	13	28	41	86	28

1993-94

Manager : Jimmy Mullen

Division Two (6th)
Promoted via play offs

Note		Date			Opponents	Result		h/t	Goalscorers/times	Opp. goal times
	1	Aug	14	h	PORT VALE	W	2-1	1-1	Joyce (2) 14, 53	35
	2		21	a	Reading	L	1-2	0-2	Eyres 85p	11, 26
	3		28	h	LEYTON O	W	4-1	2-1	Eyres 25, Deary 36, Farrell 55, Heath 90	30
	4		31	a	Rotherham U	L	2-3	1-2	Law 20og, Francis 46	16, 18, 61
	5	Sep	4	a	Bournemouth	L	0-1	0-1		13
Measham's last game	6		11	h	FULHAM	W	3-1	1-0	Randall 8, Eyres 51, Deary 64	58
	7		14	h	BRIGHTON & H A	W	3-0	2-0	Russell (2) 1, 47, Davis 31	
	8		18	a	Stockport C	L	1-2	1-0	Francis 27	66, 71
	9		25	a	Bristol R	L	1-3	0-3	Russell 81	28, 40, 45
	10	Oct	2	h	HARTLEPOOL U	W	2-0	1-0	Eyres 36, Heath 74	
	11		9	h	PLYMOUTH A	W	4-2	1-1	Eyres 8, Monington 57, Peel (2) 65, 73	10, 68
	12		16	a	Bradford C	W	1-0	1-0	Heath 10	
	13		23	h	HUDDERSFIELD T	D	1-1	0-0	Eyres 82p	69
	14		30	a	Cambridge U	W	1-0	1-0	Eyres 1	
	15	Nov	2	a	Swansea C	L	1-3	1-2	Francis 22	33, 36, 52
	16		6	h	YORK C	W	2-1	1-0	Eyres (2) 22p, 79	68
	17		20	a	Brentford	D	0-0	0-0		
	18		27	h	EXETER C	W	3-2	2-1	Russell 37, Eyres 45p, Francis 46	15, 84
	19	Dec	11	h	READING	L	0-1	0-1		26
	20		18	a	Port Vale	D	1-1	0-0	Mullin 85	73
	21		27	h	WREXHAM	W	2-1	0-1	Russell 51, Davis 65	17
	22		29	a	Barnet	D	1-1	0-0	Heath 90	85
	23	Jan	1	h	BLACKPOOL	W	3-1	1-1	Farrell 24, Russell 50, Francis 55	5
	24		3	a	Hull C	W	2-1	1-1	Davis 45, Deary 79	22
	25		15	h	BRADFORD C	L	0-1	0-0		57
	26		22	a	Plymouth A	L	2-3	0-2	Heath 66, Philliskirk 82	31, 32, 67
	27		29	h	CAMBRIDGE U	W	3-0	1-0	Randall 35, Eyres 87p, Heath 90	
	28	Feb	5	a	Huddersfield T	D	1-1	0-0	Deary 54	77
	29		12	h	CARDIFF C	W	2-0	0-0	Philliskirk 54, Francis 69	
	30		19	a	Leyton O	L	1-3	1-0	Parkinson 28	59, 62, 67
	31		26	h	BOURNEMOUTH	W	4-0	2-0	Eyres 2, Philliskirk 16, Joyce 52, Davis 58	
Monington's last game	32	Mar	1	a	Cardiff C	L	1-2	1-0	Davis 18	55, 82
	33		5	a	Fulham	L	2-3	2-1	Eyres 27, Randall 42	9, 53, 76
	34		12	h	STOCKPORT C	D	1-1	0-0	McMinn 58	55
	35		16	a	Brighton & H A	D	1-1	1-0	Davis 1	85
	36		19	h	BRISTOL R	W	3-1	1-0	Philliskirk 30, Heath 58, McMinn 90	67
	37		26	a	Hartlepool U	L	1-4	1-2	Eyres 43	10, 16, 70, 90
	38		29	h	HULL C	W	3-1	1-0	Pender 44, Eyres (2) 67p, 80	88
	39	Apr	2	a	Wrexham	L	0-1	0-0		50
	40		4	h	BARNET	W	5-0	0-0	Philliskirk (3) 47, 53, 69, Heath 80, Eyres 81	
	41		9	a	Blackpool	W	2-1	2-0	Eyres 6, Francis 43	90
	42		16	h	SWANSEA C	D	1-1	0-1	Davis 64	38
	43		23	a	York C	D	0-0	0-0		
	44		26	h	ROTHERHAM U	D	0-0	0-0		
	45		30	h	BRENTFORD	W	4-1	2-1	Eyres 21, McMinn 32, Heath 47, Randall 81	38
last league games for Farrell & Les Thompson	46	May	7	a	Exeter C	L	1-4	0-1	Joyce 46	26, 50, 54, 64

FA Cup

	Date			Opponents	Result		h/t	Goalscorers/times	Opp. goal times
1	Nov	13	h	YORK C	D	0-0	0-0		
rep		30	a	York C	W	3-2	2-1	Heath 5, Joyce 29, Eyres 89	45, 90
2	Dec	4	h	ROCHDALE	W	4-1	2-0	Jones 25og, Eyres (3) 43, 72, 88p	78
3	Jan	8	a	Charlton A	L	0-3	0-1		19, 49, 58

Final, Manchester U 4-0 Chelsea, at Wembley.

League Cup

Note		Date			Opponents	Result		h/t	Goalscorers/times	Opp. goal times
	1	Aug	17	a	Preston N E	W	2-1	1-1	Eyres 27p, Davis 77	12
agg 6-2			25	h	PRESTON N E	W	4-1	1-0	Russell 15, Eyres 46, Francis 56, Deary 65	50
	2	Sep	22	h	TOTTENHAM H	D	0-0	0-0		
agg 1-3		Oct	6	a	Tottenham H	L	1-3	1-1	Eyres 7	3, 72, 90

Final, Aston Villa 3-1 Manchester U, at Wembley.

Details of other first team games elsewhere.

Att.	Pos	Beresford	Measham	L Thompson	S Davis (2)	Pender	Joyce	Francis	Deary	Heath	K Russell	Eyres	Monington	Farrell	Randall	Mullin	Patterson	Peel	Wilson	Philliskirk	Parkinson	McMinn	Lancashire	P Smith		
12,594		1	2	3	4	5	6	7	8	9*	10	11	S*													1
5,855	12	1	2	3	4	5	6*	7	8	9	10	11	S*													2
10,133	7	1	2	3	4	5		7	8	9	10	11		6												3
5,533		1	2	3	4	5		7**	8	9	10	11	S*	6*	S**											4
5,574	13	1	2	3*	4	5		7	8	9	10	11	S*	6**	S**											5
9,021	12	1	2	3	4	5		7	8	9	10	11			6											6
8,837		1		3	4	5		7*	8	9	10	11		2	6	S*										7
5,122	9	1		3	4	5		7	8	9	10	11		2	6											8
5,732	12	1		3	4	5		7**	8	9	10	11		2*	6	S**	S*									9
9,532	8	1		3	4	5		7**	8	9	10	11	2*	S*	6			S**								10
10,488	8	1		3	4	5		7*	8	9	10	11	2		6			S*								11
9,501	6	1		3	4	5		S*	8	9	10	11	2		6			7*								12
12,011	6	1		3	4	5*		S*	8	9	10	11	2		6			7								13
4,826	3	1		3	4	5		7	8	9	10	11	2		6											14
3,358		1		3	4	5	S**	7*	8	9	10	11	2		6**			S*								15
10,236	3	1		3	4	5	6	7	8	9	10	11	2*					S*								16
6,085	6	1		3	4	5	6	7*	8	9	10	11	2		S*											17
9,040	4	1		3	4	5	6	7	8	9	10	11	2													18
11,650	7	1		3	4	5	6	7	8	9	10**	11	2*		S*	S**										19
10,710	7	1		3	4	5*	2	7	8	9	10	11		S*	6**	S**										20
15,357	5	1			4	5	2	7	8		10	11			6			9	3							21
2,360	5	1			4	5	2	7	8	9	10	11		S**	6**			S*	3*							22
18,165	4	1		3	4	5	2	7	8	9	10	11		6												23
11,232	4	1		3	4	5	2	7	8	9	10			6					11							24
13,517	5	1		3	4	5*	2	7**	8	9	10	11		S*	6			S**								25
10,595	6	1		3	4	5	2**	S*	8	9	10*	11	6	S**						7						26
10,659	5	1		3		5	S*	7	8	9		11	4		6*					10	2					27
10,634	5	1		3		5		7	8	9	S*	11	4		6					10*	2					28
11,276	4	1				5		7	8	9		11	4		6				3	10	2					29
5,201	5	1				5		7	8	9	S*	11	4		6				3	10*	2					30
10,383	5	1			4	5	8	7		9		11			6			S*	3	10*	2					31
5,469		1			4	5	8**	S*		9		11	7	S**	6				3	10*	2					32
4,943	6	1			4	5		S*	8	9		11			6				3	10*	2	7				33
13,130	7	1			4	5		S*	8	9		11			6				3	10*	2	7				34
8,021		1			4	5		S*	8	9		11			6				3	10	2	7*				35
10,651	5	1			4	5		S*	8	9		11			6				3	10*	2	7				36
2,879	7	1		3	4	5		S*	8	9		11			6					10*	2	7				37
10,574		1		3	4	5		S*	8	9		11		S**	6					10	2**	7*				38
7,253	7	1		3	4	5		S*	8*	9		11		6						10	2	7				39
10,412	7	1		3	4	5		S*	8	9		11			6					10*	2	7				40
7,956	4	1		3	4		6	9	8			11*		5	S*					10	2	7				41
10,694	6	1		3	4		6**		8			11		5	S**	9		S*		10*	2	7				42
8,642	6	1		3	4		10		8			11		5	6			S*		9*	2	7				43
10,806		1		3	4		S**		8			11		5	6	S*		9		10*	2	7**				44
11,363	6	1		3	4	5		10*	8**	9		11		S**	6						2	7	S*			45
3,155	6	1		3**	4	5	8	10		9		11		S**	6						2	7*		S*		46
Appearances		46	6	36	42	42	19	31	43	41	26	45	16	13	31	1		4	11	19	20	14				
Apps as sub							3	12			2		4	9	6	5	1	9					1	1		
Goals (79)					7	1	4	7	4	9	6	19	1	2	4	1		2		7	1	3			1	og

Att.	Pos	Beresford	Measham	L Thompson	S Davis (2)	Pender	Joyce	Francis	Deary	Heath	K Russell	Eyres	Monington	Farrell	Randall	Mullin	Patterson	Peel	Wilson	Philliskirk	Parkinson	McMinn	Lancashire	P Smith		
10,199		1		3	4	5	6	7	8	9	10**	11	2*		S*			S**								1
5,720		1		3	4	5	6	7	8	9	10	11	2													rep
11,388		1		3	4	5	6	7	8	9	10	11	2													2
8,336		1		3*	4	5	2	7	8	9	10	11		6**				S**	S*							3
Appearances		4		4	4	4	4	4	4	4	4	4	3	1												
Apps as sub															1			2	1							
Goals (7)							1			1		4													1	og

Att.	Pos	Beresford	Measham	L Thompson	S Davis (2)	Pender	Joyce	Francis	Deary	Heath	K Russell	Eyres	Monington	Farrell	Randall	Mullin	Patterson	Peel	Wilson	Philliskirk	Parkinson	McMinn	Lancashire	P Smith		
6,283		1	2	3	4	5	6	7	8		10	11		9												1
9,346		1	2	3	4	5	6*	7	8	9	10	11		S*												2nd leg
16,844		1		3	4	5		7	8	9	10	11		2	6											2
20,614		1		3	4	5		S*	8	9	10	11	2		6			7*								2nd leg
Appearances		4	2	4	4	4	2	3	4	3	4	4	1	2	2			1								
Apps as sub								1						1												
Goals (7)					1			1	1		1	3														

1994-95

They say a week is a long time in football.

Well Burnley had to wait a lot longer than a week to return to the top end of English football.

Since the steady decline of the club in the early 1970s, the Clarets have always been regarded as a sleeping giant.

After slipping out of the top flight in 1976, the club spent a lifetime in the lower reaches of the pyramid.

And even after relegation from the old Second Division in 1983, Burnley were rubbing shoulders with the likes of Chester and Aldershot, rather than Chelsea and Arsenal.

The 1993-94 season had changed all that, as Burnley ended an 11-year wait to return to the top two tiers of the English game.

But it would prove to be a fleeting appearance, as just 12 months later, the joy of that memorable day at Wembley would become a distant memory.

Hopes were high at the start of the new campaign that the Clarets really would mix it with the big boys upon their promotion.

Season ticket sales boomed, as an influx of new blood was drafted in by Jimmy Mullen.

The club transfer record had stood for 16 years, since Leighton James' £165,000 arrival from QPR in 1978, but that was consigned to the history books when £200,000 was shelled out for the services of Glasgow Rangers' England under 21 international Chris Vinnicombe.

But before the new campaign could even get underway, even that figure was bettered as attacking midfielder Liam Robinson signed on the dotted line for £250,000 from Bristol City.

Those two new arrivals were just the start of a non-stop revolving door that was Turf Moor during the 1994-95 season.

On the eve of the new season, and a trip to title favourites Middlesbrough, both Les Thompson and David Williams were given free transfers out of the club after failing to agree terms.

But while they departed, more were drafted in, as Mark Winstanley arrived from Bolton, Alan Harper signed on after a successful trial, and Gerry Harrison also arrived from Huddersfield on trial.

John Gayle also came in on a month's loan from Coventry, and made his debut in the Clarets' first home game of the season against Stoke.

A Steve Davis goal just before half-time looked set to have earned Burnley all three points, only for the visitors to equalise four minutes into injury time.

And if that wasn't heartbreaking enough, déjà vu struck in the next home game against Bristol City, with Robinson netting against his former club only for the visitors to grab an injury time leveller.

Who knows what might have happened had those two goals not gone in, and whether or not Burnley's season may have been reshaped.

But after a 1-0 home reverse to Barnsley, the Clarets did finally pick up their first win of the campaign, with Robinson netting the only goal at Luton.

And another tremendous performance at Millwall four days later saw Burnley come from behind to win 3-2.

Defeats to Wolves and West Brom saw Mullen's men firmly root themselves in the drop zone.

But in their next outing against Tranmere, Turf Moor descended into late drama of the highest order.

After John Aldridge had given the visitors the lead, a David Eyres penalty squared things up.

But deep into stoppage time, Steve Davis upended Aldridge in the area and was duly sent off for his troubles.

The referee indicated before the spot kick was taken that the final whistle would be blown immediately after the outcome.

But in front of the Bee Hole End, Marlon Beresford produced a miraculous save to deny Aldridge, and Tranmere, all three points.

A 3-2 aggregate victory in the first round of the Coca Cola Cup had led to Burnley being paired with Liverpool in round two.

But all hopes of an upset were quickly dashed, as after a 2-0 loss at Anfield, Burnley were hammered 4-1 at Turf Moor in the second leg, with only Robinson's late goal to show for their troubles.

Steve Davis (2)
Clarets' stalwart over three decades and two millennia

Back to the league, and there was controversy in a tempestuous local derby at home to Bolton.

After falling behind, Steve Davis and John Deary turned the tide in Burnley's favour.

And they were only denied maximum points by a late equaliser, which came via a somewhat ungentlemanly throw-in from John McGinlay.

But after a goalless draw at Sunderland, Burnley produced their best performance of the season to see off Charlton 2-1 at The Valley.

Notts County were also beaten, and after Jamie Hoyland had been signed from Sheffield United for £130,000, his former club were beaten 4-2 at Turf Moor in a day of history.

It was the first time ever that a Burnley league game had been televised live, with Granada showing Burnley suddenly leap up to 15th in the table thanks to goals from Robinson, Hoyland, Gayle and Davis.

Four games without a win brought them back down to earth, and back to within touching distance of the drop zone.

But New Years Eve 1994 saw the year go out with a bang, as Burnley produced their biggest win of the season at the expense of sorry Southend.

It was a game that saw debuts for both Craig Armstrong and Andy Saville, drafted in on loan from Nottingham Forest and Birmingham City respectively.

Saville was to make an instant impression, setting the ball rolling just 27 minutes into his first appearance, with the opening goal.

Gayle added another before the break, before Graham Bressington maintained what was a miserable afternoon for him with an own goal six minutes into the second period.

Not only was he on the end of a 5-1 hiding, contributing to one of them, but he was later to be sent off along with team mate Phil Gridelet and Burnley's Gerry Harrison.

Goals in the last four minutes from Steve Davis and Liam Robinson put the icing on the cake as far as Burnley were concerned.

But if 1994 had ended with a bang, 1995 began with an almighty whimper.

Eight successive league defeats followed, with the 4-1 reverse at Tranmere in late February equalling the unwanted club record set exactly a century previously in 1895.

That spell also saw stalwart John Deary leave Turf Moor after just over 200 games for the club, following on from Andy Farrell earlier in the campaign.

The demoralising run of defeats was finally ended at West Brom, with Liam Robinson netting in a 1-1 draw.

That run had seen Burnley plummet to the bottom of the table, and a position from which they were never to recover, But that didn't stop them dipping into the transfer market, as Andy Cooke was signed from League of Wales outfit Newtown for £40,000.

Cooke would stay with Newtown for the remainder of the campaign, not witnessing at first hand the downturn of fortunes that his new club had undergone.

The Clarets would not pick up another win on their travels, despite Oldham, Luton, Port Vale, Charlton and Derby all being accounted for at home.

A defeat in the reverse fixture at Port Vale virtually condemned Burnley to the drop.

But to make matters worse, their fate was sealed in front of their own supporters.

Portsmouth's 2-1 win at Turf Moor made sure Burnley would make the swiftest possible return to the Second Division.

Their season was summed up on the final day, as victory at eventual play-off winners Bolton was only denied by a last minute Mixu Paatelainen equaliser.

In the immediate wake of relegation, Mullen said: "I don't feel let down by the players at all – you've got to ask yourself could we have done a little more to help them and vice versa. I won't pass the buck on to anybody."

And at the end of the day, the buck stopped with him, as the following season would prove.

Chris Vinnicombe celebrates, with Jimmy Mullen, his winner against Oldham at Turf Moor

1994-95 - First Division

		P	W	D	L	F	A	Pts
1	Middlesbrough	46	23	13	10	67	40	82
2	Reading	46	23	10	13	58	44	79
3	Bolton W	46	21	14	11	67	45	77
4	Wolverhampton W	46	21	13	12	77	61	76
5	Tranmere R	46	22	10	14	67	58	76
6	Barnsley	46	20	12	14	63	52	72
7	Watford	46	19	13	14	52	46	70
8	Sheffield U	46	17	17	12	74	55	68
9	Derby C	46	18	12	16	66	51	66
10	Grimsby T	46	17	14	15	62	56	65
11	Stoke C	46	16	15	15	50	53	63
12	Millwall	46	16	14	16	60	60	62
13	Southend U	46	18	8	20	54	73	62
14	Oldham A	46	16	13	17	60	60	61
15	Charlton A	46	16	11	19	58	66	59
16	Luton T	46	15	13	18	61	64	58
17	Port Vale	46	15	13	18	58	64	58
18	Portsmouth	46	15	13	18	53	63	58
19	West Bromwich A	46	16	10	20	51	57	58
20	Sunderland	46	12	18	16	41	45	54
21	Swindon T	46	12	12	22	54	73	48
22	BURNLEY	46	11	13	22	49	74	46
23	Bristol C	46	11	12	23	42	63	45
24	Notts C	46	9	13	24	45	66	40

1994-95

Manager : Jimmy Mullen

Division One (22nd)
Relegated

Notes	No.	Date		Venue	Opponents	Result		h/t	Goalscorers/times	Opp. goal times
	1	Aug	13	a	Middlesbrough	L	0-2	0-2		28, 35
	2		20	h	STOKE C	D	1-1	1-0	Davis 43	90
	3		27	a	Oldham A	L	0-3	0-0		51, 81, 84
	4		30	h	BRISTOL C	D	1-1	1-0	Robinson 40	90
	5	Sep	3	h	BARNSLEY	L	0-1	0-0		53
	6		10	a	Luton T	W	1-0	1-0	Robinson 44	
	7		14	a	Millwall	W	3-2	0-0	Winstanley (2) 53, 69, Robinson 79	46, 74
	8		17	h	WOLVERHAMPTON W	L	0-1	0-0		59
	9		24	a	West Bromwich A	L	0-1	0-0		71
	10	Oct	1	h	TRANMERE R	D	1-1	0-1	Eyres 70p	26
	11		8	h	BOLTON W	D	2-2	0-1	Davis 68, Deary 72	5, 82
	12		15	a	Sunderland	D	0-0	0-0		
	13		22	a	Charlton A	W	2-1	0-0	Davis 51, Robinson 62	80
	14		29	h	NOTTS C	W	2-1	1-0	Eyres 7p, Hoyland 52	51
	15	Nov	1	h	WATFORD	D	1-1	0-1	Eyres 72	39
	16		5	a	Reading	D	0-0	0-0		
	17		20	h	SHEFFIELD U	W	4-2	1-1	Robinson 24, Hoyland 54, Gayle 71, Davis 78	45, 83
	18		23	a	Swindon T	D	1-1	0-1	Gayle 68	17
	19		26	a	Grimsby T	D	2-2	0-1	Davis 57, Parkinson 90	43, 68
	20	Dec	10	a	Stoke C	L	0-2	0-0		69, 84
	21		18	h	MIDDLESBROUGH	L	0-3	0-1		14, 64, 90
Southend goal 69m	22		31	h	SOUTHEND U	W	5-1	2-0	Saville 27, Gayle 34, Bressington 51og, Davis 86, Robinson 90	
	23	Jan	2	a	Portsmouth	L	0-2	0-1		27, 84
Deary's last game	24		14	a	Notts C	L	0-3	0-0		55, 70, 87
	25		21	h	READING	L	1-2	0-2	Parkinson 56	6, 10
	26	Feb	4	h	SWINDON T	L	1-2	0-1	Harrison 85	43, 73
	27		11	a	Watford	L	0-2	0-0		53, 71
	28		18	h	GRIMSBY T	L	0-2	0-1		25, 81
	29		21	a	Sheffield U	L	0-2	0-1		44, 90
	30		15	a	Tranmere R	L	1-4	0-1	Garnett 89og	16, 47, 78, 90
	31	Mar	4	h	WEST BROMWICH A	D	1-1	0-0	Robinson 89	63
	32		7	a	Barnsley	L	0-2	0-1		41, 89
	33		11	h	OLDHAM A	W	2-1	1-0	Nogan 7, Vinnicombe 76	47
	34		15	a	Derby C	L	0-4	0-1		28, 51, 55, 90
	35		18	a	Bristol C	D	1-1	0-1	Eyres 66	13
	36		21	h	LUTON T	W	2-1	0-0	Mullin 73, Harrison 83	61
	37		24	a	Wolverhampton W	L	0-2	0-1		11, 59
	38		28	h	PORT VALE	W	4-3	1-1	Nogan 45, Randall 60, Shaw 64, Sandeman 64og	42, 68, 84
	39	Apr	1	h	MILLWALL	L	1-2	0-1	Shaw 75	38, 57
	40		4	h	CHARLTON A	W	2-0	1-0	Eyres 24, Shaw 81	
	41		8	a	Southend U	L	1-3	0-2	Nogan 82	5, 6, 54
	42		15	h	DERBY C	W	3-1	2-0	Eyres 12, Shaw 19, Davis 70	68
	43		17	a	Port Vale	L	0-1	0-1		40
	44		22	h	PORTSMOUTH	L	1-2	0-1	Eyres 81	35, 61
	45		29	h	SUNDERLAND	D	1-1	1-1	Eyres 36p	16
	46	May	7	a	Bolton W	D	1-1	0-0	Philliskirk 61	90

FA Cup

Round	Date		Venue	Opponents	Result		h/t	Goalscorers/times	Opp. goal times
1	Nov	12	h	SHREWSBURY T	W	2-1	1-1	Heath 28, Deary 46	36
2	Dec	4	a	Chester C	W	2-1	0-0	Eyres 49p, Heath 85	76
3	Jan	7	a	Cambridge U	W	4-2	2-1	Eyres 25p, Robinson 45, Randall 73, Gayle 77	18, 86
4		28	h	LIVERPOOL	D	0-0	0-0		
rep	Feb	7	a	Liverpool	L	0-1	0-1		44

Final, Everton 1-0 Manchester U, at Wembley.

League Cup

Notes	Round	Date		Venue	Opponents	Result		h/t	Goalscorers/times	Opp. goal times
	1	Aug	16	h	YORK C	W	1-0	0-0	Joyce 73	
agg 3-2			23	a	York C	D	2-2	0-1	Robinson 64, Gayle 67	17, 73
	2	Sep	21	a	Liverpool	L	0-2	0-1		42, 84
agg 1-6		Oct	5	h	LIVERPOOL	L	1-4	0-1	Robinson 84	15, 51, 68, 75

Final, Liverpool 2-1 Bolton W, at Wembley.

Details of other first team games elsewhere.

Att.	Pos	Beresford	Parkinson	Vinnicombe	Davis	Winstanley	Joyce	A Harper	Deary	Heath	L Robinson	McMinn	Lancashire	Gayle	Harrison	W Russell	Eyres	Randall	Philliskirk	Hoyland	Francis	Dowell	Mullin	C Armstrong	Saville	Brass	Pender	Stewart	Peel	S Thompson	Nogan	Shaw	
23,343		1	2	3	4	5	6*	7	8	9	10	11	S*																				1
15,331	20	1	2	3	4	5	6*	7	S*	9	10	11		8																			2
11,310	23	1	3		4	5	6**	7	S**	9	10	11*		8	2	S*																	3
11,067		1	2	3	4	5	6	7		9	10*	11		8	S*																		4
11,968	23	1	2	3	4	5	S**	6**	8	S*	10	7		9*			11																5
6,911	21		2	3	4	5		7		9	10	11			8	1		6															6
7,375		1	2	3	4	5		7	6	9	10	11			8																		7
17,766	21	1	2	3	4	5		7	6	9	10**	11			8*		S*		S**														8
13,539	22	1	2	3	4	5		7	S**	9	10	8*			6**		11		S*														9
12,427	22	1	2	3	4	5		6		9	10	7			8*		11		S*														10
16,687	22	1	2*	3	4	5			9		10	7**		S**	S*		11	6	8														11
17,700	22	1	2	3		5		7	9	S*	10*			S**			11	6	8**	4													12
9,436	21	1	2	3	4	5		7	9		10						11	6		8													13
12,876	18	1	2	3	4	5		7	9	S*	10						11	6*		8													14
11,739		1	2	3	4	5		7**	9*	S**	10						11	6	S*	8													15
8,150	21	1	2	3**	4	5		7	9	8	10*			S*			11	6			S**												16
11,475	15	1	2		4	5		7*		8	10			S*			11	6		9		3											17
7,654		1	2		4	5		7		8	10			S*			11	6		9		3*											18
7,084	15	1	2		4	5		7		8	10**			S*			11	6		9	S**	3*											19
13,040	18	1	2		4	5**		7		8	10			9			11	6*	S**	3			S*										20
12,049	20	1	2		4	5		7*		8	10**			S*			11	6		9		3	S**										21
10,561	19	1	2		4	5			11	8	10	S*		9*	6									3	7								22
9,097	20	1	2		4	5^			11	8	9				6*	S*	10		S^					3**	7	S**							23
8,702	22	1	2		4	5		7	S**	8	10**	S*					3	6*		11					9								24
9,841	22		2		4	5		7*			10	S*		9		1	11	6		8				3**	S**								25
10,960	23	1	2		4	5		7			10**	S*			S**		11	6		8			9	3*									26
9,297	23	1	2			5		7		9	10	S*			6*		3			8			11				4						27
10,511	23	1	3			5				S*	S**	7			2**		11	6		8			10				4*	9					28
13,349		1	2		4	5		7*		9					6		3			8			11					10	S*				29
9,909	24	1	2		4			7*		9	S*				6		3			5								10		8	11		30
11,885	24	1	2		4			7*		S*	S**						11	6		5		3**						9		8	10		31
5,537		1	2	5	4	3											11	6		7								9	S*	8	10*		32
11,620	24	1	2	5	4	3											11	6		7								9		8	10		33
13,922		1	2	5	4	3											11	6		7			9*						S*	8	10		34
6,717	24		S**	5	4	3					S*				2	1	11	6**		7							10			8	9*		35
9,551				5	4	3					7				2	1	11	6					S*				10*			8	9		36
25,703				5	4	3					10*				2**	1	11	6		7						S**				8	9	S*	37
10,058				5	4	3									2*	1	11	6		10			S**			S*				8	9**	7	38
10,454	23	1	2*		4	5					S*						11	6		10			S**			3				8	9**	7	39
10,045		1	2	5	4	3					S*	11*					9	6		10										8		7	40
5,027	22	1	2	5	4	3					S**	11					9**	6		10						8					S*	7*	41
11,534	22	1	2	5	4	3					S*	7*					11	6	9	10												8	42
9,663	22	1	2	8	4	3*					S*						11	6	9	10							5				S**	7**	43
10,666	22	1	2	5	4	3					S**	7					11	6	9**	10											S*	8*	44
15,121	21	1	2	5	4	3						7*					11	6	9	10			S*								S**	8**	45
16,853	22	1	2	5	4	3											11	6	9				7							10	8		46
Appearances		40	42	29	43	44	4	27	12	21	29	17		7	16	6	38	32	7	30		5	6	4	3	2	5	6		12	11	8	
Apps as sub			1				1		4	6	10	5	1	7	3	2	1		6		2		6		1	3			3		4	1	
Goals (49)			2	1	7	2			1		7			3	2		8	1	1	2			1		1						3	4	3 ogs
9,269		1	2		4	5		7	9	8	10*						11	6			S*	3											1
4,231		1	2		4	5		7		8	10			S*			11	6		9		3*											2
6,275		1	2			5		7	S*	8	10	11*		9			3	6		4													3
20,551			2		4	5		7			10*	S*				1	3	6		8			9		11								4
32,109		1	2		4	5		7			10	S*			11*		3	6		8**			9						S**				rep
Appearances		4	5		4	5		5	1	3	5	1		1	1	1	5	5		4		2	2		1								
Apps as sub									1			2		1							1								1				
Goals (8)									1	2	1			1			2	1															
6,390		1	2		4	5	6	7	8	9	10		11									3											1
3,089		1	2	3*	4	5	6**	7	S*	9	10	11	S**	8																			2nd leg
23,359		1	2	3	4	5		7	S*	9	10**	11			8*		6		S**														2
19,032		1	2	3	4	5		6*		9	10	7**		S**	S*		11		8														2nd leg
Appearances		4	4	3	4	4	2	4	1	4	4	3	1	1	1		2		1			1											
Apps as sub									2				1	1	1				1														
Goals (4)							1				2			1																			

1995-96

It took Burnley seven years to clamber out of the Fourth Division.
English football's basement. The soccer doldrums. An unwanted place to be.
And things became so drastic that the Clarets, twice Football League Champions, came agonisingly close to dropping out of the League altogether.
Jimmy Mullen was the man to change all that, leading the Clarets out of the soccer wilderness in 1992 and to the brink of the big time.
But season 1995-96 saw Mullen wake up from his three-year dream, and into the harsh reality of a football manager.
It was a campaign where the unthinkable almost occurred.
Having took so long to pull themselves up the cellar steps, Burnley were almost pushed back down them again and back onto the lowest rung of English football's league ladder.
And if the season had gone on for another five more games or so, that may have happened.
Turf Moor was a gloomy place, with the club still smarting from losing their First Division status the previous season.
Hopes were high that the club would bounce back after a fleeting appearance in the second tier, but Mullen was to feel an angry backlash midway through the campaign.
It had all began so brightly, with David Eyres and Tony Philliskirk both on target in an opening day success over Rotherham.
But how ironic it would be, that the return game against the same opposition would be the turning point of the entire season.
Defeats at Bristol Rovers and Carlisle were minor blips on the radar, but Burnley were moulding a home record to rival anyone in the division.
Brentford, Hull, Swansea and Brighton were all accounted for, and it wasn't until Notts County came to town on 4 November that the Clarets experienced a home defeat.
Even that 4-3 reverse could have been avoided, but that was to be their only home defeat in 12 until the turn of the year.
And it wasn't as if 1996 started badly either, as Stockport were beaten in a thriller.
But things began to turn sour at Millmoor, on 20 January.
A solitary goal from Rotherham's Trevor Berry proved Burnley's undoing, just seven days after coming through that seven-goal bonanza with Stockport.
That win, thanks to goals from Chris Vinnicombe, Andy Cooke, Kurt Nogan and John Francis, put the Clarets fifth in the table, six points off an automatic promotion place.
But within three months, the face of Burnley Football Club had undergone a makeover of massive proportions.
That defeat at Rotherham was followed by one of the low points of the season at home to Oxford United on a Tuesday night.
A paltry crowd of 6,815 were in attendance that night, the lowest crowd at Turf Moor in Mullen's four-year tenure as boss.
A 2-0 victory for the visitors was their first on the road all season, and this was on the penultimate day of January.
And it triggered the home fans to vote with their feet, in a bid to vent their anger at the people running their beloved club.
Hundreds of disgruntled supporters conducted a 20-minute demonstration in the immediate aftermath of the defeat, calling for the heads of manager Mullen and chairman Frank Teasdale.
It was the most vociferous display of dissatisfaction since the stormy end of Frank Casper's reign as boss.
But it got worse just four days later, as a pitiful display at Brentford made it three successive defeats.
Three games without a point and three games without a goal prompted Mullen to move into the transfer market, shelling out £25,000 on Stockport County striker Ian Helliwell.
But he was to just make three starts for the club, with his debut coming in the home game with Crewe Alexandra.
That 1-0 defeat will always be remembered for one thing, as sections of the home faithful turned their backs on proceedings in the infamous "3:33 protest".

Kurt Nogan
top scorer with 23 goals in league and cup

It was a sight that will long be remembered in Burnley's history, and one that attracted media attention from up and down the country.
But the angry fans were to get their wish, as just 48 hours after that game, Mullen's reign as Burnley manager was over.
Ironically, his tenure in the hot seat had lasted exactly 200 league games, but the quest was on to find a suitable replacement.
A phone poll run in the Burnley Express saw Brian Flynn emerge as the firm favourite among the supporters.
Mullen's assistant Clive Middlemass was placed in temporary

charge, overseeing a 3-3 home draw with York before defeats to Hull (3-0) and Blackpool (1-0).

Steve Coppell, Mike Walker, Michael Phelan and Brian McClair were among the many names to be touted for the vacancy.

And it was Walker who was the first to express an interest in the job, commenting: "If Burnley are ambitious, they will come in for me."

It was even mooted at one point that Coppell had been interviewed for the vacancy, and that an unnamed former Claret would also be travelling to Turf Moor as his assistant.

But those rumours were to be quashed when the club's silence was broken in early March.

It was the bookies' favourite, Adrian Heath, who was handed the job, and he made an immediate impact: "I want to get Burnley Football Club back to the top.

"It is a big challenge, but I am confident I can take that challenge head on and make Burnley great again.

"In the immediate future, I want to help Burnley climb the table first, but the long term aim is to reach the Premiership inside five years.

"I have a great deal of affection for the club, and simply could not say no.

"They are an ambitious club, and I feel I am ready for the task at hand.

"I had an unbelievable rapport with the fans as a player, and hopefully that will be a big plus in turning the fortunes of the club around.

"It's a job which anyone who has ever played for Burnley would find very hard to turn down."

His first game in charge saw the Clarets register their first win since the Stockport clash, with Nogan netting the only goal of the game.

However, the rose-tinted glasses were soon flung onto the rubbish pile, as that was to be the only win in his first nine matches.

The overall record made cruel reading, with the Clarets picking up just six points from a possible 48.

And the run was so severe, that a 1-0 defeat at Brighton on 9 April put Burnley just a point and a place above the relegation zone.

Two unlikely heroes, Warren Joyce and Peter Swan, were both on target as that run was ended with a 2-1 home win over Peterborough.

But it was the 2-0 success at Wrexham, thanks to Liam Robinson and Nogan, that finally disposed of the cloud of possible relegation.

The season was ended with a bang, with a 2-1 success over Shrewsbury in front of the home faithful.

But the 24 league games since the turn of the year had yielded just 21 goals, with four of those coming in the victory over Stockport back in January.

Who knows where the club might have ended up if it wasn't for Nogan, who smashed 20 goals in an otherwise forgettable campaign.

The home win against Shrewsbury on the final day was the least the fans deserved, after a season of unbelievable turmoil, and extreme nail-biting.

But then, that's part and parcel of being a Burnley fan.

Marlon Beresford
already being compared to Colin McDonald
high praise indeed!

1995-96 - Second Division

		P	W	D	L	F	A	Pts
1	Swindon T	46	25	17	4	71	34	92
2	Oxford U	46	24	11	11	76	39	83
3	Blackpool	46	23	13	10	67	40	82
4	Notts C	46	21	15	10	63	39	78
5	Crewe A	46	22	7	17	77	60	73
6	Bradford C	46	22	7	17	71	69	73
7	Chesterfield	46	20	12	14	56	51	72
8	Wrexham	46	18	16	12	76	55	70
9	Stockport C	46	19	13	14	61	47	70
10	Bristol R	46	20	10	16	57	60	70
11	Walsall	46	19	12	15	60	45	69
12	Wycombe W	46	15	15	16	63	59	60
13	Bristol C	46	15	15	16	55	60	60
14	Bournemouth	46	16	10	20	51	70	58
15	Brentford	46	15	13	18	43	49	58
16	Rotherham U	46	14	14	18	54	62	56
17	BURNLEY	46	14	13	19	56	68	55
18	Shrewsbury T	46	13	14	19	58	70	53
19	Peterborough U	46	13	13	20	59	66	52
20	York C	46	13	13	20	58	73	52
21	Carlisle U	46	12	13	21	57	72	49
22	Swansea C	46	11	14	21	43	79	47
23	Brighton & HA	46	10	10	26	46	69	40
24	Hull C	46	5	16	25	36	78	31

1995-96

Manager : Jimmy Mullen until February 1996, Clive Middlemass until March 1996, then Adrian Heath

Division Two (17th)

	No.	Date		h/a	Opponents	Result		h/t	Goalscorers/times	Opp. goal times
	1	Aug	12	h	ROTHERHAM U	W	2-1	2-1	Eyres 25p, Philliskirk 39	10
	2		19	a	Stockport C	D	0-0	0-0		
	3		26	h	BRENTFORD	W	1-0	1-0	Nogan 11	
	4		29	a	Bristol R	L	0-1	0-0		49
	5	Sep	6	h	WALSALL	D	1-1	0-0	Joyce 90	77
	6		9	a	Carlisle U	L	0-2	0-0		52, 70
	7		12	a	York C	D	1-1	1-0	Cooke 38	71
	8		16	h	HULL C	W	2-1	1-0	Nogan 40, Allison 89og	90
Philliskirk's last game	9		23	a	Chesterfield	L	2-4	2-2	Nogan 17, Eyres 44p	27, 42, 54, 75
	10		30	h	SWANSEA T	W	3-0	1-0	Nogan 15, Joyce 53, Eyres 79	
	11	Oct	7	h	WYCOMBE W	D	1-1	1-0	Joyce 40	64
	12		14	a	Bournemouth	W	2-0	1-0	Vinnicombe 6, Nogan 78	
	13		21	h	BRIGHTON & H A	W	3-0	3-0	Eyres 4, Swan 33, Nogan 36	
	14		28	a	Bradford C	D	2-2	1-1	Harrison 24, Swan 86	22, 54
	15		31	a	Peterborough U	W	2-0	2-0	McDonald 11, Swan 33	
	16	Nov	4	h	NOTTS C	L	3-4	1-2	Nogan (2) 3, 85, Cooke 69	16, 37, 59, 74
	17		18	a	Shrewsbury T	L	0-3	0-2		8, 35, 59
	18		25	h	WREXHAM	D	2-2	0-0	Nogan 59, Joyce 65	51, 66
	19	Dec	2	h	CARLISLE U	W	2-0	1-0	Nogan (2) 38, 57	
Randall's last game	20		9	h	CHESTERFIELD	D	2-2	1-1	Nogan (2) 21, 81	43, 64
	21		16	a	Swansea T	W	4-2	1-0	Eyres 32, Nogan 54, Cooke (2) 75, 87	61, 63
McMinn's last game	22		23	h	BRISTOL C	D	0-0	0-0		
	23	Jan	13	h	STOCKPORT C	W	4-3	2-3	Vinnicombe 6, Cooke 17, Nogan 69, Francis 79	3, 11, 33
	24		20	a	Rotherham U	L	0-1	0-0		85
	25		30	h	OXFORD U	L	0-2	0-1		26, 69
	26	Feb	3	a	Brentford	L	0-1	0-0		61
	27		10	h	CREWE A	L	0-1	0-1		21
	28		17	h	YORK C	D	3-3	0-2	Winstanley 50, Francis 60, Nogan 67	12, 34, 55
	29		24	a	Hull C	L	0-3	0-1		4, 69, 83
Francis' last game	30	Mar	2	h	BLACKPOOL	L	0-1	0-0		62
	31		9	a	Bristol C	W	1-0	0-0	Nogan 84	
	32		12	a	Blackpool	L	1-3	1-1	Nogan 28	25, 59, 79
	33		16	h	SWINDON T	D	0-0	0-0		
	34		19	a	Crewe A	L	1-3	0-0	Winstanley 65	51, 57, 89
	35		23	a	Oxford U	L	0-5	0-1		37,77,80,86,90
	36		30	a	Wycombe W	L	1-4	0-2	Mahorn 54	12, 32, 82, 90
	37	Apr	2	h	BOURNEMOUTH	D	0-0	0-0		
	38		6	h	BRADFORD C	L	2-3	0-2	Robinson 54, Eyres 69p	35, 36, 90
	39		9	a	Brighton & H A	L	0-1	0-1		19
	40		13	h	PETERBOROUGH U	W	2-1	0-0	Joyce 52, Swan 66	68
	41		17	a	Swindon T	D	0-0	0-0		
	42		20	a	Notts C	D	1-1	1-0	Swan 31	65
	43		23	h	BRISTOL R	L	0-1	0-0		64
	44		27	a	Wrexham	W	2-0	2-0	Robinson 26, Nogan 45	
	45		30	a	Walsall	L	1-3	0-0	Nogan 51	52, 82, 89
Warren Joyce's last game	46	May	4	h	SHREWSBURY T	W	2-1	1-1	Weller 14, Winstanley 73	42

FA Cup

Rd	Date		h/a	Opponents	Result		h/t	Goalscorers/times	Opp. goal times
1	Nov	10	h	WALSALL	L	1-3	1-1	Eyres 25	9, 49, 57

Final, Manchester U 1-0 Liverpool, at Wembley.

League Cup

	Rd	Date		h/a	Opponents	Result		h/t	Goalscorers/times	Opp. goal times
	1	Aug	15	a	Mansfield T	W	1-0	1-0	Nogan 28	
agg 4-1			22	h	MANSFIELD T	W	3-1	1-0	Randall 8, Nogan (2) 59, 68	61
	2	Sep	20	a	Leicester C	L	0-2	0-1		26, 55
agg 0-4		Oct	3	h	LEICESTER C	L	0-2	0-0		79, 87

Final, Aston Villa 3-0 Leeds U, at Wembley.

Details of other first team games elsewhere.

Att.	Pos	Beresford	Parkinson	Vinnicombe	Swan	Pender	Randall	McMinn	Joyce	Philliskirk	Nogan	Eyres	Francis	Brass	Winstanley	A Harper	Hoyland	A Cooke	Harrison	Borland	McDonald	Heath	Weller	Adams	W Russell	L Robinson	Helliwell	Dowell	S Thompson	P Smith	Bishop	Mahorn					
10,478		1	2	3	4	5	6**	7*	8	9	10	11	S*	S**																							1
8,463	8	1	2	3	4		6	11*	8	9	10		S*		5	7																					2
9,586	5	1	2	3	4		6		8	9*	10	S*	11		5		7																				3
5,646		1	2	3	4		6		8*	9**	10	11	S*		5		7	S**																			4
8,778		1		3	4		6		S**	9*	10	11	7	2**	5		8	S*																			5
7,318	15	1		3	4		6		8	9**	10	11	S*		5		7	S**	2*																		6
4,684		1		3	4				8		10*	11	S*		5		6	9	2	7																	7
10,613	9	1		3	4*			7	8	S**	10	S*			5		6**	9	2		11																8
4,933	13	1	2*	3					6	9**	10	11	S**		5	7			4		S*	8															9
8,068	9	1	2	3			6	7	8		10	9			5				4		11																10
8,029	11	1	2	3	4		6	7*	8		10	9**	S*		5			S**			11																11
4,954	7	1	2	3	5				8		10	9*			4		6	S*	7		11																12
9,016	5	1	2	3	5			7*	8		10	9	S*		4		S**		6		11**																13
8,356	6	1	2*	3	5		S*		8**		10	9	S**		4		6	S^	7		11^																14
4,737		1	2	3	5		S*		8*		10	9			4		6		7		11																15
10,511	7	1	2**	3	5		S*	11*			10	9	S^		4		6	S**	7		8^																16
3,914	8	1	2	3*	5^		11**		8		10	9	S*	S**	4		6	S^	7																		17
8,710	8	1		3	4		11	S*	8		10	9			5		6*		2			7															18
8,297	4	1		3			6		8		10	11		2	5		4	S*				9*	7														19
8,459	6	1		3			6	S*	8		10	11^	S^	2	5		4	S**				9**	7*														20
2,078	5	1		3					8*		10	11		2	5		4	9	6				7	S*													21
9,327	5	1		3*	S^			S*	8		10	11		2	5		4	9^	6**				7	S**													22
9,113	5	1		3	4				8		10	S*	S**	2	5		7*	9	6				11**														23
4,018	6	1		3	4				8		10	11	S*	2*	5			9	6				7														24
6,815			2*	3	4				8		10	11	S*		5			9	6**				7		1	S**											25
5,195	8		2*	3					8		10	11	9		5		4		6				7		1	S*											26
9,153	11		2	3**					8		10	11	S*		5		4	S**	6				7*		1		9										27
8,731	12		2						8		10		7		5		4	S**	6				11**		1	S*	9*	3									28
4,206	15			3	4				8		10		S*		5		6		2						1	7	9*		11								29
10,082	16			3	4				8		10	11**	S^		5			S**	2				7*		1	9^			6	S*							30
6,612	15	1	2	3					8		10	11			5		S*		4*				7			S**			6	9**							31
8,941		1	2	3					8		10	11			5				4				7*			9			6	S*							32
9,360	15	1	2	3					8		10	11			5			9*	4				7						6	S*							33
3,393		1	2	3					8		10	11			5			9	4				7						6								34
6,529	18	1	2	3					8		10	11			5			9*	4				7						6	S*							35
4,921	18	1	2	3*	4						10	11			5				7			9**	S**						8		6	S*					36
7,941			2		4						10	11			5				6				7		1				8		3	9					37
9,714	20				4				6		10	11			5				2				7*		1	S*			8		3	9					38
5,954					4				6		10				5	9*			2						1	7			8	11	3	S*					39
8,393	20				4				6		10	11			5				2			S*			1	7			8		3	9*					40
10,480		1			4				6		10*	11			5				2				7			9			8		3	S*					41
5,697	20	1	2		4				6		10	11			5								7			9			8		3						42
9,368		1	2		4				6		10	11			5								7*			9**			8	S**	3	S*					43
6,664	19	1	2						6		10	11			5								7			9			8	3*	4	S*					44
3,411		1	2		4				6**		10	11			5				3				7*			9	S**		8	S*							45
9,729	17	1	2		4*				6**		10	11^			5	S^			3			S*	7			9			8	S**							46
Appearances		36	29	35	31	1	12	7	42	7	46	39	4	7	45	3	21	10	35	1	8	5	24		10	11	3	1	18	3	9	3					
Apps as sub					1		3	3	1	1		3	18	2		1	2	13			1	2	1	2		5	1			7		5					
Goals (56)				2	5				5	1	20	6	2		3			5	1		1		1			2						1				1	og

Att.		Beresford	Parkinson	Vinnicombe	Swan	Pender	Randall	McMinn	Joyce	Philliskirk	Nogan	Eyres	Francis	Brass	Winstanley	A Harper	Hoyland	A Cooke	Harrison	Borland	McDonald	Heath	Weller	Adams	W Russell	L Robinson	Helliwell	Dowell	S Thompson	P Smith	Bishop	Mahorn					
6,525		1	2	3	5		8*	11^			10	9	S^		4		6**	S**	7	S*																	1
Appearances		1	1	1	1		1	1			1	1			1		1		1																		
Apps as sub													1					1		1																	
Goals (1)												1																									

Att.		Beresford	Parkinson	Vinnicombe	Swan	Pender	Randall	McMinn	Joyce	Philliskirk	Nogan	Eyres	Francis	Brass	Winstanley	A Harper	Hoyland	A Cooke	Harrison	Borland	McDonald	Heath	Weller	Adams	W Russell	L Robinson	Helliwell	Dowell	S Thompson	P Smith	Bishop	Mahorn					
2,544		1	2	3	4	5			8	9	10	11*	S*			7				6																	1
4,673		1	2	3	4*		6		8	9	10		S*		5		7			11																	2nd leg
11,142		1	2	3					6	9	10	11			5	7			4			8															2
4,553		1	2	3			6	11	8		10	9	S*		5				4				7*														2nd leg
Appearances		4	4	4	2	1	2	1	4	3	4	3			3	2	1		2	2		1	1														
Apps as sub													3																								
Goals (4)							1				3																										

1996-97

OBITUARY
THOMAS (TOMMY) LAWTON
DIED 6 NOVEMBER 1996, AGED 77.

Arguably the greatest player ever to pull on a Burnley shirt, the pity of it was that Tommy Lawton had already moved on from Turf Moor long before reaching the age of eighteen.

Born in Bolton, he joined Burnley as a 16-year-old with a mighty reputation, having reputedly scored 570 goals in three seasons of schoolboy football. He made his League debut in March 1936 and is still the youngest player to have appeared in Burnley's first team. Only 25 appearances and 16 goals later, he was transferred to Everton for £6,500, an enormous fee for so young a player, on New Year's Day 1937. Within two seasons, he was an established England international and had a League championship medal.

Lawton's career was cruelly cut short by World War II. If it had not been, there is every chance that he would have gone on to become both the League's and England's all-time record scorer. As it was, he averaged close to a goal a game for his country. He was capable of scoring with either foot or with his head, and it was a tragedy for football that most of his peak playing years fell during the war.

Most obituaries of Tommy Lawton refer only in passing to his time at Turf Moor, but it was at Burnley where his legend was born.

RIP

We just love days where record books are rewritten.

Certain matches where, in the final stages, fans are frantically searching their memories to recall when it happened last.

Supporters everywhere clambering to get one up on the friend sat next to them.

5 October 1996 was just one of those days.

And it was Paul Barnes' name that was on everybody's lips.

Adrian Heath had brought Barnes to Turf Moor from Birmingham City for £400,000, just weeks into the new season.

He had made his debut in the 1-0 defeat at Gillingham, after the Clarets had registered two wins and two defeats in their opening four outings.

It had all started so rosy, with two wins against Luton and Walsall sending Burnley top of the tree.

But defeats to Shrewsbury and Millwall had brought them back down to earth with a bump.

Barnes would experience a rough ride in his first few months at his new club, with the fans beginning to get on his back.

His first six league games for his new club yielded no goals, and neither did the Clarets' 6-2 aggregate League Cup defeat to Charlton Athletic.

But it would come good all at once for Barnes, when Stockport County came to town.

After bringing his goalscoring drought to an end just past the half hour, he would add another just before half-time.

A third on the hour meant he had hit a hat-trick in just 29 minutes, but he wasn't finished there.

Two more in seven second-half minutes contributed to a 5-2 triumph – and incredibly Barnes had netted all five inside 46 minutes!

And afterwards, he announced his shock: "I actually had £20 on myself to score the first goal, but I never imagined going on to hit five!

"It is just superb, everything seemed to drop for me - I was even expecting one to go in off the back of my head.

"I've scored four before and had four or five hat-tricks, but five is very special.

"That ranks up there with my best times in football."

He wasn't wrong.

Barnes became the first Burnley player to score five in a game since Andy Lochhead 31 years earlier.

The feat also saw him go down as only the fifth Claret in history to net five goals in the same game.

And even the individual club record of six, set by Louis Page in a 7-1 defeat of Birmingham at St Andrews in April 1926, appeared in real danger at one stage.

And manager Adrian Heath admitted it was only what he deserved, saying: "I'm a firm believer that you get out of football what you put in.

"Paul Barnes has worked hard and has not had a lot of luck in front of goal – he so much deserved this.

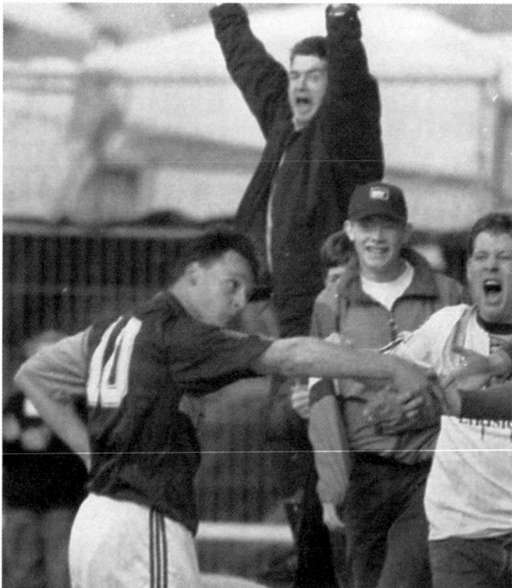

Everybody wants to shake the hand of Paul Barnes after his five goals against Stockport

"They were great finishes - when you buy a player and break the club record, you obviously hope he's going to come in and set the place alight straight away.

"I never doubted that Paul would do that at Burnley, and I was especially pleased that it was in front of our own fans.

"I can't remember too many players scoring five in a league game

"It's a strange old business the profession of a striker, isn't it?"

In the space of one match, Barnes had become the club's second leading goalscorer for the season behind Kurt Nogan.

And the moment after his fifth goal went in, when he ran

over to the North Stand and counted out each goal finger by finger, will never be forgotten.
A superb gesture from his manager saw Barnes replaced in the final minute by Andy Cooke, ensuring the five-star striker received a richly-deserved standing ovation.
And it was to be the catalyst for Barnes to be the lynchpin of a successful campaign, that almost saw the Clarets snatch a play-off spot.
Despite that feat, Barnes would only have six goals to his name come the second week of November.
The ball really began rolling for him during a 2-1 win at Bristol Rovers.
One goal either side of half-time was at the centre of a four-game winning sequence, sandwiched between home league victories over Crewe and Bournemouth.
And in the FA Cup, the Clarets progressed to the second round with a 2-1 win over Lincoln, thanks to goals from Nigel Gleghorn and Damian Matthew.
The three league successes propelled the Clarets into the play-off places, but after collecting four points against Plymouth and Wrexham, a decline set in.
But they almost caused an upset in the third round of the FA Cup, at Anfield.
Stan Collymore hit the only goal of the game just 12 minutes in, but Burnley's dogged resistance could well have produced an unlikely replay.
In and around that game, just two wins arrived from 12 outings, against Gillingham and Bury at Turf Moor.
Six games without a success saw them drop out of the play-off picture, as Burnley struggled to find any consistent form in front of goal.
But it wouldn't take a genius to work out who would bring that run of results to an end, and in what style he would do it.
Not only that, but what a place to do it.
A first win in seven came at Bloomfield Road against Lancashire rivals Blackpool, and it was Barnes at the heart of it.
After putting Burnley ahead after only six minutes, the lead was wiped out thanks to James Quinn.
But two goals in five minutes from Barnes either side of the interval earned him his first treble since that memorable day back in October.
Burnley were rolling again, and after a goalless draw at Wrexham, three wins followed.
Peterborough were hit for five at Turf Moor, but this time, Barnes helped himself to just three.
Brentford were brushed aside 3-0 at Griffin Park, while Walsall's play-off charge was halted somewhat as the Clarets brought home a 3-1 success.
Burnley were suddenly in fifth place, and had a real shot at a top six finish.
But just like the early part of the year, the Clarets would embark on a run of form that would ultimately leave them consigned to life in the Second Division for another season.
Burnley well and truly dried up in front of goal, with just two goals in their next five matches.
Not only that, but goal machine Barnes would hit only two more in the final eight matches of the campaign.

A 2-0 home defeat to Luton was followed three days later by a 2-1 reverse at Gay Meadow against Shrewsbury.
Paul Weller would net the only goal of the game to beat Millwall, but that was to be the Clarets' only win in seven.
Adrian Heath's men finally slipped put of the top six with a 1-0 loss at Stockport County – sweet revenge for Barnes' one-man mission at Turf Moor earlier in the season.
But a 5-0 hammering at Wycombe was the final nail in the coffin for Burnley's aspirations of a play-off finish.
However, their final three games of the campaign looked, on paper, to be very winnable.
Games against Rotherham and Notts County were first up, with both languishing in the relegation zone.
And a home game against Watford on the final day, themselves in freefall after a long play-off chase, was also appetising.
But Burnley shot themselves in the foot twice, as they could pick up only two points against the two bottom sides in the table.
Rotherham even managed to lead twice at Turf Moor, only for Barnes and two from Andy Cooke to rescue a point.
But Cooke was to turn villain at Notts County, sent off after just 18 minutes, as the Clarets had to rely on an injury time strike from Damian Matthew to earn a share of the spoils.
Cooke's Jekyll and Hyde end to the season continued against Watford on the final day, as he made up for his early bath in the previous game to register a second half treble.
But it wasn't enough for Burnley, who ended the season ninth in the table, and just five points off a top six slot.
Victories against the league's two bottom clubs towards the end of the season would have made for quite a final day.
But it wasn't to be, and Adrian Heath stepped down from the hotseat just weeks after the curtain came down on another campaign.

1996-97 - Second Division

		P	W	D	L	F	A	Pts
1	Bury	46	24	12	10	62	38	84
2	Stockport C	46	23	13	10	59	41	82
3	Luton T	46	21	15	10	71	45	78
4	Brentford	46	20	14	12	56	43	74
5	Bristol C	46	21	10	15	69	51	73
6	Crewe A	46	22	7	17	56	47	73
7	Blackpool	46	18	15	13	60	47	69
8	Wrexham	46	17	18	11	54	50	69
9	BURNLEY	46	19	11	16	71	55	68
10	Chesterfield	46	18	14	14	42	39	68
11	Gillingham	46	19	10	17	60	59	67
12	Walsall	46	19	10	17	54	53	67
13	Watford	46	16	19	11	45	38	67
14	Millwall	46	16	13	17	50	55	61
15	Preston NE	46	18	7	21	49	55	61
16	Bournemouth	46	15	15	16	43	45	60
17	Bristol R	46	15	11	20	47	50	56
18	Wycombe W	46	15	10	21	51	56	55
19	Plymouth A	46	12	18	16	47	58	54
20	York C	46	13	13	20	47	68	52
21	Peterborough U	46	11	14	21	55	73	47
22	Shrewsbury T	46	11	13	22	49	74	46
23	Rotherham U	46	7	14	25	39	70	35
24	Notts C	46	7	14	25	33	59	35

1996-97

Manager : Adrian Heath

Division Two (9th)

	No.	Date			Opponents	Result		h/t	Goalscorers/times	Opp. goal times
	1	Aug	17	a	Luton T	W	2-1	2-1	Thompson 24, Nogan 32	36
	2		24	h	WALSALL	W	2-1	1-1	Eyres 22, Nogan 48	44
	3		27	h	SHREWSBURY T	L	1-3	0-1	Cooke 58	19, 48, 85
	4		31	a	Millwall	L	1-2	0-0	Nogan 75	70, 79
	5	Sep	7	a	Gillingham	L	0-1	0-0		80
	6		10	h	BLACKPOOL	W	2-0	0-0	Gleghorn 65, Nogan 76	
	7		14	h	WYCOMBE W	W	2-1	2-1	Nogan (2) 25, 36	1
	8		21	a	Chesterfield	D	0-0	0-0		
	9		28	h	BRISTOL C	L	2-3	1-1	Gleghorn 44, Weller 55	12, 62, 79
	10	Oct	1	a	Bury	L	0-1	0-1		14
	11		5	h	STOCKPORT C	W	5-2	2-0	Barnes (5) 32, 45, 61, 71, 78	57, 76
	12		12	a	Rotherham U	L	0-1	0-1		42
Heath's last game	13		15	a	Watford	D	2-2	0-0	Gleghorn 28, Smith 76	39, 78
	14		19	h	NOTTS C	W	1-0	0-0	Barnes 60	
	15		26	h	PLYMOUTH A	W	2-1	1-0	Nogan 28, Eyres 47p	72
	16		27	a	Preston N E	D	1-1	0-1	Nogan 53	26
	17	Nov	2	a	York C	L	0-1	0-0		61
	18		9	h	CREWE A	W	2-0	1-0	Nogan 31, Matthew 70	
	19		19	a	Bristol R	W	2-1	1-0	Barnes (2) 32, 46	48
Vince Overson's last game	20		23	h	BOURNEMOUTH	W	1-0	1-0	Barnes 6	
	21		30	a	Plymouth A	D	0-0	0-0		
	22	Dec	3	h	WREXHAM	W	2-0	2-0	Cooke 2, Nogan 39	
	23		14	h	BRENTFORD	L	1-2	0-1	Swan 85	14, 54
	24		20	a	Peterborough U	L	2-3	1-2	Barnes 6, Matthew 83	20, 27, 60
	25		28	h	GILLINGHAM	W	5-1	1-1	Cooke (2) 24, 86, Smith 62, Barnes (2) 83p, 88	15
	26	Jan	11	a	Bristol C	L	1-2	1-1	Smith 36	19, 68
	27		17	h	BURY	W	3-1	3-1	Swan 19, Smith 25, Eyres 29	32
	28		25	h	PRESTON N E	L	1-2	1-1	Barnes 7	5, 69
	29		28	h	CHESTERFIELD	D	0-0	0-0		
	30	Feb	1	a	Crewe A	D	1-1	0-0	Barnes 88	50
	31		8	h	YORK C	L	1-2	1-1	Gleghorn 12	5, 90
	32		15	a	Bournemouth	D	0-0	0-0		
	33		22	h	BRISTOL R	D	2-2	1-1	Matthew 39, Barnes 90	13, 78
last games for Nogan & L Robinson	34		25	a	Blackpool	W	3-1	2-1	Barnes (3) 7, 43, 48	16
	35	Mar	1	a	Wrexham	D	0-0	0-0		
	36		8	h	PETERBOROUGH U	W	5-0	3-0	Barnes (3) 8, 30, 34, Cooke 56, Matthew 86	
	37		15	a	Brentford	W	3-0	3-0	Hoyland (2) 9, 34, Matthew 45	
	38		22	a	Walsall	W	3-1	1-0	Cooke (2) 26, 55, Barnes 85	90
	39		29	h	LUTON T	L	0-2	0-2		13, 39
	40	Apr	1	a	Shrewsbury T	L	1-2	0-0	Barnes 74	80, 86
	41		5	h	MILLWALL	W	1-0	1-0	Weller 13	
	42		12	a	Stockport C	L	0-1	0-0		86
Steve Thompson's last game	43		15	a	Wycombe W	L	0-5	0-4		12,29,34,42,82
	44		19	h	ROTHERHAM U	D	3-3	1-1	Cooke (2) 13, 58, Barnes 59	22, 55, 57
	45		26	a	Notts C	D	1-1	0-0	Matthew 90	66
Parkinson's last game	46	May	3	h	WATFORD	W	4-1	0-0	Cooke (3) 50, 52, 73p, Parkinson 67	88

FA Cup

	Rd	Date			Opponents	Result		h/t	Goalscorers/times	Opp. goal times
	1	Nov	16	h	LINCOLN C	W	2-1	1-0	Gleghorn 30, Matthew 75	47
	2	Dec	7	a	Walsall	D	1-1	0-0	Eyres 66	90
aet, 1-1 at 90m, won 4-2 on pens	rep		23	h	WALSALL	D	1-1	1-0	Barnes 43	74
	3	Jan	4	a	Liverpool	L	0-1	0-1		12

Final, Chelsea 2-0 Middlesbrough, at Wembley.

League Cup

	Rd	Date			Opponents	Result		h/t	Goalscorers/times	Opp. goal times
	1	Aug	20	a	Mansfield T	W	3-0	1-0	Cooke 31, Nogan 50, Eyres 74	
agg 5-0		Sep	3	h	MANSFIELD T	W	2-0	2-0	Matthew 3, Eyres 45	
	2		17	a	Charlton A	L	1-4	1-3	Eyres 7	5, 41, 45, 48
agg 2-6			24	h	CHARLTON A	L	1-2	1-1	Nogan 45	17, 90

Final, Leicester C 1-0 Middlesbrough, at Hillsborough, after a 1-1 draw after extra time, at Wembley.

Details of other first team games elsewhere.

Att.	Pos	Beresford	Parkinson	Eyres	Harrison	Winstanley	Hoyland	Matthew	S Thompson	Nogan	A Cooke	Gleghorn	L Robinson	Weller	Brass	Barnes	P Smith	W Russell	Swan	V Overson	Vinnicombe	Heath	Hodgson	Little	Huxford	Guinan	
6,484		1	2	3	4	5	6	7	8	9	10*	11	S*														1
10,322	1	1	2	3	4	5	6			9	10*	11	S*	7	8												2
9,072		1	2	3	4	5	6*		8	9	10	11	S*	7													3
9,281	9	1	2	3	4*	5	6	7	8**	9	S**	11	10		S*												4
6,116	13	1	2	3	4	5	6	7		9	S*	11			8*	10											5
13,599		1	2	3	4*	5	6	7		9	S**	11			8	10**	S*										6
9,379	7	1	2	3	4	5	6	7		9	S*	11			8	10*											7
5,529	6		2	3	4*	5	6			9**		11			10	8	7	1	S*	S**							8
9,538	11	1	2*			5	6			9	S*	11		7	4	10	8				3						9
7,557		1			2	5	6			9	10*	11		7	4	8	3					S*					10
10,332	8	1	2	3	4	5				9	S*	11		7		10*	8			6							11
4,562	12	1	2	3	4	5		S*		9**	S**	11		7*		10	8			6							12
6,450		1	2	3	4	5		7		9*	S*	11			S**	10^	8**			6		S^					13
9,372	12	1	2	3	4	S*		7		9		11				10	8			6			5*				14
9,602	10	1	2	3	4	5		7		9		11				10	8			6							15
12,652		1	2	3	4	5		7		9		11				10	8			6							16
5,958	12	1	2	3	4			7**		9	S*	11		S**	6	10*	8		5								17
9,459	10	1	2	3	4			7		9	S*	11			6	10*	8		5								18
4,123		1	2	3	4			7*		9		11		S*	6	10	8		5								19
8,564	6	1	2	3*	4				S**	9	S^	11**		7	6	10^	8		5	S*							20
6,289	8	1	2	3	4					9	10	11		7	6		8		5								21
8,587		1	2	3	4					9	10	11		7	6		8		5								22
10,575	5	1	2	3		4*		S**		9	10	11**		7	6	S*	8		5								23
5,283		1	2	3		4	5*	7		9		11			6	10	8							S*			24
10,004	7		2	3**	4		6	7*	S**		9	11		S*	5	10	8	1									25
10,013	8		2**		4					S*	9	11		S**	6	10	8	1	5		3			7*			26
10,526			2	3	4*		S*			9**	S**	11		S^	6	10	8	1	5					7^			27
16,186	7	1	2*	3	4			S**		9		11**		S*	6	10	8		5					7			28
7,903		1		3		4		7	S*			11*	9		6	10	8		5						2		29
4,734	5	1		3		4		7	S**			11**	9	S*	6	10	8		5						2*		30
8,961	5	1	2	3	4*			7**		9		11		S**	6	10	8		5						S*		31
6,021	8	1	2	3		6		7*	S*	9		11**	S^	8	4	10^			5						S**		32
8,847	8	1	2*	3		6		7	11	9				8**	4	10			5					S*	S**		33
7,331		1	2	3		6		7	11	9**			S**		4	10^	S^		5					8*	S*		34
6,947	8	1	2			6	5	7	11					S*	4	10	9				3			8*			35
8,646	6	1	2		S^	6	5	7	11		9*			8	4	10^	3**				S**			S*			36
6,624	4	1	2		S*	6	5	7	11		9			8*	4	10	3										37
6,306	5	1	2		S*	6	5	7	11*		9			8	4	10	3										38
15,490	6	1	2			6	5**	7	11*		9			8	4	10	3							S**		S*	39
4,462		1	2			6	5^	7	11*		9**			8	4	10	3				S^				S*	S**	40
9,840	6	1	2		7	6	5		11		9*			8	4	10					3					S*	41
9,187	8		2	9	7	6	5^		11**					8*	4	10	S*	1			3				S^	S**	42
5,786			2	9	7	6	5**		11^		8*				4	10	S^	1			3				S**	S*	43
7,875	9	1	2	3	7	6	5*	11			8			9	4	10	S*										44
4,591	11	1	2	3	7**	6	5*	11			8			9	4	10	S**									S*	45
8,269	9	1	2	3	7*	6	5	11			8	S*		9**	4	10	S**										46
Appearances		40	43	36	32	34	24	29	14	30	19	32	3	22	37	39	30	6	16	6	6		1	5	2		
Apps as sub					3	1	1	3	5	1	12	1	5	9	2	1	7		1	2	2	2		4	7	6	
Goals (71)			1	3			2	6	1	10	12	4		2		24	4		2								

Att.	Pos	Beresford	Parkinson	Eyres	Harrison	Winstanley	Hoyland	Matthew	S Thompson	Nogan	A Cooke	Gleghorn	L Robinson	Weller	Brass	Barnes	P Smith	W Russell	Swan	V Overson	Vinnicombe	Heath	Hodgson	Little	Huxford	Guinan	
6,484		1	2*	3	4			7		9	S**	11		S*	6	10**	8		5								1
5,031		1	2	3	4					9	10	11		7	6		8		5								2
5,799		1	2	3	4*	5	6	7				11		S**	S*	10	8							9**			rep
33,252		1	2	3	4	5	6**				S**	11		7*	9	10	8							S*			3
Appearances		4	4	4	4	2	2	2		2	1	4		2	3	3	4		2					1			
Apps as sub											2			2	1									1			
Goals (4)				1				1				1				1											

Att.	Pos	Beresford	Parkinson	Eyres	Harrison	Winstanley	Hoyland	Matthew	S Thompson	Nogan	A Cooke	Gleghorn	L Robinson	Weller	Brass	Barnes	P Smith	W Russell	Swan	V Overson	Vinnicombe	Heath	Hodgson	Little	Huxford	Guinan	
1,708		1	2	3	4	5	6	7	8*	9	10**	11	S**		S*												1
2,884			2	3		5	6	7	8	9*	S*	11**	10	S**	4			1									2nd leg
4,874		1	2	3	4	5	6	7*		9**	S**	11			8	10	S*										2
2,281			2	3		5	4			9		11		7		10	8	1		6							2nd leg
Appearances		2	4	4	2	4	4	3	2	4	1	4	1	1	2	2	1	2		1							
Apps as sub											2		1	1	1		1										
Goals (7)				3				1		2	1																

1997-98

What a rollercoaster of emotions this season turned out to be.
Burnley fans expect to experience highs and lows throughout the trials and tribulations of a football season.
They expect to have things to talk about over a pint in their local pub, at both ends of the scale.
But this particular season seemed to dish out a few too many negatives for a Claret liking.
However, it all culminated in one of the most thrilling end-of-season showdowns since a certain meeting with Orient in 1987.
Burnley went into the final game of the season knowing victory would guarantee their survival in the Second Division.
They had spent a huge percentage of the campaign in the relegation zone, and not gone higher than nineteenth at any stage.
But despite that, three points against Plymouth Argyle on the final day would see them spend another season in English football's third tier.
However, there was another ingredient to be tossed into this already overflowing cauldron.
Victory for Burnley might have kept them up – but it could have sent their opponents down.
Success for either may still not have been enough, had Brentford taken maximum points from their clash at Bristol Rovers.
And so, with the prospect of both sides being relegated, it promised to be some contest in front of what would prove to be the largest Turf Moor crowd of the decade.
Andy Cooke settled any nerves that the home crowd might have had just 12 minutes in, but the Pilgrims were back level within a similar time frame.
However, that man Cooke struck again just before the interval to make that half-time pie go down that much more smoothly.
Chances went begging for both sides after the interval, but Burnley ultimately ground out the result they desired.
The joys of victory were greeted with a mass pitch invasion from the home supporters, gathering in front of the now-despondent travelling Argyle fans.
However, the Claret hordes could have been left with egg on their faces, had Brentford done the necessary at the Memorial Stadium in Bristol.
As it was, they had lost 2-1, and Burnley fans could celebrate another incredible last day survival act.
It had all looked a forlorn task at the back end of March, following a 1-0 defeat at Millwall.
That narrow reverse had relegated Burnley back to the foot of the table.
But five wins from their nine remaining games was ultimately enough to keep them up, and save the man in charge from a catastrophic managerial campaign.
It had all begun so incredibly, on 8 July 1997.
Clarets fans up and down the country opened up their morning newspapers to find they had a new man at the helm.
But this was no ordinary man, and it would have been enough for most hardened supporters to choke on their cereal.
It was none other than Chris Waddle, a man who, throughout the 1980s, had been one of English football's shining lights.
Or was that Diamond Lights?

The new campaign kicked off a time where every Clarets supporter was champing at the bit for it to begin.
What impact would Waddle make in his first managerial role?
What kind of players would he be able to attract?
But those lofty expectations were soon quashed, as Burnley suffered one of their worst ever starts to a season.
Waddle named himself in the starting line-up for the opening game at Watford, against a side that would eventually go on to lift the title.
The fact then that they only came away from Vicarage Road with a 1-0 reverse didn't rate too low down on the end-of-season ranking list.
But it was the start of a dreadful run of early season form that would be the focal point of football fans up and down the country.
Six games into the campaign, and Burnley had quite literally taken root at the foot of the Second Division.
Six games without a goal, six games without a win, and only three goalless draws against Gillingham, Bristol Rovers and Oldham Athletic to show for their efforts.
But it was a different story in the Coca-Cola Cup, as Burnley did both in beating Lincoln City 3-2 on aggregate.
Things did improve slightly on the league front against York, in the fact that Burnley scored a goal, as Paul Barnes netted in the twelfth minute of a 3-1 defeat.

Chris Brass
long serving, reliable defender

That signalled the end of a run of 552 minutes without a league goal, but the Clarets did crash out of the League Cup at the second round stage, 6-0 on aggregate against Stoke.
It was to be another four league games before victory was tasted, but finally, at the eleventh time of asking, it happened.
Carlisle United were the ones to suffer the ignominy, going down 3-1 to a goal from Barnes, and two from Gerry Creaney.
The signing of Creaney, on loan from Manchester City, was the catalyst for a brief upturn in fortunes.
He made his debut from the bench in the 1-1 draw with Preston, before scoring his first two goals for the club in only his second start in a 2-2 draw with Wycombe.

A week later came the victory over Carlisle, followed by hard-fought draws away at both Wrexham and Plymouth.

That was followed by another 2-2 draw, this time at home to Bournemouth, where Creaney was again on target as Burnley lifted themselves off the foot of the table.That game also saw Waddle net his one and only goal for the club.

And things started to look up for both him and Burnley with two successive victories, at home to Walsall, and their first away success of the season at Luton.

Creaney's goal in the 2-1 loss at Blackpool proved to be his last for the club, as his prolific period in a Clarets shirt was brought to a conclusion.

Eight goals in nine starts had made him an instant hero with the Burnley fans, and it triggered a campaign from supporters willing for him to be signed up.

Top scorer Andy Cooke
his 16 goals included two against Plymouth
that kept the Clarets up

But it never happened, Creaney went back to Manchester City, and Burnley's run of bad form started up once more.

One win in eight league games followed, beginning with an early exit from the FA Cup, losing 3-0 at home to Rotherham United after a 3-3 draw at Millmoor.

A 2-1 home success against Northampton at the back end of November brought that sequence to a close, but five games without a win from that point on returned the Clarets to the foot of the division.

Andy Cooke scored twice to break the sequence, as Burnley secured a surprise 2-0 home win against Watford.

Andy Payton netted the only goal of the match two games later to secure success over Southend.

But the shock of the season came on the last day of January when York visited Turf Moor.

A side that couldn't score at all at the start of the season, suddenly turned into one that couldn't stop.

Burnley had notched their first goal of the season at Bootham Crescent back in September, and they moved off the foot of the table in spectacular style by knocking seven past them this time around.

The icing on the cake was applied by Andy Cooke, who netted a second half treble to cap a glorious 7-2 victory.

And not content with that, the Clarets followed it by coming from behind to beat derby rivals Preston 3-2 at Deepdale.

Things couldn't be better, but predictably for this season, a run of seven games without a win duly followed.

A 2-1 home success against Grimsby broke that trend, one of four games in the run-in where Payton netted the winner.

He also did the business against Northampton, Bristol City and Fulham, meaning Burnley went into the final game with survival to play for.

And survive they did, at the end of what had been a season of contrasting emotions.

OBITUARY

KEITH ROBERT NEWTON

DIED JUNE 1998, AGED 56.

Few former Blackburn Rovers players have been fully accepted by the Burnley faithful, but Keith Newton managed it with no problem at all.

He had already won 27 England caps and a League championship medal (with Everton) before he arrived at Turf Moor in the close season of 1972. He proved to be the final piece in the jigsaw as Jimmy Adamson built a side to return to the First Division, which they did at the end of Newton's first season.

An assured and cultured full-back, he spent most of his Turf Moor career on the left of the defence, and provided the knowhow and experience to complement the flair that Adamson's side already possessed further up front. He was one of six ever-presents in that Second Division championship campaign of 1972-73 and remained a fixture in the side over the next four seasons. He remained at Turf Moor until the summer of 1978, by which time his League career was over at the age of 36.

Born in Manchester, he spent his entire career in this part of the country, and settled in Blackburn after his retirement from football.

RIP

1997-98 - Second Division

		P	W	D	L	F	A	Pts
1	Watford	46	24	16	6	67	41	88
2	Bristol C	46	25	10	11	69	39	85
3	Grimsby T	46	19	15	12	55	37	72
4	Northampton T	46	18	17	11	52	37	71
5	Bristol R	46	20	10	16	70	64	70
6	Fulham	46	20	10	16	60	43	70
7	Wrexham	46	18	16	12	55	51	70
8	Gillingham	46	19	13	14	52	47	70
9	Bournemouth	46	18	12	16	57	52	66
10	Chesterfield	46	16	17	13	46	44	65
11	Wigan A	46	17	11	18	64	66	62
12	Blackpool	46	17	11	18	59	67	62
13	Oldham A	46	15	16	15	62	54	61
14	Wycombe W	46	14	18	14	51	53	60
15	Preston NE	46	15	14	17	56	56	59
16	York C	46	14	17	15	52	58	59
17	Luton T	46	14	15	17	60	64	57
18	Millwall	46	14	13	19	43	54	55
19	Walsall	46	14	12	20	43	52	54
20	BURNLEY	46	13	13	20	55	65	52
21	Brentford	46	11	17	18	50	71	50
22	Plymouth A	46	12	13	21	55	70	49
23	Carlisle U	46	12	8	26	57	73	44
24	Southend U	46	11	10	25	47	79	43

1997-98

Manager : Chris Waddle

Division Two (20th)

		Date			Opponents	Result		h/t	Goalscorers/times	Opp. goal times
	1	Aug	9	a	Watford	L	0-1	0-1		31
	2		16	h	GILLINGHAM	D	0-0	0-0		
	3		23	a	Southend U	L	0-1	0-1		6
	4		30	h	BRISTOL R	D	0-0	0-0		
	5	Sep	2	h	OLDHAM A	D	0-0	0-0		
	6		7	a	Chesterfield	L	0-1	0-1		2
	7		13	a	York C	L	1-3	1-0	Barnes 12	62, 64, 84
	8		20	h	PRESTON N E	D	1-1	0-1	Cooke 80	19
	9		27	a	Brentford	L	1-2	0-1	Ford 57	2, 90
	10	Oct	4	h	WYCOMBE W	D	2-2	1-1	Creaney (2) 3, 73	13, 54
	11		11	h	CARLISLE U	W	3-1	1-0	Barnes 18, Creaney (2) 67, 71	83
	12		18	a	Wrexham	D	0-0	0-0		
	13		21	a	Plymouth A	D	2-2	1-1	Eyres 7p, Creaney 57	40, 47
Eyres' last game	14		25	h	BOURNEMOUTH	D	2-2	1-0	Waddle 45, Creaney 65	58, 68
	15	Nov	1	h	WALSALL	W	2-1	1-0	Barnes 27, Cooke 80	79
	16		4	a	Luton T	W	3-2	1-2	Williams 25, Creaney 61, Barnes 66	33, 36
	17		8	a	Blackpool	L	1-2	1-1	Creaney 15	42, 85
	18		18	h	MILLWALL	L	1-2	1-1	Cooke 29	2, 62
	19		22	a	Grimsby T	L	1-4	1-1	Weller 16	19, 59, 73, 78
	20		29	h	NORTHAMPTON T	W	2-1	0-0	Moore 76, Barnes 82	50
	21	Dec	2	a	Bristol C	L	1-3	1-0	Barnes 29	48, 71p, 83
	22		13	h	WIGAN A	L	0-2	0-2		13, 44
	23		19	a	Fulham	L	0-1	0-0		89
	24		26	h	CHESTERFIELD	D	0-0	0-0		
Barnes' last game	25	Jan	3	a	Gillingham	L	0-2	0-1		10, 68
	26		10	h	WATFORD	W	2-0	2-0	Cooke (2) 13, 35	
	27		17	a	Bristol R	L	0-1	0-0		50
	28		24	h	SOUTHEND U	W	1-0	1-0	Payton 43	
York goals 35m, 77m	29		31	h	YORK C	W	7-2	2-1	Moore 40, Barras 40og, Brass 47, Cooke (3) 49, 58, 88, Payton 82	
	30	Feb	7	a	Preston N E	W	3-2	0-1	Payton 48, Cooke 57, Moore 90	34, 61
	31		14	a	Wycombe W	L	1-2	0-1	Cooke 88	33, 57
	32		21	h	BRENTFORD	D	1-1	0-0	Little 77	50
	33		24	h	WREXHAM	L	1-2	1-1	Cooke 30	11, 64
	34		28	a	Carlisle U	L	1-2	0-1	Cooke 50	18, 81
	35	Mar	7	a	Walsall	D	0-0	0-0		
	36		14	h	LUTON T	D	1-1	0-0	Payton 61	79
	37		21	a	Millwall	L	0-1	0-1		21
	38		28	h	GRIMSBY T	W	2-1	1-1	Little 12, Payton 80	16
	39	Apr	4	a	Northampton T	W	1-0	1-0	Payton 16	
	40		7	h	BLACKPOOL	L	1-2	1-1	Payton 13	45, 51
	41		11	h	BRISTOL C	W	1-0	1-0	Payton 7p	
	42		13	a	Wigan A	L	1-5	0-2	Little 48	32,42,78,81,88
Vinnicombe's last game	43		18	h	FULHAM	W	2-1	1-1	Cooke 2, Payton 83	35
Waddle's last game	44		25	a	Bournemouth	L	1-2	0-0	Matthew 72p	56p, 61
Hoyland's last game	45		28	a	Oldham A	D	3-3	3-1	Cooke 26, Weller 33, Little 43	28, 76, 78
last games for Harrison & Matthew	46	May	2	h	PLYMOUTH A	W	2-1	2-1	Cooke (2) 12, 41	25

FA Cup

1	Nov	15	a	Rotherham U	D	3-3	2-2	Cooke 24, Moore 37, Weller 55	17, 36, 65
rep		25	h	ROTHERHAM U	L	0-3	0-1		10, 68, 89

Final, Arsenal 2-0 Newcastle U, at Wembley.

League Cup

	1	Aug	12	a	Lincoln C	D	1-1	0-1	Howey 76	38
agg 3-2			26	h	LINCOLN C	W	2-1	2-1	Cooke 1, Eyres 17p	26
	2	Sep	16	h	STOKE C	L	0-4	0-1		36, 61, 68, 80
agg 0-6			24	a	Stoke C	L	0-2	0-1		34, 72

Final, Chelsea 2-0 Middlesbrough after extra time, at Wembley.

Details of other first team games elsewhere.

Att.	Pos	Beresford	Huxford	Winstanley	Williams	Blatherwick	Brass	Waddle	Ford	Eastwood	Barnes	Eyres	Matthew	Hoyland	Vinnicombe	Howey	Weller	Cooke	Duerden	Gleghorn	N Moore	Kiwomya	C Smith	Little	Harrison	Creaney	G Cowans	P Smith	Carr-Lawton	Payton	Robertson	Henderson	Woods	Mullin	Gentile		
11,155		1	2	3	4**	5	6	7	8	9*	10	11	S*	S**																							1
11,811	20	1	2	7	4	5	6^	S**	8		10**	11	S^		3*	9	S*																				2
4,218	24	1	2	3	4*	5		S**	8		10**	11	S*			6	7	9																			3
9,887	23	1	2	3		5		4	S*		10		8			6	7		9**	11*	S**																4
11,189		1		3		5	2	7*	8		S*	11	10			6	4				S**	9**															5
7,406	24	1				5	3	7*	8		10	11	4			6	2	9					S*														6
5,424	24	1			4	5	3		8		10	11	7**			6	2	9*				S*		S**													7
13,809	24	1					2	S*	8**		10	11^	4		3		7	9			6	S^			5*	S**											8
4,548	24	1					2	7	8		10*	11			3	5					6				4	9	S*										9
9,057	24	1					2*	7	8		10	11			3	5	S*				6				4	9											10
10,687	24	1		5			2	7*	8		10	11			3		S*	S**			6				4	9**											11
5,132	24	1			S*		2	7**	8		10^	11			3	5*	S**	S^			6				4	9											12
3,006		1					2	7	8		10	11			3*	5	S*				6				4	9											13
9,501	23	1			8^		2	7			10	11			3*	5	S*	S**			6			S^	4	9**											14
9,293	22	1			8	S^	2	7**			10*				3	5	11	S*			6					9^	4	S**									15
5,315		1			8	S^	2	7*			10				3	5	11	S**			6					9**	4^	S*									16
7,429	20	1			8	S*	2**	7			10				3*	5	11	S**			6					9	4										17
8,834		1			8	S*	2*				10				3**	5	7	9			6				S**		4	11									18
4,829	21	1			8	5	2	7**	S*		10						3	9			6				S**		4*	11^	S^								19
8,369	19	1				5	2	7	8		10		S**		3	9**	11*	S*			6				4												20
11,136		1				5	2	7*	8		10		S*		3**	9	11	S**			6				4												21
9,520	23	1				5*	2	7	8		10		S*		3**	6	11	9							4			S**									22
5,096		1			11*		2	S*	8		10		7**			6	3	9			5			S**	4												23
10,861	23	1			11*		2		8		10		7		3**	6		9			5			S*	4			S**									24
5,886	24	1			11**		2	S^	8^		10		7		3*	6		9			5			S**	4			S*									25
9,551	24	1		3		S*	2	7*	8				11					9			5			6	4			10									26
7,208	24	1		3			2	7	8				11*	S**							5			6**	4			10		9	S*						27
9,386	24	1		3		S**	2*	7	8				11				9**				5			6	4					10	S*						28
9,975	21	1		3			2						11	S*			7*	9			5			6	4					10	8						29
12,263	19	1		3			2						11				7	9			5			6	4					10*	8	S*					30
5,926	19	1		3		S**	2						11				7**	9			5			6	4					10	8*	S*					31
10,097	20	1		3		7	2		S*				11*					9			5			6	4					10	8						32
8,576		1		3		7	2		S*					11*			S**	9			5			6	4					10	8**						33
7,192	22	1		3		S^	2		7**					S**			11^	9			5			6	4					10	8*	S*					34
5,212	23			3			2		8						7		11*	9			5			6	4					10	S*		1				35
9,656	23			3			2		8						7**	S*	6	9			5				4*			S**		10	11		1				36
7,582	24			3**				7	8						6	S**	2	9			5				4			11		10*		S*	1				37
8,256	24			3				7*	8					S*	S**		2				5			6^	4			11**		10		S^	1	9			38
7,264	22			3				7	8								2				5			6	4			11		10			1	9			39
13,413				3				7	8*								2				5			6	4			11		10		S*	1	9			40
10,600	22			3			S^	7**					11	S**	S*		2	9			5			6^	4					10*			1	8			41
4,926	22			3			S**						11**	7			2	9			5			6	4					10*		S*	1	8			42
9,745	22			3			S**		8				11		S*		2	9			5			6**	4					10*			1	7			43
6,527	22			3			4	7	8	S*			11				2	9			5			6							10*		1				44
9,781				3			2		8	S**			11*	S*			7	9			5			6	4					10**			1				45
18,811	20			3			2		8				11				7	9			5			6	4					10			1				46
Appearances		34	4	27	13	13	37	26	32	1	24	13	21	2	20	21	32	26	1	1	38	1		19	33	9	5	8		19	8		12	6			
Apps as sub					1	8	3	5	4	2	1		6	7	3	2	7	8			2	2	1	5	2	1	1	6	1		3	7					
Goals(55)					1		1	1	1		6	1	1				2	16			3			4		8				9						1	og

Att.	Pos	Beresford	Huxford	Winstanley	Williams	Blatherwick	Brass	Waddle	Ford	Eastwood	Barnes	Eyres	Matthew	Hoyland	Vinnicombe	Howey	Weller	Cooke	Duerden	Gleghorn	N Moore	Kiwomya	C Smith	Little	Harrison	Creaney	G Cowans	P Smith	Carr-Lawton	Payton	Robertson	Henderson	Woods	Mullin	Gentile		
5,709		1			8	S**	2	7*			10				3**	5	11	9			6				S^		4^	S*									1
3,118		1			8*	5	2	7	S*		10					3	11	9			6				S**		4**										rep
Appearances		2			2	1	2	2			2				1	2	2	2			2						2										
Apps as sub						1			1																2			1									
Goals (3)																	1	1			1																

Att.	Pos	Beresford	Huxford	Winstanley	Williams	Blatherwick	Brass	Waddle	Ford	Eastwood	Barnes	Eyres	Matthew	Hoyland	Vinnicombe	Howey	Weller	Cooke	Duerden	Gleghorn	N Moore	Kiwomya	C Smith	Little	Harrison	Creaney	G Cowans	P Smith	Carr-Lawton	Payton	Robertson	Henderson	Woods	Mullin	Gentile		
3,010		1	2	7	4	5	6		8		10	11*	S*		3	9																					1
4,644		1	2	3		5		4			10	11	8			6	7	9																			2nd leg
4,175		1			4	5	3	S**	8		10	11	7**			9*	2				6			S*													2
6,041		1	S^				2	7*				11	4^		3		S*	9**			6			S**		8	10								5		2nd leg
Appearances		4	2	2	2	3	3	2	2		3	4	3		2	3	2	2			2					1	1								1		
Apps as sub			1					1					1				1							2													
Goals (3)												1				1		1																			

1998-99

It was a rant that will go down in Clarets folklore.

Stan Ternent had already made his intentions clear on becoming Burnley's new manager.

But no-one could have had any idea as to what was in store within months of him taking charge.

Ternent had arrived from Bury in June, taking over the hotseat from the departed Chris Waddle.

Major changes needed to be made after the Clarets' last gasp escape on the final day of the previous campaign.

But if anyone knew that, it was Ternent.

And just three games into his regime, Burnley fans everywhere were given a startling insight into his plans to reshape the entire playing staff.

It was the third Saturday of the season and Burnley were looking to capitalise on their opening day home success over Bristol Rovers.

Andy Payton had scored twice on that day, only for the Clarets to then suffer a brief blip in a 1-0 loss at Chesterfield.

York City arrived in town on the back of a 3-0 mauling at Preston on the opening day, and a 1-1 draw at home to Gillingham.

But they couldn't have asked for an easier three points then the ones they got at Turf Moor on 22 August.

Burnley were outplayed in every department, and the Minstermen could well have gone back to Bootham Crescent with a far more emphatic scoreline.

And it proved to be the straw that broke the camel's back for four of Ternent's inherited side.

Afterwards, he blasted: "It's not personal, it's business. Steve Blatherwick, Lee Howey, Mark Winstanley and to a lesser degree Michael Williams, because he will never win the crowd over, will not play for Burnley Football Club again.

"They are not right for Burnley and they are not coming from where I am coming from.

"They are on the transfer list - they can go on a free transfer."

Winstanley, signed from Bolton four years earlier, was playing his first game of the season having been drafted in for the injured Steve Morgan.

Morgan had picked up a knock during the 4-1 home League Cup defeat to Bury four days earlier, that had seen Burnley crash out at the first hurdle 5-2 on aggregate.

As for Blatherwick and Howey, they had both been signed in the previous close-season by Chris Waddle.

Both had started all five league and cup games of the new campaign, but like Winstanley, the York game would prove to be their last.

Ternent added: "I need to bring some new bodies into the club.

"I have got to make a move because three points out of nine does not represent a good start to the season, regardless of what's happening.

"I need some players but I will never get a better club if I live to be a million."

So that was that.

The four players singled out would still remain on the pay role at Turf Moor, and train with the rest of the squad.

But if Ternent's comments hadn't projected enough of a statement, his actions would speak louder than words.

The very next day after the York debacle, Ternent raided his former club Bury to bring in two ready-made replacements in Peter Swan, starting a second spell with the club, and Gordon Armstrong.

Both would go straight into the starting line-up to face Walsall, but despite the latter netting a debut goal, the Clarets still went down 3-1.

There was welcome relief when Millwall were beaten 2-1 at Turf Moor, before Ternent snapped up another central defender in free transfer Brian Reid.

But joy soon turned to despair once more, as the Clarets went on an unenviable run of six games without a win.

Ternent was starting to make his mark however, and that included getting the best out of one eventual Claret legend.

Andy Payton, brought to Turf Moor from Huddersfield by previous boss Chris Waddle as part of a swap deal for Paul Barnes, was starting to show his true colours.

And that was brought to the fore against Colchester, as he netted twice in the first 11 minutes to help seal a morale-boosting 4-0 win.

Rune Vindheim also netted in that game after being drafted in, and he would also pop up to score a last minute equaliser in the 1-1 home draw with Notts County.

Home victories over Oldham and Wrexham followed, before a less than favourable run of results began with a 4-1 derby defeat at Preston.

That was the catalyst for a run which saw just one win in ten,

Graham Branch at the beginning of a long Turf Moor career
Micky Mellon is in support

with that coming via a 1-0 success over Blackpool, courtesy of a Payton penalty.

And that included a humiliating defeat to Darlington in the first round of the FA Cup, as the home side scored three times in the last nine minutes to win 3-2.

A staggering win at Bristol Rovers brought an end to the run, as the Clarets went ahead four times through Steve Davis, Graham Branch, Payton and Andy Cooke, to eventually triumph 4-3.

But another dreadful run, one win in ten once more, would see them plummet into the relegation places.

New arrival Paul Cook helped to steady the ship in midfield

A 2-1 success at Millwall was their only bright spot.

And if the storm clouds hadn't already begun to gather over Turf Moor, they would certainly appear during a certain 10-day spell.

On 27 February Clarets fans watched in horror as Bob Taylor scored all five goals in a 5-0 win for Gillingham at Turf Moor.

And if that wasn't bad enough, in the next home match Manchester City went one better when they put six past Paul Crichton without reply.

After make-or-break talks with chairman Barry Kilby, Ternent blasted: "It's been business as usual since day one. I have never packed anything in in my life, and I don't intend to start now. I came to a do a job and I will do it my way."

He also insisted he was made of "sterner stuff" than previous managers Adrian Heath and Chris Waddle.

While worried about their club's plight, Burnley fans could only admire the way Ternent had stood his corner.

And all who backed him would see their feelings come to fruition over the final 12 games of the campaign.

Burnley did follow those two appalling scorelines with a 1-0 home defeat to Preston.

But amazingly, that was to be their final defeat of the season. Victories over Macclesfield, Colchester and Blackpool followed, before a quite stunning performance in a 4-1 win at Stoke.

And the size of the turnaround was amplified as Burnley beat champions-elect Fulham 1-0 at Turf Moor thanks to a goal from Ronnie Jepson.

Two draws against Wigan and Northampton brought a bewildering campaign to an end but the building blocks had been put in place for a quite incredible rescue act.

Burnley had used 38 players over the course of the season, as Ternent continued to inject fresh blood into the team.

And but for that late surge of form, the Clarets would once again, just like the previous season, have been embroiled in a relegation battle.

Within days of the season ending, Ternent again made his intentions clear, as twelve players were released from the club. They included Brian Reid, drafted in during the aftermath of the York game in August, after no agreement was reached on a deal. Ternent had certainly made his mark. Clarets fans would not have to wait long to see the results of his unique style.

OBITUARY
HAROLD MATHER
DIED 1 MARCH 1999, AGED 78.

Already 25 years old when he made his League debut in the first match of the post-war era, Harold Mather nevertheless remained part of the Burnley first-team picture longer than any of his colleagues in the renowned Clarets' side of 1946-47. He was a product of the football academy of Folds Road School, Bolton, which also produced Tommy Lawton among others, and he joined Burnley in 1938, but failed to make the first team before the outbreak of war. Afterwards, though, he was a stalwart, lining up for years at left-back alongside Arthur Woodruff, his impeccable timing making him an indispensable member of Burnley's "Iron Curtain" defence of that period. He was the first Claret to top 300 League appearances in the post-war era.

Although Burnley was his only League club as a player, he remained in the game for several years afterwards as a coach, both in England and abroad. In common with so many ex-Clarets, he returned to live in Burnley after his retirement from the game.

RIP

1998-99 - Second Division

		P	W	D	L	F	A	Pts
1	Fulham	46	31	8	7	79	32	101
2	Walsall	46	26	9	11	63	47	87
3	Manchester C	46	22	16	8	69	33	82
4	Gillingham	46	22	14	10	75	44	80
5	Preston NE	46	22	13	11	78	50	79
6	Wigan A	46	22	10	14	75	48	76
7	Bournemouth	46	21	13	12	63	41	76
8	Stoke C	46	21	6	19	59	62	69
9	Chesterfield	46	17	13	16	46	44	64
10	Millwall	46	17	11	18	52	59	62
11	Reading	46	16	13	17	54	63	61
12	Luton T	46	16	10	20	51	60	58
13	Bristol R	46	13	17	16	65	56	56
14	Blackpool	46	14	14	18	44	54	56
15	BURNLEY	46	13	16	17	54	73	55
16	Notts C	46	14	12	20	52	61	54
17	Wrexham	46	13	14	19	43	62	53
18	Colchester U	46	12	16	18	52	70	52
19	Wycombe W	46	13	12	21	52	58	51
20	Oldham A	46	14	9	23	48	66	51
21	York C	46	13	11	22	56	80	50
22	Northampton T	46	10	18	18	43	57	48
23	Lincoln C	46	13	7	26	42	74	46
24	Macclesfield T	46	11	10	25	43	63	43

1998-99

Manager : Stan Ternent

Division Two (15th)

Note	No	Date			Opponents	Result		h/t	Goalscorers/times	Opp. goal times
	1	Aug	8	h	BRISTOL R	W	2-1	2-1	Payton (2) 2, 31	8
	2		15	a	Chesterfield	L	0-1	0-0		88p
Winstanley's last game	3		22	h	YORK C	L	0-1	0-1		32
	4		29	a	Walsall	L	1-3	0-1	Armstrong 69	34, 88, 90p
	5	Sep	1	h	MILLWALL	W	2-1	2-0	Cooke (2) 21, 30	88
	6		5	a	Luton T	L	0-1	0-0		47
	7		9	a	Reading	D	1-1	0-1	Payton 77	28
	8		12	h	WYCOMBE W	D	1-1	1-1	Payton 6	36
	9		19	a	Gillingham	L	1-2	1-1	Payton 31	11, 86
	10		26	h	WIGAN A	D	1-1	0-0	Reid 67	90
	11	Oct	3	a	Manchester C	D	2-2	1-1	Payton 34, Cooke 54	8, 85
	12		9	a	Colchester U	W	4-0	2-0	Payton (2) 2, 10, Vindheim 50, Cooke 71	
	13		17	h	NOTTS C	D	1-1	0-1	Vindheim 90	8
	14		20	h	OLDHAM A	W	1-0	0-0	Cooke 75	
	15		24	a	Macclesfield T	L	1-2	0-1	Little 73	18, 86
	16		31	h	WREXHAM	W	2-1	1-0	Payton 29, 55	46
	17	Nov	7	a	Preston N E	L	1-4	1-1	Eastwood 15	23, 46, 49, 57
	18		10	h	STOKE C	L	0-2	0-0		47, 61
	19		21	a	Bournemouth	L	0-5	0-0		55,60p,69,74,90
	20		28	h	BLACKPOOL	W	1-0	0-0	Payton 67p	
	21	Dec	12	a	Fulham	L	0-4	0-2		26, 38, 57, 73
Burnley's 4000th league game	22		19	h	NORTHAMPTON T	L	0-2	0-0		70, 82
	23		26	a	York C	D	3-3	1-0	Payton (2) 23, 87, Robertson 58	54, 61, 72
	24		28	h	LINCOLN C	D	1-1	0-0	Henderson 80	72
	25	Jan	2	h	WALSALL	D	0-0	0-0		
	26		9	a	Bristol R	W	4-3	3-3	Davis 15, Branch 30, Payton 44, Cooke 54	25, 36, 45
	27		16	h	CHESTERFIELD	L	1-2	0-1	Cooke 85	30og, 65
	28		23	a	Millwall	W	2-1	1-0	Cooke 11, Davis 80	86
	29		30	a	Lincoln C	D	1-1	0-1	Reid 66	32
	30	Feb	6	h	LUTON T	L	1-2	1-1	Mellon 29	34, 87
	31		13	h	READING	D	1-1	0-0	Reid 90	54
	32		20	a	Wycombe W	L	0-2	0-0		51, 52
	33		27	h	GILLINGHAM	L	0-5	0-4		14, 27, 41, 43p, 48
Neil Moore's last game	34	Mar	9	h	MANCHESTER C	L	0-6	0-2		17,41,50,59,65,82
	35		14	h	PRESTON N E	L	0-1	0-0		61
	36		20	a	Wrexham	D	1-1	0-1	Mellon 75	14
	37		28	h	MACCLESFIELD T	W	4-3	1-2	Little 17, Cowan 57, Payton 79, Davis 90	9, 14, 63
	38	Apr	3	a	Notts C	D	0-0	0-0		
	39		5	h	COLCHESTER U	W	3-1	0-1	Johnrose 57, Payton (2) 82, 89	26
	40		10	a	Oldham A	D	1-1	0-1	Payton 52	37
	41		13	a	Blackpool	W	2-0	1-0	Payton 25, Little 57	
	42		17	h	BOURNEMOUTH	D	0-0	0-0		
	43		24	a	Stoke C	W	4-1	2-1	Pickering 5, Payton 11, Little 67, 90	30
	44	May	1	h	FULHAM	W	1-0	0-0	Jepson 82	
	45		3	a	Wigan A	D	0-0	0-0		
	46		8	a	Northampton T	D	2-2	0-1	Cook 68p, Cooke 88	7, 80

FA Cup

Note	Rd	Date			Opponents	Result		h/t	Goalscorers/times	Opp. goal times
at Riverside, Middlesbrough	1	Nov	17	a	Darlington	L	2-3	1-0	Payton (2) 37, 55p	81, 87, 90

Final, Manchester U 2-0 Newcastle, at Wembley.

League Cup

Note	Rd	Date			Opponents	Result		h/t	Goalscorers/times	Opp. goal times
	1	Aug	11	a	Bury	D	1-1	1-1	Cooke 29	17
agg 2-5			18	h	BURY	L	1-4	1-1	Payton 41	45, 51, 71, 78

Final, Tottenham H 1-0 Leicester C, at Wembley.

Details of other first team games elsewhere.

Att.	Pos	Crichton	Brass	Morgan	Ford	Blatherwick	Howey	Little	Williams	A Cooke	Payton	P Smith	C Smith	Jepson	N Moore	Ward	Robertson	Winstanley	Carr-Lawton	C Scott	Heywood	Eastwood	Armstrong	Weller	Swan	Reid	Henderson	Vindheim	Maylett	O'Kane	Hewlett	Pickering	Davis	Branch	Mellon	Johnrose	T Cowan	P Cook	Williamson	Kval	Parks	
11,781		1	2	3	4*	5	6^	7	8	9	10**	11	S*	S**	S^																											1
5,426	14		2	3		5	6	7		9*	10	11	8**	S*	4	1	S**																									2
9,715	19		2			5*	6**		7^		10	11	8		4	1		3	9	S*	S**	S^																				3
4,599	20		6					7		9	10	11		8	2	1	S*						3	4*	5																	4
8,526			6					7		9	10	11	4		2*	1	8			S*			3		5																	5
5,554	19		6					7		9	10	11		8		1	2						3		5	4																6
10,080			4					7		9	10		11*	8**		1	2		S*	S**			3		5	6																7
9,120	17		4					7		9	10		S*			1	8		11*	2			3		5	6																8
5,702	19		4					7		9	10		8			1	11			2			3		5	6																9
10,183	18		4					7		9	10	11*				1	8			2	5		3			6	S*															10
30,722	20							7		9	10	11	S*			1	8			2	5		3			6		4*														11
5,532								7		9	10**	11	S*			1	8			2	5		3			6		4*	S**													12
10,559	18							7		9	10	11*				1	8		S*		5		3		2	6		4														13
9,539								7		9	10	11*				1	8			S**	5	S*	3		2	6		4**														14
3,995	15							7		9	10		S*			1				8		5	3		2*	6		4	S**	11				2nd sub Maylett for C.Smith								15
10,109	14		8	3				7			10					1				2	5	S**	9			6		4*	S*	11				3rd sub Eastwood for Maylett								16
15,888	18		8	3	S**						10					1				2	5	7	9*			6^	S^	4**	S*	11												17
10,575			8	3	10			7								1				2	5	9*				6	S**	4**	S*	11												18
5,907	19	1	5	8	4			7		9	10						2					11*				6			S*	3												19
11,925	17	1	5		4			7		9	10						2**			S**	11	S*				6				3*	8											20
9,983	18	1	11		4					9**	10						2				5		7			6	S**		S*	3	8*											21
8,783	19	1	8		4					9	10						7*				5	S**	11			6	S*			3**		2										22
5,630	19	1	5	3	4					9	10**						7					11*	8		S*	6	S**					2										23
9,635	17	1	5	3	4					9							7*					11**	8		10	6	S**		S*			2										24
10,892	17	1		3	4					9	10						7						8		S*	6						2	5	11*								25
7,129	15	1		3						9*	10						7						8		S*	6						2	5	11	4							26
10,985	16	1	S*	3				7		9	10				S^								8*		6				S**			2**	5	11^	4							27
7,407	15	1		3	11			7		9*	10**				2								8		S*	6			S^				5	S**	4	3rd Sub Maylett for Branch						
6,361	15	1		3				7**		9	10*				2		S**						8			6			S*				5	11	4							29
10,285	16	1		3				7^		9	10*				2		S*						8		S^	6			S**				5	11**	4							30
9,366	16	1		3						9	S*				7*		S^						8			6			S**			2^	5	11**	4	10						31
5,195	18	1	4	3**						9*	8	3rd sub Heywood for Swan									S^		7		S*	6			S**			2	5	11		10						32
8,981	18	1	7**					S**		9	8			S*	5*								3			6						2		11	4	10						33
17,251		1		3	8			7			9				2*								10			6			S*				5	11	4							34
11,561	21	1	6					7			10											S*	8*									2	5	11	4		3	9				35
4,151	21	1	6					7			10												8									2	5	11	4		3	9				36
10,500	19	1	6					7			10			S**									8**									2	5	11*	4	S*	3^	9	S^			37
6,625	19	1	6					7**			10			S*									8									2	5	S**	4	11	3	9*				38
10,747	17	1	6*					7			10			S**									8			S^						2**	5	S*	4	11	3	9^				39
8,542	18	1	6							7*	10**			S**									8									2	5	S*	4	11	3	9				40
5,658		1	6					S*		9^	10**			S^									7									2	5	S**	4	11	3*	8				41
9,802	17	1	6							9				S*								S**	7									2	5	11**	4	10	3	8*				42
10,965	15	1	6					7		9	10*			S^		2nd sub Johnrose for Branch							11									2	5	S*	4	S**	3	8^				43
13,086	14	1	6					7		9				S*									11									2**	5	10*	4	S**	3	8				44
5,528		1	6					7		9**				S*									11			5			S**			2			4	10	3	8*				45
7,435	15	1	6					7		9		S**					10**						11			5			S*			2*			4		3	8				46
Appearances		29	33	17	11	3	3	32	2	36	39	11	5	3	10	17	19	1	2	9	11	6	40	1	11	30		8		8	2	21	19	14	20	9	12	12				
Apps as sub			1		1			2			1	1	5	12	2		5		2	5	2	7			6	1	7		17					6		3			1			
Goals (54)								5		9	20			1			1					1	1			3	1	2				1	3	1	2	1	1	1				

Att.	Pos	Crichton	Brass	Morgan	Ford	Blatherwick	Howey	Little	Williams	A Cooke	Payton	P Smith	C Smith	Jepson	N Moore	Ward	Robertson	Winstanley	Carr-Lawton	C Scott	Heywood	Eastwood	Armstrong	Weller	Swan	Reid	Henderson	Vindheim	Maylett	O'Kane	Hewlett	Pickering	Davis	Branch	Mellon	Johnrose	T Cowan	P Cook	Williamson	Kval	Parks	
5,059			8	11	10			7			9									2	5	3				6		4												1		1
Appearances			1	1	1			1			1									1	1	1				1		1												1		
Apps as sub																																										
Goals (2)											2																															

Att.	Pos	Crichton	Brass	Morgan	Ford	Blatherwick	Howey	Little	Williams	A Cooke	Payton	P Smith	C Smith	Jepson	N Moore	Ward	Robertson	Winstanley	Carr-Lawton	C Scott	Heywood	Eastwood	Armstrong	Weller	Swan	Reid	Henderson	Vindheim	Maylett	O'Kane	Hewlett	Pickering	Davis	Branch	Mellon	Johnrose	T Cowan	P Cook	Williamson	Kval	Parks	
3,927			2	3		5	6	7	8*	9**		11	4	10^	S*				S**								S^														1	1
5,453			2	3^		5	6**	7			10	11		9*	4		S*		S**					8			S^														1	2L
Appearances			2	2		2	2	2	1	1	1	2	1	2	1									1																	2	
Apps as sub															1		1		2								2															
Goals (2)										1	1																															

1999-2000

OBITUARY
WALTER JOYCE
DIED 29 SEPTEMBER 1999, AGED 62.

Oldham-born Walter Joyce signed professional for Burnley in 1954, but had to wait nearly six years for his League debut, firstly because of National Service when he was in the RAF, and then owing to the sheer difficulty of breaking into a side that was so successful, culminating of course in the League Championship triumph of 1960.

It was early in the season following the title win that Joyce finally made his First Division debut, and he was a regular during 1960-61, usually appearing at right-half as captain Jimmy Adamson was employed elsewhere. That was to prove his best season at the Turf, and although he appeared occasionally during the following three campaigns, his contribution to the successes of the era has often been overlooked. It was his misfortune to be around at a time when Burnley had so many top players, but he did captain the reserve side to successive Central League championships in 1962 and 1963.

He enjoyed more regular League football down the road at Blackburn after leaving Turf Moor in 1964, and later moved into management at Rochdale. He remained in the game in various capacities almost up to his death, and his son Warren played for Burnley in the 1990s.

RIP

It was the perfect end to an entire season's work.

Emotion was running high at Glanford Park on 6 May 2000.

But the few hundred or so Burnley fans that had made the trip to Scunthorpe experienced an afternoon they will never forget.

Promotion was on the line, second place was up for grabs.

It was a straight battle between the Clarets and Gillingham and prior to kick-off, the two sides were locked together on 85 points.

No-one could have predicted the rollercoaster of differing emotions that would occur over just an hour and a half.

Preston had already been crowned Champions some weeks before, while four other sides were competing for three play-off slots.

But for Burnley, it was a two-way battle with the Gills to see who would join North End in celebration, and who would have to settle for the lottery of the play-offs.

Such was the interest back home, that 7,270 fans packed into Turf Moor to watch live footage of the contest being beamed back on a big screen.

That in itself would have been the fifth highest crowd of the day in Division Two, but every supporter in attendance knew there was work to be done.

Gillingham's vastly superior goal difference meant it was they who held the upper hand prior to kick-off.

Burnley seemingly had to win at Scunthorpe, and hope that Wrexham, managed by former Clarets favourite Brian Flynn, could do them one huge favour against Peter Taylor's Gills.

And just 11 minutes into the contest, Burnley could celebrate.

News filtered through from the Racecourse Ground that Wrexham had taken the lead.

But just 10 minutes later, disaster struck at Scunthorpe as Lee Hodges bundled the ball past Paul Crichton.

Amazingly, that meant both Burnley and Gillingham were losing, and, as things stood, it would be the latter that would grab that second promotion place.

But just before half-time, once again, it was advantage Burnley, as Micky Mellon cracked a shot past Iron keeper Ross Turner.

As the second half ticked on, there were just as many Burnley fans listening to radios as there were watching proceedings unfold. Then, on 73 minutes, the ball broke to Glen Little on the edge of the Scunthorpe box, and he unleashed an unerring shot that beat Turner all ends up.

Delirium set in among the travelling hordes, but the job was not done yet.

The next 17 minutes seemed like years but, as the final whistle sounded, it was Burnley who were celebrating promotion.

Scunthorpe had been beaten, and so had Gillingham.

Afterwards, an emotional Stan Ternent said: "Every promotion is special. I've had a few in my time but Burnley is very, very special.

"There were a lot of doubting Thomases but I just felt it was our destiny.

"From towards the end of last season I knew we would be competitive if I got the players I wanted, which I did, and they have been absolutely blinding."

Ternent had labelled it as a major achievement, and, with the Clarets having collected 88 points he was absolutely right. Especially considering the position they were in after a certain Tuesday night in April 2000.

The two sides who would go on to contest that final day rollercoaster met at Turf Moor.

Burnley approached the game four points ahead of their rivals, knowing that victory would virtually rule their opponents out of the running. Alas it never happened, and the visitors went away with a thoroughly deserved 3-0 success.

Having gone into the game on the back of three straight wins against Cardiff, Notts County and Oxford, the result was a severe body blow to Burnley's promotion charge.

Millwall were next up, with Burnley surging into a 4-0 lead through Ian Cox, Andy Cooke, Steve Davis and Paul Cook.

Ian Wright salutes the Burnley fans after one of his crucial goals

And despite an almighty scare, they survived a remarkable comeback to win the game 4-3.

A 3-2 Easter Monday success over Brentford and a 2-0 win over Cambridge in the final home game of the campaign followed.

Clarets fans could then only watch on as Gillingham won their game in hand, 4-1 against Cardiff, to move ahead on goal difference.

But it was they who would end up smiling when the dust had finally settled on a truly remarkable campaign.

The season had started modestly for the Clarets, with Andy Cooke netting a second half equaliser in a 1-1 draw at Wycombe.

A 2-1 success over Chesterfield in their first home game propelled them into the top six – a position they would not relinquish during the rest of the season.

Andy Payton netted the winners against both Oldham and Stoke, before the first League defeat of the season came in a 1-0 loss at Bristol Rovers.

The Pirates were to be the talking point of the season, as they set the division alight.

But a run of just one victory in their final 10 matches meant they somehow even managed to miss out on a play-off spot.

Back with the Clarets, who followed their defeat at the Memorial Ground with just two victories in their next seven games.

Those came against Bournemouth and Colchester, both at Turf Moor, but the poor run of form failed to move them out of the top six.

Then, what a response, as three victories on the spin ended with a 5-0 thumping of Wrexham, who would go on to figure prominently in Burnley's destiny on the last day of the season.

Blackpool, Wycombe and Cardiff were all beaten in the weeks that ensued, before a surprise 4-2 defeat at Bury on Boxing Day.

And on that occasion, they were only spared a more humiliating scoreline thanks to two injury time goals from Ronnie Jepson and John Mullin. However, they put it right two days later, or rather, Payton did.

Ten years earlier, he had been the first goalscorer of the 1990s decade when netting for Hull City in a lunchtime kick-off against Sunderland.

And in a remarkable twist of fate, he would become the last goalscorer of not only the decade, but the millennium, to cap off a superb hat-trick in a 3-2 victory over Oxford at Turf Moor.

That put Payton in the spotlight, but it would be a new team-mate who would soon grab all the headlines.

On Valentine's Day, the news broke that Stan Ternent was about to pull off a major transfer coup.

And so it proved, as Arsenal legend Ian Wright was unveiled to a stunned Burnley public at a showpiece press conference.

Turf Moor was packed to the rafters for his eagerly-anticipated debut, but the gloss was taken off it somewhat in a drab goalless draw with Wigan.

But Wright would turn out to be the catalyst for the end-of-season run-in, with three of his four goals arriving at the most crucial of moments.

His first came just six minutes from time to grab a 2-2 draw at Gillingham.

And four days later he was on target again, this time in less spectacular style, as Reading were beaten 3-0.

But it was the goal against Notts County on 8 April that he will probably be best remembered for.

After Payton had given the Clarets an early lead, it seemed like two crucial points had been thrown away when Mark Stallard netted an equaliser four minutes from time.

But Ian would prove to be in the Wright place at the Wright time to net an emotional injury time winner, which sent this small part of East Lancashire into raptures.

And if Burnley fans hadn't been put through enough, in their very next game, Steve Davis and Paul Weller both netted in the final five minutes at Oxford, to turn a 1-0 deficit into a 2-1 success.

Wright came off the bench to score his last goal for the club in the 3-2 success at Brentford and he made cameo appearances in both of Burnley's final two games, including the final minutes at Scunthorpe.

Ian Wright was a signing that will always be remembered by the Clarets faithful, as will this truly remarkable season.

Glen Little thunders in the winner at Scunthorpe
the Clarets are up!

1999-2000 - Second Division

		P	W	D	L	F	A	Pts
1	Preston NE	46	28	11	7	74	37	95
2	BURNLEY	46	25	13	8	69	47	88
3	Gillingham	46	25	10	11	79	48	85
4	Wigan A	46	22	17	7	72	38	83
5	Millwall	46	23	13	10	76	50	82
6	Stoke C	46	23	13	10	68	42	82
7	Bristol R	46	23	11	12	69	45	80
8	Notts C	46	18	11	17	61	55	65
9	Bristol C	46	15	19	12	59	57	64
10	Reading	46	16	14	16	57	63	62
11	Wrexham	46	17	11	18	52	61	62
12	Wycombe W	46	16	13	17	56	53	61
13	Luton T	46	17	10	19	61	65	61
14	Oldham A	46	16	12	18	50	55	60
15	Bury	46	13	18	15	61	64	57
16	Bournemouth	46	16	9	21	59	62	57
17	Brentford	46	13	13	20	47	61	52
18	Colchester U	46	14	10	22	59	82	52
19	Cambridge U	46	12	12	22	64	65	48
20	Oxford U	46	12	9	25	43	73	45
21	Cardiff C	46	9	17	20	45	67	44
22	Blackpool	46	8	17	21	49	77	41
23	Scunthorpe U	46	9	12	25	40	74	39
24	Chesterfield	46	7	15	24	34	63	36

1999-2000

Manager : Stan Ternent

Division Two (2nd)
Promoted

		Date			Opponents	Result		h/t	Goalscorers/times	Opp. goal times
	1	Aug	7	a	Wycombe W	D	1-1	0-1	Cooke 68	27
	2		14	h	CHESTERFIELD	W	2-1	2-0	Payton 32p, Johnrose 34	65p
	3		21	a	Oldham A	W	1-0	1-0	Payton 31	
	4		28	h	STOKE C	W	1-0	0-0	Payton 75	
	5		30	a	Bristol R	L	0-1	0-1		37p
	6	Sep	3	h	BOURNEMOUTH	W	2-1	1-1	Branch 40, Davis 62	39
	7		11	a	Preston N E	D	0-0	0-0		
	8		18	h	COLCHESTER U	W	3-0	2-0	Payton (3) 10, 38p, 51	
	9		25	a	Bristol C	D	0-0	0-0		
	10	Oct	2	h	BRENTFORD	D	2-2	2-0	Payton 23, Cook 31	54, 80
	11		10	h	SCUNTHORPE U	L	1-2	0-1	Payton 58	25, 85
	12		16	a	Millwall	D	1-1	1-0	Cooke 11	70
	13		19	a	Cambridge U	W	1-0	1-0	Cooke 5	
	14		23	h	BRISTOL C	W	2-0	1-0	Cook 6, Cooke 61	
	15	Nov	2	h	WREXHAM	W	5-0	1-0	Mullin (2) 43, 70, Mellon 46, Little 49, Branch 83	
	16		6	a	Luton T	L	1-2	0-0	Cooke 50	49, 69
	17		14	h	BLACKPOOL	W	1-0	0-0	Mellon 77	
	18		23	a	Reading	D	0-0	0-0		
	19		27	a	Wigan A	D	1-1	1-1	Payton 17	42
	20	Dec	4	h	WYCOMBE W	W	1-0	0-0	Payton 78	
	21		18	h	CARDIFF C	W	2-1	1-1	Armstrong 34, Johnrose 68	15og
	22		26	a	Bury	L	2-4	0-4	Jepson 89, Mullin 90	8, 10p, 33, 41
very last goal of the Millenium	23		28	h	OXFORD U	W	3-2	1-1	Payton (3) 22p, 79, 90	3, 52
	24	Jan	3	a	Notts C	L	0-2	0-1		15, 62
	25		15	a	Chesterfield	D	1-1	1-0	Payton 4	73
	26		22	h	OLDHAM A	W	3-0	1-0	Cooke 24, Payton (2) 62, 81	
Swan's last game	27		29	a	Stoke C	D	2-2	0-0	Payton (2) 75p, 83	67, 70og
	28	Feb	5	h	BRISTOL R	W	1-0	0-0	Little 69	
	29		12	a	Bournemouth	W	1-0	1-0	Payton 32	
	30		19	h	WIGAN A	D	0-0	0-0		
	31		26	a	Colchester U	W	2-1	2-1	Davis (2) 17, 38	19
Brass' last game	32	Mar	4	h	PRESTON N E	L	0-3	0-1		2, 72, 78
	33		7	h	LUTON T	L	0-2	0-1		27, 55
	34		11	a	Wrexham	W	1-0	1-0	Payton 6	
	35		14	a	Gillingham	D	2-2	1-1	Payton 31, Wright 86	4, 68
	36		18	h	READING	W	3-0	1-0	Davis 37, Payton 52, Wright 84	
	37		21	a	Blackpool	D	1-1	0-0	Branch 69	48
	38		25	h	BURY	D	2-2	0-0	Payton 51, Jepson 90	79, 89
	39	Apr	1	a	Cardiff C	W	2-1	1-0	Davis 21, Payton 61	68og
	40		8	h	NOTTS C	W	2-1	1-0	Payton 6, Wright 90	86
	41		15	a	Oxford U	W	2-1	0-1	Davis 85, Weller 90	13
	42		18	h	GILLINGHAM	L	0-3	0-1		21, 51, 70
	43		22	h	MILLWALL	W	4-3	3-0	Cox 7, Cooke 29, Davis 42, Cook 52	60, 78, 87
	44		24	a	Brentford	W	3-2	0-1	Mullin (2) 61, 76, Wright 64	43, 90
	45		29	h	CAMBRIDGE U	W	2-0	2-0	Payton (2) 13, 31	
Wright's last game	46	May	6	a	Scunthorpe U	W	2-1	1-1	Mellon 41, Little 73	21

FA Cup

				Opponents			h/t	Goalscorers	Opp. goal times
1	Oct	31	a	Barnet	W	1-0	0-0	Cook 74	
2	Nov	20	h	ROTHERHAM U	W	2-0	0-0	Cook 67, Mullin 75	
3	Dec	11	a	Derby C	W	1-0	0-0	Cooke 62	
4	Jan	8	a	Coventry C	L	0-3	0-1		11, 70, 75

Final, Chelsea 1-0 Aston Villa, at Wembley.

League Cup

					Opponents			h/t	Goalscorers	Opp. goal times
	1	Aug	11	a	Manchester C	L	0-5	0-1		36, 48, 62p, 74, 82
agg 0-6			24	h	MANCHESTER C	L	0-1	0-0		61

Final, Leicester C 2-1 Tranmere R, at Wembley.

Details of other first team games elsewhere.

Att.	Pos	Crichton	West	Thomas	Davis	P Smith	Little	Mellon	P Cook	Mullin	Branch	A Cooke	Lee	Payton	Jepson	Armstrong	T Cowan	Johnrose	Brass	Robertson	Weller	Swan	Cox	Wright	S Grant		
6,119	9	G	D	D	D	D	M	M	M**	M*	M^	F	S*	S**	S^												1
10,615	6	G	D	D	D*		S^	M	M**			S**	F**	F^	S*	D	M	M									2
8,543	4	G	D	D		M		M	M**		S*	F*	S^	F^	S**	D	D	M									3
11,328	3	G	D	D		M	S**	M**	M^		S*		F*	F	S^	D	D	M									4
7,624	3	G	D	D			M	M	M**	S^	F			F	S**	D	D*		M	S*						3rd sub Mullin for Robertson	5
10,223		G	D	D	D	M*	M	M	M^		F**			F	S^	D	S*	S**									6
13,708	4	G	D	D	D	M^	M*	M**	M	S*	F			F		D	S^	S**									7
10,090	1	G	D	D	D	M	M^	M**	M	S^	F*		S*	F		D		S**									8
11,510	2	G	D	D	D	M	M*	M	M^	S*	F**			F	S^	D		S**									9
10,907	3	G	D	D	D	M*	M	M**	M	S**	F^	S^		F		D		S*									10
10,752	5	G	D	D	D	M	M	M*	M	S*	F^	S**		F		D**					S^						11
8,601	6	G	D	D	D	D	M*	S*	M	M	S**	F**		F				M									12
4,320		G	D	D	D	D^	M*	S*	M	M	F**	F	S**					M	S^								13
10,175	5	G	D	D	D	D	M	S**	M^	M**	S*	F*		F	S^			M									14
8,944		G		D	D		M	M	M*	M	S^	F^	S*	F**	S**	D			D								15
7,205	4	G		D	D		M	M	M	M	S**	F	S^	F**	S*	D^			D*								16
12,898	4	G	D	D	D		M	M	M	M*	S*	F		F**	S**	D											17
6,149		G	D	D	D		M	M	M	M	S*	F*	S**	F**		D											18
11,986	5	G	D	D	D		M	M	M	M	S*	F**	S**	F		D*											19
9,149	5	G	D*	D	D		M	M	M	M**	S**	F^		F	S*	D		S^									20
9,753	5	G	D*	D	D		M^	M	M	M**	S*	F^		F	S^	D		S**									21
9,115	6	G	D*		D		M	D**		F	M	F			S**	D	S*	M	M		S^						22
14,218	5	G	D*	D	D	S**	M	M	M^	M	D**	F		F	S*						S^						23
8,229	5	G	D*	D	D	S**	M	M	M	M	D**	F^		F	S^							S*					24
4,214	6	G	D	D			M		M		S^	F^		F	S**	D*	D	M	S*		M**						25
12,391	5	G	D	D	D	S*		M**	M^	S**	M*	F		F	S^	D		M									26
15,354	5	G	D*	D	D	S^	S*		M	M	M^	F		F		D		M**				S**					27
13,526	5	G		D	D		D**	S**	M^	M	S*	F		F	S^	M*		M					D				28
5,804	4	G	S^	D	D		D	S*	M**	M*	M	F		F^	S**			M					D				29
20,435	5	G	S*	D	D	S**	D*		M	M	M**	F^			S^			M					D	F			30
6,194	5	G		D	D		D		M	M*	M	F			S*			M					D	F			31
22,310	5	G	D		D	S*	M	S**	M**	M*	D	F^						M	S^				D	F			32
12,080		G		D	D	S^	D	S*	M**	M*	M^	F		S**				M					D	F			33
6,582	5	G	S*	D	D	M	D*	M	M**			F^		F	S**			M					D	S^			34
7,347		G		D	D		D	M*	M**	S*	M	F^		F	S^			M					D	S**			35
14,436	5	G		D	D		D	M*	M	S*	M	F^	S^	F**				M					D	S**			36
8,029		G		D	D		D	M*	M	S*	M	F**		F				M					D	S**			37
13,297	5	G		D	D		D	S**	M*	M	M	F**		F	S*			M					D				38
6,487	5	G	S**	D	D	M	D	S*	M	M*	F**		S^	F^				M					D				39
13,022	5	G		D	D	M	D	M	M^		F*		S*	F**	S^			M					D	S**			40
7,549	5	G	D**	D	D	M*		M	M^		F		S*	F				M			S**		D	S^			41
17,026		G	D**	D	D	M*		M	M^		F			F	S*			M			S**		D	S^			42
14,890	4	G		D	D			M	M^	M	D	F**	S*	F*	M						S^		D	S**			43
6,595	3	G		D	D		D**	M		M	M	F		F*	S**			M					D	S*			44
15,084	2	G	D	D	D		S^	M	M**	M	D	F*		F^	S**			M						S*			45
5,862	2	G	D	D	D		S*	M	M	M	D*	F**		F^	S^			M						S**			46
Appearances		46	30	44	42	17	36	33	44	27	31	33	2	39	1	22	5	28	4		1		17	4			
Apps as sub			4			7	5	9		10	13	3	13	2	30		3	7	3	1	6	2		11			
Goals (69)					7		3	3	3	5	3	7		27	2	1		2			1		1	4			

Att.	Crichton	West	Thomas	Davis	P Smith	Little	Mellon	P Cook	Mullin	Branch	A Cooke	Lee	Payton	Jepson	Armstrong	T Cowan	Johnrose	Brass	Robertson	Weller	Swan	Cox	Wright	S Grant	
2,563	G	D	D	D	D*	M^	M	M	M		F	S**	F**	S^	S*										1
8,110	G	D	D	D		M	M	M**	M	S*	F^	S^	F	S**	D*										2
23,400	G	D	D	D		M	M	M^	M	S*	F		F*	S**	D**		S^								3
22,774	G	D*	D	D		M	M	M	M	S*	F		F		D										4
Appearances	4	4	4	4	1	4	4	4	4		4		4		3										
Apps as sub										3		2		3	1		1								
Goals (4)								2	1		1														

Att.	Crichton	West	Thomas	Davis	P Smith	Little	Mellon	P Cook	Mullin	Branch	A Cooke	Lee	Payton	Jepson	Armstrong	T Cowan	Johnrose	Brass	Robertson	Weller	Swan	Cox	Wright	S Grant	
11,074	G	D	D	D		M^	M	M**		F*		S*	F	S**		D	M							S^	1
3,647	G	S*	D			M	M*			F^		F**		S**	D	D	M	M	D					S^	2nd leg
Appearances	2	1	2	1		2	2	1		2		1	1		1	2	2	1	1						
Apps as sub		1										1		2										2	
Goals (0)																									

2000-01

It was a moment Burnley fans had waited 18 years to arrive. Promotion from the Second Division meant only one thing. New grounds were to be visited, young fans had the chance to visit the likes of Bolton, Wolves, Birmingham and Nottingham Forest.

But all those were cast to the back of the minds, as one team stood out.

Not just one team, but one stadium, one rivalry, and one trip down the M65.

That's right, a certain side in blue and white would be competing at the same level as the Clarets, for the first match-up in the time it takes to become a man.

And as far as the two contests were concerned, the pitch at Turf Moor and Ewood Park would be a place for men, not boys.

While Burnley had experienced joy of the highest order with their final day promotion success over Scunthorpe, Blackburn had experienced relegation from the Premiership.

And that had occurred just five years after they had been the kings of English football, in the same year that Burnley had been relegated from the First Division.

As soon as the fixture lists were published in pre-season, every Burnley fan reached straight for the newspaper.

When were the dates? How long did they have to wait?

Four months into the season was the answer, and 17 December.

By that time, Burnley could have been anywhere in the table. If last time they experienced football at this level was anything to go by, 17 December had seen Burnley in 18th place, about to embark on a club record equalling run of eight successive league defeats.

But to some Claret fans that didn't matter, as long as they beat Blackburn, they could finish bottom of the pile with three points to their name!

However, this was a different side to the one that had come up under Jimmy Mullen six years before.

Stan Ternent had built a solid unit, with a unique blend of youth and experience across the length and breadth of the pitch.

And there was something at the back of your mind that thought, when that special date in December did come along, Burnley would not be scrapping for their lives.

Going into the first game of the season at Bolton, a travelling army of Claret supporters descended in numbers onto the Reebok Stadium.

Twelve months earlier they had kicked of the season at Wycombe, and now they were advancing through the turnstiles and into another world.

But the end result was just the same, as Phil Gray stooped to head his only goal in a Claret shirt early in the second half, to send the away contingent delirious.

Victory over Wimbledon in their first home game, thanks to a solitary Paul Weller effort, saw Burnley eighth in the table.

But this was only two games into the season, and surely the Clarets couldn't keep that rate up.

Victory over Hartlepool in the first round of the Worthington Cup, 6-4 on aggregate, saw the Clarets through to play Crystal Palace.

Despite not losing either tie against the Eagles, Andy Linighan's last gasp equaliser in the second leg at Selhurst Park saw them through on away goals.

But back in the league, the Clarets did keep up their fine run of form as, after an average run of two wins in seven games, four straight victories catapulted Ternent's troops into the play-off places.

That run started with a 3-2 win at Tranmere on a Friday evening, with Andy Payton netting a last minute winner.

Stockport – another old enemy – Sheffield Wednesday and QPR were also accounted for, but Burnley were to sample the harsh reality of football in their next outing.

A cold Wednesday evening in the Midlands, and a trip to the City Ground at Nottingham Forest.

Within four minutes, talk of "one of those nights" already began emanating from the travelling fans as Chris Bart-Williams put Forest ahead.

A goal right on half-time from Andy Johnson was cruel on Burnley, but it was to get worse in the second period.

Gareth Taylor
a potent strike force with Ian Moore

A Bart-Williams penalty, and further goals from Alan Rogers and Riccardo Scimeca saw Burnley crushed 5-0, and set up a long journey back to East Lancashire.

They needed to bounce back quickly, and did at the first attempt, beating Crewe 1-0 at Turf Moor thanks to Andy Cooke.

Graham Branch gave the Clarets the lead at West Brom in their next game, but Jason Roberts' 87th minute equaliser would prove massively decisive later on.

Defeat at Birmingham came in the middle of a run of home

wins against Sheffield United, Norwich and Forest, an Andy Payton penalty exacting revenge for the Clarets' crushing defeat at the City Ground just six weeks previously.

If the storm was to come at Turf Moor on 17 December, then the previous week at Preston was a heavy gust of wind.

Ian Moore scored in a 2-1 defeat at Deepdale, but all eyes were focused on Blackburn's trip to the Turf.

Home fans had waited a long time for this moment, and spent all week dreaming of what might be.

But unfortunately, Santa decided not to give the Burnley fans an early Christmas present.

Goals in stoppage time at the end of either half from Jason McAteer and Marcus Bent meant it was the Ewood hordes who would go home the happier.

All that wait for nothing.

There would be another chance to set the record straight later on in the year, but the less said about that the better.

The trio of derby games ended with another defeat, this time a 2-0 reverse at home to Bolton.

And further defeats to Barnsley and Wolves meant, in the words of Stan Ternent: "Christmas is cancelled until further notice".

The Clarets crashed out of the FA Cup at the first hurdle, losing on penalties to Scunthorpe after a 1-1 draw in the replay at Glanford Park.

A goalless draw at Gillingham in the league and a revenge home win over Barnsley lifted some of the gloom, but three successive defeats from that point would see the gap between the Clarets and the play-off positions grow that much wider.

Fulham were beaten at Turf Moor thanks to a late Glen Little winner, as were Huddersfield thanks to a solitary Steve Davis effort.

Two wins arrived from their next five outings, before the small matter of the second Blackburn game came up on the horizon.

But as they say on the BBC News, just before Match of the Day is screened, "if you don't want to know the score, look away now".

Blackburn showed their superiority in abundance on a glum Sunday afternoon.

Craig Short's scrappy effort, and one of the unluckiest own goals you're likely to see from Steve Davis, saw Rovers 2-0 up at the break.

Burnley did have the ball in the net only for Ian Moore's goal to be rightly ruled out for offside.

But after the interval, Matt Jansen scored twice to rub salt in the wounds, and if that wasn't enough, Craig Hignett netted in injury time to apply the iodine.

It was Burnley's second 5-0 hammering of the season, but despite that, they were still tenth.

Victories over Preston and Wimbledon suddenly made the play-offs look possible again.

And who knows what might have happened had, for the second time in the season, West Brom not come up with a late equaliser, this time thanks to Bob Taylor at Turf Moor.

A 3-2 Easter Monday win at Norwich was backed up with wins over Tranmere and Watford.

But the 2-0 defeat at Sheffield United on the penultimate weekend saw any hopes of the season being extended mathematically disappear.

Burnley ultimately finished the season just one place and two points behind a play-off place.

West Brom held sixth spot.

Remember those two late equalisers?

That just about summed it up.

Ian Moore
Burnley's first £1m man

2000-01 - First Division

		P	W	D	L	F	A	Pts
1	Fulham	46	30	11	5	90	32	101
2	Blackburn R	46	26	13	7	76	39	91
3	Bolton W	46	24	15	7	76	45	87
4	Preston NE	46	23	9	14	64	52	78
5	Birmingham C	46	23	9	14	59	48	78
6	West Bromwich A	46	21	11	14	60	52	74
7	BURNLEY	46	21	9	16	50	54	72
8	Wimbledon	46	17	18	11	71	50	69
9	Watford	46	20	9	17	76	67	69
10	Sheffield U	46	19	11	16	52	49	68
11	Nottingham F	46	20	8	18	55	53	68
12	Wolverhampton W	46	14	13	19	45	48	55
13	Gillingham	46	13	16	17	61	66	55
14	Crewe A	46	15	10	21	47	62	55
15	Norwich C	46	14	12	20	46	58	54
16	Barnsley	46	15	9	22	49	62	54
17	Sheffield W	46	15	8	23	52	71	53
18	Grimsby T	46	14	10	22	43	62	52
19	Stockport C	46	11	18	17	58	65	51
20	Crystal P	46	12	13	21	57	70	49
21	Portsmouth	46	10	19	17	47	59	49
22	Huddersfield T	46	11	15	20	48	57	48
23	Queens Park R	46	7	19	20	45	75	40
24	Tranmere R	46	9	11	26	46	77	38

2000-01

Manager : Stan Ternent

Division One (7th)

		Date			Opponents	Result		h/t	Goalscorers/times	Opp. goal times
	1	Aug	12	a	Bolton W	D	1-1	0-1	Gray 55	26p
	2		19	h	WIMBLEDON	W	1-0	1-0	Weller 27	
	3		26	a	Wolverhampton W	L	0-1	0-0		73
	4		28	h	GILLINGHAM	D	1-1	0-0	Ashby 70og	66
	5	Sep	9	a	Crystal P	W	1-0	0-0	Branch 77	
	6		12	a	Fulham	L	1-3	1-0	Cook 10	53, 64, 80
	7		16	h	GRIMSBY T	D	1-1	1-1	Cooke 18	11
	8		23	a	Huddersfield T	W	1-0	1-0	Payton 17	
	9		30	h	PORTSMOUTH	D	1-1	0-0	Weller 88	74
	10	Oct	6	a	Tranmere R	W	3-2	1-0	Davis (2) 45, 55, Payton 90	56, 63
	11		14	h	STOCKPORT C	W	2-1	2-0	Payton 20, Branch 24	57
	12		17	h	SHEFFIELD W	W	1-0	0-0	Davis 74	
	13		21	a	Queens Park R	W	1-0	0-0	Mullin 70	
	14		25	a	Nottingham F	L	0-5	0-2		4, 45, 54p, 76, 89
Cooke's last game	15		31	h	CREWE A	W	1-0	1-0	Cooke 39	
Crichton's last game	16	Nov	4	a	West Bromwich A	D	1-1	1-0	Branch 23	87
	17		11	h	SHEFFIELD U	W	2-0	0-0	Payton (2) 53p, 67	
	18		18	a	Birmingham C	L	2-3	0-0	Cox 60, Weller 89	48, 50, 85
	19		21	h	NORWICH C	W	2-0	0-0	Payton 56, Davis 65	
	20	Dec	2	h	NOTTINGHAM F	W	1-0	0-0	Payton 78p	
	21		9	a	Preston N E	L	1-2	1-0	Moore 26	51, 67
	22		17	h	BLACKBURN R	L	0-2	0-1		45, 90
	23		23	h	BOLTON W	L	0-2	0-0		54, 72
	24		26	a	Barnsley	L	0-1	0-0		89
Jepson's last game	25	Jan	1	h	WOLVERHAMPTON W	L	1-2	1-1	Branch 9	28, 85
	26		13	a	Gillingham	D	0-0	0-0		
	27		20	h	BARNSLEY	W	2-1	1-0	Johnrose 24, Payton 61	77
	28	Feb	3	a	Crewe A	L	2-4	1-3	Branch 11, Cook 59p	5, 40p, 43p, 85
	29		10	h	CRYSTAL P	L	1-2	1-0	Cook 12	74, 90
	30		17	a	Grimsby T	L	0-1	0-0		55
	31		20	h	FULHAM	W	2-1	0-0	Moore 73, Little 88	49
Mellon's last game	32		24	h	HUDDERSFIELD T	W	1-0	0-0	Davis 47	
	33	Mar	3	a	Portsmouth	L	0-2	0-0		57, 69p
	34		6	a	Stockport C	D	0-0	0-0		
	35		13	a	Watford	W	1-0	0-0	Taylor 73	
	36		17	a	Sheffield W	L	0-2	0-1		41, 70p
	37		24	h	QUEENS PARK R	W	2-1	2-0	Smith 12, Taylor 42	54
	38	Apr	1	a	Blackburn R	L	0-5	0-2		14, 28og, 55, 70, 82
	39		6	h	PRESTON N E	W	3-0	2-0	Moore 3, Ball 44, Little 73	
	40		10	a	Wimbledon	W	2-0	2-0	Taylor 2, Moore 45	
	41		14	h	WEST BROMWICH A	D	1-1	0-0	Little 47	84
	42		16	a	Norwich C	W	3-2	1-2	Ball 24, Taylor 48, Moore 63	13, 37p
	43		21	h	BIRMINGHAM C	D	0-0	0-0		
	44		24	h	TRANMERE R	W	2-1	1-1	Yates 22og, Mullin 59	20
Paul Smith's last game	45		28	a	Sheffield U	L	0-2	0-1		21, 89
	46	May	6	h	WATFORD	W	2-0	0-0	Payton 74, Mullin 90	

FA Cup

	3	Jan	6	h	SCUNTHORPE U	D	2-2	1-1	Moore 45, Johnrose 90	2, 47
aet, lost 4-5 on pens	rep		23	a	Scunthorpe U	D	1-1	0-0	Payton 73	84

Final, Liverpool 2-1 Arsenal, at The Millenium Stadium, Cardiff.

League Cup

	1	Aug	22	h	HARTLEPOOL U	W	4-1	0-1	Payton (3) 63p, 69, 90, Davis 87	37
agg 6-4		Sep	5	a	Hartlepool U	L	2-3	1-2	Cooke 18, Payton 82	30p, 38, 90
	2		19	h	CRYSTAL P	D	2-2	0-1	Cooke 67, Payton 81p	17, 46
aet, agg 3-3, lost on away goals			27	a	Crystal P	D	1-1	1-0	Cooke 45	90

Final, Liverpool 1-1 Birmingham C after extra time, at The Millenium Stadium, Cardiff, Liverpool won on pens.

Details of other first team games elsewhere.

Att.	Pos	Crichton	Cox	Davis	Thomas	Weller	Mullin	Ball	P Cook	Briscoe	A Cooke	P Gray	Little	Branch	Payton	Armstrong	Mellon	Jepson	Michopoulos	P Robinson	Johnrose	I Moore	Maylett	P Smith	Shandran	G Taylor	West			
20,662		G	D	D	D	D	M*	M	M	M	F**	F	S*	S**																1
15,124	8	G	D	D	D	D	S**	M	M	M	F^	F*	M**	S*	S^															2
20,156	11	G	D	D	D	D^	S**	M	M	M	F**	F*	M	S*	S^															3
15,611	12	G	D	D	D	D^	S^	M	M	M	F*	F**	M	S**	S*															4
18,531	8	G	D	D*	D	D	S*	M	M	M	F**	F^	M	S^	S**															5
11,863		G	D		D	D	F^	M	M*	M	F		M	S*	S**	D**	S^													6
15,413	12	G	D	D	D	D*	S*	M	M**	M	F^		M	S**	F			S^												7
14,016	11		D	D	D		S**	M	M	D	F*		M**	S*	F^		M	S^	G											8
15,494	10		D	D	D^	S*		M	M*	M	F**		D	S**	F		M	S^	G											9
10,153			D	D	D	S*	F*	M	M^	D			M	F**	S**		M	S^	G											10
16,107	7		D	D	D	S*		M	M^	D			M*	F	F**		M	S^	G	S**										11
16,372			D	D	D	M		M	M*	D	S*			F**	F^		M	S**	G		S^									12
11,427	6		D	D	D	D	S*	M	M**	M				F*	F^		M		G	S^	S**									13
17,195			D	D^	D	D	S*	M	M*	M				F**	F^		M		G	S**	S^									14
13,189			D	D	D	D	S*	M	M**		F^			M	F*		M	S^	G		S**									15
17,828	5	S*	D	D	D	D	S^	M	M**	M				F	F^		M		G*		S**									16
16,635	4		D	D	D	M*	S^	M		D			S*	F**	F^		M	S**	G		M									17
19,641	8		D	D	D	S*	S^	M		D			M*	F**	F		M^		G	S**	M									18
15,017			D	D	D	S*	S^	M	M^	M**			D*	F	F		M		G			S**								19
17,876	6		D	D	D	D	S**	M	M*					M	F**		M	S^	G		S*	F^								20
17,355	8		D	D	D	D	S**		M*						F	S^	M	S*	G		M^	F	M**							21
21,369	9		D	D	D	D	S^	M	M*					M**	F		M^		G		S*	F	S**							22
19,552	9		D	D	D	D*	F	M	M**				S*	F			M^	S^	G		S**			M						23
18,725	10		D	D	D	M		M					S*	F*	S**		M	S^	G		M	F**		D				3rd sub Jepson for Little		24
15,483	10		D		D	M	S**							M	F*	D	M	S^	G		M^	F**	S*	D						25
9,331	10		D	D	D	D	M*		M				S*	F					G		M	F		M						26
15,380	9		D	D	D	D	S**	M	M^				S*	M*	F**	S^			G		M	F								27
6,994	10			D	D	D	M**	M	M				M	D	S**				G			F^	S*	F*	S^					28
14,973	10		D	D		D	S^		M*				M	D	F^		M		G		M	F	S**	S*				2nd sub Maylett for Smith		29
6,044	10		D**	D	D	M	F^		S*				M	D	S**	M			G		M*	F	S^							30
15,737			D	D	D	M			M				D**	M		M	S*		G		S**	F*				F				31
16,191	10			D	D^	D		M*	M**				M	M	S^	D	S*		G		S**	F				F				32
12,941	10		S^	D	D	D	S**	M^	M**	S*			M	M*		D			G			F				F				33
7,087			D	D	D	M	S**	M	M	M				D	S*				G			F*				F**				34
13,653			D	D	D	M	F**	M	M*	D					S^	S*			G			F^	S**			M				35
20,184	10		D	D	D	M	M**	M*		D^			S**		S^	M			G			F		S*		F				36
14,018	10			D	D	D		M	M^				M	D	S**	S^			G			F**	S*	M*		F				37
23,442	10		D	D	D	D		M**	M				M	M*	S**	S^			G			F^		S*		F				38
16,591			D	D		M	S*	M	M				M		S**				G			F*	S^	D		F**	D^			39
6,132				D		M	S**	M	M	S*			M^		S^	D*			G			F**		D		F	D			40
18,199	9			D	S*	M	S^	M	M**	S**			M^			D*			G			F		D		F	D			41
17,507	8			D	S**	M		M	M**	S*			M		S^	D			G			F^		D*		F	D			42
17,057	8		S^	D	D	M		M		M*			M		S**	D^			G			F	S*			F	D**			43
13,717				D	D	M**	F^	M	S*	M			M		S^	D			G			F	S**				D*			44
20,013	7			D	D		M	M	M^	D*					S**	D			G			F	M**	S^		F	S*			45
18,283	7		S^	D	D	M	S**	M	M^	D			M*		S*	D			G			F**				F				46
Appearances		7	35	44	41	39	11	40	38	25	10	5	27	26	18	14	19		39		9	26	2	10		15	6			
Apps as sub		1	3		2	5	25		2	4	1		7	9	22	5	3	13		4	10	1	10	4	1		1			
Goals (50)			1	5		3	3	2	3		2	1	3	5	9						1	5		1		4			2	ogs

Att.	Pos	Crichton	Cox	Davis	Thomas	Weller	Mullin	Ball	P Cook	Briscoe	A Cooke	P Gray	Little	Branch	Payton	Armstrong	Mellon	Jepson	Michopoulos	P Robinson	Johnrose	I Moore	Maylett	P Smith	Shandran	G Taylor	West	
8,054			D^	D	D	M	M		M				S*	F*	S**		M**		G		S^	F		D				3
4,709			D	D	D	M	S^	M	M**				S**	D^	F	S*			G		M*	F						rep
Appearances			2	2	2	2	1	1	2					2	1		1		2		1	2		1				
Apps as sub							1						2		1	1					1							
Goals (3)															1						1	1						

Att.	Pos	Crichton	Cox	Davis	Thomas	Weller	Mullin	Ball	P Cook	Briscoe	A Cooke	P Gray	Little	Branch	Payton	Armstrong	Mellon	Jepson	Michopoulos	P Robinson	Johnrose	I Moore	Maylett	P Smith	Shandran	G Taylor	West	
3,319		G	D	D	D	M	S^	M	M^	D	F**	F*	M	S*	S**													1
1,090		G	D	D	D	M^		M	M	D	F**	F*	M	S**	S*								S^					2nd leg
5,889			D	D	D		M**	M	M*	D	F^			M	F		S*	S^	G				S**					2
5,720			D	D	D			M	S*		F	S^	M*	M^	F**	D	M	S**	G									2nd leg
Appearances		2	4	4	4	2	1	4	3	3	4	2	3	2	2	1	1		2									
Apps as sub							1		1			1		2	2		1	2					2					
Goals (9)				1							3				5													

2001-02

How on earth can an entire season rest on one moment? How can the outcome of a 46-game campaign rest on a few seconds of play?

Such a scenario was demonstrated at Turf Moor on 21 April 2002.

It had seemed like the most perfect of scripts to end what had been a rollercoaster campaign.

The legend that was Paul Gascoigne, signed by Stan Ternent to aid the push for the Premiership, almost became a Clarets legend with one solitary set piece.

Burnley went into the final game of the season in the play-off places by just one goal.

Victory in the final game of the season against Coventry may not have been enough, while defeat may still have seen the Clarets enter the four-team lottery.

A win for Burnley, coupled with either a defeat for Millwall, or a draw or a defeat for Birmingham, would have seen Ternent's men in the play-offs.

Alternatively, victory for Norwich by a smaller or equal margin than them would also have seen Burnley grab a play-off place.

With minutes to go, Norwich were leading 2-0 against Crewe, while Burnley only held a 1-0 advantage over the Sky Blues.

David Johnson was hacked down on the edge of the area, and up-stepped Gascoigne to score the goal that would have extended the season by a few weeks at least.

However, Clarets hopes were dashed when visiting keeper Magnus Hedman palmed his effort around the post.

Their cause looked lost, but with virtually the last kick of the game, Gascoigne was handed another chance after Glen Little was brought down.

But once again, a barrage of groans and screams greeted a quite brilliant save from Hedman as he miraculously clawed the ball away. That save was met almost immediately by the final whistle, meaning Burnley had missed out on the play-offs by just one goal.

It was as if the agony of missing out by a point the previous season hadn't been enough!

The devastation on the faces of fans on three sides of Turf Moor was as clear as you're likely to witness.

The script had been torn to shreds, and Ternent was the one who had to pick up the pieces once again.

But all that final day drama could have been avoided.

A 3-1 defeat in their penultimate game of the campaign at Grimsby sowed the seeds for their failure, and it was Lee Briscoe's late goal in that game that was keeping Burnley in the play-offs.

And ultimately, that would come back to haunt them in the cruellest way possible.

Burnley fans at the start of the season could not have dreamt that the season they were about to witness would turn out like it did.

Pre-season hopes were turned into reality by a sequence of victories that saw the Clarets take the division by storm.

The heartbreak of the previous season seemed to have given the players an extra boost, as they began with a confident 2-0 success at Sheffield Wednesday in front of the TV cameras.

That game saw Burnley without a single debutant in the starting line-up of an opening fixture for the first time in two decades.

But those players made it two out of two in their next outing with a 3-2 victory at home to Wimbledon.

If the league campaign had begun with a bang, it was soon met with a bump after the Clarets crashed out of the Worthington Cup at home to league newcomers Rushden and Diamonds.

Numerous first teamers had been rested for the seemingly bread and butter passage through to the second round.

But despite bringing on a number of big guns for the second half, the Clarets went out 3-2.

A return to winning ways at Millwall followed, but their perfect record was kicked into touch by Manchester City, who went away from Turf Moor with a 4-2 win under their belts.

Tony Ellis then grabbed an emotional winner in a superb 3-2 win at Bradford, before victories over Rotherham, Walsall and Birmingham made it seven wins from eight games.

OBITUARY

GEORGE BRAY

DIED 13 FEBRUARY 2002, AGED 83.

Like Brian Miller a generation later, George Bray was a one-club man who served Burnley in several capacities and remained at Turf Moor long after his retirement as a player. Also like Miller, his favoured position was left-half.

Born in Oswaldtwistle, he came from a footballing family, his brother Jack achieving fame with Manchester City and England. George joined Burnley in 1937, and established himself in the side in the final season before the outbreak of World War II. He played in Northern Ireland while serving there during the war, but took his place in the Clarets line-up on the resumption in 1946 and played a full part in the successes of the first post-war season, which ended with Burnley promoted and reaching the F.A. Cup final.

A solid defender, he missed very few games in the next four seasons as Burnley consolidated in the top flight. When younger blood eventually took over, he joined the Turf Moor coaching staff, and trained the "A" team, then the reserves, and finally, from 1970, the first team. His final job at the club was kit man, a position he held until 1992. He continued to live in Burnley after his retirement.

RIP

A top-of-the-table clash at Norwich followed, but Burnley were to come away empty-handed after a 2-1 reverse, as well as collecting injuries to both Glen Little and Ian Moore.

That was followed by a rollercoaster 3-3 home draw with Crewe, that had seen Burnley fight back from 2-0 and 3-2 deficits to equalise in the last minute, but two defeats followed against West Brom and Nottingham Forest.

If Turf Moor hadn't been tense enough against Crewe, another 3-3 home draw against Barnsley followed, before a solitary Paul Cook goal brought Crystal Palace's eight game winning run to a shuddering halt.

That was met by a 3-0 mauling at Wolves, but a 10-game unbeaten run then ensued to catapult Ternent's men to the summit of the table once more.

That run included six straight wins, highlighted by the Clarets completing the double over Crystal Palace, and a couple of memorable goals from Arthur Gnohere helping to seal a 3-2 win at derby rivals Preston.

However, a trip to Maine Road on 29 December would change the complexion of the entire season.

Victory there would have taken Burnley seven points above City, who at the beginning of the campaign had been the bookies' overwhelming favourites for the title.

But the Clarets couldn't have got off to a worse start, falling behind to Paulo Wanchope's goal just two minutes in.

One of the key points of the season came when Burnley were awarded a penalty, but Glen Little spurned the chance to draw the Clarets level when he shot horribly wide.

That was followed by three goals in the final 15 minutes of the first half, as Wanchope completed his hat-trick, with the Clarets going in 4-0 down at the interval.

Ian Moore did pull one back, but Darren Huckerby's last minute goal just emphasised the fact that Burnley had been completely and utterly demoralised.

Postponements meant that the next game was against Canvey Island in the FA Cup third round, but the Clarets weren't about to repeat their performance against Rushden and Diamonds earlier in the campaign.

A first Clarets hat-trick from Ian Moore highlighted a 4-1 success, before a goalless draw at Wimbledon in their first league outing since the demolition at Maine Road.

Robbie Blake was signed from Bradford, making his debut as a substitute in the 2-0 defeat at home to West Brom, but that was followed by a much-needed 2-1 success at Watford thanks to Paul Weller's last gasp winner.

However, sandwiched inbetween was defeat at Cheltenham Town, as Burnley were sent tumbling out of their second cup competition of the season by lower league opposition, managed by a certain Steve Cotterill!

Three draws followed, against Barnsley, Rotherham and Nottingham Forest, but a 2-1 victory against Crewe meant Burnley were still very much in the promotion reckoning.

However, two successive home defeats against two fellow promotion rivals in Birmingham and Norwich would ultimately blow a major hole in their fight for promotion.

The latter of those two games saw the eagerly-awaited full debut of Blake, but that 1-1 draw was the only start he would make all season.

The nosedive continued with a 1-0 reverse at second-bottom Walsall, but bottom side Stockport County were next up and a 2-0 victory was recorded thanks to Gareth Taylor and Ian Cox.

Prior to the home game with Preston, David Johnson joined from Nottingham Forest on a month's loan.

But the real headline was the signing of Gascoigne, who watched from the sidelines as Johnson ultimately netted the winner on his debut in a 2-1 derby win.

Gascoigne's debut came in a 1-1 midweek home draw against Bradford, before a trip home from Sheffield United after a 3-0 defeat saw the alarm bells begin to ring as regards hopes of a play-off slot.

Those feelings were compounded after a 3-2 home defeat to Wolves, a game that witnessed more than its fair share of controversy.

Gareth Taylor seemed to have a perfectly good goal disallowed, Alan Moore was harshly sent off, and Wolves somehow led 3-0 at half-time.

Ian Moore and Johnson did pull it back to 3-2, but in the end, it was another defeat that saw Burnley continue their appalling run of form.

A 1-1 draw at Portsmouth and a 2-0 home win against Gillingham followed, but the 3-1 defeat at Grimsby left Burnley fans wondering if they had thrown away their chance.

And so it proved, as Hedman's heroics in the final minutes against Coventry consigned Burnley to the second tier of English football for another season.

In the season's closing moments, only a fantastic save by the Coventry keeper, from **that** Paul Gascoigne free kick, kept the Clarets out of the play offs

2001-02 - First Division

		P	W	D	L	F	A	Pts
1	Manchester C	46	31	6	9	108	52	99
2	West Bromwich A	46	27	8	11	61	29	89
3	Wolverhampton W	46	25	11	10	76	43	86
4	Millwall	46	22	11	13	69	48	77
5	Birmingham C	46	21	13	12	70	49	76
6	Norwich C	46	22	9	15	60	51	75
7	BURNLEY	46	21	12	13	70	62	75
8	Preston NE	46	20	12	14	71	59	72
9	Wimbledon	46	18	13	15	63	57	67
10	Crystal P	46	20	6	20	70	62	66
11	Coventry C	46	20	6	20	59	53	66
12	Gillingham	46	18	10	18	64	67	64
13	Sheffield U	46	15	15	16	53	54	60
14	Watford	46	16	11	19	62	56	59
15	Bradford C	46	15	10	21	69	76	55
16	Nottingham F	46	12	18	16	50	51	54
17	Portsmouth	46	13	14	19	60	72	53
18	Walsall	46	13	12	21	51	71	51
19	Grimsby T	46	12	14	20	50	72	50
20	Sheffield W	46	12	14	20	49	71	50
21	Rotherham U	46	10	19	17	52	66	49
22	Crewe A	46	12	13	21	47	76	49
23	Barnsley	46	11	15	20	59	86	48
24	Stockport C	46	6	8	32	42	102	26

2001-02

Manager : Stan Ternent

Division One (7th)

Note	No.	Date		h/a	Opponents	Result		h/t	Goalscorers/times	Opp. goal times
	1	Aug	12	a	Sheffield W	W	2-0	0-0	Taylor 57, Cook 76p	
	2		18	h	WIMBLEDON	W	3-2	3-1	A.Moore 12, Cook 29p, Armstrong 40	11, 65
	3		25	a	Millwall	W	2-0	0-0	A.Moore 63, I.Moore 68	
	4		27	h	MANCHESTER C	L	2-4	1-1	Davis 25, Briscoe 50	17, 49, 61, 85
	5	Sep	2	a	Bradford C	W	3-2	0-0	Little (2) 46, 78, Ellis 85	61, 81
	6		8	h	ROTHERHAM U	W	3-0	0-0	I.Moore 47, Weller 49, Payton 89p	
	7		15	h	WALSALL	W	5-2	2-0	Taylor 31, I.Moore 45, Briscoe (2) 69, 72, Cook 79	51, 64og
	8		18	a	Birmingham C	W	3-2	2-2	Little (2) 9, 71, I.Moore 34	19, 41
	9		22	a	Norwich C	L	1-2	0-1	Armstrong 57	4, 55
	10		25	h	CREWE A	D	3-3	0-2	Taylor 61, Payton (2) 82p, 90	17, 28, 89
Mullin's last game	11		29	a	West Bromwich A	L	0-1	0-0		67
	12	Oct	13	a	Nottingham F	L	0-1	0-0		79
	13		20	h	BARNSLEY	D	3-3	2-1	Morgan 23og, Briscoe 36, Payton 86p	45p, 52, 88
	14		23	h	CRYSTAL P	W	1-0	1-0	Cook 17	
	15		28	a	Wolverhampton W	L	0-3	0-3		10og, 20, 39og
	16		30	a	Gillingham	D	2-2	1-2	Taylor 31, Little 52p	8, 15
	17	Nov	4	h	SHEFFIELD U	W	2-0	2-0	Taylor 30, Cook 33	
	18		10	h	PORTSMOUTH	D	1-1	0-0	Taylor 69	72
	19		13	h	WATFORD	W	1-0	1-0	Little 3	
	20		17	a	Coventry C	W	2-0	2-0	Taylor 11, Little 33	
	21		23	h	GRIMSBY T	W	1-0	1-0	Taylor 3	
	22	Dec	1	a	Crystal P	W	2-1	1-1	I.Moore (2) 23, 63	38
	23		9	a	Preston N E	W	3-2	2-2	Gnohere (2) 17, 61, Little 26	29, 41p
	24		15	h	STOCKPORT C	W	3-2	1-1	Little 9p, Taylor 66, I.Moore 70	11, 90p
	25		22	h	MILLWALL	D	0-0	0-0		
	26		29	a	Manchester C	L	1-5	0-4	I.Moore 60	2, 27, 37, 45, 90
	27	Jan	12	a	Wimbledon	D	0-0	0-0		
	28		19	h	SHEFFIELD W	L	1-2	0-1	Taylor 77p	33, 90
	29	Feb	3	h	WEST BROMWICH A	L	0-2	0-2		36, 40
	30		6	a	Watford	W	2-1	0-1	Cox 71, Weller 90	23
	31		9	a	Barnsley	D	1-1	1-1	Taylor 37	6
	32		12	a	Rotherham U	D	1-1	1-1	Taylor 9p	12p
	33		16	h	NOTTINGHAM F	D	1-1	0-0	Gnohere 88	67p
	34		23	a	Crewe A	W	2-1	1-0	Taylor 19, A.Moore 59	64
	35		26	h	BIRMINGHAM C	L	0-1	0-1		25
	36	Mar	2	h	NORWICH C	D	1-1	1-0	Taylor 6	55
	37		5	a	Walsall	L	0-1	0-0		52
	38		9	a	Stockport C	W	2-0	0-0	Taylor 51, Cox 82	
	39		17	h	PRESTON N E	W	2-1	2-0	I.Moore 5, Johnson 25	84
	40		20	h	BRADFORD C	D	1-1	1-0	Johnson 20	78
	41		23	a	Sheffield U	L	0-3	0-1		19, 47, 88
	42		30	h	WOLVERHAMPTON W	L	2-3	0-3	I.Moore 47, Johnson 85	9, 26, 45
	43	Apr	1	a	Portsmouth	D	1-1	1-0	Johnson 20	75
	44		6	h	GILLINGHAM	W	2-0	0-0	I.Moore 55, Johnson 62	
	45		13	a	Grimsby T	L	1-3	0-3	Briscoe 90	5, 12, 43
last games for Ball, Thomas and Gascoigne	46		21	h	COVENTRY C	W	1-0	0-0	Taylor 67	

FA Cup

Rd	Date		h/a	Opponents	Result		h/t	Goalscorers/times	Opp. goal times
3	Jan	5	h	CANVEY ISLAND	W	4-1	2-0	Little 24, I.Moore (3) 45, 78, 84	67
4		26	a	Cheltenham T	L	1-2	1-2	A.Moore 29	22, 26

Final, Arsenal 2-0 Chelsea, at The Millenium Stadium, Cardiff.

League Cup

Rd	Date		h/a	Opponents	Result		h/t	Goalscorers/times	Opp. goal times
1	Aug	21	h	RUSHDEN & D	L	2-3	0-1	A.Moore 55, McGregor 84	5, 50, 76

Final, Blackburn R 2-1 Tottenham H, at The Millenium Stadium, Cardiff.

Details of other first team games elsewhere.

Att.	Pos	Michopoulos	West	Davis	Cox	Briscoe	Little	P Cook	Weller	Armstrong	I Moore	Taylor	A Moore	Ellis	Payton	Mullin	Ball	Gnohere	Thomas	A Grant	Papadopoulos	Maylett	Johnrose	Branch	Beresford	Blake	McGregor	Johnson	Gascoigne	Cennamo							
21,766		G	D	D	D	D	M	M	M*	M	F^	F**	S*	S**	S^																						1
14,473	3	G	D	D	D	D	M	M		M	F**	F	M*	S**		S*																					2
11,903	2	G	D	D	D	D	M	M		M*	F^	F	S*	S^			M	S**																			3
19,602	4	G	D*	D	D	D^	M	M**	S**	M	F	F			S^		M	S*																			4
17,547	1	G	D	D		D	M	M	F	D	F*		M	S*			M																				5
14,820	1	G	D	D			M	M	F**	D	F*	S*	M		S**		M	D																			6
14,019	1	G	D	D		S*	M	M			F*	F^	M**	S^		S**	M	D	D																		7
18,426		G	D	D		D	M	M*		D	F**	F	M^	S^			M	S**	S*																		8
19,849	1	G	D	D		D	M^	M	S*	D	F**	F	M*	S^	S**		M																				9
13,964		G	D**	D		D		M*	M	M^	F	F			S**	S*	M	D	S^																		10
21,442	2	G	D	D	M**	D		M	M		F*	F		S^	S**	S*	M^	D																			11
24,016	2	G	D	D	M	D		M^	M		F**	F			S^		M	D*		S*	S**																12
14,690	5	G	D**	D	D	D		M*	M	S^	F^	F			S**		M			M		S*															13
14,713		G		D	D	D	S**	M*	M	S*	F^	F**			S^		M	D		M																	14
24,893	4	G	S**	D	D*	D	S*	M**	M	S^	F	F					M	D		M^																	15
8,067		G	D	D	D	D	M	M**	M		F*	F			S*		S**			M^			S^														16
13,166	9	G	D		D	D	M^	M*	M		F**	F						D		M	S**	S^	S*														17
14,123	5	G	D		D	D	M	M**	M		F*	F			S*			D		M			S**														18
13,162		G	D		D	D	M	M**	M*		F	F					S*	D		M			S**														19
16,849	1	G	D		D	D*	M	M**	M		F	F	S**				S*	D		M																	20
18,535		G	D		D		M	M**	M*		F	F^	S**		S^		S*	D		M				D													21
18,457	1	G	D		D	D	M**		M*		F		M^	S**			S*	D		M			S^	F													22
20,370	1	G	D		D	D	M**		S**		F	S*	M^				M	D		M			S^	F*													23
15,526	1	G	D		D	D	M		S*	S**	F^	F	M*				M	D			S^			M**													24
16,131	1	G	D		D	D	M		S*		F	F	M*				M	D		M																	25
34,250	1	G	D*		D	D	M				F**	F	M	S**			M	D		M	S*																26
7,675	3	G	D		D	D		M*			F		M	S**			M	D		M	S*			F							2nd sub Ellis for Papadopoulos						27
16,081	5	G	D		D	D					F**	F	M				M	D		M	S**	S*		M*													28
15,846	7		D		D	D	S*	M*	S**		F^	F	M**				M	D		M					G	S^											29
12,160			D		S**	D	M		M		F	F**					M	D		M		S^		D*	G	S*					3rd sub Maylett for Blake						30
14,411	5		D		D	D	M^		M		F**	F	S*				M	D		M*		S^			G	S**											31
9,021			D		D	D	M**		M		F*	F^	M				M	D				S**		S^	G	S*											32
15,085	5		D		D^	D	M		M	S**	S^	F	F				M	D		M*					G	S*					2nd sub Armstrong for Blake						33
6,458	5		D		D	D	M**	M	F	D*	S**	F	M				M							S*	G												34
13,504			D	S**	D**	D	M	M*	F		S*	F	M^				M							D	G	S^											35
14,679	5		D	D		D	M*		M	S**	S*	F	M^				M	D				S^			G	F**											36
5,611			D^	D	S^	D		S*	M**	M*	F	F	M				M	D				S**			G												37
6,410	6			D^	D	D		S**	M		F	F					M		M	M**		S*			G	S^	D*										38
18,388	4		D		D	D	S*	S**	M*		F^		M				M		D	M					G	S^		F**									39
19,479			D		D	D	M*				F				S^		M		D	M		S**			G	S*		F**	M^								40
19,003	4		D		D*	D			S**		M**	F	S*		S^		M		D	M					G			F	M^								41
21,823	4	G	D			D	S**		M^		S*	F*	M				M	D	D	S^								F	M**								42
18,020	4	G	D			D	S**		M^	S*	F**		M				M	D	D	M*								F	S^								43
16,236	4	G	D	D		D	M		S**		F	S*					M	D	M	M**								F*									44
9,275	6	G	D*	D		D	M**		S*		F	S^					M^	D	M	M								F	S**								45
18,751	7	G	D**	D		D	M		M		F^	S^			S**		M	D	M*									F	S^								46
Appearances		33	43	22	32	43	31	25	29	11	41	35	23				37	31	10	26				8	13	1	1	8	3								
Apps as sub			1	1	2	1	6	3	9	7	5	5	6	11	15	4	5	3	2	2	6	10	6	2		9			3								
Goals (70)				1	2	5	9	5	2	2	11	16	3	1	4			3										5								1	og

Att.	Pos	Michopoulos	West	Davis	Cox	Briscoe	Little	P Cook	Weller	Armstrong	I Moore	Taylor	A Moore	Ellis	Payton	Mullin	Ball	Gnohere	Thomas	A Grant	Papadopoulos	Maylett	Johnrose	Branch	Beresford	Blake	McGregor	Johnson	Gascoigne	Cennamo							
11,496		G	D		D	D	M**	S**	S*		F	F*	M^				M	D		M	S^																3
7,300		G*	D		D	D	M**				F^	F	M				M	D		M		S^		S**						S*							4
Appearances		2	2		2	2	2				2	2	2				2	2		2																	
Apps as sub								1	1												1	1		1						1							
Goals (5)							1				3		1																								

Att.	Pos	Michopoulos	West	Davis	Cox	Briscoe	Little	P Cook	Weller	Armstrong	I Moore	Taylor	A Moore	Ellis	Payton	Mullin	Ball	Gnohere	Thomas	A Grant	Papadopoulos	Maylett	Johnrose	Branch	Beresford	Blake	McGregor	Johnson	Gascoigne	Cennamo							
4,398		G		D	D		S*	S**			S^	F	M			M**	M	D			F^	M*					D										1
Appearances		1		1	1							1	1			1	1	1			1	1					1										
Apps as sub							1	1			1																										
Goals (2)													1														1										

2002-03

OBITUARY
JOHN (JACKIE) CHEW
DIED 19 OCTOBER 2002, AGED 82.

The regular occupant of Burnley's number seven shirt in the years following World War II, Jackie Chew formed a notable right-wing partnership with Billy Morris in the side that took the club back to the First Division and then established them in the top flight.

Blackburn-born, he was on Rovers' books as an amateur before the war, but it was Burnley who first signed him as a professional, shortly before League football resumed in 1946. A reliable crosser of the ball, he also scored a fair number of goals for a winger and was in fact Burnley's top scorer in 1948-49.

He was still a regular in the side as late as 1953, but at the end of the following season moved on to Bradford City, where he played just one season before leaving League football. He was also a fine cricketer at Lancashire League level, and turned out for Rishton long after his football career had ended. His death left his wing partner Billy Morris as the sole survivor from that famous Burnley side of 1947.

RIP

Calling all blind men on galloping horses!

However many of you there are, 2002-03 was a season for you.

Or at least that's who manager Stan Ternent focused on.

One particular August evening in Berkshire yielded one of the most abject performances seen by a Burnley team for some time.

Fans who had made the long trip down to Reading shook their heads in disbelief, as the Clarets had thrown in a performance nowhere near good enough for English football's second tier.

It had produced a second successive 3-0 defeat on the road, from their opening two away fixtures.

And it was a far cry from anyone who had been at Turf Moor almost exactly four months earlier, to see their side come agonisingly close to a play-off spot.

So bad was the performance, that Ternent seriously considered his future.

In his after-match press conference, he uttered: "I am going to have to have a chat with the chairman and see where we go from here.

"Tonight I was embarrassed to be their gaffer, because that performance is a reflection on me.

"Everyone knows the players are not performing; a blind man on a galloping horse can see that.

"A lot of people have spent a lot of money to come down here and watch that and I am embarrassed."

All this drama followed a 3-0 defeat at Wolves, just a week after the Clarets had been well and truly hammered on the opening day.

In their own back yard, Burnley had fallen 3-1 at the hands of newly-promoted Brighton and Hove Albion.

And the only shining light from that endless tunnel was Lee Briscoe's injury time consolation, a goal which the vast majority of the home crowd had missed.

That was to be their only goal in their opening five matches, with a 1-0 reverse at home to Sheffield United acting as the meat in the sandwich between the two abject away performances.

For the first time since winning promotion two seasons earlier, the Clarets found themselves bottom of the table.

Things could only get better, surely. And get better they did.

After picking up their first point of the campaign in a goalless home draw with Crystal Palace, the Clarets proceeded to win six of their next eight games.

In total, an unbeaten run stretching all of 10 games would come from that first point, with back-to-back 2-1 successes against Derby and Stoke the catalyst.

A totally unique scene for many at Turf Moor came with the visit of Millwall.

The Lions had not been allowed to bring any fans with them to East Lancashire, and so each of their two goals on the night was met with a deadly hush.

Ian Moore was the man to rescue a point with a late equaliser at 2-2 and it was the same scoreline at Bradford four days later.

However, this story told a different tale, as against nine men, Ternent's troops somehow contrived to lose a 2-1 lead to a late stoppage time leveller.

Five victories then followed, four in the league and one in the cup against Huddersfield, before another 2-2 draw, this time at Ipswich, and another late equaliser.

This time, however, it came in Burnley's favour, as Dimi Papadopoulos became the hero of the hour.

Richard Chaplow demonstrating that the Turf Moor production line is still flourishing

But after a 3-0 loss at home to eventual champions Portsmouth, the season's other talking point could begin.

29 October 2002, and a chilly Tuesday night in Grimsby.

There have been a few "I was there" moments for Burnley fans over the years, but none quite like this.

Gareth Taylor scored two goals, as did Robbie Blake, and Ian Moore was the other name on the scoresheet.

And yes, every one of those goals was at the right end.

But despite scoring five away from home, Burnley still managed to board the bus back home empty-handed.

And incredibly, the Clarets never once found themselves in the lead in a game they eventually lost, 6-5.
If there had been disbelief at Reading two months earlier, this was shock on a whole new level.
But Clarets fans had seen nothing yet.
Defeat to Preston four days later was followed by a terrific victory over Tottenham in the League Cup.
And that was preceded by home victories over Coventry, Norwich and Nottingham Forest, sandwiching a goalless draw at Rotherham and defeat at Watford.
There was also the small matter of Manchester United coming to town, as the prize for knocking Tottenham out of the League Cup.
Ole Gunnar Solksjaer and Diego Forlan both netted to avoid an upset, but 10 days later, Burnley were making headlines again.
Former Clarets pair Alan Lee and John Mullin both lined up against their former club for Rotherham, and both netted twice as the Millers surged into a 4-0 lead.
Steve Davis did net twice himself to pull it back to 4-2, and had Mike Pollitt not made a quite superb save, the script might have been different.
As it was, Darren Byfield came off the bench to grab two himself, as the Clarets were humbled 6-2 in front of their own fans.
A 4-2 reverse at Gillingham followed immediately after, before Gareth Taylor netted undoubtedly one of Burnley's goals of the season in a 2-1 success over Wolves.
And three successive draws were brought to an end by the next chapter of Burnley's forgotten art of defending.
Remember that performance at Reading earlier in the season? Well the Royals were at it again, this time at Turf Moor, as five more goals were added to the growing 'goals against' tally.
Two games earlier, Drissa Diallo had arrived from Belgian Club Mechelen to make a solid debut in a 1-1 draw with Ipswich.
But against Reading, he must have wished he was back in Belgium.
Three successive wins did arrive, against Coventry, Derby and Stoke, but prior to the Derby clash, there was the small matter of Fulham in the FA Cup.
A surprise 1-1 draw in the first leg meant the Cottagers were brought back to Turf Moor.
And goals from Gareth Taylor, Ian Moore and Drissa Diallo helped humble the Premiership side 3-0.
And after a point at Millwall in the league, the Clarets were live to the nation once more in their biggest game in recent memory.
The quarter-finals of the FA Cup, and, on paper, the easiest tie they could have hoped for, against Watford at Vicarage Road.
But Burnley just never turned up, and it was a case of 'what if' as they succumbed 2-0.
Back to the league, and with the Clarets in 11th place, despite everything that had happened, amazingly they were still within shouting distance of the top six.
But a run of seven games without a win put paid to that, ending with another quite shambolic Turf Moor afternoon against their old friends from the cup, Watford.
The game yielded a hat-trick from a Burnley player.
Gareth Taylor was the man in question, and he didn't even get the matchball.
That was to end up on the mantelpiece of Michael Chopra, who went one better, bagging four as the Hornets travelled home with an incredible 7-4 victory.
The Clarets did attempt to set the record straight with a 2-0 home win over Preston, followed by a similar success against Gillingham.

Paul Weller (left)
almost eleven years at Turf Moor

But in their last home game of the season against Sheffield Wednesday, the Burnley supporters were given a final reminder of a quite staggering campaign.
Already-relegated Wednesday made the footballing world stand up, as Burnley were hit for seven on their own patch for a second time in three weeks.
A final score of 7-2 spoke for itself, and made the magic of the cup run fade away into the depths of people's minds.
The season couldn't get any worse – that is apart from ending with a 2-1 defeat at Wimbledon.

2002-03 - First Division

		P	W	D	L	F	A	Pts
1	Portsmouth	46	29	11	6	97	45	98
2	Leicester C	46	26	14	6	73	40	92
3	Sheffield U	46	23	11	12	72	52	80
4	Reading	46	25	4	17	61	46	79
5	Wolverhampton W	46	20	16	10	81	44	76
6	Nottingham F	46	20	14	12	82	50	74
7	Ipswich T	46	19	13	14	80	64	70
8	Norwich C	46	19	12	15	60	49	69
9	Millwall	46	19	9	18	59	69	66
10	Wimbledon	46	18	11	17	76	73	65
11	Gillingham	46	16	14	16	56	65	62
12	Preston NE	46	16	13	17	68	70	61
13	Watford	46	17	9	20	54	70	60
14	Crystal P	46	14	17	15	59	52	59
15	Rotherham U	46	15	14	17	62	62	59
16	BURNLEY	46	15	10	21	65	89	55
17	Walsall	46	15	9	22	57	69	54
18	Derby C	46	15	7	24	55	74	52
19	Bradford C	46	14	10	22	51	73	52
20	Coventry C	46	12	14	20	46	62	50
21	Stoke C	46	12	14	20	45	69	50
22	Sheffield W	46	10	16	20	56	73	46
23	Brighton & HA	46	11	12	23	49	67	45
24	Grimsby T	46	9	12	25	48	85	39

2002-03

Manager : Stan Ternent

Division One (16th)

Note	No.	Month	Date	Venue	Opponents	Result		h/t	Goalscorers/times	Opp. goal times
	1	Aug	10	h	BRIGHTON & H A	L	1-3	0-1	Briscoe 90	29, 65, 68
	2		17	a	Wolverhampton W	L	0-3	0-1		2, 49, 88
	3		24	h	SHEFFIELD U	L	0-1	0-1		35
	4		27	a	Reading	L	0-3	0-0		55, 87, 90
	5		31	h	CRYSTAL P	D	0-0	0-0		
	6	Sep	7	a	Derby C	W	2-1	0-1	Blake 51p, Barton 55og	8
	7		14	h	STOKE C	W	2-1	0-0	Gnohere 76, Papadopoulos 81	74
	8		17	h	MILLWALL	D	2-2	1-1	West 18p, I.Moore 85	31, 64
	9		21	a	Bradford C	D	2-2	0-1	Blake 57, Taylor 76	17, 90
	10		28	h	WIMBLEDON	W	1-0	0-0	Little 51	
	11	Oct	5	a	Sheffield W	W	3-1	1-0	Taylor 8, Little 57, I.Moore 60	67
	12		12	h	WALSALL	W	2-1	1-0	Blake 42, Davis 69	79
	13		19	a	Leicester C	W	1-0	0-0	I.Moore 55	
	14		22	a	Ipswich T	D	2-2	1-2	Gnohere 6, Papadopoulos 90	2, 16
	15		26	h	PORTSMOUTH	L	0-3	0-1		21, 58, 86
	16		29	a	Grimsby T	L	5-6	3-4	Taylor (2) 22, 49, I.Moore 31, Blake (2) 45, 83p	3,28,31,36,56p,72
	17	Nov	2	a	Preston N E	L	1-3	0-1	Taylor 51	3, 62, 66
	18		9	h	COVENTRY C	W	3-1	2-0	Blake 15p, Grant 35, Davenport 86og	66p
	19		16	a	Rotherham U	D	0-0	0-0		
	20		23	h	NORWICH C	W	2-0	0-0	McGregor 59, Little 85	
	21		30	a	Watford	L	1-2	0-1	Taylor 76	40, 72p
	22	Dec	7	h	NOTTINGHAM F	W	1-0	1-0	Briscoe 28	
	23		14	h	ROTHERHAM U	L	2-6	0-3	Davis (2) 67, 78	12,27,30,59,84,89
	24		21	a	Gillingham	L	2-4	1-3	Taylor 28, Blake 76p	17, 41, 45, 64
	25		26	h	WOLVERHAMPTON W	W	2-1	2-0	Taylor 24, West 32	85
	26		28	a	Brighton & H A	D	2-2	1-0	Little 44, I.Moore 71	88, 89
	27	Jan	11	h	IPSWICH T	D	1-1	0-1	Blake 66p	22
	28		18	a	Crystal P	D	1-1	1-0	Taylor 44	62p
	29	Feb	1	h	READING	L	2-5	0-2	I.Moore 55, West 90	37, 45, 52, 79, 90
	30		8	a	Coventry C	W	1-0	1-0	Cox 35	
	31		22	h	DERBY C	W	2-0	2-0	I.Moore 8, Taylor 23	
	32	Mar	1	a	Stoke C	W	1-0	0-0	West 56	
	33		4	a	Millwall	D	1-1	1-0	I.Moore 18	84
	34		12	a	Sheffield U	L	2-4	0-2	Taylor 64, Blake 90	17, 36, 66, 72
Cox's last game	35		15	a	Walsall	L	2-3	0-2	Blake 74p, Little 90	24, 33, 66
	36		18	h	LEICESTER C	L	1-2	0-0	Sinclair 90og	79, 83
	37		22	h	GRIMSBY T	D	1-1	0-1	A.Moore 52	43
Cook's last game	38		25	h	BRADFORD C	L	0-2	0-1		18, 89
	39	Apr	5	h	WATFORD	L	4-7	4-5	Taylor (3) 15, 39, 45, Davis 35	13,16,26,29,40,61,90
	40		8	h	PRESTON N E	W	2-0	1-0	Papadopoulos 42, Blake 61	
Briscoe's last game	41		12	a	Norwich C	L	0-2	0-1		3, 67
	42		15	a	Portsmouth	L	0-1	0-0		73
	43		19	h	GILLINGHAM	W	2-0	1-0	Taylor 28, Diallo 60	
	44		21	a	Nottingham F	L	0-2	0-0		75, 90
Michopoulos' last game	45		26	h	SHEFFIELD W	L	2-7	1-3	Blake (2) 42, 53	3,5,32,47,66,73og,80
last games for Davis, Taylor, Beresford & Armstrong	46	May	4	a	Wimbledon	L	1-2	1-0	Taylor 27	55, 81

FA Cup

Note	Rd	Month	Date	Venue	Opponents	Result		h/t	Goalscorers/times	Opp. goal times
	3	Jan	4	a	Grimsby T	D	2-2	2-0	A.Moore 14, Weller 18	57p, 87
Payton's last game	rep		14	h	GRIMSBY T	W	4-0	1-0	I.Moore (2) 25, 90, Little 79, Blake 86p	
	4		25	a	Brentford	W	3-0	0-0	Blake 52, Cook 86, Little 89	
	5	Feb	15	a	Fulham	D	1-1	1-1	A.Moore 4	45
	rep		26	h	FULHAM	W	3-0	2-0	Taylor 27, I.Moore 35, Diallo 52	
	6	Mar	9	a	Watford	L	0-2	0-0		64, 80

Final, Arsenal 1-0 Southampton, at The Millenium Stadium, Cardiff.

League Cup

Note	Rd	Month	Date	Venue	Opponents	Result		h/t	Goalscorers/times	Opp. goal times
	1	Sep	10	h	BLACKPOOL	W	3-0	1-0	West 13, Papadopoulos (2) 63, 75	
after extra time	2	Oct	1	a	Huddersfield T	W	1-0	0-0	Papadopoulos 104	
	3	Nov	6	h	TOTTENHAM H	W	2-1	0-1	Blake 57, Davis 61	17
	4	Dec	3	h	MANCHESTER U	L	0-2	0-1		35, 65

Final, Liverpool 2-0 Manchester U, at The Millenium Stadium, Cardiff.

Details of other first team games elsewhere.

Att.	Pos	Michopoulos	West	Davis	Gnohere	Branch	Little	A Grant	Blake	Briscoe	I Moore	Taylor	Cox	Weller	Papadopoulos	McGregor	P Cook	A Moore	Johnrose	Payton	Beresford	Armstrong	Maylett	Diallo	O'Neill	Chaplow	Waine	Rasmussen		
14,738		G	D	D	D	D*	M	M	M**	M	F^	F	S*	S**	S^															1
25,031	24	G	D	D	D		M^			F	S*	F	S**	M**	S^	D	M	M*												2
12,868	24	G	D			S*	M			D*	F	F	D	M**		D	M	M^	S**	S^										3
12,009		G	D				M	F	S^	D	S*	F	D	S**		D	M*	M^	M**											4
12,407	24	G	D				M*	M		D	S**	F	D	M	F**	D		S*	M											5
22,343	23		D		D		S*	M	F	D	F		D	M		M			M*		G									6
14,244	20		D		D		M	M	F**	D	F^	S**	D		S^	M*		S*	M		G									7
11,878			D		D		M**	M	S**	D	S^	F	D		F		S*	M^	M*		G									8
14,561	20		D	S^	D^		M	M	S**	D		F	D		F**	M*	M	S*			G									9
12,259	18		D*	D	D		M	M	F^	D	S**	F	M		S^	S*		M**			G									10
17,004	11		D	D	D	D	M		M^		F*	F	M		S*	S^	M**				G	S**								11
12,907	9		D	D	D	D	M	S*	F^	S^	F		M	M**			M*				G		S**							12
26,254	8		D	D	D	D	M*	S^	M^	M	F**	F	M	S*	S**						G									13
22,736			D	D	D	D	M*		M	M	F**	F	M	S*	S**						G									14
15,788	10		D	D	D	D**	M		M	M	F*	F	M^	S*	S^						G		S**							15
5,620			D	D	D*	D	S**		M	M	F**	F		M	S^	M^		S*			G									16
16,046	14		D	D	D		M	S*	M	D**	F^	F	M*	M	S^			S**			G									17
13,470	11		D	D	D	D	M**	M	F*	M	S^	F^		M	S*						G		S**							18
7,575	11		D		D	D			M^	M	F	F*		M	S**	D	M	S^			G		S*						2nd sub Papadopoulos for Maylett	19
16,282	9		D		D	D**	M	S*	F	M	F			M	S**	D	M*				G									20
13,977	9		D	S^	D	D	M	M	F*		F**	S*		M	S**	D		M^			G									21
13,869	9		D	D	D	D	M^		F*	M	S^	F**		M	S*		M	S**			G									22
14,121	13		D	D		D	M	S^	F	M^		F	D**	M	S*		M*	S**			G									23
7,905	15		D		D^	D	M	M**	M		F*	F	S^	M	S**	D		S*			G									24
18,641	13		D		D		M*	M	F**		S*	F	D	M	S**	D		M			G									25
6,502	12		D		D		M	M	F**		S*	F	D	M	S**	D		M*			G									26
15,501	14	G			D	D	M	M	F		F				S*	D	M	M*						D						27
16,344	16		D		D	D		M^	M*	M	F	F			S*	S^	M**	S**			G			D						28
14,420	16		D		D		S*	M	M**	M^	F	F			S**	D	M*	S^			G			D						29
13,659	15	G	D			D		M	M*		F	F	D		S*		M	M**				S**		D						30
15,063	11		D			D		M		M	F	F	D	S**		S*	M*	M**			G			D						31
12,874	11		D			D		M		M	F	F	D	S*		S**	M**	M*			G			D						32
6,045			D			D	S*	M	S^	M	F*	F	D	S**			M**	M^			G			D						33
17,359			D*	D		D	M^	S**	S*	M**	F	F	M	M			S^				G			D						34
6,327	12			S*		D	S^	M^	S**		F**	F	D*	M		D	M	M			G			D						35
14,554			D	M	D^		M	S*	F	D*	F			M	S^		M**	S**			G			D						36
13,445	15		D	M	D		M	S^	F*	D	F			M	S**		M^	S*			G			D					2nd sub Papadopoulos for A.Moore	37
11,095			D	M	S**	D	M	S*	S^	D^	F	F		M			M*				G			D**						38
10,208	17		D	M	S*	D**		M*	M	D	F	F		M	S**	D^					G				S^					39
12,245		G	D	M		D		S*	M	D	F	F		M	M*	D														40
20,026	16	G	D	M		D			M	D*	F	F		M	M^	D						S*			S^	S**			2nd sub Chaplow for Armstrong	41
19,221		G	D	M	D^	D			M		F	F		M	M*	D							S*		S**	S^			2nd sub O'Neill for Maylett	42
14,031	15	G		M	D	D			M**		F	F		M*		D								D	M^	S*	S**	S^		43
25,403	16	G		M	D	D			M		F	F			M**	D						S*		D*	S**	M		S^	3rd sub Rasmussen for Armstrong	
17,435	16	G**		D	D	D		M	M		F	F				D*					S**	S^	M^		S*	M				45
1,972	16		D	M**		D		M	M		F*	F			S**	D					G	D			M		S*			46
Appearances		13	41	25	31	31	28	24	34	32	35	38	23	26	7	25	21	14	5		33	1	1	14	2	2				
Apps as sub				3	2	1	5	10	7	1	9	2	3	8	27	5	2	13	1	1	1	5	5		5	3	2	2		
Goals (65)			4	4	2		5	1	13	2	8	16	1		3	1		1						1					3	ogs

Att.	Pos	Michopoulos	West	Davis	Gnohere	Branch	Little	A Grant	Blake	Briscoe	I Moore	Taylor	Cox	Weller	Papadopoulos	McGregor	P Cook	A Moore	Johnrose	Payton	Beresford	Armstrong	Maylett	Diallo	O'Neill	Chaplow	Waine	Rasmussen	
5,350					D	D		M	F		M		D	M*	F**	D	S*	M			G	S**							3
5,436		G	D*		D	D	M	M	F**		F		S*		S^	D	M	M^		S**									rep
9,563			D		D	D	S**	M	F**	M	M*	F					M	S*			G			D					4
13,062			D			D		M		M	M	F	D	S*		S**	M**	F*			G			D					5
11,635			D			D	S**	M^		M	M	F	D	S*		S^	M*	F**			G			D					rep
20,336			D	S**		D	S*	M^	S^	M	M	F	D				M**	F*			G			D					6
Appearances		1	5		3	6	1	6	3	4	6	4	4	1	1	2	5	5			5			4					
Apps as sub				1			3		1				1	2	1	2	1	1		1		1							
Goals (13)							2		2		3	1		1			1	2						1					

Att.	Pos	Michopoulos	West	Davis	Gnohere	Branch	Little	A Grant	Blake	Briscoe	I Moore	Taylor	Cox	Weller	Papadopoulos	McGregor	P Cook	A Moore	Johnrose	Payton	Beresford	Armstrong	Maylett	Diallo	O'Neill	Chaplow	Waine	Rasmussen	
7,448			D		D		M*	M	F**	M	F^	S**	D	M	S^	D		S*			G								1
5,887				M	D	S**		M^	F*	D	F	M	D		S*	D	S^	M**			G								2
13,512			D	M	D	D	S*	M	F**	M^		F		M	S**	D*	S^				G								3
22,034			D	D	D^	D	M	S*	F	M**		F		M	S**		M*	S^			G								4
Appearances			3	3	4	2	2	3	4	4	2	3	2	3		3	1	1			4								
Apps as sub						1	1	1				1			4		2	2											
Goals (6)			1	1					1						3														

2003-04

OBITUARY
WILLIAM (BILLY) MORRIS
DIED 31 DEC 2002, AGED 84

Just two months after the death of Jackie Chew, Billy Morris passed away, the last link with one of the all-time great Burnley sides, the promotion winners of 1947. He first made his mark at Turf Moor in the season just before the war, but it was afterwards that his career blossomed, despite being already 28 when League football resumed after the hostilities. Small in stature (only 5'4"tall), Morris was a fast and tricky inside-forward with a good eye for goal, and his performances for Burnley brought him international recognition for Wales. He remained a more or less automatic choice at Turf Moor until well into his thirties, and enjoyed something of an Indian summer in the 1951-52 season when he finished top scorer with 18 League goals. That last full season also saw him regain his place in the Welsh side.

He remained at Turf Moor until 1960 as coach and "A" team trainer, and later had two spells as manager of Wrexham. He remained in Wales following his retirement.

RIP

Stan Ternent's legacy was hauling the club up by its bootstraps and putting it back on an upward curve.

In six years, he was largely responsible for ending the barren years in the lower leagues and breathing new life into the Clarets.

And looking back, life under Ternent could never be described as dull!

However, it was still a bombshell when, with just a week remaining of the 2003-04 season, chairman Barry Kilby announced he was seeking a new direction.

The tough decision had been made and Ternent's contract was unceremoniously cancelled following a turbulent campaign.

And for many, the 'highlight' of Stan's final year in charge at Turf Moor will forever be the emotionally charged scenes on the final day of the season.

Boyhood heroes Sunderland were fitting opponents for Ternent's curtain call on 9 May 2004.

And what a send off he received at the end of a season that never really hit the heights of previous campaigns.

Burnley struggled to make a mark from the off and three successive defeats in August saw them plummet to the foot of the table, with Crystal Palace, West Brom and Wigan all accounting for the Clarets.

There was a spectacular early contender for Goal of the Season in the opening day 2-3 defeat to Palace, with Lee Roche's piledriver deserving of more than mere consolation.

A first win of the season at Gillingham was quickly followed by two more victories, against Crewe and Stoke, and all of a sudden, Burnley were tenth.

But false dawns have been aplenty at Turf Moor and this one followed suit, with only two victories coming in the subsequent 13 league outings.

The low point came with a 1-6 hammering at Ipswich on a dismal Tuesday night in Suffolk. Already 0-5 down at half time, out of sight and a long, long way from home, this was arguably the night where the reality of a long, hard season sunk in.

Lying 18th by late November, Burnley finally halted their slide down the table with a welcome 3-0 win over upwardly mobile Reading, the goals coming from Robbie Blake, Richard Chaplow and Luke Chadwick.

But as winter drew in the Clarets were already eliminated from the Carling Cup, losing 0-2 at Wolves in the third round after accounting for Chesterfield on penalties, and then Scunthorpe.

Ian Moore helped grab a point at Sunderland, and was on target again alongside two Blake strikes in a 3-2 home success over Sheffield United.

But there was to be no festive cheer for Ternent and his troops and four successive defeats in December meant the year ended on a miserable note.

That quartet of setbacks included a memorable Lancashire derby at Preston that yielded eight goals, with Ricardo Fuller

Brian Jensen in action
an ever present record for 'the Beast' in his first season

the chief tormentor in a 3-5 defeat for the Clarets.

Such unpredictable scorelines were becoming commonplace in the latter part of Ternent's reign. And although the floodgates were slowed to a mere leaking of goals in the New Year, Burnley would still not do enough at the right end of the field to pick up another league win until the first week of February, when Glen Little ended an eight-game winless streak with the only goal to make it a double over Gillingham.

There was some joy in the FA Cup, with Mansfield beaten 2-0 in the third round at Field Mill and Gillingham, by now sick of the sight of Burnley, routinely despatched in round four.

A fifth round trip to Millwall looked no less daunting and suddenly, murmurings of another FA Cup run could be heard around town.

But when Valentine's Day broke, the Lions broke Burnley hearts and it was a day reminiscent of the quarter final defeat at Watford the previous season.

The Clarets never really showed up and slipped quietly out of the competition with a 0-1 defeat.

The 4-2 victory over Ipswich the following weekend showed true character – but recalling the Portman Road annihilation back in October, the return leg was only the Clarets fourth win in 25 Championship outings and only six points kept them above the drop zone.

Bizarrely, given the league position, the league defeat at Millwall on February 28 was the first since January dawned.

But the die had been cast and by the time a first away success since early September came in a 2-1 win at Bradford - thanks to goals from Robbie Blake and a priceless last minute winner from Ian Moore - it was two wins in 16 games.

But for Moore's strike, only goal difference would have kept Burnley out of the bottom three.

And when title-chasing Norwich City pitched up at Turf Moor a week later and chalked up a 5-3 victory, that two point safety net was looking mighty precarious.

A decisive day at Walsall in early march saw Robbie Blake's penalty earn victory at the Bescot Stadium and widened the gap to four points with five games remaining.

But two days later, the Clarets turned in probably their worst performance of the entire campaign in a 2-3 Easter Monday home defeat by Watford.

Defeat at Cardiff the following weekend meant that one solitary goal was keeping the Clarets afloat.

Cue a sequence of two of the most important wins in years, which began with Graham Branch netting a priceless opener in a re-arranged home clash with Wimbledon.

That helped drag Burnley away from the drop zone, and Branch repeated the trick four days later as fellow relegation rivals Derby County were beaten 1-0 at Turf Moor.

Those unlikely six points had done the trick and with safety virtually assured, the Clarets flopped over the finishing line.

After six memorable seasons in charge, it would have perhaps been fitting for Ternent to go out on a high.

But the final away game of the campaign was a disaster as the Clarets were humbled 0-3 at Rotherham.

Chairman Kilby spent the weekend mulling over the situation before finally reaching his historic decision and news of Ternent's departure broke to coincide with the final week of the season.

Turf Moor was therefore packed to the rafters for the visit of Sunderland and with Glen Little – another set to leave Turf Moor in the summer – fittingly leading out the side and scoring the opener early in the game, the script looked to have been heaven sent.

The epitaph had a sting in the tail though as Sunderland came from behind to take the three points back to the North East.

But on this occasion the supporters had come to honour, not their team, but the man who was in charge for the very last

Robbie Blake salutes the Turf Moor crowd after one of his 22 goals in league and cup

time. And at the final whistle, the very final act saw Ternent take in a lap of appreciation with tears in his eyes before exiting his arena for the last time.

He later admitted: "It's a sad day, but in many ways, the reception that myself and Sam (Ellis) had at the end is something that will live in my memory forever.

"I said when I came that I would leave the club better than I found it. I think I've done that and I wish Burnley Football Club every success in the future."

It was the end of an era and the search for Ternent's successor was on.

The list of applicants would prove to be just one more measure of how much Stan Ternent had put Burnley back on the map.

2003-04 - First Division

		P	W	D	L	F	A	Pts
1	Norwich C	46	28	10	8	79	39	94
2	West Bromwich A	46	25	11	10	64	42	86
3	Sunderland	46	22	13	11	62	45	79
4	West Ham U	46	19	17	10	67	45	74
5	Ipswich T	46	21	10	15	84	72	73
6	Crystal P	46	21	10	15	72	61	73
7	Wigan A	46	18	17	11	60	45	71
8	Sheffield U	46	20	11	15	65	56	71
9	Reading	46	20	10	16	55	57	70
10	Millwall	46	18	15	13	55	48	69
11	Stoke C	46	18	12	16	58	55	66
12	Coventry C	46	17	14	15	67	54	65
13	Cardiff C	46	17	14	15	68	58	65
14	Nottingham F	46	15	15	16	61	58	60
15	Preston NE	46	15	14	17	69	71	59
16	Watford	46	15	12	19	54	68	57
17	Rotherham U	46	13	15	18	53	61	54
18	Crewe A	46	14	11	21	57	66	53
19	BURNLEY	46	13	14	19	60	77	53
20	Derby C	46	13	13	20	53	67	52
21	Gillingham	46	14	9	23	48	67	51
22	Walsall	46	13	12	21	45	65	51
23	Bradford C	46	10	6	30	38	69	36
24	Wimbledon	46	8	5	33	41	89	29

2003-04

Manager : Stan Ternent

Division One (19th)

		Date			Opponents	Result		h/t	Goalscorers/times	Opp. goal times
	1	Aug	9	h	CRYSTAL P	L	2-3	2-2	Blake 10, Roche 19	6, 32p, 67
	2		16	a	West Bromwich A	L	1-4	1-1	Blake 27	31, 58, 87, 88
	3		23	h	WIGAN A	L	0-2	0-1		13, 77
	4		25	a	Gillingham	W	3-0	2-0	I.Moore 27, West 30, Blake 77	
	5		30	h	CREWE A	W	1-0	0-0	Chaplow 52	
	6	Sep	6	a	Stoke C	W	2-1	2-0	May 18, Chadwick 27	53
	7		13	a	Norwich C	L	0-2	0-0		58, 90
	8		16	h	NOTTINGHAM F	L	0-3	0-1		7, 76, 82
	9		20	h	BRADFORD C	W	4-0	1-0	I.Moore 42, Chadwick (2) 54, 60, Blake 68	
	10		27	a	Wimbledon	D	2-2	2-0	Blake (2) 21, 37	66, 71
	11		30	a	Watford	D	1-1	0-1	Chadwick 53	45
	12	Oct	4	h	WALSALL	W	3-1	1-1	Facey (3) 4, 83, 87	23
	13		14	a	Ipswich T	L	1-6	0-5	Facey 49	19,21,24,30,40og,90
	14		18	a	West Ham U	D	2-2	1-1	Facey 39, I.Moore 81	21, 86
	15		25	h	MILLWALL	D	1-1	0-0	I.Moore 60	53
	16	Nov	1	h	CARDIFF C	D	1-1	0-0	Chaplow 52	75
	17		8	a	Sheffield U	L	0-1	0-1		44
	18		15	a	Derby C	L	0-2	0-1		19, 90p
	19		22	h	ROTHERHAM U	D	1-1	1-0	Blake 35	51
	20		25	h	READING	W	3-0	1-0	Blake 5, Chaplow 47, Chadwick 54	
	21		29	a	Sunderland	D	1-1	0-1	I.Moore 72	39
	22	Dec	6	h	SHEFFIELD U	W	3-2	3-2	Blake (2) 17, 45p, I.Moore 34	24, 30
	23		13	h	COVENTRY C	L	1-2	0-2	Blake 53	8, 40og
	24		20	a	Preston N E	L	3-5	1-1	I.Moore 24, Gnohere 64, Blake 78p	18, 60, 71, 82, 88
Gnohere's last game	25		26	a	Crewe A	L	1-3	0-1	Blake 89p	37, 55, 90
	26		28	h	STOKE C	L	0-1	0-0		52
	27	Jan	10	a	Crystal P	D	0-0	0-0		
	28		17	h	WEST BROMWICH A	D	1-1	0-0	Blake 68	73
	29		31	a	Wigan A	D	0-0	0-0		
	30	Feb	7	h	GILLINGHAM	W	1-0	0-0	Little 83	
	31		21	h	IPSWICH T	W	4-2	2-0	Little 26, May 28, Chaplow 61, Blake 90	65, 88
	32		24	a	Reading	D	2-2	1-1	I.Moore 23, May 69	19, 90
	33		28	a	Millwall	L	0-2	0-1		12, 52
	34	Mar	2	h	WEST HAM U	D	1-1	1-1	Branch 31	36p
	35		6	h	PRESTON N E	D	1-1	1-0	Blake 19	58p
	36		13	a	Coventry C	L	0-4	0-3		10, 33, 39p, 78
	37		17	a	Nottingham F	D	1-1	1-0	Chaplow 15	80
West's last game	38		27	a	Bradford C	W	2-1	1-1	Blake 8, I.Moore 90	18
	39	Apr	3	h	NORWICH C	L	3-5	3-2	Wood 7, May 30, Blake 38	14, 32, 51, 62, 89
	40		10	a	Walsall	W	1-0	0-0	Blake 56p	
	41		12	h	WATFORD	L	2-3	1-1	McGregor 30, Adebola 86	39p, 55, 84
	42		17	a	Cardiff C	L	0-2	0-0		78p, 80
Alan Moore's last game	43		20	h	WIMBLEDON	W	2-0	2-0	Branch 26, Ntimban-Zeh 45og	
	44		24	h	DERBY C	W	1-0	1-0	Branch 42	
	45	May	1	a	Rotherham U	L	0-3	0-2		15, 39, 85p
last games for Little, Weller & May	46		9	h	SUNDERLAND	L	1-2	1-1	Little 11	37, 66

FA Cup

3	Jan	3	a	Mansfield T	W	2-0	1-0	I.Moore (2) 30, 73	
4		24	h	GILLINGHAM	W	3-1	2-0	I.Moore 30, Blake (2) 33, 64	71
5	Feb	14	a	Millwall	L	0-1	0-0		70

Final, Manchester U 3-0 Millwall, at The Millenium Stadium, Cardiff.

League Cup

aet, won 3-2 on pens	1	Aug	12	a	Chesterfield	D	0-0	0-0		
	2	Sep	23	a	Scunthorpe U	W	3-2	2-1	Chadwick 22, Blake 42, I.Moore 77	32, 85
	3	Oct	28	a	Wolverhampton W	L	0-2	0-0		48, 81

Final, Middlesbrough 2-1 Bolton W, at The Millenium Stadium, Cardiff.

Details of other first team games elsewhere.

Att.	Pos	Jensen	Roche	Branch	Gnohere	Camara	Chadwick	Weller	Chaplow	Little	A Moore	Blake	A Grant	West	O'Neill	May	I Moore	Todd	Farrelly	Facey	McGregor	McEveley	Wood	Orr	P Scott	Townsend	Adebola	Johnrose	Pilkington		
12,976		G	D	D	D	D	M	M*	M**	M	F^	F	S*	S**	S^																1
22,489	24	G	D**	D		D	M	M	S*	F	M*	F	M	S**		D															2
13,231	24	G		D	S**	D	M^	M	S*	M	S^	F**	M*	D		D	F														3
7,645	19	G		D		D	M**	M	S**	M	S*	F	M	D		D	F*														4
11,495	15	G		D	S**	D	M		M**	M	S*	F	M	D		D	F*														5
14,867	10	G		M		D	M	S*				F	M	D		D	S**	D	M*	F**											6
16,407	13	G	S*	M**		D	M					F	M	D*		D	S**	D	M	F											7
12,530		G	D*	S^		D	M	S*	S**			F^	M			D	M	D	M**	F											8
12,719	12	G		S**		D	M	S*	S^			F	M*	D		D**	M	D	M^	F											9
5,639	11	G		S*		D	M**	M	S**			F*		D		D	M	D	M	F											10
11,573		G		S**		D	M	M	S*			F		D		D**	M	D	M*	F											11
10,532	8	G		D		D	M	M	M			F		D			M	D		F											12
22,048		G	D	D		D		M	M			F		D			M		M	F											13
31,474	13	G		D	D	D	M	M*	M			F**	S*	D			M		S**	F											14
10,435	16	G		D	D**	D	M	M*	M			F	S*	D			M		S**	F											15
10,886	15	G		D	D	D	S*		M	M**		F*	M	D			M		S**	F											16
20,967	18	G	S^	D*	D	D	M**		M			S**	M	D			F		M	F^	S*										17
21,960	18	G	S**	S*	D	D			M	M		F	M	D**		D	F		M*												18
12,928	18	G		M	D	D			M	M		F	M	D		D	F*			S*											19
9,473		G		M*	D	D	S*	S**	M**	M		F	M	D		D	F			S^										3rd sub Facey for Chadwick	20
29,852	16	G	S**			D	M*	S*	M	M		F	M	D**		D	F				D										21
11,452	14	G	D		D	D	M*	S*	M	M		F	M	S**			F				D									2nd sub West for Weller	22
10,358	16	G	D**		D	D	M^	M		M		F	M	S**		S*	F				D*	S^									23
18,802	18	G		S**	D	D^	S*	M*	M	M		F	M	D**		D	F				S^										24
9,512	19	G		D	D	D	S*	M	M**	M*		F	M	D^			F				S^	S**									25
12,812	21	G		D		D**	M*	M	M			F	M	D	S**	D	F					S*									26
15,276	20	G	D	S**		D	M*	M	M**	S*		F	M			D	F				D										27
13,106	19	G	D	M**		D	M*			M	S**	F	M	S*		D	F				D										28
11,147	19	G	D			D			M	M*		F	M			D	F				D		M	S*							29
10,400	19	G	D			D	S*		M	M	M*		M			D	F				D		F								30
12,418	17	G	D			D		M*	M	M		F	M			D	F				D			S*							31
10,543		G	D			D		M	M*	M		F	M			D	F				D			S*							32
10,148	18	G	D^	S*		D	S**			M**	M*	F		S^		D	F				D		M	M							33
12,440		G	D*	M		D	M**			M	S**	F	M	S*		D	F				D										34
15,837	18	G		M*		D			M	M	S*	F	M	D		D	F				D										35
12,953	21	G						M	M	M	D**	F	M	D^		D*	F				D		S*		S**	S^					36
26,885		G		D		D		S*	M	M		F	M**	D		D	F				S**		M*								37
13,677	19	G		D		D		S**	M*	M		F**	M	D		D	F						M				S*				38
12,417	20	G	D	D		D	S*	M*	S**	M	S^	F	M^			D	F						M**								39
7,769	19	G	D	D		D	S^	M*	S*	M		F	M				F^				D		M					S**		2nd sub Johnrose for Chaplow	40
11,413	20	G	D	D		D	S**	M*		M		F	M				F				D		M**				S^	S*		3rd sub Adebola for Chadwick	41
13,525	21	G	D	F		D	M		M	M		F	M*			D					D							S*			42
13,555		G	D	F		D	S^	M*	M**	M	S*	F^				D					D							M	S**		43
16,189	17	G	D	F		D	S**	M	M	M*		F**				D					D		S*					M			44
9,157	19	G	D*	F		D**	S**	M	M^	M		F			S^	D					D						S*	M			45
18,852	19	G		D		D^	S*	M*	M**	M		F			S**	D	F				D				S^			M			46
Appearances		46	21	30	12	45	23	25	30	33	5	44	34	25		34	38	7	9	12	20		8	1				4			
Apps as sub			4	8	2		13	8	9	1	8	1	3	7	4	1	2		3	2	3	4	2	3	2	1	3	3	1		
Goals (60)			1	3	1		5		5	3		19		1		4	9			5	1		1				1			1	og

Att.		Jensen	Roche	Branch	Gnohere	Camara	Chadwick	Weller	Chaplow	Little	A Moore	Blake	A Grant	West	O'Neill	May	I Moore	Todd	Farrelly	Facey	McGregor	McEveley	Wood	
8,290		G	D			S*	M**	M	M		S**	F	M			D	F				D	D*		3
9,735		G	D	S*		D			M	M	M*	F	M			D	F				D			4
10,420		G	D**			D	S**	S*	M	M	S^	F*	M			D	F				D^		M	5
Appearances		3	3			2	1	1	3	2	1	3	3			3	3				3	1	1	
Apps as sub				1		1	1	1			2													
Goals (5)												2					3							

Att.		Jensen	Roche	Branch	Gnohere	Camara	Chadwick	Weller	Chaplow	Little	A Moore	Blake	A Grant	West	O'Neill	May	I Moore	Todd	Farrelly	Facey	
2,928		G	D	D**	D	D	M	M	S*	F	M*	F	M	S**							1
2,915		G				D	F	M				M		D		D	M	D	M	F	2
18,548		G	S*	D	D	D			M**	M		F	M	D*			M		S**	F	3
Appearances		3	1	2	2	3	2	2	1	2	1	3	2	2		1	2	1	1	2	
Apps as sub			1						1					1					1		
Goals (3)							1					1					1				

2004-05

The winds of change were once again whistling through the corridors and halls of Turf Moor.

It had been six years since the managerial merry-go-round last spun at Turf Moor.

But following Stan Ternent's shock dismissal all talk was of who would jump aboard as the first new manager of the 21st century.

Numerous names were bandied around in the local media, but the lengthy list of candidates was slowly and ever so carefully whittled down to one and that man was Steve Cotterill.

The former Cheltenham Town and Stoke City manager, a highly qualified coach, had proven pedigree and fitted in perfectly with chairman Barry Kilby's blueprint of appointing a young, hungry manager.

Cotterill instantly hit the ground running after ending the previous season coaching with Leicester City following his departure from Sunderland, where he was in situ as Howard Wilkinson's assistant.

Within days, John McGreal had become the Clarets' first summer signing, arriving from Ipswich on a free transfer.

And before the season got underway four more, in the shape of fellow defenders Frank Sinclair and Michael Duff, goalkeeper Danny Coyne and midfielder Micah Hyde, also put pen to paper in East Lancashire.

Hyde was to make an immediate impact, notching the first goal of the new season in a 1-1 home draw with Sheffield United on the opening day.

His only other goal that season, seven months later, would go down in Burnley folklore.

But a memorable night at Ewood Park was still some time away and Cotterill was about to enjoy a honeymoon period.

Victories at Watford in the Championship and at Bury in the Carling Cup helped made it five games unbeaten for the new man at the helm.

West Ham and Gillingham inflicted the first defeats, but the Clarets steeled themselves and embarked on an eight-game unbeaten run.

Unfortunately, six of those games ended all square, keeping the reins on a slow, but steady climb up the league table.

The two wins, at home to Crewe and Cardiff, were complemented by progress in the Carling Cup, where a Brian Jensen–inspired Burnley ousted Wolves at Turf Moor on penalties.

Following an unbeaten September a defeat at Derby County in October, which ended the unbeaten run, was instantly forgotten as Burnley put in one of their performances of the season in the Carling Cup third round.

Premiership side Aston Villa arrived at Turf Moor as firm favourites, but goals from Mo Camara, Graham Branch and Jean-Louis Valois earned the Clarets a deserved 3-1 victory and plenty of column inches.

Cotterill's side were already carving out a reputation as something of a cup team, a suggestion that would gather further momentum later in the campaign, and also in his second season at Turf Moor.

But with a fourth round place secured and confidence building, a return to league action brought a 2-1 victory at once-mighty Leeds United, despite falling behind inside 12 seconds.

Burnley's Carling Cup dream was shattered with the visit of Tottenham, as new manager Martin Jol guided Spurs to a comfortable 3-0 win.

But there was no shame and following the canny capture of Aston Villa defender Gary Cahill on loan, the Clarets showed their mettle with three straight league wins over Nottingham Forest, Brighton and Millwall.

Incredibly, the hat-trick of 1-0 wins all came courtesy of Robbie Blake, as the striker took his tally for the season to 11.

Now sitting eighth in the Championship, it was becoming apparent that Blake was key to Burnley's success.

However, his goals had caught envious glances from elsewhere and after adding to his growing reputation with a match-winning brace against Preston, in turn passing the half-century mark for the club, Blake's Turf Moor days were becoming numbered.

Fans soon discovered that Wigan were keen to land the £1m signing and after three unsuccessful bids, rumours of his departure intensified when Blake was omitted from the squad that faced the Latics at Christmas.

It's on its way
Micah Hyde launches his "goal of the season" to equalise in the FA Cup at Ewood Park

Blake had now stated his desire to leave Turf Moor and join the Latics' charge for the Premiership.

And in early January, Burnley's leading light and leading scorer finally quit Turf Moor ..... bound for Birmingham City!

A club record £1.25m finally swayed the Burnley board and Wigan fans were left feeling nearly as deflated as their Burnley counterparts, who were soon reeling from a double whammy.

The euphoria over the FA Cup third round victory over Liverpool, courtesy of a bizarre moment of madness from

Liverpool's Djimi Traore, had hardly died down when former Centre of Excellence starlet Richard Chaplow made the £1.5m transfer deadline day move to West Brom, in turn smashing the outgoing transfer record for the second time in weeks.

League form was by now patchy, perhaps understandably so since the FA Cup fourth round victory over Bournemouth had landed the Clarets a plum fifth round tie at home to old adversaries Blackburn Rovers. A 2-0 win at Coventry in early February was Burnley's only victory in a barren, but incident-packed month that effectively ended all hopes of a play off push.

But all eyes were now on the FA Cup and a highly-charged Turf Moor clash live on television ended goalless and signalled a trip to Ewood Park 10 days later.

In the hiatus, Burnley finally spent £600,000 of the cash generated from their two high-profile departures, ending their search for Blake's replacement by bringing Ade Akinbiyi to Turf Moor from Stoke City on a three-and-a-half year deal.

However, Akinbiyi was unavailable as the Clarets made the short journey down the M65 for a spine-tingling evening that left 7,000 travelling Burnley fans with a memory to treasure and dreaming of what might have been.

The Clarets trailed until just before the break when a seemingly routine throw in led to those once-in-a-lifetime moments.

Hyde, who had not scored since August, received the ball on the right hand corner of the penalty area, controlled it on his knee and swivelled.

Spotting Brad Friedel marginally off his line, the Jamaican unleashed a howitzer that flew into the top corner and sent the visiting support into raptures.

It was a sublime moment of individual brilliance, the first time Burnley had scored on their greatest rivals' patch for over a generation – 22 years to be precise.

Cruelly, it would ultimately count for nothing.

Rovers grabbed an undeserved winner less than five minutes from time to deny Burnley at least another 30 minutes their battling performance had more than merited.

But the scenes following the final whistle, where Cotterill marched his players out into the centre of a sodden Ewood Park for an impromptu huddle, at least gave the travelling army one last image to treasure.

Cup excitement over for another year, Burnley still had Akinbiyi's Clarets' debut to look forward to.

Much had been written of the powerful striker's physical attributes. And with over £12m of transfer fees behind him, there remained an outside hope that the nine-point gap to the play offs was not insurmountable.

But the physical side of Akinbiyi's game made the headlines for all the wrong reasons as Burnley's 'gentle giant' was uncharacteristically sent off for an off-the-ball incident caught on camera just three minutes after making his bow as a second half substitute in the 0-2 defeat at home by Sunderland.

The ensuing three-match ban left Burnley toothless and the season quickly ran out of steam. Indeed, only four wins came in the last 12 games.

Back-to-back 2-0 victories over QPR and Plymouth in the final two home games did bring some sunshine as Spring sprung.

Ian Moore (left) and Lee Roche celebrate Djimi Traore's og in the FA Cup win against Liverpool months later the Reds lifted the Champions League trophy

But in truth, Burnley never really recovered from the sale of Blake in the New Year. Thirteen goals in the first half of the season had offered hope that the Clarets could forge a play off push.

At the time of his departure, they lay just six points off the pace and the loss of the talismanic goalscorer was a blow to manager and fans alike.

It was becoming a familiar tale. Under the previous manager top scorer Gareth Taylor was sold off while the club was making serious inroads and looking to push to the next level. Now Cotterill got an immediate taste of life at a club that was providing rich pickings for others.

Unfortunately, it was a situation that would soon rear its ugly head again.

2004-05 - Championship

		P	W	D	L	F	A	Pts
1	Sunderland	46	29	7	10	76	41	94
2	Wigan A	46	25	12	9	79	35	87
3	Ipswich T	46	24	13	9	85	56	85
4	Derby C	46	22	10	14	71	60	76
5	Preston NE	46	21	12	13	67	58	75
6	West Ham U	46	21	10	15	66	56	73
7	Reading	46	19	13	14	51	44	70
8	Sheffield U	46	18	13	15	57	56	67
9	Wolverhampton W	46	15	21	10	72	59	66
10	Millwall	46	18	12	16	51	45	66
11	Queens Park R	46	17	11	18	54	58	62
12	Stoke C	46	17	10	19	36	38	61
13	BURNLEY	46	15	15	16	38	39	60
14	Leeds U	46	14	18	14	49	52	60
15	Leicester C	46	12	21	13	49	46	57
16	Cardiff C	46	13	15	18	48	51	54
17	Plymouth A	46	14	11	21	52	64	53
18	Watford	46	12	16	18	52	59	52
19	Coventry C	46	13	13	20	61	73	52
20	Brighton & HA	46	13	12	21	40	65	51
21	Crewe A	46	12	14	20	66	86	50
22	Gillingham	46	12	14	20	45	66	50
23	Nottingham F	46	9	17	20	42	66	44
24	Rotherham U	46	5	14	27	35	69	29

2004-05

Manager : Steve Cotterill

Championship (13th)

	No	Date			Opponents	Result		h/t	Goalscorers/times	Opp. goal times
	1	Aug	7	h	SHEFFIELD U	D	1-1	1-0	Hyde 16	52
	2		10	a	Rotherham U	D	0-0	0-0		
	3		14	a	Watford	W	1-0	0-0	Moore 64	
	4		21	h	WOLVERHAMPTON W	D	1-1	1-1	Blake 24	15
	5		28	a	West Ham U	L	0-1	0-0		62
	6		30	h	GILLINGHAM	L	1-2	0-1	Moore 87	5, 69
	7	Sep	11	h	CREWE A	W	3-0	2-0	McGreal 12, Blake 42, Chaplow 49	
	8		14	a	Wigan A	D	0-0	0-0		
	9		18	a	Leicester C	D	0-0	0-0		
	10		25	h	STOKE C	D	2-2	2-1	Moore 3, Blake 19p	34, 50
	11		28	h	CARDIFF C	W	1-0	0-0	Chaplow 88	
	12	Oct	2	a	Reading	D	0-0	0-0		
	13		16	a	Ipswich T	D	1-1	1-0	Blake 19	90
	14		19	h	COVENTRY C	D	2-2	0-0	Blake 65p, Branch 73	62, 70
	15		22	h	DERBY C	L	0-2	0-0		57, 63
	16		30	a	Queens Park R	L	0-3	0-3		13p, 16, 24
	17	Nov	3	a	Leeds U	W	2-1	2-1	Roche 10, Duffy 31	1
	18		6	h	IPSWICH T	L	0-2	0-1		15, 65
	19		13	h	NOTTINGHAM F	W	1-0	1-0	Blake 6	
	20		20	a	Brighton & H A	W	1-0	0-0	Blake 70	
	21		27	h	MILLWALL	W	1-0	0-0	Blake 61p	
	22	Dec	4	a	Plymouth A	L	0-1	0-0		90p
	23		11	h	PRESTON N E	W	2-0	1-0	Blake (2) 45, 85	
Blake's last game (of 1st spell)	24		18	a	Sunderland	L	1-2	1-1	Branch 36	35, 52
	25		28	h	WIGAN A	W	1-0	1-0	Branch 24	
	26	Jan	3	a	Stoke C	W	1-0	0-0	Cahill 79	
	27		15	h	READING	D	0-0	0-0		
	28		22	a	Cardiff C	L	0-2	0-1		13, 74
	29	Feb	5	h	LEEDS U	L	0-1	0-0		66
	30		12	a	Coventry C	W	2-0	0-0	Oster 64, Moore 69	
	31		15	a	Crewe A	D	1-1	0-1	Grant 53	18
	32		23	a	Derby C	D	1-1	1-0	Valois 34	70
	33		26	a	Preston N E	L	0-1	0-0		82p
	34	Mar	4	h	SUNDERLAND	L	0-2	0-1		26, 89
	35		8	h	LEICESTER C	D	0-0	0-0		
	36		12	h	ROTHERHAM U	W	2-1	2-1	Grant 11, Sinclair 14	4
	37		15	a	Wolverhampton W	L	0-2	0-1		38, 60
Ian Moore's last game	38		19	a	Sheffield U	L	1-2	0-1	Akinbiyi 84	29, 49
	39	Apr	2	h	WATFORD	W	3-1	2-0	Bowditch 20, O'Connor 43, Valois 90	77
	40		5	h	WEST HAM U	L	0-1	0-0		83
	41		9	a	Gillingham	L	0-1	0-0		56
	42		16	h	BRIGHTON & H A	D	1-1	1-0	Akinbiyi 23	52
	43		19	h	QUEENS PARK R	W	2-0	1-0	Akinbiyi (2) 43, 81	
Roche's last game	44		23	a	Nottingham F	L	0-1	0-0		70
	45		30	h	PLYMOUTH A	W	2-0	0-0	Valois 87p, O'Connor 90	
Cahill, Camara, Grant - last games	46	May	8	a	Millwall	D	0-0	0-0		

FA Cup

	Rd	Date			Opponents	Result		h/t	Goalscorers/times	Opp. goal times
	3	Jan	18	h	LIVERPOOL	W	1-0	0-0	Traore 51og	
Chaplow's last game	4		29	h	BOURNEMOUTH	W	2-0	1-0	Moore (2) 17, 90	
	5	Feb	20	h	BLACKBURN R	D	0-0	0-0		
	rep	Mar	1	a	Blackburn R	L	1-2	1-1	Hyde 42	31, 86

Final, Arsenal 0-0 Manchester U after extra time, at the Millenium Stadium, Cardiff, Arsenal won on pens.

League Cup

	Rd	Date			Opponents	Result		h/t	Goalscorers/times	Opp. goal times
	1	Aug	24	a	Bury	W	3-2	2-2	Mattis 17og, Blake (2) 33p, 52	12, 18
aet, 1-1 at 90m, won 4-2 on pens	2	Sep	21	h	WOLVERHAMPTON W	D	1-1	0-1	Blake 50	45
	3	Oct	26	h	ASTON VILLA	W	3-1	1-0	Branch 9, Camara 65, Valois 86	81
	4	Nov	9	h	TOTTENHAM H	L	0-3	0-1		31, 52, 58

Final, Chelsea 3-2 Liverpool after extra time, at The Millenium Stadium, Cardiff.

Details of other first team games elsewhere.

Att.	Pos	Coyne	Duff	McGreal	Sinclair	Camara	Chaplow	A Grant	Hyde	Branch	I Moore	Blake	Roche	Valois	O'Neill	Pilkington	Duffy	Sanokho	J O'Connor	Jensen	Cahill	Oster	Whittingham	Akinbiyi	Bowditch		
16,956		G	D	D	D	D	M	M*	M	M	F	F	S*														1
6,243		G	D	D	D	D	M	M	M	M	F	F															2
12,048	6	G	D	D	D	D	M*	M	M	M	F	F	S*														3
13,869	10	G	D	D	D	D	M	M	M	M	F	F															4
22,119	11	G	D	D	D	D	M	M	M	M*	F	F	S*														5
11,574	14	G	D	D	D	D	M	M	M	M	F	F															6
11,274	12	G	D	D	D	D	M**	M		M	F	F^	M*	S*	S**	S^											7
9,746		G	D	D	D	D	M	M		M	F	F	M*	S*													8
22,495	14	G	D	D	D	D	M	M		M	F	F		M													9
12,981	14	G	D	D	D	D	M	M*	M	M	F	F					S*										10
7,200		G		D	D	D	M	M*	S*	M	F	F		M**			D	S**									11
15,400	11	G	D	D	D	D	M		M	M	F	F		M													12
23,183	10	G	D*	D	D	D	M^	M	M	M	F**	F	S**	S^			S*										13
10,919		G	D	D	D	D	M**	S**	M	M	F	F	S*	M*													14
13,703		G	D	D	D	D	M**	S*	M	M	F	F		M*			S**										15
15,638	17	G**	D	D	D	D	S^	M	M	M*		F	F	M^					S*	S**							16
27,490			D	D**	D	D		M	M			F	F		S*		M*	S**	M	G							17
11,969	16			D	D*	D		M	M	M		F	F				D	S*	M	G							18
11,622	14		D	D		D		M	M**		S*	F	F	M*			S**		M	G	D						19
6,109	12		D		D	D		M		M	F	F	M						M	G	D						20
11,471	8		D		D	D		M		M	F	F	M						M	G	D						21
13,508	11		D	S*	D	D		M		M	F	F	M*						M	G	D						22
15,318	11		D		D	D		M*	M		F	F	M	S*					M	G	D						23
27,102	12		D	D		D	S**		M	M**	F	F	S*	M*					M	G	D						24
16,485	11		D	D		D	S*	M	M	M	F		F*						M	G	D						25
15,689	11		D*	D	M	D	S**	M	M	F	F		S*						M**	G	D						26
11,392	10		D*	D	M	D	M	M		F**	F		S*	S**					M	G	D						27
11,562	13			D	D*	D	S**	M	M	S*	F		F	M**					M	G	D						28
17,789	16			D	D	D		M	M	M	F		F	S*						G	D	M*					29
13,236	12		D	D		D		M	M	M	F		S*	M						G	D	F*					30
7,718			D	D	D	D		M	M	M*	S*			M						G		F	F				31
23,701			D			D		M	M	S*	F*		D	M						G	D	M	F				32
18,202	13		D			D		M		M	F		D	M						G	D	M	F				33
12,103			D**		D	D		M*	M	M	F		S*	M						G	D		F	S**			34
10,933			D	D	D				M	M	F			M						G	D	M	F				35
10,539	13		S^	D	D	D		M	M	S*	S**			M**						G	D	M	F*		F^		36
24,336			S^	D	D	D		M	M	S**	S*			M*						G	D	M	F**		F^		37
19,374	14		D		D	D			M	M*	S**		M	S*						G	D	M**		F	F		38
11,507	14		S**	D	D	D		S*	M	M**				S^					M	G	D	M^		F	F*		39
12,209		G	S*	D	D^	D		S^	M	M				S**					M		D	M**		F	F*		40
9,447	14		D	D		D		S**	M	M				M*					M	G	D	F**		F	S*		41
11,611	14	G	D*	D		D		M	M	M			S*						M		D			F	F		42
10,396			D	D		D		M**	M	M			S*	S^					M	G	D	S**		F^	F*		43
24,165	14	G	D	D		D		M**	M	F^			M*	S^					M		D	S*		F	S**		44
12,893	13		S*	D	D	D		M**	M	M				S**					M	G	D*	S^		F	F^		45
12,171	13	G	D	D	M	D		M	M	F									M		D			F			46
Appearances		20	37	38	36	45	16	37	37	39	30	24	17	18			3		20	26	27	12	7	9	8		
Apps as sub			5	1			5	5	1	4	5		12	12	2	1	4	3	1	1		3		1	2		
Goals (38)				1	1		2	2	1	3	4	10	1	3			1		2		1	1		4	1		

Att.	Coyne	Duff	McGreal	Sinclair	Camara	Chaplow	A Grant	Hyde	Branch	I Moore	Blake	Roche	Valois	O'Neill	Pilkington	Duffy	Sanokho	J O'Connor	Jensen	Cahill	Oster	Whittingham	Akinbiyi	Bowditch		
19,033			D	D	D	M	M	M		F		M	F						G	D						3
9,944			D	D	D	M**	M	M	M	F^		S*	S**		S^				G	D	F*					4
21,468		M	D**	D*	D		M	M	S^	F^		S**	M						G	D	S*	F				5
28,691		D		D	D		M*	M**	S*	F		S**	M						G	D	M	F				rep
Appearances		2	3	4	4	2	4	4	1	4		1	3						4	4	2	2				
Apps as sub									2			3	1		1						1					
Goals (4)								1		2															1	og

Att.	Coyne	Duff	McGreal	Sinclair	Camara	Chaplow	A Grant	Hyde	Branch	I Moore	Blake	Roche	Valois	O'Neill	Pilkington	Duffy	Sanokho	J O'Connor	Jensen	Cahill	Oster	Whittingham	Akinbiyi	Bowditch		
3,648	G	D	D	D	D	M	M	M*	M	F	F	S*														1
5,013		D	D*	S*	D	M	M	D	M	F	F		M						G							2
11,184	G	D	D		D		M	M	M		F	D	F			M										3
10,639		D			D		M	M	F*		F	D	S*		S**	M	M		G	D					2nd sub Pilkington for Valois	4
Appearances	2	4	3	1	4	2	4	4	4	2	4	2	2			2	1		2	1						
Apps as sub				1								1	1		1											
Goals (7)					1				1		3		1												1	og

2005-06

If selling the ace in your pack once could be deemed careless, then doing so twice in two seasons could be construed as reckless.

Thank heavens then that the manager did not follow suit when the opportunity arose, or the whole pack of cards could have come tumbling down.

This tale of another season is yet another story of what might have been at Turf Moor.

The departure of Robbie Blake must still have rankled Steve Cotterill as he rebuilt for another tilt at the Championship; a league he was now describing as "Premiership Two" given the growing number of former top-flight teams in competition for a place back at the top table of English football.

Thankfully, Ade Akinbiyi stepped into the limelight, scoring 14 goals in a blistering first half of the season.

Predictably, it all ended in tears once again as Burnley's main man smashed the outgoing transfer record for the third time in a year, taking with him another season's hopes and dreams.

Building for the new season, Cotterill was again busy in the transfer market, raiding the south coast for Bournemouth trio Wade Elliott, Garreth O'Connor and John Spicer. He then completed a whirlwind summer with a day trip to Florida to secure the signing of Stoke defender Wayne Thomas, who joined team mate Gifton Noel-Williams at Turf Moor.

Sheffield United defender Jon Harley and Arsenal youngster Danny Karbassiyoon ensured there would be plenty of new faces around when the season kicked off at Crewe.

Two successive defeats got the season off to the worst possible start. Noel-Williams' debut goal at Gresty Road was mere consolation, while Sheffield United beat the Clarets 2-1 in the first home game.

The mood was lightened in dramatic style, as Cotterill recorded his biggest win as Burnley boss in a 4-0 thumping of Coventry at Turf Moor.

Akinbiyi netted twice in the rout, and there was even time for Noel-Williams to blaze a penalty so far into the visiting fans, that the ball came back with a Sky Blue shirt on it!

Controversy followed at Watford where Burnley lost 1-3 following an injury to Brian Jensen that resulted in a Hornets' goal.

Jensen missed the League Cup victory over Carlisle, which prompted a wretched league run of just four points from the next 18 on offer.

A 3-0 victory over Barnsley in the League Cup broke up that winless streak, while a similar success over Ipswich, and a solitary Garreth O'Connor strike at Wolves, live on Sky, got the Clarets' campaign back on track.

Only a solitary goal win at Leicester yielded any points from the next four outings, and there was revenge for Aston Villa, who defeated the Clarets by a single goal in the third round of the League Cup to avenge their defeat at Turf Moor 12 months earlier.

At that stage, Burnley sat a lowly 16th in the Championship table. But fortunes were about to change for the better and Akinbiyi's winner against Hull restored confidence and led to a further victory over Millwall.

That set up an eventful Bonfire Night clash at Luton, where Akinbiyi was truly on fire!

An incredible 90 minutes at Kenilworth Road saw the striker complete his first hat-trick, earn the 10-man Clarets a remarkable victory and give new meaning to the phrase 'remember, remember the fifth of November!'

Unbeaten on their own patch, Town fell behind to two stunning Akinbiyi strikes – the second a Goal of the Season contender.

But just before half time, Jensen raced out of his goal to deny Steve Howard and, after carrying the ball over the whitewash was instantly show the red card.

With no substitute goalkeeper on the bench, the task was volunteered for by midfielder John Spicer, who later admitted he had he never played there before.

Predictably, Town pulled a goal back before the break and both sets of fans doubtless spent the interval expecting the inevitable comeback.

However, 10 minutes into the second period, Akinbiyi raced clear and went down under a challenge to earn a penalty, which he coolly converted past former Clarets stopper Marlon Beresford.

Luton reduced the arrears once more, leading to a frantic final half an hour before Burnley could celebrate an against-all-odds victory.

And in scenes reminiscent of the previous season's cup defeat at Blackburn, the final whistle brought the inevitable huddle, complete with Akinbiyi clutching his match ball!

Ever-present James O'Connor (right) celebrates one of his goals with Kyle Lafferty

That win catapulted the Clarets up to eighth place after 18 games, separated from the top six only by goal difference.

And they would enter the play-off places on merit just seven days later with Spicer, restored to his midfield role, netting the only goal in a home win and league double over Leicester.

Four victories came to a shuddering halt at Leeds, who completed their own double over the Clarets with a 2-0 win at Elland Road.

And a mixed bag of results sent the Clarets back down to

11th place in the table before one of the results of the season arrived just eight days before Christmas.

Watford were already mounting their own promotion campaign, but they were humbled 4-1 at Turf Moor to slump to only their second away defeat of the season.

A solitary Akinbiyi goal accounted for his old club Stoke on Boxing Day and suddenly, with Burnley leapfrogging the Potters into fifth place, Christmas was a joyous time at Turf Moor.

But disaster lay just around the corner and that goal would prove to be Akinbiyi's last in his first spell with the club.

Sheffield United manager Neil Warnock – a man with an eye on the Premiership and a penchant for signing strikers galore – entered the January transfer market and, following protracted negotiations, finally landed the Clarets striker for a fee totalling £1.75m.

Akinbiyi finally left following the 0-2 home defeat to Preston, bringing the curtain down on a dismal month of five defeats in six games, including an FA Cup third round defeat at Derby.

That run could be no coincidence following all the rumblings and uncertainty over Akinbiyi's future, as well as that of the manager himself!

In late January, former club Leicester City expressed an interest in talking to the Clarets' boss about the vacant manager's job at the Walkers Stadium, an approach that was swiftly rebuffed by Burnley chairman Barry Kilby.

Amid all this chaos, Burnley still lay 10th and the play offs remained a possibility.

In practice though, the cutting edge was blunted for the second successive season and any hope was more of a pipe dream.

Cotterill brushed off all talk of leaving and denied a rift with Kilby, insisting: "I'd like to thank Leicester for approaching me but a lot has been built here in the last 18 months.

"I have a great relationship with the chairman and supporters of our club and I'm staying."

Backing those words with action, former England and Bolton striker Michael Ricketts had already been drafted in as a loan replacement for his main striker.

And although Ricketts contributed with a winner on his home debut against Plymouth – ending a run of seven games without a win – and scored again the following week at Ipswich, the die had been cast.

In Akinbiyi's absence the goals had well and truly dried up and Ricketts' strike at Portman Road was the only goal scored in six successive defeats.

The season had fizzled out like many before it and, on the back of the worst run of the season, Burnley slumped as low at 18th.

Already, Cotterill was looking for another goalscorer to spearhead the attack the following season.

He found the answer in Andy Gray, who had endured a nightmare spell at Sunderland.

In March, the well-travelled hitman joined the Clarets along with former Sporting Lisbon and Blackburn Rovers midfielder Alan Mahon.

And Gray wasted no time hitting the ground running, scoring in back-to-back home games against Norwich and Southampton to settle into his new surroundings.

Ade Akinbiyi on the ball
top scorer in 2005-06

Gray even scored for a third successive home game to earn all three points against QPR in early April.

But tellingly, that was only the third win since the Boxing Day victory over Stoke City.

The season was ending in a whimper, with just 16 points gleaned from 19 league games since welcoming in 2006.

2005-06 - Championship

		P	W	D	L	F	A	Pts
1	Reading	46	31	13	2	99	32	106
2	Sheffield U	46	26	12	8	76	46	90
3	Watford	46	22	15	9	77	53	81
4	Preston NE	46	20	20	6	59	30	80
5	Leeds U	46	21	15	10	57	38	78
6	Crystal P	46	21	12	13	67	48	75
7	Wolverhampton W	46	16	19	11	50	42	67
8	Coventry C	46	16	15	15	62	65	63
9	Norwich C	46	18	8	20	56	65	62
10	Luton T	46	17	10	19	66	67	61
11	Cardiff C	46	16	12	18	58	59	60
12	Southampton	46	13	19	14	49	50	58
13	Stoke C	46	17	7	22	54	63	58
14	Plymouth A	46	13	17	16	39	46	56
15	Ipswich T	46	14	14	18	53	66	56
16	Leicester C	46	13	15	18	51	59	54
17	BURNLEY	46	14	12	20	46	54	54
18	Hull C	46	12	16	18	49	55	52
19	Sheffield W	46	13	13	20	39	52	52
20	Derby C	46	10	20	16	53	67	50
21	Queens Park R	46	12	14	20	50	65	50
22	Crewe A	46	9	15	22	57	86	42
23	Millwall	46	8	16	22	35	62	40
24	Brighton & HA	46	7	17	22	39	71	38

2005-06

Manager : Steve Cotterill

Championship (17th)

	Date			Opponents	Result		h/t	Goalscorers/times	Opp. goal times
1	Aug	6	a	Crewe A	L	1-2	0-1	Noel-Williams 67	44, 89
2		9	h	SHEFFIELD U	L	1-2	0-2	Akinbiyi 72	5, 40
3		13	h	COVENTRY C	W	4-0	2-0	G.O'Connor 28, Thomas 37, Akinbiyi (2) 87, 90	
4		20	a	Watford	L	1-3	1-2	G.O'Connor 16p	11, 30, 83
5		27	h	DERBY C	D	2-2	0-1	Akinbiyi 46, Noel-Williams 53	30, 90
6		29	a	Reading	L	1-2	1-1	Akinbiyi 42	7, 70
7	Sep	10	h	CARDIFF C	D	3-3	2-2	Elliott (2) 1, 23, J.O'Connor 89	8, 45, 72p
8		13	a	Preston N E	D	0-0	0-0		
9		17	a	Plymouth A	L	0-1	0-0		46
10		24	h	BRIGHTON & H A	D	1-1	1-1	G.O'Connor 34p	25
11		27	h	IPSWICH T	W	3-0	1-0	J.O'Connor 33, G.O'Connor 72, McCann 87	
12		30	a	Wolverhampton W	W	1-0	1-0	G.O'Connor 23	
13	Oct	15	h	LEEDS U	L	1-2	0-0	G.O'Connor 60p	71, 75
14		18	a	Leicester C	W	1-0	0-0	Akinbiyi 64	
15		22	a	Crystal P	L	0-2	0-1		38, 78
16		28	h	HULL C	W	1-0	1-0	Akinbiyi 29	
17	Nov	1	h	MILLWALL	W	2-1	0-1	Dyer 76, Elliott 80	1
18		5	a	Luton T	W	3-2	2-1	Akinbiyi (3) 15, 31, 54p	43, 60
19		19	h	LEICESTER C	W	1-0	1-0	Spicer 40	
20		22	a	Leeds U	L	0-2	0-0		55p, 70
21		26	h	CREWE A	W	3-0	1-0	Spicer (2) 27, 68, Dyer 72	
22	Dec	3	a	Southampton	D	1-1	0-1	Akinbiyi 66	34p
23		10	a	Sheffield U	L	0-3	0-2		29, 34, 81
24		17	h	WATFORD	W	4-1	2-0	Branch 32, Harley (2) 42, 77p, J.O'Connor 79	62
25		26	h	STOKE C	W	1-0	0-0	Akinbiyi 56	
26		28	a	Norwich C	L	1-2	0-2	Safri 73og	16, 39
27		31	h	SHEFFIELD W	L	1-2	0-1	G.O'Connor 84p	5, 56
28	Jan	2	a	Queens Park R	D	1-1	1-1	McCann 10	45
29		14	a	Cardiff C	L	0-3	0-0		58, 60, 63
30		21	h	PRESTON N E	L	0-2	0-1		13, 86p
31		31	a	Brighton & H A	D	0-0	0-0		
32	Feb	4	h	PLYMOUTH A	W	1-0	1-0	Ricketts 24	
33		11	a	Ipswich T	L	1-2	1-0	Ricketts 45	62, 83p
34		14	h	WOLVERHAMPTON W	L	0-1	0-1		15
35		25	a	Coventry C	L	0-1	0-0		54
36	Mar	4	h	READING	L	0-3	0-1		10, 55, 90
37		11	a	Derby C	L	0-3	0-3		19, 29, 34
38		18	a	Stoke C	L	0-1	0-0		52
39		24	h	NORWICH C	W	2-0	1-0	Gray 18, Branch 51	
40		28	h	SOUTHAMPTON	D	1-1	1-1	Gray 9	1og
41	Apr	1	a	Sheffield W	D	0-0	0-0		
42		8	h	QUEENS PARK R	W	1-0	0-0	Gray 79	
43		15	a	Hull C	D	0-0	0-0		
44		17	h	CRYSTAL P	D	0-0	0-0		
45		22	a	Millwall	L	0-1	0-1		45
46		30	h	LUTON T	D	1-1	0-1	Lafferty 78	42

FA Cup

3	Jan	7	a	Derby C	L	1-2	1-1	G.O'Connor 29	18, 67

Final, Liverpool 3-3 West Ham U after extra time, at The Millenium Stadium, Cardiff, Liverpool won on pens.

League Cup

1	Aug	23	h	CARLISLE U	W	2-1	0-0	Duff 52, Akinbiyi 90	74
2	Sep	20	h	BARNSLEY	W	3-0	1-0	Lowe 28, Akinbiyi 52, Spicer 59	
3	Oct	25	a	Aston Villa	L	0-1	0-1		22

Final, Manchester U 4-0 Wigan A, at The Millenium Stadium, Cardiff.

Details of other first team games elsewhere.

Att.	Pos	Coyne	Sinclair	McGreal	Thomas	Branch	Elliott	J O'Connor	G O'Connor	Hyde	Akinbiyi	Noel-Williams	Lafferty	Jensen	Duff	McCann	Bermingham	Harley	Lowe	Spicer	Courtney	Dyer	L Grant	Karbassiyoon	Ricketts	Bardsley	Gray	Mahon		
8,006		G	D	D	D	D	M	M	M*	M	F	F	S*																	1
11,802			D*	D	D	D	M	M	M	M	F	F	S*	G																2
11,683	16			D	D	D	M*	M	M	M	F	F	S**	G	D	S*													2nd sub Lafferty for McCann	3
16,802	19	S**	D*			D		M	M	D	F	F	S*	G**	D	M	M													4
12,243	18	G		D	D	M		M	M	M	F	F*			D			D	S*											5
14,027	19	G		D	D**	M		M	M	M*	F	F			D			D	S**	S*										6
10,431	20	G	D^	D		M*	M**	M		M	F	F			D		S**	D	S^	S*										7
17,139		G		D		S*	M*	M		M	F	F			D			D	D	M										8
11,829	23	G		D		S*	M*	M		M	F	F			D			D	D	M										9
11,112	23	G*	S^	D^		M**		M	M	M	F	F		S*	D			D	D	S**										10
10,496			D			M		M	M	M	F**			G	D	S*	S**	D	D	F*										11
21,747			D	D		M		M	M	M	F**			G	D	S*	S**	D		F*										12
16,174	18		D	D		M*	S^	M	M	M	F	S**		G	D	S*		D		F^									2nd sub Noel-Williams for McCann	13
23,326			D	D			M*	M	M^	M	F	S^		G	D			D	S*	F**	S**									14
20,127	17		D	D			M**	M	M	M	F	S*		G	D			D		F*	S**									15
11,701			D				M**	M	M^	M	F	S*		G	D	S^		D	D	F*	S**									16
10,698			D				M^	M	M	M	F	S*		G	D**			D	D	F*	S^	S**								17
8,518	8		D	D			M**	M	M*	M	F	S*		G				D	S**	F	D									18
12,592	6			D			M**	M	M*	M	F				D	S*		D	D	F	S**		G							19
21,318			D	D			S*	M		M	F			G	D*			M	D	F**		M		S**						20
11,151	6		D	D*			S**	M	M^	M	F			G	D			D	S*	F		M**		S^						21
21,592	7		D			D	M	M	M	M	F	S*		G				D	D	F*										22
23,118	11		D	D		S**	S^	M	M**	M	F	S*		G	D^				D	F*		M								23
13,815	8		D	D	S**	F**	S^	M		M	F	S*		G	D			D		M*		M^								24
17,912	5		D	D	S*	M*	M	M		M	F	F		G	D			D												25
25,204	7		D	D	M**	S**	S*	M	S^	M	F	F^		G	D			D		M*										26
14,607	9		D	D*	S*	M**	M	M	S**	M	F	F		G	D			D^						S^						27
12,565	8		D	D	S**	S*	F**	M	M*	M	F			G	D	M		D												28
10,872	9		D	D	D	S*	F^	M	M**	M	F	S**		G		M*		D		S^										29
17,220	10		D	D	D*	F	M	M	M**	M^		F		G	S*			D		S^				S**						30
6,267			D	D		F	M*	M	M**	M				G	D	S*		D		S**					F					31
11,292	10		D	D		M	S*	M	M*	M		F		G	D			D							F					32
24,482	11			D	D	M*	S^	M		M		F**		G	D	S*		D		M^	S**				F					33
11,056				D		S*	D	M		M		F		G	D	M*		D		M					F					34
19,641	14		D			D*	M**	M^		M		S^	S**	G	D	M		D		F				S*	F					35
12,888	15		D	D	D		S*	M		M			F	G	F	M		D		M*										36
23,292	17		D^	D	D	S**	F	M*	M	M**				G	S^	M		D		S*					F					37
12,082	18				D	M^	S*	M	M*			S**		G	D	M**		D		S^					F	D	F			38
11,938			D			M^	M**	M					S^	G	D	M		D		S**					F*	D	F	S*		39
10,636			D			M		M**		S**			S*	G	D	M		D							F*	D	F	M		40
24,485	17		D			M		M						G	D	M		D		S*					F*	D	F	M		41
11,247	15		D	S^		M**	S*	M		S**				G	D	M^		D							F*	D	F	M		42
19,926	16		D	S*		M		M					F**	G	D	M		D		S**						D*	F	M		43
11,449	14		D	D		F		M		M			S*	G	D	M*		D									F	M		44
7,780	16		D	D*		M	S**	M		M				G	D			D		S*					F**		F	M		45
12,473	17		D			M**	S*	M	S**				F^	G	D	M		D		D					S^		F	M*		46
Appearances		7	36	33	12	29	23	46	26	39	29	17	3	38	39	15	1	41	10	22	1	4	1		12	6	9	7		
Apps as sub		1	1	2	4	8	13		3	2		12	8	1	2	8	3		6	12	6	1		5	1			1		
Goals (46)					1	2	3	3	7		12	2	1			2		2		3		2			2		3		1	og

Att.	Pos	Coyne	Sinclair	McGreal	Thomas	Branch	Elliott	J O'Connor	G O'Connor	Hyde	Akinbiyi	Noel-Williams	Lafferty	Jensen	Duff	McCann	Bermingham	Harley	Lowe	Spicer	Courtney	Dyer	L Grant	Karbassiyoon	Ricketts	Bardsley	Gray	Mahon	
12,713			D	D	S*	S**	F*	M	M	M	F			G	D**	M		D											3
Appearances			1	1			1	1	1	1	1			1	1	1		1											
Apps as sub					1	1																							
Goals (1)									1																				

Att.	Pos	Coyne	Sinclair	McGreal	Thomas	Branch	Elliott	J O'Connor	G O'Connor	Hyde	Akinbiyi	Noel-Williams	Lafferty	Jensen	Duff	McCann	Bermingham	Harley	Lowe	Spicer	Courtney	Dyer	L Grant	Karbassiyoon	Ricketts	Bardsley	Gray	Mahon	
5,114		G		D	D	D		M	M	M	F	F	S*		D*	M													1
4,501		G	S*	D		M		M	M	M^	F**	S**			D	S^		D	D*	F									2
26,872			D				M**	M	M		F	S*		G	D	M^		D	D	F*	S^			S**					3
Appearances		2	1	2	1	2	1	3	3	2	3	1		1	3	2		2	2	2									
Apps as sub			1									2	1			1					1			1					
Goals (5)											2				1				1	1									

2006-07

How quickly the fortunes of football management can change. One minute you are celebrating the award for Manager of the Month, the next your team is in freefall and about to post the worst run of league form in living memory.

Such was the tale of Burnley's 125th anniversary season, when the usual hope and expectation gave way to the unexpected, mind-numbing reality of a 19-game winless streak.

Nobody could have foreseen the four-month wait for an elusive victory.

And as was becoming the norm, the absence of the Clarets top goalscorer midway through the season played a huge part in the tailspin, albeit this time through an untimely injury to 10-goal Andy Gray.

Manager Steve Cotterill had again planned meticulously for the campaign, bedding in the likes of Gray and Alan Mahon at the business end of the previous season and adding to his numbers with Crewe Alexandra duo Steve Jones and Stephen Foster.

And the Clarets got off to a flyer, with Jones bagging a debut brace against QPR and Gray opening his account with an impressive winner at Leicester.

A hard-fought 1-1 draw at Sheffield Wednesday meant that Burnley sat proudly on top of the Championship three games in.

Things took a turn for the worse with their first defeat of the season at home to Wolves, and a disappointing first round Carling Cup exit to League Two Hartlepool.

Another defeat to newly-promoted Colchester made it three Turf Moor losses on the trot, but that ended in style against Barnsley thanks to Gifton Noel-Williams.

With Burnley 0-2 down early in the game, the gangly striker came off the bench to single-handedly inspire a second half fightback, netting his first goal in over a year just after the interval and going on to become the first Burnley substitute ever to net a league hat-trick in a remarkable 4-2 win.

Andy Payton remains the only other Claret to score a hat-trick as a sub, which he achieved in the League Cup against Hartlepool in 2000.

Inspired, the Clarets went on a roll and as October arrived Norwich City fell to another formidable performance, hammered 4-1 on their own patch at Carrow Road, in a game beamed live to the nation.

Hull City were the next to be swept aside and by the time the month ended with more impressive victories against Lancashire rivals Preston and Luton Town, Burnley were back up to third place.

A run of six unbeaten games caught the eye of Football League bosses and for the first time in his Burnley career, Cotterill won the coveted Coca Cola Championship Manager of the Month award.

The dreaded curse of the trophy failed to materialise as a last-gasp Chris McCann header against Ipswich kept Burnley flying high and just two points behind leaders Cardiff.

But the last unbeaten away record in the division finally fell in mid-November when Cardiff City won the battle to go top of the league with a 1-0 Ninian Park victory.

Wounded, Burnley lost two successive games to Birmingham and West Brom before bouncing back to winning ways against Leeds United at Turf Moor.

But the three points came at a great cost as free-scoring Gray, who scored the winner against his former club, fractured his foot in a late challenge that ruled him out of action for the majority of the remainder of the campaign.

And his absence cruelly coincided with the beginning of an unforeseen run of results that would blow apart Burnley's play off aspirations.

Fourth place following that victory, it was four whole months and 19 matches, including an FA Cup third round defeat at Premiership Reading in January, that turned a potential promotion campaign into a frightening brush with relegation. Throughout, it seemed the harder Burnley tried, the worst things became. Three defeats and three draws in December were initially considered little more than a blip.

The New Year's Day signing of Ade Akinbiyi, who cost £1m less than when he had crossed the Pennines one year earlier to join Sheffield United, meant Gray's sorry absence had been addressed. Surely normal service would be resumed. Sadly not.

Player of the Year Wade Elliott in full flight

January followed in the same vein, with just one point coming from three league outings against Southampton, Stoke City and Derby County.

February was a flop and March brought more misery. The shortest month dragged its feet, with two points gleaned from five games despite the unexpected return of Gray from injury.

And the shoots of a spring recovery failed to materialise as the Clarets suffered a fourth month of disastrous results.

When Southend scored a galling injury time winner, many supporters feared the worst and defeat at Preston the following week meant just two points kept the Clarets out of the relegation places.

A welcome return to Turf Moor therefore had Burnley fans billing the clash with struggling Luton Town as a classic six pointer, do or die, win or bust.
The Hatters lay second bottom of the Championship on the back of their own horrendous run, four points from safety.
Defeat was unthinkable, but Burnley had found the net just once in five games and the barren run went on following a dour goalless draw. Turf Moor was a restless place at the final whistle after the 19th attempt to register a victory fell flat.
There was understandable trepidation three days later when supporters braved another home game against Plymouth, who had recently exited the FA Cup following a brave run.
Cotterill was in no mood for a wake, however, and fists pumping and arms flailing, he emerged from the players tunnel with the intention of rousing the fans.
They, and in turn the players, responded – and how!
Thirteen minutes in Michael Duff headed in Wade Elliott's free kick and seven minutes later a recovering Gray, whose premature return to the side had not yet paid dividends, flicked the ball on for loanee Paul McVeigh to double the lead.
Steve Jones made it three before half-time and with the shackles now released Wade Elliott completed an incredible 4-0 scoreline by smashing the ball into the net.
The hoodoo was banished and the relief was tangible from all four corners of Turf Moor.
Cotterill later emphasised that he had retained confidence in his players during the winter of discontent, insisting the main problem had not been the overall play, but merely a chronic lack of goals.
But even the ever-scrutinising manager could not have expected his players to follow up their first three points since November with a stunning smash-and-grab raid on promotion chasing Birmingham the following weekend.
Cardiff City were soon unable to halt a hat-trick of successes and suddenly, all fears of relegation had been all but banished in a remarkable seven April days.
A defeat away to crisis club Leeds United did cause one or two more flutters, but all doubts were dispelled as the Clarets made it 15 points from 18 with comprehensive victories over Norwich City, the first and only league double of the season, and West Brom.
That meant Burnley could relax as they headed for a spine-tingling televised game at Sunderland.
Roy Keane's side had enjoyed the very reverse of Burnley's season, starting awfully and steadily improving to eye one more victory that would put them within touching distance of promotion.
Over 44,000 supporters flocked to the Stadium of Light with plans already being made for the Premiership, but Burnley gave the Champions-elect the biggest fright of their lives.
After the Clarets fell behind early in the game, Gray equalised with Burnley's first penalty award in 66 league and cup games, stretching back 16 months to New Year's Eve 2005.
Elliott then conjured up a quite stunning strike from distance to put Burnley ahead and threaten to spoil the party.
But the Black Cats rode their luck and, showing title form, hit back themselves to claim the spoils in a five-goal thriller.
Burnley had made their point, however. Determined to show that they were not the push overs their mid-season results

Top scorer Andy Gray celebrates one of his 14 goals

might have suggested to outsiders, they ended their 125th season sitting 15th in the Championship.
It was not the campaign everyone had hoped for.
It was certainly not a roller-coaster campaign that anyone could have predicted.
But in a division jam-packed full of former top-flight clubs, awash with far greater revenue streams and millions of pounds worth of controversial Premiership parachute payments, the Clarets were still in there fighting.
And in the modern era, that had been as much a mark of success as any longed-for promotion.

2006-07 - Championship

		P	W	D	L	F	A	Pts
1	Sunderland	46	27	7	12	76	47	88
2	Birmingham C	46	26	8	12	67	42	86
3	Derby C	46	25	9	12	62	46	84
4	West Bromwich A	46	22	10	14	81	55	76
5	Wolverhampton W	46	22	10	14	59	56	76
6	Southampton	46	21	12	13	77	53	75
7	Preston NE	46	22	8	16	64	53	74
8	Stoke C	46	19	16	11	62	41	73
9	Sheffield W	46	20	11	15	70	66	71
10	Colchester U	46	20	9	17	70	56	69
11	Plymouth A	46	17	16	13	63	62	67
12	Crystal P	46	18	11	17	59	51	65
13	Cardiff C	46	17	13	16	57	53	64
14	Ipswich T	46	18	8	20	64	59	62
15	BURNLEY	46	15	12	19	52	49	57
16	Norwich C	46	16	9	21	56	71	57
17	Coventry C	46	16	8	22	47	62	56
18	Queens Park R	46	14	11	21	54	68	53
19	Leicester C	46	13	14	19	49	64	53
20	Barnsley	46	15	5	26	53	85	50
21	Hull C	46	13	10	23	51	67	49
22	Southend U	46	10	12	24	47	80	42
23	Luton T	46	10	10	26	53	81	40
24	Leeds U	46	13	7	26	46	72	36

*** - Leeds United deducted 10 points for entering administration**

2006-07

Manager : Steve Cotterill

Championship (15th)

		Date			Opponents	Result		h/t	Goalscorers/times	Opp. goal times
	1	Aug	5	h	QUEENS PARK R	W	2-0	0-0	Jones (2) 59, 69	
	2		8	a	Leicester C	W	1-0	1-0	Gray 45	
	3		12	a	Sheffield W	D	1-1	0-0	J.O'Connor 82	67p
	4		19	h	WOLVERHAMPTON W	L	0-1	0-1		19
	5		26	a	Crystal P	D	2-2	1-0	Mahon 23, Lafferty 52	48, 74
	6	Sep	9	h	COLCHESTER U	L	1-2	0-1	Gray 88	26, 54p
	7		12	h	BARNSLEY	W	4-2	1-2	Harley 42, Noel-Williams (3) 57, 83, 90	21, 32
	8		16	a	Stoke C	W	1-0	1-0	Gray 1	
	9		23	h	SOUTHAMPTON	L	2-3	2-1	Jones 4, Gray 33	18, 54, 73
	10	Oct	1	a	Norwich C	W	4-1	2-0	J.O'Connor 32, Gray (2) 45, 64, Mahon 89	82
	11		14	h	HULL C	W	2-0	2-0	Duff 10, Noel-Williams 13	
	12		17	h	SOUTHEND U	D	0-0	0-0		
	13		21	a	Plymouth A	D	0-0	0-0		
	14		27	h	PRESTON N E	W	3-2	1-0	J.O'Connor 44, St.Ledger 82og, Gray 89	77, 80
	15		31	a	Luton T	W	2-0	2-0	Gray (2) 31, 36	
	16	Nov	4	h	IPSWICH T	W	1-0	0-0	McCann 90	
	17		11	a	Cardiff C	L	0-1	0-1		23
	18		18	a	West Bromwich A	L	0-3	0-3		5, 7, 45
	19		25	h	BIRMINGHAM C	L	1-2	1-1	McCann 4	15, 83
	20		28	h	LEEDS U	W	2-1	0-0	Noel-Williams 67, Gray 69	87
	21	Dec	2	a	Ipswich T	D	1-1	0-0	Lafferty 86	90p
	22		9	a	Coventry C	L	0-1	0-1		31p
	23		16	h	SUNDERLAND	D	2-2	1-0	Lafferty (2) 9, 52	80, 90
	24		23	h	DERBY C	D	0-0	0-0		
	25		26	a	Barnsley	L	0-1	0-1		30
Hyde's last game	26		30	a	Hull C	L	0-2	0-2		6, 23p
	27	Jan	13	a	Southampton	D	0-0	0-0		
Sinclair's last game	28		23	h	STOKE C	L	0-1	0-1		24
	29		31	a	Derby C	L	0-1	0-1		4
	30	Feb	3	a	Queens Park R	L	1-3	1-1	McCann 18	13, 55, 72
	31		10	h	SHEFFIELD W	D	1-1	0-0	Elliott 55	58
	32		17	a	Wolverhampton W	L	1-2	0-2	McCann 53	5, 40
	33		20	h	LEICESTER C	L	0-1	0-0		67og
	34		24	a	Colchester U	D	0-0	0-0		
	35	Mar	3	h	CRYSTAL P	D	1-1	1-1	Akinbiyi 38	15
McGreal's last game	36		13	a	Southend U	L	0-1	0-0		90
Branch's last game	37		17	a	Preston N E	L	0-2	0-1		33, 75
	38		31	h	LUTON T	D	0-0	0-0		
	39	Apr	3	h	PLYMOUTH A	W	4-0	3-0	Duff 13, McVeigh 20, Jones 38, Elliott 61	
	40		7	a	Birmingham C	W	1-0	0-0	Spicer 80	
	41		9	h	CARDIFF C	W	2-0	1-0	Jones 4, McVeigh 48	
	42		14	a	Leeds U	L	0-1	0-1		21
	43		17	h	NORWICH C	W	3-0	1-0	Akinbiyi 30, Gray 86, Elliott 89	
	44		23	h	WEST BROMWICH A	W	3-2	1-2	Gray (2) 15, 48, McCann 87	6, 8
	45		27	a	Sunderland	L	2-3	1-1	Gray 39p, Elliott 50	14, 54p, 80
	46	May	6	h	COVENTRY C	L	1-2	0-1	McVeigh 62	41, 55

FA Cup

				Opponents	Result		h/t	Goalscorers/times	Opp. goal times
3	Jan	8	a	Reading	L	2-3	0-2	Akinbiyi 69, G.O'Connor 90	27, 37, 55

Final, Chelsea 1-0 Manchester U after extra time, at Wembley.

League Cup

				Opponents	Result		h/t	Goalscorers/times	Opp. goal times
1	Aug	22	h	HARTLEPOOL U	L	0-1	0-0		78p

Final, Chelsea 2-1 Arsenal, at The Millenium Stadium, Cardiff.

Details of other first team games elsewhere.

Att.	Pos	Jensen	Sinclair	Thomas	Duff	Harley	Mahon	McCann	J O'Connor	Jones	Gray	Lafferty	Hyde	Elliott	G O'Connor	Foster	Noel-Williams	McGreal	Branch	Spicer	Coyne	Pollitt	Djemba-Djem.	Akinbiyi	Gudjonsson	Caldwell	Coughlan	McVeigh		
12,190		G	D	D	D	D	M^	M	M*	M	F	F**	S*	S**	S^															1
19,035		G	D	D	D	D	M**	M	S*	M	F^	S**	M	F*		S^														2
22,425	2	G	D	D	D	D	M*	M	S**	M^	F	S*	M	F**		S^														3
12,245	7	G	D	D	D	D	M^	M	S*	M		F	M*	F**		S^	S**													4
16,396	6	G	D		D	D	M		M	M**	F	F^	M			S*	S^	D*	S**											5
10,039	11	G	D^	D	S^	D	M		M	M*	F	F**	M	S**			S*	D												6
10,304	6	G		D	D	D	M*	S**	M	M**	F	S^	M	F			S*	D											3rd sub Lafferty for N-Williams	7
12,247	3	G	S**	D	D	D		S*	M	M^	F	S^	M	M**			F*	D												8
13,051	7	G	S*	D	D	D	S^	S**	M	M**	F		M^	M*			F	D												9
24,717	3	G	D		D	D	S*	S**	M	M**	F	S^	M	M*			F^	D												10
11,530	2	G	D		D	D	S*	S^	M	M**	F		M^	M*	S**		F	D												11
10,461	5	G	D		D	D	S^		M	M^	F		M	M**	S**	S*	F	D*												12
12,817	4	G	D		D	D	S**		M	M	F	S*	M	M**		D	F*													13
14,871	4	G	D	D**	D	D	S^		M	M	F	S*	M	M^		S**	F*													14
7,664	3	G	D		D	D		S*	M	M*	F	F	M	M		D														15
11,709	3	G	D		D	D	S*	D	M	M**	F	S^	M	M*			F^			S**										16
15,744	4	G	D	D	D	D	S*	M	M	M	F	S**		M*			F**													17
18,707	4	G	D	D	D	D**	S*	M	M	M	F	S^	S**	M*			F^													18
12,889	5	G		D	D	D	S**	M**	M	M	F	S*	M			D	F*													19
15,061	4			D	D	D	S**	S*	M	M	F^	S^	M*	M**			F	D			G									20
22,254	6		S**	D	D	D		M	M	M**		F	S*	M*			F	D			G									21
18,362	7			D	D	D	S**	M	M**	M^		F		M*		S^	F	D	S*		G									22
14,798	9			D	D		M	D		M		F	M	M*			F**	D	S**	S*	G									23
12,825	9	S*		D	D	D		M	M	M		F		M		D	F				G*									24
12,842	10	G		D	D	D*	S**	M	M	M^		F**	S*	M	S^	D	F													25
17,731	11	G		D	D	D*	S^	M^	M**	F		S**	M	M		D	F	S*												26
20,486	13			D	D	D		M	M			F		M				D				G	M	F						27
12,109	13		D	D	D	D		M*	M			S*		M^	S^		F					G	M**	F	S**					28
23,122	15			D*	D	D^	S**	S^	M			F		M**		S*		D				G	M	F	M					29
10,811	15				D	D	M**	M	M	S**	S*	F				D^		D				G		F	M*	S^				30
12,745	14				D	D		S^	M	M^	F*	S*		M				D			G		S**	F	M**	D				31
19,521	15				D^	D		S*	M	M**	F	S**		M		S^		D			G			F	M*	D				32
10,274	16			D		D^		M	M	S*	F	S^		M*				D			G		S**	F	M**	D				33
4,934	17			D*	S*	S^		D^	M		F	M		M**				D	S**		G			F	M	D				34
10,659	18				D	D		M*	M	S*	F**			M	S**			D			G			F	M	D				35
8,855	18				D	D		M	M		F	S**		M		S*		D*		S^	G			F	M**	D			3rd sub Spicer for Foster	36
17,666	18				D	D		D	M**	F		M		M					S*	S**	G		M	F		D*				37
11,088	19	G		D		D		M	S**	M**	F	S*			S^								M	F*		D	D	M^		38
9,793	18	G		D	D	D		S*	M*	M	F^			M**	S**								M	S^		D		F		39
28,777	17	G		D	D	D			M	M**	F^			M						S*			M	S^		D	S**	F*		40
11,347	17	G		D	D	D		S*	M	M	F^			M**						S^			M	S**		D		F*		41
23,528	17	G		D	D	D			M**	M	F			M*						S**			M	S*		D		F		42
9,681	16	G		D	D	D		S**	M	M**	F^	S*		M						S^			M	F*		D				43
12,500	15	G		D	D	D		S*	M*	M	F			M^						S^			M	F**		D		S**		44
44,448	15	G		D	D	D		M*		M**	F			M^						S^			M	S**	S*	D		F		45
12,830	15	G		D	D	D	M*			S*	F			M						S^			M	F**	M^	D		S**		46
Appearances		30	16	33	42	44	10	24	39	37	34	15	19	40		7	19	21			12	4	13	15	9	16	1	6		
Apps as sub		1	3		2	1	15	14	4	4	1	20	4	2	8	10	4	1	5	11			2	5	2	1	1	2		
Goals (52)					2	1	2	5	3	5	14	4		4			5			1				2				3	1	og

	Jensen	Sinclair	Thomas	Duff	Harley	Mahon	McCann	J O'Connor	Jones	Gray	Lafferty	Hyde	Elliott	G O'Connor	Foster	Noel-Williams	McGreal	Branch	Spicer	Coyne	Pollitt	Djemba-Djem.	Akinbiyi	Gudjonsson	Caldwell	Coughlan	McVeigh	
	G		D		D	S**	M	M	M**		S*		M^	S^	D	F*	D						F					3
Appearances	1		1		1		1	1	1				1		1	1	1						1					
Apps as sub						1					1			1														
Goals (2)														1									1					

	Jensen	Sinclair	Thomas	Duff	Harley	Mahon	McCann	J O'Connor	Jones	Gray	Lafferty	Hyde	Elliott	G O'Connor	Foster	Noel-Williams	McGreal	Branch	Spicer	Coyne	Pollitt	Djemba-Djem.	Akinbiyi	Gudjonsson	Caldwell	Coughlan	McVeigh	
	G	S^	D	D	D	M^	M*	M	M	F	F	S*	S**		D**													1
Appearances	1		1	1	1	1	1	1	1	1	1				1													
Apps as sub		1										1	1															
Goals (0)																												

Players 1882 to 1888

This section lists players who are known to have appeared for Burnley FC during the period between August 1882 and June 1888. Burnley played around 300 games in those first six seasons, mostly "friendlies", but unfortunately many team line-ups went unrecorded. Some players, although not many, would have appeared in more than a hundred games, others would have been a first team regular for perhaps just a single season, or for a dozen games, and many others would have turned out just once.
Some of the names shown here will also appear in the record of players who appeared in League football from September 1888.
All played some part in the formative years of Burnley Football Club.

Abrahams	Jack
Arthurs	
Aspden	
Avery	George
Balshaw	
Barlow	
Bateson	
Beattie	Jack
Beverley	J
Birley	Arthur
Birnie	
Birtwistle	
Bone	
Bradshaw	Harry
Brown	J
Brown	William
Bryce	Tom
Bury	T
Bury	William H
Caulfield	Dan
Chase	R.B.
Clegg	
Clegg	G
Conway	
Crabtree	
Crawford	
Crombie	
Cross	Tom
Culpan	Harry
Dewhurst	Tom
Dobson	
Dowds	
Drummond	
Duckworth	John
Duckworth	
Eastwood	Charles W
Edwards	
Elston	Robert
Forrest	James
French	Tom
Friel	Dannie
Fulton	C
Gair	Jack
Gair	W
Gallocher	Pat
Gemmell	
Goodall	
Hargreaves	
Hargreaves	J
Hargreaves	Samuel
Harper	James
Harling	
Hartley	Joseph W
Hay	Tag
Heap	
Hind	
Hibbert	Jack
Holden	
Holker	
Horne	John Kay
Horsfield	
Haworth	John Henry
Howett	
Hunter	
Jackson	
Jacobs	
Jones	Alfred
Kay	Robert
Keenan	Jack
Kennedy	
Lang	Alex (Sandy)
Lathom	W.R.
Leighton	
Lofthouse	Joseph Morris
Logan	Peter
Lord	Simeon
Lucas	
McAleese	
McCallum	P
McClelland	
McClintock	Alex
McConnell	James
McCrae	Robert
McFetridge	William
McIntyre	Hugh
McKay	George
McNee	J
Mackereth	
Marshall	
Marsland	J
Metcalfe	Leonard
Midgeley	J
Midgley	Tom
Miller	
Moorhouse	W.H.
Newsome	
Parker	
Parkinson	
Pilkington	
Place	Walter (senior)
Poland	Fred
Ramsey	
Rawlinson	
Reid	
Robinson	Bethel
Ronaldson	William
Ross	Nicholas
Secker	Fred
Shields	Jack
Shorrock	
Slater	F
Smith	Harry
Smith	William S
Southworth	James
Strachan	Tot
Struthers	
Sugg	Frank
Sutcliffe	Charles
Suter	Fergie
Taylor	
Thompson	
Tillotson	H
Tomlinson	
Towler	F
Towneley	William
Trafford	
Turner	
Waddington	George C.
Waddington	J
Waddington	Samuel
Walkinshaw	
Walmsley	
Walton	Harry
Warburton	
Ward	
Waugh	David
Whitehead	
Whiteside	
Whittaker	
Whittaker	
Whittaker	
Whitworth	
Wigglesworth	J
Wilkinson	Jonathan
Wilkinson	Tom
Whittaker	W.J
Woods	James
Worthington	
Wrigley	
Yates	James
Young	J

Players 1888 to 1915

"Other" appearances are test matches and the FA Charity Shield of 1921
This section covers all players who made their League debuts between September 1888 and May 1915
It also includes players who just played in the FA Cup prior to September 1888.
Appearances and goals are grouped together for players with more than one spell at Turf Moor

		Born	Date	from/prev club	date	League		FA Cup		Other		Total		to/next club	date
						apps	gls	apps	gls	apps	gls	apps	gls		
Abbott	Walter	Birmingham	7 Dec 1877	Everton	May 1908	57	15	8	3			65	18	Birmingham	Aug 1910
Abrahams	Jack				Sep 1885	13	1	3	0			16	1	Bly Union Star	1889
Almond	James			Nelson	Nov 1896	1	0					1	0	Swindon T	Feb 1897
Arnott	James			Hapton	Oct 1897	12	0					12	0		1899
Ashworth	John			Lowerhouse	Aug 1888	2	2					2	2		1890
Aspden	Thomas E		1881	Kettering	Aug 1903	29	4	2	0			31	4	Brighton	Aug 1904
Atkinson	George	Appleby			Aug 1904	14	0					14	0		1905
Bamford	Thomas F	Horwich		Darwen	Apr 1909	137	0	20	0			157	0	Rochdale	Sep 1920
Bannister	William	Burnley	1879	Earby	Aug 1899	55	4	3	1			58	5	Bolton W	Nov 1901
			2nd spell	Leicester C	Aug 1910									Crewe A	May 1912
Barron	Fred	Stockton	7 Jun 1879	Stockton S M	Jun 1898	400	13	23	1			423	14	Released	May 1911
Bates	Charles	West Bromwich	1889		May 1910	15	5					15	5	Asst trainer	Aug 1912
Beard	Arthur H				Aug 1904	1	0					1	0		1904
Beddows	Jonathon H	Burton on Trent	1885	Manchester U	Jul 1907	16	7					16	7		1909
Bell	Arthur	Burnley	Nov 1882	Bly Belvedere	Feb 1902	101	28	3	1			104	29	Retired	1909
Bellamy	James	Barking	Oct 1881	Motherwell	Oct 1912	21	3	1	0			22	3	Fulham	Jul 1914
Beveridge	David			Albion R	Aug 1896	20	0	4	1	4	0	28	1	Grimsby T	May 1899
Birchall	Joseph				Jan 1902	12	1					12	1	Preston N E	Feb 1903
Birnie				Bly Wanderers	Sep 1886			2	0			2	0	Brierfield	1887
Black	David G		29 Mar 1896	Wolves	Dec 1896	12	5	1	0			13	5	Tottenham H	May 1897
Boden	Roland			Earlestown	May 1909	5	0					5	0	Witton A	Aug 1910
Bolton	William			Walk Mill	Apr 1915	1	0					1	0		1916
Booth	Jerry			Bly Belvedere	Oct 1903	1	0					1	0		1903
Bowes	William	Armadale	1870	Broxburn	Feb 1891	269	79	18	4	8	1	295	84	Released	May 1901
Boyd	Henry	Lanchester	1866	Sunderland Alb.	Aug 1892	4	1					4	1	West Brom	Oct 1892
Boyle	Thomas W	Hoyland	29 Jan 1888	Barnsley	Sep 1911	210	36	25	7	1	0	236	43	Wrexham	Apr 1923
Bradshaw	Ernest	Padiham	1887	Padiham	Jun 1911	8	0					8	0	Released	Apr 1914
Bradshaw	William	Burnley		Burton U	Jun 1907	11	1					11	1		1907
Brady	Arthur			Broxburn	Mar 1893	24	9					24	9	Released	May 1894
Brady	Alexander	Cathcart		Partick T	Aug 1888	20	7					20	7	Sunderland	Feb 1889
Brady	W			Renton	Dec 1888	9	2	2	2			11	4	Newcastle W E	1889
Brae	James				Aug 1896	6	0					6	0	Released	Nov 1896
Brewis	Robert		1885	Lincoln C	Jun 1908	2	0					2	0	Released	May 1909
Brierley	Herbert J				Mar 1899	2	0					2	0	Released	Apr 1899
Brodie	John C	Kilmarnock		Kilmarnock	Nov 1890	2	0					2	0	Kilmarnock	Mar 1891
Brown	David C				Aug 1896	4	0					4	0	Released	Nov 1896
Brown	Harry			Local juniors	Mar 1902	7	0					7	0	Released	Apr 1902
Brown	Jonathon	Clayton le Moors		Gt Harwood	Dec 1913	1	0					1	0	Wartime fatality	
Brown	Robert N	Cambuslang	Aug 1870	Bolton W	Mar 1897	4	1			4	0	8	1	on loan until	Apr 1897
Brunton	Matthew	Burnley	20 Apr 1878	Accrington	Aug 1901	30	8	2	0			32	8	Accrington	Aug 1902
Buchanan	Robert	Johnstone	1868	Sunderland Alb.	Aug 1892	40	12	2	0			42	12	Woolwich A	Sep 1894
Bury	William H	Darwen	1865	Padiham	Mar 1887	43	0	6	1			49	1	Nelson	Jun 1891
Caldow	G				Aug 1889	6	0					6	0	Released	Nov 1889
Campbell	J			Darwen	May 1889	14	3	1	0			15	3		1890
Campbell	T Fred	Burnley		Queens Park	Oct 1905	9	0	1	0			10	0	Queens Park	Nov 1907
Carr	Zacharious			Preston Hornets	Apr 1890	1	0					1	0		1890
Cawthorne	Rupert			Clitheroe	May 1906	24	0					24	0	Clitheroe	Aug 1907
			2nd spell	Clitheroe	Jul 1908									Released	Apr 1910
Chadburn	Joseph	Halifax	1885	Bradford C	Nov 1908	9	4					9	4		1910
Chadwick	W Edgar	Blackburn	1870	Everton	May 1899	31	10	1	0			32	10	Southampton	Aug 1900
Chambers	Thomas			Hearts	Oct 1892	26	9	2	0			28	9	Hearts	1893
			2nd spell	Hearts	Apr 1896									St Bernards	Jan 1897
Charlton	Thomas	Middlesbrough		Stockport C	Mar 1913	7	3					7	3	Blackpool	Nov 1913
Clarke	George				Mar 1909	3	0					3	0		1909
Collins	Henry	Wynlaton	1876	Hebburn A	Jun 1900	30	0	3	0			33	0	Queens Park R	Aug 1901
Cox	W			Hibernian	Nov 1888	26	0	2	0			28	0	Everton	Jan 1890
Coyle	B			Glasgow Hibs	Nov 1889	2	0					2	0	Released	Jan 1890
Crabtree	James W	Burnley	23 Dec 1871	Local juniors	1888	72	9	5	0			77	9	Rossendale U	Apr 1890
			2nd spell	Heywood	Aug 1892									Aston Villa	May 1895
Crawford	James	Stirling		Kings Park	Aug 1902	45	4	3	1			48	5	Colne	Jan 1904
Cretney	Jonathon	Workington		Newcastle U	Jun 1905	167	8	10	2			177	10	Gainsborough	Jun 1911
Crossley	Thomas H				1891	1	0					1	0		1891
Davidson	Andrew			Clyde	Jul 1905	47	10	1	0			48	10	Croyden	Aug 1907
Davidson	James	Edinburgh	25 Oct 1873	Celtic	Aug 1895	65	7	2	0			67	7	Lincoln C	Mar 1897
			2nd spell	Brighton U	Apr 1900									Released	Apr 1902
Dawson	Arthur	Rishton	1882	Nelson	Jul 1908	1	0					1	0	Accrington	Aug 1909
Dawson	Jeremiah	Cliviger	18 Mar 1888	Cliviger	Feb 1907	522	0	46	0	1	0	569	0	Coach/scout	1929
Dawson	Jonathon				Aug 1906	1	0					1	0		1907
Dickinson	H James	Padiham			Sep 1901	2	0					2	0	Padiham	Jan 1902
Dixon	Arthur	Barrowford	5 Oct 1879	Local juniors	Aug 1900	175	8	8	0			183	8	Tottenham H	May 1907
Dodd	Robert	Blackburn		Clitheroe	Aug 1910	5	0					5	0		1911
Dollins	J W	Fleetwood		Fleetwood	Apr 1909	8	0					8	0	Fleetwood	Sep 1910
Donaghey	Bernard				Jul 1907	5	2					5	2	Released	1908
Dougan	Patrick		1889	East Fife	Feb 1910	1	0					1	0	Released	Apr 1910
Drabble	Frank	Southport	8 Jul 1888	Nottingham F	Dec 1911	2	0					2	0	Bradford	Jun 1913
Driver	Fred				Aug 1900	17	2					17	2	Trawden	May 1903
Duckworth	Harry				Oct 1900	9	3					9	3	Released	Apr 1903
Duckworth	Robert W			Royal Swifts	Aug 1888	5	1					5	1	Rossendale U	Apr 1890
Duerden	John		1873		1890	3	0					3	0	Rossendale U	Aug 1891
Dunn	Thomas		1871	Wolves	Dec 1896	7	0					7	0	Released	Nov 1897
Edmondson	William			Briercliffe R	Jan 1903	2	0					2	0	Released	1903
Egan	T William	Chirk	1872	Ardwick	Feb 1894	10	2					10	2	Ashton	May 1895
Elston	Robert				Jun 1887		2	0				2	0	South Shore	1888

		Born	Date	from/prev club	date	League		FA Cup		Other		Total		to/next club	date
						apps	gls	apps	gls	apps	gls	apps	gls		
Espie	John	Hamilton	1868	Burnbank Swifts	Dec 1891	93	9	2	0			95	9	Manchester C	Feb 1896
Fairburn	James			Darlington	May 1899	1	0					1	0	Released	Mar 1900
Ferguson	William			Celtic	Mar 1897	33	7	2	1	2	1	37	9	Manchester C	Nov 1899
Freeman	Bertram C	Handsworth	Oct 1885	Everton	Apr 1911	166	103	23	12			189	115	Wigan B	cs 1921
Friel	Daniel			Accrington	Oct 1883	27	1	6	1			33	2	Nelson	Nov 1889
Fulton	C			Local juniors	1883			1	0			1	0	Released	1887
Galbraith	Hugh			Middlesbrough I	Nov 1891	5	2					5	2	Luton T	Nov 1892
Gallocher	Patrick	Johnston	1864	Padiham	Aug 1886	20	6	4	3			24	9	Accrington	Mar 1889
Goodison	Percy	Burnley	1891	Emmotts	Sep 1911	1	0					1	0	Accrington	Jun 1912
Goodwin	Fred				Nov 1906	1	0					1	0		1906
Graham	William				May 1891	24	3	2	0			26	3	Lincoln C	Apr 1893
Green	Benjamin H	Penistone	23 Feb 1883	Birmingham	Sep 1909	71	29	6	4			77	33	Preston N E	May 1911
Green	William	Gravesend	1882	Brentford	May 1903	147	0	6	0			153	0	Bradford	Dec 1908
Greenwood	Jonathon W	Todmorden		Local juniors	Jun 1905	11	0					11	0	Nelson	May 1906
Greenwood	Thomas			Local juniors	Aug 1899	1	0					1	0	Released	1899
Grice	Reuben	Ruddington	1890	Rotherham C	May 1914	2	0					2	0		1914
Gunton	Samuel	Norwich		Gainsborough T	Feb 1913	1	0					1	0	Armed Forces	1914
Haddow	David	Dalserf	12 Jun 1869	Motherwell	Dec 1895	38	0	5	0	4	0	47	0	New Brighton T	Aug 1898
Halley	George	Cronberry	29 Oct 1887	Bradford	Mar 1913	137	4	16	1			153	5	Southend U	Nov 1922
Hampson	Walker	Radcliffe	24 Jul 1889	Colne	Feb 1914	4	0					4	0	South Shields	Sep 1919
Hannigan	Richard			Woolwich	Dec 1899	8	3					8	3		1900
Haresnape	Robert	Blackburn	1866	Blackburn R	May 1889	27	8	1	0			28	8	Irwell Springs	Nov 1891
Hargreaves					1888			1	0			1	0		1889
Hargreaves	A				Oct 1894	3	0					3	0	Released	May 1895
Hargreaves	A				Nov 1905	1	0					1	0		1906
Hargreaves	Ellis			Local juniors	Dec 1892	1	0					1	0		1897
Harris	Joshua	Glasgow	5 Nov 1891	Ashfield	Sep 1901	57	5	5	0			62	5	Bristol C	May 1912
Hartley	Abraham	Dumbarton	8 Feb 1872	Woolwich A	Dec 1899	13	5					13	5		1900
Hartley	James			Sunderland	Nov 1896	1	0					1	0	Lincoln C	Mar 1897
Henderson	Robert			Bee Hole	May 1904	10	0					10	0	Clitheroe	Jul 1905
Heyes	L			Darwen	May 1889	11	2	1	0			12	2	Hyde U	Feb 1890
Heys	Stephen	Accrington		Colne	May 1906	1	0					1	0	Haslingden	May 1909
Hibbert	Jack	Darwen		Local juniors	May 1888	1	0					1	0		1889
Hill	James	Paisley		St Mirren	Dec 1889	151	37	11	5			162	42	Stoke	Jan 1897
Hillman	Jack	Tavistock	30 Jun 1870	Local juniors	1890	175	0	9	0	4	0	188	0	Everton	Feb 1895
			2nd spell	Dundee	Mar 1898									on loan until	May 1898
			3rd spell	Dundee	Oct 1898									Manchester C	Jan 1902
Hodgson	Edward	Chorley	1886	Chorley	Sep 1911	120	53	17	9			137	62	Deceased	Aug 1911
Hogan	Cornelius			Watford	Nov 1901	43	17	3	2			46	19	Released	Apr 1903
Hogan	James	Nelson	16 Oct 1882	Rochdale	Oct 1903	50	12	2	0			52	12	Fulham	Oct 1905
Holden	T H				Sep 1906	1	0					1	0		1907
Howarth					Sep 1886			1	0			1	0		1887
Howarth	William			Accrington	Dec 1899	14	0					14	0	Released	Apr 1903
Howarth	William				Feb 1908	9	0	1	0			10	0	Southport	Aug 1909
Husband	William	Kilmarnock		St Mirren	May 1912	39	7	6	0			45	7	Hamilton A	Aug 1914
Hutchinson	William			Alston	Aug 1904	1	0					1	0		1904
Jackson					Oct 1886			1	0			1	0		1887
Jackson	William			Barrow	Aug 1903	22	6	2	4			24	10		1904
Jeffrey	William	Dalderby	1868	Gainsborough T	Aug 1891	7	0					7	0	Woolwich A	Mar 1892
Jenkinson	William	Burnley		Local juniors	Jan 1897	50	12	4	2			54	14	West Ham U	Aug 1901
			2nd spell	West Ham U	May 1903									Colne	May 1904
Johnson	David			Barrow	Dec 1906	4	0					4	0	Released	Apr 1907
Johnson	E			Glentoran	Feb 1894	9	0	1	0			10	0	Glentoran	Apr 1895
Jones	S Clifford	Rotherham		Gainsborough T	Feb 1913	82	0	3	0			85	0	Accrington	Dec 1922
Kavanagh					1887	1	0					1	0	Nelson	Dec 1888
Kay	Robert				Aug 1884	5	0	2	0			7	0		1888
Kaye	Archibald	Glasgow	1869	Glasgow Thistle	Jan 1890	28	0					28	0		May 1891
Keenan	Jack	Clitheroe	1864	Clitheroe	Aug 1884	68	0	10	1			78	1	Retired	1893
Kelly	Robert	Ashton in Mak	16 Nov 1894	St Helens	Nov 1913	277	88	21	9	1	0	299	97	Sunderland	Dec 1925
Kenyon	Joseph			Failsworth	May 1906	29	0	1	0			30	0	Released	Apr 1907
King	George	Dunblane		Sunderland Alb.	Aug 1892	33	2	2	0			35	2	Millwall	Aug 1894
Lambie	Claude	Glasgow	1868	Glasgow Thistle	Jan 1890	29	21	2	1			31	22	Clyde	Mar 1891
			2nd spell	Highland Lt Infantry	Dec 1892									on leave for a month	
Lambie	William A			Hamilton A	Oct 1901	1	0					1	0	Released	Oct 1901
Lang	Alexander	Bridge of Weir	1864	Padiham	Sep 1885	123	2	11	1			134	3	Released	Apr 1895
Leake	Alexander	Small Heath	11 Jul 1871	Aston Villa	Dec 1907	81	2	9	0			90	2	Wednesbury	Jun 1910
Lee	Edward				Aug 1902	26	3	1	0			27	3	Released	Apr 1903
Lester	Edmund			Fleetwood R	Mar 1898	1	0					1	0	Released	May 1899
Lindley	Richard	Bolton		Oswaldtwistle	Mar 1908	137	42	15	4			152	46	Bradford C	May 1920
Lindsay	James	Stockton	1879	Newcastle U	May 1900	30	0	3	0			33	0	Bury	Apr 1901
Lindsay	James J	Glasgow		Glentoran	Jul 1914	74	18	6	3			80	21	Larne	Jul 1923
Lindsay	Neil		1875	Thornliebank	Apr 1895	2	0					2	0	Clitheroe	Oct 1895
Livingstone	Archibald	Bothwell	9 Nov 1877	Third Lanark	Mar 1893	169	3	8	0	4	0	181	3	Nelson	Aug 1900
Lockhart	George	Barrhill	1877	Bolton W	Mar 1900	93	0	5	0			98	0	Released	Aug 1903
Lomas	William	Pendleton	1891	Heywood U	Apr 1909	36	21	1	0			37	21	Bury	Feb 1911
Longair	William	Dundee		Sunderland	Nov 1896	12	0	1	0			13	0	Dundee	May 1897
Lovett	Jonathon			Local Juniors	Jan 1906	1	0					1	0		1906
Lowe	Luke	Wigan	1889	Eccles B	Dec 1911	1	0					1	0	Accrington	Feb 1912
Lowe	Robert H			Congleton	Jan 1904	3	0					3	0		1904
McCallum	Charles		1888	Workington	Dec 1910	4	0					4	0	Renton	Sep 1911
McColl	William	Drymen	1865	Morton	Dec 1889	9	2	1	0			10	2	Released	Mar 1890
McConnell	James			Padiham	Aug 1886	1	0	5	0			6	0	Brierfield	1890
McCrae	Robert			Vale of Leven	Sep 1884	2	0	5	0			7	0	Bly Union Star	Aug 1889
McEleny	Charles	Glasgow	6 Feb 1872	Celtic	Nov 1895	15	1	3	0			18	1	Celtic	May 1896
McFarlane	Dugald	Barrow	24 Aug 1880	Barrow	Aug 1903	121	34	4	0			125	34	Tottenham H	Jul 1908
McFetridge	William	Govan	1862	Padiham	Aug 1886	85	2	10	2			95	4	Retired	Nov 1892
McInnes	Angus			St Bernards	Mar 1898	38	4	2	0			40	4		1899
			2nd spell		Aug 1902									Padiham	Oct 1903
McKay	William	Edinburgh			Nov 1888	5	4					5	4	Newcastle W E	May 1889
McKnight	John			Darwen	May 1894	22	6					22	6	Released	Apr 1895
McLardie	Alexander	Paisley	1868	St Mirren	Mar 1890	43	24	4	2			47	26	Paisley A	Jun 1892

		Born	Date	from/prev club	date	League		FA Cup		Other		Total		to/next club	date
						apps	gls	apps	gls	apps	gls	apps	gls		
McLaren	William	Glasgow		Cowdenbeath	Dec 1910	63	0	10	0			73	0	Huddersfield T	Dec 1913
McLean	James T	Inverness	1881	Bradford C	Nov 1908	41	0	8	0			49	0		May 1910
McLintock	Thomas	Maybole		Kilmarnock	Aug 1893	233	15	13	0	8	0	254	15	Kilmarnock	Dec 1903
McLoughlin	William		1888	Darwen	Mar 1909	6	0					6	0	Released	May 1910
McMahon	Ross			Erin R	Nov 1888	2	0	2	0			4	0		1889
McMillan	William			Southampton	Jun 1898	3	0					3	0	Released	Mar 1900
McNab					Feb 1906	1	0					1	0		1906
McNab	William	Glasgow	1870	Glasgow N	Sep 1892	14	5	2	1			16	6	Woolwich A	Dec 1893
McVean	Malcolm	Jamestown	7 Mar 1871	Liverpool	Mar 1897	4	0			4	0	8	0	Dundee	May 1897
Mackay				Cambuslang	Dec 1888	9	2					9	2	Released	May 1889
Marr	Robert				Nov 1890	9	4					9	4	Released	cs 1891
Marshall	Thomas			Bolton W	Oct 1904	23	4	2	2			25	6		1906
Matthew	James	Dundee		Lincoln	Aug 1891	26	1	2	0			28	1	Accrington	Mar 1893
Mayson	Thomas	Whitehaven	8 Dec 1886	Walker C	Dec 1907	67	14	4	3			71	17	Grimsby T	Oct 1911
Midgley	Thomas			Burnley Rovers	Aug 1882	1	0					1	0		1889
Miller	John	Maryhill	1878	Birtley	Nov 1899	18	2	1	0			19	2		1900
Milligan	George	Glasgow	1891	Ashfield	Nov 1911	2	0					2	0	Clyde	May 1914
Minion	Fred			Bacup	May 1907	2	0					2	0	Released	May 1909
Moffat	Hugh	Congleton	Jan 1885	Congleton T	Jan 1904	201	13	13	0			214	13	Oldham A	Dec 1910
Mole	George	Stockton	1879	Newcastle U	Aug 1900	9	2	3	1			12	3		1901
Mooney	Joseph				Apr 1906	1	0					1	0	Released	Apr 1906
Morley	Jonathon B	Carlisle	1885	Sunderland	Jun 1908	96	15	12	2			108	17	Preston N E	Mar 1912
Morrison	Thomas		1874	Glentoran	Feb 1894	179	26	11	2	5	0	195	28	Glentoran	Sep 1895
			2nd spell	Celtic	Feb 1897									Manchester U	Dec 1902
			3rd spell	Manchester U	Aug 1906									Glentoran	1907
Mosscrop	Edwin	Southport	16 Jun 1892	Southport C	Jul 1912	176	19	21	1	1	0	198	20	Retired	Nov 1922
Mountford	Harry W	Hanley	1886	Everton	Apr 1911	28	10	1	0			29	10	Third Lanark	Nov 1913
Mudie				Dundee	Dec 1888	1	0					1	0		1889
Mullineaux	James E	Blackburn	1872	Lincoln C	Mar 1892	26	0	3	0			29	0	Burton W	Sep 1894
Munn	Stuart	Glasgow	22 Aug 1873	Third Lanark	Aug 1894	2	0					2	0	Grimsby T	Jul 1895
Murphy	Bernard			Duntocher	Jul 1905	6	2					6	2		1905
Murray	T			Dundee Harp	Oct 1889	7	1					7	1	Released	Feb 1890
Napier	Walter				May 1895	1	0					1	0	Released	Nov 1895
Nash	Joseph	Uxbridge		Uxbridge	Aug 1889	5	0	2	0			7	0	Nelson	Mar 1893
Nesbitt	William	Todmorden	1892	Portsmouth R	Sep 1911	172	19	19	1	1	0	192	20	Bristol C	Oct 1923
Newton	Frank L		1883	Bradford	Jan 1911	6	2	3	0			9	2	Released	May 1911
Nicol	Alfred			Stockton	Jun 1898	2	0					2	0	Released	Apr 1899
Nicol	Thomas	Linlithgow	1870	Mossend Swifts	Feb 1891	140	42	9	2			149	44	Blackburn R	Dec 1896
Nunnick	William	Colne	1877	Trawden F	Oct 1898	1	0					1	0	Nelson	1899
Ogden	Arthur	Burnley		Local juniors	Aug 1906	45	12	7	6			52	18	Bacup	Sep 1910
O'Rourke	Peter	Newmilns	22 Sep 1874	Celtic	May 1897	18	1					18	1	Lincoln C	May 1899
Oswald	John	Greenock		Notts C	Aug 1890	15	1	1	1			16	2	Sunderland Alb	Feb 1891
Parker	Jonathon	Barrow		Barrow St M	May 1905	32	1					32	1	Bradford	Nov 1908
Parker	Samuel			Hurlford	Oct 1894	5	0					5	0	Southport C	Feb 1895
Parkinson	William				Feb 1901	2	0					2	0	Released	May 1901
Paterson	Thomas	Quarter	1874	Motherwell	Nov 1895	7	3					7	3	Released	Apr 1896
Patterson	T				Nov 1890	2	0					2	0	Released	Jan 1891
Picken	Jonathon B	Hurlford	1881	Manchester U	Dec 1911	18	10	1	0			19	10	Bristol C	Oct 1913
Pickering	William	Glasgow			Aug 1912	13	6	1	0			14	6	Wartime fatality	Nov 1917
Pinnell	Archibald			Chorley	Jun 1898	5	0	1	0			6	0	New Brompton	Jul 1899
Place	Walter junior	Burnley	1872	Local juniors	1893	172	32	9	4	6	0	187	36	Woolwich A	May 1900
Place	Walter senior	Burnley	22 Mar 1870	Local juniors	Oct 1886	116	6	9	3	4	0	129	9	Colne	1886
			2nd spell	Bly Union Stars	Apr 1890									Retired	1900
Poland	Fred			Dundee Harp	Apr 1888	9	5					9	5	Emigrated	Nov 1888
Porterfield	Alfred		1869	Kings Park	Apr 1895	2	0					2	0	Released	Apr 1895
Provan	John		1874	West Calder	Jun 1895	4	0					4	0	Released	Apr 1896
Reid	Robert	Newtongrange		Cowdenbeath	Aug 1910	84	0	5	0			89	0	Huddersfield T	Oct 1914
Reynolds	Jeremiah			Celtic	May 1895	107	0	9	0	8	0	124	0	Released	Apr 1900
Ridsdale	George				Aug 1901	3	0					3	0	Released	Apr 1902
Ridsdale	J				Aug 1888	1	0					1	0	Brierfield	1889
Riley	James E				Jan 1906	3	0					3	0	Released	May 1907
Riley	Richard	Padiham		Colne	Aug 1912	3	2					3	2	Third Lanark	Oct 1913
Robertson	Hugh	Wishaw		Millwall	Jun 1895	40	15	3	2	3	0	46	17	Lincoln C	Jun 1897
Robertson	Peter			Polton Vale	Apr 1895	1	0					1	0	Released	Nov 1895
Ross	Andrew	Hurlford	17 Feb 1878	Barrow	Sep 1904	24	2	2	0			26	2	Released	May 1905
Ross	Henry	Brechin	1881	Brechin Harp	Mar 1899	106	2	5	0			111	2	Fulham	May 1904
Ross	James D	Edinburgh	28 Mar 1866	Liverpool	Mar 1897	51	30	5	2	7	1	63	33	Manchester C	Feb 1899
Ryan	William				Sep 1892	1	0					1	0	Padiham	Nov 1894
Savage	James	Withnell	12 May 1876	Nelson	Apr 1899	36	11	5	0			41	11	Trawden F	Jun 1902
Sawers	Alexander			Clyde	Sep 1892	2	0	1	0			3	0		1893
Sawley	Alfred				1900	13	1					13	1	Trawden F	May 1903
Seeburg	Max P	Leipzig	19 Sep 1884	Leyton	Jul 1910	17	0	1	0			18	0	Grimsby T	Jun 1911
Sewell	W Ronald	Wingate	19 Jul 1890	Gainsborough T	Feb 1913	23	0	4	0			27	0	Blackburn R	Feb 1920
Short	William		1886	Bacup	May 1907	3	0					3	0	Nelson	Jul 1908
Smethams	J Charles	Congleton	1886	Congleton T	Sep 1907	60	4	9	2			69	6	Blackburn R	Aug 1910
Smith	Albert	Burnley		Local juniors	Oct 1905	105	21	2	0			107	21	Bradford	Nov 1908
Smith	Harry			Local juniors	1882			2	0			2	0		1887
Smith	Joseph			Keswick	May 1904	15	2	1	1			16	3		1905
Smith	Philip		1886	Chelsea	Sep 1910	7	0					7	0	Crewe A	Jun 1911
Smith	Richard	Workington	29 Oct 1877	Workington	Sep 1904	174	70	11	5			185	75	Workington	Jul 1910
Smith	William S	Haggate		Haggate	Oct 1885	7	0					7	0		1895
Snowden	Thomas H	Jarrow	1887	South Shields	Oct 1911	14	0	1	0			15	0	Released	Apr 1912
Spiers	Daniel	Ayrshire	1868	St Mirren	Dec 1889	27	1					27	1		1891
Splitt	Thomas	Lochgelly	1886	Cowdenbeath	Dec 1909	47	0	1	0			48	0	Halifax T	Jun 1913
Stewart	Alexander	Greenock	1869	Morton	Dec 1899	66	7					66	7	Everton	Dec 1892
			2nd spell	Northampton T	Aug 1901									Leicester C	Oct 1902
Stirling	James			Polton Vale	Apr 1895	2	0					2	0	Released	Oct 1895
Storey	Cuthbert W			Bly Belvedere	Jan 1903	4	1					4	1		1903
Sugden	Thomas				Dec 1901	7	0					7	0		1902
Sugg	Frank H	Ilkeston	11 Jan 1862		Aug 1885			3	0			3	0	Bolton W	Feb 1888
Sutherland	James	Inverness	1881	Inverness C	Dec 1899	11	1					11	1		1901

		Born	Date	from/prev club	date	League		FA Cup		Other		Total		to/next club	date
						apps	gls	apps	gls	apps	gls	apps	gls		
Sutherland	Malcolm			Darwen	May 1894	1	0					1	0	Released	Nov 1894
Swain	Joseph				Feb 1904	1	0					1	0		1904
Swainston	Henry	Richmond	16 Jan 1876	Darlington	May 1899	2	0					2	0	Released	Mar 1900
Swift	Henry	Accrington		Accrington	Apr 1910	64	2	4	0			68	2	Third Lanark	May 1913
Tait	William			Newton Heath	Aug 1888	5	5					5	5	Released	Oct 1888
Tatham	William	Burnley		Local juniors	Feb 1895	51	0	2	0			53	0	Nelson	Sep 1901
Tattersall	William			Heywood	1895	5	0					5	0	Nelson	Mar 1897
Taylor	David	Bannockburn	5 Aug 1884	Bradford C	Dec 1911	221	5	28	0	1	0	250	5	St Johnstone	May 1924
Taylor	Joseph	Burnley		Bacup	Nov 1893	323	12	21	2	8	0	352	14	Retired	May 1907
Thorpe	Levy	Seaham Harbour	18 Nov 1889	Blackpool	Oct 1913	72	3	7	2			79	5	Blackburn R	Feb 1920
Tillotson	Stephen	Brierfield		Blackpool	Aug 1909	9	0					9	0	Released	Oct 1911
Toman	Wilfrid	Bishop Auckland	1873	Victoria U	Dec 1896	63	30	6	1	5	4	74	35	Everton	Apr 1899
Towler	Edwin				Nov 1902	23	0	1	0			24	0		1904
Trainer	Stephen	Coatbridge			Jun 1906	3	0					3	0	Released	May 1907
Tranter	Richard A	Bolton	1894	Padiham	Jan 1914	5	0					5	0	Armed Forces	1914
Turnbull	Peter			Third Lanark	Mar 1893	46	21	2	0			48	21	Bolton W	Mar 1895
Valentine	Fred			Earlestown	Jul 1907	18	3					18	3	Accrington	Jul 1910
Walders	David	Barrow	1884	Barrow	Jul 1903	93	3	4	3			97	6	Oldham A	May 1906
Walders	Jonathon	Barrow		Barrow	May 1904	48	2	1	0			49	2	Oldham A	May 1906
Walker	John				Aug 1890	40	0	2	0			42	0	Clyde	Jul 1892
Warburton	T				Nov 1895	1	0					1	0	South Shore	Jun 1897
Watkins	William			Trawden	Jun 1898	44	7					44	7	Trawden F	Jun 1902
Watson	David			Annbank	Aug 1893	2	0					2	0	Released	May 1894
Watson	William	Birkdale	11 Sep 1890	Southport C	Mar 1909	346	18	33	2	1	0	380	20	Accrington	cs 1925
Waugh	David			Padiham	1886			2	1			2	1	Everton	Aug 1888
Weightman	David		1890	Baillieston	Dec 1909	4	0					4	0		1910
			2nd spell	Royal Albert	Nov 1911									Released	Apr 1912
Welsh	Fred			Bacup	Aug 1902	1	0					1	0		1902
Whitaker					Oct 1886			2	0			2	0		1887
White	E Thomas	Uxbridge		Uxbridge	Apr 1889	21	0	1	0			22	0	Retired	1890
Whiteley	Charles	Burnley		Local juniors	Jun 1905	3	0					3	0	Clitheroe	Aug 1907
Whittaker	Edgar			Bly Belvedere	Nov 1902	1	0					1	0		1902
Whittaker	Fred	Nelson		Local juniors	Mar 1905	60	21	1	1			61	22	Bradford C	Nov 1908
Whittam	Arthur			Local juniors	Oct 1903	4	1					4	1		1904
Wilcox	Herbert	Bolton	1884	Bury	May 1907	3	0					3	0	Released	May 1909
Wilde	James	Sheffield		Rotherham U	Jun 1914	1	0					1	0	Reading	Aug 1920
Williams	Henry	Bolton		Bolton W	Aug 1903	32	8	2	0			34	8	Manchester U	May 1904
Wolstenholme	Thomas			Bolton W	Jun 1907	38	0	1	0			39	0	Bradford	Jun 1908
Wood	Alfred	Workington		Blackpool	Jun 1905	5	1	1	0			6	1	Workington	May 1906
Woods	James				Jan 1885	1	0					1	0		1889
Woods	Jonathon	Workington	1889	Workington	Jan 1911	2	0					2	0		1912
Woodward	Harry		1887	Hednesford T	Oct 1908	3	0					3	0		1910
Woolfall	Thomas	Darwen		Darwen	Aug 1899	33	0	1	0			34	0	Bolton W	May 1900
Wright	Robert			Everton	Jun 1907	2	0					2	0		1907
Wynne	Fred	Todmorden			Jun 1902	10	0					10	0		1902
Yates	John	Blackburn	1861	Accrington	Aug 1888	29	7	2	0			31	7	Released	Apr 1894
Own goals October 1885 to April 1915							22		1				23		
Untraced goals October 1885 to April 1915							23		5				28		

FA Cup winners 1914
Back: Ernest Edwards (trainer), Tom Bamford, Ronnie Sewell, David Taylor,
Middle: Willie Nesbitt, Richard Lindley, Bert Freeman, Teddy Hodgson, Eddie Mosscrop,
Front: George Halley, Tommy Boyle, Willie Watson.

Players 1915 to 1919

During the four seasons of the First World War, September 1915 to April 1919
Appearances and goals recorded here are limited to the Wartime Football Leagues and the main knockout cup competitions
Many players were guest players from other clubs, shown where known, or just amateurs of varying ability
The Burnley players shown were first teamers, reserves or juniors.

	Club	1915-16	1916-17	1917-18	1918-19	TOTAL
T.Adamson	Crewe A		3	9-2gls		**12-2gls**
Atkinson				1	1	**2**
Aunger				1		**1**
T.Bamford	Burnley	34		1	2	**37**
Barber			10-2gls		1	**11-2gls**
Beech					1	**1**
J.Bellamy	Ex Burnley				2-1gl	**2-1gl**
G.Benson	Ex Burnley Res			3	2	**5**
Bertinshaw	Ex Stockport				2	**2**
T.Bibby					1	**1**
J.Birch	Blackburn R		2			**2**
W.Bolton	Ex Burnley		1			**1**
Booth	Stockport			1		**1**
T.Boyle	Burnley	32-8gls	21-3gls	1	9-2gls	**63-13gls**
E.Bradshaw	Padiham/Ex Burnley	1			1	**2**
Briggs				1-1gl		**1-1gl**
Broom			1			**1**
Broome	Soldier				1	**1**
J.Brown		11	1			**12**
W.Brown	Ex Burnley		1	1	5	**7**
W.Brownhill					3	**3**
Bullen					1	**1**
Burrell	Scottish youth				1	**1**
P.Cawtherley			1	1		**2**
G.Chapman	Blackburn R	3-3gls				**3-3gls**
Chatto	Birmingham Small Arms			1		**1**
J.Clarkson	Cliviger youth				18-1gl	**18-1gl**
W.Clarkson		1	2	1	3-1gl	**7-1gl**
Cliff	Soldier				1-1gl	**1-1gl**
Cocker	Blackpool		1			**1**
W.Cook	Oldham/Ex Bly cricketer		7-1gl			**7-1gl**
H.Cowgill					1	**1**
Cornthwaite	Ex Accrington S			9-1gl		**9-1gl**
A.Cowell	Blackburn R	5				**5**
B.Cross	Liverpool			1		**1**
Cunningham	Local amateur				7-2gls	**7-2gls**
J.Dawson	Burnley	34	28	3	13	**78**
Dickinson			1			**1**
Dixon	Ex Nelson				2	**2**
R.Duckworth	Blackburn R		1	1		**2**
Dunn				1		**1**
Duxbury	Local amateur			4		**4**
Edwards	Wigan youth			23-5gls		**23-5gls**
W.Ellis	Accrington S	4-1gl				**4-1gl**
Emmott	Local amateur				5	**5**
Ewart				2		**2**
W.Finney	Ex Accrington S			22	8	**30**
Floyd					1	**1**
B.Freeman	Burnley	11-6gls	16-5gls	18-9gls	31-19gls	**76-39gls**
Garnett	Local amateur			2		**2**
R.Glendenning	Bolton W		1			**1**
W.Grant					4-1gl	**4-1gl**
Green			1			**1**
Greenwood	Local amateur				4	**4**
G.Halley	Burnley	1-1gl	4-4gls			**5-5gls**
Halstead				1		**1**
Hampson				2		**2**
W.Hampson	Burnley	5-1gl			1	**6-1gl**
Hancock	Cliviger youth/Bly Res		5-4gls			**5-4gls**
C.Hargreaves	Soldier			1		**1**
H.Hastie	Padiham	7-3gls	34-2gls	30	1	**72-5gls**
Hayes	Preston N E			1		**1**
Hendry			3			**3**
Henshaw				1		**1**
T.Heslop	Bolton W		6	23-3gls		**29-3gls**
W.Hibbert	Newcastle U		4			**4**
J.Hillman	Burnley trainer	2		1		**3**
Hilton					1	**1**
A.Hinton	Crewe A			7		**7**
Hobson				11	1	**12**
E.Hodgson	Burnley	36-23gls	14-5gls	1-1gl	11-10gls	**62-39gls**
Hodgson				2		**2**
Jenkins	Local youth			1		**1**
G.Johnson	Atherton youth		14-4gls	8-1gl	15-3gls	**37-8gls**
R.Jones			1	18	2	**21**

	Club	1915-16	1916-17	1917-18	1918-19	TOTAL
W.Kellock	Plymouth A		21-14gls			**21-14gls**
Kelly	Everton Res			1		**1**
R.Kelly	Burnley	31-7gls	20-9gls	1	20-10gls	**72-26gls**
Kempster	Everton Res			1		**1**
Kite	Ex Accrington S				2	**2**
Lawson			1-1gl			**1-1gl**
A.Lee	Manchester youth				5	**5**
Lees	Ex Stockport			1		**1**
R.Lindley	Burnley	32-13gls	33-17gls	36	31-7gls	**132-37gls**
Littlefair					1	**1**
Lockett			4-1gl			**4-1gl**
W.Lomas	Ex Burnley				1	**1**
Lord			1			**1**
Lovatt				1		**1**
Lucas	Blackburn youth				1	**1**
McGuire					1	**1**
McLoughlin	Scottish youth				1	**1**
Malkin	Port Vale			1		**1**
Mallinson	Altrincham youth				1	**1**
Marr	Ex Burnley Res			2		**2**
W.Marrs	Ex Bradford C				1	**1**
W.Mellor	Newton le Willows youth				3	**3**
J.	Burnley Res	1		4		**5**
Monaghan				1		**1**
Moorcroft	Liverpool youth			1		**1**
E.Mosscrop	Burnley	25-5gls	1-1gl		9	**35-6gls**
W.Nesbitt	Burnley	25-19gls	19-1gl	9-1gl	20-2gls	**73-23gls**
Neston					1	**1**
A.Newton	Ex Manchester C			5	23-2gls	**28-2gls**
F.Newton				2	1	**3**
G.Newton				1		**1**
H.Newton	Local youth			1		**1**
W.Newton	Manchester C		2	5-1gl	19	**26-1gl**
Norman			2-2gls			**2-2gls**
P.Norris	Salford youth				1-1gl	**1-1gl**
O'Brien	Soldier/Padiham youth			3		**3**
J.Ormerod					1	**1**
M.Ormerod					8	**8**
J.Orr	Blackburn R	5-3gls				**5-3gls**
F.Pearson	Local Amateur				1	**1**
Percival	Local Amateur	1				**1**
G.Pickles	Worsthorne youth		4			**4**
Pollard	Ex Burnley Res			6		**6**
Pollitt	Army cadet			3		**3**
Pritchard	St Helens youth			1		**1**
C.Quinn	Hurst youth			2		**2**
Riley				1-1gl		**1-1gl**
K.Roberts			6-1gl			**6-1gl**
Robinson				1		**1**
W.R.Sewell	Burnley				1	**1**
H.Shaw	Ex Burnley Res				1	**1**
Sinclair	Todmorden youth				1	**1**
Smallwood	Birmingham Small Arms			1		**1**
A.Smith					1	**1**
L.Smelt	Rotherham		3	1	10	**14**
A.Spencer				1		**1**
H.Spencer	Acc. S/Lowerhouse cricketer			8		**8**
J.Spencer	Ex Burnley Res			5	1	**6**
T.Splitt	Halifax T				8	**8**
A.Stewart	Son of ex Burnley player		1			**1**
H.Stuttard	Soldier				2	**2**
Tattersall	Local amateur			3		**3**
A.Taylor	Manchester youth			1		**1**
D.Taylor	Burnley	33-1gl	1	1	2	**37-1gl**
H.Taylor					4	**4**
S.Taylor	Ex Huddersfield				1-2gls	**1-2gls**
W.Taylor	Nottingham youth				21-1gl	**21-1gl**
B.Thomas			3-1gl			**3-1gl**
Thompson	Oldham A			1-1gl		**1-1gl**
L.Thorpe	Burnley	3-1gl	3	4	1	**11-1gl**
S.Tillotson	Ex Burnley			8		**8**
R.Tranter	Burnley	1				**1**
D.Walders	Ex Burnley	1	1			**2**
A.Walmsley	Blackburn R	21-1gl				**21-1gl**
Wareing			11			**11**
H.Watson	Nelson		1			**1**
W.Watson	Burnley	30-4gls		2	12	**44-4gls**
A.Wellings	Salford youth			1		**1**
Whittaker	Padiham youth/soldier			1-1gl		**1-1gl**
W.Whittle					1	**1**
T.Wilcox	Exeter		3	3	1	**7**
H.Wilde			1			**1**
James Wilde	Burnley		13		8	**21**

	Club	1915-16	1916-17	1917-18	1918-19	TOTAL
Joseph Wilde			27	1		**28**
F.Willetts	Birmingham youth			1		**1**
Williams			1		1	**2**
Wood	Rochdale				1	**1**
E.Woods				32-4gls	1	**33-4gls**
R.Woods	Local collier			1		**1**
F.Woodward	Wigan youth		2-3gls	11-3gls		**13-6gls**
J.Yates	Accrington S		25-1gl		2-1gl	**27-2gls**
Own goals				2gls		**2gls**

Players 1919 to 1939

"Other" appearances are just in the FA Charity Shield game in May 1921
This section covers all players who made their senior debuts between August 1919 and April 1939
It also incorporates the full career records of all players who appeared both before and after World War 1, and both before and after World War 2
Appearances and goals are grouped together for players with more than one spell at Turf Moor

		Born	Date	from/prev club	date	League		FA Cup		Other		Total		to/next club	date
						apps	gls	apps	gls	apps	gls	apps	gls		
Adams	Edward F	Anfield	30 Nov 1906	Southport	Feb 1936	111	0	7	0			118	0	Retired	1943
Alderman	Albert E	Alvaston	30 Oct 1907	Derby C	Aug 1934	19	2					19	2	Released	May 1935
Anderson	Joseph	Bishopton	1895	Clydebank	Mar 1920	121	64	4	8	1	0	126	72	Clydebank	Oct 1923
Armitage	John H	Chapeltown	21 Aug 1897	Mexborough	May 1924	44	1					44	1	Oldham A	May 1926
Ashbridge	Kenneth	Burnley	12 Nov 1916	Local juniors	Oct 1935	1	0					1	0	Halifax T	Sep 1938
Ashcroft	Gordon	Lea	7 Sep 1902	Coppull	Nov 1925	1	0					1	0	Burscough	Aug 1927
Astin	James	Hapton	16 Aug 1900	Army	Sep 1921	13	0					13	0	Grimsby T	Sep 1923
Bassnett	Alfred	St Helens	10 Apr 1893	Eccles	Jun 1919	147	5	9	0	1	0	157	5	Lincoln C	Nov 1926
Beel	George W	Bracebridge H	26 Feb 1900	Chesterfield	Apr 1923	316	179	21	9			337	188	Lincoln C	Feb 1932
Bellis	George A	Kirkee, India	8 Jun 1904	Wolves	Dec 1932	86	0	5	0			91	0	Bournemouth	Jun 1935
Bennie	Peter	Larkhall	10 Jun 1898	Albion R	Jun 1923	36	7	7	0			43	7	Bradford C	Sep 1924
Bennion	S Raymond	Wrexham	1 Sep 1896	Manchester U	Nov 1932	31	0	4	0			35	0	Coach	Aug 1934
Billingham	Jack	Daventry	3 Dec 1914	Bristol C	May 1938	93	36	3	0			96	36	Carlisle U	Sep 1949
Birchenough	Frank	Crewe		West Ham U	Aug 1920	2	0					2	0	Released	Apr 1921
Blinkhorn	Fred	Bolton	2 Aug 1901	Horwich RMI	May 1925	15	0					15	0	Retired	May 1928
Bowsher	Stanley J	Newport	3 Oct 1899	Newport C	Jan 1929	82	2	3	0			85	2	Rochdale	Mar 1933
Boyle	Thomas W	Hoyland	29 Jan 1888	Barnsley	Sep 1911	210	36	25	7	1	0	236	43	Wrexham	Apr 1923
Bray	George	Oswaldtwistle	11 Nov 1918	Gt Harwood	Oct 1937	241	8	18	1			259	9	Coach	1952
Brocklebank	Robert E	Barnet	23 May 1908	Aston Villa	Mar 1936	121	33	7	5			128	38	Chesterfield	Sep 1945
Brophy	Thomas	St Helens	8 Jan 1897	St Helens T	Sep 1920	3	0					3	0	St Helens T	May 1922
Brown	George	Mickley	22 Jun 1903	Aston Villa	Oct 1934	35	24	6	3			41	27	Leeds U	Sep 1935
Brown	James	Motherwell	1907	East Fife	May 1927	228	5	13	0			241	5	Manchester U	Jun 1935
Bruton	Jack	Westhoughton	21 Nov 1903	Horwich RMI	Mar 1925	167	42	9	2			176	44	Blackburn R	Dec 1929
Burley	George M	West Ham	23 Dec 1900	Chester	Oct 1926	4	0					4	0	Colwyn Bay	Jul 1929
Carson	James	Clydebank	1912	Crystal P	May 1936	6	0					6	0	Alloa A	Aug 1937
Chambers	Robert	Newcastle	11 Dec 1899	Lincoln C	Mar 1922	4	0					4	0	Rotherham U	Jun 1923
Chambers	William T	Wednesbury	10 Aug 1906	Darlaston	May 1929	2	0					2	0	Released	May 1930
Chedgzoy	Sydney	Liverpool	17 Feb 1912	Everton	May 1933	5	1					5	1	Millwall	May 1934
Chester	Thomas H	Glasgow	7 Nov 1907	Bury	Mar 1937	51	1	3	0			54	1	Notts C	Jun 1939
Clacher	John	Kirkcaldy	1912	Altrincham	May 1934	30	1					30	1	Darlington	May 1937
Clarkson	William	Padiham	1891	Nelson	Aug 1914	2	0					2	0	Rotherham	Aug 1920
Clayton	James G	Sunderland	May 1913	Aston Villa	Oct 1938	16	10					16	10	Retired	1942
Comrie	Malcolm	Denny		Manchester C	May 1934	8	0					8	0	Crystal P	Jun 1935
Conway	Herman	Gainsborough	11 Oct 1908	Gainsborough	Feb 1930	81	0	6	0			87	0	West Ham U	Jun 1934
Conway	Thomas	Belfast		Willowfield	May 1928	3	0	1	0			4	0	Northampton T	Jul 1932
Cragg	Richard	Burnley	1893	Army	May 1919	15	5	2	1			17	6	Stockport C	Sep 1920
Crompton	Wilfred	Blackburn	1 Apr 1908	Blackburn R	May 1932	31	8	4	0			35	8	Gillingham	Jun 1934
Cross	Benjamin	Birkenhead	20 Aug 1898	Runcorn	Apr 1920	237	57	17	4	1	0	255	61	Retired	1928
Cunliffe	Arthur	Blackrod	5 Feb 1909	Middlesbrough	Apr 1937	9	0					9	0	Hull C	Jun 1938
Dawson	Jeremiah	Cliviger	18 Mar 1888	Cliviger	Feb 1907	522	0	46	0	1	0	569	0	Retired	May 1929
Devine	Joseph	Motherwell	8 Aug 1905	Bathgate	May 1925	114	27	7	2			121	29	Newcastle U	Jan 1930
Dixon	Ernest	Pudsey	10 Jul 1901	Halifax T	Mar 1924	3	0					3	0	Halifax T	Dec 1924
Dobinson	Harold	Darlington	2 May 1898	Durham C	Jan 1922	2	0					2	0	Queens Park R	Jun 1923
Dougall	Peter	Denny	21 Mar 1909	Denny Pace	Oct 1926	6	2					6	2	Clyde	Feb 1929
Dougall	William	Denny	25 Oct 1895	Falkirk	Feb 1926	60	1	3	0			63	1	Retired	1929
Douglas	George H	Stepney	18 Aug 1893	Leicester C	Feb 1921	5	0					5	0	Oldham A	May 1922
Douglas	Thomas A	Ayr	11 Sep 1910	Blackpool	Sep 1933	63	13	2	0			65	13	Witton A	May 1936
Down	William	Ryhope	22 Jan 1898	Doncaster R	Sep 1927	80	0	2	0			82	0	Released	May 1930
Downes	Percy	Langold	12 Sep 1904	Stockport C	May 1934	61	6	8	0			69	6	Oldham A	May 1936
Drinnan	James M	Harthill	28 May 1906	Luton T	Jun 1930	6	2					6	2	Released	Apr 1931
Drummond	Robert G	Dalmeny	1898	Bathgate	May 1924	3	0					3	0	Pembroke Dock	May 1925
Dryden	John	Broomhill	1911	Bristol C	May 1938	4	2					4	2	Peterborough	May 1939
Earle	Edwin	Newbiggin	17 Jun 1905	Nelson	Dec 1926	3	1					3	1	Boston U	Jul 1928
Edwards	Reginald T	Coseley	1912	Brierley Hill	Jun 1931	18	5					18	5	Walsall	Sep 1933
Emerson	William	Eniskillen	1891	Glentoran	Mar 1922	44	0	1	0			45	0	Glentoran	Sep 1924
Evans	James H	Rhyl	29 Dec 1894	Southend U	Apr 1923	20	0					20	0	Swansea T	Jul 1925
Fairhurst	Richard	St Helens	5 Sep 1911	Skelmersdale	Nov 1931	23	3					23	3	Hartlepools	Aug 1934
Fergus	Alexander	Kirkintilloch	1899	Bathgate	May 1924	38	0	3	0			41	0	Coventry C	Mar 1927
Fisher	John	Hodthorpe	4 Aug 1897	Chesterfield	Mar 1922	32	3	1	0			33	3	Chesterfield	Apr 1923
Fisher	Peter	Glasgow	1915	Watford	Jan 1937	23	2					23	2	Dunfermline	Aug 1939
Fitton	Frederick	Bury	1906	Adlington	May 1928	15	2					15	2	Oldham A	Jun 1930
Flack	Hugh	Belfast	1903	Crusaders	May 1927	3	0					3	0	Swansea T	May 1929
Fletcher	Charles A	Homerton	28 Oct 1905	Brentford	Feb 1936	62	21	3	1			65	22	Plymouth A	Nov 1937
Forrest	Alexander	Hamilton	2 Apr 1908	Bo'ness	Mar 1927	108	4	8	0			116	4	Chesterfield	Jun 1933
Freeman	Albert	Preston	21 Oct 1899	Leyland	Mar 1923	78	19	4	0			82	19	Swansea T	May 1929
Freeman	Bertram C	Handsworth	Oct 1885	Everton	Apr 1911	166	103	23	12			189	115	Wigan B	Sep 1921
Gallacher	William	Dalmuir		Renton	Jan 1920	4	0					4	0	Released	Mar 1920
Gardner	Thomas	Huyton	28 May 1910	Aston Villa	Apr 1938	39	3	1	0			40	3	Wrexham	Dec 1945
Gastall	John W H	Oswaldtwistle	25 May 1913	Bacup	May 1936	21	7					21	7	Accrington S	May 1938
Gee	Harold	Haydock	25 Dec 1895	Newton C	Aug 1921	5	0					5	0	New Brighton	Jul 1923
Gillatt	Ernest	Wensley		Clapton O	Sep 1923	1	0					1	0	Released	Oct 1923
Graham	William	Hetton le Hole	3 Oct 1914	Blyth S	Sep 1932	5	2					5	2	Bury	May 1935
Greenhalgh	John S	Bolton	1898	Leyland	Oct 1921	7	0					7	0	Barrow	May 1923
Haddow	Andrew	Glasgow		Greenock M	May 1927	1	0					1	0	Clyde	Feb 1929
Hall	John	Hetton le Hole		Hetton Juniors	Aug 1930	38	4	3	0			41	4	Released	1932
Halley	George	Cronberry	29 Oct 1887	Bradford	Mar 1913	137	4	16	1			153	5	Southend U	Nov 1922
Hampson	Thomas	Burg	20 May 1898	West Ham U	Dec 1925	6	0					6	0	Released	Apr 1926
Hancock	Edward	Rotherham	29 Mar 1907	Liverpool	Feb 1933	112	24	11	7			123	31	Luton T	Nov 1936
Hargreaves	Harold	Higham	3 Feb 1899	Tottenham H	Mar 1926	26	6					26	6	Rotherham U	May 1928
Harker	William	Brierfield	1911	Nelson	May 1931	24	6	2	1			26	7	Torquay U	Jun 1933
Hastie	Henry	Padiham		Local juniors	Jul 1919	7	0					7	0	Released	May 1920
Heap	Clifford	Burnley	14 Feb 1906	Juniors	Aug 1925	5	0					5	0	Thames	Jul 1930
Henderson	Robert		1910	Clackmannan	Sep 1929	1	0					1	0	Released	May 1930
Henderson	Willam L	Willington Quay	1905	Thames	Sep 1930	2	0					2	0	Released	Apr 1931
Heslop	Archibald	Durham		Annfield Plain	Dec 1927	24	4	1	0			25	4	Luton T	May 1930

		Born	Date	from/prev club	date	League apps	League gls	FA Cup apps	FA Cup gls	Other apps	Other gls	Total apps	Total gls	to/next club	date
Hill	John H	Hetton le Hole	2 Mar 1897	Plymouth A	May 1923	184	13	14	0			198	13	Newcastle U	Oct 1928
Hillam	Charles E	Burnley		Clitheroe	May 1932	19	0	2	0			21	0	Manchester U	May 1933
Hindmarsh	John S	Ashington	1913	Sheffield W	Jun 1935	39	1	2	0			41	1	Notts C	May 1937
Hornby	Ronald	Rochdale	13 Apr 1914	Stalybridge C	May 1934	123	16	12	3			135	19	Retired	1949
Hubbick	Henry	Jarrow	12 Nov 1914	Spennymoor	Mar 1935	58	1	5	0			63	1	Bolton W	Feb 1937
Hughes	Alexander	Hetton le Hole		Hetton Juniors	Aug 1931	3	0					3	0	Accrington S	Aug 1933
Hughes	Leonard	Edmonton	1899	Leyton	Dec 1924	28	1	2	0			30	1	Accrington S	Sep 1926
Hunt	Patrick	Glasgow		Hamilton	Nov 1928	8	0	3	0			11	0	Belfast C	Dec 1930
Hutchinson	Alexander	Musselburgh	1908	Bo'ness	Oct 1929	5	2					5	2	Blackpool	Oct 1930
Jackson	Thomas	Sunderland	1896	Sunderland W E	Feb 1920	1	0					1	0	Dundee	Jan 1921
Jeavons	William H	Woodhouse	9 Feb 1912	Chesterfield	Jun 1932	1	0					1	0	Accrington S	Jun 1933
Jenkins	Evan T	Ynyshir	28 Feb 1904	Lincoln C	May 1930	66	16	4	1			70	17	Lincoln C	Sep 1933
Jennings	Samuel	Nottingham	18 Dec 1898	Stockport	Jan 1932	6	2					6	2	Released	May 1932
Johnson	Robert E O	Fencehouses	25 Oct 1911	B Auckland	Sep 1934	78	0	7	0			85	0	Nelson	Aug 1949
Jones	S Clifford	Rotherham	13 Dec 1890	Gainsborough	Feb 1913	82	0	3	0			85	0	Accrington S	Dec 1922
Jones	Thomas W	Shrewsbury	23 Mar 1907	Oakengates	Nov 1930	94	24	5	0			99	24	Blackpool	Sep 1933
Kelly	John	Hetton le Hole	2 Mar 1913	Hetton Juniors	Oct 1930	30	12					30	12	Newcastle U	Apr 1933
Kelly	Robert	Ashton in M	16 Nov 1894	St Helens T	Nov 1913	277	88	21	9	1	0	299	97	Sunderland	Dec 1925
Kilcar	Stephen	Bo'ness	1910	Chester	May 1935	24	7	2	0			26	7	Bournemouth	Sep 1936
Knight	George	Bolton	12 May 1921	Holdens Temp	May 1938	9	2					9	2	Retired	1948
Knox	William			Bathgate	May 1927	23	0					23	0	Luton T	May 1930
Lancaster	Wilfred	Backbarrow	1904	Dick Kerr's	Dec 1924	4	0					4	0	Released	Apr 1925
Lane	John	Birmingham	29 May 1898	Cradley Heath	Dec 1920	5	0					5	0	Chesterfield	Jul 1923
Lawton	Jack	Bolton	1912	Manchester N E	Apr 1934	3	0					3	0	Altrincham	Jul 1936
Lawton	Thomas	Bolton	6 Oct 1919	Junior	Feb 1935	25	16					25	16	Everton	Dec 1936
Liggins	John G	Altrincham	26 Mar 1906	Leicester C	Nov 1935	4	1					4	1	Shrewsbury	Jun 1936
Lindley	Richard	Bolton		Oswaldtwistle	Mar 1908	137	42	15	4			152	46	Bradford C	May 1920
Lindsay	James J	Glasgow	1891	Glentoran	Jul 1914	74	18	6	3			80	21	Larne	Jul 1923
Lumsden	Frank	Sunderland	1914	Queens Park R	May 1937	1	0					1	0	Released	Apr 1938
McCluggage	Andrew	Larne	1 Sep 1900	Bradford	May 1925	204	22	9	2			213	24	Dundalk	Sep 1931
McGrory	Robert	Bishopton	17 Oct 1895	Dumbarton	Aug 1920	3	0					3	0	Stoke C	Apr 1921
Manns	Thomas	Rotherham		Eastwood WMC	May 1931	10	0					10	0	Manchester U	May 1933
Mantle	Joseph	Hetton le Hole	9 May 1908	Hetton Juniors	Mar 1926	50	22	2	0			52	22	Plymouth A	Mar 1931
Marshall	Jack G	Bolton	29 May 1917	Bacup B	Nov 1936	26	0	1	0			27	0	Retired	1948
Martindale	Leonard	Bolton	30 Jun 1920	Rossendale U	Jul 1937	69	2	4	0			73	2	Accrington	Dec 1951
Mays	Albert W	YnYshir	12 Mar 1902	Notts C	May 1930	2	0					2	0	Walsall	Jan 1931
Mee	George W	Bulwell	12 Apr 1900	Derby C	Sep 1932	18	3	3	2			21	5	Mansfield T	Jul 1933
Meechan	John S	Falkirk		St Mirren	Jul 1933	2	0					2	0	Falkirk	Sep 1933
Merrick	Charles	Pendleton		Walsden	Sep 1930	12	0					12	0	Swindon T	Jun 1933
Miller	Thomas H	Hamilton	1910	Oakengates	Apr 1932	5	1					5	1	Released	Feb 1934
Miller	William	Bainsford	1910	Everton	Oct 1936	74	18	3	1			77	19	Tranmere R	Nov 1938
Moorwood	Leonard	Wednesbury	1888	West Brom	Oct 1920	18	0					18	0	Weymouth	Oct 1924
Morgan	William	Burnley	16 Dec 1896	Juniors	Mar 1920	28	0	6	0			34	0	Released	Aug 1925
Morris	William	Llandulas	30 Jul 1918	Llandudno	Jan 1939	211	47	19	6			230	53	Coach	1952
Mosscrop	Edwin	Southport	16 Jun 1892	Southport C	Jul 1912	176	19	21	1	1	0	198	20	Retired	1923
Mustard	John	Bold on Tyne	1905	Preston N E	Mar 1933	15	4					15	4	Southend U	Dec 1933
Nesbitt	William	Todmorden	1892	Portsmouth R	Sep 1911	172	19	19	1	1	0	192	20	Bristol C	Oct 1923
Nevin	George W	Lintz	16 Dec 1907	Sheffield W	May 1935	26	0					26	0	Lincoln C	May 1937
Nisbet	Gavin		1906	Preston N E	Sep 1935	2	0					2	0	Accrington	Jun 1936
Norris	Patrick	Broughton		Salford	Aug 1919	2	0					2	0	Stockport	Aug 1920
O'Beirne	Joseph	Waterford		Stalybridge C	Aug 1923	5	0					5	0	Nelson	Jun 1924
O'Dowd	J Peter	Halifax	26 Feb 1908	Blackburn R	Mar 1930	65	8	2	0			67	8	Chelsea	Nov 1931
O'Grady	Harry	Tunstall	16 Mar 1907	Leeds U	May 1933	13	7	2	0			15	7	Bury	May 1934
Oliver	John	Gateshead	1915	Stoke C	May 1935	3	0					3	0	Released	Apr 1937
Page	Louis A	Kirkdale	27 Mar 1899	Northampton T	May 1925	248	111	11	4			259	115	Manchester U	Mar 1932
Page	Samuel	Blackheath	1901	Halesowen	Nov 1921	12	0	1	0			13	0	St Johnstone	Jan 1925
Pake	Ralph R	Tynemouth	1913	Newcastle U	May 1936	5	1					5	1	Released	Apr 1937
Parkin	George	Hunslet	20 Aug 1903	Halifax T	Mar 1924	125	2	3	0			128	2	Chester	Sep 1929
Pearson	John C	Dudley	14 Mar 1896	Cradley H	Feb 1921	1	0					1	0	Brentford	Aug 1923
Pinkerton	Henry	Glasgow		Port Vale	May 1936	3	0					3	0	Falkirk	Aug 1938
Pollard	Walter	Burnley	26 Sep 1906	Juniors	Sep 1924	20	4					20	4	West Ham U	Jun 1929
Prest	Thomas W	Darwen	1910	Darwen	Jan 1930	80	16	2	1			82	17	Brighton	Jun 1935
Rayner	Frank	Goldthorpe		Mexborough	Mar 1935	79	7	4	0			83	7	Notts C	Jun 1939
Readett	Harold	Darwen	1913	Hurst	May 1934	3	0					3	0	Wrexham	May 1936
Reid	Andrew	Aberdeen		Bo'ness	Mar 1927	3	0					3	0	Bradford	Jul 1928
Reynolds	Walter	Sheffield	24 Nov 1906	Leeds U	Jun 1932	19	3	1	0			20	3	Newport C	Jul 1933
Richards	Percy	Manchester	15 May 1905	New Mills	Feb 1926	9	8					9	8	Plymouth A	Jan 1928
Richardson	Arthur	Wigan	1914	Calderstones	Oct 1936	11	2	4	1			15	3	Chesterfield	Jul 1938
Richardson	George	Horden		Horden A	Aug 1920	9	5					9	5	Derby C	May 1923
Richmond	Gilbert	Bolton	2 Apr 1909	Clitheroe	May 1932	176	1	17	1			193	2	Released	Sep 1939
Roberts	Lawrence			Renton	Feb 1920	1	0					1	0	Hamilton	Feb 1920
Roberts	W Thomas	Handsworth	29 Nov 1898	Preston N E	Oct 1924	49	28	1	1			50	29	Preston N E	Jul 1926
Robinson	Alick	Leigh	17 Apr 1906	Bury	Oct 1933	204	8	17	1			221	9	Retired	1945
Robinson	James W	Ruyton		Durham	Aug 1923	4	0					4	0	Nelson	Jul 1925
Robson	William P	Newcastle	14 Jan 1908	Stoke	Oct 1937	10	2	2	1			12	3	Released	Apr 1939
Schofield	John	Waterfoot	1913	Bacup	Aug 1931	9	0					9	0	Accrington S	May 1935
Scott	R Alexander	Liverpool	29 Oct 1913	Liverpool	May 1933	57	0	8	0			65	0	Wolves	Feb 1936
Sellars	William	Sheffield	7 Oct 1907	Southport	Jul 1933	19	0	1	0			20		Bradford	Jun 1934
Sewell	W Ronald	Wingate	19 Jul 1890	Gainsborough	Feb 1913	23	0	4	0			27	0	Blackburn R	Feb 1920
Sims	Stephen	Bedminster	11 Dec 1895	Bristol R	Jul 1922	11	0					11	0	Weymouth	Jul 1924
Smelt	Leonard	Rotherham	7 Dec 1890	Gainsborough	Mar 1919	229	0	18	0	1	0	248	0	Barrow	Jun 1926
Smith	Ernest	Shirebrook	1912	Sutton Junction	Nov 1931	7	1					7	1	Released	May 1934
Smith	F Cecil	Marchwiel	30 Oct 1904	Stalybridge C	Jun 1932	106	48	13	5			119	53	Cardiff C	May 1936
Smith	Wilfred	Sheffield	28 Mar 1910	Blackpool	Sep 1933	29	0	2	0			31	0	Crystal P	Jul 1935
Smith	William S	South Shields	22 Oct 1903	Crystal P	May 1936	53	0	3	0			56	0	Accrington S	Jun 1939
Sommerville	George	Glasgow	1901	Hamilton	Jul 1926	118	0	6	0			124	0	Bristol C	Aug 1932
Spargo	Stephen	Burnley	29 Dec 1903	Juniors	Nov 1924	3	0	1	0			4	0	Nelson	Aug 1929
Stage	William	Edinburgh	22 Mar 1893	Bury	Jun 1928	25	1	3	0			28	1	Southampton	Jul 1930
Steel	John	Denny	Oct 1901	Hamilton	Nov 1925	145	5	7	0			152	5	Released	Apr 1931
Stein	James	Coatbridge	7 Nov 1907	Everton	Oct 1936	42	8	5	2			47	10	New Brighton	Jun 1938
Storer	Harry	West Derby	2 Feb 1898	Derby C	Feb 1929	52	5	2	0			54	5	Coventry C	May 1931
Storey	Thomas	Foulridge	23 Nov 1914	Nelson	Oct 1935	35	7	1	0			36	7	Accrington S	Sep 1938
Syme	Robert	Queensferry		Manchester C	Jul 1934	9	0					9	0	Dunfermline	Feb 1935

		Born	Date	from/prev club	date	League apps	League gls	FA Cup apps	FA Cup gls	Other apps	Other gls	Total apps	Total gls	to/next club	date
Taylor	Archibald			Cambuslang R	May 1937	3	1					3	1	Reading	Jun 1939
Taylor	David	Bannockburn	5 Aug 1884	Bradford C	Dec 1911	221	5	28	0	1	0	250	5	St Johnstone	May 1924
Taylor	Fred	Burnley	24 Feb 1920	Local juniors	Mar 1937	49	7	1	0			50	7	New Brighton	Jul 1948
Taylor	William	Southwell	1886	Notts C	Apr 1919	17	2	2	0			19	2	Oldham A	Nov 1920
Thompson	George	Ashington	1895	Bedlington U	Apr 1914	5	0					5	0	Rotherham U	Jun 1921
Thorpe	Levy	Seaham	18 Nov 1889	Blackpool	Oct 1913	72	3	7	2			79	5	Blackburn R	Feb 1920
Toll	Jack P	Bradford	7 Feb 1914	Bridlington	Nov 1935	20	9	3	3			23	12	Released	Apr 1939
Tonner	James	Glasgow	1900	Bo'ness	Oct 1924	37	2					37	2	Hamilton	Oct 1926
Tresadern	Jack	Leytonstone	26 Sep 1890	West Ham U	Oct 1924	22	0	1	0			23	0	Northampton T	May 1925
Twiss	James	Haydock	1897	Skelmersdale	Dec 1919	4	1					4	1	Wigan B	Jul 1920
Twist	Richard	Hindsford		Hindsford	Nov 1931	10	0	1	0			11	0	Preston N E	Oct 1932
Wadsworth	Samuel J	Darwen	13 Sep 1896	Huddersfield T	Sep 1929	7	0					7	0	Lytham	Dec 1931
Wallace	James	M of Campsie		Clyde	Jan 1929	39	8					39	8	Chester	Oct 1930
Wallace	Thomas H	Jarrow	1911	Sunderland	May 1933	61	1	6	0			67	1	Released	May 1936
Waller	William	Bolton		Nelson	Jul 1922	1	0					1	0	Scunthorpe U	Aug 1923
Warburton	Arthur	Bury	30 Oct 1903	Manchester U	Nov 1933	25	4	2	0			27	4	Nelson	Aug 1934
Waterfield	George	Swinton	2 Jun 1901	Mexborough	Oct 1923	371	5	23	0			394	5	Crystal P	Jun 1935
Watson	William	Birkdale	11 Sep 1890	Southport C	Mar 1909	346	18	33	2	1	0	380	20	Accrington S	May 1925
Weale	Thomas J	Merthyr	1911	Crewe A	Feb 1934	15	2					15	2	Released	May 1936
Weaver	Robert S			Altrincham	Dec 1930	6	0					6	0	Released	May 1932
Weaver	Walter	Birkenhead	9 Nov 1898	South Liverpool	Aug 1919	106	15	10	3			116	18	Everton	Dec 1924
Weston	John M	Halesowen	1904	Halesowen	Apr 1926	2	1					2	1	Northampton T	Jul 1928
Wheelhouse	Benjamin	Rothwell	23 Sep 1902	Halifax T	Mar 1924	13	0					13	0	Released	Apr 1925
Whitty	Ernest		1911	Skelmersdale	Dec 1931	2	0					2	0	Skelmersdale	Feb 1932
Williams	John	Pendleton	1901	Rossendale U	May 1924	4	2	1	0			5	2	Released	May 1926
Willighan	Thomas	Belfast	1903	Willowfield	Mar 1928	59	0	2	0			61	0	Retired	May 1934
Wood	William	Blackburn		Blackburn R	Mar 1933	7	0					7	0	Mansfield T	Jan 1934
Wood	William H	Mereclough	5 Apr 1910	Juniors	Apr 1930	32	0					32	0	Yeovil	May 1934
Woodruff	Arthur	Barnsley	12 Apr 1913	Bradford C	Jun 1936	271	0	21	0			292	0	Workington	Jul 1952
Own goals August 1919 to April 1939							15		1				16		

Football League Champions 1920-21
Back: Alf Bassnett, Len Smelt, David Taylor, Charlie Bates (Trainer), Jerry Dawson, Cliff Jones, Walter Weaver,
Middle: Billy Nesbitt, Bob Kelly, Joe Anderson, Benny Cross, Eddie Mosscrop,
Front: George Halley, Tommy Boyle, Willie Watson.

Players 1939 to 1946

Players records during the seven seasons of the Second World War, the period September 1939 to May 1946
Appearances and goals recorded here are limited to the Wartime Football Leagues
and the main knockout cup competitions. The FA Cup in 1945-46 is not included
Many players were guest players from other clubs, shown where known, or just amateurs of varying ability
The Burnley players shown were first teamers, reserves or juniors

	Club	1939-40	1940-41	1941-42	1942-43	1943-44	1944-45	1945-46	TOTAL
E.Adams	Burnley	13	6						**19**
Allen					1				**1**
Ancell								2	**2**
R.Attwell	West Ham							15-1gl	**15-1gl**
J.Bannister					2				**2**
Barker	Aston Villa				1				**1**
Batty						1			**1**
G.Bentley	Burnley	6	3	4	1	2			**16**
J.Billingham	Burnley	4-1gl							**4-1gl**
Birch	Notts C				1				**1**
Bowden	Arsenal							1	**1**
Bradford	Preston N E						12		**12**
G.Bray	Burnley	16	2	4	3	3	10	18	**56**
J.Bray	Manchester C							1	**1**
J.Breedon	Burnley							4	**4**
Brereton							1		**1**
R.Bright	Burnley		17-6gls	12-2gls	18-8gls	2-2gls	3-1gl		**52-19gls**
J.Brindle					2-1gl	1			**3-1gl**
R.Brocklebank	Burnley	25-9gls	36-17gls	37-19gls	20-2gls	33-16gls	38-14gls		**189-77gls**
Brooks							18-11gls	1-1gl	**19-12gls**
Bunker	Fulham							1	**1**
Burns						1-1gl	5-2gls	5	**11-3gls**
Campbell								1	**1**
Carter	Bury				1				**1**
J.Chew	Blackburn							25-2gls	**25-2gls**
Clarkson							1		**1**
J.Clayton	Burnley	4-5gls		1-1gl		1			**6-6gls**
F.Coates	Preston N E		14-6gls	2					**16-6gls**
H.Conway	Ex Burnley		15				1		**16**
Cook						1			**1**
Cooke	Fulham		5-4gls						**5-4gls**
C.Crawshaw	Exeter C				5-4gls				**5-4gls**
K.Crowther	Burnley						1	7-2gls	**8-2gls**
B.Crossland	Burnley			1	1		2		**4**
Deverall				1					**1**
N.Dougall	Burnley colt	4	13		1	3	1		**22**
G.Drury	Arsenal						6-2gls	9-2gls	**15-4gls**
J.Dryden	Burnley						5-4gls		**5-4gls**
Edwards							1		**1**
Edwardson						1			**1**
A.Emptage	Manchester C	1							**1**
J.Fairbrother	Preston N E		6						**6**
G.Foxcroft	Burnley							1	**1**
F.Gallimore	Preston N E						25		**25**
Gallon	Swansea T					2			**2**
T.Gardner	Burnley	25-1gl	36-1gl	36-10gls	31-7gls	36-12gls	38-15gls	14	**216-46gls**
J.Gastall	Ex Burnley			1					**1**
Geddes	Stockport C					6			**6**
Gibson				1					**1**
G.Haigh	Burnley							20-1gl	**20-1gl**
Hargreaves	Burnley					1			**1**
Harrison				6				2	**8**
J.Hays	Burnley	1						23-8gls	**24-8gls**
T.Henderson	Burnley						3		**3**
T.Hetherington	Ex Burnley	1							**1**
Hobson								5	**5**
Hodgeon	Burnley						1	2	**3**
O.Hold	Aldershot							8-4gls	**8-4gls**
G.Holdcroft	Preston N E		5	27	31				**63**
K.Holden	Burnley				1	3	6		**10**
Holdsworth	Burnley						1		**1**
R.Hornby	Burnley	25-11gls	36-5gls	29-5gls	12-2gls	7-2gls		3-1gl	**112-26gls**
Horner						1			**1**
Horton	Aldershot				1				**1**
R.Hulbert	Bury	5							**5**
Innard								3	**3**
H.Jackson	Burnley		3	8-5gls	9-6gls	6-7gls	10-9gls	29-18gls	**65-45gls**
P.Jackson			1	1					**2**
W.Jeavons	Ex Burnley		1						**1**
R.Johnson	Burnley	1	2	3		4		26	**36**
Jones				1					**1**
G.Keighley					9	3			**12**
Kinghorn							12-6gls		**12-6gls**
F.P.Kippax	Burnley	1	25-16gls	22-13gls	4-3gls	8-1gl	13-2gls	24-9gls	**97-44gls**
N.Kirkman	Burnley		2	25	4		7		**38**

	Club	1939-40	1940-41	1941-42	1942-43	1943-44	1944-45	1945-46	TOTAL
G.Knight	Burnley	23-12gls	19-6gls	1	1	2			**46-18gls**
J.Knight	Burnley							2	**2**
Lawson				1					**1**
J.Lomax		3	14	15	8				**40**
Looms							2		**2**
J.Loughran	Burnley	3	17			1		11	**32**
McBain	Hamilton A							2	**2**
McCavana							1		**1**
W.McEwan	Queens Park R				1-2gls				**1-2gls**
McFarlane	Falkirk					2-1gl			**2-1gl**
McGahie						3			**3**
McIntosh		1							**1**
McNee	Rangers					1			**1**
Makin	Everton						3		**3**
Manning	Huddesfield T				7-2gls				**7-2gls**
Mansley	Preston N E					2			**2**
N.Marsden	Burnley		1	6	1				**8**
J.Marshall	Burnley	16	20			4	3		**43**
L.Martindale	Burnley	8	3-2gls	3	1		44-9gls	2	**61-11gls**
H.Mather	Burnley	26	35	1	3	16	16	35	**132**
Meek								3	**3**
Mignot	Burnley						1-1gl		**1-1gl**
Milner								3	**3**
W.Moir		1-1gl							**1-1gl**
H.Morton	Burnley	6							**6**
W.Morris	Burnley	3-3gls						22-12gls	**25-15gls**
Moss	Burnley						2		**2**
Mulvaney								3	**3**
Newsham	West Brom A				2				**2**
F.Nuttall	Bly Colt	2-2gls	2						**4-2gls**
H.O'Donnell	Blackpool				17-4gls				**17-4gls**
E.Owens								2	**2**
Patterson							21-8gls		**21-8gls**
H.Potts	Burnley		1			3-2gls	4-3gls	1	**9-5gls**
T.Prest	Ex Burnley			1					**1**
Readay	Leicester C					3			**3**
H.Readett	Ex Burnley			4	7				**11**
Reid	Queens Park R					19-3gls	1-1gl		**20-4gls**
Reynolds						1			**1**
G.Richmond	Ex Burnley			2					**2**
H.Riddeough	Blackburn R				1				**1**
J.Roach	Manchester U				1			1	**2**
A.Robinson	Burnley		14	20	24-3gls	21-3gls	17		**96-6gls**
N.Rose						1			**1**
H.Rudman	Burnley				15	28-2gls	14-3gls	18	**75-5gls**
Russell	Sheffield W					3			**3**
L.Salmon							3-1gl		**3-1gl**
Sagar				1					**1**
F.Sargent	Tottenham H					21-2gls			**21-2gls**
Scott	Preston N E					1			**1**
J.Shields	Celtic				1				**1**
Shorthouse					1				**1**
Shreeve								7	**7**
Sibley	Luton T					1			**1**
C.Sidlow	Wolves							2	**2**
Slingsby						1			**1**
G.Smith	Manchester C	1					3-1gl		**4-1gl**
T.Smith	Burnley	18		1	1	5			**25**
Sneddon								2	**2**
R.Snowden	Burnley		13	30	19	5-2gls			**67-2gls**
F.Soo	Stoke C							3	**3**
H.Spencer	Burnley	1				2	1	1	**5**
J.Strong	Walsall			2		30	41	30	**103**
C.Sutcliffe	Burnley			4					**4**
A.Taylor			1						**1**
F.Taylor	Burnley	12-5gls		3	1			1	**17-5gls**
H.Taylor							2		**2**
J.Taylor	Blackburn R				1	5			**6**
Tonge							2		**2**
R.Waddington	Burnley			9-3gls	14-6gls				**23-9gls**
Walmsley	Preston N E					2			**2**
F.Ward	Burnley			9	1	1			**11**
Watson					13	23-5gls	2		**38-5gls**
R.Webster	Sheffield U				19-1gl	25	36-1gl		**80-2gls**
H.Whalley				17-4gls					**17-4gls**
Whittaker							3		**3**
E.Wigglesworth					3			4	**7**
Wlkinson	Burnley colt		3-2gls						**3-2gls**
Williams						1			**1**
Wilson								15	**15**
J.Wood		6-6gls							**6-6gls**
A.Woodruff	Burnley	24	36	36	30	36	39	42	**243**
Wyles	Everton						2-1gl		**2-1gl**
Own goals				2gls	1gl	2gls		2gls	**7gls**

Players 1946 to 1976

See elsewhere for "other" competitions covered
This section covers all players who made their senior debuts between August 1946 and April 1976
It also includes all players who appeared both before and after World War 2 and incorporates the full career records of players who appeared before, and returned to Turf Moor after, May 1976

Sub appearances are shown in brackets

		Born	Date	from/prev club	date	League		FA Cup		FL Cup		Other		Total		to/next club	date
						apps	gls	apps	gls	apps	gls	apps	gls	apps	gls		
Adamson	James	Ashington	4 Apr 1929	Juniors	Jan 1947	426	17	52	1	3	0	5	0	486	18	Coach	Sep 1964
Aird	John	Glencraig	18 Feb 1926	Jeanfield Sw	Aug 1948	132	0	11	0					143	0	emigrated NZ	Sep 1955
Angus	John	Amble	2 Sep 1938	Juniors	Sep 1955	438(1)	4	45	0	25	0	12	0	520(1)	4	retired	May 1972
Appleby	James	Shotton	15 Jun 1934	Wingate W	Feb 1953	1								1		Blackburn R	Feb 1958
Attwell	Reginald	Oakengates	23 Mar 1920	West Ham U	Oct 1946	244	9	25	2					269	11	Bradford C	Oct 1954
Bellamy	Arthur	Blackhill	5 Apr 1942	Juniors	Jun 1959	204(13)	29	9	0	16	0	7(1)	0	236(14)	29	Chesterfield	Jul 1972
Billingham	Jack	Daventry	3 Dec 1914	Bristol C	Jul 1937	93	36	3	0					96	36	Carlisle U	Sep 1947
Binns	Eric	Halifax	13 Aug 1924	Goole T	May 1949	15	0							15	0	Blackburn R	May 1955
Blacklaw	Adam	Aberdeen	2 Sep 1937	Juniors	Oct 1954	318	0	44	0	12	0	9	0	383	0	Blackburn R	Jul 1967
Blant	Colin	Rawtenstall	7 Oct 1946	Rossendale U	Aug 1964	46(7)	7	2	1	7	1			55(7)	9	Portsmouth	Apr 1974
Bradshaw	Paul	Sheffield	2 Oct 1953	Apprentice	Oct 1970	11(2)	2	1	0	2	0	0(1)	0	14(3)	2	Sheffield W	Sep 1976
Bray	George	Oswaldtwistle	11 Nov 1918	Gt Harwood T	Oct 1937	241	8	18	1					259	9	Coach	1952
Breedon	Jack	Barnsley	29 Nov 1907	Manchester U	Oct 1945			1	0					1	0	Released	May 1946
Brennan	Ian	Easington	25 Mar 1953	Apprentice	Oct 1970	173(2)	11	10	0	13	1	14	2	210(2)	14	Bolton W	Dec 1980
Brown	Alan	Consett	26 Aug 1914	Huddersfield T	Feb 1946	88	0	10	0					98	0	Notts C	Oct 1948
Brown	Joseph	Cramlington	26 Apr 1929	Middlesbrough	Apr 1946	6	0							6	0	Bournemouth	Jun 1954
Brown	William	Falkirk	5 Feb 1950	Juniors	Feb 1967	0(1)	0							0(1)	0	Carlisle U	Jul 1969
Burke	Robert	Ballymena	5 Nov 1934	Albertville	Sep 1955	19	5	1	0					20	5	Chester	Jun 1958
Butterfield	Jack	Barnsley	30 Aug 1922	Tamworth	Feb 1946	3	0							3	0	Scout	Nov 1949
Buxton	Michael	Corbridge	29 May 1943	Juniors	Jun 1960	16(2)	0			1	0			17(2)	0	Halifax T	Jun 1968
Cargill	David	Arbroath	21 Jul 1936	Juniors	Jul 1953	5	0							5	0	Sheffield W	Sep 1956
Casper	Frank	Barnsley	9 Dec 1944	Rotherham U	Jun 1967	230(7)	74	11	5	22	9	5	1	268(7)	89	Coach	Feb 1976
Cheesebrough	Albert	Burnley	17 Jan 1935	Juniors	Jan 1952	142	35	16	5					158	40	Leicester C	Jun 1959
Chew	Jackie	Blackburn	13 May 1920	Blackburn R	Mar 1946	225	39	23	2					248	41	Bradford C	Jun 1954
Clarke	Alf	Hollinwood	23 Aug 1926	Crewe A	Dec 1948	24	6	3	1					27	7	Oldham A	Aug 1952
Cliff	Eddie	Liverpool	30 Sep 1951	Apprentice	Oct 1968	21	0			3	0			24	0	Notts C	Jul 1973
Coates	Ralph	Hetton le Hole	26 Apr 1946	Apprentice	Jun 1963	214(2)	26	12	1	22(2)	2	9	3	257(4)	32	Tottenham H	May 1971
Collins	Douglas	Newton	28 Aug 1945	Grimsby T	Sep 1968	172(15)	18	9	0	12(1)	0	7(1)	1	200(17)	19	Plymouth A	May 1976
Connelly	John	St Helens	18 Jul 1938	St Helens T	Nov 1956	215	85	38	15	7	2	5	2	265	104	Manchester U	Apr 1964
Corr	Pat	Derry	31 Mar 1927	Coleraine	Oct 1951	1	0							1	0	Released	May 1953
Cummings	Tommy	Castledown	12 Sep 1928	Stanley U	Oct 1947	434	3	38	0	6	0	1	0	479	3	Mansfield T	Mar 1963
Dixey	Richard	Leicester	2 Sep 1956	Enderby T	Dec 1974	3	0							3	0	Kettering T	Aug 1976
Dobson	J Martin	Rishton	14 Feb 1948	Bolton W	Aug 1967	406(4)	63	31	7	34	4	22	2	493(4)	76	Everton	Aug 1974
Dobson	J Martin		2nd spell	Everton	Aug 1979											Bury	Mar 1984
Docherty	Michael	Preston	29 Oct 1950	Apprentice	Oct 1947	149(4)	0	5	0	9(2)	0	5	1	168(6)	1	Manchester C	Apr 1976
Elder	Alex	Glentoran	25 Apr 1941	Glentoran	Jan 1959	271	15	39	2	11	0	9	0	330	17	Stoke C	Aug 1967
Elliott	William	Bradford	20 Mar 1925	Bradford	Aug 1951	74	14	8	2					82	16	Sunderland	Jun 1953
Fenton	Ronald	South Shields	2 Sep 1940	Juniors	Sep 1957	11	1			4	2			15	3	West Brom A	Nov 1962
Finn	Michael	Liverpool	1 May 1954	Apprentice	Dec 1971	4	0	1	0					5	0	Released	May 1976
Flavell	Bobby	Berwick	7 Mar 1956	Apprentice	Mar 1973			1	0					1	0	Halifax T	Feb 1976
Fletcher	Paul	Bolton	13 Jan 1951	Bolton W	Mar 1971	291(2)	71	16(1)	7	18	1	24	7	349(3)	86	Blackpool	Feb 1980
Flynn	Brian	Port Talbot	12 Oct 1955	Apprentice	Oct 1972	193(9)	19	18	2	18(2)	4	10	2	239(11)	27	Leeds U	Nov 1977
			2nd spell	Leeds U	Mar 1982											on loan until	Mar 1982
			3rd spell	Leeds U	Nov 1982											Cardiff C	Nov 1984
Foxcroft	George				1945			1	0					1	0	Released	May 1946
France	Garry	Stalybridge	5 May 1946	Stalybridge C	Apr 1966	1(2)	0			2	1			3(2)	1	Bury	Jul 1968
Furnell	James	Clitheroe	23 Nov 1937	Juniors	Nov 1954	2	0			1	0			3	0	Arsenal	Feb 1962
Gray	William	Durham	24 May 1927	Chelsea	Aug 1953	120	30	10	2					130	32	Nottingham F	Jun 1957
Haigh	Gordon	Barnsley	18 Aug 1921	Ransoms	Nov 1945	18	3	2	0					20	3	Bournemouth	Apr 1950
Hankin	Raymond	Wallsend	2 Feb 1956	Apprentice	Feb 1973	110(2)	37	6	2	12	4	9	4	137(2)	47	Leeds U	Sep 1976
Hapgood	Anthony	Kettering	13 Jun 1930	Blackburn R	Mar 1948	7	2							7	2	Watford	Jul 1953
Harris	Gordon	Worksop	2 Jun 1940	Firbeck C	Jan 1958	258	69	30	5	16	5	9	2	313	81	Sunderland	Jan 1968
Harrison	Raymond	Boston	21 Jun 1921	Boston U	Apr 1946	60	20	10	6					70	26	Doncaster R	Dec 1949
Hayes	William	Cork	7 Nov 1915	Huddersfield T	Feb 1950	12	0							12	0	Released	May 1952
Hays	Jack	Ashington	12 Dec 1918	Bradford	May 1939	146	12	8	1					154	13	Bury	Sep 1951
Henderson	Tommy	Burnley	1 Oct 1927	Juniors	Aug 1945	2	0							2	0	Released	May 1951
Holden	William	Bolton	1 Apr 1928	Trialist	Aug 1950	187	74	12	4					199	78	Sunderland	Dec 1955
Hornby	Ronald	Rochdale	13 Apr 1914	Stalybridge C	May 1934	123	16	12	3					135	19	Retired	May 1949
Ingham	William	Stakeford	22 Oct 1952	Apprentice	Nov 1969	181(30)	22	14(2)	1	12(1)	3	26	5	233(33)	31	Bradford C	Aug 1980
Irvine	Willie	Carrickfergus	18 Jun 1943	Juniors	Jun 1960	124(2)	78	9(1)	9	8(1)	8	3	2	144(4)	97	Preston N E	Mar 1968
Jackson	Harry	Blackburn	30 Dec 1918	Darwen	Dec 1940			2	1					2	1	Manchester C	Jun 1946
Jakub	Yanek (Joe)	Falkirk	7 Dec 1956	Apprentice	Dec 1973	203(2)	8	19	0	11	0	20	1	253(2)	9	Bury	Oct 1980
			2nd spell	Chester C	Aug 1988											Chester C	Jul 1993
James	Leighton	Llwchwyr	16 Feb 1953	Apprentice	Feb 1970	331(5)	66	17	2	22	8	23(1)	5	393(6)	81	Derby C	Nov 1975
			2nd spell	Queens Park R	Sep 1978											Swansea C	May 1980
			3rd spell	Newport C	Jul 1986											Released	May 1989
Johnson	Robert	Fencehouses	25 Oct 1911	B Auckland	Sep 1934	78	0	7	0					85	0	Nelson	Aug 1949
Jones	Peter	Ellesmere Port	25 Nov 1949	Apprentice	May 1967	2	0			2	0			4	0	Swansea C	Jul 1971
Jones	Rodney	Ashton	23 Sep 1945	Rotherham U	Mar 1967	9	0			1	0			10	0	Rochdale	Jun 1971
Joyce	Walter	Oldham	10 Sep 1937	Juniors	Nov 1954	70	3	8	0	7	0	4	0	89	3	Blackburn R	Feb 1964
Kennerley	Kevin	Chester	26 Apr 1954	Arsenal	May 1972	6	1							6	1	Port Vale	May 1976
Kindon	Steven	Warrington	17 Dec 1950	Apprentice	Dec 1967	175(10)	46	10(1)	2	14(2)	2	13	8	212(13)	58	Wolves	Jul 1972
			2nd spell	Wolves	Nov 1977											Huddersfield T	Dec 1979
Kinsella	Leonard	Alexandria	14 May 1946	Apprentice	May 1963	7(6)	0			0(1)	0			7(7)	0	Carlisle U	Sep 1970
Kippax	Peter	Burnley	17 Jul 1922	Juniors	1940	32	6	11	1					43	7	Liverpool	Jan 1949
Kirkham	Reginald	Ormskirk	8 May 1919	Wolves	Mar 1947	13	1	2	0					15	1	Released	May 1952
Knight	George	Bolton	12 May 1921	Holdens Temp	May 1938	9	2							9	2	Retired	1948
Knight	Jack	Bolton	12 Sep 1922	Juniors	Aug 1945	26	5	1	0					27	5	Preston N E	Dec 1948
Lancaster	Desmond	Burnley	16 Jul 1937	Juniors	Aug 1954	1	0							1	0	Darlington	Mar 1958
Latcham	Leslie	Stanley	22 Dec 1942	Juniors	Jun 1960	149(4)	10	6(1)	1	18(1)	0	5	1	178(6)	12	Plymouth A	Jul 1971
Lawson	Ian	Onslow	24 Mar 1939	Juniors	Mar 1956	23	7	5	8	2	0			30	15	Leeds U	Mar 1962
Lochhead	Andrew	Millgie	9 Mar 1941	Renfrew Juns	Dec 1958	225(1)	101	19	12	15	9	6	6	265(1)	128	Leicester C	Oct 1968
Loggie	David	Newbiggin	31 May 1957	Apprentice	Jun 1974	6(1)	0	0(1)	0	0(1)	0	2(1)	0	8(4)	0	York C	Jun 1978

Sub appearances are shown in brackets

		Born	Date	from/prev club	date	League		FA Cup		FL Cup		Other		Total		to/next club	date
						apps	gls	apps	gls	apps	gls	apps	gls	apps	gls		
Loughran	Joseph	Consett	12 Aug 1915	Luton T	Jul 1939	65	0	8	0					73	0	Southend U	Sep 1949
Lyons	Terence	Bradford	14 May 1929	Juniors	Oct 1949	12	3							12	3	Bradford	Sep 1951
McDonald	Colin	Tottington	15 Oct 1930	Hawkshaw	Oct 1948	186	0	15	0					201	0	Retired	May 1961
McIlroy	James	Lambeg	25 Oct 1931	Glentoran	Mar 1950	439	116	50	13	3	1	5	1	497	131	Stoke C	Mar 1963
McKay	Peter	Newburgh	23 Feb 1925	Dundee U	May 1954	60	36	6	2					66	38	St Mirren	Jan 1957
McLaren	Andrew	Larkhall	24 Jan 1922	Preston N E	Dec 1948	3	1	1	1					4	2	Sheffield U	Mar 1949
McNulty	Joseph	Dundalk	17 Jul 1923	Ards	May 1949	8	0							8	0	Sheffield U	Jun 1952
Marshall	Jack	Bolton	29 May 1917	Bacup B	Nov 1936	26	0	1	0					27	0	Retired	1948
Marshall	William	Bolton	11 Jul 1936	Distillery	Oct 1953	6	0			3	0			9	0	Oldham A	Aug 1962
Martindale	Leonard	Bolton	30 Jun 1920	Juniors	Jul 1937	69	2	4	0					73	2	Accrington S	Dec 1951
Mather	Harold	Bolton	24 Jan 1921	Juniors	May 1938	301	0	28	0					329	0	Nelson	Feb 1955
Mellor	Peter	Prestbury	20 Nov 1947	Witton A	May 1969	69	0	4	0	8	0			81	0	Fulham	Feb 1972
Meredith	Trevor	Kidderminster	25 Dec 1936	Kidderminster	Nov 1957	37	8			1	0			38	8	Shrewsbury T	Apr 1964
Merrington	David	Newcastle	26 Apr 1945	Apprentice	Jun 1962	96(2)	1	9(1)	0	13	0	5	1	123(3)	2	Bristol C	Jul 1971
Miller	Brian	Hapton	19 Jan 1937	Juniors	Feb 1954	379	29	50	4	13	1	13	3	455	37	Coach	Apr 1967
Milner	James	Newcastle	3 Feb 1933	Blyth S	Dec 1952	1	0							1	0	Darlington	Dec 1957
Morgan	William	Glasgow	2 Oct 1944	Juniors	Oct 1961	195(1)	19	13	1	15	2	8	0	231(1)	22	Manchester U	Aug 1968
			2nd spell	Manchester U	Jun 1975											Bolton W	Mar 1976
Morley	Anthony	Ormskirk	26 Aug 1954	Preston N E	Feb 1976	83(13)	5	3(2)	1	3(1)	1	2	0	91(16)	7	Aston Villa	Jun 1979
			2nd spell	West Brom	Oct 1988											on loan until	Nov 1988
Morris	Colin	Blyth	22 Aug 1953	Apprentice	Aug 1971	9(1)	0	0(1)	0			3	0	12(2)	0	Southend U	Jan 1977
Morris	William	Colwyn Bay	30 Jul 1918	Llandudno T	Jan 1939	211	47	19	6					230	53	Coach	1952
Murray	John	Newcastle	2 Mar 1948	Juniors	Mar 1965	20(2)	6			4(1)	4			24(3)	10	Blackpool	Mar 1970
Newlands	Douglas	Edinburgh	29 Oct 1931	Aberdeen	Mar 1955	98	21	6	2					104	23	Stoke C	Jul 1959
Newton	Keith	Manchester	23 Jun 1941	Everton	Jun 1972	209	5	14	1	14	1	16	0	253	7	Released	May 1978
Noble	Peter	Newcastle	19 Aug 1944	Swindon T	Jun 1973	241(2)	63	15	1	19	8	24	8	299(2)	80	Blackpool	Jan 1980
Nulty	Geoffrey	Prescot	13 Feb 1949	Stoke C	Jul 1968	123(7)	20	9	0	4(1)	1	8(1)	3	144(9)	24	Newcastle U	Dec 1974
O'Neil	Brian	Bedlington	4 Jan 1944	Juniors	Jan 1961	231(4)	22	18	1	21(1)	1	7	1	277(5)	25	Southampton	May 1970
O'Neill	William	Cork	29 Dec 1919	Chelmsford C	Jan 1949	1	1							1	1	Walsall	Jan 1951
Parker	Derrick	Wallsend	7 Feb 1957	Apprentice	Feb 1974	48(1)	12	3	1	2	0	1	1	54(1)	14	Southend U	Feb 1977
			2nd spell	Oldham A	Oct 1985											Released	May 1987
Parton	Jeffrey	Swansea	24 Feb 1953	Apprentice	Mar 1970	3	0							3	0	Northampton T	Jul 1975
Pashley	Terry	Chesterfield	11 Oct 1956	Apprentice	Oct 1973	16(2)	0					0(2)	0	16(4)	0	Blackpool	Aug 1978
Peyton	Gerry	Birmingham	20 May 1956	Atherstone T	May 1975	30	0	1	0	1	0	2	0	34	0	Fulham	Dec 1976
Pilkington	Brian	Leyland	12 Feb 1933	Leyland M	Apr 1951	300	67	33	7	3	1	4	2	340	77	Bolton W	Mar 1961
Pointer	Raymond	Cramlington	10 Oct 1936	Dudley W	Aug 1957	223	118	35	12	7	2	5	0	270	132	Bury	Aug 1965
Potts	Harry	Hetton le Hole	22 Oct 1920	Juniors	Nov 1937	165	47	16	3					181	50	Everton	Oct 1950
Price	John	Easington	25 Oct 1943	Horden CW	Nov 1960	21	2	1	0					22	2	Stockport C	May 1965
Probert	Eric	South Kirby	17 Feb 1952	Apprentice	Feb 1969	62(5)	11	1	0	2	0	2	0	67(5)	11	Notts C	Jul 1973
Robinson	Peter	Ashington	4 Sep 1957	Juniors	Jun 1976	48(7)	3	4	0	3	0	4	0	59(7)	3	Sp Rotterdam	Jul 1980
Robson	James	Pelton	23 Jan 1939	Juniors	Jan 1956	202	79	29	14	6	4	5	3	242	100	Blackpool	Mar 1965
Rodaway	William	Liverpool	26 Sep 1954	Apprentice	Sep 1971	245(2)	3	13	0	18	0	25	0	301(2)	3	Peterborough	Jul 1981
			2nd spell	Tranmere R	Aug 1986											Released	May 1987
Rudman	Harold	Whitworth	4 Nov 1924	Juniors	Dec 1942	71	0	4	0					75	0	Rochdale	Jul 1957
Samuels	Leslie	Oldham	8 Dec 1928	Juniors	Dec 1949	2	0							2	0	Exeter C	Jul 1953
Scott	Derek E	Gateshead	8 Feb 1958	Apprentice	Feb 1975	277(8)	24	23	0	24	3	26	2	350(8)	29	Bolton W	Jul 1985
Scott	James	Hetton le Hole	7 Sep 1934	Juniors	Sep 1951	3	0			2	0			5	0	Oldham A	Jun 1961
Seith	Robert	Coatbridge	9 Mar 1932	Juniors	Mar 1949	211	6	27	0					238	6	Dundee	Aug 1960
Shackleton	Alan	Padiham	3 Feb 1934	Juniors	May 1954	31	18	1	0					32	18	Leeds U	Oct 1958
Shannon	Leslie	Liverpool	12 Mar 1926	Liverpool	Nov 1949	263	39	19	5					281	44	Released	May 1959
Simpson	Peter	Sunderland	21 Sep 1940	Juniors	Nov 1957	3	0							3	0	Bury	Aug 1963
Smith	David	Dundee	22 Sep 1933	Juniors	Sep 1950	99	1	8	0	1	0			108	1	Brighton	Jul 1961
Smith	Fred	West Sleekburn	25 Dec 1942	Juniors	Dec 1959	84	1	10	0	8(1)	0	4	0	106(1)	1	Portsmouth	May 1970
Spencer	Harold	Burnley	30 Apr 1919	Juniors	Sep 1937	4	1							4	1	Wrexham	Jul 1950
Spencer	Jack	Bacup	24 Aug 1920	Bacup	Jun 1948	37	8	6	3					43	11	Accrington S	Jun 1951
Stephenson	Roy	Crook	27 May 1932	Juniors	Jun 1949	78	27	2	1					80	28	Rotherham U	Sep 1956
Stevenson	Alan	Staveley	6 Nov 1950	Chesterfield	Jan 1972	438	0	33	0	36	0	36	0	543	0	Rotherham U	Aug 1983
Strong	G James	Morpeth	7 Jun 1916	Walsall	Jan 1946	264	0	21	0					285	0	Released	May 1954
Summerbee	Michael	Cheltenham	15 Dec 1942	Manchester C	Jun 1975	51	0	1	0	6	0	3	0	61	0	Blackpool	Dec 1976
Talbut	John	Oxford	20 Oct 1940	Juniors	Oct 1957	138	0	14	0	5	1	3	0	160	1	West Brom	Dec 1966
Taylor	Fred	Burnley	24 Feb 1920	Juniors	Mar 1937	49	7	1	0					50	7	New Brighton	Jul 1948
Ternent	Raymond	Blyth	9 Sep 1948	Apprentice	Sep 1965	13	0	1	0	1	0			15	0	Southend U	May 1971
Ternent	F Stanley	Gateshead	16 Jun 1946	Apprentice	Jun 1963	5	0							5	0	Carlisle U	May 1968
Thomas	David	K'by in Ashfield	5 Oct 1950	Apprentice	Oct 1967	153(4)	19	4	0	16	4	2	0	175(4)	23	Queens Park R	Oct 1972
Thompson	Desmond	Southampton	4 Dec 1928	York C	Nov 1952	62	0	7	0					69	0	Sheffield U	May 1955
Thomson	Harry	Edinburgh	25 Aug 1940	Bo'ness U	Aug 1959	117	0	5	0	15	0	4	0	141	0	Blackpool	Jul 1969
Thomson	James	Glasgow	1 Oct 1946	Chelsea	Sep 1968	294(3)	3	23	1	21	1	23	1	361(3)	6	Released	May 1981
Todd	Samuel	Belfast	22 Sep 1945	Glentoran	Sep 1962	108(8)	1	0(1)	0	7(1)	1	3	0	118(10)	2	Sheffield W	May 1970
Towers	Ian	Blackhill	11 Oct 1940	Juniors	Oct 1957	43(1)	12	6	1	1	1			50(1)	14	Oldham A	Jan 1966
Waiters	Anthony	Southport	1 Feb 1937	Liverpool	Jul 1970	38	0	1	0	1	0	2	0	42	0	Coventry C	Dec 1971
Waldron	Colin	Bristol	22 Jun 1948	Chelsea	Oct 1967	308	16	14	0	23	0	11	2	356	18	Manchester U	Jun 1976
Walker	David	Colne	15 Oct 1941	Juniors	May 1959	38	1	1	0	1	0			40	1	Southampton	May 1965
Walton	John	Horwich	21 Mar 1928	Bury	Feb 1954	18	2							18	2	Coventry C	Oct 1956
Welch	Ronald	Chesterfield	26 Sep 1952	Apprentice	Oct 1969	1	0							1	0	Brighton	Dec 1973
West	Alan	Hyde	18 Dec 1951	Apprentice	Dec 1968	41(4)	3	2	0	3	0	1(2)	0	47(6)	3	Luton T	Oct 1973
White	William	Liverpool	13 Oct 1936	Juniors	Jan 1954	9	4	2	0	1	0			12	4	Wrexham	Mar 1961
Wilson	Charles			RAF	1945			1	0					1	0	Released	May 1946
Wilson	David	Wolverhampton	4 Oct 1944	Walsall	Sep 1969	10(3)	0	3	0					13(3)	0	Chesterfield	Jun 1971
Wilson	Harry	Hetton le Hole	29 Nov 1953	Apprentice	Dec 1970	12	0							12	0	Brighton	Dec 1973
Wilson	Ian	Fife	11 Feb 1923	Preston N E	Jun 1948	19	1	2	1					21	2	Leicester C	Mar 1950
Wilson	William	Portadown	23 Sep 1936	Portadown	Sep 1955	2	0							2	0	Released	May 1958
Winton	Douglas	Perth	6 Oct 1929	Jeanfield Sw	Sep 1947	183	1	15	0					198	1	Aston Villa	Jan 1959
Woodruff	Arthur	Barnsley	12 Apr 1913	Bradford C	Jun 1936	271	0	21	0					292	0	Workington	Jul 1952
Wrigley	Wilfred	Clitheroe	4 Oct 1949	Juniors	Jul 1968	6	1			2	0			8	1	Released	Sep 1970
Own goals August 1946 to May 1976							38		4		2				44		

Players 1976 to 2007

See elsewhere for "other" competitions covered
This section covers all players who made their senior debuts between Aug 1976 and May 2007
It also incorporates the full career records of players who made their seniordebuts before May 1976, then left and later returned to Turf Moor
Appearances and goals are grouped together for players with more than one spell at Turf Moor

Sub appearances are shown in brackets

		Born	Date	from/prev club	date	League		FA Cup		FL Cup		Other		Total		to/next club	date
						apps	gls	apps	gls	apps	gls	apps	gls	apps	gls		
Adams	Derek W	Aberdeen	25 Jun 1975	Aberdeen	Jan 1995	0(2)	0							0(2)	0	Released	1996
Adebola	Bamber(Dele)	Lagos, Nigeria	23 Jun 1975	Coventry C	Mar 2004	0(3)	1							0(3)	1	on loan until	Apr 2004
Akinbiyi	Adeola O (Ade)	Hackney	10 Oct 1974	Stoke C	Feb 2005	53(6)	18	2	1	3	2			58(6)	21	Sheffield U	Jan 2006
			2nd spell	Sheffield U	Jan 2007											current player	Jun 2007
Allen	Mark S	Newcastle	18 Dec 1963	Apprentice	Dec 1981	0(2)	1					0(1)	0	0(3)	1	Tranmere R	Aug 1983
Anderson	Colin R	Newcastle	26 Apr 1962	Apprentice	Apr 1980	3(3)	0					2	0	5(3)	0	Released	May 1982
Arins	Anthony F	Chesterfield	26 Oct 1958	Apprentice	Jul 1976	29	2			1	0	2	0	32	2	Leeds U	May 1980
Armstrong	S Craig	South Shields	23 May 1975	Nottingham F	Dec 1994	4	0							4	0	on loan until	Feb 1995
Armstrong	Gordon I	Newcastle	15 Jul 1967	Bury	Aug 1998	88(17)	4	3(3)	0	2	0			93(20)	4	Accrington S	Jun 2003
Atkinson	Paul G	Pudsey	14 Aug 1961	Oldham A	Jul 1988	18(4)	1	6	0	3	0	2	0	29(4)	1	Released	May 1990
Baker	Stephen	Newcastle	16 Jun 1962	Southampton	Feb 1984	10	0					2	1	12	1	on loan until	Apr 1984
Ball	Kevin A	Hastings	12 Nov 1964	Fulham	Jul 2000	77(5)	2	3	0	5	0			85(5)	2	Released	May 2001
Bardsley	Philip A	Salford	28 Jun 1985	Manchester U	Mar 2006	6	0							6	0	on loan until	Apr 1976
Barnes	Paul L	Leicester	16 Nov 1967	Birmingham C	Sep 1996	63(2)	30	5	1	5	0			73(2)	31	Huddersfield T	Jan 1998
Bent	Junior A	Huddersfield	1 Mar 1970	Huddersfield T	Nov 1989	7(2)	3							7(2)	3	on loan until	Feb 1990
Beresford	Marlon	Lincoln	2 Sep 1969	Sheffield W	Aug 1992	286(1)	0	25	0	22	0	16	0	349(1)	0	Middlesbrough	Mar 1998
			2nd spell	Middlesbrough	Jan 2002											York C	Aug 2002
			3rd spell	York C	Oct 2002											Bradford C	Sep 2003
Bermingham	Karl J K	Dublin	6 Oct 1985	Manchester C	Aug 2005	1(3)	0							1(3)	0	on loan until	Sep 2005
Biggins	Wayne	Sheffield	20 Nov 1961	Matlock T	Feb 1984	78	30	3	1	6	1	7	5	94	37	Norwich C	Oct 1985
Bishop	Charles D	Nottingham	16 Feb 1968	Barnsley	Mar 1996	9	0							9	0	on loan until	Apr 1996
Blake	Robert J	Middlesbrough	4 Mar 1976	Nottingham F	Jan 2002	103(17)	42	6(1)	4	11	5			120(18)	51	Birmingham C	Jan 2005
Blatherwick	Steven S	Nottingham	20 Sep 1973	Nottingham F	Jul 1997	16(8)	0	1(1)	0	5	0	3	0	25(9)	0	Chesterfield	Dec 1998
Borland	John R	Lancaster	28 Jan 1977	Trainee	Jul 1995	1	0	0(1)	0	2	0			3(1)	0	Scunthorpe U	Aug 1996
Bowditch	Dean P	Bishops Stortford	15 Jun 1986	Ipswich T	Mar 2005	8(2)	1							8(2)	1	on loan until	Apr 2005
Branch	Graham	Liverpool	12 Feb 1972	Stockport C	Dec 1998	208(56)	17	9(8)	0	14(3)	1	1	0	232(67)	18	Released	May 2007
Brass	Christopher P	Easington	24 Jul 1975	Trainee	Jul 1993	120(14)	1	6(1)	0	8(1)	0	8(2)	0	142(18)	1	York C	Mar 2001
Bray	Ian M	Neath	6 Dec 1962	Huddersfield T	Jul 1990	15(2)	0			4	0	4(1)	1	23(3)	1	Released	Apr 1992
Briscoe	Lee S	Pontefract	30 Sep 1975	Sheffield W	Jul 2000	100(6)	7	6	0	7	0			113(6)	7	Preston N E	Jul 2003
Britton	Ian	Dundee	19 May 1954	Blackpool	Aug 1986	102(6)	10	1(2)	0	7	0	11(1)	0	121(9)	10	Released	May 1989
Buckley	Neil A	Hull	25 Sep 1968	Hull C	Mar 1990	5	0							5	0	on loan until	Apr 1990
Burke	Marshall	Glasgow	26 Mar 1959	Apprentice	Mar 1977	22(2)	5	2	0	1(1)	0			25(3)	5	Leeds U	May 1980
Busby	Martyn G	Slough	24 Mar 1953	Queens Park R	Feb 1980	4	1							4	1	on loan until	Mar 1980
Cahill	Gary J	Dronfield	19 Dec 1985	Aston Villa	Nov 2004	27	1	4	0	1	0			32	1	on loan until	May 2005
Caldwell	Stephen	Stirling	12 Sep 1980	Sunderland	Jan 2007	16(1)	0							16(1)	0	current player	Jun 2007
Camara	Mohamed	Guinea	25 Jun 1975	Wolves	Jul 2003	90	0	6(1)	0	7	1			103(1)	1	Celtic	Jun 2005
Campbell	David A	Eglinton	2 Jun 1965	West Brom A	Mar 1993	7(1)	0							7(1)	0	Wigan A	Jul 1994
Carr-Lawton	Colin	South Shields	5 Sep 1978	Trainee	Jan 1997	2(3)	0			0(2)	0	1(1)	0	3(6)	0	Berwick R	Jun 1999
Cassidy	Thomas	Belfast	18 Nov 1950	Newcastle U	Jul 1980	70(2)	4	8(1)	1	8(2)	2	7	1	93(5)	8	Released	May 1983
Caughey	Mark	Belfast	27 Aug 1960	Hibernian	Feb 1987	8	0							8	0	on loan until	Mar 1987
Cavener	Philip	North Shields	2 Jun 1961	Apprentice	May 1979	55(14)	4	5(1)	0	6(1)	0	8	1	74(16)	5	Released	May 1983
Cennamo	Luigi	Germany	11 Feb 1980	Olympiakos	Jul 2001			0(1)	0					0(1)	0	Released	Apr 2002
Chadwick	Luke H	Cambridge	18 Nov 1980	Manchester U	Jul 2003	23(13)	5	1(1)	0	2	1			26(14)	6	on loan until	May 2004
Chaplow	Richard D	Accrington	2 Feb 1985	Trainee	Sep 2003	48(17)	7	5	0	3(1)	0			56(18)	7	West Brom A	Jan 2005
Chilton	Anthony J	Maryport	7 Sep 1965	Sunderland	Feb 1985	1	0							1	0	Whitley Bay	1985
Chippendale	Brian A	Bradford	29 Oct 1964	York C	Jul 1985	6(2)	0							6(2)	0	Preston N E	Oct 1985
Clayton	John	Elgin	20 Aug 1961	Volendam	Aug 1992	3	1			1	0			4	1	Retired	May 1994
Cochrane	G Terence	Killyleagh	23 Jan 1953	Coleraine	Oct 1976	62(5)	13	4(1)	0	7	4	6	1	79(6)	18	Middlesbrough	Oct 1978
Comstive	Paul T	Southport	25 Nov 1961	Wrexham	Jul 1987	81(1)	17	2	0	8	3	11	3	102(1)	23	Bolton W	Sep 1989
Conroy	Michael K	Glasgow	31 Dec 1965	Reading	Jul 1991	76(1)	31	9(1)	4	4	1	9(1)	5	98(3)	41	Preston N E	Aug 1993
Cook	Paul A	Liverpool	22 Feb 1967	Stockport C	Mar 1999	140(7)	12	11(2)	3	5(4)	0			156(13)	15	Accrington S	Jun 2003
Cooke	Andrew R	Shrewsbury	2 Jan 1974	Newtown	May 1995	134(37)	51	7(3)	2	8(2)	6	9(2)	2	158(44)	61	Stoke C	Dec 2000
Coughlan	Graham	Dublin	18 Nov 1974	Sheffield W	Mar 2007	1(1)	0							1(1)	0	on loan until	May 2007
Courtney	Duane	Oldbury	7 Jan 1985	Telford U	Aug 2005	1(6)	0			0(1)	0			1(7)	0	Released	May 2006
Cowan	Thomas	Bellshill	28 Aug 1969	Huddersfield	Mar 1999	17(3)	1			2	0	0(1)	0	19(4)	1	Cambridge U	Jul 2000
Cowans	Gordon S	Cornforth	27 Oct 1958	Stockport C	Aug 1997	5(1)	0	2	0	1	0			8(1)	0	Retired	May 1998
Cox	Ian G	Croydon	25 Mar 1971	Bournemouth	Feb 2000	107(8)	5	8(1)	0	7	0			122(9)	5	Gillingham	Aug 2003
Coyne	Daniel	Prestatyn	27 Aug 1973	Leicester C	Aug 2004	39(1)	0			4	0			43(1)	0	Released	May 2007
Creaney	Gerard T	Coatbridge	13 Apr 1970	Manchester C	Sep 1997	9(1)	8			1	0			10(1)	8	on loan until	Nov 1997
Crichton	Paul A	Pontefract	3 Oct 1968	West Brom A	Aug 1998	82(1)	0	4	0	4	0	2	0	92(1)	0	on loan until	Aug 1998
			2nd spell	West Brom A	Nov 1998											Norwich C	Jun 2001
Daley	Steven	Barnsley	15 Apr 1953	Golden Bay E	Nov 1983	20(3)	4	2(2)	0			4	1	26(5)	5	San Diego	May 1984
Daniel	Peter W	Hull	12 Dec 1955	Lincoln C	Jul 1987	40(1)	0	1	0	6	0	4	0	51(1)	0	Retired	May 1989
Davis (1)	Steven P	Birmingham	26 Jul 1965	Crewe A	Oct 1987	147	11	9	0	7	0	18	1	181	12	Barnsley	Jul 1991
Davis (2)	Stephen M	Hexham	30 Oct 1968	Southampton	Nov 1989	321(6)	42	24(1)	1	19	4	17	0	381(7)	47	on loan until	Jan 1990
			2nd spell	Southampton	Aug 1991											Luton T	Jul 1995
			3rd spell	Luton T	Dec 1998											Blackpool	Jul 2003
Deakin	Raymond J	Liverpool	19 Jun 1959	Bolton W	Jul 1985	212(1)	6	7	0	15	0	12	0	246(1)	6	Released	May 1991
Deary	John S	Ormskirk	18 Oct 1962	Blackpool	Jul 1989	209(6)	23	20(1)	2	13(3)	1	23	1	265(10)	27	Rochdale	Jan 1995
Devaney	Philip C	Huyton	12 Feb 1969	Apprentice	Feb 1987	8(5)	1					0(1)	0	8(6)	1	Released	May 1988
Devenney	Michael P	Bolton	8 Feb 1980	Trainee	Jul 1998							0(1)	0	0(1)	0	Released	2000
Devine	Peter	Blackburn	25 May 1960	Blackburn R	Jun 1984	46(10)	4	3	4	0(1)	0	4(2)	2	53(13)	10	Chorley	1987
Diallo	Drissa	Mauretania	4 Jan 1973	KV Mechelen	Jan 2003	14	1	4	1					18	2	Ipswich T	Jun 2003
Dixon	Lee	Manchester	17 Mar 1964	Apprentice	Jul 1982	3	0							3	0	Chester C	Feb 1984
Dixon	Paul K	Londonderry	22 Feb 1960	Apprentice	Jun 1978	23(1)	1	5	0			4	0	32(1)	1	Released	May 1983
Djemba-D	Eric D	Cameroon	4 May 1981	Aston Villa	Jan 2007	13(2)	0							13(2)	0	on loan until	May 2007
Dobson	J Martin	Rishton	14 Feb 1948	Bolton W	Aug 1967	406(4)	63	31	7	34	4	22	2	493(4)	76	Everton	Aug 1974
			2nd spell	Everton	Aug 1979											Bury	Mar 1984
Donachie	William	Glasgow	5 Oct 1951	Portland T	Nov 1982	60	3	12	0	4	0	4	1	80	4	Oldham A	Jul 1984
Donovan	Terence C	Liverpool	27 Feb 1958	Aston Villa	Feb 1985	13(2)	6	0(2)	0	0(1)	0			13(5)	6	Rotherham U	Sep 1983
Donowa	B Louie	Ipswich	24 Sep 1964	Birmingham C	Jan 1993	4	0					2	0	6	0	on loan until	Jan 1993
Dowell	Wayne A	Durham	28 Dec 1973	Trainee	Mar 1993	6	0	2	0	1	0			9	0	Rochdale	Jul 1996
Duerden	Ian C	Burnley	27 Mar 1978	Trainee	Jul 1996	1	0							1	0	Halifax T	Aug 1998
Duff	Michael J	Belfast	11 Jan 1978	Cheltenham T	Jul 2004	118(9)	2	3	0	8	1			129(9)	3	current player	Jun 2007
Duffy	Richard M	Swansea	30 Aug 1985	Portsmouth	Sep 2004	3(4)	1			2	0			5(4)	1	on loan until	Oct 2004
Dyer	Nathan A J	Trowbridge	29 Nov 1987	Southampton	Oct 2005	4(1)	2							4(1)	2	on loan until	Nov 2005

Sub appearances are shown in brackets

						League		FA Cup		FL Cup		Other		Total			
		Born	Date	from/prev club	date	apps	gls	apps	gls	apps	gls	apps	gls	apps	gls	to/next club	date
Eastwood	Philip J	Blackburn	6 Apr 1978	Trainee	Jul 1996	7(9)	1	1	0			1	0	9(9)	1	Released	May 1999
Edwards	Neil R	Liverpool	2 Jul 1967	Liverpool	Aug 1985	0(1)	0							0(1)	0	Released	May 1986
Eli	Roger	Bradford	11 Sep 1965	Northwich V	Jul 1989	70(29)	20	7(5)	5	4(2)	0	15	6	96(36)	31	Released	Jun 1994
Elliott	Wade P	Eastleigh	14 Dec 1978	Bournemouth	Jul 2005	63(15)	7	2	0	1(1)	0			66(16)	7	current player	Jun 2007
Ellis	Anthony J	Salford	20 Oct 1964	Rochdale	Jul 2001	0(11)	1							0(11)	1	Released	Apr 2002
Entwistle	Wayne P	Bury	6 Aug 1958	Bolton W	Aug 1986	6(2)	2			1(1)	0			7(3)	2	on loan until	Oct 1986
Eyres	David	Liverpool	26 Feb 1964	Blackpool	Jul 1993	171(4)	37	14	8	17	7	9	3	211(4)	55	Preston N E	Oct 1997
Facey	Delroy M	Huddersfield	22 Apr 1980	Bolton W	Sep 2003	12(2)	5			2	0			14(2)	5	on loan until	Nov 2003
Farrell	Andrew J	Colchester	7 Oct 1965	Colchester U	Aug 1987	237(20)	19	19(2)	0	17(4)	1	28(4)	3	301(30)	23	Wigan A	Sep 1994
Farrelly	Gareth	Dublin	28 Aug 1975	Bolton W	Sep 2003	9(3)	0			1(1)	0			10(4)	0	on loan until	Nov 2003
Flynn	Brian	Port Talbot	12 Oct 1955	Apprentice	Oct 1972	193(9)	19	18	2	18(2)	4	10	2	239(11)	27	Leeds U	Nov 1977
			2nd spell	Leeds U	Mar 1982											on loan until	Mar 1982
			3rd spell	Leeds U	Nov 1982											Cardiff C	Nov 1984
Ford	Mark S	Pontefract	10 Oct 1975	Leeds U	Jul 1997	43(5)	1	1(1)	0	2	0	5(1)	0	51(7)	1	Torquay U	Jul 2000
Foster	Stephen J	Warrington	10 Sep 1980	Crewe A	Aug 2006	7(10)	0	1	0	1	0			9(10)	0	current player	Jun 2007
France	M Paul	Holmfirth	10 Sep 1968	Bristol C	Jul 1990	7(1)	0	1	0	1	0			9(1)	0	Released	May 1992
Francis	John A	Dewsbury	21 Nov 1963	Sheffield U	Jan 1990	143(34)	37	12(2)	1	9(4)	1	17(5)	7	181(45)	46	Cambridge U	Aug 1992
			2nd spell	Cambridge U	Mar 1993											Released	May 1996
Futcher	Ronald	Chester	25 Sep 1956	Port Vale	Nov 1989	52(5)	25	8(1)	3	2	1	5	1	67(6)	30	Released	Jul 1991
Gallagher	Joseph A	Liverpool	11 Jan 1955	West Ham U	Jul 1983	46(1)	3	1	0	3	0	3	0	53(1)	3	Released	May 1987
Gardner	Stephen G	Middlesbrough	3 Jul 1968	Manchester U	Jul 1987	93(2)	0	2	0	7	0	11	0	113(2)	0	Released	May 1990
Gascoigne	Paul J	Gateshead	27 May 1967	Everton	Mar 2002	3(3)	0							3(3)	0	Released	Apr 2002
Gayle	John	Bromsgrove	30 Jul 1964	Coventry C	Aug 1994	7(7)	3	1(1)	1	1(1)	1			9(9)	5	Stoke C	Jan 1995
Gentile	Marco	Holland	24 Aug 1968	Maastricht	Jul 1997					1	0			1	0	Released	Oct 1997
Gleghorn	Nigel W	Seaham	12 Aug 1962	Stoke C	Jul 1996	33(1)	4	4	1	4	0	2	0	43(1)	5	Altrincham	Jun 1998
Glendon	Kevin W	Manchester	21 Jun 1961	Hyde	Dec 1983	4	0							4	0	Released	May 1984
Gnohere	D Arthur	Ivory Coast	20 Nov 1978	SM Caen	Aug 2001	74(7)	6	5	0	7	0			86(7)	6	Queens Park R	Feb 2004
Gow	Gerald	Glasgow	29 May 1952	Rotherham U	Aug 1983	8(1)	0	1	0					9(1)	0	Released	May 1984
Grant	Stephen H	Birr	14 Apr 1977	Stockport C	Aug 1999					0(2)	0			0(2)	0	Released	Sep 1999
Grant	Anthony J	Liverpool	14 Nov 1974	Manchester C	Oct 2001	121(20)	3	15	0	9(1)	0			145(21)	3	Bristol C	Aug 2005
Grant	Lee A	H. Hempstead	27 Jan 1983	Derby	Nov 2005	1	0							1	0	on loan until	Dec 2005
Gray	Philip	Belfast	2 Oct 1968	Luton T	Jul 2000	5	1			2(1)	0			7(1)	1	Oxford U	Nov 2000
Gray	Andrew D	Harrogate	15 Nov 1977	Sunderland	Mar 2006	43(1)	17			1	0			44(1)	17	current player	Jun 2007
Grewcock	Neil	Leicester	26 Apr 1962	Shepshed C	Jun 1984	180(22)	27	10	1	12(1)	2	16(1)	2	218(24)	32	Released	May 1991
Gudjonsson	Johannes (Joey)	Iceland	25 May 1980	AZ Alkmaar	Jan 2007	9(2)	0							9(2)	0	current player	Jun 2007
Guinan	Stephen A	Birmingham	24 Dec 1975	Nottingham F	Mar 1997	0(6)	0							0(6)	0	on loan until	Apr 1997
Haddock	Peter M	Newcastle	9 Dec 1961	Newcastle U	Mar 1986	7	0							7	0	on loan until	Apr 1986
Hall	Brian W	Glasgow	22 Jan 1946	Plymouth A	Nov 1977	39(4)	3	3	0			5	0	47(4)	3	Released	May 1980
Hamilton	David	South Shields	7 Nov 1960	Chester C	Aug 1989	11(4)	0	0(1)	0	4	1	2	0	17(5)	1	Chorley	1992
Hamilton	William R	Belfast	9 May 1957	Queens Park R	Nov 1979	200	58	23	10	16	5	12	4	251	77	Oxford U	Aug 1984
Hampton	Peter J	Oldham	12 Sep 1954	Stoke C	Jul 1984	116(2)	2	4	0	8	0	4	0	132(2)	2	Rochdale	Aug 1987
Hancock	Anthony E	Manchester	31 Jan 1967	Stockport C	May 1989	9(8)	0	1(2)	0	0(1)	0	1	0	11(11)	0	Preston N E	Jan 1990
Hansbury	Roger	Barnsley	26 Jan 1955	Eastern A (HK)	Aug 1983	83	0	8	0	6	0	6	0	103	0	Cambridge U	Jul 1985
Hardy	Jason P	Manchester	14 Dec 1969	Apprentice	Jul 1988	38(6)	1	3(2)	1			2	0	43(8)	2	Released	Apr 1992
Harley	Jonathan (Jon)	Maidstone	26 Sep 1979	Sheffield U	Aug 2005	85(1)	3	2	0	3	0			90(1)	3	current player	Jun 2007
Harper	Steven J	Newcastle-u-Lyme	3 Feb 1969	Preston N E	Jul 1991	64(5)	8	10	3	1(2)	0	9	1	84(7)	12	Doncaster R	Aug 1993
Harper	Alan	Liverpool	1 Nov 1960	Luton T	Aug 1994	30(1)	0	5	0	6	0			41(1)	0	Released	May 1996
Harrington	Philip	Bangor	20 Nov 1963	Blackpool	Nov 1985	2	0							2	0	on loan until	Nov 1985
Harris	Jason M	Bacup	26 Dec 1969	Apprentice	Jul 1988	4	0					2	0	6	0	Burnley B H	1989
Harris	Mark A	Reading	15 Jul 1963	Crystal P	Aug 1989	4	0			2	0			6	0	on loan until	Sep 1989
Harrison	Gerald R	Lambeth	15 Apr 1972	Huddersfield T	Aug 1994	116(8)	3	6(2)	0	5(1)	0	7(1)	0	134(12)	3	Sunderland	Jul 1998
Heath	Adrian P	Stoke	11 Jan 1961	Stoke C	Aug 1992	110(10)	29	12	6	8(1)	0	7	0	137(11)	35	Sheffield U	Dec 1995
			2nd spell	Sheffield U	Mar 1996											Everton	Jun 1997
Heesom	Darren L	Warrington	8 May 1968	Apprentice	Dec 1985	36(2)	1	2(1)	0			4	0	42(3)	1	Released	May 1987
Heggarty	James P	Larne	4 Aug 1965	Brighton & H A	Jul 1985	33(3)	1	2	0	2	0	1	0	38(3)	1	Released	Oct 1986
Helliwell	Ian	Rotherham	7 Nov 1962	Stockport C	Feb 1996	3(1)	0							3(1)	0	Ilkeston T	Jun 1998
Henderson	Kevin M	Ashington	8 Jun 1974	Morpeth T	Dec 1997	0(14)	1			0(2)	0	0(4)	1	0(20)	2	Hartlepool U	Jul 1999
Hewlett	Matthew P	Bristol	25 Feb 1976	Bristol C	Nov 1998	2	0					1	0	3	0	on loan until	Dec 1998
Heywood	Matthew S	Chatham	26 Aug 1979	Trainee	Jul 1998	11(2)	0	1	0			1	0	13(2)	0	Swindon T	Jan 2001
Higgins	Robert J	Bolsover	23 Dec 1958	Apprentice	Jul 1976	3	0							3	0	Released	May 1980
Hird	Kevin	Colne	11 Feb 1955	Leeds U	Jul 1984	83	23	5	4	6	2	6	1	100	30	Released	May 1986
Hodgson	Douglas J	Frankston, Aus.	27 Feb 1969	Sheffield U	Oct 1996	1	0							1	0	on loan until	Oct 1996
Holden	Richard W	Skipton	9 Sep 1964	Carnegie College	Mar 1986	0(1)	0							0(1)	0	Halifax T	Sep 1986
Holt	David	Padiham	26 Feb 1952	Oldham A	Jul 1980	84	1	5	0	10	2	11	1	110	4	Retired	1983
Hooper	Stuart R	St Annes	16 Jun 1970	Apprentice	Jul 1988	0(1)	0							0(1)	0	Released	May 1989
Hoskin	J Ashley	Accrington	27 Mar 1968	Apprentice	Dec 1985	72(16)	11	3(1)	0	2(1)	0	8(2)	2	85(20)	13	Released	May 1989
Howarth	Neil	Farnworth	15 Nov 1971	Trainee	Jul 1990	0(1)	0							0(1)	0	Released	May 1994
Howey	Lee M	Sunderland	1 Apr 1969	Sunderland	Aug 1997	24(2)	0	2	0	5	1	0(1)	0	31(3)	1	Northampton T	Nov 1998
Hoyland	Jamie W	Sheffield	23 Jan 1966	Sheffield U	Oct 1994	77(10)	4	7	0	5	0	5(1)	0	94(11)	4	Scarborough	Aug 1998
Hutchison	Thomas	Cardenden	22 Sep 1947	Bulova (HK)	Aug 1983	92	4	8	0	6	0	8	1	114	5	Swansea C	Jul 1985
Huxford	Richard J	Scunthorpe	25 Jul 1969	Bradford C	Jan 1997	2(7)	0					1	0	3(7)	0	Dunfermline	Feb 1998
Hyde	Micah A	Newham	10 Nov 1974	Watford	Jul 2004	95(7)	1	5	1	6(1)	0			106(8)	2	Peterborough U	Jan 2007
Jakub	Yanek (Joseph)	Falkirk	7 Dec 1956	Apprentice	Dec 1973	203(2)	8	19	0	11	0	20	1	253(2)	9	Bury	Oct 1980
			2nd spell	Chester C	Jul 1989											Released	May 1993
James	Leighton	Llwchwyr	16 Feb 1953	Apprentice	Feb 1970	331(5)	66	17	2	22	8	23(1)	5	393(6)	81	Derby C	Nov 1975
			2nd spell	Queens Park R	Sep 1978											Swansea C	May 1980
			3rd spell	Newport C	Jul 1986											Released	May 1989
Jensen	Brian	Copenhagen	8 Jun 1975	West Brom A	Jul 2003	140(3)	0	9	0	7	0			156(3)	0	current player	Jun 2007
Jepson	Ronald F	Stoke	12 May 1963	Oldham A	Jul 1998	4(55)	3	0(3)	0	2(4)	0			6(62)	3	Coach	2001
Johnrose	Leonard	Preston	29 Nov 1969	Bury	Feb 1999	55(30)	4	1(2)	1	2	0	1	0	59(32)	5	Bury	Oct 2002
			2nd spell	Swansea C	Mar 2004											Retired	May 2004
Johnson	David A	Jamaica	15 Aug 1976	Nottingham F	Feb 2002	8	5							8	5	on loan until	Apr 2002
Jones	David	Harrow	3 Jul 1964	Leyton O	Feb 1989	4	0							4	0	Released	May 1989
Jones	Stephen G	Derry	25 Oct 1976	Crewe A	Aug 2006	37(4)	5	1	0	1	0			39(4)	5	current player	Jun 2007
Joyce	Warren G	Oldham	20 Jan 1965	Plymouth A	Jul 1993	65(5)	9	4	1	8	1	8	1	85(5)	12	Hull C	Jul 1996
Karbassiyoon	Daniel	Virginia, USA	10 Aug 1984	Arsenal	Jul 2005	0(5)	0			0(1)	0			0(6)	0	Released	May 2006
Kendall	Mark	Blackwood	20 Sep 1958	Swansea C	Dec 1991	2	0	1	0					3	0	on loan until	Jan 1992
Kennedy	Stephen	Audenshaw	22 Jul 1965	Apprentice	Jul 1983	18	0	1(1)	0	0(1)	0	2	0	21(2)	0	Released	1987
Kilner	Andrew W	Bolton	11 Oct 1966	Apprentice	Jul 1984	2(3)	0							2(3)	0	Released	May 1986
Kindon	Stephen M	Warrington	17 Dec 1950	Apprentice	Dec 1967	175(10)	46	10(1)	2	14(2)	2	13	8	212(13)	58	Wolves	Jul 1972
			2nd spell	Wolves	Nov 1977											Huddersfield T	Dec 1979
Kiwomya	Andrew D	Huddersfield	1 Oct 1967	Bradford C	Sep 1997	1(2)	0							1(2)	0	on loan until	Sep 1997
Kval	Frank P	Bergen, Norway	17 Jul 1974	Brann Bergen	Oct 1998			1	0					1	0	Released	May 2000
Lafferty	Kyle	Enniskillen	16 Sep 1987	Trainee	Dec 2005	18(28)	5	0(1)	0	1(1)	0			19(30)	5	current player	Jun 2007

Sub appearances are shown in brackets

						League		FA Cup		FL Cup		Other		Total			
		Born	Date	from/prev club	date	apps	gls	apps	gls	apps	gls	apps	gls	apps	gls	to/next club	date
Lancashire	Graham	Blackpool	19 Oct 1972	Trainee	Jun 1991	11(20)	8	2(2)	1	1(1)	0	3(4)	1	17(27)	10	Preston N E	Dec 1994
Lawrence	Leslie O	Rowley Regis	18 May 1957	Rochdale	Nov 1984	22(9)	8					2(2)	1	24(11)	9	Peterboro' U	Jul 1986
Laws	Brian	Wallsend	14 Oct 1961	Apprentice	Oct 1979	125	12	15	1	14	2	6	0	160	15	Huddersfield T	Aug 1983
Lee	Alan D	Galway	21 Aug 1978	Aston Villa	Jul 1999	2(13)	0	0(2)	0	1(1)	0	1	1	4(16)	1	Rotherham U	Sep 2000
Leebrook	Peter D	Saltburn	18 Sep 1968	Apprentice	May 1987	52	0			4	0	3	0	59	0	Released	Jun 1988
Little	Glen M	Wimbledon	15 Oct 1975	Glentoran	Nov 1996	211(35)	32	11(6)	3	11(4)	0	4(1)	1	237(46)	36	Reading	May 2004
Lowe	Keith S	Wolverhampton	13 Sep 1985	Wolves	Aug 2005	10(6)	0			2	1			12(6)	1	on loan until	Dec 2005
McAdam	Steven	Portadown	2 Apr 1960	Portadown	May 1978	5	0							5	0	Released	Aug 1980
McCann	Christopher J	Co. Meath	21 Jul 1987	Trainee	Jan 2006	39(22)	7	2	0	3(1)	0			44(23)	7	current player	Jun 2007
McDonald	Paul T	Motherwell	20 Apr 1968	Southampton	Sep 1995	8(1)	1					2	0	10(1)	1	on loan until	Nov 1995
McEveley	James (Jay) M	Liverpool	11 Feb 1985	Blackburn R	Dec 2003	0(4)	0	1	0					1(4)	0	on loan until	Jan 2004
McGee	Paul G	Sligo	19 Jun 1954	Preston N E	Nov 1981	33(1)	9	2	2	5	4			40(1)	15	on loan until	Dec 1981
			2nd spell	Preston N E	Mar 1982											Released	May 1983
McGreal	John	Liverpool	2 Jun 1972	Ipswich T	Aug 2004	92(4)	1	5	0	5	0			102(4)	1	Released	May 2007
McGregor	Mark D T	Chester	16 Feb 1977	Wrexham	Jul 2001	46(8)	2	5(2)	0	4	1			55(10)	3	Blackpool	Jul 2004
McGrory	Shaun P	Coventry	29 Feb 1968	Coventry C	Jul 1987	34(12)	2	5	0	2	0	4(1)	0	45(13)	2	Released	May 1990
McKay	Paul W	Banbury	28 Jan 1971	Trainee	Nov 1989	8(4)	0	1(1)						9(5)	0	Released	May 1993
McKenzie	Paul A	Aberdeen	4 Oct 1969	Peterhead	Jan 1992	1(3)	0					0(2)	0	1(5)	0	Released	May 1994
McMinn	Kevin C (Ted)	Castle Douglas	29 Sep 1962	Birmingham C	Mar 1994	38(8)	3	2(2)	0	4	0	3(1)	0	47(11)	3	Released	Apr 1996
McVeigh	Paul F	Belfast	6 Dec 1977	Norwich C	Mar 2007	6(2)	3							6(2)	3	on loan until	May 2007
Mahon	Alan J	Dublin	4 Apr 1978	Wigan A	Mar 2006	17(16)	2	0(1)	0	1	0			18(17)	2	current player	Jun 2007
Mahorn	Paul G	Leyton	13 Aug 1973	Tottenham H	Mar 1996	3(5)	1							3(5)	1	on loan until	Apr 1996
Malley	Philip	Felling on Tyne	1 Nov 1965	Hartlepool U	Mar 1984	91(4)	5	3	1	5	0	7(3)	0	106(7)	6	Released	May 1988
Marriott	Andrew	Sutton in Ashfield	11 Oct 1970	Nottingham F	Aug 1991	15	0					2	0	17	0	on loan until	Nov 1991
Matthew	Damian	Islington	23 Sep 1970	Crystal P	Jul 1996	50(9)	7	2	1	6(1)	1	3	0	61(10)	9	Northampton T	Jul 1998
May	David	Oldham	24 Jun 1970	Manchester U	Aug 2003	34(1)	4	3	0	1	0			38(1)	4	Released	May 2004
Maylett	Bradley	Manchester	24 Dec 1980	Trainee	Feb 1999	3(42)	0	0(1)	0	1(2)	0	1	0	4(45)	0	Swansea C	Jun 2003
Measham	Ian	Barnsley	14 Dec 1964	Cambridge U	Nov 1988	181(1)	2	19	0	8	0	21	0	229(1)	2	Doncaster R	Sep 1993
Mellon	Michael J	Paisley	18 Mar 1972	Tranmere R	Jan 1999	72(12)	5	5	0	3(1)	0			80(13)	5	Tranmere R	Mar 2001
Michopoulos	Nikalaos	Greece	20 Feb 1970	PAOK Salonika	Aug 2000	85	0	5	0	3	0			93	0	Retired	Jun 2003
Miller	David B	Burnley	8 Jan 1964	Apprentice	Jan 1982	31(5)	3	1	0	2	0	3(2)	0	37(7)	3	Tranmere R	Jul 1985
			2nd spell	Preston N E	Feb 1989											on loan until	Mar 1989
Monington	Mark D	Bilsthorpe	21 Oct 1970	Trainee	Mar 1989	65(19)	5	4(1)	1	5	0	5(2)	0	79(22)	6	Rotherham U	Nov 1994
Mooney	Brian J	Dublin	2 Feb 1966	Sunderland	Sep 1992	6	0							6	0	on loan until	Oct 1992
Moore	Neil	Liverpool	21 Sep 1972	Norwich C	Aug 1997	48(4)	3	2	1	3(1)	0	4	0	57(5)	4	Macclesfield T	Dec 1999
Moore	Ian R	Birkenhead	26 Aug 1976	Stockport C	Nov 2000	170(22)	37	17	12	6(1)	1			193(23)	50	Leeds U	Mar 2005
Moore	Alan	Dublin	25 Nov 1974	Middlesbrough	Jul 2001	42(27)	4	8(3)	3	3(2)	1			53(32)	8	Released	May 2004
Morgan	Stephen A	Oldham	19 Sep 1968	Wigan A	Aug 1998	17	0	1	0	2	0			20	0	Hull C	Jul 1999
Morley	Anthony W	Ormskirk	26 Aug 1954	Preston N E	Feb 1976	83(13)	5	3(2)	1	3(1)	1	2	0	91(16)	7	Aston Villa	Jun 1979
			2nd spell	West Brom A	Oct 1988											on loan until	Nov 1988
Muir	Ian J	Coventry	5 May 1963	Queens Park R	Oct 1982	1(1)	1							1(1)	1	on loan until	Oct 1982
Mullin	John M	Bury	11 Aug 1975	Trainee	Aug 1992	51(50)	10	7(1)	1	2(1)	0	1	0	61(52)	11	Sunderland	Aug 1995
			2nd spell	Sunderland	Mar 1998											on loan until	Apr 1998
			3rd spell	Sunderland	Jul 1999											Rotherham U	Oct 2001
Mumby	Peter	Bradford	22 Feb 1969	Leeds U	Jul 1989	36(10)	9	3(2)	2	4	2	2(1)	0	45(13)	13	Released	Apr 1992
Murphy	Philip	Liverpool	21 Nov 1960	Witton A	Nov 1986	12(3)	5					3	2	15(3)	7	Released	May 1987
Neenan	Joseph P	Manchester	17 Mar 1959	Scunthorpe U	Jan 1985	90	0	3	0	4	0	7	0	104	0	on loan until	Mar 1985
			2nd spell	Scunthorpe U	Jul 1985											Peterboro' U	Jul 1987
Noel-Williams	Gifton R E	Islington	21 Jan 1980	Stoke C	Jul 2005	36(16)	7	1	0	1(2)	0			38(18)	7	Real Murcia	Jan 2007
Nogan	Kurt	Cardiff	9 Sep 1970	Brighton & H A	Feb 1995	87(5)	33	3	0	8	5	5	4	103(5)	42	Preston N E	Mar 1997
O'Connell	Brendan	Waterloo	12 Nov 1966	Exeter C	Jun 1988	62(2)	17	3	1	6	3	5	2	76(2)	23	Barnsley	Mar 1990
O'Connor	James K	Dublin	1 Sep 1979	West Brom A	Oct 2004	105(5)	8	2	0	4	0			111(5)	8	on loan until	Jan 2005
			2nd spell	West Brom A	Mar 2005											current player	Jun 2007
O'Connor	Garreth	Dublin	10 Nov 1978	Bournemouth	Jul 2005	26(11)	7	1(1)	2	3	0			30(12)	9	Released	May 2005
Oghani	George W	Manchester	2 Sep 1960	Bolton W	Jun 1987	73(1)	21	2	0	8	3	9	3	92(1)	27	Released	Apr 1989
O'Kane	John A	Nottingham	15 Nov 1974	Everton	Oct 1998	8	0							8	0	on loan until	Dec 1998
O'Neill	Matthew P	Accrington	25 Jun 1984	Trainee	Jul 2003	2(11)	0							2(11)	0	Released	May 2005
O'Rourke	William J	Nottingham	2 Apr 1960	Apprentice	Feb 1978	14	0	2	0			1	0	17	0	Chester C	Mar 1984
Orr	Bradley J	Liverpool	1 Nov 1982	Newcastle U	Jan 2004	1(3)	0							1(3)	0	on loan until	Feb 2004
Oster	John M	Boston	8 Dec 1978	Sunderland	Jan 2005	12(3)	1	2(1)	0					14(4)	1	Reading	Aug 2005
Overson	Richard J	Kettering	3 Jun 1959	Apprentice	Jun 1977	5(1)	0							5(1)	0	Hereford U	May 1980
Overson	Vincent D	Kettering	15 May 1962	Apprentice	Nov 1979	213(6)	6	19	0	10	1	15(1)	0	257(7)	7	Birmingham C	Jun 1986
			2nd spell	Stoke C	Aug 1996											Halifax T	Aug 1998
Painter	P Robert	Ince	26 Jan 1971	Maidstone U	Mar 1992	16(10)	2	1	0	2	0			19(10)	2	Darlington	Dec 1993
Palin	Leigh G	Worcester	12 Sep 1965	Hull C	Sep 1992	1	0							1	0	Halifax T	Oct 1992
Palmer	Geoffrey	Cannock	11 Jul 1954	Wolves	Nov 1984	34	0	3	0	2	0	4	0	43	0	Wolves	Dec 1985
Papadopoulos	Demitrios	Kazakhstan	20 Sep 1981	Akratitos	Jul 2001	7(33)	3	1(2)	0	1(4)	3			9(39)	6	Panathanaikos	Jun 2003
Parker	Derrick H	Wallsend	7 Feb 1957	Apprentice	Feb 1974	48(1)	12	3	1	2	0	1	1	54(1)	14	Southend U	Feb 1977
			2nd spell	Oldham A	Oct 1985											Released	May 1987
Parkinson	Gary A	Thornaby	10 Jan 1968	Bolton W	Jan 1994	134(1)	4	10	0	12	0	6	1	162(1)	5	Preston N E	May 1997
Parks	Anthony	Hackney	28 Jan 1963	Blackpool	Aug 1997					2	0			2	0	Barrow	Oct 1997
Patterson	Ian	Chatham	4 Apr 1973	Sunderland	Aug 1993	0(1)	0							0(1)	0	Wigan A	Mar 1994
Payton	Andrew P	Whalley	23 Oct 1967	Huddersfield T	Jan 1998	115(41)	69	6(2)	3	4(2)	6	6	3	131(45)	81	Released	May 2003
Peacock	Dennis M	Lincoln	19 Apr 1953	Doncaster R	Sep 1985	8	0							8	0	on loan until	Nov 1985
Pearce	Christopher L	Newport	7 Aug 1961	Wrexham	Jul 1987	181	0	15	0	16	0	24	0	236	0	Released	Apr 1992
Peel	Nathan J	Blackburn	17 May 1972	Sheffield U	Sep 1993	4(12)	2	0(3)	0	1	0	1(2)	0	6(17)	2	Released	May 1996
Pender	John P	Luton	19 Nov 1963	Bristol C	Sep 1990	171	8	17	1	11	1	23	1	222	11	Wigan A	Aug 1995
Penney	Stephen A	Ballymena	16 Jan 1964	Hearts	Jul 1992	10(1)	3	3	0	2	0			15(1)	3	Retired	Jan 1994
Phelan	Michael C	Nelson	24 Sep 1962	Apprentice	Jul 1980	166(2)	9	16	0	16	2	14	2	212(2)	13	Norwich C	Jul 1985
Philliskirk	Anthony	Sunderland	10 Feb 1965	Peterboro' U	Jan 1994	33(7)	9			4(1)	0			37(8)	9	Cardiff C	Dec 1995
Pickering	Nicholas	Newcastle	4 Aug 1963	Darlington	Mar 1993	4	0							4	0	Released	Jun 1994
Pickering	Albert (Ally) G	Manchester	22 Jun 1967	Stoke C	Dec 1998	21	1							21	1	Cambridge U	Dec 1999
Pilkington	Joel T	Accrington	1 Aug 1984	Trainee	Jul 2003	0(2)	0	0(1)	0	0(1)	0			0(4)	0	Released	May 2005
Pollitt	Michael F	Farnworth	29 Feb 1972	Wigan A	Jan 2007	4	0							4	0	on loan until	Feb 2007
Potts	Eric T	Liverpool	16 Mar 1950	Preston N E	Sep 1980	48(8)	5	4(1)	1	2	1	4	0	58(9)	7	Released	May 1982
Powell	Barry I	Kenilworth	29 Jan 1954	Bulova (HK)	Jul 1984	9(2)	0	2	2	2	0			13(2)	2	Swansea C	Feb 1985
Randall	Adrian J	Amesbury	10 Nov 1968	Aldershot	Dec 1991	105(20)	8	8(2)	1	6	1	3	0	122(22)	10	York C	Dec 1995
Rasmussen	Mark A	Newcastle	28 Nov 1983	New Hartley	Jul 2001	0(2)	0							0(2)	0	Released	2003
Ray	Philip	Wallsend	21 Nov 1964	Apprentice	Nov 1982	1	0					2	0	3	0	Released	May 1985
Reeves	David E	Birkenhead	19 Nov 1967	Sheffield W	Nov 1987	16	8					2	1	18	9	on loan until	Mar 1988
Reeves	Kevin P	Burley	20 Oct 1957	Manchester C	Aug 1983	20(1)	12	5	3	2	0			27(1)	15	Retired	Aug 1984
Regis	Robert A	Huddersfield	24 Jan 1967	Huddersfield T	Feb 1986	3(1)	1	0(1)	0					3(2)	1	Released	Mar 1987
Reid	Brian R	Paisley	15 Jun 1970	Morton	Sep 1998	30(1)	3	1	0			1	0	32(1)	3	Dunfermline	Jul 1999
Rhodes	Mark N	Sheffield	26 Aug 1957	Rotherham U	Mar 1985	12(1)	0					1	0	13(1)	0	Released	Nov 1985

Sub appearances are shown in brackets

		Born	Date	from/prev club	date	League		FA Cup		FL Cup		Other		Total		to/next club	date
						apps	gls	apps	gls	apps	gls	apps	gls	apps	gls		
Ricketts	Michael B	Birmingham	4 Dec 1978	Leeds U	Jan 2006	12(1)	2							12(1)	2	on loan until	Apr 2006
Robertson	Stuart	Glasgow	29 Sep 1959	Apprentice	Jul 1977	30(2)	0			1	0			31(2)	0	Exeter C	Mar 1982
Robertson	Mark W	Sydney, Aus.	6 Apr 1977	Marconi	Mar 1997	27(9)	1			1(1)	0	3(2)	0	31(12)	1	Dundee	Mar 2001
Robinson	Andrew C	Oldham	10 Mar 1966	Manchester U	Oct 1985	5	1							5	1	on loan until	Nov 1985
Robinson	S Liam	Bradford	29 Dec 1965	Bristol C	Jul 1994	43(20)	9	5	1	5(1)	2	1(1)	0	54(22)	12	Scarborough	Aug 1997
Robinson	Paul D	Sunderland	20 Nov 1978	Wimbledon	Oct 2000	0(4)	0							0(4)	0	on loan until	Nov 2000
Roche	Lee P	Bolton	28 Oct 1980	Manchester U	Jul 2003	38(16)	2	4(3)	0	3(2)	0			45(21)	2	Wrexham	Jul 2005
Rodaway	William V	Liverpool	26 Sep 1954	Apprentice	Sep 1971	245(2)	3	13	0	18	0	25	0	301(2)	3	Peterboro' U	Jul 1981
			2nd spell	Tranmere R	Aug 1986											Released	May 1987
Rowell	Gary	Seaham	6 Jun 1957	Carlisle U	Aug 1988	8(11)	1			2	0			10(11)	1	Released	May 1990
Russell	Kevin J	Portsmouth	6 Dec 1966	Stoke C	Jun 1993	26(2)	6	4	0	4	1	1	1	35(2)	8	Bournemouth	Feb 1994
Russell	Wayne L	Cardiff	29 Nov 1967	Ebbw Vale	Oct 1993	22(2)	0	1	0	2	0			25(2)	0	Released	May 1997
Sanokho	Amadou	France	1 Sep 1975	Sanguistese	Sep 2004	0(3)	0			1	0			1(3)	0	Oldham A	Mar 2005
Saville	Andrew V	Hull	12 Dec 1964	Birmingham C	Dec 1994	3(1)	1	1	0					4(1)	1	on loan until	Jan 1995
Scott	Christopher J	Burnley	12 Feb 1980	Trainee	Jul 1998	9(5)	0	1	0					10(5)	0	Released	2000
Scott	Paul D	Burnley	29 Jan 1985	Trainee	2003	0(2)	0							0(2)	0	Released	2005
Shandran	Anthony M	Newcastle	17 Sep 1981	Trainee	Nov 2000	0(1)	0							0(1)	0	Released	May 2003
Shaw	Paul	Burnham	4 Sep 1973	Arsenal	Mar 1995	8(1)	4							8(1)	4	on loan until	Apr 1995
Sinclair	Frank M	Lambeth	3 Dec 1971	Leicester C	Jul 2004	88(4)	1	5	0	2(3)	0			95(7)	1	Huddersfield T	Feb 2007
Slawson	Stephen M	Nottingham	13 Nov 1972	Notts C	Feb 1993	5	2							5	2	on loan until	Mar 1993
Smith	Malcolm	Stockton on Tees	21 Sep 1953	Middlesbrough	Sep 1976	82(3)	17	4(1)	0	5	0	7	3	98(4)	20	York C	Aug 1980
Smith	Nigel	Leeds	21 Dec 1969	Leeds U	Jul 1989	6(6)	0					0(1)	0	6(7)	0	Released	May 1991
Smith	I Paul	Easington	22 Jan 1876	Trainee	Jul 1994	79(33)	5	6(1)	0	3(1)	0	5	0	93(35)	5	Hartlepool U	Nov 2001
Smith	Carl P	Sheffield	15 Jan 1979	Trainee	Sep 1997	5(6)	0			1	0			6(6)	0	Worksop T	Jun 1999
Sonner	Daniel J	Wigan	9 Jan 1972	Wigan A	Jul 1990	1(5)	0			0(1)	1	0(1)	0	1(7)	1	Released	May 1993
Southern	Michael	Lytham St Annes	31 Oct 1968	Apprentice	1986							1	0	1	0	Released	May 1987
Spicer	John W	Romford	13 Sep 1983	Bournemouth	Aug 2005	22(23)	4			2	1			24(23)	5	current player	Jun 2007
Steven	Trevor M	Berwick	21 Sep 1963	Apprentice	Sep 1981	74(2)	11	13	4	10	1	3	0	100(2)	16	Everton	Jul 1983
Stewart	Paul A	Manchester	7 Oct 1964	Liverpool	Feb 1995	6	0							6	0	on loan until	Mar 1995
Swan	Peter H	Leeds	28 Sep 1966	Plymouth A	Aug 1995	58(10)	7	3	0	2	0	6	0	69(10)	7	Bury	Aug 1997
			2nd spell	Bury	Aug 1998											York C	Mar 2000
Tate	Jeffrey	Blyth	11 May 1959	Wallsend YC	Aug 1978	5	1							5	1	Morecambe	1980
Taylor	Alan D	Hinckley	14 Nov 1953	Hull C	Jun 1984	60(4)	23	3	3	5	3	3	3	71(4)	32	Bury	Jun 1986
Taylor	Steven J	Royton	18 Oct 1955	Mansfield T	Jul 1980	118(13)	43	14	5	14(2)	1	18(1)	3	164(16)	52	Wigan A	Aug 1983
			2nd spell	Preston N E	Aug 1987											Rochdale	Mar 1989
Taylor	Gareth K	Weston S M	25 Feb 1973	Manchester C	Feb 2001	88(7)	36	6	1	4(1)	0			98(8)	37	Nottingham F	Aug 2003
Thomas	Mitchell A	Luton	2 Oct 1964	Luton T	Jul 1999	95(4)	0	6	0	6	0	1	0	108(4)	0	Released	Apr 2002
Thomas	Wayne J R	Gloucester	17 May 1979	Stoke C	Jul 2005	45(4)	1	1(1)	0	2	0			48(5)	1	current player	Jun 2007
Thompson	Leslie	Cleethorpes	23 Sep 1968	Maidstone U	Jul 1992	38(1)	0	4	0	4(1)	0	5	0	51(2)	0	Released	Aug 1994
Thompson	Steven J	Oldham	2 Nov 1964	Leicester C	Feb 1995	44(5)	1			2	0	1(1)	0	47(6)	1	Rotherham U	Jul 1997
Todd	Andrew J J	Derby	21 Sep 1974	Blackburn R	Sep 2003	7	0			1	0			8	0	on loan until	Oct 2003
Townsend	Ryan M G	Tameside	2 Sep 1985	Trainee	2003	0(1)	0							0(1)	0	Released	2004
Tueart	Dennis	Newcastle	27 Nov 1949	Stoke C	Dec 1983	8(7)	5	2	0			0(2)	0	10(9)	5	Released	May 1984
Valois	Jean-Louis	France	15 Oct 1973	Clyde	Sep 2004	18(12)	3	3(1)	0	2(1)	1			23(14)	4	Released	May 2005
Vindheim	Rune	Norway	15 May 1972	SK Brann	Oct 1998	8	2	1	0			1	0	10	2	Hartlepool U	Sep 1999
Vinnicombe	Christopher	Exeter	20 Oct 1970	Rangers	Jun 1994	90(5)	3	2	0	9	0	7(1)	1	108(6)	4	Wycombe W	Aug 1998
Waddle	Christopher R	Felling	14 Dec 1960	Sunderland	Jul 1997	26(5)	1	2	0	2(1)	0			30(6)	1	Torquay U	Sep 1998
Waine	Andrew P	Manchester	24 Feb 1983	Trainee	Jul 2002	0(2)	0							0(2)	0	Released	2003
Waldron	Malcolm	Emsworth	6 Sep 1956	Southampton	Sep 1983	16	0	3	1					19	1	Portsmouth	Mar 1984
Walker	J Nicol	Aberdeen	29 Sep 1962	Hearts	Feb 1992	6	0					1	0	7	0	on loan until	Mar 1992
Walsh	Michael T	Blackley	20 Jun 1956	Everton	Dec 1982	3	0							3	0	on loan until	Jan 1983
Ward	Gavin J	Sutton Coldfield	30 Jun 1970	Bolton W	Aug 1998	17	0							17	0	on loan until	Nov 1998
Wardrobe	Michael	Newcastle	24 Mar 1962	Apprentice	Mar 1980	0(1)	0	1	0					1(1)	0	Stockport C	Aug 1981
Weller	Paul A	Brighton	6 Mar 1975	Trainee	Nov 1993	199(53)	11	8(6)	2	12(2)	0	7(1)	0	226(62)	13	Rochdale	Sep 2004
West	Dean	Morley	5 Dec 1972	Bury	Jul 1999	145(13)	5	11	0	6(2)	1	1	0	163(15)	6	Lincoln C	Jul 2004
Wharton	Andrew	Rossendale	21 Dec 1961	Apprentice	Dec 1979	63(2)	6	6(3)	1	7	2	3	0	79(5)	9	Chester C	Feb 1984
Whatmore	Neil	Ellesmere Port	17 May 1955	Oxford U	Aug 1984	8	1			1	0			9	1	Mansfield T	Nov 1984
White	E Winston	Leicester	26 Oct 1958	Colchester U	Oct 1988	93(11)	14	10	3	6	1	6(2)	3	115(13)	21	West Brom A	Mar 1991
Whittingham	Peter M	Nuneaton	8 Sep 1984	Aston Villa	Feb 2005	7	0	2	0					9	0	on loan until	Mar 2005
Williams	David P	Liverpool	18 Sep 1968	Oldham A	Mar 1988	24	0			2	0	2	0	28	0	Cardiff C	Aug 1994
Williams	Michael A	Bradford	21 Nov 1969	Sheffield W	Jul 1997	15(1)	1	2	0	3	0	1	0	21(1)	1	Oxford U	Mar 1999
Williamson	John B	Derby	3 Mar 1981	Trainee	1998	0(1)	0							0(1)	0	Released	1999
Wilson	Paul A	Bradford	2 Aug 1968	Halifax T	Feb 1993	31	0	0(1)	0					31(1)	0	York C	Oct 1994
Winstanley	Mark A	St Helens	22 Jan 1968	Bolton W	Aug 1994	151(1)	5	8	0	13	0	8(1)	0	180(2)	5	Preston N E	Mar 1999
Wood	Ian T	Radcliffe	15 Jan 1948	Oldham A	May 1980	14(3)	0			2(1)	0	3	0	19(4)	0	Released	Nov 1981
Wood	Neil A	Manchester	4 Jan 1983	Manchester U	Jan 2004	8(2)	1	1	0					9(2)	1	on loan until	Apr 2004
Woods	Christopher C E	Boston	14 Nov 1959	Sunderland	Jul 1997	12	0					2	0	14	0	Retired	Aug 1998
Woodworth	Anthony D	Manchester	5 Mar 1968	Apprentice	Mar 1986	1	0							1	0	Released	May 1987
Wright	William H	Corbridge	4 Nov 1962	Trialist	Jan 1981							1	0	1	0	Released	May 1983
Wright	Ian E	Woolwich	3 Nov 1963	Celtic	Feb 2000	4(11)	4							4(11)	4	Retired	May 2000
Yates	Mark J	Birmingham	24 Jan 1970	Birmingham C	Aug 1991	9(9)	1	0(2)	0	1	0	2(1)	0	12(12)	1	Doncaster R	Jul 1993
Young	Kevin	Sunderland	12 Aug 1961	Apprentice	May 1979	114(6)	11	17(1)	0	10(1)	1	5(2)	0	146(10)	12	Bury	Jul 1984
Zelem	Peter	Manchester	13 Feb 1962	Wolves	Aug 1987	17(2)	2	1	0	3	0	2(1)	0	23(3)	2	Released	May 1989
Own goals August 1976 to May 2007							43		4		7		3		57		

Substitutes

The option of using one substitute was first introduced into English League football ready for the start of the 1965-66 season, initially with the stipulation that the use of a substitute should be only to replace an injured player. In the early days a player coming on to the field in such circumstances had the option of wearing a number 12 shirt or an un-numbered shirt. Burnley's first named substitute for a League match was Sammy Todd, who was not called upon during the opening match of the season, at Chelsea, on 21 August 1965. The first Burnley sub to enter the field of play was Ian Towers who replaced Willie Irvine at the start of the second half of the 2-2 draw with Arsenal at Turf Moor on 28 August 1965. It was Towers' only League game of the season and his last League appearance in a Burnley shirt. Len Kinsella was the first Claret to make his League debut as a substitute when he replaced John Angus against Aston Villa on 20 November 1965. Kinsella was also Burnley's first League Cup substitute, coming on for Ralph Coates at Sheffield United on 5 October 1966. Burnley's first FA Cup substitute was Sammy Todd who replaced broken leg victim Willie Irvine during the third round replay with Everton, at Goodison Park, on 31 January 1967.

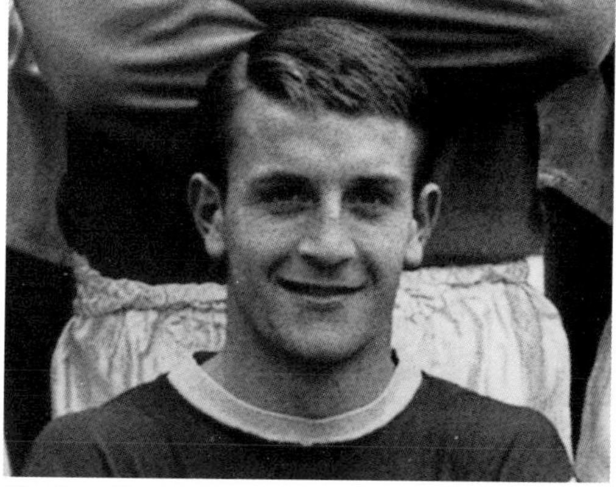

The first Clarets substitute to score in a senior competitive match was Willie Irvine (above), who replaced Martin Dobson and then went on to hit the equaliser in Burnley's 1-1 draw with Nottingham Forest at Turf Moor on 7 October 1967. The first Burnley player to score whilst making his debut as a substitute was Dennis Tueart in the 5-0 victory against Scunthorpe at Turf Moor on New Years Eve 1983.

Two substitutes were first allowed in the FA Cup for the 1986-87 season with most clubs, including Burnley, adopting the number 14 for any second sub used. Darren Heesom was the first Claret to wear 14, coming on for Peter Hampton during Burnley's ignominious 0-3 defeat at Telford in the first round tie at Bucks Head on 15 November 1986. The option of two League substitutes was introduced the following campaign, 1987-88, with Steve Gardner the first Burnley player to wear 14 in a League match. Gardner came on for his Clarets' League debut, replacing Shaun McGrory during the opening game of the season against Colchester at Turf Moor on 15 August 1987.

On 16 March 1991 Andy Farrell made his own little piece of Burnley FC history when he came off the bench and scored twice against Carlisle to turn a 0-1 deficit into a 2-1 victory. Farrell replaced Neil Grewcock after 56 minutes, headed the equaliser after 68 minutes, then crashed a free kick into the Cumbrians' net after 80 minutes. Surprisingly Farrell's two goals in twelve minutes of that match were his only goals of the season.

The concept of a third substitute was introduced for season 1993-94, although until 1995 the third sub named was specifically a goalkeeper, with most clubs, including Burnley, adopting number 13. During 1993-94 David Williams sat on the bench for 59 League and Cup matches and never once got his shirt, (or shorts or boots!), dirty.

Burnley's first-ever substitute goalkeeper was Wayne Russell who took over between the sticks at Oldham on 27 August 1994 when Marlon Beresford was sent off for handling outside the penalty area. Russell, who nominally replaced Ted McMinn, became the first Clarets' keeper to make his League debut as a substitute and also the first Burnley player to wear number 13 in a League match. Russell took over in goal again, this time replacing Gerry Harrison, when Beresford was sent off at Portsmouth on 2 January 1995, the occasion when three Burnley substitutes were used for the first time.

Three outfield substitutes were seen for the first time in a Burnley League side on 28 October 1995, when Adrian Randall, John Francis and Andy Cooke replaced Gary Parkinson, Warren Joyce and Paul McDonald in a 2-2 draw at Bradford City.

More Clarets' history was made on 22 August 2000 when Andy Payton (above) became the first Clarets substitute to score three goals in a senior competitive match. Hartlepool were the victims in a first round League Cup tie at Turf Moor and Payton scored his hat-trick in the second half after replacing Andy Cooke at half time.

Gifton Noel-Williams wrote the latest page of Burnley FC history on substitutes when he replaced Alan Mahon after 34 minutes against Barnsley at Turf Moor on 12 September 2006. With the Clarets 0-2 down, Jon Harley pulled one back then Noel-Williams took over, scoring a second half hat-trick with the Clarets going on to win 4-2 with Gifton becoming the first Burnley substitute ever to score three goals in a League match.

1959 to 2007

Other first team matches (friendlies and/or as detailed)

A number of team line-ups (eg various Lancashire Cup ties and some friendlies) are a combination of senior and reserve players
Friendlies, particularly early season, often include trialists

1959-60

								Goalscorers	Opp goals
friendly re Alex Elder transfer	Aug	17	a	Glentoran	W	8-1		Robson (4), Pilkington, Pointer, Connelly, McIlroy	
new floodlights	Sep	30	a	Folkestone	W	3-1		Connelly (2), White	
benefit for Neil Dougall, Billy's son	Oct	5	a	Plymouth A	W	6-1		White, Harris, Pointer (3), Pilkington	
		19	h	BRITISH OLYMPIC XI	W	5-0		McIlroy (2), Connelly (2), White	
Lancs Cup	Nov	23	h	MANCHESTER C	W	5-1		White, Fenton, Towers, Lochhead, Harris	
Lancs Cup	Jan	13	a	Chester	W	3-1		Meredith, Harris (2)	
Lancs Cup semi	Mar	22	a	Preston N E	W	3-0		Lochhead, Simpson, Harris	
Lancs Cup final	Apr	12	h	MANCHESTER U	W	4-2		Joyce, Lochhead (2), Harris	
in New York	May	28	n	Bayern Munich	W	3-0		Pointer, Pilkington, Miller	
in New York	Jun	1	n	Kilmarnock	L	0-2			
in New York		4	a	New York Americans	D	3-3		Pointer, Robson (2)	
in Montreal		7	a	Montreal Cantalia	L	1-2		Pointer	
in Toronto		9	n	Heart of Midlothian	W	2-1		Pointer (2)	
in New York		11	n	Glenavon	W	6-2		Pilkington (3), Miller (2), Harris	
in Jersey City		19	n	Nice	W	4-0		Pilkington, Lawson (2), Robson	

1960-61

FA Charity Shield	Aug	13	h	WOLVERHAMPTON W	D	2-2	1-0	Miller 15, Connelly 88	55, 87
Lancs Cup	Nov	8	h	SOUTHPORT	W	1-0		Lochhead	
European Cup		16	h	REIMS	W	2-0	2-0	Robson 1, McIlroy 22	
Euro Cup, 2nd leg, in Paris		30	a	Reims	L	2-3	1-0	Robson 32, Connelly 75	50, 57, 76
European Cup	Jan	18	h	HAMBURG	W	3-1	1-0	Pilkington (2) 7, 60, Robson 75	85
Lancs Cup	Feb	21	h	ROCHDALE	W	3-0		Lochhead (2), Meredith	
European Cup , 2nd leg	Mar	15	a	Hamburg	L	1-4	0-2	Harris 55	8, 42, 58, 61
Lancs Cup semi	Apr	17	h	BURY	W	2-0		Towers, Lawson	
Lancs Cup final		25	h	BLACKBURN R	W	1-0	1-0	Lawson	
in Lisbon	May	24	a	Belenenses	D	1-1		unknown	
in Lisbon		27	a	Sporting Club	W	2-1		unknown (2)	

1961-62

at Easter Road	Aug	5	a	Edinburgh Select XI	W	7-4		Connelly, Robson (3), Pointer (3)	
		12	a	Glentoran	W	7-1		Pointer, Harris (2), Lawson (2), Adamson, Connelly	
new floodlights	Oct	4	a	Oldham A	D	3-3		Harris, Robson, Lawson	
Lancs Cup		17	a	Preston N E	W	2-1		Lochhead (2)	
		24	a	Folkestone	W	5-2		Lochhead (3), Fenton, Lawson	
Lancs Cup semi	Apr	30	h	BLACKBURN R	W	3-2		Irvine (2), Morgan	
Cathedral festival	May	10	a	Coventry C	W	4-2		Robson, Price, Pointer (2)	
Lancs Cup final		11	h	LIVERPOOL	W	2-1	1-1	Towers (2)	
		17	a	Norrkoping	L	0-2			
		21	a	Djurgaarden	W	3-0		Pointer (3)	
in Copenhagen		24	a	Danish XI	W	5-3		Towers (3), Harris, McIlroy	
		27	a	Gothenburg XI	D	2-2		Towers, Fenton	

1962-63

at Tynecastle	Aug	4	a	Edinburgh Select XI	W	4-2		Connelly, Robson (2), Harris	
		11	a	Bradford C	D	3-3		Pointer (2), Harris	
new floodlights	Oct	10	a	Portsmouth	D	1-1		Miller	
Lancs Cup		17	a	Everton	W	1-0		Robson	
Colin McDonald testimonial	Nov	6	h	ALL STARS XI	L	4-6		Connelly, Harris, Lochhead, Pointer	
new floodlights	Feb	26	a	Peterborough U	W	3-1		Pointer, Harris, Robson	
	Mar	16	a	Hull C	D	1-1		Lochhead	
Lancs Cup	Apr	3	a	Blackpool	L	1-3		Robson	

1963-64

	Aug	9	a	Bury	L	0-2			
		17	h	BURY	W	4-0		Lochhead (2), Irvine, Connelly	
Lancs Cup	Nov	4	a	Manchester U	L	2-5		Irvine, Price	
Tommy Cummings testimonial		12	h	ALL STARS XI	D	10-10		Harris, Lochhead, Robson (2), Meredith (2), Connelly (3), Miller	

1964-65

								Goalscorers	Opp goals
	Aug	8	a	Newcastle U	D	1-1		Towers	
		15	h	NEWCASTLE U	L	0-1			
Lancs Cup	Oct	28	a	Chester	D	0-0			
Lancs Cup replay	Dec	15	h	CHESTER	W	8-1		Robson (3), Pointer (3), Bellamy (2)	
Lancs Cup	Mar	9	a	Everton	W	3-1		Robson, Latcham, Hill og	
Lancs Cup semi		30	h	PRESTON N E	W	5-1		Latcham (3), Coates, Price	
Lancs Cup final	Apr	14	h	SOUTHPORT	W	2-0	0-0	Pointer, Towers	
Ken Hiley family benefit		26	h	EX CLARETS XI	D	5-5		Morgan, Elder (2) 1p, O'Neil, Harris	

1965-66

	Aug	6	a	Austria Vienna	D	0-0			
		10	a	Lausanne Sports	W	2-1		Irvine, Morgan	
		13	a	Servette Geneve	D	0-0			
Lancs Cup	Nov	23	a	Chorley	D	1-1		Thomson	
Lancs Cup replay	Dec	21	h	CHORLEY	W	4-0		Latcham, Blant, Murray, Smith	
Lancs Cup	Jan	31	h	Preston N E	W	1-0		Kinsella	
Lancs Cup semi	Apr	14	h	ROCHDALE	W	2-0		Latcham, Kinsella	
Lancs Cup final	May	16	a	Barrow	W	4-0	3-0	Latcham, Bellamy, Kinsella, Blant	

1966-67

	Aug	3	a	Hannover	D	1-1		Coates	
		6	a	Offenbach Kickers	D	1-1		Miller	
		8	a	Munich 1860	L	0-5			
Inter Cities Fairs Cup (1)	Sep	20	a	Stuttgart	D	1-1	1-0	Irvine 17	50p
Fairs Cup (1), 2nd leg		27	h	STUTTGART	W	2-0	0-0	Coates 58, Lochhead 70	
Inter Cities Fairs Cup (2)	Oct	19	a	Lausanne Sports	W	3-1	2-1	Coates 30, Harris 45, Lochhead 87	16
Fairs Cup (2), 2nd leg		25	h	LAUSANNE SPORTS	W	5-0	2-0	Lochhead (3) 26, 32, 74, O'Neil 49, Irvine 52	
Lancs Cup	Nov	1	a	Blackburn R	D	0-0			
Inter Cities Fairs Cup (3)	Jan	18	h	NAPOLI	W	3-0	2-0	Coates 3, Latcham 21, Lochhead 51	
Fairs Cup (3), 2nd leg	Feb	8	a	Napoli	D	0-0	0-0		
Lancs Cup replay	Mar	7	h	BLACKBURN R	L	0-2			
Inter Cities Fairs Cup (4)	Apr	4	a	Eintracht Frankfurt	D	1-1	0-1	Miller 55	36
Fairs Cup (4), 2nd leg		18	h	EINTRACHT FRANFURT	L	1-2	0-1	Miller 86	33, 72

1967-68

	Aug	5	a	Stockport C	L	0-1			
		9	a	Aston Villa	D	0-0			
		11	a	Crystal P	W	3-2		Bellamy (2), Blant	
Lancs Cup	Oct	17	h	PRESTON N E	W	5-0		S.Ternent, Murray, Brown (3) 1p	
Lancs Cup	Mar	5	h	CHORLEY	W	2-0		Buxton p, Irvine	
		8	a	Preston N E	D	2-2		Lochhead, Morgan	
Lancs Cup semi	Apr	29	h	BARROW	W	1-0		Casper	
Lancs Cup final	May	13	a	Morecambe	L	1-2	1-1	Dobson	

1968-69

opening of new stand	Jul	29	a	Southport	W	2-1		O'Neil p, Murray	
	Aug	2	a	Bury	L	0-1			
Lancs Cup	Oct	22	h	LIVERPOOL	L	0-1			
Div 1 fixture aban 45m, snow	Mar	31	h	SUNDERLAND	aban	1-0		Casper p	

1969-70

	Jul	26	a	Tranmere R	W	4-0		Casper, Thomas, Kindon (2)	
		30	a	Bolton W	D	1-1		Collins	
opening of Cricket Field stand	Aug	2	h	MIDDLESBROUGH	D	1-1		Kindon	
Lancs Cup		24	h	ROCHDALE	W	2-0		Nulty, Murray	
Lancs Cup	Dec	9	h	BURY	W	2-0		Casper, R.Ternent	
Lancs Cup semi	Mar	18	h	OLDHAM A	W	4-0		Latcham, Nulty (2), Kinsella	
Lancs Cup final	Apr	9	h	BARROW	W	3-2	0-1	Nulty, Arrowsmith og, Kinsella p	

1970-71

								Goalscorers	Opp goals
	Aug	1	a	Middlesbrough	D	2-2		Nulty, Spraggon og	
		3	a	Scarborough	W	4-3		Nulty (2), Kindon, Thomson	
		5	a	Doncaster R	D	2-2		Kindon, Nulty	
		8	a	Luton T	W	2-1		Nulty, Waldron	
Texaco Cup	Sep	15	h	HEART OF MIDLOTHIAN	W	3-1	2-0	Docherty 2, Merrington 16, Kindon 56	80
Lancs Cup		16	h	ROCHDALE	D	1-1		West	
Lancs Cup replay		23	a	Rochdale	L	0-1			
Texaco Cup, agg 4-5		30	a	Heart of Midlothian	L	1-4	0-2	Casper 80	14, 43, 50og, 71
	Jan	23	a	Blackburn R	L	0-2			

1971-72

	Jul	31	a	Bolton W	L	0-1			
	Aug	7	a	Oldham A	D	1-1		Casper	
Lancs Cup	Sep	7	h	BARROW	W	2-0		Probert (2) 1p	
Lancs Cup	Dec	7	h	SOUTHPORT	D	2-2		Fletcher, Kindon	
Lancs Cup replay		14	a	Southport	W	2-1		Thomson, Kindon	
Lancs Cup semi	Mar	29	h	LIVERPOOL	W	1-0		West	
Lancs Cup final	Apr	20	a	Manchester U	D	2-2	1-1	Kindon, Bellamy	
Lancs Cup final replay	May	2	h	MANCHESTER U	W	3-0	1-0	Dobson, James (2)	

1972-73

	Jul	22	a	Swansea C	W	2-1		Casper, Ingham	
		24	a	Newport C	D	1-1		James	
Watney Cup		29	a	Lincoln C	W	1-0	0-0	James 89	
Watney Cup	Aug	2	h	BRISTOL R	L	0-2	0-1		16, 48
		5	a	Blackpool	L	0-2			
Lancs Cup	Oct	10	a	Blackpool	L	0-2			
John Angus testimonial	May	1	h	MILLIONAIRE XI	W	4-3		Fletcher, Dobson, Hankin (2)	
Warwick Rimmer testimonial		2	a	Bolton W	L	1-3		Nulty	

1973-74

	Aug	11	a	Penzance	W	4-0		Casper (2), Dobson, Nulty	
		14	a	Torquay U	W	3-0		Casper, Ingham (2)	
		15	a	Kettering T	D	2-2		Noble, Atkinson og	
FA Charity Shield		18	a	Manchester C	W	1-0	0-0	Waldron 66	
Texaco Cup	Sep	18	h	EAST FIFE	W	7-0	5-0	Noble 8, Nulty (2) 12, 31, Fletcher (3) 27, 37, 76, James 65	
Texaco Cup, agg 10-2	Oct	3	a	East Fife	W	3-2	0-1	Fletcher 70, Hankin 74, Noble 88	2, 67
Lancs Cup		23	h	MANCHESTER U	D	0-0			
Texaco Cup		24	a	Heart of Midlothian	W	3-0	0-0	Noble 51, Dobson 61, James 90	
Texaco Cup, agg 8-0	Nov	6	h	HEART OF MIDLOTHIAN	W	5-0	2-0	Collins 14, Nulty 17, Fletcher 74, Hankin (2) 79, 82	
Texaco Cup semi		27	h	NORWICH C	W	2-0	1-0	James 33p, Noble 81	
Texaco Cup semi, agg 5-2	Dec	12	a	Norwich C	W	3-2	0-1	Hankin 84, Noble 87, Waldron 89	21, 77
Lancs Cup replay	Apr	4	a	Manchester U	L	1-3		Morris	
Texaco Cup final, aet, 1-1 at 90m	Apr	24	a	Newcastle U	L	1-2	1-1	Fletcher 25	31, 102
	May	29	a	Martinique	L	3-4		Fletcher, Waldron, James	
		30	a	St Lucia	W	5-0		Fletcher (2), James (2) 1p, Nulty	

1974-75

in Stavanger	Jul	31	a	Viking	L	1-2		Ingham	
in Oslo	Aug	7	a	Valerengen	W	2-0		Dobson (2)	
in Bergen		9	a	Brann Sports	W	2-0		Dobson, Fletcher	
	Jan	25	a	Sheffield W	W	3-1		Hankin (2), James	
in Madeira	May	21	n	Maritimo	D	3-3		Collins, Morris, Thomson	

1975-76

	Aug	5	a	Plymouth A	W	1-0		James	
		9	a	Swindon T	L	1-3		Hankin	
		12	h	BLACKBURN R	W	1-0		Hankin	
	May	9	a	Bermuda Select XI	W	4-3		Fletcher, Hankin, Noble, Ingham	
		16	a	Bermuda National XI	W	3-0		Hankin (2), Parker	

1976-77

Anglo Scottish Cup	Aug	7	a	Blackburn R	D	1-1	1-0	Flynn 42	83
Anglo Scottish Cup		11	a	Blackpool	L	1-2	0-2	Noble 89	1, 4
Anglo Scottish Cup		14	h	BOLTON W	W	1-0	1-0	Ingham 25	
	Nov	13	a	Sheffield W	L	1-2		Fletcher	
Div 2 fixture aban 45m, frost	Dec	11	a	Notts C	aban	0-0			
in Palma	May	29	a	Real Mallorca	D	3-3		Loggie (2), Smith	

1977-78

								Goalscorers	Opp goals
Anglo Scottish Cup	Aug	2	h	BLACKBURN R	W	2-1	1-0	Smith 8, Ingham 60	75
Anglo Scottish Cup		6	a	Bolton W	L	0-1	0-1		41
Anglo Scottish Cup		9	h	BLACKPOOL	L	0-4	0-2		36, 44, 51, 66
Frank Casper testimonial	Sep	20	h	CASPER'S XI	L	2-4		Fletcher (2)	

1978-79

Anglo Scottish Cup	Aug	5	h	PRESTON N E	W	3-2	2-0	Kindon 5, Ingham 43, Fletcher 72	48, 70
Anglo Scottish Cup		8	h	BLACKPOOL	W	3-1	2-0	Ingham 21, Smith 34, Cochrane 82	52
Anglo Scottish Cup		12	a	Blackburn R	D	1-1	1-1	Smith 2	9
Anglo Scottish Cup	Sep	12	h	CELTIC	W	1-0	0-0	Kindon 56	
AS Cup, 2nd leg, agg 3-1		27	a	Celtic	W	2-1	2-0	Brennan 21, Kindon 26	68p
Anglo Scottish Cup semi	Oct	31	a	Mansfield T	W	2-1	0-1	Kindon 79, James 82	31
2nd leg, aet, agg 2-2, 8-7 pens	Nov	7	h	MANSFIELD T	L	0-1	0-1		30
Anglo Scottish Cup final	Dec	5	a	Oldham A	W	4-1	2-0	Kindon (2) 1, 75, Noble 3, Thomson 67	86
AS Cup final, 2nd leg, agg 4-2		12	h	OLDHAM A	L	0-1	0-1		41

1979-80

Anglo Scottish Cup	Aug	4	a	Blackburn R	D	2-2	1-0	Kindon 1, Metcalfe 68og	51, 79
Anglo Scottish Cup		7	a	Blackpool	L	2-3	0-0	Noble 58p, Ingham 90	48, 50, 79
Anglo Scottish Cup		11	h	PRESTON N E	L	1-2	0-0	Brennan 62	67, 74
on the Isle of Wight	Mar	16	a	Newport	L	0-2			

1980-81

Anglo Scottish Cup	Jul	29	a	Bury	L	1-2	0-0	Dobson 58p	48, 78
Anglo Scottish Cup	Aug	2	h	OLDHAM A	W	3-1	0-1	Scott 51, Taylor 58, Cavener 84	6
Anglo Scottish Cup		5	h	SHREWSBURY T	D	1-1	1-1	Cassidy 1	10

1981-82

Football League Group Cup	Aug	15	h	CARLISLE U	W	4-2	4-2	Hamilton (2) 2, 29, Taylor (2) 28, 40	10, 41
Football League Group Cup		18	a	Preston N E	W	1-0	1-0	Hamilton 14	
Football League Group Cup		22	a	Blackpool	D	0-0	0-0		
Football League Group Cup	Dec	8	h	WATFORD	W	2-1	2-0	Scott 18, Holt 23	57
F League Group Cup semi	Feb	16	a	Wimbledon	L	0-5	0-2		27, 38, 51, 57, 70
Alan Stevenson testimonial	Mar	24	h	MANCHESTER C XI	D	3-3		Young, Casper, Laws	

1982-83

aban 79m, floodlight failure	Aug	3	a	Folkestone	aban	0-1			
at Folkestone		5	n	Maidstone U	W	3-0		Scott, Hamilton, Steven	
at Folkestone		6	n	Queens Park R XI	D	1-1		Cassidy	
Lancs Cup		14	h	OLDHAM A	D	1-1		Hamilton	
Lancs Cup		17	a	Rochdale	D	0-0			
Lancs Cup		21	h	BURY	D	0-0			

1983-84

IOM tournament, in Ramsey	Aug	5	n	St Mirren	W	2-1		Scott (2)	
IOM tournament, in Douglas		7	n	Sunderland	L	0-1			
IOM tournament, in Douglas		9	a	Isle of Man	W	6-0		Flynn, Young, Donovan, Scott, Reeves (2) 2p	
Lancs Cup		13	a	Preston N E	W	2-1		Reeves p, Wharton	
Lancs Cup		16	h	BLACKURN R	D	1-1		Scott	
Lancs Cup		20	h	BLACKPOOL	D	0-0			
	Feb	6	a	Torquay U	L	0-2			
Associate Members Cup		21	h	BOLTON W	W	2-1	1-0	Donachie 7, Biggins 84	62
Associate Members Cup	Mar	13	h	DARLINGTON	W	2-1	0-1	Biggins 50, Baker 70	12
A M Cup, aet, 1-1 at 90m		20	a	Doncaster R	W	3-1	1-1	Flynn 28, Daley 101, Biggins 105	45
A M Cup, aet, 0-0 at 90m	Apr	17	a	Tranmere R	L	0-2	0-0		93, 98
Norman Bell testimonial	May	16	a	Blackburn R	L	1-3		Biggins	

1984-85

	Aug	3	a	Great Harwood T	W	2-0		Powell, Flynn	
		5	a	Morecambe	L	0-1			
Lancs Cup		11	h	BLACKPOOL	W	1-0		Hird	
Lancs Cup		14	a	Rochdale	L	0-1			
Lancs Cup		18	h	WIGAN A	L	1-2		Scott	
Freight Rover Trophy (ex AMC)	Jan	29	h	STOCKPORT C	W	5-1	3-0	Biggins (2) 22, 28, Devine 31, Phelan 58, Hutchison 72	66
FRT 2nd leg, agg 6-1	Feb	4	a	Stockport C	W	1-0	0-0	Hird 61	
FRT aet, 1-1 at 90m, 4-5 pens	Mar	19	a	Tranmere R	D	2-2	0-0	Devine 85, Phelan 103	65, 98
FRT aet, 1-1 at 90m, 3-5 pens	Apr	10	a	Mansfield T	D	1-1	1-0	Taylor 29	81

1985-86

								Goalscorers	Opp goals
	Jul	27	h	LIVERPOOL	L	1-5		Taylor	
Wayne Biggins transfer match		30	a	Matlock T	W	5-3		Overson, Biggins (2), Lawrence, Taylor	
Lancs Cup	Aug	3	h	BURY	L	1-3		Taylor	
Lancs Cup		6	a	Rochdale	W	7-0		Hampton, Biggins (3), Grewcock (2), Chippendale	
Lancs Cup		10	h	BOLTON W	W	4-0		Grewcock, Biggins (3)	
Lancs Cup final		13	a	Blackburn R	L	0-1	0-0		
Freight Rover Trophy	Jan	21	a	Chesterfield	W	2-1	1-1	Lawrence 25, Taylor 46	10
Freight Rover Trophy	Mar	13	h	DARLINGTON	D	1-1	1-1	Taylor 13	18

1986-87

								Goalscorers	Opp goals
Lancs Cup	Aug	9	a	Wigan A	D	1-1		Hoskin	
Lancs Cup		12	h	BOLTON W	L	2-3		Hoskin, Heggarty	
Lancs Cup		16	h	PRESTON N E	D	0-0			
	Dec	6	h	MANCHESTER U XI	L	0-4			
Freight Rover Trophy		9	a	Blackpool	W	3-2	2-1	Hoskin 3, Murphy (2) 36, 83	9, 68
Freight Rover Trophy		16	h	BOLTON W	L	0-2	0-1		22, 81
FRT fixture, aban 45m, fog	Jan	20	a	Bolton W	aban	1-1		Grewcock	
Freight Rover Trophy		27	a	Bolton W	L	1-2	0-1	Parker 56	37, 74

1987-88

								Goalscorers	Opp goals
Lancs Cup	Aug	1	h	BLACKPOOL	L	0-2			
Lancs Cup		4	h	BLACKBURN R	W	2-1		Comstive, Britton	
Lancs Cup		7	a	Bolton W	D	1-1		Oghani	
Sherpa Van Trophy (ex FRT)	Oct	27	a	Tranmere R	W	2-1	1-0	Oghani 4, Grewcock 68	47
Sherpa Van Trophy	Nov	24	h	ROCHDALE	W	3-2	2-0	Grewcock 7, Reeves 43, Farrell 77	73, 76
	Dec	5	h	PRESTON N E	W	3-1		Reeves, Hooper, Britton	
Sherpa Van Trophy	Jan	19	h	CHESTER C	W	1-0	0-0	Oghani 80	
		30	h	HUDDERSFIELD T	D	1-1		Taylor	
Sherpa Van Trophy	Feb	9	a	Bury	W	1-0	1-0	Comstive 37p	
SV Trophy, aet, 5-3 on pens	Mar	8	h	HALIFAX T	D	0-0	0-0		
SV Trophy northern final	Apr	12	h	PRESTON N E	D	0-0	0-0		
2nd leg, aet, agg 3-1		19	a	Preston N E	W	3-1	1-0	Oghani 32, Hoskin 93, Comstive 117	66
SV Trophy final, at Wembley	May	29	n	Woverhampton W	L	0-2	0-1		22, 51

1988-89

								Goalscorers	Opp goals
Lancs Cup	Aug	6	h	PRESTON N E	L	0-1			
Lancs Cup		9	h	BLACKBURN R	L	1-3		Comstive p	
Lancs Cup		13	a	Blackpool	L	1-2		Oghani	
Sherpa Van Trophy	Nov	22	a	York C	W	2-0	1-0	O'Connell 8, Comstive 60p	
Sherpa Van Trophy		29	h	HARTLEPOOL U	W	3-0	1-0	Davis 8, White 57, O'Connell 76	
SVT, aet, 2-4 on pens	Jan	17	h	CREWE A	D	1-1	0-1	Macowat 57og	30
in Cheltenham	Feb	19	a	Endsleigh XI	W	7-2		O'Connell (2), Miller (2), Grewcock, Oghani, White	

1989-90

								Goalscorers	Opp goals
	Jul	26	a	Gloucester C	L	1-3		McGrory	
		28	a	Worcester C	L	0-3			
	Aug	1	h	HIBERNIAN	L	0-1			
Lancs Cup		5	h	BOLTON W	D	2-2		Mumby, Farrell	
Lancs Cup		8	h	BLACKBURN R	L	0-2			
Lancs Cup		12	h	WIGAN A	L	0-2			
Leyland DAF Cup (ex SVT)	Nov	7	a	Preston N E	L	0-3	0-1		24, 83, 84
Leyland DAF Cup		28	h	STOCKPORT C	L	0-2	0-1		39, 88
in Cheltenham	Dec	4	a	Endsleigh XI	W	5-1		Francis (3), Deary, McKay	

1990-91

								Goalscorers	Opp goals
	Aug	2	a	Emley	W	1-0		Eli	
		7	h	COVENTRY C	L	0-2			
Lancs Cup		11	h	BLACKPOOL	D	2-2		Francis, Futcher	
Lancs Cup		14	h	WIGAN A	W	3-1		Farrell, Futcher, Francis	
Lancs Cup		18	a	Bolton W	L	0-3			
Leyland DAF Cup	Nov	6	h	CREWE A	W	2-1	1-0	White 43, Francis 89	60
	Dec	17	h	DYNAMO BREST	W	1-0		Deakin	
Leyland DAF Cup	Jan	8	a	Stockport C	D	1-1	1-1	Farrell 23	8
LDC replay, aet, 2-2 after 90m		22	h	STOCKPORT C	W	3-2	1-1	Eli 20, Jakub 58, White 112	37, 69
Leyland DAF Cup		29	a	Bradford C	W	1-0	0-0	Futcher 72	
Leyland DAF Cup	Feb	19	a	Preston N E	L	1-6	0-4	Bray 84	2,25,26,38,55,78
Play off semi	May	19	a	Torquay U	L	0-2	0-1		5, 83
Play off semi, 2nd leg, agg 1-2		22	h	TORQUAY U	W	1-0	0-0	Evans 90og	

1991-92

								Goalscorers	Opp goals
	Jul	25	a	Dynamo Stavropol	D	1-1		Conroy	
in Kidlovsk		29	a	Asmaral	D	1-1		Francis	
Lancs Cup	Aug	3	h	BURY	L	0-2			
Lancs Cup		6	h	BLACKBURN R	D	1-1		Conroy	
Jimmy Holland testimonial		8	h	OLDHAM A	L	1-2		Lancashire	
Lancs Cup		10	a	Preston N E	L	1-5		Deary	
Div 4 fixture, later expunged		24	h	ALDERSHOT	W	2-0	0-0	Conroy 46p, Francis 49	
Autoglass Trophy (ex LD Cup)	Oct	22	a	Blackpool	W	3-1	3-1	Francis 32, Eli (2) 36, 41	16
Autoglass Trophy	Nov	19	h	DONCASTER R	W	2-0	2-0	Francis 28, Eli 44	
	Dec	3	h	DYNAMO STAVROPOL	W	4-3		Conroy, Francis, Sonner (2)	
Div 4 fixture, later expunged		21	a	Aldershot	W	2-1	0-0	Harper 72, Lancashire 79	88
FA Cup tie aban 76m, fog	Jan	14	a	Derby C	aban	0-2			
AT tie aban 90m, frost		21	h	SCARBOROUGH	aban	0-0			
Autoglass Trophy	Feb	4	h	SCARBOROUGH	W	3-1	0-0	Conroy 56, Deary 63, Eli 87	71
AT aet, 1-1 at 90m, 4-2 pens		18	a	Rotherham U	D	1-1	1-0	Francis 10	71
Autoglass Trophy	Mar	17	h	HUDDERSFIELD T	W	2-0	2-0	Conroy 9p, Eli 24	
AT northern final	Apr	7	h	STOCKPORT C	L	0-1	0-1		33
2nd leg, agg 1-3		15	a	Stockport C	L	1-2	1-1	Pender 22	6, 73
	May	19	h	AJAX	L	0-1			

1992-93

								Goalscorers	Opp goals
	Jul	24	a	Burnley Bank Hall	W	4-1		Lancashire, Monington, McKenzie (2)	
Lancs Cup		29	h	PRESTON N E	W	5-1		Randall (2), Conroy, Painter, Deary	
Lancs Cup	Aug	1	a	Blackpool	D	1-1		Conroy	
		4	h	CHELSEA	W	1-0		Conroy	
		7	h	DYNAMO MOSCOW	L	2-4		Harper, Conroy	
LC final, won 4-3 on pens		11	h	BURY	D	2-2	1-1	Randall, Painter	
Autoglass Trophy	Jan	19	a	Blackpool	W	3-1	0-1	Conroy (2) 62, 78, Farrell 76	25
Autoglass Trophy	Feb	2	a	Chesterfield	L	0-3	0-2		26, 45, 87

1993-94

								Goalscorers	Opp goals
Lancs Cup	Jul	24	h	BLACKPOOL	W	4-3		Heath, Eyres, Conroy (2)	
Lancs Cup		27	h	BOLTON W	L	0-1			
Lancs Cup		31	a	Rochdale	L	1-4		Francis	
new floodlights	Aug	4	a	Morecambe	L	1-2		Heath p	
Billy Urmson testimonial		6	a	Oldham A	L	1-4		Painter	
		7	h	LIVERPOOL	L	0-4			
Autoglass Trophy	Oct	19	a	Preston N E	L	1-2	0-0	Eyres 87	68, 75
Autoglass Trophy	Nov	9	h	CARLISLE U	L	1-2	0-1	Russell 51	41, 90
Play off semi	May	15	h	PLYMOUTH A	D	0-0	0-0		
Play off semi, 2nd leg, agg 3-1		18	a	Plymouth A	W	3-1	2-1	Francis (2) 29, 31, Joyce 81	15
Play off final, at Wembley		29	n	Stockport C	W	2-1	1-1	Eyres 29, Parkinson 66	2

1994-95

							Goalscorers
	Jul	10	a	Mauritius XI	L	0-3	
Lancs Cup		23	h	BURY	L	1-2	Mullin
Lancs Cup		26	h	MANCHESTER U XI	L	2-3	Deary, Peel
Lancs Cup		30	a	Rochdale	W	2-0	Eyres (2) 2p
	Aug	6	a	Falkirk	D	1-1	Robinson
Penrith FC centenary	Nov	3	a	Penrith	W	6-2	Flodstrom (2), Mullin (3), Francis
Div 1 fixture aban 65m, flood	Dec	26	h	PORT VALE	aban	1-2	McMinn

1995-96

								Goalscorers	Opp goals
Lancs Cup	Jul	22	a	Southport	L	0-1			
Lancs Cup		25	h	WIGAN A	L	0-3			
		29	a	Cardiff C	D	0-0			
		31	a	Ebbw Vale	D	1-1		Philliskirk	
	Aug	5	h	MANCHESTER C	W	2-1		Nogan, Francis	
AW Shield (ex A'glass)	Oct	17	a	Rotherham U	D	1-1	1-0	Nogan 44	67
Auto Windscreens Shield	Nov	7	h	CHESTER C	D	1-1	1-0	Nogan 43	54
AWS after sd extra time		29	a	Crewe A	W	1-0	0-0	Nogan 105	
Auto Windscreens Shield	Jan	6	a	Carlisle U	L	0-5	0-3		12, 14, 30, 49, 89

1996-97

								Goalscorers	Opp goals
behind closed doors	Jul	22	h	OLDHAM A	W	2-0		Nogan, Gleghorn	
		27	a	Coleraine	W	4-0		Eyres, Thompson, Hoyland, Boer	
		29	a	Ards	W	5-0		Bambo, Gleghorn, Eyres, Boer, Nogan	
		30	a	Glenavon	D	0-0			
	Aug	1	a	Glentoran	W	4-0		Nogan (2), Smith, Gleghorn	
		3	a	Crusaders	D	0-0			
		5	a	Chester C	L	0-2			
		12	h	LIVERPOOL	L	0-4			
Auto Windscreens Shield	Dec	10	a	Hartlepool U	W	2-0	1-0	Nogan 14, Eyres 55	
FAC tie aban 45m, f'light failure		17	h	WALSALL	aban	0-1			
Auto Windscreens Shield	Feb	4	h	STOCKPORT C	L	0-1	0-1		18

1997-98

	Jul	19	a	Crusaders	D	2-2		Barnes p, Eyres	
		22	a	Linfield	W	2-1		Barnes (2)	
		24	a	Glenavon	D	1-1		Barnes	
		26	a	Glentoran	W	4-1		Cooke (2), Matthew, Weller	
		31	h	GREMIO	W	1-0		Cooke	
	Aug	2	h	MANCHESTER C	L	0-3			
Auto Windscreens Shield	Jan	27	h	NOTTS C	W	2-0	1-0	Little 22, Cooke 61	
Auto Windscreens Shield	Feb	3	h	CARLISLE U	W	4-1	1-0	Payton 17, Vinnicombe 61, Cooke 74, Henderson 90	55
Auto Windscreens Shield		17	h	PRESTON N E	W	1-0	1-0	Payton 39	
AWS northern final	Mar	10	a	Grimsby T	D	1-1	1-0	Payton 23	78
AWS nf, 2nd leg, agg 1-3		17	h	GRIMSBY T	L	0-2	0-1		10, 57

1998-99

	Jul	18	a	Dawlish T	W	4-0		Payton p, Cooke, Carr-Lawton, Smith	
		21	a	Elmore	W	4-0		Little (2) 1p, Payton, Smith	
		25	a	Halifax T	D	3-3		Blatherwick, Cooke, Sertori og	
		28	a	Morecambe	L	0-1			
	Aug	1	a	Rochdale	W	1-0		Monington og	
Auto Windscreens Shield	Dec	8	h	PRESTON N E	L	0-1	0-0		57

1999-2000

	Jul	22	h	EVERTON	W	1-0		Lee	
		25	h	SUNDERLAND	L	0-2			
		27	a	Rochdale	W	1-0		Little	
		31	a	Carlisle U	W	2-1		Cooke, Lee	
AWS, after sd extra time	Dec	7	a	Wigan A	L	1-2	1-1	Lee 27	38p, 114

2000-01

IOM tournament, in Douglas	Jul	23	n	Oldham A	L	1-3		Mellon	
IOM tournament, in Douglas		26	a	Isle of Man XI	L	0-1			
IOM tournament, in Douglas		28	n	Darlington	W	3-2		Cooke (2) 1p, Mullin	
		31	h	NEWCASTLE U	L	0-1			
	Aug	2	h	MANCHESTER C	W	2-1		Gray, Mullin	
		4	a	Rochdale	L	0-1			
closed doors, at Carrington	Jan	10	a	Manchester U XI	L	1-7		Little	

2001-02

IOM tournament, in Douglas	Jul	22	n	Wrexham	W	2-0		Davis, Taylor	
IOM tournament, in Ramsey		24	a	Isle of Man XI	W	1-0		Payton	
IOM, in Douglas, 5-6 pens		25	n	Oldham A	D	1-1		Taylor	
IOM final, in Douglas		28	n	Wrexham	L	0-1			
		31	h	EVERTON	L	0-1			
	Aug	4	h	CHELSEA	L	1-2		I.Moore	

2002-03

IOM, in Douglas, 4-3 pens	Jul	21	n	Wrexham	D	3-3		Gnohere, Taylor, Davis	
IOM tournament, in Douglas		23	n	Luton T	L	1-3		Blake p	
IOM tournament, in Ramsey		26	a	Isle of Man XI	W	5-0		Blake (2), Papadopoulos, Payton, Davis	
		31	h	BOLTON W	D	1-1		Taylor	
	Aug	4	a	Bury	D	1-1		Grant	

2003-04

IOM, in Douglas, 4-3 pens	Jul	20	n	Blackpool	D	1-1		Taylor p	
IOM tournament, in Peel		22	n	Wrexham	L	1-4		I.Moore	
IOM tournament, in Douglas		25	n	Rotherham U	W	2-0		Blake, Little	
		27	h	LEEDS U	W	4-2		Chaplow, I.Moore (2) 1p, Blake p	
		30	a	Accrington S	D	1-1		I.Moore	
	Aug	2	h	BIRMINGHAM C	D	2-2		I.Moore, Blake p	

2004-05

							Goalscorers	Opp goals
	Jul	10	a	Accrington S	W	2-1	Moore, Yates	
		17	h	DUNDEE U	L	1-2	Blake	
		22	h	EVERTON	D	1-1	Blake	
in Vocklabruck, Austria		27	a	Wacker Burghausen	D	1-1	Branch	
in Freilassing, Austria		31	a	Munich 1860	D	1-1	Sinclair	
Stan Ternent testimonial	Aug	17	h	MANCHESTER U XI	L	1-3	Pugh	
Champ. fixture aban 19m, flood	Jan	1	h	LEICESTER C	aban	0-0		

2005-06

	Jul	16	a	Cheltenham T	D	0-0		
		20	a	Accrington S	W	3-0	McGreal, Branch, Elliott	
		23	h	MALAGA	D	0-0		
in Abtenau, Austria		26	n	PAOK Salonika	D	1-1	G.O'Connor	
in Bad Wimsbach, Austria		31	n	Wacker Burghausen	D	1-1	J.O'Connor	

2006-07

	Jul	8	a	Accrington S	W	3-2	Gray, Jones, Mahon	
		18	a	Bury	D	0-0		
		22	h	BOLTON W	W	2-1	Gray, Hyde	
in Garda, Italy		25	a	Selezione Verona	W	7-0	Jones (4), Gray, Lafferty, Cristofoli og	
in Garda, Italy		29	n	Alense Vivaldi	W	4-1	Jones, Gray (2), McCann	
Graham Branch testimonial	May	7	h	EX CLARETS	W	6-4	Lafferty, Mahon, Jones, Rodriguez, Jensen (2)	

The FA Charity Shield at Turf Moor in August 1960
Brian Miller (left) scored Burnley's first goal against Wolves in a 2-2 draw

Other senior line ups

Other senior team line ups not included in the seasonal pages.
Apart from the FA Cup ties shown, these are all the competitions that constitute "other" matches in the schedules of players' appearances and goals.

FA CUP

(campaigns not within Football League seasons)

1885-86

Round 1

17 Oct 1885 v Darwen Old Wanderers (a), lost 0-11

Burnley's first ever FA Cup tie was not treated with the importance it deserved.

With professionals then ineligible for the FA Cup and having already arranged a first team fixture for that date, the club fielded a team of reserves at Darwen and suffered what is still Burnley FC's record defeat in senior peacetime football.

Unfortunately the Burnley team that lined up on that historic day does not appear to be recorded anywhere.

1886-87

Round 1

23 Oct 1886 v Astley Bridge (a), drew 3-3

There are various versions of this team line up depending upon which newspaper report is consulted. Believe it or not there are even different versions of the final score which has been confirmed by the Football Association to be 3-3.

McConnell, Whittaker, Birnie, McFetridge, H.Smith, Keenan, McCrae, Place senior, Friel, Sugg, Howarth.

Scorers : Place senior (2), unknown

Replay

30 Oct 1886 v Astley Bridge (h), drew 2-2

McConnell, Whittaker, Birnie, Keenan, Jackson, H.Smith, McCrae, Place senior, Friel, Fulton, McFetridge

Scorers : unknown, Keenan

Both Burnley and Astley Bridge subsequently withdrew from the competition

1887-88

Round 1

15 Oct 1887 v Darwen Old Wanderers (h), won 4-0

McConnell, Bury, Lang, Abrahams, Sugg, McFetridge, Friel, McCrae, Waugh, Elston, Gallocher.

Scorers : Friel, McFetridge (2), unknown

Att : 2,000

Round 2

5 Nov 1887 v Accrington (a), lost 2-3

McConnell, Bury, Lang, Abrahams, Sugg, Keenan, Friel, McCrae, Waugh, Elston, Gallocher.

Scorers : Unknown, Waugh

Att : 7,000

1945-46

Round 3, first leg

5 Apr 1946 v Stoke C (a), lost 1-3

Foxcroft, Woodruff, Mather, Martindale, Johnson, Loughran, Hays, Morris, Jackson, Haigh, Kippax.

Scorer : Morris

Second leg

7 Apr 1946 v Stoke C (h), won 2-1, agg 3-4

Breedon, Woodruff, Mather, Wilson, Johnson, Loughran, Hays, Morris, Jackson, Haigh, Kippax.

Scorers : Jackson, Kippax p

TEST MATCHES/PLAY OFFS

1896-97

19 Apr 1897 v Newton Heath (h), won 2-0

Haddow, Reynolds, McLintock, Place senior, Brown, Taylor, McVean, Ross, Robertson, Bowes, Ferguson.

Scorers : Bowes, Ferguson

Att : 10,000

21 Apr 1897 v Newton Heath (a), lost 0-2

Haddow, Reynolds, McLintock, Place senior, Brown, Taylor, Morrison, McVean, Robertson, Bowes, Ferguson.

Att : 7,000

24 Apr 1897 v Notts C (a), drew 1-1

Haddow, Reynolds, McLintock, Place senior, Brown, Taylor, McVean, Ross, Toman, Bowes, Place junior.

Scorer : Brown

Att : 15,000

26 Apr 1897 v Notts C (h), lost 0-1
Haddow, Reynolds, McLintock, Place senior, Brown, Taylor, McVean, Ross, Robertson, Bowes, Place junior.
Att : 11,000

1897-98
21 Apr 1898 v Blackburn R (a), won 3-1
Hillman, Reynolds, McLintock, Beveridge, Taylor, Livingstone, Morrison, Ross, Toman, Bowes, Place junior.
Scorers : Toman (3)
Att : 8,000

23 Apr 1898 v Blackburn R (h), won 2-0
Hillman, Reynolds, McLintock, Beveridge, Taylor, Livingstone, Morrison, Ross, Toman, Bowes, Place junior.
Scorers : Toman, Ross
Att : 12,000

26 Apr 1898 v Stoke (h), lost 0-2
Hillman, Reynolds, McLintock, Beveridge, Taylor, Livingstone, Morrison, Ross, Toman, Bowes, Place junior.
Att : 9,000

30 Apr 1898 v Stoke (a), drew 0-0
Hillman, Reynolds, McLintock, Beveridge, Taylor, Livingstone, Morrison, Ross, Toman, Bowes, Place junior.

1990-91
Semi final, first leg
19 May 1991 v Torquay U (a), lost 0-2
Pearce, Measham, Bray, Hamilton, Pender, Davis, Farrell, Deakin (Grewcock), Francis, Jakub, Eli.
Att : 5,600

Second leg
22 May 1991 v Torquay U (h), won 1-0, agg 1-2
Pearce, Measham, Bray, Deary, Pender (Sonner), Davis, Farrell, Futcher, Francis, Jakub, Eli.
Scorer : Evans og
Att : 13,620

1993-94
Semi final, first leg
15 May 1994 v Plymouth A (h), drew 0-0
Beresford, Parkinson, Thompson, Davis, Pender, Joyce, McMinn (Lancashire), Deary, Heath, Francis, Eyres.
Att : 18,794

Second leg
18 May 1994 v Plymouth A (h), won 3-1, agg 3-1
Beresford, Parkinson, Thompson, Davis, Pender, Joyce (Farrell), McMinn, Deary, Heath, Francis (Peel), Eyres.
Scorers : Francis (2), Joyce
Att : 17,515

Final
29 May 1994 v Stockport C (at Wembley), won 2-1
Beresford, Parkinson, Thompson, Davis, Pender, Joyce, McMinn, Deary, Heath, Francis (Farrell), Eyres.
Scorers : Eyres, Parkinson
Att : 44,806

FA CHARITY SHIELD

1920-21
16 May 1921 v Tottenham H (a), lost 0-2
Dawson, Smelt, Taylor, Bassnett, Boyle, Watson, Nesbitt, Kelly, Anderson, Cross, Mosscrop.
Att : 20,000

1960-61
13 Aug 1960 v Wolverhampton W (h), drew 2-2
Blacklaw, Angus, Elder, Adamson, Cummings, Miller, Connelly, McIlroy, Pointer, Robson, Pilkington.
Scorers : Connelly, Miller
Att : 20,000
(Trophy shared, each club retaining it for six months)

1973-74
18 Aug 1973 v Manchester C (a), won 1-0
Stevenson, Docherty, Newton, Dobson, Waldron, Thomson, Nulty, Casper, Fletcher, Collins, James.
Scorer : Waldron
Att : 23,988

FOOTBALL LEAGUE MATCHES IN THE ABANDONED 1939-40 SEASON (WORLD WAR II)

26 Aug 1939 v Coventry C (h), drew 1-1
Adams, Robinson, Marshall, Gardner, Woodruff, Bray,
Hays, Brocklebank, Clayton, Dryden, Hornby.
Scorer : Hornby
Att : 11,661

2 Sep 1939 v Birmingham (a), lost 0-2
Adams, Robinson, Marshall, Gardner, Woodruff, Bray,
Hays, Brocklebank, Clayton, Dryden, Hornby.
Att : 18,001

EUROPEAN CUP

1960-61
Round 2, first leg
16 Nov 1960 v Reims (h), won 2-0
Blacklaw, Angus, Elder, Joyce, Adamson, Miller,
Connelly, McIlroy, Pointer, Robson, Pilkington.
Scorers : McIlroy, Robson
Att : 36,742

Second leg
30 Nov 1960 v Reims (a), lost 2-3, agg 4-3
Blacklaw, Angus, Elder, Joyce, Adamson, Miller,
Connelly, McIlroy, Pointer, Robson, Pilkington.
Scorers : Connelly, Robson
Att : 45,000

Round 3, first leg
18 Jan 1961 v SV Hamburg (h), won 3-1
Blacklaw, Angus, Elder, Joyce, Adamson, Miller,
Connelly, McIlroy, Pointer, Robson, Pilkington.
Scorers : Pilkington 2, Robson
Att : 47,000

Second leg
15 Mar 1961 v SV Hamburg (a), lost 1-4, agg 4-5
Blacklaw, Angus, Elder, Joyce, Adamson, Miller,
Connelly, McIlroy, Pointer, Robson, Harris.
Scorer : Harris
Att : 71,000

INTER-CITIES FAIRS CUP

1966-67
Round 1, first leg
20 Sep 1966 v VfB Stuttgart (a), drew 1-1
Blacklaw, Angus, Elder, O'Neil, Miller, Bellamy,
Morgan, Lochhead, Irvine, Harris, Coates.
Scorer : Irvine
Att : 74,000

Second leg
27 Sep 1966 v VfB Stuttgart (h), won 2-0, agg 3-1
Blacklaw, Angus, Miller, Bellamy, Talbut, Todd,
Morgan, Lochhead, Irvine, Harris, Coates.
Scorers : Lochhead, Coates
Att : 23,716

Round 2, first leg
19 Oct 1966 v Lausanne-Sports (a), won 3-1
Blacklaw, Angus, Elder, O'Neil, Talbut, Miller,
Morgan, Lochhead, Bellamy, Harris, Coates.
Scorers : Coates, Harris, Lochhead
Att : 4,000

Second leg
25 Oct 1966 v Lausanne-Sports (h), won 5-0, agg 8-1
Blacklaw, Angus, Elder, Bellamy, Talbut, Miller,
Morgan, Lochhead, Irvine, Harris, O'Neil.
Scorers : Lochhead (3), O'Neil, Irvine
Att : 18,573

Round 3, first leg
18 Jan 1967 v Napoli (h), won 3-0
Thomson, Angus, Smith, O'Neil, Miller, Todd,
Morgan, Lochhead, Coates, Harris, Latcham.
Scorers : Lochhead, Latcham, Coates
Att : 24,519

Second leg
8 Feb 1967 v Napoli (a), drew 0-0, agg 3-0
Thomson, Smith, Todd, O'Neil, Miller, Merrington,
Morgan, Lochhead, Coates, Harris, Latcham.
Att : 60,000

Round 4, first leg

4 Apr 1967 v Eintracht Frankfurt (a), drew 1-1

Thomson, Smith, Angus, O'Neil, Miller, Merrington, Morgan, Bellamy, Coates, Harris, Latcham.

Scorer : Miller

Att : 25,000

Second leg

18 Apr 1967 v Eintracht Frankfurt (h), lost 1-2, agg 2-3

Thomson, Smith, Elder, O'Neil, Miller, Merrington, Morgan, Bellamy, Coates, Harris, Latcham.

Scorer : Miller

Att : 25,161

FOOTBALL LEAGUE TROPHY / GROUP CUP / ASSOCIATE MEMBERS CUP. ALSO, FREIGHT ROVER / SHERPA VAN / LEYLAND DAF / AUTOGLASS / AUTO WINDSCREENS, ETC (VARIOUS GUISES)

1981-82

Group

15 Aug 1981 v Carlisle U (h), won 4-2

Stevenson, Laws, Holt, Scott, Overson, Dobson, Cavener, Taylor, Hamilton, Cassidy, Potts.

Scorers : Taylor (2), Hamilton (2)

Att : 2,305

Group

18 Aug 1981 v Preston N E (a), won 1-0

Stevenson, Laws, Holt, Scott, Phelan, Dobson, Cavener, Taylor, Hamilton, Cassidy, Potts.

Scorer : Hamilton

Att : 5,269

Group

22 Apr 1981 v Blackpool (a), drew 0-0

Stevenson, Laws, Holt, Scott, Phelan, Dobson, Cavener, Taylor, Hamilton, Cassidy (Overson), Young.

Att : 3,464

Quarter final

8 Dec 1981 v Watford (h), won 2-1

Stevenson, P. Dixon, Holt, Scott, Overson, Phelan, Cavener, Potts, Taylor, Anderson, Young

Scorers : Scott, Holt

Att : 2,658

Semi final

16 Feb 1982 v Wimbledon (a), lost 0-5

O'Rourke, Miller, Ray, Holt, P. Dixon, Anderson, Scott, Cavener, Wright (Allen), Potts, Young.

Att : 1,267

1983-84

Round 1

21 Feb 1984 v Bolton W (h), won 2-1

Hansbury, Dobson, Donachie, Phelan, Overson, Flynn, Miller, Daley, Scott, Biggins, Hutchison.

Scorers : Donachie, Biggins

Att : 3,355

Round 2

13 Mar 1984 v Darlington (h), won 2-1

Hansbury, Baker, Donachie, Phelan, Overson, Flynn (Tueart), Daley (Miller), Scott, Hamilton, Biggins, Hutchison.

Scorers : Baker, Biggins

Att : 1,978

Northern quarter final

20 Mar 1984 v Doncaster R (a), won 3-1

after extra time

Hansbury, Baker, Donachie, Phelan, Overson, Flynn, Daley, Miller (Tueart), Hamilton, Biggins, Hutchison.

Scorers : Biggins, Daley, Flynn

Att : 3,504

Northern semi final

17 Apr 1984 v Tranmere R (a), lost 0-2

after extra time

Hansbury, Kennedy, Donachie, Phelan, Overson, Flynn, Daley, Scott, Hamilton, Biggins, Hutchison.

Att : 3,928

1984-85

Round 1, first leg

29 Jan 1985 v Stockport C (h), won 5-1

Neenan, Palmer, Hampton, Phelan (Malley), Overson, Hird, Grewcock, Kennedy, Devine, Biggins, Hutchison (Lawrence).

Scorers : Biggins (2), Phelan, Hutchison, Devine

Att : 1,432

Second leg

4 Feb 1985 v Stockport C (a), won 1-0

Neenan, Palmer, Malley, Phelan, Overson, Hird, Grewcock, Gallagher, Devine (Lawrence), Biggins, Hutchison.

Scorer : Hird

Att : 1,568

Round 2

19 Mar 1985 v Tranmere R (a), drew 2-2,
after extra time, Burnley lost 4-5 on pens
Hansbury, Palmer, Hampton, Phelan, Overson, Hird, Grewcock, Gallagher, Devine, Biggins, Hutchison.
Scorers : Devine, Phelan
Att : 1,325

Northern quarter final

10 Apr 1985 v Mansfield T (a), drew 1-1,
after extra time, Burnley lost 3-5 on pens
Hansbury, Palmer, Malley, Phelan, Overson, Hird (Devine), Rhodes, Scott, Taylor, Grewcock, Hutchison.
Scorer : Taylor
Att : 2,540

1985-86

Group

21 Jan 1986 v Chesterfield (a), won 2-1
Neenan, Hird, Heesom, Malley, Overson, Deakin, Grewcock, Devine, Taylor, Lawrence, Hampton.
Scorers : Taylor, Lawrence
Att : 1,053

13 Mar 1986 v Darlington (h), drew 1-1
Neenan, Hird, Hampton, Malley, Overson, Heggarty, Grewcock (Devine), Deakin, Taylor, Lawrence, Hoskin.
Scorer : Taylor
Att : 1,138

1986-87

Group

9 Dec 1986 v Blackpool (a), won 3-2
Neenan, Leebrook, Heesom, Rodaway, Gallagher, Deakin, Grewcock, Harris, Murphy, James (Malley), Hoskin.
Scorers : Murphy (2), Hoskin
Att : 1,448

16 Dec 1986 v Bolton W (h), lost 0-2
Neenan, Leebrook, Heesom, Rodaway, Southern, Deakin, Britton, Harris, Murphy, Malley, Hoskin.
Att : 1,465

Round 1

27 Jan 1987 v Bolton W (a), lost 1-2
Neenan, Leebrook, Heesom, Rodaway, Malley, Deakin, Grewcock, Parker, Murphy, James, Hoskin.
Scorer : Parker
Att : 3,698

1987-88

Group

27 Oct 1987 v Tranmere R (a), won 2-1
Pearce, Daniel, Malley, James, Zelem, Gardner, Farrell, Grewcock, Oghani, Comstive, Taylor (Britton).
Scorers : Oghani, Grewcock
Att : 1,801

24 Nov 1987 v Rochdale (h), won 3-2
Pearce, Farrell, Deakin, Davis, Zelem, Gardner, Britton, Grewcock (Hoskin), Reeves, Comstive, Taylor (Devaney).
Scorers : Grewcock, Farrell, Reeves
Att : 2,677

Round 1

19 Jan 1988 v Chester C (h), won 1-0
Pearce, Farrell, Deakin, Britton, Davis, Gardner, Hoskin, Grewcock, Oghani, Comstive, Taylor.
Scorer : Oghani
Att : 3,436

Northern quarter final

9 Feb 1988 v Bury (a), won 1-0
Pearce, Daniel, Deakin, Britton, Davis, Gardner, Farrell, Reeves, Taylor, Comstive, Hoskin.
Scorer : Comstive pen
Att : 4,672

Northern semi final

8 Mar 1988 v Halifax T (h), drew 0-0,
after extra time, Burnley won 5-3 on pens
Pearce, Daniel, Deakin, Britton, Davis, Gardner (McGrory), Farrell, Oghani, Taylor, Comstive, Grewcock (Hoskin).
Att : 10,222

Northern final, first leg

12 Apr 1988 v Preston N E (h), drew 0-0
Pearce, McGrory, Deakin, Britton, Davis, Gardner, Farrell, Oghani, Taylor, Comstive, Hoskin.
Att : 15,680

Second leg

19 Apr 1988 v Preston N E (a), won 3-1,
after extra time, agg 3-1
Pearce, McGrory, Deakin, Britton, Davis, Gardner, Farrell (Malley), Oghani, Taylor, Comstive, Hoskin.
Scorers : Oghani, Hoskin, Comstive
Att : 17,592

Final

29 May 1988 v Wolverhampton W (at Wembley), lost 0-2
Pearce, Daniel, Deakin, Britton, Davis, Gardner, Farrell, Oghani, Taylor, Comstive, McGrory (James).
Att : 80,841

1988-89

Group

22 Nov 1988 v York C (a), won 2-0
Pearce, Measham, Farrell, Britton, Davis, Gardner, Morley, Oghani, O'Connell, Comstive, Atkinson.
Scorers : Comstive pen, O'Connell
Att : 1,648

29 Nov 1988 v Hartlepool U (h), won 3-0
Pearce, Measham, Farrell, Britton, Davis, Gardner, White, Oghani, O'Connell, Comstive, Atkinson.
Scorers : White, Davis, O'Connell
Att : 3,478

Round 1

17 Jan 1989 v Crewe A (h), drew 1-1,
after extra time, Burnley lost 2-4 on pens
Pearce, Measham, Farrell, Britton, Davis, Gardner, White (Taylor), Oghani, O'Connell, Comstive, James (Zelem).
Scorer : Macowat og
Att : 6,392

1989-90

Group

7 Nov 1989 v Preston N E (a), lost 0-3
Pearce, Measham, Hardy (McGrory), Deary, Eli, Davis, White, Mumby, O'Connell, Jakub, Farrell.
Att : 5,241

28 Nov 1989 v Stockport C (h), lost 0-2
Pearce, Measham, Hardy, Farrell, Davis, Hancock (Mumby), White, Futcher, O'Connell, Jakub, McGrory (Smith).
Att : 3,352

1990-91

Group

6 Nov 1990 v Crewe A (h), won 2-1
Pearce, Measham, Deakin, Deary, Pender, Davis, White, Francis, Mumby, Jakub, Grewcock.
Scorers : White, Francis
Att : 3,481

8 Jan 1991 v Stockport C (a), drew 1-1
Williams, Measham, Deakin, Deary, Pender, Davis, White, Futcher, Francis, Jakub, Farrell.
Scorer : Farrell
Att : 1,707

Round 1

22 Jan 1991 v Stockport C (h), won 3-2,
after extra time
Pearce, Measham, Deakin, Deary, Pender, Davis, Farrell, Futcher (White), Eli, Jakub, Grewcock.
Scorers : Eli, Jakub, White
Att : 3,378

Northern quarter final

29 Jan 1991 v Bradford C (a), won 1-0
Pearce, Measham, Deakin, Deary, Pender, Davis, Farrell, Futcher (Francis), Eli, Jakub, Grewcock.
Scorer : Futcher
Att : 5,432

Northern semi final

19 Feb 1991 v Preston N E (a), lost 1-6
Williams, Measham, Deakin, Deary, Pender, Davis, Farrell, Francis, Eli (Bray), Jakub, Grewcock (White).
Scorer : Bray
Att : 12,016

1991-92

Preliminary round

22 Oct 1991 v Blackpool (a), won 3-1
Marriott, Measham, Jakub, Davis, Pender, Farrell, Harper, Deary, Lancashire (Conroy), Eli, Francis.
Scorers : Francis, Eli (2)
Att : 2,805

19 Nov 1991 v Doncaster R (h), won 2-0
Marriott, Measham, Jakub, Davis, Pender, Farrell, Harper, Deary, Francis (Yates), Conroy (Lancashire), Eli.
Scorers : Francis, Eli
Att : 2,590

4 Feb 1992 v Scarborough (h), won 3-1
Marriott, Measham, Jakub, Davis, Pender, Farrell, Harper, Deary, Lancashire (Conroy), Eli, Francis.
Scorers : Conroy, Deary, Eli
Att : 2,956

Northern quarter final

18 Feb 1992 v Rotherham U (a), drew 1-1,
after extra time, Burnley won 4-2 on pens
Marriott, Measham, Jakub, Davis, Pender, Farrell, Harper, Deary, Francis, Conroy, Eli (Lancashire).
Scorer : Francis
Att : 2,578

Northern semi final

17 Mar 1992 v Huddersfield T (h), won 2-0
Walker, Measham, Jakub, Monington, Pender, Farrell, Harper (Lancashire), Deary, Francis, Conroy, Eli.
Scorers : Conroy pen, Eli
Att : 10,775

Northern final, first leg

7 Apr 1992 v Stockport C (h), lost 0-1
Pearce, Farrell, Jakub, Davis, Pender, Monington, Yates, Deary, Lancashire, Bray (McKenzie), Eli.
Att : 13,259

Northern final, second leg

15 Apr 1992 v Stockport C (a), lost 1-2, agg 1-3
Pearce, Farrell, Jakub, Davis, Pender, Yates, Harper (McKenzie), Deary, Francis, Conroy, Eli (Monington).
Scorers : Pender
Att : 8,260

1992-93

Round 2

19 Jan 1993 v Blackpool (a), won 3-1
Beresford, Measham, Jakub, Davis, Pender, Deary, Donowa, Randall (Farrell), Eli, Conroy, Harper.
Scorers : Conroy (2), Farrell
Att : 2,979

Northern quarter final

2 Feb 1993 v Chesterfield (a), lost 0-3
Beresford, Measham, Jakub, Davis, Pender, Deary, Donowa (Monington), Farrell, Heath, Conroy, Harper.
Att : 3,314

1993-94

First round

19 Oct 1993 v Preston N E (a), lost 1-2
Beresford, Monington, Thompson, Davis, Pender, Randall, Peel, Deary, Heath, Joyce (Francis), Eyres.
Scorer : Eyres
Att : 4,485

9 Nov 1993 v Carlisle U (h), lost 1-2
Beresford, Monington, Thompson, Davis, Pender, Joyce, Francis, Deary, Heath (Peel), Russell, Eyres.
Scorer : Russell
Att : 4,674

1995-96

First round

17 Oct 1995 v Rotherham U (a), drew 1-1
Beresford, Parkinson, Vinnicombe, Winstanley, Swan, Hoyland, Harrison, Joyce, Cooke (Francis), Nogan, McDonald.
Scorer : Nogan
Att : 1,539

7 Nov 1995 v Chester C (h), drew 1-1
Beresford, Parkinson, Vinnicombe, Winstanley, Swan, Hoyland, Harrison (Robinson), Randall, Eyres (Cooke), Nogan, McDonald (Francis).
Scorer : Nogan
Att : 3,225

29 Nov 1995 v Crewe A (a), won 1-0,
after sudden death extra time (golden goal)
Beresford, Brass, Vinnicombe, Swan, Winstanley, Harrison, Weller, Joyce, Heath (Cooke), Nogan, Eyres.
Scorer : Nogan
Att : 2,596

Northern quarter final

7 Jan 1996 v Carlisle U (a), lost 0-5
Beresford, Brass, Vinnicombe, Hoyland, Winstanley, Harrison, Weller (Francis), Joyce, Swan, Nogan, Cooke (McMinn).
Att : 5,169

1996-97

Round 1

10 Dec 1996 v Hartlepool U (a), won 2-0
Beresford, Parkinson, Eyres, Overson (Harrison), Swan, Brass, Weller (Little), Smith, Nogan, Cooke, Gleghorn (Thompson).
Scorers : Nogan, Eyres
Att : 921

Round 2

4 Feb 1997 v Stockport C (h), lost 0-1
Beresford, Huxford, Eyres, Thompson, Swan, Brass, Matthew (Winstanley), Smith, Robinson (Carr-Lawton), Weller, Gleghorn.
Att : 4,251

1997-98

Round 2

27 Jan 1998 v Notts C (h), won 2-0

Beresford, Weller, Winstanley, Hoyland, Blatherwick, Little, Robertson, Ford (Vinnicombe), Cooke, Payton, P. Smith.

Scorers : Little, Cooke

Att : 2,442

Northern quarter final

3 Feb 1998 v Carlisle U (h), won 4-1

Beresford, Williams (Brass), Vinnicombe, Harrison, Moore, Little, Hoyland, Ford (Weller), Cooke, Payton (Henderson), P. Smith.

Scorers : Payton, Vinnicombe, Cooke, Henderson

Att : 4,573

Northern semi final

17 Feb 1998 v Preston N E (h), won 1-0

Beresford, Brass, Winstanley, Harrison (Hoyland), Moore, Little, Blatherwick, Robertson, Cooke, Payton (Henderson), Matthew (Ford).

Scorer : Payton

Att : 10,079

Northern final, first leg

10 Mar 1998 v Grimsby T (a), drew 1-1

Woods, Brass, Winstanley, Harrison, Moore, Little, Vinnicombe, Ford, Cooke, Payton (Robertson), Matthew (Howey).

Scorer : Payton

Att : 6,064

Second leg

17 Mar 1998 v Grimsby T (h), lost 0-2, agg 1-3

Woods, Brass, Winstanley, Robertson (Henderson), Moore, Vinnicombe, Weller, Ford, Cooke, Payton P. Smith.

Att : 10,257

1998-99

Round 1

8 Dec 1998 v Preston N E (h), lost 0-1

Crichton, Brass, Vindheim (Devenney), Ford, Heywood, Reid, Maylett, Hewlett, Cooke (Henderson), Carr-Lawton, Eastwood.

Att : 3,366

1999-2000

Round 1

7 Dec 1999 v Wigan A (a), lost 1-2,

after sudden death extra time (golden goal)

Crichton, West (Robertson), Branch, Weller (Brass), Davis, Thomas, Little, Johnrose, Lee (Cowan), Payton, Mullin.

Scorer : Lee

Att : 2,085

WATNEY CUP

1972-73

Round 1

29 Jul 1972 v Lincoln C (a), won 1-0

Stevenson, Docherty, Newton, Dobson, Waldron, Thomson, Ingham, Casper, Fletcher, Probert (West), James.

Scorer : James

Att : 7,428

Round 2

2 Aug 1972 v Bristol R (h), lost 0-2

Stevenson, Docherty, Newton, Dobson, Waldron, Thomson, Ingham (Bradshaw), Casper, Fletcher, Probert (West), James.

Att : 10,589

TEXACO CUP

1970-71

Round 1, first leg

15 Sep 1970 v Heart of Midlothian (h), won 3-1

Waiters, Merrington, Angus, Docherty, Waldron, Thomson, Thomas, Coates, Casper, Collins, Kindon (Bellamy).

Scorers : Docherty, Merrington, Kindon

Att : 10,106

Second leg

30 Sep 1970 v Heart of Midlothian (a), lost 1-4, agg 4-5

Waiters, Latcham, Merrington, Docherty, Waldron, West, Thomas, Coates, Casper, Bellamy, Collins.

Scorer : Casper

Att : 16,500

1973-74

Round 1, first leg

18 Sep 1973 v East Fife (h), won 7-0

Stevenson, Noble, Newton, Ingham, Waldron, Thomson, Nulty, Hankin, Fletcher, Collins (Pashley), James.

Scorers : Fletcher (3), Nulty (2), James, Noble

Att : 10,374

Second leg

3 Oct 1973 v East Fife (a), won 3-2, agg 10-2

Stevenson, Noble, Newton, Dobson, Waldron, Thomson, Nulty, Hankin, Fletcher, Ingham, James.

Scorers : Fletcher, Noble, Hankin

Att : 2,000

Round 2, first leg

24 Oct 1973 v Heart of Midlothian (a), won 3-0

Stevenson, Noble, Newton, Dobson, Thomson, Rodaway, Nulty, Hankin, Fletcher, Ingham, James.

Scorers : Dobson, Noble, James

Att : 22,000

Second leg

6 Nov 1973 v Heart of Midlothian (h), won 5-0, agg 8-0

Stevenson, Ingham, Newton, Dobson, Waldron, Rodaway, Nulty, Hankin, Fletcher, Collins, James.

Scorers : Hankin (2), Fletcher, Collins, Nulty

Att : 9,063

Round 3, first leg

27 Nov 1973 v Norwich C (h), won 2-0

Stevenson, Noble, Newton, Dobson, Waldron, Thomson, Nulty, Ingham, Fletcher, Collins, James.

Scorers : James, Noble

Att : 4,858

Second leg

12 Dec 1973 v Norwich C (a), won 3-2, agg 5-2

Stevenson, Noble, Newton, Dobson, Waldron, Ingham, Nulty, Hankin, Fletcher, Collins, James.

Scorers : Hankin, Waldron, Noble

Att : 11,797

Final

24 Apr 1974 v Newcastle U (a), lost 1-2

after extra time

Stevenson, Noble, Newton, Dobson (Collins), Waldron, Rodaway, Nulty, Hankin, Fletcher, Ingham, James.

Scorer : Fletcher

Att : 34,540

ANGLO-SCOTTISH CUP

1976-77

Preliminary group

7 Aug 1976 v Blackburn R (a), drew 1-1

Peyton, Scott, Newton, Noble, Thomson, Rodaway, Morris, Hankin, Ingham, Flynn (Loggie), Summerbee.

Scorer : Flynn

Att : 11,012

11 Aug 1976 v Blackpool (a), lost 1-2

Stevenson, Scott, Newton, Noble, Thomson, Rodaway, Morris, Fletcher, Hankin, Flynn, Summerbee.

Scorer : Noble

Att : 9,386

14 Aug 1976 v Bolton W (h), won 1-0

Peyton, Scott, Newton, Noble, Thomson, Rodaway, Morris, Ingham, Hankin, Flynn, Summerbee.

Scorer : Ingham

Att : 9,028

1977-78

Preliminary group

2 Aug 1977 v Blackburn R (h), won 2-1

Stevenson, Newton, Brennan, Noble, Robinson, Rodaway, Ingham, Smith, Fletcher, Flynn, Cochrane.

Scorers : Ingham, Smith

Att : 8,119

6 Aug 1977 v Bolton W (a), lost 0-1

Stevenson, Newton, Brennan, Noble, Robinson, Rodaway, Ingham, Smith, Loggie, Flynn, Cochrane.

Att : 8,250

9 Aug 1977 v Blackpool (h), lost 0-4
Stevenson, Newton, Brennan, Noble (Pashley), Robinson, Rodaway, Ingham, Smith, Loggie, Flynn, Cochrane.
Att : 5,515

1978-79
Preliminary group
5 Aug 1978 v Preston N E (h), won 3-2
Stevenson, Scott, Brennan, Noble, Thomson, Rodaway, Cochrane, Ingham, Fletcher, Kindon, Smith.
Scorers : Ingham, Kindon, Fletcher
Att : 7,456

8 Aug 1978 v Blackpool (h), won 3-1
Stevenson, Scott, Brennan, Noble, Thomson, Rodaway, Cochrane, Ingham, Fletcher, Kindon, Smith.
Scorers : Ingham, Cochrane, Smith
Att : 4,750

12 Aug 1978 v Blackburn R (a), drew 1-1
Stevenson, Scott, Brennan, Noble, Thomson, Rodaway, Morley, Ingham, Fletcher, Kindon, Smith.
Scorers : Smith
Att : 9,791

Quarter final, first leg
12 Sep 1978 v Celtic (h), won 1-0
Stevenson, Scott, Brennan, Noble, Thomson, Rodaway, Cochrane, Hall, Fletcher, Kindon, James.
Scorer : Kindon
Att : 30,000

Second leg
27 Sep 1978 v Celtic (a), won 2-1, agg 3-1
Stevenson, Scott, Brennan, Noble, Thomson, Rodaway, Smith, Ingham, Fletcher, Kindon, James.
Scorers : Brennan, Kindon
Att : 28,000

Semi final, first leg
31 Oct 1978 v Mansfield T (a), won 2-1
Stevenson, Scott, Brennan, Noble, Thomson, Rodaway, Hall, Ingham, Fletcher, Kindon, James.
Scorers : Kindon, James
Att : 5,517

Second leg
7 Nov 1978 v Mansfield T (h), lost 0-1,
after extra time, agg 2-2, Burnley won 8-7 on pens
Stevenson, Scott, Brennan, Noble, Thomson, Rodaway, Hall, Ingham, Fletcher, Kindon, James.
Att : 6,871

Final, first leg
5 Dec 1978 v Oldham A (a), won 4-1
Stevenson, Arins, Brennan, Noble, Thomson, Rodaway, Hall, Ingham, Fletcher, Kindon, James.
Scorers : Kindon (2), Thomson, Noble
Att : 10,456

Second leg
12 Dec 1978 v Oldham A (h), lost 0-1, agg 4-2
Stevenson, Arins, Brennan, Noble, Thomson, Rodaway, Hall, Ingham, Fletcher, Kindon, James.
Att : 10,865

1979-80
Preliminary group
4 Aug 1979 v Blackburn R (a), drew 2-2
Stevenson, Scott, Jakub, Noble, Thomson, Rodaway, Ingham, Dobson, Fletcher, Kindon, James.
Scorers : Kindon, Metcalfe og
Att : 7,749

7 Aug 1979 v Blackpool (a), lost 2-3
Stevenson, Scott, Brennan, Noble, Robinson, Rodaway, Ingham, Dobson, Fletcher, Kindon, James.
Scorers : Noble, Ingham
Att : 5,003

11 Aug 1979 v Preston N E (h), lost 1-2
Stevenson, Scott, Brennan, Noble, Thomson, Rodaway, Ingham, Dobson, Fletcher, Kindon, James.
Scorer : Brennan
Att : 6,171

1980-81
Preliminary group
29 Jul 1980 v Bury (a), lost 1-2
Stevenson, Wood, Holt, Dobson, Dixon, Rodaway, Cavener, Cassidy, Hamilton, Taylor, Ingham (Young).
Scorer : Dobson
Att : 3,887

2 Aug 1980 v Oldham A (h), won 3-1
Stevenson, Wood, Holt, Scott, Overson, Thomson, Cassidy, Dobson, Hamilton, Taylor, Cavener.
Scorers : Scott, Taylor, Cavener
Att : 4,083

5 Aug 1980 v Shrewsbury T (h), drew 1-1
Stevenson, Wood, Holt, Scott, Overson, Dixon, Cassidy (Young), Dobson, Hamilton, Taylor, Cavener.
Scorer : Cassidy
Att : 3,354

David Eyres and Gary Parkinson
Heroes of Wembley 1994

ALDERSHOT GAMES IN 1991-92

Aldershot resigned mid-season having played Burnley twice. Their League record was subsequently expunged.

24 Aug 1991 v Aldershot (h), won 2-0
Pearce, Measham (Farrell), Bray, Davis, Pender, Monington, Eli, Deary, Francis, Conroy, Hamilton.
Scorers : Conroy pen, Francis
Att : 5,877

21 Dec 1991 v Aldershot (a), won 2-1
Pearce, Measham, Jakub, Davis, Pender, Farrell, Harper, Deary, Francis, Conroy, Lancashire.
Scorers : Harper, Lancashire
Att : 2,574

Record against other clubs

Burnley's record against other clubs in senior competition

Some clubs have changed names over the years, the current or most recent name is used here
Points won have not been included, 2 points for a win until 1980-81, 3 points for a win 1981-82 onwards
Games on neutral grounds shown at the end are included in the totals under the appropriate section
Away games played on, or switched to, other venues have been shown as away games

Football League

	Home						Away						Total					
	P	W	D	L	F	A	P	W	D	L	F	A	P	W	D	L	F	A
Accrington	5	2	2	1	9	8	5	1	2	2	8	9	10	3	4	3	17	17
Aldershot	4	1	1	2	4	3	4	2	1	1	5	4	8	3	2	3	9	7
Arsenal	43	21	10	12	67	50	43	9	9	25	46	94	86	30	19	37	113	144
Aston Villa	47	28	8	11	113	71	47	7	12	28	47	109	94	35	20	39	160	180
Barnet	2	2	0	0	8	0	2	0	2	0	1	1	4	2	2	0	9	1
Barnsley	26	16	6	4	60	28	26	8	8	10	28	38	52	24	14	14	88	66
Birmingham City	40	24	10	6	77	39	40	13	6	21	50	68	80	37	16	27	127	107
Blackburn Rovers	41	20	7	14	70	60	41	13	6	22	71	96	82	33	13	36	141	156
Blackpool	53	31	11	11	94	51	53	17	17	19	63	65	106	48	28	30	157	116
Bolton Wanderers	55	29	12	14	96	56	55	13	17	25	56	97	110	42	29	39	152	153
AFC Bournemouth	9	4	5	0	16	6	9	2	3	4	6	11	18	6	8	4	22	17
Bradford	18	9	6	3	33	24	18	6	4	8	25	34	36	15	10	11	58	58
Bradford City	25	9	8	8	40	30	25	8	6	11	33	39	50	17	14	19	73	69
Brentford	11	5	4	2	19	13	11	2	4	5	11	18	22	7	8	7	30	31
Brighton & Hove A	9	4	3	2	16	8	9	2	3	4	7	11	18	6	6	6	23	19
Bristol City	18	5	7	6	27	24	18	6	5	7	23	26	36	11	12	13	50	50
Bristol Rovers	13	6	6	1	19	8	13	2	3	8	12	23	26	8	9	9	31	31
Burton Swifts	1	1	0	0	2	0	1	1	0	0	2	0	2	2	0	0	4	0
Burton United	7	5	2	0	14	4	7	3	1	3	9	11	14	8	3	3	23	15
Bury	22	9	8	5	35	24	22	2	8	12	27	47	44	11	16	17	62	71
Cambridge United	11	6	2	3	19	13	11	5	1	5	15	16	22	11	3	8	34	29
Cardiff City	32	18	7	7	58	35	32	6	8	18	32	61	64	24	15	25	90	96
Carlisle United	14	11	2	1	29	14	14	2	6	6	18	22	28	13	8	7	47	36
Charlton Athletic	22	13	4	5	39	19	22	3	7	12	23	42	44	16	11	17	62	61
Chelsea	39	21	11	7	79	35	39	15	5	19	50	61	78	36	16	26	129	96
Chester City	4	4	0	0	8	0	4	1	1	2	1	7	8	5	1	2	9	7
Chesterfield	25	7	13	5	30	22	25	7	5	13	23	44	50	14	18	18	53	66
Colchester United	9	5	1	3	12	9	9	4	3	2	14	9	18	9	4	5	26	18
Coventry City	17	7	7	3	28	18	17	7	3	7	19	23	34	14	10	10	47	41
Crewe Alexandra	12	7	3	2	19	6	12	2	2	8	11	24	24	9	5	10	30	30
Crystal Palace	11	5	4	2	16	12	11	4	4	3	11	11	22	9	8	5	27	23
Darlington	3	2	0	1	5	3	3	0	1	2	4	8	6	2	1	3	9	11
Darwen	3	3	0	0	20	2	3	2	1	0	7	2	6	5	1	0	27	4
Derby County	42	20	9	13	74	53	42	8	8	26	43	87	84	28	17	39	117	140
Doncaster Rovers	11	6	2	3	22	9	11	4	0	7	12	16	22	10	2	10	34	25
Everton	49	21	14	14	86	64	49	8	14	27	61	97	98	29	28	41	147	161
Exeter City	10	8	2	0	24	7	10	2	3	5	10	18	20	10	5	5	34	25
Fulham	40	29	6	5	87	33	40	8	9	23	47	77	80	37	15	28	134	110
Gainsborough T	13	10	2	1	29	11	13	4	2	7	9	18	26	14	4	8	38	29
Gillingham	16	7	3	6	25	23	16	2	6	8	15	24	32	9	9	14	40	47
Glossop	14	9	3	2	28	14	14	4	4	6	14	21	28	13	7	8	42	35
Grimsby Town	23	16	6	1	47	14	23	4	2	17	24	47	46	20	8	18	71	61
Halifax Town	7	6	0	1	13	6	7	3	3	1	11	8	14	9	3	2	24	14
Hartlepool United	8	5	3	0	13	1	8	0	4	4	7	16	16	5	7	4	20	17
Hereford United	8	4	3	1	14	14	8	1	2	5	4	14	16	5	5	6	18	28
Huddersfield Town	28	14	6	8	43	34	28	10	4	14	23	37	56	24	10	22	66	71
Hull City	23	13	5	5	40	20	23	7	6	10	26	39	46	20	11	15	66	59
Ipswich Town	14	8	2	4	23	15	14	1	4	9	13	33	28	9	6	13	36	48
Leeds United	32	14	7	11	56	43	32	7	9	16	40	60	64	21	16	27	96	103
Leicester City	44	25	12	7	93	45	44	12	14	18	63	75	88	37	26	25	156	120
Leyton Orient	23	14	4	5	48	18	23	8	2	13	22	38	46	22	6	18	70	56
Lincoln City	23	16	4	3	44	20	23	6	4	13	26	41	46	22	8	16	70	61
Liverpool	37	18	9	10	61	51	37	8	10	19	34	66	74	26	19	29	95	117
Loughborough Town	1	1	0	0	9	3	1	1	0	0	2	0	2	2	0	0	11	3
Luton Town	23	11	7	5	37	25	23	10	3	10	35	40	46	21	10	15	72	65
Macclesfield Town	1	1	0	0	4	3	1	0	0	1	1	2	2	1	0	1	5	5
Maidstone United	3	2	1	0	5	3	3	2	0	1	3	2	6	4	1	1	8	5
Manchester City	42	20	11	11	74	63	42	7	11	24	46	94	84	27	22	35	120	157
Manchester United	51	26	8	17	91	64	51	13	8	30	66	116	102	39	16	47	157	180
Mansfield Town	4	4	0	0	8	3	4	1	2	1	3	5	8	5	2	1	11	8
Middlesbrough	24	14	7	3	59	24	24	4	7	13	28	56	48	18	14	16	87	80
Millwall	25	14	6	5	41	24	25	4	10	11	25	36	50	18	16	16	66	60

Football League

	Home						Away						Total					
MK Dons	6	4	1	1	9	6	6	2	3	1	9	5	12	6	4	2	18	11
New Brighton	1	1	0	0	2	1	1	0	0	1	1	2	2	1	0	1	3	3
Newcastle United	47	27	6	14	77	60	47	14	10	23	60	83	94	41	16	37	137	143
Newport County	6	5	1	0	12	4	6	3	1	2	7	4	12	8	2	2	19	8
Northampton Town	7	6	0	1	19	7	7	3	2	2	9	10	14	9	2	3	28	17
Norwich City	14	10	3	1	30	11	14	3	1	10	15	29	28	13	4	11	45	40
Nottingham Forest	44	23	14	7	85	45	44	8	10	26	39	89	88	31	24	33	124	134
Notts County	25	15	7	3	41	18	25	2	7	16	19	64	50	17	14	19	60	82
Oldham Athletic	23	13	4	6	44	24	23	4	7	12	22	41	46	17	11	18	66	65
Oxford United	7	2	4	1	9	9	7	3	2	2	9	10	14	5	6	3	18	19
Peterborough United	8	3	3	2	15	8	8	1	2	5	8	19	16	4	5	7	23	27
Plymouth Argyle	22	12	6	4	33	21	22	5	8	9	22	33	44	17	14	13	55	54
Portsmouth	23	15	4	4	45	24	23	5	3	15	24	43	46	20	7	19	69	67
Port Vale	18	9	6	3	47	22	18	3	9	6	24	30	36	12	15	9	71	52
Preston North End	59	32	15	12	103	69	59	12	11	36	74	134	118	44	26	48	177	203
Queens Park R	12	9	2	1	19	9	12	3	1	8	10	25	24	12	3	9	29	34
Reading	13	4	3	6	23	18	13	1	6	6	11	21	26	5	9	12	34	39
Rochdale	7	4	0	3	8	6	7	2	1	4	8	8	14	6	1	7	16	14
Rotherham United	14	5	6	3	27	20	14	1	5	8	10	20	28	6	11	11	37	40
Scarborough	5	2	1	2	9	6	5	1	0	4	4	9	10	3	1	6	13	15
Scunthorpe United	9	2	3	4	11	9	9	2	3	4	11	17	18	4	6	8	22	26
Sheffield United	51	30	10	11	106	60	51	4	15	32	35	98	102	34	25	43	141	158
Sheffield Wednesday	41	26	5	10	94	48	41	11	8	22	43	74	82	37	13	32	137	122
Shrewsbury Town	4	1	1	2	4	6	4	1	0	3	3	8	8	2	1	5	7	14
Southampton	20	13	3	4	42	21	20	1	9	10	13	35	40	14	12	14	55	56
Southend United	8	4	2	2	15	10	8	2	1	5	13	15	16	6	3	7	28	25
Stockport County	25	17	6	2	60	27	25	6	7	12	27	38	50	23	13	14	87	65
Stoke City	43	21	9	13	69	49	43	10	8	25	52	90	86	31	17	38	121	139
Sunderland	48	24	11	13	89	49	48	8	14	26	62	98	96	32	25	39	151	147
Swansea City	17	9	7	1	30	12	17	4	4	9	18	34	34	13	11	10	48	46
Swindon Town	7	1	2	4	4	9	7	4	2	1	9	5	14	5	4	5	13	14
Torquay United	6	4	2	0	9	3	6	2	1	3	5	8	12	6	3	3	14	11
Tottenham Hotspur	44	24	13	7	87	50	44	10	9	25	51	109	88	34	22	32	138	159
Tranmere Rovers	7	3	4	0	14	9	7	3	0	4	11	12	14	6	4	4	25	21
Walsall	15	9	4	2	26	13	15	4	4	7	18	24	30	13	8	9	44	37
Watford	11	8	1	2	27	14	11	3	2	6	10	18	22	11	3	8	37	32
West Bromwich A	60	27	14	19	106	76	60	16	12	32	67	122	120	43	26	51	173	198
West Ham United	35	22	9	4	83	47	35	7	7	21	43	64	70	29	16	25	126	111
Wigan Athletic	8	2	2	4	6	8	8	0	5	3	3	10	16	2	7	7	9	18
Wolverhampton W	56	21	14	21	91	88	56	10	9	38	49	128	112	31	23	59	140	216
Wrexham	15	8	3	4	27	16	15	7	4	4	23	15	30	15	7	8	50	31
Wycombe Wanderers	5	2	3	0	7	5	5	0	1	4	3	14	10	2	4	4	10	19
York City	10	4	4	2	24	12	10	1	4	5	10	16	20	5	8	7	34	28

FA Cup

	Home						Away						Total					
	P	W	D	L	F	A	P	W	D	L	F	A	P	W	D	L	F	A
Accrington							1	0	0	1	2	3	1	0	0	1	2	3
Altrincham	1	1	0	0	6	1							1	1	0	0	6	1
Arsenal	4	2	0	2	10	11	1	0	0	1	0	2	5	2	0	3	10	13
Astley Bridge	1	1	0	0	2	2	1	0	1	0	3	3	2	1	1	0	5	5
Aston Villa	6	2	1	3	8	9	4	1	1	2	3	6	11	3	2	6	11	18
Barnet							1	1	0	0	1	0	1	1	0	0	1	0
Barnsley	1	1	0	0	2	0							1	1	0	0	2	0
Birmingham City	2	2	0	0	5	2	2	1	0	1	2	1	4	3	0	1	7	3
Bishop Auckland							1	1	0	0	3	2	1	1	0	0	3	2
Blackburn Rovers	2	0	2	0	3	3	5	2	0	3	5	8	7	2	2	3	8	11
Blackpool							2	0	0	2	0	2	2	0	0	2	0	2
Bolton Wanderers	2	1	0	1	3	1	1	0	0	1	1	2	3	1	0	2	4	3
AFC Bournemouth	3	3	0	0	10	0	1	0	1	0	1	1	4	3	1	0	11	1
Bradford							2	0	0	2	0	3	2	0	0	2	0	3
Bradford City	1	1	0	0	5	0	1	0	1	0	2	2	2	1	1	0	7	2
Brentford	1	0	1	0	1	1	3	2	0	1	7	4	4	2	1	1	8	5
Brighton & Hove A	1	1	0	0	2	0	1	0	1	0	3	3	2	1	1	0	5	3
Bristol Rovers	1	0	0	1	2	3	2	1	1	0	6	4	3	1	1	1	8	7
Bury	4	2	1	1	6	3	4	1	1	2	4	5	8	3	2	3	10	8
Cambridge United							1	1	0	0	4	2	1	1	0	0	4	2
Canvey Island	1	1	0	0	4	1							1	1	0	0	4	1
Cardiff City	1	0	0	1	0	2	1	0	1	0	2	2	2	0	1	1	2	4
Carlisle United	1	1	0	0	3	1	1	0	1	0	2	2	2	1	1	0	5	3
Charlton Athletic	1	1	0	0	2	1	1	0	0	1	0	3	3	1	0	2	2	5

FA Cup

	Home						Away						Total					
Chelsea	2	0	1	1	2	4	4	0	2	2	6	11	9	0	5	4	10	19
Cheltenham Town							1	0	0	1	1	2	1	0	0	1	1	2
Chester City	1	0	0	1	0	2	1	1	0	0	2	1	2	1	0	1	2	3
Chesterfield	3	3	0	0	11	2	2	0	1	1	4	5	5	3	1	1	15	7
Coventry City	3	3	0	0	9	0	1	0	0	1	0	3	4	3	0	1	9	3
Crewe Alexandra	1	1	0	0	4	2							1	1	0	0	4	2
Crystal Palace	2	2	0	0	10	0	2	0	2	0	0	0	4	2	2	0	10	0
Darlington							1	0	0	1	2	3	1	0	0	1	2	3
Darwen							1	0	0	1	0	2	1	0	0	1	0	2
Darwen Old Wand	1	1	0	0	4	0	1	0	0	1	0	11	2	1	0	1	4	11
Derby County	4	2	1	1	8	9	3	1	0	2	2	4	7	3	1	3	10	13
Doncaster Rovers	1	0	1	0	1	1	1	1	0	0	3	1	2	1	1	0	4	2
Everton	4	2	1	1	5	4	3	1	0	2	5	5	7	3	1	3	10	9
Exeter City	1	1	0	0	2	0							1	1	0	0	2	0
Fulham	2	1	1	0	3	0	4	2	1	1	7	3	8	4	3	1	13	5
Gainsborough T	1	1	0	0	4	1							1	1	0	0	4	1
Gillingham	1	1	0	0	3	1							1	1	0	0	3	1
Grimsby Town	2	2	0	0	7	1	2	1	1	0	4	2	4	3	1	0	11	3
Halifax Town	1	1	0	0	3	1							1	1	0	0	3	1
Hartlepool United	1	1	0	0	1	0							1	1	0	0	1	0
Huddersfield Town	5	3	1	1	9	4	2	1	0	1	4	4	7	4	1	2	13	8
Hull City							1	0	0	1	0	3	1	0	0	1	0	3
Hyde United							1	1	0	0	2	0	1	1	0	0	2	0
Keswick							1	1	0	0	8	0	1	1	0	0	8	0
Leeds United							1	1	0	0	3	2	1	1	0	0	3	2
Leicester City							1	1	0	0	7	3	1	1	0	0	7	3
Leyton Orient	1	0	1	0	1	1	1	1	0	0	1	0	2	1	1	0	2	1
Lincoln City	4	2	2	0	7	4	3	1	1	1	4	4	7	3	3	1	11	8
Liverpool	5	2	3	0	4	1	6	0	0	6	2	12	14	4	4	6	8	13
Luton Town	2	2	0	0	6	1	1	0	1	0	0	0	3	2	1	0	6	1
Manchester City	3	1	0	2	3	2							3	1	0	2	3	2
Manchester United	4	3	0	1	16	7	2	0	1	1	1	2	6	3	1	2	17	9
Mansfield Town	1	1	0	0	4	2	1	1	0	0	2	0	2	2	0	0	6	2
Middlesbrough	2	2	0	0	4	1	1	0	1	0	1	1	3	2	1	0	5	2
Millwall							1	0	0	1	0	1	1	0	0	1	0	1
MK Dons	1	0	0	1	0	1	1	0	0	1	1	3	2	0	0	2	1	4
New Brighton	1	1	0	0	9	0							1	1	0	0	9	0
Newcastle United	1	0	1	0	1	1	2	0	0	2	1	3	4	0	1	3	2	6
Newport County	1	1	0	0	2	1							1	1	0	0	2	1
Nottingham Forest	1	1	0	0	3	0	1	0	1	0	0	0	2	1	1	0	3	0
Notts County							4	1	0	3	6	7	4	1	0	3	6	7
Nuneaton Borough							1	1	0	0	3	2	1	1	0	0	3	2
Old Westminsters	1	1	0	0	4	3							1	1	0	0	4	3
Oldham Athletic							1	1	0	0	4	1	1	1	0	0	4	1
Oxford United	1	0	1	0	0	0	2	0	0	2	1	5	3	0	1	2	1	5
Penrith							1	1	0	0	9	0	1	1	0	0	9	0
Port Vale	3	2	1	0	6	2	2	0	0	2	1	4	5	2	1	2	7	6
Portsmouth	2	2	0	0	4	1	1	0	1	0	1	1	3	2	1	0	5	2
Queens Park R	2	2	0	0	10	3							2	2	0	0	10	3
Reading	1	1	0	0	1	0	3	0	1	2	3	5	4	1	1	2	4	5
Rochdale	1	1	0	0	4	1							1	1	0	0	4	1
Rotherham United	4	2	1	1	5	4	4	2	1	1	8	9	8	4	2	2	13	13
Runcorn	1	0	1	0	0	0	1	1	0	0	2	1	2	1	1	0	2	1
Scarborough	2	2	0	0	3	1							2	2	0	0	3	1
Scunthorpe United	3	1	2	0	8	3	2	0	2	0	3	3	5	1	4	0	11	6
Sheffield United	5	2	2	1	9	8	5	1	1	3	6	8	12	4	4	4	16	16
Sheffield Wednesday	3	2	1	0	6	2	5	0	2	3	1	8	9	2	3	4	7	13
Shrewsbury Town	2	1	1	0	3	2	2	1	0	1	2	2	4	2	1	1	5	4
South Shields	2	2	0	0	6	3							2	2	0	0	6	3
Southampton							1	0	0	1	1	2	1	0	0	1	1	2
Southend United	1	1	0	0	6	0							1	1	0	0	6	0
Stafford Rangers							1	1	0	0	3	1	1	1	0	0	3	1
Stockport County	1	0	1	0	1	1	2	2	0	0	5	2	3	2	1	0	6	3
Stoke City	5	3	1	1	7	5	2	0	0	2	2	10	7	3	1	3	9	15
Sunderland	4	2	2	0	6	3	7	1	1	5	4	9	13	3	4	6	12	15
Swansea City	3	3	0	0	10	3	1	0	1	0	0	0	4	3	1	0	10	3
Swindon Town	4	2	1	1	9	7	3	1	1	1	5	5	7	3	2	2	14	12
Telford United							1	0	0	1	0	3	1	0	0	1	0	3
Thorneycrofts	1	1	0	0	5	0	1	0	1	0	0	0	2	1	1	0	5	0
Tottenham Hotspur	1	1	0	0	3	1	4	1	1	2	6	6	7	2	1	4	10	13
Walsall	2	0	1	1	2	4	2	0	1	1	1	2	4	0	2	2	3	6

FA Cup

	Home						Away						Total					
Watford							1	0	0	1	0	2	1	0	0	1	0	2
West Bromwich A							1	0	0	1	1	5	1	0	0	1	1	5
West Ham United	1	0	0	1	1	3	1	0	0	1	2	3	2	0	0	2	3	6
Wolverhampton W	1	1	0	0	3	0							1	1	0	0	3	0
Wrexham	1	1	0	0	1	0							1	1	0	0	1	0
York City	1	0	1	0	0	0	1	1	0	0	3	2	2	1	1	0	3	2

Football League Cup

	Home						Away						Total					
	P	W	D	L	F	A	P	W	D	L	F	A	P	W	D	L	F	A
Arsenal	1	0	1	0	3	3	1	0	0	1	1	2	2	0	1	1	4	5
Aston Villa	2	1	1	0	4	2	3	0	1	2	2	5	6	1	2	3	7	9
Barnsley	1	1	0	0	3	0							1	1	0	0	3	0
Birmingham City	1	1	0	0	3	2							1	1	0	0	3	2
Blackpool	2	1	0	1	3	1	1	0	1	0	2	2	3	1	1	1	5	3
Bradford City	1	0	1	0	1	1	1	1	0	0	3	2	2	1	1	0	4	3
Brentford	1	1	0	0	2	1	1	0	1	0	1	1	2	1	1	0	3	2
Brighton and Hove A	1	0	0	1	1	3							1	0	0	1	1	3
Bury	3	2	0	1	6	6	4	2	1	1	12	11	7	4	1	2	18	17
Cardiff City	2	2	0	0	5	3	2	1	1	0	6	2	4	3	1	0	11	5
Carlisle United	2	1	1	0	3	2	1	0	0	1	1	4	3	1	1	1	4	6
Charlton Athletic	1	0	0	1	1	2	1	0	0	1	1	4	2	0	0	2	2	6
Chester City	1	1	0	0	2	0	1	0	0	1	0	1	2	1	0	1	2	1
Chesterfield							1	0	1	0	0	0	1	0	1	0	0	0
Coventry City							2	2	0	0	3	1	2	2	0	0	3	1
Crewe Alexandra	2	0	0	2	4	6	2	1	0	1	3	1	4	1	0	3	7	7
Crystal Palace	2	1	1	0	4	2	1	0	1	0	1	1	3	1	2	0	5	3
Doncaster Rovers							1	1	0	0	4	0	1	1	0	0	4	0
Grimsby Town	1	1	0	0	6	0	1	0	1	0	1	1	2	1	1	0	7	1
Hartlepool United	2	1	0	1	4	2	1	0	0	1	2	3	3	1	0	2	6	5
Hereford United							1	1	0	0	4	1	1	1	0	0	4	1
Huddersfield Town							1	1	0	0	1	0	1	1	0	0	1	0
Hull City							1	1	0	0	2	1	1	1	0	0	2	1
Ipswich Town	1	0	0	1	1	2							1	0	0	1	1	2
Leeds United							1	0	0	1	0	4	1	0	0	1	0	4
Leicester City	3	2	0	1	6	2	1	0	0	1	0	2	4	2	0	2	6	4
Lincoln City	1	1	0	0	2	1	1	0	1	0	1	1	2	1	1	0	3	2
Liverpool	3	2	0	1	3	4	3	0	1	2	1	6	6	2	1	3	4	10
Luton Town	1	0	0	1	0	1	1	0	1	0	1	1	2	0	1	1	1	2
Manchester City	1	0	0	1	0	1	1	0	0	1	0	5	2	0	0	2	0	6
Manchester United	4	0	1	3	0	6	4	0	1	3	3	9	8	0	2	6	3	15
Mansfield Town	2	2	0	0	5	1	2	2	0	0	4	0	4	4	0	0	9	1
Middlesbrough	2	1	0	1	3	4	1	0	1	0	1	1	3	1	1	1	4	5
Norwich City	2	1	1	0	4	2	1	0	0	1	0	1	3	1	1	1	4	3
Nottingham Forest	3	2	0	1	5	2	1	0	0	1	1	4	4	2	0	2	6	6
Peterborough United							1	0	0	1	0	4	1	0	0	1	0	4
Plymouth Argyle	1	0	0	1	1	2							1	0	0	1	1	2
Preston North End	1	1	0	0	4	1	1	1	0	0	2	1	2	2	0	0	6	2
Queens Park R							1	1	0	0	2	1	1	1	0	0	2	1
Reading							1	1	0	0	2	1	1	1	0	0	2	1
Rochdale	2	1	0	1	3	4	2	0	2	0	4	4	4	1	2	1	7	8
Rotherham United	1	1	0	0	2	0	1	0	1	0	1	1	2	1	1	0	3	1
Rushden and D	1	0	0	1	2	3							1	0	0	1	2	3
Scunthorpe United							1	1	0	0	3	2	1	1	0	0	3	2
Sheffield United							1	0	0	1	0	2	1	0	0	1	0	2
Shrewsbury Town	1	1	0	0	5	0	1	0	1	0	1	1	2	1	1	0	6	1
Southampton	1	1	0	0	3	2	1	1	0	0	4	2	2	2	0	0	7	4
Stockport County	1	0	0	1	0	1	1	1	0	0	2	0	2	1	0	1	2	1
Stoke City	2	1	0	1	2	5	3	1	1	1	2	2	5	2	1	2	4	7
Swindon Town	1	0	0	1	1	2	1	1	0	0	2	1	3	2	0	1	5	6
Torquay United							1	0	0	1	0	1	1	0	0	1	0	1
Tottenham Hotspur	3	1	1	1	2	4	2	1	0	1	5	4	5	2	1	2	7	8
Tranmere Rovers	1	0	1	0	3	3	1	0	0	1	2	4	2	0	1	1	5	7
West Ham United	1	0	0	1	0	2	1	0	0	1	0	4	2	0	0	2	0	6
Wigan Athletic	1	0	0	1	2	3	1	0	0	1	1	3	2	0	0	2	3	6
Wolverhampton W	2	0	2	0	2	2	2	0	0	2	0	4	4	0	2	2	2	6
Workington							1	1	0	0	1	0	1	1	0	0	1	0
Wrexham	2	2	0	0	5	1	2	1	0	1	3	2	4	3	0	1	8	3
York City	1	1	0	0	1	0	1	0	1	0	2	2	2	1	1	0	3	2

Other competitive matches

	Home						Away						Total					
	P	W	D	L	F	A	P	W	D	L	F	A	P	W	D	L	F	A
Blackburn Rovers	6	3	1	2	8	8	5	1	3	1	7	6	11	4	4	3	15	14
Blackpool	6	2	2	2	6	9	7	3	1	3	13	11	13	5	3	5	19	20
Bolton Wanderers	6	3	1	2	11	8	4	0	1	3	2	7	10	3	2	5	13	15
Bradford City							1	1	0	0	1	0	1	1	0	0	1	0
Bristol Rovers	1	0	0	1	0	2							1	0	0	1	0	2
Bury	2	0	1	1	1	3	2	1	0	1	2	2	4	1	1	2	3	5
Carlisle United	3	2	0	1	9	5	1	0	0	1	0	5	4	2	0	2	9	10
Celtic	1	1	0	0	1	0	1	1	0	0	2	1	2	2	0	0	3	1
Chester City	2	1	1	0	2	1							2	1	1	0	2	1
Chesterfield							2	1	0	1	2	4	2	1	0	1	2	4
Crewe Alexandra	2	1	1	0	3	2	1	1	0	0	1	0	3	2	1	0	4	2
Darlington	2	1	1	0	3	2							2	1	1	0	3	2
Doncaster Rovers	1	1	0	0	2	0	1	1	0	0	3	1	2	2	0	0	5	1
East Fife	1	1	0	0	7	0	1	1	0	0	3	2	2	2	0	0	10	2
Eintracht Frankfurt	1	0	0	1	1	2	1	0	1	0	1	1	2	0	1	1	2	3
Grimsby Town	1	0	0	1	0	2	1	0	1	0	1	1	2	0	1	1	1	3
Halifax Town	1	0	1	0	0	0							1	0	1	0	0	0
SV Hamburg	1	1	0	0	3	1	1	0	0	1	1	4	2	1	0	1	4	5
Hartlepool United	1	1	0	0	3	0	1	1	0	0	2	0	2	2	0	0	5	0
Heart of Midlothian	2	2	0	0	8	1	2	1	0	1	4	4	4	3	0	1	12	5
Huddersfield Town	1	1	0	0	2	0							1	1	0	0	2	0
Lausanne Sports	1	1	0	0	5	0	1	1	0	0	3	1	2	2	0	0	8	1
Lincoln City							1	1	0	0	1	0	1	1	0	0	1	0
Manchester City							1	1	0	0	1	0	1	1	0	0	1	0
Manchester United	1	1	0	0	2	0	1	0	0	1	0	2	2	1	0	1	2	2
Mansfield Town	1	0	0	1	0	1	2	1	1	0	3	2	3	1	1	1	3	3
MK Dons							1	0	0	1	0	5	1	0	0	1	0	5
Napoli	1	1	0	0	3	0	1	0	1	0	0	0	2	1	1	0	3	0
Newcastle United							1	0	0	1	1	2	1	0	0	1	1	2
Norwich City	1	1	0	0	2	0	1	1	0	0	3	2	2	2	0	0	5	2
Notts County	2	1	0	1	2	1	1	0	1	0	1	1	3	1	1	1	3	2
Oldham Athletic	3	1	1	1	4	3	1	1	0	0	4	1	4	2	1	1	8	4
Plymouth Argyle	1	0	1	0	0	0	1	1	0	0	1	3	2	1	1	0	1	3
Preston North End	7	2	2	3	5	6	6	3	0	3	8	13	13	5	2	6	13	19
Reims	1	1	0	0	2	0	1	0	0	1	2	3	2	2	0	1	4	3
Rochdale	1	1	0	0	3	2	3	1	1	1	7	1	4	2	1	1	10	3
Rotherham United							2	0	2	0	2	2	2	0	2	0	2	2
Scarborough	1	1	0	0	3	1							1	1	0	0	3	1
Shrewsbury Town	1	0	1	0	1	1							1	0	1	0	1	1
Stockport County	5	2	0	3	8	7	3	1	1	1	3	3	9	4	1	4	13	11
Stoke City	1	0	0	1	0	2	1	0	1	0	0	0	2	0	1	1	0	2
VfB Stuttgart	1	0	1	0	1	1	1	1	0	0	2	0	2	1	1	0	3	1
Torquay United	1	1	0	0	1	0	1	0	0	1	0	2	2	1	0	1	1	2
Tottenham Hotspur							1	0	0	1	0	2	1	0	0	1	0	2
Tranmere Rovers							3	1	1	1	4	5	3	1	1	1	4	5
Watford	1	1	0	0	2	1							1	1	0	0	2	1
Wigan Athletic	3	1	0	2	4	5	2	0	1	1	2	3	5	1	1	3	6	8
Wolverhampton W	1	0	1	0	2	2							2	0	1	1	2	4
York City							1	1	0	0	2	0	1	1	0	0	2	0

Matches on neutral grounds (included in totals above)

	FA Cup						Football League Cup						Other					
	P	W	D	L	F	A	P	W	D	L	F	A	P	W	D	L	F	A
Aston Villa	1	0	0	1	0	3	1	0	0	1	1	2						
Charlton Athletic	1	0	0	1	0	1												
Chelsea	3	0	2	1	2	4												
Fulham	2	1	1	0	3	2												
Liverpool	3	2	1	0	2	0												
Newcastle United	1	0	0	1	0	2												
Sheffield United	2	1	1	0	1	0												
Sheffield Wednesday	1	0	0	1	0	3												
Stockport County													1	1	0	0	2	1
Sunderland	2	0	1	1	2	3												
Swindon Town							1	0	0	1	2	3						
Tottenham Hotspur	2	0	0	2	1	6												
Wolverhampton W													1	0	0	1	0	2

	FA Cup	Football League Cup	Other
Aston Villa	Bramall Lane (1924)	Old Trafford (1961)	
Charlton Athletic	Wembley (1947)		
Chelsea	St Andrews, Highbury, White Hart Lane (all 1956)		
Fulham	Villa Park, Filbert Street (both 1962)		
Liverpool	Crystal Palace (1914), Ewood Park, Maine Road (both 1947)		
Newcastle United	Hillsborough (1974)		
Sheffield United	Old Trafford, Goodison Park (both 1914)		
Sheffield Wednesday	Villa Park (1935)		
Stockport County			Wembley (1994)
Sunderland	Bramall Lane, St Andrews (both 1913)		
Swindon Town		The Hawthorns (1968-69)	
Tottenham Hotspur	Villa Park (1961), Wembley (1962)		
Wolverhampton W			Wembley (1988)

Third Division Champions 1981-82
Back: Billy Hamilton, Alan Stevenson, David Holt, Billy O'Rourke, Paul Dixon, David Miller, Vince Overson, Lee Dixon, Andy Wharton, Steve Taylor, Billy Wright,
Front: Mike Phelan, Derek Scott, Phil Cavener, Brian Laws, Trevor Steven, Paul McGee, Frank Casper (coach), Brian Miller (manager), Martin Dobson (captain).

Football League Record

Burnley in the Football League 1888-89 to 2006-07

	P	W	D	L	F	A	Pts	Pos		Top scorer (League only)
Football League										
1888-89	22	7	3	12	42	62	17	9 of 12	Re-elected	7 - Alec Brady
1889-90	22	4	5	13	36	65	13	11 of 12	Re-elected	6 - Robert Haresnape
1890-91	22	9	3	10	52	63	21	8 of 12		16 - Claude Lambie
1891-92	26	11	4	11	49	45	26	7 of 14		17 - Tom Nicol
Division One										
1892-93	30	13	4	13	51	44	30	6 of 16		8 - Bowes/Buchanan
1893-94	30	15	4	11	61	51	34	5 of 16		15 - Peter Turnbull
1894-95	30	11	4	15	44	56	26	9 of 16		11 - Tom Nicol
1895-96	30	10	7	13	48	44	27	10 of 16		10 - Hugh Robertson
1896-97	30	6	7	17	43	61	19	16 of 16	Relegated (after test matches)	11 - Billy Bowes
Division Two										
1897-98	30	20	8	2	80	24	48	1 of 16	Champions/promoted (after test matches)	23 - Jimmy Ross
Division One										
1898-99	34	15	9	10	45	47	39	3 of 18		11 - Wilf Toman
1899-1900	34	11	5	18	34	54	27	17 of 18	Relegated	10 - Edgar Chadwick
Division Two										
1900-01	34	20	4	10	53	29	44	3 of 18		11 - Bowes/Jenkinson
1901-02	34	10	10	14	41	45	30	9 of 18		10 - Cornelius Hogan
1902-03	34	6	8	20	30	77	20	18 of 18	Re-elected	7 - Cornelius Hogan
1903-04	34	15	9	10	50	55	39	5 of 18		8 - McFarlane/Williams
1904-05	34	12	6	16	43	52	30	11 of 18		13 - Dugald McFarlane
1905-06	38	15	8	15	42	53	38	9 of 20		10 - Dugald McFarlane
1906-07	38	17	6	15	62	47	40	7 of 20		16 - Dick Smith
1907-08	38	20	6	12	67	50	46	7 of 20		24 - Dick Smith
1908-09	38	13	7	18	51	58	33	14 of 20		13 - Dick Smith
1909-10	38	14	6	18	62	61	34	14 of 20		18 - Benny Green
1910-11	38	13	15	10	45	45	41	8 of 20		11 - Benny Green
1911-12	38	22	8	8	77	41	52	3 of 20		32 - Bert Freeman
1912-13	38	21	8	9	88	53	50	2 of 20	Runners-up/promoted	31 - Bert Freeman
Division One										
1913-14	38	12	12	14	61	53	36	12 of 20		16 - Bert Freeman
1914-15	38	18	7	13	61	47	43	4 of 20		19 - Teddy Hodgson
World War One										
1919-20	42	21	9	12	65	59	51	2 of 22	Runners-up	12 - Bert Freeman
1920-21	42	23	13	6	79	36	59	1 of 22	Champions	25 - Joe Anderson
1921-22	42	22	5	15	72	54	49	3 of 22		20 - Joe Anderson
1922-23	42	16	6	20	58	59	38	15 of 22		17 - Bob Kelly
1923-24	42	12	12	18	55	60	36	17 of 22		19 - George Beel
1924-25	42	11	12	19	46	75	34	19 of 22		15 - Tom Roberts
1925-26	42	13	10	19	85	108	36	20 of 22		26 - Louis Page
1926-27	42	19	9	14	91	80	47	5 of 22		24 - George Beel
1927-28	42	16	7	19	82	98	39	19 of 22		35 - George Beel
1928-29	42	15	8	19	81	103	38	19 of 22		30 - George Beel
1929-30	42	14	8	20	79	97	36	21 of 22	Relegated	15 - Louis Page
Division Two										
1930-31	42	17	11	14	81	77	45	8 of 22		25 - George Beel
1931-32	42	13	9	20	59	87	35	19 of 22		12 - George Beel
1932-33	42	11	14	17	67	79	36	19 of 22		16 - Tom Jones
1933-34	42	18	6	18	60	72	42	13 of 22		17 - Cecil Smith
1934-35	42	16	9	17	63	73	41	12 of 22		21 - George Brown
1935-36	42	12	13	17	50	59	37	15 of 22		10 - Cecil Smith
1936-37	42	16	10	16	57	61	42	13 of 22		12 - Charles Fletcher
1937-38	42	17	10	15	54	54	44	6 of 22		14 - Bob Brocklebank
1938-39	42	15	9	18	50	56	39	14 of 22		10 - John Clayton
World War Two										
1946-47	42	22	14	6	65	29	58	2 of 22	Runners-up/promoted	15 - Harry Potts

Burnley in the Football League 1888-89 to 2006-07 continued

	P	W	D	L	F	A	Pts	Pos		Top scorer (League only)
Division One										
1947-48	42	20	12	10	56	43	52	3 of 22		14 - Harry Potts
1948-49	42	12	14	16	43	50	38	15 of 22		11 - Jackie Chew
1949-50	42	16	13	13	40	40	45	10 of 22		11 - Harry Potts
1950-51	42	14	14	14	48	43	42	10 of 22		12 - Bill Holden
1951-52	42	15	10	17	56	63	40	14 of 22		18 - Billy Morris
1952-53	42	18	12	12	67	52	48	6 of 22		22 - Bill Holden
1953-54	42	21	4	17	78	67	46	7 of 22		19 - Billy Gray
1954-55	42	17	9	16	51	48	43	10 of 22		14 - Bill Holden
1955-56	42	18	8	16	64	54	44	7 of 22		25 - Peter McKay
1956-57	42	18	10	14	56	50	46	7 of 22		13 - Jimmy McIlroy
1957-58	42	21	5	16	80	74	47	6 of 22		16 - Jimmy McIlroy
1958-59	42	19	10	13	81	70	48	7 of 22		27 - Ray Pointer
1959-60	42	24	7	11	85	61	55	1 of 22	Champions	20 - John Connelly
1960-61	42	22	7	13	102	77	51	4 of 22		25 - Jimmy Robson
1961-62	42	21	11	10	101	67	53	2 of 22	Runners-up	25 - Ray Pointer
1962-63	42	22	10	10	78	57	54	3 of 22		19 - Andy Lochhead
1963-64	42	17	10	15	71	64	44	9 of 22		11 - Andy Lochhead
1964-65	42	16	10	16	70	70	42	12 of 22		22 - Willie Irvine
1965-66	42	24	7	11	79	47	55	3 of 22		29 - Willie Irvine
1966-67	42	15	9	18	66	76	39	14 of 22		18 - Andy Lochhead
1967-68	42	14	10	18	64	71	38	14 of 22		14 - Frank Casper
1968-69	42	15	9	18	55	82	39	14 of 22		13 - Frank Casper
1969-70	42	12	15	15	56	61	39	14 of 22		17 - Steve Kindon
1970-71	42	7	13	22	29	63	27	21 of 22	Relegated	5 - Eric Probert
Division Two										
1971-72	42	20	6	16	70	55	46	7 of 22		18 - Frank Casper
1972-73	42	24	14	4	72	35	62	1 of 22	Champions/Promoted	15 - Paul Fletcher
Division One										
1973-74	42	16	14	12	56	53	46	6 of 22		13 - Paul Fletcher
1974-75	42	17	11	14	68	67	45	10 of 22		16 - Leighton James
1975-76	42	9	10	23	43	66	28	21 of 22	Relegated	13 - Hankin/Noble
Division Two										
1976-77	42	11	14	17	46	64	36	16 of 22		13 - Peter Noble
1977-78	42	15	10	17	56	64	40	11 of 22		12 - Steve Kindon
1978-79	42	14	12	16	51	62	40	13 of 22		14 - Peter Noble
1979-80	42	6	15	21	39	73	27	21 of 22	Relegated	7 - Billy Hamilton
Division Three										
1980-81	46	18	14	14	60	48	50	8 of 24		16 - Steve Taylor
1981-82	46	21	17	8	66	45	80	1 of 24	Champions/Promoted	11 - Billy Hamilton
Division Two										
1982-83	42	12	8	22	56	66	44	21 of 22	Relegated	13 - Billy Hamilton
Division Three										
1983-84	46	16	14	16	76	61	62	12 of 24		18 - Billy Hamilton
1984-85	46	11	13	22	60	73	46	21 of 24	Relegated	18 - Wayne Biggins
Division Four										
1985-86	46	16	11	19	60	65	59	14 of 24		16 - Alan Taylor
1986-87	46	12	13	21	53	74	49	22 of 24		10 - Leighton James
1987-88	46	20	7	19	57	62	67	10 of 24		14 - George Oghani
1988-89	46	14	13	19	52	61	55	16 of 24		13 - Brendan O'Connell
1989-90	46	14	14	18	45	55	56	16 of 24		7 - Futcher/White
1990-91	46	23	10	13	70	51	79	6 of 24	Play-off semi finals	18 - Ron Futcher
1991-92	42	25	8	9	79	43	83	1 of 22	Champions/promoted	24 - Mike Conroy

Burnley in the Football League 1888-89 to 2006-07 continued

	P	W	D	L	F	A	Pts	Pos		Top scorer (League only)
New Division Two										
1992-93	46	15	16	15	57	59	61	13 of 24		20 - Adrian Heath
1993-94	46	21	10	15	79	58	73	6 of 24	Promoted via play-offs	19 - David Eyres
Division One										
1994-95	46	11	13	22	49	74	46	22 of 24	Relegated	8 - David Eyres
Division Two										
1995-96	46	14	13	19	56	68	55	17 of 24		20 - Kurt Nogan
1996-97	46	19	11	16	71	55	68	9 of 24		24 - Paul Barnes
1997-98	46	13	13	20	55	65	52	20 of 24		16 - Andy Cooke
1998-99	46	13	16	17	54	73	55	15 of 24		20 - Andy Payton
1999-2000	46	25	13	8	69	47	88	2 of 24	Runners-up/promoted	27 - Andy Payton
Division One										
2000-01	46	21	9	16	50	54	72	7 of 24		9 - Andy Payton
2001-02	46	21	12	13	70	62	75	7 of 24		16 - Gareth Taylor
2002-03	46	15	10	21	65	89	55	16 of 24		16 - Gareth Taylor
2003-04	46	13	14	19	60	77	53	19 of 24		19 - Robbie Blake
Championship										
2004-05	46	15	15	16	38	39	60	13 of 24		10 - Robbie Blake
2005-06	46	14	12	20	46	54	54	17 of 24		12 - Ade Akinbiyi
2006-07	46	15	12	19	52	49	57	15 of 24		14 - Andy Gray

SUMMARY

					Goals			
	P	**W**	**D**	**L**	**F**	**A**	**Pts**	
1st tier	**1982**	**784**	**447**	**751**	**3163**	**3157**	**2015**	**51 seasons**
2nd tier	**1586**	**602**	**390**	**594**	**2217**	**2254**	**1731**	**39 seasons**
3rd tier	**506**	**186**	**150**	**170**	**703**	**652**	**690**	**11 seasons**
4th tier	**318**	**124**	**76**	**118**	**416**	**411**	**448**	**7 seasons**
Totals	**4392**	**1696**	**1063**	**1633**	**6499**	**6474**	**4884**	**108 Football League seasons**

Second Division Champions 1972-73
Back: Jim Thomson, Colin Waldron, Alan Stevenson, Jeff Parton, Keith Newton,
Middle: Mike Docherty, Doug Collins, Alan West, Geoff Nulty, Harry Wilson, David Thomas, Leighton James,
Front: Billy Ingham, Frank Casper, Paul Fletcher, Martin Dobson (captain), Eric Probert, Paul Bradshaw

Internationals

Burnley's full internationals 1882 to May 2007

Surname	First name	caps & goals	Country	Date	Opponent	Score	Goals	Venue		
Aird	**John**	4	Scotland	5 May 1954	Norway	1-0		Hampden Park		
				19 May 1954	Norway	1-1		Oslo		
				16 Jun 1954	Austria	0-1		Zurich		**WCF**
				19 Jun 1954	Uruguay	0-7		Basle		**WCF**
Angus	**John**	1	England	27 May 1961	Austria	1-3		Vienna		
Also Football League										
Bannister	**William**	1	England	18 Mar 1901	Wales	6-0		Newcastle		
Also Football League		*(2 full caps in all)*								
Blacklaw	**Adam**	3	Scotland	4 Jun 1963	Norway	3-4		Bergen		
				13 Jun 1963	Spain	6-2		Madrid		
				7 Dec 1965	Italy	0-7		Naples		
Bowsher	**Stan**	1	Wales	2 Feb 1929	Northern Ireland	2-2		Wrexham		
Boyle	**Tommy**	1	England	15 Feb 1913	Ireland	1-2		Belfast		
Also Football League										
Bruton	**Jack**	3	England	17 May 1928	France	5-1		Paris		
Also Football League				19 May 1928	Belgium	3-1		Antwerp		
				13 Apr 1929	Scotland	0-1		Hampden Park		
Cassidy	**Tommy**	4	Northern Ireland	15 Oct 1980	Sweden	3-0		Belfast		
		(24 full caps - 1 goal in all)		19 Nov 1980	Portugal	0-1		Lisbon		
				18 Nov 1981	Israel	1-0		Belfast		
				25 Jun 1982	Spain	1-0		Valencia	sub	**WCF**
Coates	**Ralph**	2	England	21 Apr 1970	Northern Ireland	3-1		Wembley		
Also Football League		*(4 full caps in all)*		21 Apr 1971	Greece	3-0		Wembley	sub	
Cochrane	**Terry**	4	Northern Ireland	19 May 1978	Wales	0-1		Wrexham	sub	
		(26 full caps - 1 goal in all)		20 Sep 1978	Rep of Ireland	0-0		Dublin	sub	
				25 Oct 1978	Denmark	2-1		Belfast		
				29 Nov 1978	Bulgaria	2-0		Sofia		
Connelly	**John**	10 - 4gls	England	17 Oct 1959	Wales	1-1		Cardiff		
Also Football League		*(20 full caps - 7 goals in all)*		28 Oct 1959	Sweden	2-3	1gl	Wembley		
				18 Nov 1959	Northern Ireland	2-1		Wembley		
				19 April 1960	Scotland	1-1		Hampden Park		
				14 Oct 1961	Wales	1-1		Cardiff		
				25 Oct 1961	Portugal	2-0	1gl	Wembley		
				4 Apr 1962	Austria	3-1		Wembley		
				9 May 1962	Switzerland	3-1	1gl	Wembley		
				21 Nov 1962	Wales	4-0	1gl	Wembley		
				27 Feb 1963	France	2-5		Paris		
Cox	**Ian**	4	Trinidad & Tobago	25 Feb 2001	Cayman Islands	3-0		Trinidad		
		(16 full caps in all)		28 Feb 2001	Jamaica	0-1		Kingston		
				24 Mar 2001	Guatemala	3-1		Trinidad		
				28 Mar 2001	Costa Rica	0-3		Costa Rica		
Coyne	**Danny**	10	Wales	9 Feb 2005	Hungary	2-0		Cardiff		
		(15 full caps in all)		26 Mar 2005	Austria	0-2		Cardiff		
				30 Mar 2005	Austria	0-1		Vienna		
				17 Aug 2005	Slovenia	0-0		Swansea		
				3 Sep 2005	England	0-1		Cardiff		
				7 Sep 2005	Poland	0-1		Warsaw		
				6 Feb 2007	Northern Ireland	0-0		Belfast		
				24 Mar 2007	Republic of Ireland	0-1		Dublin		
				28 Mar 2007	San Marino	3-0		Cardiff		
				26 May 2007	New Zealand	2-2		Wrexham		
Crabtree	**James**	3	England	1 Mar 1894	Ireland	2-2		Belfast		
Also Football League		*(14 full caps in all)*		9 Mar 1895	Ireland	9-0		Derby		
				6 Apr 1895	Scotland	3-0		Goodison Park		

Dawson	**Jerry**	2	England	22 Oct 1921	Ireland	1-1		Belfast	
Also Football League				8 Apr 1922	Scotland	0-1		Villa Park	
Dobson	**Martin**	4	England	3 Apr 1974	Portugal	0-0		Lisbon	
Also Football League		*(5 full caps in all)*		29 May 1974	East Germany	1-1		Leipzig	
				1 Jun 1974	Bulgaria	1-0		Sofia	
				5 Jun 1974	Yugoslavia	2-2		Belgrade	
Duff	**Michael**	14	Northern Ireland	18 Aug 2004	Switzerland	0-0		Zurich	sub
		(17 full caps in all)		7 Sep 2005	England	1-0		Belfast	sub
				8 Oct 2005	Wales	2-3		Belfast	
				12 Oct 2005	Austria	0-2		Vienna	
				1 Mar 2006	Estonia	1-0		Belfast	
				21 May 2006	Uruguay	0-1		New Jersey	
				26 May 2006	Romania	0-2		Chicago	
				16 Aug 2006	Finland	2-1		Helsinki	sub
				2 Sep 2006	Iceland	0-3		Belfast	sub
				6 Sep 2006	Spain	3-2		Belfast	
				7 Oct 2006	Denmark	0-0		Copenhagen	
				6 Feb 2007	Wales	0-0		Belfast	
				24 Mar 2007	Liechtenstein	4-1		Vaduz	
				28 Mar 2007	Sweden	2-1		Belfast	
Elder	**Alex**	34 - 1gl	Northern Ireland	6 Apr 1960	Wales	2-3		Wrexham	
		(40 full caps - 1goal in all)		8 Oct 1960	England	2-5		Belfast	
				26 Oct 1960	West Germany	3-4		Belfast	
				9 Nov 1960	Scotland	2-5		Hampden Park	
				12 Apr 1961	Wales	1-5		Belfast	
				3 May 1961	Greece	1-2		Athens	
				10 May 1961	West Germany	1-2		Berlin	
				7 Oct 1961	Scotland	1-6		Belfast	
				17 Oct 1961	Greece	2-0		Belfast	
				22 Nov 1961	England	1-1		Wembley	
				10 Oct 1962	Poland	2-0		Katowice	
				20 Oct 1962	England	1-3		Belfast	
				7 Nov 1962	Scotland	1-5		Hampden Park	
				28 Nov 1962	Poland	2-0		Belfast	
				3 Apr 1963	Wales	1-4		Belfast	
				30 May 1963	Spain	1-1		Bilbao	
				15 Apr 1964	Wales	3-2		Swansea	
				29 Apr 1964	Uruguay	3-0		Belfast	
				3 Oct 1964	England	3-4		Belfast	
				14 Oct 1964	Switzerland	1-0		Belfast	
				14 Nov 1964	Switzerland	1-2		Lausanne	
				25 Nov 1964	Scotland	2-3		Hampden Park	
				17 Mar 1965	Netherlands	2-1		Belfast	
				31 Mar 1965	Wales	0-5		Belfast	
				7 Apr 1965	Netherlands	0-0		Rotterdam	
				7 May 1965	Albania	4-1		Belfast	
				2 Oct 1965	Scotland	3-2		Belfast	
				10 Nov 1965	England	1-2		Wembley	
				24 Nov 1965	Albania	1-1		Tirana	
				30 Mar 1966	Wales	4-1		Cardiff	
				22 Jun 1966	Mexico	4-1	1gl	Belfast	
				22 Oct 1966	England	0-2		Belfast	
				16 Nov 1966	Scotland	1-2		Hampden Park	
				12 Apr 1967	Wales	0-0		Belfast	
Elliott	**Billy**	5 - 3gls	England	18 May 1952	Italy	1-1		Florence	
Also Football League				25 May 1952	Austria	3-2		Vienna	
				4 Oct 1952	Northern Ireland	2-2	1gl	Belfast	
				12 Nov 1952	Wales	5-2		Wembley	
				26 Nov 1952	Belgium	5-0	2gls	Wembley	
Emerson	**William**	5	Northern Ireland	1 Apr 1922	Wales	1-1		Belfast	
		(11 full caps - 1 goal in all)		21 Oct 1922	England	0-2		The Hawthorns	
				3 Mar 1923	Scotland	0-1		Belfast	
				14 Apr 1923	Wales	3-0		Wrexham	
				20 Oct 1923	England	2-1		Belfast	

Surname	First name	Caps	Country	Date	Opponent	Score	Goals	Venue	Notes
Flack	**Hugh**	1	Northern Ireland	23 Feb 1929	Scotland	3-7		Belfast	
Flynn	**Brian**	34 - 3gls	Wales	20 Nov 1974	Luxembourg	5-0		Swansea	sub
		(66 full caps - 7 goals in all)		16 Apr 1975	Hungary	2-1		Budapest	sub
				1 May 1975	Luxembourg	1-1		Luxembourg	sub
				17 May 1975	Scotland	2-2	1gl	Cardiff	
				21 May 1975	England	2-2		Wembley	
				23 May 1975	Northern Ireland	0-1		Belfast	
				19 Nov 1975	Austria	1-1		Wrexham	
				24 Mar 1976	England	1-2		Wrexham	
				24 Apr 1976	Yugoslavia	0-2		Zagreb	
				8 May 1976	England	0-1		Cardiff	
				14 May 1976	Northern Ireland	1-0		Swansea	
				22 May 1976	Yugoslavia	1-1		Cardiff	
				6 Oct 1976	West Germany	0-2		Cardiff	sub
				17 Nov 1976	Scotland	0-1		Hampden Park	
				30 Mar 1977	Czechoslovakia	3-0		Wrexham	
				28 May 1977	Scotland	0-0		Wrexham	
				31 May 1977	England	1-0		Wembley	
				3 Jun 1977	Northern Ireland	1-1		Belfast	
				6 Sep 1977	Kuwait	0-0		Wrexham	
				20 Sep 1977	Kuwait	0-0		Kuwait City	
				12 Oct 1977	Scotland	0-2		Anfield	
				15 Dec 1982	Yugoslavia	4-4	1gl	Totograd	
				23 Feb 1983	England	2-1		Wembley	
				27 Apr 1983	Bulgaria	1-0		Wrexham	
				28 May 1983	Scotland	0-2		Cardiff	
				31 May 1983	Northern Ireland	1-0		Belfast	
				12 Jun 1983	Brazil	1-1	1gl	Cardiff	
				21 Sep 1983	Norway	0-0		Oslo	
				12 Oct 1983	Romania	5-0		Wrexham	
				16 Nov 1983	Bulgaria	0-1		Sofia	
				14 Dec 1983	Yugoslavia	1-1		Cardiff	
				28 Feb 1984	Scotland	1-2		Hampden Park	
				6 Jun 1984	Norway	0-1		Trondheim	
				10 Jun 1984	Israel	0-0		Tel Aviv	
Freeman	**Bert**	3 - 2gls	England	10 Feb 1912	Ireland	6-1	1gl	Dublin	
Also Football League		*(5 full caps - 3 goals in all)*		11 Mar 1912	Wales	2-0	1gl	Wrexham	
				23 Mar 1912	Scotland	1-1		Hampden Park	
Gray	**Phil**	3	Northern Ireland	2 Sep 2000	Malta	1-0		Belfast	sub
		(26 full caps - 6 goals in all)		7 Oct 2000	Denmark	1-1		Belfast	sub
				11 Oct 2000	Iceland	1-0		Reykyavik	sub
Hamilton	**Billy**	34 - 5gls	Northern Ireland	16 May 1980	Scotland	1-0	1gl	Belfast	
		(41 full caps - 5 goals in all)		20 May 1980	England	1-1		Wembley	
				23 May 1980	Wales	1-0		Cardiff	
				11 Jun 1980	Australia	2-1		Sydney	
				18 Jun 1980	Australia	2-1		Adelaide	
				15 Oct 1980	Sweden	3-0		Belfast	
				19 Nov 1980	Portugal	0-1		Lisbon	
				25 Mar 1981	Scotland	1-1	1gl	Hampden Park	
				29 Apr 1981	Portugal	1-0		Belfast	
				19 May 1981	Scotland	0-2		Hampden Park	
				3 Jun 1981	Sweden	0-1		Stockholm	
				14 Oct 1981	Scotland	0-0		Belfast	
				18 Nov 1981	Israel	1-0		Belfast	
				23 Feb 1982	England	0-4		Wembley	
				27 May 1982	Wales	0-3		Wrexham	
				17 Jun 1982	Yugoslavia	0-0		Zaragoza	**WCF**
				21 Jun 1982	Honduras	1-1		Zaragoza	**WCF**
				25 Jun 1982	Spain	1-0		Valencia	**WCF**
				11 Jul 1982	Austria	2-2	2gls	Madrid	**WCF**
				4 Jul 1982	France	1-4		Madrid	**WCF**
				13 Oct 1982	Austria	0-2		Vienna	
				17 Nov 1982	West Germany	1-0		Belfast	
				15 Dec 1982	Albania	0-0		Tirana	
				27 Apr 1983	Albania	1-0		Belfast	
				24 May 1983	Scotland	0-0		Hampden Park	
				28 May 1983	England	0-0		Belfast	

Surname	First name	Caps	Country	Date	Opponent	Score	Goals	Venue	
Hamilton (continued)				31 May 1983	Wales	0-1		Belfast	
				21 Sep 1983	Austria	3-1	1gl	Belfast	
				12 Oct 1983	Turkey	0-1		Ankara	
				16 Nov 1983	West Germany	1-0		Hamburg	
				13 Dec 1983	Scotland	2-0		Hampden Park	
				4 Apr 1984	England	0-1		Wembley	
				22 May 1984	Wales	1-1		Swansea	
				27 May 1984	Finland	0-1		Pori	
Harris Also Football League	**Gordon**	1	England	5 Jan 1966	Poland	1-1		Goodison Park	
Hill Also Football League	**Jack**	8 *(11 full caps in all)*	England	28 Feb 1925	Wales	2-1		Swansea	
				17 Apr 1926	Scotland	0-1		Old Trafford	
				20 Oct 1926	Northern Ireland	3-3		Anfield	
				2 Apr 1927	Scotland	2-1		Hampden Park	
				11 May 1927	Belgium	9-1		Brussels	
				26 May 1927	France	6-0		Paris	
				22 Oct 1927	Northern Ireland	0-2		Belfast	
				28 Nov 1927	Wales	1-2		Turf Moor	
Hillman Also Football League	**Jack**	1	England	18 Feb 1899	Ireland	13-2		Sunderland	
Hyde	**Micah**	4 - 1gl	Jamaica	18 Aug 2004	USA	1-1		Kingston	
				4 Sep 2004	Panama	1-2		Kingston	
				8 Sep 2004	El Salvador	3-1	1gl	San Salvador	
				9 Oct 2004	Panama	1-1		Panama City	
Irvine	**Willie**	17 - 6gls *(23 full caps - 8 goals in all)*	Northern Ireland	3 Apr 1963	Wales	1-4		Belfast	
				30 May 1963	Spain	1-1	1gl	Bilbao	
				14 Nov 1964	Switzerland	1-2		Lausanne	
				25 Nov 1964	Scotland	2-3	1gl	Hampden Park	
				17 Mar 1965	Netherlands	2-1		Belfast	
				31 Mar 1965	Wales	0-5		Belfast	
				7 Apr 1965	Netherlands	0-0		Rotterdam	
				7 May 1965	Albania	4-1		Belfast	
				2 Oct 1965	Scotland	3-2	1gl	Belfast	
				10 Nov 1965	England	1-2	1gl	Wembley	
				24 Nov 1965	Albania	1-1	1gl	Tirana	
				30 Mar 1966	Wales	4-1	1gl	Cardiff	
				22 Jun 1966	Mexico	4-1		Belfast	
				22 Oct 1966	England	0-2		Belfast	
				16 Nov 1966	Scotland	1-2		Hampden Park	
				22 Nov 1967	England	0-2		Wembley	
				28 Feb 1968	Wales	0-2		Wrexham	
James	**Leighton**	23 - 3gls *(54 full caps - 10 goals in all)*	Wales	27 Oct 1971	Czechoslovakia	0-1		Prague	
				24 Nov 1971	Romania	0-2		Bucharest	
				24 May 1972	Scotland	0-1		Hampden Park	sub
				15 Nov 1972	England	0-1		Cardiff	
				24 Jan 1973	England	1-1		Wembley	
				28 Mar 1973	Poland	2-0	1gl	Cardiff	
				12 May 1973	Scotland	0-2		Wrexham	
				15 May 1973	England	0-3		Wembley	
				19 May 1973	Northern Ireland	0-1		Goodison Park	
				26 Sep 1973	Poland	0-3		Chorzow	
				11 May 1974	England	0-2		Cardiff	
				14 May 1974	Scotland	0-2		Hampden Park	
				18 May 1974	Northern Ireland	1-0		Wrexham	
				4 Sep 1974	Austria	1-2		Vienna	
				30 Oct 1974	Hungary	2-0		Cardiff	
				20 Nov 1974	Luxembourg	5-0		Swansea	
				16 Apr 1975	Hungary	2-1		Budapest	
				1 May 1975	Luxembourg	3-1	2gls	Luxembourg	
				17 May 1975	Scotland	2-2		Cardiff	
				21 May 1975	England	2-2		Wembley	
				23 May 1975	Northern Ireland	0-1		Belfast	
				19 Nov 1975	Austria	1-0		Wrexham	
				29 Nov 1978	Turkey	1-0		Wrexham	

Player		Caps	Date	Opponent	Score	Goals	Venue		
Jones	**Steve**	3 Northern Ireland	16 Aug 2006	Finland	2-1		Helsinki	sub	
		(27 full caps - 1 goal in all)	7 Oct 2006	Denmark	0-0		Copenhagen	sub	
			24 Mar 2007	Liechtenstein	4-1		Vaduz	sub	
Kelly	**Bob**	11 - 6gls England	10 Apr 1920	Scotland	5-4	2gls	Hillsborough		
Also Football League		*(14 full caps - 8 goals in all)*	23 Oct 1920	Ireland	2-0	1gl	Sunderland		
			14 Mar 1921	Wales	0-0		Cardiff		
			9 Apr 1921	Scotland	0-3		Hampden Park		
			13 Mar 1922	Wales	1-0	1gl	Liverpool		
			8 Apr 1922	Scotland	0-1		Villa Park		
			14 Apr 1923	Scotland	2-2	1gl	Hampden Park		
			20 Oct 1923	Ireland	1-2		Belfast		
			22 Oct 1924	Ireland	3-1	1gl	Goodison Park		
			28 Feb 1925	Wales	2-1		Swansea		
			4 Apr 1925	Scotland	2-0		Hampden Park		
Lafferty	**Kyle**	10 - 1gl Northern Ireland	21 May 2006	Uruguay	0-1		New Jersey	sub	
			26 May 2006	Romania	0-2		Chicago	sub	
			16 Aug 2006	Finland	2-1	1gl	Helsinki	sub	
			2 Sep 2006	Iceland	0-3		Belfast	sub	
			6 Sep 2006	Spain	3-2		Belfast		
			7 Oct 2006	Denmark	0-0		Copenhagen		
			11 Oct 2006	Latvia	1-0		Belfast		
			6 Feb 2007	Wales	0-0		Belfast		
			24 Mar 2007	Liechtenstein	4-1		Vaduz		
			28 Mar 2007	Sweden	2-1		Belfast	sub	
McCluggage	**Andy**	11 - 2gls Northern Ireland	26 Feb 1927	Scotland	0-2		Belfast		
		(13 full caps - 2 goals in all)	9 Apr 1927	Wales	2-2		Cardiff		
			22 Oct 1927	England	2-0		Belfast		
			4 Feb 1928	Wales	1-2		Belfast		
			25 Feb 1928	Scotland	1-0		Hampden Park		
			22 Oct 1928	England	1-2		Goodison Park		
			2 Feb 1929	Wales	2-2	1gl	Wrexham		
			23 Feb 1929	Scotland	3-7		Belfast		
			1 Feb 1930	Wales	7-0	1gl	Belfast		
			20 Oct 1930	England	1-5		Bramall Lane		
			22 Apr 1931	Wales	2-3		Wrexham		
McDonald	**Colin**	8 England	18 May 1958	USSR	1-1		Moscow		
Also Football League			8 Jun 1958	USSR	2-2		Gothenburg		**WCF**
			11 Jun 1958	Brazil	0-0		Gothenburg		**WCF**
			15 Jun 1958	Austria	2-2		Boras		**WCF**
			17 Jun 1958	USSR	0-1		Gothenburg		**WCF**
			4 Oct 1958	Northern Ireland	3-3		Belfast		
			22 Oct 1958	USSR	5-0		Wembley		
			26 Nov 1958	Wales	2-2		Villa Park		
McIlroy	**Jimmy**	51 - 10gls Northern Ireland	6 Oct 1951	Scotland	0-3		Belfast		
Also Football League		*(55 full caps - 10 goals in all)*	20 Nov 1951	England	0-2		Villa Park		
			19 Mar 1952	Wales	0-3		Swansea		
			4 Oct 1952	England	2-2		Belfast		
			5 Nov 1952	Scotland	1-1		Hampden Park		
			15 Apr 1953	Wales	2-3		Belfast		
			3 Oct 1953	Scotland	1-3		Belfast		
			11 Nov 1953	England	1-3		Goodison Park		
			31 Mar 1954	Wales	2-1		Wrexham		
			2 Oct 1954	England	0-2		Belfast		
			3 Nov 1954	Scotland	2-2		Hampden Park		
			20 Apr 1955	Wales	2-3		Belfast		
			8 Oct 1955	Scotland	2-1		Belfast		
			2 Nov 1955	England	0-3		Wembley		
			11 Apr 1956	Wales	1-1		Cardiff		
			6 Oct 1956	England	1-1	1gl	Belfast		
			7 Nov 1956	Scotland	0-1		Hampden Park		
			16 Jan 1957	Portugal	1-1		Lisbon		
			10 Apr 1957	Wales	0-0		Belfast		
			25 Apr 1957	Italy	0-1		Rome		
			1 May 1957	Portugal	3-0	1gl	Belfast		
			5 Oct 1957	Scotland	1-1		Belfast		
			6 Nov 1957	England	3-2	1gl	Wembley		

Player		Caps	Country	Date	Opponent	Score	Goals	Venue		
McIlroy (continued)				4 Dec 1957	Italy	2-2		Belfast		
				15 Jan 1958	Italy	2-1	1gl	Belfast		
				16 Apr 1958	Wales	1-1		Cardiff		
				8 Jun 1958	Czechoslovakia	1-0		Halmstad		**WCF**
				11 Jun 1958	Argentina	1-3		Halmstad		**WCF**
				15 Jun 1958	West Germany	2-2		Malmo		**WCF**
				17 Jun 1958	Czechoslovakia	2-1		Malmo		**WCF**
				19 Jun 1958	France	0-4		Norrkoping		**WCF**
				4 Oct 1958	England	3-3		Belfast		
				15 Oct 1958	Spain	2-6	1gl	Madrid		
				5 Nov 1958	Scotland	2-2	1gl	Hampden Park		
				22 Apr 1959	Wales	4-1	1gl	Belfast		
				3 Oct 1959	Scotland	0-4		Belfast		
				18 Nov 1959	England	1-2		Wembley		
				6 Apr 1960	Wales	2-3		Wrexham		
				8 Oct 1960	England	2-5		Belfast		
				26 Oct 1960	West Germany	3-4		Belfast		
				12 Apr 1961	Wales	1-5		Belfast		
				3 May 1961	Greece	1-2	1gl	Athens		
				10 May 1961	West Germany	1-2	1gl	Berlin		
				7 Oct 1961	Scotland	1-6		Belfast		
				17 Oct 1961	Greece	2-0		Belfast		
				22 Nov 1961	England	1-1	1gl	Wembley		
				9 May 1962	Netherlands	0-4		Rotterdam		
				10 Oct 1962	Poland	2-0		Katowice		
				20 Oct 1962	England	1-3		Belfast		
				7 Nov 1962	Scotland	1-5		Hampden Park		
				28 Nov 1962	Poland	2-0		Belfast		
Michopoulos	**Nik**	2	Greece	12 May 2002	Romania	3-2		Alexandroupoli	sub	
				15 May 2002	Cyprus	3-1		Rhodes	sub	
Miller	**Brian**	1	England	27 May 1961	Austria	1-3		Vienna		
Also Football League										
Morgan	**Willie**	1	Scotland	21 Oct 1967	Northern Ireland	0-1		Belfast		
		(21 full caps - 1goal in all)								
Morris	**Billy**	5	Wales	16 Apr 1947	Northern Ireland	1-2		Belfast		
				10 Nov 1948	England	0-1		Villa Park		
				20 Nov 1951	Scotland	1-0		Hampden Park		
				5 Dec 1951	Rest of UK	3-2		Cardiff		
				19 Mar 1952	Northern Ireland	3-0		Swansea		
Morrison	**Tom**	4	Northern Ireland	4 Mar 1899	Wales	1-0		Belfast		
		(7 full caps in all)		24 Feb 1900	Wales	0-2		Llandudno		
				1 Mar 1902	Scotland	1-3		Belfast		
				22 Mar 1902	England	0-1		Belfast		
Mosscrop	**Eddie**	2	England	16 Mar 1914	Wales	2-0		Cardiff		
Also Football League				4 Apr 1914	Scotland	1-3		Hampden Park		
Page	**Louis**	7 - 1gl	England	12 Feb 1927	Wales	3-3		Wrexham		
Also Football League				2 Apr 1927	Scotland	2-1		Hampden Park		
				11 May 1927	Belgium	9-1	1gl	Brussels		
				21 May 1927	Luxembourg	5-2		Luxembourg		
				26 May 1927	France	6-0		Paris		
				22 Oct 1927	Northern Ireland	0-2		Belfast		
				28 Nov 1927	Wales	1-2		Turf Moor		
Papadopoulos	**Demi**	1	Greece	20 Nov 2002	Rep of Ireland	0-0		Athens	sub	
Pilkington	**Brian**	1	England	2 Oct 1954	Northern Ireland	2-0		Belfast		
Also Football League										
Pointer	**Ray**	3 - 2gls	England	28 Sep 1961	Luxembourg	4-1	1gl	Highbury		
Also Football League				14 Oct 1961	Wales	1-1		Cardiff		
				25 Oct 1961	Portugal	2-0	1gl	Wembley		

Surname	First name	Caps	Country	Date	Opponent	Score	Goals	Venue	
Taylor	**Gareth**	4	Wales	27 Mar 2002	Czech Republic	0-0		Cardiff	sub
		(15 full caps - 1gl in all)		21 Aug 2002	Croatia	1-1		Varadzin	sub
				12 Feb 2003	Bosnia-Herzog.	2-2		Cardiff	sub
				26 May 2003	USA	0-2		San Jose	
Todd	**Sammy**	8	Northern Ireland	22 Jun 1966	Mexico	4-1		Belfast	sub
		(11 full caps in all)		22 Oct 1966	England	0-2		Belfast	
				28 Feb 1968	Wales	0-2		Wrexham	
				3 May 1969	England	1-3		Belfast	
				6 May 1969	Scotland	1-1		Hampden Park	
				10 May 1969	Wales	0-0		Belfast	
				10 Sep 1969	USSR	0-0		Belfast	
				18 Apr 1970	Scotland	0-1		Belfast	
Waterfield	**George**	1	England	12 Feb 1927	Wales	3-3		Wrexham	
Watson	**Willie**	3	England	5 Apr 1913	Scotland	1-0		Chelsea	
Also Football League				14 Feb 1914	Ireland	0-3		Middlesbrough	
				25 Oct 1919	Ireland	1-1		Belfast	
Willighan	**Tommy**	2	Northern Ireland	7 Dec 1932	Wales	1-4		Wrexham	
				16 Sep 1933	Scotland	2-1		Hampden Park	
Yates	**Jack**	1 - 3gls	England	2 Mar 1889	Ireland	6-1	3gls	Anfield	

WCF = World Cup Finals

Also played for the Football League whilst with Burnley;
Jimmy Adamson, Reg Attwell, Alan Brown, Frank Casper, Benny Cross, Tommy Cummings, Teddy Hodgson, Peter Kippax, Hugh Moffat, Brian O'Neil, Alick Robinson, Wilf Toman, Arthur Woodruff.

Won "B" international caps whilst with Burnley;
John Aird, Jimmy Adamson, Tommy Cummings, Alex Elder, Bill Holden, Billy Marshall, Brian Pilkington, Les Shannon, Billy Wilson, Doug Winton

Burnley's amateur internationals;
Arthur Bell, Peter Kippax

Burnley's under 23 internationals;
England : John Angus, Albert Cheesebrough, Ralph Coates, John Connelly, Martin Dobson, Paul Fletcher, Ray Hankin, Gordon Harris, Brian Miller, Brian O'Neil, Ray Pointer, Jimmy Robson, Alan Stevenson, John Talbut, David Thomas, Alan West.
also Richard Chaplow won caps at both under 21 and under 20 level.
Northern Ireland : Alex Elder, Willie Irvine, Sammy Todd,.
Scotland : Adam Blacklaw, Andy Lochhead, Willie Morgan.
Wales : Brian Flynn, Leighton James, Jeff Parton.

An Irish international squad in training in the seventies
Standing: Sammy Todd - 2nd left, Alex Elder - 4th left
Kneeling: Willie Irvine - far right, George Best - far left.

Welsh wizards Leighton James and Brian Flynn -
James (left) watches as Flynn tangles with the keeper

Most appearances & goals

Most appearances

Players with 250 or more senior appearances
In sequence of most League starts
(sub apps in brackets)

	League		Total	
	apps	goals	apps	goals
Jerry Dawson	522	0	569	0
Jimmy McIlroy	439	116	497	131
John Angus	438(1)	4	520(1)	4
Alan Stevenson	438	0	543	0
Tommy Cummings	434	3	479	3
Jimmy Adamson	426	17	486	18
Martin Dobson	406(4)	63	493(4)	76
Fred Barron	400	13	423	14
Brian Miller	379	29	455	37
George Waterfield	371	5	394	5
Willie Watson	346	18	380	20
Leighton James	331(5)	66	393(6)	81
Joe Taylor	323	12	352	14
Steve Davis	321(6)	42	381(7)	47
Adam Blacklaw	318	0	383	0
George Beel	316	179	337	188
Colin Waldron	308	16	356	18
Harold Mather	301	0	329	0
Brian Pilkington	300	67	340	77
Jim Thomson	294(3)	3	361(3)	6
Paul Fletcher	291(2)	71	349(3)	86
Marlon Beresford	286(1)	0	349(1)	0
Derek Scott	277(8)	24	350(8)	29
Bob Kelly	277	88	299	97
Alex Elder	271	15	330	17
Arthur Woodruff	271	0	292	0
Billy Bowes	269	79	295	84
Jimmy Strong	264	0	285	0
Les Shannon	263	39	281	44
Gordon Harris	258	69	313	81
Louis Page	248	111	259	115
Billy Rodaway	245(2)	3	301(2)	3
Reg Attwell	244	9	269	11
Peter Noble	241(2)	63	299(2)	80
George Bray	241	8	259	9
Andy Farrell	237(20)	19	301(30)	23
Benny Cross	237	57	255	61
Tom McLintock	233	15	254	15
Brian O'Neil	231(4)	22	277(5)	25
Frank Casper	230(7)	74	268(7)	89
Andy Lochhead	225(1)	101	265(1)	128
Ray Pointer	223	118	270	132
David Taylor	221	5	250	5
John Connelly	215	85	265	104
Ralph Coates	214(2)	26	257(4)	32
Vince Overson	213(6)	6	257(7)	7
Glen Little	211(35)	32	237(46)	36
John Deary	209(6)	23	265(10)	27
Keith Newton	209	5	253	7
Graham Branch	208(56)	17	232(67)	18
Arthur Bellamy	204(13)	29	236(14)	29
Joe Jakub	203(2)	8	253(2)	9
Billy Hamilton	200	58	251	77
Paul Weller	199(53)	11	226(62)	13
Brian Flynn	193(9)	19	239(11)	27
Billy Ingham	181(30)	22	233(33)	31

Leading goalscorers

Players with 50 or more senior goals
In sequence of most League goals

	League	Total
	goals	goals
George Beel	179	188
Ray Pointer	118	132
Jimmy McIlroy	116	131
Louis Page	111	115
Bert Freeman	103	115
Andy Lochhead	101	128
Bob Kelly	88	97
John Connelly	85	104
Jimmy Robson	79	100
Billy Bowes	79	84
Willie Irvine	78	97
Frank Casper	74	89
Bill Holden	74	78
Paul Fletcher	71	86
Dick Smith	70	75
Gordon Harris	69	81
Andy Payton	69	81
Brian Pilkington	67	77
Leighton James	66	81
Joe Anderson	64	72
Peter Noble	63	80
Martin Dobson	63	76
Billy Hamilton	58	77
Benny Cross	57	61
Teddy Hodgson	53	62
Andy Cooke	51	61
Cecil Smith	48	53
Billy Morris	47	53
Harry Potts	47	50
Steve Kindon	46	58
Steve Taylor	43	52
Robbie Blake	42	51
David Eyres	37	55
Ian Moore	37	50

Burnley Managers

In the very early days after Burnley FC was founded in 1882, the concept of a football manager, as we would know it today, would have been completely unheard of. Although players would be put through their paces by a trainer, who may or may not have been qualified, or even suitable, to train players for important matches, team selection itself would invariably have been in the hands of the club committee or board of directors.

Reference works on early Burnley "managers" have invariably designated Arthur Sutcliffe as the first encumbent of such a position, but more recent research tells us that Sutcliffe was appointed purely as the new club secretary following the resignation of secretary and former player Thomas White in the summer of 1892. There is no doubt that team selection, together with decisions on the introduction, as well as the departure, of players would have been firmly in the hands of the club committee, although the secretary would have had a contribution to make in such decisions.

Beginning with Harry Bradshaw, some of the early club secretaries combined their duties with that of team manager, although Bradshaw himself was initially appointed as team manager only.

Harry Bradshaw

Born: Burnley, 1853
Died: Wimbledon, 28 September 1924
Manager: August 1894 to June 1899
Secretary/manager from March 1897

The summer of 1894 was a watershed in the management of Burnley FC when it was decided to follow the lead of other clubs and appoint a team manager, although later he also assumed secretarial duties. Harry Bradshaw had been involved with the club since the change from rugby to association football in 1882 and a committee member since 1887. In 1893 Bradshaw made available his gents oufitters shop in the centre of town, to be used as a Burnley FC office for members to pay for and collect tickets. He later converted rooms over his shop into a social club for the Burnley players. Harry Bradshaw was the successful applicant when the position as the club's first team manager was advertised in the local press.

Bradshaw had hoped to build on Burnley's best-ever season in 1893-94, a fifth place finish, but he was unfortunate to preside over a steady decline which led to bottom place and relegation for the first time in 1897.

Towards the end of that disastrous campaign Bradshaw had tempted the inspirational Jimmy Ross to Turf Moor and he and centre forward Wilf Toman scored the goals that took the Clarets back to the top flight, as Second Division Champions, after only one season.

Bradshaw had brought big Jack Hillman back to the club, and introduced young full back Fred Barron to the defence for the first campaign back in the top flight. 1898-99 started promisingly and for a time there was the real possibility that the First Division crown may come to Turf Moor for the first time. Alas it didn't happen but it had been a successful season, third in the top flight representing the club's highest ever League placing.

In the summer of 1899, Harry Bradshaw was ready for a new challenge, resigned as Burnley manager, and accepted the position as manager of Second Division Woolwich Arsenal. Within five years he had taken the Gunners from the verge of bankruptcy and built a team which won promotion to the First Division in 1904.

He left Plumstead for Southern League Fulham the same year, and guided the Cottagers to Football League status in 1907 and an FA Cup semi final in 1908. Bradshaw left Craven Cottage in 1909 to take up the position of secretary of the Southern League, a position he held until his death in 1924, aged 71.

One of Harry Bradshaw's sons, Burnley-born William, joined his home town club in 1907, and played a few games at senior level.

After the departure of Harry Bradshaw, first team affairs remained in the hands of the Burnley Directors until the appointment of Ernest Mangnall.

J.Ernest Mangnall

Born: Bolton
Died: St Annes, 13 January 1932
Secretary/manager: March 1900 to October 1903

Ernest Mangnall, a former goalkeeper at Lancashire County level, was a director at Bolton Wanderers before he came to Turf Moor in 1900 to take over as secretary/manager from the departed Harry Bradshaw.

Mangnall inherited a struggling team who had certainly not

consolidated upon their excellent campaign in 1898-99 despite the introduction of a number of new faces, notably the former England inside forward Edgar Chadwick, signed from Everton.

By the time Mangnall arrived at Turf Moor relegation seemed almost inevitable and his new team managed just two victories, both 1-0. The last match of that disappointing campaign was at Nottingham Forest and after Burnley's relegation had been confirmed following a 0-4 defeat, the news broke that goalkeeper Jack Hillman had tried to bribe the Forest team to "take things easy".

Back in the Second Division after just two years in the top flight, the club were hit by the 12-month ban handed out to Hillman. To replace him Ernest Mangnall signed Henry Collins from Hebburn Argyle, having already bought full backs James Lindsay and George Lockhart.

Although third place in the Second Division was achieved in 1901, even relative success was short-lived. The decline was swift and at the end of the calamitous 1902-03 season, arguably the club's worst-ever, even allowing for 1986-87, Burnley suffered the ignominy of finishing at the very bottom of the Second Division and having to apply for re-election.

Despite the team's less than spectacular record under his control, early in the 1903-04 campaign Mangnall suddenly left Turf Moor having been appointed as manager at Second Division Manchester United, as the man to build a promotion-winning side.

He surpassed expectations by gaining promotion in 1906 and bringing two League Championships to Old Trafford, in 1908 and 1911, as well as an FA Cup Final triumph in 1909.

After being instrumental in the formation of the Central League in 1911, Ernest Mangnall left Old Trafford to join arch rivals Manchester City in 1912, where he stayed until leaving League football in 1924.

He also helped found the Football Managers' Association, and upon his retirement from the game, he was awarded an FA long-service medal and a testimonial game, when a combined Manchester team met Liverpool.

He died in 1932.

Spencer (Spen) Whittaker

Born: Oswaldtwistle, 1871
Died: Crewe, 16 April 1910
Secretary/manager: October 1903 to April 1910

The Burnley Board moved swiftly to appoint a successor to Ernest Mangnall and the man chosen was Spencer Whittaker, known as 'Spen', who had developed something of a reputation in local football in Accrington.

Whittaker immediately introduced numerous new players to try to seek a swift improvement on the field. David Walders came from Barrow, goalkeeper Billy Green from Brentford, and Dugald McFarlane, also from Barrow.

The most inspired early signing however, was that of Hugh Moffat from Congleton, who was a versatile player and a valuable servant to the club for a number of years.

Things did start to improve over the next few seasons, then in February 1907, Whittaker signed a young apprentice blacksmith who was to be the first member of the first great Burnley side and who would be around the Turf Moor scene for many years to come.

His name, of course, was Jerry Dawson.

The next key signing at Turf Moor was probably that of Alex Leake from Aston Villa in December 1907. Not destined to stay long enough to share in glories to come, former international Leake was an inspiration to the team during his time at the club, a natural leader and a man who was very popular with the supporters

Then in April 1910 tragedy struck.

Spen Whittaker was on his way to London by overnight train to register the signing of a new player, Harry Swift from Accrington.

When the train stopped at Crewe, it was reported that a man had fallen from a carriage some distance outside the town. The area was searched and Spen Whittaker was found lying on the track, having suffered terrible injuries. He died shortly afterwards.

A benefit match was held at Turf Moor for Whittaker's wife

and family, with Manchester United providing the opposition for a Football League Xl that included a number of Burnley players.

Following the death of Spen Whittaker, Burnley director and former chairman Richard Wadge temporarily assumed the club's secretarial duties until the end of the season, with team affairs in the hands of the directors.

John Haworth

Born: Accrington, 1876
Died: Burnley, 4 December 1924
Secretary/manager: July 1910 to December 1924

The Turf Moor directors once again looked to the town of Accrington to build upon the promising foundations laid by Spen Whittaker.

John Haworth was brought up in a sporting family, his uncle, George Haworth, winning five England caps and skippering Accrington FC when, along with Burnley, they were founder members of the Football League in 1888.

Haworth was a full back in his playing days with the Meadow Bank team, but soon gave up competitive football, becoming the club's secretary. He joined Accrington Stanley, then in the North East Lancashire Combination, as a committee man in early 1897 and became club secretary later in the year.

With Haworth as secretary, Stanley won the Lancashire Combination in 1902-03 and again in 1905-06, and it was from this background that he came to Turf Moor in 1910.

One of Haworth's first signings was Charlie Bates, initially as a player, but who, as assistant trainer, then first team trainer, would share in the club's triumphs over the next dozen years.

In that first summer in charge, he also broke new ground by bringing Burnley's first overseas player to Turf Moor, German Max Seeburg.

Around this time, also, John Haworth made his mark by suggesting that the club changed the colours of their shirts from green, which the new manager considered unlucky.

The Burnley director agreed and it was decided to change to the colours of the current League Champions, the claret and blue of Aston Villa.

Towards the end of his first season in charge, Haworth made his first major signing, a real coup when he persuaded the great Bert Freeman to come to Turf Moor from Everton.

The following September came the coup de grace when Tommy Boyle was signed from Barnsley.

Haworth knew that Boyle was the man that the team needed most of all, literally the pivot around which the achievements to come would revolve.

Steady progress, rather than spectacular success, followed and, after a near miss in 1912, promotion was achieved in 1913, together with a run to the FA Cup semi final.

Then in November 1913, another major signing was engineered by John Haworth when Bob Kelly arrived from St Helens Town.

The events surrounding the FA Cup triumph of 1914 are well documented, and the following season, the last before League football was suspended, was a magnificent one.

Burnley, by now, truly 'the Clarets' finished in fourth position, only three points from the title.

Better was to come in 1919-20, when Burnley were runners-up to West Brom as John Haworth and Charlie Bates planned the club's assault on the League Championship that they knew was within the team's capabilities.

After a disappointing start, the 1920-21 season was a triumph for all concerned.

There was the magnificent unbeaten run of 30 League matches, with many of the players reaching their peak at the same time, superbly led by Tommy Boyle, Haworth's lieutenant on the field.

Undoubtedly the key to the success however, was the mastermind, John Haworth, who knew every player inside out and knew how to get the very best from each one.

Third position followed in 1921-22 but the great days were coming to an end and a period of mediocrity was in store for Burnley Football Club.

Sadly John Haworth contracted pneumonia and he became the second successive Burnley manager to die in office, when he passed away in 1924 aged only 48.

Haworth was a man who never played football above junior level and had never before experienced management at a senior level, yet he guided the Clarets to the top honours in the game.

His contribution to Burnley Football Club's success is enormous and will never be forgotten.

Albert Pickles

Born: Burnley, 1877
Died: Read, 12 September 1958
Secretary/manager: January 1925 to August 1932
Team manager only from May 1931

Following the death of the enormously successful John Haworth, the club looked within to appoint his successor, local man Albert Pickles, who had been elected to the board of directors in 1918.

Pickles was an outstanding schoolboy athlete as well as a promising amateur footballer in his younger days with Burnley Belvedere.

As a 17-year-old in the late 1890s, he was offered a trial by Aston Villa at the instigation of the great James Crabtree, but parental consent was not forthcoming and a possible professional career in the game was lost.

Pickles faced a daunting task in trying to emulate his illustrious predecessor. The Championship side had all broken up, attendances were falling and prospects of lasting success looked slim.

Jack Bruton was Pickles' first signing, from Horwich RMI in March 1925. The youngster had been much sought after and was soon blooded into the first team.

Relegation was safely avoided and plans were laid for the new season.

Of course, the 1925-26 campaign was the time of a change in the offside law, and with new signings Joe Devine, Andy McCluggage and the lightning fast winger Louis Page, the team approached the new season with confidence.

That confidence evaporated somewhat on the opening day of the season when Burnley suffered a 0-10 defeat at the hands of Aston Villa.

Shortly afterwards, the great Bob Kelly left the club and it was mostly downhill after that, with only the one-man Louis Page show at Birmingham in April saving Burnley that season.

Relegation inevitably came in 1930 and, after two undistinguished Second Division campaigns, both George Beel and Louis Page left Turf Moor in 1932.

Two games into the 1932-33 season, after a heavy defeat at Preston, Pickles offered his resignation, which was 'reluctantly' accepted by the board.

Tom Bromilow

Born: Liverpool, 7 October 1894
Died: Nuneaton, 4 March 1959
Secretary/manager: October 1932 to July 1935
Team manager from November 1932

Tom Bromilow was the first Burnley manager to have played football at a professional level, and one of the minority not promoted from within the club.

He joined Liverpool from Army football in 1918 and went on to become a cultured wing half, and a prominent figure in the Anfield club's League Championship successes in 1922 and 1923.

He played over 300 League games for the Reds and won five England caps, the last in 1925, before leaving to coach in Amsterdam in 1930.

Neither Bromilow nor his wife could settle in Holland and he returned to England to take up his appointment with Burnley in 1932.

His success at Turf Moor was limited, as after inheriting a struggling team and with crowds dwindling and interest waning, he faced an uphill struggle.

New players came and went with regularity, although one of Bromilow's early achievements was to sign Ray Bennion from Manchester United. Bennion would be part of the Turf Moor success story in the years ahead from behind the scenes, but initially he became a first team regular at right half. Bromilow also persuaded another experienced wing half, old campaigner Alick Robinson, to transfer his allegiance from Bury in 1933.

Robinson became Burnley's club captain and provided a degree of stability to the defence right up until the outbreak of war.

In October 1934, Bromilow created a stir by signing George Brown from Aston Villa. Brown, a former England player, had starred in the great Huddersfield Town side under Herbert Chapman in the 1920s and brought a fearsome goalscoring reputation with him.

He did not let the Clarets down either, with his 21 goals in his first season helping the club to a respectable 12th place in 1935.

After growing speculation in the summer of 1935, linking Bromilow with numerous positions including that of manager at Tottenham, he eventually replaced former Burnley star Jack Tresadern as manager of Crystal Palace.
He had two spells in charge at Selhurst Park before the war, and during the early part of World War Two he managed Leicester City, guiding them to the League South title and the Midland Cup.
He returned to the game in 1948 as manager of Newport County, but stayed for only a short time and later scouted for Leicester.
Tom Bromilow died in 1959, aged 64.

Selection Committee 1935 to 1939

Following the departure of Tom Bromilow the Burnley directors decided not to appoint a team manager. The decision was made for economical reasons as much as anything, with team affairs to become a joint effort between Chairman Tom Clegg, secretary Alf Boland and senior trainer Billy Dougall.
Clegg had been a member of the Burnley board since 1923, in the Chair since 1934, and was an engineer by trade. Boland had played for the club's junior teams in 1930 and was working in a local textile mill when he was appointed assistant secretary to Albert Pickles in July 1932. At only 21 he had been the Football League's youngest secretary when he was thrust into the secretary's office following Pickles' sudden resignation just five months later. The selection committee was completed by Billy Dougall, the only real football man amongst the trio. Dougall's playing career had ended at Turf Moor in 1928 and after studying physiotherapy and beginning a long career in coaching, had returned to Burnley as assistant trainer in 1933. He had replaced Charlie Bates as senior trainer in 1934.
The selection committee approach continued into the late 1930s, the period that saw the foundations starting to be built of the Burnley team that would taste success after the war. Arthur Woodruff arrived in 1936 and George Bray in 1937, before the architect of later Burnley success, Harry Potts, came to the club in November 1937 as one of the very first arrivals in Burnley's famous youth policy. Billy Morris and Jack Billingham also appeared in Burnley's first team before events in Poland in 1939 abruptly ended, for the time being, the team rebuilding plans.

Clifford Samuel Britton

Born: Bristol, 29 August 1909
Died: Hull, 1 December 1975
Manager: May 1945 to September 1948

The appointment of former England international Cliff Britton as Burnley's first post-war manager was evidence of the fierce determination of the club's directors to bring success back to Turf Moor after too many lean years.
At the club's annual general meeting of February 1946, Britton announced to an impressed audience that he had developed a promotion programme which, if successful, would lead to First Division football at Turf Moor within three years. He achieved it after just one season with a wonderful FA Cup run to Wembley into the bargain.
After playing junior football in Bristol Cliff Britton signed for Bristol Rovers as an amateur in 1926, turning professional in 1928. He was transferred to Everton in 1930 for a substantial fee but took some time to establish himself in the League side at Goodison Park.
When he did, he was in the team to stay and at the end of 1932-33, his first season as a regular, he won an FA Cup Winners' medal, Everton defeating Manchester City 3-0 at Wembley. Cliff Britton's cultured and stylish play at wing half brought him his first England cap in 1934 against Wales and he won nine altogether in the years leading up to World War Two. He also played in many wartime Internationals alongside Stan Cullis and Joe Mercer, a mighty half back line indeed.

He had a reputation as a dour man with a strict disciplinary code and it was said that his ideal team would be made up of 11 tee-total, non-smoking bachelors. His success at Burnley was certainly built around the formidable "iron curtain" defence and his message to his players was an unequivocal "when not in possession, be in position!"
After steering Burnley back into the top flight, Britton spent just one more season at Turf Moor, guiding the Clarets to a very respectable third position in 1948 before leaving to return to Everton.
The Merseysiders were relegated to Division Two in 1951 but regained their top-flight status in 1954, winning promotion as runners-up to Leicester City.
In 1956 Britton resigned as Everton's manager after a series of disagreements with the club's directors. He was appointed as the manager of Preston later than year, replacing Frank Hill, whom he had preceded at Turf Moor.
After nearly five years at Deepdale he resigned in April 1961 after North End's relegation from Division One. He became Hull City's manager later that summer, and in 1966, steered the Tigers to the Championship of the Third Division.
He became City's general manager in 1969 and retired from football in October 1971. Cliff Britton died in 1975 at the age of 66.

Frank Robert Hill

Born: Forfar, 21 May 1906
Died: Luton, June 1970
Manager: October 1948 to August 1954

By the time Frank Hill took over as Burnley manager from Cliff Britton the Clarets had also lost "the iron man" Alan Brown, who had signed for Notts County.

Hill was another former International, who had also tasted success at the very pinnacle of English club football, winning three consecutive League Championship medals with the fabulous Arsenal sides of the 1930s.

A wing-half, he began his career with Forfar Athletic, his home town club, in 1924, before being transferred to Aberdeen in 1928. While at Pittodrie he won three full Scottish caps and played for the Scottish League, before a £3,000 move to Highbury in 1932.

After four years in London, the success continued at Blackpool, Hill captaining the Seasiders to promotion from Division Two in 1936-37, his only season at Bloomfield Road. After spells at Southampton and as a trainer at Preston, he was appointed player/manager of Crewe in 1944 and it was from Gresty Road that he came to Turf Moor in 1948.

In six years at Burnley, Frank Hill did a solid job in consolidating the Clarets' position back in the top flight of English football. He was responsible for bringing to Turf Moor many of the players who would go on to become household names including, of course, the greatest of them all, Jimmy McIlroy.

On the eve of the 1954-55 season, Hill suddenly accepted an invitation to return to Preston as manager, staying at Deepdale for two years. Early in 1957 he took up the offer of a coaching position in Iraq, returning to England to take over from Tommy Lawton as Notts County manager in October 1958. Relegation from Division Three in 1959, was followed by immediate promotion in 1960 but, in November 1961, Hill moved up into the Second Division as the manager of Charlton.

He retired in 1965, later working as a scout for Manchester City until his death in 1970, aged 64.

Alan Brown

Born: Consett, 26 August 1914
Died: Barnstaple, 9 March 1996
Manager: August 1954 to July 1957

Alan Brown was the iron man of Burnley Football Club immediately after the Second World War, the centre-half and captain of a formidable team with a reputation for giving nothing away in defence.

He played both rugby and football in his schoolboys on the banks of the Tyne and quite often turned out for his school rugby team on Saturday mornings before playing with his local junior team, Spen Black and White, in the afternoons.

He signed for Huddersfield Town in 1933 and immediately modelled himself on Alf Young, the Terriers' classic stopper centre-half who played for England before the war. It was Young's consistency however that was to restrict Alan Brown's progress at Leeds Road.

He spent some time in the Police Force during the 1930s and by the time war broke out in 1939 had not really established himself in Huddersfield's side. During the war he guested for Liverpool, Manchester United and Notts County as well as playing for the RAF in inter-services matches. In 1945 he was selected as a reserve for the England team to play Scotland at Villa Park.

In February 1946, Cliff Britton, newly appointed Burnley manager, saw Alan Brown as the keystone of his plan to bring success to Turf Moor. Although Brown was 31, Britton was shrewd enough to know that here was a man born to lead.

The skipper and driving force from the centre of defence, Alan Brown was an ever-present as he led the Clarets to promotion from the Second Division and to Wembley as FA Cup Runners-Up to Charlton in 1947. The success of the team was certainly built round the defence, the 29 goals conceded has been bettered just once in the club's history and that was in Victorian times from a programme of just 30 games!

Alan Brown won his only representative honour when he captained the Football League to a 4-3 victory against the Irish League in Belfast in 1948. Arthur Woodruff was also in the League side for that match.

In October 1948, with the Clarets firmly established back in the top flight, Brown was suddenly transferred to Third Division Notts County for £12,500, a considerable fee for a 34-year-old. Ambitious County were attempting to build a promotion side around the legendary Tommy Lawton and, although it had worked by 1950, Alan Brown had lasted only three months before leaving Meadow Lane.

He joined Sheffield Wednesday as a coach in 1951 then, in the summer of 1954, returned to Turf Moor, scene of his best days as a player, to replace the departed Frank Hill as Burnley manager.

He enjoyed three moderately successful years in charge before leaving for Sunderland in 1957, his first season at Roker Park ending in relegation from the top flight, the club's first since joining the League in 1890!

He moved to Sheffield Wednesday as manager in 1964 and his four years at Hillsborough included defeat by Everton in the epic FA Cup Final of 1966. He returned to Roker Park in 1968, later coached in Norway and, after returning to England, assisted Plymouth before retiring.

Before his death in 1996 aged 81, Alan Brown wrote a book on his coaching methods. Such was his popularity still and such was his influence on those he coached, many of the top names in football management of that era provided financial assistance to make sure the book was published.

William Dougall

Born: Denny, 25 October 1895
Died: Burnley, 15 November 1966
Manager: July 1957 to January 1958

Billy Dougall's career with Burnley spanned five decades and he was one of the club's finest-ever servants as player, trainer, coach, physiotherapist and manager.

His football career began when he left his job as a miner to join Hibernian as a junior, before his transfer to Falkirk in 1921. Five years later, in February 1926, a transfer fee of £3,000 took him to Turf Moor where, in the years ahead, he was to play a unique role in the development of many of Burnley's most famous players.

He immediately became a regular at wing-half in the Clarets' First Division side but his playing career was ended abruptly on Christmas Day 1928 when he suffered severe cartilage damage in a match at Leicester.

He returned home to Scotland to study physiotherapy in Glasgow, before taking up his football career again in London. In 1930 he joined Thames FC, then in the Third Division South, as trainer, before moving to Charlton as assistant trainer.

Billy Dougall's heart had remained at Burnley, however, and in 1932 he returned to Turf Moor as reserve team trainer going on to succeed Charlie Bates as first team trainer in 1934. Following the resignation of manager Tom Bromilow in 1935, Dougall was invited by Clarets' Chairman Tom Clegg to be part of a selection committee alongside Clegg himself and club secretary Alf Boland, an arrangement that lasted until the outbreak of World War Two.

In 1938 Billy Dougall's expertise was acknowledged by the County FA when he was also given the role of official coach to Lancashire Schools.

He remained at Burnley throughout the club's rise from an unfashionable Second Division side to one of the foremost football powers in the land. Chairman, Bob Lord described Billy Dougall's contribution to the Clarets' progress as impossible to overstate and paid tribute to him and reserve coach Ray Bennion as two jewels, the finest servants a football club could possible have.

Billy Dougall was 61-years-old when he was invited to take over as manager from Alan Brown in July 1957. He accepted, but even then was not enjoying the best of health, and, in November 1957, responsibility for first team affairs passed to Ray Bennion while Dougall underwent hospital treatment.

He resigned the manager's post on medical advice early the following year and was immediately appointed physiotherapist. He held that position throughout the club's glory days of First Division Championship, European campaigns, FA Cup Final and on into the 60s, before his well-earned retirement in 1965.

He died at his home in Burnley the following year, aged 71.

Harry Potts

Born: Hetton-le-Hole, 22 October 1920
Died: Burnley, 16 January 1996
Manager: January 1958 to February 1970
Also: February 1977 to October 1979

Harry Potts was one of Burnley Football Club's finest servants.

As a player he was instrumental in the club's post-war revival and as manager was the man at the helm when the Football League Championship, the game's ultimate measure of

Harry Potts with the League Championship Trophy

achievement, came to Turf Moor in 1960.

His love affair with Burnley began in 1937 when, as a 16-year-old, he was one of the pioneers of the Turf Moor youth system. He travelled from his home in County Durham, after the offer of a trial, and first turned out in a midweek junior league game against Blackpool.

Harry Potts was into his stride at once and an impressive performance led to his being taken on to Burnley's ground staff and, later in the year, after turning 17, signing as a professional.

After establishing himself in Burnley's Central League side, Potts was ready for contention for league football, when his prospects were cruelly dashed following the outbreak of war in 1939.

After serving with the RAF in India, Potts returned to Turf Moor after hostilities ended, and, in 1946, was ready to begin his career in earnest. Like more than half the Burnley team, he made his Football League debut in the opening match of the first post-war season.

Potts missed just two games during that momentous season that ended with promotion back to the top flight and an FA Cup Final appearance at Wembley against Charlton. He was the Clarets' top scorer as he was in all but one of his four full seasons at Turf Moor, but it was his inside forward combination with Billy Morris that will best be remembered during the boom years of the late 1940s. Potts was known as the General of the Burnley team, his more defensive qualities complementing perfectly the attacking instincts of Welsh international Morris.

As with many players of Potts' generation, however, his late start in league football, because of the war, meant that his age caught up with him all too quickly. In 1950 he became unsettled and, though still a regular, was placed on the transfer list at his own request.

Cliff Britton, manager of struggling Everton, and Potts' former mentor at Turf Moor, sensed a bargain and paid a record £20,000 in October 1950 to take him to Goodison Park. The move was not an overwhelming success for Potts, just turned 30, or Everton, who were relegated at the end of the season.

After his first campaign on Merseyside, Harry Potts was unable to claim a regular first team place and began to coach Everton's juniors. He was released in 1956 to take up a coaching post at Wolves and, in the summer of 1957, he was appointed as the manager of Shrewsbury Town. It was to be a short apprenticeship to a long career in management.

After just half a season at Gay Meadow he saw an opportunity to return to Burnley following the resignation, through illness, of Billy Dougall, who had himself only been in the hot seat a matter of months. On 21 February 1958, Harry Potts returned to Turf Moor ready to begin a new chapter in Burnley FC's success story.

He would have been the first to admit that he inherited an excellent team both on the field and behind the scenes. Billy Dougall, continuing as the club's physiotherapist and trainer, Ray Bennion had both been tremendously influential on Potts' own playing career and were to play a vital part in the success to come.

Of the championship side, only Alex Elder had yet to arrive, although many of the players who were to become heroes in a very short time were only just starting to make their impact on the First Division. Harry Potts was to be the catalyst who would turn a good team into a great one.

After a sixth place finish in 1958 and seventh in 1959, the Clarets embarked upon their season of destiny in August 1959 with a narrow victory at Leeds.

On the same day, a young man called Trevor Meredith was playing for Burnley Reserves against Leeds Reserves at Turf Moor when he fractured a shin.

How that young man's luck was to change at the sharp end of the season, bringing glory to himself, to Burnley ... and to Harry Potts!

Throughout the season the Clarets were always in touch with the leaders, with Tottenham in pole position for much of the campaign until Wolves overtook them with three weeks to go. Burnley had games in hand, but had never actually topped the table at all as the dramatic finale was played out.

Wolves and Tottenham both finished their fixtures as scheduled on the last Saturday of the season as Burnley could only manage a disappointing goalless draw with Fulham at Turf Moor. With one game still to play, against Manchester City at Maine Road, postponed from FA Cup Sixth Round day, the Clarets were third, with Wolves a point ahead and Tottenham level on points, both with superior goal averages. Only a Burnley victory would bring the title to Turf Moor.

Nearly 66,000 people saw Brian Pilkington score after just four minutes, only for City to equalise soon afterwards. With half an hour gone, Trevor Meredith crashed in the crucial goal to leave the Clarets with an hour to hang on for the victory.

City pounded away and the Blues' fans roared them on, joined by the entire Wolves team sat in the stands, together with what seemed like half the population of Wolverhampton!
It was to no avail. The Clarets held firm and as the final whistle sounded, emerged at the head of the pack for the very first time that season. Harry Potts had masterminded the ultimate triumph in only his second season in charge. Burnley were the Champions of the First Division!
1960-61 was to be another successful season for the Clarets, but this time there was to be no slip up by the magnificent Tottenham Hotspur. Burnley were very much one of the supporting cast as Spurs achieved the League and Cup Double, the first time by any club during the 20th century. For Burnley, it was fourth in the league and a semi-final in both the FA Cup and the inaugural Football League Cup.
Domestic activity was interrupted by the Clarets' first ever European Cup campaign with a two-legged victory against Stade de Reims and a narrow but honourable defeat against the mighty Hamburg. It was during the away leg against Reims that Harry Potts almost caused a diplomatic incident when incensed by the French team's constant "pinching" of yards at free kicks, ran on to the pitch and moved the ball back. He was subsequently fined by the football authorities and banned from the touchline for the rest of the season.
1961-62 has, of course, gone down in Turf Moor history as the season when the Clarets themselves were set for football immortality by winning the double. For the first two-thirds of the season they were virtually invincible and were performing even better than in the championship season two years earlier.
It all went wrong as March began but, even after only two wins in the next 11 league games, Burnley would still have clinched the double had they won their last three matches of the season. It didn't happen, of course, Ipswich Town swept past to claim the title and old foes Tottenham triumphed over the Clarets in a classic Wembley FA Cup Final.
Then, in 1963, almost overnight, Harry Potts turned from hero and favourite uncle to villain and wicked stepfather. He and Burnley chairman Bob Lord became public enemies number one and two when it was announced to a stunned Burnley public that Jimmy McIlroy had been placed on the transfer list. "Sack Potts" was the clamour by graffiti everywhere.
Post McIlroy, the club prospered, however, and Harry Potts continued at the helm even though the very great days had gone and a marvellous team was breaking up. League positions were more than acceptable, there was another European campaign in 1966-67 and another League Cup semi-final in 1968.
It became progressively more difficult for the small town clubs however, and early in 1970 Harry Potts decided to step aside. He became Burnley's general manager with his protege Jimmy Adamson stepping up to take over responsibility for team affairs.
There were hard times ahead and after the Clarets' relegation in 1971, a season of steadying the ship was followed in the summer of 1972 by Harry Potts decision to leave Turf Moor. After a spell out of football, he was appointed as the manager of Blackpool in December 1972 and, inevitably, the fates had decreed that the opponents for his first match in charge, at Bloomfield Road, would be Burnley.
In a turbulent Boxing Day Lancashire derby, his new charges were no match for a Clarets' side on their way to the Second Division Championship. The Seasiders had two players sent off and Burnley took the points in a 2-1 win.
It was a revenge victory by Blackpool over Burnley at Bloomfield Road in an FA Cup tie in January 1976, that ended Jimmy Adamson's career as Burnley manager.
Just four months later however, after three not unsuccessful seasons in charge, Potts himself was out of a job, sacked by the Blackpool board along with youth team coach Ray Pointer.
In July 1976, Potts renewed his connection with Burnley, replacing Dave Blakey as chief scout. The following February, with the Clarets in dangerous waters in Division Two, manager Joe Brown was dismissed and Harry Potts was reappointed in his place, almost 40 years after first arriving at Turf Moor.
There was to be one last triumph in store for Potts. In 1978 the Clarets were triumphant in the Anglo-Scottish Cup with two memorable victories over Celtic undoubtedly the highlight of that success, triggered by the return to Turf Moor of prodigal son, Leighton James.
In October 1979, with the Clarets at the foot of the Second Division, and without a league win, he was replaced as manager by Brian Miller, another of the 1960 championship side that Potts himself had nurtured. His days at Burnley Football Club had come to an end.
He later became part of the success story of top non-league side Colne Dynamoes, scouting for new talent, before its sudden demise in 1990.
Harry Potts passed away in 1996 aged 75. He was undoubtedly one of the major influences on post-war events at Turf Moor and will forever have a place in the annals of Burnley Football Club.

James Adamson

Born: Ashington, 4 April, 1929
Manager: February 1970 to January 1976

Jimmy Adamson was one of Turf Moor's very favourite sons whose overall career at Burnley spanned four decades and who is arguably the best uncapped player in English football during the post-war period.
Adamson was born in the mining community of Ashington, the sixth child of a colliery worker. Like thousands of football mad youngsters in the north-east of the thirties, the narrow ill-lit alleys forming murky corridors between the terraced houses were the first football pitches the young Adamson knew. His ball skills were finely honed during endless hours of constant practice on the uneven cobbled surface.
At school, Jimmy Adamson was a centre half and his ability and undoubted class would have won him many honours at schoolboy level, but for the war. After leaving school he joined Ashington YMCA and switched from the centre half position to inside forward.
It was while playing for East Chevington juniors that he was spotted by Turf Moor scout Jackie Dryden, an ex-Claret who

was as shrewd a judge of natural talent as they come, and the young Adamson was soon on his way to East Lancashire.

After joining the ground staff Adamson's career at Turf Moor was carefully mapped out. However, after only two weeks, the youngster became homesick and caught the train back to Ashington. He was soon back in the fold and signed his first professional contract in January 1947, still only 17 years of age.

It must be said that his early years at Turf Moor were something of a struggle. Still playing as an inside forward he graduated through the junior teams and the reserve team, but it was only after his conversion to wing half that his true potential started to be realised.

Even then, he was almost 22-years-old when he made his league debut at Bolton in February 1951. He replaced the great Reg Attwell at right half and performed well enough to keep Attwell out of the team for the remainder of the season. Adamson had arrived in earnest and, along with Tommy Cummings and Jimmy McIlroy, was even now laying the foundations for the League Championship triumph still almost a decade away.

He had been a revelation since moving to the right half position and, although never the fastest of players, his lovely control and his superb reading of the game eventually brought recognition by the International selectors. In March 1953, he was chosen to represent England B in the first ever meeting with Scotland B in Edinburgh. Tommy Cummings and Bill Holden were also in the England side with Jock Aird in opposition.

In 1955, Bobby Seith staked his claim for a regular place in the Burnley side at right half and Jimmy Adamson was happy enough to accommodate him, moving to centre half in place of the injured Tommy Cummings. It is perhaps surprising to note that Adamson only rarely wore the number four shirt from then on until the championship was almost secured in 1960. John Angus had made the right back position his own, Alex Elder made the breakthrough during the title-winning season and Brian Miller had also made his presence felt.

Tommy Cummings re-established himself early in 1960 and, with Adamson moving back to the right half position for which he is best remembered, it was the unfortunate Bobby Seith that missed out on the triumphant run-in which ended at Maine Road, Manchester in May 1960.

In October that year Adamson, by now 31-years-old, received another belated honour when he was chosen for the Football League side to play the Irish League at Blackpool. Team-mates, Jimmy McIlroy, John Connelly and John Angus were also in that line-up which beat the Irish 5-2.

1961-62 of course was the season when Burnley were on course to win the league and cup double, a feat that would surely have meant immortality for this small town club. It was not to be, the Clarets were pipped at the post by Ipswich for the League Championship and beaten by Tottenham at Wembley in the FA Cup Final.

In recognition of Burnley's magnificent achievement, captain, Jimmy Adamson was voted "Footballer of the Year" with Jimmy McIlroy the runner-up. At 33, Adamson was included in the England squad for the 1962 World Cup in Chile and was appointed assistant to manager Walter Winterbottom.

When Winterbottom resigned, Jimmy Adamson was offered the position of England manager, but although he was a fully qualified FA coach, he felt he could not accept the position because of his lack of managerial experience. Alf Ramsey stepped in and went on to mastermind England's World Cup win in 1966.

During 1962-63 Adamson's place in the Burnley team came under more and more pressure with Walter Joyce, David Walker and later Brian O'Neil getting the nod. He was the man back in possession at the start of the following campaign but, in February 1964, played his final game for the Clarets, a 1-1 draw at Blackpool.

He joined the Turf Moor coaching staff and was seen as the natural successor to manager Harry Potts, taking over the reins in 1970. His "team of the seventies" was relegated in 1971, but Adamson plotted a triumphant return to the top flight in 1973 and all seemed set for a return to glory days after two good years back in the First Division.

1975-76 was a season of struggle however and, just as Bloomfield Road had been the scene of his final game as a Burnley player back in 1964, it also marked his last game as Burnley manager when the Clarets were dispatched from the FA Cup by the Seasiders at the third round stage.

After a coaching spell in Holland he replaced FA Cup hero Bob Stokoe as manager of Sunderland in 1976, but failed to prevent their relegation from Division One. He took over from Jock Stein as Leeds manager in 1978 and in two years at Elland Road guided United to a place in the UEFA Cup. It was a short-lived success story however, and, after a poor start to the 1980-81 season he resigned, and left the game for good.

Jimmy Adamson now lives quietly in Burnley and is not involved with football at all. As the last Burnley player to captain a First Division Championship side as well as the last Claret to lead an FA Cup Final team out at Wembley, he undoubtedly ranks, along with Tommy Boyle, as the club's most influential captain of all time.

Joseph Brown

Born: Cramlington, 26 April, 1929
Manager: January 1976 to February 1977

From a playing point of view, Joe Brown would no doubt be classed as a vintage Cherry rather than a vintage Claret, all but a handful of his Football League appearances being during his days at Bournemouth in the 1950s.

However, Brown was instrumental in one of Burnley Football Club's proudest achievements, the lifting of the FA Youth Cup in 1968. His vast experience as the man in charge of that side ensured that a fine crop of young talent, Steve Kindon, David Thomas, Alan West and Mike Docherty amongst others, was harvested at just the right time.

Joe Brown was spotted by Middlesbrough, playing junior football in Seaton Delaval near Whitley Bay and joined the Ayresome Park ground staff at 15. He signed as a professional on his 17th birthday in 1946, but it was not until 1949 that he was given a chance in Boro's First Division side.

Brown began almost immediately to be troubled by back problems, which continued to plague him throughout his playing days and almost certainly prevented him from enjoying a long career at the very top level.

After arriving at Turf Moor in 1952, he replaced the great Reg Attwell in the Burnley side, but a slipped disc put paid to his hopes of First Team football. After a long spell in hospital and an extended run in the reserves he was transferred to Bournemouth in the summer of 1954.

During his six years at Dean Court, all spent in the old Third Division South then the Third Division, Joe Brown qualified as an FA coach. After a spell coaching in South Africa he returned to England joining Aldershot in 1960 only for his back problems to flare again, forcing his retirement.

He returned to Burnley as third team coach in 1961, going on to mastermind the FA Youth Cup win of 1968, still vividly remembered by most fans of that era. He became Burnley's assistant manager under Jimmy Adamson and then replaced him when Adamson resigned in 1976.

Joe Brown's stint at the Turf Moor helm was not an auspicious one. Relegation in the summer of 1976 was followed by a poor Second Division season and he was sacked in February 1977 to make way for the return of Harry Potts.

The parting of the ways for Burnley and Joe Brown meant the start of a new career, and he was appointed Youth Development Officer by Manchester United, a position he held for many years until retiring to live quietly in Burnley.

Harry Potts

Manager: February 1977 to October 1979

Brian Miller

Born: Hapton, 19 January 1937
Died: Burnley, 7 April 2007
Manager: October 1979 to January 1983
Also: July 1986 to January 1989

Only a relatively small number of players born in Burnley have gone on to represent their home town club as a professional. Hardly any have given such stalwart and unstinting service as player, coach, manager and chief scout, as Brian Miller who first arrived at Turf Moor as a 15-year-old amateur in 1952.

Miller was brought up in Hapton and had been spotted by a Burnley director playing in a Schoolboy Cup Final in Blackburn. He was soon recruited to the office staff and made steady progress through the junior teams before signing as a professional in 1954.

He made his first team debut at wing-half, deputising for Les Shannon during the FA Cup marathon with Chelsea in February 1956 and scored his first goal in senior football, in only his second League appearance, shortly afterwards. Up against a formidable trio like Shannon, Jimmy Adamson and Bobby Seith, and with the sidelined Tommy Cummings waiting to come back from injury, the young Miller did well to force himself into the reckoning as the title-winning side began to come together.

Force himself into it he did, however and, over the next few years his rugged, hard-tackling style was a key factor in the team's success, and he played in every league and cup game during the momentous championship season of 1959-60. His consistency was further rewarded that summer with three England under 23 appearances, the first in a 4-1 win in Berlin against East Germany.

Following another successful season for Burnley in 1960-61, Brian Miller won what proved to be his only full cap in May 1961 against Austria in Vienna. Team-mate John Angus also made his first and last appearance for the full England side in that match, which England lost 3-1. It can't have helped either the team's cause or the future international prospects of the two Burnley players that both men played out of position, Angus at left-back and Brian Miller at right-half.

Miller continued to be an automatic choice for Burnley on into the mid-sixties. Although he didn't score at all in the League during his last season, 1966-67, he netted both the Clarets' goals in the two-legged European Fairs Cup quarter-final against Eintracht Frankfurt in April 1967. Just days later, however, in a League match at Villa Park, so often an unlucky ground for Burnley, a badly twisted knee signalled the end of a marvellous playing career. With the exception of John Angus, he was the last member of the First Division Championship side.

Miller joined the Turf Moor coaching staff in 1967 and became reserve team trainer and later trainer for the first team under both Jimmy Adamson and Harry Potts. He replaced Potts as Burnley manager in 1979 but was unable to prevent the Clarets sliding into Division Three for the first time ever at the end of his first season in charge.

He masterminded the Third Division Championship campaign of 1981-82, but it was a short-lived success. With the team struggling at the wrong end of Division Two in January 1983, he was dismissed to make way for Frank Casper on the eve of the Clarets' spectacular 4-1 win at Tottenham in the League Cup quarter-final.

Brian Miller returned to the hot seat in the summer of 1986 with the Clarets, by then, in Division Four and about to embark upon the most traumatic season in the club's history. As the campaign unfolded, a poor season began to deteriorate into a desperate struggle for survival. It began to become a real possibility that Burnley would be the first team to suffer automatic relegation to the Football Conference.

Media speculation was intense during the last few weeks of that awful season and, as the final game, "The Orient Game", approached, Brian Miller was the man who had to rally his troops to one last gargantuan effort to prevent what could have been the death of this great club. He succeeded - just. The unthinkable was avoided. The clouds rolled away and the building for the future began.

Brian Miller kept the momentum going the following season with a modest League campaign backed up by a run to Wembley in the Sherpa Van Trophy. Although the Clarets lost to Wolves, themselves starting to recover from hard times, the crowd at the final of nearly 81,000, was testimony to the phenomenal latent support of this small town club.

In January 1989 Miller was again replaced as Burnley manager by Frank Casper, taking up a new role as Chief Scout, the position he held until his retirement in 1996.

Brian Miller, the classic example of the one-club man, passed away after a short illness in 2007, aged 70.

Frank Casper

Born: Barnsley, 9 December 1944
Caretaker manager: January 1983 to June 1983
Manager: January 1989 to October 1991

Frank Casper was a splendid servant to Burnley Football Club, certainly on the field where he was a firm crowd favourite. Unfortunately he was never quite able to make the transition between a successful player and a consistently successful manager.

The young Casper was a dashing winger at school in Barnsley but was converted to inside-forward when playing for Barnsley Schoolboys and Yorkshire Schoolboys. After a trial for the England Schoolboy side, Casper was invited to Blackpool for a trial and was seriously considering signing for the Seasiders when Rotherham manager Tom Johnston stepped in first. After playing for United's Reserve team at 15, he was given an early chance in Rotherham's Second Division side, scoring on his League debut against Derby County in 1962. He also had an early introduction to Burnley, scoring in the Millers 1-1 draw at Turf Moor in the FA Cup third round of January 1964.

When Frank Casper crossed the Pennines to join Burnley for £30,000 in June 1967 his transfer, especially the fact that there was a fee involved, was an event in itself. Burnley simply did not spend money to buy players, and the amount paid for Casper was the first time, other than very nominal sums, since Alex Elder had arrived from Glentoran in 1959.

He scored on his Clarets' debut against Coventry with the

Burnley Express coining the immortal phrase "A rasper from Casper!" and, in fact, scored five goals in his first five Burnley games. He was top scorer in each of his first two seasons at Turf Moor and also found the net on the only occasion he won a representative honour, playing for the Football League in a 3-1 victory against the Scottish League at Hampden Park in March 1969. All seemed set for a return to glory at Turf Moor as Harry Potts handed the managerial reins to Jimmy Adamson in February 1970.

Frank Casper was one of the key players around whom Adamson was going to build his "Team of the Seventies" at Burnley. Relegation in 1971 however, after 24 years in the top flight, seemed to mean the end of the dream, until Casper, among others, found his shooting boots again during the two-year struggle for promotion.

He was top scorer again in 1971-72 as the Clarets first promised much, withered but finished strongly. Then the clouds rolled away during the 1972-73 campaign as Burnley played some magnificent football on their way to the Second Division Championship and a return to the First Division.

Season 1973-74 was a turning point in Frank Casper's football career. The Clarets were off to an unbeaten start back in the top flight and continuing the flowing football when Casper was the subject of a crunching tackle by Tottenham's Cyril Knowles. He was out of the side until February, returning just in time to score the goal against Wrexham that ensured Burnley's place in the FA Cup semi-final against Newcastle.

The week before that historic day, Casper was again on the receiving end of a shuddering tackle, this time by Leeds United's Norman Hunter at Elland Road. Although he played in the semi-final it was his last game for 18 months until he returned against Queens Park Rangers in October 1975.

He took the field to a tremendous reception from the fans and, with a sense of true theatre, scored the only goal of the game, the 100th and last of a memorable career. He appeared in Burnley's team again briefly but, as the Clarets once again slid out of the top flight, announced his retirement as a player.

He joined the Turf Moor backroom staff in 1976, first coaching the youth team and later the reserves and first team. Burnley fans will vividly remember events in January 1983 when Casper was suddenly thrust into the managerial hot-seat replacing Brian Miller just before the Clarets trip to Tottenham for the League Cup Quarter-Final.

After the famous 4-1 victory, and fighting performances against Liverpool in both semi-finals, it only needed Second Division survival to ensure that the caretaker/manager role would be made permanent. It was not to be however, and the following summer as the Clarets contemplated life in the Third Divison once again, Frank Casper was out and John Bond was in.

After a spell at Bury as assistant manager to ex-Claret Martin Dobson, he returned to Turf Moor as manager in 1989, again replacing Brian Miller. By now Burnley were in the Fourth Division and not yet showing any real sign of beginning the long road back.

Within two years however the Clarets were flirting with success with a controversial defeat by Torquay over two legs in the play-off semi-finals, a sign that the revival had begun at last.

For Casper however the long awaited recovery was not quite quick enough. After a particularly inept performance by the Clarets, at Scarborough in September 1991, he resigned amid mounting criticism from the terraces and was replaced by assistant manager Jimmy Mullen.

Frank Casper then began a successful business career in partnership with former Turf Moor Commercial Manager Joyce Pickles, running a thriving sportswear company based in Burnley.

He still lives in Burnley and, although still very much a Claret, is now working for Bury FC where one of his sons, Chris Casper, is the manager.

John Frederick Bond

Born: Colchester, 17 December 1932
Manager: June 1983 to August 1984

Almost certainly Burnley's most controversial manager ever, John Bond was the first "outsider" to manage the club in nearly 30 years when the directors decided that a change of policy was needed after relegation to the Third Division in 1983.

Whatever his faults, there is no doubt that during Bond's time at Turf Moor the Clarets were always newsworthy and, but for the injury that ended the career of Kevin Reeves, John Bond's legacy might have been very different.

After schoolboy football in Essex he joined West Ham from Colchester Casuals in 1949 and enjoyed a long career at Upton Park after becoming the Hammers' first choice right-back. He won a Second Division Championship medal in 1958 and collected an FA Cup Winners' medal in 1964 as West Ham beat Preston at Wembley after overcoming the Clarets in the quarter-final. He also appeared twice for the Football League.

His playing career ended at Torquay in 1969 and, after coaching at Gillingham, took on his first managerial role at

Bournemouth in 1970. Success came immediately and he guided the Cherries to promotion from the Fourth Division in 1971, narrowly missing out on a second successive promotion in 1972.

A bigger stage beckoned, and in November 1973 he was appointed manager of First Division Norwich, although the Canaries were destined for relegation at the end of his first season in charge. Bond showed he still had the golden touch however, guiding Norwich back to the top flight in 1975 as well as to the League Cup Final against Aston Villa.

Carrow Road was still enjoying First Division football when Bond accepted the challenge to join Manchester City in October 1980, taking the Canaries' youth coach, John Benson with him as his assistant. The Blues were bottom of the First Division without a win, but the Bond magic worked again in his first season with a mid-table finish, an FA Cup Final appearance against Tottenham and a League Cup semi-final against Liverpool.

After a good start to the 1982-83 season however, City faltered badly, and Bond resigned in February 1983 with Second Division football looming for Maine Road at the end of the season.

His arrival at Turf Moor came with many fans expecting caretaker/manager, Frank Casper to be given the job on a permanent basis after his efforts the previous season. The mould was broken however and Essex man breezed into the club with plenty of ideas of how to put the Clarets back on the football map.

John Bond's main strategy was to surround himself with players he knew well from former clubs, Tommy Hutchison, Roger Hansbury, Kevin Reeves and Gerry Gow. His new backroom staff had also worked with him before, John Benson, his assistant manager and John Sainty, his coach.

Out went Trevor Steven, Brian Laws, Lee Dixon, Andy Wharton and mid-season, Martin Dobson, after the club captaincy had very quickly passed to Tommy Hutchison.

The season started brightly enough with Reeves combining very well with Billy Hamilton, the pair hitting 31 goals between them in League and Cup before Reeves was injured at the turn of the year. From a position challenging for promotion, the Clarets faded to mid-table and in the last month of the season with many of his players suffering a crisis in confidence and form, Bond was travelling the country planning more rebuilding.

Suddenly, five days before the start of the new season, he was gone, and one of the most turbulent periods in the history of Burnley FC was over.

He later managed Swansea and Birmingham where he struggled to make an impression and was sacked on each occasion. He returned to the game in 1990 as assistant manager to Asa Hartford at Shrewsbury, later replacing Hartford as manager before he resigned in 1993.

Bond spent some time assisting his son Kevin at Stafford Rangers before a spell as manager of Witton Albion. In 1999 he teamed up again with John Benson, then manager of Wigan Athletic, but left the JJB Stadium when Benson himself left in 2000.

John Harvey Benson

Born: Arbroath, 23 December, 1942
Manager: August 1984 to May 1985

Not for the first time in his career, John Benson stepped into the shoes of John Bond when he was appointed Burnley manager on the eve of the 1984-85 season.

A wing half, Benson's League career began in the First Division with Manchester City in 1962 before his move to Torquay in 1964. He played over 200 League games for the Gulls, helping them to promotion from the Fourth Division in 1966, and it was at Plainmoor that he first played alongside John Bond.

He joined Bournemouth in 1970, shortly after Bond had taken over as manager, and in 1973 moved to Norwich as player/coach, again following John Bond. He returned to Dean Court in 1975 as player/manager, a position he held until 1979.

After another spell at Norwich, as youth coach, John Benson followed Bond to Manchester City in October 1980 as his assistant manager. The duo enjoyed some success at Maine Road but it was short-lived, and when Bond resigned in February 1983, Benson took over as manager with City in mid-table but on the slide.

By the end of the season City had been relegated and John Benson lost his job. He teamed up with John Bond yet again, at Burnley, and after a modest season in the Third Division, stepped from the Turf Moor shadows into the limelight after Bond's departure.

His season in charge was not an auspicious one although there were highlights, including a 9-0 victory at Penrith in the FA Cup first round, equalling the club's highest ever score in peacetime.

There was also a 7-0 win against Rotherham at Turf Moor in February 1985 but by then the Clarets were on the edge of the Third Division relegation zone and showing little sign of recovery.

At the end of the season Fourth Division football was

beckoning for the first time ever and just days after the final match, Benson resigned, with youth development officer John Doherty placed in charge of players' affairs.
John Benson worked as chief scout for Barnsley, later coaching in Dubai and Kuwait before returning to assist John Deehan at Norwich City. He followed Deehan to Wigan in 1995 and, after initially declined the manager's role when Deehan was sacked, eventually took over when his replacement Ray Mathias lost his job in 1999. He resigned in 2000 after Wigan's defeat in the play-offs but became General Manager, then Youth Development officer before joining Birmingham City, although he later returned to the JJB.

Martin McLean Buchan

Born: Aberdeen, 6 March 1949
Manager: June 1985 to October 1985

Martin Buchan's appointment was very well received by the Burnley faithful. A well-respected player who had performed at the highest level for his club and his country, cutting his managerial teeth at a club desperately in need of success. Sadly, he left Turf Moor after just four months, unable to adapt to the change from player to manager.
After joining Aberdeen in 1965, Buchan soon became a regular first team player, quickly being appointed as captain. He skippered the Dons to victory in the 1970 Scottish Cup Final against Celtic and his mature displays won him the Scottish Player of the Year award in 1971 aged only 22.
Already with youth, under 23 and full International honours behind him, he joined Manchester United in March 1972 for £125,000, immediately becoming an automatic choice. Although the early 70s were not vintage years at Old Trafford, Martin Buchan's performances for United and for Scotland were invariably of the highest standard.
After relegation in 1974, Buchan won a Second Division Championship medal in 1975 and an FA Cup runners-up medal in 1976 as United were beaten by underdogs Southampton. It was back to Wembley in 1977 and this time there was no mistake as Buchan himself lifted the FA Cup in triumph after the victory over Liverpool. The Reds were back at Wembley once more in 1979, this time going down to Arsenal.
After over 450 first team games for United and with 34 full Scottish caps, Buchan moved to Oldham in the summer of 1983 ending his playing career at Boundary Park.
He seemed a natural for football management, but it was not to be and Martin Buchan's short stay at Turf Moor was his only spell behind the manager's desk.
He later worked for a well-known sports equipment company before accepting an advisory role at the Professional Footballers Association.

Thomas H. Cavanagh

Born: Liverpool, 29 June 1928
Died: March 2007
Manager: October 1985 to June 1986

Tommy Cavanagh appeared as a guest player for Preston during the war, signing as a professional at 21 years-old in 1949. He joined Stockport in 1950 and played briefly in County's Third Division North side before a move to Second Division Huddersfield in May 1952.
He was a regular during his time at Leeds Road as the Terriers won promotion back to the top flight in 1953 and finished third in Division One in 1954, Tommy Cavanagh contributing nine goals from inside forward.
In 1956 he was transferred to Doncaster, then in the Second Division, but suffered two successive relegations in 1958 and 1959. After a season with Bristol City, Cavanagh's League career ended with Carlisle in 1961.
After a spell as player/manager with Cheltenham Town he joined Brentford as trainer, taking over as the Bees' manager in 1965. He left in 1966, moving to Nottingham Forest as trainer/coach, Forest finishing as First Division runners-up in 1967.
Following a period as coach at Hull he joined Manchester United as trainer in 1972 being appointed assistant manager

by Tommy Docherty in 1977. He remained at Old Trafford until 1980 and, of course, his time at United coincided with the development of Martin Buchan as a player of the highest class and a natural leader.

Buchan appointed Tommy Cavanagh as his trainer after his own arrival at Turf Moor in 1985, and it was Cavanagh who took over after Buchan abruptly resigned just three months into the season.

1985-86 was a desperate season for the Clarets and in reality, no matter who had been in charge, the campaign would, in all probability, still have been purely one of consolidation and, indeed, survival. Early in 1986, the club was reported as being £800,000 in debt losing a further £10,000 a month and up for sale.

Tommy Cavanagh tried to focus his mind and that of his players purely on football and invited Brian Kidd to help out with training.

At the end of the season a 14th place finish looked acceptable but in June 1986 Cavanagh resigned quoting health problems after a hip operation. He later worked at the FA School of Excellence at Lilleshall until retirement in 2002.

Tommy Cavanagh died in 2007 aged 78.

Brian Miller

Manager: July 1986 to January 1989

Frank Casper

Manager: January 1989 to October 1991

James Mullen

Born: Jarrow, 8 November 1952
Manager: October 1991 to February 1996

When Jimmy Mullen took over as manager from Frank Casper, the Clarets were 11th in Division Four and looking like they would complete yet another Fourth Division season out of the running for honours. Less than three months later they were at the top of the League with the look of promotion certainties after a complete transformation.

Mullen spent 10 years with Sheffield Wednesday, his first club, after joining the Owls as an apprentice, turning professional in 1970. His first season as a regular in Wednesday's defence was 1972-73 and Burnley fans of that era will remember his first encounter with the Clarets in October 1972.

Still unbeaten and leading the Second Division, Burnley won 1-0 at Hillsborough thanks to a stunning long range effort from Leighton James which had the 30,000 fans in raptures. Following Wednesday's relegation in 1975 the rest of Jimmy Mullen's Hillsborough career was spent in the Third Division, and when he left in August 1980 he had played over 250 senior games for the club.

He captained Rotherham to the Third Division Championship in 1981 and, after joining Cardiff in March 1982, also led the Bluebirds to promotion from the Third Division in 1983 as runners-up to Portsmouth.

After a spell as assistant manager at Ninian Park, he joined Newport as player/manager, ending his playing career at Somerton Park. Following another short period with Cardiff he joined Aberdeen as assistant manager to Ian Porterfield in 1987.

He replaced Sam Ellis as Blackpool manager in April 1989 but his only season at Bloomfield Road ended in relegation from Division Three and he was sacked in May 1990.

Jimmy Mullen arrived at Turf Moor in August 1990 as Frank Casper's assistant following the departure of Mick Docherty to Hull. The combination worked well and, at the end of the season, the Clarets fell just short of promotion after losing to Torquay in the play-off semi-final.

Mullen's start as the Clarets' manager was little short of sensational. Nine straight League victories and nine successive wins away from home, included the memorable 6-2 triumph at Wrexham, in only his second game at the helm, Burnley's best League win on foreign soil in over 30 years.

At the end of his first season in charge the prayers of the Turf Moor faithful had been answered and the Fourth Division had been left behind after seven long years. The scenes at York on that marvellous night in April 1992 will long remain in the memory, as will the festivities at Turf Moor a few days later as the Championship Trophy was presented.

1992-93 was a season of consolidation in the new Second Division but even that campaign started with a success, Burnley collecting the Lancashire Senior Cup, and ended with the Clarets sharing another championship party, this time as guests of Stoke City.

For sheer drama there has been little (Orient excepted!) in recent years to compare with the climax of the 1993-94 season. After a good, but perhaps not an exceptional, campaign the Clarets qualified for the play-offs in sixth position, 12 points adrift of Plymouth, who finished third.

After a goalless draw at Turf Moor against the Pilgrims, the Mullen magic worked again with a 3-1 victory at Home Park and the Clarets were at Wembley to face Stockport in the play-off final.

If volume of support was a yardstick, the match itself need not have taken place, such was the overwhelming degree that the Burnley fans outnumbered those of Stockport County who, incidentally, had also finished 12 points clear of the

Clarets that season!

The story of the match itself has passed into Turf Moor history and is well-documented elsewhere in this volume. Suffice to say that Jimmy Mullen's achievement in guiding the Clarets to two promotions in three years is unique in club history.

Sadly the bubble was about to burst and it was a terrible anti-climax when Burnley lost their hard-won First Division status after just one season. The momentum had somehow been lost and, of course, in a very short time, Jimmy Mullen had changed from hero to villain.

The alarming slide continued during 1995-96 and, for a time, there was a real possibility that the Clarets were heading towards a second successive relegation. To give the Burnley Directors due credit they certainly tried to remain loyal to the man who had brought long awaited success to Turf Moor. Eventually however, in the face of mounting criticism from Burnley fans, Jimmy Mullen and Burnley FC parted company in February 1996. Mullen's last game in charge was the 0-1 defeat by Crewe at Turf Moor, on the day of the infamous 3.33 protest by disgruntled Clarets' supporters.

After a spell as manager of Sligo Rovers he worked with Neville Southall assisting the Welsh FA before a number of non league managerial appointments.

For much of his time at Turf Moor Jimmy Mullen enjoyed an excellent relationship with the fans, his obvious passion for the game, and for Burnley, made him a popular figure. The wonderful start to his spell in the Clarets' hot seat helped of course and guiding his team to the Fourth Division Championship, followed by a second promotion just two years later, ensured him a permanent place in Turf Moor folklore. It seems strange that he never really enjoyed anything like his Burnley success before he came to Turf Moor, and his career has never hit similar heights since he left.

Adrian Heath

Born: Stoke-on-Trent, 11 January 1961
Player/manager: March 1996 to June 1997

There was a certain inevitability about Adrian Heath's appointment to the Turf Moor hot seat in March 1996.

In December the previous year he had left Turf Moor to team up with former boss Howard Kendall at Sheffield United.

But as the Turf Moor door closed behind him he said: "Who knows, one day I may be back as manager."

When the Clarets journeyed to Adams Park for the first time, to play Wycombe Wanderers on 30 March 1996, it meant that they had visited every other club then in the Football League or the Premiership.

The purists could claim perhaps that technically, clubs that had changed grounds since Burnley's previous visit, such as Middlesbrough or even Wimbledon, might nullify that record.

What is certainly not in doubt however, is the other page of Burnley FC history that Adrian Heath wrote that day at Wycombe when he took his place in the starting line-up. He became the first Burnley manager ever to play in a competitive game for the club.

Adrian Heath had graduated from a prolific production line of young talent at Stoke City in the late 1970's. He flourished at the Victoria Ground under the watchful eye of player/coach Howard Kendall and the two would go on to work together on a number of occasions in the years to come. Heath made his senior debut for the Potters in 1979 and immediately became a First Division regular, effectively replacing his mentor when Kendall left for Ewood Park in the summer of 1979. Still only 20 he rejoined Kendall at Everton for a record fee early in 1982 and it was at Goodison Park where Adrian Heath achieved his greatest success. He was an FA Cup winner in 1984 but was injured for the latter part of Everton's League Championship campaign of 1984-85. The Blues finished as runners-up to Liverpool in both League and FA Cup in 1986, but in 1987 won the First Division Championship again with Adrian Heath, this time playing a key role alongside former Claret Trevor Steven. Heath then played in Spain then had a short spell at Aston Villa before linking up once again with Howard Kendall, this time at Manchester City. After another brief period at Stoke, he made the move to Turf Moor in the summer of 1992, with Burnley manager Jimmy Mullen undoubtedly clinching one of the shrewdest transfers of his career

For the first time since very early in his career, Heath played

as an out and out front man under Mullen and he was soon among the goals, hitting 20 in his first season at Turf Moor, easily the best of his league career.

He was a key figure in the run to promotion via the play-offs in 1994, still with energy and enthusiasm to spare as he lent his support to new goalscoring hero, David Eyres.

1994-95 was not a vintage season for the Clarets and it ended with Adrian Heath injured and on the sidelines as First Division football slipped away from Turf Moor.

After relegation he was very much on the fringe of first team action and in December 1995, accepted the challenge of the position of assistant manager at Sheffield United. The new manager at Bramall Lane, replacing the long-standing Dave Bassett, was none other than Howard Kendall.

Meanwhile, back at Turf Moor, a disappointing season was

fast turning into a crisis as a second successive relegation started to become a distinct possibility.

Finally, in February 1996, Jimmy Mullen was relieved of his position. After a short spell with Clive Middlemass in charge of team affairs, the new Burnley manager was confirmed as, the man who had overwhelmingly been voted the fans' choice, Adrian Heath.

The team responded with a victory at Bristol City in his first game in charge, but didn't win again for five weeks as the trap door loomed large.

It all ended happily enough however, relegation avoided, a new era ushered in and a favourable impression created by the new man in charge. Turf Moor was now ready for the new challenge that lay ahead.

Few could imagine that his reign would last for just one more season.

It was a season that promised much, but in the end delivered very little. A season of stop-starts, the Clarets hit top spot in the early days of the campaign, but eventually, after a typical Turf Moor rollercoaster, petered away to a ninth-place finish and more disappointment.

Paul Barnes emerged as a goalscoring hero, but Kurt Nogan's prowess diminished and, as one win in the last five games saw the Clarets end up as also-rans, rumours were soon rife that Heath would be on the way out of the door again.

Sure enough, once again the lure of Howard Kendall was too strong, as was the pull of Goodison Park, and in June 1997 Adrian Heath left Turf Moor to work with Howard Kendall once again, this time as assistant manager at Everton.

Heath's time at Goodison was relatively short and in 1999 he succeeded Steve Bruce for a brief spell as Sheffield United manager, eventually moving aside after the arrival of Neil Warnock.

In 2006 he was caretaker manager at Coventry City before being replaced by Ian Dowie.

Christopher Waddle

Born: Hedworth, 14 December 1960
Player/manager: July 1997 to May 1998

Although as a youngster he trained with Newcastle, Chris Waddle was not offered an apprenticeship and spent time as a trainee with Coventry before being released. After returning to his native north east he eventually found a job in a sausage factory whilst playing football in the Northern League for Tow Law Town.

They say that what goes around comes around and Waddle was eventually spotted by Sunderland, who offered him a trial. That led nowhere but the Black Cats' loss was the Magpies' gain and Newcastle United snapped him up, again, this time for a transfer fee of £1000, in the summer of 1980. Under Arthur Cox his progress was swift and, after a League debut in October 1980 Chris Waddle soon became a regular, and a star, in United's Second Division side alongside Kevin Keegan and, amongst others, Glenn Roeder. In 1983-84 he was an ever present as Newcastle won promotion back to the top flight and in March 1985, after winning England under 21 honours, he collected his first full international cap in a 2-1 win for England against the Republic of Ireland at Wembley.

He left for Tottenham in 1985 and was a member of the England World Cup squad in 1986 in Mexico and again in 1990 in Italy. England fans will never let him forget the penalty he ballooned over the crossbar in the semi final defeat by Germany in Turin.

By then Waddle was playing in the French League with Marseilles, having helped them to the first of three domestic Championships. In 1991 he starred as Marseilles reached the Champions League final against Red Star Belgrade in Bari, only for the journey to end in disappointment, as Red Star triumphed on penalties after a goalless draw. It's perhaps interesting to note that Chris Waddle was not one of Marseilles' penalty takers.

In 1992 he returned to England and joined Sheffield Wednesday where he was a key figure in Wednesday's runs to Wembley in both the FA Cup and League Cup. Both finals were lost to Arsenal but such was the impression that Chris Waddle had made, he was voted the Football Writers Player of the Year.

He left Hillsborough in 1996 and during 1996-97 played for Falkirk, Bradford City and finally Sunderland before being released.

The excitement around Turf Moor, following his appointment as Burnley manager, was so strong you could almost reach out and touch it.

The brilliance of a player capable of giving an international masterclass coupled with the experience of assistant manager Glenn Roeder had all the hallmarks of a truly great managerial partnership.

On day one they claimed that they had never been in the Second Division before and already felt they had been there a day too long.

Unfortunately, it took a dramatic last day win over Plymouth Argyle to stop the Waddle-Roeder partnership taking Burnley out of the Second Division – in the wrong direction. Waddle made some memorable signings, but he also made some poor ones.

Fringe players from Premiership clubs never seemed to settle down to life in the Second Division with the exception of goalkeeper Chris Woods who came as a coach but ended up playing the final quarter of the season following the dramatic sale of Marlon Beresford to Middlesbrough.
Waddle's brief reign as boss, therefore, saw the end of one of the most notable Turf Moor careers of the last two decades. But it also saw the birth of another. With the Clarets in trouble he made the decisive move to bring Andy Payton from Huddersfield in a swap deal for fellow striker Paul Barnes.
The season itself was a quarter old before the first league win came along.
It had taken the Clarets seven games to net their first goal and it took something like promotion form for the remaining 36 games for Waddle to avoid relegation in what proved to be his only season in professional management.
A disappointing draw at Oldham in the penultimate game meant that the Clarets had to beat Plymouth on the final day and then hope for the right results elsewhere.
Two crucial goals from Andy Cooke ensured all that was achieved, but just days later Waddle resigned. He played briefly for Torquay then began coaching at Sheffield Wednesday before leaving Hillsborough in 2000.
These days he can be heard as a regular broadcaster and match summariser on Radio Five Live.

Francis Stanley Ternent

Born: Gateshead, 16 June 1946
Manager: June 1998 to June 2004

Stan Ternent spent six years at Turf Moor after joining the Clarets as an apprentice in the summer of 1962 and signing as a professional a year later. He was very fit, hard-working and an extremely versatile player but found it almost impossible to break into Burnley's First Division side.
When he finally made it, the experience was a sobering one as the Clarets were hammered 0-7 at Sheffield Wednesday in May 1967, the final away game of the season. After appearing briefly during 1967-68, a season of transition at Turf Moor, he joined Carlisle United for £4,000 in May 1968.
Ternent immediately became a regular at Brunton Park, all his time in Cumbria being spent in the Second Division, and he contributed to the club's promotion to the First Division for the first time ever in 1974, before being released.
After two years at Sunderland without a first team appearance, he joined Blackpool as a coach to work under Bob Stokoe, as he had at both Carlisle and Sunderland. He ultimately replaced Stokoe, to take up his first managerial appointment with the Seasiders in August 1979.
His reign at Bloomfield Road was brief and he was sacked after just eight months. After a spell out of the game he joined Bradford City as a coach and became assistant manager to Steve Coppell at Crystal Palace in 1989. Later that year he was appointed as Hull City's manager but was dismissed in 1991.
He joined Bury in 1994, assisting former Claret Mike Walsh and when Walsh departed from Gigg Lane in September 1995, Ternent took over as manager.
Operating just around the corner from Turf Moor, a ground he could still see from his family home, Ternent caught the eye as he worked miracles at Gigg Lane and took the Shakers from Division Three to Division One.
He had been linked with the Turf Moor job at each of the previous two vacancies and when Chris Waddle departed, Stan Ternent was the choice of the Burnley board.
Then followed six of the most sensational seasons of recent times as Ternent helped the Clarets write all kinds of headlines.

Ternent did not like the squad he had inherited and immediately set about breaking it up and bringing in familiar faces from his other spells in management.
But it was a struggle until the penultimate game of his first season when Ronnie Jepson scored a winner against promoted Fulham and the Clarets were safe.
Having successfully completed that part of his job, he set about the bigger mission – getting the Clarets promoted.
And that was a feat he accomplished at the end of his second season in charge.
That season saw promotion achieved on the last day of the season, as the Clarets came from behind to beat Scunthorpe, and Gillingham failed to beat Wrexham.
But the biggest headlines had come along just a few short months earlier when Ternent pulled off the unthinkable and signed former Arsenal legend and England striker Ian Wright. That signing caught everyone's attention and the Clarets were back in the promised land with an eye on the Premiership.
In each of the next two seasons the Clarets went close to the play-offs missing out on goal difference in the first season and by a single point the next, the signing of another former England idol Paul Gascoigne not quite working the oracle on the second occasion.
Ternent also gave the Clarets their first ever seven-figure signings with the arrival of both Ian Moore and Robbie Blake.

But the second half of his reign at Turf Moor was blighted by the after-effects of the collapse of the ITV Digital television company and the subsequent loss of revenue.

Two successful battles were fought against relegation, but then, in the final week of the 2003-04 campaign, Burnley Chairman Barry Kilby sensationally announced that Stan Ternent was to leave the club. There were emotional scenes at Turf Moor on that final day against Sunderland as the Burnley fans paid a generous tribute to one of their own.

Six months later he was back in the game as manager of Gillingham, drafted in to fight another relegation battle, but it proved to be a short-term appointment and he left the Priestfield Stadium after the Gills lost their place in the Football League Championship.

Stephen Cotterill

Born: Cheltenham, 20 July 1964
Appointed manager: June 2004

In five years at the helm at Cheltenham Town, Steve Cotterill took the Robins from the Southern League to Division Three, winning the Conference Championship and the FA Trophy along the way.

As a player, Cotterill featured for non League Alvechurch and Burton Albion before joining Premiership Wimbledon in 1989, making his Dons' debut alongside Lawrie Sanchez, Dennis Wise, John Fashanu....and Vinnie Jones! He later played for Brighton, Bournemouth, where he was top scorer in 1993-94, and Hereford, before a knee injury ended his senior playing career. He took the first tentative steps into management when he followed former "Crazy Gang" team-mate Sanchez into the Sligo Rovers job.

In 1997 he returned to manage Cheltenham and over 250 games in charge of his home-town club saw him achieve a cult status at Whaddon Road.

But then events took a couple of twists that temporarily halted one of the most promising young managerial careers in the domestic game.

In 2002 he was lured away to manage Stoke City but after a very brief stay former Leeds boss Howard Wilkinson asked him to become his assistant at the Stadium of Light. His spell on Wearside was equally short and the managerial team was sacked in March 2003 after just five months with the Black Cats heading for relegation from the Premiership.

Out of the game for a spell, he then spent some time on the coaching staff at Leicester City before emerging as the front-runner to replace Stan Ternent at Turf Moor.

One of his games as Cheltenham Town boss had been an FA Cup win over the Clarets in January 2002. He caught chairman Barry Kilby's eye that day, and less than three years later he was the new man at Turf Moor.

He inherited just the nucleus of a squad, but brought in some seasoned professionals and looked set to reignite a Claret and Blue tilt at the Premiership.

But each of his first three seasons in charge saw progress halted in mid-term. The first campaign saw the dual sale of Richard Chaplow and leading scorer Robbie Blake, the pair becoming the first-ever seven-figure sales, the goals dried up and the season petered away.

The second saw the sale of crowd favourite Ade Akinbiyi with similar consequences and the third saw leading scorer Andy Gray injured just before the half-way point. Then followed a 19-match winless run that saw the Clarets drop from promotion hopefuls to relegation battlers.

Fortunately Gray returned in time, the battle was won and the return of Akinbiyi brought new belief.

That belief was further strengthened in the close season of 2007 as Blake returned and other new signings included international goalkeeper Gabor Kiraly, international winger Besart Berisha and Premiership defender Stephen Jordan.

With ambitious plans for the redevelopment of Turf Moor in the pipeline, the future under Steve Cotterill looked very bright as the 125th season ended and a new era dawned.

Abandoned matches

12 Dec 1891, Burnley v Blackburn R (3-0)
65 minutes, snow.
Although this match was indeed abandoned after the Blackburn players left the field, strictly speaking it does not constitute an abandoned match as it was not replayed and the result was allowed to stand.
It is included here for information as it is probably Burnley's most famous abandonment, alongside the "stop the game, it's snowing" FA Cup tie against Manchester United in 1909.

28 Dec 1895, Burnley v Sheffield U (1-0)
65 minutes, heavy rain.
Tatham, Tattersall, McLintock, McEleny, Taylor, Livingstone, Nicol, Davidson, Robertson, Bowes, Place jun.
Scorer : Davidson.
Replayed 3 Feb 1896, Burnley 5-0 Sheffield Utd (Division One).

25 Jan 1896, Burnley v Stoke (4-0)
74 minutes, fog.
Tatham, Reynolds, McLintock, Place sen, McEleny, Taylor, Nicol, Hill, Provan, Bowes, Place jun.
Scorers : Opp og, unknown (3)
Replayed 16 Mar 1896, Burnley 2-0 Stoke (Division One)

7 Jan 1899, Burnley v Stoke (1-2)
69 minutes, fading light
Hillman, Reynolds, McLintock, Barron, Taylor, Livingstone, Morrison, Ross, Toman, Bowes, Place jun.
Scorer : Bowes
Replayed 17 Apr 1899, Burnley 1-1 Stoke (Division One)

24 Nov 1900, Barnsley v Burnley (0-2)
82 minutes, fading light.
Collins, Lindsay, Lockhart, Barron, Bannister, Taylor, Morrison, Watkins, Jenkinson, Davidson, Savage.
Scorers : Savage, Davidson.
Replayed 5 Apr 1901, Barnsley 2-1 Burnley (Division Two)

21 Feb 1903, Burslem PV v Burnley (0-0)
13 minutes, heavy rain & wind.
Towler, Ross, Lockhart, Barron, Taylor, Dixon, Crawford, Duckworth, Hogan, Driver, McInnes.
Replayed 30 Mar 1903, Burslem PV 3-1 Burnley (Division Two)

5 Dec 1903, Woolwich A v Burnley (1-0)
63 minutes, fog.
Green, Ross, Dixon, Barron, Walders, Taylor, Jackson, Hogan, Whittam, McFarlane, Williams.
Replayed 29 Feb 1904, Woolwich A 4-0 Burnley (Division Two)

9 Sep 1905, Burnley v Leicester F (1-0)
75 minutes, waterlogged pitch.
Green, Dixon, Moffatt, Barron, D.Walders, Cretney, J.Walders, Wood, R.Smith, Davidson, Murphy.
Scorer : Wood
Replayed 2 Oct 1905, Burnley 0-2 Leicester F (Division Two)

4 Nov 1905, Leeds C v Burnley (1-1)
53 minutes, fog.
Green, Greenwood, Campbell, Barron, D.Walders, Moffatt, Marshall, Davidson, R.Smith, McFarlane, Cretney.
Scorer : Marshall.
Replayed 3 Feb 1906, Leeds C 1-1 Burnley (Division Two)

6 Mar 1909, Burnley v Manchester U (1-0)
72 minutes, snow, blizzard.
Dawson, Barron, McLean, Cretney, Leake, Moffatt, Morley, Ogden, R.Smith, Abbott, Smethams.
Scorer : Ogden
Replayed 10 Mar 1909, Burnley 2-3 Manchester U (FA Cup fourth round)

11 Jan 1913, Leeds C v Burnley (2-4)
50 minutes, snow.
Dawson, Bamford, Taylor, McLaren, Boyle, Watson, Mosscrop, Lindley, Freeman, Hodgson, Husband.
Scorers : Hodgson, Boyle, Freeman (2).
Replayed 15 Jan 1913, Leeds C 2-3 Burnley (FA Cup first round)

7 Jan 1956, Bury v Burnley (2-2)
65 minutes, fog.
McDonald, Rudman, Winton, Seith, Cummings, Shannon, Gray, Walton, McKay, Cheesebrough, Pilkington.
Scorer : McKay (2)
Replayed 10 Jan 1956, Bury 0-1 Burnley (FA Cup third round)

24 Jan 1959, Blackburn R v Burnley (0-0) 45 minutes, frozen pitch.
McDonald, Cummings, D.Smith, Seith, Miller, Adamson, Connelly, McIlroy, Pointer, Robson, Pilkington.
Replayed 28 Jan 1959, Blackburn R 1-2 Burnley
(FA Cup fourth round)

31 Mar 1969, Burnley v Sunderland (1-0) 45 minutes, snowstorm.
Thomson, Angus, Latcham, Dobson, Waldron, Blant, Thomas, Coates, Casper, Probert, Collins, sub O'Neil.
Scorer : Casper (pen)
Replayed 23 Apr 1969, Burnley 1-2 Sunderland
(Division One)
Note - the abandoned match was itself a postponed fixture.

11 Dec 1976, Notts C v Burnley (0-0) 45 minutes, frost/frozen pitch.
Stevenson, Newton, Brennan, Noble, Robinson, Rodaway, Cochrane, Flynn, Smith, Morley, Summerbee.
Replayed 2 Mar 1977, Notts C 5-1 Burnley
(Division Two)

20 Jan 1987, Bolton W v Burnley (1-1) 45 minutes, fog.
Woodworth, Leebrook, Heesom, Rodaway, Malley, Deakin, Grewcock, Parker, Murphy, James, Hoskin, subs Britton, Gallagher.
Scorer : Grewcock
Replayed 27 Jan 1987, Bolton W 2-1 Burnley
(Freight Rover Trophy first round)

14 Jan 1992, Derby C v Burnley (2-0) 76 minutes, fog.
Kendall, Measham, Jakub, Davis, Pender, Farrell, Harper, Deary, Francis, Conroy, Eli.
Replayed 25 Jan 1992, Derby C 2-0 Burnley
(FA Cup third round replay)

21 Jan 1992, Burnley v Scarborough (0-0) 90 minutes, frozen pitch.
Pearce, Measham, Jakub, Davis, Pender, Farrell, Harper, Deary, Francis, Conroy, Lancashire.
Replayed 4 Feb 1992, Burnley 3-1 Scarborough
(Autoglass Trophy first round [N])

26 Dec 1994, Burnley v Port Vale (1-2) 65 minutes, waterlogged pitch.
Beresford, Parkinson, Dowell (Harrison), Davis, Winstanley, Randall, Hoyland, Heath, Gayle, Robinson, McMinn.
Scorer : McMinn.
Replayed 28 Mar 1995, Burnley 4-3 Port Vale
(Division One)

17 Dec 1996, Burnley v Walsall (0-1) 45 minutes, floodlight failure.
Beresford, Parkinson, Eyres, Winstanley, Swan (Hoyland), Brass, Weller, Smith, Nogan, Barnes, Gleghorn.
Replayed 23 Dec 1996, Burnley 1-1 Walsall, after extra time, 4-2 on pens (FA Cup second round replay)
This was the first ever Burnley match abandoned for any reason other than adverse weather conditions.

1 Jan 2005, Burnley v Leicester C (0-0) 19 minutes, waterlogged pitch
Jensen, Duff, Sinclair, McGreal, Camara, Roche, Grant, J. O'Connor, Hyde, Branch, I. Moore.
Replayed 8 Mar 2005, Burnley 0-0 Leicester C
(Championship)

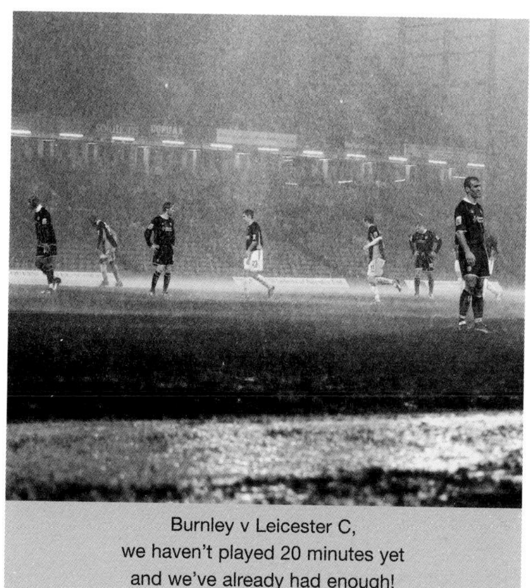

Burnley v Leicester C,
we haven't played 20 minutes yet
and we've already had enough!

Burnley FC Reserves

Burnley Reserves 1890-91 to 2006-07

	Season	P	W	D	L	F	A	Pts	Pos	
North East Lancs League										
	1890-91	20	12	3	5	70	39	27	2 of 12	Runners-up
	1891-92	22	15	4	3	99	36	34	2 of 12	Runners-up
	1892-93	22	16	6	0	112	23	38	1 of 12	Champions
	1893-94	18	17	1	0	119	15	35	1 of 10	Champions
Lancs Combination										
	1894-95	24	10	4	10	64	45	24	7 of 13	
	1895-96	26	11	7	8	66	54	29	6 of 14	
	1896-97	28	12	6	10	64	44	30	7 of 15	
	1897-98	30	9	4	17	61	82	22	13 of 16	
	1898-99	28	17	5	6	75	30	39	4 of 15	
	1899-1900	30	18	4	8	66	49	40	4 of 16	
	1900-01	34	13	7	14	61	56	33	11 of 18	
	1901-02	34	9	5	20	42	99	23	16 of 18	
	1902 to 1904				No reserve team					
North East Lancs Combination										
	1904-05	24	14	2	8	68	42	30	3 of 13	
Lancs Combination										
Div 2	1905-06	36	16	5	16	59	55	37	10 of 19	
Div 2	1906-07	38	20	2	16	93	68	42	8 of 20	
Div 2	1907-08	38	26	4	8	130	52	56	2 of 20	Runners-up
Div 1	1908-09	38	17	12	9	92	66	46	5 of 20	
Div 1	1909-10	38	13	11	14	66	69	37	9 of 20	
Div 1	1910-11	38	15	5	18	62	69	35	16 of 20	

All the Football League clubs with reserve teams in the Lancs Combination resigned en bloc to form the Central League

	Season	P	W	D	L	F	A	Pts	Pos
Central League									
	1911-12	32	13	5	14	66	62	31	12 of 17
	1912-13	38	22	4	12	87	47	48	3 of 20
	1913-14	38	16	6	16	57	72	38	11 of 20
	1914-15	38	21	5	12	80	41	47	4 of 20
World War One									
	1919-20	42	15	5	22	66	71	35	18 of 22
	1920-21	42	18	7	17	84	73	43	9 of 22
	1921-22	42	21	6	15	77	79	48	4 of 22
	1922-23	42	18	10	14	70	63	46	6 of 22
	1923-24	42	8	13	21	41	81	29	21 of 22
	1924-25	42	8	9	25	62	95	25	22 of 22
	1925-26	42	17	8	17	87	77	42	13 of 22
	1926-27	42	14	6	22	71	99	34	19 of 22
	1927-28	42	15	5	22	71	115	35	19 of 22
	1928-29	42	19	9	14	88	76	47	6 of 22
	1929-30	42	14	8	20	80	109	36	16 of 22
	1930-31	42	12	10	20	66	95	34	18 of 22
	1931-32	42	12	4	26	68	140	28	21 of 22
	1932-33	42	15	7	20	78	94	37	17 of 22
	1933-34	42	10	11	21	73	102	31	18 of 22
	1934-35	42	18	3	21	84	109	39	15 of 22
	1935-36	42	12	14	16	58	73	38	15 of 22
	1936-37	42	24	5	13	97	71	53	3 of 22
	1937-38	42	16	11	15	71	68	43	7 of 22
	1938-39	42	15	4	23	60	85	34	21 of 22
World War Two									

Burnley Reserves 1890-91 to 2006-07 continued

		P	W	D	L	F	A	Pts	Pos	
Central League										
	1946-47	42	22	8	12	77	50	52	3 of 22	
	1947-48	42	18	7	17	57	50	43	9 of 22	
	1948-49	42	24	12	6	72	32	60	1 of 22	Champions
	1949-50	42	21	11	10	78	53	53	3 of 22	
	1950-51	42	19	14	9	62	32	52	2 of 22	Runners-up
	1951-52	42	18	5	19	63	61	41	8 of 22	
	1952-53	42	23	5	14	70	62	51	5 of 22	
	1953-54	42	24	8	10	68	48	56	2 of 22	Runners-up
	1954-55	42	22	8	12	94	59	52	4 of 22	
	1955-56	42	15	11	16	72	76	41	11 of 22	
	1956-57	42	13	9	20	58	78	35	17 of 22	
	1957-58	42	15	7	20	58	77	37	16 of 22	
	1958-59	42	14	7	21	58	72	35	16 of 22	
	1959-60	42	18	7	17	66	68	43	11 of 22	
	1960-61	42	23	7	12	91	64	53	4 of 22	
	1961-62	42	30	7	5	113	40	67	1 of 22	Champions
	1962-63	42	27	7	8	101	34	61	1 of 22	Champions
	1963-64	42	23	9	10	77	42	55	4 of 22	
	1964-65	42	19	13	10	76	50	51	6 of 22	
	1965-66	42	18	9	15	70	71	45	9 of 22	
	1966-67	42	13	14	15	60	60	40	13 of 22	
	1967-68	42	17	12	13	52	51	46	10 of 22	
	1968-69	42	15	13	14	64	58	43	10 of 22	
	1969-70	42	23	9	10	76	51	55	4 of 22	
	1970-71	42	18	15	9	77	61	51	5 of 22	
	1971-72	42	16	8	18	61	73	40	12 of 22	
	1972-73	42	15	8	19	57	60	38	16 of 22	
	1973-74	42	12	5	25	38	65	29	20 of 22	
	1974-75	42	13	13	16	64	68	39	14 of 22	
	1975-76	42	15	10	17	64	71	40	13 of 22	
	1976-77	42	11	14	17	55	64	36	16 of 22	
	1977-78	42	11	12	19	51	67	34	19 of 22	
	1978-79	42	15	9	18	42	56	39	14 of 22	
	1979-80	42	18	10	14	46	49	46	9 of 22	
	1980-81	42	16	12	14	45	45	44	9 of 22	
	1981-82	42	7	11	24	42	88	25	21 of 22	League re-structured
Div 2	1982-83	30	14	8	8	49	41	36	4 of 16	Promoted
Div 1	1983-84	30	5	9	16	19	45	24	16 of 16	Relegated
Div 2	1984-85	34	6	4	24	41	74	22	17 of 18	
Div 2	1985-86	34	6	6	22	36	74	24	17 of 18	
	1986 to 1989				Did not compete					
Div 2	1989-90	34	7	3	24	30	69	24	18 of 18	
Div 2	1990-91	34	13	11	10	53	48	50	8 of 18	
Div 2	1991-92	34	14	6	14	48	52	48	7 of 18	
Div 2	1992-93	34	11	8	15	46	56	41	13 of 18	
Div 2	1993-94	34	16	4	14	55	49	52	7 of 18	
Div 2	1994-95	34	15	6	13	67	68	51	9 of 18	
Div 2	1995-96	34	11	10	13	62	68	43	12 of 18	League re-structured
Div 2 (3rd tier)	1996-97	24	9	5	10	46	41	32	8 of 13	semi final in League Cup
Div 2 (3rd tier)	1997-98	24	14	5	5	56	29	47	1 of 13	Champions
Div 2 (2nd tier)	1998-99	24	6	8	10	20	35	26	12 of 13	League re-structured
Premier Div	1999-2000	22	6	9	7	29	34	27	10 of 12	
Premier Div	2000-01	24	12	3	9	44	43	39	4 of 13	
Premier Div	2001-02	24	11	6	7	43	40	39	5 of 13	
Premier Div	2002-03	20	8	1	11	35	37	25	9 of 11	
Premier Div	2003-04	22	4	4	14	26	52	16	12 of 12	Relegated
Div 1 west (2nd tier)	2004-05	22	5	11	6	24	21	26	7 of 12	
Div 1 west (2nd tier)	2005-06	18	5	5	8	26	31	17	9 of 10	3 pts deducted
	2006-07				Did not compete					

FA Youth Cup results

FA Youth Cup results 1954 to 2007

1954-55	Round 1	Blackpool	away	lost	0-1	
1958-59	Round 2	BLACKBURN R	home	lost	1-2	
1961-62	Round 1	Manchester C	away	lost	2-3	
1962-63	Round 2	Leeds U	away	won	2-0	
	Round 3	GRIMSBY T	home	won	5-1	
	Round 4	LIVERPOOL	home	drew	1-1	
	replay	Liverpool	away	lost	0-4	
1963-64	Round 2	Manchester C	away	lost	1-4	
1964-65	Round 2	LIVERPOOL	home	won	4-1	
	Round 3	Blackpool	away	drew	2-2	
	replay	BLACKPOOL	home	drew	2-2	
	2nd replay	Blackpool	away	won	2-1	
	Round 4	Everton	away	lost	0-4	
1965-66	Round 2	BOLTON W	home	won	4-0	
	Round 3	Bradford C	away	won	2-1	
	Round 4	LEEDS U	home	drew	1-1	
	replay	Leeds U	away	lost	0-4	
1966-67	Round 2	Blackpool	away	won	3-0	
	Round 3	PRESTON N E	home	lost	1-2	
1967-68	Round 2	YORKSHIRE AMS	home	won	7-1	
	Round 3	MANCHESTER C	home	won	4-3	
	Round 4	Manchester U	away	drew	0-0	
	replay	Manchester U	home	won	2-1	
	Round 5	Sheffield U	away	won	2-0	
	Semi final	Everton	away	drew	0-0	
	2nd leg	EVERTON	home	won	3-2	agg 3-2
	Final	Coventry C	away	lost	1-2	
	2nd leg	COVENTRY C	home	won	2-0	agg 3-2

FA Youth Cup winners 1967-68
Back: Pat Dooney, Steve Kindon, Wilf Wrigley, Gerry McEvoy, Eddie Cliff, George Coppock,
Front: Alan West, Eric Probert, Michael Docherty, David Hartley, Peter Jones, David Thomas.

FA Youth Cup results 1954 to 2007 continued

1968-69	Round 2	PRESTON N E	home	lost	1-3	
1969-70	Round 2	MANCHESTER C	home	won	3-1	
	Round 3	Stoke C	away	lost	1-3	
1970-71	Round 2	Liverpool	away	won	2-0	
	Round 3	BLACKBURN R	home	won	4-1	
	Round 4	MANCHESTER U	home	won	2-0	
	Round 5	Hull C	away	won	2-0	
	Semi final	CARDIFF C	home	drew	1-1	
	2nd leg	Cardiff C	away	drew	0-0	agg 1-1
	replay	CARDIFF C	home	lost	1-3	after extra time
1971-72	Round 2	MANCHESTER C	home	won	1-0	
	Round 3	Oldham A	away	lost	0-1	
1972-73	Round 2	MANCHESTER C	home	drew	1-1	
	replay	Manchester C	away	won	4-1	
	Round 3	Bolton W	away	lost	0-3	
1973-74	Round 2	Rotherham U	away	won	2-0	
	Round 3	Huddersfield T	away	drew	1-1	
	replay	HUDDERSFIELD T	home	lost	1-2	
1974-75	Round 2	SHREWSBURY T	home	drew	1-1	
	replay	Shrewsbury T	away	won	2-0	
	Round 3	Blackburn R	away	drew	1-1	
	replay	BLACKBURN R	home	won	3-0	
	Round 4	Tottenham H	away	lost	0-3	
1975-76	Round 2	Blackburn R	away	drew	0-0	
	replay	BLACKBURN R	home	lost	1-2	
1976-77	Round 2	Sheffield U	away	drew	0-0	
	replay	SHEFFIELD U	home	won	1-0	
	Round 3	Liverpool	away	lost	0-3	
1977-78	Round 2	Manchester C	away	won	2-1	
	Round 3	LIVERPOOL	home	won	3-2	
	Round 4	Plymouth A	away	won	1-0	
	Round 5	MIDDLESBROUGH	home	won	2-0	
	Semi final	ASTON VILLA	home	lost	1-3	
	2nd leg	Aston Villa	away	lost	0-1	
1978-79	Round 2	MIDDLESBROUGH	home	lost	0-1	
1979-80	Round 2	MIDDLESBROUGH	home	lost	0-1	
1980-81	Round 1	HULL C	home	drew	1-1	
	replay	Hull C	away	won	1-0	
	Round 2	ROCHDALE	home	won	7-0	
	Round 3	Newcastle U	away	lost	0-2	
1981-82	Round 1	HARTLEPOOL U	home	won	1-0	
	Round 2	Blackpool	away	won	1-0	
	Round 3	Coventry C	away	drew	0-0	
	replay	COVENTRY C	home	won	2-1	
	Round 4	Queens Park R	away	lost	0-3	
1982-83	Round 2	WIGAN A	home	won	4-0	
	Round 3	Barnsley	away	lost	0-3	
1983-84	Round 2	SUNDERLAND	home	drew	1-1	
	replay	Sunderland	away	lost	0-2	

FA Youth Cup results 1954 to 2007 continued

1984-85	Round 2	BOLTON W	home	won	2-0
	Round 3	Birmingham C	away	lost	1-3
1985-86	Round 2	MANCHESTER U	home	lost	0-2
1986-87	Round 2	GRIMSBY T	home	lost	0-1
1987-88	Round 1	York C	away	won	2-1
	Round 2	Newcastle U	away	lost	0-2
1988-89	Round 2	LEEDS U	home	lost	1-2
1990-91	Round 1	Wigan A	away	won	3-0
	Round 2	Doncaster R	away	lost	0-4
1991-92	Round 1	SHEFFIELD U	home	lost	0-2
1992-93	Round 1	BARNSLEY	home	drew	2-2
	replay	Barnsley	away	lost	0-3
1993-94	Round 1	Newcastle U	away	drew	1-1
	replay	NEWCASTLE U	home	won	3-0
	Round 2	LEEDS U	home	won	3-0
	Round 3	Wimbledon	away	won	4-3
	Round 4	ARSENAL	home	lost	0-1
1994-95	Round 1	Tranmere R	away	lost	0-5
1995-96	Round 1	Southport	away	won	2-1
	Round 2	STOKE C	home	won	1-0
	Round 3	Norwich C	away	lost	1-2
1996-97	Round 1	Newcastle U	away	won	2-1
	Round 2	Liverpool	away	lost	2-5
1997-98	Round 1	WREXHAM	home	won	2-0
	Round 2	Hull C	away	lost	0-1
1998-99	Round 1	Oldham A	away	lost	0-2
1999-2000	Round 1	Mansfield T	away	drew	1-1
	replay	MANSFIELD T	home	lost	1-3
2000-01	Round 3	SHEFFIELD W	home	lost	0-6
2001-02	Round 3	Manchester C	away	lost	0-3
2002-03	Round 3	CRYSTAL P	home	lost	0-2
2003-04	Round 3	Sheffield U	away	lost	1-4
2004-05	Round 3	NORWICH C	home	lost	1-2
2005-06	Round 3	Hull C	away	won	3-2
	Round 4	FULHAM	home	won	2-1
	Round 5	LIVERPOOL	home	lost	0-3
2006-07	Round 3	MILTON KEYNES D	home	won	3-2
	Round 4	LUTON T	home	won	2-0
	Round 5	Swindon T	away	lost	1-3

Stories between the sticks

A collection of custodian chronicles down the years.

3 Nov 1888
Burnley 1-7 Blackburn R
After 31 goals are conceded in the previous 8 games, centre forward Fred Poland is tried between the sticks. Enough said.

7 Jan 1893
West Brom 7-1 Burnley
En route to the Hawthorns, Jack Hillman contrives to get left behind on a railway station platform in Stockport. When he arrives at West Bromwich it is half time and 10 man Burnley are already 1-4 down, with Billy Bowes having spent the first half in goal.

18 Nov 1893
Blackburn R 3-2 Burnley
25 Nov 1893
Everton 4-3 Burnley
Walter Place senior demonstrates his all round versatility by playing, and performing competently, in goal in both these games. He replaces Jack Hillman who is unavailable.

26 Sep 1896
Preston N E 5-3 Burnley
Willie Tatham eventually has to leave the field after taking a severe blow to the chest early on. He is replaced in goal by Walter Place senior who keeps a clean sheet in his 20 minutes between the sticks, also saving two penalties.

28 Apr 1900
Nottingham F 4-0 Burnley
One of the most infamous games in Burnley's history. After the match Jack Hillman is accused by the Forest players of offering bribes for them to "take things easy" to ensure the Turfites avoid relegation. Hillman is subsequently banned from football for a complete season.

13 Feb 1909
Burnley 2-0 Grimsby T
Burnley are awarded a total of four penalties, three of which are saved by the Grimsby keeper, Walter "Buns" Scott.

12 Sep 1910
Darwen 0-1 Burnley
When Jerry Dawson is replaced in goal by defender Hugh Moffat for this East Lancashire Charity cup tie, speculation is rife that Dawson has signed for Blackburn Rovers. It eventually emerges that Dawson missed his train and will be between the Burnley sticks for a little while yet.

4 Feb 1911
Burnley 2-0 Barnsley
After Barnsley's Tommy Boyle handles, Clarets' keeper Jerry Dawson is entrusted with the spot kick. His effort is parried by the keeper, only for the rebound to be put away by Jonathan Morley.

Jun 1912
After approval by the FA Council, the decision is taken at the Football League annual meeting that goalkeepers may only handle the ball in their own penalty area. Previously they could handle anywhere in their own half!

18 Apr 1914
Manchester C 4-1 Burnley
Just a week before Burnley's FA Cup final date with Liverpool, Jerry Dawson is injured early on and is eventually replaced in goal by full back David Taylor. Dawson is already suffering the effects of an injury received in the first FA Cup semi final with Sheffield United, and this latest setback continues a chain of events that become part of Burnley FC folklore.

16 Dec 1925
Bury 8-1 Burnley
In only his second match for Burnley, Tommy Hampson is carried off just 20 minutes in, after a collision with a Bury player. With the score at 1-1, centre half Jack Hill dons the gloves for the rest of the first half, conceding two goals but saving a penalty. Wing half Len Hughes is between the sticks for the whole of the second half.

5 Nov 1927
Bolton W 7-1 Burnley
After 28 minutes, with the Clarets just one goal down, George Sommerville suffers a broken collar bone after a collision with a Bolton forward. Centre half Jack Hill goes in goal until half time with inside forward Paddy Freeman donning the gloves in the second half.

25 Dec 1928
Burnley 3-2 Liverpool
A wonderful Turf Moor reception for Jerry Dawson as he turns out for his last senior game at the age of 40.

26 Dec 1928
Liverpool 8-0 Burnley
What a contrast in emotions as George Sommerville appears in his first League game for more than a year.

9 Nov 1929
Blackburn R 8-3 Burnley
After half an hour Billy Down is injured in a collision with Rovers' Bob Crompton. He bravely carries on until the final whistle but is severely restricted in his movement. After the match Down is rushed to hospital where a ruptured kidney is diagnosed. For a while there is concern for his life but he eventually recovers although he never plays for Burnley again.

21 Feb 1953
Derby C 1-3 Burnley
Des Thompson is injured as Derby score their only goal just before half time. Harold Mather replaces him between the sticks but Thompson is fit enough to continue after the break.

15 Dec 1956
Chelsea 2-0 Burnley
After an hour, with Chelsea leading 1-0, Colin McDonald cracks a bone in his ankle and has to leave the field. Left back Jock Winton takes over between the posts for the rest of the contest.

17 Mar 1959
League of Ireland 0-0 Football League
The end of an era for both Burnley and England as Colin McDonald suffers a badly broken leg. The senior football career of one of the Clarets' finest servants is over.

8 Feb 1967
Napoli 0-0 Burnley
Arguably the most celebrated performance by a Burnley goalkeeper in the club's history. "God in a green jersey" Harry Thomson is simply unbeatable in the notorious "Battle of Naples"

22 Mar 1969
Coventry C 4-1 Burnley
The score is still 0-0 just after half time when Rodney Jones injures his ankle. Jones carries on but conceded three goals he might have expected to save before going off to be replaced by Les Latcham.

9 Aug 1969
Derby C 0-0 Burnley
With just four minutes remaining of an impressive Burnley debut, Peter Mellor injures his hand and has to leave the field. Once again Les Latcham deputises.

27 Dec 1980
Burnley 4-1 Blackpool
Alan Stevenson becomes the first-ever Clarets' goalkeeper to be sent off, as he is dismissed in the last minute after inexplicably kicking out at ex-Claret Colin Morris as the Seasiders score their consolation goal. Full back Brian Laws takes over between the posts for the short time left.

11 Dec 1982
Burnley 2-4 Leicester C
Burnley are leading 2-1 when Alan Stevenson is sent off after 55 minutes for a foul on Gary Lineker. Paul McGee faces, but is beaten by, the spot kick and is immediately replaced between the sticks by Brian Laws (the shortest goalkeeping career on record?)
McGee later takes, but misses, a penalty of his own.

26 Jan 1991
Burnley 3-2 Stockport C
Chris Pearce is sent off just three minutes from the end of normal time, following a fracas with County's David Frain, who is also dismissed. Andy Farrell dons the gloves for the last three minutes plus an extra four minutes added time, but there are no more goals.

8 May 1993
Stoke C 1-1 Burnley
Marlon Beresford has to leave early from the Potters' Championship celebration party with blood pouring from a face injury. Mark Monington proves to be a more than competent deputy and keeps a clean sheet, with Adrian Randall securing a point for the Clarets.

27 Aug 1994
Oldham A 3-0 Burnley
After Marlon Beresford is sent off for handball outside the area, his replacement is Wayne Russell, the first Burnley keeper ever to make his debut as a substitute.

2 Jan 1995
Portsmouth 2-0 Burnley
Wayne Russell once more deputises for Beresford who is again dismissed for handling the ball outside the penalty area.

5 Nov 2005
Luton T 2-3 Burnley
With the Clarets 2-0 ahead, Brian Jensen is sent off for hand ball. Midfield man John Spicer performs heroically as his replacement between the sticks, while an Ade Akinbiyi hat-trick ensures all three points are on their way to Turf Moor.

Mark Monington in unfamiliar garb, ready to face Second Division Champions Stoke City

Famous Fans

A group of well-known Burnley fans share their passion and confess how they became hooked.

Name: Andy Hodgson
Occupation: Auctioneer and Presenter of digital channel Bid-up.tv
Earliest Memory: "My first game at Turf Moor was an England youth international and I remember sitting in the Bob Lord Stand in awe of the Longside. I then went with a mate to see Burnley play York and stood in the away end in the Longside. I was stunned by the support on the other side of the fence, and wished I was on the Burnley side as York got thrashed 6-0, but I was hooked on the Turf from that point."
Interesting Fact: "I helped launch the new home kit on the channel for the 2004-05 season. I had an assistant called Jenny....but her nickname was Jennoir, as she came from the French valleys! The club had the new shirt made up for her with her name 'Jennoir' on the back. We spent the evening pretending she'd signed for the club and Burnley FC thought they'd signed a big French superstar to follow in the footsteps of Arthur Gnohere. We didn't sell much that night, but Hunters and Burnley FC got a lot of free advertising!"

Name: John Kettley
Occupation: Weatherman for TV and Radio
Earliest Memory: "I started watching them just after they won the title in 1960, because despite hailing from Todmorden, they were still my local side. It was nice to be close to such a big club, but my first game was a 4-3 defeat to Sheffield Wednesday at the Turf. It was pouring down with rain, but I remember the atmosphere being something that I wanted to sample again and again.
"It was the late 1960s when I started watching them on a regular basis. I remember watching them against Lausanne and Frankfurt, and savouring the atmosphere that was being generated around me – that was something special and something that won't ever leave me."
Interesting Fact: "When I'm doing the weather reports on television or radio, I always try and drop Burnley in as often as I can – you have to don't you, really! I also help Birmingham City's groundsman out with forecasts, but despite me not being able to get up to Burnley as often as I'd like these days, they are always at the front of my mind."

Name: Phil Willis
Occupation: MP for Harrogate and Knaresborough

Earliest Memory: "My father was born and bred in Burnley, and started taking me on Turf Moor in the early 1940s. I lived in Rosegrove, and while I was there, Tommy Cummings moved in across the road and Jimmy McIlroy did likewise around the corner.

"I remember the match against Newcastle when Tommy scored 'that goal', because I immediately ran home and waited hours for him to get home so I could get his autograph.

"It was fantastic in those days, I used to love queuing for tickets, especially for the European game at the Parc Des Princes to play Reims. They were great years and very enjoyable, and even now, some of my memories of going to see Burnley have remained the happiest memories of my life."

Interesting Fact: "When my dad first took me on the Turf he worked as a postman. His round saw him deliver the post to Bob Lord, and when his Christmas bonus came round, Bob paid him in sausages!"

Name: Amy Lame
Occupation: Broadcaster, Writer and Entertainer

Earliest Memory: "Not a lot of people believe me when I say I'm a Burnley fan, because I'm a lady from New Jersey. My partner's dad took me to my first game on Boxing Day a few years ago against Wolves, when I'd never been to a game before.

"I was just swept away by the emotion and ferocity in which everyone was supporting the team, it was just an amazing atmosphere. I'd never experienced anything like it before – I love spectacles, I like being in an arena, and Turf Moor was just a special place to be in."

Interesting Fact: "A year after my first match I did Celebrity Fit Club, and we did some football training. My father-in-law got me a Burnley shirt to wear while I was doing it, and that was what made a lot of people realise I was a fan. It was at the time when there was a lot of fundraising going on, and I made sure I did my bit by donating money for every pound I lost – which unfortunately wasn't much!"

Name: Allan "Boff" Whalley
Occupation: lead guitarist with band Chumbawamba

Earliest Memory: "I was nine when I went on my first game, which was an FA Cup replay against Chelsea at Turf Moor in 1970.

"We got beat 3-1, but as soon as I walked in the ground I thought it was fantastic. I went on with my dad and at the time was supporting anyone successful – I wanted to see Peter Osgood but he was injured, but that only made me concentrate on Burnley.

"I tried to get on as many as I could, and when I was at university in Maidstone I went to a few away games – including the 7-0 defeat at QPR in 1979, which seemed to be repeated on Match Of The Day for ever and a day!"

Interesting Fact: "When 'Tubthumping' was released it was an anthem that seemed to be adopted by football clubs all over the country, because it was an anthem. But the first time I went on Turf Moor and realised Burnley were running out to it, I had goosebumps. It was an amazing feeling, and I thought it suited us!"

Name: Richard Moore
Occupation: Actor, best known for 'Jarvis' on Emmerdale
Earliest Memory: "My granddad and dad used to take me on, and we used to go in what is now the Cricket Field Stand because we would always go behind the goal.

"I know I started going on in the early 1950s, but I can't for the life of me remember when my first game was. The earliest one that springs to mind was when Burnley beat Manchester United 5-3.

"I used to attend Holy Trinity Junior School just up the road, and they used to play midweek games on a Tuesday afternoon. I still remember me and friends sat next to an open window, listening for the cheers from the ground so we could keep tabs on the score."

Interesting Fact: "I went on to attend an amateur drama group called the Highcliffe Players, and remember playing a show on the day Burnley won the First Division Championship at Manchester City. The place was full, but they were more interested in the score than they were on our performance!"

Name: Eric Knowles
Occupation: Antiques Dealer
Earliest Memory: "I used to stand at the back of the Longside, and my first game was against Blackpool in 1963. I remember the masses of people, and my dad had made me a portable stool to stand on! But when my brother started coming on, my dad had to add an extension to it. I'll always remember the rattles, and the fact that if you were late you didn't get much of a view.

"There used to be someone who, before mascots were around, used to walk around the pitch wearing a mortarboard, to symbolise Burnley being the university of English football.

"I remember going on a game against Leeds in 1968 - their side included players like Billy Bremner and Norman Hunter. We ended up absolutely hammering them 5-1, which was a wonderful feeling."

Interesting Fact: "I remember coming into contact with a Burnley shirt from the 1914 cup final, along with a medal. A Jimmy McIlroy shirt from the game with Reims has also come across my path before, and it was nice to see that they were all bought by the club."

Name: Alastair Campbell
Occupation: Former Director of Communications and Strategy to the Prime Minister
Earliest Memory: "I've tried many times to pinpoint my first game, but have been unable to do so. I know I started going on when I was four years old, when they were league champions, and have clear memories of playing a few teams like Chelsea and West Ham.

"I remember singing my first ever song - we've got Willie Morgan – and remember standing right at the front of the old Brunshaw Road Stand, because you were so close to the players it was unbelievable.

"Because we lived in Keighley we used to go and watch a few clubs, but Burnley were always the one I wanted to support because of the distinguishable colours and atmosphere."

Interesting Fact: "I took Tony Blair to see a Burnley game at Hartlepool once, and we lost 4-1. He has never been to a game since, but I've lost count of how many times I've tried to get him on Turf Moor. He hasn't been yet, but I'm determined to get him there."

Name: Tony Livesey
Occupation: Journalist and Broadcaster
Earliest Memory: "My first game was a 1-1 draw with Birmingham in 1971, but I remember playing Manchester United at home, where there were about 200 kids sat on the wall at the front of the Longside. I fell off and caused every one of them to fall onto the pitch!

"The one that really stands out is when we played Preston away in 1972-73 – we got a 1-1 draw to clinch the Second Division title, and it was like the entire town of Burnley had moved to Preston.

"I went with my uncle, and that day I thought Burnley was the biggest football team in the world. We had taken over the town, and I'm getting goosebumps just talking about it"

Interesting Fact: "When Burnley beat Orient to stay in the Football League, I couldn't attend because I was working for a newspaper in Dubai. At the time of the result it was 2 a.m. over there, so I altered the back page to read 'Burnley Stay Up'. My editor wasn't best pleased in the morning, because no one had ever heard of Burnley over there!"

Name: Rachel Brown
Occupation: Footballer with Everton and England
Earliest Memory: "My first ever match was the Sherpa Van Trophy Final at Wembley, which we unfortunately lost. But that experience convinced me that I wanted to become a footballer.

"I remember going down on the train with my flat cap on and scarf, and still remember the experience to this day because it was amazing.

"I only had a season ticket for a couple of seasons, but Ted McMinn and Marlon Beresford were my two heroes more than any others. I loved watching Marlon play, and he was definitely a massive influence in me wanting to become a goalkeeper."

Interesting Fact: "As a Burnley supporter, in was a fantastic honour for me to play for England against Australia at Turf Moor. I've played in lots of big stadiums, both in England and abroad, but that was the best game I have played in by a mile. The build up and the atmosphere made me immensely proud, I received a fabulous reception from the crowd and all my family was there to watch me. It was something I will never forget, and would love to experience again in my career."

Name: Sam Aston
Occupation: Actor, best known for 'Chesney' on Coronation Street
Earliest Memory: "I started going on in primary school about 1992, because all my brothers and sisters were Burnley fans. I've not a good memory of games back then, but certain games do stick out, like the 0-0 draw with Blackburn in the FA Cup recently.

"It's not often that I can get to games – we film six days a week and I have Saturdays off, but on Saturdays I go to a drama group so I can't get to games. My mates are always telling me to pretend I'm sick so I can go on the Turf, but I've never plucked up the courage to do it."

Interesting Fact: "I was asked to present an award to Gary Cahill at the end of last season, which was really nerve wracking. But it wasn't as bad as doing the half-time draw – I don't think I've ever been as nervous in my life, and that includes the audition for Coronation Street!

"There isn't really much rivalry on the set because they are all Manchester United and City fans, but there is a costume designer who is a Blackburn fan. My character is a Manchester City fan, but I think I'm going to try and convert him slowly and see if the writers notice."

Turf Moor the early days

Turf Moor has been the scene of sporting activity in Burnley since at least 1833 when Burnley Cricket Club was founded and played their early matches there.

When the members of Burnley Football Club decided to move their home ground to Turf Moor, adjacent to the cricket ground, what they were moving to was little more than a field. They had what they needed to at least begin playing football however and, just two weeks after their final match at Calder Vale, the club prepared to welcome their first visitors to their new home.

Conditions for that historic encounter with Rawtenstall, on 17 February 1883, were not ideal for football - "a high wind making correct play impossible". The Rawtenstall players didn't seem to mind the conditions however, they got on with the game and emerged as winners 6-3.

After that disappointing first match the members got to work on the pitch, ensuring it was properly drained "under the direction of Mr Charles Riley," committee member and self appointed first groundsman.

In those early days Turf Moor attendances were generally, at most, a few thousand but for a local derby against Padiham in 1884, almost 12,000 squeezed in to see "the Pads", then a force in the area, win a thrilling encounter 4-2.

Within a short time work began on accommodating spectators more comfortably and by 1885 the first wooden grandstand had been built on the Brunshaw Road side of the ground.

In 1886 of course, Turf Moor played host to Royalty when Prince Albert Victor, grandson of Queen Victoria, was almost certainly the first member of the Royal Family to visit a senior football ground. A match against Bolton had been specially arranged as part of the Prince's visit to Burnley to open the town's new Victoria Hospital, to be named in Her Majesty's honour. The front of the stand was given a new coat of paint for the Royal visit and more than 9,000 people turned up to see Bolton edge home by the odd goal after the proverbial seven-goal thriller.

A sketch of Turf Moor in the 1890's

In 1891 Burnley Union Stars FC, who had been one of Burnley's most serious, and bitter, rivals in pre League days, was disbanded. The Stars, had had their own ground at Daneshouse, complete with grandstand, and the Burnley committee immediately bought the stand and moved it to Turf Moor. It was erected on what, in later years, would come to be known as the Longside.

In March 1891 Turf Moor staged its first floodlit football match when the Burnley committee decided to experiment. Sixteen lamps were placed on poles at intervals around the ground, fuelled by creosote oil and "the illumination was said to be equivalent to 50,000 candles". Spectators reported that the sides of the ground were lit well enough but there was a dark patch in the centre of the pitch. Nevertheless the crowd of over 3,000 enjoyed the novelty of the occasion, as well as a 4-2 victory over local rivals Nelson.

For the purists, although this was the first association football match at Turf Moor, a floodlit rugby match had taken place on the cricket field some 13 years earlier. In November 1878 Burnley Rovers played a match against Bacup under just three lamps powered by a small engine.

The Burnley Express was lukewarm in its reporting of the occasion -

"only one light could be said to be effective, the other two flickering and going out in the most spasmodic manner. A local band played selections and this, to a great extent, relieved the monotony of the proceedings"

For the record Bacup won the match watched by an estimated crowd of over 3,000, although many more people were able to witness the historic event from the hill at the back of Turf Moor.

In 1898 it was decided that the old "Stars" stand had had its day and it was duly demolished. It was replaced by a new grandstand "to increase accommodation and comfort" for the Burnley spectators. In 1903 another storey was added to the Brunshaw Road stand to accommodate the club's offices and in September 1903 the annual meeting was able to be held at the ground for the first time.

In 1909 Burnley had their first real FA Cup run and in the quarter final were drawn against League Champions Manchester United at Turf Moor. In readiness for what was anticipated to be a huge crowd, teams of men "worked night and day" to extend what was still referred to as the "Stars" stand, building an enclosure, erecting new barricades and turnstiles and increasing the banking around the ground. When the day of the match dawned, the weather was awful, snow began to fall early in the morning and, by kick off time, it was "scarcely fit to turn out". Nevertheless almost 16,000 people braved the weather, but it had been estimated that, but for the atrocious weather, the attendance would have been around 30,000. This was, of course the famous "stop the game it's snowing" match and, after 72 minutes, it was abandoned with Burnley 1-0 in front.

Turf Moor 1905, viewed from the Bee Hole end

In the spring of 1911 plans were announced for a new Brunshaw Road stand with the architect to be none other than one of Burnley's former star players, Arthur Bell.

A rail strike delayed the arrival of steelwork for the roof but even so, spectators were still able to use the new stand for Burnley's first home match of the season in September 1911, against Leeds. Not so the players, the new dressing rooms were not ready and they had to change in the cricket pavilion next door!

The cost of the work on the new stand was put at £5,000, and it would provide capacity for 5,500 people, 2,200 seated with 3,300 more in the enclosure at the front. With 1,400 seats in the "Stars" stand and space for around 34,000 in the rest of the ground, Turf Moor's total capacity was just under 41,000.

In 1913 it was decided to demolish what locals still called the "Stars" stand even though the original that had been erected in 1891, had been replaced in 1898.

Also in 1913 the Brunshaw stand was extended to run the full length of the pitch and in 1914 a roof was added to the Cricket field end, increasing the capacity of the ground to around 50,000.

In March 1914 Turf Moor was awarded its first senior representative match when the Football League hosted the Scottish League. Burnley had three players in the Football League team, Tommy Boyle, Teddy Hodgson and Eddie Mosscrop but it was the Scottish League side that emerged with a 3-2 victory.

In 1922 there were over 46,000 at Turf Moor to see the ground stage its only FA Cup semi final, Huddersfield Town beating Notts County 3-1. The FA insisted that the Turf Moor pitch be lengthened by four yards to 115 yards for the tie, although afterwards it was returned to its normal dimensions.

In February 1924 Huddersfield were again the Turf Moor visitors in an FA Cup tie when the ground attendance record of 54,778 was set. The Clarets made it a memorable, if tightly packed, day for their fans with an epic 1-0 victory against a team on its way to the first of three successive League Championships.

In 1927 England played their only full international fixture at Turf Moor, Clarets' captain Jack Hill leading his country, with Louis Page also in the England side. Once again Turf Moor proved to be an unlucky ground for a national team, with Wales winning 2-1 and Hill scoring an own goal.

In 1932 Burnley's first supporters club was established and the group immediately set about fundraising Their plans included, amongst other improvements, a roof for the Beehole end and although that never materialised, they did provide their own hut and a scoreboard at the back of the Beehole embankment.

In 1938 there were already tentative plans in place to provide terracing and a roof on what would become the Longside. Events in Europe however would put plans for Turf Moor, and just about everywhere else in Britain, on hold for the foreseeable future.

Turf Moor 1929

Turf Moor
the Albert Maddox years

Almost 60 years since he first walked into the Turf Moor offices, and with more than 50 years of experience behind the scenes at Burnley Football Club, who better than Albert Maddox to tell the story of Turf Moor since World War Two

Albert Maddox being presented with an amateur football trophy in 1947 by Burnley captain Alan Brown

Albert was born in Oswaldtwistle in 1921 and worked for a firm of textile machine exporters from the age of 15. He was a promising schoolboy footballer and at the age of 17 was offered a trial at Wolverhampton Wanderers. Events in the days before he was due to travel to Molineux rather interfered with the plans of the young Maddox, it was the outbreak of the Second World War!

Albert joined the RAF in 1941 and served in the Middle East where he managed to play some football, also appearing for Accrington Stanley when home on leave. He was demobbed in 1946 and went along to Turf Moor for a trial, but soon realised he was up against stiff competition, and he was not taken on as a professional.

However Albert did eventually join the Turf Moor staff, in October 1947 he was appointed as assistant secretary to Henry Smith. He succeeded Smith as club secretary in July 1961 and in 1968, after 21 years at Turf Moor, he was presented with the Football League long service medal.

In 1982, at the age of 60 he decided to retire, only to return four years later following the illness and untimely death of his successor, and friend, Bob Bradshaw. Albert continued to work hard in the secretary's office at his beloved Burnley FC, either as the man in charge or providing valuable assistance, until 1997 until he finally handed over the reins of assistant secretary to Cathy Pickup..... who just happened to be Albert's daughter!

Albert takes up the story of Turf Moor...

Most people will have been told tales of bygone days by their grandparents.

Stories of war, strife and toil, and how life was so different back when they were young.

That said, life is all about change, whichever part or segment of it you look at.

And unsurprisingly, football is no different.

Rules of the game, wages, transfer fees – everything about the beautiful game is constantly being updated for the modern day.

And the life of the stadiums in which the sport is hosted from week to week is another side of football that is forever being brought up to speed with the 21st century.

Today, Turf Moor is one of the oldest football league grounds still in use, second only to Preston North End's Deepdale home.

And like many others, it has undergone wholesale changes during its lifetime.

Drastic changes off the pitch have also been transmitted onto the pitch, with the famous old ground playing host to almost every level of the professional game.

From an England international and top flight league football, to the LDV Vans Trophy on a cold Tuesday night and to 1,696 fans for a Fourth Division encounter with Colchester United.

Turf Moor has seen it all since its inaugural match against Rawtenstall in February 1883, and one man has seen more than most.

Albert Maddox first arrived through the front doors of the club back in 1947.

There, he worked as an assistant to Secretary Henry Smith, under the club management of Cliff Britton.

Turf Moor Longside in the 1940's

And he detailed how the place changed during his four decades at the club, and how he expects it to carry on improving for many years to come.

Speaking fondly, Maddox said: "When I first joined, what is now the Bob Lord Stand was the Brunshaw Road Stand, which comprised of a centre stand, Stand A, and two wing stands, which were B and C.

"It could hold about 3,150 seats and it comprised everything, including the players' dressing rooms, board rooms, offices, medical rooms and everything you could imagine.

"The players came out in the centre, because in front of the stand itself there were two enclosures divided by the players' tunnel. These held 6,000 people, so on that side you could accommodate nearly 9,500 people. These enclosures were very popular – it was only a shilling and they were popular for the people who wanted to be near to the players coming out."

Also when he first arrived, Turf Moor boasted a terraced version of the current Cricket Field Stand, which as Maddox detailed, was popular with the masses: "Around the late 1940s, the old Cricket Field Stand comprised of wooden sleepers or railway sleepers as terracing, and it was a very popular place for crowds to gather.

"One of my best friends, who was a policeman from Rawtenstall, used to tell me he dreaded being on duty at that end of the ground, because people relieved themselves in the open!

"We had a major building programme going on at that time, when the Cricket Field Stand was terracing. First of all we acquired some land from the cricket field to extend the stand and to take it further back, by giving them some cash and building them a new pavilion.

"The old stand itself was heated by a massive boiler which we had purchased as well – I'm not sure if that is still there but it could well be, because it was such a massive thing I doubt whether they could get it out!

"The idea was, not only for it to heat the stand, but the provision was made to heat the pitch by the way of undersoil heating. There was a huge pipe laid right down the centre of the pitch, linking up to the boiler in the Cricket Field Stand, but due to economical reasons, that undersoil heating never came into operation.

"At the same time we were having the pitch done up, which was done by a firm called Cambridge Soil Services. They were meant to be the experts, but you looked at it and wondered how on earth grass would grow on it because it was like a desert.

"It was a massive job, because there were all the pipes laid for drainage and heating as well with a view to working, but it never came into operation.

"Coinciding with that was the price of oil, because when we first got the boiler installed the price of oil was 11d (less than 5p) per gallon, and it rocketed up so high that it became uneconomical to heat the stand and the pitch, and the whole project went kaput.

"The Cricket Field Stand at that point was terracing, as was the Longside and the Bee Hole End, and before segregation came into it you could walk into the ground at any entrance and walk all the way round. We had many gates over 50,000 and we could empty the ground in no time at all, but getting in was a different matter."

One fine example of those masses of support came in an FA Cup tie with Manchester United in January 1954 -

"We had a ticket office but with no special staff, and there are two mates in particular that I remember vividly where gates are concerned. The Manchester United game was a match that sticks in my mind, because the gate was huge.

"It was well over 50,000, but a lot of people would turn up late – this was one of the best cup matches one could possibly see, and after six minutes it was 2-2! There were hundreds, if not thousands that never saw the first four goals – it ended up 5-3 but I still remember the crowds outside that missed the four goals."

And as far as memories go, another one jumps to the front of Maddox's mind more than any other: "When we played Bradford City in an FA Cup tie in February 1960, we were the premier team in this area. That included the main part of Yorkshire, because teams like Leeds United were insignificant in those days.

"A massive amount of support used to come across from Yorkshire, and when we played Bradford City at Bradford in the cup, we were the top team and were expected to walk it.

"But lo and behold, not long before the finish of the game, we were 2-0 down and managed to equalise late. We brought them back to Burnley for a replay on the following Tuesday – obviously we had no provision for tickets because we hadn't the time – and 52,850 went through the turnstiles!

"5,000 or so were locked out – they simply couldn't get in – and the police were turning them back at Halifax!

"We used to have two turnstiles, A and B, which were where the Cricket Field Stand is, and we had two checkers, Jim Thompson and Harry Wakefield. There was always a lot of rivalry between those two as to who could take the most, but fortunately, on this particular night, the admission fee was only half a crown, which was one coin.

"That meant there was no change to be given, so they had their foot on the turnstile constantly. Each turnstile took over 3,000 spectators, which I don't think will ever be beaten.

"We obviously have the top attendance against Huddersfield in the 1920s, but that might have been passed once or twice because we used to get a lot climbing over the wall at the Bee Hole End and jumping the turnstile.

Albert Maddox and Chairman Frank Teasdale, 1988

"In those days the turnstile was only waist high – we had over 50,000 on quite a number of occasions, including against Arsenal in 1937 who we played in a cup tie when the queues for that game went right up past the fire station."

At the time of the new surface in the late sixties, it was heralded as a state-of-the-art system designed to rival even Wembley.

But despite that, it proved to be unlucky for the Clarets, as within two seasons, they dropped out of the First Division for the first time in 24 years.

End of an era - 1996

Burnley fans had to get used to the changes on the pitch, but they also witnessed numerous other changes away from the grass.

Maddox explained: "We built two new stands in a very short period of time, the Bob Lord Stand and the new Cricket Field Stand. These were, to a large degree, only made possible due to the sale of players – in fact some fans called the Bob Lord Stand the Martin Dobson Stand!

"The Bob Lord Stand and the Cricket Field Stand were opened within a few years of each other and these were big steps forward for the club, the building of these stands, but with seated stands and segregation, the capacity crowd came down and down.

"The Bob Lord Stand was initially affected by subsidence, and it was decided – rightly or wrongly – that it had to be replaced. But the board decided we would build the Cricket Field Stand first, to move all the changing rooms across as a temporary thing.

"Then the old Brunshaw Road Stand was demolished then rebuilt, and probably we had to cut our cloth in terms of finance because the changing rooms were never moved back.

"I think it was due to finance that there were no players dressing rooms incorporated into it, and consequently you still have them coming out at the old Cricket Field Stand end. I much prefer how it was before, and I don't think there are many grounds that have the players' tunnel at one end of the ground, but a lot of it was down to expense."

While the two new seated stands had been built, the Longside and Bee Hole End still remained.

The Longside would go down in folklore as the heartbeat of Turf Moor, until its demolition in 1996, and Maddox recalled memories of its use when he first arrived at the club: "I used to come on a lot to watch my friend, George Bray, around the time of the war, and the Longside used to be all cinders and hardcore. There was no terracing initially, but when it was done, it was covered by a roof and railings were put up to segregate the Bee Hole End – we used to have a turnstile where you could transfer your ticket from one to the other so you could be under cover.

"In the early days, we used to have a scoreboard at the back of the Bee Hole End, where they used to put the scores on with metal plates. Then, later on, we had the broadcast box for the announcements, which was a sort of wood cabin, and then it was extended so much as it was raised up on stilts."

And he recalled one such moment regarding the Bee Hole End which sticks out: "There was one game, it was an FA Cup tie against Sunderland, where a lot of people arrived late because they had been in the pubs and arrived at the last minute.

"I think the gate had been shut at the Bee Hole End, because we used to have a maximum number of people after having given every turnstile a finishing number. There was a big rush, and I think they forced the gates at the Bee Hole End and the perimeter wall actually gave way. There was only one injury, a young lad from Burnley, who hurt his back, but the game was stopped for a short period."

He added: "Then of course there was segregation, which came in after the Taylor Report following the disaster at Hillsborough. There had been railings put up before then, and when we played Celtic in the Anglo-Scottish Cup, a lot of the Celtic fans used these railings as spears!

"There's no doubt that segregation has reduced the capacity of most grounds, but I liked the old enclosures. A lot of people want to stand, but it is all about safety now and you can't run football clubs like you used to do.

"It was quite an emotional time when both the Longside and Beehole terraces were demolished in the mid-nineties. The new stands are magnificent but I definitely prefer how it was in the old days, I hope we get back to how it was back then, but I very much doubt it will ever happen. From a safety point of view I doubt whether terracing will ever come back."

Shortly after completing this interview with Phil Simpson, Albert Maddox passed away at the grand old age of 85.

Albert Maddox 1921-2007
RIP

Turf Moor the neutral matches

As well as senior and representative matches involving other teams, many schools and local matches have been staged at Turf Moor over the years, but only those with special significance or are the first of many (eg Hospital Cup final, Keighley Cup final) are mentioned here.

29 Nov 1878
Burnley Rovers v Bacup
Played under rugby rules on the cricket field, the first game of any kind ever played under artificial light in Burnley.

15 Apr 1882
Blackburn Rovers 3-1 Accrington,
Lancashire FA Cup final
The first association football match ever played at Turf Moor. This was almost certainly the game that provided the final inspiration for the rugby-playing members of Burnley Rovers to change codes to association football.

11 Jun 1883
Burnley 2-1 Burnley Ramblers,
The first Hospital Cup final
The Burnley Medical Officer of Health, Dr Thomas Dean, inaugurated what is believed to be the oldest amateur football tournament in the world, with all the profits being used for the benefit of Burnley's hospitals. Dr Dean later presented his own cup to Burnley FC secretary George Waddington and the final of the competition, when it has been staged, has traditionally been held at Turf Moor ever since.

19 Dec 1885
Lancashire 5-0 North Wales.
Burnley players Jack Keenan and Danny Friel were included in the Lancashire team, Friel scoring twice.

24 May 1886
Burnley District 0-0 Padiham
In aid of hospital funds.
The Burnley District side was made up of players from a number of Burnley teams, including Burnley's Jack Keenan, Danny Friel and Bob McCrae, against Padiham, then the strongest team around.

27 Nov 1886
Lancashire 7-1 Nottinghamshire
Representative match.
Four Burnley players were selected for Lancashire, Jack Keenan, who captained the team, William McFetridge, David Waugh and Pat Gallocher, who scored one of the goals.

17 Apr 1893
North East Lancs League 2-0 Lancs Combination.

16 Feb 1895
McLintock's Xl 3-0 Crabtree's Xl.
Described as a trial match for local talent

Apr 1902
An agreement was reached with Burnley FC to play all Burnley Belvedere's home matches at Turf Moor for the next two years. Belvedere were members of the Lancashire Amateur League.

31 Jan 1903
Lancashire Amateurs 5-2 Cheshire Amateurs
Arthur Bell and Fred Campbell, Belvedere players also registered to play for Burnley, were both included in the Lancashire side.

4 Apr 1903
Burnley Belvedere 3-1 Padiham Reserves
N E Lancs Combination Shield final

7 Dec 1907
Nelson 3-1 Colne
Lancashire Junior Cup final

16 Nov 1908
Accrington S 1-0 Colne
FA Cup third round, second replay

27 Apr 1910
Football League X1 4-1 Manchester United Xl
Benefit match for the family of Spen Whittaker, the late Burnley Manager, who had died in tragic circumstances. Burnley players Jerry Dawson, Jonathan Cretney and Hugh Moffat all featured in the Football League side.

20 Apr 1912
Mauldeth 4-8 Rest of North of England League
Exhibition lacrosse match, 25 minutes each way before Burnley v Huddersfield T

21 Mar 1914
Football League 2-3 Scottish League.
Three Burnley players were included in the Football League side, Tommy Boyle, Teddy Hodgson and Eddie Mosscrop. The Burnley trio made an early impact, Hodgson scored after 7 minutes following a goalmouth scramble, then Mosscrop was tripped in the penalty area, with the ensuing spot kick expertly dispatched by Boyle. After just ten minutes the Football League were 2-0 up and coasting but three goals in the second half turned it completely around. To make it worse for the Burnley contingent, it was later decided that Hodgson's goal was an own goal by Scottish defender Peter Nellies! The Football League trainer for the match was Burnley's Ernest Edwards

22 Sep 1919
Burnley X1 1-5 Football League X1
Benefit match for the family of Teddy Hodgson, pre war Burnley star, who had died as a result of war wounds. The Burnley team included guests Billy Meredith (Manchester C), Ted Vizard (Bolton W) and Harold Walden (Bradford C). Walden scored the goal for the Burnley Xl.

23 Mar 1920
Dick Kerr's Ladies 5-0 Liverpool Ladies
In aid of discharged Soldiers and Sailors Association

23 Nov 1920
Dick Kerr's Ladies 7-0 Verdin Cooke Ladies.
Ladies exhibition match to raise funds for Burnley CC

28 Feb 1921
The North 6-1 England
England trial Bob Kelly, Billy Nesbitt and Cliff Jones all played for England, with Jack Hillman acting as the trainer for the North team.

7 Sep 1921
St Helens Girls 4-1 Barnes Girls
In aid of the local YMCA
Ladies football was becoming more and more popular but shortly after this game the Football Association asked the senior clubs not to stage any more ladies matches at their grounds.

25 Mar 1922
Huddersfield T 3-1 Notts C
FA Cup semi final (attendance 46,323) The only FA Cup semi final to be staged at Turf Moor. The FA insisted that the pitch be lengthened by four yards to 115 yards for the tie, although afterwards it was returned to its original length.

1923
The beginning of a famous Burnley tradition when the Chairman of Burnley Education Committee, Alderman Elijah Keighley, inaugurated a football competition to be played for by all Burnley's elementary schools, with the winners to receive a cup.

3 April 1923
Alderman Keighley, a former mayor of the town, presented his trophy to the captain of Stoneyholme Council School after St Mary Magdelene's were beaten 2-1 in the first of many Keighley Cup finals at Turf Moor.

21 Dec 1923
Dick Kerr's Ladies 5-1 Heys Bradford Ladies
Played on the cricket ground to get round the FA sanction.

17 May 1924
England 1-2 Scotland
Under 14 schoolboy international

27 Apr 1925
Lancashire Xl 3-4 Yorkshire Xl.
Benefit match for the family of the late Burnley secretary/manager John Haworth. The Yorkshire side included Bradford full back Andy McCluggage who was signed by Burnley just a week later. This game was one of the trial matches for the proposed new offside law, introduced at the beginning of the 1925-26 season.

28 Nov 1927
England 1-2 Wales
The only full international ever played at Turf Moor, with Burnley players Jack Hill and Louis Page in the England side, Hill being the captain. There were also two future Burnley players on view, George Brown of England and Ray Bennion of Wales. Neither of the Clarets were at their best, with Hill scoring an own goal, and neither played for their country again.
The acting England manager was former Burnley Chairman Charles Sutcliffe, then the President of the Football League and England's trainer for the match was the Burnley trainer Charlie Bates. One of the linesmen was Harry Hull from Burnley.

2 May 1933
Burnley Xl 2-8 International Xl
Benefit match for the family of Len Smelt, who had just passed away. Cecil Smith and Jack Mustard scored the Burnley Xl goals. Former Clarets Bob Kelly, Louis Page and Jack Bruton were included in the international line up.

17 Mar 1937
England Probables 2-0 England Possibles
International trial match.
The Probables trainer was Billy Dougall with Billy's assistant, Frank Hudspeth looking after the Possibles. One of the linesmen was Mr J. Mayo of Burnley. The Probables side included Cliff Britton and Jack Bray (George's brother) and in the Possibles team was a certain Stanley Matthews as well as James Clayton, then of Wolves, but who later joined Burnley from Aston Villa. This was one of the first occasions in England when the players wore numbered shirts (each team 1-11) and certainly the very first time the experiment had been seen at Turf Moor.

21 Aug 1943
Burnley Xl 2-5 Police & Civil Defence Xl
For the benefit of local war charities Tommy Lawton guested for Burnley Xl, goals by Lawton and Tom Gardner

19 Aug 1944
Burnley X1 3-2 National Police & Civil Defence X1,
For the benefit of local war charities Burnley team with guests, goals by Gardner (2) and Reid (QPR player)

27 Jun 1945

Prime Minister Winston Churchill visited Burnley and, frequently giving his V for victory sign and smoking the inevitable cigar, he addressed a sizeable crowd within Turf Moor. He was said to have been greatly impressed by his reception as he thanked the people of Burnley for their efforts during the War. Just days later he was voted out of office at a General Election.

9 Apr 1949
Lancashire Schoolboys 2-3 Yorkshire Schoolboys
First schoolboy match to be broadcast on radio.

15 Oct 1949
Burnley Reserves 2-1 Central League Xl
Challenge match, Burnley were Central League Champions in 1948-49. Stephenson and Attwell scored for Burnley, Les Shannon, then with Liverpool but later to sign for Burnley, scored for the Central League.

28 Apr 1956
Lancashire 0-3 Yorkshire West Riding
Northern Counties Amateur Championship final

10 Nov 1961
Lancashire Schoolboys 2-3 Yorkshire Schoolboys
Abandoned after 48 minutes

26 Apr 1965
Burnley Xl 5-5 Select Xl
Benefit for the family of Ken Hiley, a local referee tragically killed in a car crash on his way to referee a match at Carlisle. A Burnley team made up of established players and up and coming stars, took on a team of ex Clarets and more up and coming stars. Burnley goalscorers were Elder p, O'Neil, Morgan, Irvine, Harris. Select scorers were Shannon (2), Coates, Pointer and Burnley-born David Wilson. It was preceded by a match
Burnley Select Amateur Xl 1-1 West Lancs League Xl.

22 Mar 1969
England 0-2 Scotland
"Victory Shield" schoolboy international (under15)
Harry Wilson was in the England side, he was then on Burnley's books as an associate schoolboy.

2 May 1972
England 5-2 Scotland
Schoolboy international

4 Feb 1975
Lancashire 1-0 Merseyside
Northern Counties under 15 Schools Championship, Turf Moor's new £30,000 floodlights used for the first time.

9 May 1982
Ex Clarets 3-7 All Stars
Promotion special. First match ever played on a Sunday at Turf Moor

13 May 1983
Czechoslovakia 3-1 West Germany
European Youth Championships

29 Mar 1987
Fylde Falcons 12-31 Leeds Cougars
American Football game

28 Feb 1992
England 2-2 Wales
Under 15 schoolboy international

14 Nov 1993
Accrington S 2-3 Scunthorpe U
FA Cup first round
Former Claret Ashley Hoskin was in the Accrington side

7 Jun 1995
England 4-0 Latvia
UEFA under 21 Championship.

4 Sep 2003
England 1-0 Australia
Women's international.
Burnley-born Rachel Brown in goal for England

9 Oct 2005
England 2-2 Holland
Under 20 international.
Ex Clarets Gary Cahill and Richard Chaplow both in the England team, with Chaplow captaining the side.

25 May 2007
England 'B' 3-1 Albania
The final major fixture at Turf Moor of the first 125 years. There were no Clarets' connections in the England side (although Phil Neville's father was Burnley's commercial manager for a short period in the 1980's!). However the Albanian line-up included Hamburg's Besart Berisha who was the visitors' most impressive player and scored their only goal, an excellent individual effort. Steve Cotterill was obviously impressed, Berisha signed for Burnley soon afterwards.

Left: Michael Owen leads out England 'B' against Albania
Right: Besart Berisha tangles with England's Gareth Barry

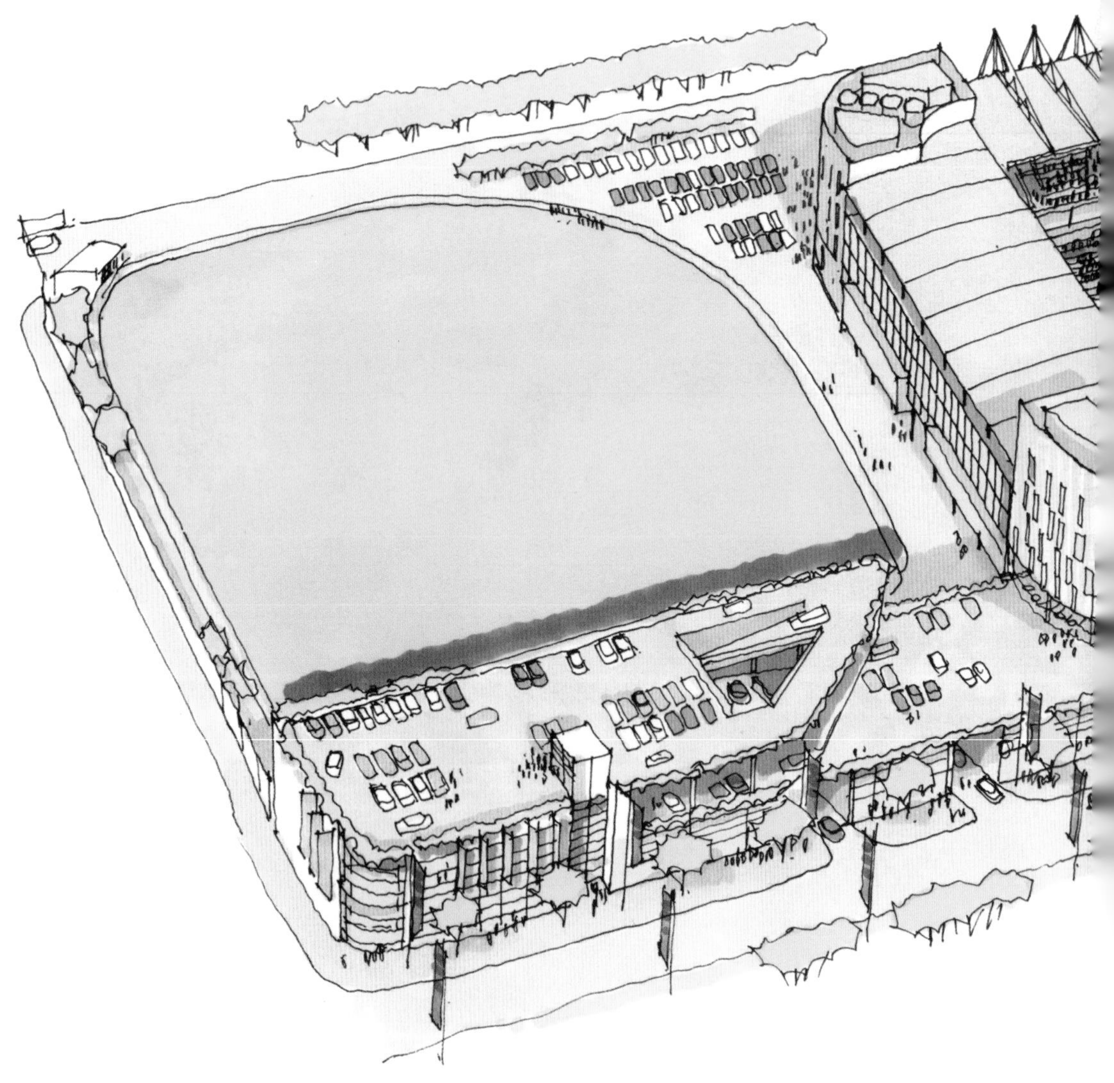

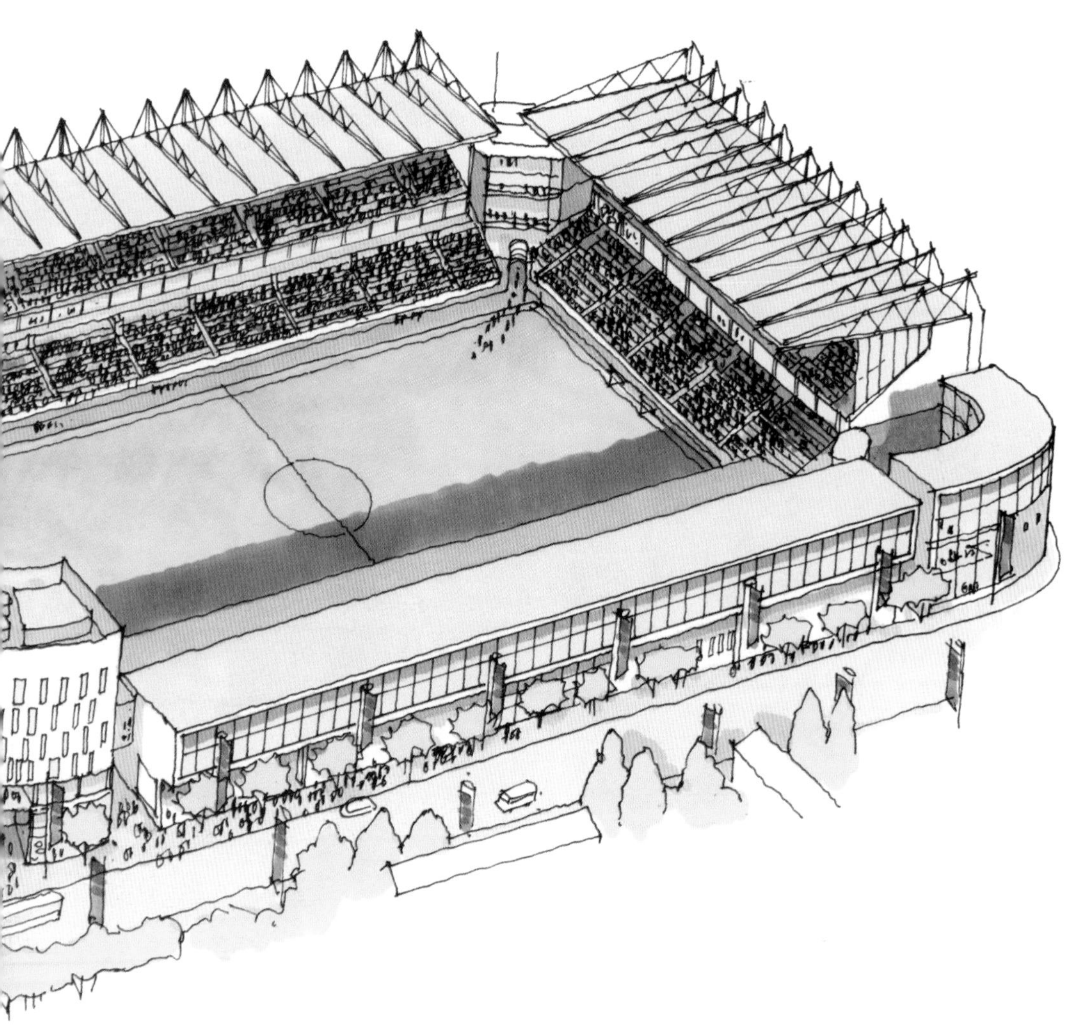

And finally...

The Future...

The new Millennium had brought renewed hope to Burnley fans. Promotion back to the second tier of English football in 2000 was a huge step in the right direction.

Undoubtedly, enthusiasm wavered as the Clarets' initial challenge for promotion to the Premiership, and the pot of riches it entails, quickly gave way to a series of credible, yet frustrating mid-table finishes.

Season ticket holders with dreams dashed began to gradually ebb away, leaving an average crowd of just under 12,000 by the time Burnley, along with Lancashire neighbours Preston, became the longest inhabitants of the Championship in 2007.

The 2006-07 season also saw the first murmurings of discontent among the loyal supporters, following an unprecedented and unfathomable 19-game winless streak.

To the eternal credit of the Burnley board of directors, in a results-driven industry, they took the brave decision to keep faith with manager Steve Cotterill, who in his defence had spent three years toiling to build a squad, only to see the family silver sold off at each crucial turn.

Burnley has always been a selling club, and as gems such as Robbie Blake, Richard Chaplow and Ade Akinbiyi shone, their worth became such that predatory clubs with cash to splash inevitably pounced.

Yet suddenly, in December 2006, all that changed.

Rossendale-born businessman Brendan Flood, a lifelong fan, was voted onto the board of directors after Chairman Barry Kilby, pro-actively seeking new investment, removed the restriction on the number of directors.

Brendan had made his fortune as a Manchester-based shopping centre owner and developer and instantly set about making his mark at Turf Moor.

Along with Kilby, and with the absolute backing of the remaining eight directors, plans were quickly made to totally transform the football club.

This culminated in an announcement in July 2007, of a dramatic £20million re-development of Turf Moor and the Gawthorpe training facility was unveiled.

Around the town and surrounding area jaws could be heard dropping in unison.

The master plan included the demolition of the ageing Cricket Field Stand, built in the early 1970s and which was deemed unsafe for a short spell in early 2007 after sections of the roof finally gave way to the elements.

A total facelift of Harry Potts Way was another integral part of the plans, opening up exciting new retail outlets with the aim of driving up revenues and including a hotel and multi-story car park.

Crucially, a club with a proud history of unearthing and nurturing young talent – especially during the halcyon days of the 1960s - was also to see its Centre of Excellence upgraded to Academy status.

The excitement was tangible, with the re-development programme set to start early in 2008 and last for approximately three years.

The legacy would be a 22,000 all-seater stadium, fit for top flight football with an infrastructure to support a hoped-for upturn in the supporter base and encompassing a whole host of social, leisure and commercial ventures to become a sporting and enterprise hub, and breathe new life into the local community.

All this coincided with the club's 125th anniversary and, in many ways it signalled a re-birth: a chance to start afresh and take this magnificent football club forward with renewed optimism and expectation.

Those plans are detailed in full here.

Roll on the next 125 years.

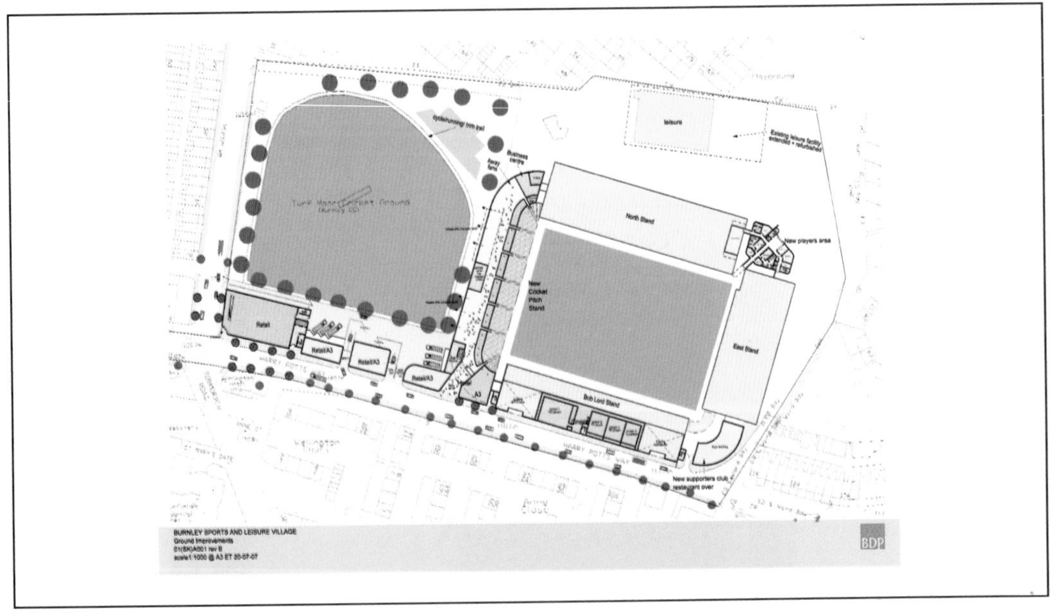

A MASTER PLAN FOR BURNLEY FOOTBALL CLUB SPORTS & LEISURE VILLAGE

The six phases of the massive redevelopment progamme, many running concurrently, are as follows:

Phase One (2008)

The new players' dressing rooms and hospitality block will be built between the Jimmy McIlroy and James Hargreaves Stands at a cost of approximately £1.25m. This three tier, glass-fronted building will be the hub of match days and house Premiership facilities and a fully furnished media suite.

Phase Two (Summer 2008)

The ageing David Fishwick (Cricket Field) Stand is to be demolished and replaced by a £10million, single tier stand housing corporate boxes, a hotel, business centre, gymnasium and cricket pavilion within the new stand. A multi-storey car park is to be built on Harry Potts Way, with access to a concourse linking all amenities.

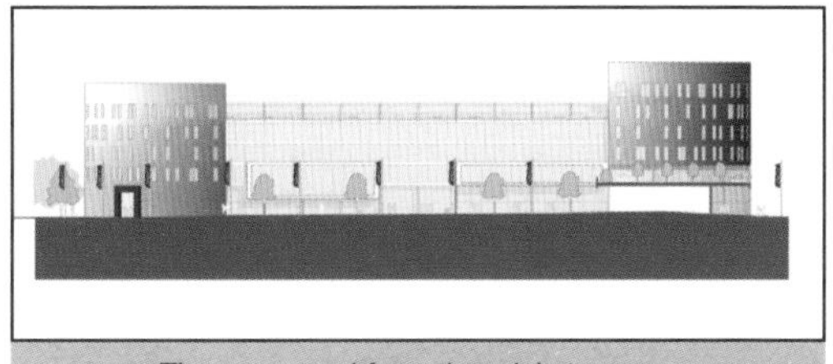

The new stand from the cricket square

Phase Three (Summer 2008)

The building of a two-storey retail sports store on the approach to Turf Moor on Harry Potts Way. This will replace the existing club superstore, which will be later redeveloped. Harry Potts Way will benefit from the planting of trees to freshen and enliven the approach from the town centre. This tree-lined avenue is to be extended down to Centenary Way with the financial help and support of Burnley Borough Council and Government agencies.

Phase Four (Summer 2008)

The exciting development of a Burnley Football Club Academy at the Gawthorpe training ground in Padiham, costing around £2million. This state-of-the-art facility will enable the club to attract and further nurture young talent to compete with the biggest clubs in England.

Phase Five (Summer 2009)

The internal refurbishment and external redevelopment of the Bob Lord Stand at an estimated cost of £3.75million. The wooden seating is to be replaced and a new façade to the existing stand on Harry Potts Way will encompass a multi-screen digital cinema, restaurants, new club offices and modern hospitality suites.

Phase Six (Summer 2009)

A new £1million bar and restaurant for use by supporters is to be built on the site of the former club offices and shop, with commercial offices above.
Allied to the recently announced build in the Jimmy McIlroy Stand void, which commences shortly as an 'Enterprise Haven' for start-up businesses, these new developments, in conjunction with the Community Sports Trust, will transform Turf Moor into a thriving sports, entertainment, business and educational centre and help to regenerate the entire town.
The club intends to encourage start up businesses and academic bodies to expand within the new commercial offices and Business Centre to create a unique Enterprise Park. The total cost of the above is approximately £20million and completion is estimated at Summer 2010.

The new hotel from Harry Potts Way

Why Clarets?

We are all proud to support Burnley FC, "the Clarets", and claret and blue has been synonymous with Burnley since......well, for ever, hasn't it?

Actually, no it hasn't, it's less than 100 years, 1910 to be precise, since the club first registered a change of colours to claret and blue, and even in the years since then, other club colours have sometimes been used for home matches.

When Burnley Rovers Rugby Club metamorphosised into Burnley Football Club in 1882, the playing members continued to turn out in narrow blue and white stripes and these colours were used until 1890 when the first change came. An all blue shirt was adopted for the start of the1890-91 season but this change was short-lived as blue was deemed to be "too sombre" so mid-season, the team changed to all-white.

It was in the summer of 1891 that claret first appeared on the Burnley shirts although claret and blue was still some way off. The new registered strip was broad vertical stripes in claret and amber.

In 1894, in their wisdom, the Burnley committee opted for another change, still stripes, but this time it was a rather daring pink and white. Believe it or not, that strip was also short-lived and, in 1895, the amber stripes returned, this time paired with black. The club was certainly keeping the shirt makers on their toes and changed again in 1896, once more in mid-season, to all red.

Red was still around until a few matches into the start of the 1900-01 campaign when green shirts suddenly appeared, and green remained as the colours of Burnley FC for the next decade.

Turf Moor success in the Edwardian era was almost non-existent and, in the summer of 1910, with green considered by many to be unlucky, there was a feeling that it was perhaps time for another change.

Burnley's new manager John Haworth certainly thought so. Haworth took as his inspiration the current (1910) League Champions, Aston Villa, who had won the title six times altogether, more than any other club since the League was founded in 1888. Villa played in claret and blue, so claret and blue became the new colours of Burnley FC.

The Clarets were born!

Had John Haworth been appointed a year earlier, things might well have been rather different, Newcastle United were League Champions in 1909 for the third time in five years!

Whether Burnley's green shirts had played any part in the club's years in the doldrums is for others to decide but Turf Moor's fortunes certainly improved over the following years. Eighth place in Division Two in 1911 was followed by 3rd position in 1912 and promotion to the First Division in 1913 as runners-up to Preston. Burnley also reached the FA Cup semi final in 1913.

The Clarets wasted no time in collecting their first major honour, building on the previous year with their epic FA Cup triumph against Liverpool in 1914. In 1915, now an established First Division force, they finished fourth, just three points from the Championship.

After the Great War had re-focused people's priorities, football again became important and, in 1920, Burnley, still on the rise, finished as runners-up to West Brom.

Then in 1921 came the pinnacle of achievement for Burnley FC, the Football League Championship, the ultimate prize in club football. Not only that, within that magnificent campaign, the Clarets established a record of 30 top flight League games in a single season without defeat. That feat that has only just been bettered, by Arsenal in 2003-04, more than eighty years later!

Burnley also finished third in 1922, but the golden age at Turf Moor was just about coming to an end.

In 1934, Burnley's colours suddenly changed again, still claret and blue but reversed, with light blue the prominent colour. In 1935 it was changed once more, this time to white with black trim, with the trim disappearing in 1937, leaving an all-white shirt.

Once again success was conspicuous by its absence but Burnley continued to play mostly in white during the Second World War, although claret and blue was often used as a change strip

In wasn't until as late as June 1946, and then almost as an afterthought, that the club decided to re-register their colours as claret and blue, and even that was partly due to readers' letters to the "Burnley Express."

It was probably just a co-incidence that Burnley, once again in claret and blue, won promotion in 1947 and reached the FA Cup final, heralding the beginning of another golden age at Turf Moor.

More than sixty years on there have been a number of relatively minor variations, although the introduction of the "V" shirt in 1975 was looked upon as fairly radical!

Nevertheless we are still in claret and blue, after that momentous change nearly a century ago.

It is difficult to imagine a scenario that would prompt another change, not least because one suspects that the fans would be "up in arms".

The Clarets we are, and the Clarets we will stay.

UP THE CLARETS!

Subscribers

Presentation Copy Number 1 Burnley Football Club

2 Ray Simpson - Proud to be Burnley FC's Historian
3 Phil Simpson - Thanks dad. Here's to the next joint effort!
4 Darren Bentley - In memory of Terry Bentley
5 Wallace Chadwick - Dedicated to all the Clarets featured within these pages - but possibly to some more than others!
6 Edward Lee - Proud to be involved in such a great book.
7 Glenys Simpson - My labour of love!
8 Barry Kilby, Chairman, Burnley FC
9 Steve Cotterill, Manager, Burnley FC
10 Jimmy McIlroy
Most people would agree, Burnley FC's greatest-ever player
11 The Burnley Express - the town's newspaper
12 The Lancashire Telegraph - Proud to cover Burnley Football Club
13 Empics/PA Photos
14 Alastair Nayler
15 Nayler Group Limited
16 Adam Riding
17 Chris Boden and Suzanne Geldard
18 Albert Maddox - a truly wonderful man. RIP
19 Mrs Margaret Potts and family, in memory of Harry Potts
Remembering with pride his achievement as Burnley's manager in the First Division Championship season of 1959-60
20 In memory of Brian Miller A true gentleman and a great servant of a great club.
21 In memory of Luke Smith "CRILL", my best mate, who passed away far too soon on 10th April 2007, aged 21.
Never forget you - Phil.
22 The Football League
23 The Football Association
24 The Lancashire Football Association
25 The Professional Footballers Association
26 For Helen Kay Simpson, my beautiful daughter, love Dad. X
27 Joseph Peter Tickle - in memory of my grandad, Richard Henry Clough, a true Burnley fan.
28 Craig Ford
29 Andrew Sisson
30 Brendan Flood, Operational Director, Burnley FC
31 Liz and Terry Butterworth - Accrington Clarets for life
32 Dave & Harriet Thomas for John Fielden
33 Nigel P.N. Lambert
34 Christian & David Farrar. Clarets 4 ever
35 In loving memory of Sue Frankland
36 Dean & Deb Trotter - Southend Clarets since 1999
37 Gordon Elliman, I'm proud to be associated with Burnley F.C.
38 Simon Mahrous
39 Alan Bullock - Born and bred a Claret
40 Chloe Tyler - Burnley is my religion, Turf Moor is my church
41 Steve Tyler - 50 years a Claret
42 Peter, James & Lucy Brunskill, Keighley Clarets
43 Bill Mellor, Happy birthday, lots of love, Jean XX
44 Chris Emmerson - Claret & Blue through and through
45 Neil Pollard, Nailsea, Somerset
46 Derek Forbes Stackhouse
47 Albert L.J. Comber. Through thick and thin always a Claret
48 Christopher Coxhead. Memories of a lifetime Dad, Rich.
49 Matthew Harrison
50 Roger David Bentley
51 John, Scott & Elliott Riley
52 George Brown
53 To Robert Holmes, lots of love from your wife Jane.
54 Stephen John Jackson, lifetime Claret.
55 Michael Bullen
56 Richard Mellor
57 Best wishes to Mike Bailey
58 Mark & Nick Calvert, Chesterfield
59 Christopher, James and the late Alan Sharples
60 "John Parker" - To dad, a fine Claret at 60
61 Norman Edmondson
62 Mike Smith - Congratulations Clarets and here's to the next 125.
63 Ian, Lydia, Jack and Ruth Fletcher, Rossendale.
64 Brian King - love from Heather X
65 Loyal Clarets supporter - Jeff Acreman
66 Matthew Gilmartin - A Claret forever
67 Martin Pickering - Claret forever!
68 Tim Blackledge - Once a Claret, always a Claret
69 June Watson - Don't stop me now!
70 Garry Morris
71 David Kilburn - 40 years a Claret
72 Michael Kilburn - Once a Claret, always a Claret
73 Sammy Rosenberg - Up the Brooklyn Clarets!
74 Derek Brotherton. Turf Moor - a gateway to heaven
75 Ian Chase and family - Loyal Clarets for 125 years
76 Chris Hampson - Claret and Blue 'til I die
77 Lee Michael Holt
78 Daniel James Holt
79 Neil Kay
80 Paul Hind
81 Gareth Murphy
82 Geoff Salter - Forever Claret and Blue
83 Cliff & Lorna Hacking
84 Exile makes the heart grow fonder - Forever Claret, Dan Milner
85 Happy Birthday Kristin
86 Mark Ashworth - 4 ever Claret
87 Forever Clarets - Ian, Anne, Brent & Damon Bannister
88 A proud supporter for 47 years - Mr. Adrian Ashworth
89 Roy Milner, 45 years a Claret and still proud to follow Burnley FC
90 Barrie Gallagher (Oldham Claret)
91 Charles Ingham
92 Jonathan Ingham
93 No nay never forever - Richard
94 For Steven & James - True Clarets
95 Rob Yeates - Forever a Claret
96 Jon Kennett - Preston Claret since 1993
97 Peter Mulligan
98 John Cox - Remembering all the Clarets greats
99 Julian Booth - Congratulations on 125 years - A Claret forever!
100 Stuart L. Marshall - A proud supporter of our local team, Come on you Clarets!
101 Mrs. S.J. Walker
102 Always Claret, never Blue, Roger Fielding since 1952
103 Joe Vella, Il glorja tal-passat trid terggha tigi!
104 John R. Sharpe - How to make a supporter happy!
105 Rob - Little extra 2007 - Up the Clarets, love Dad.
106 Over 55 years a supporter - Robert Barker
107 Over 55 years a supporter - Michael Barker
108 To Keith Baxter (our daddy) with love from Kyle and Natasha
109 Paul Rhodes - Happy birthday, love from Mum and Tony.
110 John Philip Ramsden
111 Phil Doyle - 125 years of history, some great memories
112 Lynz will always be a Claret
113 To Drew - Happy birthday, lots of love always, your Jodes
114 To Dave - A lifelong supporter
115 Andrew Burnhill
116 To Roger with best wishes
117 Craig Edmondson
118 Alan Leaver - A Claret forever
119 Rick - Forty-five years a Claret
120 Martin Barnes - "When the Ball Moves" Editor

121 To Arthur, a long time Claret supporter. Happy birthday.
122 Andy Lord
123 John Pedley - His book
124 David Pedley - His book
125 Julie Walker - A lifelong Claret, from Nick + Mooro.
126 To Peter Smith, a Claret since 1959
127 Graham Wilkinson - Always a Claret!
128 Andrew Shaw
129 Peter Leonard Hodson - Up the Clarets!
130 Stephen Hartley - Come on Burnley, onwards and upwards!
131 David J. Hulme from 1958/59. Forever Claret
132 Carl Pickering. Burnley 'til I die
133 John Mark. I left Burnley in 1956 but will be a Claret for life
134 Steve Harris - Claret and proud since 1964
135 Lois M. Benyon
136 Francis Woodward - Always a Claret whatever the weather.
137 In memory of Harold and Allan Dyson by Adrian Fletcher
138 Martin Golightly "Forever Burnley"
139 John Rowling - True Claret and fantastic father
140 Chris Rowling - Loyal Claret, brother and son.
141 Tony Scholes - In memory of my mum and dad.
142 Clarets Mad Website supporting youth football at Turf Moor
143 Michael Scholes
144 Graham Coxall
145 Richard Whately
146 To Adrian with all my love, Nicky X
147 Rod Harling, true Claret from 1959 to the last breath I breathe.
148 Jeremy Chadwick: 1 game and 1 goal at Turf Moor
149 Richard Price
150 Alan Whittaker
151 Peter, Adam and Zara Towne, supporting the Clarets
152 Peter, Adam and Zara Towne, supporting the Clarets
153 Nigel Standige
154 Richard Moore - Actor - A Claret for 50 years plus
155 William Watson - Adored as one of Burnley's all-time greats.
156 Nigel Hartley. All way a Clarets' supporter all his life
157 Rob Harmer - still Claret after all these years!
158 Once a Claret, always a Claret - Ian Brookes
159 I am Clarets mad! - James Brookes
160 Come on you Clarets! - Katie Brookes
161 Fiona L. Miller - Forever Claret!
162 Claret and Blue through and through - J. Michael Varley
163 Harry Hurren - A true Claret
164 For Becky Brown
165 Thanks dad for taking me to the Turf in 1961 - Martin Clarke
166 Olav Gjesteland - Long distance and time support
167 Andrew and Maya Ings, Ashbourne, Derbyshire.
168 Paul Laurence Walsh. A Claret since 1960
169 To Paul, love Ceara
170 Ernest Foster
171 Paul Anthony Schofield and Daniel John Schofield, born 17th November, 2006.
172 Gary Chadwick
173 Eddie Simmons, A true Claret
174 Terence & James Denslow - True lifelong Clarets
175 Mr. E.K. Hartley, celebrating 60 Claret years
176 Geoff Watson
177 Keep the faith Pat, we will be Champions again.
178 David Broom - Come on you Clarets!
179 John and Andy Ritchings
180 In memory of Jack Riley - A true Burnley legend
181 Paul & Andrew Haworth, Clarets born and bred
182 Kevin Green, Christopher Green, Peter Green.
183 Keith Sladen
184 For Burnley Ben
185 William, Richard & Sean - Three generations of supporters
186 David Nuttall - Bacup Claret
187 Margaret Spencer, who first took me on in 1957, and Tim, who continues.
188 Roy Hickey "I have a dream......"(M.L. King Jnr.)
189 Kenneth Goldie - Jimmy McIlroy's best pal.
190 Chris, Shirley and Zach Cave - Southport Clarets
191 Pete Ellis. Claret & Blue in my blood. First idol of many Jimmy Mac.
192 To Rob, from Dad. "Happy birthday!"
193 Arthur Charles Stammers
194 Mark Inger - Wembley '88
195 Chris Gorman - born in Burnley, believe in Burnley FC.
196 Rupert Booth (Mr. Longsider) Happy 125th BFC.
197 Terry Hephrun
198 To Doug for your 65th birthday. Hope this brings back memories.
199 Dave Coyle - Lifetime Claret
200 Wayne Blackledge - Always a Claret!
201 Peter W. Bibby
202 Jonathan Peter Bibby
203 Simon James Bibby
204 Catherine Jane Bibby
205 Bob Watson
206 David Watson
207 Ged Coyle - 2 FA Cup Finals - 3rd time lucky?
208 Alan Butterworth
209 Jim Fallon - Born a Claret, die a Claret
210 Keith Bullough and Nathaniel Bullough
211 Henry Metcalfe - A Yorkshire Claret
212 Stephen W. Wells, a faithful fan, stood, sat and shouted.
213 Dave McManus - Born a Claret, always a Claret
214 Martin Spiers - BFC, the heart of the town
215 David Rockliffe
216 Billy Mortimer was here, R.I.P. from Neil
217 Chris, Harry and Joseph Smith - Moss Bank, St. Helens
218 John Smith - Waterfoot, Rossendale
219 Lee Wilkinson - A Claret for life
220 Peter B. Toner, born in Blackburn, live in Preston, always a Claret
221 Happy Birthday Grandad, Love from Tom & Ellie
222 Gerald Edgar Maden Riley
223 Phil Wilcock - Proud to be a Claret!
224 Jeff Smith - A loyal Burnley fan since 1960
225 Anne Whalley - A Huddersfield Claret
226 Jim Park - Best wishes on your 54th birthday
227 Rappo - In memory of Jimmy Rapson and New Year's Day 1966
228 Steve Hawkes and Yvonne Lucas - Together forever Clarets
229 Neil Glenister - Claret forever
230 Barry Heagin
231 Loyal supporter 50 years - Steve Neary
232 Michael John Pownall
233 For my boys - Adam & Ross
234 Thanks mate for making me laugh - Stephen Hargreaves
235 David Wilkinson - Dad, enjoy the memories, with love.xx
236 John Smith - Longing to return to the top flight!
237 Saw my first match in 1936 - Doug Nicolson
238 Long may the Clarets prosper - Michael E. Benyon
239 Ian Carson - Dedicated to my beautiful family
240 To Grandad with love, Millie and Jessica.

241 To Chris, Andrew & Anthony Hill - Always be true Clarets. Dad
242 Fred Bates
243 To Chris, a true Claret. Love Mel.
244 Colin Robinson - In memory of Dad, Neil.
245 Bryan Catlow - Supporter since 1945
246 William Thornton
247 Martin Jennings - This is my 60th year.
248 To James and Steven - Two true Clarets
249 William Proctor
250 For Jason Brian Mount, with love from your proud parents.xx
251 William and George Irvine, grandsons of a legend.
252 Mark Butterworth
253 Stephen Foster
254 Michael Ashworth
255 Paul B. French
256 Phil Bird "Up the Clarets"
257 Forever and always a Claret - Steven Heaton
258 66/67 season 40 years of passion of BFC - Mick Hornby
259 Being a Claret helps to define me - Bob Nicholson
260 Peter J. Clough
261 For John, Happy birthday, love Sandra
262 Best wishes for the next 125yrs - Penrith Clarets
263 Catherine, Ian, Heather and Graham Shutt - A Claret family
264 Catherine, Ian, Heather and Graham Shutt - A Claret family
265 Catherine, Ian, Heather and Graham Shutt - A Claret family
266 Dave Mack (Ashton under Lyne)
267 Colin, Peter and Alexander Milner
268 To Stephen, my nephew and lifelong Claret supporter
269 Graham and Andy Veevers
270 Happy 50th Dad, from Chris (still 75 behind Burnley)
271 Martin and Helena Wilkinson, Loughborough Clarets
272 Ralph Wilkinson, Grange-over-Sands
273 To Dad, with love, Liv & Colum
274 Tony, Kathryn and Mark Pickin
275 Jan Gedzielewski
276 Julia Bullock - Harrogate's No. 1 Claret
277 Louise Bullock - Stoke Mandeville's No. 1 Claret
278 Dave Burnley - One day our time will come! Keep the faith!
279 Keith and Rosa Edwards - Proud to be Claret!
280 Marc, Liz, Cameron and Freya Edwards - Proud to be Claret!
281 Glyn Barry Jones
282 To No. 1 Burnley fan - Alan Heap
283 Howard Bracewell, BFC - Passion, tradition & history
284 Michael Timberlake
285 Richard Joseph Logan
286 Thanks to my dad, John Cornforth, for taking me to Burnley
287 Dave O'Connell
288 Iain - Happy birthday - Love from Lesley XX
289 Eric Knowles - Proud to be a Clarets' fan
290 David Holden - A Claret since 1946, still going strong!
291 The Frost Family - Forever Clarets
292 Dear James, A dissertation on Burnley FC! You must be mad!
293 Steven Tomlinson
294 Martyn John Brassington - Keep the dream alive!
295 Julian Etherington - Once a Claret, always a Claret.
296 To Stephen Ormerod
297 Alan Barnes - "Happy Retirement",
love Jess, Jayne, Taj and Pauline.
298 Forever a Claret - Andrew Astin
299 Keep the faith - Peter Astin. N.Z.
300 Mark Atkinson - 50 years and still a Claret

301 Michael Moore - A Kiwi Claret forever
302 John Davis - You'll always be a Claret
303 Mick Davis - A Claret for life
304 Peter Haworth - Proud to be a Claret
305 Phillip Sutcliffe - Once a Claret, only a Claret
306 Joseph Sutcliffe -2006/07, my first season, aged 12 weeks.
307 To Lucas Alexander Ward, lots of love, Mum, Dad & Morgan
308 For my dad, Stephen Dent - 50 years a Claret
309 Steven Coles
310 David M. Timberlake - A Claret for over 50 years
311 Oshcosh Clarets, we are here
312 To Peter Law, Happy 60th birthday
313 John Greenwood
314 Tony Dickinson - 50 years a Claret
315 Happy birthday Elizabeth - Jack & Gillian
316 Peter Francis - A lifelong Clarets' fan
317 To Alan, with fond memories of Les - a true Burnley fan
318 Michael Evans - Up the Clarets
319 William Nathan Brooks - Up the Clarets, long may they reign
320 Graham Cottam - A lifetime in Claret and Blue
321 Andrew Hartley
322 Luke Hartley
323 Mick Garman - Forever and ever a Claret
324 David Longley - Lifelong Clarets' fan
325 John C. Tomlinson
326 For Alan - THE football professor
327 Stephen Lee - A Claret for 50 years, thanks to my dad, Tom Lee
328 Matthew Smith
329 Boy to man, Burnley till I die - Barry Hornsby
330 Thanks for the memories! Phil Willis M.P.
331 Andrew Brown - Wakefield Claret
332 David Brown - Lifelong Claret
333 Andy Waterworth - 'Tyneside Clarets'
334 David and Peter O'Keeffe
335 In memory of Harry Anderton
336 Robert Nutter, Datchet, Berkshire
337 Ken & Christa, Immer Ein Claret, Stuttgart
338 Phil Halshaw - Always a Claret
339 Michael John Redfearn, Wolves Sept.26th,1970. 2-3
340 Ian Thwaite
341 Andrew Preston Pitman
342 Nick, Jake & Thomas Barrett
343 Ted Barrett
344 Mike Stokes of Peterborough (Posh Claret)
345 To Dad, a true Claret - From Tracy, Andrew & Vicki
346 Trevor Slack - Cheshire's No. 1 Claret
347 Geoffrey Mann
348 Many congratulations! Thanks, it's been great - Steve Wells
349 Many congratulations! Thanks, it's been great - Steve Wells
350 St. John's C of E Primary School, Cliviger
351 Pendle Vale College
352 Stephen Hodgson - A true Claret
353 Jim Hodgson - A Claret forever
354 For Ben, with love, Dad
355 Carl J. Taylor - Shanghai Clarets
356 Julie Szwec
357 To Nicola Fawley, from Aunty Judith & Uncle Alan
358 To David Fawley, from Aunty Judith & Uncle Alan
359 Beatrice Waddington Aged 90 - Loved the Clarets since 1928
360 Ian Gregory

361 Adam Gregory - from Dad
362 David Wildman + Brian & Alan - Clarets forever
363 To Ken - Happy 60th,
with best wishes from your work colleagues
364 Rev. David Wiseman - 3rd generation Wiseman Clarets!
365 Christian Wiseman - 4th generation Wiseman Clarets!
366 Burnley College
367 Gunnar Lorgen
368 Dad, Happy Birthday, from Chris & Johnny
369 Home from home forever - Ian Brogden
370 Mick G. - Rotherham Claret
371 Happy birthday Chris, with love from your very own Claret X
372 Nigel Madigan
373 The Pollards, Fieldens & McCourts - 5 generations of Clarets
374 Onwards to success in the next 125 years - Peregrine Towneley
375 Onwards to success in the next 125 years - Peregrine Towneley
376 Robert Woodmore - The ultimate trip down memory lane,
back to 1960 for me.
377 Tony Jagger
378 Mr. E. Dowling. Once a Claret, always a Claret,
man and boy from 1950
379 Alex Travis - Yorkshire Claret
380 Sarah Clegg - Yorkshire Claret
381 Harold Rudman - Ex Claret
382 Pete Scanlon - for Chris, Ben & Big Enty - Clarets daft!
383 Pauline & Patrick - Forever Clarets
384 Happy 50th birthday Dixie
385 Padiham St. Leonards C of E Primary School
386 Peter Pike - Happy 70th birthday 26/6/07.Carol. X
387 The Premier League beckons - Ronnie McMeekin
388 In loving memory of Graham Wells, a true Claret to the end
389 David Roberts
390 Burnley ' til I die - Christopher McNabb
391 Always be a Claret - Jonathan McNabb
392 Eric Vickery
393 To Allan Kay, a lifelong Claret
394 Keith Cassidy, for Kathy,Jane, Julie and family
395 Paul "Chief" McMylor, the Oldham Claret
396 Kev Day, a wonderful son-in-law and even better Burnley fan
397 Derek Hamilton. Number 1 Claret, all my love always, Liz
398 Jake, to me you are what Harry Potts is to football
- A hero! Love Mum.
399 Tony Carden - A lifetime in Claret and Blue
400 Worsthorne Primary School
401 For David - Happy birthday to a lifelong supporter.
402 Mr. Stephen Cain - Up the Clarets!
403 To Mick, you will always be a Claret. Love Sandra
404 Towneley Hall, Art Gallery and Museum
405 Clive Spencer - For Dad (Ronnie Spencer 1932-2001)
406 Mrs. Joyce Hindle
407 Chris Flynn - Supporting the Clarets from New York City
408 Happy birthday daddy, with love from Charlie
409 Dave & Liz - Clarets for 40 years
410 John Sullivan - Director BFC. Clarets for Premiership.
411 Adam Sullivan - Isle of Wight Clarets fan
412 Gemma Sullivan - Blackpool Clarets fan
413 Paul Sullivan - Blackpool Clarets and Rams fan
414 Chris Sullivan - Auckland N.Z. Clarets fan
415 Caitlin Sullivan - Sheffield Clarets fan
416 Pete and Chris Marsden - BFC Forever
417 Colin, Deborah, Charlotte and Dominic Potts
418 Mark Donnelly - Always be a Claret
419 50 years, 4 divisions, 1000 memories - Bernard Ferguson
420 To Richard - True Claret
421 John and Margaret Connolly - Here's to the next 125
422 Ruth and David Roe, in memory of Sydney Roe
423 Carl Bayliffe - View the world through Claret-tinted glasses
424 To Bill, happy 60th birthday. From Sue
425 Ian Belford - Once a Claret. Always a Claret
426 Andy Murphie
427 To Andrew - We saw this and thought of you, Love mum and dad.
428 Jordan Croisdale - Claret forever
429 Phil Lea
430 To Lawrie Pearson, founder member Dunnington Clarets
431 To Derek Hughes, supporter since 1945
432 Donald Speak - supporting the Clarets since 1943
433 Lancashire County Libraries
434 Lancashire County Libraries
435 Lancashire County Libraries
436 Lancashire County Libraries
437 Lancashire County Libraries
438 Lancashire County Libraries
439 Lancashire County Libraries
440 Lancashire County Libraries
441 Lancashire County Libraries
442 Lancashire County Libraries
443 Lancashire County Libraries
444 Lancashire County Libraries
445 Lancashire County Libraries
446 Michael Duffy & Andrew Duffy (Preston Clarets)
447 Chris Ellis-Brown. Born in Portsmouth, belongs to Burnley
448 Andrew Sladen
449 Gordon Small - Burnley Union Star remembered
450 Matt and Daniel Barnes
451 Lee Turner - Claret until I die
452 Sarah Clinkard - Donegal/Burnley
453 To Dad, Happy 70th birthday, love Julie, Joe & Sam
454 Martin O'Connell - Claret through and through
455 Derek Ainsworth at R.B.H. sends best wishes to the Clarets
456 For my dad, Sid - A true Claret. Thanks, Len
457 Andrew D.M. Smith
458 To Aaron, Happy birthday, love Mum and Dad
459 Neil Towler, a lifelong Claret
460 To No.1 Burnley fan, David Lord, NSW.Aus. From the Whittakers
461 Jim Powers
462 To Danielle, my gorgeous girlfriend. Love Tim XX
463 Mark Horsfall
464 Claire & Howard Jones - Long live the Clarets!
465 Greta & James Jones - Clarets 4 ever. Love C+H. X
466 Simon Bain, award-winning business journalist fan from 1960
467 Andrew Morgan
468 Susan Williams
469 Robert Edward Smith
470 Colin, Paul, Rachel & Liam Cavanagh
471 Colin, Paul, Rachel & Liam Cavanagh
472 Allan Taylor - The good times are coming back
473 BFC - Thank you for 20yrs of memories, David Pilling
474 Stuart, Rob and Rick Elliott, the Clarets - it's a family affair.
475 Rob, Rick and Stuart Elliott, the Clarets - it's a family affair.
476 Rick, Rob and Stuart Elliott, the Clarets - it's a family affair.
477 Many happy memories for the Aggett family
478 Tommy Aspinall - Clarets is the name, football is the game
479 Stephen Aspden - Remembering Ritchie, love to Suzi
480 To Peter Catlow, a lifelong Claret

481 P.I. & R.D. Pomeroy
482 Remembering Harry Howarth and Jack Oldham
483 Great memories of the past, great hopes for the future - Tony Lister
484 Donald Copeman
485 For Andrew, Derek, Mary, David & Gary McCluggage - True Clarets
486 Anthony Riley, loyal supporter, always and forever a Claret
487 Philip N Murphie
488 James Philip Murphie
489 To Simon Barrett - a very fine Claret! From his sons Josh and Kai.
490 Nicola Helen Neilson - Proud to be a Claret.
491 Happy birthday Bill
492 Happy birthday Shaun - From Ruth and Bill
493 Dear Nicky, happy 25th birthday, love Chloe.
494 Forty years and counting to a love supreme. Graham S.
495 In memory of Joe Cooper, from Gordon, Adam and Johnny
496 Dad, up the Clarets! Love from Jonathan and Henry
497 3 generations of Schofields adding their continued support.
498 3 generations of Schofields adding their continued support.
499 3 generations of Schofields adding their continued support.
500 Barrie James Oliver
501 Christopher J. Rawson
502 In memory of Jack, Michael and Dale Clancy
503 Happy Christmas Steven Holden, from Mum and Dad
504 Jim Marriott - supporting Burnley since 1927
505 Tom and Jim Howarth
506 To Mel Summers, a fan through highs and lows
507 In memory of John O'Brien - Simon + Judith O'Brien
508 To Dave Rogan, a lifelong Clarets & Rossy supporter. Luv Karen
509 Mark Corrigan.ATB! Mick,Gabs,Josh,Joe & Lydia
510 David Alexander
511 Stuart Hardacre
512 Gwen McNally and Jorge
513 John Lightfoot - Always a Claret
514 All the best, Clarets forever, Sue and Ian Ormrod
515 Martin Cosgrif - October 2007
516 Barney & Ali. Melbourne, Australia.
517 Shaun McArdle-Watson lives for football
518 To Philippos Hadjiioannou, in memory of your great-great grandfather, Albert Jobling.
519 To Milo Hatfield, in memory of your great-great grandfather, Albert Jobling
520 John and Julia Hatfield, in memory of grandfather Albert Jobling, Burnley FC's first chairman.
521 Pat Keightley
522 Mr. J.A. Quinn
523 Only "the Clarets" for me. Thanks dad. Baz Grimshaw.
524 John Pilling
525 To Dad, happy birthday, love William
526 Philip Grimshaw
527 "Thanks for the memories and the hope" Andrew James Morris
528 Julian Ambrose - older, wiser, but still at every home game!
529 To Chris, from Burnley FC 2007
530 John G. Quinn
531 Pauline Lockwood - In memory of Harry and Ivy Lockwood
532 Harry & Dorothy Lockwood & family (Northants)
533 To Ethan Rundle, my greatest grandson, from grandad Malcolm
534 Neil Pilling - Cumbria Claret
535 James Hodgkin will always be a distant follower of the Clarets
536 Brian Holgate, Youth team Claret and lifelong fan.
537 John Marshall, Claret and Blue through and through.
538 David Sagar
539 David, Elaine and Susan Watson
540 Cliff Lomax, Northumberland exile, 60th birthday.
541 For a true football fan, Burnley through and through - David Isherwood
542 For Andrew, Derek, Mary, David & Gary McCluggage - True Clarets
543 From the low point to possibly the Promised Land soon, quite a ride at close quarters. Clive Holt
544 Antony, Chantal, Emily and Amy Wilson
545 Jack - Claret & Blue through & through, Love from Mum & Dad
546 John - Happy 40th birthday, love from Paul, Carole & Jack.
547 To Martin Dandy, love from Mum & Dad
548 To Billy & Margaret, love from Philip & Family
549 To Philip, Dawn & Boys, love from the Family
550 In memory of Margaret Noonan - a lovely woman, from Raymond Dillon, and best wishes to the Dyce Reds.
551 Pete Smith
552 Chris Smith
553 Ben Smith
554 Mark Jackson, fan since 1960
555 John Feane - "60's in Belvedere Rd. to Bradford-on-Avon, Wilts now"
556 Richard Guilfoyle - Skipton
557 Michael, Wendy, Tom & Lee Guilfoyle - Skipton Clarets
558 Craig Schofield - first match 4. 1.1975
Louis Schofield - first match 23.11.2002
559 Colin Shuttleworth
560 To Tony - Clarets fan forever!
561 Clarets forever - John, Anthony, Daniel and Ruben O'Hara
562 Kevin Lumb & Family - Burnley supporters forever
563 Geoffrey Maynard Jones
564 John Hargreaves - A lifetime supporter, love from Harriet and Katie
565 Good luck to the Clarets in the future - Lynn Lonsdale
566 Many more years of supporting Clarets Mark
567 Kevin Walton
568 Tony Foulds - Always a Claret
569 Craig Foulds - Forever a Claret
570 Sarah Foulds - Forever a Claret
571 Chris Green - Forever a Claret, love you lots, Sarah.
572 Happy first birthday to George Auty.
573 Here's to the next 125 years - Les Hargreaves
574 The Malcolm Family - Proud supporters of Burnley FC
575 Arthur, Freda and Michael Thompson
576 To Gill, love David Badminton
577 Happy 30th Jon, from all at M.S.I.F.- Come on you Clarets!
578 Stewart Knapton - Clarets fan since 1948."Very tolerant wife"
579 Burnley Football Club - the best ever - Aaron and Callum Phelan
580 Alan Ashworth - A lifelong Claret!
581 The Chases - Claret and Blue since 1882 - Geoff Chase
582 Paul Bentley(PEB) Once a Claret, always a Claret
583 4-1 at Southend - What a trip! AL Graham & Sons, Lancaster
584 Peter Birtwistle - Happy birthday Daddy.
585 Colin W. Hopkins - "A fantastic club with a great history".
586 To hat-trick hero Arthur, from Andy, Sara, Gary & Fiona Crossley
587 To Tony Crossley, love from Mum and Dad - Up the Clarets!
588 Rev. Ralph Thomas and Rob Thomas
589 Robin Sharphouse. For bringing me to Turf Moor, thanks Dad.
590 Ian Thompson, Bradford
591 Jon and Susan Hart - Clarets since 1973 & forever will bee!
592 Keiron Sagar
593 Happy Christmas, love Paul and Cath.
594 Happy Christmas Dad
595 Paul Sagar
596 Michael A Wood, In memory of my late father Edwin, a true Claret
597 Christopher Quinn
598 Mr. D. Carr - Claret for fifty years
Keep up the good work Mr. Cotterill!
599 Other than playing myself I have watched Burnley 76 years
Had 3 trials myself under Cliff Britton - R. Wills.
600 Ex-Clarets In Sport

601 Jacqueline Victoria Lawrence
602 Lee Edward Lawrence Jnr.
603 In loving memory of James Edward Lawrence
604 Stephen Berry, Cowling, West Yorkshire.
605 John Steele
606 Matthew Steele
607 Ric Collinge
608 Vic Collinge, Border Bookshop, Todmorden
609 To Steven and Andrew, from Grandad Baldwin
610 Keith Patchett of Hayle, Cornwall
611 Jack G. Davies - Clarets fan in Turkey
612 T. David Anforth, Clarets fan since 1947
613 Barry Fothersgill has been a fan for 58 years
614 Peter Graham Irving
615 Gavin Bradshaw
616 Trevor, James and Luke Wilde - Up the Clarets!
617 Philip Heyworth, Clarets forever!
618 Andy Gee - Number one club
619 Colin Gee - Many thanks to Brian O'Neil
620 Harold Gee - Watched 'em for 64 years and still sane! (I think)
621 Clarets forever - Joe Cronshaw
622 John Stuart Livingstone
623 Miss Lucy Ransom
624 Miss Barbara Perrott
625 Mr. Frank Albert Tetlow
626 Mr. William A Powell (Hemel Hempstead)
627 Carl Sanderson
628 Peter Mackay - Just like a fine wine,
the "Clarets" get better every year.

**A special thank you
to all the pre-publication subscribers
from everybody involved in the Clarets Chronicles**

The Football League Championship
The ultimate measure of sucess in domestic club football

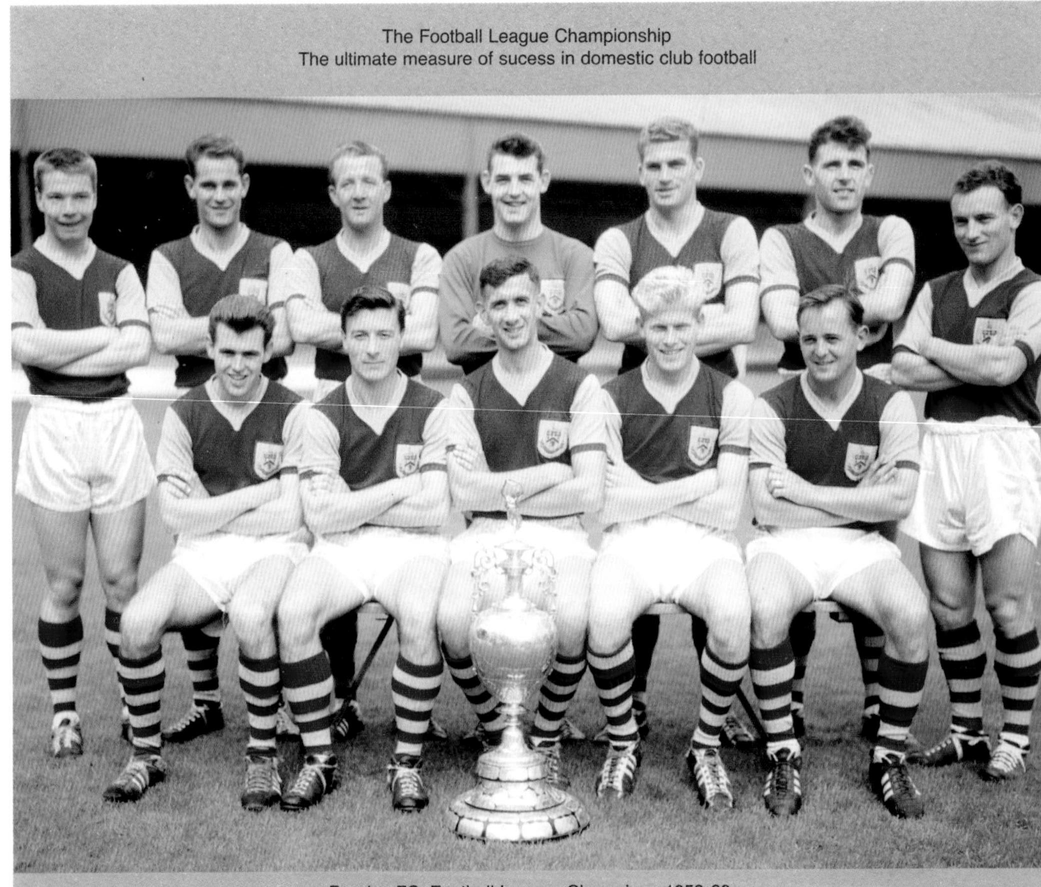

Burnley FC, Football League Champions 1959-60
Back: Alex Elder, Jimmy Robson, Tommy Cummings, Adam Blacklaw, Brian Miller, John Angus, Trevor Meredith,
Front: John Connelly, Jimmy McIlroy, Jimmy Adamson, Ray Pointer, Brian Pilkington.